Concepts
and Theories
of Human
Development

Concepts and Theories of Human Development

THIRD EDITION

Richard M. Lerner
Tufts University

Routledge
Taylor & Francis Group

LONDON AND NEW YORK

Originally published 1976.

Published 2002 by Lawrence Erlbaum Associates, Inc.

Published 2014 by Routledge
2 Park Square, Milton Park, Abingdon, Oxfordshire OX14 4RN
711 Third Avenue, New York, NY 10017

First issued in paperback 2014

Routledge is an imprint of the Taylor and Francis Group, an informa business

Library of Congress Cataloging-in-Publication Data

Lerner, Richard M.
Concepts and theories of human development / Richard M. Lerner. — 3rd ed.
p. cm.
Includes bibliographical references and index.
ISBN 0-8058-2798-6
1. Developmental psychology. I. Title.

BF713 .L47 2001
155—dc21

2001040282

ISBN 13: 978-0-8058-2798-9 (hbk)
ISBN 13: 978-1-138-01245-5 (pbk)

To Sam Goldfarb, Sam Korn, and Sam Karson

CONTENTS

4   The Nature–Nurture Controversy: Implications of the Question How?   86

5   The Continuity–Discontinuity Issue   106

8   Developmental Systems Theory: The Sample Case of Developmental Contextualism   195

9   Life-Span, Action Theory, Life-Course, and Bioecological Perspectives   218

15   Stage Theories of Development   360

16   The Differential Approach   409

17   The Ipsative Approach to Development   438

PREFACE to the Third Edition

Ten years elapsed between the first and second edition of this book and, now, 15 years have passed between the second and third. Given this rate of revision, I approach the writing of this Preface fairly certain that I will not be the person writing a fourth edition of this text, should one be produced. As such, I want to be certain I explain both the features of this edition and my hopes for it.

Readers familiar with the first two editions of *Concepts and Theories* will find much that is familiar to them in this edition. The emphasis remains on philosophical and historical bases of the key conceptual issues in the field, the centrality of the nature–nurture issue, the importance of understanding the dynamics between continuity and discontinuity across the life span, the ways in which stances on the nature–nurture and continuity-discontinuity issues frame theories of human development, and on the associations among philosophy, concepts, theories, methods, and applications of developmental science. In addition, I believe my own theoretical position has evolved. I have come to understand that the theoretical approach I use to frame my own research, developmental contextualism, is an instance of a broader set of dynamic, person–context relational models termed *developmental systems theory*. Nevertheless, my theoretical viewpoint is still very much the same one I presented in the second edition.

However, the field of human development, as well as I, have progressed in the past 15 years. Developmental systems theories have taken center stage in contemporary developmental science and have provided compelling alternatives to reductionistic theoretical accounts having either a nature or a nurture emphasis. Moreover, at this writing, developmental systems models serve as productive bases for innovation in developmental methodology and for important applications aimed at promoting positive individual development across the life span and strengthening family and community contexts.

I have sought to reflect this current status of the field in the third edition of *Concepts and Theories*. To accomplish this, I have expanded the book substantially in comparison to the second edition.

Prior chapters have been significantly rewritten and new chapters have been added.

For example, as in the second edition, there are separate chapters on definitional issues pertinent to the nature–nurture issue, the continuity–discontinuity issue, and the contributions of T. C. Schneirla. As before, there are also separate chapters on stage theories, and the differential and ipsative approaches to the conceptualization and study of human development. However, the present edition now includes a separate chapter on the historical roots of concepts and theories of human development, philosophical models of development, and developmental contextualism. In addition, two new chapters surround the discussion of developmental contextualism, one on developmental systems theories, wherein several exemplars of such models are discussed and, in turn, a corresponding chapter wherein key instances of such theories—life-span, life-course, bioecological, and action theoretical theories—are presented. Moreover, another new chapter, on cognition and development, contrasts developmental systems' approaches to cognitive development with neo-nativist perspectives.

Similarly, a more differentiated treatment of nature-oriented theories of development is present in this edition. There are separate chapters on behavior genetics, the controversy surrounding the study of the heritability of intelligence, and the work on instincts by Konrad Lorenz. In addition, a new chapter on sociobiology is included in this edition.

Finally, as in other editions, a chapter on methodological issues is included. However, a new chapter of the application of developmental science has been added.

If this edition of *Concepts and Theories* is successful, it will accomplish four things. First, it will convince readers that the concepts and theories involved in the study of human development are vital, rich, and of great importance for scholarship and society. The concepts and theories one uses in the study of human development frame both science and the application of that science for public policy and social programs.

My second and third hopes pertain specifically to developmental systems theories. I hope that readers will be persuaded that such approaches to theory and research are the most conceptually sound and empirically productive means through which to conduct developmental science. In turn, and as I note at the end of the book, I hope that this volume will serve to underscore the oft-quoted observation of Kurt Lewin (1943), that there is nothing as practical as a good theory.

At this writing, I believe that the need has never been greater in history for an approach to developmental science that can significantly enhance the life chances of the world's diverse infants, children, adolescents, and adults across their life spans. I believe that such an application of developmental scholarship may best be pursued through work associated with developmental systems theories. More than just wanting to underscore the importance of concepts and theories in general for society, my hope is that this book will contribute to the use of developmental systems theories in such efforts.

My fourth hope is personal. Over the course of my career, I have had the great good fortune and privilege to profit from the intellectual stimulation, guidance, support, and collegiality of numerous colleagues and former and current students. I have also had the gift of a loving and supportive family. I hope that all of these colleagues, friends, and loved ones will be pleased by my certain belief that their contributions enabled this book to be written.

To offer appropriate thanks to all the people who shaped this book, and my work that enabled it, would significantly extend an already quite long volume. However, I believe I must take this opportunity to thank several of these colleagues specifically because of their direct involvement with this edition of the book. Five colleagues—Gerald Adams, Gilbert Gottlieb, Jerry Hirsch, Lawrence Schiamberg, and Gwendolyn T. Sorell—read all or most of the manuscript for this edition. Their tremendous efforts and their always sage comments and suggestions are deeply valued. They improved the volume enormousbly.

William Damon influenced enormously my ability to write this book. The opportunity he gave me to join him in editing Volume 1 of the fifth edition (1998) of the *Handbook of Child Psychology*, on "Theoretical models of human development," and the numerous conversations we had about the manuscripts that eventually comprised the chapters of the volume, were the professional and intellectual events that most significantly shaped my work on this edition of *Concepts and Theories*. I must add that the other members of the editorial team for the other volumes of the *Handbook*—Nancy Eisenberg, Deanna Kuhn, Robert Siegler, Irving Sigel, and Anne Renninger—as well as Paul Mussen, the Editor of the prior two editions of the *Handbook*, also were invaluable and stimulating colleagues.

In addition, it will be clear to any reader of this book that there are numerous colleagues whose scholarship shaped my own thinking enormously. Many of these colleagues contributed chapters to Volume 1 of the *Handbook* and/or collaborated with me in theoretical and empirical work that is reflected in this edition of *Concepts and Theories*. Chief among these wonderfully supportive and brilliant colleagues are: Paul B. Baltes, Margret Baltes, Joan Bergstrom, Jochen Brandtstädter, Gilbert Brim, Urie Bronfenbrenner, Peter Benson, Jack Block, Marc Bornstein, Jeanne Brooks-Gunn, Robert Cairns, Maya Carlson, Stella Chess, Thomas Chibucos, Anne Colby, Andrew Collins, Roger A. Dixon, Felton Earls, Ann Easterbrooks, Jacquelynne Eccles, Glen Elder, David Elkind, Doris Entwisle, David Featherman, David Henry Feldman, Marcus Feldman, Hiram Fitzgerald, Kurt Fischer, Celia Fisher, August Flammer, John Flavell, Donald T. Floyd, Donald Ford, Alexandra Freund, Cynthia Garcia Coll, Calvin Gidney, Arthur Goldberger, Gilbert Gottlieb, Stephen J. Gould, Gary Greenberg, Tilmann Habermas, John Hagen, Beatrix Hamburg, David Hamburg, Stephen Hamilton, Stuart T. Hauser, Penny Hauser-Cram, Jutta Heckhausen, Karen Hein, Donald Hernandez, E. Mavis Hetherington, Jerry Hirsch, Kathryn Hood, Frances Degen Horowitz, David Hultsch, Francine Jacobs, Jerome Kagan, Theodora Kalikow, Leon Kamin, Bernard Kaplan, Philip Kendall, Maureen Kenny, Sam J. Korn, Kurt Kreppner, Michael Lamb, David Layzer, Jacqueline V. Lerner, Michael Lewis, Richard C. Lewontin, Lynn S. Liben, Ulman Lindenberger, Lewis P. Lipsitt, Rick R. Little, Eleanor Maccoby, David Magnusson, Harriette McAdoo, Susan McHale, Marvin McKinney, Julia R. Miller, Jayanthi Mistry, John Modell, John Murray, Rolf Muuss, John R. Nesselroade, Gil Noam, Charles Ostrom, Willis Overton, David Palermo, Anne C. Petersen, Karen J. Pittman, Penny Ralston, Hayne W. Reese, Barbara Rogoff, Fred Rothbaum, Sandra Scarr, George Scarlett, Robert Selman, Lonnie R. Sherrod, Coby Simerly, Linda Smith, Rainer Silbereisen, Lou Anna Simon, Michael A. Smyer, Gwendolyn T. Sorell, Elizabeth Sparks, Graham B. Spanier, Margaret Spencer, Ursula Staudinger, Lawrence Steinberg, Stephen Suomi, Ruby Takanishi, Carl S. Taylor, Esther Thelen, Alexander Thomas, Linda S. Thompson, Ethel Tobach, Francisco A. Villarruel, Alexander von Eye, Fred Von-dracek, James Votruba, Douglas Wahlsten, Mary Walsh, Seymour Wapner, Richard A. Weinberg, Donald Wertlieb, Wendy Wheeler, Sheldon White, Ellen Winner, Joachim Wohlwill, Maryanne Wolf, and Robert Zucker.

I want to acknowledge also the enormous support of my colleagues in the Eliot-Pearson Department of Child Development at Tufts University. Their collegiality, stimulation, and encouragement were critical contributions to my efforts in writing this book. I also want to note my great appreciation for the superb contributions of my current graduate students (Pamela Anderson, Cathrine Barton, Tamara Bates, Aida Bilalbegovic, Deborah Bobek, Shireen Boulos, Jana Chaudhuri, Imma De Stefanis, Elizabeth Dowling, Kimberly Howard, Susanna Lara Roth, and Nicole Simi) and support staff (Lisa Marie DiFonzo and Holly Maynard). I have been fortunate over the years to have graduate students who stimulated and challenged me, and who enabled my thinking and scholarship to advance substantially. Many of those individuals who were students when the second edition appeared are now accomplished professors and professionals at the publication of the third edition: Nancy Busch-Rossnagel, Domini Castellino, Roger Dixon, Patricia East, Melissa Freel, Nancy Galambos, Laura Hess, Karen Hooker, Lauren Jaconson, Jasna Jovanovic, Margie Lachman, Kathleen Lenerz, Laurie McCubbin, Patricia Mulkeen, Kathleen Nitz, Christine Ohannessian, Daniel Perkins, Jacqueline Schwab, Carol Ryff, John Schulenberg, Judy Shea, Gwendolyn T. Sorell, Ron Spiro, Jonathan Tubman, and Michael Windle. I

am grateful for all of their continuing collegiality, collaboration, and friendship over the years.

I am grateful to the publisher of the third edition, Lawrence Erlbaum Associates, for all the professionalism and quality efforts made on behalf of the book. In particular, I would like to thank the two editors who helped me over the course of the development of this edition, Judi Amsel and Bill Webber. Their support and enthusiastic collaboration were essential and greatly appreciated. I also greatly appreciate the superb work of Donna King, who expertly guided the production of this edition. I want to express my special thanks to Larry Erlbaum. We first met at about the time the first edition of this book went into production. In the quarter century in which we have worked together—on this book, more than a dozen others, and two journals—Larry's friendship, generosity, great humor, sense of perspective, commitment to quality, wisdom and—most of all—humaneness have been remarkable gifts to me and hundreds of other scholars.

As at the close of the Preface of the Second Edition of *Concepts and Theories*, I express my deep gratitude to my wife, Jacqueline, and our children—Justin, Blair, and Jarrett—not only for their support and affection but also for their forbearance during the hours I spent writing this book. For a person of words, it is only accurate to say there are not ones sufficient to express all my love for them.

R.M.L.
Medford, Massachusetts
June 2001

PREFACE to the Second Edition

Ten years have passed since the publication of the first edition of *Concepts and Theories of Human Development*. During that time, there has been considerable activity among developmentalists in regard to the philosophical, conceptual, and theoretical issues pertinent to human development. Although the basic organization and orientation of the second edition of *Concepts and Theories of Human Development* remain consistent with those found in the first edition, the revision has profited immensely from the literature of the last decade.

The goals of the book remain the same: to discuss the philosophical and historical bases of the key ideas found in the study of human development; to indicate how these bases relate to the core conceptual issues of development—the nature–nurture controversy, the continuity–discontinuity issue, and the issue of stability–instability in development; to discuss how these issues influence the formulation of different theories of development; to present overviews of instances of the major types of developmental theories, in order to indicate the links among philosophy, concepts, theory, and research; to evaluate research associated with different theories of development in order to appraise the usefulness of a given theory and the soundness of its stance on core issues of development; and to discuss the implications of philosophy, concepts, and theory for the research methods and research designs employed in the study of human development.

Moreover, my orientation toward these presentations remains the same. In both editions, it is clear that I favor an approach to development which in the first edition was labeled organismic-interactional, or probabilistic-epigenetic, and which in the second edition is additionally denoted by such terms as organismic-contextual and developmental-contextual.

The introduction of these new terms may suggest that my thinking has evolved. I hope that it has, and that the changes are evident in the second edition.

In the ten years since the publication of the first edition, I have spent considerable time thinking and writing: about the usefulness of a contextual philosophy for developmental theory; about the nature of developmental processes across the life span; and about the usefulness of the life span view of human development as a general orientation in trying to understand the character of developmental processes and the relations between individuals and contexts that may underlie these processes. These interests are reflected throughout the second edition, and have led to broadened discussions of:

- the philosophical and historical bases of the study of human development (Chapters 1 and 2);

- the nature–nurture controversy (Chapter 3), its manifestation in the debate about the heritability of intelligence and of racial differences in IQ (Chapter 4), and its possible "resolution" in regard to developmental theory through the adoption of a probabilistic-epigenetic, or developmental-contextual, orientation (Chapter 5);

- the continuity–discontinuity issue, its relationship to the issue of stability–instability in development, and the issue of the nature of plasticity across the life span (Chapter 6);

- the character of the different theoretical approaches to development, and their relationship to the key conceptual issues of development (Chapter 7);

- major instances of stage theories (Chapter 8), of differential approaches (Chapter 9), of ipsative approaches (Chapter 10), and of empirical- or theoretical behavioristic approaches (Chapter 11), and an evaluation of empirical literatures associated with each; and

- the implications of philosophy, concepts, and theory for developmental research methodology and design, and some of the key features, problems, and potentials of developmental research methods (Chapter 12).

The useful expansions of and changes in my thinking that are reflected in the second edition derive from the contributions to the literature made by many colleagues. Their writings and their discussions with me not only have helped me grow intellectually but also have set a standard of excellence to which I can only aspire. Thus, I am deeply grateful to: Margaret M. Baltes, Paul B. Baltes, Albert Bandura, Jack Block, Sandor B. Brent, Orville G. Brim, Jr., Urie Bronfenbrenner, Jeanne Brooks-Gunn, Nancy Busch-Rossnagel, Stella Chess, Anne Colby, W. Edward Craighead, Roger A. Dixon, Sanford Dornbusch, Judith Dunn, Glen H. Elder, Jr., David L. Featherman, Nancy L. Galambos, Arthur S. Goldberger, Eugene Gollin, Gilbert Gottlieb, William T. Greenough, Ruth T. Gross, Norma G. Haan, Beatrix A. Hamburg, Sara Harkness, Willard W. Hartup, Christopher Hertzog, E. Mavis Hetherington, Jerry Hirsch, Karen Hooker, David F. Hultsch, Saburo Iwawaki, Jerome Kagan, Bernard Kaplan, Philip C. Kendall, John R. Knapp, Sam J. Korn, Gisela Labouvie-Vief, Michael E. Lamb, P. Herbert Leiderman, Jacqueline V. Lerner, Michael Lewis, Lynn S. Liben, Gardner Lindzey, Lewis P. Lipsitt, David Magnusson, Gerald E. McClearn, Harry McGurk, Susan M. McHale, John A. Meacham, John W. Meyer, Dale T. Miller, Walter Mischel, Paul H. Mussen, John R. Nesselroade, Willis F. Overton, David S. Palermo, Ross D. Parke, Marion Perlmutter, Anne C. Petersen, Robert Plomin, Hayne W. Reese, M. Bernadette Reidy, Klaus F. Riegel, Matilda W. Riley, Carol D. Ryff, Sandra Scarr, K. Warner Schaie, Ellin K. Scholnick, Martin E. P. Seligman, Virginia S. Sexton, Lonnie Sherrod, Alexander W. Siegel, Ellen Skinner, M. Brewster Smith, Gwendolyn T. Sorell, Graham B. Spanier, Laurence D. Steinberg, Charles Super, Alexander Thomas, Ethel Tobach, Fred W. Vondracek, Alexander von Eye, Franz E. Weinert, Sheldon H. White, Sherry Willis, Michael Windle, and Joachim Wohlwill.

I also wish to thank my excellent graduate students, who were always ready to read and discuss my drafts and always capable of pointing out places where my writing—and my thinking—could be improved. I thank for all their help: Athena Droogas, Patricia L. East, Wendy Gamble, Marjorie B. Kauffman, Joseph S. Kucher, and Kathleen Lenerz. I am grateful to Joy Barger, Teresa Charmbury, and Kathleen Hooven for their expert and professional secretarial assistance. I thank Colleen Kearns and Leslie Parkes for their help in compiling the references and indices.

Finally, during the long gestation period for this second edition, I have been fortunate to receive the support of several institutions. I began planning and writing the second edition while I was a 1980–1981 Fellow at the Center for Advanced Study in the Behavioral Sciences. I am grateful for financial support provided by National Institute of Mental Health Grant #5-T32-MH14581-05 and by the John D. and Catherine T. MacArthur Foundation, and for the assistance of the center's staff. Since leaving the center and through this writing, my work has been funded in part by grants from the John D. and Catherine T. MacArthur Foundation and from the William T. Grant Foundation, and I am grateful for this support. I completed the writing of the second edition during the 1983–1984 academic year, which I began as a Visiting Scientist at the Max-Planck Institute for Human Development and Education in Berlin, and which I ended by being once again in residence, throughout the summer, at the Center for Advanced Study in the Behavioral Sciences. I appreciate greatly the support for my work provided by both institutions.

Finally, the institution to which I owe my greatest debt is my family. From Jacqueline Lerner and our children, Justin and Blair, I received all the emotional support and the diversions I needed to keep returning to my task until it was completed.

R.M.L.
University Park, Pennsylvania
September 1985

PREFACE to the First Edition

In this text, I have attempted to provide the student with a general introduction to core concepts and major theories in developmental psychology. An integration is made of such concepts and theories, along with their philosophical bases, within a framework that presents divergent points of view about these ideas. However, the Organismic, Interactionist developmental viewpoint is clearly given major emphasis. While discussions of the views and research of learning-oriented developmentalists, for example, are presented and evaluated, as is the work of particular ethological writers, these positions are contrasted with the Organismic developmental notions of such theorists as Piaget, Werner, Schneirla, Kohlberg, and Thomas. The work of these latter theorists is representative of an orientation to developmental psychology which is viewed as being the most tenable and useful conceptual synthesis currently available. In essence then, the text attempts to integrate and evaluate core concepts, major theories, and research in developmental psychology from an Organismic, Interactionist perspective.

The format of this text stands in contrast to most other human development texts which primarily emphasize research findings. Of course, I believe that such "facts" are necessary for students. But the meaning of such information, and indeed what we actually consider to be factual, is constantly altered in the face of empirical advances and new theoretical integrations. Hence, I believe that students will appreciate and assimilate the facts of development if they are acquainted with the "meanings" attached to these facts by developmental psychologists. For this reason, and because of historical trends within the field which have now come to stress the primacy of theoretical integration, I have written this book to emphasize such integrations. Students are still given "facts," but first they are given some bases for interpreting the possible "meanings" of these facts.

Three interrelated bases for understanding human development are offered. First, the Mechanistic and the Organismic philosophies of science are shown to provide both contrasting views

of "humans" and alternative approaches to the major conceptual issues of psychological development. Second, various ways of formulating these issues (the nature-nurture and the continuity–discontinuity controversies) are discussed, and recent empirical research and debate about them are evaluated. For instance, the relevance of the nature–nurture controversy to concerns about the sources of racial differences in IQ scores is indicated. Similarly, the relation between the continuity–discontinuity issue and debates about the ontogenetic (and phylogenetic) generalizability of laws of learning and of life-span changes in intellectual functioning is discussed. Finally, ways are described in which the core conceptual issues of development may provide a basis for understanding the formulation of the major types of theoretical points of view in developmental psychology. The Stage, Differential, Ipsative, and Learning approaches are discussed, and major theories and research within each approach are introduced. Thus, the Stage approaches of Piaget, Kohlberg, and Freud, the Differential theoretical formulations of Erikson, the differential empirical work of Kagan and Moss, and the life-span, multivariate, sequential research approaches of Schaie, Baltes, and Nesselroade are presented. In addition, the Ipsative research, involved in the New York Longitudinal Study, of Thomas, Chess, Birch, Hertzig, and Korn, and the Learning-oriented work of Bijou and Baer and of Mischel are evaluated. Finally, the interrelation of developmental theory and research is presented along with a discussion of its social relevance.

While it is of course possible to provide the student with an integration of theory and fact by combining numerous readings and lecture materials, such a combination would not provide the student with what I consider to be a major asset of this book, which is the organization and integration of this material within what I hope is a convincing and useful framework from which to understand human development. This Organismic, Interactionist point of view, interrelated with its conceptual alternatives, permits an introduction to the study of developmental psychology that is, in my opinion, both pedagogically appropriate and more closely aligned with current emphases in the discipline than is any other single treatment.

During the course of writing the text, my ideas have been challenged and honed by the numerous colleagues with whom I have discussed the material and who have read various portions of several drafts of the book. Specifically, I would like to thank John Knapp, Joseph Fitzgerald, Samuel Karson, Henry Orloff, and Stuart Karabenick, all of Eastern Michigan University, and the many reviewers provided by the publisher. In addition, I am in great debt to the people who provided my training: Harry Beilin, Samuel Messick, Joseph Church, Elizabeth Gellert, and of course, Sam Korn. The diverse contributions of these people have sharpened my ideas, strengthened my arguments, and improved my presentation. Any limitations that remain stem totally from me. I am also grateful to Cathy Gendron for her excellent drawings of psychologists. I am also indebted to the hundreds of students who have listened semester after semester to lectures that attempted to present the material contained in this book and who have read and used various drafts of this book as their course text. Here I would especially like to thank Michael Karson for his thorough work and useful criticisms. My students' enthusiasm, comments, and interactions with me—and likewise the lack of these things—have led to substantial alterations in the format and style of presentation of various text sections.

R.M.L.
Ypsilanti, Michigan
January 1976

About the Author

Richard M. Lerner is the Bergstrom Chair in Applied Developmental Science at Tufts University. A developmental psychologist, Lerner received a Ph.D. in 1971 from the City University of New York. He has been a fellow at the Center for Advanced Study in the Behavioral Sciences and is a fellow of the American Association for the Advancement of Science, the American Psychological Association, and the American Psychological Society. Prior to joining Tufts University, he was on the faculty and held administrative posts at Michigan State University, Pennsylvania State University, and Boston College, where he was the Anita L. Brennan Professor of Education and the Director of the Center for Child, Family, and Community Partnerships. During the 1994–1995 academic year, Lerner held the Tyner Eminent Scholar Chair in the Human Sciences at Florida State University. Lerner is the author or editor of 42 books and more than 280 scholarly articles and chapters. He edited Volume 1, on "Theoretical models of human development," for the fifth edition of the *Handbook of Child Psychology*. He is the founding editor of the *Journal of Research on Adolescence* and of the journal, *Applied Developmental Science*. He is known for his theory of, and research about, relations between life-span human development and contextual or ecological change. He has done foundational studies of adolescents' relations with their peer, family, school, and community contexts, and is a leader in the study of public policies and community-based programs aimed at the promotion of positive youth development.

Concepts
and Theories
of Human
Development

1 | *Human Development: Facts or Theory?*

STUDENTS AND BASIC COURSES IN SCIENCE: FACTS VERSUS THEORY

Well, I've learned a lot of facts, but what do they all *mean?*

A typical comment from a college student? I believe so. Many students believe that college professors are only concerned with fact memorization. It is generally believed by students and professors alike that facts (perhaps crammed into one's head the night before an exam) are soon forgotten. On the other hand, general concepts are retained for a much longer time. Still, many basic college courses require the student to memorize a lot of facts.

With today's explosion of scientific research, there certainly are more facts to know than ever before. Thus, to get an overview of a field like child or human development, a student must become acquainted with such information. Therefore, as more and more data are collected each year, rapid clarifications, refinements, and advancements are made in factual knowledge (Ghiselli, 1974).

Examples of the Impermanence of Psychological "Facts"

There are many examples of the idea that what is considered factual—in the sense of being permanent, immutable, or universal—may be ephemeral or, at least, substantially modifiable as a consequence of new information being obtained. Some of the examples of this point are derived from what has become classic research in human development.

The Visual World of the Newborn

For instance, before the work of Fantz and colleagues (e.g., Fantz, 1958; Fantz, Ordy, & Udelf, 1962), it was believed that a newborn infant's visual world was comprised of blurry images, ei-

ther due to incomplete maturation of the visual system or too few appropriate visual experiences.

However, Fantz was able to demonstrate that, even in the first few weeks of life, infants are capable of accommodating to nearby visual stimulation and also to seeing patterns. Thus, the "fact" that infants could only see diffuse light-and-dark stimulation was found not to be a fact at all. Through use of the methods he devised, Fantz was able to clarify, refine, and advance our factual knowledge of infants' visual perception.

Intellectual Changes and Aging

Similarly, other such "facts" of psychological development have fallen by the wayside in the face of new research findings. For instance, for many decades a basic belief about intellectual development concerned the decreases in functions that were assumed to characterize the later years of life. It was held that, as people progressed through adulthood to old age, there was an accelerating decline in their mental functioning (e.g., see Horn, 1970; Schaie, Labouvie, & Buech, 1973). These decrements were supposed to represent a certain "fact" of psychological development and functioning across the life span as shown by the data in Figure 1.1.

New techniques for the measurement of age changes in intellectual development and functioning across the life-span were devised through the work of K. Warner Schaie, Paul B. Baltes, and colleagues (e.g., Baltes, Dittmann-Kohli, & Dixon, 1984; Baltes & Schaie, 1974; Nesselroade, Schaie, & Baltes, 1972; Schaie, 1965; Schaie, Labouvie, & Buech, 1973; Schaie & Strother, 1968). The application of these techniques in several studies indicates that there may not be a general decline in intellectual functioning throughout the later years after all. Rather, the results of some of these studies (e.g., Baltes, Lindenberger, & Staudinger, 1998; Baltes, Staudinger, & Lindenberger, 1999; Schaie, Labouvie, & Buech, 1973) indicated that for *some*

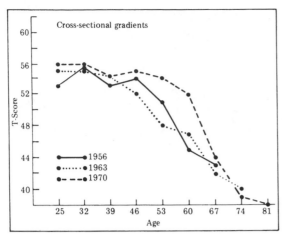

FIGURE 1.1

Age changes in intellectual ability, as revealed by conventional, cross-sectional research techniques. Note the *decreases* in intellectual ability that occur with increases in age.

Source: K. W. Schaie, G. B. Labouvie, and B. U. Buech (1973). Generational and cohort-specific differences in adult cognitive functioning: A fourteen-year study of independent samples, *Developmental Psychology* 9. Copyright © 1973 by the American Psychological Association. Reprinted by permission.

measures of intellectual functioning there is no age-associated decrease. In fact, for some measures, there seems to be an increase.

K. Warner Schaie

In 1956, Schaie (Baltes & Schaie, 1974; Schaie, 1965; Schaie & Strother, 1968) began to study 500 people ranging in age from 21 (young adulthood) to 70 (the aged years). He administered two tests of cognitive ability, the Thurstone and Thurstone Primary Mental Abilities Test and Schaie's Test of Behavioral Rigidity. Seven years later, 301 of the people were retested with the same instruments. Using such statistical techniques as factor analysis, Schaie and his colleagues found that four different types of cognitive abilities were being assessed by these tests:

1. *Crystallized intelligence,* which measures knowledge attained through education and socialization (e.g., verbal comprehension and number skills). This is the type of intelligence measured by most traditional tests (Baltes & Schaie, 1974).

2. *Cognitive flexibility,* which measures the ability to shift from one way of thinking to another.

3. *Visual-motor flexibility,* which measures a similar shifting ability, but in tasks requiring a coordination between visual and muscular movements.

4. *Visualization,* which measures the ability to organize and process visual information.

Schaie found that, depending on how his data were analyzed, differential support was found for the presence of intellectual decline. Specifically, when he analyzed his data in accordance with the requirements of a specific type of research design, less evidence was found for decline.

There are two frequently used ways to design research pertinent to the measurement of development. Cross-sectional studies measure different age groups of people (e.g., 5-, 10-, and 15-year-olds) at one point in time (e.g., in 1995). In longitudinal studies, a group of people all born at one point in time (e.g., in 1980) are measured at different points in time (e.g., in 1985, 1990, and 1995, when they are 5, 10, and 15 years old respectively).

Thus, both techniques give information about how people of a particular age perform at a given point in time. However, the two procedures make different use of *birth cohorts.* A *cohort* is a group of people who have commonly experienced a particular event. For instance, a birth cohort is a group of people who share a common time of birth (e.g., the same year). In cross-sectional studies, people from groups born in different years (i.e., from different birth cohorts) are studied. In longitudinal studies, people from the same birth cohort (i.e., people born in the same year) are studied.

A third type of design for developmental research was developed by Schaie, Baltes, and Nesselroade (Baltes, 1968; Nesselroade & Baltes, 1974; Nesselroade, Schaie, & Baltes, 1972; Schaie, 1965; Schaie & Strother, 1968). This type of design is termed *sequential,* and it combines both cross-sectional and longitudinal components. For example, in one instance of a longitudinal sequential design, a cross section of people (i.e., people from different birth cohorts) is longitudinally (repeatedly) studied over the course of several times of measurement.

When Schaie and his colleagues analyzed their data cross-sectionally, they saw the adolescent-to-adulthood decline typically seen in such studies. However, when they looked at the longitudinal data within each of the birth cohort groups in their sequential design, they found a decline on only one of the four measures (visual-motor flexibility). In fact, for the mental abilities most linked to high-level intellectual functioning—those involved in crystallized intelligence (Baltes & Schaie, 1974) and visualization—a systematic *increase* in scores for all age groups was seen. Even those people over 70 years of age improved from the first testing to the second. Thus, as seen in Figure 1.2, older people scored lower than younger people on the four measures of intelligence in both 1956 and 1963.

However, for both crystallized intelligence and visualization, scores increased between these two times of testing, even for the older groups.

Similarly, data from a study by Schaie, Labouvie, and Buech (1973) show that many scores increase when members of the same cohort are tested at succeeding times. Yet, if these within-cohort curves are not analyzed and only cross-sectional curves are considered, the typical adolescent-to-adult decline will be seen. The graphs in Figure 1.3 illustrate these findings.

The course of intellectual change from young adulthood onward is clearly not just an age-related phenomenon. The aforementioned data indicate that differences in scores and patterns of change in scores from one time of measurement to another are mainly associated with membership in different birth cohort groups. In other words, how well a person performed at any one time, and whether that performance was stable, was associated more with cohort differences than with chronological age. It also appears that, as far as the absolute level of ability scores is concerned, the measured intelligence of the general population is increasing across history. Perhaps because of better educational techniques that are more geared at the cognitive attributes current tests measure, members of younger birth cohorts are

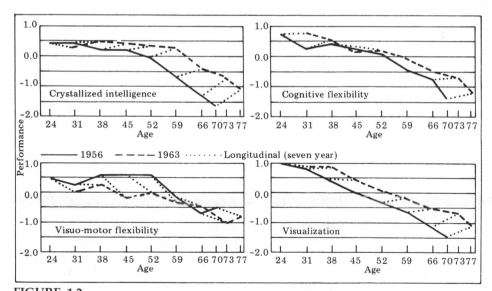

FIGURE 1.2

Age, time, and cohort components of change for four types of cognitive abilities: The solid lines slope downward, indicating that in 1956 and 1963 older people scored lower than younger ones on various dimensions of intelligence. However, the dashed lines, which show how a given age group's performance changed from the first test to the second, reveal that in older groups crystallized intelligence and visualization go up, not down.

Source: Adapted from Baltes and Schaie (1974).

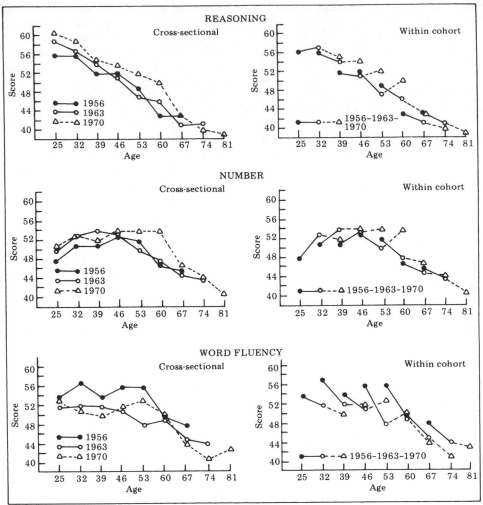

FIGURE 1.3

Cross-sectional (*left*) and within-cohort sequential (*right*) curves for scores on ability tests for reasoning, number, and word fluency, respectively.

Source: Adapted from Schaie, Labouvie, and Buech (1973).

more likely to achieve higher absolute scores than are members of older birth cohorts.

Today's young adults not only have a higher level of cognitive ability than members of older birth cohorts (as measured by tests such as those used by Schaie, Baltes, Nesselroade, Labouvie, and colleagues), but they are also, as is the case with members of all cohorts, likely to maintain much of this level of functioning across their life-span (Baltes et al., 1998, 1999). On the basis of findings from sequential studies, one may expect that many of the levels and types of ability present in earlier life will be maintained or enhanced in the adult and aged years. In short, through the application of innovative measurement designs, Schaie and associates were able to demonstrate

that a long-held "fact" about cognitive development across the human life-span was not a fact after all. Moreover, research by Baltes, Dittmann-Kohli, and Dixon (1984), Baltes and Kliegl (1992), and Baltes and Willis (1982) further indicated that even if intellectual decline is seen in the aged, it does not represent an unchangeable feature of their functioning. Baltes and Willis (1992) devised several training techniques intended to enhance the intellectual functioning of aged people (i.e., people in their seventh and eighth decades of life). These techniques were successful in increasing aged people's performance on intelligence tests, both immediately and in relatively long-term (several months) follow-up tests.

Adolescents and the Universal Experience of "Storm and Stress"

There are numerous other examples that illustrate the impermanence of "facts." For instance, the idea that adolescence is a developmental period invariably characterized by storm and stress is found both in scientific accounts of the period (Davis, 1944; Freud, 1969; Hall, 1904; McCandless, 1970) and in the popular media. Many writers have romanticized or dramatized the adolescent experience in novels, short stories, or news articles. It is commonplace to survey a newsstand and find a magazine article describing the stormy years of adolescence, the new crazes or fads of youth, or the explosion of problems with teenagers such as crime or sexuality. In addition, many people hold a stereotype about adolescence (Anthony, 1969) that suggests, because of the supposed rebelliousness and close contact of adolescents with their friends, parents must be more controlling and restrictive of their children during this time.

However, over the course of the three to four decades when medical, biological, and social scientists began to study the adolescent period intensively, sound scientific information that countered these romantic characterizations of adolescence as inevitably and universally stormy and stressful began to accumulate (Laursen, 1995; Lerner & Galambos, 1998; Petersen, 1988). This research demonstrated that youth undergo many different types of changes throughout the adolescent years. Although some youth do experience personal and interpersonal storm and stress, such young people represent only a small minority of adolescents. While there are problems of life associated with all developmental periods, adolescence is not an especially problematic period for the majority of young people. Moreover, the research shows that although adolescents do spend more time with their friends than with their parents, most youth have healthy relationships with their parents and continue to be positively influenced by their parents (e.g., in regard to their goals for education and employment).

Bandura (1964) observed that, by adolescence, most children had so thoroughly adopted parental values and standards that parental restrictions were actually reduced. In addition, Bandura noted that although the storm and stress idea of adolescence implies a struggle by youth to free themselves of dependence on parents, parents begin to train their children in childhood to be *independent*. Finally, Bandura found that adolescents' choice of friends was not a major source of friction between adolescents and parents. Adolescents tended to form friendships with those who shared similar

Albert Bandura

values. As such, the peers tended to support those standards of the parents that had already been adopted by the adolescents.

Bandura pointed out, however, that these observations do not mean that adolescence is a stressless, problemless period of life. He was careful to note that *no* period of life is free of crisis or adjustment problems, and that any period of life may present particular adjustment problems for some people and not for others. Thus, one has to be careful about generalizing problems seen in one group of adolescents to all adolescents. Bandura, in a portion of his study, observed a sample of antisocial boys. Their excessive aggression did lead to their adolescence being associated with storm and stress. However, Bandura found that one could not appropriately view their problems as solely resulting from adolescence. Their problem behaviors had been present throughout their childhood. However, when the boys were physically smaller, their parents were able to control the boys' aggressive behavior better than they could during adolescence.

From Bandura's study, it may be concluded that:

1. Even when storm and stress is seen in adolescence, it is not necessarily the result of events in adolescence but may instead be associated with developments prior to adolescence.

2. Storm and stress is not necessarily characteristic of the adolescent period—many possible types of adolescent development can occur.

The existence of such different paths through adolescence is supported by the results of other studies.

Offer (1969) found three major routes through the adolescent period. He noted that there is a *continuous growth* type of development involving smooth changes in behavior. Adolescents showing such development were not in any major conflict with their parents and did not feel that parental rearing practices were inappropriate or that they themselves did not share parental values. Most adolescents fell into this category. Such a pattern is like the one described by Bandura. A second type of pattern is *surgent growth,* with development involving an abrupt change without the turmoil associated with storm and stress. Finally, however, Offer identified a *tumultuous growth* type of adolescent development. Here, crisis, stress, and problems characterize the period, and for such adolescents, storm and stress aptly characterizes the nature of their change.

Thus, the adolescent period is only characterized by storm and stress for some people. Based on the Bandura and Offer studies, it may be assumed that only a minority of adolescents experience such a tumultuous period. This conclusion is supported by the data of Douvan and Adelson (1966). In their study, as in the previously noted studies, most adolescents shared the basic values of their parents and were satisfied with their family life and the style of treatment by their parents. We may see, then, that available data are inconsistent with the stereotype that adolescence is a *generally* stressful and stormy period.

Conclusions: From Facts to Theory

The data provided from studies of infant perception, adolescent personality and social development, and intellectual changes in the adult and aged years allow us to recognize that, in an active science such as human development, the status of our knowledge will rapidly and continually be altered. It is possible—perhaps even likely—that what is a "fact" when a particular student begins a basic college course may no longer be a "fact" by the end of the course.

I do not simply intend to be irreverent about the role of facts in science. Facts are absolutely essential in any active scientific enterprise. But, to paraphrase Ludwig von Bertalanffy (1933), a biologist noted for his theoretical contributions to that science, "A collection of data no more makes a science than does a heap of bricks make a house!"

What, then, builds the bricks of a science into a house? I believe it is the conceptual and theoretical issues of a science. Certainly the listings in a telephone directory are facts. But a knowledge of the names in the phone book would certainly be, to quote singer–songwriter Bob Dylan (1964), "useless and pointless knowledge." However, if one could relate such data to some conceptual framework, then perhaps some meaning could be provided.

Let us suppose that I have a hypothesis, perhaps derived from some theory in social psychology, that predicts that a person with a particular ethnic background would tend to live in a neighborhood with other people having that same ethnic background. To test my hypothesis, I spread out a large street map of the city and cut out each name and address in the phone book and place it on the appropriate place on the map. After a while, a pattern begins to emerge. People with Italian names seem to cluster in one area, people with Irish names in another area, and people with Jewish names in yet another area. This example not only supports the hypothesis, but also illustrates the point that a conceptual orientation provides a way of organizing a seemingly meaningless or obscure body of data into a meaningful and perhaps, important body of factual knowledge.

A major function of theory is to integrate existing facts; to organize them in such a way as to give them meaning. A second function of theory is to provide a framework for the generation of new information. A theory may be defined as a system of statements that integrate existing information and lead to the generation of new information.

Human development scientists may often have numerous facts available to them (e.g., facts relating to children's thinking at various ages). The results of empirical studies might indicate that young children tend to use relatively general, global, and concrete categories to organize their thinking, but older children use more differentiated, specific, and abstract categories. For instance, younger children might label all furry, four-legged creatures as "doggies," while older children might have different labels (e.g., "dogs," "cats," and "horses") and a shared, superordinate label ("animals"). Older children might also recognize that all these creatures share the common but abstract quality of "life." While such facts are interesting in and of themselves, their meaning is not obvious; certainly the implications of such facts for more general psychological development and functioning are not clear.

Thus, when a scientist such as Jean Piaget (1950, 1970) offers a theory of the development of thought that allows such facts to be integrated and understood, and, moreover, specifies the empirically testable implications of such theoretical integrations for other areas of psychological development, the importance is obvious. Such theories are useful to developmental psychology because they integrate existing factual knowledge and lead to the generation of new information that advances understanding.

The point is that although facts are important, they alone do not make a science. The development of science, I would argue, also relies on the advancement of theory. As a survey of the history of developmental psychology bears witness (Looft, 1972), the scientific study of human development has itself evolved through an increasing emphasis on theory and conceptual integration. In Chapter 2, we review this history and not only see the changing role of theory, but are also able to introduce many of the key concepts of human development (concepts we repeatedly discuss throughout this book). These concepts have had a long history of influence on thinking about human development. As we move in our historical account from the prescientific, philosophical discussions of development to today's current theoretical discussions, we see that issues pertinent to a few key concepts continue to be central.

Yet, although the scientific status of theory per se and the need for and roles of theory remain essentially invariant, across this history of developmental science, we cannot ignore research. If there were no research, theories would be empty exercises. If there were no way to test a given theoretical integration, the formulation would be scientifically useless. Although we discuss the role of research in developmental psychology at length in Chapter 18, as well as at other points throughout the book, it is appropriate to indicate here some of the important interrelations that exist between research and theory.

Research is often done to try to answer the questions raised by science. Such issue-based research results in data, as does all research. A theory may exist or be devised to integrate the facts of a science—the first role of a theory—and to lead to the generation of new facts—the second role of a theory. Someone, however, may think that these same facts can be integrated in another way—that is, with another theory. Theoretical arguments come about from such differences. Yet, because each different theory attaches different meanings to the same facts, research is done in order to clarify the differing theoretical interpretations. Even if such theoretical differences did not exist, research would be done to see whether ideas (i.e., hypotheses) derived from the theory could be shown to be empirically supported. In either case, research is needed to show the integrative usefulness of a theory or its usefulness in leading to new facts.

Thus, in the abstract, theory and research are inextricably bound; nevertheless, some concrete interrelational problems exist. Because of the complexity and abstractness of many of the controversies of a science, the interrelation of research and theoretical issues is not often evident or unequivocal. A common complaint of many people working in science is that there seems to be a widening gap between theory and research. Although there is some truth in this statement, I suggest that if one looks at the relation between research and theory at a more basic level, an interrelation may be seen.

PHILOSOPHY, THEORY, AND RESEARCH

Everything a scientist does depends on three points:

1. *Assumptions* about the nature of the subject matter.

2. Preferences for the *topic* of study within the subject matter.

3. Preferences for the *methods* of study.

Many psychologists are interested in studying how human behavior develops. If I assume, for purposes of illustration, that all behavioral development can be regarded as the acquisition of a series of responses, then I would look for the stimuli in a person's environment that evoke these responses. Consistent with Point 1, I would assume that even complex adult behaviors could be understood on the basis of these stimulation-produces–responding relationships, and that my job as a scientist would be to tease out the basic stimulus–response relations. Accordingly, and in terms of Point 2, the topics that my work would bear on could, perhaps, be best subsumed by the terms *learning* or, more precisely, *conditioning*. Moreover, as suggested by Point 3, the methods I would employ would be those involved with, for instance, classical or operant conditioning. I would probably prefer not to study topics such as "alterations in the balance among the id, ego, and superego in determining changes in the development of people's object relations" (e.g., Freud, 1954), or "the need for the development of a sense of trust in the first year of life in order for healthy personality development to proceed" (e.g., Erikson, 1959). The methods used to study these nonpreferred topics (e.g., clinical interviews and retrospective verbal reports) would not rank very high on my method preference list.

If someone asked me how my work related to general issues in psychological development, I would point out that all scientific research, no matter what topic it bears, is underlain by a particular philosophy of science or of *human beings*. One could ask where my assumption—that behavioral development can be viewed as the cumulative acquisition of responses—came from. Could other assumptions be made, for example, that there is something inborn (innate) in human beings that serves to shape their behavioral development? The answer is yes. The point here is that the particular assumptions I make are influenced by the philosophical views I hold about the nature of human development (e.g., Kagan, 1980, 1983; Kuhn, 1962; Overton & Reese, 1973; Pepper, 1942; Reese & Overton, 1970).

These assertions lead to a second response to the question of how my work is related to general conceptual issues in development. We have seen how research is underlain by theory and, more primarily, by a philosophy of science or humanity. Therefore, my work *would* be related to general conceptual issues in that it would lead to a determination of the tenability (the defensibility) of my position. As I continued to work from a particular point of view, I would eventually be able to see how well this viewpoint accounted for the phenomena of behavioral development. I would be able to see if my research, based as it is on an underlying philosophical premise, continued to account for these phenomena. For instance, was my theory useful? Did it lead to statements or hypotheses that helped explain substantial amounts of the differences among—the variance in—the scores constituting a particular set of data? Ultimately, I would learn whether the variables I was studying were capable of explaining behavioral development or whether other variables necessarily entered the picture.

I would learn whether the exclusive study of the functioning of environmentally based variables—stimuli and responses—can explain behavioral development. If I found this not to be the case—if I found, for example, that hereditary mechanisms seem to play a crucial role—I would be forced either to give up my initial philosophical/theoretical position and adopt another one or to revise my position so that it could account for the functioning of these other variables in terms consistent with my original philosophical/theoretical position.

In a third way, too, the outcome of my research can be seen to have general theoretical relevance. This third way, however, can be indirect, and its relevance to general issues or theory may not even be intended. Someone else might be able to use the facts that another researcher has found. To explain this third way more completely, let us consider some of the reasons a scientist might conduct a research study.

Some Reasons for Doing Research

The reason why particular scientists conduct particular studies may be idiosyncratic and, in general, diverse. However, three reasons illustrate the ways in which the outcomes of research can have conceptual relevance.

First, a person may be interested in illuminating some theoretical controversy. For instance, as previously discussed, there may be an observed phenomenon that is accounted for by two different theoretical positions. In adolescent development, for example, it is typically found that there is a marked increase in the importance (saliency) of the peer group. Why does this occur? Both Freud (1969) and Erikson (1968) have devised theories. Consistent with the work of her father, Anna Freud takes what is termed a *psychosexual* position and ties this occurrence primarily to a biological change in the person (i.e., the emergence of a genital drive). Erikson, however, diverges somewhat from strict psychoanalytic (i.e., Freudian) theory and explains it in what he terms a *psychosocial* position, by specifying some possible relations between the developing person and his or her society.

Which theory can best account for the empirical facts? This question constantly arises in the course of scientific inquiry. A clever researcher may be able to devise a study that would put the two different interpretations to a so-called *critical* or *crucial* test—a study whose results would provide support for one theoretical position and nonsupport for the other. If the results came out one way, Theory "A" would be supported; if they came out another way, Theory "B" would be supported.

It is important to note, however, that whether a scientist can perform a crucial test of two theories, or only of specific competing hypotheses derived from these theories, is *itself* a controversial issue. According to Hempel (1966), a philosopher of science, two hypotheses derived from two different theories can neither be proved nor disproved in any absolute sense. Hempel argues that this is true even if many tests of these two hypotheses are performed by the most sophisticated researchers using the most careful and extensive methods available to them, and even if all test outcomes result in completely favorable results for one hypothesis and completely unfavorable results for the other. Such results would not establish any absolute, conclusive validity for one hypothesis, but rather only relatively strong support for it. It is always possible that future tests of the two hypotheses would result in favorable outcomes for the previously unfavored hypothesis and in unfavorable outcomes for the previously favored one. In addition, it is also possible that if other hypotheses were derived from the two different theories, tests of these two new competing hypotheses would result in favorable outcomes for the theory that was not supported when the first set of derived hypotheses was tested. Thus, as Hempel argues, in an absolutely strict sense, a crucial test is impossible in science.

But the results of testing two competing theoretical positions may be "crucial" (and extremely useful) in a less strict sense. Results of tests of two rival positions can indicate that one theory is *relatively* untenable, while the other position is *relatively* tenable. This contrast may arise because the theories are found to be differentially useful in explaining (accounting for) the findings of research. For instance, *all* the differences among the scores (e.g., of children on a test of reading ability) in a particular set of data (e.g., the data derived from a study of 100 third-grade children) equal, by definition, 100% of the variance in a data set. One of two tested theories ("A") may account for substantially more (a greater proportion) of the variance (e.g., 55% as compared to 30%) in this data set, and this result means that in this case Theory "A" was more useful.

In other words, because tests of Theory "A" resulted in (more) favorable outcomes (i.e., more variance was accounted for), it is more tenable; it may be considered more *useful*. That is, the theory appears best able to account for existing facts. Because of the theory's demonstrated usefulness, it might play a more prominent role in any further work in the field. However, even if one construes crucial tests in a relatively unstrict way (i.e., in respect only to relative use), they are few and far between in human development. Still, they remain a potentially important and useful impetus for research.

A second reason for doing research is to test ideas (hypotheses) derived from a theory. Such deductions are made in order to see whether they can be empirically supported through research. Researchers would start by saying that if their theory is making appropriate statements, then certain things should necessarily be the case. Let us say, for example, that my theory is that, as children develop, the conceptual categories they can actively use to designate certain classes of things in their environment become more differentiated. For instance, returning to an earlier-used example, I might suspect that no matter what animal I showed a 2-year-old, the child would respond by saying "doggie" (or some equivalent term, such as "woof-woof"). I might also suspect that if I looked at a somewhat older child, say a 4- to 5-year-old, I would see the ability not only to correctly classify different animals (dogs, cats, and elephants) but also the ability to correctly classify different types of dogs (collies, German shepherds, and poodles). Thus, in accordance with my theory, I might hypothesize (predict) that as the children I study increase in age, their ability to correctly classify different animals will also increase. If my theory is defensible, my hypothesis, deduced from my theory, should be supported by the results of my study.

By testing deductions, researchers can provide support or refutation for their theory. Research based on such *deductive reasoning* is an important component of scientific thinking, and it will be discussed in further detail below.

However, I have said that there is a third way in which research can be found to be relevant to theory. Sometimes a researcher may conduct a study just to find out what exists. A person may have no theoretical issue in mind but may only be interested in describing the characteristics of a certain phenomenon or aspect of behavioral development, or in seeing what will be the behavioral result of a certain manipulation.

Let us say that a person works as a psychologist in a summer camp for children and adolescents and finds that there is a problem with some youth taking the possessions of another youth with whom they are sharing living quarters. Faced with such a problem, the psychologist might reason that, in order to design an effective strategy to prevent or reduce such behavior, it would be useful to know the reasons that the 5- through 15-year-old campers might give to explain why a person should not steal from friends. The psychologist might then ask groups of 5- and 15-year-old campers to give their reasons for not stealing from friends. The results might be that 5-year-olds' reasons seem to be rather concrete, reflecting a fear of punishment and an orientation toward obedience. A 5-year-old might say you should not steal because your friend will hit you or your camp counselor will punish you for doing something they say is wrong. The 15-year-old's reasons might be more abstract, reflecting the notion that stealing from a friend violates implicit rules of mutual trust and respect, or that as a member of society, one implicitly has to respect the rights of others. Researchers might find this result of such interest that they report it in some formal way (e.g., through a presentation at a professional meeting or in a journal article), and this adds additional facts to the literature of the science.

Although researchers may not intend to relate their facts to any theories, the theoretical relevance of the facts can be found after the research is done. In attempting to ascertain the validity of a particular theory, someone may be able to use the facts as a means to support that theory. Thus, the facts reported in the aforementioned example could, after their communication, be seen to fit into a theoretical formulation. In fact, Kohlberg (1963a, 1963b) formulated a theory of moral development (discussed in Chapter 15) that could incorporate the hypothetical findings.

In sum, although a fact may now be "loose"—not related to a theory—this does not exclude the possibility that, at some later time, it may be seen as related to or consistent with a general concept. Many facts not initially intended to be directly related to a theory do eventually find their way into one. This takes place through another major type of scientific thinking process: *inductive reasoning*. In this process, a scientist will start with sets of facts and then try to find some conceptual formulation to organize and perhaps explain them. A scientist using such reasoning proceeds from observed facts to integrative concepts or theories.

In the various ways outlined above, the outcome of *all* research does bear on the general conceptual and theoretical issues of a science. Although a researcher's reasons for undertaking the study of a topic may not relate to these general considerations, it is important to be aware of this perspective if only to gain an appreciation of the cumulative and dynamic aspects of a science such as human development. From this perspective, a student will be able to see several things:

1.   *Why some people study one topic while others investigate another.* Differences in underlying philosophies of science and/or humanity lead to differences in the assumptions a scientist makes about the nature of the subject matter. As we have seen, this leads scientists to look at different aspects of development and, hence, to investigate different topics.

2.   *Why abstract theoretical debates occur.* When scientists assume a particular philosophical or theoretical point of view, they become committed to it; they attempt to defend it, to show its tenability (e.g., Kuhn, 1962). They will attempt to justify their positions through logic and empirical research. Commitments to different theoretical points of view may cause one scientist to interpret a given fact one way, and another scientist to interpret the same fact a different way (Overton & Reese, 1973; Reese & Overton, 1970).

3.   *Why an understanding of these theoretical concepts is crucial for an adequate understanding and appreciation of the research, data, and facts of a science.* If students are given this conceptual perspective, they will know not only some implications of the results of one or more research studies but also the meaning and relevance of research as it bears on the general concepts of a science.

TEXTBOOKS IN HUMAN DEVELOPMENT

Unfortunately, it seems that many students do not develop this orientation to and appreciation of theory in many basic science courses. Some students report that studying the textbooks for such courses is like studying the telephone directory. Why is this often the case?

Numerous child development textbooks capably and clearly describe the dimensions and characteristics of a child's development. They also do a good job of acquainting the reader with the presumed or known processes underlying development. Thus, the authors of these texts present to the readers summaries of both the appropriate empirical research and the relevant theoretical notions of child development (e.g., those of Bronfenbrenner, Erikson, Freud, Piaget, and Vygotsky). However, these theoretical accounts are necessarily somewhat limited. Full explications of any of these theorists' ideas would fill (and have filled) books of their own. Moreover, there is not often the space available in such texts to explain the connections between philosophy, theory, and key conceptual issues (e.g., whether heredity or experience is more involved in a particular aspect of development). Nevertheless, for the reasons discussed in the preceding section, I believe that a greater emphasis needs to be put on theory and concepts.

The main purpose of most survey texts is not to communicate either theory by itself or theory joined with the core conceptual issues involved in the study of human development. Rather, these texts emphasize research and empirical generalizations based on these findings. The point here is one of emphasis; most texts do include discussions of theories, but generally in limited amounts. While most current texts do an outstanding job of presenting empirical results and trends in these findings, such presentations do not directly provide students with an integrative conceptual framework from which to view the field. Because the instructor often does not have the time to supply this framework, many students, after reading such a text, feel that they have interacted with a large mass of complex and often disjointed information, and many of them struggle to understand what it all means.

I believe that many incipient human development scientists are lost due to this problem. Never realizing the intellectual excitement that the instructor feels—because the instructor is well aware both of empirical trends and the conceptual implications of the research findings—the student may be "turned off" by a delineation of the details of particular studies. Thus, in failing to see the whole picture, the student does not understand the overall importance of the things he or she does learn about the subject.

This Text's Approach

How do I think this book represents a significant departure from the typical text used in an introductory science course? First and foremost, I must admit that I am biased. I have certain beliefs about how best to teach and try to understand a science: I believe that a science should be approached from integrated, philosophical, conceptual, and theoretical points of view.

As suggested previously, there are two major ways to go about studying the phenomena of a science: inductively or deductively. The characteristics and uses of these processes are complex, and because a full explication of these topics is beyond the goals of the present discussion, a brief overview will suffice. A more detailed, but still introductory, presentation of these topics can be found in Hempel (1966).

If one follows the inductive method, one starts with facts. Scientists will first look at some set of data. Then, in an attempt to integrate these facts, they will try to devise some general principles. In other words, one first focuses on facts and then tries to formulate a concept that will integrate those facts. Although the inductive approach is certainly a valid, important, and useful way of studying the phenomena of a science, it has been argued that this approach can lead to the compiling of a "heap of bricks" rather than a "house." In other words, this approach can lead to much data being collected without any clear a priori reason; that is, without any preceding, explicitly articulated, and theoretically considered rationale. Many facts might be gathered, but their general significance might be unknown or difficult to ascertain. As an alternative, I elect to take a deductive approach. I prefer to begin my scientific research from the theoretical end of the data—theory continuum.

As noted earlier, a theory can be defined as a group of statements (e.g., concepts and principles) that integrate existing facts and lead to the generation of new ones. Similarly, Hempel (1966) suggests that a theory explains empirical uniformities that have been previously discovered and usually predicts new regularities of similar kinds. To be consistent with this definition, I would use theory in the following way within the deductive approach:

1.   To be considered sound and tenable, my theory should be able to integrate existing facts. That is, my theory should be able to account for the established empirical findings on which it has been established. For example, operationally, to be useful, my theory should be able to account for the differences (the variance) in a set of data. To be *more* useful than other approaches, my theory should account for further variance (i.e., the theory would possess greater "deployability"), and should do so more readily, with more precision (i.e., with fewer statements, assumptions, and positing of unobservable constructs), and in greater scope (i.e., it is useful for a greater number of data sets than are other theories). The usefulness of theories may be evaluated in regard to its attributes of precision, scope, and deployability (see Baltes & Nesselroade, 1973; Baltes, Reese, & Nesselroade, 1977; Overton & Reese, 1973).

2.   Moreover, based on my theory, I should be able to devise some statements that—if found to be borne out by research—would provide support for my theory (and if found false, would refute it). Put in more formal terms, I should be able to generate testable *hypotheses* from my theory. My theory

should be open, then, to falsification (Popper, 1959) through empirical tests. The hypotheses I would test would usually take the form of "if–then . . ." propositions; that is, "if my theory is appropriate in saying so and so, then such and such should be the case." I would be reasoning that if my theory were useful, my deduction, which was open to either falsification or verification, should be supported by the outcome of my research.

3.   It is essential, then, that I put my deduction to an *empirical test,* by making some sort of relevant observation, for example, within an experimental or correlational study. If the results yield the predicted findings, then this new fact, developed through deductive reasoning, will be appropriately placed within my theoretical system. This fact will be a brick added to my house rather than piled onto my heap.

In sum, by emphasizing a deductive theoretical perspective, I can see how well my facts fit together as a cohesive, understandable whole. Moreover, I can see what sort of information is needed to fill the gaps in my theory or to clarify and refine it. The facts I derive from my deductive approach will not be useless or random. Rather, they will contribute to my theoretical edifice. My deductively produced facts will support, clarify, or falsify my theoretical position.

Cattell's Inductive-Hypothetico-Deductive Model

Of course, as scientists function in their day-in–day-out endeavors, such idealized deductive theoretical reasonings may not occur, and in fact, such sharp textbook divisions between inductive and deductive reasoning are typically not maintained (Cattell, 1966). Rather, as a given scientist attempts to establish "general laws which can be empirically tested and which lead to deductions extending our theoretical understanding and practical control" (Cattell, 1966, p. 11), and thus tries to fulfill the function of science, both inductive and deductive reasoning may typically be used. As indicated previously, there may be several reasons for doing a particular research study, and at different times the same scientist may do a particular study for any of these reasons. Thus, research, as it occurs in the real world, may not have deductively derived hypotheses as its starting point (Cattell, 1966). For instance, the initial impetus for research may be the observation of a curious empirical phenomenon or regularity.

We have drawn a distinction between induction and deduction in order to emphasize the point of view that science best advances when facts are gathered with an eye toward eventual integration with theory. This distinction may not necessarily characterize the scientific reasoning of the "real-life," practicing research psychologist. All scientists should work toward formulating general principles from which testable deductions are derived (Cattell, 1966). However, this endeavor does not necessarily have to begin with a hypothesis. Research may be hypothesis-searching (or "exploratory") as well as hypothesis-testing.

As we have seen, research may begin with interesting observations of empirical reality obtained while the scientist is working in the general context of a theoretical orientation. For example, believing in a theory specifies that all behavior is a response to stimulation, the scientist may present a novel stimulus to a 3-year-old child (e.g., a slice of purple bread) just to see what sorts of responses are elicited. From this empirical observation, the researcher might induce that a fact (e.g., the child responds with a negative facial expression to the purple bread) is representative of some more general regularity (e.g., color is an important aspect of food stimuli, and atypical colors are disliked). As a consequence, the researcher might formulate a hypothesis to test the validity of this induction (e.g., if I present food stimuli that are typically colored, such as an orange tangerine, to a young child, then more positive reactions will be elicited than will be the case if I present atypically-colored food stimuli, such as a blue tangerine). Then, the researcher might deduce what empirical consequences would have to be obtained in order for the hypothesis to be confirmed (e.g., children may smile and reach for orange tangerines and may frown and withdraw from blue ones). Accordingly, the researcher may make another, higher-order empirical observation, and the whole process would start anew.

What we see then is that in actuality the method that perhaps best characterizes the reasoning of the practicing scientist is neither purely deductive nor purely inductive. Rather, it may be what Cattell (1966) terms *inductive-hypothetico-deductive* in nature. As illustrated in Figure 1.4, this method begins with some empirical observation, which in turn serves as the basis for the induction of some empirical regularity. This induction needs to be subjected to empirical verification; however, in order to ascertain its validity, a hypothesis is derived from the induction, and the empirical consequences

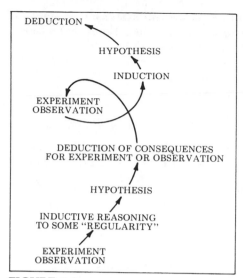

FIGURE 1.4
Cattell's notion of the inductive-hypothetico-deductive spiral.

Source: R. B. Cattell, ed. (1966). *Handbook of multivariate experimental psychology*, Diagram 1.1, p. 16. Copyright © 1966 by Rand McNally & Company, Chicago. Reprinted by permission of Rand McNally College Publishing Company.

of this hypothesis are deduced and tested. The result of this test is, of course, another empirical observation, which continues the inductive-hypothetico-deductive spiral again.

In sum, then, although the conceptual distinction between the inductive and deductive methods of scientific reasoning is a valid one, we must recognize that in actuality the practicing research scientist often uses both techniques. Yet, it still remains the case that *inevitably* deductions from general organizing principles must eventually be drawn and tested in order for theory, and hence understanding, to be advanced. It is for this ultimate reason that I prefer and emphasize the deductive approach to science. Thus, the first way in which this book will depart from others (aside from having an *admittedly* biased author) is that the primary orientation will be conceptual and theoretical.

To this end, I first describe the history of the conceptual and theoretical ideas that have been used in the study of human development. I then acquaint you with the basic philosophies of science underlying the core conceptual issues of human development (Chapter 3). We later turn our attention to these key conceptual issues them-

selves—the nature–nurture issue (Chapter 4) and the continuity–discontinuity issue (Chapter 5). In this latter discussion, we review the interrelated problem of stability–instability. In turn, several chapters are devoted to illustrating and, as much as is feasible, to resolving the conceptual issues involved in understanding the role of nature and nurture in human development (Chapters 6 through 9) and in continuities and discontinuities that are involved in developmental change across the life-span. For instance, we discuss the concept of instinct and the critical-periods hypothesis, and consider how contemporary views of the relations that exist between nature and nurture variables (e.g., heredity and environment) resolve some of the logical and empirical problems linked with these ideas. Throughout Chapters 6 through 9, a theoretical approach that integrates both nature and nurture and continuous and discontinuous processes of development—developmental system theory—is presented as a useful means to resolve the key conceptual issues involved in the study of human development.

However, after these chapters, we consider (in Chapters 10 through 17) other theoretical approaches to human development. In Chapters 10 through 14, we discuss instances of nature-based theories of human development, ranging from extreme hereditarian (genetic reductionist) models to theories subscribing to a modified view of the role of nature in human development (ideas subsumed under the label of "neonativism"). In turn, in Chapters 15 through 17, we discuss, respectively, stage, differential, and ipsative (i.e., within-person) approaches to developmental theory.

Throughout Chapters 6 through 17, we interrelate the core conceptual issues of development with these theoretical approaches, and the major emphasis is on the interrelation of concepts and theories. However, this does not mean that research methods, research findings, or the applications of developmental science are ignored. Research is integrated into the conceptual discussions throughout the book. However, rather than attempt to review all the research literature bearing on a particular issue, we discuss a key study or two that illustrate, clarify, or refine the issues. Moreover, Chapter 18 is devoted to a presentation of the methodological and ethical implications of concepts and theories of human development. In turn, throughout the book and, in particular, in Chapter 19, we discuss applied developmental science and the importance of developmental scholarship for improving human development across the life-span and for contributing productively to civil society.

DEVELOPMENTAL CONTEXTUALISM AS AN INSTANCE OF DEVELOPMENTAL SYSTEMS THEORY

As I have previously noted, and as will become quite clear to readers of this book, I have a preferred theoretical orientation toward human development. This position combines features of a philosophical position that has been termed *organicism* and of another philosophical view that has been termed *contextualism* (Pepper, 1942). In addition, this approach to theory has been labeled in many ways: *probabilistic epigenesis* (Gottlieb, 1970, 1983), *organismic contextualism* (Overton, 1983), or simply, *developmental contextualism* (Lerner & Kauffman, 1985).

Developmental contextualism is an instance of a more general approach to developmental theory, one termed *developmental systems* (Ford & Lerner, 1992; Lerner, 1998b; Sameroff, 1983; Thelen & Smith, 1998). In Chapters 6, 7, 8, and 9, I shall discuss developmental systems more fully and chapter 8 will be devoted specifically to a presentation of the details of developmental contextualism. Here, however, let me note that I believe that developmental contextualism and developmental systems theory generally provide a useful theoretical integration of important ideas of human development. A brief overview of the developmental contextual position may illustrate this use.

The Focus of Developmental Contextualism

What is a person? What sort of changes characterize people as they develop? Where do these changes come from? How do they relate to human development? Questions such as these are inevitably involved in any theoretical consideration of human development. The developmental contextual theoretical perspective has its own specific answers to these questions.

Essentially, developmental contextualism asserts that human beings are active rather than passive. Developmental contextualism also stresses that the world around the developing person—both the physical and the social ecology of human life—is active. According to developmental contextualism and other instances of developmental systems theory, the basic process of development involves the integration or fusion (Tobach & Greenberg, 1984) of these instances or "levels" (the person and the context or ecology) of human development. Specifically, then, in developmental contextualism, the

integration of (a) the actions of people in and on their world, and (b) the actions of the world on people, shape the quality of human behavioral and psychological functioning (Brandtstädter, 1998, 1999; Brandtstädter & Lerner, 1999; Lerner & Busch-Rossnagel, 1981).

Sources of Action in Human Development

Where do the actions that propel human development come from? It is clear that in a general sense the only sources of behavior are people's genetic inheritance (nature) and his or her environmental experience and contextual influences (nurture). However, consistent with its conceptualization of the character of human life—of focusing on the integration of levels of organization—developmental contextualism stresses that the source of the actions involved in human development is derived from *dynamic* interactions between nature and nurture. That is, the biological (organismic) characteristics of the individual affect the context. Adolescents who look differently as a consequence of contrasting rates of biological growth (earlier versus later maturation), for example, elicit different social behaviors from peers and adults (Brooks-Gunn, 1987; Lerner, 1987; Petersen, 1988). At the same time, contextual variables in the organism's world affect its biological characteristics. For example, girls growing up in nations or at times in history with better health care and nutritional resources reach puberty earlier than girls developing in less advantaged contexts (Katchadourian, 1977; Tanner, 1991).

In other words, individuals have characteristics that act on the environment and, simultaneously, they lives in an environment that acts on his or her characteristics. Given that individuals are at the center of these reciprocal actions (or dynamic interactions), he or she, through his or her actions, a source of his or her own development (Lerner, 1982; Lerner & Busch-Rossnagel, 1981; Lerner & Walls, 1999). Therefore, in developmental contextualism, there is a "third source" of development—the individual (cf. Schneirla, 1957).

These dynamic changes may involve both *quantitative* and *qualitative* changes in the processes of development. For instance, processes involved with a person's perceptual, motivational, or cognitive development undergo changes in kind or type (quality), and in amount, frequency, magnitude, or duration (quantity). This conception of change does not deny that there are some aspects of a person that remain the same throughout life; rather, it asserts that human development is a synthesis between changes and processes and variables that remain constant (Brim & Kagan, 1980b; Lerner, 1985).

Due to the integration of the organizational levels of human life, developmental contextualism asserts that the *laws* that govern the functioning of both constancy and change are related both to an organism's biology (e.g., heredity) and to its environment (e.g., experience). Hempel (1966) defines a law as a statement asserting some invariant characteristics about a phenomenon or process; we will also grant the status of law to statements that apply only approximately, with certain qualifications, under certain specifiable conditions, or with a given level of probability.

These two sets of factors (heredity and environment) *interact* to account for behavioral development. Logically, there are several possible ways that heredity and environment can be related (Overton, 1973; Lerner, 1985). First, it is possible that either heredity or environment might act alone as a source of behavioral development. Second, the contribution of heredity may be added to the contribution of the environment. Third, heredity and environment may be related to each other in a multiplicative, or interactionist, manner.

Thus, many different types of interaction may occur. Lerner and Spanier (1980) and Lerner (1985) have identified three such types, labeling them weak, moderate, and strong. (I explain these different types of interaction in Chapter 3.) Here, however, it is useful to note that in a strong interaction the components of a relation are part of an enmeshed system. Components cannot exist apart from, and in fact are defined by, their relation to (integration in) the system (Gollin, 1981; Gottlieb, 1997; Tobach & Greenberg, 1984). Clearly, given its levels of integration focus, strong interactions are the ones emphasized in developmental contextualism. For instance, strong interactions involving the reciprocal (bidirectional) influences between people and their contexts have been emphasized by Riegel (e.g., 1975, 1976a, 1976b) and by adherents of the life-span perspective (e.g., Baltes, 1987; Baltes et al., 1998, 1999).

The mode of interaction between biological and contextual variables involves (a) the action of environmental variables (e.g., nutrition, health care, and disease) on the individual's characteristics (e.g., the person's unfolding maturational processes, body build, and temperament); and (b) the action of such organismic characteristics on aspects of the person's environment (e.g., on how parents, teachers, or peers react to a child whose temperament is active versus passive, or whose height and weight are substantially above or below averages for his or her age and sex). Given this potetial influence of

people's characteristics of organismic individuality on their social world, we may see the important connection between strong interactions and the dynamic, bidirectional person–context actions that enable (from a developmental contextual perspective) people to play an active, contributory role in their development. In short, people do not merely wait while the environment acts to govern their development. Rather, in addition to being shaped by the environment, people act to shape their world and thus play an active, contributory role in their development.

Contrary to the position espoused by such behaviorist theorists as Skinner (1956), Bijou (1976), Baer (1970), and Bijou and Baer (1961)—who maintain that behavioral development is essentially controlled by the environment—developmental contextual-oriented developmentalists consider the role of the person's activity as a central source of development. Hence, just as much as the environment and its agents (e.g., parents) influence the child, the child's characteristics influence these environmental agents (see Bell, 1968; Lerner, 1982; Lerner & Busch-Rossnagel, 1981; Schneirla, 1957; Thomas, Chess, Birch, Hertzig, & Kolz, 1963). We have noted, however, that developmental contextualists also emphasize the significance of context in shaping an individual's characteristics. I have stressed that it is the integration of these actions that is central in developmental contextual thinking.

A major goal of this book is to expand and clarify the developmental contextual position and to detail how it provides a conceptual framework from which to view human development. I also illustrate how this point of view allows an interrelation and understanding of the nature–nurture, continuity–discontinuity, and critical-periods issues.

However, as previously suggested, there are major theoretical approaches to human development that are philosophically distinct from those associated with developmental contextualism or with other instances of developmental systems theory. These alternatives are linked with versions of what may be termed *organismic-based* or *mechanistic-based* theories (Overton & Reese, 1973; Reese & Overton, 1970). Chapter 3 includes a presentation of the major philosophical models that have been used to form theories of human development. Here, however, it is useful to note that, across the chapters in this book, I proceed from the philosophy of science to concepts, theories, and eventually to issues of application and research pertinent to human development. It is useful to frame this set of discussions by an appraisal of the meaning of the term *development*.

DEFINING THE CONCEPT OF DEVELOPMENT

The meaning of the term development has engaged, and continues to engage, psychologists and sociologists in philosophical and theoretical debate (e.g., Collins, 1982; Featherman, 1985; Ford & Lerner, 1992; Harris, 1957; Kaplan, 1966, 1983; Lerner, 1976, 1985; Overton & Reese, 1973; Reese & Overton, 1970). The existence of the debate is itself indicative of a key feature of the meaning of the term. That is, development is not an empirical concept. If it were, inspection of a set of data would indicate to any observer whether development was present.

However, different scientists can look at a data set and disagree about whether development has occurred. This is because development is a theoretical concept. It is, as Kaplan (1966, 1983) put it, a concept of postulation. One's study of development begins with some implicit or explicit concept of what development is. Then, when one inspects a given set of data, it can be determined whether the features of the data match, or fit with, one's concept.

In other words, a given scientist's concept of development serves as a conceptual template. For instance, if one believes that developmental changes are *only* changes that reflect an alteration from global, or undifferentiated, functioning (e.g., labeling any four-legged creature with the verbal label "doggie") to differentiated functioning (e.g., responding to such creatures with labels appropriate to their species, such as doggie, kitty, and mouse), then if and only if a given change conforms with this format will it be labeled a *developmental* change. Scientists would use such a template when they look at data. Observations that coincide with the structure of the template are labeled developmental ones; observations that do not match the template are judged nondevelopmental.

Debates among scientists about the meaning of development arise because different scientists have different templates. These conceptual differences exist because different scientists are committed to distinct philosophical and theoretical beliefs about the nature of the world and human life. For instance, some scientists find it useful to view the world as analogous to a machine and to study humans in terms of the energies needed to set the discrete parts of the machine in motion. Other scientists do not find it useful to use the machine metaphor. Instead, they conceive of humans as integrated wholes, and they study how the structure or the organization of this whole changes over time.

Despite the philosophical and theoretical differences that exist among scientists in their conception of development, there is some agreement about the minimal features of any concept of development. In its most general sense, development refers to change. But clearly, *change* and *development* are not equivalent terms. If they were, there would hardly be a need for the more abstract term *development,* and there would seem to be little reason for the philosophical and theoretical debates about the meaning of the term. Thus, although whenever development occurs there is change, not all changes are developmental ones.

The ups and downs of one's checkbook balance, for example, involve changes, but few if any scientists would label such changes as developmental. In addition, random, chaotic, completely disorganized, or totally dispersive changes cannot readily be construed as developmental. Changes must have a systematic, organized character in order for them to be labeled developmental.

But systematicity, or organization, does not suffice to define development. An office organized by one head secretary may run by one system, while another office, organized by another head secretary, may run by a completely different system. If the first secretary leaves his job and is replaced by the second secretary, the latter may change the former secretary's system into the one she prefers. A system, or an organization, exists during the tenure of the first secretary and then during the tenure of the second. Yet, the second system is not an outgrowth of the first; there is no necessary connection between the two. In fact, if the first secretary returns to his job, the first system can be reinstated, and in such a case, there would again be no necessary connection between the two organizations. Thus, although change occurred and although a system existed at the two points in time across which change was observed there was no connection between the two systems. The character of the first system in no way influenced the character of the second. Accordingly, the change in the office was not developmental, although it did involve an organized systematic structure.

For organized, or systematic, changes to be developmental, they have to have a *successive* character. The idea of successive changes indicates that the changes seen at a later time are at least in part influenced by the changes that occurred at an earlier time, if only to the extent that the range of changes probable at the later time is limited by earlier occurrences. In short, in a most general sense, the concept of development implies systematic and successive changes over time in an organization.

Virtually without exception, however, developmental scientists go considerably beyond this minimum definition. For instance, historically the concept of development is biological (Harris, 1957). As such, the unit of concern (or analysis) for most psychologists is typically an individual organism. Furthermore, because the intellectual roots of the concept of development lie in biology, developmental changes are held to be only those systematic, successive changes over time in the organization of an organism *that are thought to serve an adaptive function* (i.e., to enhance survival; Schneirla, 1957). Often, when a change results in increased adaptation, it is regarded as a progressive change (Ford & Lerner, 1992; Nisbet, 1980).

However, other developmental scientists postulate that organized, successive changes must have a specific form in order for one to say that a *developmental progression* exists. In other words, only when the structure of an organization changes in a particular sequence is development said to occur. For example, building on the illustration of a template for development change that I provided earlier, we may note that Werner (1948, 1957), Werner and Kaplan (1956), and Kaplan (1983) postulate that development exists when a system changes from being organized in a very general or global way (wherein few, if any, differentiated parts exist) to having differentiated parts that are organized into an integrated hierarchy. Werner and Kaplan label this concept of development the *orthogenetic principle* and indicate that only those structural changes that coincide with this sequence of globality to differentiated and integrated parts fulfill the requirements for a developmental progression (Werner & Kaplan 1956, 1963).

The point of these examples is that, despite a relatively high degree of consensus about development being a theoretical concept, that, at the least, connotes systematic and successive change in an organization, there is a good deal of disagreement among developmental scientists about what particular ideas need to be added in order to define the term adequately. These differences in definitions are associated with philosophical and theoretical differences which also divide scientists. The theoretical differences among scientists are ultimately based on their commitments to different philosophical positions (Kuhn, 1962; Pepper, 1942). As a consequence, it is useful to discuss the historical bases of the different philosophical positions and theoretical orientations that have influenced and continue to influence developmental scientists. We discuss this in the next chapter.

2 | *Historical Roots of Human Development: Concepts and Theories*

Have people always believed that humans develop? Have people always said that infants are different from children and that both are different from adolescents? Have "special" portions of the life span, such as adolescence or the aged years, always existed? Have people always believed that there is such a phenomenon as human development, and if not, when and why did such a belief arise?

Focusing on the Western world, we may note that many of the central questions and controversies about human development are quite old, with roots in ancient Greece and the traditions of Western philosophy. Throughout both the 2,000 years of this philosophy and approximately 125 years of pertinent science, the ideas advanced to explain human development have revolved around the same few issues. These issues represent the core concepts in any discussion of development, and differences among philosophers and scientists can be understood by looking at the stances they take in regard to such basic conceptual issues. These issues pertain most directly to one issue: the *nature–nurture controversy.* Although definable in several ways, this controversy relates to the relative roles of inborn characteristics and experiential influences in human development. Thus, in order to organize and understand the evolution involved in the history of development, it is necessary to introduce briefly some definition of the nature–nurture issue.

THE HISTORICAL ROLE OF THE NATURE–NURTURE ISSUE

The very first idea ever elaborated concerning human development involved what is still the most basic issue in development today: the nature–nurture issue. This issue pertains to the source of human behavior and development. A question is raised about where behavior and development come from. As soon as the very first ideas were formulated about what human behavior was and where it came from, a stance was taken in regard to this issue.

In its most extreme form, the issue pertains to whether behavior and development derive from *nature* (or in modern terms, *heredity, maturation,* or *genes*) or, at the other extreme, whether behavior and development derive from *nurture* (or in modern terms, *environment, experience,* or *learning*). However, whatever terms are used, the issue raises questions about how inborn, intrinsic, native, or, in short, nature characteristics (e.g., genes) may contribute to development and/or, in turn, how acquired, socialized, environmental, experienced, or, in short, nurture characteristics (e.g., stimulus–response connections, education, or socialization) may play a role in development. Table 2.1 lists some terms used in this and later chapters that pertain to nature and nurture contributions, respectively. This table will be useful to refer to in much of the presentation that follows.

The separation, or split, between nature and nurture illustrated in the table reflects a key distinction made by philosophers and scientists about the bases of human development. The separation between nature and nurture is an exemplar of the tendency in modern thought to approach the study of people with concepts that reflect conceptual "splits." That is, realities about development are discussed or debated in either/or terms.

Such bifurcation of concepts of development can be traced in modern philosophy, at least, to the ideas of Rene Descartes, a seventeenth-century philosopher. Here, however, we may note

TABLE 2.1
Terms Associated with the Nature or Nurture Conceptions of Development

Nature terms	Nurture terms
Genetic	Acquired
Heredity	Education
Inborn	Empiricism
Innate	Environment
Instinct	Learning
Intrinsic	Socialization
Maturation	
Nativism	
Preformed	

that human development and, more specifically, developmental psychology are fields wherein fundamental conceptual issues have been framed traditionally as Cartesian splits (Overton, 1998). That is, the conceptual issues that are regarded as foundational for the fields are cast as controversies involving distinct conceptual entities. In Chapter 5, for instance, we will discuss issues such as continuity versus discontinuity, stability versus instability, and constancy versus change. As illustrated in Table 2.1, the fundamental character of the nature–nurture split may be illustrated by the several manifestations of this controversy in the developmental psychology literature.

These issues, however, represent controversies because they cast the fundamental nature of development into a split frame of reference. The split is illustrated by the categorical either/or form of the questions. With this split frame, all fundamental questions ask "Which one?" Thus, this conceptual prejudice advances the argument that one or the other member of the pair necessarily constitutes the "real" feature of development, and the opposite member is only apparently real. For example, Rowe's (1994) approach to understanding the role of the family, and of socialization agents more generally, on child development involves splitting nature from nurture, and results in a belief that the family and all societal variables are really genetic in character. Therefore, Rowe considers "socialization" influences to be more apparent than real. To Rowe, what seem to be family or social influences are really inherited, genetic propensities to behave in particular ways in the presence of particular social settings.

Once the analysis of development is framed in such a split fashion, it is generally further assumed that some set of empirical investigations will ultimately record a definitive answer to the either/or question. The simple empirical observation that generations of empirical investigations have failed to resolve any of these issues demonstrates the inadequacy of this assumption. Nevertheless, the fundamental conceptual prejudice continues to hold the controversies in place as controversies (Overton, 1998).

Split positions assign either/or explanatory values to the segregated individual elements. Traditionally, the elements are treated as "causes," and the two broad classes of elements used to explain change are "biological" causes or factors and "social–cultural" causes or factors. As discussed more fully in Chapter 4, it is assumed within a split position that all change can be totally explained by one position or the other, or by some *additive combination* of the two elementary foundational factors (Anastasi, 1958; Schneirla, 1956, 1957).

In contrast to split positions, there exist relational conceptions. These concepts pertain to a set, or "family," of theories labeled (from Chapter 1) developmental systems perspectives. These theories are discussed again briefly in this chapter, but are the focus of discussion in Chapters 6 through 9.

The explanatory categories generated by split positions stand in contrast to those generated by relational positions (Overton, 1998). Relational positions aim to "heal" the biological and social–cultural split:

1. By offering categories that describe the biological and the social–cultural as alternative ways of viewing the same whole (Gollin, 1981; Gottlieb, 1992; Lerner, 1986; Overton, 1973, 1994a, 1998; Tobach, 1981).
2. By suggesting that action constitutes a broad-based mechanism of development that itself differentiates into biological and social–cultural manifestations (Brandtstädter, 1998, 1999; Brandtstädter & Lerner, 1999; Eckensberger, 1989; Oppenheimer, 1991a, 1b; Overton, 1994b, 1998).

Philosophers and scientists advanced ideas about development that pertain to nature, to nurture, or to some combination of the two. They often use terms other than those listed in Table 2.1. The relational, and hence integrative and systems, perspective about nature and nurture evolved out of these debates about the source of development. It is argued that all ideas about development relate to the nature–nurture issue and, in turn, that all other issues of development derive from the nature–nurture issue.

Although a fuller discussion of the relation of the nature–nurture issue to these other core issues of development (e.g., the continuity–discontinuity issue and the critical periods hypothesis) is found in later chapters, the present discussion of the philosophical and scientific concern with the concept of development points to the prominence across time of the nature–nurture issue. In fact, one can regard this historical review as involving the swinging of a pendulum, a pendulum moving from conceptions of human development stressing nature, to conceptions stressing nurture, to—at this writing—conceptions stressing that neither extreme is appropriate. It is now thought that notions such as interactions, relationism, fusion, integration, or systems need to be used in order to understand how the bases of human development combine to foster systematic change across the life span (Lerner, 1998b).

PHILOSOPHICAL ROOTS

The beginning of concern with the phenomena in the world around us can be traced to the first philosophers. Philosophical statements consist of attempts to speculate about the elements in the world. This speculation first occurred more than 2,500 years ago. It is estimated that in about 600 B.C., a Greek named Thales of Miletus (640–546 B.C.) became the first philosopher through his attempts to speculate about the nature of the universe in order to predict a solar eclipse (Clark, 1957).

This event indicates that, when humans first turned their attention to the nature of phenomena in their world, they were concerned with the characteristics of the universe and not the characteristics of humans themselves. Philosophical concerns about the character of the universe pertain to cosmology, and this topic remained the predominant focus of thinkers for several hundred years.

Ideas about the nature of humans, not to mention human development, were not historically the first ideas considered by philosophers. In fact, it was about 200 years later that the first major philosophical statement pertinent to the nature of humans was presented. Plato made this contribution.

Plato (427–347 B.C.)

From Plato's ideas one can derive statements relevant to human development. Yet many of these derivations are indirect. Plato's writings, and those of philosophers for centuries following him, do not reflect a primary concern with human development, although ideas about human change across the life span were apparent. The portion of Plato's writing from which one can derive his major ideas relevant to development essentially deals with the mind–body problem.

This problem—a major concern to philosophers for over 2,000 years—inquires into the relation between the physical, spatial, and temporal body and the nonphysical, nonspatial, and nontemporal mind (or in Plato's term, "soul"). How does something that does not take up matter, space, or time (a soul) relate to something that does (a body)?

Plato reasoned that souls are eternal. He philosophized that there is a "realm of ideas," a spiritual place where souls reside. At birth, however, the body "traps" a particular soul. The soul remains in the body for the life of the person and returns to the realm of ideas when the person dies. Since the soul resides in the realm of ideas, it enters the body with these ideas at birth. That is, the person is born with *innate ideas,* with preexisting, preformed knowledge.

Thus, Plato's idea about the relation between mind and body not only represented the first major statement about what humans are like but also represented a stance in regard to the nature–nurture issue. Humans are not the way they are primarily because of experience or education. They do not have to learn their knowledge. Rather, their knowledge is built into them; it is innate. This first major statement about human behavior supported the nature stance. In short, Plato said that humans are the way they are (i.e., having innate ideas) because they have a soul, and that this soul is a nature-based phenomenon.

In addition, Plato believed that the soul was divided into three layers, and that these layers also had implications for a view of human development. The lowest layer of the soul involved humans' desires and appetites. There, passions, emotions, lusts, and physical needs were found (Muuss, 1975a). A parallel can be seen between this layer of the soul and what another man, more than 2,000 years later, called a structure of the personality: Plato's first layer corresponds to the construct of the id in Sigmund Freud's (1949) theory.

Plato labeled the second layer of the soul the spirit. There, courage, endurance, and aggressiveness originated (Muuss, 1975a). Although humans and animals both had the first and second layers, only humans had the third layer. The third layer was the true, or real, soul. It was, Plato said, reason. It was immortal and, as already noted, only resided temporarily in the body.

What makes this layer idea relevant to a conception of development is that Plato did not believe that the attributes of each layer of the soul were immediately seen from birth. That is, people exercised the attributes of each layer successively, and Plato noted that, although reason was certainly present in all humans, the exercise of reason was not achieved by all people (Muuss, 1975a). Humans had to be trained in order to have their reasoning abilities drawn from them, and such training was what was involved, of course, in the Socratic method of education. This is the method where existing knowledge is drawn from a person on the basis of questions asked by the teacher.

In sum, Plato's ideas provided the first major statement relevant to human development. This first conception of human development placed the basis of human functioning in the nature conceptual "camp." Moreover, many of Plato's ideas are compatible with ideas expressed in theories of human development devised thousands of years later (e.g., Freud, 1949). Furthermore, although not an explicit theory of development, Plato's ideas of the layers of the soul did directly suggest that people differ across their lives in the attributes they manifest. Plato's ideas about the soul indirectly influenced others to speculate about the makeup of the soul and how its attributes were manifested. One person whose ideas were so influenced by Plato was his most famous student: Aristotle. Stimulated by his teacher's thinking, Aristotle revised Plato's ideas about the soul and about its relation to the body and, most important, devised ideas explicitly relevant to understanding development.

Aristotle (384–322 B.C.)

Aristotle was also interested in the mind–body problem. His position differed from Plato's, however. Aristotle proposed the *hylomorphic doctrine,* which said that spirit (*hylo*) and matter (*morph*) were inseparable, although distinct. The soul was present in all living organisms and gave life to matter. Aristotle philosophized that this occurred because there was a nonphysical, nonspatial, and nontemporal "force" that "breathed life" into matter. He called this force an *entelechy.* In short, Aristotle proposed the idea of *vitalism.* According to the idea of vitalism, there is a nonempirical, but vital (i.e., life-giving), entity present in any living organism that imparts life to that organism and directs its functioning.

Although an entelechy was present in all organisms, not all organisms had the same sort of entelechy. Like Plato, Aristotle postulated that layers of the soul existed. But in anticipation of Charles Darwin (1859), who wrote more than 2,000 years later, Aristotle conceived of these levels in a biological–evolutionary manner (Muuss, 1975a). Aristotle also believed there were three layers of the soul, but he identified them as a plant-like layer, an animal-like layer, and a human-like layer. The plant layer was associated with life functions related to reproduction and nourishment. Although animals and humans had this layer as part of their souls, plants only had this layer. Animals had their additional second layer, which was associated with functions such as locomotion, sensation, and perception; animals did not have the third layer of the soul.

The third layer was found only in humans, who, of course, had the other two layers as well. The human layer was associated with thinking and reasoning, and it was the possession of these attributes that Aristotle believed set humans apart from animals and plants. In essence then, Aristotle believed that humans innately possess functions relating to three layers of the soul, and that the layer-related functions pertain to characteristics of life throughout the biological world. Accordingly, while Aristotle's postulation is a notion of development, it is a notion of *phylogeny,* not of *ontogeny.*

Ontogeny is concerned with the development of an individual from conception to death. Phylogeny is also concerned with development, but here the concern is how a particular species came to exist in the first place, or how it came to have the characteristics it possesses today. It is a concern with evolutionary or *phylogenetic* (or *phyletic*) roots (origins; Hodos & Campbell, 1969). In short, one may talk about either ontogeny or phylogeny and still be concerned with development. When one talks about the latter, however, one speaks of the history of the development of one or more species from their simpler ancestral to their more complex contemporary forms.

Thus, Aristotle's idea of the layers of the soul was related to the idea of phylogenetic development. It considered human attributes vis-à-vis the attributes of other (presumably less elaborated) forms of life. Later in this chapter, in our discussion of the ideas of Charles Darwin, Ernst Haeckel, and G. Stanley Hall, I note that there are important distinctions between Aristotle's position and a view of phyletic development based on current scientific understanding of evolution. Nevertheless, given this important qualification, one may recognize Aristotle's ideas as the first statement directly pertinent to development, albeit less to ontogenetic development than to phyletic development.

However, Aristotle *did* offer ideas about ontogeny. First, like Plato, Aristotle believed that the functions associated with each layer of the soul emerged in a sequence from lower to higher. Aristotle was more explicit than Plato about this progression and divided the maturation of the human being into three stages of seven years each.

The first seven years were labeled infancy, and Aristotle saw humans of this age and animals as being alike. Both were ruled by their desires and emotions. Thus, in this first period, Aristotle saw phyletic consistency between humans and animals. The next period of development Aristotle labeled boyhood, while the last period of development was termed young manhood. (By today's standards, Aristotle's language would be considered sexist.) After the end of this last stage, development was presumably complete. The 21-year-old person was a mature adult.

One measure of Aristotle's continuing influence through history is his belief that maturity was reached at age 21—a belief carried over to modern society. (Until relatively recently, the age of majority in the United States was 21. This arbitrary number was influenced by Aristotle's writings.) Aristotle's influence was even greater than this. Because his philosophy regarding the mind–body problem was adopted by Saint Thomas Aquinas (1225–1274), and then subsequently by the Catholic Church, Aristotle's views became almost canonized. They became the only acceptable dogma of the church (Misiak & Sexton, 1966; Misiak & Staudt, 1954).

Aristotle's philosophy also provided an instance of one of the two sides of a one-key manifestation of the nature–nurture debate among philosophers, biologists, and behavioral and social scientists: preformationism versus epigenesis. This manifestation of the nature–nurture debate involves disputes about whether the course of development is formed by innate characteristics (preformationism), as Aristotle suggested, or, on the other hand, by processes that arise through probabilistic exchanges between the organism and its context (epigenesis; Gottlieb, 1992, 1997).

Aristotle's philosophical hegemony emphasized the preformationist side of the debate. Indeed, until the Protestant Reformation, begun in the sixteenth century by Martin Luther (1483–1546), Aristotle's philosophy remained largely unchallenged. Because the Catholic Church was, during these several centuries, a truly catholic (i.e., universal) institution, and because of the prominence of religion in the lives of people during this period, challenging the dogma of the church was a dangerous act. A challenge to the dogma could lead to excommunication, and if expelled from the church, there was no place else to go. Accordingly, because any one part of Aristotle's philosophy might be seen as related to another, no part was challenged until the Protestant Reformation provided an alternative to Catholicism. Until the sixteenth century, then, no view of development other than Aristotle's, regarding either ontogeny or phylogeny, was put forth. At this time, however, another idea relevant to development was advanced.

The Medieval Christian Era

As exemplified by John Calvin (1509–1564) and the American Puritans (e.g., the Pilgrims of the ship *Mayflower*), the medieval Christians had a religious philosophy that stressed the innate characteristics of humans. Based on portions of the Bible's *Book of Genesis*, this philosophy stressed the idea of original sin. Humans were said to be born with sin in them, or born basically evil. A second belief was that humans were basically depraved, and that their innate sin would be compounded by the inborn tendency to continue to commit sinful acts. In short, the medieval Christian view of human development was, like the others we have thus far encountered, a nature view.

The nature orientation of this position is best illustrated by the reason given for the presence of innate sin and for innate tendencies toward continued badness. Medieval Christianity believed in the *homunculus* idea of creation. The reason for innate sin was that a homunculus—a full-grown but miniature adult—was present from birth in the newborn's head. Instantly created with the child, this homunculus contained the sin and the basic depravity.

Of course, from this view, parents could apply harsh rules and stern punishments to their children. The children—having a preformed adult in them—were only different from other adults in terms of size. Hence, when children were bad, it was not because they did not know better—any adult knew how to act—it was because the "devil," the homunculus, made them misbehave.

While this medieval Christian view does represent a conception of development different from Aristotle's, it still represents a nature view. In fact, in this concept, children do not have to develop at all (except in size), since they had preformed adults within them. Thus, the ideas of Plato, Aristotle, and the medieval Christians give us a concept of human development that stresses that any real change across ontogeny comes from nature, from inborn tendencies. Furthermore, insofar as the medieval Christian view is concerned, there is no need for a theory of development. However, a philosophical position relevant to a concept of development did arise, and in the span of another 150 years led to a scientific view of development. To reach this philosophical position, it is useful to first consider the impact of another view.

René Descartes (1596–1650)

Theological changes resulted in the loss of universal acceptance of Aristotelian philosophy and allowed philosophers to return to issues that had remained unaddressed for hundreds of years. A Frenchman, René Descartes, led this movement. He reconsidered the mind–body problem, and his work marks the beginning of the era of modern philosophy.

In trying to formulate a proof for the existence of God, Descartes found it necessary to once again raise the issue of the relation between the physical body and the spiritual soul. He saw the two as separate (dual) entities. As noted earlier, this view meant that modern philosophy was launched with a "split" view of reality (Overton, 1998). That is, Descartes proposed that soul and body exist as two separate "lines" that cross at a particular location in the body, that is, the pineal gland (a small gland near the pituitary gland). Descartes termed this dualistic view of mind and body *interactionism*.

Moreover, in a manner similar to that of Plato, Descartes said that when the soul interacts with the body at the pineal gland, it gives the body knowledge. Thus, like Plato, Descartes believed in innate ideas. As such, although he was the first modern philosopher—by virtue of readdressing long-unconsidered issues—Descartes returned to a nativistic (nature) conception of human functioning first put forth by Plato. However, Descartes' ideas stimulated other philosophers to reconsider these "old" issues. Other views of the mind–body issue arose. While accepting Descartes' dualism, other philosophers rejected his idea of mind–body interaction (Misiak & Sexton, 1966).

One major reason for this rejection was Descartes' attempt to "prove" statements about the mind on the basis of assertions that stressed innate characteristics—characteristics that were said to be "just there," independent of any *empirical* (observable) proof. A group of philosophers who rejected Descartes nativism argued that the only way to explain the existence of a phenomenon—for example of the mind—was through the formulation of ideas based on empirical events (i.e., events capable of observation). Together, these philosophers formed a school of thought that evolved in Great Britain in the seventeenth century. One may understand the views of this group, and how they led to a concept of development, by focusing on the contributions of one leading thinker in what has been termed the British "school" (as in "school of thought") of empiricism.

John Locke (1632–1704)

Several British philosophers held similar ideas about the need to use empirical proof (e.g., Thomas Hobbes, James Mill, John Stuart Mill, David Hume, David Hartley, Alexander Bain, and John Locke). We focus on Locke's ideas as an example of the British school's position, and also because of the continued influence of his ideas on later scientific thinking.

Locke rejected the idea that the mind is composed of innate ideas. Instead, he believed that at birth the mind was like a blank slate or, to use his (Latin) term, a *tabula rasa*. Any knowledge that the mind obtained was derived from experience. Experience made its impression on the mind—it wrote on the blank slate—by entering the body through the senses. Thus, because we experienced, or sensed, certain observable events—for example, visual, auditory, and tactile stimulation—our mind changed from having no ideas to having knowledge.

Accordingly, here we have a philosophical statement about ontogenetic development that emphasized, for the first time, nurture. Experiences from the environment provided the basis of development. The newborn was different from the adult because the newborn had no knowledge and the adult did. Thus, there was development—change in knowledge in this case—and the development was based on nurture.

In stressing the role of nurture variables such as sensory stimulation in shaping behavior (or knowledge), Locke provided a philosophical view quite consistent with a major theory in the history psychology: the Behavioristic, learning approach to development. People like Skinner (1938), Bijou (1976), Bijou and Baer (1961), and Gewirtz and Stingle (1968) stress that behavioral changes can be understood in terms of environmentally based stimulus–response relations. In this regard, modern learning theorists are quite like Locke, a point that is returned to later in the chapter.

Locke's influence, however, extended beyond providing a philosophical and historical basis of learning theory. In fact, his ideas had two more general impacts. First, Locke's stress on the environment caused other philosophers to begin to consider the potential role of the environment. One major figure so influenced was Jean Jacques Rousseau (1712–1778). Rousseau combined both nativistic and environmental ideas in his philosophy—one quite pertinent to a notion of development—and, in so doing, became the first philosopher to explicitly take the view that a nature–nurture interaction provided the basis of human development. Rousseau said that all children are born innately good (a nature statement); however, in interaction with civilization (their experience, or nurture), they become corrupt. Hence, he argued for a "return to nature" in order to avoid the unfavorable effects of civilized experience.

Thus, Locke's emphasis on the environment did influence other philosophers to consider nurture, with the fortunate additional result of leading such philosophers to devise other ideas of ontogenetic development. Locke's ideas also had a second (more indirect but nevertheless more important) influence. A concern with empiricism, with observation, promotes a concern with science. All science rests on empiricism, and, therefore, the most basic characteristic of science is observation. Science could not exist if the statements made by its practitioners (i.e., by scientists) could not be falsified or supported through observations. In promoting interest in empirical concerns among philosophers and other intellectuals, Locke was—albeit indirectly—promoting interest in scientific concerns among these people.

During this time, the intellectuals in society were also the leaders of society (i.e., the ones with the resources and power to get an education). Developments in such intellectual areas as philosophy, literature, and science were common and popular topics of social conversation. Knowledge of such developments was a mark of the status of being an educated and (usually) rich and powerful person. As such, Locke's influence promoted a general concern with science among the educated. Whenever new events in science took place, news of them would not only reach other scientists but would also be likely to get the attention of all educated people. Such information, then, if important enough, could not only influence scientists but also could have implications for all areas of intellectual concern.

By the middle of the century following Locke's death, an event occurred in science that had great impact. It influenced not only the area of science it pertained to, but also all areas of science and intellectual concern (e.g., education, theology, law, and medicine). The event was the publication of a book by a then relatively unknown British naturalist. The book—representing a theory derived

Charles Darwin

from observations made while the author was on a trip to the Galapagos Islands (which are in the Pacific, on the equator, and off the coast of Ecuador)—was *The Origin of Species by Means of Natural Selection,* and the author was Charles Darwin. Published in 1859, it represents the transition from philosophical to scientific concern with the idea of development. As had been launched by Aristotle about 2,000 years earlier, the preformationism–epigenesis debate remained prominent across the history of scientific concern with the concept of development (Gottlieb, 1992).

SCIENTIFIC ROOTS OF DEVELOPMENT

Locke's empiricism promoted the influence of science, and as such, provided one basis for the impact of Darwin's ideas. Yet, there is a historical irony. Locke's ideas stressed a nurture view of ontogenetic development. However, the scientific view of development that Darwin devised stressed a nature view of phylogenetic development. With the transition from philosophy to science, the nature–nurture pendulum swung back to nature. However, as in philosophy, the pendulum did not stay there. A consideration of Darwin's work is useful in seeing these swings in science.

Charles Darwin (1809–1882)

There are several key ideas in Darwin's theory of evolution. The environment in which a type of animal (a species) exists places demands on that animal. If the only food for an animal in a given environment is the leaves of tall trees, then the animal must be able to reach the leaves in order to survive. The environment "demands" that the animal possess some characteristic that will allow it to reach the high leaves. If the animal has that characteristic, it will fit in with its environment, get food, and survive. It will live and be able to reproduce, and thus pass on to its offspring those characteristics that enabled it to meet the demands for survival. If it is not fit, it will die. It will not live to reproduce. Its characteristics, which did not enable the meeting of the demands of nature, will not be passed on. As other individuals of the species with such nonfit characteristics similarly fail to survive and reproduce, the species and its characteristics will become extinct.

Imagine, for example, that there were two species of giraffe, one with a long neck (as is the case) and the other with a short neck. Because the long-necked giraffe has the characteristics that fit in with the demands of the particular environment, it would (and does) survive; the short-necked giraffe would not. Of course, if the setting changed—if, for example, only food very low on the ground were available—the characteristics of the short-necked giraffe might best fit the environment and the outcome would be reversed. The point Darwin stressed is that the characteristics of the natural setting determined which organism characteristics will lead to survival and which ones will not. Thus, it was the natural environment that selected organisms for survival. This is termed *natural selection*.

Darwin used the idea of *survival of the fittest,* a concept introduced by Herbert Spencer (Gottlieb, 1992). Organisms that possess characteristics that fit the survival requirements for a particular environmental setting will survive. In other words, certain characteristics in certain settings have *fundamental biological significance*—they allow the organism to survive (and have the opportunity to reproduce and pass on the characteristics to offspring). Characteristics shaped by natural selection that meet the demands of the environment (and allow survival) are *adaptive* characteristics.

The giraffe example stresses that various physical characteristics of an organism may be *functional*. In an evolutionary sense, something is functional if it is adaptive, if it aids survival. In other words, "adaptive" means fit by virtue of natural selection (Gould & Vrba, 1982). Thus, the *structure* of an organism (its physical makeup, constitution, and morphological or bodily characteristics) may be functional. However, while Darwin in 1859 emphasized the function of physical structures of species, he later (1872) pointed out that behavior, too, had survival value. Showing fear when a dangerous bear approaches, being able to learn to avoid certain stimuli (snakes) and to approach other stimuli (food) are examples of behaviors that are adaptive; they aid survival.

The function of behavior became the focus of much social scientific concern. Those interested in the phylogeny of behavior were not the only ones concerned with the function of behavior. In addition, the idea was promoted that the behavioral changes characterizing ontogeny could be understood on the basis of adaptation. Thus, the adaptive role of behavior became a concern providing a basis for all of American psychology (White, 1968). This concern plays a major part in the ideas of theorists as diverse as Hall (1904), Freud (1949), Piaget (1950), Erikson (1959), and Skinner (1938, 1950). However, before the role of ontogenetic changes in adaptation—and, hence, in survival—can be completely discussed, it is useful to return to Darwin's ideas about survival and see how they reflect a concern not with ontogeny but with phylogeny.

Not all species survive. There are several reasons why this might happen. The natural environment might change, putting different demands on species. Species members that have adaptive characteristics will pass them on to their offspring and, therefore, the species will continue. Other species, lacking adaptive characteristics, will not be fit to survive and they will die out. Another reason one species might survive instead of another is that some change in the genetic material (e.g., through mutation or cross-breeding) might give rise to new characteristics that favor survival. In either of these illustrations, however, evolution would proceed on the basis of the transmission of adaptive characteristics from parents to offspring. Species would evolve—change with history—as a consequence of natural selection, of survival of the fittest.

The basis of an organism's survival, then, does not primarily depend on what it acquires over the course of its ontogeny that may be adaptive.

Rather, its potential for adaptive functioning is transmitted to it by the parents. Adaptation is a hereditary, or nature, phenomenon. On the basis of evolution—the history of changes in a species, its phylogenetic development—a member of a species either will or will not be born with adaptive characteristics. Thus, Darwin's theory is a nature view of phylogenetic development.

In summary, based on his observations, Darwin presented the first major scientific theory of development. As noted, this evolutionary view of species development had profound effects on areas of concern other than science. But it is possible to remain within the scientific realm in order to gauge the impact of Darwin's ideas on those concerned not only with nature and phylogenetic issues, but also with issues pertinent to ontogeny and, finally, human development. Darwin's ideas were a major influence on the person who both founded the field of developmental psychology and devised the first scientific theory of human development. This man was G. Stanley Hall, and a consideration of his work brings our discussion—after more than 2,000 years—to a scientific concern with human ontogenetic development.

G. Stanley Hall (1844–1924)

G. Stanley Hall (1844–1924) organized the American Psychological Association and became its first president. Hall and William James are the only two people ever elected twice to this post. Hall also started the first American journal of psychology, aptly called *The American Journal of Psychology,* as well as the first scientific journal devoted to human development (first entitled *Pedagogical Seminary,* and then given its present name, *The Journal of Genetic Psychology*). Hall (1883) contributed one of the earliest papers on child psychology and also wrote the first text on adolescence (a two-volume work titled *Adolescence,* 1904). His often overlooked text on old age (*Senescence,* 1922) attests to the ground-breaking life-span perspective he brought to the study of human development.

One of the most prominent and influential psychologists at the turn of the century, Hall had his most specific influence on developmental psychology. Hall saw development from a nativist point of view. Although not many scholars adopted his specific nature-based theory of development as such, some of his students—including Arnold L. Gesell (1929, 1931, 1934, 1939, 1946, 1948, 1954) and Lewis M. Terman (1916, 1925; Terman & Tyler, 1954), who were among the most prominent developmentalists during the first several decades of the twentieth century—did follow the general, nativistic developmental orientation Hall espoused.

In devising his nature viewpoint, Hall was profoundly influenced by Darwin. In fact, fancying himself the "Darwin of the mind" (White, 1968),

G. Stanley Hall

Arnold Gesell

Lewis Terman

Hall attempted to translate Darwin's phylogenetic evolutionary principles into conceptions relevant to ontogeny. He did this by adapting ideas derived from those of the embryologist, Ernst Haeckel.

The contributions of Ernst Haeckel. Ernst Haeckel (1834–1919) was a famed biologist, Darwinist, and theoretician. Haeckel's work was a major intellectual force in bringing Darwin's work into European and, particularly, German scholarship and in creating the German *Social Darwinist* movement (Richards, 1987; Stein, 1987). Social Darwinism was an attempt to use Darwin's ideas of evolution to understand the organization of society *and* to create a new, or to legitimate an existing, social order (Tobach, Gianutsos, Topoff, & Gross, 1974). In other words, Haeckel's goal was to provide scientific legitimization for the romantic vision of the German people *(Volk)* as a group who have singularly met the test of succeeding in the struggle *(Kampf)* for survival imposed by nature and, consequently, having been selected for hegemony (i.e., domination or rule) over other races, and, indeed, over the world.

In this synthesis of his biologically determinist version of Darwinian evolutionary principles and volkish philosophy, Haeckel (1876, 1891) forged a viewpoint that was as much a political movement as it was science. According to Stein (1987), Haeckel's views

> combined an almost mystical, religious belief in the forces of nature (i.e., natural selection as the fundamental law of life) with a literal, and not analogical, transfer of the laws of biology to the social and political arena. It was, in essence, a romantic folkism

Sheldon White

Ernst Haeckel

synthesized with scientific evolutionism. It included the standard Darwinian ideas of struggle (*Kampf*) and competition as the foundation for natural, and therefore social law, with a curious "religion" of nature which implied a small place for rationalism, the lack of free will, and happiness as submission to the eternal laws of nature. *Blut und Boden* were the reality of human existence. (p. 259)

In 1906, joined by several prominent German scientists, theologians, literary critics, novelists, and politicians, Haeckel formed the Monist League, the aim of which was to organize both scientific and political support for Haeckel's Social Darwinist ideas. The belief uniting the members of the Monist League was that all of life—human and nonhuman—could be unified through use of Haeckel's Social Darwinist principles (Richards, 1987; Stein, 1987). Haeckel and his colleagues in the Monist League believed that one set of ideas could integrate not only the understanding of human evolution but also politics, religion, morality, and ethics. The multiple disciplines and professions that were united within the perspective forwarded by Haeckel could, therefore, provide a compelling frame to a scholar such as Hall, who was interested in integrating Darwinian biological ideas with the study of human development.

The features of Haeckel's work that were associated with Hall proposing just such an integration pertained to Haeckel's ideas about *recapitulation*. Haeckel (1891) believed that an embryo's ontogenetic progression mirrored the phylogenetic history—the evolution—of its species. Thus, when one looks at the changes characterizing an individual member of a species as it progresses across its embryological period, one sees a recapitulation of the evolutionary changes of the species.

By recapitulation, Haeckel meant that the mechanism of evolution was a change in the timing of developmental events such that there occurred a universal acceleration of development that pushed ancestral (adult) forms into the juvenile stages of descendants (Gould, 1977). For example, Haeckel (1868) interpreted the gill slits of human embryos as characteristics of ancestral adult fish that had been compressed into the early stages of human ontogeny through a universal mechanism of acceleration of development rates in evolving lines. In short, Haeckel was the author of the notion that "ontogeny recapitulates phylogeny."

Hall's recapitulationist theory. Hall applied to postnatal life the recapitulationist idea that Haeckel used for prenatal, embryological development. Hall believed that the changes characterizing the human life cycle were a repetition of the sequence of changes a person's ancestors followed during their evolution. Arguing that during the years from birth to sexual maturity a person was repeating the history of the species, as had been done prenatally. Hall believed that the postnatal recapitulation was somewhat more limited than the prenatal (Gallatin, 1975). In fact, according to Gallatin (1975), Hall believed that:

> Rather than repeating the entire sweep of evolution, childhood was supposed to proceed in stages, each of which mirrored a primitive stage of the human species. Very early childhood might correspond, Hall speculated, to a monkey-like ancestor of the human race that had reached sexual maturity around the age of six. The years between eight and twelve allegedly represented a reenactment of a more advanced, but still prehistoric form of mankind, possibly a species that had managed to survive by hunting and fishing. (pp. 26–37)

Furthermore, Hall believed that adolescence represented a specific period in ontogeny after childhood. Hall was the first person, within a scientific theory of development, to conceive of adolescence as a distinct portion of the life span (the term had, however, initially appeared in the first half of the century; Muuss, 1975a). Moreover, Hall's demarcation of adolescence as a distinct period of ontogeny was discussed in a manner consistent with a life-span view of human development. That is, Hall saw the capacities and changes of childhood continuing into adolescence, but at a more rapid and heightened pace.

In addition, Hall saw adolescence as a period of transition between childhood and adulthood. That is, the stages of life previous to adolescence stressed the innate characteristics that humans held "in common with the animals" (Hall, 1904, I, p. 39). However, the stage of life following adolescence was said to raise a human "above them [i.e., animals] and make him most distinctively human" (Hall, 1904, I, p. 39). In short, adolescence was a period of transition from being essentially beast-like to being essentially human-like (i.e., civilized and mature).

The native endowment provided by human evolution, Hall believed, moved the person through the adolescent ontogenetic period, and, thus, put the person in the position of being able to contribute to humans' highest level of evolutionary attainment: civilization. Hence, Hall (1904, II, p. 71) said that "early adolescence is thus the infancy of man's higher nature, when he receives from the great all-mother his last capital of energy and evolutionary momentum." However, because of the acceleration and heightened capacities emerging in adolescence, and also because of the difficulty in casting off the characteristics of animal-like behavior and in simultaneously acquiring the characteristics of civilization, the adolescent period was necessarily a stressful, difficult time of life. Adolescence was, according to Hall, a universal period of storm and stress.

Criticisms of recapitulationist theory. Hall extended the concept of human development beyond childhood and, in so doing, placed the period of adolescence within a perspective that encompassed the entire life span. However, the recapitulationist theoretical frame within which he forwarded his view of human development was not generally accepted by either his students or his colleagues. Considerable conceptual and empirical criticism was leveled against Hall's, and, therefore, Haeckel's, recapitulationist application of Darwinian evolutionary ideas (Gottlieb, 1992). It should be noted that Darwin, too, was a recapitulationist, but just not as explicit so as was Haeckel (Gottlieb, 1992).

In light of the critiques of their respective views, it seems clear that neither Haeckel nor Hall appropriately represented the evolutionary process through their respective recapitulationist ideas. Even as an analogy, a recapitulationist description of human ontogeny is inappropriate. As initially pointed out by Thorndike (1904), and reemphasized by Gallatin (1975), by age two to three years a human child has already exceeded the cognitive capacities of all other species—living (e.g., monkeys or apes) or extinct (e.g., humans' prehominid ancestors; Johanson & Edey, 1981). Sensorimotor, verbal, and social behaviors, for instance, are all more advanced in the three-year-old human than in adults of any of these other species. In addition, there is no evidence that the developmental events of adolescence are a mirror of the history of civilization.

The legacy of Hall's recapitulationism: The contributions of Terman and Gesell. Hall's most prominent students were Lewis Terman and Arnold Gesell. Their contributions illustrate much of the interest in ontogenetic development through the first three decades of the twentieth century. Terman was interested in mental measurement. The first intelligence test was constructed by Binet (Binet & Simon, 1905a, 1905b) in Paris. Terman was one of the first to translate this test into English. (H. H. Goddard in 1910 was the first.) Terman, a professor at Stanford University, published the test as the Stanford–Binet (1916) and adopted the intelligence quotient (IQ), suggested by the German psychologist William Stern, to express people's performance on the test (IQ = mental age divided by chronological age, multiplied by 100 to remove the fraction).

Terman's interest in measuring intellectual ability was only in part based on a concern with describing how people differ (i.e., individual differences). His interest was also theoretical. He believed that intelligence was mostly (if not exclusively) a nature characteristic. Accordingly, not only did he develop an instrument to describe individual differences in intelligence but he also carried out research to try to determine the genetic component of intelligence. One such study was his *Genetic Studies of Genius,* a longitudinal study of intellectually gifted children from 1921 onward (Terman, 1925; Terman & Oden, 1959). (As noted earlier, a longitudinal study is one in which the same persons are repeatedly measured over time. Terman's was one of the first begun in this country; Sears, 1975.)

Although it did not prove that intelligence is genetically determined (for reasons we explore in later chapters), Terman's work, involving nearly 50 years of study and reported in five published volumes over this span (see Terman & Oden, 1959), was quite important for several reasons. First, it encouraged several other longitudinal studies of human development. These provided data relevant to changes in development across the life span. Second, Terman's findings did much to dispel myths about the psychological and social characteristics of intellectually gifted people. Although such people were sometimes stereotyped as weak, sickly, maladjusted, or socially inept, Terman provided data showing them to be healthy, physically fit, athletic, and personally and socially adjusted.

Third, Terman's work did much to make developmental psychology a descriptive, normative discipline. His work with the IQ test and his descriptions of the development of gifted people involved making *normative* statements. (A *norm* is an average, typical, or modal characteristic for a particular group.) If nature is the source of human development and environment plays no primary role, then to deal with information pertinent to the inevitable (because of its biological, nature basis) pattern of ontogeny, one only needs to describe the typical development of people. We see in later chapters that there are serious problems with this reasoning. However, Hall's other prominent student, Arnold Gesell, based his work even more explicitly on this reasoning than did Lewis Terman, and did even more to make developmental psychology a normative, descriptive field.

Arnold Gesell was convinced of the importance of biological influences on development but was not an avid supporter of Hall's recapitulationist ideas (Dixon & Lerner, 1999; Kessen, 1965). For example,

Gesell's positive regard for Darwin's impact on developmental psychology can be read in his article "Charles Darwin and Child Development" (Gesell, 1939, 1948). Here, Gesell acknowledged Darwin's "perception of the gradual genesis of all living things, including the genesis of the human mind" (1948, p. 44) and argued that Darwin's developmental perspective had a profound impact on the understanding of childhood. Gesell also pointed to the influence of Darwin's ideas on both Hall and him. But it was this common influence that Gesell emphasized, not Hall's specific "translation" of this influence into a (recapitulationist) theory of human development (Dixon & Lerner, 1999).

Thus, Gesell proposed a theory that can be understood by his term *maturational readiness*. This nature-based theory claimed that maturational changes were independent of learning (Gesell's conception of what nurture amounted to). Sensorimotor behavior and even many cognitive abilities (e.g., vocabulary development) were under the *primary* control of maturation. This meant that their pattern of development was maturationally determined. Thus, an individual would develop when it was maturationally ready to, and attempts to teach a child before this time could not be helpful.

In his writing and research (Gesell, 1929, 1931, 1934, 1946, 1954), Gesell stressed the need for the careful and systematic cataloging of growth norms. His work provided science with much useful knowledge about the expected sequence and times of emergence of numerous physical and mental developments of children from particular demographic backgrounds. These descriptions would allow people to know, he believed, the nature-based sequence and timing of development and, as such, the point at which a person was maturationally ready for learning. While such a belief is evaluated in succeeding chapters, the present point is that Gesell's theory and research did much to make developmental psychology not only a nature-based discipline but also one whose major, if not exclusive, focus was descriptive. However, a nurture-based theory of behavior arose to counteract the predominant nature focus.

Behaviorism and Learning Theory

Just as the pendulum swung between nature and nurture in philosophy, one may argue that it moved similarly in science. In the second decade of the twentieth century and continuing through the 1950s, American psychology as well as other areas of social science (e.g., sociology; Homans, 1961) came to be quite strongly influenced by a particular conceptual–theoretical movement: a Behavioristic,

learning-theory view of behavior. Although this movement was not developed from a primary concern with children or human development, it was extensively applied to human development. In fact, no learning theory has ever been devised on the basis of information derived primarily from children (White, 1970). Nevertheless, philosophically consistent with Locke's empiricist views, this movement stressed that in order for psychology to be an objective science, ideas about behavior had to be derived from empirically verifiable sources.

John B. Watson, emphasizing this orientation, developed his point of view under the label *behaviorism* (Watson, 1913, 1918). He stressed that stimuli and responses combined under certain lawful, empirical conditions—the laws of *classical* and *operant conditioning*—types of learning that are discussed in later chapters. By focusing on how environmental stimuli gained control over the behavior of organisms, one could know how behavior was acquired and, by implication, developed. Development was seen as the cumulative acquisition of objective and empirical stimulus–response relations. All one had to understand, in order to deal with human development, was the way the laws of conditioning controlled behavior. Watson applied these ideas to children, both in his research (Watson & Raynor, 1920) and in his prescriptions for child care (Watson, 1928).

John B. Watson

The nurture view of behaviorism gave psychologists a position that allowed them to be viewed as objective scientists, like their colleagues in the natural sciences. As such, behaviorism and its variants and extensions (Hull, 1929; Skinner, 1938) became the predominant conceptual focus in American psychology. As with Watson's work, applications of ideas and principles derived not primarily from humans but from other organisms—usually rats (Beach, 1950; Herrnstein, 1977)—were made to humans, and ideas pertinent to human development arose. Thus, ideas about how humans acquire behavior consistent with the rules of society, that is, how they are *socialized* were formulated. Such *social-learning* theories were not only pertinent to a nurture view of development but also, at times, involved some attempt to reinterpret nature conceptions of development (e.g., those of Freud, 1949) in nurture terms (Dollard, Doob, Miller, Mowrer, & Sears, 1939; Miller & Dollard, 1941).

However, in its major impact this nurture view of development was quite distinct from *integration* with nature concerns about development. Through the early 1940s, there was little integration of efforts by nature- and nurture-oriented workers. The learning-oriented workers were doing *manipulative* studies—that is, they conducted experiments that varied stimuli to ascertain the effect on responses. Their work tended to concentrate on readily observable aspects of behavioral development (e.g., aggressive behaviors). This work constituted an elaborate and fairly precise compendium of how variations in given stimulus characteristics were related to variations in the responses of certain groups of children—basically white, middle-class children of highly educated parents (Graham, 1992).

Thus, into the 1940s, proponents within the nature *or* nurture camps continued to work, but usually with little concern for integration with each other's endeavors. A major historical event served to alter this and to move developmental science from a primarily descriptive to a primarily theoretical, explanatory-oriented field. The event was the Second World War.

World War II

The events surrounding World War II irrevocably altered the nature of American social science. First, the effects of events in Europe were felt even before the United States entered the war in December 1941. Nazi persecution led many Jewish intellectuals to flee Europe, and many sought refuge and a new start for their careers in the United States. Great pains were taken by Americans to find positions in universities and associated institutions for the refugees, despite the fact that many of them held ideas counter to those predominating in the American academic scene (i.e., behaviorism and learning theory).

For instance, although Freud himself settled in London (and died there in 1939), many psychoanalytically oriented people—some trained by Freud and/or his daughter Anna—came to this country. Some of them, for example, Peter Blos, and most notably, Erik Erikson, brought psychoanalytic ideas about human development with them.

Once America entered the war and numerous soldiers had to be treated for psychological as well as physical trauma, the federal government gave universities large amounts of money to train clinical psychologists. This opened the door for many professionals with psychoanalytic orientations to become faculty members at universities previously dominated by behaviorists (Misiak & Sexton, 1966). These people had the backgrounds appropriate for teaching clinical skills to the large new groups of future clinicians that were needed.

Thus, one impact of World War II was to encourage psychoanalytic thinking in many psychology departments. This orientation represented the introduction of nature-based thinking into departments where behaviorists previously resided in total control of the intellectual domain (Gengerelli, 1976). Additionally, it represented just one of many different theoretical accounts of human functioning—accounts that stressed either nature or both nature and nurture as sources of behavior and development—that were making inroads into American thinking.

As such, nativistic ideas about perception and learning—introduced by psychologists who believed in what were termed the holistic aspects of behavior—were juxtaposed with the learning ideas of the behaviorists. The *gestalt* (meaning "totality") views represented by these Europeans (people like Max Wertheimer, Kurt Koffka, Wolfgang Kohler, and Kurt Lewin) were also shown to be pertinent to areas of concern such as brain function, group dynamics, and social problems (Sears, 1975).

Ideas explicitly relevant to development were also introduced. For example, Heinz Werner (1948) presented to Americans a view of development involving continual nature–nurture interactions and a concept—orthogenesis (which is discussed more fully in Chapter 5)—that was held to be a general, regulative principle depicting the character of all developmental change.

The developmental theory of the Russian psychologist, Lev S. Vygotsky (1927/1982, 1933/1966) serves as another example of the increasing influence of non-American ideas on the study of human development. Vygotsky, like his contemporary Jean Piaget (they were both born in 1896, but whereas Piaget lived until 1980, Vygotsky died in 1934 at age 38), saw development as progressing through stages of development. We discuss Piaget's ideas again later in this chapter and also focus on them in Chapter 15. We may note here, however, that although both Piaget and Vygotsky presented theories that pertained to broad changes in the nature of a child's mental life, Vygotsky placed more emphasis than did Piaget on language and, especially, on culture in individual development (Cairns, 1998; Keil, 1998; Valsiner, 1998).

Vygotsky's theory drew on a broad range of ideas, from disciplines as varied as psychology, comparative ethology, art, cultural analysis, language, and neuroscience (Keil, 1998). Vygotsky's interest in these multiple disciplines, and the levels of organization within the ecology of human development to which they pertained, was associated with his devising a theory that stressed the social and cultural origins of individual (e.g., cognitive or personality) development and the idea that a person's instrumental activity (the actions a person takes to reach goals within a given situation) were enabled by social life (Cairns, 1998; Overton, 1998).

Lev S. Vygotsky

Illustrating this emphasis on person–context relations, we may refer to a key concept within Vygotsky's theory, the *zone of proximal development.* To understand this concept, it is useful to recognize that Vygotsky's theory integrated (a) the individual's actions; and (b) his or her thoughts and language (cognitive processes through which the person makes meaning in the world); with (c) his or her embeddedness in a specific "whole field," that is, the context or setting within which the person is acting (Valsiner, 1998). To Vygotsky, the person was an active agent in his own development, and selected within the field the specific goals of his or her actions and identified the means to reach them (Valsiner, 1998).

Some goals are available to the developing person through emitting actions already in his or her repertoire and by recruiting resources (means) available to him or her. For example, although a young child may not be able to reach a cookie on the kitchen counter by standing on his or her toes, he or she may be able to move a chair close to the counter, stand on it, and reach the cookie. However, some goals are not available to the child. A cookie placed on top of a refrigerator may not be able to be reached by him or her, even if standing on a chair. However, a child can be educated about the skills needed to recruit a taller person (e.g., an adult) to provide aid, and get the cookie for him or her (e.g., "Be polite," "say please," etc.). In addition, the child can be taught to either safely place a book on the chair and then stand on it, or the child can be instructed in the use of a step stool.

Thus, the field within which the child exists can be divided into a "zone" within which the child can fend for himself or herself and a "zone" within which the child requires education or instruction. The zone of proximal development constitutes, then, "the difference between what a child can accomplish with guidance, and what he or she can achieve through individual effort and solo performance" (Valsiner, 1998, p. 207). By engaging in actions within this zone, Vygotsky believed that the child develops through a process in which he or she "transcends his or her present level of development through constructive play" (Valsiner, 1998, p. 207).

In sum, whether due to interest in Werner's (1948) ideas about the format of developmental change, or in Vygotsky's (1927/1982, 1933/1966) theory about person–context developmental processes, the outcome of these changes in the complexion of intellectual ideas about development, fostered in the United States by events relating to World War II, was a pluralism of ideas about development. Now there were numerous interpretations of behavior and development, interpretations that were based on substantially different conceptions of the sources of human behavior and development. Any given behavior, then, could be interpreted according to quite different alternatives, and these alternatives were advanced by respected advocates often working in the same academic contexts. The simultaneous presentation of diverse interpretations promoted a move away from a focus on mere description and toward a primary concern with theoretical interpretations of development. This focus on explanation was heightened in the post-World War II era, throughout the 1950s and 1960s.

The 1950s and 1960s

Because of the pluralism of perspectives promoted by the events surrounding World War II, developmentalists became less concerned with just collecting descriptive data. Rather, they focused more on the interpretation—the meaning—of development. As such, they became primarily concerned with the comparative use and evaluation of various theories in putting the facts of development together into an understandable whole. One index of this change of focus was the rediscovery of the theory of Jean Piaget.

Piaget's theory of the development of cognition was known in America in the 1920s (Piaget, 1923). Yet, because of the "clinical" nature of his research methods, his nonstatistical style of data analysis, the abstract constructs with which he was concerned, and his use of terms not then common in American psychological science (e.g., assimilation, operations)—all of which ran counter to predominant trends in the United States—his theory and research were not given much attention until the late 1950s. At that time, however, due to postwar European intellectual influences, Americans were turning greater attention to the intellectual resources in Europe. Thus, the Swiss scientist, Piaget, was rediscovered. It can be fairly said that concern with the abstract and conceptual ideas of his theory came to dominate American developmental psychology throughout the 1960s. In fact, his influence continues to this writing, both as a result of further study of his ideas and of the promotion of discussions of alternative theoretical conceptualizations (Brainerd, 1978; Liben, 1983; Kuhn & Siegler, 1998; Siegel & Brainerd, 1977).

Interest in adult development and aging also began to grow rapidly in the 1960s. As explained by Baltes (1979a), this interest provided a major impetus to the current concern with development across the life span, because studies of adult development and aging moved scientific interest

Bernice L. Neugarten

beyond the childhood and adolescent years. Major research and theoretical contributions to the study of adult development and aging were provided by Bernice Neugarten (1964, 1968; Neugarten & Gutmann, 1958; Neugarten, Havighurst, & Tobin, 1968) and Robert Havighurst (1951, 1953, 1956, 1957; Havighurst, Neugarten, & Tobin, 1968) at the University of Chicago, in their longitudinal research beginning in the 1950s.

However, as Havighurst (1973) himself pointed out, this work had an intellectual debt to some earlier work done in the 1930s and 1940s. Except for one early work—an article by Sanford (in the

Robert J. Havighurst

American Journal of Psychology, 1902) called "Mental Growth and Decay"—interest in life-span changes and in researching the nature of life-span development did not really exist before the 1920s. In fact, except for Hall's (1922) text, *Senescence,* and a book by H. L. Hollingworth (1927), it was the 1930s that saw the growth of interests related to development across the entire life span. At this time, Else Frenkel-Brunswik began a series of studies at the University of California (Berkeley) on the basis of an interest in life-span development; the work of Charlotte Bühler (1933) in Germany was published and began to become well known; and a book by Pressey, Janney, and Kuhlen (1939) was published. The scientists involved in these respective endeavors worked largely in isolation from one another, often unaware of (or at least not making reference to) the contributions of the others (Baltes, 1979a).

It was not until the 1950s, when the work of Neugarten and Havighurst really began, and the intellectual climate in the United States favored conceptual integration and pluralism, that these seeds of life-span interest really took hold. It was the fostering of research and theory in adult development and aging at that time that laid another portion of the foundation for the trends in human development seen in the decades following the 1950s and 1960s, trends that emphasized that multiple pathways of change exist across the life span (e.g., Lachman & James, 1997). Nevertheless, even before that period there was a long historical tradition behind the perspective that is today labeled the life-span view of human development (Baltes, 1979a, 1979b, 1987; Baltes et al., 1998; Baltes et al., 1999; Baltes, Reese, & Lipsitt, 1980).

By the 1960s, concern with development involved a focus on various theories of development, an interest in development into the adult and aged years, *and* a concern with internal and/or mental phenomena of development (e.g., the cognitive or thinking changes studied by Piaget, or the emotional changes of interest to Sigmund Freud and Erik Erikson), and not only on overt, behavioral changes. Bronfenbrenner (1963), in a review of the history of developmental science, similarly notes that from the 1930s to the early 1960s there was a continuing shift from studies involving the mere collection of data toward research concerned with abstract processes and constructs. Accordingly, in depicting the status of the field in 1963, Bronfenbrenner said that "first and foremost, the gathering of data for data's sake seems to have lost favor. The major concern in today's developmental research is clearly with inferred processes and constructs" (p. 257).

Paul H. Mussen

Similarly, in a review a decade later, Looft (1972) found a continuation of the trends noted by Bronfenbrenner. Looft's review, like Bronfenbrenner's, was based on an analysis of major handbooks of developmental psychology published from the 1930s through the time of the review. Each handbook represented a reflection of the current content, emphasis, and concerns of the field. Looft found that in the first handbook (Murchison, 1931) developmental psychology was largely descriptive. Consistent with our analysis and with Bronfenbrenner's conclusions, Looft saw workers devoting their time essentially to the collection of norms. However, a shift toward more general integrative concerns was seen by 1946, and this trend continued through 1963 (Bronfenbrenner, 1963) to 1972 (Looft, 1972). Indeed, as a case in point, we may note that the editor of the 1970 edition of the *Handbook of Child Psychology,* Paul H. Mussen, pointed out that "the major contemporary empirical and theoretical emphases in the field of developmental psychology . . . seem to be on *explanations* of the psychological changes that occur, the mechanisms and processes accounting for growth and development" (Mussen, 1970, p. vii).

In commenting on Mussen's 1970 edition, William Damon (1998), the editor-in-chief of the fifth, 1998 edition of the *Handbook of Child Psychology,* noted that:

> As for theory, Mussen's Handbook was thoroughly permeated with it. Much of the theorizing was organized around the approaches that, in 1970, were

William Damon

known as the "three grand systems": (a) Piaget's cognitive-developmentalism, (b) psychoanalysis, and (c) learning theory. Piaget was given the most extensive treatment. He reappeared in the Manual, this time authoring a comprehensive (and some say, definitive) statement of his entire theory, which now bore little resemblance to his 1931/1933 sortings of children's intriguing verbal expressions. In addition, chapters by John Flavell; by David Berlyne; by Martin Hoffman; and by William Kessen, Marshall Haith, and Philip Salapatek, all gave major treatments to one or another aspect of Piaget's body of work. Other approaches were represented as well. Herbert and Ann Pick explicated Gibsonian theory in a chapter on sensation and perception, Jonas Langer wrote a chapter on Werner's organismic theory, David McNeill wrote a Chomskian account of language development, and Robert Le Vine wrote an early version of what was soon to become "culture theory."

With its increased emphasis on theory, the 1970 Manual explored in depth a matter that had been all but neglected in the Manual's previous versions: the mechanisms of change that could account for, to use Murchison's old phrase, "the problem of how the infant becomes an adult psychologically." In the process, old questions such as the relative importance of nature versus nurture were revisited, but with far more sophisticated conceptual and methodological tools. (p. xv)

In sum, it may be seen that a multiplicity of theories, and a concern with the explanation of the processes of development, came to be predominant foci by the beginning of the 1970s. Such concerns lead to the recognition that there is not just one way (one theory) to follow when attempting to put together the facts (the descriptions) of development. Rather, a pluralistic approach to such integration is needed. When followed, it may indicate that more descriptions are necessary. Thus, although observation (*empiricism*) is the basic feature of the *scientific method,* theoretical concerns guide descriptive endeavors. One gathers facts because one knows they will have a meaning within a particular theory. Moreover, since such theory-based research may proceed from any theoretical base, the data generated must be evaluated in terms of their use in advancing understanding of developmental change processes.

The 1970s and 1980s

The prominence of theory, the evaluation of theories by criteria of their usefulness in integrating the facts of development, and findings that developmental changes take many different forms at different points in time (and that such changes need to be understood from a diverse array of explanatory stances) led, in the 1970s, to an increasingly abstract concern with understanding the character of development. Consequently, the 1970s and 1980s were characterized by the elaboration of numerous models of the association between the context of human life and the character of individual development.

As the same time, these models of person–context relations were being developed as frames for actual research about the linkages between individuals and their complex, multitiered settings. This research served as both a product and a producer of the enhancement of theories of person–context relations and of more nuanced understandings of the nature of the process through which human development was propelled by the associations individuals have with the ecology of human development. Throughout the 1970s researchers studying the infant years often provided foundational contributions to the development of person–context relational models.

Infancy research and theory. The work of Michael Lewis (e.g., 1972; Lewis & Feiring, 1978; Lewis & Lee-Painter, 1974; Lewis & Rosenblum, 1974a; Pervin & Lewis, 1978) is an exemplar of the role that scholars of infant development played in devising models of person-context relations and of demonstrating their usefulness in research on human development. Building on the insights of Bell (1968) about the potential

Michael Lewis

presence in correlational data about socialization of bidirectional influences between parents and children, Lewis and his colleagues launched a program of work that integrated model development with empirical research about infant–parent interaction.

For instance, in a book—*The Effect of the Infant on Its Caregiver* (Lewis & Rosenblum, 1974a)—that represents a watershed event in the history of the study of human development through the use of person–context relational models, Lewis argued that "Not only is the infant or child influenced by its social, political, economic and biological world, but in fact the child itself influences its world in turn" (Lewis & Rosenblum, 1974b, p. xv) and maintained that "only through interaction can we study, without distortion, human behavior (Lewis & Lee-Painter, 1974, p. 21). In his research with Lee-Painter, Lewis provided data supporting the use of a flow model of interaction in understanding, for instance, sequences of exchanges involving maternal and infant vocalizations as well as touch, looking, smiling, and play behaviors (e.g., Lewis & Lee-Painter, 1974, pp. 34–45).

Envisioning the relational, dynamic developmental systems models that would come to the fore in the study of human development a quarter century later, Lewis and Lee-Painter (1974) foresaw that:

> What we need to develop are models dealing with interaction . . . or with the interaction independent of the elements . . . This relational position not only requires that we deal with elements in interaction but also requires that we not consider the static

quality of these interactions. Rather, it is necessary to study their flow with time. . . Exactly how this might be dome is not at all clear. It may be necessary to consider a more metaphysical model, a circle in which there are neither elements nor beginnings/ends. (pp. 46–47)

Lewis himself continued across the ensuing quarter century, and through this writing, to contribute theory and research that forwarded and empirically tested the dynamic models he envisioned in 1974 (e.g., Lewis, 1983, 1987, 1990, 1997; Pervin & Lewis, 1978). His scholarship fostered an intellectual climate among other infancy researchers to reconceptualize phenomena of infant development within the sorts of dynamic personal–context relational models he championed.

One key instance of this influence arose in regard to the study of infant attachment. Here, the theory and research of Michael Lamb is a prime example of the use of person–context relational models in the study of infant attachment. Lamb and his colleagues (e.g., Lamb, 1977a, 1977b, 1977c, 1978a, 1978b; Lamb, Thompson, Gardner, & Charnov, 1985; Thompson & Lamb, 1986) approached the study of infant attachment within the context of the assumptions that:

1. Children have an influence on their "socializers" and are not simply the receptive foci for socializing forces.

2. Early sociopersonality development occurs in the context of a complex family system rather than in the context of the mother–infant dyad.

3. Social and psychological development is not confined to infancy and childhood but is a process that continues from birth to death (Lamb, 1978, p. 137).

Within this conceptual framework, Lamb and his colleagues (e.g., Lamb et al., 1985) found that prior interpretations of infant attachment, which included "an emphasis on the formative significance of early experiences, a focus on unidirectional influences on the child, a tendency to view development within a narrow ecological context, and a search for universal processes of developmental change" (Thompson & Lamb, 1986, p. 1) to be less powerful in accounting for the findings of attachment research than an interpretation associated with the sorts of person–context relational models burgeoning during the 1970s and 1980s. Accordingly, in a review of attachment research conducted through the mid-1980s, Lamb and his colleagues concluded that "reciprocal organism–environment influences, developmental plasticity, individual patterns of

Michael Lamb

developmental change and broader contextual influences on development can better help to integrate and interpret the attachment literature, and may also provide new directions for study" (Thompson & Lamb, 1986, p. 1).

Lamb's work challenged the field of infancy to study the early years of life *not* through the use of narrow conceptions of the exclusive influences of heredity or early experiences or of simplistic views of proximal dyadic relationships acting in isolation from the fuller and richer ecology of human development. He provided, instead, a vision for the understanding of infancy as part of the entire life span of the individual and of all of the other people in the infant's world and for appreciating this complex set of social interactions as reciprocal exchanges in and with a multilevel and dynamic context (e.g., see Lamb, 1977a, 1077b, 1977c, 1978a, 1978b; Lamb et al, 1985).

In fact, and as was the case with Lewis (e.g., 1997), Lamb continued through the next quarter century and, as well, through this writing, to contribute research that studied infant development within the context of a dynamic, person–context relational model (e.g., Campbell, Lamb, & Hwang, 2000; Lamb, 1998, 2000). In essence, then, stimulated by scholars of infancy such as Michael Lewis and Michael Lamb, the study of human development during the 1970s and 1980s became increasingly focused on developing models, and

conducting research, that enabled understanding of interactions, reciprocal influences, or bidirectional relations between individuals and the complex contexts within which they developed.

Damon (1998), characterizing these trends as they were represented in the 1983 edition of the *Handbook of Child Psychology* (Mussen, 1983) noted that:

> The grand old theories were breaking down. Piaget was still represented by his 1970 piece, but his influence was on the wane throughout the other chapters. Learning theory and psychoanalysis were scarcely mentioned. Yet the early theorizing had left its mark, in vestiges that were apparent in new approaches, and in the evident conceptual sophistication with which authors treated their material. No return to dust-bowl empiricism could be found anywhere in the set. Instead, a variety of classical and innovative ideas were coexisting: ethology, neurobiology, information processing, attribution theory, cultural approaches, communications theory, behavioral genetics, sensory-perception models, psycholinguistics, sociolinguistics, discontinuous stage theories, and continuous memory theories all took their places, with none quite on center stage. Research topics now ranged from children's play to brain lateralization, from children's family life to the influences of school, day care, and disadvantageous risk factors. There also was coverage of the burgeoning attempts to use developmental theory as a basis for clinical and educational interventions. The interventions usually were described at the end of chapters that had discussed the research relevant to the particular intervention efforts, rather than in whole chapters dedicated specifically to issues of practice. (pp. xv–xvi)

In order to understand the nature of changes in concepts and theories of human development that occurred across the 1970s and 1980s, and how these changes resulted in the focus in the 1990s on elaborating further developmental systems theories of human development, it will be important to focus on both the theoretical and empirical work conducted during these two decades

The role of philosophical models. Reese and Overton (1970; Overton & Reese, 1973), among others (e.g., Lerner, 1976, 1978; Riegel, 1973, 1975) pointed out that just as the facts and methods of science are to be understood as shaped by theory, scientific theories, in turn, are shaped by superordinate philosophies. Throughout the 1970s, repeated discussions occurred about how two major philosophical positions—what we learn in Chapter 3 are termed the *mechanistic* and the *organismic models*—shaped developmental theories (e.g., Lerner, 1976, 1978, 1979; Overton, 1973; Overton & Reese, 1973; Reese & Overton, 1970; Riegel,

1975, 1976a, 1976b; Sameroff, 1975). Each of these philosophical positions led to a different set, or "family," of theories.

For example, many mechanistic-type theories stress that even quite complex levels of human behavior can be reduced to rather simple elements: basic stimulus–response (S–R) connections acquired through the "laws," or principles, of classical and operant conditioning (Baer, 1970, 1980; Bijou, 1976; Bijou & Baer, 1961; Skinner, 1938, 1950). Other mechanistic theories (Plomin, 1986; Rowe, 1994) seek to reduce social phenomena (e.g., parent–child relations and socialization) and psychological functioning (e.g., personality traits, temperament style, or intelligence) to genetic inheritance (i.e., to the compliment of genes received at conception, the *genotype*).

Many organismic-type theories stress that as people develop, they pass through a universal and unchangeable sequence of qualitatively different phases, levels, or "stages," of development (Erikson, 1959, 1963, 1968; Freud, 1949, 1954; Piaget, 1950, 1970). Since each stage of development is different in kind from all others, organismically oriented developmentalists would disagree with mechanistically oriented ones about the appropriateness of reducing different levels (e.g., society, the family, and the individual) or different stages (e.g., the sensorimotor, preoperational, concrete operational, and formal operation stages posited by Piaget, 1960, 1970) to either one level (e.g., that of biology or, more specifically, genes), or to a common set of elements (e.g., stimulus–response connections formed through the "laws" of classical and operant conditioning), respectively.

The discussions prompted by the work of Reese and Overton (1970) involved, as well, consideration of the "family of theories" associated with each model. Although there are differences among family members (e.g., Freud, in his organismic theory, emphasized emotional and personality development whereas Piaget, in his organismic theory, emphasized cognitive development), there is greater similarity among the theories within a family (e.g., the common stress on the qualitative, stage-like nature of development) than there is between theories associated with different families (e.g., mechanistically oriented Behavioristic theorists, such as Bijou and Baer, 1961, would deny the importance, indeed the reality, of qualitatively different stages in development). Due to the philosophically based differences between families of theories derived from the organismic and the mechanistic models, the 1970s and 1980s involved several discussions about the different stances held by members of one or another theoretical "family" regarding an array of key conceptual issues of development. Examples are the nature and nurture bases of development (Lehrman, 1970; Lerner, 1978; Overton, 1973) the quality, openness, and continuity of change (Brim & Kagan, 1980a, 1980b; Looft, 1973); appropriate methods for studying development (Baltes, Reese, & Nesselroade, 1977); and ultimately, the alternative truth criteria for establishing the "facts" of development (Dixon & Nesselroade, 1983; Reese & Overton, 1970).

This awareness of the philosophical bases of developmental theory, method, and data contributed to the consideration of additional models appropriate to the study of psychological development. In part, this consideration developed as a consequence of interest in integrating assumptions associated with theories derived from organismic and mechanistic models (Looft, 1973). For instance, Riegel (1975, 1976a, 1976b) attempted to apply a historical model of development that seemed to include some features of organicism (e.g., the active organism) and some features of mechanism (e.g., the active environment). In turn, Riegel's interest in continual, reciprocal relations between an active organism and its active context (and not in either element per se), and the concern with these relations as they exist on all phenomenal levels of analysis, formed a basis for his proposing a dialectical model of human development (Riegel, 1975, 1976a, 1976b). Other developmentalists, also

Klaus F. Riegel

focusing on the implications for theory of viewing distinct levels of analysis as reciprocally interactive, proposed related models, ones termed *transactional* (Sameroff, 1975), *relational* (Looft, 1973), or *developmental–contextual* (Lerner, 1978, 1984, 1986). This philosophically driven interest in bidirectional organism-context relations led several theorists to explore the application of a change-oriented contextual model to the collection and interpretation of developmental (and other psychological) data. (See especially the volumes on contextualism edited by Hayes, Hayes, Reese, & Sarbin, 1993, and by Rosnow & Georgoudi, 1986.) This last feature of the recent history of the field of human development is also linked to the second basis for the growing interest in the context of human development.

The discussions about the influence of the organismic and the mechanistic models led developmental psychologists to recognize that the stances scientists took in regard to key issues of human development—such as whether, because of the appropriateness of reducing all behavior to common elements, there is a sameness, or continuity, across life *or* whether, because of the existence of new stages, there is change, or discontinuity, across life—depended ultimately on philosophical positions. That is, developmentalists recognized that a main (if not the ultimate) reason scientists had different positions regarding concepts and theories of development was that they were committed to different philosophies (see Kuhn, 1962; Overton, 1998). In other words, differences about these issues were underlain by nonempirical, philosophical differences and could not, therefore, be readily decided on the basis of data. Indeed, Reese and Overton (1970; Overton & Reese, 1973) pointed out that developmentalists working from different philosophical positions would have different truth criteria for establishing the "facts" of development because what is a fact to one scientist may not be accepted as a legitimate or relevant fact by another. As a consequence, because of basic philosophical disagreements, disputes across philosophical positions could not be settled by facts.

In short, the interest that arose in the 1970s and developed across the 1980s in the philosophical bases of theories of development also led many developmentalists to explore the potential use of philosophies other than the organismic and the mechanistic. The considerations of these ideas resulted in revised ways of thinking about the linkages between the developing individual and his or her changing context.

It is useful here to consider three significant instances of the theoretical models of human development that emerged from scholars' efforts to devise new, and more integrative, ways of thinking about individual–context relations. These instances of human development theory—the dialectical view championed by Klaus Riegel, the bioecological view developed by Urie Bronfenbrenner, and the life-span perspective developed by Paul B. Baltes, John R. Nesselroade, K. Warner Schaie, and their colleagues—continued to develop after the 1980s. Together, the influence of their continued elaboration was, in the 1990s, to help crystallize the emphasis in developmental theory on understanding individual–context relations in relation to integrative, developmental systems (Lerner, 1998a).

The dialectical model. In many ways, Klaus F. Riegel (1975, 1976a, 1976b) was both the intellectual leader of and catalyst for the exploration in the 1970s of the use of alternative models for the study of human development. This was the case, first, because he was a prolific and passionate writer—his book, *Psychology Mon Amour: A Countertext* (Riegel, 1978), being an excellent case in point—and, second, because he was editor of the journal *Human Development,* the prime outlet for theoretical scholarship in the field of human development.

Of the many important contributions of Riegel's scholarship, two are particularly pertinent to the present discussion. First, his dialectical model emphasized that the primary goal of a developmental analysis was the study of change, not stasis. Second, his model stressed that any level of organization—from inner–biological, through individual–psychological and physical–environmental, to the sociocultural—influences and is influenced by all other levels. Thus, Riegel (1975, 1976a, 1976b) "developmentalized" and "contextualized" the study of the person by embedding the individual within an integrated and changing matrix of influences derived from multiple levels of organization.

Riegel (1973, 1975, 1976a, 1976b) proposed that dialectical philosophy could be used to devise a unique theory of development, one that did not only focus on the organism (and, for instance, its genes or its maturationally guided progression through stages), or only on the environment (as, for instance, the source of the stimulation that provided the basis of S–R connections). Instead, Riegel (1975, 1976a, 1976b) hoped to forge a dialectical psychology that focused on the *relations* between developing organisms and their changing environments. Riegel emphasized that such relations involved continual conflicts among variables from several levels of "being" (or levels of organization of life phenomena). For example, he assumed that development involved constant changes among the multiple, reciprocally related inner–biological, individual–psychological, physical–environmental, and sociocultural levels of analysis.

Riegel's model of dialecticism was an important instance of the growing interest during this period in the interactive role of the changing physical and social context for human behavior and development. Riegel's ideas, as well as those of Sameroff (1975), Looft (1973), Lerner (1978, 1979), and others (Bronfenbrenner, 1977, 1979), were similar in their emphasis on change and context— and, to this extent, may be interpreted as being part of a common "family" of models. However, as scholarship about this family advanced, it became increasingly clear that important distinctions existed among family members.

Riegel's (1975, 1976a, 1976b) ideas on context and change differed from those of other family members with respect to the format of change. The nature of dialectical change, which is always in the same direction, that of a synthesis between two "conflicting" opposites (termed thesis and antithesis), may be more compatible with the view of change found in organicism than that of the philosophical position termed *contextualism* (Dixon, Lerner, & Hultsch, 1991a, 1991b). As we discuss in Chapter 3, contextualism promotes a view of change that is dispersive, that is, that can occur in innumerable directions (Pepper, 1942). On the other hand, organismic change is always unidirectional; it is directed to a single endpoint or goal (Pepper, 1942). When applied to the life span, Riegel's (1976b) dialectical view may have had more in common with contemporary organismic views (e.g., Alexander & Langer, 1990; Chapman, 1988a, 1988b; Piaget, 1970) than with contemporary contextual ones.

To counter this criticism, Riegel (1976b) tried to argue that dialecticism constituted a model of development distinct from organicism. In his view, the dialectical theory of cognitive development differed from the one of Piaget (1950, 1970). For example, whereas Piaget proposed that, after the development of the last stage of development in his theory—a stage he termed *formal operations* (see Chapter 15)—no new cognitive structure emerged. Riegel argued that the dialectic resulted in a fifth, open-ended stage of cognitive development. However, given that both the organismic model of Piaget and his dialectic model emphasized a single format and direction for developmental change, it was difficult for Riegel to maintain that at its core—in regard to the character of the main process of developmental change—the two positions were different.

Moreover, Riegel did not attend to the similarities and differences between his dialectical model and theories that stressed the contextual philosophy or world view, although both sets of ideas stress change through individual–context relations. Given the problem of discriminating Riegel's dialectical model from organicism, and the availability of a model for theory—contextualism— which afforded a different, and more plastic view of change, the dialectical model of Riegel did not remain a conception of prime focus among developmental scholars beyond the 1970s and early 1980s. Nevertheless, attention to Riegel's ideas did facilitate the interest of the community of developmental scholars in other theoretical models of change through individual–context relations. Thus, at least in this respect, Riegel's dialectical model can be seen as compatible with the attention paid, during these two decades, to contextualism (Hultsch & Hickey, 1978; Lerner, Skinner, & Sorell, 1980).

In contextualism, developmental changes occur as a consequence of reciprocal (bidirectional) relations between the active organism and the active context. Just as the context changes the individual, the individual changes the context. As such, by acting to change a source of their own development—by being both products and producers of their context—individuals affect their own development (Bell, 1968; Bell & Harper, 1977; Lerner, 1982; Lerner & Busch-Rossnagel, 1981; Lewis & Rosenblum, 1974; Schneirla, 1957).

Contextualism found many adherents among developmentalists during the 1970s (Lerner, Hultsch, & Dixon, 1983) as well as many critics (e.g., see Capaldi & Proctor, 1999, for a review and Kendler, 1986, as an example). Nevertheless, because of the potential to provide ideas that could more usefully understand (e.g., account for more variance pertinent to) the dynamic (i.e., the multilevel and bidirectional) relationships between the developing individual and variables associated with his or her biological, interpersonal, societal, cultural, and historical contexts, developmental scholars continued to explore the use of models of person–context relations associated with contextualism (if not specifically Riegel's dialecticalism). As I have noted, two major examples of such approaches were the bioecological view of human development (Bronfenbrenner, 1977, 1979) and the life-span developmental psychology perspective (e.g., Baltes, et al., 1980).

Bronfenbrenner's bioecological view of human development. The leading formulator of the bioecological approach to human development was

Urie Bronfenbrenner (1977, 1979, 1983; Bronfenbrenner & Crouter, 1983; Bronfenbrenner & Morris, 1998). Bronfenbrenner argued that much of developmental research involved studying children under artificial "experimental" conditions. Thus, he argued, "Much of contemporary developmental psychology is the science of the strange behavior of children in strange situations with strange adults for the briefest possible periods of time" (1977, p. 513). Bronfenbrenner asserted that only "experiments created as real are real in their consequences" (1977, p. 529), and he stressed that research should begin to focus on how children develop in settings representative of their actual world (i.e., in *ecologically valid* settings). Instead of studying children only in the laboratory, one should study them in their homes, schools, and playgrounds.

Bronfenbrenner also argued that developmental psychologists needed a much more precise and differentiated view of the actual ecology of human development; it would not suffice just to view all features of a person's context as merely representing the "stimulus environment." The context of human development was composed of different levels, or systems, of organization; although the systems were interrelated—often in a reciprocal manner (Belsky & Tolan, 1981)—they were, nevertheless, sufficiently distinct to necessitate discrimination among them.

Bronfenbrenner proposed four systems within the ecology of human development. The first system he labeled the *microsystem,* and he noted that this portion of the context is composed of "the complex of relations between the developing person and environment in an immediate setting containing the person" (Bronfenbrenner, 1977, p. 515). For example, the family is one major microsystem for infant and child development (Belsky, 1982; Belsky & Tolan, 1981); it involves interactions between the child, his or her parents, and any siblings that are present in the home. Other microsystems of early life include the day care, nursery, or school setting, involving both child–teacher and child–peer interactions; and the playground, most often involving child–peer interactions.

A child's microsystems may be interrelated. What occurs in the school may affect what happens in the family, and vice versa. Bronfenbrenner noted that such microsystem interrelations constitute a second ecological system. He termed this the *mesosystem,* and he defined it as "the interrelations among major settings containing the developing person at a particular point in his or her life" (Bronfenbrenner, 1977, p. 515).

Often, what happens in a microsystem (e.g., in an interaction between a child and a parent within the family context) may be influenced by events that occur in systems in which the child takes no part. For example, an adult who is a parent also has other social roles, for instance, as a worker. The child is probably not part of his or her parents' workplace interactions, but events that affect the parents at work can influence how they treat the child. For instance, if a parent has a particularly bad or tiring day at work, he or she may punish the child more severely than usual for some disapproved act. Thus, because the people with whom the child lives interact in—and are affected by—contexts other than those containing the child, the child may be affected by settings in which he or she plays no direct role. Bronfenbrenner saw such influences as constituting a third system within the ecology of human development. He labeled this system the *exosystem,* and he defined it as "an extension of the mesosystem embracing . . . specific social structures, both formal and informal, that do not themselves contain the developing person but impinge upon or encompass the immediate settings in which the person is found, and thereby delimit, influence, or even determine what goes on there" (Bronfenbrenner, 1977, p. 515).

Finally, Bronfenbrenner noted that there exists a *macrosystem* within the ecology of human development. This system is composed of historical events (e.g., wars, floods, and famines) that may affect the other ecological systems, as well as cultural values and beliefs that influence the other ecological systems. Natural disasters may destroy the homes, schools, or other microsystems of a person or a group of developing people, and/or they may make certain necessities of life (e.g., food or fresh water) less available. Cultural values can influence the developing child in many ways. For example, cultural beliefs about the appropriateness of breastfeeding and about when weaning from the breast should occur can affect not only the nutritional status of the child but, because mother's milk may make some children less likely to develop allergies later in life, it can also affect their health status. Values about child rearing, and indeed the value or role of children in society, can affect the behaviors developed by a child (e.g., see Baumrind, 1971, 1972) *and* can even have implications for whether the child survives.

A particularly dramatic example of how cultural values about the importance of children can affect a child's survival may be taken from information about the culture that existed in the ancient Near

East in Carthage. That is, it seems clear that Carthaginian society, which flourished from about 800 to 150 B.C.

> attached particular importance to the small child though the manifestation of this importance was gruesome, indeed horrendous. Punic religious beliefs demanded the sacrifice of the children of the nobility to the gods . . . the ancient Carthaginians believed they were handing over to the gods their precious possessions. One has only to spend an hour or so in one of the two infant Necropolises excavated in Carthage and to consider the thousands of tiny grave stelae that mark the sacrifice of each child to sense the potency of the forces that drove the Carthaginians to kill their children, many of whom were as much as three years old when they were delivered up to the gods. (French, 1977, pp. 7–8)

The life-span developmental psychology perspective. A second major instance of a contextually oriented perspective that became increasingly prominent during the 1970s has been labeled (as noted earlier) life-span developmental psychology or the life-span view of human development (Baltes, 1979b; Baltes et al., 1980; Lerner, Hultsch, & Dixon, 1983). The major formulators of this perspective were Paul B. Baltes, K. Warner Schaie, John R. Nesselroade, Hayne W. Reese, and Orville G. Brim, Jr. As is discussed more fully in later chapters, this perspective emphasizes the potential for systemic change across life and sees this potential as deriving from reciprocal influences, of people on their contexts as well as of contexts on people.

As Baltes (1979b) has indicated, there are two rationales for this emphasis on person–context relations as central to developmental change:

> One is, of course, evident also in current child development work. As development unfolds, it becomes more and more apparent that individuals act on the environment and produce novel behavior outcomes, thereby making the active and selective nature of human beings of paramount importance. Furthermore, the recognition of the interplay between age-graded, history-graded, and nonnormative life events suggests a contextualistic and dialectical conception of development. This dialectic is further accentuated by the fact that individual development is the reflection of multiple forces that are not always in synergism, or convergence, nor do they always permit the delineation of a specific set of endstates. (p. 2)

Based on this view of developmental change, life-span developmental psychology (Baltes, Lindenberger, & Staudinger, 1998a, 1998b; Baltes, Reese, & Lipsitt, 1980) became crystallized as a set of interrelated ideas about the nature of human development.

In their combination, these ideas present a set of implications for theory building, methodology, and scientific collaboration across disciplinary boundaries. Among the key ideas emanating from this perspective are that, across life, development involves the integration of gains–losses (e.g., we gain facility in our native language but, with development, lose the capacity to be as fluent as a "native" speaker in other languages), embeddedness (individual development occurs within a social, physical, cultural, and historical context, with which it is reciprocally interactive), and plasticity (due to the relations between individuals and this complex context there are multiple pathways, or directions, that developmental change may take) (Baltes, 1987). An interrelated set of implications may be derived from these propositions, these propositions and implications constitute the key concepts in current life-span thinking.

The life-span perspective is often associated with a call for interdisciplinary research in human development (Dixon & Lerner, 1999). That is, attempts have been made to integrate ideas from the many disciplines involved in the study of human lives (e.g., anthropology, biology, and sociology). This integration is important because change across life occurs on multiple levels (e.g., biological, psychological, and social), and changes on one level often influence changes on other levels.

Although the life-span perspective forwarded by Baltes, Nesselroade, and Schaie is often associated with scholarly publications during the late 1960s (e.g., Baltes, 1968; Schaie, 1965; Schaie & Strother, 1968), several historical analyses (e.g., Baltes, 1979a, 1983; Dixon & Lerner, 1999; Dixon & Nesselroade, 1983; Havighurst, 1973; Mijller-Brettel & Dixon, 1990) have identified salient earlier contributions from both Europe and the United States: for example, Bühler (1933), Sanford (1902), Hall (1922), Havighurst (1948), Hollingworth (1927), Neugarten (1964), and Pressey, Janney, and Kuhlen (1939). In turn, however, during the 1970s and 1980s, the life-span perspective was advanced significantly by a series of conferences at West Virginia University on conceptual, methodological, and empirical issues (e.g., Baltes & Schaie, 1973; Datan & Ginsberg, 1975; Datan & Reese, 1977; McCluskey & Reese, 1984; Nesselroade & Reese, 1973), as well as by a series of volumes on life-span research (e.g., Baltes, 1978; Baltes & Brim, 1984; Baltes, Featherman, & Lerner, 1986; Featherman, Lerner, & Perlmutter, 1994).

In sum, from the life-span perspective, the potential for developmental change is seen to be present across all of life; the human life course is held to be potentially multidirectional and necessarily multidimensional. In addition, the sources of the potentially continual changes across life are seen to involve both inner–biological and outer–ecological levels of the context within which the organism is embedded. The growth of life-span developmental psychology in the 1970s led to a view of human development that suggested that individual changes across life are both products and producers of the multiple contextual levels in which a person is embedded.

Other instances of contextual theorizing in the 1970s and 1980s. In addition to the bioecological and the life-span perspectives, which were of most importance to developmental psychologists, other noteworthy instances of the influence of contextual thinking arose in the 1970s. Coming from a remarkably diverse array of intellectual traditions, these instances suggested that contextualism both offered a conceptual framework for asking ecologically meaningful questions and suggested methodological strategies for doing new and potentially more useful empirical research.

For example, in 1974 James J. Jenkins rejected the mechanistic model he had used to guide his associationistic view of memory. He suggested that instead of this traditionally American approach to the study of memory, a contextual approach be adopted (Jenkins, 1974). He argued that "what memory is depends on context" (Jenkins, 1974, p. 789), and defended this view by presenting the results of several empirical studies (Jenkins, 1974) that demonstrated that:

> What is remembered in a given situation depends on the physical and the psychological context in which the event was experienced, the knowledge and skills that the subject brings to the context, the situation in which we ask for evidence for remembering, and the relation of what the subject remembers to what the experimenter demands. (p. 793)

Jenkins (1974, p. 787) noted that to deal adequately with all these sources of variation means that "being a psychologist is going to be much more difficult than we used to think it to be." In part, this difficulty arises because there is no one mode of analysis, or methodological strategy, that is always useful in assessing all the levels of analysis involved in the memory process at all historical moments. Thus, not only is methodological pluralism promoted from this contextual perspective, but also the criterion of usefullness must be employed when deciding if a particular methodological strategy is appropriate. One must decide: "What kind of an analysis of memory will be useful to you in the kinds of problems you are

facing? What kinds of events concern you?" (Jenkins, 1974, p. 794). In other words, Jenkins (1974) believes that:

> The important thing is to pick the right kinds of events for your purposes. And it is true in this view that a whole theory of an experiment can be elaborated without contributing in an important way to the science because the situation is artificial and nonrepresentative in just the senses that determine its peculiar phenomena. In short, contextualism stresses relating one's laboratory problems to the ecologically valid problems of everyday life. (p. 794)

Thus, Jenkins (1974) reaches a conclusion quite compatible with the one Bronfenbrenner (1977) stressed.

A model of psychological functioning with marked similarity to Riegel's (1975, 1976a, 1976b) dialectical one, as well as to features of the life-span perspective, is Sarbin's (1977) *dramaturgical model*. This is a technique that, through use of the notion of employment, attempts to capture the sequence of reciprocal events between individuals and their changing social contexts. Sarbin (1977) applied his contextualist model to the analysis of data sets pertinent to the genesis of schizophrenia, the nature of hypnosis, and the characteristics of imagination, in order to illustrate the integrative utility of contextually derived ideas. His presentation serves to illustrate that contextual ideas can be useful in understanding an array of psychological processes, ranging from those associated with cognition and affect to those traditionally labeled as personality and social processes. Moreover, Sarbin stressed that the interrelation among processes cannot only be integrated by contextual thinking but, in fact, needs to be appreciated if both adaptive and nonadaptive outcomes of person–context relations are to be understood. For example, Sarbin (1977) suggested that in the understanding of the bases of schizophrenia the contextualist would, as opposed to the mechanist, take

> as his unit, not schizophrenia, not improper conduct, not the rules of society, but as much of the total context as he can assimilate. His minimal unit of study would be the man who acted as if he believed he could travel unaided through space *and* the person or persons who passed judgment on such claims. (p. 25)

Thus, as in Riegel's (1976a) model of crises being generated by conflicts among different developmental levels, Sarbin (1977) searched for the bases of adaptive and maladaptive functioning *not* within the realm of individual ("personological") functioning, but rather within the domain of the conflicts and crises created by the degrees of "goodness of fit" (Thomas & Chess, 1977) a person experiences in his or her relations with the social context. Sarbin also saw the relevance of his ideas to those put forth in other calls for contextualist thinking. In fact, he saw Jenkins (1974), as well as Cronbach (1975) and Gergen (1973), as making consonant appeals.

Indeed, these latter two papers are not the only instances of appeal for contextualism in the 1970s; other prominent examples may be cited. The *American Psychologist* is the journal of the American Psychological Association, designed to publish articles of current and broad interest to psychologists. The previously discussed articles by Jenkins (1974), Bronfenbrenner (1977), and Riegel (1977) were published in the *American Psychologist,* and in the last three years of the 1970s, three additional articles appeared in the *American Psychologist* that, in different ways, made an appeal for contextualism. Walter Mischel (1977), arguing for considering the role of context in understanding personality, suggested that unless one considered the changing and bidirectional relations between people and their worlds, an adequate understanding of consistency and change in the person could not be attained. Petrinovich (1979) promoted *probabilistic functionalism*—an idea drawn from Egon Brunswik's notion of ecological validity—which called for an array of methodological strategies not dissimilar in intent to those suggested in calls for methodological pluralism put forth by contextual thinkers such as Bronfenbrenner (1977) and Jenkins (1974), among others (Lerner, Skinner, & Sorell, 1980). Most interestingly, Albert Bandura (1978) reconceptualized his social-learning theory as involving causal processes that are based on reciprocal determinism. That is, consistent with key emphases in contextualism, Bandura asserted that, "from this perspective, psychological functioning involves a continuous reciprocal interaction between behavioral, cognitive, and environmental influences" (Bandura, 1978, p. 344).

The empirical study of individual–context relations. As noted earlier, one basis of the development, during the 1970s and 1980s, of the use of contextual ideas about human development was the empirical findings pertinent to person–context relations that were generated. These findings were both products and producers of person–context developmental models because they proved quite problematic to interpret when viewed from extant organismic- or mechanistic-derived theories. Consequently, scholars sought to evaluate the use of dialectical and/or contex-

tual–philosophical, or metatheoretical, models for such interpretations.

As is discussed in greater detail in Chapter 5, Brim and Kagan (1980) reviewed evidence about the influence of early experience on the life course. To illustrate the sort of findings discussed by Brim and Kagan (1980b), we may again note the research of Schaie (1979) (see, too, Chapter 1), which reported that the direction of age changes in intellectual aging are related to variables associated with birth cohort membership. Members of one birth cohort might show negatively accelerated changes in levels of cognitive abilities during their aged years; another cohort might show stability in these abilities during this period; and still another cohort might show continued growth in abilities during their aged years. The particular pattern depended on educational and pedagogical variables present in the context of a given cohort during the particular time in history when its members were educated.

Data generated during this period suggested that not only may contextual variables exist which differentiate people born at given times in history (and thereby influence the particular direction of their ontogenetic changes) but also there may be contextual variables, present only at specific times of measurement, which may "cut across" cohorts and influence the direction of change of people from different cohorts. For instance, Nesselroade and Baltes (1974) studied about 1,800 West Virginia male and female adolescents in 1970, 1971, and 1972. These adolescents were from birth cohorts 1954 to 1957, and, thus, ranged in age at the time of first measurement from 13 to 16. Personality questionnaires and measures of intelligence were administered to these adolescents. Contrary to what is stressed by those theorists who focus on personological components of adolescent development (e.g., Anna Freud, 1969), Nesselroade and Baltes found that change at this time of life was quite responsive to sociocultural–historical influences. In fact, age by itself was not found to be a very influential contributor to change. Rather, for these groups of adolescents, developmental change was more influenced by cultural changes over the two-year historical period than by age-related sequences. For instance, adolescents as a whole, despite their age or birth cohort, decreased in "superego strength," "social–emotional anxiety," and achievement during the 1970–1972 period. Moreover, most adolescents, regardless of age or cohort, increased in independence during this period.

The Nesselroade and Baltes (1974) data showed that it was the time at which all these differently aged adolescents were measured that was most influential in their changes. Perhaps due to the events in society of that time—for example, events associated with the Vietnam War—all adolescents scored similarly in regard to these personality characteristics. Despite where they were chronologically (i.e., their age) upon "entering" the 1970–1972 historical era, members of different cohorts changed in similar directions, presumably due to events surrounding them at the times they were tested.

Perhaps, the best example of how the changing social context provides a basis of individual development was derived from Elder's (1974) longitudinal study of the development of people who were children and adolescents during the Great Depression in the United States. Elder reported that among a group of 84 males and 83 females born 1920 or 1921, characteristics of the historical era produced alterations in the influence of education on achievement, affected later adult psychological health for youths from working-class families suffering deprivation during this era, and enhanced the importance of children in later adult marriages for youths who suffered hardships during the depression.

Other components of a person's context that can influence individual development are the physical and social characteristics of the school environment. Simmons, Rosenberg, and Rosenberg (1973) found that changes in the school context may influence personality. In a study of about 2,000 children and adolescents, they found that, in comparison to 8- to 11-year-old children, early adolescents—particularly those 12 and 13 years of age—showed more self-consciousness, greater instability of self-image, and slightly lower self-esteem. However, they discovered that contextual rather than age-associated effects seemed to account for these findings. Upon completion of the sixth grade, one portion of the early-adolescent group had moved to a new school—a local junior high school—whereas the remaining portion of the early adolescents stayed in the same school (which offered seventh- and eighth-grade classes). The group of early adolescents who changed their school setting showed a much greater incidence of the personality changes than did the group that remained in the same school. Corresponding findings were reported by Simmons and Blyth (1987). Thus, variables related to changes in the school context seem to influence the personality development of young people.

Empirical findings emerging throughout the 1970s and 1980s indicated that organism-centered models of developmental change could not account for the multidirectionality of ontogenetic change. Instead, the context of human development needed to be incorporated into any adequate analysis of the diversity of developmental trajectories that was seen to characterize the life course. This context was not, however, the simplistic, S–R environment of learning theorists (White, 1970) or of those taking a behavior–analytic approach to development (Bijou, 1976; Bijou & Baer, 1961).

The multiple levels of the context, which seem linked to the organism level over the course of the life span, cannot be reduced to the molecular elements of any extant mechanistic–behavioristic theory (Lerner & Kauffman, 1985). Instead, organism and context may be seen as two distinct, yet inextricably linked, components of the system of relationships comprising the ecology of human life (Bronfenbrenner, 1979; Ford, 1987).

Thus, and in support of the contention that research and theory during the 1970s and 1980s were mutually influential, the empirical findings about individual–context relations meshed quite well with the view of organism and context being forwarded in the dialectical, bioecological, and life-span views of human development. The view of human development that emerged from this empirical–theoretical synergy was one wherein theoretical reductionism was eschewed in favor of models that depicted changing, synthetic relations among qualitatively distinct levels of analysis. Thus, the combined influence of research and theory during these two decades was to set the stage for the elaboration, in the succeeding decade, of theories that viewed individual and context as integrated systemically across life.

Conclusions

In sum, as the decade of the 1980s ended, Paul Mussen's (1970) view of developmental science at the beginning of the 1970s—that the field placed its emphasis on explanations of the process of development—was both validated and extended. Mussen alerted developmentalists to the burgeoning interest—not in either structure, function, or content per se— but to change, to the processes through which change occurs, and thus on the means through which structures transform and functions evolve over the course of human life. His vision of and for the field presaged what emerged in the 1990s to be at the cutting-edge of contemporary developmental theory: A focus on the process through which the individual's engagement with their context constitutes the basic process of human development.

THE 1990s THROUGH TODAY: THE EMERGENCE OF DEVELOPMENTAL SYSTEMS

The interest that had emerged by the end of the 1980s in understanding the dynamic relation between individual and context was, during the 1990s, brought to a more abstract level, one concerned with understanding the character of the integration of the levels of organization comprising the context, or bioecology, of human development (Lerner, 1998a, 1998b). This concern was represented by reciprocal or dynamic conceptions of process, of how structures function and how functions are structured over time and, interestingly, by the elaboration of theoretical models that were not necessarily tied to a particular content domain but rather were focused on understanding the broader developmental system within which all dimensions of individual development emerged (e.g., Ford & Lerner, 1992; Gottlieb, 1992, 1997; Sameroff, 1983; Thelen & Smith, 1994, 1998). In other words, although particular empirical issues or substantive foci (e.g., motor development, successful aging, wisdom, extraordinary cognitive achievements, intentional behavior and goal pursuit, language acquisition, the self, psychological complexity, or concept formation) lent themselves readily as exemplary sample cases of the processes depicted in a given theory (Lerner, 1998a), the theoretical models that were forwarded within the 1990s were superordinately concerned with elucidating the character of the individual–context (relational, integrative) developmental system (1998b).

For example, as illustrated by most of the chapters in volume 1 of the fifth edition of the *Handbook of Child Psychology* (Damon, 1998), a volume titled "Theoretical Models of Human Development" (Lerner, 1998a), the theories forwarded by contributors illustrated that the interest and, arguably, the power of these instances of contemporary developmental theories lied in their ability not to be limited by (or, perhaps better, not to be confounded by an inextricable association with) a unidimensional portrayal of the developing person (e.g., the person seen only from the vantage point of stimulus–response connections; emotions, or cognitions, e.g., see Bijou & Baer, 1961, Freud, 1949; Piaget, 1970; respectively). In these theories the person was neither biologized, psychologized, nor sociologized. Rather, the individual was "systemized," that is, his or her development was conceptualized as embedded within an integrated matrix of variables derived from multiple levels of organization. Across

these theories, development was conceptualized as deriving from the dynamic relations among the variables within this multitiered matrix.

Moreover, the theories represented in volume 1 of the *Handbook* (Lerner, 1998a) did not use the polarities that engaged developmental theory in the past, most notably nature–nurture. The theories did not employ "split" depictions of developmental processes along what were argued to be conceptually implausible and empirically counterfactual lines (Gollin, 1981; Overton, 1998); the theories did not force counterproductive choices between false opposites. Rather, the theories were united by a common interest in gaining insight into the integrations that exist among the multiple levels of organization involved in human development (e.g., see Baltes et al., 1998; Brandtstädter, 1998; Bronfenbrenner & Morris, 1998; Cairns, 1998; Csikszentmihalyi & Rathunde, 1998; Elder, 1998; Fischer & Bidell, 1998; Fisher, Jackson, & Villarruel, 1998; Gottlieb, Wahlsten, & Lickliter, 1998; Lerner, 1998b; Magnusson & Stattin, 1998; Overton, 1998; Shweder et al., 1998; Thelen & Smith, 1998; Valsiner, 1998; Wapner & Demick, 1998).

These integrative, systems-oriented developmental theories articulated during the 1990s and today, then, are certainly more complex than their organismic or mechanistic predecessors. However, they are also more nuanced, more flexible, more balanced, and less susceptible to extravagant, or even absurd, claims (e.g., that "nature," split from "nurture" can shape the course of human development; that there is a gene for altruism, militarism, intelligence, and even television watching; or that when the social context is demonstrated to affect development, the influence can be reduced to a genetic one; Lorenz, 1966; Plomin, 1986; Plomin et al., 1990; Rowe, 1994; Rushton, 1987, 1988).

As a summary of the status of developmental theory at the end of the 20th century, we may note the views of William Damon. Characterizing the theories represented in the fifth edition of the *Handbook of Child Psychology*, Damon (1998) indicated that:

> Among the formidable models and approaches that the reader will find in this *Handbook* are the dynamic system theories, the life-span and life-course approaches, cognitive science and neural models, the behavior genetics approach, person–context interaction theories, action theories, cultural psychology, ecological models, neo-Piagetian and neo-Vygotskian models. Although some of these models and approaches have been in the making for some time, my impression is that they are just now coming into their own, in that researchers now are drawing on them more directly, taking their implied assumptions

and hypotheses seriously, using them with specificity and with full control, and exploiting all of their implications for practice. (p. xvi)

The range of efforts Damon notes is discussed in this book.

CONCLUSIONS

By the end of the twentieth century, then, the conceptually split, mechanistic, and atomistic views, that had been involved in so much of the history of concepts and theories of human development, had been replaced by theoretical models that stressed relationism and integration across all the distinct but fused levels of organization involved in human life. This dynamic synthesis of multiple levels of analysis is a perspective having its roots in systems theories of biological development (Cairns, 1998; Gottlieb, 1992; Kuo, 1930, 1967, 1976; Novikoff, 1945a, 1945b; Schneirla, 1956, 1957; von Bertalanffy, 1933), and allows development to be understood as a property of systemic change in the multiple and integrated levels of organization (ranging from biology to culture and history), comprising human life and its ecology.

Moreover, as noted by Cairns (1998), the interest in understanding person–context relations within an integrative, or systems, perspective has a rich history within developmental psychology as well as in developmental biology. For example, James Mark Baldwin (1897a, 1897b) expressed interest in studying development-in-context, and, thus, in understanding integrated, multilevel, and interdisciplinary scholarship (Cairns, 1998). These interests were also shared by Lightner Witmer, the founder, in 1896, of the first psychological clinic in the United States (Cairns, 1998; Lerner, 1977). Cairns describes the conception of developmental processes—as involving reciprocal interaction, bidirectionality, plasticity, and biobehavioral organization (all quite modern emphases)—as integral in the thinking of the founders of the field of human development. Wilhelm Stern (1914; see Kreppner, 1994) stressed the holism that is associated with a developmental systems perspective

about these features of developmental processes. In addition, other contributors to the foundations and early progress of the field of human development (e.g., John Dewey, 1916; Kurt Lewin, 1935, 1954; John B. Watson, 1928) stressed the importance of linking child development research with application and child advocacy—a theme of very contemporary relevance (Lerner, Fisher, & Weinberg, 1997, 2000a, 2000b; Zigler, 1999).

In short, there has been a history of visionary scholars interested in exploring the use of ideas associated with developmental systems theory for understanding the basic process of human development and for applying this knowledge within the actual contexts of people to enhance their paths across life. Developmental systems theory has emerged from its historical roots to become, today, the overarching conceptual frame associated with contemporary concepts and theories of human development.

In the succeeding chapters of this book, I (as is noted in Chapter 1) emphasize these developmental systems theories of human development. On the other hand, I do not neglect detailed consideration of theoretical positions that differ in their emphases from those associated with a developmental systems perspective. This book also considers, therefore, organismically oriented developmental theories (e.g., those associated with Sigmund Freud, Jean Piaget, and Lawrence Kohlberg) and viewpoints that involve a split concept of nature and nurture, for example, mechanistic theories associated with behavior genetics (e.g., Plomin, 1986; Rowe, 1994), sociobiology (e.g., Rushton, 1987, 1988a, 1988b), or behavioral–functional analysis approaches (e.g., Bijou & Baer, 1961).

This book discusses and evaluates the stances of both developmental systems and nondevelopmental systems theories in regard to the core conceptual issues involved in the study of human development (nature–nurture and continuity–discontinuity). This presentation rests, however, on an understanding of the key philosophical issues involved in the understanding of concepts and theories of human development. Accordingly, these philosophical issues are considered in the next chapter.

3 | *Philosophical Models of Development*

Scientists do not initiate their research without implicit and explicit assumptions. Often these assumptions take the form of theories that guide the selection of hypotheses, methods, data analysis procedures, and so on. Scientists use a specific set of rules to determine reality. Through making observations—the fundamental task of scientists—they quantitatively and/or qualitatively measure phenomena objectively under particular conditions. Then, scientists attempt to identify regularities among observations. Such regular, predictable relationships among variables are called *laws*. Finally, a *theory*—a set of statements (e.g., propositions) consisting of defined and interrelated constructs integrating these laws—is developed. Besides integrating knowledge, a theory serves the function of guiding further research.

Even though we can appraise our universe by relying on an empirical approach to knowledge, and can delineate what steps—observations, laws, and theories—are involved, a glance at the scientific literature shows that scientists do not agree about their observations, laws, and theories. This is the case primarily because they make different philosophical assumptions about the nature of the world (Kuhn, 1962; Overton, 1998; Pepper, 1942). Thus, in addition to the relatively empirical facts of science, scientists also hold *preempirical beliefs* or *presuppositions* (Kagan, 1980). These are beliefs that are not open to empirical test.

These beliefs may also be explicit or implicit (Watson, 1977). They may take the form of a presupposition about the nature of a specific feature of life—for example, that there is an inevitable connection between early experience and behavior in later life (Kagan, 1980, 1983). In addition, these beliefs may take the form of a more general "paradigm" (Kuhn, 1962, 1970), "model" (Overton & Reese, 1973; Reese & Overton, 1970), "world view" (Kuhn, 1962) or "world

hypothesis" (Pepper, 1942). These terms all pertain to a philosophical system of ideas that serves to organize a set, or a "family" (Reese & Overton, 1970), of scientific theories and associated scientific methods.

These philosophical models of the world have quite a pervasive effect on the scientific positions they influence: They specify the basic characteristics of humans, and of reality itself, and thus function either to include or exclude particular features of humans and/or of the world's events in the realm of scientific discourse. Hence, science is relative rather than absolute. Facts are not viewed as naturally occurring events awaiting discovery. According to Kuhn (1962), science

> seems an attempt to force nature into [a] preformed and relatively inflexible box . . . No part of the aim of normal science is to call forth new sorts of . . . phenomena; indeed those that will not fit the box are often not seen at all. Nor do scientists normally aim to invent new theories, and they are often intolerant of those invented by others. (p. 24)

A full understanding of human development cannot be obtained from any one theory or methodology, nor can it be obtained from a cataloging of empirical "facts." The integration of philosophy, theory, method, and research results is required to attain a complete understanding of an area of scientific scholarship. Within such an integration theory and research are given meaning. They are developed and interpreted within the context of a given philosophical perspective. Thus, we need to understand the different philosophical assumptions on which the study of development can be based. We need to examine the models, or world views, that are used today in the study of human development.

Since the early 1970s, Hayne W. Reese and Willis F. Overton have written a series of essays (Overton, 1984, 1991a, 1991b, 1991c, 1991d, 1994a, 1994b, 1994c, 1998; Overton & Reese, 1973, 1981;

Willis F. Overton

Reese, 1982, 1993, 1995; Reese & Overton, 1970) that explain the ways in which theory and method are influenced by philosophical issues pertinent to the study of human development. For instance in chapter 1, we reviewed Overton's (1998) discussion of "split" versus relational issues in philosophy. We saw how the former type of concept was linked to theories which involved the separation of nature- and nurture-related processes; within such split conceptions one process (nature or nurture) is regarded as "real," or at least of primary influence, and the other type of process is seen as pseudophenomenal or derivative (in regard to influencing development). In turn, Overton (1998) explained how theories associated with relational philosophical ideas (e.g., developmental systems theories such as developmental contextualism; Lerner, 1991, 1996, 1998b) took an integrated view of nature and nurture processes, and saw them as fused and reciprocally interactive over the course of life.

Prior to Overton's (1998) discussion of split-versus-relational ideas in philosophy, Overton and Reese (1973, 1981; Reese & Overton, 1970) focused their attention on the import for theory and method in human development of two world views—the mechanistic and the organismic—which, historically, have been central in influencing theories of development. Although, as we shall discuss later in this chapter, many theories of development associated with mechanism and organicism were *similar* in adopting split views of nature and nurture,

Reese and Overton significantly advanced the understanding of human development by describing the different "families" (related, or consonant, groups) of theories and methodological traditions associated with mechanistic- and organismic-related theories.

The work of Reese and Overton was seminal in promoting, among other developmental psychologists, an interest in exploring the potential role of other world hypotheses in shaping theories of development. For instance, as noted in chapter 2, Riegel (1975, 1977a, 1977b) discussed the potential use of a "dialectical" model of development, and Lerner (1984, 1985; Lerner, Hultsch, & Dixon, 1983; Lerner & Kauffman, 1985, 1986), as well as Reese and Overton (Reese, 1982; Overton, 1984; Overton & Reese, 1981), discussed the ways in which a "contextual" world hypothesis (Pepper, 1942) could be used to devise a theory of development. As I noted in Chapter 2, the dialectical model emphasizes syntheses among the conflicts arising from the interactions among variables from different levels of analysis (e.g., the inner–biological, individual–psychological, physical–environmental, and sociocultural; Riegel, 1975, 1976a, 1976b). We saw in Chapter 2 that

Hayne W. Reese

contextualism stresses the continually changing context of life, the bidirectional interactions among individuals and the context, and that the timing of these interactions shapes the direction and outcome of development (Pepper, 1942).

As Overton (1984) has made clear, however, these latter models (i.e., the dialectical and the contextual ones) do not readily provide a useful set of ideas for the derivation of scientifically adequate theories of development *unless* they are integrated into mechanistic or organismic conceptions. Indeed, as both Overton (1984) and Lerner and Kauffman (1985) argue, and as we again note later in this chapter, the dispersive nature of the contextual world hypothesis does not provide a useful frame for understanding the systematic, organized, and successive (or progressive) character of change that is the defining feature of development (see Chapter 1; Ford & Lerner, 1992). Thus, although Pepper (1942) claimed that it was not philosophically permissible to "mix metaphors" and combine mechanistic, organismic, and contextual world views, I believe one may do just this. Arguing on the basis of criteria of usefulness (e.g., in regard to developing statements that, in comparison to those of other positions, account for more variance in developmental data sets, lead to more novel discoveries than do ideas associated with other positions, or integrate a broader range of phenomena pertinent to development than is the case with other positions), Overton (1984) and Lerner and Kauffman (1985) advanced the notion of combining organicism and contextualism to frame a new approach to developmental theory. Overton (1984) pointed out the possibility of integrating contextualism with either mechanism *or* organicism to produce such a new theory. Similarly, Reese (1993; Hayes, Hayes, Reese, & Sarbin, 1993) discusses ways in which mechanism and contextualism are related. However, I shall argue that the mechanistic view has too many conceptual limitations for use as a model for development. In fact, I will explain that a key conceptual problem is that mechanistic theories of development inevitably follow a split view of reality, and, thus, involve a false division between nature and nurture processes (Overton, 1973, 1984, 1998). I will argue for a synthesis of organicism and contextualism (as did Overton, 1984), and will suggest that, just as contextualism needs organicism to enhance its use, so does organicism need contextualism. To begin to develop this argument, it is useful to turn to a presentation of the mechanistic, the organismic, and the contextual models.

THE MECHANISTIC– PHILOSOPHICAL MODEL

Pepper (1942) noted that each of the "world hypotheses," or philosophical models, he described (formism, mechanism, organicism, and contextualism) could be associated with a core, or root, metaphor—a concept which captured the essence of the philosophy. In mechanism, the root metaphor is a machine. As explained by Reese and Overton (1970), the mechanistic–philosophical model

> represents the universe as a machine, composed of discrete pieces operating in a spatiotemporal field. The pieces—elementary particles in motion—and their relations form the basic reality to which all other more complex phenomena are ultimately reducible. In the operation of the machine, forces are applied and there results a discrete chain-like sequence of events. These forces are the only efficient or immediate causes; purpose is seen as a mediate or derived cause. Given this, it is only a short trip to the recognition that complete prediction is in principle possible, since complete knowledge of the state of the machine at one point in time allows inference of the state at the next, given a knowledge of the forces to be applied. (p. 131)

As summarized by Anderson, this philosophical position states that "the workings of our minds and bodies, and of all the animate or inanimate matter of which we have any detailed knowledge, are assumed to be controlled by the same set of fundamental laws, which except under certain extreme conditions we feel we know pretty well" (1972, p. 393). A key assumption of the mechanistic position is that the events of all sciences can be uniformly understood by the same set of laws.

For instance, proponents of this viewpoint often hold that physics and chemistry are the basic natural sciences; they often believe that the laws of these two disciplines are the one set of fundamental laws alluded to by Anderson (1972). That is, although several different meanings of the term *mechanism* have been used by philosophers and scientists, one major version of the mechanistic position is an interpretation of biological (or psychological) phenomena in physical and chemical terms (von Bertalanffy, 1933). This interpretation provides an apt illustration for our discussion, and we focus on it to explain the position.

In this interpretation, it is the laws of chemistry and physics—the rules that depict the mechanisms by which atoms and molecules function—that are the fundamental laws of the real world. Everything involves atoms and molecules; nothing exists in the natural world that is not basically made up of these things. If one understands the mechanisms by which atoms and molecules combine and function, then one understands the laws basic to everything. The mechanics of chemistry and physics then become the ultimate laws of all events.

These basic laws that govern all natural events and phenomena, whether organic or inorganic, are held to apply to all levels of phenomenal analysis. Consistent with Nagel (1957), we define a *level* as a state of organization of matter, or life, phenomena. For example, chemistry, with its particular set of concepts and principles, represents one level of organization, while psychology, with its own set of terms, represents another. One can describe behavior at its own level or in terms of the principles of another level. We can study how children at various age levels develop the ability to perform in certain situations (e.g., on classroom tests) by attempting to discern the social relationships (between teachers and students) and the psychological factors (e.g., cognitive ability or motivation) involved in such behavior. Alternatively, these very same behaviors may be described and studied at another level. The children's performance certainly involves the functioning of their physiological systems (e.g., the central nervous system and the endocrine system), a lower level (in the sense of underlying the behavioral level) of analysis. Ultimately, of course, the functioning of their physiological systems involves the functioning of the atoms and molecules that form the basic matter of living, organic material.

These other levels—psychology or physiology—are only "derivative." That is, *in reality,* they are nothing more than levels derived from combinations of the constituent elements, the atoms and molecules governed by the laws of chemistry and physics. Hence, the split in mechanism between the real- and the pseudo-phenomena of existence is apparent.

By splitting existence into the "real" level versus the "apparent but derivative" levels, mechanists can thus seek to understand psychological and social functioning by reference to the laws of physics and chemistry. These mechanisms represent the most fundamental level of analysis that can be reached. Because this level is invariably involved in any other level, we can certainly seek to understand psychology by reference to chemistry and physics. These basic physical laws are just as applicable to human development as they are to physiology, or for that matter, to any other event or phenomenon in the natural world. Everything living or nonliving is made up of atoms and molecules. Ultimately, then, if we understand the rules by which atoms and molecules function, we can understand the components of all things in the natural world. All we must do to understand biology, psychology, sociology, or the movement of the stars is to bring each down to its most basic constituent elements, to the most fundamental level of analysis: the physical–chemical level. The events and phenomena of all sciences—of everything in the natural world—may be uniformly understood through the mechanisms involved in atoms and molecules.

Proponents of the mechanistic–philosophical viewpoint would not seek to explain the phenomena of human development per se; this is not the appropriate level of analysis. Rather, they would attempt to reduce these phenomena of physiological, psychological, and social functioning to the fundamental level of analysis—the laws of chemistry and physics. The basic epistemological point of this mechanistic position, then, is *reductionism.* That is, to gain knowledge of a level of phenomenal organization, the route to take is to reduce the phenomena of a given (higher) level to the elemental, fundamental (lower, or molecular) units that comprise it.

Thus, it is believed that there is nothing special about the complex pattern of events we call physiological, psychological, or social functioning. In the final analysis, these events involve the functioning of the very same atoms and molecules that are involved in the workings of a liver, a kidney, or a shooting star. Thus, like everything else, physiological, psychological, or social phenomena are governed by the laws of chemistry and physics and, upon appropriate reduction, may be understood in terms of those laws. From this standpoint, then, if we knew enough about chemistry and physics, we could eliminate the sciences of human development, physiology, psychology, or sociology completely. For example, Homans (1961) proposed a stimulus–response view of social functioning that attempted to reduce the phenomena studied by sociology to the elemental units of classical and, especially, operant conditioning. In turn, Wilson (1975) proposed a genetic reductionist view of social functioning (termed *sociobiology,* discussed in Chapter 13) which was aimed at eliminating the need for the sciences of psychology, sociology, and even anthropology. Thus, as pointed out by Bolles (1967, p. 5), this reductionistic assumption involves "the doctrine that all natural events have physical causes, and that if we knew enough about physical and mechanical systems we would then be able to explain, at least in principle, all natural phenomena."

Reductionism directly implies a *continuity* position. No new laws are needed to explain the phenomena of a given level of study; rather, the same exact laws apply at all levels. Since natural phenomena at any and all levels can be reduced to the phenomena of the fundamental physical–chemical level, these same laws are continuously applicable to all levels of phenomena. Since no new, additional, or different laws are needed to account for or to understand the phenomena that may be thought to characterize any particular level, continuity by definition exists. As we have seen, psychological or social functioning may be reduced to the level of chemistry and physics *because* the latter level is invariably present in anything that exists.

What this means, then, is that the "real" laws governing any and all events in the world are really the laws of chemistry and physics. There is again, then, a split: The only real laws are those that pertain to the "to-be-reduced-to-level" (i.e., chemistry and physics). "Laws" about other levels do not reflect the reality of the true, causal phenomena of the natural world. In essence, the mechanistic position holds that in the final analysis one must inevitably deal with certain fundamental laws in order to completely, accurately, and ultimately understand any and all living and nonliving matter in the natural world. And, as Anderson (1972) has commented, once this concept is accepted:

> It seems inevitable to go on uncritically to what appears at first sight to be an obvious corollary of reductionism: That if everything obeys the same fundamental laws, then the only scientists who are studying anything really fundamental are those who are working on those laws. In practice, that amounts to some astrophysicists, some elementary particle physicists, some logicians and other mathematicians, and few others. (p. 393)

Because of the belief that reductionism will lead to fundamental knowledge, and because of the associated postulation of continuity in the laws and mechanisms that are involved in an appropriate consideration of natural phenomena, two events may ultimately occur. First, the phenomena in the world labeled psychological or social would no longer be a focus of scientific concern; these phenomena are not fundamental—they must be reduced to be appropriately understood. Second, the people in the world labeled physiologists, psychologists, sociologists, or human developmentalists would no longer be necessary; these people are not studying fundamental phenomena of the natural world.

What would replace psychology, sociology, and, in fact, all sciences other than the "fundamental" ones, would be a consideration of the basic mechanisms of the physical–chemical level of analysis. To understand every event and phenomenon in the natural world one must understand the mechanisms of physics and chemistry. This statement highlights another major attribute of the mechanistic position. Adherents of this position conceptualize the functioning of the components (the atoms and molecules) of the most fundamental level of analysis within the framework of a machine. As we have seen, according to this model, biological or psychological phenomena are only seemingly complicated constellations of physical and chemical processes. In principle, once we know the mechanisms of physical and chemical functioning, we know all we have to know about the world. In other words, because the fundamental level of analysis functions mechanistically, all the world is seen as functioning mechanistically.

Since physics and chemistry are machine-like sciences, all that must be done in order to move from one level of analysis to another is to specify the mechanism by which the basic elements of physics and chemistry combine. Since the molecular (physical–chemical) laws apply at the higher (physiological, psychological, or social) level, it is necessary only to discern the mechanisms by which these molecular elements are quantitatively added. In other words, to go to a higher level, all one must do is add these elements to what was present at the lower level.

If, by analogy, the nervous system was made up of 10 oranges, the circulatory system of 18 oranges, the respiratory system of 6 oranges, etc., all that would be necessary for moving up to the psychological–behavioral level would be to add all the oranges together. Thus, the only difference between levels is a quantitative one, a difference in amount, size, magnitude, and so on.

The mechanistic position is diagrammatically illustrated in Figure 3.1. Two levels of analysis are represented; Level 1, for example, could be the biological level, and, Level 2, the psychological level. Both are comprised of the same basic thing, in this case, oranges. To move from one level to another all one must do is add more oranges. Thus, between the two levels there is a continuity in the basic elements that make up each level; each level can be reduced to the same basic elements.

In summary, when the mechanistic philosophy of science is used as a framework from which to

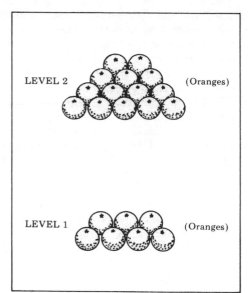

FIGURE 3.1
Mechanistic position: Each level is comprised of the same basic elements.

devise a theory of development, adherents of the mechanistic model would view psychology, sociology, or human development as branches of natural science (e.g., see Bijou, 1976; Bijou & Baer, 1961). They would seek to reduce the phenomena of psychological or social functioning to basic mechanical laws (e.g., stimulus–response relations, as in Bijou & Baer, 1961, or Homans, 1961, or to the combinations of chemicals involved in the activity of genes, as in Plomin, 1986; Rowe, 1994). They would attempt such reductions because they believe that these laws continuously apply to all phenomenal levels. In this view, the phenomena of psychology or sociology are not unique in nature but are, rather, controlled by the laws that govern all events and phenomena in the natural world. The position thus holds that there are basic and common laws that govern all things in the universe. Neither biology, psychology, sociology, nor any science (other than physics or chemistry), for that matter, really has its own special laws; in a basic sense, all sciences—and more important, all events and phenomena in the real world—are controlled by a common set of principles. It is believed that the phenomena, or events, that all sciences study can be uniformly subsumed (unified) and understood by one common set of natural-science principles (see Harris, 1957).

Thus, the basic characteristics of the mechanistic position are as follows:

1. It is a *natural-science* viewpoint.

2. It is a *reductionist* viewpoint.

3. It is a *continuity* viewpoint.

4. It is a *unity-of-science* viewpoint.

5. It is a *quantitative* viewpoint.

6. It is an *additive* viewpoint.

Translating the Mechanistic Philosophy Into a Theory of Development

As I have briefly illustrated, when the mechanistic model is transformed, or translated, into a set of ideas pertinent to human development, a reactive, passive, or "empty-organism" model of humans results (Reese & Overton, 1970). From this perspective, the human is inherently passive; his or her activity results from the action of external forces, ones placed *on* the person through environmental stimulation or *in* the person through genetic inheritance. In either case, it is not the individual's own action that is the basis of his or her development. Rather, it is the force of nature (genes) *or* nurture (the stimulus environment) that is the real basis of the behavior of the developing person.

For example, in one behavioristic instance of this mechanistic position, stimuli are held to evoke a response from a passive organism. The works of Skinner (1938), Bijou (1976), Baer (1982), Bijou and Baer (1961), and Gewirtz (1961) are representative of this position. These authors try to formulate the determining mechanisms of human behavioral development according to a natural-science model (Bijou & Baer, 1961). They attempt to discern the empirical (observable) and quantifiable parameters of environmental stimulation that fit this model (Gewirtz & Stingle, 1968).

As is discussed in detail in Chapter 10, the nature, mechanistic–developmental theory of Rowe (1994) claims to eliminate the need for "socialization science" by reducing all psychological and social phenomena to genes. Viewing behavior as a quantitative addition of discrete elements that combine, analogously, in the mechanical manner of chemistry and physics, nature or nurture mechanistic theorists appropriately look to elements other than the individual as the source of human development. A machine is passive until extrinsic energy activates it. Human beings, viewed as machines, are also passive until environmental stimulation (nurture) or the genes inherited at conception (nature) causes them to act. Thus, human development becomes just the historical, "mechanical mirror" (Langer, 1969) of environmental stimulation or genetic determination. Moreover, as Reese and Overton (1970) explain, *changes* in the "products of the machine," that is, changes over time in the behavior of organisms, do *not* result from phenomena intrinsic to their "own" (individual) level (i.e., their psychological, behavioral, or social relationship level); rather, again, changes result from (can ultimately be reduced to) alterations in the stimuli impinging on them or the genes placed in them.

Thus, those committed to such a mechanistic position would, in their psychological theorizing, try to explain behavioral development in terms of the principles of classical and operant conditioning (e.g., Baer, 1982; Bijou, 1976; Bijou & Baer, 1961; Gewirtz & Stingle, 1968); the principles of genetic inheritance (e.g., Plomin, 1986; Rowe, 1994); or the purported principles of genetic reproduction (such as gametic potential and inclusive fitness; Dawkins, 1976). Given that much of chapters 10 through 13 is devoted to a discussion of these latter, nature, mechanistic positions, it is useful to illustrate the "translation" of mechanistic philosophy into a theory of human development by focusing on instances of nurture, mechanistic theories.

A Nurture, Mechanistic Theory of Development

All mechanistic theories have a split ontology. They must split nature from nurture and hold that only one of these domains of potential influence is actually real. Since the epistemology of mechanists is to reduce all phenomena to one common constituent level, it cannot be logically maintained that there are two *different* and real levels (sources) of influence on the person's development, nature *and* nurture. Either one level has to be reduced to another (as Rowe, 1994, does when he reduces family and other social influences to the activity of genes), or the other level has to be accepted as materially real but not functionally (efficiently) real (or relevant) in the determination of behavior and development. This latter split is the type typically adopted within nurture, mechanistic theories of human development.

In such viewpoints, humans are, at their core and/or initially in their ontogeny, basically passive entities, awaiting stimulation from the environment in order to act, or more accurately, to respond. How does such stimulation bring human behavior under control?

Many mechanistic–behavioristic theorists would suggest that the principles of classical (respondent) conditioning and of operant (instrumental) conditioning can explain it. The former set of principles can account for stimulation-produced responding ($S \rightarrow R$) while the latter can account for response-produced stimulation ($R \rightarrow S$). Given the broad applicability of these types of conditioning in the natural world, they should be able to account for the acquisition of the responses of organisms (Bijou, 1976; Bijou & Baer, 1961). Such mechanistic–behavioristic theorists deal with the generic human being—the general case of humanity. The laws of conditioning are ubiquitous in their applicability to all human behavior and, for that matter, to the behavior of all organisms (see Skinner, 1938). External stimulation provides the material and efficient cause of behavior and development.

From a mechanistic–behavioristic perspective, organisms differ across their life span only in the quantitative presence of qualitatively identical behavioral units (i.e., elements of the behavioral repertoire acquired by the causally efficient laws of conditioning; e.g., Bijou, 1976; Bijou & Baer, 1961). As such, the organism is seen as a host (Baer, 1976) of these elements, and even the most complex human behavior is believed to be reducible to these identically constituted units (Bijou, 1976). The only constraint on behavioral change in a consequent period of life is imposed by past (i.e., antecedent) reinforcement history; that is, the repertoire of behaviors present in an organism at any point in time may moderate the efficiency by which current stimuli can extinguish or otherwise modify any particular behavior in the repertoire. The meaning of "past reinforcement history," however, may be such as to preclude any strong view of the potential for developmental change beyond the earliest periods of life.

From the mechanistic, behavior perspective, no strong (i.e., idealized) view of development is present. Instead, the concept of development is reduced to a concept of change in the elements of the behavioral repertoire; therefore, change is brought about by processes that either add to or subtract from the behavioral repertoire via conditioning. Consequently, change at any point in life becomes a technological matter that occurs with regard to past reinforcement history, and pertains to such issues as management of stimulus contingencies and of reinforcement schedules (e.g., in regard to building up, reducing, or rearranging a behavioral "chain" of stimulus–response connections).

Interindividual differences in response to a stimulus or interindividual differences in intraindividual change may become particularly problematic from this perspective. The only way in which such differences may be accounted for is by reference to differences in past reinforcement history, a history that may be typically uncharted among humans. Indeed, two organisms exposed to the same stimulus history, who nevertheless, react differently to the same immediate stimulus would present a formidable interpretative problem for this perspective (since an internal organizing structure independent of past stimulus history is not part of this model). Thus, since humans from quite similar backgrounds (e.g., identical twins reared together) may not behave in exactly the same way, scientists functioning from this perspective are forced to account for such differences by postulating some unseen but efficiently causal difference in stimulus history, or by arguing that such behavioral differences arise merely as a consequence of errors of measurement. Alternatively, such differences may be ignored.

Given the belief in the continuous and exclusive applicability of, and only of, functional (which in this perspective means efficient, and, in some cases, material; Skinner, 1966) stimulus–behavior relations, *only* the most simplistic view of the context is found in this perspective (e.g., Bijou, 1976). I do not use the term "simplistic" in any pejorative sense; rather, it serves to indicate that, in the behavioristic tradition, one can use only those features of the context—that is, the stimulus environment in the terms of this perspective—that can be translated into stimulus–response units. Features of the context that cannot be translated (i.e., reduced) into such units are invisible in this approach. For instance, sociopolitical historical events or emergent qualitative changes in social structures must either be reduced to elementaristic, behavioral terms or ignored. Moreover, because of a necessarily unequivocal commitment to reduce to efficiently causal antecedents, a strict mechanistic–behavioral position (e.g., the functional–analysis position of Baer, 1982) must be committed to the views (a) that early (indeed the earliest) stimulus–response experience is prepotent in shaping the rest of life; and (b) that, therefore, there can be no true novelty or qualitative change in life. Taken literally, a belief that any current behavior or event can be explained by or reduced to an antecedent efficient cause or a stimulus, means—in behavioral terms—that all of life must ultimately be explainable by the earliest experience of such antecedent–consequent relations. Any portion of "later" life must be explained by efficiently causal prior events. Thus, nothing new or qualitatively distinct can, in actuality, emerge consequent to these initial events.

Zukav (1979) explains this feature of mechanistic thinking (in regard to Newtonian physics) by noting that:

> If the laws of nature determine the future of an event, then, given enough information, we could have predicted our present at some time in the past. That time in the past also could have been predicted at a time still earlier. In short, if we are to accept the mechanistic determination of Newtonian physics—if the universe really is a great machine—then from the moment that the universe was created and set in motion, everything that was to happen in it already was determined. According to this philosophy, we may seem to have a will of our own and the ability to alter the course of events in our lives, but we do not. Everything, from the beginning of time has been predetermined, including our illusion of having a free will. The universe is a prerecorded tape playing itself out in the only way it can. (p. 26)

In short, the nurture, mechanistic–behavioral position represents a "translation" into psychological theory of the natural science, efficiently causal philosophy that Zukav (1979) describes in regard to Newtonian physics; that is, the first physical antecedent–consequent relation is transformed into the first, or at least quite an early, stimulus–response connection. Although it is not emphasized in many discussions of mechanistic–behavioral views, such as the functional-analysis perspective (Baer, 1982; Reese, 1982), the early proponents of this view were quite clear in their belief that early experience was prepotent in shaping all of life (see Kagan, 1983).

John B. Watson (1928) argued that "at three years of age the child's whole emotional life plan has been laid down, his emotional disposition set" (p. 45). Moreover, Watson (1924) boasted that:

> Give me a dozen healthy infants, well-formed, and my own specified world to bring them up in and I'll guarantee to take any one at random and train him to become any type of specialist I might select—doctor, lawyer, artist, merchant—chief and yes, even beggarman and thief, regardless of his talents, penchants, tendencies, abilities, vocations, race of his ancestors. (p. 82)

However, what often goes unrecognized is that Watson (1924) knew that this assertion about the efficacy of the application of radical behavioristic ideas in shaping behavior was quite overstated. That is, he admitted that:

> I am going beyond my facts and I admit it, but so have the advocates of the contrary and they have been doing it for many thousands of years. (p. 82)

Nevertheless, Watson, and other behaviorists, in seeking to counter what they regarded as the similarly overstated claims of nativists, continued to insist on the primacy of early experience. For example, Edward Thorndike (1905) contended that:

> Though we seem to forget what we learn, each mental acquisition really leaves its mark and makes future judgment more sagacious . . . nothing of good or evil is ever lost; we may forget and forgive, but the neurones never forget or forgive . . . It is certain that every worthy deed represents a modification of the neurones of which nothing can ever rob us. Every event of a man's mental life is written indelibly in the brain's archives, to be counted for or against him. (pp. 330–331)

Such views constitute a belief that the potential changes able to be induced in the person by later experience are quite limited, and that the potential for plasticity in later childhood, adolescence, and in the adult and aged years is markedly constrained by "early experience," by "past reinforcement history."

The point of the present discussion is to make clear the general nature of the translation of the mechanistic, reductionistic–philosophical position into the psychological theoretical position of such nurture, mechanistic–behavioristic psychologists as Bijou (1976), Bijou and Baer (1961), and Baer (1982). To such psychologists, all behavioral functioning is a consequence of stimulation. To understand behavior at any and all points in development, all one must do is understand the laws by which a person's responses come to be under the control of environmental stimulation.

Scientists functioning from this viewpoint often contend that there are two sets of laws that describe and explain how responses come under environmental stimulation: those of classical and operant conditioning. Because all behavior is ultimately controlled by the stimulus world, and because this world exerts its control through the functioning of a fundamental set of laws of conditioning, all behavior may be understood by reducing it to these same basic laws of stimulus–response relations. All behavior—whether of two different species of animals (rats and humans) or of two different age-groups of children (5- and 15-year olds)—is composed of the same basic stimulus–response elements, and these same basic elements are always associated on the basis of the same laws. Hence, seemingly complex behavior may be understood by reducing it to the same basic constituent elements that make up any and all behavior. Because all behavior may be so reduced, the same laws must, therefore, be applicable to explain behavior at any (animal or human age) level at which it occurs. Continuity in the laws of conditioning, in

the rules that account for behavioral functioning, is another aspect of this approach.

Thus, to completely understand behavioral functioning and development, one must simply know the mechanisms by which stimuli in a person's world come to control that person's behavior at all points in the life span. Once these mechanisms are known, one can reduce behavior at different points in life to common constituent elements. In turn, because the same elements comprise behavior at each level, one can account for any differences in behavior between points in the life span merely by reference to the quantitative difference in the stimulus–response relations in the person's behavior repertoire. If behavior is composed totally of the stimulus–response relations a person has acquired over the course of life as a function of conditioning, then the difference between behavior at any two points in life could only be a quantitative one in the number of associations acquired. One could move from lower to higher levels of behavior analysis simply by adding on the similarly acquired stimulus–response associations.

By this point, then, the way in which the nurture, mechanistic model becomes translated into a theoretical view of human development should be clear. Although the mechanistic position is an abstract philosophical view of the nature of the real world, the position is not without its influence in science in general and human development in particular. One basis for this influence in human development is that behavioral phenomena traditionally associated with behaviorism (e.g., classical and operant conditioning, desensitization, and behavioral shaping) depict important features of behavioral *change,* if not behavioral development. Thus, the mechanistic position frames what are, descriptively, important means through which person–context relations (typically reduced, of course, to stimulus–response connections) may change.

Accordingly, in providing the philosophical basis of the empirical–behavioral or the functional–analysis (Baer, 1982; Bijou, 1976; Reese, 1982) approach to human development, the mechanistic position presents what has been an influential philosophical–psychological view of the nature of humanity. Naturally, the position has had significant criticisms leveled at it. In fact, one may view the organismic position as a culmination of the objections raised about the assumptions and assertions of the mechanistic position (Bertalanffy, 1933). As a means of transition to our discussion of the organismic position, let us first consider some of the important problems of the mechanistic position.

Problems of the Mechanistic Model

We have seen that the core conceptual basis of the mechanistic model is reductionism. We have also seen that the belief in reductionism is predicated on the assertion that, because all matter is made up of basic (e.g., physical–chemical) components, the only appropriate, necessary, and sufficient approach to investigating the fundamental laws of natural world is to study these basic components. Hence, the adherent of the mechanistic model asserts that to understand any and all levels of phenomena in the real world, these higher levels must be reduced to the laws of the fundamental constituent level. However, Anderson (1972) in describing the reductionistic component of the mechanistic position, also sees the viewpoint as advancing an argument containing a logical error:

> The main fallacy in this kind of thinking is that the reductionist hypothesis does not by any means imply a "constructionist" one: The ability to reduce everything to simple fundamental laws does not imply the ability to start from those laws and reconstruct the universe. In fact, the more the elementary particle physicists tell us about the nature of the fundamental laws, the less relevance they seem to have to the very real problems of the rest of science, much less to those of society. (p. 393)

But why does the ability to reduce from a higher, seemingly more complex, level of analysis to the lower level not necessarily imply the reverse? Why does such reductionistic ability not imply that one can move from the lower to the higher levels—and thereby construct the universe—by simply adding more of the same constituent elements onto what already exists at a lower level? Why, when we attempt to do this, and when we concomitantly learn more and more about the fundamental level, do we seem to be missing an understanding of the important problems and phenomena of the higher levels? Why does the reductionist fail when attempting to also be a constructionist? Again, we may turn to Anderson (1972):

> The constructionist hypothesis breaks down when confronted with the twin difficulties of scale and complexity. The behavior of large and complex aggregates of elementary particles, it turns out, is not to be understood in terms of a simple extrapolation of the properties of a few particles. Instead, *at each level of complexity entirely new properties appear,* and the understanding of the new behaviors requires research which I think is as fundamental in its nature as any other. That is, it seems to me that one may array the sciences roughly linearly in a hierarchy, according to the idea: The elementary entities of science X obey the laws of science Y.

X	Y
Solid-state or many-body physics	Elementary particle physics
Chemistry	Many-body physics
Molecular biology	Chemistry
Cell biology	Molecular biology
.	.
.	.
Psychology	Physiology
Social sciences	Psychology

> But this hierarchy does not imply that science X is "just applied Y." *At each stage entirely new laws, concepts, and generalizations are necessary,* requiring inspiration and creativity to just as great a degree as in the previous one. Psychology is not applied biology, nor is biology applied chemistry. (p. 393, italics added)

What Anderson is saying, therefore, is that the constructionist hypothesis fails because, simply, "more is different." In other words, as one studies levels of higher and higher complexity, one concomitantly sees that new, qualitatively different characteristics come about—or emerge—at each of these levels. The new characteristics are not present at the lower, fundamental level and are, therefore, not understandable by reduction to the lower level. One cannot move from higher to lower levels (and back again) merely by adding or subtracting more of the same, because as one combines more of the same into a higher level of complexity, this combination has a quality that is not present in the less complex constituent elements as they exist in isolation. Thus, the reductionist–mechanistic position fails because reductionism does not mean constructionism, and in turn, constructionism fails because of the presence of qualitatively new properties emerging and characterizing each higher level of analysis.

Reductionism also fails for other reasons. Reductionism is predicated on the belief that reference to the constituent elements comprising all matter can suffice in accounting for the nature of phenomena at all levels of analysis. However, we have seen that this continuity assumption is weak. If new, qualitatively different phenomena characterize each higher level of analysis, then, by definition, continuity does not exist. If something new does exist, this clearly means that just the same thing as existed before does not exist. One may not explain all natural phenomena by reference to one common set of continuously applicable fundamental laws. In other words, the shortcomings of the reductionistic–mechanistic position— whether it is a nature or a nurture version of such a view—also include the inadequacy of its continuity assumption. Thus, this philosophical position is unable to explain all natural phenomena through reduction to one set of fundamental laws. Reductionism cannot be used to explain successfully all levels of phenomena in the natural world because (Eacker, 1972):

> This conception appears to ignore the additional fact that once the behavior has been explained physiologically, the physiology still remains to be explained (cf. Skinner, 1950). Furthermore, if physiology in turn is to be explained by biochemistry and it by physics, how physics is to be explained poses an enduring problem because there are no sciences left. In short, this type of explanation leads to a finite regression with one science left unexplained, unless, of course, it is self-explanatory; no one is likely to admit that of physics. (p. 559)

We see, then, that there are many problems with the mechanistic model. It fails to suffice in accounting for the nature of the phenomena present at all levels of analysis because at each level of analysis there exist qualitatively new, and, hence, discontinuous, phenomena. One should perhaps resort to a point of view that emphasizes these phenomena. What is being alluded to is the fact that the very objections raised about the mechanistic position seem, in their explication, to suggest the necessary characteristics for a point of view that would successfully counter the po-sition. Specifically, mechanistic constructionism fails because new phenomena emerge to characte-rize higher levels of analysis; therefore, the first component of a successful alternative position would be one positing the emergence of qualitatively discontinuous changes as characterizing development. This notion of emergence would be introduced to counter the problems of reductionism, while the idea of qualitative discontinuity would be raised to address the inability of a mechanistic constructionist position to account for all phenomena present at all levels. In essence, a developing organism would be viewed as a creature passing through qualitatively different levels (e.g., phases or stages) of development, periods made different because of the presence of new (lawfully distinct) phenomena emerging to characterize that portion of the life span.

These alternative views of the nature of differences between levels of analysis, or between portions of the ontogeny of an organism, are represented in the organismic philosophy of science. Let us consider the ways in which this second position offers a view of the world in contrast to mechanism.

THE ORGANISMIC MODEL

As explained by Reese and Overton (1970), the organismic model has as its basic metaphor "the organism, the living, organized system presented to experience in multiple forms" (p. 132). Moreover, Reese and Overton (1970) go on to note that:

> The essence of substance is activity rather than the static elementary particle proposed by the mechanistic model. . . . In this representation, then, the whole is organic rather than mechanical in nature. The nature of the whole, rather than being the sum of its parts, is presupposed by the parts and the whole constitutes the condition of the meaning and existence of the parts . . . the important point here is that efficient cause is replaced by formal cause (i.e., cause by the essential nature of a form). (p. 133)

Adherents of one or another version or instance of the organismic philosophy of science (e.g., Bertalanffy, 1933; Schneirla, 1957; Tobach, 1981) reject the reductionism of mechanism and maintain that at each new level of phenomenal organization there is an emergence of new phenomena that cannot be reduced to lower levels of organization. They hold that one cannot appropriately make a quantitative reduction to a lower organizational level and hope to understand all phenomena at the higher organizational level. This inability to reduce occurs because, at each higher organizational level, something new comes about, or emerges (Novikoff, 1945a, 1945b). Thus, a change in quality and not merely in quantity characterizes the differences between one level of analysis and another. If one reduces to the lower level, one eliminates the opportunity of dealing with the new characteristic (which is actually the essential characteristic) of the higher level, the very attribute that defines the difference between the lower and higher levels.

For example, going from one animal level to another, or from one stage of human life to another, would be analogous to changing from an orange into a motorcycle. How many oranges comprise a motorcycle? Obviously this is a ludicrous question, because here we have a change in kind, type, or quality, rather than merely in amount, magnitude, or quantity.

The above argument—the irreducibility of a later form to an earlier one—is the essence of the *epigenetic viewpoint,* the view that human development is characterized by the emergence of new forms across ontogeny. One cannot reduce a qualitative change, something new, to a precursory form. Epigenesis denotes that at each higher level of complexity there emerges a new characteristic, one that simply was not present at the lower organizational level and, thus, whose presence is what establishes a new level as just that—a stage of organization qualitatively different from a preceding one. Thus, according to Gottlieb (1970, p. 111), epigenesis connotes that patterns of behavioral activity and sensitivity are not immediately evidenced in the initial stages of development. Since development is characterized by these qualitative emergences, then by definition the various new behavioral capacities that develop are not actually present until they do in fact emerge.

The doctrine of epigenesis asserts that development is characterized by qualitative "emergences." Simply, new things come about in development. Newness means just that: Something now exists that was not present before, either in smaller or even in precursory form. Epigenesis asserts that development is represented by the emergence of characteristics at each new stage of development that were not present in any precursory form before their time of appearance.

The presence of qualitatively new characteristics at each higher stage indicates that reduction to lower levels is inappropriate—if full understanding of the new stage is sought. For instance, the behavior of a three-month old may *perhaps* be understood by reference to relatively simple stimulus–response, reflexlike associations; yet, when the child reaches about two years of age there may emerge a new symbolic function—language (as an example of the ability to represent physical reality through use of nonphysical symbols). Thus, as one consequence of this representational ability, the child may now show behaviors (e.g., being able to imitate some person or event long after the time of actual viewing) that can best be understood by reference to this emergent symbolic ability; trying to reduce this two-year-old's behavior to the functioning shown at an earlier age would be inappropriate because the representational ability that enables one to account for the two-year-old's behavior was simply not present at the earlier age.

Thus, an antireductionist view is maintained because the qualitative change that depicts a higher stage of development cannot be understood, since it does not exist, at the lower level. Because the nature of what exists changes from stage to stage, and because there is qualitative change from stage to stage, there cannot be complete continuity between stages. New things—variables, processes, and/or laws—represent the differences between stages; hence, such qualitative change means that discontinuity (at least in

part) characterizes differences between stages. Such differences are in *what* exists and not just in *how much* exists. Thus, to the organismic thinker, laws of the psychological level of analysis are unique in nature—they are not merely reducible to the laws of physics and chemistry. Similarly, each different phyletic or ontogene-tic level is viewed as having features qualitatively discontinuous from every other.

This aspect of the organismic position is represented in Figure 3.2, which shows qualitative discontinuity between the two levels represented. Because something new has emerged at the higher level, one cannot reduce one level to another. Level 1 is comprised of oranges and Level 2 is a motorcycle. One cannot hope to understand the functioning of a motorcycle through even an intensive study of oranges!

But, on what basis do proponents of the organismic viewpoint assert that qualitative discontinuity characterizes development? How do organismic thinkers explain their assertion that epigenesis—qualitative discontinuity—represents differences between levels?

Organismic thinkers would be in agreement with an idea borrowed from Gestalt psychology, that the whole (the organism) is more than the sum of its parts. That is, a human organism is more than a liver added to two kidneys, to one spinal cord, to one brain, to one heart, and so on. Organismic thinkers would reject the additive,

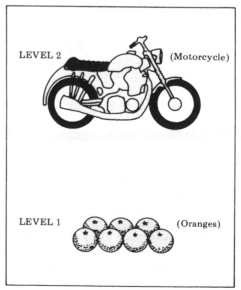

FIGURE 3.2
Organismic position: Qualitative discontinuity exists between levels.

and implicitly splitting assumption underlying the mechanistic position, and, instead, maintain that a fused, integrative, and holistic type of combination would be more accurate. They would argue that organisms, as organized and relational systems, show in the integrations among their constituent elements (their parts) properties that cannot be reduced to physical and chemical terms.

One may reach a physical and chemical understanding of a kidney, a brain, and a liver. However, properties will be seen in the organism considered as a whole that derive not from the separate organ systems per se but from their relations (integrations) with each other. When parts combine they produce a property that did not exist in the parts in isolation. The parts do not merely add up (e.g., 2 + 3 = 5), but multiplicatively interact (e.g., 2 × 3 = 6; hence, one more unit is present here than with the additive combination). This interaction brings about the emergence of a new property.

In essence, the organismic viewpoint asserts that the basis of the epigenetic (qualitatively discontinuous) emergences that characterize development lies in the multiplicative interactions of the constituent parts of the organism. When the parts combine, they produce a new complexity, a characteristic existing only as a product of the interaction of these parts. This new property does not exist in any of the constituent parts—or in any of the lower organizational levels—even in precursory form.

Ludwig von Bertalanffy (1933), a leading formulator of the organismic viewpoint, suggested that nothing can be learned about the organism as such from a study of its parts in isolation. He believed that this inability existed because an organism, in its natural state, viewed as a whole being (and not just as a bunch of constituent parts), shows phenomena that are so different from physical, mechanistic ones that entirely new concepts are needed to understand them.

Thus, if one accepts the epigenetic, organismic point of view; a mechanistic, reductionistic view of organisms is entirely inappropriate. The characteristics of a whole living organism have nothing in common with the characteristics or structures of a machine (or a kidney, liver, or other organ split off from the whole organism). Such distinctions occur because the characteristics—or parts—of a machine can be separated without a change in their basic properties. For instance, a car's carburetor will still be a carburetor, and will still have the same properties, regardless of whether it is

Ludwig von Bertalanffy

attached to a car. But, according to the organismic position, this is not the case with living organisms. With living organisms, at each new level of analysis an emergence takes place; with every step building up to the whole living organism, from an atom to a molecule to a cell to a tissue to an organ, new phenomena occur that cannot be derived from the lower, subordinate levels.

Thus, knowledge of the functioning of the various subsystems that make up an organism does not lead to an understanding of the whole organism. For example, water has an emergent quality (its liquidness) that cannot be understood by reducing water to its constituent (and gaseous) elements (hydrogen and oxygen). Similarly, human beings have unique characteristics (or qualities), such as being able to love, being governed by abstract principles of moral and ethnical conduct, or showing high levels of "need achievement," that emerge as ontogenetically distinct (qualitatively discontinuous) features and cannot be understood by mere reduction to underlying neural, hormonal, and muscular processes. As I have already noted, a basis for this position, which is put forward by organismic theorists, is a belief in epigenetic processes—a belief that at each new level of behavioral organization there emerge qualitatively new (discontinuous) phenomena that cannot be reduced to lower levels.

In summary, the basic characteristics of the organismic position are:

1. It is an *epigenetic* viewpoint.

2. It is an *antireductionist* viewpoint.

3. It is a *qualitative* viewpoint.

4. It is a *discontinuity* viewpoint.

5. It is an *integrative relational*, or *multiplicative* interactionist viewpoint.

Translating the Organismic Model Into a Theory of Development

When the organismic model is translated into a set of ideas pertinent to human development, an active organism model of humans results. From this perspective, the human is inherently active; that is, it is the human who provides a source of its behaviors in the world, rather than the world providing the source of the human's behaviors. Humans, by virtue of their structure, give meaning to their behavior; that is, they provide it with organization—with form—by virtue of integrating any given behavior into the whole. Thus, humans, by virtue of their activity and organization, are *constructors* of their world rather than passive responders to it. Moreover, as a consequence of the inherent activity of humans, change or development is accepted as given (Reese & Overton, 1970). In other words, change may not be reduced to efficient or material causes, although such causes may impede or facilitate change. Rather, the structure or configuration of mental or behavioral life, the integrated lattice of relationships, or simply the form of the whole, is the basis of the individual's development. In short, formal cause is basic in the organismic perspective (Reese & Overton, 1970).

From the organismic perspective, development of a given process (e.g., cognition) is an idealized and goal-directed intraorganism phenomenon. As explained by Pepper (1942):

> With organicism, no ordinary common-sense term offers a safe reference to the root metaphor of the theory. The common term "organism" is too much loaded with biological connotations, too static and cellular, and "integration" is only a little better. Yet there are no preferable terms. With a warning we shall accordingly adopt these [p. 280] . . . The categories of organicism consist, on the one hand, in noting the steps involved in the organic process, and, on the other hand, in noting the principal features in the organic

structure ultimately achieved or realized. The structure achieved or realized is always the ideal aimed at by the progressive steps of the process [p. 281]. . . . The pivotal point in the system . . . is the goal and final stage of the progressive categories and it is the field for the specification of the ideal categories. (p. 283)

Qualitative change, forged by the inevitable synthesis of contradictions, as is, for example, represented by emergent structural reorganization (Piaget, 1970) or focal reorientation in the mode of dealing with the world or with gratifying one's emotions (e.g., Erikson, 1959; Freud, 1954), is seen as the key feature of development. Thus, the organismic approach is a holistic one, one wherein *formal* cause, and in its "purest" philosophical formulation also *final* cause (also termed teleological, or goal-directed cause, which we discuss again later) provides the basis of developmental explanation (Nagel, 1957; Pepper, 1942). In organicism, there is a goal for development: To achieve the form the organism is inherently destined to take. This goal serves to direct the development of the organism, literally pulling the individual toward his or her final end state. By analogy, the ideal of the full flower in bloom—for instance, the rose—pulls the seed, the bud, etc. in the direction of this future form. Such teleology, or goal-directedness, means that future idealizations of the organism—its final, fully developed form—direct change within the individual during the present, shaping the organism in manners that enable it to attain the final form (e.g., the formal operational stage or the genital stage) that is the goal of development.

However, given this formal and final explanatory orientation, especially when it is cast within a teleologically idealized view of developmental progression, material and efficient causative agents—for instance, as derived from the context enveloping the organism—are seen as irrelevant to the sequence of development, and as such to the form the organism takes at any point in this sequence. Said in another way, the inherent and goal-directed form of the organism is the basis of development, and any other potential source of influence on change across ontogeny is, at best, of only secondary importance. Thus, the context can inhibit or facilitate (i.e., speed up or slow down) developmental progression, but it cannot alter the quality of the process or its sequential universality. If a contextual variable does alter the quality or sequence of an organism's progression, then by definition that feature of functioning was not a component of development.

Ironically, then, although constituting an alternative to the nature–nurture split conceptions of mechanism, the "classic" (Reese & Overton, 1970) developmental version of organicism becomes also a split position! Although not involving as complete a split as in mechanism, wherein only one domain—nature *or* nurture—can be real, classic organicism (e.g., as in the developmental psychologies of Jean Piaget or psychoanalysis; Wolff, 1960) sees nature as of primary importance in life. This importance exists because nature provides the formal cause of developmental change. Nurture variables exist as well, however, in the view of classic organicists. The contribution of nurture variables to development is only secondary, in that their only influence is to moderate features of primarily intrinsic trends (e.g., such as pace of progression to the teleologically directed final form of development).

Gottlieb (1970) has labeled this version of organicism *predetermined epigenesis*. An early version of Victor Hamburger's (1957) organismic position epitomizes this view:

> The architecture of the nervous system and the concomitant behavior patterns result from self-generating growth and maturation processes that are determined entirely by inherited, intrinsic factors, to the exclusion of functional adjustment, exercise, or anything else akin to learning. (p. 56)

It should be noted, however, that Hamburger (1973) later repudiated this view of epigenesis and adopted a position akin to an alternative view, one labeled *probabilistic epigenesis* (Gottlieb, 1970, 1983, 1997).

The features of probabilistic epigenesis are associated with developmental systems theories (Ford & Lerner, 1992; Gottlieb, 1991, 1992, 1997; Same-roff, 1983; Thelen & Smith, 1994, 1998), such as developmental contextualism (e.g., Lerner, 1978, 1998b). This correspondencc is noted again in this chapter, in the context of a discussion of how ideas associated with the mechanistic and the organismic models pertain to several key issues of development. The rationale for this presentation is that, as was the case with the mechanistic position, there are several problems we may identify with the organismic position. These problems come to the fore when comparing the mechanistic and the organismic models' positions in regard to the developmental issues we discuss. However, I argue that many of these problems can be usefully addressed by adopting a probabilistic epigenetic, rather than a predetermined epigenetic, view of organicism.

But, as I also argue, such an adoption, in actuality, constitutes a divorce from "pure" organicism. In fact, such an adoption creates a "marriage" (an integration) between organicism and another model useful in devising an approach to development: a contextual model. As I point out in various portions of the next section, organicism and contextualism are, philosophically, often intimately, related (Overton, 1984; Pepper, 1942). Thus, the "marriage" I propose is one between quite compatible models. Thus, by introducing some of the compatibilities between organicism and contextualism in the next section, and also by developing the argument for the usefulness of probabilistic epigenesis in the context of a comparative discussion of mechanism and organicism, and of the uses and problems with each, I am setting the stage for both a direct treatment of the contextual model and a discussion of its uses and limitations; therefore, I am preparing us for my proposal about an integration of the organismic and the contextual models—an integration that I labeled in chapter 1 as developmental contextualism, an instance of developmental systems theory.

MECHANISTIC AND ORGANISMIC MODELS AND ISSUES OF DEVELOPMENT

It is useful to begin this section by reiterating some of the key features of the mechanistic and organismic models. The mechanistic model stresses the continuous applicability of a common set of laws or principles. Continuity exists because even quite complex behavior may be reduced to common elements (e.g., stimulus–response connections in nurture, S–R, behavioristic theories, or genes in nature, behavioral genetics or sociobiological theories), elements whose linkage is controlled by forces external to or placed into (through inheritance) the essentially passive, reactive organism. Thus, the task of developmental psychologists, from this perspective, is to identify the efficient antecedents (e.g., the environmental stimuli or genes) controlling consequent behaviors.

The organismic model stresses the integrated structural features of the organism. If the parts making up the whole become reorganized as a consequence of the organism's active construction of its own functioning, the structure of the organism may take on new meaning; thus, qualitatively distinct principles may be involved in human functioning at different points in life.

These distinct, or new, levels of organization are typically termed *stages* in this perspective (Lerner, 1976; Reese & Overton, 1970). The task of developmental psychologists within organicism is to assess the different functions of the organism that are associated over time with its changing structure.

From these general distinctions between the two models, there arise several other issues pertinent to understanding development. Reese and Overton (1970; Overton & Reese, 1973) and Lerner (1978, 1985) have identified several of these issues. These ideas serve to highlight the distinctions that we have already drawn. In addition, their discussion leads us to a presentation of a third model, contextualism.

Elementarism Versus Holism

The mechanistic model is an elementaristic one. Human functioning is reduced to its core constituent elements (e.g., S–R connections and genes) and, in turn, the laws that govern the functioning of these elements are applicable continuously across life. Consequently, there is no true qualitative discontinuity, no newness, no emergence, and no epigenesis within this perspective. Only quantitative differences may exist.

The organismic model is a holistic one. As Reese and Overton (1970) explain, "The assumption of holism derives from the active organism model. More particularly, it derives from the representation of the organism as an *organized* totality, a system of parts in interaction with each other, such that the part derives its meaning from the whole" (p. 136). Reese and Overton also note that the idea of holism within organicism has been most clearly articulated by Werner and Kaplan (1963), who indicated that the idea

> maintains that any local organ or activity is dependent upon the context, field or whole of which it is a constitutive part: its properties and functional significance [meaning] are, in larger measure, determined by the larger whole or context. (p. 3)

As will become clear when we discuss the world hypothesis of "contextualism" (Pepper, 1942), a similar emphasis is placed on the role of the context in providing meaning for the parts of which it is constituted. Thus, as we have already implied and as Pepper (1942) and Overton (1984) have explained, there is considerable similarity between the organismic and the contextual models. However, the two models are distinct in significant ways, ways which lead us to find contextualism of

use in surmounting some of the limitations that exist in the traditional (classic) organismic model. These limitations are explained as we further discuss some of the issues that divide organicism and mechanism. These discussions lead us toward an integration of organicism and contextualism as a means to formulate a concept of development that adequately remedies problems found in exclusively organismic or mechanistic (or contextualistic, for that matter) views.

Antecedent–Consequent Versus Structure–Function Relations

The mechanistic model stresses efficient (and material) causes and is thereby concerned with identifying the necessary and sufficient antecedents of a behavior. Behavior is reduced, then, to an analysis of a qualitatively unchanging, continuous, and unbroken chain of cause–effect (e.g., S–R or gene-behavior) relations. In organicism, however, the emphasis is on determining the functions associated with the actively constructed structures of the organism. Qualitative changes in structures can occur as the active organism constructs—or better, reconstructs—its organization. Thus, novelty, newness, qualitative discontinuity, or epigenesis occurs as a consequence of changing structure–function relations.

But if structure leads to function, what accounts for structure? One answer is simply function. That is, the active organism shapes its structure, which in turn influences the organism's function, and so on, in a continuous and bidirectional (reciprocal) manner (e.g., Gottlieb, 1976a, 1976b, 1983; Kuo, 1967; Tobach, 1981). This answer is only one of several possible replies and is in fact quite controversial. Kohlberg (1968), Reese and Overton (1970), Overton (1973), Gottlieb (1976a, 1976b), and Lerner (1976, 1986) have noted that there exist several formulations about the source of an organism's structure. These formulations divide on the basis of their relative emphases on nature based processes (e.g., nativistic, preformed, and innate variables) and nurture-based processes (e.g., conditioning, the physical ecology of one's context, and the social events of one's context) in accounting for structure. As such, these formulations divide in respect to what I have suggested (in Chapter 1) is perhaps the key issue of human development—the nature–nurture issue, or the controversy surrounding the source of any facet of human behavioral development.

For instance, nurture-based, mechanistic formulations about the character of psychological structure have tended to emphasize the role of environmentally based processes (e.g., the laws of classical and operant conditioning) in building up a response repertoire (and/or mediation processes) within the organism (e.g., Bijou, 1976; Bijou & Baer, 1961). Thus, from this perspective, structure is imposed from outside the organism.

In turn, there exist several formulations associated with the organismic model. Several nature-based views stress the role of nativistic variables and indicate that such variables exert a predetermined influence on an organism's structure—an influence independent of any role of nurture variables. Examples are from Chomsky (1965, 1966) and McNeill (1966), who maintain that psychological (linguistic) structures are completely present at birth, and Hamburger (1957), who was cited earlier as maintaining that the inherent structure of the nervous system directly determines various behavioral functions. Given that the character and course of changes in such structures are believed to be so thoroughly shaped by nativistic variables, it may be apparent why Gottlieb (1970) has labeled such views predetermined–epigenetic.

Some formulations associated with the organismic view emphasize that an *interaction* between nature and nurture variables provides the basis of structure. However, as is discussed again later, the concept of interaction is itself a complex, controversial one. Indeed, one's concept of interaction—the components one sees as interrelating within the organismic whole—determines whether one remains committed to an exclusively organismic model or to a position that integrates organicism and contextualism (Lerner, 1985; Lerner & Kauffman, 1985).

For instance, Piaget (1968, 1970) maintained that while there existed an innate (congenital) structure, or organization, structures consequently develop through an interaction between the innate organization and the ongoing activity of the person (Reese & Overton, 1970). Note, however, that this concept of interaction sees the focal point, the locus, of interaction *within* the organism. The interaction is between the existing internal organization and the active organism's constructionist functions on or with that organization. While this organismic, internal version of interaction stands as the converse of the nurture, mechanistic, more extrinsic notion of interaction (as a relation between past reinforcement history and present stimulus conditions), the Piagetian (1968, 1970) notion of interaction is distinct from those we discuss as being associated with the contextual model. That is, to preview that discussion,

a *strong* concept of organism–environment interaction (Lerner & Spanier, 1978, 1980; Overton, 1973), transaction (Sameroff, 1975), or dynamic interaction (Lerner, 1978, 1979, 1985) is associated with a contextual perspective. This concept rejects a split between nature and nurture, or even between organism and environment, and stresses that a fused relationship exists among all components of the developmental system (Schneirla, 1956, 1957). As such, organism and context are always embedded each in the other (Lerner, Hultsch, & Dixon, 1983). The context is composed of multiple levels changing interdependently across time (i.e., historically) and, because organisms influence the context that influences them, they are efficacious in playing an active role in their own development (Lerner & Busch-Rossnagel, 1981).

But, as is also emphasized in organicism (Werner & Kaplan, 1963), because of the mutual embeddedness of organism and context, a given organismic attribute will have different implications for developmental outcomes in the milieu of different contextual conditions; this relativism exists because the organismic attribute is only given its functional meaning by virtue of its relation to a specific context. If the context changes, as it may over time, the same organismic attribute will have a different import for development. In turn, the same contextual condition will lead to alternative developments, in that different organisms interact with it. Thus, to draw quite a subtle distinction in somewhat strong terms, in the type of interactions stressed in contextualism a given organismic attribute only has meaning for psychological development by virtue of its timing of interaction—its relation to a particular set of time-bound contextual conditions. The import of any set of contextual conditions for psychosocial behavior and development can only be understood by specifying relations of the context to the specific, developmental features of the organisms within it. This central role of the timing of organism–context interactions in the determination of the nature and outcomes of development provides, as we shall see, a time- (or timing-) dependent, probabilistic component of epigenesis (Gottlieb, 1970; Scarr, 1982; Scarr & McCartney, 1983). As such, a distinctive feature of an approach to development that draws on contextual philosophical ideas is the treatment of the concepts of time and timing.

Although this probabilistic epigenetic perspective gains its potential for providing an approach to developmental theory distinct from organicism (by drawing from issues associated with the contextual treatment of the concepts of time and timing), it can only do so by building on organicism. This relation is highlighted in the next developmental issue we discuss.

Behavioral Versus Structural Change

What is it that develops, that changes, with development? Does this development have any necessary direction? As Reese and Overton (1970) explain, the answers to these questions provide human development with perhaps the most important distinctions between the mechanistic and the organismic (and, we may also note the contextual) positions.

Within the mechanistic model, qualitatively identical elements may be added to or subtracted from the machine. For instance, in the nurture, behavioristic translation of the model, lawfully identical S–R connections may be added to or subtracted from the response repertoire. Development is thus a matter of quantitative constancy or change, with elements being added to or subtracted from the organism's repertoire in accordance with, for instance, the laws of conditioning (Bijou & Baer, 1961).

With decreases or increases possible in the number of S–R connections in the repertoire, development may be said to be multidirectional within this perspective. In short, in this exemplar of the mechanistic model in human development, what changes in development is the number of S–R connections in the organism's repertoire, and there is no a priori direction to such change.

Quite a different set of ideas exists within the organismic model. Reese and Overton (1970) noted that this model emphasizes changes in structures and functions, and they stressed that these changes are specified a priori to move toward a final goal or end state. That is, as I noted earlier in this chapter, development is *teleological* within this view; it is goal-directed. Indeed, Reese and Overton (1970) indicated that within the organismic model, the definition of development is "changes in the form, structure, or organization of a system, such changes being directed towards end states or goals" (p. 139).

Reese and Overton (1970) explained that development within this view is an a priori concept; that is, the general function of development—the end state or goal (e.g., "maturity," "ego integrity," "genital sexuality," or "formal operations"—is postulated in advance and acts as a principle for ordering change. In short, in the organismic perspective, structure–function relations develop and these

changes are, in a final sense, unidirectional—they move toward a final end state.

But, although development is thus seen to be an a priori, idealized ordering of structure–function relations, and development is therefore continuous in the sense of always being directed by the final end state, there may be—and typically are—qualitative changes in structure–function relations over the course of development. The possibility of structure–function changes of a qualitative character raises two other key developmental issues on which the models provide divergent perspectives.

Continuity Versus Discontinuity

Continuity means constancy or a lack of change in some feature of development. For example, a given personality trait (e.g., dependency) may be continuously present within a person across his or her life, or a child's growth rate (e.g., two inches a year) may remain constant across the childhood years. Discontinuity means change. Dependency may be altered or transformed into independence, and with puberty and the adolescent growth spurt, an individual's growth rate may increase dramatically.

Both the mechanistic and the organismic models speak of continuity and discontinuity. In the nurture, mechanistic model, the number of S–R connections (elements) in the response repertoire may be continuous; and in organicism, a given structure–function relation may be continuous for a specific period of the person's life. Thus, ideas of continuity may be derived from both models.

However, the models divide clearly when the issue of discontinuity is raised. Quantitative discontinuity is only possible within the translations of mechanism present in human development. However, within organicism, the active organism may construct—or better, revise—its structure, and in so doing a new structure–function relation will exist. Thus, qualitative discontinuity is possible within organicism. Such a change constitutes not just more of a previously or already existing structure; rather, it constitutes something new, something that cannot be reduced to a prior state or status of the organism. Such changes are said to be emergent ones, and such qualitative discontinuity is termed epigenesis.

The possibility that life is characterized by qualitatively distinct phases of structure–function relations raises another key developmental issue. This is the issue of stages.

Stages of Development

Like many of the other concepts we have been discussing, the concept of stage is a complex and controversial one (e.g., Brainerd, 1978; Flavell, 1980; Kessen, 1962; Lerner, 1980; McHale & Lerner, 1985; Overton & Reese, 1973; Reese & Overton, 1970; Wohlwill, 1973). Here, we need to note only that the models clearly divide on the basis of the way the term *stage* is used as a theoretical construct. In nurture, mechanistic, and behavioristic positions (e.g., Bijou, 1976), a stage summarizes the presence of some set, or some quantity, of S–R connections. However, there is nothing qualitatively different about organisms at one or another stage of life.

In organismically derived theories, however, a stage denotes a qualitatively distinct level of organization (e.g., Reese & Overton, 1970; Schneirla, 1957); that is, a stage is an organizational structure qualitatively discontinuous with those of prior or later periods. As Reese and Overton (1970) explain:

> Within the active organism model, change is in structure–function relationships or in organization. As organization changes to the extent that new system properties emerge (new structures and functions) and become operational, we speak of a new level of organization which exhibits a basic discontinuity with the previous level. (p. 143)

Sources of Development

The mechanistic position, when translated into a developmental theory, will typically take the form of either a nature or nurture position. Resting on an additive and a mechanistic assumption, the mechanistic position tries to explain behavioral development in terms of a single set of source determinants. Because they are committed to a continuity position, mechanistic thinkers would, by definition, be committed to the view that the same set of laws can always account for behavior. If continuity is asserted, it is then most difficult to draw one's explanations of behavioral development from different sources of development. (Of course, it may be possible to argue that nature and nurture laws may be reduced to the same laws and are thus not different sources after all; but this type of appeal really begs the question because, once again, we are back to one common set of laws.)

As we have seen, mechanistic–behavioristic theorists view the environment (nurture) as the source of the determinants of behavior. Human beings are seen as machines; they are energized to respond by stimulation that derives solely from the environment. Hence, humans are seen as essentially passive. They must await energizing stimulation that evokes behavior. Human behavior is seen as amorphous, as having no (initial) shape or form. It is held that all human behavior is derived from a stimulus environment that is independent of human beings, who have no original form; their form is shaped completely by the environment, and, hence, processes or variables not involved with such environmental stimulation really do not contribute at all to the shaping of behavior. Thus, heredity (nature) is never systematically incorporated into these theorists' ideas, and the environment is considered the material and efficient source of the shaping of human behavior.

In mechanistic, nature theories (e.g., Freedman, 1979; Plomin, 1986; Rowe, 1994) behavioral development is seen as deriving from a single source; but in this case, the source would be nature. Behavioral development would thus be the continuous unfolding of preformed genetic givens. Prior to the behavior genetic theories of Plomin (1986) and Rowe (1994) or the sociobiological theories of Dawkins (1976), Freedman (1979), and Rushton (1987, 1999), William Sheldon's (1940, 1942) constitutional psychology position was a view consistent with a mechanistic nature formulation, as was the work of some of the European animal behaviorists (ethologists such as Lorenz, 1965; see Chapter 12). Sheldon viewed body type as the essential determinant of personality or temperament. He maintained that body type—whether essentially fat, muscular, or thin—is primarily genetically determined; hence, he views personality as essentially derived from a single source—genetic inheritance. Lorenz (1965) may also be seen as a mechanistic–nature theorist. As is discussed in greater detail in Chapter 12, Lorenz believed that in some animals there existed behavior patterns called instincts, entities whose structures were inherited. Such instincts, therefore, were totally unavailable to any environmental influence. The validity of ideas such as those of Sheldon and specifically of Lorenz is evaluated in subsequent chapters.

The present point is that mechanistic theorists typically emphasize either a nature or nurture viewpoint. Although some (if not most) nurture, mechanist theorists do explicitly admit, for example, that nature may provide an important contributory source of human functioning (e.g., see Bijou & Baer, 1961), this admission never seems to lead to any systematic consideration of the role of this other source in the development of behavior. Because changes in behavior are held to be continuous and additive instead of multiplicative, only one source of behavior (nature or nurture) is systematically taken into account. The combination of influences from nature and nurture occurs, however, as one of the predominant points of view within the organismic philosophy of science.

Although all organismic–epigenetic positions have the basic characteristics listed earlier, I have noted that the precise basis of the determinants of epigenesis is itself a controversial issue among organismic thinkers. What determines when and how the constituent parts comprising the whole organism interact to produce qualitative discontinuity? The basic issue involved in this question is the nature–nurture problem, and relates to the concept of interaction discussed earlier. The question becomes simply, "Does the source of epigenesis lie in nature, nurture, or a combination of the two?" On the one hand, there are those thinkers who maintain that epigenesis is predetermined through genetic inheritance (e.g., Erikson, 1959). Maturation, for instance, is held to play the key role in the order and timing of the qualitative emergences that define epigenesis (Erikson, 1959). In other words, development is seen as going through qualitative changes, and some epigenetic thinkers argue that these changes are completely determined by genes; the environment in which these genes exist is seen to play no role in producing the qualitative changes that characterize development (in this regard, such epigenetic thinkers are indistinguishable from the nature, mechanistic theorists such as Lorenz, 1965). Thus, these epigenetic changes are predetermined by invariant maturational factors, such as growth and tissue differentiation, which are held simply to unfold in a fixed sequence—a sequence that arises independent of any experiential context. As noted before, this predetermined–epigenetic viewpoint is well illustrated by the early views of Hamburger (1957). According to Gottlieb (1983) this version of epigenesis, as it is expressed in the early views of Hamburger (1957) and others, means that:

The development of behavior in larvae, embryos, fetuses, and neonates can be explained entirely in terms of neuromotor and neurosensory maturation (i.e., in terms of proliferation, migration, differentiation, and growth of neurons and their axonal and dendritic processes). In this view, factors such as the use or exercise of muscles, sensory stimulation, mechanical agitation, environmental heat, gravity, and so on, play only a passive role in the development of the nervous system. Thus, according to predetermined epigenesis, the nervous system matures in an encapsulated fashion so that a sufficiently comprehensive account of the maturation of the nervous system will suffice for an explanation of embryonic

and neonatal behavior, the key idea being that structural maturation determines function, and not vice versa. (p. 11)

As is demonstrated in Chapter 4, this nature–epigenetic viewpoint has rather severe conceptual limitations (akin to those involved in the type of view represented by Lorenz). In my view, the alternative conception of the source of epigenesis—*probabilistic epigenesis*—appropriately deals with the conceptual issues inherent in a consideration of human development. Moreover, this view represents, in opposition to both the mechanistic and the predetermined–epigenetic views, the notion that developmental changes are determined by a multiplicative interaction—or, better, a fusion, a complete, systemic integration—of two sources of development, nature and nurture. Since the probabilistic–epigenetic position views development as qualitatively discontinuous, and further views this discontinuity as arising from such a strong interaction, it is understandable that two different sources of development (hereditary and environmental sources) can be seen to provide the basis of the multiplicative interaction or fusion that defines and brings about the qualitative discontinuity.

T. C. Schneirla (1957), the eminent comparative psychologist, argued that no behavior is predetermined or preformed. The role of the environment must always be taken into account in trying to understand the qualitative changes that characterize epigenesis. Specifically, one must consider the experience of various stimulative events acting on the organism throughout the course of its life span. These stimulative events may occur in the environment outside the organism (exogenous stimulation) or in the environment within the organism's own body (endogenous stimulation). No matter where they occur, however, the influence of patterns of environmental stimulation upon the contribution that genes make toward behavior must always be considered.

Genes must exist in an environment. They do not just float in nothingness. Changes in the environment may help or hinder the unfolding (better, the contribution) of the genes. In other words, the experiences that take place in the environment will play a role in what contribution genes can make. If X-rays invade the environment of the genes, if oxygen is lacking, or if poisonous chemicals enter this environment, the role of the genes in contributing to behavior will certainly be different from their role if such environmental stimulative events did not occur. In addition to toxic or noxious influences, the internal and external environments provide essential signals for gene expression during the course of normal development (Gottlieb, 1991, 1992, 1997).

To illustrate the interaction of genes and external environment (i.e., the environment outside the organism), it is useful to consider the results of experiments testing how exposure to enriched, as opposed to impoverished, environments alters the most basic chemical constituent of genes: DNA. Uphouse and Bonner (1975) assessed the transcription of RNA from DNA in the brains or livers of rats exposed to:

1. High environmental enrichment (i.e., living in a cage with eleven other rats and having "toys" and mazes available for exploration).

2. Low environmental enrichment (i.e., living in a cage with one other rat but no exploration materials).

3. Isolation (i.e., living in a cage alone and with no exploration materials).

The RNA from the brains of the environmentally enriched rats showed a level of transcription of DNA significantly greater than that of the other groups. No significant differences were found with liver RNA.

Grouse et al. (1978) also found significant differences between the brain RNA of rats reared in environmentally rich versus environmentally impoverished contexts. In addition, Grouse, Schrier, and Nelson (1979) found that the total complexity of brain RNA was greater for normally sighted kittens than for kittens who had both eyelids sutured at birth. However, the RNAs from the nonvisual cortices and from subcortical structures were not different for the two groups. Grouse, Schrier, and Nelson (1979) concluded that the normal development of the visual cortex, which is dependent on visual experience, involves a greater amount of genetic expression than occurs in the absence of visual experience. Given such findings about the contextual modifiability of genetic material, it is possible to assert that genes are appropriate targets of environmental influence.

Moreover, one cannot say with total certainty what type of environmental stimulative influences will always occur or whether the environment will interact with genes to help or hinder development. Rather, one may say only that certain types of environmental influences will *probably* occur (as they do with the average organism of a certain species) and/or that a given emergence will *probably* take place if the gene–experience interaction proceeds as it usually does.

Thus, in order for development to proceed normally (i.e., in the appropriate sequence typical for the species), environmental stimulative events must operate on (interact with) the maturing organism at specific times in the organism's development. Since epigenesis is determined by both hereditary (genetic) and experiential sources, experience must interact with hereditary-linked processes (e.g., maturation) at certain times in the organism's development in order for specific emergences to occur. If the emergence of a particular behavioral development is determined by a maturation–experience interaction, and if for a particular species this interaction usually occurs at a certain time in the life span (e.g., at about six months of age), then if the particular experience involved in this interaction occurs either earlier or later for a given member of the species, there will be a change in the emergent behavioral capacity. Thus, the species-typical timing of maturational–experiential interactions is essential in order for the emergences that characterize development to occur normatively.

However, the timing of these interactions is not invariant. One can never expect with complete certainty that these interactions will occur at their typical times for all members of a species. Some individuals in a given species may undergo these interactions earlier than others, while others may undergo them at a later-than-average time. For instance, in humans, adolescents differ in the timing of their pubertal maturation, with some youth attaining a particular point in their maturation (e.g., menarche) earlier than their age-mates, and other youth reaching this point later than average (Brooks-Gunn & Petersen, 1983). These differences may or may not lead to significantly different, or substantially altered, characteristics in the resulting behavioral capacity. For instance, early maturing boys enjoy greater peer popularity than do late maturing boys, whereas the reverse set of associations occurs during early- and mid-adolescence for early- and late-maturing girls (Brooks-Gunn & Petersen, 1983; Petersen, 1987, 1988).

The point is that although emergent behavioral developments find their source in the interaction between maturation and experience, one cannot expect the timing or functional significance of these interactions always to be the same for all individuals in a species. As illustrated by early- and late-maturing adolescents, alterations in the timing of these interactions, if extreme enough, could lead to changes in the behavioral characteristics that develop as a consequence of the interactions. Thus, one can say that certain emergences will probably occur, given fairly typical timing of maturation–experience interactions. Hence, the probabilis-tic–epigenetic position recognizes that:

1. Both experience and maturation are invariably involved in determining the qualitative changes that characterize development.

2. The timing of the interactions between maturation and experience is a factor of critical importance in the determination of behavioral development.

3. Since these interactions cannot be expected to occur at exactly the same time for every organism within a given species, one can only say with a given level of confidence that certain emergences will probably occur.

The probabilistic formulation of epigenesis should appear more complicated than its predeterministic counterpart because it is! Development is an exceedingly complex phenomenon and any accurate conceptualization of it would have to take this complexity into account. Thus, Schneirla (1957), recognizing both the complexity of behavioral development and the failure of predetermined–developmental notions to acknowledge that complexity, illustrates the probabilistic–epigenetic viewpoint by stating:

> The critical problem of behavioral development should be stated as follows: (1) to study the organization of behavior in terms of its properties at each stage from the time of egg formation and fertilization through individual life history; (2) to work out the changing relationships of the organic mechanisms underlying behavior; (3) always in terms of the contributions of earlier stages in the developmental sequence; and (4) in consideration of the properties of the prevailing developmental context at each stage. (p. 80)

As I have indicated, I believe that this probabilistic–epigenetic viewpoint offers the most appropriate conceptualization of development. Indeed, as is discussed in later chapters, this perspective provides the basis of developmental systems notions of human development (e.g., Ford & Lerner, 1992; Gottlieb, 1991, 1992, 1997; Gottlieb, Wahlsten, & Lickliter, 1998).

Conclusions

The mechanistic model stresses a passive organism in an active world; it emphasizes reductionism, continuity of laws governing development, only quantitative behavioral change across life, potential multidirectionality of change, elementarism, and antecedent–consequent relations; and it eschews the idea of stages as qualitatively distinct periods of life. The organismic model stresses an active organism in a relatively passive world, and it emphasizes emergence; qualitative change in structure–function relations across life; unidirectional, teleological, goal-directed change; holism; and the appropriateness of the idea of stages as qualitatively distinct levels of organization.

Each of these two models has led to a set of theories—sets that we have noted that Reese and Overton (1970) termed a "family of theories." These families are of use in the study of all or part of the life span. For instance, the behavioristically oriented, functional–analysis approach of Bijou and Baer (1961; Bijou, 1976) exemplifies the translation of a nurture, mechanistic model into a theory of development. However, other family members include the social-learning theories of Miller and Dollard (1941), Davis (1944), and McCandless (1970). The theories of Werner (1948), Piaget (1950, 1968, 1970), Freud (1954), and Erikson (1959, 1963, 1968) exemplify the translation of the organismic model into developmental theories.

Both mechanistically and organismically derived orientations encounter problems when attempting to formulate a useful concept of development. Mechanistically derived conceptions cannot, as we have noted, deal directly with novelty or with qualitatively distinct levels of being. In the former case, novelty must be interpreted as reducible to common constituent elements; in the latter case,

Sidney Bijou

Donald Baer

have characteristics that as much shape their world as their world shapes them (Bell, 1968; Bell & Harper, 1977; Lerner, 1982; Lerner & Busch-Rossnagel, 1981; Lewis & Rosenblum, 1974) *and* that these organismic characteristics cannot be adequately interpreted as merely derivative of the organism's conditioning history or experience-independent genetic inheritance (Gottlieb, 1992, 1997; Gottlieb et al., 1998; Schneirla, 1957; Tobach, 1981; Tobach & Schneirla, 1968).

For these reasons, I am oriented more to formulating an organismically derived concept of development than a mechanistically derived one. There are, however, major conceptual problems with organicism that diminish its usefulness for derivation of a concept of development. Among these are:

1. The need in organicism to "deal mainly with historic processes even while it consistently explains time away" (Pepper, 1942, p. 280).

2. The fact that "organicism takes time lightly or disparagingly" (Pepper, 1942, p. 281; and, as an instance, see Kaplan, 1983).

3. The teleological features of organicism, wherein for the "fragments" of an organic whole there is "inevitability of connections among fragments . . . [an] implication of wholeness contained in them" (Pepper, 1942, p. 292), "an internal drive toward the integrations which complete them" (Pepper, 1942, p. 291), and where, although the particular path to a goal is not predetermined it is, nevertheless, the case that "the goal was predetermined in the structure of the facts" (Pepper, 1942, p. 295).

the influence of cultural, sociological, and physical ecological variables, for instance, must also be reduced to common (e.g., behavioristic) principles in order for their influence to have a place (i.e., an efficient causal influence) in the continuity perspective of mechanism. Often, such reduction is quite forced and/or artificial and, as such, variables from distinct levels of analysis may end up being ignored. Moreover, despite the possibility of multidirectionality in development, we have seen that, in practice, mechanistically derived conceptions often adopt a position involving the continuous applicability of early experience to later life (e.g., Thorndike, 1905; Watson, 1928). In fact, in nature, mechanistic theories that stress the role of genes as the material and efficient causes of behavioral development (e.g. Plomin, 1986; Rowe, 1994; Rushton, 1987, 1999) *the very first experience—conception—*is the key experience in human life. It is at conception that the genotype is received, and it is held that this inheritance is the major source of structure and function across the life span. Moreover, we have noted that Zukav (1979) argued that the view of antecedent–consequent relations held by mechanists logically requires such a proscription against discontinuity or change in later life. Finally, there is mechanism's insistence on a passive model of the organism. Such a conception, especially when translated into a theory of human development, is unable to account for the evidence that organisms

These key features of "pure" organicism fail to deal with the point that the timing of interaction of causal developmental variables is probabilistic (Gollin, 1981; Gottlieb, 1970; 1976a, 1976b, 1991, 1992, 1997; Scarr, 1982; Scarr & McCartney, 1983; Schneirla, 1956, 1957; Tobach, 1981; Tobach & Schneirla, 1968). As a consequence, there is a lack of concern with the implication that such differences in time may mean that, while the process of development may remain invariant across history (e.g., while an orthogenetic progression in structure–function relations may exist), the ongoing features of developmental trajectories may show considerable interindividual variability, *and* there may be no universally inevitable end state for a developmental progression. In other words, there may be a probabilistic, rather than a predetermined, pattern to epigenetic change.

Moreover, as with mechanistically derived conceptions, the use of "pure" organismic conceptions of development is diminished in light of several sets of findings for which extant organismic views cannot devise adequate interpretations. That is, as opposed to mechanistic conceptions, which encountered difficulty as a consequence of failures to treat adequately organismic features of the person, organismic conceptions have encountered difficulty as a consequence of not being able to test effects on the person ultimately associated with variables derived from the context enveloping the person (e.g., Baltes et al., 1998, 1999; Elder, 1998; Shweder et al., 1998).

Attempts to use a biological model of growth, one based on an organismic conception of development (e.g., Cumming & Henry, 1961), to account for data sets pertinent to the adult and aged years have not been completely successful (Baltes, Reese, & Lipsitt, 1980; Baltes & Schaie, 1973). Viewed from the perspective of this organismic conception, the adult and aged years were necessarily seen as periods of decline (Cumming & Henry, 1961). However, all data sets pertinent to age changes (e.g., in regard to intellectual performance) during these periods were not consistent with such a unidirectional format of change. For example, as is noted in Chapter 1, increasingly greater between-people differences in within-person change were evident in such data sets (Baltes, 1983; Baltes & Schaie, 1974, 1976; Schaie, Labouvie, & Buech, 1973). Simply put, as people developed into the adult and aged years, differences between them increased.

On the basis of such data, Brim and Kagan (1980b, p. 13) concluded that "growth is more individualistic than was thought, and it is difficult to find general patterns." Factors associated with the historical time within which people were born (i.e., with membership in particular birth cohorts) and/or with events occurring at particular historical times appeared to account for more of these changes, particularly with respect to adult intellectual development, than did age-associated influences (Baltes et al., 1980). Data sets pertinent to the child (Baltes, Baltes, & Reinert, 1970) and the adolescent (Elder, 1974, 1980, 1998; Nesselroade & Baltes, 1974) that considered these birth-cohort and time-of-measurement effects also supported their saliency in developmental change. These findings led scientists to induce conceptualizations useful for understanding the role of these nonage-related variables in development (e.g., Baltes, Cornelius, & Nesselroade, 1977; Baltes et al., 1998,

1999; Brim & Ryff, 1980). These conceptualizations have been interpreted as being consistent with a developmental contextual view of development (Baltes, 1979b; Lerner, 1982, 1998b; Lerner, Hultsch, & Dixon, 1983).

Brim and Kagan (1980b) have summarized the character of this developmental–contextual view by noting that this

> conception of human development . . . differs from most Western contemporary thought on the subject. The view that emerges . . . is that humans have a capacity for change across the entire life span. It questions the traditional idea that the experiences of the early years, which have a demonstrated contemporaneous effect, necessarily constrain the characteristics of adolescence and adulthood . . . there are important growth changes across the life span from birth to death, many individuals retain a great capacity for change, and the consequences of the events of early childhood are continually transformed by later experiences, making the course of human development more open than many have believed. (p. 1)

Given the interest and importance attached to ideas linked to contextualism in the scholarship summarized by Brim and Kagan (1980), it is appropriate to evaluate the usefulness of this model for the derivation of an adequate concept of development. While contextualism does have many attractive conceptual features, similar to mechanism and organicism, it also has significant problems, Indeed, these problems are of sufficient scope to obviate the use of "pure" contextualism in deriving an adequate concept of development. However, contextual views may be combined with organismic ones. I shall argue that such a synthesis provides a quite useful basis for deriving a concept of development, one that eliminates many of the problems found in the two models taken separately.

THE CONTEXTUAL MODEL

According to Pepper (1942), the main metaphor of contextualism is neither the machine nor the whole organism. It is the historic event. "The real historic event, the event in its actuality, is when it is going on *now*, the dynamic dramatic active event" (Pepper, 1942, p. 232). In contextualism, every behavior and incident in the world is a historic event, and, thus, change and novelty are accepted as fundamental. A contextual model assumes (a) *constant change* of all levels of analysis;

and (b) *embeddedness* of each level with all others—changes in one level promote changes in all levels. The assumption of constant change denotes that there is no complete uniformity or constancy. Rather than change being a phenomenon to be explained, a perturbation in a stable system, change is a given (Overton, 1978). Thus, the task of the scientist is to describe, explain, and optimize the parameters and trajectories of *processes* (i.e., variables that reflect the *relations* among the levels of the system and that show time-related changes in their quantity and/or quality).

The second assumption of contextualism stresses the interrelation of all levels of analysis. Because phenomena are not seen as static but rather as change processes, and because any change process occurs within a similarly (i.e., constantly) changing world (of processes), any target change must be conceptualized in the context of the other changes within which it is embedded. Thus, change will constantly continue as a consequence of this embeddedness.

There is an organism in the contextual perspective, but it is conceived of as an "organism in relation" (Looft, 1973) or an "organism in transaction" (Dewey & Bentley, 1948; Lerner, 1991, 1996; Pervin, 1968; Sameroff, 1975, 1983) with its context. These relations are the focus of developmental analysis. They constitute the *basic process* of human development. As such, the timing of the interaction between organism and context is critical in contextualism. Indeed, as implied earlier, the fact that the timing of interaction plays a central role in contextualism serves to provide a key distinction between contextualism and organicism. As Pepper (1942) explains:

> Organicism takes time lightly or disparagingly; contextualism takes it seriously. . . . The root metaphor of organicism always does appear as a process, but it is the integration appearing in the process that the organicist works from and not the duration of the process. When the root metaphor reaches its ultimate refinement the organicist believes the temporal factor disappears. (p. 281)

Although emphasizing that the transaction or "dynamic interaction" (Lerner, 1978, 1979, 1980) between organism and context is what develops in development, it is important to note that, because of its admittance of multiple causative "agents" (formal, efficient, material, but not final), into developmental explanation, contextually derived perspectives do not exclude features associated with organismic–developmental theories. A major example is the use made by contextually

oriented theorists (e.g., Lerner, & Busch-Rossnagel, 1981) of the orthogenetic principle (Werner, 1957) to describe the nature of change in the relations between individuals and their contexts; in fact, this principle has been used in even broader contextually related analyses—those pertinent to the relations among large-scale systems in the universe (Prigogine, 1978, 1980).

In short, a contextual perspective, when used to devise a concept of development (and, thus, when synthesized with features of organismic thinking), need not, should not, and typically *does* not (Lerner, 1984, 1985) avoid the use of universalistic, and, thus, constantly applicable, principles of development. Instead, the emphasis in such approaches is on the *relation* between the structural and functional characteristics of the organism and the features (e.g., the demands or presses) of the organism's context. Indeed, particular attention is paid to the mutual constraints and opportunities provided by both elements in the relation—organism and context (Lerner, 1984, 1991). Rather than seeing ideas such as "orthogenesis," which have traditionally been used primarily to depict intra-organism development (e.g., see Siegel, Bisanz, & Bisanz, 1983), in reference to the individual psychological level of analysis alone, the use of such ideas is made in reference to a "unit of analysis"—the "organism in transaction"—linking individual and context.

However, it is at this point that major problems arise with the use of "pure" contextualism as a paradigm from which to derive a concept of development. Contextualism is at its core (Overton, 1984) a dispersive paradigm. That is, there is no necessary connection or relation among the parts of the whole, either within or across time. Relations at one point in time (e.g., among thoughts, feelings, personality, and behavior) may or may not exist at another point in time. In pure contextualism, there is simply no prediction possible from one point in life (or history) to the next. In other words, a purely contextual approach sees the components of life as completely dispersive (Pepper, 1942)—as lacking any necessary across-time organization, systemic connection, or successive patterning. Pepper (1942) believed that it was the dispersive character of contextualism that was the key idea making it a world view distinct from the organismic one, a world view in turn marked, according to Pepper (1942), by integration. As I argued in Chapter 1, if the term development is to have meaning beyond that of mere change, it must imply, at the very least, systematic and successive changes in the organization of an organism or, more generally, a system. Thus, a world view that stressed only the dispersive, chaotic, and disorganized character of life would not readily lend itself to the derivation of a theory of development.

But, although contextualism may not suffice in and of itself as a model from which an adequate concept of development may be derived, there is a way to combine features of this model with organicism—with which we have seen that contextualism is closely aligned (Pepper, 1942)—to forge such a concept. As I suggested earlier, this "marriage" is possible by reference to the ideas associated with the probabilistic–epigenetic view of organicism.

Contextualism and Probabilistic Epigenesis

A major point of contrast between organicism and contextualism arises because the contextual perspective excludes any notion of final cause (e.g., see Nagel, 1957; Pepper, 1942), and, thus, leads to a belief in the potential plasticity of the organism across life. However, this view of plasticity is one derived from the contextual concept of dispersiveness, and, thus, is a notion that involves, in effect, limitless, unconstrained, and unpredictable plasticity. Such a notion is clearly counterfactual (Lerner, 1984).

Accordingly, whereas the "pure" contextual view of plasticity is not empirically or logically useful, when teleology is rejected and/or a state of tension (or a "contradiction"; Tobach, 1981) is postulated between influences that promote multidirectional changes and influences that promote integration, a developmental contextual conception is reached. This view emphasizes not the intrinsically preformed or inevitable timetables and outcomes of development, but rather that the influence of the changing context on development is to make the trajectory of development less certain with respect to the applicability of norms to the individual (Gottlieb, 1970). Thus, developmental contextual conceptions emphasize the probabilistic character of development and in so doing admit of more plasticity in development than do predetermined–epigenetic conceptions.

In other words, the developmental contextual view of human development reflects the ideas in the position labeled "probabilistic epigenetic organismic" by Gottlieb (1970), and developed by Gottlieb (1976a, 1976b), and earlier by Schneirla (1956, 1957) and Tobach and Schneirla (1968). Overton (1984) termed this conception *organismic–contextual* and, in turn, Gottlieb (1991, 1992, 1997; Gottlieb et al., 1998) described this position as a developmental psychobiological systems view.

However it is labeled, "probabilistic epigenesis" designates (Gottlieb, 1970):

> The view that the behavioral development of individuals within a species does not follow an invariant or inevitable course, and, more specifically, that the sequence or outcome of individual behavioral development is probable (with respect to norms) rather than certain. (p. 123)

Moreover, Gottlieb (1970) explains that this probable, and not certain, character of individual development arises because:

> Probabilistic epigenesis necessitates a bidirectional structure–function hypothesis. The conventional version of the structure–function hypothesis is unidirectional in the sense that structure is supposed to determine function in an essentially nonreciprocal relationship. The unidirectionality of the structure–function relationship is one of the main assumptions of predetermined epigenesis. The bidirectional version of the structure–function relationship is a logical consequence of the view that the course and outcome of behavioral epigenesis is probabilistic: it entails the assumption of reciprocal effects in the relationship between structure and function whereby function (exposure to stimulation and/or movement of musculoskeletal activity) can significantly modify the development of the peripheral and central structures that are involved in these events. (p. 123)

In essence, as compared to predetermined epigenesis, where the key assumption (Gottlieb, 1983)

> holds that there is a unidirectional relationship between structure and function whereby structural maturation determines function (structural maturation → function) but not the reverse, probabilistic epigenesis assumes a bidirectional or reciprocal relationship between structural maturation and function whereby structural maturation determines function and function alters structural maturation (structural maturation ←→ function). (p. 12)

Most important for the formulation of a useful concept of development, the changes depicted in this probabilistic–epigenetic formulation of development are not completely dispersive. As does Overton (1984), I believe that when features of organicism—for instance, its regulative ideas about integrative change across ontogeny (e.g., as illustrated through the concept of orthogenesis; Siegel, Bisanz, & Bisanz, 1983; Wapner & Demick, 1998; Werner, 1957)—are synthesized with the probabilistic nature of contextual change, a useful *development contextual* conception is created, one that reflects the ideas described in Chapter 1 as linked to developmental systems theory.

Developmental Contextualism and the Issue of Dispersion

As noted, Pepper (1942) emphasizes that the dispersive nature of contextualism is the feature that is the key to its being a world view distinct from organicism. He argues that:

> The historic event which is the root metaphor of contextualism is a nearer approximation to the refined root metaphor of organicism than any common-sense term. This is so true that it is tempting to regard these two theories as species of the same theory, one being dispersive and the other integrative. It has occasionally been said that pragmatism is simply idealism with the absolute left out, which in our terms would be to say that contextualism is simply dispersive organicism. But, the insistence on integration which is characteristic of organicism makes so great a difference that it is wiser to consider them as two theories. (p. 280)

In being completely dispersive, a "pure" contextualism would not be suitable for use as a philosophical model from which to derive a concept of development. However, as I have explained, a "pure" organicism would also be limited as a paradigm from which to derive a useful concept of development (e.g., because of teleology and, thus, the insistence on an inevitable unidirectional end course to development).

Mechanism cannot be used as an alternative to either of these two paradigms because there is really no concept of developmental change, qualitative discontinuity, or even of newness or novelty that can be derived from this paradigm. Thus, either some new paradigm must be adopted or, as Overton (1984) suggested, it may be possible and *empirically useful*—despite Pepper's (1942) and others' (e.g., Kendler, 1986) protestations—to merge ideas from contextualism and organicism. Overton (1984) termed this merger *contextual organicism*. My own preference is for the term suggested by Gottlieb (1970): probabilistic epigenesis. The term developmental contextualism may be used *if* sight is not lost of the fact that one is still referring to an organismic, epigenetic process. That is, it is not just that the context produces alterations in development. Instead, since the context is influenced as well as constrained by the organism's characteristics, we must keep in mind the need to define development in terms of organism—context reciprocal, or dynamic–interactional (Lerner, 1978, 1979, 1982, 1984) relations (Brandtstädter, 1998, 1999; Brandtstädter & Lerner, 1999; Ford & Lerner, 1992; Lerner & Walls, 1999). In developmental contextualism or, more broadly, in developmental systems theories, the

concept of development is really one of probabilistic epigenesis, of a synthesis between organismic processes and changes and contextual ones (e.g., Gottlieb et al., 1998; Sameroff, 1983; Thelen & Smith, 1998). Let us consider more fully the nature and implications of this concept of development.

THE CONCEPT OF DEVELOPMENT IN DEVELOPMENTAL CONTEXTUALISM

Gollin (1981) explained that probabilistic developmental change is not dispersive because the living system—the organism—has organization and internal coherence, and these features constrain the potentials of the *developmental context* to affect the system. Gollin (1981) says:

> The determination of the successive qualities of living systems, given the web of relationships involved, is probabilistic. This is so because the number of factors operating conjointly in living systems is very great. Additionally, each factor and subsystem is capable of a greater or lesser degree of variability. Hence, the influence subsystems have upon each other, and upon the system as a whole, varies as a function of the varying states of the several concurrently operating subsystems. Thus, the very nature of living systems, both individual and collective, and of environments, assure the presumptive character of organic change. Living systems are organized systems with internal coherence. The properties of the parts are essentially dependent on relations between the parts and the whole (Waddington, 1957). The quality of the organization provides opportunities for change as well as constraints upon the extent and direction of change. Thus, while the determination of change is probabilistic, it is not chaotic. (p. 232)

Gollin's position illustrates that one needs to understand that development occurs in a multilevel context, and that the nature of the changes in this context leads to the probabilistic character of development. However, one also needs to appreciate that the organism shapes the context as much as the context shapes the organism (Lerner & Busch-Rossnagel, 1981; Lerner & Walls, 1999).

Tobach (1981), Scarr (1982), and Scarr and McCartney (1983) made similar points. For example, Tobach (1981) indicated that:

> Three processes (contradictions) intercept in time to bring about qualitative changes in the individual (development, which includes growth and maturation): (a) the inner contradiction of the organism; (b) the inner contradiction of the environment; and (c)

Sandra Scarr

is the course of human development directed primarily by structures in the environment that are external to the person or is development guided principally by the genetic program within? Second, is development primarily continuous or discontinuous? (p. 852)

Answering the first question bears on the idea of probabilistic epigenesis; answering the second relates to the concept of plasticity. In regard to the first issue, Scarr (1982) explained:

Answers to the first question have shifted in recent years from the . . . empiricist position to the . . . nativist view. Neonativist arguments, however, do not assume the extreme preformism of the early century. Development does not merely emerge from the precoded information in the genes. Rather, development is the probabilistic result of indeterminate combinations of genes and environments. Development is genetically guided, but variable and probabilistic because influential events in the life of every person can be neither predicted nor explained by general laws. Development, in this view, is guided primarily by the genetic program through its multilevel transactions with environments that range from cellular to social. The genetic program for the human species has both its overwhelming commonalties and its individual variability because each of us is both human and uniquely human. (pp. 852–853)

In regard to the second question, Scarr (1982) suggested that as a consequence of an organism's biological contributions and the probabilistic transactions this biology has with its multilevel context, neither complete consistency nor complete change characterizes the human condition. Instead:

Human beings are made neither of glass that breaks in the slightest ill wind nor of steel that stands defiantly in the face of devastating hurricanes. Rather, in this view, humans are made of the newer plastic—they bend with environmental pressures, resume their shapes when the pressures are relieved, and are unlikely to be permanently misshapen by transient experiences. When bad environments are improved, people's adaptations improve. Human beings are resilient and responsive to the advantages their environments provide. Even adults are capable of improved adaptations through learning, although any individual's improvement depends on that person's responsiveness to learning opportunities. (p. 53)

In other words (Scarr & McCartney, 1983), there exists:

A probabilistic connection between a person and the environment. It is more likely that people with certain genotypes will receive certain kinds of

the outer contradiction between the organism and the environment. Some of the inner contradictions would be the metabolic cycle, and neurohormonal cycles; these have characteristics of negative and positive feedback that bring about continuous change with more or less stability in the organism. The environment expresses its own contradictions in diurnal and seasonal variations, faunal and floral interrelations, and so on. Given different lighting conditions (environmental contradictions), the effects on the hormonal function (intraorganismic contradictions) bring about changes in the organism's activity that bring it into changing relationships with the abiota or biota, and particularly with conspecifics (contradiction between organism and environment). The intersect of these three processes (contradictions) brings about developmental change in the organism. The organism may act on the environment (the social aspect), resulting in copulation, bringing about a new developmental stage. (pp. 60–61)

In turn, Scarr (1982) noted:

Two big questions have occupied developmental theorists from antiquity to the present day . . . First, parenting, evoke certain responses from others, and select certain aspects from the available environments; but nothing is rigidly determined. The idea of genetic differences, on the other hand, has seemed to imply to many that the person's developmental fate was preordained without regard to experience. This is absurd. By involving the idea of genotype → environment effects, we hope to emphasize a probabilistic connection between genotypes and their environments. (p. 428)

Similarly, Gollin (1981) noted that:

The relationships between organisms and environments are not interactionist, as interaction implies that organism and environment are separate entities that come together at an interface. Organism and environment constitute a single life process. . . . For analytic convenience, we may treat various aspects of a living system and various external environmental and biological features as independently definable properties. Analytical excursions are an essential aspect of scientific inquiry, but they are hazardous if they are primarily reductive. An account of the *collective behavior* of the parts as an organized entity is a necessary complement to a reductive analytic program, and serves to restore the information content lost in the course of the reductive excursion. . . . In any event, the relationships that contain the sources of change are those between organized systems and environments, not between heredity and environment. (pp. 231–232)

In a related vein, Tobach (1981) noted:

Gene function is expressed in enzymes and proteins that are fundamental and ubiquitous to all aspects of molecular function and derivatively in physiological integration. However, the preeminence of societal factors in human development in determining the significance of these biochemical processes is also never lost. If the child is discovered to have an enzyme deficiency that is corrected through dietary supplementation, the outcome will depend on whether the child is in a society in which such knowledge is not available, or if the knowledge is available, whether the treatment is available to the individual child. Extremes in chromosomal structures and function such as trisomy-21, despite their demonstrated molecular base, are also variably vulnerable to societal processes. (p. 50)

A final point about the developmental contextual/probabilistic–epigenetic view needs to be highlighted. Although both contextual and mechanistic–behavioral perspectives make use of the context enveloping an organism in attempts to explain development, it is clear that they do so in *distinctly* different ways. Contextually oriented theorists do not adopt a reflexively reductionistic approach to conceptualizing the impact of the context. Instead, because of a focus on organism–context transactions, and thus a commitment to using an interlevel, or relational, unit of analysis (Lerner, Skinner, & Sorell, 1980), the context may be conceptualized as being composed of multiple, qualitatively different levels (e.g., the inner–biological, the individual–psychological, the outer–physical, and the sociocultural) (Riegel, 1975, 1976a, 1976b).

Moreover, although both the mechanistic and the developmental contextual perspectives hold that changes in the context become part of the organism's intraindividually changing constitution, the concept of "organism" found in the two perspectives is also quite distinct. In developmental contextualism, the organism is not merely the host of the elements of a simplistic environment. Instead the organism is itself a qualitatively distinct level within the multiple dynamically interacting levels forming the context of life. As such, the organism has a distinct influence on that multilevel context that is influencing the organism. As a consequence, the organism is, in short, not a host of S–R connections but an active contributor to its own development (Lerner, 1982; Lerner & Busch-Rossnagel, 1981).

How may such organism–context interactions occur? In other words, how may an organism make an active contribution to its own development? One answer to this question is found in the "goodness of fit" model of person–context relations (e.g., Lerner & Lerner, 1983, 1989; Lerner et al., 1995). Just as a person bring their characteristics of physical, emotional, and behavioral individuality to a particular social setting, there are demands placed on the person by virtue of the social and physical components of the setting. These demands may take the form of:

1. Attitudes, values, or stereotypes held by others regarding the person's attributes.

2. The attributes (usually behavioral) of others with whom the person must coordinate, or fit, for adaptive interactions to exist.

3. The physical characteristics of a setting (e.g., the presence or absence of access ramps for the handicapped) that require the person to possess certain attributes (again, usually behavioral) for the occurrence of efficient interaction.

The person's characteristics of individuality, in differentially meeting these demands, provide a basis for the feedback he or she gets from the socializing environment. For example, considering the second type of contextual demands that exist—those that arise as a consequence of the behavioral characteristics of others in the setting—problems of fit might occur when a child who is highly irregular in his biological functions (e.g., eating, sleep–wake cycles, and toileting behaviors) interacts in a family setting composed of highly regular and behaviorally scheduled parents and siblings.

Lerner and Lerner (1983, 1989) and Thomas and Chess (1977; Chess & Thomas, 1984, 1999) believed that adaptive psychological and social functioning do not derive directly from either the nature of a person's characteristics of individuality per se or the nature of the demands of the contexts within which the person functions. Rather, if a person's characteristics of individuality match (or "fit") the demands of a particular setting, adaptive outcome in that setting will accrue. Those people whose characteristics match most of the settings within which they exist should receive supportive or positive feedback from the contexts and should show evidence of the most adaptive behavioral development. In turn, of course, mismatched people, whose characteristics are incongruent with one or most settings, should show alternative developmental outcomes.

In sum, the present point is that to probabilistic–epigenetic theorists, behavioral development becomes, at least in part, a matter of self-activated generation. These theorists view development as arising essentially from the multiplicative interaction or, better, the fusion of two qualitatively different sources—heredity and environment. Hence, it is a logical next step to focus on the meeting place of those factors lying primarily within the organism (hereditary) and those lying primarily outside (environmental). This meeting place is, of course, the organism itself. By focusing on the contributions that the organism's own characteristics (e.g., its type of behavioral style and its physical appearance) make toward its own further development, developmental–contextual theorists are essentially studying the continual accumulations of the interacting contributions of nature and nurture. This focus brings about a concern with what roles various aspects of the organism play in shaping the individual's own behavior. A fuller explication of this aspect of the probabilistic–epigenetic, or developmental–contextual, viewpoint is made in Chapter 8.

Developmental Contextualism as a "Compromise" Conception

We have discussed the notion that developmental contextualism constitutes an integration, or "compromise" position derived from several different philosophical models or world views. For instance, we have noted that Overton (1984) suggested that organicism may be integrated with either contextualism or mechanism in order to formulate a synthetic position which capitalizes on the useful features of the mechanistic and the organismic positions. While I have argued that mechanism in and of itself is not useful for forging a true developmental theory, following Overton (1984), I suggest that within developmental contextualism there exists at least two ways of synthesizing some of the potentially useful features of mechanism and, of course, organicism.

The levels-of-organization hypothesis. The first of these means of synthesis has been implied in much of what we have previously discussed. It is termed the *levels-of-organization hypothesis* and is illustrated by the work of Schneirla (1957). The compromise notes that there are different levels of organic and/or phenomenal organization and that the laws of the lower levels (e.g., physics and chemistry) are implied in the laws of the higher (e.g., the psychological) level. Yet, the laws of the higher level cannot be reduced to or predicted from the laws of the lower level. This is true because such reduction will not lead to an understanding of the emergent quality of the higher level. Clearly, this assertion has been presented as a basic part of the organismic–epigenetic viewpoint. The water example provided earlier in this chapter is an illustration of this compromise. Another illustration is that although certain neural, hormonal, and muscular processes certainly underlie (are implied in) a person's being in love, reduction of love to these lower levels—or to the still-lower levels of chemistry and physics—is unlikely to result in an understanding of this phenomenon.

An example of the application of the levels-of-organization compromise may be seen by reference to some classic findings in the literature on children's problem-solving behavior. Kendler and Kendler (1962) devised a way to study problem-solving behavior in various species of organisms (e.g., rats and humans), as well as in humans of various ages (e.g., nursery-school children and college students). In the procedure they devised, children are presented first with two large squares and two small squares. One of each type of square is painted black and one of each type is painted white. Thus, there are a large black and a large white square, and a small white and a small black square. The children's task is to learn to respond either to the color dimension (thus, ignoring the size) or to the size dimension (thus, ignoring the color). For example, a child may be presented with a large black and a small white square on one trial and then perhaps a large white square and a small black square on another. Now, if size is the aspect of the stimuli that should be responded to and, further, if a response toward the bigger of the two squares will always lead to a reward, the child should choose the large stimulus in each trial, no matter what the color. In other words, the child first learns that size is the relevant aspect of the stimuli; therefore, the subject learns to respond to the difference in size and to ignore (not respond to) differences in color of the squares.

Rats, nursery-school children, and college students can all learn this first problem-solving task. The interesting thing about this type of problem solving is what happens when the rules about the relevant aspect of the stimuli are changed. In the first problem-solving task, size was the relevant dimension (the big squares were rewarded and the small squares were not). Without directly cueing the children that this rule has changed, it is still possible to keep the size of the stimuli as the relevant dimension (and the color as the nonrelevant dimension), but to make choice of the *small* squares the response that will be rewarded. Thus, the same dimension of the stimuli (size) is still

relevant, but there has been a reversal as to which *aspect* of size (from large to small) will lead to a reward. Kendler and Kendler called this type of alteration a *reversal shift;* the same stimulus dimension is still related to reward, but which of the two stimuli within this same dimension is positive and which is negative is reversed.

A second type of shift may occur, however, in the second problem-solving task. Instead of size being the reward-relevant dimension, color can be. Now, response to the black squares (regardless of their size) will lead to a reward, and response to the white squares (regardless of their size) will not. This type of change involves a shift to the other dimension of the stimuli and is not within the same dimension. Hence, the Kendlers termed this second type of possible change a *nonreversal shift*. Figure 3.3 illustrates the reversal and the nonreversal shifts. In all cases, the stimuli toward which a response will lead to a reward are marked "+," while the stimuli toward which a response will not be rewarded are marked "−."

Kendler and Kendler (1962) reviewed the studies of reversal and nonreversal problem solving done with rats, nursery-school children, and college stu-

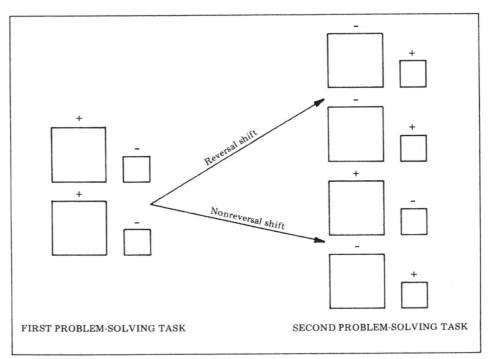

FIRST PROBLEM-SOLVING TASK   SECOND PROBLEM-SOLVING TASK

FIGURE. 3.3
Examples of a reversal and a nonreversal shift.
Source: H. H. Kendler and T. S. Kendler (1962). Vertical and horizontal processes in problem solving. *Psychological Review,* 69. Copyright © 1962 by the American Psychological Association. Reprinted by permission.

dents. After learning the first problem (e.g., after making 10 correct responses to the large-size stimuli), would it then be easier to learn a reversal shift or a nonreversal shift (again using the learning criterion of 10 consecutive correct responses)? The Kendlers' review indicated that rats learn a nonreversal shift more easily than a reversal shift. Moreover, so do most nursery-school children. As do rats, these human children reach the criterion for making a nonreversal shift faster than they reach the criterion for making a reversal shift. However, somewhat older children, as well as college students, find a reversal shift easier.

The Kendlers interpreted these age changes by suggesting that in development there emerges a new mental process in children such that they move from rat-like responses to (college) student-like responses; this new mental process, not present at earlier ages (e.g., efficient language processes), alters children's problem-solving behavior so that a reversal shift becomes easier than a nonreversal shift. Whereas children's problem-solving behavior at the nursery-school level can be accounted for by reference to processes apparently also identifiable in rats, their later behavior may be explained by the emergence of a new mental process.

Certainly, the processes present in the nursery-school children provided a developmental basis for the processes seen among the older children.

That is, it would be unlikely to find older children who now functioned like college students but never functioned like younger children (or rats, too, in this case). Yet, these former processes are not sufficient to account for the behavior of the older children. The type of problem-solving behavior changes, and this alteration appears related to the emergence of a new mental function. Any attempt to reduce the laws of the later level to those of the earlier level will avoid dealing with the important emergent processes that apparently characterize the older age level. Thus, although other interpretations of these findings have been offered (see Esposito, 1975), the present point is that the work reported by the Kendlers (1962) illustrates the level-of-organization compromise. The laws of the lower level may be involved in those of the higher one, but because those of the higher involve emergent qualities, the former laws will not suffice to account for the phenomena of the higher level if any attempt at reduction is made.

The levels-of-organization compromise is presented diagrammatically in Figure 3.4. Here, we see that at Level 1 two gases, hydrogen and oxygen, are present; at Level 2, however, the two gases combine to produce a substance (water) that has a property (liquidness) that did not exist in either of the Level-1 elements in isolation. Although the presence of the lower level's phenomena is certainly implied in the phenomena of the higher level, the latter level still has phenomena (e.g., liquidness) that cannot be understood through reduction to those of the lower level.

The general-and-specific-laws compromise. The second compromise between the mechanistic and the organismic positions maintains that there are general and specific laws that govern development: Certain general laws apply to any and all levels of psychological functioning. Yet, each specific level of psychological development is also governed by specific laws. Such a compromise is often found in the work of organismic theorists (e.g., Heinz Werner and Jean Piaget) (see Chapters 5 and 15, respectively). Like other organismic developmental theorists who stress the concepts of stage in their ideas, Piaget viewed development as involving two processes: First, a general, continuous process (the "equilibration" process) that is present at all levels, and, in fact, is used to account for the continual development of children through the various stages of cognitive development; and second, specific qualitatively distinct phenomena (e.g., preoperational thinking), which actually serve as the definitional basis of the various stages of development at which they occur.

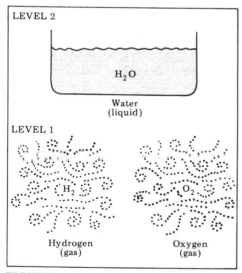

FIGURE 3.4
Levels-of-organization compromise between the mechanistic and the organismic positions.

Sigmund Freud, also an organismic theorist, similarly made use of a compromise between general and specific laws of development. Freud viewed sexual functioning as passing through various "psychosexual stages of development" (1949). However, he saw this development as being energized by a finite amount of mental energy ("libido") present in every individual at birth. This mental energy passed through the body of a person in a prescribed sequence and became concentrated at particular locations of the body (e.g., the mouth during the "oral stage") at specific periods of the person's life. Although this same mental energy was seen as always being involved in emotional ("psychosexual") functioning at all times in a person's life—and as such represents a general law of development—the manner in which emotional functioning was expressed was dependent on exactly where the mental energy was centered. Thus, to Freud, psychosexual functioning involved the combined contribution of a continuously applicable mental energy and a specific area (or zone) of the body where this mental energy happened to be located at a certain time in development. This specific characteristic of psychosexual functioning determined the mode of expression of one's emotions. Hence, Freud's view of psychosexual development, which is discussed again in Chapter 15, is an example of how organismic developmentalists may utilize the general-and-specific-laws compromise in their theories.

The general-and-specific-laws compromise is represented in Figure 3.5. At both Level 1 and Level 2, we see that a general law, G, exists. However, at Level 1, there is also present a specific law, S_1, but at Level 2, there is present a different specific law, S_2.

If at each new developmental level of organization there is an emergence of new phenomena that cannot be reduced to lower organizational levels, how may the laws governing—or the variables involved in—these new phenomena be understood? Typical of other organismically oriented theorists, Schneirla (1957) maintained that to understand this emergence one must look at the specific contribution of that developmental level's genetic inheritance (nature) and its environment or experience (nurture). The sources of behavior must lie within these two domains, and one must look at how each level's nature and nurture dynamically interact to produce the qualitatively new phenomena that characterize it. This type of interactive view of the process of development has many uses, several of which will be focused on in succeeding chapters. Here, however, I should note that, as with organicism, mechanism, and

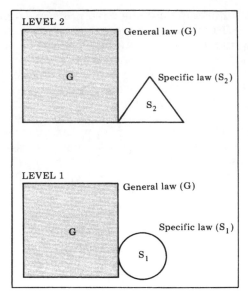

FIGURE 3.5
General-and-specific-laws compromise between the mechanistic and the organismic positions.

contextualism, the developmental–contextual integration I propose also has problems and limitations. Let us consider some of the key ones.

LIMITS AND PROBLEMS OF A DEVELOPMENTAL–CONTEXTUAL PERSPECTIVE

The concepts of organism, of context, and of the relations between the two found in a probabilistic–epigenetic, developmental–contextual perspective are, as a set, quite distinct from those associated with organismic and mechanistic conceptions. Such a developmental–contextual perspective leads to a multilevel concept of development, one in which the focus of inquiry is the dynamic organism–environment relation or transaction. Further, such a developmental contextual orientation places an emphasis on the potential for intraindividual change in structure and function—for plasticity across the life span. Yet, several conceptual and derivative methodological problems must be confronted in order:

1. To move such a developmental contextual orientation from merely being a "perspective" to being useful for the derivation of theory (Baltes, 1979b).

2. To usefully employ developmental contextualism as a framework within which to study dynamic individual–context relations.

First, substantively, we must recognize that despite the great amount of evidence that exists for human plasticity (Baltes et al., 1998, 1999; Gollin, 1981; Gottlieb, 1997; Lerner, 1984), we still cannot answer several fundamental questions about the contextual, dynamically interactive parameters of plasticity. Are different levels of analysis and/or different targets within levels differentially plastic? For example, it may be the case that selected features of our genotype (e.g., the number of chromosomes that we possess) cannot be altered (without, at least, severely damaging our organismic integrity) no matter what the nature of our organism–context relations may be. On the other hand, more molar, behavioral features of functioning may not be subject to such restrictions.

For instance, are there limits to the number of random digits a person can learn to recall or to the number of locations a person may recall? Current evidence indicates that such limits are quite variable, and that even among very old people—for example, those in their eighth or ninth decade of life—there are training techniques that can capitalize on their still-available (albeit diminished, relative to earlier age periods) "reserve" of plasticity in order to enhance performance on such tasks (e.g., see Baltes, 1987, 1997; Baltes et al., 1998, 1999).

In addition to not fully knowing the limits of plasticity that currently characterize levels of analysis, we do not know what further substantive and technological advances may imply for the future character of these limits. If we take the idea of probabilistic epigenesis seriously, and if we recognize that science and technology represent natural parts of the human ecology, then we cannot anticipate where future scientific advances may lead.

For example, the geneticist Brown (1981) noted that in the 1970s scientists could not *imagine* how a gene could ever be isolated. Yet, Nobel laureate Paul Berg (1981) indicated that by the 1980s such identification was quite routine, and that in just a few years the growth in the application of recombinant DNA methods had been truly explosive. For instance, he indicated that:

> Molecular cloning provides the means to solve the organization and detailed molecular structure of extended regions of chromosomes and eventually the entire genome, including man. Already, investigators have isolated a number of mammalian and human genes, and in some instances determined their chromosomal arrangement and even their detailed nucleotide sequence. (p. 302)

As Toulmin (1981) put the issue:

> And as for the possibilities open to future, more complex cultures, there too we must be prepared to speculate open-mindedly. There, perhaps, people generally will take pride in having overcome the "illusions" of material conservation and Euclidean space alike, and may come to talk about everyday material objects with the same conceptual sophistication we ourselves display toward such un-everyday things as electrons. (p. 261)

For instance, can microcomputers implanted in the brain enhance cognitive (e.g., memory) capacities? Might other microcomputers, implanted in the nervous and muscular systems return aged people to former levels of physical agility or, for paralyzed individuals, enable them to again use their limbs? At this writing, these technological advances exist in developmental form. Before this book is 10 years old, such technology will certainly be more common. Thus, current limits of plasticity are not necessarily future ones. These limits are themselves plastic and are likely to change in a direction that, for some of us, lies beyond our imagination.

But recognition that the limits of plasticity can change over time raises a developmental issue. The actualization of plasticity, of course, involves change, and change can only be identified over time. Numerous questions exist about the rates of change of plastic processes at the several levels of analysis that are integrated to provide the bases of behavior. First, it is clear that there is a "non-equivalent temporal metric" across the various levels of analysis (Lerner, Skinner, & Sorell, 1980) involved in person–context transactions. That is, all levels of the context change over time, but time may not have an identical meaning at all the levels.

One way to understand this is to note that the smallest meaningful division of time to detect change differs among levels. If time is one's X axis, with the Y axis reflecting levels of one's target process, then sensible X-axis divisions to detect infant neuromuscular changes may be as small as weeks. However, the smallest sensible division to detect changes in society brought about by new public policies regarding the availability of food for the poor may be a year. As such, the effects of such a policy change on infant growth might need to be assessed not by studying changes *within* a group if infants but, instead, by comparing differences *across* different infant birth cohorts.

For example, one could understand through such a comparison if, say, 36-week-old infants have greater neuromuscular maturity, as a group, one or two years after the policy than was the case for groups studied one or two years before the policy. In other words, because it may take a year or more to detect changes due to macro-level alterations, within-person changes (which may occur over weeks or months) may "fall between the cracks," that is, between the year-by-year (or larger) divisions of the X axis. Indeed, if an attempt is made to verify the existence of such macro (e.g., policy) influences, it may be that a long-term, perhaps intergenerational, perspective needs to be taken; or in a within-cohort analysis, it may be that only interindividual differences in intraindividual change, and not intraindividual change itself, can be assessed.

In addition, even within a given level, time may not have an equivalent meaning at different points in development. For example, on the level of the individual, a one-year separation between birthdays may seem a vast length of time to a five-year-old; to someone experiencing his or her thirty-ninth birthday, the one-year period until the fortieth birthday may seem quite short; and to an 85-year-old, a one-year wait for some important event may, again, seem quite long.

Complicating this issue is that even though the effects of a biological intervention on society may take a long time to detect, there is not necessarily symmetry of influence. That is, "upper level" societal alteration and social change may quite visibly, and relatively rapidly affect "lower level" individual and biological processes. For example, changes in federal government funding programs for school lunch programs for poor children; welfare support to working, single mothers; or Medicare and Medicaid for the elderly can rapidly affect an individual's health, and cognitive and familial functioning variables (Lerner, Sparks, & McCubbin, 1999, 2000).

The issues of the nonequivalent temporal metric, and of the asymmetry of interlevel influences, can be seen to lead to other ones. First, given the rates of change of different levels, one needs to know how processes at different levels connect to one another: How do interlevel influences occur? One answer to this question may be to explore the use of a "goodness of fit" model of person–context relations (e.g., Eccles, 1991; Eccles & Midgley, 1989; Lerner & Lerner, 1983, 1999). Here, individual behavioral characteristics that are congruent with pertinent behavioral presses are studied for their import for adaptive person–immediate–social context (e.g., peer group) exchanges.

Of course, the goodness-of-fit model is not the only conception of person–context relations that may be derived from a developmental–contextual orientation. Indeed, an infinity of interlevel relations may perhaps occur, and there exists a potentially similarly large array of ways to model them. Scholars need to devote more thought and empirical energies to their investigation.

Methodology and Issues for Intervention

Interventions represent attempts to:

1. Ameliorate or prevent undesired or problematic features of individual and/or group behavior.

2. Enhance or optimize an individual's or a group's behavior or social situation in the direction of some desired or valued end (e.g., better health or improved self-concept).

A developmental–contextual view of person–context relations, and of plasticity, raises several issues pertinent to intervention. First, the issue of asymmetry of interlevel influences raises largely unaddressed concerns about efficiency and about cost–benefit ratios. For instance, with an intervention targeted at the cognitive–behavioral level (e.g., the modification of academic achievement) is it more efficient to institute a "bottom-up strategy" (e.g., intervening at the biological level), a "parallel-level strategy" (e.g., intervening by cognitive–behavioral means), or a "top-down" strategy (intervening by instituting or changing social programs)? Which strategy leads to the most benefits, relative to economic, social, and personal costs? We simply do not know the answers to these questions for many of the potential targets of intervention.

A decision about the level of analysis on which to focus one's intervention efforts is complicated by the fact that all levels of analysis are developing or changing over time. While this feature of the human condition permits both *concurrent* (same time or immediate) and *historical* (long-term or delayed) interventions, it again raises questions of efficiency and cost–benefit ratios. For example, when during the life span is it best to intervene to optimize a particular target process (and, of course, on what level is it best to focus one's efforts)? Are periods of developmental transition (e.g., puberty or retirement) or periods of *relatively* more stability (e.g., midlife; Lachman & James, 1997), better times to focus one's efforts? Moreover, do some intervention goals, for example the elimination of fetal alcohol syndrome, or FAS (Streissguth et al., 1980), require an intergenerational–developmental rather than an ontogenetic–developmental approach? In the case of FAS, for instance, might it be of more benefit to intervene with women who are at risk for excessive alcohol use during pregnancy—*before* they become pregnant? Again, for most potential targets, intervention issues such as these have remained relatively unaddressed.

A final relatively unaddressed issue relates to direct and indirect intervention effects and to planned and unplanned effects. If an individual's plasticity both derives from and contributes to the other levels of analysis within which he or she transacts, one must anticipate that actualizing the potential for plasticity at any one level of analysis will influence changes among other variables, both at that level and at others. From this perspective, one should always expect that any direct and/or intended effect of intervention will have indirect and often unintended consequences (Willems, 1973).

This recognition leads to two points. First, interventions should not be initiated without some conceptual or theoretical analysis of potential indirect and unintended consequences. One needs to consider the developmental system when planning an intervention. For instance, changing a spouse's assertiveness may be the direct intended effect of a cognitive–behavior therapist's efforts. However, the changed assertiveness might lead to a diminution of marital quality and, in addition, to a divorce. Such indirect effects might have been unintended by the therapist and undesired by either therapist or client. Thus, my view is that one must think quite seriously about the broader, contextual effects of one's intervention efforts. Clearly, a developmental–contextual perspective would be of use in this regard. It would sensitize one to the general possibility, and perhaps some specific instances, of the indirect effects of one's intervention efforts. Such reflection is useful in several ways, a major instance of which is that some undesirable indirect effects may be anticipated. If so, the issue of cost–benefit ratios can be addressed before intervention begins.

Of course, the fact that undesired effects may arise from intervention efforts raises the point that plasticity is a double-edged sword: A system open to enhancement is also open to deterioration. That is, plasticity permits interventions to be planned in order to improve the human condition, but indirect effects may also cause a deterioration in a target person's life condition and/or

the condition of the context. This problem is also complicated by recognizing that as a consequence of people being transactionally related to their multilevel contexts, a failure to intervene (to alter the context of life) is *itself* an intervention; that is, it keeps the context on a trajectory from which it might have been shifted if one had acted. Thus, one must assess the cost–benefit ratio not only of one's actions but also of one's failure to act.

Conclusions

I have pointed to some of the key conceptual and methodological issues that remain to be resolved if a developmental–contextual perspective is to be successfully used not only to study individual–context relations but also to intervene to enhance such relations. Pessimism because of the presence of these problems is unwarranted. Every approach to human development has limitations, as I hope I have made clear in this chapter. Thus, the fact that there are problems to be resolved about developmental contextualism, or about developmental systems theories in general, does not single these views out from other developmental paradigms. Indeed, given that it was only in the 1970s that this view of contextualism came to the fore, the clarity with which the problems have been articulated, the methodological advances that have already been made (e.g., see Nesselroade, 1988; Nesselroade & Baltes, 1979; Nesselroade & Ghisletta, 2000; Nesselroade & von Eye, 1985; von Eye, 1990a, 1990b), and the several data sets that speak to the empirical use of this contextual perspective (e.g., Baltes et al., 1980, 1998, 1999; Brim & Kagan, 1980) are reasons for great optimism for the future.

Developmental contextualism has influenced and will continue to influence scientific activity. Indeed, all the models we have considered in this chapter have such an influence. Let us conclude this chapter, then, with a brief discussion of the implications of the models for scientific activity.

IMPLICATIONS OF PHILOSOPHICAL MODELS OF DEVELOPMENT FOR SCIENTIFIC ACTIVITY

Philosophical models are not capable of being evaluated in terms of whether they are correct (Overton, 1998; Reese & Overton, 1970). Nevertheless, they shape the theories that scientists use to interpret the facts they derive from their studies of the "real" world. Moreover, in shaping theories, world views shape the very questions scientists ask in their study of the real world. The questions that follow from different theories are likely to be quite different, and in turn, the data generated to answer these contrasting questions are unlikely to provide comparable answers.

For instance, a nurture, mechanistic theorist who derives a theory of human development may try to reduce behavior to learning principles common to people of all ages. Thus, he or she might seek to discover those environmental–behavioral reactions that remain identical from infancy through adolescence and adulthood. Alternatively, an organismically oriented theorist would attempt to find those phenomena that are unique to and representative of particular age periods. In turn, a developmental–contextualist theorist might look at the relation of an event to others at earlier times in the life cycle, as well as to current cultural, environmental, and long-term historical influences. The reciprocal nature of these interactions would also be considered.

The point is that scientific activity derived from alternative world views asks different questions about development. Consequently, scientists committed to alternative world views may collect data on different topics. One scientist is not necessarily functioning correctly and another incorrectly. The issue is not one of deciding which theory is best, or which leads to truth and which does not. Theories from different world views asks different questions because the very nature of reality is conceived of differently. Thus, what is a true depiction of reality for one world view may be irrelevant for another (e.g., see Kuhn, 1962).

One major implication of the nature of this philosophy–science relationship is that a criterion other than truth must be used to evaluate interpretations of development. Earlier in this chapter and in Chapter 1 as well, I forwarded "usefulness" as one such criterion (e.g., in regard to accounting for more variance in developmental data sets, leading to more novel discoveries, or integrating a broader range of phenomena pertinent to development than is the case with other positions), and explained that such dimensions of utility could be summarized by the concepts of precision, scope, and deployability. When theories have precision, scope, and deployability, they are useful for the description of developmental phenomena, for the explanation of development, and for devising ways to optimize human behavior and development.

Of course, such deployability is not the sole province of science. Using theory and research to enhance human life requires collaboration between scholars and the societal institutions and individuals their work is aimed at serving (Lerner et al., 1994; Lerner & Simon, 1998a, 1998b). Scholars cannot ethically deploy their theories and research to enhance human life without the agreement and collaboration of the community, broadly writ (Chibucos & Lerner, 1999; Fisher & Tyron, 1988, 1990; Lerner & Simon, 1998b). In addition, such application requires not only scholar–community collaboration but also the financial support of public and private funders (e.g., the federal government, and businesses or foundations, respectively). Deployability is a political issue as much as it is a scientific one and, as such, issues of policy and policy engagement become a central concern to scholars interested in the application of developmental science (Fisher & Lerner, 1994a, 1994b; Lerner, Fisher, & Weinberg, 2000a, 2000b).

In sum, since any theory might be used to pursue understanding of human development or to influence public policy, I have suggested that theories should be evaluated on the basis of their usefulness and indicated that a developmental–contextual perspective may be particularly useful in regard to description, explanation, and optimization. Of course, these uses depend on the meaning attached to the concepts of description, explanation, and optimization.

Theories differ in regard to the features of behavioral or mental life they deem important to describe. Nevertheless, there is consensus that description per se pertains to the depiction or representation of the phenomena of interest in a given theory. However, as is noted in Chapter 1, considerably less consensus exists in regard to the explanation of development. For instance, as noted earlier in this chapter, mechanistically oriented organismically oriented, and contextually oriented theorists differ in respect to whether cause–effect, formal, or configural information is regarded as essential for explanation. When theories differ in regard to how development is explained, they also vary in their ideas for what variables need to be engaged in interventions aimed at optimizing development.

In Chapter 5, we focus on the issues of description, explanation, and optimization as they pertain to the topic of continuity–discontinuity in development. Throughout the succeeding chapters, we return to the various ideas about description, explanation, and optimizations associated with different theories of human development. For instance, in Chapter 8, we discuss the features of developmental contextualism and its ideas about description, explanation, and optimization. As can be readily inferred from my presentation in this chapter, this discussion pertains to a great extent on a consideration of the nature–nurture controversy and on an indication of the specific stances taken by developmental contextualism in regard to this key issue of human development. As such, it is important to turn, in Chapter 4, to a discussion of this issue.

4 | The Nature–Nurture Controversy: Implications of the Question How?

A child is born, and may seem to have few distinguishable capabilities. Soon, however, rather well-coordinated sensorimotor behaviors begin to develop. Later, other, more complicated motor patterns emerge. Still later, the child's vocalizations turn into words.

A baby goose (a gosling), moments after it breaks through its shell, begins to walk after its mother. From then on, the goose will attach itself to other geese in all its social behaviors.

A newborn human baby, just a few hours after birth, sucks on a nonnutritive nipple more when the sucking is followed by a recording of their mother's voice than when the sucking is followed by a recording of another female voice.

What is the basis of these diverse behaviors? In fact, what is the basis of any behavior at any point in development? Some scientists have interpreted the emergence of behaviors such as these in a way that suggests that experience seems to play a minimal role, if any, and that innate, maturational, or hereditary factors are what seem to account for the appearance of such behaviors. Yet other scientists claim just the opposite. Observing the same behaviors, their interpretations emphasize environmental factors. Still other scientists (myself included) attempt to interpret such behaviors in a way that takes into account both the contributions of biological and experiential factors.

Where does the truth lie? Perhaps all positions have elements of truth in them, but the arguments about where the bases of behavior lie are by no means resolved. From the discussions in Chapters 1, 2, and 3, it may be seen that the basic issue in human development is the nature–nurture controversy. Indeed, this controversy has been and remains to be very much an issue.

For example, as indicated in Chapter 2, some psychologists interested in the study of perceptual processes (the Gestalt school) claimed that nativistic factors were most important in determining a person's perception, while others (e.g., Hebb, 1949) took an empiricist point of view. In the area of personality, some (e.g., Sheldon, 1940, 1942) stressed what they claimed to be innate sources of a person's temperamental–behavioral functioning, whereas others (e.g., McCandless, 1967, 1970) maintained that acquired, socially learned responses were the source of such functions. In looking at certain types of animal behavior (e.g., social attachments made by newborn birds, such as ducklings, to other members of their own species), some writers (e.g., Lorenz, 1965) postulated preformed, innate mechanisms to account for such behaviors, whereas others (e.g., Gottlieb, 1970, 1983; Kuo, 1967; Lehrman, 1953; Schneirla, 1957) took a probabilistic–epigenetic approach. Some researchers interested in verbal development stressed the primacy of maturation (Gesell & Thompson, 1941), whereas others who viewed the same sort of behaviors offered interpretations that stressed learning (Gagné, 1968). Finally, some psychologists interested in intelligence—or more specifically in IQ scores (see Chapter 2) suggested hypotheses that stressed the primacy of heredity factors (e.g., Herrnstein, 1971; Herrnstein & Murray, 1994; Jensen, 1969, 1974, 1980), whereas others pointed to the role of the environment (Hebb, 1970; Kagan, 1969) and/or to gene–environment interaction (Lewontin, 1976, 2000; Lewontin, Rose, & Kamin, 1984).

Indeed, and in respect to the last instance of the continuing concern with the nature–nurture issue, the renewal of controversy about the nature and nurture of intelligence seemingly opened up a Pandora's box regarding the contributions of nature and nurture to such topics as sexism, militarism, social Darwinism, racism (Tobach et al., 1974), educability (Jensen, 1973), and sex differences in personality (e.g., Carlson, 1972; Maccoby, 1998), to name just some of the areas of concern. In fact, as evidenced by contributions to the literatures of several disciplines (e.g., Feldman & Lewontin, 1975;

Gottlieb, 1997; Gottlieb et al., 1998; Herrnstein & Murray, 1994; Lewontin, 1976; Lewontin et al., 1984; Loehlin, Lindzey, & Spuhler, 1975; Wilson, 1975), not only has the debate regarding the contributions of nature and nurture to human functioning not been resolved to date, but it has also evolved as a concern of multidisciplinary relevance.

Perhaps the best example of the multidisciplinary dimensions of this debate arose in 1975 with the publication of E. O. Wilson's *Sociobiology: The New Synthesis*. As noted in Chapter 3 and as is more fully discussed in Chapter 13, sociobiology, as promoted by Wilson (1975) and others (e.g., Trivers, 1971), attempts to integrate through biological reductionism not only the biological sciences but also the social sciences and the humanities. As pointed out by the philosopher Caplan (1978, p. 2), this approach is "the latest and most strident of a series of efforts in the biological sciences to direct scientific and humanistic attention toward the question of what is, fundamentally, the nature of human nature." Consistent with the metatheoretical assumptions, discussed in Chapter 3, as being associated with those adopting a predetermined–epigenetic position, many sociobiologists construe nature as making a predetermined, immutable contribution to behavior. That is, whatever the proportion of variance in human social behavior with a genetic basis, it is that proportion that is genetically constrained and generally unavailable to contextual influence.

The criticisms of sociobiology have come from the several disciplinary quarters that sociobiologists seek to digest (e.g., see Caplan, 1978; Hubbard, 1990; Lerner, 1992; Lerner & von Eye, 1992; Lewontin, 2000; Lips, 2001). Within the biological and social sciences, criticisms have generally been associated with the conceptualizations that stress that sociobiologists do not appreciate the plasticity of genes, organisms, or contexts; and that just as genes influence their contexts, the reverse is also the case (e.g., see Gottlieb, 1991, 1992, 1997; Gottlieb et al., 1998; Grouse et al., 1978, 1979; Uphouse & Bonner, 1975).

In this debate about the usefulness of sociobiological thinking, a key influence on the differences of opinion expressed by participants is the philosophical differences among them. Those who favor sociobiological thinking are essentially arguing from a predetermined–epigenetic viewpoint (see Gottlieb, 1983, 1997). In turn, those who reject this conceptualization argue from a metatheoretical stance that emphasizes strong, or dynamic, interactions between heredity and environment (e.g., Gould, 1976; Lerner, 1976, 1978, 1992a; Lerner & von Eye, 1992; Lewontin, 1976; Lewontin et al., 1984; Overton, 1973, 1998). Thus, this viewpoint is consonant with the developmental–contextual position discussed in earlier chapters. Again, philosophical division characterizes this instance of the nature–nurture debate.

The details of each of the above controversies need not be specified here in order to make the point that the field of human development in no way takes a place behind philosophy in the intensity of its debate over the nature–nurture issue. In all cases, the essence of each debate is always the same—the relative contributions of nature and nurture variables in providing a source of behavior.

TOWARD A RESOLUTION OF THE NATURE–NURTURE CONTROVERSY

By this time, you are probably wondering how a controversy that has engaged so many bright men and women for so many years can still remain unresolved. Can the issues not be detailed in such a way as to somehow diminish the seemingly endless division of opinion? I think they can. Rather than discuss here all the details of such controversies which often led to what I believe were conceptual dead ends, let me turn to a review of various scholars' formulations that were offered in an attempt to resolve the nature–nurture controversy. I begin my analysis with a review of the seminal ideas of a famous psychologist, a former president of the American Psychological Association, Anne Anastasi. I then use Anastasi's formulations as a general framework within which to begin to consider the issues necessary for my reconceptualization of the nature–nurture controversy. To illustrate the application of this conceptualization, I (in Chapter 11) consider as a sample case the nature–nurture issue as it has occurred, and continues to exist, in the study of intelligence.

The Position of Anne Anastasi

Anne Anastasi's classic article, which first appeared in the *Psychological Review* in 1958, represents a most lucid and well-considered treatment of the nature–nurture controversy. The essential problem in appropriately conceptualizing the nature–nurture controversy, as Anastasi saw it, was that psychologists were asking the wrong questions. Therefore, they obviously could not get the right answers. Anastasi attempted to show why previous inquiries led to dead ends and to identify the appropriate question.

Anne Anastasi

As we have seen in Chapter 2, the first way that philosophers—as well as psychologists—inquired into this problem was to ask, "Which one?" Based on a Cartesian split conception of reality (Overton, 1998; see Chapter 2), the question was framed as "Does heredity or environment, nature or nurture, provide the determining source of behavior?" Those who posed the issue in this way were assuming the reality of only one source of behavior; that is, in splitting the world into the real and the pseudo-phenomenal, the assumption was made that that the independent, isolated action of one or the other domain provided a source of a behavior. However, we should reject this split way of posing the problem, because it is basically illogical. To explain, let us use the terms focused on by Anastasi: That is, nature is *heredity* and nurture is *environment*.

The "which one?" question assumes that heredity and environment are independent, separable sources of influence, and as such, that one can exert an influence in isolation from the other. But Anastasi pointed out that such a split assumption was illogical. This was true because there would be no one in an environment without heredity, and there would be no place to see the effects of heredity without environment. Genes do not exist in a vacuum. They exert their influence on behavior in an environment. At the same time, however, if there were no genes (and consequently no heredity), the environment would not have an organism in it to influence. Accordingly, nature and nurture are inextricably tied together. In life, they never exist independent of the other. As such, Anastasi argued that *any* theory of development, in order to be logical and to accurately reflect life situations (i.e., to have *ecological validity*), must stress that nature and nurture were always involved in all behavior, and it was simply not appropriate to ask "which one?" because they were both completely necessary for any organism's existence or for the existence of any behavior.

Some psychologists (e.g., Hebb, 1949; Lehrman, 1953; Schneirla, 1956, 1957), however, had recognized the inappropriateness of the "which one?" question even before Anastasi's (1958) article was published. Yet, others had asked another question that, according to Anastasi, was also inappropriate. It also led to a conceptual dead end. These psychologists put the issue this way: Granted that nature and nurture are always involved in any behavior, that both of them are always needed, *how much* of each is needed for a given behavior? For intelligence, do you need 90% heredity and 10% environment, or is intelligence perhaps only two parts heredity and eight parts environment? Or some might ask: For personality, can it be 50% of each, whereas for perception it is seven parts of one, three parts of the other? In essence, psychologists asking this question would attempt to ascertain how much of each source was needed for a given type of behavior.

But this question also leads to a fruitless end, because it—like the "which one?" question—is based on the same split and inappropriate underlying assumption. In the case of the "how much?" question, the instantiation of the split assumption may be termed the *independent, additive-action assumption*. It suggests that the way in which nature and nurture are related to each other is that the contribution of one source is added to the contribution of the other to provide the behavior. We can see that this solution puts the nature-nurture relation into the terms of a recipe: Add one part of X to some part of Y; add some unknown part of nature to an unknown part of nurture to get behavior.

However, such a question raises many others. For example, for the 80% of intelligence that might be thought to be nature, one may ask where that 80% exerts its influence if not in an environment. For the 20% of intelligence thought to be nurture, how is that 20% acted on if an organism does not first have inherited genes? Does not the nature part play a role with the nurture part? If not, then what can that nurture possibly contribute to? And what of the (unknown) contributory part of nature? Can it contribute to behavior without any environmental support? Where does it contribute if not in an environment? Thus, the "how much?" question soon leads to separating out (splitting) the independent, isolated effects of nature and nurture, a conceptual route we have just taken by means of the "which one?" question. We rejected the route, with its split notions of either heredity or environment, because we saw that nature and nurture are always inextricably bound. Thus, we must also reject the "how much?" route because it really does not take us beyond the "which one?" path. In fact, the "which one?" question can be seen to be just a special case of the "how much?" question. That is, the former question implies a 100%/0% (or a 0%/100%) split between nature and nurture, respectively, while the latter implies some percentage split less than that.

Thus, we see that a conceptualization of the independent action of either source (in either an isolated or an additive manner) will lead us to a conceptually vacuous dead end. We should conclude, then, that two assertions directly follow from this argument. First, nature and nurture are always completely involved in all behavior. Put another way, 100% of nature and 100% of nurture always make their contributions to all behavior. Any method of inquiry into the source of behavioral development that does not take cognizance of this statement and that seeks to make artificial distinctions between nature and nurture can lead only to conceptual confusion and an empirical blind alley. Second, since independent-action conceptualizations of the contributions of nature and nurture similarly lead to conceptual dead ends, an alternative conceptualization of their contributions, that of (*dynamically*) *interactive*, or *fused, action,* seems more appropriate.

This alternative, which seems useful from the perspective of our previous considerations (and see Chapter 3), indicates that both nature and nurture interact dynamically (as components, or dimensions, of a fused, developmental system) to provide a source of behavioral development. Because both sources have been seen to be necessarily completely present and because we have seen that it is inappropriate to speak of their contributions as adding to each other, then it seems that we should ask: *How* do nature and nurture dynamically interact to produce behavioral development? *How* do the effects of each multiply (or reciprocally interrelate within a fused, developmental system) to provide a source of development? Thus, the

probabilistic–epigenetic version of organism, with its notion of a multiplicative, or dynamic, interaction between nature and nurture as providing the basis of development, is the view associated with this question.

This third question—the question of "how?"—leads to what I regard as the appropriate route of investigation into the contributions of nature and nurture. This, Anastasi argued, is the appropriate way to formulate the issue, because it takes cognizance of the logical necessity of the material existence of both domains for a living organism (or living system; Ford & Lerner, 1992). That is, this question denies a split between nature and nurture based on the contention that one domain is real and the other is pseudo-phenomenal (e.g., as in Rowe, 1994). Rather, the question is based on what we may term the *interactive, multiplicative-action assumption,* which implies

1. That nature and nurture are both fully involved in providing a source of any behavioral development.

2. That they cannot, therefore, function in isolation from one another but must always interact (be systemicallly fused) in their contributions.

3. That interaction (which, as we have seen, cannot be appropriately construed to mean addition) can be conceptualized as a multiplicative type of interrelation—that is, a type of relation in which the full presence of each source is completely intertwined with the other.

In other words, from this view heredity and environment do not add together to contribute to behavior, but rather development is seen as a *product* of nature–nurture interaction.

An analogy helps illustrate this. The area of a rectangle is determined by a formula that multiplies the length by the width (area = length × width). To know the area of a given rectangle, one has to look at the product of a multiplicative relation. It is simply incorrect to ask which one, length or width, determines the area, because a rectangle would not exist unless it had both length and width. Similarly, it is incorrect to ask how much of each is necessary to have area, because the two dimensions cannot merely be added; they must be multiplied in order to produce a rectangle.

Of course, although length and width must always be completely present in order to have a rectangle, different values of each will lead to different products (or areas). Thus, in determining a particular product (a given area) of a length × width interaction, one must ask *how* a specific value of length in interaction (in multiplication) with a specific value of width produces a rectangle of a given area. More generally, one must recognize that the same width would lead to different areas in interaction with varying lengths and, in turn, the same length would lead to different areas in interaction with varying widths.

By moving from this analogy back to the question "how?" in regard to the nature–nurture issue, it may be seen that comparable statements may be made. There would be no product—no behavioral development—if nature and nurture were not 100% present. Thus, the assumption of a split that underlies the "which one?" and "how much of each?" questions are rejected, and it is recognized that any behavioral development is the result of a multiplicative, interactive relation between specific hereditary and environmental influences. Moreover, it should be noted that this means that the same hereditary influence will lead to different behavioral products in interaction with varying environments; furthermore, the same environment will lead to varying behavioral outcomes in interaction with different hereditary influences.

This means that heredity and environment *never* function independently of each other. Nature (e.g., genes) never affects behavior directly; it always acts in the context of internal and external environments. Environment (e.g., social stimulation) never directly influences behavior; it will show variation in its effects depending on the heredity-related characteristics of the organism on which it acts.

These statements about the reciprocal interdependence of nature and nurture are not just casual matters. In Chapter 2, we saw that major philosophers and scientists have tried to conceptualize behavior and development in terms that are inconsistent with the view reflected by the interactive action conception. Succeeding chapters consider theorists who emphasize that various components of development (e.g., cognition or personality) can be understood by ideas that stress *either* nature or nurture (i.e., the "which one?" question). Thus, it is important to point out that others do not necessarily agree that the formulation I favor is the best or most useful one. Nevertheless, I believe that the question "how?" leads the human developmentalist to a consideration of the interactive effects of nature and nurture in providing a basis of development. It seems that, of the questions discussed by Anastasi (1958), only this question casts aside fruitless polemics and

allows developmental scientists to begin to unravel the decidedly complex interactions of nature and nurture.

HEREDITY–ENVIRONMENT DYNAMIC INTERACTIONS

Assuredly, if Anastasi had ended her article after making some of the above points, her contribution to the conceptual clarification of the nature–nurture controversy would have been considered substantial. Anastasi's article provided additional ideas, however. After indicating that the appropriate way to conceptualize the nature–nurture controversy is in terms of *how* these two sets of sources interact, Anastasi suggested how each basis, heredity and environment, may provide a basis of behavioral development.

Nature Effects Are Indirect

Let us focus first on hereditary factors. Anastasi argued that the effects of heredity on behavior were diverse and always indirect. That is, no psychological function is ever inherited as such; heredity always relates to behavior in an indirect way. At the very least, any hereditary influence on behavior must be mediated by—must occur in the context of—a supportive, facilitative internal as well as external environment. This assertion is derived from the rationale that was used to object to the reality-splitting (Overton, 1998) "which one?" question: You need internal and external environments to see the effects of heredity; there would be no place to see the contribution of nature if there were no environmental context. Accordingly, the specific contribution of heredity to behavior will depend on the specific environment in which that contribution occurs. Consistent with the probabilistic–epigenetic position discussed in Chapter 3, we may assert that any hereditary contribution must occur in an environmental context, and the particular expression of the hereditary contribution that will eventually be seen will depend on the specific characteristics of the environment in which it occurs.

To illustrate, let us represent hereditary contributions by the letter "G" (for genes), environmental contributions by the letter "E," and behavioral outcomes by the letter "B." As shown in Figure 4.1, it is possible to conceptualize the contribution of heredity to behavior as being direct. Hence, in this formulation, a particular combination of genes (G_1) will invariably lead to a particular behavioral

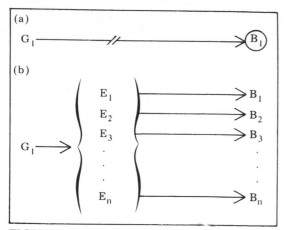

FIGURE 4.1

(a) Heredity (*G*) does not directly lead to behavior (*B*). (b) Rather, the effects of heredity on behavior will be different under different environmental (*E*) conditions. Since the early 1900s, this phenomenon has been known in biology as the "norm of reaction."

Source: (Gottlieb, (1992); Hirsch (1970).

outcome (B_1). However, it has been argued that this conceptualization is not appropriate. As such, an interactive idea of nature and nurture, illustrated in Figure 4.1, has been advanced. Here, the same hereditary contribution (G_1) can be linked with an infinity of behavioral outcomes (B_1 to B_n) as a consequence of interaction in the infinity of environments (E_1 to E_n) that could exist.

Consider as an example the case of a child born with Down syndrome. The genetic material—the DNA—of genes is arranged on stringlike structures present in the nucleus of each cell. These structures are chromosomes. The typical cells of the human body have 46 chromosomes, divided into 23 pairs. The only cells in the body that do not have 46 chromosomes are the gametes—the sex cells (sperm in males and ova in females). These cells carry only 23 chromosomes, one of each pair. This arrangement assures that when a sperm fertilizes an ovum to form a zygote, the new human so created will have the number of chromosome pairs appropriate for the species. However, in a child born with Down syndrome, a genetic anomaly exists. There is an extra chromosome in the twenty-first-pair—three chromosomes instead of two.

Thus, children with Down syndrome have a specific genetic inheritance. The complement of genes transmitted to people at conception by the union of the sperm and ovum is termed the *genotype*. This is what constitutes our genetic inheritance.

At least insofar as the extra chromosome is concerned, the Down syndrome child has a specific genotype. Yet, even though the genotype remains the same for any such child, the behavioral outcomes associated with this genotype differ.

As recently as 40 to 50 years ago, Down syndrome children, who are typically recognized by certain physical (particularly facial) characteristics, were expected to have life spans of no more than about 12 years. They were also expected to have quite low IQ scores. They were typically classified into a group of people who, because of low intelligence, required custodial (usually institutional) care. Today, however, Down syndrome children often live well beyond adolescence. Additionally, they lead more self-reliant lives. Their IQs are now typically higher, often falling in the range allowing for education, training, gainful employment, and even accomplishments in the creative or performing arts (e.g., writing or acting).

How did these vast differences come about? Certainly, the genotype did not change. Rather, what changed was the environment of these children. Instead of invariably being put into institutions, different and more advanced special education techniques were provided, often on an outpatient basis. These contrasts in environment led to variation in behavioral outcomes despite the same heredity, that is, despite *genotypic invariance*.

That heredity always exerts its effects indirectly through environment in the development of physical as well as behavioral characteristics may also be illustrated. First, consider the disease *phenylketonuria* (PKU). This disorder, involving an inability to metabolize fatty substances because of the absence of a particular digestive enzyme, led to the development of distorted physical features and severe mental retardation in children. It was discovered that the lack of the necessary enzyme resulted from the absence of a particular gene and, as such, PKU is another instance of a disease associated with a specific genotype.

Today, however, many people—perhaps even some college students reading this book—may have the PKU genotype without having either the physical or the behavioral deficits formerly associated with the disease. Researchers discovered that if the missing enzyme is put into the diets of newborns identified as having the disease, all negative effects can be avoided (Scriver & Clow, 1980a, 1980b). Again, change in the environment has changed the outcome. In fact, researchers also found that at about 1 year of age the PKU child no longer needs the added enzyme since the body either no longer needs it to metabolize fat or produces the enzyme in another way (Scriver & Clow, 1980a, 1980b). Here, again, it may be seen that the same genotype will lead to alternative outcomes, both physical and behavioral, when it interacts in contrasting environmental settings.

Another example illustrates this point still further and, more important, provides a basis for specifying the variety of environmental characteristics within which hereditary contributions are embedded. First, imagine that an experiment (improbable for ethical and technological reasons) were done — say a mother was pregnant with *monozygotic* (identical) twins. These are twins who develop from the same fertilized egg—the same zygote—which splits after conception. Hence, the two zygotes have the same genotype. But, importantly, because the zygotes implant on somewhat different parts of the wall of the uterus, there exist somewhat different environments. Imagine further that it was possible, immediately after the zygote split into two, to take one of them and implant it in another woman who would carry the organism through to birth. Finally, imagine that the first woman, "Mother A," has lived for the last several years on a diet of chocolate bars, potato chips, and soda pop, smoked two packs of cigarettes a day, and consumed a pint of alcohol each evening. On the other hand, say the second woman, "Mother B," has consumed a well-balanced diet and neither smoked nor drank. In all other respects, the women are alike.

Here is a situation wherein two genotypically identical organisms are developing in quite different uterine environments. Such differences are known to relate to *prenatal, perinatal* (birth), and *postnatal* behavior on the part of the offspring, and even to have implications for the mother. Thus, despite the genotype identity, the offspring of Mother A would be more likely to be born anemic (because of the mother's poor diet) and to be smaller, less alert, and more hyperactive (because of the mother's smoking habit and alcohol intake) than the offspring of Mother B.

Although this study with Mother A and Mother B is imaginary, the influence of the uterine environment on the offspring is not at all fanciful. The imaginary example was used to illustrate that variations in the environment will cause significant physical and behavioral changes in an offspring despite the genotype. As we discuss in more detail later, even physical characteristics such as eye or skin color may be influenced by environmental variations (albeit extreme ones) no matter what genes are inherited. If mothers are exposed to extreme radiation or dangerous chemicals (as in the case of mothers in the 1950s who took the tranquilizer *thalidomide*), pigmentation of the eyes or the skin can be radically altered and/or limbs can be severely deformed.

In sum, then, I believe that in order to understand the contributions of heredity to development one needs to recognize that genes influence physical and behavioral characteristics indirectly, by acting in a specific environment. If the same genetic contribution were to be expressed in an environment having other specific characteristics, the same genes might be associated with an alternative behavioral outcome. Accordingly, in order to completely specify the interactions of nature with nurture, one should know all the ways in which the environment can vary (and, as is argued in the following section it is also the case that one must know how genes vary to specify the interactions of nurture with nature).

There is an infinity of possible environmental variations; and today, one cannot even begin to identify all the chemical, nutritional, psychological, social, and physical ecological variables that may vary in the environment, much less identify the ways in which they provide a significant context for development. Nevertheless, one may note at this point that the environment may be thought of as existing at many levels. One can look at the environment in molecular terms—and talk of chemicals in the body of the mother. Or one can use molar terms—and talk of noise and air pollution levels in particular settings (e.g., urban ones). Consequently, it is useful to specify levels of the environment because it allows discussion about where the variables that provide the context for nature–nurture dynamic interactions may lie. As such, we now consider levels of environmental variation.

Levels of the Environment

An organism does not exist independent of an environment, and as much as the organism is shaped by the environment, the organism *shapes* the environment (Lerner, 1982; Lerner & Busch-Rossnagel, 1981; Lerner & Walls, 1999). As a consequence of this interdependency, both organism and environment may continually change, and this change involves multiple levels of analysis. These levels—the inner–biological, individual–psychological, physical–environmental, and sociocultural–historical (Riegel, 1975, 1976a)— denote the types of nurture-related variables that may provide the context for nature interactions.

The inner–biological level. The genotype is first expressed in utero, in the mother's body. Hence, the chemical and physical makeup of the mother can affect the offspring. Chemicals in the mother's bloodstream can enter that offspring through the umbilical cord, the attachment between mother and offspring. As already noted, poor nutrition, excessive smoking, alcohol use, and other drug ingestion can affect the unborn child. In addition, diseases (e.g., rubella) can lead to malformations of the heart and limbs and can affect the development and function of sensory organs (the eyes or ears).

The work of Phelps, Davis, and Schartz (1997) illustrated that even among monozygotic (MZ) twins, internal biological influences occurring prenatally can affect development. For instance, MZ twins may differ in regard to whether they share a single placenta and chorion or have separate placentas and chorions. Phelps et al. (1997) report that MZ twins who share a chorion can be more dissimilar than MZs who do not share a chorion in regard to physical and medical variables (e.g., birth weights) and more similar in regard to some psychological characteristics (e.g., variables related to personality or intelligence).

The individual–psychological level. Independent of her diet, smoking or drinking habits, and physical health status, the psychological functioning of the mother can affect the unborn child. Excessive maternal stress (e.g., "nervousness" about the pregnancy) can affect the offspring. Mothers who have excessive stress in about the third month of pregnancy are more likely to have children with certain birth defects (such as cleft palate or harelip) than are mothers who are not as stressed (Sutton-Smith, 1973). To illustrate the interrelation among all the levels of the environment), it may be that maternal stress exerts an influence on the unborn child by altering the chemicals (e.g., adrenaline) in the blood—at the inner–biological level—at a time in the embryological period when specific organs are being formed.

In addition, previous child-rearing experiences can play a part on the individual–psychological level. Experienced parents (those who already have a child) are not the same people they were before they had an offspring. Firstborns, in this sense, have different parents than latter-borns, even though the parents involved may be biologically the same. Thus, a mother may be less likely to be stressed by a second pregnancy. Not only might this affect the chemicals in her bloodstream but also, in being less "nervous," she might be less likely to engage in "nervous" behaviors (e.g., smoking).

Of course, as more information about prenatal care becomes available in society (e.g., about the dangers of a woman drinking during pregnancy), and as cultural values change (e.g., toward showing general approbation for drinking during pregnancy), effects on maternal stress and "nervous" behaviors will change. Thus, one level of environment is related to another, the individual–psychological to the sociocultural–historical. Before turning to the latter level, however, let us consider the physical–environmental level.

The physical–environmental level. Physical settings differ in such variables as air quality, water purity, noise levels, population density, and general pollution of the environment. Such variables can affect the inner–biological functioning of a person by producing variations in the likelihood of contracting certain diseases (Willems, 1973), and can also affect the individual–psychological level by producing various levels of stress (Gump, 1975). In turn, the quality of the physical setting may be seen as both a product of the values and behaviors of the culture of a society and a producer of changes in the sociocultural setting across time. If values regarding industrialization in the United States had not existed as they did in the early 1960s, and if high levels of industrial waste had not polluted air, land, water, and wildlife, there would have been no basis for the general emergence of countervailing values in the late 1960s and 1970s regarding environmentalism, ecology, and the reduction of pollution. The physical–environmental level is not independent of the sociocultural–historical level.

The sociocultural–historical level. Attitudes toward smoking, knowledge about prenatal health care, and values and public policies (e.g., prohibiting smoking in public buildings) about secondhand smoke may change across time to influence the unborn child. Thus, with advances in education (remember the example of children with Down syndrome), medicine, and science (remember the example of children with PKU), and changes in attitudes, values, mores, behaviors, and policies (e.g., regarding smoking, drinking, drug use, and pollution of the environment), the outcome of any given hereditary contribution to development will be altered.

In sum, it may be seen that a variety of behavioral outcomes may result from nature interactions with a multilevel environment. Development is thus an outcome of hereditary contributions "dynamically interacting" with changes in the environmental setting (Lerner, 1978, 1979). Thus, a genotype is not a blueprint for a final behavioral outcome (Gottlieb, 1992, 1997; Gottlieb et al., 1998; Hirsch, 1970). There is no one-to-one relation between genotype (our genetic inheritance) and *phenotype* (the observed outcome of development, the outcome of a specific genotype–environment interrelation). Rather, numerous phenotypes can result from the same genotype. The range of potential outcomes that could result from a given genotype's potentially infinite interactions with environments is termed the *norm of reaction* (Hirsch, 1970), a concept we turn to later in this chapter.

Here, we should note that the indirectness of hereditary effects means that we cannot a priori specify what behavioral effect a particular hereditary contribution will have. Hereditary contributions can express themselves only within the context of their interaction with a complex (i.e., multilevel and systemically changing) mediating environment. Without knowing how this environment will mediate the hereditary effects, we can make no before-the-fact statement about what specific behaviors will result from a particular hereditary contribution. (This is a particularly essential point; in Chapter 6, it is seen as an important feature of the probabilistic–epigenetic view of the nature–nurture controversy.)

Thus, there can be no preformed, direct, or invariant hereditary contribution to behavior. As I indicated in Chapter 3, in our discussion of the probabilistic–epigenetic viewpoint, the most accurate way of conceptualizing the contribution of nature factors to behavioral development is

1. To recognize the necessary and crucial role that nurture factors play in providing a dynamically interactive context for nature factors.

2. To recognize that the time at which these factors interrelate will play an important role in shaping development; that is, the interactive contribution of one factor to the other will not be the same at different points in development.

Because the characteristics of nature and nurture factors as well as their time of interaction cannot be expected to occur at exactly the same time or in exactly the same way for every organism, before the fact one can say only that certain things will probably occur. Because of our recognition of Points 1 and 2, the best we can do is take a guess, with some degree of confidence in our chances of being correct (i.e., we can make a probabilistic statement), about what sort of specific behavioral development will eventually result from a particular hereditary contribution. Said another way, *behavioral development is a probabilistic outcome of the fusion of particular instances (e.g., states) of variables that exist at multiple, integrated levels of organization* (e.g., Gottlieb, 1997; Tobach, 1981).

Any statement that in effect says that a given hereditary contribution will invariably (in all environmental contexts) result in a certain specific behavior is simply incorrect. Therefore, we can make several statements about the indirect effects of heredity on behavior. First, the following points should be clear:

1. The same hereditary influence can be expected to have a different behavioral effect in different environmental conditions.

2. Alternatively, the reverse may also be true—different hereditary influences can lead to the same behavioral development in varying environmental situations.

   To be complete, we should also point out that:

3. The same environmental effect may be expected to lead to different behavioral outcomes under differing hereditary contributions.

4. Different environments can lead to the same outcome in the context of varying hereditary contributions.

Together, these points mean that the sources of behavior interact with each other in complex ways. And any analysis of behavioral development that attempts to be appropriate in its recognition of this complexity must always attempt to understand the varying status of the interactions of both nature and nurture factors.

The Continuum of Indirectness

Given heredity's indirect contribution to behavior, Anastasi conceptualized the contributions of heredity to behavior as varying along a "continuum of indirectness," a hypothetical line whose endpoints are "least indirect" and "most indirect." Such a hypothetical continuum is represented in Figure 4.2. The left end represents those hereditary contributions to a person that are *least indirect* (or most direct) in their influence. One may speculate that such effects may be represented by such physical characteristics as eye color or eventual shape of the nose. But be careful to remember that even these least indirect hereditary effects need, at the very least, the supportive, facilitative influence of the environment. That is, "least indirect" effects are those that will tend to arise despite a wide range of contextual variation. However, at the extremes of this variation (e.g., involving highly toxic chemical influences or high

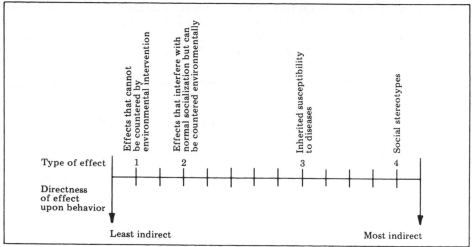

FIGURE 4.2
Contributions of heredity to behavioral development vary along a continuum of indirectness. Numbers 1 through 4 refer to some points along this continuum. See the text for an explanation of the uses and limits of this figure.

dosages of radiation occurring at particular times in ontogeny such as during the embryonic period of prenatal development), even "least indirect" effects will show context-dependent variation.

The right end of the continuum represents those hereditary contributions to a person that are *most indirect*. Here the possible number or types of interrelations with the environment increases and, accordingly, the range of resulting behavioral outcomes are much more numerous. Thus, as hereditary influences become more indirect, the range of possible behavioral outcomes of the interaction between heredity and environment similarly increases.

What are some possible illustrations of the range of indirect hereditary contributions to behavior? Anastasi suggested four points along the continuum of indirectness to illustrate this range of effects. These four hypothetical points are ordinal in nature; they are ordered consecutively from "least indirect" effect through "most indirect" effect, although no exact specification of the location of these points can be made. Thus, although we may be sure that these effects are ordered appropriately, we are sure of neither their exact locations along the continuum nor of the relative distances between them.

Moreover, it is essential to note that Points 1 and 2 in the figure refer to genetic deficits (i.e., situations wherein the genes are not working either because they are absent; because they are anomalous such as in Down syndrome, wherein extra genetic material is present; or because there is a lack of the appropriate signals for genetic expres-

sion, such as in the disease cystic fibrosis). These two points in the figure do not reflect the character of heredity–environment interaction within normal genetic complement. Despite the limitations of Figure 4.2, Anastasi's specification of the points along the continuum serves to usefully illustrate the range of heredity's indirect effects on behavior.

Hereditary effects that in no way can be countered through any known environmental intervention. Hereditary contributions to behavior that cannot be ameliorated through the use of any known intervention or environmental manipulation are considered to make up the class of hereditary effects that are least indirect in relation to behavior. Although, as previously noted, these effects need a supportive, facilitative environment in which to exert their contribution; once they make their contribution to behavior there is nothing that one can *presently* do, through changing the environment, to change that contribution.

For example, let us again consider the inheritance of a chromosome trisomy; that is, the inheritance that is associated with Down syndrome. As noted earlier, such a child has rather distinctive physical (particularly facial) characteristics and may have moderate-to-severe mental retardation. Thus, after the inheritance of such a chromosomal anomaly, there is nothing we can do through environmental intervention, with our current state of knowledge, to avert the inevitability of the child's mental retardation. Although we can certainly attempt to train the child to maximize his or her potential, we cannot now raise that potential to the level it might have reached had the child not inherited a trisomy of Chromosome Pair 21. This inheritance thus represents the least indirect contribution of heredity to behavior, a contribution that cannot *presently* be countered through environmental manipulation.

Of course, future scientific advances, for instance in recombinant DNA technology (Berg, 1981), may result in knowledge allowing antenatal repair of a flawed human genome (McKusick, 1981). Thus, as we saw with PKU, the effect of a given genetic deficit on behavior can be altered, given appropriate scientific advances (Scriver & Clow, 1980a, 1980b). As such, an effect once classified as "least indirect"—such as was once the case with PKU—may not remain so for all time.

Hereditary deficits that interfere with normal socialization but can be countered through environmental intervention.   Moving a little further along on the continuum of indirectness brings us to a second class of indirect hereditary effects. These are more indirect in their contribution to behavior because their contribution can be somewhat ameliorated by changes in the environment. Thus, although effects of this second class may interfere with the process by which a child acquires the behaviors that society may define as being necessary and appropriate, such interference may at least be somewhat counteracted by appropriate environmental modifications.

For example, let us say that because of a genetic anomaly a child is born blind or deaf. Certainly, such a handicap would retard the development of the child's communication skills and in this way interfere with normal socialization. Because the child cannot see or hear, the process by which the child develops the behaviors that society designates as necessary or appropriate will not be as efficient as it will be for a child who is not disabled. However, the fact that such an unfortunate inheritance interferes with the development of one's communication skills and socialization in general does not mean that these developments are lost forever. As is dramatically illustrated in the play, *The Miracle Worker,* the story of Helen Keller and her teacher, the handicaps of blindness and deafness can be counteracted. Thus, although a hereditary effect can interfere with socialization, certain environmental modifications can be instituted to modify or possibly even eliminate the effects of that hereditary contribution to behavior.

Inherited susceptibility to disease.   A third, still more indirect hereditary contribution to behavior is that type of inheritance that may predispose a person to contracting certain diseases. Let us say that as part of a person's inherited physical characteristics he or she develops relatively weak musculature in one chamber of the heart. This hereditary contribution may or may not exert any influence on the person's behavior. But certain environmentally based characteristics the person may possess (e.g., being overweight, lacking regular exercise, having a poor diet, and being middle-aged) may interact with the person's constitution and make him or her very likely to have a heart attack. Yet, in another person not similarly predisposed but having the same environmentally based characteristics, heart disease may never develop.

Similarly, consider hay fever. If we argue that this disease is hereditarily based, then we can see that our inherited susceptibility may or may not lead to a behavioral effect, depending on the specific environment in which we live. If we live in an area where the pollen count is extremely low, our susceptibility to this disease may never affect our behavior. In fact, because there would be little if any pollen to precipitate an attack, we might never even know that we have the disease. But if we live in an area in which the pollen count varies seasonally, and at certain times of the year, it reaches high levels, then our behavior will certainly be affected. We will sneeze, our eyes will water, and we will try to seek the comfort and release provided by antihistamines and air-conditioned rooms. Our behavior might be affected even at times of the year when no pollen is present in the air. We might, for example, find ourselves going to a physician all winter to get weekly or monthly desensitization injections that will diminish the effects of pollen during the late summer. This third point along the continuum of indirectness well illustrates a point made earlier: The same hereditary contribution will have a different effect on behavior under different environmental conditions.

Social stereotypes.   A final point along the hereditary continuum of indirectness, certainly representing the *most* indirect effect, may be termed *social stereotypes.* This may seem somewhat paradoxical: How can social stereotypes be a hereditary effect, albeit the most indirect one, on behavior? Let us follow the reasoning underlying this classification carefully, not only to demonstrate its tenability but also to illustrate the complex interactions between heredity and environment that provide the source of behavioral development.

As we previously noted, physical characteristics may be among the least indirect hereditary contributions to a person. Thus, certain physical characteristics such as sex, eye color, or skin pigmentation are to a great extent very directly hereditarily determined. The range of variation in these characteristics, despite environmental differences, is not as great as that of other types of characteristics.

How may such physical characteristics lead to social stereotypes? In attempting to function efficiently, people find ways to reduce the complexity of the situations around them. In the real world, we are literally bombarded by stimulation coming from numerous, diverse sources. Obviously, we cannot respond to all these stimuli simultaneously or even successively. If we did so we would never get anything done, and this certainly would not make us very adaptive organisms. We would devote the major share of our lives to processing all the nuances of all the dimensions of the world before we acted as a consequence of stimulation. Consequently, we attend to some stimuli in our environment and disregard others, depending in part on what information most richly, reliably, and validly tells us what we need or want at that time and in that situation. In this way, we can be economical and efficient in our social interactions.

A person is one type of stimulus object we encounter in our environment. But a person is also a complex stimulus having many dimensions (sex, age, race, style of dress, apparent status, etc.), and we cannot respond to all characteristics of a person at once if we are to be efficient and economical. So, in order to be economical, we are likely to attend to as few dimensions of a person as possible. Depending in part, for example, on the type of information we need in order to function efficiently at that moment, we attend only to certain stimulus attributes, or cues. On the basis of these cues, we place people in certain categories; that is, we associate people's specific stimulus attributes with specific categories of information, behavioral characteristics, or social attributes. By doing this, we need only respond to a certain few dimensions and this reduction in complexity allows us to function efficiently and economically.

This process of categorization is a very basic one, permeating all our interactions. For example, if we were lost in a big city, it might be a successful, but relatively inefficient, strategy to stop and ask various people how to get to a certain location. But if we perceive a person wearing a uniform and a badge standing by an intersection, we might respond by placing that person in the category of police officer. We would then attribute to that person the possession of certain information (e.g., knowledge of directions); we would ask for this information, reliably receive it, and then be on our way.

Thus, we see that whenever we perceive other people:

1. We respond to certain stimulus attributes, or cues, they possess (in order to maintain economical interpersonal relations).

2. On the basis of these cues, we place these people in certain categories.

3. On the basis of this categorization, we attribute to these persons the possession of certain information or characteristics of behavior.

Anastasi suggested—and from much accumulated evidence (e.g., see Lerner & Korn, 1972; Secord & Backman, 1964) it seems clear—that one major type of cue that people readily use in organizing their interpersonal perceptions and interactions is physical characteristics that are least indirectly hereditarily determined. Thus, it is probable that in some societies (and here I am intentionally understating my argument) people are categorized on the basis of certain inherited physical characteristics. If this occurs, we will probably make certain invariant personality attributions and maintain certain invariant behavioral expectancies for all people placed in that category. We will do this because, after all, the reason that we categorize in the first place is to tell us efficiently what to expect about that class of people-stimuli. It would defeat the purpose of economical categorization processes to admit exceptions to our attributions.

What may be the effects of categorizing people on the basis of inherited physical characteristics? In answering this question we will see how such inherited characteristics provide the most indirect hereditary source of behavior: social stereotypes. To address this question, though, let us offer a not-too-imaginary example.

Suppose that there is a society that has, as a most salient cue for the categorization of people, a certain inherited physical characteristic: skin color. Now, for argument's sake, let us further imagine that one of the two skin-color groups in this society is categorized unfavorably. That is, people in that group, when put into this physically cued category, receive negative behavioral expectations and personality attributions—for example, they are thought of as lazy and shiftless and unable to profit very much from educational experiences. Certainly, at least some people in this imaginary category could probably benefit from education and are not lazy, but it is likely that such categorizations would be maintained despite experience of such exceptions. If this is the case—that our categorization involves an overgeneralized belief or attitude—then we may term such a categorization a *stereotype*. Thus, it is possible that in response to a physical attribute we place a person in a category and in so doing maintain stereotyped expectations about that person.

If a skin-color group were stereotyped as uneducable and lazy, it would not make sense to put much effort into attempting to educate people of that group. Because we would not expect them to learn too much, we would not spend much money on their schooling. In fact, such a group might have a history of going to inferior schools where there were inadequate facilities and poorly qualified teachers. Thus, because of the stereotype, this skin-color group would experience inadequate, inferior, or substandard educational opportunities.

Finally, years later, a researcher might come along and decide to see if the categorization of these people involves an overgeneralization. He or she finds that this group does not seem to be doing very well educationally that many people in this group do not score high scholastically, do not seem to have intellectual aptitudes as high as those of members of the other skin-color group, often do not go on to higher education, and accordingly do not often enter into the higher-prestige, higher-salary, and higher-socioeconomic-status professions. Thus, the person doing this study might conclude that the facts show that this skin-color group cannot profit to any great degree from educational experiences. Many of those in the favored skin-color group of this imaginary society, who may often have made such an attribution about those in the less-favored skin-color group, might say that they "knew it all along."

But our analysis of the situation is certainly different. What occurred with this stereotyped skin-color group was as follows:

1. On the basis of their relatively direct inheritance of a physical characteristic—their skin color—people in this group were placed in a specific unfavorable category.

2. In turn, on the basis of this categorization, specific negative behavioral expectations were invariably attributed to members of this category. (We might suggest here that a basis of both the initial categorization and the concomitant attributions and expectations might lie in the social and economic history of this group.)

3. These attributions were associated with differential experiences and opportunities (different when compared to the society's other skin-color group).

4. These differential situations delimited the range of possible behaviors that this group could develop. In other words, the group was channeled into a selected, limited number of behavioral alternatives—the very same behaviors they were stereotypically held to have.

5. Finally, many members of the group developed these behaviors because of the above channeling. That is, the end result of the physically cued social stereotype was a *self-fulfilling prophecy*.

In sum, we see that on the basis of a physically cued categorization, we may make a stereotypic attribution and, accordingly, channel the people of that category into certain behavioral patterns by creating social situations within which they cannot do other than develop along the lines of the social stereotype. Our social stereotypes about directly inherited physical cues may have a very profound effect on behavior. They may result in self-fulfilling prophecies.

Unfortunately, of course, the example that we have just considered is not imaginary at all. Although this social-stereotype effect on behavior can obviously function either favorably or unfavorably for the categorized people, this illustration reflects the most pernicious example of the effect of social stereotypes. From our analysis, we can see that a strong argument can be made that the people of color in the United States have perhaps experienced the most unfortunate effects of this most indirect type of hereditary contribution to behavior—social stereotypes. Thus, it may be that African Americans for many years have been involved in an educational and intellectual self-fulfilling prophecy in the United States. This possibility is an important concept in Chapter 11 when the controversy about the nature and nurture of racial differences in intelligence is discussed (e.g., Gould, 1980, 1981; Hebb, 1970; Herrnstein, 1971; Herrnstein & Murray, 1994; Jensen, 1969, 1973, 1980; Layzer, 1974).

At this point, however, it suffices to say that social stereotypes certainly seem to represent a potent source of behavioral development. Although this is the most indirect hereditary contribution to behavior, it does, nonetheless, appear to play a ubiquitous role in our behavioral development. We have used the example of skin color to illustrate the effects of physically cued social stereotypes, but other, more subtle or more obvious, examples could be mentioned—for example, sex, hair texture, shape of nose, breast size in women, or body build and physical attractiveness. In fact, the effects of social stereotypes about body build and physical attractiveness are a topic to which I have addressed much research (e.g., Jovanovic, Lerner, & Lerner, 1989; Lerner, 1969, 1972, 1973, 1979, 1982; Lerner & Brackney, 1978; Lerner et al., 1980; Lerner & Gellert, 1969; Lerner & Karabenick, 1974; Lerner, Karabenick, & Meisels, 1975a, 1975b; Lerner, Karabenick, & Stuart, 1973; Lerner, Knapp, & Pool, 1974; Lerner & Korn, 1972; Lerner & Lerner, 1977; Lerner, Lerner, & Jovanovic, 1996; Lerner, Orlos, & Knapp, 1976; Lerner & Schroeder, 1971a, 1971b; Lerner, Sorell, & Brackney, 1981; Padin, Lerner, & Spiro, 1981; Perkins & Lerner, 1995), and the interested reader may consult these references to see that the processes involved in the social stereotyping of body build and attractiveness appear to be the same as those involved in the social stereotyping of skin color. With both types of cues, people seem to be channeled into a self-fulfilling prophecy by their society (see, too, Jovanovic et al., 1989; Langlois & Stephan, 1981; Sorell & Nowak, 1981).

Up to this point, we have considered the implications of Anastasi's suggested four points along her theoretical continuum of indirectness, the continuum along which heredity contributes to behavior. But the major implication of the question "how?" is that nature interacts with nurture to affect all behavior. We must, then, consider the ways in which the environment contributes to behavioral development. In so doing, we can continue to use Anastasi's (1958) paper as a model. Thus, we now look at another continuum—the environmental continuum or, as Anastasi conceptualizes it, the "continuum of breadth."

Nurture: The Continuum of Breadth

Turning our attention to environmental factors, we may note that, just as the effects of heredity on behavior can best be understood in relation to environment, the effects of the environment on behavior can best be understood in relation to the nature of the organism. Anastasi conceived of the environment as making its contribution to behavioral development along a continuum of breadth. In other words, environmental factors vary in terms of their pervasiveness of effect on behavior. Some environmental factors, then, may be seen to have very broad, pervasive effects on a person, relating to many dimensions of functioning and

enduring in their contributions for relatively long periods of time. Alternatively, other environmental factors may have narrow, minimal effects, making their contributions only to small or limited segments of a person's behavior and exerting their influence for relatively short, transitory periods. Such a continuum of breadth is illustrated in Figure 4.3. Those environmental effects that are derived from the left end of the continuum exert narrow, minimally pervasive effects on behavior, while those at the right end are broad and maximally pervasive in nature.

But what are examples of environmental effects? Just what sort of variables are there in the environment that contribute to behavioral development along such a continuum of breadth? Anastasi suggested two general categories of environmental effects.

Organic effects. The first category of environmental effects may be labeled *organic*. There are some environmental occurrences that lead to changes in the makeup of the organism; they affect what the organism has and how it functions. In short, these factors change the constitution of one's physical and/or physiological processes.

Typically, one may adventitiously encounter environmental variables that affect the organic makeup of one's body either through contracting a disease or having an accident. However, the eventual behavioral outcomes of such organic changes may, in turn, be either broad or narrow in nature. For example, losing half of one's cerebral cortex in an auto crash, or an arm or a leg, or having permanent facial scars after a fire may all be considered environmentally mediated changes in a person's organic makeup that will have obviously pervasive, enduring effects on behavior. Alternatively,

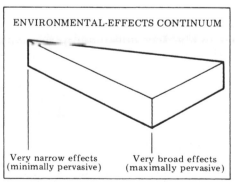

ENVIRONMENTAL-EFFECTS CONTINUUM

Very narrow effects (minimally pervasive)   Very broad effects (maximally pervasive)

FIGURE 4.3
The contributions of environment to behavioral development vary along a continuum of breadth.

loss of a single finger or toe, while being an organic change, would probably not have as great an effect. Moreover, accidents such as stubbing one's toe certainly affect behavior, but in an obviously more trivial, narrow, and transitory way.

Disease may also be broad or narrow in its behavioral contributions. Contracting a disease such as polio, sickle cell anemia, or muscular dystrophy would certainly have a very pervasive effect on a child's behavioral development and functioning. The range of behaviors in which children with such disorders can engage differs greatly from that of children not so affected. On the other hand, some diseases, although affecting the makeup of the organism, do so only in limited or short-term ways. Thus, catching a cold or contracting a childhood disease such as chicken pox would affect behavior, but only for a minimal amount of time and probably in not too pervasive ways.

Of course, the environment can contribute to behavioral development through organic changes in ways that do not have to be construed as negative. Environmentally based organic changes that facilitate or improve behavioral functioning, rather than deteriorating it, can be induced. Such factors as changes in diet, climate, physical regimen, or medical treatments can result in changes in organic makeup that may have positive effects on behavioral functioning and development.

Stimulative effects. The second category of environmental effects on behavior may be termed *stimulative*. These are environmental events that act as direct stimulative influences on behavioral responses. Here, too, such variables may be broad or narrow in their contributions to behavior. Perhaps the broadest stimulative environmental variable is culture. Differences among cultures may pertain to variation in values, modes of living, technology, language, religion, presence of material goods, and availability of educational opportunities. For example, a child growing up in an industrialized, Western nation is exposed to vastly different qualitative and quantitative experience stimuli than is a child living in a "Third World," developing nation. The differential resources and experiences associated with these contrasting cultural settings permeate all aspects of the developing child's world, and serve to shape his or her varying behavioral repertoires.

A somewhat narrower, less pervasive stimulative influence may be, for example, the college experience. Events in this specific environment certainly evoke intellectual, attitudinal, and behavioral repertoires among students, and such cognitive and behavioral repertoires are, in turn, probably different in nature from those found among young people

not exposed to the college experience (Hamilton, 1994; Sherrod, Haggerty, & Featherman, 1993). Finally, some stimulative influences are exceedingly narrow, trivial, and of short duration in their contributions to behavior. Such minimally pervasive effects are numerous, occurring daily in our interactions in the real world. Thus, having a particularly rude, discourteous cabdriver or salesperson may affect us momentarily, but probably not to any great, enduring extent.

In sum, then, Anastasi suggested that the effects of the environment on our behavioral development vary in their pervasiveness. Whether these effects are organic or stimulative in type, they present a range of environmental influences that will interact with indirect hereditary contributions to provide the source of our development. But, as was the case with hereditary influences on behavior, such environmental effects do not have direct impact on development. Rather, just as the effects of nature on behavior are influenced by nurture, environmental contributions to behavior are influenced by the nature of the organism. From this view, the same environmental event (e.g., contraction of a disease or exposure to a particular college course) or group of events (e.g., those associated with middle-class as opposed to upper-class membership) will lead to different behavioral outcomes depending on the nature of the organism.

Using the same symbols as in Figure 4.1, one may see this view illustrated in Figure 4.4. As shown in Figure 4.4a, it is possible to conceptualize the contribution of environment to behavior as being direct. Thus, a particular environmental event or set of events (E_1) is seen as directly leading to a particular behavioral outcome (B_1). However, as with the former argument regarding nature contributions, this view is not tenable. I have argued for a dynamic interactional view of nature and nurture, and the environmental contribution component of this view is illustrated in Figure 4.4b. Here the same environmental contribution (E_1) can be associated with an array of behavioral outcomes (B_1 to B_n) as a consequence of interaction with organisms having different natures (G_1 to G_n). A basis of *plasticity* (the potential for systematic change) in development is thus promoted, and this may be illustrated in several ways.

First, consider a very general set of experiential events associated with being a child of upper-middle-class parents. Imagine that such parents had two children who were *dizygotic twins,* also termed *fraternal twins.* Such siblings are born of the same pregnancy but are from two separate ova

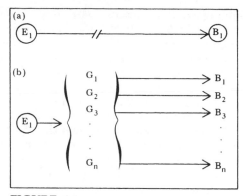

FIGURE 4.4

(a) Environment (E) does not directly lead to behavior (B). (b) Rather, the effects of environment on behavior (B) will be different in interaction with organisms having different heredities (G).

that are fertilized at the same time. Thus, although born together, these siblings have different genotypes (unlike monozygotic twins). If one of these twins was born with the genetic anomaly discussed earlier (Down syndrome) but the other was born with a normal complement of genes, a situation would result wherein children born of the same parents at the same time would potentially be exposed to the same environmental events.

However, regardless of the experiences encountered by the Down syndrome twin, the effects of those experiences could not be expected to result in behaviors falling within a range identical to that of the sibling. Despite advances in special education noted earlier, one would not expect a Down syndrome child to have the same level of intellectual aptitude or achievement potential as his or her sibling. For instance, one would not expect the Down syndrome child to attain a vocation such as physicist, neurosurgeon, or professional football player. Such expectations might, however, be appropriately maintained in regard to the sibling born with the normal genotype. Thus, the hereditary nature of the organism imposes limits on the possible contributions of environment.

Other illustrations of this interaction may be drawn from the information presented above about the prenatal maternal environment. It was noted that if the mother contracted rubella during pregnancy, adverse physical and functional outcomes for the infant might follow. However, this same experience (contraction of rubella) may or may not lead to these outcomes depending on the maturational level of the organism. If the experience occurs during the embryological period,

these negative effects are likely to occur; if it happens in the late fetal period, they are not likely to happen. Similarly, excessive maternal stress will or will not be more likely to lead to certain physical deformities (like cleft palate) depending on the maturational level of the organism. Thus, here again, the nature of the organism moderates the influence of experience on development.

It may be concluded, then, that even if one is talking about very narrow sorts of environmental experiences (e.g., meeting a specific person in a brief social encounter) or very broad types of experiences (e.g., those associated with membership in one culture versus another), the effects of these environmental influences would not be the same if they interacted with hereditarily (genotypically) different organisms. Nor would the effects be the same even if it were possible to ensure that the different organisms had identical experiences. As long as the nature of the organism is different, the contributions of experience will vary.

It is important to note that all humans are genotypically unique. A conservative estimate is that there are over 70 *trillion* potential genotypes (Hirsch, 1970, p. 73; McClearn, 1981). This means that no two living humans share the same genotype, with the possible exception of identical twins. However, even for these people, the differences in the experiences they encountered—differences that began as soon as their respective zygotes implanted at different points on their mother's uterine wall—contribute to their diversity. It should be noted, however, that overall genotype uniqueness exists simultaneously with a great deal of genetic commonality across *all* people. Any two people taken at random from the world's population will differ only in about three of 1,000 base pairs of DNA (Gottlieb, 1998; Gottlieb et al., 1998). Accordingly, human heredity involves an integration of genetic commonality and genetic uniqueness.

This argument is underscored by noting that a genotype immediately becomes a phenotype at the moment of conception. The genotype is expressed in one and *only* one environment. Hence, although a norm of reaction exists for the genotype, that is, for any given genotype, there is a range of possible phenotypes that may arise from it, once the genotype is expressed in one particular context, all the other alternative phenotypes that *could* have resulted from the given genotype are excluded. Thus, even identical twins become (at least slightly) phenotypically different from each other at the moment of implantation.

Conclusions

Because of genotypic uniqueness, all individuals will interact with their environments (be they the same or different) in unique, specific ways. Thus, the environment always contributes to behavior, but the precise direction and outcome of this influence can only be completely understood in the context of an appreciation of the genetic individuality of the person. In turn, individual differences in genetic makeup do not in and of themselves directly shape behavior. Interaction with an environment, itself having a host of distinctly individual features, has to be taken into account.

In other words, heredity and environment, nature and nurture, are always present and involved in providing a source of our development. The specific indirect contribution of nature can be understood only in the context of the particular broad-to-narrow contribution of nurture with which it is interacting. In turn, an exact understanding of how a certain environmental contribution affects behavior can be reached only by understanding how it interrelates with the organism's nature. Thus, in trying to conceptualize how nature and nurture interact, Anastasi relied—as have we—on the *norm-of-reaction* concept as a useful one in conceptualizing the interacting influences of nature and nurture. Let us consider this concept in greater detail.

THE NORM OF REACTION

The concept of norm of reaction has been a popular and useful one for geneticists since it was introduced in the early part of the twentieth century by Woltereck (Dunn, 1965). To understand the concept, we must first recall that what we inherit from our parents, what they transmit to us when fertilization occurs, is a particular set of genes. This genetic endowment, or genotype (Hirsch, 1963), represents the hereditary–developmental potential for all our eventual physical, physiological, and behavioral characteristics. However, there is not a one-to-one relation, an *isomorphism,* between our genotype and the eventual characteristics we do develop. That is, our genotype does not represent a genetic blueprint; we cannot specify how a particular genetic contribution will manifest itself behaviorally merely by knowledge of the genotype. As we have pointed out, no psychological trait is ever directly inherited. So, the eventual manifestation of our genotype—how the genotype will express itself when behavior develops—depends on the interaction of that genotype with the environment. And of course, this expression will vary under different environmental conditions.

Thus, what we see in the developed or developing person is the product of the interaction of the environment with the person's genotype. As noted already, what we see is the phenotype. Therefore, despite genotypic invariance, because phenotypes can be expected to be different in varying environmental conditions, what our genetic inheritance actually represents is not a predetermined, inevitable blueprint of our eventual characteristics. Our phenotype is neither a mere replica of our genotype nor is it isomorphic with it. Rather, our genetic inheritance represents *a range of potential outcomes,* and the developmental outcome that eventually manifests itself will occur due to the interaction of the environment within this range of genetic potential.

This, then, is the norm-of-reaction concept: "The same genotype can give rise to a wide array of phenotypes depending upon the environment in which it develops" (Hirsch, 1970, p. 73). In other words, our genotype—our heredity—gives us a range, or sets the limits, for the development of our characteristics; but the environment, interacting within these limits, plays an essential role in determining what will eventually be developed, or what our phenotype will be. In short, the norm-of-reaction concept asserts that our genetic inheritance sets the broad limits—the upper and lower boundaries—for our behavioral development, but the eventual behavioral outcome (our phenotype) will depend on the specifics of the environment interacting within our hereditary limits.

Before assessing some of the implications of this concept, let us use an example to illustrate its meaning. We have suggested that the genotype may be conceived of as a range of potential behavioral outcomes, as the hereditary upper and lower limits for the development of a particular psychological characteristic. Now, let us suppose that a given child's genotype for intelligence has a range from a low of 40 to a high of 160 IQ points. What will the child's IQ be? In other words, what will the phenotypic IQ be?

This outcome will depend, of course, on the specifics of the environment in which the child is reared. If we reared the child for the first 12 years of his or her life in a clothes closet and then measured the child's IQ, we might suppose that the phenotypic IQ would fall near the lower limit set by the child's genotype, most likely near 40. However, we would expect a different phenotypic IQ if we took another child with the same exact genotype and reared him or her in a more stimulating environment, say in the home of a professional couple who provided facilitative general learning tools and excellent language models, and who fostered high achievement motivation (see Bloom, 1964). A child reared in such an environment would be likely to have a measured IQ near the upper limit of his or her norm of reaction.

Thus, although both children in our example had the same exact genotypic intelligence, their phenotypic intelligence would be quite different because of their markedly varied rearing environments. In essence, then, we see that the phenotype for any observed psychological characteristic does not depend solely on the person's genotype, or genetic endowment; rather, the phenotype is the end result of a complex interaction of the environment within the genotypic range of potentials represented by that person's norm of reaction.

Psychologists other than Anastasi (e.g., Hirsch, 1963, 1970; Schneirla, 1957) recognized the utility of the norm-of-reaction concept in conceptualizing the nature of heredity–environment interactions. Hebb (1949), for instance, offered a conceptualization of intelligence consistent with the notions implicit in the norm-of-reaction concept. He suggested that humans were endowed with a range of intellectual potential, a genotypic intelligence. He termed this inherited range of intellectual potential *intelligence A*. However, psychology has not devised a means of assessing intelligence A; that is, there is no existing technique to appraise a person's genotypic intelligence. Rather, what can be measured is what Hebb termed *intelligence B*—the outcome of an individual's history of environmental interactions within the context of the person's norm of reaction. Thus, this phenotypic intelligence, intelligence B, is a measurement of the result of an interaction between environment and hereditary endowment.

To the extent, then, that Hebb's (1949) notions are tenable, the norm-of-reaction concept as it applies to this conceptualization of intelligence suggests the following:

1. We are all born with a genotypic intelligence (intelligence A), which represents a range of potential intellectual developments.

2. However, psychologists do not measure intelligence A when administering an IQ test; no means exist to measure this hypothetical construct (see Layzer, 1974).

3. Another type of intelligence exists, which is the product of an interaction between the person's environmental history and genotypic intelligence. This second type of intelligence (intelligence B) represents the phenotypic intelligence of the person.

4. This phenotypic intelligence is what is measured by IQ tests.

5. However, the genotype–phenotype intelligence correlation remains unknown; that is, if the genotype represents a range of possible intellectual outcomes, then whether the phenotype represents a low, middle, or high point within this range remains unknown. The person has been endowed with a specific genotype, and through environmental interaction this genotype has provided a basis for the person's phenotype; however, whether this environmental interaction led to a phenotype that is expressive of the high or low part of the person's genotype cannot be assessed (again, see Layzer, 1974, for detailed mathematical reasons).

6. Finally, all this suggests that given another environmental history, the same genotype could be expected to have led to a different phenotype. Still, however, the portion of the norm-of-reaction to which this new phenotype related would remain unknown.

These points illustrate how one psychologist—Hebb (1949)—used the norm-of-reaction concept in relation to a specific psychological construct: intelligence. In Chapter 11, we review in greater detail the implications of the norm-of-reaction concept for the topic of intelligence. However, for the moment let us continue our analysis of the norm-of-reaction concept.

The last implication of Hebb's ideas about intelligences A and B (Point 6 mentioned earlier) is that, although we may expect the same genotype to lead to different phenotypes in different environments, what portion of the genotype is reflected by a specific phenotype remains unknown. This suggests that the norm-of-reaction concept has limitations, and it is important that these limitations be made clear.

Limitations of the Norm-of-Reaction Concept

The relation between genetic endowment and behavior has been a continuing research and theoretical concern of Jerry Hirsch. In several papers (e.g., Hirsch 1970, 1981), he argued that although there was a norm of reaction associated with the observable outcomes of an individual's ontogenetic development (i.e., a person's phenotype), this range was not predictable in advance. In other words, before the person has developed, it is impossible to say that, because of his or her genotype, given certain environmental manipulations one type of phenotype will develop, while given other environmental circumstances another phenotype will result. In essence, at the human level there is really no way to directly assess the expected range of phenotypes that can be associated with a given genotype. At best, we can only make statements about particular genotype–environment interactions *after* they have occurred.

In fact, at any level of life organization, the norm of reaction remains largely unknown in most cases (Hirsch, 1970). This is so because in order to be able to exactly specify the norm of reaction for any living animal (or plant, for that matter), one must be able to reproduce exactly—to clone—an individual, specific genotype many times. In effect, one must be able to reproduce several genetically identical organisms. These replicated (cloned) genotypes must then be exposed to as diverse an array of environments as possible. The range of phenotypes that develop from these exposures would give an estimate of the norm of reaction for that specific genotype. Ideally, this exposure should be totally inclusive of all possible environmental conditions to which the genotype might be exposed. Of course, in reality such an infinite exposure could only at best be approximated, so the most that can be done is to offer an approximation of the norm of reaction for any one genotype.

We can agree, then, with Hirsch's (1970) conclusion:

> Even in the most favorable materials only an approximate estimate can be obtained for the norm of reaction, when, as in plants and some animals, an individual genotype can be replicated many times and its development studied over a range of environmental conditions. The more varied the conditions, the more diverse might be the phenotypes developed from any one genotype. (pp. 69–70)

Further clarifications of the norm-of-reaction concept need to be made. Hirsch pointed out that different genotypes should not be expected to have the same norm of reaction. The norm of reaction associated with each individual genotype can be expected to be differentially unique—that is, differentially broad or narrow. Therefore, the range of phenotypes that would develop from a specific genotype under varying environmental conditions can he expected to differ from individual to individual. The point here is that each and every person who walks this earth (possibly, but not assuredly, with the exception of identical—monozygotic—twins) has his or her own individual norm of reaction.

To illustrate how our genetic endowment provides a basis of the uniqueness of each human life and provides substance for the claim that all humans have a unique heredity–environment interactive history (Hirsch, 1970; Lerner, 1978, 1979; McClearn, 1981), consider that estimates of the

number of structural genes (i.e., genes that code for proteins) in humans range between 50,000 and 100,000 (e.g., Bodmer & Cavalli-Sforza, 1976; Gottlieb, 1998; Stern, 1973). Although, as we have emphasized above, humans are much more genetically similar than dissimilar, it is also the case that if one considers how much genotypic variability can be produced by the reshuffling process of meiosis occurring with 100,000 genes, then the potential for variability is so enormous that "it is next to impossible that there have ever been two individuals with the same combination of genes" (McClearn, 1981, p. 19).

Indeed, we have noted already the estimate by Hirsch (1970) that there are over 70 trillion potential human genotypes. Bodmer and Cavalli-Sforza (1976) provided further information about the genetic variability associated with each human by putting forward the estimate that each human had the capacity to generate 10^{3000} different eggs or sperm. In comparison, they estimated that the number of sperm of all men who had ever lived was *only* 10^{24}. Accordingly, McClearn (1981) noted:

> If we consider 10^{3000} possible eggs being generated by an individual woman and 10^{3000} possible sperms being generated by an individual man, the likelihood of anyone ever—in the past, present, or future having the same genotype as anyone else (excepting multiple identical births, of course) becomes dismissably small. (p. 19)

Moreover, the character of human genetic variability is highlighted if we recognize that "genetic" does not mean "congenital"; that is, that the "total genome is not functioning at fertilization, at birth, or at any other time of life" (McClearn, 1981, p. 26). The expression of any individual human genotype is a developmental phenomenon, influenced in regard to the turning on and/or off of genes by the endogenous and exogenous components of the individual's genotype–environment interaction history (Jacob & Monod, 1961; McClearn, 1970, 1981; Schaie et al., 1975). For instance, McClearn (1981) notes:

> Different genes are decoded and come into play at various times during the lifetime of a particular organism. One illustration of this phenomenon is the differential production of certain kinds of hemoglobin during various phases of development. For example, production of the beta chain accelerates at the time of birth and peaks after a few months, whereas production of the alpha chain rises prenatally and maintains a high level. (p. 26)

As Hirsch (1970, 1999) explained, across the life span norms of reaction will individualize even identical genotypes (see, too, Phelps et al., 1997), and given the evidence we have just reviewed, even if one simplifies the situation enormously in order to make an estimate, we can assume, then, that few people will have the same genotype—much less identical norms of reaction across life (Hirsch, 1970, 1999; Jensen, 1973).

Because of this uniqueness, all individuals will interact with their environments in unique, specific ways. This assertion points to the necessity of trying to determine individual laws of human behavior—laws that account for the individual's unique pattern of development within his or her environment. Alternatively, Hirsch's argument suggests the futility of attempting to specify general "laws of environmental influence" or of attempting to account for all the variations in human behavior merely by recourse to invariant, overt environmental stimuli and responses.

There are two important implications here: First, that each individual is genotypically unique and will interact differently in a given environment than will other, genotypically unique people; and, therefore, second, that a complete focus on the environment in an attempt to account for all behavioral variation is both misguided and incorrect. These implications will be relevant to our discussions of organismic and mechanistic theories in subsequent chapters, as well as to our analysis of the ipsative theoretical approach to human development. Thus, our subsequent discussions of the nature and nurture issue will lead us to stress the inescapable fact of human uniqueness. This fact is derived from an appropriate understanding of the genetic basis (or contribution) of individuality.

At this point, then, we can summarize our discussion of the norm-of-reaction concept by stating what it does and does not tell us about how nature and nurture interact to produce behavioral development.

1. Heredity alone does not determine behavior. An isomorphism does not exist between a genotype and a phenotype.

2. Rather, the way that genes function is to provide a range of possible outcomes of development. These outcomes will result from the varying specifics of the interactions of the environment with the genotype, and different phenotypes can be expected to result from different interactions.

3. However, the norm of reaction cannot be predicted in advance and, on the human level, it cannot even be well estimated or approximated.

4. Therefore (and this is a crucial point), in actuality, those limits set by our hereditary endowment, by our genotype, can never be specified (Hirsch, 1979, p. 70). We cannot reproduce individual human genotypes and expose them to all possible environmental situations. Because of this fact, we cannot know any given individual's range of genetic potential.

5. But what we *can* do is recognize that the norm of reaction is unique with each individual and, therefore, since it can be expected to vary from one individual to another, individuals will interact differently with their environments. This process will result in basic phenotypic uniqueness among people.

Thus, the norm-of-reaction concept highlights the necessity of focusing on the interaction of nature and nurture in order to understand behavioral development. This concept's implications illustrate that "extreme environmentalists were wrong to hope that one law or set of laws described universal features of modifiability. Extreme hereditarians were wrong to ignore the norm of reaction" (Hirsch, 1970, p. 70).

In sum, in this chapter, we have considered general concepts in the nature–nurture controversy and have dealt with some of their rather broad implications. At the beginning of this chapter, however, I indicated that the nature–nurture issue is very much alive today and still "rears its head" in many currently researched and contested content areas of human development. In order to illustrate how these general concepts may be appropriately applied to specific topics, we turn in subsequent chapters to discussion of several of these topics—intelligence, the notion of instincts, and the ideas associated with the area of sociobiology. The discussions in these chapters is preceded by—or framed within—a fuller explication of the approach to the nature–nurture issue that we have termed probabilistic–epigenetic or developmental–contextual, and by an account of how this approach fits within the broader sets of ideas associated with developmental systems theories.

However, prior to these illustrative discussions, we need to turn first, in Chapter 5, to a second key issue involved in understanding the nature–nurture controversy, that is, the continuity–discontinuity issue. This issue—which is one of understanding the relation of constancy and change in human development—raises ideas that interrelate with those linked to the nature–nurture issue. Our treatment of these ideas allows us to understand how developmental systems theory enables us to address and resolve controversies about nature and nurture found in the literatures pertinent to intelligence, instinct, and sociobiology.

5 | *The Continuity–Discontinuity Issue*

A second major issue in developmental psychology can be derived from the nature–nurture issue. Granted that there are laws governing development and that these laws lie within the province of nature and nurture, how do they function across the life span of a species? Do the laws involved in determining development remain the same or do they change in their functioning across ontogeny? In turn, do the psychological functions of the person and/or the variables involved in his or her behavior stay the same or change across life?

If the same laws and/or variables are involved in development at different times in the ontogeny of a species, this is *continuity*. Alternatively, if different laws account for, and/or there are different psychological functions involved in development at different times in the ontogeny of a species, this is *discontinuity*. This, then, is the second central conceptual issue that pervades the study of human development—that is, the continuity–discontinuity issue.

DEFINING THE ISSUE

In a general way, one may say that if things stay the same, *continuity* exists, and if things change, *discontinuity* exists. However, greater precision and clarification of the continuity–discontinuity issue are necessary. Within human development, the continuity–discontinuity issue pertains to issues of the description and explanation of within-person change.

Description of Intraindividual Change

In seeking to systematically represent the changes a person goes through across time, that is, in trying to describe intraindividual change, one may ask whether the behavior being described takes the same form across time. Simply, does the behavior look the same? When engaging in peer-group relations, do a child, an adolescent, and an adult do the same things? If behavior seen at one point in the life span can be represented or depicted in the same way as behavior at another point, then *descriptive continuity* exists. If behavior seen at one point in the life span cannot be represented or depicted in the same way as behavior at another point, then *descriptive discontinuity* exists.

The former situation would exist if what a person did with his or her peers in order to "have fun" were the same in adolescence and adulthood, while the latter situation would exist if the person engaged in different activities during these two times. Further illustration of descriptive continuity and discontinuity is seen in Figure 5.1. Part (a) of the figure illustrates no change in intraindividual status (continuity), whereas Part (b) shows change in intraindividual status (discontinuity).

Explanation of Intraindividual Change

Changes in the description of behavior across a person's life can occur for many reasons. In fact, even the *same* change, regardless of whether it is continuous *or* discontinuous, can be explained by many reasons. If the same explanations are used to account for behavior across a person's life, then this means that behavior is interpreted as involving unchanging laws or rules. In this case, there is *explanatory continuity*. If, however, different explanations are used to account for behavior across a person's life, then there is *explanatory discontinuity*. In other words, if the variables used to account for developmental processes do not vary from Time 1 to Time 2 in a person's life, explanatory continuity exists; if the variables used to account for developmental processes do vary from Time 1 to Time 2 in a person's life, explanatory discontinuity exists.

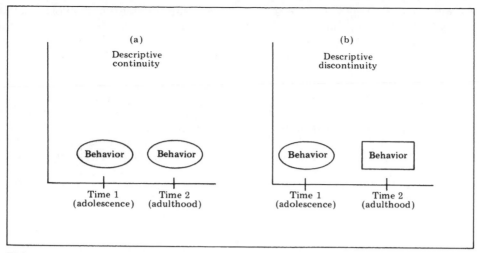

FIGURE 5.1
(a) If behavior can be represented in the same way at two times in the individual's life span, then descriptive continuity exists between these two points. (b) If behavior cannot be represented in the same way at two times in the individual's life span, then descriptive discontinuity exists between these two points.

On the other hand, if the same laws account for the behavior of a person at Time 1 and Time 2 in life, this would be termed *explanatory continuity*. If different laws account for the behavior of a person at Time 1 and Time 2, this would be termed *explanatory discontinuity*. Simply, then, if the laws governing behavior remain the same with time, continuity exists; if the laws governing behavior change with time, discontinuity exists. These relations are illustrated in Figure 5.2.

Descriptive and Explanatory Combinations

It is possible to have any combination of descriptive continuity–discontinuity and explanatory continuity–discontinuity. For instance, suppose

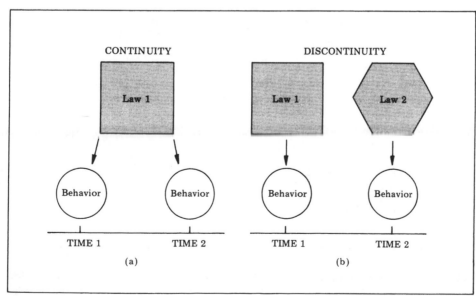

FIGURE 5.2
An illustration of (a) continuity and (b) discontinuity in development.

one were interested in accounting for a person's recreational behavior at different times in his or her life and tried to explain this behavior through the use of motivational ideas. There might or might not be changes in the main recreational behaviors (e.g., bicycle riding or aerobic exercise) from childhood to adolescence. There might be descriptive continuity or discontinuity. In either case, however, one might suggest a continuous or a discontinuous explanation.

For instance, it might be argued that recreational behavior—whatever specific form it may take—is always motivated by curiosity. Bike riding in childhood and adolescence, or bike riding in the former period and aerobic exercise in the latter, may just be determined by the person's curiosity about seeing where the bike ride can take him or her (in the former case) or about learning new exercise regimens (in the latter case). Thus, one would be accounting for behavior based on an explanatory continuous interpretation.

Alternatively, it might be argued that recreational behavior in adolescence is determined not by curiosity motivation but rather by sexual motivation. That is, although curiosity led to bike riding in childhood, the adolescent goes to aerobic exercise classes to meet possible dating partners. Here, then, one would be accounting for behavior based on an explanatory discontinuous interpretation.

Further illustration of explanatory continuity and explanatory discontinuity is presented in Figure 5.3. Part (a) is an illustration of no intraindividual change in the explanations for behavior over time (continuity). Part (b) shows intraindividual change in the explanations for behavior over time (discontinuity). In both portions of the figure, the behavior being described is continuous; as previously indicated, however, descriptive continuity or discontinuity and explanatory continuity or discontinuity can occur. Intraindividual change may take a form fitting into any of the quadrants shown in Figure 5.4.

With Change Form 1, descriptions of behavior would remain the same (e.g., the person engages in recreational activities by doing the same thing); similarly, the reasons used to explain why the behavior did not change would also remain the same (e.g., the same motive is present). Change Form 2 would involve the same descriptions of behavior (e.g., bike riding as the major form of recreation) across time, but the explanation for the identical behavior would change from Time 1 (e.g., the person rides to master a motor skill) to Time 2 (e.g., the person rides to meet possible dating partners). Change Form 3 would involve the behavior changing from Time 1 (e.g., bike riding) to Time 2 (e.g., aerobic exercise), but the explanation for behavior would remain the same (e.g., motivation to master motor skills). Finally, Change Form 4 involves the

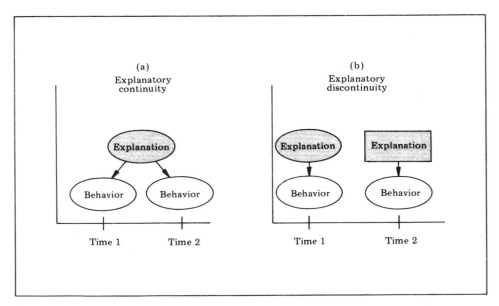

FIGURE 5.3
(a) If behavior can be accounted for in the same way at two times in the person's life span, then explanatory continuity exists between these two points. (b) If behavior cannot be accounted for in the same way at two times in the individual's life span, then explanatory discontinuity exists between these two points.

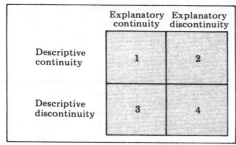

FIGURE 5.4
Intraindividual change may take a form reflecting any combination of descriptive and explanatory continuity or discontinuity.

behavior being understood on the basis of different reasons (e.g., Time 1 behavior involves a motor-skill motive and Time 2 involves an interest in dating).

Quantitative Versus Qualitative Changes

Descriptions or explanations of development can involve quantitative or qualitative changes. Descriptively, quantitative changes involve differences in how much (or how many) of something exists. For example, in adolescence quantitative changes occur in such areas as height and weight because there is an adolescent growth spurt and these changes are often interpreted as resulting from quantitative increases in the production of growth-stimulating hormones.

In turn, descriptive qualitative changes involve differences in what exists, in what sort of phenomenon is present. The emergence in adolescence of a drive-state never before present in life—that is, a reproductively mature sexual drive (Freud, 1969)—and the emergence in adolescence of new and abstract thought capabilities not present in younger people—that is, formal operations (Piaget, 1950, 1970)—are instances of changes interpreted as arising from qualitative alterations in the person. It is believed that the person is not just "more of the same"; rather, the person is seen as having a *new* quality or characteristic.

Explanations of development can vary also in regard to whether one *accounts* for change by positing quantitative changes (e.g., increases in the amounts of growth hormone present in the bloodstream) or by positing a new reason for behaviors (e.g., an infant's interactions in his or her social world are predicated on the need to establish a sense of basic trust in the world, whereas an adolescent's social interactions involve the need to establish a sense of identity, or a self-definition). In other words, it is possible to offer an explanatory

discontinuous interpretation of development involving *either* quantitative or qualitative change. For instance, when particular types of explanatory discontinuous qualitative changes are said to be involved in development, the critical-periods hypothesis discussed in Chapter 6 is often raised (e.g., Erikson, 1959, 1964; see Chapter 16 of this book). The point is that on the basis of adherence to a particular theory of development (e.g., a predetermined–epigenetic, or nature, theory), qualitative changes are believed to characterize ontogeny, and because of this, discontinuous explanations of change are needed.

We may see, then, that virtually any statement about the character of intraindividual development involves, explicitly or implicitly, taking a position in regard to three dimensions of change: descriptive continuity–discontinuity, explanatory continuity–discontinuity, and the quantitative versus the qualitative character of one's descriptions and explanations—that is, the quantitative–qualitative dimension pertains to both description and explanation. This situation is illustrated in Figure 5.5. As suggested by this figure, one may have descriptive quantitative discontinuity coupled with explanatory qualitative continuity, or descriptive

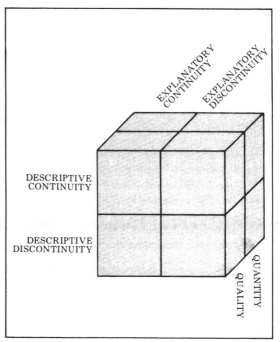

FIGURE 5.5
The intraindividual change box. Intraindividual development involves change along three dimensions—descriptive continuity–discontinuity; explanatory continuity–discontinuity; and a quantitative–qualitative dimension.

qualitative continuity coupled with explanatory quantitative discontinuity, and so forth.

For example, a feature of personality (e.g., a component of temperament such as mood) may remain descriptively the same over time. It may be represented or depicted isomorphically at two different temporal points (e.g., positive mood may be represented by the percentage of facial expressions per unit time which are scored as indicative of smiling). Such cases, therefore, may be an instance of descriptive qualitative continuity. However, *more* of this qualitatively invariant phenomenon may exist at Time 2 (e.g., there may be more smiles per unit time), and thus descriptive quantitative discontinuity may be coupled with descriptive qualitative continuity.

Moreover, both descriptive quantitative discontinuity and descriptive qualitative continuity may be explained by the same ideas, such as by continuous explanatory principles. Smiling may be assumed to be released across life by biogenetically based physiological mechanisms. Alternatively, descriptive continuity or descriptive discontinuity may be explained by different ideas, such as by discontinuous explanatory principles. For instance, smiling may be assumed to be biogenetically released in early infancy and mediated by cognitively and socially textured processes across subsequent developmental periods. Indeed, if different explanations are, in fact, invoked, they may involve statements that constitute either quantitatively or qualitatively altered processes.

In short, the particular couplings that one posits as involved in human life will depend on the substantive domain of development one is studying (e.g., intelligence, motivation, personality, or peer-group relations) and, as we shall see, primarily on one's theory of development. That is, any particular description or explanation of intraindividual change is the result of a particular theoretical view of development. This implies that commitment to a theory that focuses only on certain variables or processes will restrict one's view of the variety of changes that may characterize development. Indeed, theory, not data, is the major lens through which one "observes" continuity or discontinuity in development.

CONTINUITY–DISCONTINUITY AS A THEORETICAL ISSUE

For a long time, many developmentalists held continuity–discontinuity to be an empirical issue. They contended that the existence of continuity or discontinuity for the development of a given psychological process could be determined only from the results of research. Of course, this position has a degree of validity. Whether one sees continuity or discontinuity in behavioral development is partially dependent on research data. The point is, however, that the results of research are not the only determining factor for the existence of continuity or discontinuity. There are other, more important factors, and these are primarily theoretical.

The Role of Theory

It may be seen that a change can take any one of several forms, and that even the same descriptive change can be interpreted (explained) in different ways. The primary reason that people interpret a given change in contrasting ways is that theoretical differences exist among them. For instance, if one adopts a theoretical position stressing the progressive, hierarchical integration of the organism (e.g., Gagné, 1968), one will necessarily view development as essentially continuous. On the other hand, if one stresses the progressive differentiation of the organism, one will view development as essentially discontinuous.

Accordingly, a given theoretical position might lead one to interpret a given piece of empirical evidence in one way (e.g., as consistent with a continuity position), while someone with a different theoretical position might interpret that same empirical fact in another way (e.g., as consistent with a discontinuity position). To illustrate, whether one views babbling as continuous or discontinuous with speech depends on one's particular theoretical perspective. Similarly, the events of adolescence may be interpreted as continuations of processes present in earlier ontogenetic periods or as results of processes especially present in adolescence. Thus, Davis (1944) explained storm-and-stress behavior in adolescence (behavior that, by the way, was regarded as descriptively discontinuous) by proposing social-learning principles applicable to earlier ontogenetic periods. That is, he used an explanatory continuous idea to account for descriptive changes in the behaviors of children versus adolescents. As can be recalled from Chapter 2, Hall (1904), however, coupled descriptive discontinuity with explanatory discontinuity, and argued that the adolescent period recapitulated a distinct portion of phylogeny.

The point of recasting the ideas of Davis and Hall into continuity–discontinuity terms is to indicate that whether a given behavior is seen as continuous or discontinuous is not primarily an empirical issue. It is a theoretical issue (Langer, 1970; Werner, 1957). Furthermore, since theoretical differences affect the ways in which one collects and analyzes data, even descriptions of behavior as continuous or discontinuous are primarily matters of theoretical interpretations and not of empirical "reality."

Suppose that a researcher wants to study the level of aggression in the play situations of children from the ages of 6 through 11. The researcher develops a measure of aggression that is applicable to children throughout this age range, studies groups of children at each age level, and obtains scores for each child. Now, let us imagine that the researcher has a theory about the development of aggression that predicts that aggression in children of this age range should be discontinuous. Thus, the researcher might specifically expect to see abrupt changes in the levels of aggression, and he or she accordingly graphs the results of the study so that any year-by-year fluctuations in aggression levels would be evident. Such a graph is seen in Figure 5.6a. The graphed results would reveal abrupt fluctuations in measured aggression levels in play situations within the age range studied, and the researcher could use these results to support the notion that aggression in play situations is a discontinuous phenomenon in children.

On the other hand, the researcher's theory might hold that aggression is a continuous phenomenon in children of this age range. Accordingly, the researcher might not expect any abrupt changes in levels of aggression with age; instead, he or she might expect such development to be a gradual process. Thus, for ease and clarity in the analysis and presentation of the results of the study (and/or because the aggregation of data may lead to a more reliable estimation of data points), the researcher might use the average scores for a combination of the 6- and 7-year-olds as one data point on the graph, the average scores for a combination of the 8- and 9-year-olds as another data point, and so on; such a graph is seen in Figure 5.6b. The researcher could now use these results to support the contention that aggression in play situations decreases rather gradually over time with children and that such aggression is therefore a continuous phenomenon.

As another example, suppose one researcher believed in a theory that specified that learning in childhood involved general laws leading to smooth, continuous, incremental learning. Suppose, in turn, that another scholar used a theory that suggested that childhood learning was discontinuous—that it involved jumps or spurts in knowledge and that different children spurted ahead at different times. Both researchers might do the same experiment to test their respective views, but the way they handled their data—and what their data purportedly proved—would reflect more about their theoretical biases than factual reality.

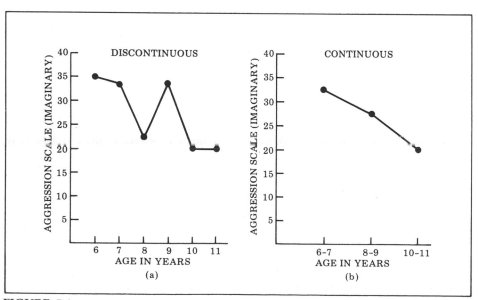

FIGURE 5.6
How one handles data may contribute to whether one views development as being discontinuous (a) or continuous (b).

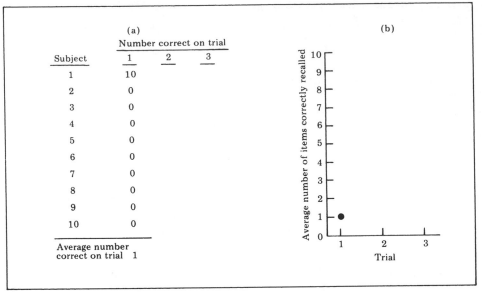

FIGURE 5.7
Results of a study of learning in childhood—the data collected and graphed for the group for Trial 1.

Suppose that, to study learning in children, 10 elementary-school students were selected on the basis of those factors that might influence their ability to learn (e.g., their IQs, ages, educational levels, etc.). Each student would be given a list of 10 nonsense syllables—two consonants and a vowel—for which no previous knowledge existed. Syllables like "guz," "wog," or "zek" might be used. After seeing the list, the students would be asked to recall the items, and the number of words correctly recalled on each of the trials would be the score the researcher would record for each student.

A researcher who believed in general laws and continuity might decide to pool the responses across students because of the belief that learning was generally the same for all children (and because of the relation between aggregation and reliability of estimation noted earlier). Thus, in graphing the results, the researcher might use the group average for number of items correct on Trial 1 (see Figure 5.7a). Suppose that on Trial 1, Participant 1 recalled all items correctly but all other participants recalled no items. The total number of items recalled for this Trial would be 10, and the average number for the 10 participants would be 1. Thus, the point on the graph of Figure 5.7b would be entered. If we further suppose that on Trial 2, Participant 1 continued to recall all 10 items correctly, and that Participant 2 did the same—whereas all others continued to score zero—then the situation in Figure 5.8 would

occur. The total number of correct items would be 20, the average would be 2, and the second point on the graph (see Figure 6.8b) would be entered. Similarly, if on the third trial Participant 3 recalled all 10 items—as Participants 1 and 2 continued to do—but all others still scored zero, a situation like that in Figure 5.9 would occur.

If such patterns continued and the researcher connected the points in the figure, he or she would see evidence that learning was smooth and continuous. Because of the belief in general laws of learning (i.e., that all people learn in the same manner), the researcher might not look at the individual differences in the participants' learning, and the data graphed would be group scores. Thus, in this example (which is intentionally extreme to make a point about the theoretical basis of continuity–discontinuity decisions), the group data would support a continuity view of learning. Yet, if analyzed differently, the very same data could support a discontinuity interpretation.

If a researcher who believed in discontinuity graphed the data shown in Figures 5.7, 5.8, and 5.9, he or she would emphasize the individuality of learning processes—that children show discontinuous spurts in learning after varying lengths of time in which no learning is evidenced. Thus, from the same data, a graph like that of Figure 5.10 could be drawn, and as such, the individual data would now support the discontinuity view of learning.

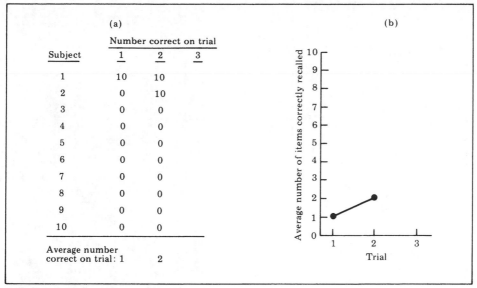

FIGURE 5.8
Results of a study of learning in childhood—the data collected and graphed for the group for Trial 2.

I have already stated that this example is extreme. Experienced, competent researchers would invariably be sensitive to such major trends in their data. However, this is precisely the point. Most often, trends in data are *considerably* more subtle than those in Figures 5.7 through 5.10. As such, the impact of a theoretical orientation on the collection and handling of data is not as readily obvious. This situation not only requires vigilance about how researchers—because of their biases—may affect the nature of the "realities" they "discover"; it also highlights the need to be aware of how depictions of data relate primarily to theoretical issues and not to empirical ones.

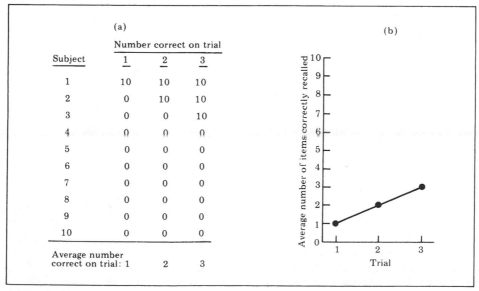

FIGURE 5.9
Results of a study of learning in childhood—the data collected and graphed for the group for Trial 3.

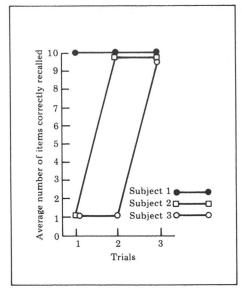

FIGURE 5.10
Results of a study of learning in childhood—the data collected are the same as those of Figures 5.7, 5.8, and 5.9, but here they are graphed to show individual (as opposed to group) performances across trials.

In sum, both in explaining and describing intraindividual change as continuous or discontinuous, one's theoretical perspective is a major determinant of what particular change format (see Figure 5.5) is advanced as representative of development. Furthermore, it is important to note that even among those who agree that development must be explained by discontinuous terms, there are important differences in the discontinuities they specify as being involved in change. But here, too, the basis of these differences involves theoretical contrasts. With theoretical issues so central, then, in the continuity–discontinuity issue, it may be of considerable use to have a means to organize these issues systematically. To do so, we consider the work of Heinz Werner.

THE CONTRIBUTIONS OF HEINZ WERNER

The conceptual factors that influence the continuity–discontinuity issue have been usefully specified by Heinz Werner (1948, 1957). Like T. C. Schneirla, and other major contributors to developmental psychology such as Piaget, Werner conceptualized development from an organismic point of view. Werner's writings, and those of his

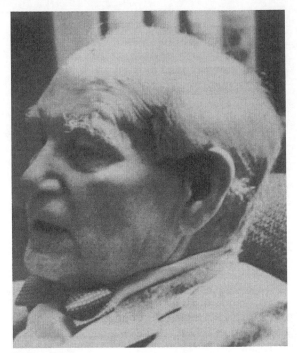

Heinz Werner

colleagues (e.g., Seymour Wapner, Bernard Kaplan, and Jonas Langer), have contributed immeasurably to the advancement of organismic theory as well as to the appropriate conceptualization of the continuity–discontinuity issue.

Bernard Kaplan

Jonas Langer

Werner (1957) saw that considerable confusion existed among human developmentalists over the continuity–discontinuity issue and that at the crux of this confusion was a lack of understanding about two different aspects of change. He saw that developmental processes could change quantitatively or qualitatively. I have already indicated (see Figure 5.5) that this dimension of change must always be considered in discussions of descriptive and explanatory continuity–discontinuity. However, Werner (1948, 1957) explained the superordinate conceptual importance of the qualitative–quantitative dimension of change.

Quantitative Change

In regard to the quantitative aspect of development, there is change in a feature of development in regard to how much of something exists. Quantitative change is an alteration in the amount, frequency, magnitude, or amplitude of a developmental variable or process. For example, imagine that a person's weight had been measured at the same time during each of his eighth through thirteenth years. He weighed 125 pounds when he was measured at ages 8, 9, 10, 11, and 12; but he weighed 150 pounds when he was measured at age 13. Thus, a quantitative change occurred in how much weight existed between the times of measurement occurring at 12 and 13 years of age.

This example is illustrated in Figure 5.11. Here, we see that quantitative change is abrupt. There are no intermediate steps by which the person's weight gradually moved from one level (amount) to the next. In measuring this change, there is a gap between one point in the measurement curve and another; that is, the curve representing the different measurements is not smooth (as in Figure 5.12) but, rather, has an abrupt change in its direction (as in Figure 5.11). There is a "gappiness" in the curve—a lack of an intermediate stage between the earlier and later levels of a variable (Werner, 1957, p. 133). The occurrence of an abrupt change is *quantitative discontinuity*.

Alternatively, the child's change in weight could have been gradual, as is illustrated in Figure 5.12. By gaining 5 pounds a year, the child gradually goes from 125 to 150 pounds between his eighth and thirteenth years. With gradual quantitative changes the rate of change stays the same—it is continuous—from one measurement time to the next. This is *quantitative continuity*.

Qualitative Change

The second aspect of change that Werner specified is the qualitative one. Here, we are primarily concerned not with *how much* of something exists but with *what* exists—what kind or type of thing exists. We are concerned with whether a new quality has come to characterize an organism, whether

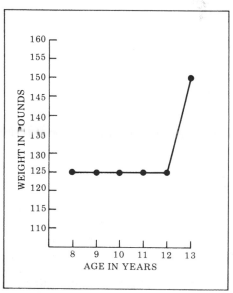

FIGURE 5.11
An example of an abrupt change (quantitative discontinuity).

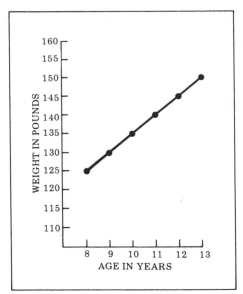

FIGURE 5.12
An example of a gradual quantitative change.

something new has emerged in development. When we are considering qualitative change, we are dealing with *epigenesis,* or emergence.

In Chapter 3, we considered the central role of epigenesis in organismic conceptions of development. In distinguishing between quantitative and qualitative aspects of change, Werner highlighted a core conception of the organismic position. Some of the types of changes that comprise development are emergent changes. These are changes in what exists rather than in how much of something exists. Something new comes about in development, and because it is new—because it is qualitatively different from what went before—it cannot be reduced to what went before. Hence, consistent with the analogy we presented in Chapter 3, if at Time 1 we can be represented by 10 oranges and at Time 2 we can be represented by a motorcycle, we cannot reduce our Time 2 motorcycle status to our Time 1 orange status.

To take another example, before puberty a person may be characterized as being (in part) comprised of several drives (e.g., a hunger drive, a thirst drive, a drive to avoid pain, and perhaps a curiosity drive). With puberty, however, a new drive emerges (or, at least, emerges in a mature form)—the sex drive. With this emergence, the adolescent begins to have new feelings, thoughts, and behaviors, which may be interpreted as being a consequence of this new drive (Freud, 1969). The emergence of this new drive is an instance of

qualitative discontinuity. The sex drive cannot be reduced to hunger and thirst drives, for instance.

Qualitative changes are by their very nature discontinuous. A qualitative, emergent, epigenetic change is *always* an instance of discontinuity. Moreover, not only is an emergent change an irreducible change, but it is a change characterized by gappiness. Developmental gappiness occurs when there is a lack of an intermediate level between earlier and later levels of development. It should be clear that gappiness must also be a part of an emergent change. The presence of an intermediate step between what exists at Time 1 and the new quality that emerges at Time 2 would suggest that the new quality at Time 2 could be reduced through reference to the intermediate step. Because we have just seen that an emergent change is defined in terms of its developmental irreducibility to what went before, it is clear that gappiness must also be a characteristic of any emergence.

In sum, then, the characteristics of emergence and gappiness are needed to describe qualitatively discontinuous changes in development; on the other hand, the characteristic of gappiness (abruptness) alone seems to suffice for characterizing quantitatively discontinuous changes. Thus, as Werner (1957) stated:

> It seems that discontinuity in terms of qualitative changes can be best defined by two characteristics: "emergence," i.e., the irreducibility of a later stage to an earlier; and "gappiness," i.e., the lack of intermediate stages between earlier and later forms. Quantitative discontinuity on the other hand, appears to be sufficiently defined by the second characteristic. . . . To facilitate distinction and alleviate confusion, I would suggest substituting "abruptness" for quantitative discontinuity, reserving the term "discontinuity" only for the qualitative aspect of change. (p. 133)

What Werner provided us with, then, is a clarification of the concepts involved in appropriately considering the continuity–discontinuity issue. He gave us the conceptual means by which to discriminate between quantitative continuity–discontinuity and qualitative continuity–discontinuity.

Which of these two concepts (continuity or discontinuity) best characterizes the changes comprised by development? In a sense, Werner's answer to this question is that *both* concepts characterize developmental changes. That is, Werner provided us with a concept that allows us to see the interrelation of continuity and discontinuity in development and to see, again, that the continuity–discontinuity issue is primarily theoretical. Werner's ideas allow us to understand that whether one posits continuity or discontinuity as characterizing development rests primarily on the implicit theoretical assumptions and the explicit theoretical positions one maintains. The concept that allows us to see this state of affairs quite clearly is one we have discussed in preceding chapters—the orthogenetic principle. Here, we consider its use in organizing the key conceptual concerns involved in the continuity–discontinuity issue.

THE ORTHOGENETIC PRINCIPLE

Werner postulated that developmental psychology had one general regulative principle of development. This principle, which he termed the *orthogenetic principle,* states that "whenever development occurs it proceeds from a state of relative globality and lack of differentiation to a state of increasing differentiation, articulation, and hierarchic integration" (Werner, 1957, p. 126).

Thus, whenever development occurs, the changes that characterize it follow a specified sequence. At Time 1 in development, a particular psychological process, or variable, would be relatively global—general, or undifferentiated. At Time 2 in development, however, this same psychological process would have become relatively differentiated—more specific. In addition, the differentiated status of the process would exist in the form of a hierarchy.

An illustration of the orthogenetic principle helps us to understand its meaning. Consider a relatively young child, for example, a child of about 16 months of age. We spend a day with the child and decide to take a short walk. While doing so we see a dog. The child points and says "doggie." We smile, perhaps, and say, "Yes, that's a doggie." But soon we see a cat and the child also points and says "doggie." Similarly, when the child sees a picture of a raccoon in a magazine, he or she also says "doggie."

We might conclude, then, that this child has a relatively global (undifferentiated) concept of animals. The child calls any furry creature with four legs and a tail a doggie. In other words, this child's conceptual development, at least insofar as animals are concerned, is in a state of globality, or lack of differentiation. Now, suppose that we visited this same child about a year or so later. On the basis of Werner's orthogenetic principle, we would expect that if the child's animal concepts had developed, they would be relatively less global—they would be more differentiated. The child might now say "dog" only when a dog is, in fact, in view, and "cat," "raccoon," "horse," and so on when appropriate.

On another, still later visit we might notice some other things. The child might show evidence of

knowing that all dogs, cats, horses, and so on are animals and, in turn, that animals are different from trees. We would see that the child's animal concepts had not only become more differentiated but had also formed into a hierarchy—that is, cats, dogs, and horses had all become instances of the class "animals." Still later, perhaps, we would see that increasing differentiation and hierarchical organization had occurred. The child would have developed a concept not only of dog but also of different breeds of dogs and, in addition, might be able to show evidence of knowing that within each breed there are puppies and adults and/or males and females of that breed. Moreover, the child might be able to differentiate among types of plants (e.g., trees from flowers from vegetables) and might know that both plants and animals are in a similar, higher-order class (living things) and are different from nonliving things.

Thus, what we would see with the development of the child's animal concepts is a change from having relatively global, undifferentiated concepts to having concepts organized into a hierarchical structure. This development is illustrated in Figure 5.13, which shows that the orthogenetic principle can be used to describe the nature of developmental change. This principle holds that all developmental changes should proceed from globality to differentiation and hierarchical organization. Thus, Werner asserted that the orthogenetic principle was a general, regulative law of all development. The principle describes the nature of developmental change and in so doing gives one a framework within which to consider the continuities and discontinuities that may compose a particular psychological development. Let us see how.

The Orthogenetic Principle and the Continuity–Discontinuity Issue

Jonas Langer (1970), an eminent former student of Heinz Werner, contributed to clarifying how the orthogenetic principle helps us to understand the continuity–discontinuity issue. He pointed out that *both* continuity and discontinuity may be considered to characterize development. Discontinuity occurs as the relatively global organization of earlier times in development becomes differentiated. On the other hand, continuity occurs as the differentiated organism is hierarchically integrated. One stresses developmental continuity by pointing out that earlier developments will become subsumed under later ones—that what went before will be subordinated to later, superordinate developments.

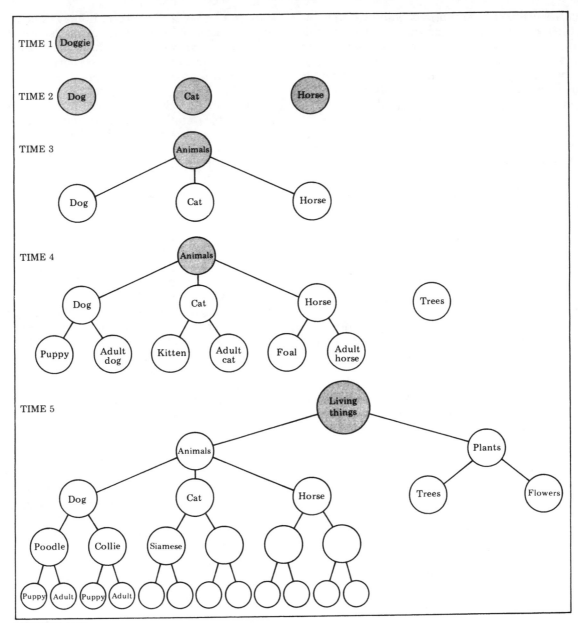

FIGURE 5.13
An illustration of the orthogenetic principle. The child's concepts of animals develop from a state of globality and lack of differentiation (Time 1) to a state of differentiation and hierarchical organization (Time 5).

Hence, development is characterized by a *synthesis,* an interweaving, of two opposing tendencies. First, there is the tendency to become more differentiated. This involves the tendency for new characteristics to emerge from previous global characteristics, the tendency for global characteristics to become different, specific characteristics. This differentiation is thus discontinuity. Second, there is the tendency to become hierarchically organized,

the tendency for earlier developments to be continuously subsumed under later ones. This hierarchical organization is thus continuity.

In short, what Langer (1969, 1970) and Werner (1957) suggested was that there were *both* continuous and discontinuous aspects of development. To maintain an appropriate perspective about development, therefore, one must recognize that the organism develops in accord with both of these perhaps seemingly opposed processes. If one focuses exclusively, however, on one or the other of these two different processes, one will miss the nature of the synthesis that characterizes psychological development, and, accordingly, one will have an incomplete view. Thus, if one focuses exclusively on discontinuity, one might incorrectly view development as quite a disorderly process. Alternatively, if one focuses exclusively on continuity, one will not understand the qualitative changes of the interacting, developing organism (Langer, 1970, p. 733). Langer and Werner opted for a view of development that recognized the existence of both general (continuous) and specific (discontinuous) laws of development. This general-and-specific-laws position has been outlined in Chapter 3; we see in Chapter 15 that Piaget, too, opted for this position and, thus, took a theoretical stance quite similar to Werner's organismic position.

The orthogenetic principle highlights the fact that one must consider both the continuous and the discontinuous aspects of development. Both can be seen to characterize developmental changes in that development proceeds from a state of globality and lack of differentiation to a state of differentiation (hence, discontinuity) and integrated, hierarchical organization (hence, continuity). In other words, development is actually a *dialectical* process, a synthesis between thesis and antithesis. Throughout the life span there is a dialectical integration—a synthesis—between discontinuous differentiation (thesis) and continuous hierarchicalization (antithesis).

However, despite the apparent tenability of these assertions, arguments over whether continuity or discontinuity characterizes phylogenetic and/or ontogenetic development still occur. One such debate has centered around whether the laws governing the phylogenetic development of learning are continuous or discontinuous. It is useful to consider this controversy. First, the specifics of this debate serve to illustrate a particular and important instance of the continuity–discontinuity issue. Second, the information is essential for our consideration of the continuity–discontinuity issue as it is applied to ontogenetic development.

THE PHYLOGENY OF LEARNING: CONTINUITY OR DISCONTINUITY?

Learning is a complex phenomenon. Although psychologists have spent a considerable amount of time and energy studying the learning process (e.g., see Hilgard, 1956; Kimble, 1961; Kuhn, 1995;

Lerner, 1995b), there is no consensus about the nature of learning. Different theorists define learning in different ways and advance different notions about what processes make up learning (see Kuhn, 1995). For the purposes of our present discussion, we may consider learning the acquisition of relations between environmental stimulation and behavioral responses, or simply, the acquisition of certain types of stimulus–response relations. If an animal acquires a bar-pressing response in the presence of a red light or a response of turning to the right at various points in a maze in order to obtain food, we may say that learning has occurred. Although this definition certainly does not allow us to point to all the complexities involved in a consideration of learning (Kuhn, 1995), it is not our goal to deal with all these issues; rather, we will focus on a particular aspect of the controversies involved in the study of learning, the issue of whether learning is a phylogenetically continuous or discontinuous phenomenon. Are the laws governing learning the same for all species? Or must we posit new laws to account for the learning of animals of different phylogenetic levels?

In the history of this controversy, M. E. Bitterman played a central, clarifying role. In three important papers (1960, 1965, 1975), Bitterman presented arguments and empirical evidence that served to clarify the continuity–discontinuity issue in learning. Bitterman (1960) noted that many psychologists interested in studying learning in different animals adopted as a working assumption the notion that learning processes are essentially the same in all animals. This assumption, he pointed out, had its basis in the ideas of no less eminent a figure than Charles Darwin. Darwin (1872) believed that differences among species in capacities such as learning are differences in amount (degree) and not in type (kind). Thus, relying perhaps on Darwin, many psychologists just assumed that the laws governing the learning of one phyletic level were qualitatively identical to those governing the learning of other phylogenetic levels.

This working hypothesis was extremely useful. Its adoption facilitated the experimental analysis of the learning process, because once continuity was assumed, psychologists could study one species and then apply the resulting data to other species. Hence, because it was easier to manipulate the stimulus–response relationships of laboratory rats (e.g., as compared with children), rats virtually came to be the exclusive organism studied. Any laws found with rats could be *assumed* to apply to humans, because the only difference between these species was in quantity, not quality, of learning. The laws of rat learning could be used to understand how humans learn. In other words, by focusing on how the rat learned one could readily discover the universal laws of learning, the laws that applied to all organisms.

As Bitterman (1960, p. 485) pointed out, however, many "learning psychologists" (those psychologists interested in the study of learning) soon lost sight of the fact that their working assumption was only just that—an assumption—and that it needed to be put to empirical tests. One needed to see if the laws of learning for one species were in fact applicable to all species. This, of course, could not be done if learning psychologists continued to focus research interest almost exclusively on the laboratory rat.

Unfortunately, many learning psychologists never did put this assumption to the test, and soon many transformed this working assumption into an article of faith, an untested belief (Bitterman, 1960). Accordingly, we find such an early, famous learning psychologist as J. B. Watson saying that "in passing from the unicellular organisms to man no new principle is needed" (1914, p. 318). Similarly, later learning theorists, such as Dollard and Miller (1950), maintained that "any general phenomena of learning found in rats will also be found in people" (p. 63). Indeed, one of the most prominent psychologists ever identified with the psychology of learning, B. F. Skinner, espoused an identical position. He, too, turned the working assumption that began with Darwin into an article of faith.

In 1956, Skinner published an article that contained the graph seen in Figure 5.14, which shows what we may term *learning curves* (i.e., the cumulative records of changes in responses as a function of learning trials or time), obtained by Skinner from the responses of a rat, a pigeon, and a monkey. But which curve belongs to which one of these three quite different animals? Skinner's answer to this question was, "It doesn't matter" (1956, p. 230). As Bitterman (1960) pointed out, Skinner did not present these curves to show that the learning processes of these animals were identical; rather, he assumed this. Although we can see that the behavioral products of these animals— their learning curves—are markedly similar, this does not necessarily mean that it does not matter which curve belongs to which animal. By asserting this position on the basis of functional (response) similarity, one is assuming that the processes, or structures, underlying these functions are identical.

Skinner asserted that it did not really matter what processes underlie an animal's behavioral

B. F. Skinner

capability so long as one could demonstrate that one could shape the animal's behaviors in certain ways in specific situations. If one could make an animal emit a certain response, and make another species of animal emit an identical response, then it was irrelevant that the processes by which these animals came to develop their response capabilities were different. As long as one could control the stimulus–response relations of animals and thereby demonstrate that different organisms could be made to respond in identical ways in these situations, other differences among the animals

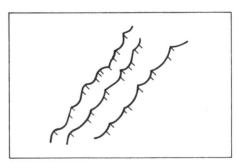

FIGURE 5.14
Learning curves for a pigeon, a rat, and a monkey.

Source: B. F. Skinner (1956). A case history in scientific method. *American Psychologist*, 11.

were irrelevant. They were irrelevant because in demonstrating that one could make different animals do the same things (e.g., learn to press a bar in a given pattern), one had demonstrated that these animals were essentially the same.

In Chapter 6, we see that such an argument is inconsistent with Schneirla's (1957) probabilistic–epigenetic view of behavioral development and of the changing character of the relations between structure and function. To preview that discussion, we may note some of the pitfalls of the position Skinner espoused: Simply, just because we have techniques with which to manipulate the behavior of two different animals so as to make them emit markedly similar responses in similar situations does not necessarily mean that the developmental laws governing the acquisition of their response capabilities are therefore the same, or that the different animals will typically show identical responses in all other situations. To show that we can make an animal do something through the use of a particular experimental manipulation does not mean that this is the way the animal comes to behave in its natural environment (cf. McCall, 1981). Thus, to summarize the essential difference between Skinner's continuity position and Schneirla's probabilistic–epigenetic position, we may offer an anecdote told about one of Schneirla's most eminent students, Daniel Lehrman (Korn, S. J., personal communication, 1967). Once, at a symposium held at the New York Academy of Sciences, Lehrman was called on to summarize the essential differences between the positions of Skinner and Schneirla, who had just presented lectures to the assembled group. He did so in one sentence: "Professor Skinner is interested in finding out how animals come to do what he wants them to do, while Professor Schneirla is interested in finding out how animals come to do what *they* want to do!"

In addition, according to Bitterman (1960), Skinner's reasoning is unwarranted. First, demonstrating that different animals can be made to do the same things does not necessarily prove that they learn in the same way. Again, we have seen that the assumption that even identical behaviors are underlain by identical laws is not logically necessary. Second, as previously implied, demonstrating that animals can be made to acquire *certain* stimulus–response relations in specific situations does not prove that they acquire *all* their stimulus–response relations in *all* of their life situations in that same way. Third, demonstrating that *some* animals can be made to perform the same way in a certain situation does not prove that *all* animals can be made to perform identically. For example, we know

that rats, pigeons, and some apes can be made to perform identically in some situations, but what about fish, elephants, pigs, 3-year-old humans, and 70-year-old humans? In fact, when some researchers *have* compared such other animals (e.g., pigs, raccoons, and chickens) on similar learning tasks, they have found that similar behaviors cannot necessarily be made to take place (Breland & Breland, 1961).

A simple demonstration of similar learning curves among different species does not demonstrate any universal laws of learning. The applicability of any law of learning to all species needs empirical verification, and Bitterman (1960) emphasized that such testing had by no means been provided by Skinner or any other learning psychologist. Thus, the assumption of phylogenetic continuity remains just an assumption.

Bitterman did not merely point to the need for testing this assumption. He also began a series of important experiments designed to determine whether the laws of learning were continuous across the phylogenetic scale. Accordingly, he chose as research participants species of animals other than laboratory rats. In a paper published in 1965, Bitterman reported on some of the results of his studies, as well as studies by other researchers.

In some of the studies, the learning capabilities of a particular species of fish were compared with rat learning. When he compared the learning of these two types of animals in four different learning situations, Bitterman found that the laws governing the learning of this type of fish appeared to be different from the laws governing rat learning. For example, Figure 5.15 (adapted from Bitterman, 1965), shows that the performance of rats on one of these four learning tasks clearly improved with time. As the rats were trained, they made fewer and fewer errors. On the other hand, the performance of the fish clearly did not improve. In fact, from the curve we can see that their performance seemed to get worse. The more practice they had on the task, the more errors they seemed to make. Thus, for a given type of learning task, one species improved with practice and the other species seemed to get worse. Clearly, the laws governing the learning for these two species are not the same.

In addition, Bitterman compared the performance of the rats and the fish on the four types of learning tasks with the performances of other species on these four types of tasks. Not only did he again find evidence for discontinuity in the laws of learning, but he also found that on some tasks some species learned like rats, and on other tasks these same species learned in a manner

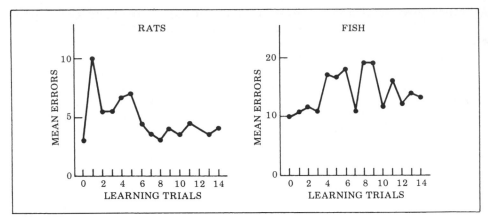

FIGURE 5.15
Performance of (a) rats and (b) fish on a specific type of learning task.

Source: Adapted from M. E. Bitterman (1965). Phyletic differences in learning. *American Psychologist,* 20. Copyright © 1965 by the American Psychological Association. Reprinted with permission.

similar to fish. Thus, whereas some species (e.g., monkeys) always learned in the way that the rats learned and others seemed to learn in the way fish learned, some animals learned some problems the way rats did and other problems the way fish did. These findings by Bitterman are summarized in Table 5.1, adapted from his 1965 article.

In summary, Bitterman argued against the seemingly well-ingrained assumption that there were universal laws of learning and only these universal laws, and thus that the laws of learning were necessarily continuous along the phylogenetic scale. He believed that the laws of learning

of one species could not necessary be assumed to apply to all species. We have seen that his assessments of different species of animals on different types of learning tasks allow us to conclude that, simply, the same laws of learning do not seem to apply to all species. Thus, the import of Bitterman's work is to demonstrate the necessity of testing crucial developmental issues and not simply assuming that one's position on the issue is correct. Moreover, Bitterman provided developmental science with evidence against the notion that all phylogenetic levels are the same in regard to psychological or behavioral functioning. Bitterman indicated that one common set of laws may not suffice to account for all the behavior of all species, and that instead there were qualitative differences among species. That is, there were differences in kind as well as in degree. A key implication of Bitterman's work was that discontinuity as well as continuity may characterize the phylogeny of learning.

If there are differences among animals in the laws governing learning, may it also be possible that there are differences *within* a given species? That is, may ontogenetic development also be characterized by discontinuity in the laws governing learning?

TABLE 5.1
Behavior of a Variety of Animals in Four Types of Learning Problems Expressed in Terms of Whether Their Learning Was Similar to That of the Rat or of the Fish

| Animal | Learning problem | | | |
	1	2	3	4
Monkey	Rat	Rat	Rat	Rat
Rat	Rat	Rat	Rat	Rat
Pigeon	Rat	Rat	Fish	Fish
Turtle	Fish	Fish	Fish	Fish
Fish	Fish	Fish	Fish	Fish
Cockroach	Fish	Fish	—	—
Earthworm	Fish	—	—	—

Note. Adapted from M. E. Bitterman (1965). Phyletic differences in learning. *American Psychologist,* 20, 396–410. Copyright © 1965 by the American Psychological Association. Adapted with permission.

ONTOGENETIC IMPLICATIONS OF THE CONTINUITY–DISCONTINUITY ISSUE

In 1980, Orville G. Brim, Jr., and Jerome Kagan edited a book (*Constancy and Change in Human*

Development) that reviewed evidence from several disciplines about whether early experience provided a virtually immutable shaper of the entire life course—in other words, about whether events in early life necessarily constrained developments later on (see, too, Bruer, 1999, for a more recent review of these issues). With the publication of the Brim and Kagan (1980) volume, the issue of continuity–discontinuity across life came to the fore of developmental psychological concern.

The authors brought together in the Brim and Kagan volume reviewed studies that indicated that features of the person's historical setting often shaped personality, social, and intellectual functioning to a much greater extent than maturational- or age-associated changes (Elder, 1974; Nesselroade & Baltes, 1974; Schaie, 1979). General historical events such as wars, economic privations, or political upheavals, as well as personal events such as marriage, divorce, illness, death, or career change, were often seen to provide potent shapers of the quantity of life changes and of the quality of the life course (e.g., Elder, 1974, 1979, 1980, 1998). These studies also indicated that there were multiple paths through life. As people age they become increasingly different from each other, and these different life paths are again linked to general historical or personal events

Jerome Kagan

Orville G. Brim, Jr.

(Baltes 1987, 1997; Baltes et al., 1980, 1998, 1999; Brim & Ryff, 1980).

On the basis of such findings, Brim and Kagan (1980) concluded that the potential for change existed across life; that as a consequence of active people reciprocally interacting in a changing world, the life course was always characterized by the potential for *plasticity*—that is, systematic changes within the person in his or her structure and/or function. While not denying that constancies and continuities could and did characterize much of many people's life courses, and that plasticity is therefore not limitless, Brim and Kagan (1980) suggested that many such features of life were not necessary ones. They contended that change and the potential for change characterized life because of the plasticity of the processes involved in people's lives.

These conclusions were controversial. One key reason for the controversy was a consequence of the fact that many of the scientific disciplines devoted to the study of human behavior, its evolution, and its development across the life span have historically been influenced by a "presupposition of limits" (Gould, 1981).

The Presupposition of Limits and the Presupposition of Plasticity

A presupposition is a culturally deep-rooted, pre-empirical idea about the nature of reality. It is an idea held even before data are collected pertinent to the idea. Presuppositions function in a manner comparable to the ideas discussed earlier in regard to theories; that is, a presupposition, like a theory, may lead to differential treatment of data, and such treatment may result in the "discovery" in the data of evidence for the truth of the presupposition.

The term *presupposition of limits* is meant to summarize a general position or class of arguments in philosophy, one that has many instances (see Toulmin, 1981). This presupposition involves the view that human functioning is unalterably constrained by one factor or by a circumscribed set of factors (e.g., genes and early experience); that is, the view is that there is a necessary "connection" (Kagan, 1980, 1983) between what is given by these causal variables and a consequent form or function, and that this connection is unavailable for manipulation or alteration (Lehrman, 1970). In other words, this view implies that there is one (or a limited few) developmental pathway(s), and that an individual's trajectory along a path is determined by causal factors that permit no deviation.

Although most current conceptions of development do not manifest this presupposition in terms as strong as those I have outlined, there are, nevertheless, several influential theoretical statements consistent with the presupposition of limits (e.g., Eysenck & Kamin, 1981a, 1981b; Herrnstein & Murray, 1994; Lorenz, 1965; Rowe, 1994). For instance, Klaus and Kennell (1976) introduced a notion of maternal–infant bonding that stressed that the quality of the bond established between the mother and the infant in the first few minutes or hours after the infant's birth imposed a potent constraint on the rest of the newborn's social and affective development. Klaus and Kennell (1976) indicated:

> We strongly believe that an essential principle of attachment is that there is a *sensitive period* in the first minutes and hours after an infant's birth which is optimal for the parent–infant attachment. (pp. 65–66)

Klaus and Kennell (1976) explained that one of their principles of attachment was that:

> early events have long-lasting effects. Anxieties a mother has about her baby in the first few days after birth, even about a problem that is easily resolved, may affect her relationship with the child long afterward. (p. 52)

Klaus and Kennell (1976) concluded:

> This original mother–infant bond is the wellspring for all the infant's subsequent attachments and is the formative relationship in the course of which the child develops a sense of himself. Throughout his lifetime the strength and character of this attachment will influence the quality of all future bonds to other individuals. (pp. 1–2)

A theoretical position consistent with the implicit stance taken by Klaus and Kennell (1976) in regard to the presupposition of limits was presented by Fraiberg (1977). She contended that throughout the life span, every instance of and/or type of expression of the emotion of love was necessarily connected to a bond that originated in the first year of life. Fraiberg (1977) argued that:

> Love of a partner and sensual pleasure experienced with that partner begin in infancy, and progress to a culminating experience, "falling in love," the finding of a permanent partner, the achievement of sexual fulfillment. In every act of love in mature life, there is a prologue which originated in the first year of life. (pp. 31–32)

In addition to these formulations, Bruer (1999) reviewed other arguments that perpetuated what he termed the *myth of the first three years,* that is, the belief that brain development in the first three years of life determine, in an all-or-none, once-in-a-lifetime manner, the success of a child's development across the entire life span. Bruer (1999) noted that as a consequence of this myth, parents might have believed that by the time their children entered kindergarten all the brain developments crucial to their success in life were behind them. Although I have more to say in Chapter 6 about such "critical period" ideas, we may note that Bruer provided considerable neurobiological and behavioral evidence to indicate that the brain remains an instrument for learning and development across life and, indeed, there are data pertinent to very old age (e.g., from the Berlin Study of Aging; Baltes et al., 1998, 1999) that indicates that cognitive development and learning can occur in the ninth and tenth decades of life!

On the basis of such data, Nelson (1999) concluded that:

> First, given the protracted nature of synapse formation, given that the cultivation of some synaptic circuits depend heavily on experience, and given the multitude of experiences a child has in his or her lifetime, we should be telling parents that no single experience, good or bad, will likely have much influence on their child's development (although there will be

Charles Nelson

caveats to this suggestion, e.g., whether the child has been spared perinatal or genetic injury). Similarly, given the long evolutionary history our species enjoys, many of the so-called enriched experiences some parents seem to intent on providing their children with will likely not matter later in life. Thus, whether the child has the "right" mobile positioned above the crib or the right music or foreign language tape playing in the background will likely prove inconsequential in the long run; that is, the child might have a facility for languages or music (although even this is uncertain), but these experiences will not impact development broadly defined. This, in turn, should take the pressure off parents to be perfect. Third, our species would not have survived as long as it has if all of our development depended heavily on specific experiences occurring at precise points in time. Moreover, even those systems whose development is tied to sensitive or critical periods (e.g., our sensory system) provide for some flexibility both in the quality and the timing of certain experiences. Thus, so long as our visual system receives general patterned information, we will develop pattern vision. The lesson here, of course, is that we, as parents, teachers, and role models, can make a few mistakes. Lastly, as dramatic as brain development is in the first few years, we should think of these years as analogous to building a foundation for a house. However, unless construction continues, the house will be incomplete, and its owners may never be satisfied with the final product—nor may its neighbors. Based on my perspective as a neuroscientist and developmental psychologist, I argue that

our responsibility to our children must be distributed throughout the course of their lives, not focused on just the first 3 years. To do otherwise would be not only short-sighted, it would not be good science. (p. 237)

Despite the good sense and the good science that is reflected in the views of Nelson (1999) and Bruer (1999), the fact that they had to make their arguments two decades after Brim and Kagan (1980) had also presented evidence supporting just such ideas about plasticity across the life span suggests that notions about the lack of plasticity in human development—or, in other words, notions predicated on the presupposition of limits—are difficult to eliminate, even when they are shown to be counterfactual. Indeed, there has been across the history of the study of human development formulations that were fairly explicitly associated with the presupposition of limits.

For example, the nineteenth-century craniology of Broca (1861, 1862a, 1862b, 1862c) involved the assumption that the size of the human skull was the factor limiting an individual's or a social group's intellectual capacity (Gould, 1981). Similarly, genetic deterministic theories of both the nineteenth and twentieth centuries assumed that one's biology—received at conception and represented by the genotype—constrained one's moral (Lorenz, 1940), cognitive–intellectual (Goddard, 1912, 1914; Herrnstein & Murray, 1994), or vocational (Terman, 1916) developments (cf. Gould, 1981). In short, the presupposition of limits is a preempirical—and in my view unduly pessimistic—belief in the irremediable character of human nature. It holds that for better or for worse, we are a direct, unalterable product of our evolution, biology, genes, and early experiences. There can be no intervention to prevent, ameliorate, or enhance this "natural order." Simply, this "biology is destiny" argument leaves little room for ontogenetic adaptation.

However, a presupposition of limits may be contrasted with one of plasticity. Such a presupposition involves the belief that there may be change within a person over time, change in his or her physical, psychological, and social structures and functions. This potential for change is thought to exist because of the constant irrevocable relation that exists between a person and his/her world. In other words, the presupposition of plasticity rests on the idea that the person always exists in a world that he or she both influences and is influenced by (Lerner, 1982; Lerner & Busch-Rossnagel, 1981; Lerner & Walls, 1999). Changes in people affect changes in their physical and social worlds—worlds that, as they are thus altered, promote further changes in people. Because of the reciprocal relations between people and their worlds, one may be optimistic that there now are (or may eventually be) ways to better the human condition. One may, therefore, countenance the hope that experiences at one time in life need not constrain possibilities later or—that at least some early problems, deficits, or insults to the integrity of the organism may be ameliorated (Lerner, 1984, 1993a; Scarr, 1982; Sigman, 1982).

To contrast the implications of the presupposition of limits versus the presupposition of plasticity in regard to optimism versus pessimism about changing human functioning, we may note that beliefs in (or the presence of) fixity in human functioning and development suggest that humans are resistant to change, that they are static, immutable organisms. Beliefs in (or evidence for) plasticity suggest by definition that there is some potential for within-person (intraindividual) change, and these beliefs promote a scientific stress on studying processes fostering or constraining change. In addition, the existence of plasticity in the functioning and development of humans permits an optimistic orientation to intervention. In addition to preventative strategies, techniques aimed at ameliorating, or even enhancing, the human condition may appropriately be instituted (Clarke & Clarke, 1976; Lerner, 1995a). Without plasticity, humans who possess undesired or undesirable characteristics would be, simply, without remediation (Hunt, 1961). Humans would be unable to adapt to any significant types of social changes such as those that have occurred in the domain of gender roles in the past several decades (e.g., Block, 1973; Maccoby, 1998).

What could be done with such people? If there is a belief that personal and social behaviors and health are fixed by genes or, in turn, by experiences in very early life experiences that are presumed to have unmodifiable connections to functioning in later life (Kagan, 1980, 1983), then rather severe treatment policies can be instituted. Brim and Kagan (1980) depicted such perspectives by noting:

> The belief that early experiences create lasting characteristics, like the belief in biological and genetic determinism, makes it possible to assume that attempts to improve the course of human development after early childhood are wasted and without consequence. If society believes that it is all over by the third year of life, it can deal harshly with many people in later life because nothing more can be done, and social programs designed to educate, redirect, reverse, or eliminate unwanted human characteristics cannot be justified. Policies of racial, ethnic, and sex discrimination, incarceration rather than rehabilitation of criminals, ignoring urban and rural poverty, and isolation of the elderly have found shelter in the belief in the determinism of the early years of life. (p. 21)

Simply, the presence of plasticity holds the promise of potentially enhancing human life and the presence of fixity or immutability does not. The empirical existence of plasticity is, therefore, not a point of minor practical significance. Simply, if all levels of life are available to be changed, then there is great reason to be optimistic about the ability of intervention programs to enhance human development. However, as Brim and Kagan (1980) indicated, we, too, should emphasize that optimism about plasticity must be tempered in light of the need to understand the presence of both continuity and discontinuity—of both constancy and change—in ontogeny. As we shall see, Werner's (1957) ideas again help us to understand this point.

Plasticity and Probabilistic Epigenesis

If discontinuity in development exists along with continuity, then any plasticity that arises as a consequence of discontinuity must be understood as a *relativistic* phenomenon. As a consequence of this relativity, the issue for the study of human development is to learn the organismic and contextual conditions that promote and/or constrain systematic change in structure and/or function. A similar call for the need to understand how the processes that promote plasticity also promote constraints on change has been made by Gollin (1981), who also adopted a relativistic view of the bases of an organism's plasticity across life. Moreover, we have noted in Chapter 3 that Gollin (1981) believed that the variables from these bases afford plasticity because of the probabilistic character of their confluence (see also Gottlieb, 1970, 1997; Lerner, 1978, 1984, 1993a, 1998b).

An emphasis on probabilistic–epigenetic development indicates that the processes that give humans their individuality and their plasticity are the same ones that provide for human commonality and constancies (cf. McClearn, 1981). Indeed, Jack Block (personal communication, 1982) made this point eloquently, cautioning that when using the term plasticity one must not also imply that within the malleable system there is not a structure or structures. He noted that "if individuals are self-initiating, self-organizing systems, responsive in dynamic ways to changing contexts, this is because they have within them various ego structures, cognitive structures, perceptual structures, [and] action or knowledge structures through which experience is apprehended, processed and behavior is forged."

In essence, processes of development are plastic in that they continually involve probabilistic–epigenetic transactions between organism and context. The outcomes (ontogenetic products) of these developmental progressions are internal and behavioral structures affording a human the ability to change self and/or context to meet the demands of life, the ability to attain a good fit or match with the context.

But, as I have indicated, plasticity is not limitless. Human behavior is always influenced by past events, by current conditions, and by the specific features of the individual's organismic constitution. As noted in Chapter 3, a notion of complete or limitless plasticity is antithetical to any useful concept of development (Baltes, Dittmann-Kohli, & Dixon, 1984; Kaplan, 1983; Lerner & Busch-Rossnagel, 1981; Lerner & Walls, 1999; Sroufe, 1979; Sroufe & Waters, 1977), and is, therefore, unwarranted on philosophical, theoretical, and methodological—as well as on empirical—grounds (e.g., see Block, 1982).

On the other hand, any view that stresses complete constraints, necessary connectivity across life periods, or irremediable limits placed on later behavioral organization by antecedent experiences is similarly unwarranted. Such a view would ignore the demonstrations that at least some behavioral flexibility can be shown across all of life (Baltes, 1987, 1997; Baltes & Baltes, 1980; Baltes et al., 1998, 1999; Baltes & Willis, 1982; Brim & Kagan, 1980; Bruer, 1999; Greenough & Green, 1981; Lerner, 1984, 1998b; Nelson, 1999; Willis, 1982; Willis & Baltes, 1980) and that there is evidence for the plasticity of the processes producing such capability.

The point I want to emphasize here is that the intellectual agenda promoted by an analysis of the plasticity concept, at least insofar as one follows the probabilistic epigenetic model discussed in Chapter 3, is not one of determining whether constancy or change, or whether stereotypy or plasticity, characterize development. *Both do.*

Let me reiterate that a key feature of Werner's (1948, 1957) orthogenetic principle is that a developmental change is *defined* as one wherein processes promoting discontinuity (i.e., those promoting differentiation) are synthesized with those promoting continuity (i.e., those promoting hierarchic integration). From this orthogenetic perspective, developmental change is not only lawful and a synthesis of constancy and change, but developmental change is also thereby consistent with the features of ontogeny that we have seen are

highlighted by a probabilistic epigenetic conception of development. Thus, the task for developmental analysis is one of determining the individual and contextual conditions under which one will see constancy or change (cf. Block, 1982; Lerner, 1979).

For instance, what developmental processes lead to a child developing a given level of "ego resiliency" (Block & Block, 1980), and what conditions constrain the development of such a level of flexibility? In order to address such questions we must be concerned with the life-span character of the relation between constancy and change, of plasticity and constraints on plasticity. Some features of this character are discussed in the next section.

Plasticity as a Ubiquitous but Declining Phenomenon

An organism's plasticity does not remain at a constant level across its life span. There are several lines of work pertinent to this point.

First, MacDonald (1985), in an essay integrating the concept of sensitive period (discussed in Chapter 6) with the literature pertinent to early experience effects, made several points that led to the conclusion that plasticity is a ubiquitous but declining phenomenon across the life span. A sensitive period is one within which the development of specific features of the organism's structure or function (e.g., the development of native language facility during the first 5 years of life) is most responsive to stimulation (e.g., from a person emitting, or modeling, the native language) particularly pertinent to that feature of development. MacDonald (1985) pointed out that the idea of sensitive period is best understood as a notion pertaining to the efficiency of environmental influences. He indicated that the two key parameters of a sensitive-period concept were the age of the organism and, although usually ignored, the intensity of the environmental stimulus needed to modify the age effect. He explained that the sensitive-period concept therefore meant that deprivation or stimulation would be most efficient at producing effects at particular ages and that attempts to override these effects outside the sensitive period would require relatively large investments of time or energy (MacDonald, 1985).

For example, injection of testosterone propionate into newborn female mice results in greater masculinization than does injection at Day 12 of life (Bronson & Desjardins, 1970). If injection is delayed until Day 30, a longer injection period is needed in order to obtain the same level of masculinization (Edwards, 1970). Similar findings were reported by Barraclough (1966). A progressively larger dose of testosterone propionate was needed to induce acyclicality in female rats at later ages. For instance, at 5 days of age, only 5 mg were needed to lower the proportion of cycling females to 56%. However, at 10 days of age, 1,250 mg were needed to achieve a similar percentage. Thus, Mac-Donald (1985) indicated that a larger dose or more intensive treatment was needed at later ages; that is, the organism was increasingly refractory to modification by environmental stimulation.

MacDonald (1985) reviewed other nonhuman (e.g., Bateson, 1964; Hoffman & Rattner, 1973; Immelmann & Suomi, 1981) and human (e.g., Flint, 1978; McKay et al., 1978) data that support the previously described roles of the age and environmental-stimulus-intensity parameters of the sensitive period notion. Together these data suggest that while the organism can be changed across its life, it becomes increasingly more difficult to effect change; change requires a more intensive environmental stimulus. In other words, MacDonald argued that plasticity was present across life, albeit to an increasingly narrower or more circumscribed extent (cf. Baltes & Baltes, 1980; Greenough & Green, 1981). Thus, MacDonald (1985) concluded that:

> We have come a long way from supposing that behavior is absolutely fixed at an early age by genetic factors or that after a sensitive period it is impossible to change behavior. Nevertheless, there are too many data showing otherwise to reject the idea that there are important constraints on plasticity for human or animal behavior. This fact does not, of course, prevent us from finding ways to intervene with individuals who have suffered early environmental insults. Indeed, the theory of sensitive periods suggests that the intensity of an ecologically appropriate stimulus can, at least up to a point, overcome the organism's declining plasticity . . . The fact of declining plasticity merely indicates what we already know, that successful interventions are not at present easily come by. (p. 116)

Plasticity and Constancy in Development

Of course, the fact that one does not see a change in behavior over time cannot be taken as proof of the absence of plasticity (MacDonald, 1985). Constancy in the individual can result from consistency in the demands and/or constraints of the environment within which the individual is functioning and to which the individual must adapt (cf. Wohlwill, 1980). In addition, and especially among humans, the developing individual's progressive ability to be competent in self-regulation means that the individual becomes better able to

self-select and shape the context within which he or she interacts and thereby to produce and/or maintain his or her constancy (Brandtstädter, 1998, 1999; Freund, Li, & Baltes, 1999; Heckhausen, 1999; Lerner, 1982; Lerner & Busch-Rossnagel, 1981; Mischel, 1977; Snyder, 1981). Given that the contextual pressures could be changing while such individual production processes are occurring, the maintenance of individual constancy in such a case would be evidence of considerable flexibility on the part of the individual.

Unfortunately, however, neither the enviromental nor the individual sources of constancy have been well studied (MacDonald, 1985; Wohlwill, 1980). Cairns and Hood (1983) presented, however, a discussion of five factors that gave rise to individual continuity in development. They noted that, first, individually specific biological variables may contribute to continuity in an individual's behavior. Such variables included genetic processes that might endure over several developmental periods, hormonal processes, and morphology (Cairns & Hood, 1983). However, Cairns and Hood (1983) cautioned that:

> *Biological factors are rarely translated directly into differences in social interaction patterns*. The linkages between psychobiological processes and social behavior patterns *need to be examined at each of the several points in ontogeny*. It cannot be safely assumed that biological or genetic-based differences will persist, unmodified by social encounters or interchanges in which the individual engages. (p. 309, italics added)

The second factor that Cairns and Hood (1983) identified as potentially contributing to the continuity of behavior included the social network in which development occurs. They believed that, if all other factors were equal, similarities in behavior from one time to the next would be greatest when the social network in which development occurred remained constant. This may be especially true of isolated people (Wahler, 1980). The third factor Cairns and Hood (1983) identified was behavioral consolidation. Here, based on social learning of interactional learning experiences, diverse behaviors became part of an integrated behavioral repertoire or sequence. For example, one may learn how to "put together" efficiently all the diverse behaviors involved in hosting a dinner party.

The fourth and fifth factors noted by Cairns and Hood (1983) were ones we have seen suggested before. "Social evocation and mutual control" allow individuals to contribute to the continuity of their own behavior by virtue of their being involved in a "circular function" (Schneirla, 1957). That is, by

Robert J. Cairns

virtue of their individual physical and behavioral characteristics, people evoke different reactions in others, reactions that involve (a) classification of the person–stimulus into categories (e.g., attractive, overweight, male, and black); and (b) category-specific feedback to the person (Lerner, 1976; see also Kendall, Lerner, & Craighead, 1984). Cairns and Hood (1983) noted:

> To the extent that some stimulus properties of the individual remain relatively constant over time, the social actions contingent upon the actions of others may themselves remain relatively similar. (p. 310)

Finally, Cairns and Hood (1983) noted that individuals may actively promote their own continuity. Especially as self-regulatory competency increases, individuals show choices and preferences and take actions that preserve their social network and their social relations, and maintain their environmental setting (cf. Brandtstädter, 1998, 1999; Freund et al., 1999; Heckhausen, 1999; Kendall, Lerner, & Craighead, 1984; Mischel, 1977; Snyder, 1981).

The point involved in the Cairns and Hood (1983) presentation is that there are several processes that may maintain constancy in an organism's behavior, and that none of these processes pertains to the lasting or constraining effects of early experience or speaks directly to the level of plasticity prototypic of organisms across their development. In other words, the presence of constancy across development is not in and of itself evidence against (or for) the view that organisms remain plastic across life (Cairns & Hood, 1983; MacDonald, 1985; Wohlwill, 1980).

Conclusions

Plasticity not only represents a ubiquitous but declining phenomenon across life but also because an instance of plasticity may involve the organism's actively and creatively maintaining a context within which it can remain constant, the presence of plasticity may be difficult to verify. Indeed, in this view, the presence of constancy may be an index of plasticity. Thus, the outcomes of effects of plasticity may be difficult to disentangle from other phenomena leading to constancy or change, to continuity or discontinuity in development (e.g., see the discussion in Chapter 3 about how the parameters of plasticity may vary acroxss history).

When the continuity–discontinuity issue is raised in regard to development across the human life span, it draws us into discussions of descriptions, explanations, and quantitative versus qualitative constancy or change. In addition, we are led into a consideration of issues of plasticity, of constraints on development, and of the nature–nuture controversy. However, just as the continuity–discontinuity issue is related to the nature–nurture issue, another key issue of development is closely linked to that of continuity–discontinuity: the issue of stability–instability. We consider this issue next.

THE STABILITY–INSTABILITY ISSUE

The study of continuity and discontinuity in an organism's development is really an appraisal of how descriptions and/or explanations of change may apply across ontogeny. Such appraisals necessarily involve consideration of what happens to a person as a function of the variables affecting his or her development. In other words, consideration of the continuity–discontinuity issues is, in effect, an assessment of how the character of the variables influencing development result in quantitative and/or qualitative differences within a person over the course of his or her life. Simply, the continuity–discontinuity issue is one of intraindividual (within-person) change.

However, not all people undergo intraindividual change in precisely the same way. There are differences *between* people in how they change intraindividually. Thus, in addition to asking questions about within-person change, one may also ask what happens to a person relative to other people as the relations among the variables that affect development change or remain the same.

People may obviously be placed in reference groups such as sex, age, race, ethnicity, or religion. What happens to the person's position in a reference group as the variables affecting the person function?

For example, let us consider the most common reference group in developmental psychology, an age group. Suppose that we have measured the IQ of every member of a 5-year-old age group. We would expect that different people would get different IQ scores. In fact, we could rank every member of the age group from high to low, and any given person would, therefore, have a position in the age group. What happens to this person when the variables that affect behavior function? The person's position could change, or it could remain the same, relative to the other people in the age group.

Thus, whenever we consider the continuity–discontinuity issue, a second, subsidiary issue is also raised—that of *stability–instability*. The stability–instability issue describes differences that arise between people within groups as a consequence of within-person change. Thus, two types of alterations involving people are occurring simultaneously. People may be changing over time, and because not all people change in the same way or at the same rate, people's locations relative to others may also alter. In order to understand all dimensions of a person's alteration over time, both aspects of change should be considered simultaneously. Only through such a

joint, simultaneous focus can development across the life span best be portrayed.

If a person's position relative to his or her reference group changes with development, this is *instability*. Alternatively, if a person's position relative to his or her reference group remains the same with development, this is *stability*. These terms describe a person's ranking relative to some reference group. These relations are illustrated in Figure 5.16.

Notice, however, that in this figure both examples of the IQ of the person in question (the target person) *increased* from Time 1 to Time 2 in development. This is an important point. Whether stability or instability occurs says nothing whatsoever about whether any *absolute* change took place. A person can change, and this change may still be labeled stability. This could occur if others in the reference group also changed and if the target person remained in the same relative position. On the other hand, a person could remain the same from Time 1 to Time 2 and yet his or her position relative to the reference group could be termed instable. This could occur if others in the group changed while the target person did not. Hence, we should see that the terms *stability* and *instability* describe *relative,* not absolute, changes.

Let us illustrate this point. The concept of IQ, or intelligence quotient, is relative; it expresses a measure of a person's intelligence relative to his or her age group. As noted in Chapter 2, for example, one way of expressing IQ is through use of the intelligence–quotient formula (i.e., IQ = MA/CA × 100, where MA = mental age, CA = chronological age, and 100 is used to avoid fractions). Thus, if you are as bright as a 5-year-old (MA = 5 years) and you are 5 years of age (CA = 5 years), your IQ

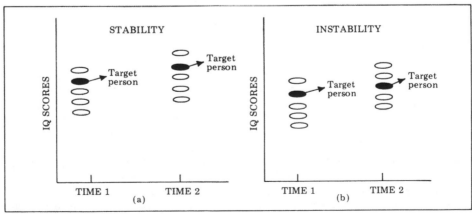

FIGURE 5.16
Examples of (a) stability and (b) instability in development.

will equal 100. Similarly, if you are 8 years old and you are as bright as an 8-year-old, your IQ will also equal 100. In this way, we see that IQ is a relative concept. It expresses one's intelligence relative to one's age (reference) group.

If a 5-year-old has an IQ of 120 and an 8-year-old has an IQ of 100, it would be clear that the 5-year-old is brighter than the 8-year-old, because the 5-year-old knows more relative to his or her age group than the 8-year-old knows relative to his or her age group. Certainly, if one could construct some imaginary scale of absolute knowledge, the 8-year-old would probably have more absolute knowledge than the 5-year-old. Yet, we say that the 5-year-old is brighter because IQ is a relative concept, and the younger child has a higher ranking in the 5-year-old reference group than does the older child in his or her reference group.

A person's absolute knowledge may change, but if the person's age group keeps pace, then his or her IQ would be stable. Conversely, even if a person's absolute knowledge remains the same from Time 1 to Time 2, his or her IQ could (a) remain the same if the age group did not change; (b) be instable and even decrease if the age group increased in its level of absolute knowledge; or (c) be instable and even increase if the age group decreased in its level of absolute knowledge.

As another example, consider the distribution of scores that would be obtained if people were measured on the characteristic of "height at puberty." Not all people would be the same height at puberty. Some would be shorter, some taller, and some of average height. People with different scores (in this case, heights) would have different positions (or locations) in the group.

When the group is tested a second time (e.g., height measured at the end of the final growth spurt in adolescence), heights may have changed for most, if not all, people. However, each person's relative position in the group could have stayed the same. If Persons A, B, and C each grew 4 inches, and all the other people in their group did as well, then despite the absolute increase in height, their relative positions in the group would have stayed the same. Despite intraindividual change, there were no interindividual differences in such change. This illustration is an example of stability. However, if a person's rate of change relative to the others in the group changes over time, if Person C grew 8 inches in height whereas everyone else grew only 4 inches, then Person C would have changed more than those in his or her group, and instability (for this person) would have occurred. As with the IQ illustrations,

notice again that in the present illustrations of both stability and instability for height, the score of the person in question increased between Time 1 and Time 2.

The terms *stability* and *instability* describe *relative,* not absolute, changes. Again, the terms relate to whether differences present among people in a group at Time 1 persisted at Time 2 (and, hence, stability occurred) or were altered, with the group distributed differently the second time (and, hence, instability occurred).

We can see that developmental stability and/or instability can be obtained in several ways. Stability between two times in a person's development can occur when (a) the person remains the same and so does the reference group or (b) the person changes and so does the reference group to corresponding extents. On the other hand, instability between two times in a person's development can occur when (a) the person remains the same but the reference group changes or (b) the person changes but so do members of the reference group to extents not corresponding with the person's degree of change. These instances of stability and instability are illustrated in Figure 5.17, where we see the relative changes that comprise stability and instability in reference to a given target person in each instance.

Relation of Continuity and Discontinuity to Stability and Instability

What we have seen is that the concepts of stability and instability describe the relative position of a developing person, whereas continuity and discontinuity pertain to the intraindividual manifestation of the functioning of the laws affecting development. In traditional (or classic) psychometric (or test) theory, stability refers to the maintenance across time of interindividual differences; instability refers to the alteration over time in these between-people differences. While stability–instability is a methodological issue (pertinent to the reliability of measurement) in classic test theory, the issue is a substantive one in the study of human development. In order to understand and describe the types of changes that characterize human development, one can and must deal simultaneously with two issues—continuity–discontinuity and stability–instability (e.g., see Baltes & Nesselroade, 1973; Emmerich, 1968). The processes that determine a person's development may be either continuous or discontinuous (in regard to both description and explanation), and the

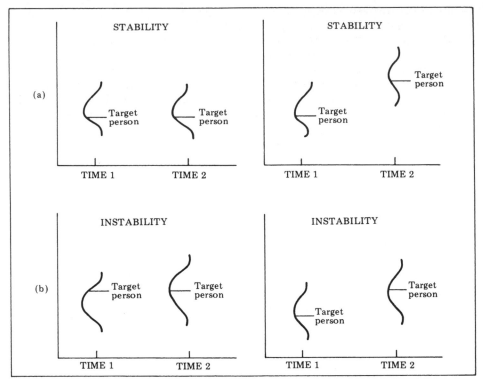

FIGURE 5.17
Two instances of the relative changes comprising (a) stability and (b) instability.

functioning of these processes may result in a person's stability or instability relative to his or her reference group.

To illustrate in respect to explanation, a developmental change may be of one of four types: (1) continuity and stability; (2) continuity and instability; (3) discontinuity and stability; or (4) discontinuity and instability. These four types of changes are indicated in Figure 5.18. In Box 1, we see continuity and stability. A change that is both continuous and stable is a change in which the laws governing behavior remain the same between two points in development and the rank-ordering of people in a reference group affected by the continuous functioning of these laws remains the same. Thus, the variables involved in the determination of these people's behavior do not change, and the people's relative positions in the group also remain the same.

In Box 2, we see a second type of developmental change, continuity and instability. In this case, although the laws affecting development remain the same over time (continuity), people's relative positions in their reference group change with development. Changes of this sort would comprise no alterations in the variables affecting development

but only changes in the ranking of people in a reference group.

In Box 3, we see discontinuity and stability. Here, the laws affecting development are altered with time, but people's relative positions in their reference group remain the same. Such changes are constituted by the nature of the variables involved in development changing over time

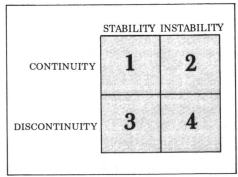

FIGURE 5.18
The interrelation of continuity–discontinuity and stability–instability.

(discontinuity) but people's rank-ordering in their reference group remaining the same (stability).

Finally, in Box 4, we see a fourth type of developmental change, discontinuity and instability. In this instance, the laws governing behavioral development change, and so do the relative positions of people in a reference group affected by these changed laws. In this kind of change the variables involved in development are altered, and the rankings of people in a reference group affected by the discontinuous functioning of these variables are also changed.

An important conclusion to draw from Figure 5.18 is that phenomena of continuity–discontinuity are distinct from those of stability–instability. Continuity does not imply stability and discontinuity does not imply instability; continuity may just as readily be coupled with instability as with stability, and discontinuity may just as readily be coupled with stability. All these relations are possible because the concepts of continuity and discontinuity pertain to the description and explanation of intraindividual change, while the concepts of stability and instability refer to interindividual differences; these latter concepts pertain to whether interindividual differences— for example, the rank-order of people along some

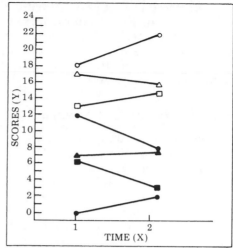

FIGURE 5.20
Another illustration of the distinction between stability and intraindividual change. The rank-order location of the group along the Y axis remains unchanged across time, indicative of complete stability, and yet all members of the group undergo intraindividual change across time.

dimension—remain the same (stability) or change (instability) across time.

It is crucial that these distinctions be kept in mind in order to avoid making mistaken inferences about the absence or presence of intraindividual change on the basis of information about stability (Baltes & Nesselroade, 1973; Baltes, Cornelius, & Nesselroade, 1977). The scores of a group of individuals may show complete stability. For example, the correlation between scores on two occasions of measurement may be perfect; the rank-order of a group in regard to their scores on a dimension may not change from Time 1 to Time 2; or the average (mean) score for the group may remain the same from Time 1 to Time 2.

Nevertheless, considerable intraindividual change may exist in regard to most if not all of the people in the group. This possibility is illustrated in Figure 5.19, where, for a group of three people, there is complete stability in regard to rank-order and mean level and yet considerable intraindividual change exists in regard to two of the three people in the group. Indeed, the directions of development (the trajectories of intraindividual change) are different for each of the people in this group. Another illustration of the distinction between stability as intraindividual change is presented in Figure 5.20, but here for a group

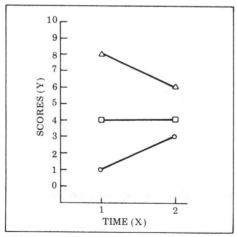

FIGURE 5.19
An illustration of why stability does not mean the absence of intraindividual change. The rank-order position along the Y axis of all people studied at Times 1 and 2 remains stable, as does the group mean; however, this stability says nothing about whether intraindividual change has occurred or about the directions (the trajectories) of intraindividual change, which in this illustration are all different.

larger than depicted in Figure 5.19; again, despite complete stability in regard to their rank-order placement at two times of measurement, each member of this group shows evidence of intraindividual change, and, in addition, several different change trajectories are present.

Changes Characteristic of Development

A person may show stability of location when in one group (e.g., distributions formed by measuring height at 17 years of age and at age 21 years of age), but may show instability when considered in the context of another (e.g., a distribution formed by measuring knowledge of calculus at 17 years of age and at age 21 years of age). Not only does this underscore the point that stability–instability is a group consideration and not the property of a person, but it also suggests that when different mesures of characteristics are taken, different statements about stability–instability may appropriately be made.

Within the same portion of the life span, people may show stability in regard to measures of some processes and instability in others. Any of these differences may, of course, involve either continuity or discontinuity. One cannot speak of a given period of life as including just one particular type of change. In the large and complex data sets typically analyzed by human development researchers, the conceptual distinctions between continuity–discontinuity and stability–instability must be kept in mind because the differences between these constructs may not be readily discernible just by an inspection of some aggregate scores, such as means and correlations.

Any statements about the nature of change depend on the particular change process on which one focuses. More important, however, because the same change phenomenon (e.g., storm and stress in adolescence) may be understood and measured in different ways, depending on the theoretical orientation of the researcher, statements about the nature of change relate primarily to theoretical issues.

In order to fully describe the types of changes that may characterize any portion of the life span, one should pay attention to all the levels at which change can exist, and to the way in which concepts drawn from theories pertaining to processes at all these levels together may provide a more complete picture of development across life. In turn, it is possible to see theory as a key "protection" against interpreting a given data set as indicative of one versus another form of continuity versus discontinuity (and/or stability versus instability). This

"buffer" is the a priori metatheoretical presuppositions (Kagan, 1980, 1983) and theoretical assumptions (Lerner, 1986) that proscribe and prescribe particular formats, or instances, of continuity or discontinuity. To illustrate, it is useful to discuss the instances of continuity and/or discontinuity that are prototypically included or excluded in theories associated with the organismic, mechanistic, and developmental–contextual models of development.

CONTINUITY AND DISCONTINUITY IN DEVELOPMENT: METATHEORETICAL AND THEORETICAL PROSCRIPTIONS AND PRESCRIPTIONS

Theories embedded within a given model of development are not all alike. For example, while the nature-oriented theories of Gesell (1946) and Erikson (1959) emphasized an ontogenetic, maturational "ground plan" as constituting the key process explaining developmental change, Hall's (1904) nature-oriented theory explained ontogenetic changes by positing a biogenetic recapitulation in ontogeny of phylogenetic changes (see Haeckel, 1868). In turn, the nurture mechanistic theory of Bijou (1976) emphasized proximal stimuli as the material and efficient causes shaping behavior. This formulation is vague or mute, however, regarding how distal sociocultural institutional influences are translated into such stimulation. In contrast, some mechanistic, sociological views (e.g., Dannefer, 1984; Homans, 1961; Meyer, 1988) discussed the distal, age-graded channeling of behavior by societal institutions, but did not discuss the links between these entities and proximal stimulation.

However, as we discussed in Chapter 3, despite such differences, theories within a metatheoretical "family" (Reese & Overton, 1970) are more similar to one another than are theories associated with other metatheories or world hypotheses (see Pepper, 1942). Consequently, it is possible to describe, at least for the general case, the prototypic views regarding continuity and discontinuity associated with theories from the organismic, mechanistic, and developmental–contextual/developmental systems metatheoretical families (remembering of course that subtle individual differences may nevertheless exist among "family members"). Table 5.2 summarizes these prototypic views.

As can be seen from this table, theories associated with any model can accomodate the presence,

TABLE 5.2

Prototypic Views of Theories Associated With the Organismic, Mechanistic, and Developmental–Contextual Models of Development

Model of development	Representative theories associated with model	Descriptive continuity[a]	Descriptive discontinuity[a]	Explanatory continuity[a]	Explanatory discontinuity[a]
Organismic	Gesell (1946); Freud (1940/1949); Erikson (1959)	Yes/yes	Yes/yes	No/yes	No/yes
Mechanistic	Bijou & Baer (1961); Bijou (1976); Dannefer (1984)	Yes/yes	Yes/no	Yes/no	Yes/no
Developmental–Contextual	Gottlieb (1983, 1987); Lerner & Lerner (1987); Baltes (1987); Featherman & Lerner (1985)	Yes/yes	Yes/yes	Yes/yes	Yes/yes

[a]Quantitative–qualitative.

Note. From R. M. Lerner & J. Tubman (1989). Conceptual issues in studying continuity and discontinuity in personality development across life." *Journal of Personality, 57,* 343–373. Copyright © 1989 by Blackwell Publishers. Reprinted with permission.

at a descriptive level, of both quantitative and qualitative continuity. This acceptance, however, is nothing more than admitting that things may stay the same across at least some portions of life. That is, there may be ontogenetic stasis. Quantitatively, this may mean that identical scores for a construct are present across time or that rates of growth remain constant (e.g., throughout the middle-childhood years). Qualitatively, stasis can occur when there is no numerical or structural change in the components of the behavioral repertoire or personality (e.g., traits).

Differences among the models exist, however, for the remaining instances of continuity and discontinuity. Both organismic- and developmental–contextual-based theories recognize that, descriptively, both quantitative and qualitative discontinuities can occur in development. However, descriptive quantitative discontinuities are largely irrelevant to organismic theorists, whose interests focus almost exclusively on qualitative structural variation across ontogeny (e.g., Erikson, 1959; Piaget, 1950). In mechanistic theories of development, no true descriptive qualitative discontinuity can exist; no novelty can exist in development (von Bertalanffy, 1933). Given the mechanist's commitment to reduce all developmental phenomena to a common set of constituent elements (e.g., in nature, mechanistic theories to genes and in nurture, mechanistic theories to S–R connections; see Chapter 3), lightly scratching the surface of any claim of newness or novelty in development will readily reveal that the operationalization of such terms is made via recourse to the quantitative

combinations (additions) of identically constituted elements. The treatment by the nurture, mechanistic theorists Bijou and Baer, of personality in childhood, which is interpreted as being reducible to chains of S–R connections, is a case-in-point. Similarly, the ideas of the nature, mechanist Rowe (1994), that all of socialization in human development can be reduced to the genes inherited at conception, is another example of such a perspective.

In regard to explanatory continuity and discontinuity, all models are distinct (see Overton, 1991). With respect to continuity, organismic theories do not typically explain development by reference to quantitatively invariant laws. Instead, qualitative invariance is stressed (i.e., to explain within-stage consistency or across-stage décalages; e.g., Levinson, 1978; Neugarten & Guttmann, 1968; Piaget, 1950). The reverse of these emphases is found in mechanistic theories. That is, quantitative invariance is emphasized. In developmental contextualism, or in developmental systems theory more generally, development may be explained by either quantitative or qualitative continuity. In regard to quantitative invariance, Haan and Day (1974) accounted for the maintenance of adults' style of engagement with their context by reference to a quantitative invariance over time in their scores for activity level. Schaie and Geiwitz (1982) accounted for the maintenance of adult personality structure by noting that adults select contexts to interact that provide a goodness of fit with their already established personality structure and, as such, do not provide demands for qualitative change in personality.

Finally, while organismic theories do not discuss quantitative discontinuity as an explanation for development, in mechanistic theories, qualitative discontinuity in the explanations of development is not possible. Within developmental contextualism or developmental systems theory, both qualitatively and quantitatively discontinuous explanations may be used. For example, while Elder (1974) and Schaie (1984) both drew on the link between individuals and features of the historical epoch within which they lived to explain individual differences in personality development, they did so by positing different types of influences. Elder (1974) argued that individual differences in achievement, health, and degrees of commitments to family values were influenced by whether a person experienced a qualitatively distinct historical event (the Great Depression) in his or her childhood or adolescence. Thus, one age group's experience of an individual–context relation that is qualitatively discontinuous from that of a succeeding cohort is used by Elder (1974) to account for individual (in this case, cohort) differences in features of personality development.

Schaie (1984) posited that such cohort differences in personality development were explained by quantitative differences across historical eras in the accumulation of life events (e.g., epidemics, wars, unemployment, inflation, and technological innovations). To Schaie, it was not the nature of the events per se which explained interindividual differences in personality development. Instead, these differences occured because of historical quantitative discontinuities in the cumulative number of events that comprised the context of a given cohort.

Theories associated with the organismic, mechanistic, and developmental–contextual models differ in the instances of continuity–discontinuity they see as possible. These differences underscore, then, the idea that continuity–discontinuity is not only an empirical concern but also a metatheoretical issue. In other words, the issue of continuity–discontinuity in human development is an empirical question, but *only* within the constraints of the variables considered relevant by the researcher's theory or metatheory; adopting alternative metatheories may introduce new variables that show a different empirical pattern. Moreover, this theoretical embeddedness of continuity–discontinuity leads us to note one key feature of our discussion of the categorizations made in Table 5.2: No instance of continuity or discontinuity is necessarily excluded within developmental–contextualism/developmental systems theory.

Acceptance of all possibilities may seem like uncritical eclecticism, but I believe that such an appraisal is not correct. Developmental systems theories do not maintain that all instances of continuity–discontinuity occur within and across developmental periods. Instead, the point is that several instances may happen. The empirical implication of this view is that developmental systems-derived theories seek to identify the organismic and contextual conditions within which any particular instance of continuity–discontinuity occurs (Baltes, 1987; Lerner, 1984).

This search for the organismic and contextual conditions of continuity–discontinuity has a long tradition in the study of human development, especially as it has been practiced by researchers who have conducted major longitudinal studies of multiple cohorts of people (e.g., Block, 1971; Eichorn, Clausen, Haan, Honzik, & Mussen, 1981; Elder, 1974; Nesselroade & Baltes, 1974; Schaie, 1979, 1984; Thomas & Chess, 1977). In fact, the attempts to make sense out of the plethora of combinations of continuity–discontinuity—of multiple directions in the course of human lives—were a major impetus to the creation of the developmental–contextual model (Dixon & Lerner, 1988; Lerner, Hultsch, & Dixon, 1983), of the life-span view of human development associated with this model (Baltes, Reese, & Lipsitt, 1980; Brim & Kagan, 1980; Lerner, 1986), and of theoretical formulations associated with developmental contextualism (e.g., Baltes, 1987; Featherman, 1985; Lerner & Lerner, 1989) or developmental systems theory more generally (Lerner, 1998b).

In the search for the organismic and contextual conditions of continuity–discontinuity, developmentalists, whose work is developmental contextual in character, would tend to agree with one implication of the orthogenetic principle of Heinz Werner (1957). The human life course is a synthesis of processes which, at one and the same time, make us both (a) similar to ourselves, at other points in time, and to others as well (these are nomothetic processes, ones affording continuity at both descriptive and explanatory levels—global and hierarchically integrated processes to Werner); and (b) *different* from ourselves, at other points in time, and from others as well (these are idiographic processes, ones affording discontinuity at both descriptive and explanatory levels—differentiating processes to Werner).

In other words, to developmental contextualists the search for the conditions of continuity and discontinuity may be translated into a search for nomothetic change processes (i.e., processes general to all of human development; processes that all people experience) and idiographic change processes (i.e., processes specific to the development on a particular individual). The integrative presence of both nomothetic and idiographic processes make all people, at one and the same time, both similar and different. The search to identify both sorts of processes is admittedly quite complex, certainly more difficult than one involving the a priori theoretical exclusion of particular instances of continuity–discontinuity.

We have noted in Chapter 3 that, to address this complexity, developmental contextualism takes a synthetic approach to development, one which, as implied in Table 5.2, integrates features of the active organism and of the active context. As such, developmental contextualism must take an open stance in regard to the instances of continuity–discontinuity that are possible. In addition, however, by thereby remaining open to the possibility that processes that promote intra- and interindividual continuity may exist along with ones that promote intra- and interindividual discontinuity, developmental contextualism fosters a second synthesis: The conditions of continuity and discontinuity—of constancy and change—may derive from a synthesis of nomothetic and idiographic processes. As such, developmental contextualism involves the idea that processes that create similarity and constancy may also act to foster dissimilarity or change. Within developmental contextualism there is, then, a synthetic view of the character and bases of continuity and discontinuity across life.

CONCLUSIONS

Any developmental change may be characterized as being either continuous or discontinuous *and* either stable or instable, and different theories of development proscribe and prescribe the character of the changes that may be involved in human development. Theories that vary in their commitment to

nature, to nurture, or to nature–nurture interactional or synthetic ideas may be contrasted, then, in regard to their inclusion of ideas pertinent to qualitative and quantitative, descriptive and explanatory continuity and discontinuity.

Thus, the two core issues involved in the study of human development—the nature–nurture and the continuity–discontinuity controversies—are both involved in different theories of development. The connection between these controversies in various theories of human development will be evident as we begin, in Chapter 6, to consider the details of the different theoretical positions in human development.

We begin this discussion by reviewing the theoretical ideas of the comparative psychologist T. C. Schneirla. We consider how his probabilistic-epigenetic theories of development involve an integration of: (a) the multiple levels of organization involved in the biological-through-sociocultural and physical ecological influences on behavior and development; (b) the variables linked to (what are regarded as fused) nature- and nurture-related processes; and (c) the dynamic relations between organism and context associated with constancy and change, with continuity and discontinuity, across life.

Schneirla's ideas constitute a foundation for the developmental contextual and, more generally, the developmental systems theoretical positions we have described in prior chapters. As such, Schneirla's work provides a frame for us to understand how the ideas one uses to address, if not resolve, the nature–nurture controversy shape the theories of development to which one adheres. His ideas will serve as a template for us to compare different theories of human development in regard to their stance in respect to the bases of human development and how these bases may propel change across the life span.

6 | *Resolving the Nature–Nurture Controversy: T. C. Schneirla and the Concept of "Levels of Integration"*

T. C. Schneirla (1902–1968) was trained in comparative psychology, receiving a Doctor of Science degree from the Department of Psychology at the University of Michigan in Ann Arbor. He left Ann Arbor in 1927 to take a position at New York University, and remained on the faculty of that institution until his death. However, beginning in 1943, he also became a member of the staff (starting as an associate curator) of The American Museum of Natural History. His theoretical and empirical work at both NYU and the museum provided developmental science with important conceptual tools for understanding how an integration of multiple—biological through ecological—levels of organization are integrated within a developmental system that propels an organism across the course of life. As such, Schneirla's theoretical ideas constituted a foundation for understanding the dynamic fusion of nature and nurture variables in development. Schneirla's ideas

1. Frame a discussion of probabilistic–epigenetic (or developmental–contextual) ideas about human development.

2. Provide a means to critique theoretical ideas that split nature from nurture and/or stress the primacy of either biological or contextual influences in human development (Overton, 1998).

To understand the contributions of Schneirla's ideas, it is useful to recall that in Chapter 2 we discussed that, historically, there have been instances in which theorists have emphasized the independent, isolated action of either hereditary mechanisms (Sheldon, 1940, 1942) or environmental mechanisms (Skinner, 1938; Watson, 1913, 1918) for some selected subset of an organism's behavioral repertoire. Although, today, due to the impact of essays not only by Schneirla (1956, 1966, 1967; Tobach & Schneirla, 1968) but also by Anastasi (1958), Kuo (1967, 1976), Gottlieb (1970, 1973, 1983, 1991, 1992, 1997, 1998); Lehrman (1953, 1970), Tobach (1981), and Overton (1973, 1998), most developmentalists acknowledge that variables from both nature and nurture sources contribute to development.

Agreement about the contribution of both nature and nurture to development, however, may be more apparent than real. Differences of opinion exist about the modes of contribution among variables derived from each of these sources; about the meaning and constitution of the contributing sources; and about how these differences are related to the alternative philosophical models to which human developmentalists may be committed. Indeed, as we shall now see, although the concept of interaction is invoked by many theorists to indicate how variables providing the source of development relate to each other, the concept is itself highly controversial. How one defines the concept also depends on one's philosophical and concomitant theoretical orientation. Understanding the various philosophical and theoretical stances one may take in regard to the concept of interactions enables us to see the importance of T. C. Schneirla's contributions to the resolution of the nature–nurture controversy.

T. C. Schneirla

THE CONCEPT OF INTERACTION

It is possible to discuss the range of concepts involved in the use of the term *interactions* by placing ideas about interaction along a continuum that ranges from "weak" to "strong." Points along the continuum reflect differences in the extent to which one source of development (nature **or** nurture) is accorded primacy as an influence on development. The greater the emphasis placed on one source of development as the "prime" mover of change across ontogeny, the weaker is the concept of interaction that is invoked. It is useful to begin the discussion of concepts of interaction, then, by considering such weak interaction notions.

Weak Interactions

To understand weak interactions, it is useful to consider the concept of interaction found in the nurture, mechanistic–behavioral view. Some psychologists, for example, Bijou (1976), argue that a person's development derives from an interaction between past reinforcement history and the current reinforcement context. Because the organism is the "host" (Baer, 1976), or locus, of the past reinforcement history, Bijou construes his concept of interaction as pertaining to *organism*–environment relations. Nevertheless, Bijou's (1976) view is that the organism is a largely passive component in the swirl of past and present

reinforcements surrounding it. The organism plays no primary role in shaping the context that influences it.

In essence, Bijou (1976) follows Skinner's (1971, p. 211) view that "a person does not act upon the world, the world acts upon him." Moreover, to underscore the idea that the stimulus environment is the cause of human behavior—in both a phylogenetic and an ontogenetic sense—Skinner (1971, p. 214) went on to say that "An experimental analysis shifts the determination of behavior from autonomous man to the environment—an environment responsible for both the evolution of the species and the repertoire acquired by each member." Thus, to Skinner (1971, p. 205), "A scientific analysis of behavior dispossesses autonomous man and turns the control he has been said to exert over to the environment."

The components of the environment that, within this perspective, are in total control of human behavior, interact only in the sense that past and present stimulus-contingencies additively combine to influence behavior. Because these environmental influences are not qualitatively distinct, and because of the restricted role delegated to the organism in this form of organism–environment interaction, some reviewers (Lerner, 1978, 1985; Overton, 1973) have characterized the type of interaction illustrated by Bijou's (1976) position as a *weak* interaction.

The type of interaction found in many predetermined organismic-stage theories may, as with the mechanistic–behavioristic tradition, be characterized as being of the weak variety. This is somewhat ironic because organismic developmental theory has been termed a *strong* developmental position (Overton & Reese, 1973; Reese & Overton, 1970). This weak interaction is the opposite of the one forwarded by Bijou (1976), because nature—not nurture—is the main force in this interaction. Although variables associated with both organism and context are said to be involved in the interactions associated with developmental (i.e., stage) progression, environmental (contextual) variables are only seen to facilitate or inhibit trajectories of primarily intrinsic (i.e., maturational) origin (Emmerich, 1968). Contextual variables cannot alter the direction, sequence, or quality of developmental change.

Moreover, in the predetermined epigenetic version of the organismic perspective, the maturational timetable (Erikson, 1959) or other biological phenomena (e.g., the movement of libido to particular areas of the body; Freud, 1954), that are believed to control the nature of developmental progressions, are all construed to be impervious to environmental influence—insofar as their impact on the quality of development is concerned. The organism is no more an influence on such biological variables than it is a determinant of the array of genes it receives at its conception. Thus, although the prime locus of developmental change lies within the organism, the organism is no more of an active agent in the interaction of this internal basis of development with the external environment than it is in nurture, mechanistic–behavioral theories such as those of Bijou (1976; Bijou & Baer, 1961).

Moderate Interactions

Another concept of interaction is found in the developmental literature. It can be labeled as *moderate* (Lerner & Spanier, 1978, 1980). Here, both organism and environment are (conceptually) equally weighted as influences on developmental outcomes. But the nature of these sources' relation while interacting may be conceptualized as analogous to the interaction term in the analysis of variance. Although organism- and environment-associated variables combine (in an additive manner, one describable by the general linear model) to influence developmental outcomes, each is construed to exist independent of (uninfluenced by) the other before (and presumably after) their interaction, and to be unchanged by the other during their interaction.

The concept of moderate interaction is not typically articulated as a feature of a particular theory of human development. Instead, it is found in the perspective to studying behavior that Gollin (1965) labeled the *child psychology approach*. This perspective is characterized by an ahistorical "subjects [participants] X tasks" approach to the analysis of behavior, and it is contrasted by Gollin (1965) with the historical "subjects X tasks-levels" approach characteristic of what he termed the *child development perspective*. In the child psychology approach, the goal is to determine the empirical contribution to variation in a dependent variable of organism-related variables (often vaguely represented by using age or sex as a factor), and environment-related variables (typically represented operationally by a specific task or manipulation), separately and in additive combination (i.e., "interactively") with organism-related variables. In other words, the concept of moderate interaction is typically expressed as a methodological component of what is also termed the *experimental child psychology approach* (Reese & Lipsitt, 1970). This approach views the treatment of subject and task, or of organism and environ-

ment (or of heredity and environment, in the analogous analysis of variance approach involved in determining what, in Chapter 10, is discussed as "heritability"), as necessarily separate, independent factors whose interaction effect or contribution is linear and additive. The interaction effect itself may combine two sources in a nonlinear, multiplicative way. That effect, however, adds linearly to the total variability.

Strong Interactions

Finally, a *strong* concept of organism–environment interaction (Lerner & Spanier, 1978, 1980; Overton, 1973), or a concept of dynamic interaction (Lerner, 1978, 1979), is associated with a probabilistic–epigenetic, developmental–contextual, or developmental–systems perspective (Ford & Lerner, 1992; Gottlieb, 1983, 1991, 1992, 1997; Kuo, 1967; Thelen & Smith, 1998). As noted in our previous discussions of probabilistic epigenesis, this concept stresses that organism and context are always embedded each in the other (Lerner, Hultsch, & Dixon 1983); the context is composed of multiple levels of organization, with variables associated with each level changing interdependently across time (i.e., historically). Because organisms influence the context that influences them, they are thus efficacious in playing an active role in their own development (Lerner & Busch-Rossnagel, 1981a, 1981b; Lerner & Walls, 1999).

Moreover, as discussed in Chapter 3, the mutual embeddedness of organism and context means that any attribute of the individual (e.g., a physical characteristic such as body build or a behavioral attribute such as a rhythmic temperamental style) will have different implications for developmental outcomes under different contextual conditions (e.g., in regard to different cultural ideas of bodily attractiveness or in regard to the requirements placed by different parents on their children in regard to the regularity of their sleep–wake cycles). The individual characteristic is given its functional meaning only by virtue of its relation to a specific context and, since contexts vary (among themselves and each across time), the same characteristic will have a different import for development. In turn, the same contextual condition will lead to alternative developments because different individuals interact with it. Thus, as I have noted earlier, a given characteristic of individuality only has meaning for human development by virtue of its timing of interaction; that is, its relation to a particular set of time-bound contextual conditions. In turn, the import of any set of contextual conditions for psychosocial behavior and development can only be understood by specifying the context's relations to the specific developmental features of the individuals within it. As discussed in Chapter 3, this central role for the timing of individual–context interactions in the determination of the nature and outcomes of development is, of course, the probabilistic component of probabilistic epigenesis (Gottlieb, 1970; Scarr, 1982; Scarr & McCartney, 1983).

To illustrate the nature of organism–context relations described in this view with an example that is returned to in Chapter 17, consider the implications of a child's temperamental individuality for his or her personality development. It may be argued that the significance of this individuality lies not in any organismic association between particular features of temperament (e.g., high activity level or low regularity or rhythmicity of biological functions) and specific aspects of personality (e.g., adjustment). Instead, it has been suggested (e.g., in Chapter 3), that what temperament implies for personality development lies in the level of congruence, match, or "goodness of fit" (Lerner & Lerner, 1983, 1989) between a particular aspect of temperament and the demands or presses of the psychosocial and physical contexts. For instance, some parents may desire or demand highly regular eating, sleeping, and toileting behaviors from their children, whereas for other parents such biological rhythmicity may be irrelevant (see Super & Harkness, 1981). A child who is biologically arrhythmic would not match the former type of demands, and as such, the import of this feature of temperament might be to promote poor parent–child relations; a consequence of a history of such relations might be poor adjustment.

Three features of this illustration are important to note here:

1. The import of the person's organismic characteristics for development is explained by reference to the *relation* between the organismic characteristics and the characteristics of the context.
2. Therefore, the presses and demands of the organism's context must be understood to be part of the explanation of individual development, and it should be emphasized that such demands vary across societies, cultures, and history (Lerner & Lerner, 1983, 1989; Super & Harkness, 1981). Thus, the multilevel influences on development—the person, the immediate context, and the broader societal, cultural, and historical settings—are apparent (cf. Bronfenbrenner, 1977, 1979; Bronfenbrenner & Morris, 1998).

3. Finally, despite the importance of the context, it is the organism's characteristics—in providing a fit or a lack thereof—that establish the adaptive, maladaptive, or neutral link between organism and setting. Thus, any contextual theory that aspires to take a *developmental* perspective in attempting to understand the possibilities for change provided by the context (Lerner, 1984, 1985), must not ignore the structural and functional nature and characteristics of the organism. As has been noted in previous chapters and is stressed again later in this chapter, this point has been emphasized by theorists forwarding "probabilistic–epigenetic, organismic" ideas of development (Gottlieb, 1970, 1976a, 1976b, 1983, 1991, 1992, 1997; Kuo, 1967, 1976; Lerner, 1976, 1978, 1979, 1980, 1982, 1984, 1991, 1996, 1998b; Schneirla, 1956, 1957).

In short, several human developmentalists have maintained that, as a consequence of person–context interdependency, a potential for plasticity exists across the life span. That is (as noted in Chapter 5, in our discussion of continuity–discontinuity across life), if intraindividual development is a synthesis of intraorganism and contextual variables, and if the context does and/or can be made to change, then the person's developmental trajectory can, at least in part, be altered. It follows that constraints on development—for example, those imposed by genes or early experience—are not so great as advocates of noncontextual orientations have previously argued (Brim & Kagan, 1980a, 1980b; Bruer, 1999; Lerner 1984; Nelson, 1999).

In contemporary human development, there are several perspectives that are consistent with the probabilistic–epigenetic conception of interaction found in a developmental systems view (of which developmental contextualism is but one instance: see Lerner, 1998a). For instance, in the fifth edition of the *Handbook of Child Psychology* (Damon, 1998), Volume 1 was devoted to "Theoretical models of human development" (Lerner, 1998a). The majority of the 19 chapters in this volume (i.e., Baltes et al., 1998; Brandtstädter, 1998; Bronfenbrenner & Morris, 1998; Cairns, 1998; Csikszentmihalyi & Rathunde, 1998; Elder, 1998; Fisher & Bidell, 1998; Fisher, Jackson, & Villarruel, 1998; Gottlieb et al., 1998; Lerner, 1998b; Magnusson & Stattin, 1998; Overton, 1998; Shweder et al., 1998; Thelen & Smith, 1998; Valsiner, 1998; Wapner & Demick, 1998) advanced ideas consistent with developmental systems theory. As such, these positions are compatible with the view that nature and nurture, organism and context, heredity and environment, relate to each other in dynamically interactive manners; that is, the variables involved in development interact in a manner reflective of fused levels of organization, of integrative levels within a developmental system (Ford & Lerner, 1992; Schneirla, 1956, 1957; Tobach, 1981).

In the remainder of this chapter, we explore in some detail the ideas involved in understanding the structure and function of the integrated levels that Schneirla described as providing the basis of the dynamic interactions found in the developmental system. Schneirla's ideas provided not only a useful framework for understanding the role of the developmental system in fostering continuity and discontinuity across the course of life, but also they afforded a basis for elaborating a life-span view of human development (Baltes, 1987, 1997; Baltes et al., 1998, 1999) and other theoretical models that stress the reciprocity of person–context relations across life (i.e., action theory; Brandtstädter, 1999; Brandtstädter & Lerner, 1999).

THE CONTRIBUTIONS OF T. C. SCHNEIRLA

The work of T. C. Schneirla and his colleagues (Ethel Tobach, Daniel Lehrman, Herbert G. Birch, and Howard Moltz) represents an attempt to deal systematically with the problems of behavioral development without resorting to facile solutions. That is, Schneirla rejected, as naive and overly simplistic, theoretical conceptions that stressed the exclusive (split) role of either nature (hereditarily preformed or predetermined mechanisms) or nurture (shaping of behavior solely by environmental stimulation). Thus, consistent with the arguments presented in Chapter 3, Schneirla focused on a dynamic interaction between nature and nurture factors in attempting to find the sources of behavioral development. Because he rejected the notion that development is a simple process, he also rejected the idea that methods used to study this process can be simple. Hence, in commenting on the relation between a nature-based variable, maturation, and a nurture-based variable, experience, Schneirla (1956) said:

> It would seem to be the prevalence of an intimate, dynamic relationship between the factors of maturation and experience that renders analytical study of

behavioral ontogeny so difficult. Methods must be devised appropriate to the complexity and subtlety of these processes. In such work, little may be expected from attempts to estimate the specific or the proportionate contributions of the innate vs. the acquired in ontogeny. (p. 407)

Thus, Schneirla presented a theoretical position consistent with what we have said about probabilistic–epigenetic conceptions of development. Let us turn, then, to a more detailed analysis of the ideas of Schneirla and his associates so that we may evaluate the extent to which such conceptions provide a fruitful, integrative framework with which to consider concepts of development pertinent to the role of developmental systems in human development.

Structure–Function Relations

One of Schneirla's major concerns as a comparative psychologist was with the relation between an organism's functioning (e.g., its motor behavior in its ecological niche) and the structure underlying the function (e.g., the neural and hormonal processes involved in such behavior). This concern arises because, in comparative psychology, one is interested in learning whether the relation between structure and function is similar or different in different species (i.e., across phylogenetic levels).

Schneirla (1957) argued that the relationship between structure and function is not always the same for organisms of different phylogenetic levels. The same functions (e.g., learning) may be present in both a rat and a human or in an infant human and an adult human. Moreover, this function may play an analogous role for each of these organisms. That is, it may allow the organism to adapt to its environment, to survive. However, the presence of this analogous function in and of itself in no way indicated that the underlying structure of learning is the same for an infant versus an adult, or for a rat versus a person.

Schneirla suggested, on the contrary, that the relation between structure and function is exceedingly complex and—more important—that it will occur with varying degrees of directness at different phylogenetic and ontogenetic levels (cf. Bitterman, 1965, 1975, discussed in Chapter 5). Thus, the degree of directness of relation between the two would be different for the ant, bird, rat, dog, ape, and human being.

Schneirla noted (1956) that behavioral patterns often reached similar developments in different phylogenetic levels as a result of parallel adaptive, evolutionary process. To some, such a similarity indicates equivalent underlying organization, or structure. But such an assumption is neither empirically universal nor logically necessary because the attainment of equivalently adaptive developments says nothing whatsoever about the antecedent developmental processes that brought about these adaptive functions. All mammals learn; but it is not necessarily correct to assert that, because both a rat and a human being develop this adaptive function, the laws, or structures, underlying their learning are the same (again, see the discussion in Chapter 5 of the work of Bitterman, 1965, 1975, in regard to phyletic differences in learning). The developmental processes by which learning comes about may be totally different for these two organisms. That is, antecedent developmental processes may be completely disparate for two different types of organisms, despite the fact that both demonstrate a similarly adaptive function. Thus, as Schneirla pointed out, these processes "may involve complex anticipations, as in a socialized human being, or may be reflex-like and automatic, as in a lower invertebrate" (1956, p. 392).

In essence, Schneirla suggested that the underlying structure of even evolutionarily similar behavioral developments is different for different phylogenetic levels. Although certainly not denying that structure underlies function, he emphasized, rather, that one must expect the relationship between structure and function to be differentially direct at different phyletic levels. Each level must be understood in and of itself, because the structure–function relationships of other phylogenetic levels will not hold for another level in question. In other words, the laws of one phyletic level will not apply to another, since the same structure–function relationships do not hold. Therefore, one cannot completely understand one phyletic level by merely reducing it to another. Schneirla also viewed ontogenetic development in a manner analogous to phylogenetic development. That is, ontogenetic processes proceed through levels just as phylogenetic processes do. Accordingly, structure–function relations between different ontogenetic levels can also be expected to be different.

It should be clear, then, that Schneirla took a now-familiar viewpoint. He advanced the probabilistic–epigenetic organismic notion of qualitative discontinuity between levels: Each different phylogenetic level has its own structure–function relationship or, in other words, its own law (Novikoff, 1945a, 1945b). Within this perspective

(Novikoff, 1945a), levels are conceived of as integrative organizations. That is:

> The concept of integrative levels recognizes as equally essential for the purpose of scientific analysis both the isolation of parts of a whole and their integration into the structure of the whole. It neither reduces phenomena of a higher level to those of a lower one, as in mechanism, nor describes the higher level in vague nonmaterial terms which are but substitutes for understanding, as in vitalism. Unlike other "holistic" theories, it never leaves the firm ground of material reality. . . . The concept points to the need to study the organizational interrelationships of parts and whole. (p. 209)

Moreover, Tobach and Greenberg (1984) stressed that:

> The interdependence among levels is of great significance. The dialectic nature of the relationship among levels is one in which lower levels are subsumed in higher levels so that any particular level is an integration of preceding levels. . . . In the process of integration, or fusion, *new* levels with their own characteristics result. (p. 2)

Thus, because of its own laws, each different level is qualitatively different from the next. This is true, Schneirla asserted, if one is talking of different phylogenetic levels—which he called *psychological levels*—and if one is talking of different ontogenetic levels—which he called *functional*

Ethel Tobach

orders—because "on each further psychological level, the contribution of individual ontogeny is a characteristically different total behavior pattern arising in a different total context" (Schneirla, 1957, p. 82).

In addition to adopting the probabilistic–epigenetic, organismic viewpoint, Schneirla also adopted the levels-of-organization compromise discussed in Chapter 3. Schneirla asserted that knowledge of the structural basis of function is not sufficient for understanding behavioral developments at any given psychological level or functional order. Structure does not simply give you function because "something else" is needed, and as such, each different level must be studied in its own terms. That "something else" is, of course, the environmental, or experiental, context within which the organism develops. Structure–function relationships can be understood only in interrelation with their environmental context. Thus, Schneirla asserted that, to understand development, one must conceive of the nature–nurture interaction in a dynamic way (cf. Thelen & Smith, 1994, 1998).

Hence, we may restate the levels-of-organization compromise—discussed in Chapter 3—in terms of Schneirla's position: For any given psychological level or functional order, the laws (variables) of the structural (lower) level are involved with (implied in) the laws of the functional, behavioral (higher) level, but function cannot be understood merely through an understanding of structure. Knowledge of structure alone is insufficient for understanding function. This is the case because function develops out of a complex (dynamic) interaction between an organism's structure and the environmental variables impinging on it, an interaction that produces a qualitatively different developmental context at each different level.

In sum, Schneirla saw phyletic and ontogenetic development as involving, at least in part, qualitative discontinuity. He saw different structure–function relationships at different levels. He maintained that the same psychological function may thus be underlain by different processes at different points in development. Thus, Schneirla took a position that is central in developmental theory and is shared by many other organismically oriented developmental theorists (e.g., Piaget, Werner, and Kohlberg). The same behavior is often determined by different variables—by qualitatively different phenomena (e.g., by features of different stages of development; see Chapter 15)—at different points in ontogeny (or phylogeny).

Behavioral Stereotypy Versus Behavioral Plasticity

Schneirla suggested that psychological levels differ qualitatively from one another because different organisms have qualitatively different structure–function relationships. These relationships are based on different organismic structure–experience interactions. But what is the nature of these different interrelationships? What is the basis of the differences between different psychological levels? This question has been a critical one in comparative psychology and evolutionary biology, and it pertains to the nature of species' evolutionary changes, the character of interspecies differences in species' evolutionary changes, and the task of providing criteria for discriminating among species levels. In addressing these issues, many evolutionary biologists and comparative psychologists have made use of the concept of *anagenesis* (Yarczower & Hazlett, 1977). Although it is not an uncontroversial idea (Capitanio & Leger, 1979; Yarczower & Yarczower, 1979), most scientists agree that "anagenesis refers to the evolution of increased complexity in some trait" (Capitanio & Leger, 1979, p. 876). For example, Dobzhansky et al. (1977) note that "Anagenetic episodes commonly create organisms with novel characters and abilities beyond those of their ancestors" (p. 236), or simply, that anagenesis is an "evolutionary advance or change." Similarly, Jerison (1978) noted that an evolutionary analysis of progress from earlier to later species "is called 'anagenetic' and is about progressive evolution," and indicated that in such an analysis "the objective is to identify grades in evolution" (pp. 1–2). Thus, an anagenetic (evolutionary) advance would place a species at a different evolutionary grade (Gould, 1976), and location of a species at a different grade would mark interspecies differences in evolutionary changes (i.e., anagenesis; Dobzhansky et al., 1977; Jerison, 1978).

However, it is clear that an advance in complexity is often difficult to identify, for example, what specific structural and behavioral criteria need to be met (cf. Capitanio & Leger, 1979)? This difficulty is especially problematic when human social behavior is involved (Yarczower & Hazlett, 1977; Yarczower & Yarczower, 1979; see also Sampson, 1977). However, Schneirla (1957, 1959; Tobach & Schneirla, 1968), among others (e.g., Birch & Lefford, 1963; Sherrington, 1951; Tobach, 1978, 1981), provided a useful framework.

Schneirla (1957) proposed the use of a behavioral *stereotypy–plasticity continuum* to differentiate the levels of complexity representative of different species. If an organism's behavioral development is stereotyped, there is a relatively fixed relation between the stimulation the organism receives and the concomitant responses it emits; that is, an almost unchanging relation exists between what goes in (stimulation) and what goes out (response). What we see is little, if any, variability in response to stimulation. Thus, if we deprive a normal frog of food for some time and then present a fly to the frog in its immediate field of vision, we will inevitably see the frog flick out its tongue to catch the fly. Assuming that we take no steps to intervene in this interaction, and that the frog continues to exist in its natural habitat, we will see little variation in the response to this stimulation.

As discussed in Chapter 5, plasticity, on the other hand, refers to the ability to show varying responses to the same stimulus input (Lerner, 1984). That is, a more variable relation exists between what goes in and what will come out.

To illustrate, some people may be in the habit of "flicking out" their tongues whenever their favorite food goes by (e.g., dessert). However, at times a reprimand from our spouse (e.g., "If you get any fatter, you won't fit through the door.") will result in our varying our response to the dessert stimulus; we may take a smaller helping than usual, or perhaps none at all. Although it would be relatively easy to train a rat to find its way in a maze, it would be more difficult to train it to develop a large and flexible repertoire of

alternate routes that it could efficiently introduce when more habitual routes were blocked. Humans, however, develop this alternate-route repertoire quite readily. Hence, as illustrated in Figure 6.1, if our most direct—and, thus, habitual—route for driving from home to the market is suddenly blocked one day, we can quite efficiently adopt an alternate route.

An organism that shows stereotypy in its ontogeny develops little behavioral variability in response to stimulation. Alternatively, an organism that shows plasticity develops a relatively considerable degree of variability in response to stimulation. Moreover, as we might expect, organisms with differing degrees of plasticity or stereotypy are on different psychological levels; the more plasticity shown in an organism's development, the higher the organism's psychological level. Thus, as Schneirla stated, "The appearance of behavioral stereotypy through ontogeny, if found characteristic of a species, indicates a lower psychological level, whereas the systematic plasticity through experiences indicates a high level" (1956, p. 83).

Of course, neither plasticity nor stereotypy is an all-or-none thing. One cannot say that the behavior of a particular species is either all stereotyped or all plastic. Rather, we may think of stereotypy and plasticity as forming a continuum, with stereotyped and plastic behavior at either end. Different psychological levels will fall at different points along this continuum, and the closer any species is to the plasticity end, the higher its

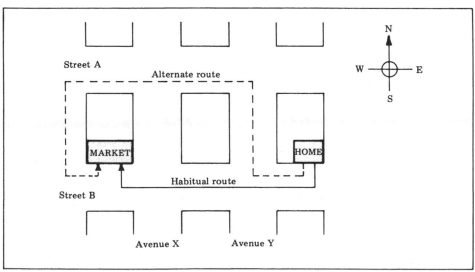

FIGURE 6.1
An illustration of human plasticity.

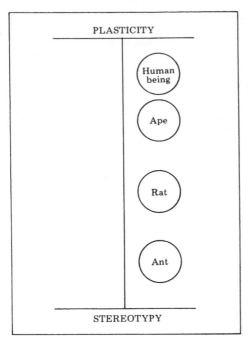

FIGURE 6.2
An illustration of a hypothetical stereotypy–plasticity continuum.

psychological level. A hypothetical example of the ordering of species of different psychological levels along this continuum is presented in Figure 6.2. Ants are at the lower end because their behavior is less plastic than that of any other represented species. Human beings are closest to the plasticity end because human behavior is more plastic than that of the other represented species, and, accordingly, the human psychological level is higher than that of any of the other species.

Hebb's A/S Ratio

What is the structural contribution to these contrasting functional capabilities? For example, what nervous system structures may contribute to the plasticity or stereotypy of different psychological levels? One answer to this question might lie in a concept found in Donald O. Hebb's (1949) writings.

The cerebral cortex of the brain of mammals (e.g., rats, monkeys, dogs, or human beings) has various sections. One section is comprised of nerve cells (neurons) that constitute the cerebral centers for sensory information—information that comes from the outside world through our receptors (e.g., the rods and cones of the retina of the eye) and into our bodies. Another area of the cerebrum is comprised of neurons that constitute our motor

cortex—that part of our cerebral cortex that sends messages to our muscles and thus allows us to behave. Still another section of our cortex is comprised of association neurons, cells that integrate and associate information from various parts of the brain. For example, one role of the association cortex is to integrate information from the sensory cortex—pertaining to what is stimulating us—with information from the motor cortex, relating to our (motor, or muscular) actions, or our behavior.

Now, it seems clear that the more association cortex we have, the more connections we can have between a given stimulus input and a behavioral output. That is, the more association fibers that exist, the more variable should associations be to any stimulus, and, accordingly, behavior should be more variable in relation to stimulus input. In 1949, Hebb proposed to express the relation between the amount of sensory cortex and the amount of association cortex in a species in terms of a ratio. This ratio was termed *the association cortex/sensory cortex ratio,* or simply the A/S ratio.

Some organisms have a low A/S ratio, expressed as A/S ratio <1.0; simply, they have more sensory cortex than association cortex. For such organisms, sensory input will be more directly related to response than it will for organisms with higher A/S ratios. With organisms that have

D. O. Hebb

relatively little association cortex in comparison with their sensory cortex, sensory input (stimulation) will more directly determine behavior. Such organisms can be called *sense-dominated*. Because such organisms have few association fibers with which to integrate their sensory input, their behavior in response to sensory input will be less variable. It will be stereotyped. It will be, relatively, directly controlled by environmental stimulation.

Animals with higher A/S ratios will, however, show relatively less sense domination. Animals with more association fibers relative to sensory fibers (animals whose A/S ratio ≥ 1.0) will integrate their sensory input with the information provided by their association fibers and thus demonstrate more variable behavior in response to stimulation. The behavior of such organisms will be more a product of an interrelation between their association cortex and their sensory cortex than would be the case with organisms having a low A/S ratio. Accordingly, their behavior will be more variable in response to stimulus (sensory) input. It will be more plastic.

Thus, differences in A/S ratios may account for different degrees of plasticity and stereotypy among different psychological levels. Consistent with Schneirla's views, Hebb (1949, p. 125) suggested that, for widely differing phylogenetic levels, a hierarchy of psychological complexity can be assumed that corresponds to gross differences in the proportion of sensory to association neurons. Similarly, Schneirla (1956, p. 411) pointed out that a deficiency in the brain's association capacity seems to be a prime condition for certain fixed responses to specific stimuli, since stereotyped response tendencies are strongest in animals with the lowest supply of association neurons.

In sum, we see that Hebb's notions allow us to speculate about a structural basis for the functional differences in stereotypy–plasticity seen on different psychological levels. Animals with more sensory cortex than association cortex are more stereotyped in their behavioral development than are animals with more association cortex relative to their sensory cortex. These latter animals are more plastic in their behavioral development than are the former. Thus, the higher an animal's A/S ratio, the more functionally plastic its behavioral development. Conversely, the lower an animal's A/S ratio, the more functionally stereotyped its behavior development. To make an analogy, then, low A/S ratios are to stereotypy (and low psychological levels) as high A/S ratios are to plasticity (and high psychological levels).

Ontogenetic Implications of Stereotypy–Plasticity and of the A/S Ratio

As might be surmised, Hebb (as well as Schneirla) maintained an active interest in the developmental implications of his ideas. Accordingly, Hebb qualified his notions about the A/S ratio by pointing out differences in the ontogeny of animals with different A/S ratios. We see that Schneirla, concerning stereotypy–plasticity, reached conclusions similar to those of Hebb.

Animals with low A/S ratios are more stereotyped in their eventual behavioral development and, accordingly, are on low psychological levels. Yet, such animals reach their final level of functional organization—of behavioral functioning—much sooner in their development than do animals with high A/S ratios. Animals with few association fibers compared to sensory fibers progress through their ontogeny relatively rapidly; they reach their final, albeit stereotyped, level in a relatively short time in their development.

One way of understanding this is to realize that such animals have comparatively few association-area cortex fibers that have to be organized through their development; they have relatively few associations that can be developed. Thus, they organize their association cortex comparatively rapidly. But at the same time, because of their comparatively limited association capacity, their behavior can never develop much variability, and hence it will be relatively stereotyped.

On the other hand, animals with high A/S ratios are comparatively more plastic in their eventual behavioral development and are, therefore, on higher psychological levels. However, such animals develop toward their final level of development relatively slowly. These high A/S ratio animals reach their final level of functional capacity—of behavioral organization—much later in their development than do low A/S ratio animals. High A/S ratio animals have more association cortex compared to their sensory cortex, and they progress through their ontogeny relatively slowly. These animals reach a higher, more plastic psychological level, but it takes them a longer time to do so.

In sum, lower A/S ratio animals develop more rapidly, but their behavior remains relatively stereotyped; it is sense-dominated and shows little variability. On the other hand, higher A/S ratio animals develop more slowly, but their eventual behavioral development will be relatively plastic; it will show considerable variability. For example, a rat is on a lower psychological level than is a human being. Similarly, the rat has a lower A/S ratio than does a human being. But, in the time span of just a few weeks, a rat may be considered to be fully developed, whereas a human infant after only a few weeks of life is not at all, of course, like an adult human in terms of behavioral or cognitive functioning. The human infant will take years to reach a level analogous to the one that the rat reaches in just a few short weeks. Yet, the human, when an adult, will be capable of considerably more complex, plastic behavior than any adult rat will ever be able to produce. In fact, this will be true of the not yet fully developed human; the human will surpass the adult rat while still a child.

An empirical instance of the point can be found in the results of a classic study by Kellogg and Kellogg (1933). The Kelloggs reared a newborn ape in their home and attempted to treat it like their own newborn child, who, by the way, also happened to be living there at the time. They diapered both infants and prompted their behavioral development, including language, in the ways that parents typically do. At first, the ape was ahead of their child in terms of behavioral development. Soon, however, the child overtook the ape and was never bested again.

Other lines of research support Schneirla's ideas about ontogenetic changes in stereotypy and plasticity. In order to illustrate this support, let us consider some issues in the development of perception.

Intersensory Integration: An Illustration

All species of animals have available processes that are adaptive; that is, every living species, by virtue of its existence, has processes that allow it to adapt to its environment. All species have ways of taking in food and eliminating waste products. I have noted that this similarity does not mean that all species have the same processes available to them. Although all species take in food and eliminate wastes, they may do these things in different ways. Thus, organisms at different psychological levels may use different processes to serve the same function. Both the one-celled amoeba and human beings take in food and eliminate wastes, but they certainly perform these adaptive functions in different ways. This is because there are new processes available at different psychological levels; there is qualitative discontinuity across psychological levels.

Accordingly, although all psychological levels have the capacity to react to stimulation, it is not appropriate to attribute the capacity of perception to all psychological levels. All psychological levels must have the ability to react to stimulation in order to survive, what Schneirla (1957) termed the capacity for *sensation*. Even one-celled protozoa have this capacity. Yet, it is not until we look at a much higher psychological level that we see the capacity for *perception*—that is, the ability to sense with meaning. Thus, at higher psychological levels a qualitatively discontinuous capacity emerges—perception—which allows the organisms of that level to adapt to their environment. These organisms have the ability, for example, to make associations with their sensations, to integrate their purely sensory information with other information available to them. Such organisms can show different responses to the same stimulus; they can associate a different output with the same input. Thus, through their association capacity (e.g., underlain by their A/S ratio), they sense with meaning.

If the capacity of higher psychological levels is qualitatively different from that of lower psychological levels, it follows that these differences should be reflected not in the degree to which different psychological levels can organize sensory information, but in the kind of organization they achieve (Schneirla, 1957, p. 96). That is, these differences should be represented not only in how much sensory information can be handled but also in what is done with that information. Higher psychological levels should show greater associative variability—greater plasticity—than should lower levels.

Accordingly, Schneirla suggested that as one moves to higher psychological levels, one will see that sensory experiences result not merely in the *fixation* of the effects of experience—that is, in the organism being able to develop a "trace effect" of a particular sensory input–reaction experience—but also in the *correlation* of these trace effects. In other words, organisms at higher psychological levels have the capacity for a kind of organization of sensory information that is different from the capacity of phylogenetically lower organisms. They have the ability to correlate or associate information coming from one sense modality (e.g., vision) with information coming from another sense modality (e.g., touch).

Thus, at higher psychological levels, organisms have the capacity of *intersensory integration,* the ability to transduce (i.e., transfer or transform) information from one sense modality to another. With this capacity, sensory input from vision, for example, may be "equated" with sensory input from touch; thus, the sensory input from the two different modalities (modes of sensing) can come to mean the same thing to the organism. For example, we can recognize a quarter by feeling or seeing the coin. We can recognize an ice cube by touching or seeing it. The sensations from either of these objects can mean the same thing to us even though they are delivered through different modalities.

Hence, as we move up the phylogenetic scale from lower psychological levels to higher psychological levels, we see perceptual ability emerging not because of new senses being present—not because higher psychological levels have more senses with which to fixate the trace effects of sensory experience than do lower levels—but because as we move to higher psychological levels better liaison emerges among existing senses. We see advances in the capacity to correlate information among the senses. We see increased intersensory integrative ability. Thus, as Birch and Lefford (1963) pointed out, "In the emergence of the mammalian nervous system from lower forms, the essential evolutionary strategy has been the development of mechanisms for improved interaction among the separate sensory modalities" (p. 3). Similarly, Sherrington (1951, p. 289) stated, "Not new senses, but better liaison between old senses is what the developing nervous system has in this respect stood for."

Accordingly, an organism of a high psychological level—for instance, a human—has the capacity to develop considerable intersensory integrative ability, to make considerable gains through sensory experiences. However, we have also seen that humans, with their high psychological level, correspondingly have a high A/S ratio. This means that although human beings are capable of high levels of behavioral development, it takes them a relatively long period of time, as opposed to animals, to reach this developmental level—the highest point of their functional order. In essence, we can expect human beings, although capable of considerable intersensory integrative ability, to develop this ability over several years in the course of their ontogeny. Simply, we may hypothesize that human intersensory integrative ability is a developmental phenomenon.

This hypothesis was tested in a classic study by Birch and Lefford (1963) of the ability of children of different ages (ranging from 5 to 11 years of age) to integrate information from three different sense modalities—vision, active touch (or the haptic sense), and passive touch (or the kinesthetic sense). Birch and Lefford used geometric forms such as blocks in the shapes of circles, squares, triangles, stars, and crosses as stimuli for the children. Two blocks were presented at a time. Sometimes, the same object was presented for each child to see and touch; at other times,

different objects were presented. In either case, each child was asked to judge whether the two blocks were the same or different.

Figure 6.3 depicts some of the results of this study. In support of the hypothesis that intersensory integrative ability increases with age (that it is a developmental phenomenon), Birch and Lefford (1963) found that "the ability to make the various intersensory judgments clearly improved with age" and concluded that "the findings strongly indicate that information received by young children through one avenue of sense is not directly transduced to another sensory modality. . . . In fact, it may perhaps be argued that the emergence of such equivalence is developmental" (p. 45).

In essence, Birch and Lefford (1963) provided strong evidence in support of the notion that the intersensory integrative ability of human beings reaches its eventual high level only after years of development. However, they also found that even their youngest research participants—the 5-year-olds—had relatively well-developed intersensory integrative ability. They suggested, however, that at younger ages (at about 3 years of age), this ability would be markedly inefficient but would rapidly improve.

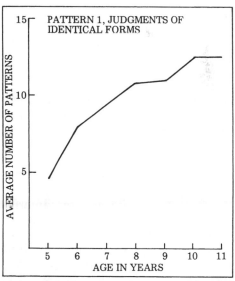

FIGURE 6.3

Some of the results of the Birch and Lefford study: Correct judgments for all intersensory pairings made when judging identical forms at different ages.

Source: Intersensory Development in Children. Copyright © 1963 by The Society for Research in Child Development. Reprinted with permission.

In a similar experiment, Abravanel (1968) studied intersensory integrative development in children ranging in age from 3.3 to 14.2 years. He found that the base level (the lowest level) for performing the various intersensory equivalencies occurred at about 3 years of age. After this time, however, integrative ability improved greatly through 7 years of age, when it reached a high level of efficiency. Thus, consistent with the notions we have derived from Schneirla's' ideas (1957) about perceptual development, we see that both the Birch and Lefford (1963) and the Abravanel (1968) studies provided findings that support the hypothesis that humans' ability to transduce information from one modality to another increases with age—that it is a developmental phenomenon.

Abravanel (1968) provided us with further findings that support some of Schneirla's other concepts about development, those pertaining to the role of the organism's own activity as a source of its own development (see, too, Chapter 9, where action theories of human development are discussed in greater detail; Brandtstädter, 1998, 1999; Brandtstädter & Lerner, 1999; Heckhausen, 1999). Abravanel found that increases in intersensory integrative ability were associated with changes in the type of exploration activity the children showed when actively touching the stimulus. Specifically, younger, less accurate children explored the stimuli by either gross or passive movements. Alternatively, older, more accurate children used finer and more articulated movements, exploring with the fingertips, for instance, rather than with the palms.

The role of the organism's activity in the development of its own plasticity has been identified in other human data sets reported by Piaget (1961, Piaget & Inhelder, 1956) and by Birch and Lefford (1967). In addition, experimental research with animals (Held & Hein, 1963) confirmed this role of the organism's activity. Littermate kittens were or were not allowed to make motor adjustments as they traversed a circular route. Those animals making the active motor adjustments later performed better on a test of depth perception—that is, on a visual cliff apparatus—than did the restricted animals.

Thus, the idea that human plasticity is a developmental phenomenon, advanced by Schneirla (1957) as well as by Hebb (1949), Piaget (1961; Piaget & Inhelder, 1956), Bühler (1928), and Baldwin (1897a, 1897b), finds empirical support. In addition, support for the notion that the organism itself actively provides a basis of this progression is evident.

Conclusions

Animals of low psychological levels will develop much more rapidly than will animals of high psychological levels. However, the gains that these two levels of animals will make through their ontogeny will be quite different. Animals on a low psychological level will be able to gain little behavioral variability through their ontogeny because the nature of their development is restricted by their structural limitations, by their low A/S ratio. Animals on a high psychological level will be able to gain considerable behavioral variability through their ontogeny because their development occurs within the context of broader structural capabilities, their high A/S ratio.

Schneirla's (1957) ideas have relevance, then, for both the phylogenetic and the ontogenetic changes of humans. Human evolution should be able to be characterized by progressively greater potentials for plasticity (Gould, 1977). In turn, however, although evolution has led to the presence of this potential, its basis in structure requires organization over the course of ontogeny (Gould, 1977; Johanson & Edey, 1981). As such, normative patterns of human ontogeny should be able to be characterized by the progressively greater presence of plasticity. There are data supporting these ideas.

In evolutionary biology, Lewontin and Levins (1978) provided evidence for the link between anagenesis, complexity, plasticity, and what they term *coupling–uncoupling* phenomena. Lewontin and Levins (1978) cite Hegel's warning "that the organism is made up of arms, legs, head, and trunk only as it passes under the knife of the anatomist," and note that "the intricate interdependence of the parts of the body . . . permit[s] survival when they function well, but in pathological conditions produce[s] pervasive disaster" (p. 79). However, such interdependence of parts is neither phylogenetically nor ontogenetically static. Relations among parts change over the course of evolution; often this involves the rapid evolution of some characteristics, or traits, and the relative constancy of others. In other words, whereas various aspects of an organism may be bound together as traits, if they are either units of development or selection they may lose their cohesion and evolve independently if the direction of selection is altered (Lewontin & Levins, 1978).

Indeed, there are several aspects of adaptation that suggest that tight integration of traits—or in Lewontin and Levins' terms, coupling—is disadvantageous. In considering this point, imagine that muscular strength, running speed, visual acuity, intellectual ability, eye color, handedness (whether one is right- or left-handed), and ability to digest specific foods (e.g., milk) were traits that were highly bound together in evolution. That is, imagine that these traits were coupled in the sense that selection pressures on one trait (e.g., decreasing the fitness, and, hence, likelihood of survival, of individuals who could not digest milk) would influence all the other characteristics equally (i.e., that the lack of survival of individuals who could not digest milk would mean that the traits of muscular strength, running speed, intellectual ability, etc. would be lost as well). Clearly, in such a situation a high degree of coupling would be a disadvantage.

Lewontin and Levins pointed out that if there is not high coupling a given characteristic may be subject to alternative selection pressures. If the optimal states of the characteristic under the separate pressures are not vastly different, then adaptation would be best served by a "compromise in which the part in question is determined by" all the presses. However, as illustrated by the imaginary example involving the digestion of milk, the uncoupling of traits may advantageous "as the number of interacting variables and the intensity of their interaction increases" (Lewontin & Levins, 1978, pp. 83–84). This is so because, in the face of these increases, it becomes increasingly difficult for selective pressures to increase fitness. Thus, species with very tight coupling will be unable to adapt as readily as those in which the different components that increase fitness are more autonomous. Indeed, the more strongly coupled and interdependent the traits of an organism, the more pervasive the damage done to an organism when some stressor overwhelms one particular trait.

Accordingly, what has occurred over the course of evolution is that the advantages of coordinated functioning and mutual regulation have come to oppose the disadvantages of excessive constraint and, hence, vulnerability; and that, at least at the human level, organisms may have the capacity to couple and uncouple traits successively. Ontogenetically, then, it may be that the most adaptive organisms are those that have the potential to develop the capacity to couple and uncouple traits as the context demands. We may suggest, therefore, that the direction of evolution at the human level has been to move toward providing the substrate for the coupling–uncoupling of traits. This is what may be involved in anagenesis. That is, if higher evolutionary grades are defined as being more complex, and if greater complexity means greater plasticity, a key instance of plasticity would be the

capability to couple, uncouple, and couple anew — either through recoupling or with ontogenetically unique couplings. This facility should become progressively established across ontogeny, as the physiological substrate of the psychological level of analysis becomes organized. Thus, we again reach the view that evolutionary and ontogenetic progression involves progressive change toward greater plasticity of functioning.

CONCEPTS REPRESENTING DEVELOPMENT

From this consideration of stereotypy–plasticity, it is clear that Schneirla was just as concerned with the problems of ontogeny as he was with those of phylogeny. He viewed both as progressing through a series of qualitatively different levels; he drew a distinction between the progression from one phylogenetic level to another, and the progression from one ontogenetic level to another, by his concepts of *psychological levels* and *functional orders,* respectively. Using Piaget's (1950, 1970) stage theory as an example (see Chapter 15), the first 2 years of life may correspond to the first part of the functional order of a human; the next 5 years to another, separate portion of the functional order; and the following 5 years to still another part of this functional order.

We have seen how the concepts of stereotypy and plasticity serve to differentiate between different psychological levels, and how the relative degree of stereotypy–plasticity may serve to characterize the psychological level of a particular animal species. Let us now turn to a consideration of Schneirla's concepts characterizing the functional order of a species.

A Definition of Development

To Schneirla (1957), *development* referred to successive changes in the organization of an organism, an organism that was viewed as a functional and adaptive system throughout its life. Providing, then, a forerunner of contemporary developmental systems theories (Ford & Lerner, 1992; Gottlieb, 1991, 1992, 1997; Gottlieb et al., 1998; Sameroff, 1983; Thelen & Smith, 1994, 1998; Wapner & Dimick, 1998), Schneirla's definition denoted that development involves successive change within a living, functioning, adaptive, individual system. By continually functioning in an adaptive manner, this system develops through successive changes throughout the life span.

But what are the characteristics of this system? What are the processes that comprise the determinants of the organism's development? Schneirla (1957, p. 86) suggested that two broad concepts represent the complex factors that make up the successive changes of development.

Maturation. The first of these two concepts is maturation. To Schneirla, maturation meant growth and differentiation of the physical and physiological systems of an organism. *Growth* refers to changes in these systems by way of tissue accretion, that is, tissue enlargement. *Differentiation* refers to changes in the structural aspects of tissues with age, that is, alterations in the interrelationship among tissues, organs, or parts of either of these.

For example, at specific points in the development of the embryo, different layers of cells exist. These cells mature not only via accretion (growth) but also through differentiation. Thus, when the embryo is in its blastula stage of development, it is divided into three layers of cells. One of these layers is termed the *mesoderm*. Eventually, as the embryo goes through changes and the cells of the mesoderm grow larger and differentiate, these cells will come to form the muscles and bones of the body. Hence, maturation refers to changes in the organism that results from the growth and differentiation of its tissues and organs.

Schneirla cautioned, however, against thinking that maturation could occur in any way independent of environmental contribution. Consistent with what we discussed in Chapter 3 about the probabilistic–epigenetic position on the nature–nurture issue (Gollin, 1981; Gottlieb, 1970, 1983, 1991, 1992, 1997; Tobach, 1981), Schneirla emphasized that maturational pro-cesses must *always* occur within the context of a supportive, facilitative environment; because of this interdependence, the exact path that maturation will take will be affected by what is happening in the environmental context of the organism. Just as maturation is not independent of environment, structure is not independent of function. Hence, as Schneirla (1957) stated:

> Maturation is neither the direct, specific representative of genetic determination in development, nor is it synonymous with structural growth. Much as an environmental context is now recognized as indispensable to any development, students of behavioral development . . . emphasize the roles of structure and function as inseparable in development. (p. 86)

Experience. The second concept needed to represent the complexity of the factors comprising developmental changes is therefore *experience*. To Schneirla, experience referred to all stimulus influences that act on the organism throughout the course of its life. Experience is a very broad, all-encompassing concept in his view. Any stimulative influence, any stimulus that acts on the organism in any way, is part of experience; and this stimulative influence can occur at any time in the organism's journey from womb to tomb. Experience may affect the organism at any time in its ontogeny.

It is clear, then, that experience can affect the organism before it is born. For example, stimulative influences may act on the fetus in the form of chemicals, drugs, or disease entities. Thus, a baby whose mother contracts German measles (rubella) during the early part of her pregnancy can be acted on in an adverse way. The effects of such an experience may be a deformed heart or blindness. Similarly, experience will obviously affect the organism after it is born. This may also take the form of diseases or accidents, but it can include experiences such as the type of care the infant receives and the support he or she has for positive, healthy development.

In sum, experience is a term representing any and all stimulative influences acting on the organism as it develops. These influences may result from events taking place within the organism's body (endogenous stimulative influences) or outside the organism's body (exogenous stimulative influences; influences of the context or the ecology of human development). In either case, experience acting on the organism provides one of the two interacting factors determining development. Let us look, then, at how experience interacts with maturation to affect development.

The role of maturation–experience interaction in developmental progress. Experience is necessary for any and all developments throughout ontogeny. Experience always has an effect on the organism, and in a specific way. Experience results in *trace effects*. To Schneirla (1957), trace effects are organismic changes that resulted from experience and that, in turn, influenced future experience. Experience effects changes in the organism, and these changes—these trace effects—influence how future experience will act on the organism. In other words, when experience acts on the organism, it will leave a trace of its action, and this trace effect becomes part of the organism and, thus, changes the organism's character. Hence, any later experience that acts on the organism will act on a *different* organism—an organism that now has a residual effect, a trace effect, of its previous experience. The second experience will result in an effect different from what would have happened had the previous experience not acted.

For example, a young child may have an experience that results in a physical disability (e.g., lack of mobility in his or her limbs). Because of this condition, which changes the character of the organism, future experiences (e.g., exposure to a physical education program) will influence the child differently than if the child had not had that previous experience.

However, the possible effects of experience are limited by the maturational status of the organism. The effect of the same experience will be different at different points in the organism's development because the organism will be at different levels of growth and differentiation at those times. Thus, because the organism's sensory, association, and motor portions of the nervous system mature with time, the effects of experience are limited.

For example, an infant is capable of perception and can form trace effects resulting from some types of perceptual experience (e.g., involving a mobile hanging over his or her crib) (Bower, 1966). At later developmental stages, the same child will be capable of developing trace effects as a result of the perceptual experiences involved in reading. However, these later experiences would not have resulted in the same trace effects had they been presented to the relatively physiologically immature infant. Alternatively, the trace effects that obtain as a result of the perceptual experiences involved in reading could never have occurred when they did had the child not had a particular series of perceptual experiences since infancy (e.g., becoming familiar with the forms or shapes in the mobile), resulting in trace effects. In sum, the nature of the behavioral gains that can result from experience are limited by the relative physiological maturation of the organism (Schneirla, 1957, p. 90).

However, maturation also has limits. These limits are imposed by experience. Consistent with the probabilistic–epigenetic, interactionist view he espouses, Schneirla (1957, p. 90) pointed out that the limitation of experience imposed by maturation is in turn limited by the developmental level of the organism—by the attained functional order the organism has reached in its ontogeny. The growth and differentiation of maturation do not occur without the supportive, facilitative effects of experience. This experience, leaving its trace effects on the organism, provides the milieu within which maturation occurs. Inappropriate experiences—such as loss of oxygen supply during the perinatal period—will not allow maturation to proceed as it would have had the inappropriate experience not occurred. Thus, maturation must interact with experience in order for development to proceed, and, in turn, the effects of experience are constrained or framed by their interaction within the limits imposed by the organism's maturational status.

Hence, a complex interaction between experience and maturation provides the basis of behavioral development. This dynamic interaction is represented schematically in Figure 6.4. Experience results in trace effects, but the nature of the trace effects is limited by the maturational status of the organism. In addition, this interaction determines what behavior the organism can develop at any particular time in its ontogeny. The experience–maturation interaction provides the basis for the developmental stage reached at a particular time in an organism's ontogeny. In turn, this developmental stage, comprising the result of the interaction between experience and maturation, provides (a) the milieu within which further maturation proceeds, does not proceed, or proceeds at a different rate; and (b) the milieu that determines what trace effects will result from further experiences. In sum, Schneirla said: "The nature of the gains made through experience is both canalized and limited by the relative

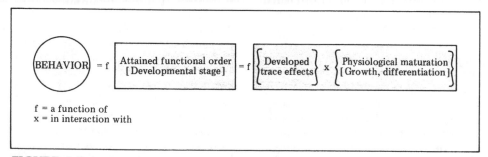

FIGURE 6.4
A complex interaction between experience and maturation provides the basis of behavioral development.

maturity of species-typical afferent, neural, and efferent mechanisms, in dependence upon the developmental stage attained" (1957, p. 90).

What we have seen to this point, then, is that behavior emerges through the course of development as a function of an interaction between experience and maturation. If appropriate experiences do not occur or, conversely, if inappropriate experiences occur, maturation will not proceed as it otherwise would have; accordingly, the behavior that would have developed will not, therefore, develop at that time. In other words, if inappropriate experiences occur (such as disease, loss of oxygen supply, or loss of a mother's nurturance), or if appropriate experiences occur but do so at a time too late for typical development to proceed, then maturation will not develop typically. It follows that the behavior that would usually have developed will be altered.

Conversely, if maturation does not proceed as it typically does (because of a lack of supportive, facilitative experiences), then the effects of experience—the trace effects—will be altered; in turn, the behavior that emerges at a particular point in time will be different. What we see, then, is that the ordered emergence of behavior in development depends centrally on the nature and timing of experience–maturation interactions. The attainment of developmental stages is dependent on the quality and timing of the variables involved in this dynamic interaction.

Conclusions

Thus, it seems clear that Schneirla's viewpoint is an exemplar of the probabilistic–epigenetic position discussed in Chapter 3. Schneirla emphasized that the nature and timing of interactions between maturation and experience are central in determining behavioral development. Moreover, the nature and timing of this interaction cannot necessarily be predicted in advance for every organism within a species. At best, we can say only that if the nature and timing of the maturation–experience interaction occur in certain ways, then behavior will probably develop along certain lines.

Accordingly, norms for development, which are statements about when in people's lives a particular behavior is typically seen, can be used only as general guidelines for considering development. Statements such as "babies will sit up at 6 months of age" "babies will say their first word at 11 months of age," or "babies will walk at 14 months of age" can be considered only as statements that apply in general terms. They may apply to a given group as a whole, but they may not necessarily

apply to any individual in that group. That is, such norms do not mean that babies must do these things at these times in order to be considered normal. Rather, they mean only that for a given large group of babies, an average time exists for the emergence of a particular behavior. At the same time that this norm exists, however, differences among individuals (i.e., interindividual differences) also *necessarily* exist. Different people show a behavior either before or after the norm for their group. In fact, we would expect all people *not* to reach the same level of development at the same time.

In sum, to Schneirla any behavioral development that occurs is obtained through a bidirectional (reciprocal) interaction between maturational and experiential factors. Thus, the emergence of any behavior at any time in an organism's development is dependent on the nature and timing of this interaction. In other words, behavioral development is not dependent on maturation or experience alone. This is because "factors of maturation may differ significantly in their influence upon ontogeny, both in the nature and in the timing of their effects, according to what relations to the effects of experience are possible under existing conditions" (Schneirla & Rosenblatt, 1963, p. 288). Hence, from Schneirla's theoretical point of view, any notion of behavioral development that stresses the exclusive contribution of either maturational or experiential factors (or biological or contextual, or nature or nurture factors) is incorrect.

Of course, Schneirla's model of development, reflecting a stress on the developmental system as causal in human development, and linked to philosophical notions that integrate probabilistically the views of organicism and contextualism, is not the only theoretical conception that is used to understand human development. Although Schneirla's ideas are conceptually compelling, and have a strong empirical foundation in biology, and comparative and developmental psychology (Aronson, Tobach, Lehrman, & Rosenblatt, 1970, 1972; Gottlieb, 1997; Gottlieb et al., 1998; Tobach & Greenberg, 1984), we have emphasized in Chapter 3 that there exist theories that derive from other philosophical positions and that do not stress nature–nurture fusion but, instead, stress either nature, nurture, or weak or moderate nature–nurture interactions.

On the one hand, Schneirla's ideas constitute historical and conceptual bases for other theories that stress how the integration of levels of biological-through-contextual/ecological organization provide a basis of human development. Accordingly, in several following chapters (Chapters 7 through 9 and 14), we consider such theories. That is, we discuss developmental systems theory in general and several specific instances of such an approach to human development (e.g., developmental contextual, life span, and action theories).

Schneirla's theory—and the developmental systems theories elaborated after it—constitute a counterpoint to theories that emphasize nature, nurture, or weak or moderate interactional views. Historically, it is arguably the case that Schneirla's ideas provided the strongest voice countering nature theories across much of the twentieth century (Aronson et al., 1970, 1972; Gottlieb, 1992, 1997). For instance, during this period, Schneirla and his colleagues (Lehrman, 1953; Tobach, Gianutsos, Topoff, & Gross, 1974; Schneirla, 1966) stood as the clearest alternative to nature theories of phylogenetic and ontogenetic change that were forwarded (e.g., Lorenz, 1965).

Regardless of how convincing one may find developmental systems theories, nature-oriented conceptions remain on the scholarly scene through this writing (e.g., Hernstein & Murray, 1994; Plomin, 1986; Rowe, 1994; Rushton, 1999; Spelke & Newport, 1998). After reviewing the noted instances of developmental systems theories, we discuss such nature-oriented theories in Chapters 10 through 14. Admittedly, after describing these nature-oriented positions, I use ideas that have their foundation in Schneirla's probabilistic–epigenetic conceptions—and that are more generally associated with developmental systems theory—to critique the nature-oriented positions.

However, to help prepare for this "point–counterpoint" approach to the presentation and analysis of developmental systems versus nature models of human development, respectively, it is useful to consider two concepts that provide exclusively nature explanations of behavioral development—the *critical-periods* hypothesis and the notion of *instinct* (or innate behavior). The critique of these concepts engaged much of Schneirla's attention during his scholarly career. Discussion of these concepts enables us to understand how Schneirla's views allow one to effectively counter views that suggest that nature variables alone can account for human development. Let us first turn to the critical-periods hypothesis.

THE CRITICAL-PERIODS HYPOTHESIS

The notion of critical periods in development was formulated in embryology. Within that area of science, the idea was advanced that the various parts of the whole organism (e.g., various organs or organ systems) emerge in a fixed sequence; more importantly, it was held that the parts that develop in a fixed sequence do so with just a certain amount of time allowed for each part to develop. It was believed that there was an overall timetable of development, and each part of the whole organism had its own fixed time of emergence, set by maturation. Each part had a critical period in which to develop.

This perspective holds that a part of the organism that is in its critical period can easily be stimulated. Such a part is highly responsive to both facilitating and disruptive influences. Thus, if the part does not develop normally or appropriately during its critical period, it will never have a second chance. Because the time limits of development are invariably fixed by maturation, even if the part does not develop, the focus of development will switch. It will shift to another organ system, in accordance with the predetermined timetable of development, and that different organ system will then be in its critical period of development. Hence, any part that does not develop during its own critical period will not have another chance.

Similarly, in human development such a critical period idea refers to a time in the ontogeny of a species during which it is crucial for a particular feature of development to emerge. The period is crucial because certain maturational processes then occurring would allegedly place time limits on the development (Schneirla & Roseblatt, 1961). For example, as we see in Chapter 16, Erik H. Erikson divides the human life span into eight stages, each of which may be interpreted as consistent with the definition of a maturationally based critical period (see Sorell & Montgomery, in press, for an alternative interpretation). In my view, the eight stages in Erikson's theory may be regarded as critical periods because each emerges in accordance with a maturational "ground plan," a developmental scheme that is built into the person (Erikson, 1959). Thus, Erikson maintains that, in the first year of life, the infant must develop a certain degree of a "sense of trust." If the infant does not develop this feeling at the time when it is supposed to develop, not only will there never be another chance but also the rest of that person's development will be unfavorably altered.

Clearly, the critical-periods hypothesis places primary dependence for healthy development on an intrinsic, maturationally determined timetable. What this formulation clearly indicates, then, is that maturation in and of itself sets critical time limits for development; there are maturationally circumscribed periods in an organism's development, and the time limits of these periods are somehow not related to experiential factors. However, from Schneirla's and others' probabilistic–epigenetic position (Gottlieb, 1970, 1983, 1991, 1992, 1997; Gottlieb et al., 1997; Tobach, 1981; Tobach & Greenberg, 1984), we can see that such a conception of critical periods is untenable. Rather than emphasizing the independent contribution of maturation, Schneirla would opt to investigate the process by which maturation and experience interact to enable a specific development to take place at a given time in ontogeny.

Schneirla did not say that certain developments were not critical for some later developments. He would agree to some extent with other researchers concerned with the critical-periods notion for (e.g., Scott, 1962) that there are critical phases of life, for instance for the development of learning. He would agree that what is learned at a certain time in an organism's ontogeny may be critical for whatever follows (Schneirla & Rosenblatt, 1963; Scott, 1962). But all this really says is that what happens at "Time 1" in a person's life may be very important—in fact, foundational or even essential—for what can or will happen at "Time 2." Such an assertion merely describes a relation between events that occur at two different times in ontogeny; it makes no statement about whether the first event was determined by maturation alone or by an interaction between maturation and experience (Bateson, 1983).

It is the source of the "criticalness" in development about which Schneirla argued. Simply, maturationally fixed time limits for development, arising without the contribution of experience, are inconsistent with his probabilistic–epigenetic position. Rather, Schneirla proposed a theory that placed "emphasis upon the fusion of maturation (growth-contributed) and experience (stimulation-contributed) processes at different stages in behavior ontogeny, together with the . . . contributions both of maturation and experience . . . , as well as the interrelations of these contributions. . . ." (Schneirla & Rosenblatt, 1963, p. 288). Indeed, Howard Moltz, a leading student of Schneirla's found experimentally that the time limits of certain purportedly critical periods (e.g., involving the immediately-after-hatching "following" behaviors of some species of birds) *could* be altered through specific manipulations of the birds' early visual experiences (e.g., Moltz & Stettner, 1961).

Weak and Strong Versions of the Hypothesis

Of course, Schneirla's view is not the only one that exists in regard to the meaning and bases of the concept of critical periods in development. Indeed, over the course of numerous reviews of the concept (e.g., Bateson, 1979, 1983; Colombo, 1982; Connolly, 1972; Hess, 1973; Hinde, 1962; Nash, 1978; Scott, 1962; Thorpe, 1961), several definitions of critical period have been forwarded. These definitions may be divided in several ways. For instance, Krashen (1975) distinguished between strong and weak versions of the critical-periods hypothesis. Consistent with McGraw (1943), the hypothesis by Colombo (1982) states in its weak form that:

> A critical period is a time during the life span of an organism in which the organism may be affected by some exogenous influence to an extent beyond that observed at other times. Simply, the organization is more sensitive to environmental stimulation during a critical period than at other times in its life. (p. 261)

Similarly, in Krashen's (1975) view, the weak version of the hypothesis states that there are periods in life when the development of a system can best be furthered by particular stimulation but that the system's development can, nevertheless, still occur after such a period.

In essence, then, in the weak form of the hypothesis, the critical period is really only a *sensitive period,* one wherein particular experiences may most readily or efficiently promote development of a system (e.g., cognition, vision, or language); nevertheless, similar or perhaps distinct experiences can foster the system's development after such a period, albeit with the requirement that the experience (the stimulus) be more intense in order to result in comparable development (MacDonald, 1985). Thus, this form of the hypothesis indicates that critical periods are not so critical after all, and that they are little more than labels applied to the well-known and hardly controversial observations that:

1. When a system is developing it needs stimulation to allow it to adequately do so (e.g., if we were totally deprived of light stimulation our visual system would not develop; Hebb, 1949), or simply that, as Schneirla (1957) explained, our systems need to be active to function adequately.

2. It is easier to influence a system—for better or worse—when it is in a state of development than after it has been fully organized (MacDonald, 1985).

In sum, in the weak form of the critical-periods hypothesis, particular experiences play a "noncontingent" (Moltz, 1973) role in development; although they are not absolutely necessary for adequate or healthy development to occur, particular experiences can enhance development due to the greater efficiency of their influence at a particular time. Thus, with such not-quite-critical critical periods, developmental deficits produced by the lack of a particular experience (e.g., language deficits due to the absence of an adequate language model) may be overcome by experiences in later life. If recovery of function can occur, this means that while a given period may be *optimal* (Moltz, 1973) for the development of a particular function, it is not a critical time for this development. As Bateson (1983, p. 8) puts it, "Once the mechanisms protecting behavior from change are stripped away by suitable treatment, change resulting from renewed plasticity is once again possible."

But we have noted that there is also a strong form of the critical periods hypothesis. In this version of the hypothesis, particular stimulation is needed at a particular time in order for normal development to proceed; in other words, if the appropriate stimulation does not occur when it is supposed to in life, then what will occur is "an irrevocable result not modifiable in subsequent development" (Scott, 1962). Thus, in such a formulation the organism *needs* certain stimulation for its continued normal development, and given inappropriate experience, it is *vulnerable to,* or *at risk for,* abnormal development during such a period (Colombo, 1982). Simply, for such a period, no recovery of function by later experience is possible (Krashen, 1975) and, as such, experience during this period has a "contingent" role (Moltz, 1973); that is, it is absolutely necessary for normal development.

The original instance of the strong version of the critical-periods hypothesis derives from the work of Konrad Lorenz (1937, see, too, Chapter 12). Lorenz introduced the concept of "imprinting" to describe what he believed to be an irrevocable social bond, or attachment, formed by newly hatched precocial birds (e.g., birds such as ducks or geese, that immediately after birth can move sufficiently to follow other animals). These birds followed the first moving object they saw (usually their mothers) during the first hours after birth. Although we have noted that Moltz and Stettner (1961) were able to manipulate (i.e., extend) the time period for imprinting through altering the visual experience of such birds (by placing a hood over their eyes that, while allowing light to come through, did not enable them to see any patterns or shapes), Lorenz (1937, 1965) claimed, nevertheless, that these first few hours were the critical period for imprinting to occur.

One may question the evidence that exists to support the reality of such strong critical periods. Colombo (1982) summarized data pertinent to the existence of strongly defined critical periods in regard to four areas of research: imprinting in birds, social development in rhesus monkeys, language acquisition in humans, and binocular vision development in mammals. Colombo (1982) noted:

> Nearly every demonstration of a critical period in behavioral development during the past 50 years has been followed by a demonstration of some behavioral recovery from the effects of critical period exposure or deprivation. The first example was with avian imprinting, in which Lorenz's (1937) claims of a tightly bounded period during which a permanent parent–offspring relationship was formed were rigorously tested. Subsequent evidence suggested that the critical period was not as temporally distinct (Brown, 1974) nor were the effects of stimulation within it as irreversible (e.g., Ratner & Hoffman, 1974; Salzen & Meyer, 1968) as Lorenz had originally thought (Bateson, 1966).

> After observing the results of social isolation during the first year of life, Harlow (1959, 1965) suggested the existence of a critical period for the development of social behavior in the rhesus monkey lasting (in one version) from birth to 250 days. The critical stimulus was apparently what he called "contact comfort," the absence of which during this early period resulted in permanent social/psychological maladjustment. Later, however, a series of experiments (Mason & Kenney, 1974; Novak & Harlow, 1975; Suomi & Harlow, 1972) demonstrated that with special interventions and patience, the adverse effects of deprivation during this period could be overcome.

> Language acquisition was another major developmental process to which critical period theory was applied, only to have that application subsequently questioned. Elaborating on a suggestion by Penfield and Roberts (1959) and through the use of data on early and late unilateral brain damage (e.g., Basser, 1962; Landsell, 1969) and the development of language in retardates (Lenneberg, Nichols, & Rosenberger, 1964), Lenneberg (1967, 1969) hypothesized a period of receptiveness to language lasting from ages 2 to 12. Language could be most easily acquired during this period; after this period, acquisition of a first language would be extremely difficult, if not impossible. The absolute irreversibility of the period's effects has been somewhat disconfirmed by subsequent investigation of acquisition after linguistic deprivation (Curtiss, 1977; Curtiss et al., 1975; Fromkin et al., 1974) and of second language learning (McLaughlin, 1977).

In initial studies of the critical period for the development of binocular vision, during which monocular deprivation resulted in anatomical degeneration of the deprived eye's pathways, complete domination of cortical physiology by the deprived eye, and apparent blindness of the deprived eye (e.g., Hubel & Wiesel, 1970) no recovery of function was reported (Blakemore & Van Sluyters, 1974; Hubel & Wiesel, 1970; Wiesel & Hubel, 1965b). Subsequent studies, however, demonstrated that recovery in at least the behavioral aspects of visual function could be obtained after the end of the period (e.g., Baxter, 1966; Chow & Stewart, 1972; Cynader, Berman, & Hein, 1976; Mitchell, Cynader, & Movshon, 1977; Timney, Mitchell, & Griffin, 1978; Mitchell, 1978). It is worth noting, however, that this recovery has yet to be demonstrated in primates (Crawford et al, 1975; von Noorden, Dowling, & Ferguson, 1970). (pp. 268–269)

Moreover, Colombo (1982) reviewed additional evidence that both the presumed onsets and terminations of critical periods—that is, the times in life when these periods are believed to begin and end—are influenced by variables both endogenous and exogenous to the organism. Thus, the time limits of these periods are neither as fixed and sudden as Lorenz (1937, 1965), for instance, maintained nor as impervious to contextual influences as Lorenz also believed. Colombo (1982) indicated that rather than a sudden and dramatic onset of sensitivity to a specific stimulus, sensitivity rises gradually to a peak and then gradually declines. These changes can be manipulated, for example, in regard to binocular visual development, by altering the amount of light in the rearing environment. We have noted that similar perceptual stimulation manipulations can alter the imprinting period in birds (e.g., Moltz & Stettner, 1961). In addition, pharmacological manipulations can extend the imprinting period of birds or even prevent it from occurring at all (Colombo, 1982).

Conclusions

There is no good evidence to support the strong version of the critical-periods hypothesis, as for instance advanced by Lorenz (1937, 1965). Nature variables *do not* prescribe fixed time limits within the life span wherein certain stimulation must occur for normal development to proceed. Rather, as a given system develops it is responsive to influences by variables outside the system but endogenous to the organism, and by variables exogenous to the organism. Indeed, Colombo's (1982) conclusions regarding the character of critical periods in development are comparable to those we would

expect from the basis of Schneirla's (1956, 1957) perspective. Colombo noted that "the emergence of a critical period . . . is based on, and may be predicted by . . . , the interaction of dynamic, developing systems, and as much effort should be directed toward identifying those systems and their interactions as toward identifying the period itself" (Colombo, 1982, p. 270).

Let us now turn to a second concept that, when also presented in its strong form, indicates that nature is the sole determinant of features of development. This is the concept of instinct, or innate behavior. As we discuss in greater detail in Chapter 12, this concept is centrally related to Lorenz's notions regarding the critical period for imprinting, and it is, in fact, Lorenz who made the most prominent contribution to the concept of instinct.

INSTINCT: INNATE BEHAVIOR

The notion of instinct, or instinctive behavior, is today perhaps most often associated with the work of Konrad Lorenz. Beginning in the 1930s, Lorenz, an Austrian-born zoologist and physician, studied certain types of behavior he termed *instinctive behavior*. By this term, Lorenz seemed to mean behavior that is preformed in the genotype. He contended that we inherit a genotype, and built into this genotype is a "limited range of possible forms in which an identical genetic blueprint can find its expression in phylogeny" (Lorenz, 1965, p. 1). In essence, then, Lorenz contended that there is an isomorphism between certain genetic inheritance and certain behaviors, and this is what he meant by instinctive behavior. Certain behaviors are preformed, or at least predetermined, and, thus, they are innate; they are built into the organism through genetic inheritance (the genotype) and, thus, are simply unavailable to any environmental influence.

More specifically, Lorenz saw certain inherited properties of nervous system structures as innate. Certain groups of neurons, he claimed, had built into them specific, distinctive properties (Lehrman, 1970). They obtained these properties directly from the genotype, with experience having no influence. For example, as Lehrman (1970, p. 24) pointed out, one such innate property of a given neural structure is "its ability to select, from the range of available possible stimuli, the one which specifically elicits its activity, and thus the response seen by the observer." That is, in the view of Lorenz, certain nervous system structures come with the innate ability to select out certain stimuli from the environment; these are the stimuli that elicit (bring forth) the built-in (predetermined) functional component of the structure, that is, the response (Lorenz, 1965).

Since, as Lorenz (1965) contended, experience plays no role in the presence of this instinctive behavior, one does not have to bother with the issue of how the relation between the stimuli and the responses comes to be established. All one has to say is that the behavior is there because it is innate. Then, one simply "explains" that innate behavior comes this way. Thus, to Lorenz, no further analysis was needed. In advancing this argument, Lorenz "solved" the problems of behavioral development by simply avoiding them—by defining them away.

In essence, then, Lorenz (1940, 1965) argued that genetic inheritance represented a "blueprint" for the development and final level and form of behavior; that is, it represented a set of directives that were unalterable by environment, experience, learning, socialization, and so on (cf. Lehrman, 1953, 1970). This genetic inheritance was believed to be able to circumscribe behavior so severely because it led directly to the formation of an instinct"—a predetermined, innate, and unmodifiable pattern of behavior specific to the species within which it exists. The behaviors associated with this instinct are then not capable of environmental, experiential modification.

Thus, behavior is constrained by instincts; variation in behavior beyond the limits imposed by the genetically fixed instinct is not possible. Such a conception of genetic influence precludes, then, a process analysis of the ways in which genetic and environmental variables contribute to behavioral development. In other words, Lorenz's (1940, 1965) conception of instinct precludes a consideration of how organismic and/or contextual processes may contribute to the development and organization of behavior. His conception eliminates any use for studying how behavior may be altered or enhanced.

From Schneirla's (1956, 1957, 1966) perspective, there are several problems inherent in Lorenz's ideas about instincts. By making a distinction between what is innate and what comes about through the environment and by implying that there exists a genetic blueprint that imposes fixed constraints on development, Lorenz opted for the "which one?" (nature or nurture) question, which we rejected as inadequate in Chapter 4. Thus, from our knowledge of Schneirla's probabilistic–

epigenetic position and from our discussion of the norm-of-reaction concept (in Chapter 4), we know that the notion of innate, or instinctive, behavior as formulated by Lorenz (1965) is not tenable for the following reasons:

1. Nature and nurture are inextricably bound; it is inappropriate to assert that genes can directly give you behavior. Nature variables need the supportive, facilitative influence of experiential factors in order to contribute to behavior. In turn, of course, experience needs nature variables with which to interact.
2. Because of this interdependency, it is inappropriate to speak of "innate" as meaning developmentally fixed—that is, to speak of certain behavior as being unavailable to environmental influence or to say that an organism must develop certain behaviors because it inherited a certain genotype (Lehrman, 1970, p. 23). The interdependence of the nature–nurture interaction is more complex. Because genes exert their influence through experiential interactions, and because the outcome of their influence will be different under different environmental (experiential) conditions (remember the norm of reaction), it is, therefore, incorrect to speak of a genetic blueprint. Simply, there is no isomorphism between genotype and eventual behavior.

Conclusions

Lorenz used the terms *innate* or *instinctive* to refer to behavior that is genetically fixed and, therefore, unavailable to environmental influence. However, from our knowledge of the probabilistic–epigenetic position we can reject such notions as being overly simplistic, as being based on faulty logic, and most important, as ignoring the problems and issues of behavioral development. To study the problems of behavioral development we must avoid terms such as *innate* (at least as employed by Lorenz 1940, 1965, 1966). Such terms end scientific investigation by simply saying that a behavior develops in a certain way because the organism is built that way. Thus, use of the terms *innate* or *instinctive* avoids assessing the processes by which behavior develops and, hence, is of little, if any, scientific use.

Perhaps, the most succinct summary of the criticisms that can be leveled against Lorenz's use of these terms was made by another one of Schneirla's students, Daniel Lehrman. In a classic paper, published in 1953, Lehrman noted:

The "instinct" is obviously not present in the zygote. Just as obviously it is present in the behavior of the animal after the appropriate age. The problem for the investigator who wishes to make a closer analysis of behavior is: How did the behavior come about? The use of "explanatory" categories such as "innate" and "genetically fixed" obscures the necessity of investigating developmental *processes* in order to gain insight into the actual mechanisms of behavior and their interrelations. The problem of development is the problem of the development of new structures and activity patterns from the resolution of the interaction of *existing* structures and patterns, within the organism and its internal environment, and between the organism and its outer environment. At any stage of development, the new features emerge from the interactions within the *current* stage and between the *current* stage and the environment. The interaction out of which the organism develops is *not* one, as is often said, between heredity and environment. It is between *organism* and environment! And the organism is different at each stage of its development. (p. 345).

Although the theoretical position of Lorenz is egregiously flawed conceptually and is, as well, empirically counterfactual, his ideas have had great influence (e.g., he was awarded the Nobel Prize in Medicine or Physiology in 1973), especially among nativistically oriented theorists. For instance, his ideas provided a major basis for sociobiological interpretations of human development (see Chapter 13). In that such nativistic interpretations are still forwarded at this writing (e.g., Rushton, 1999), the ideas of Lorenz merit greater scrutiny. This analysis is warranted also because, arguably, more so than any other nature-oriented theorist about human development, Lorenz's views were used (intentionally by Lorenz) to further the political agenda of the Nazi regime in Germany during the 1930s and 1940s (see Eisenberg, 1972; Kalikow, 1978, 1983; Lerner, 1992).

Accordingly, we have important reasons involving human development theory and its application to turn (in Chapter 12) to a fuller presentation and critique of the ideas of Lorenz. To enhance our ability to offer a persuasive developmental systems alternative to his nature, reductionistic position it is useful to consider yet another key concept associated with Schneirla's ideas. This concept helps us to go beyond the simplistic split of nature and nurture, on which ideas such as those of Lorenz rely, and, instead, to elaborate an action-oriented, dynamic view of the individual. In the view we now present, the individual—by being the organismic focus (or locus) of the integration of nature and nurture—is a key agent in its own development.

CIRCULAR FUNCTIONS AND SELF-STIMULATION IN DEVELOPMENT

From our previous discussion, we may see how Schneirla's theoretical position provides a way to conceptualize the dynamically interactive influences of nature and nurture in behavioral development. However, Schneirla suggested that there was a "third source" of development. In addition to the interaction of nature and nurture, Schneirla said, there was another source of an organism's development: the organism itself.

A "Third Source" of Development

As the organism develops, it attains certain behavioral characteristics through the effects of the maturation–experience interaction. These individual behavioral characteristics of the organism stimulate aspects of its environment (e.g., the organism's parents). This stimulated aspect then responds to the organism and this, in turn, again stimulates the organism. This is a *circular function*. The organism acts on its environment in a specific manner, and because of this particular action the environment acts on the organism in a specific way.

In other words, the organism develops distinct individual behavioral characteristics as a result of the specific maturational–experiential interaction influencing it, and as a function of these particular behavioral capabilities the organism behaves in an individually distinct manner in its environment. This action on the organism's environment provides a differential stimulus for reactions *from* the environment. The organism's individual characteristics of behavior may differentially stimulate other similarly aged organisms, the organism's parents, or even itself. The individualistic stimulation will evoke differential responses, which in turn will serve to stimulate the organism in a manner specific to it. This individualized pattern of stimulation (i.e., this specific feedback) becomes part of the experience that shapes the further individually distinct development of the organism (and, thus, the continuation of the circular reactions). In this way, the circular stimulative process, initiated by the organism's own individually distinct characteristics and actions, creates a source of the organism's own further, individual development.

Hence, the organism provides an important, ever-present source of its own development. This source must be considered as important as the other sources of the organism's behavior—those that influenced the behavior that originally initiated these circular functions. In commenting on the importance of this third source of development, Schneirla (1957) said:

> An indispensable feature of development is that of circular relationships of self-stimulation in the organism. The individual seems to be interactive with itself throughout development, as the processes of each stage open the way for further stimulus–reaction relationships depending on the scope of the intrinsic and extrinsic conditions then prevalent. (p. 86)

An illustration of the important role of circular functions and self-stimulation in the development of the organism may be offered. Because of the specifics of his maturation–experience interaction, one child develops a certain style of behavior as an infant, consisting of the following:

1. This baby's behavior lacks regularity. For example, the child might sleep for 2 hours, wake for 5, sleep for 3 hours, and then wake for 7. Sometimes, the baby might eliminate almost immediately after feeding, whereas at others there might be a considerable length of time between feeding and elimination.

2. The child, when awake, might show a considerably high activity level.

3. This might be combined with a relatively negative mood; when awake, the child cries or screams quite often.

4. When the baby does cry and scream, the child does so with a high intensity.

5. Finally, all of this high activity and loud crying and screaming seems to be set off by very minimal stimulation. That is, the child has a low threshold for responding.

Now, a second child may develop quite a different style of behavior as a result of the specifics of the child's maturation–experience interaction:

1. For example, this second child, in contrast with the first, might be regular; the child wakes, sleeps, and eliminates in predictable cycles.

2. When the child is awake, the child's activity level is of moderate magnitude.

3. This child has a positive mood; the child smiles and laughs a lot.

4. In addition, such behavior is of a moderate intensity.

5. Finally, the child maintains a moderate threshold for responding.

What we have, then, are two markedly different sets of individual behavioral characteristics. Both sets resulted from the specifics of each child's maturation–experience interaction; yet the implications of each set of characteristics for the development of the respective children are quite disparate (Chess & Thomas, 1984, 1999; Lerner & Lerner, 1983, 1989; Thomas & Chess, 1977). One might easily agree that the former child would present obvious difficulties for this child's parents. The child would stimulate reactions that would be quite different from those stimulated in the parents of the latter child. Compared with the former child, the latter would be easy to interact with and would not create any serious problems for the child's parents.

If parents could choose, before the fact, either of the above sets of characteristics for an expected child, I believe they would almost without exception choose the second set. They would rather have a predictable, smiling, moderately active baby than an unpredictable, loudly crying, highly active one; but parents cannot choose their baby's behavioral characteristics. The first baby's behavioral characteristics would create reactions in the child's parents, and these reactions would in turn stimulate the baby and become part of the child's experience. For instance, the parents of such a child might find it difficult to handle the baby for long lengths of time, and so they might make their interactions with the child relatively short and abrupt (cf. Brazelton, Koslowski, & Main, 1974). Alternatively, however, if the baby's behavioral characteristics had been like those of the second child, the baby would have evoked different reactions in the child's parents, and in turn would have had different stimulation become part of his or her experience. Thus, if the baby had been easier to handle, the baby's parents might have sought to extend their interactions with the baby. Moreover, the interactions might have been of a different quality (e.g., the interactions might have been warmer; Chess & Thomas, 1999).

From this example we can see that an organism's own behavioral characteristics do provide an important source of its own development, through the processes of circular functions and self-stimulation in development. In fact, the above illustration of this circular process is not quite imaginary. As cited above, it is based on the research findings of Thomas and Chess (1977; Chess & Thomas, 1984, 1999) and their colleagues (e.g., J. Lerner, 1983, 1984; Thomas et al., 1963), who—basing their work on Schneirla's conceptions about circular functions in development (Thomas & Chess, 1970)—studied the implications of behavioral individuality for the development of more than 100 children over the course of their infant-through-adolescent years. Their work is a focus of our discussion in Chapter 17.

Conclusions

Schneirla highlighted the necessity of focusing on the organism and its own actions in trying to understand the sources of behavioral development. His notions of circular functions and self-stimulation illustrate and emphasize a central idea in the probabilistic–epigenetic conception of development: The organism is central in its own development (Brandtstädter, 1998, 1999; Brandt-städter & Lerner, 1999; Gottlieb, 1983, 1997; Lerner, 1982, 1984; Lerner & Busch-Rossnagel, 1981; Lerner & Walls, 1999; Scarr & McCartney, 1983). An organism does not just sit passively; it does not just wait for maturation and experience to interact in order for its behavior to develop; and it certainly does not just passively wait for the environment to stimulate it to respond. Rather, the organism is always active, and its own activity provides an important source of its own development. Thus, development is in part a self-generated phenomenon.

Simply, then, the idea of an active organism dynamically relating to an active context is a central idea in Schneirla's view of development *and* in the developmental systems theoretical approach to human development for which it provides both a historical and a conceptual foundation. Accordingly, as noted earlier in this chapter, we turn, beginning in Chapter 7, to a discussion of developmental systems theory, to other theoretical positions associated with it (developmental contextualism, the life-span view of human development, and action theory), and to some of the nature-oriented theories (e.g., behavior genetics, instinct theory, or sociobiology) to which Schneirla's ideas and developmental systems conceptions provide a counterpoint.

Developmental Systems Theories

The explanatory categories generated by split positions stand in contrast to those generated by these relational positions (Overton, 1998). Relational positions aim to heal the biological/ social–cultural split both by offering categories that describe the biological, individual–psychological, and the sociocultural and physical–ecological levels of organization as alternative ways of viewing the same whole (see Gollin, 1981; Gottlieb, 1992, 1997; Lerner, 1986; Overton, 1973, 1994a, 1998; Tobach, 1981) and by suggesting that the integration of *action*—of the individual on the context and of the multiple levels of the context on the individual—constitutes the process of development (Overton, 1994b, 1998).

There are many theoretical instances of these relational positions (see Lerner, 1998a, for a presentation of the range of contemporary instances of these perspectives). As explained in prior chapters, based on ideas associated with probabilistic epigenesis, it is possible to group these relational theoretical alternatives to nature–nurture split positions under the label of developmental systems theories (e.g., Ford & Lerner, 1992; Gottlieb, 1997, Gottlieb et al., 1998; Sameroff, 1983; Thelen & Smith, 1994, 1998; Tobach & Greenberg, 1984).

There are several ways to begin to elucidate the key features of developmental systems theories. However, to build on our prior discussions of the work of T. C. Schneirla, it is useful to consider first the "psychobiological systems" view (Gottlieb et al., 1998) of another comparative psychologist: Gilbert Gottlieb.

When the history of developmental comparative science during this century is written, Gilbert Gottlieb's work—along with that of such eminent colleagues as T. C. Schneirla, Zing-Yang Kuo, Ethel Tobach, and Daniel S. Lehrman—will be seen as the most creative, integrative, generative, and important scholarship in the field (cf. Gariépy, 1995). For more than a quarter of a century, Gilbert Gottlieb (1970, 1997, Gottlieb et al., 1998) has given insightful theoretical, and ingenious empirical,

voice to the view that "an understanding of heredity and individual development will allow not only a clear picture of how an adult animal is formed but [also] that such an understanding is indispensable for an appreciation of the processes of evolution as well [and that] the persistence of the nature–nurture dichotomy reflects an inadequate understanding of the relations among heredity, development, and evolution, or, more specifically, the relationship of genetics to embryology" (Gottlieb, 1992, p. 137).

As illustrated by the brief descriptions of Gottlieb's ideas that have been noted in earlier chapters, he attempts to heal the nature–nurture split in biological and social science with the sort of relational conception depicted by Overton (1998) and others (e.g., Horowitz, 1987; Lerner, 1998b). He presented an integrative systems conception of development and of causality, and argued that "The cause of development—what makes development happen—is the relationship of the components, not the components themselves. Genes in themselves cannot cause development any more than stimulation in itself can cause development" (Gottlieb, 1997, p. 91). Similarly, he noted that "Because of the emergent nature of epigenetic development, another important feature of developmental systems is that causality is often not 'linear' or straightforward" (Gottlieb, 1997, p. 96). Gottlieb offered, then, a probabilistic conception of epigenesis that constitutes a compelling alternative to views of development that rest on a split nature–nurture conception.

GILBERT GOTTLIEB'S VIEW OF EPIGENESIS

Gottlieb (1992) presented a developmental systems perspective within which changing gene–context or organism–context *relations* are the key foci of both developmental and evolutionary analysis. As

Gilbert Gottlieb

such, he built on the work of Garstang (1922), de-Beer (1930, 1958), and Goldschmidt (1933), and noted that "Phylogeny is thus not the cause but the product of a succession of different ontogenies" (Gottlieb, 1992, p. 90). In other words, variation in development—for instance, behavioral novelty arising through the plasticity of dynamic organism–context relations (Lerner, 1984)—produces evolution; evolution does not produce development. "Ontogeny in each generation is a consequence of the coaction of hereditary or genetic factors and many different local environmental circumstances that determine the expression of the phenotype during the course of development" (Gottlieb, 1992, p. 95). In essence, then, Gottlieb agreed with Goldschmidt (1933, p. 543) that "The nature and working of the developmental process of the individual then should, if known, permit us to form certain notions regarding the possibilities of evolutionary changes." And what is the character of the developmental process as envisioned by Gottlieb?

Gottlieb's conception of the developmental process "is one of a totally interrelated, fully coactional system in which the activity of genes themselves can be affected through the cytoplasm of the cell by events originating at any other level in the system, including the external environment" (Gottlieb, 1992, pp. 144–145). Accordingly, based on the work of Schneirla (e.g., 1957), Kuo (1976), Lehrman (1970), and others (e.g., Tobach, 1981, and of course Gottlieb himself, 1970, 1976, 1983, 1991), Gottlieb (1992) provided a new definition of epigenesis:

Individual development is characterized by an increase of complexity of organization—i.e., the emergence of new structural and functional properties and competencies—at all levels of analysis (molecular, subcellular, cellular, organismic) as a consequence of horizontal and vertical coactions among its parts, including organism–environment coactions. (pp. 159–160)

Moreover, Gottlieb explained that, within the developmental system of coactions that he described, there existed both horizontal and vertical coactions. The former sort of coactions "are those that occur at the same level (gene–gene, cell–cell, tissue–tissue, organism–organism), whereas vertical coactions occur at different levels (gene–cytoplasm, cell–tissue, behavioral activity–nervous system) and are reciprocal, meaning that they can influence each other in either direction, from lower to higher, or from higher to lower, levels of the developing system" (Gottlieb, 1992, pp. 160–161).

In presenting his views of a developmental systems conception of development, Gottlieb noted that when one spoke of coaction between genes and the other levels of the system as being at the "heart of developmental analysis or causality what we mean is that we need to specify some relationship between at least two components of the developmental system" (Gottlieb, 1992, pp. 162–163). Indeed, Gottlieb (1992) contended that this systems view of individual development was the *only* "way to envisage the manner in which development must occur if a harmoniously functioning, fully integrated organism is to be its product" (pp. 165–166) . . . "[G]enes are part of the developmental system in the same sense as other components (cell, tissue, organism), so genes must be susceptible to influence from other levels during the process of individual development" (Gottlieb, 1992, p. 167).

The theory and data Gottlieb (1997; Gottlieb et al., 1998) marshalled in support of this developmental systems view are compelling. Many of these examples involve integrated, multilevel exchanges of material (e.g., nutritional and hormonal) or energy (e.g., light) variables. Gottlieb explained that such evidence underscored that the action of genes (gene expression) was "affected by events at other levels of the [developmental] system" (Gottlieb, 1991, p. 5), that "all levels of the system may be considered potentially equal" (Gottlieb, 1991, p. 6), and, therefore, that "genetic activity does not by itself produce finished traits such as blue eyes, arms, legs, or neurons. The problem of anatomical and physiological differentiation remains unsolved, but it is unanimously recognized as requiring influences above the strictly cellular level" (Gottlieb, 1991, p. 5). Thus, intraorganism variables making up the proximal context of the gene, as well as extraorganism contextual variables, are shown in Gottlieb (1991a, 1991b), as well as in the literature he cited (e.g., Edelman, 1987, 1988; Grouse, Schrier, Letendre, & Nelson, 1980; Kollar & Fisher, 1980; Uphouse & Bonner, 1975; see also Lerner, 1984), to exist in a reciprocally influential relation with genes.

Given this evidence, one conclusion is inescapable: The idea, that genes are impenetrable and fixed entities that direct a person's development in a manner independent of the supragenetic, organismic, and environmental (contextual) levels of organization within which the genes are embedded, is absurd (Ho, 1984; Strohman, 1993). No feature of biology is so encapsulated, so automated, and so invulnerable to moderation by the context that it can stand as an example of such an impenetrable entity. Simply, then, just as genes may influence supragenetic levels, both within and outside of the organism, these levels of organization influence genes. It is these multilevel coactions that produce development, and that are embodied in Gottlieb's (1992) new definition of epigenesis noted earlier.

Thus, the developmental systems framework of Gottlieb (1991, 1992, 1997) indicates that all organismic characteristics (e.g., genes, cells, tissues, and organs), as well as the whole organism itself, function in a bidirectional, reciprocal, or "dynamic interactional" (Lerner, 1978) relation with the contexts within which the organism is embedded. With the dimension of time, it is this multilevel, integrated functioning which constitutes the course of individual development.

Gottlieb's (1991, 1992) examples of dynamic interactions involve integrated, multilevel exchanges of material (e.g., nutritional and hormonal) variables, energy (e.g., light) variables, or informational (i.e., psychological and behavioral) variables. Within the human development literature, examples of dynamic interactions have most often involved integrated, multilevel exchanges involving the latter type of variables (Ford & Lerner, 1992; Lerner, 1991). Although these types of examples refer to exchanges having contents which are qualitatively different, their structure and function can be integrated within a common, developmental systems perspective, such as the one forwarded by Gottlieb (1991, 1992; see, too, Ford & Lerner, 1992). Indeed, whether illustrated by data from the field of comparative psychology or from the field of human development, the developmental systems model underscores the idea that the basic process

of development is a relational one (Overton, 1998). That is, the basic process of development is changing relations between the organism and the multilevel context comprising the ecology of the organism's development.

Moreover, the reciprocity between organism and context, and the temporality that derives from the embeddedness of all levels of this system in history, provides a change component to the organism, to the context, and to the relation between the two. In addition, the singularity of the array of variables from the multiple, integrated levels that characterizes an organism across its life span, assures that lawful individual difference (i.e., individuality that is neither mere error variance nor substantively trivial) characterizes the course of ontogeny. Thus, as Gottlieb (1992) pointed out:

> Ontogeny in each generation is a consequence of the coaction of hereditary or genetic factors and many different local environmental circumstances that determine the expression of the phenotype during the course of development. (p. 95)

Accordingly, the key features of Gottlieb's developmental systems perspective provide an intellectually important and societally timely frame for the study of human development. These features include:

- Changing organism–context coactions.
- Focus on the actual physical and social ecology within which the organism develops.
- Individual differences (or, as they are now more often labeled within the human development field, "diversity").
- A sensitivity to the entire life span as a legitimate frame within which to study interactions and individuality.

In short, within the context of Gottlieb's developmental systems view, epigenesis is a probabilistic process of individual development and "The most important feature of the developmental systems view is the explicit recognition that the genes are an integral part of the system and their activity (i.e., genetic expression) is affected by events at other levels of the system, including the environment of the organism" (1997, p. 82). Indeed, Gottlieb emphasized that "The principal ideas concern the epigenetic characterization of individual development as an emergent, coactional, hierarchical system" (Gottlieb, 1997, p. 89).

Gottlieb (1997) drew a distinction between the probabilistic view of epigenesis and the predetermined version of epigenesis discussed in Chapter

3. The latter "viewpoint holds that behavioral epigenesis is predetermined by invariant organic factors of growth and differentiation (particularly neural maturation), and the . . . [former] . . . viewpoint holds that the sequence and outcome of prenatal behavior is probabilistically determined by the critical operation of various endogenous and exogenous stimulative events" (Gottlieb, 1970, p. 111). These intraindividual and extraindividual (contextual) events are parts of the organism's experience.

Within the relational perspective forwarded by Gottlieb, experience represents, then, a concept that is central in attempts to distinguish between an integrative, developmental systems perspective and a split conception. Akin to the views advanced by Schneirla (1957), Gottlieb stated that, ". . . experience should be broadly defined to include activity produced within the organism itself (endogenous motor as well as sensory-system activity). . . . It is only by denying (or not acknowledging) the role of spontaneous endogenous activity within the nervous system as playing a formative role in neural and behavioral development that the outmoded nature versus nurture conception can be kept alive" (Gottlieb, 1997, p. 55). Indeed, by explaining the various roles of experience in development, Gottlieb "forces us to think in a new way about the role of experience in the development of behavior that is thought of as instinctive" (1997, p. 76). Thus, it is useful to discuss Gottlieb's conception of the roles of experience within developmental systems.

Modes of Experiential Contribution

Gottlieb (1997) presented a conception of experience that is rich and nuanced. He noted that:

> The invitation to search for nonobvious experiential bases of unlearned behavior, implicit and explicit in the writings of Kuo (1976), Schneirla (1956), and Lehrman (1953) has been largely ignored. As de Santillana has written, "But nothing is so easy to ignore as something that does not yield freely to understanding" (de Santillana & von Dechend, 1977, p. xii). (p. 76)

Yet, Gottlieb's scholarship does document the various roles of experience in individual development—involving inductive experiences, facilitating experiences, and maintenance experiences. He demonstrated that experience provides nonobvious, but compelling, bases of behavior. In the absence of often subtle analysis, these behaviors are naively attributed to predetermined or instinctive bases. To illustrate, in the context of his discussion

of the roles of experience, Gottlieb explained his conception of the place of canalization, and of its "alternative" process—malleability or plasticity—in development. Gottlieb (1997) noted that canalization and malleability are subtypes of induction, in that they require inductive experiences to occur.

> Canalization is a narrowing of responsiveness as a consequence of experience. (pp. 57–58) . . . This experiential canalization process is very similar to what happens in the developing nervous system: The initially 'exuberant' (i.e., very large) number of synaptic contacts is pruned by experience. This is a cardinal feature of Gerald Edelman's (1987) notion of 'neural Darwinism'. (p. 59) . . . [Canalization is thus] a fourth role of experience, with experience being defined broadly to signify the contribution of *functional activity* at the behavioral and neural levels of analysis, whether the activity arises from external or internal sources. (p. 59) . . . [Experiences can also] lead to an enhanced malleability or plasticity (the opposite of the narrowing of responsiveness brought about by canalizing experiences). (p. 59)

Thus, in the discussion of his concept of canalization, Gottlieb provided developmental science with a theoretically corrective and an empirically productive account of a key feature of organism change. That is, his presentation offered important theoretical and empirical distinctions between his and Waddington's (1942, 1957, 1971) use of the concept of canalization. Gottlieb showed Waddington's concept to be both theoretically and empirically vacuous. In turn, Gottlieb's concept of canalization is testable, and thus falsifiable, and provides an instance of the inductive role of experience. Gottlieb (1997) criticized

> the developmental geneticist Waddington's (1942) notion that early normal or species-typical physiological and anatomical development can withstand great assaults or perturbations and still return to (or remain on) its usual developmental pathway, thus producing the usual or normal phenotype. Waddington's concept of canalization says that usual developmental pathways are so strongly buffered (by genes—Waddington, 1957, p. 36, Fig. 5) that normal or species-typical development can be only temporarily derailed. Waddington (1968) used the term *chreod* to express his ideas more succinctly: A chreod, according to Waddington, is a "fated" or predetermined developmental pathway. (p. 80)

Gottlieb (1997) noted that Waddington apparently relied on the seeming face validity of this version of the concept of canalization. That is, Waddington presented no empirical support for this concept. Instead, the process purportedly involved in this concept is depicted in figurative or metaphorical terms (Gottlieb, 1997), that is, as a ball rolling down the valleys of an "epigenetic landscape" that varies in shape and in the height of the valley walls (Waddington, 1942, 1953, 1957, 1968).

Given the lack of actual empirical referents for this concept, Waddington's notion is, therefore, both conceptually and operationally empty (Gottlieb, 1997). His concept corresponds directly with a nativist, genetic determinist view of development. For example, Waddington (1957, 1971) claimed that:

> The epigenetic feed-back mechanisms on which canalization depends can, of course, be regarded as examples of gene interactions. (p. 131) . . . The degree to which each pathway is canalized or self-establishing is dependent on the particular alleles of the genes involved in it. (pp. 20–21).

In contrast to nativist notions, such as those forwarded by Waddington (1957, 1971), and to further illustrate the character of experiential influences within the developmental system, Gottlieb offered several examples of the nonobvious role of experience in individual development. For instance, he explained how experiential factors (such as social interactions, the introduction of particular gasses into the proximal atmosphere of the developing individual, or changing day length) may influence physiological functioning (e.g., hormone secretions) which, in turn, may result in the turning on of genes, that is, in the activation of DNA transcription in the cell nucleus. Outcomes of such experiences may involve effects as dramatic as the development of teethlike structures in chickens, sex reversals in coral reef fish, and a second set of wings in otherwise normal fruitflies (Gottlieb, 1997). In fact, there is now so much evidence for the fact that experience (e.g., sensory stimulation) can activate DNA in the individual that the phenomenon has a name: immediate early gene expression (Gottlieb, 1997).

These examples and the others provided by Gottlieb (1997) about the role of experience in individual development, derived from his and others research, underscore that coactions, among the integrated levels of organization of the developmental system, provide the basis of ontogenetic change (Gottlieb et al., 1998). As such Gottlieb noted that "when certain scientists refer to behavior or any other aspect of organismic structure or function as being 'genetically determined,' they are not mindful of the fact that genes synthesize protein (not behavior) and that they do so in the context of a developmental system of higher influences" (1997, p. 93). Indeed, such genetic determinist (nature–nurture split) conceptions (e.g.,

Plomin, 1986; Rowe, 1994; Rushton, 1997) "have provided impediments to thinking clearly about the need for conceptual and empirical analysis at all levels of the developmental systems hierarchy" (Gottlieb, 1991, p. 7).

To document the character of the contribution of these higher influences, Gottlieb presented comparative data indicating that, first, there is no relationship between morphological complexity and genome size. For example, although the haploid genome size (nucleotide pairs) of mammals is *less* than that of frogs and toads, salamanders, angiosperms, gymnosperms, pterosids (ferns), and even algae, mammals exceed all of these species in their approximate number of cell types and in the approximate number of descriptive morphological types they possess. In turn, second, Gottlieb documented that there is no relationship between the number of genes coding for protein and the number of neurons in the nervous system. For instance, among chordates, both *Mus musculus* and *Homo sapiens* have approximately 70,000 genes. Yet, the former organisms have about 40 million neurons whereas the latter organisms have approximately 85 billion neurons; similarly, whereas, among nematodes, *Caenorhabdhitis elegans* have about 14,000 genes and, among arthropods, *Drosophila melanogaster* have about 12,000 genes, the former organisms have approximately 302 neurons and the latter about 250,000. Given these data, it is clear that a developmental system involving coactions of genes with other levels of organization with which they are integrated within this system, provide the basis for individual development. As such, Gottlieb concluded that "there is good reason to seek the answer to evolution above the level of the genes, in the total developmental system" (1997, p. 147).

What Maintains the Split in the Study of Human Development?

Gottlieb's scholarship has been a visible and influential force in the field of developmental psychology, and of human development more specifically, for some time (e.g., Gottlieb, 1970, 1976, 1983, 1991, 1992, 1997). Moreover, his perspective converges with that found in the scholarship of other long-term leaders of developmental comparative science (e.g., Kuo, 1967, 1976; Lehrman, 1953; Schneirla, 1956; Tobach, 1971). The prominence of this work creates a puzzle: The conceptualization of genes and, superordinately, of nature as separable from nurture, found within disciplines such as behavior genetics (see Chapters 10 and 11) and sociobiology (see Chapters 12 and 13) is known—at least among geneticists and developmental comparative scientists—to be counterfactual (Ho, 1984; Lewontin, Rose, & Kamin, 1984; Müller-Hill, 1988; Strohman, 1993). How is it then that the disciplines associated with this conceptual mistake flourish?

Scholars in the field of human development must, therefore, confront several questions as a consequence of this curious situation: How did the biological, social, and behavioral sciences that attempt to contribute to the understanding of human behavior and development arrive at this point? Why do not these fields declare that the "emperor has no clothes?" Why, instead, are grants awarded and scientific journal space allocated to work having this fatal conceptual flaw? Most important, why do scholars allow such mistaken reductionistic and mechanistic thinking to influence both science policy and social policy? In turn, why is there not a more general embracing in the field of human development and in the policy arena of the scientifically valid alternative models of the role of biology–context relations, models associated with the compelling theoretical ideas and convincing empirical evidence of a group of scholars who synthesize animal comparative and human development research and forward a developmental systems, relational perspective in their scholarship?

I believe that the search for answers to these questions must encompass not only issues of the science of human development but also of the sociology of this science. In addition, the "politics" of this science, that is, the use of the science to further extrascientific ideological agendas, cannot be ignored (e.g., see Kamin, 1974; Lerner, 1992).

I believe it is clear that these questions are not merely "academic" in character. Science and public policy continues to be influenced by biologically reductionistic, split conceptions of nature and nurture. For instance, Frederick K. Goodwin, the former director of the National Institute of Mental Health (NIMH), in a speech he delivered in 1992 at a meeting of the NIMH Advisory Mental Health Council, generalized from primate studies of violence to account for violence among urban males (Psychological Science Agenda, 1992). He noted that "maybe it isn't just the careless use of the word when people call certain areas of certain cities jungles . . . we may have gone back to what might be more natural, without all of the social controls that we have imposed upon ourselves as a civilization over thousands of years in our own evolution" (Psychological Science Agenda, 1992).

As but one illustration (see Lerner, 1992, for others) of the long history of the thinking represented by Goodwin, it is important to note remarks made by Francis Galton more than 100 years earlier.

Exemplifying the sharp division between nature and nurture that is his "dubious intellectual legacy" (Gottlieb, 1992, p. 49), *and* the racist overtones often historically associated with this dichotomy, Galton contended that "When nature and nurture compete for supremacy on equal terms . . . the former proves the stronger. It is needless to insist that neither is self-sufficient; the highest natural endowments may be starved by defective nurture, whereas no carefulness of nurture can overcome the evil tendencies of an intrinsically bad *physique,* weak brain, or brutal disposition (Galton, 1975, pp. 9–10) . . . The Negro now born in the United States has much the same natural faculties as his distant cousin who is born in Africa; the effect of his transplantation being ineffective in changing his nature" (Galton, 1892, p. xxiv).

This position is not that discrepant from the one forward much more recently by Rowe (1994), who argued

> that social class may capture not variation in rearing and environmental social background, but instead variation in genes. This idea returns genes to socialization science by a back door—by the very variable (social class) thought to have liberated social science from hereditarian thinking! (p. 135)

And how do genes create those environmental characteristics marked by the term *social class*? To Rowe (1994):

> The answer is that the genes may construct a nervous system—and that hormones and neurotransmitters may then motivate behaviors resulting in dramatic redesign of an environment. The way a beaver will restructure its environment is as genetically shaped as its flat tail and keen hearing. (p. 90)

Thus, Rowe's answer, which is his description of a process termed *niche picking,* illustrates the reductionism of the nature–nurture split position and, as well, the acontextual, asystemic, and nonrelational thinking about developmental process that is associated with such a position. Simply, then, as illustrated by Rowe (1994), the intellectual debate between proponents of split and relational positions is very much a part of the contemporary landscape of the field of human development. It continues, as well, to play a role in the discussion of how developmental science may be applied to public policies affecting the social context of human life.

Conclusions

Overton (1998) explained that the casting of "our fundamental understanding of development into an inclusive relational frame has profound implications for the concepts and theories, as well as the methodology and methods, of developmental inquiry" (p. 114). We would, in addition, reiterate a point made in Chapters 3 and 5 regarding the notion of plasticity, when considered within a developmental systems view; that is, that a developmental systems perspective supports optimism about the potential efficacy of developmentally appropriate public policies and of preventive and optimizing developmental interventions and, in turn, the enactment and evaluation of such policies and programs serve as a way of testing or demonstrating this systems perspective (cf. Brim & Kagan, 1980; Gottlieb, 1997, p. 138; Lerner, 1995). Accordingly, to test the limits of this relational perspective for enhancing theory, methodology, research, and application, Gottlieb pointed science in the direction of pursuing methodological reduction—as opposed to theoretical reductionism (cf. von Bertalanffy, 1933, 1962). Gottlieb (1997) explained that:

> Theoretical reductionism seeks to explain the behavior of the whole organism by reference to its component parts—a derivative of the older, additive physical concept of mechanism—whereas methodological reductionism holds that not only is a description of the various hierarchically organized levels of analysis of the whole organism necessary but also that a depiction of the bidirectional traffic between levels is crucial to a developmental understanding of the individual. (p. 132)

In short, Gottlieb expressed the hope that "the immense gap between molecular biology and developmental psychology will one day be filled with facts as well as valid concepts" (1997, p. 100).

I believe there is a strong basis for such hope. However, to realize this goal, it is requisite to understand that the major point in casting out fundamental understanding of development into an inclusive relational frame is that it has profound implications for the concepts and theories, as well as the methodology and methods, of developmental inquiry (Overton, 1998). As such, to understand how things really work will require knowledge far beyond that that could be gained from partitioning variance into genetic and environmental components. We will need knowledge about all the levels of organization that comprise the ecology of human development and, as well, and perhaps most critically, about the dynamic system of developmental relations that comprise this ecology.

To obtain such knowledge, we must go beyond the limits of any one area of scholarship. Indeed, we will have to go beyond the limits of academe. How things really work in the real world involves people from all walks of life. In the end, then, each

of our perspectives is limited. To effect important and sustained social changes through our actions, communities of scholars in concert with communities of citizens will have to coalesce in order to learn how desired individual, family, and societal changes can be created.

In essence, then, relationism and systems, not splits into counterfactual domains of isolated acting entities, is a frame for productive science and for applications that may serve to advance the human condition. Gottlieb's (1997; Gottlieb et al., 1998) scholarship sounds the "death knell" for the nature–nurture dichotomy. His work provides a scholarly and scientific legitimization of innovative, relational answers to key questions about science and policy. For those concerned with using the best of science to inform the policies and programs affecting the quality of human development within and across the nations of our world, Gottlieb's theory and research can serve as a template through which scholars may develop or extend other approaches to using developmental systems to understand and enhance human development. To illustrate the relevance, then, of Gottlieb's scholarship to other developmental systems' approaches, we turn to a presentation of several instances of such models; that is, we consider the developmental systems perspectives forwarded by Thelen and Smith (1994, 1998), Magnusson (1980, 1985, 1990, 1995; Magnusson & Stattin, 1998), Wapner (1981, 1987, 1995; Wapner & Demick, 1998), and Ford and Lerner (1992).

THELEN AND SMITH'S DYNAMIC SYSTEMS THEORY

Thelen and Smith (1998) noted that their version of developmental systems theory—which they termed dynamic systems theory—derived from both systems thinking in biology and psychology and the study of complex and nonlinear systems in physics and mathematics. They explained that, in its simplest sense, the idea of dynamic systems refer to changes over time among elements that are interrelated systemically.

Although this idea can be extended more technically or formally, through specific mathematical equations, Thelen and Smith (1998) noted that there are two key features of any physical or biological system:

1. Development can only be understood as the multiple, mutual, and continuous interaction of all levels of the developing system, from the molecular to the cultural.

Esther Thelen

2. Development can only be understood as nested processes that unfold over many time scales, from milliseconds to years. (p. 563)

To Thelen and Smith (1998), dynamic systems theory could be applied to different species, age levels, or domains of development (e.g., from "molecular" patterns of motor functioning involved in walking or reaching to "molar" changes in cognition that may be gained through the integration of humans' actions on their context and the context's actions on them).

The Development of Novel Forms Across Life

Thelen and Smith (1994, 1998) believe that dynamic systems theory affords understanding of what they regard as the defining feature of development: the creation of new forms. That is, consistent with our discussions in prior chapters of the definition of development, Thelen and Smith contend that the essence of those changes termed *developmental*—the property of change that enables one period of life to be designated as involving a distinct point in development—is qualitative discontinuity, emergence, epigenesis, or simply, novelty. Once such novelty has been described,

however, a central explanatory issue becomes evident: "Where does this novelty come from? How can developing systems create something out of nothing?" (Thelen & Smith, 1998, p. 564).

As we discussed in Chapter 3, answers to these questions have been associated with nature, nurture, and interactionist perspectives. Not surprisingly, Thelen and Smith rejected both nature and nurture explanations and, implicitly, those interactionist positions we have discussed as representative of weak or moderate views of interaction. Instead, consistent with the ideas of Gottlieb (1997; Gottlieb et al., 1998) previously discussed Thelen and Smith (1998) noted that:

> The tradition we follow, that of *systems theories of biological organization,* explains the formation of new forms by processes of *self-organization.* By self-organization we mean that *pattern and order emerge from the interactions of the components of a complex system without explicit instructions,* either in the organism itself or from the environment. Self-organization—processes that by their own activities change themselves—is a fundamental property of living things. (p. 564)

For instance, we have discussed how both Gottlieb (1997), in his view of the coactions that are involved in epigenesis, and Schneirla (1957), in his notion of circular functions and self-stimulation in ontogeny, provide examples of these self-organizational processes.

Linda Smith

In turn, Thelen and Smith (1998) discussed evidence from embryology and morphology that indicates how highly complicated structural patterns arise within dynamic systems *not* from information specifically coded in genes but, instead, from simple initial conditions. For instance, they explained that neither the spots of leopards nor the striped tails of raccoons are derived from genes for these bodily features. Rather, these features are constructed during development when specific chemical and metabolic attributes of these animals—each one mutually facilitating and constraining the others—spontaneously organize themselves into patterns (Thelen & Smith, 1998).

Similarly, behavioral characteristics and patterns can emerge in development without the requirement of specific genetic coding for them, as is held in the field of behavior genetics (Plomin, 1986; Rowe, 1994; see Chapter 10), or as forwarded in concepts such as instinct (Lorenz, 1937, 1965; see Chapters 5 and 12). The processes that produce such developmental change are again those associated with the probabilistic–epigenetic view of organism–context relations associated with the work of Schneirla, Gottlieb, Tobach, Lehrman, and others. For instance, Thelen and Smith (1998) pointed to the work of Zing-Yang Kuo (1967, 1970, 1976) as exemplifying this dynamic interactionist view of the development of novel forms of behavior across the life span:

> Ontogenesis of behavior is a process of modification, transformation, or reorganization of the existing patterns of behavior gradients in response to the impact of new environmental stimulation; and in consequence a new spatial and/or serial pattern of behavior gradients is formed, permanently or temporarily ("learning") which oftentimes adds to the inventory of the existing patterns of behavior gradients previously accumulated during the animal's developmental history . . . Thus, in every stage of ontogenesis, every response is determined not only by the stimuli or stimulating objects, by also by the total environmental context, the status of anatomical structures and their functional capacities, the physiological (biochemical and biophysical) condition, and the developmental history up to that stage. (Kuo, 1970, p. 189)

In short, then, Thelen and Smith (1998) drew on the evidence provided by the scholarship of embryologists, and by comparative psychologists taking a probabilistic–epigenetic perspective, to assert that the basis for novelty in development arises from the integrated relation of intraorganism and extraorganism levels of organization— and not from either genetic or environmental "instructions" for such change.

The Dynamics of the Developmental System

The probabilistic–epigenetic character of the developmental process meant, to Thelen and Smith (1998), that the duality, or split (Overton, 1998), between individual and context, or between structure and function, should be eliminated from scientific discourse. In their view, contextual levels of organizations (e.g., culture) do not just support the course of development, they "are the very stuff of development itself" (Thelen & Smith, 1998, p. 572). Thelen and Smith (1998) explained the essential difference between the developmental systems perspective they favored

> and more individual-centered approaches is that the levels are conceptualized as *more* than just interacting; instead they are seen as integrally fused together. Behavior and its development are melded as ever-changing sets of relationships and the history of those *relationships* over time. (p. 572)

Thelen and Smith (1998) believed that, because of this fusion, we must reject linear systems of causality—wherein there is a direct, unidirectional line from an antecedent, "causal" event or structure (e.g., the possession of a gene) to a consequent behavior (e.g., a particular motor behavior, personality attribute, or cognitive capacity, that is, where "X" → "Y"). In the place of such linear notions of causality, developmental systems theories suggest a configural view of causality (Ford & Lerner, 1992), wherein bidirectional relations within and across fused levels of organization change interdependently across time. One depiction of such a coactional, configural view of causality within the developmental system has been offered by Gottlieb (1991) and is shown in Figure 7.1.

The causal system presented in this figure coincides with the view of causality conceived of by Thelen and Smith (1998), wherein the key features of developing individuals—self-organization, nonlinearity, openness, stability, complexity, wholeness, the emergence of novelty, and change are produced by the fused, multilevel influences comprising the developmental system. The outcomes of development—"form"—are products of this process of bidirectional relations (Thelen & Smith, 1998, p. 586).

Thelen and Smith (1998) indicated that the key feature of dynamic systems is that the many heterogeneous parts of the system (e.g., the different cells, tissues, and organs within the individual and the various individuals, institutions, and physical features of the context of any person) are free to combine in a virtually infinite number of ways. Theoretically at least, there is no limit to

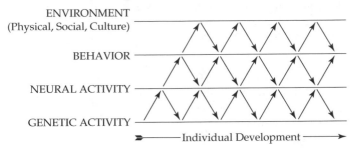

FIGURE 7.1
A developmental–psychobiological systems framework.
Source: From Gilbert Gottlieb (1991). Individual development and evolution: The genesis of novel behavior. Copyright © 1991 by Oxford University Press, Inc. Reprinted by permission.

the actual number of combinations that might occur. However, in actuality, the patterns of relations that are seen are far less. As we discussed in Chapter 5, in regard to the notion of "relative plasticity," the relation among the multiple parts of the system are sources of constraints as well as of variability. Thus, because of this relative plasticity, an order (a pattern) emerges from the complexity of the system as, through the relations within the system, the system organizes itself.

Thelen and Smith (1998) explained that order emerges from disparate parts because human development is an *open system;* that is, a system wherein energy is taken into the system and is used to increase order within it. Such a system stands in contrast to a *closed system,* wherein there is no infusion of energy into the system.

In that an open, human development system increases its organization over time, it exists in "violation" of the second law of thermodynamics (Brent, 1978; Prigogine, 1978). According to this law, a system changes in the direction of greater disorganization, termed *entropy.* However, some systems—open ones—can show *negentropy,* that is, changes in the direction of greater organization.

The Nobel laureate chemist, Ilya Prigogine (1978), has shown that negentropic change can occur because an open system draws energy from its context to increase its internal order. Prigogine demonstrated that such use of energy within an open system does result in an overall dissipation in order outside of it, that is, in the universe as a whole; thus, in the broader system, there is an increase in entropy, and the second law is then, in actuality, not violated.

Thelen and Smith (1998) noted that when the parts involved in an open system interrelate in a nonlinear manner (e.g., as shown in Figure 7.1) in-

tegration (i.e., a pattern, an organization, and structural relations) emerges. Such integration enables the system to be described via reference to fewer dimensions, or parameters, than was the case at the beginning of the development of the system. For example, in Chapter 5, we discussed Werner's (1948, 1957) concept of orthogenesis as an example of a general principle of systematic change in developing organisms wherein the globality of the individual's organization is reduced through the emergence of hierarchic integration. Later in this chapter, we return to this idea in our discussion of Wapner's (1995; Wapner & Dimick, 1998) developmental systems theory. In turn, Thelen and Smith (1998) noted that the integrative variables that emerge within an open system to reduce its dispersion and increase its organization, or pattern, may be termed either *collective variables* or *order parameters.*

The emergence of such collective variables not only reduces the theoretically infinite number of combinations within a dynamic (open) system to some much smaller actual subset but, in so doing, the integration reflected by the collective variables provides continuity and stability within the system. As Thelen and Smith (1998) explained:

> The system "settles into" or "prefers" only a few modes of behavior. In dynamic terminology, this behavioral mode is an *attractor* state, because the system—under certain conditions—has an affinity for that state. Again in dynamic terms, the system prefers a certain location in its *state,* or *phase* space, and when displaced from that place, it tends to return there. . . . All the initial conditions leading to a particular fixed point attractor are called *basins of attraction.* (p. 588)

Thelen and Smith (1998) described one type of attractor, the *chaotic* attractor, that seems to be involved in many biological systems (e.g., involving changes in heart rate, the sense of smell, and *in utero* motor movements during the fetal period). Within dynamic systems, chaos describes a situation wherein the relation among the parts of a system seem random (i.e., lacking any pattern or order). However, when the time period used for viewing a state space is extended over a significantly long time period, nonrandomness—order—is evident. In fact, chaotic change is represented by highly elaborate geometric patterns (Gleick, 1987).

Stability and Change in Dynamic Systems

Thelen and Smith (1998) noted that, in the study of human development, the most important characteristics of an attractor is its relative stability, that is, by the likelihood that the system will exist in a given state (or show a specific behavioral pattern) as compared to other ones. The presence of relative stability means that there is a higher statistical probability of one specific behavioral pattern than another and that, as well, if the system is dislodged from its preferred state it will return back to it. Moreover, the system will "work" to maintain the preferred state. Thus, as discussed in Chapter 5, in regard to the idea that continuity of behavior can be underlain by dynamic interactions between the individual and the context (Cairns & Hood, 1984), the relative stability of a developmental system does not gainsay the fact that dynamic exchanges are occurring within it.

The relative stability of a system is related to the relative plasticity of the course of development. In our discussion of plasticity and its linkage to continuity–discontinuity in development (Chapter 5), we noted that although organisms—through their dynamic interactions with their context—maintain the capacity for systematic change across the life span (Baltes et al., 1998, 1999; Lerner, 1984), these same organism–context relations constrain the variability in functional change that can be seen; as a consequence, plasticity—although ubiquitous—is relative, not absolute. Similarly, Thelen and Smith (1998, p. 626) observed that, "adaptive systems live in quasi-stability; reliable enough to make predictions about what is appropriate in a context, but flexible enough to recruit different solutions if the situation changes."

The ontogenetic changes that exist in plasticity mean that, at advanced developmental levels, when the reserve capacity for plasticity has narrowed (Baltes, 1997; Baltes et al., 1998, 1999), change is still possible but a larger than previously necessary level of intervention would be required to produce

it (Lerner, 1984; MacDonald, 1985). Similarly, Thelen and Smith (1998) noted that, "Very stable attractors take very large pushes to move them from their preferred positions, but they are dynamic and changeable nonetheless" (p. 590). In other words, the system is not fixed, with hardwired, immutable connections; rather it is *softly assembled.*

Such soft assembly is the essence of plasticity in human development and, to Thelen and Smith (1998), the defining feature of a dynamic view of development. The presence of soft assembly means that the concept that human development involves the functioning of permanent, immutable structures is not valid. Rather, developmentalists must view the development of the person as involving a dynamic linkage between (a) the stability of the system, conceived of as the resistance to change existing among the collective states; and (b) the fluctuations around the stable states, changes that provide the functional source of novelty within the system.

Transitions in Systems

Fluctuations within the system, as well as changes from the context that impinge on the system, can alter the patterns of the system. In either case, the system will change in a manner that increases order, that enhances coherence. The parts of the system will interact, or "cooperate," in the terms of Thelen and Smith (1998, p. 590), in the occurrence of a "phase shift" or, in other terms, a "nonlinear phase shift." To illustrate, Thelen and Smith (1998) indicated that:

> For example, we can walk up hills of various inclines, but when the steepness of the hill reaches some critical value, we must shift our locomotion to some type of quadrupedal gait—climbing on all fours. . . . In dynamic terminology, the slope change acted as a *control parameter* on our gait style. The control parameter does not really "control" the system in traditional terms. Rather, it is a parameter to which the collective behavior of the system is sensitive and that thus moves the system through collective states. (pp. 590–591)

Thelen and Smith (1998) noted that the "disappearance" of the newborn stepping response (i.e., stepping movements made by the newborn when he or she is held upright), which occurs after a few months of life, occurs in relation to the gain in weight, and especially in body fat, during this period. As the infants' legs get heavier across these months, there is no corresponding increase in muscle mass. As a consequence, infants have difficulty lifting their legs—not because of a neuronal change within the brain that "suppressed" the reflex—but because they do not have the muscles to do this when in the biomechanically difficult upright position (Thelen & Smith, 1998). Thus, underscoring the coherence of the changing dynamic system, one wherein patterns emerge through self-organization among components, Thelen and Smith (1998, p. 591) noted that, "Body fat deposition is a growth change that is not specific to leg movements, yet it affected the system such that a qualitative shift in behavior resulted."

Times Scales Within Dynamic Systems

The time frame for the phase shift involved in the infant stepping response involves several months within the early life of humans. One important temporal parameter of dynamic systems illustrated by this example is that the state of the system in regard to stepping when upright at a later time in ontogeny (e.g., when a lot of body fat had been gained) was related to the system state at the prior time (when the ratio of body fat to muscles afforded stepping while upright). This temporal linkage is an example of the point that the condition of the system at any one point in time provides the basis for the condition of the system at the next immediate point in time.

Thus, as discussed (in Chapter 1) in regard to the notion of successive change as being a core component of the definition of development, Thelen and Smith (1998) noted that there is always a successive character to change within a dynamic system; that is, the state of the system at Time 1 shapes the state of the system at Time 2, and the state of the system at Time 2 determines the state at Time 3, etc. Thelen and Smith (1998) noted, then, that dynamic systems are *reiterative;* that is, each state with the system is shaped by the prior state of the system.

Moreover, the time scale dividing the successive influences may vary considerably. Times 1, 2, and 3 may be divided (e.g., along the "X" axis of a graph) by seconds, days, weeks, months, years, etc. Nevertheless, the same sort of successive interdependency of states, and, therefore, the same linkages across time, will be evident, whether the state-to-state observational interval is months (as in the example of the infant stepping response) or years (as may be seen in regard to changes in IQ scores; Bloom, 1964). Thelen and Smith (1998) explained that there is a self-similarity of the system across many different levels of temporal observation. They noted that, in the terms of dynamic systems, time scales are said to be *fractal.*

However, because different components of the system have their own developmental course and, consequently, because the relations among components continuously change the time scale used within developmental studies to observe the system and make judgments about its stability or fluctuation is critical. For example, in attempting to understand the connections between the state of the system in early infancy, in regard to the presence and disappearance of the stepping response, appraisal of fat-to-muscle ratios across a monthly time parameter may be useful; however, if the interest is the emergence within the system of the ability to run efficiently, then neither such ratios nor a month-by-month perspective would be useful (Thelen & Smith, 1998). Instead, different system components (involving, e.g., the development of muscle coordination and lung vital capacity) and different time divisions (e.g., years) may be required to see the reiterative character of the system and the bidirectional influences across levels within it.

Conclusions

Thelen and Smith (1998) offered a rich and nuanced conception of the dynamic character of the human developmental system. Their theory underscored the important role of dynamic interactions—fusions, in human development—and the centrality of plasticity—of softly assembled systems—in providing within-person variability across life and between-person differences in such life-span changes. Their theory and the impressive data they marshal in support of it (Thelen & Smith, 1994, 1998), thus, highlights the active role of the individual as a central agent in his or her own development and fosters an integrative, holistic understanding of the individual and his or her context. Thelen and Smith (1998) see important and singular promise for their dynamic systems theory:

> Only a dynamic account captures the richness and complexity of real-life human behavior. The issue is not just how people learn to think in formal, logical, and abstract terms, but how they can do that *and* all the other things people do in this society: use tools, operate sophisticated machinery, find their way around, play sports and games, create art and music, and engage in complex social interactions. These activities require active perception, precisely timed movements, shifting attention, insightful planning, useful remembering, and the ability to smoothly and rapidly *shift* from one activity to another as the occasion demands. They happen in time and they recruit all the elements in the system. The challenge for developmentalists is to understand the developmental origins of this complexity and flexibility. Only dynamics, we believe, is up to the task. (p. 626)

I agree with the appraisal of Thelen and Smith about the challenge that may be met, and the potential benefits of meeting them through the use of the dynamic, developmental systems theory they forward. Other developmentalists agree as well, and, in addition, have proposed theories consonant with the one forwarded by Thelen and Smith (1998). One very significant instance of such a theory has been formulated by David Magnusson who, over the course of more than a quarter century, has made innovative and articulate contributions to scholarship about developmental systems.

MAGNUSSON'S HOLISTIC PERSON–CONTEXT INTERACTION THEORY

David Magnusson, the renown Swedish developmental psychologist, has provided singularly creative and historically influential scholarly and professional leadership facilitating and integrating the research and applied activities of developmental scientists from across the world. Magnusson's theoretical formulations and research programs

David Magnusson

have emphasized the fundamental role of context in human behavior and development (e.g., Magnusson, 1981, 1988, 1995, 1996, 1999a, 1999b; Magnusson & Stattin, 1998; Stattin & Magnusson, 1990). His intellectual vision includes a compelling conceptual rationale and substantive basis for internationally contextualized, comparative scholarship (e.g., Magnusson, 1995, 1999a, 1999b; Magnusson & Allen, 1983), and is built on four conceptual pillars: interactionism, holism, interdisciplinarity, and the longitudinal study of the person.

These themes emerge in Magnusson's theory, which stresses the synthesis, or fusion, of the person–environment system. Magnusson seeks to understand the structures and processes involved in the operation of this system and the way in which the individual behaves and develops within it. Given this integrative emphasis on person and context, Magnusson (1995) termed his theory a *holistic approach.* Magnusson and Stattin (1998) stated that:

> The individual is an active, purposeful part of an integrated, complex, and dynamic person–environment system. Furthermore, within this person–environment system, the individual develops and functions as an integrated, complex, and dynamic totality. Consequently, it is not possible to understand how social systems function without knowledge of individual functioning, and it is not possible to understand individual functioning and development without knowledge of the environment. (pp. 685–686)

As do Thelen and Smith (1998), Magnusson saw the fusions among cognitive, biological, and behavioral subsystems, and their complex interplay with the levels of the environment within which they are embedded, as involving nonlinear and probabilistic relations. The probabilistic character of the changes occurring across the life span, and the fact these changes take place in reciprocal interdependence with a multilevel, changing world, meant, to Magnusson (1995, 1996, 1999a, 1999b), as it did to Thelen and Smith (1998), that the course of human development is characterized by the emergence of "novel foci of individual functioning" (Magnusson & Stattin, 1998, p. 687).

Causality in Holistic Interactionism

To Magnusson, then, as was also seen in respect to the theories of Schneirla (1957), Kuo (1967, 1976), Gottlieb (1997) and Thelen and Smith (1998), the cause of development—the emergence of novel forms across life—is an outcome of the coactions of the components of the dynamic, person–context system. This self-organizational source of developmental change stands in contrast to either the unidirectional, single source (nature or nurture), or the weak or moderate interactional, ideas regarding the causes of development.

In what Magnusson termed the *modern interactionist perspective,* or the *holistic interactionist viewpoint,* the basis of development lies in two types of interaction: Inner interactions, involving bidirectional relationships among biological, psychological, and behavioral characteristics; and outer, person–context interactions, involving continual exchanges between the person and his or her environment. Magnusson explained that holistic interaction builds and extends the ideas of interactionism found in what he termed "classical interactionism" (Magnusson & Stattin, 1998, p. 694). As detailed by Magnusson and Stattin (1998):

> The classical interactionistic formulations emphasize that (a) an individual and his or her environment form a total system in which the individual functions as the active, purposeful agent; and (b) a main characteristic of the causal relations is reciprocity rather than unidirectionality. (p. 692)

Holistic interactionism expands on this classic conception of interaction by, first, placing greater emphasis on the dynamic, integrated character of the individual within the overall person–environment system and, second by stressing both biological and behavioral action components of the system. Thus, and drawing on many of the same literatures relied on by Gottlieb (e.g., in regard to neuropsychology and developmental biology; e.g., Damasio & Damasio, 1996; Rose, 1995) and by Thelen and Smith (e.g., in regard to chaos and general systems theory; e.g., Gleick, 1987; von Bertalanffy, 1968), and buttressed by what Magnusson (1995, 1996, 1999a, 1999b) saw as the growing importance of holistically oriented longitudinal studies of human development (e.g., Cairns & Cairns, 1994; Magnusson, 1988; Stattin & Magnusson, 1990), Magnusson and Stattin (1998) specified the four basic propositions of holistic interaction:

1. The individual functions and develops as a total, integrated organism.

2. Individual functioning within existing mental, biological, and behavioral structures, as well as developmental, change, can best be described as complex, dynamic processes.

3. Individual functioning and development are guided by processes of continuously ongoing, reciprocal interaction among mental, behavioral, and biological aspects of individual functioning, and social, cultural, and physical aspects of the environment.

4. The environment, including the individual, functions and changes as a continuously ongoing process of reciprocal interaction among social, economic, and cultural factors. (p. 694)

Features of the Person–Environment System

The holistic interactionist theory has profound implications for the conduct of developmental science. Indeed, the far-reaching character of these implications extends to even the role of the concept of "variable" in developmental research.

Magnusson and Stattin (1998) noted that, in most approaches to developmental science, the concept of "variable" is embedded within a theoretically reductionistic model of humans (see Chapter 3). Within this perspective, the "variable" becomes the unit of analysis in developmental research. However, within the context of what they term *the holistic principle,* Magnusson and Stattin (1998) forwarded a person–centered view of development and, as such, forwarded the individual—the whole person—as the core unit of developmental analysis. That is, the holistic principle "emphasizes an approach to the individual and the person–environment system as organized wholes, functioning as totalities. . . . The totality derives its characteristic features and properties from the interaction among the elements involved, not from the effect of each isolated part on the totality" (Magnusson & Stattin, 1998, p. 698).

Accordingly, if the totality, the whole person or—better—the person–environment relation, characterizes the essence of developmental change, then developmental analyses that assess single aspects of the system (e.g., single variables) are necessarily incomplete. Only a distorted view of development can be derived from appraising variables divorced from the context of other, simultaneously acting variables (Magnusson & Stattin, 1998). It is this integration of variables from across the person–environment system that constitutes the core process of human development and, as such, the necessary focus of developmental science.

Indeed, within the holistic interactionist theory, the developmental *process* involves a continual flow of integrated, reciprocally related events. Thus, time becomes a fundamental feature of individual development given that, within the probabilistic–epigenetic view taken by Magnusson (1995, 1996, 1999a, 1999b) of the interrelation of the constituent events comprising the process of development, the same event occurring at different times in ontogeny will have varying influences on behavior and development. As a consequence, "A change in one aspect affects related parts of the subsystem and, sometimes, the whole organism. At a more general level, the restructuring of structures and processes at the individual level is embedded in and is part of the restructuring of the total person–environment system" (Magnusson & Stattin, 1998, p. 700).

Thus, to Magnusson (1995, 1999a, 1999b; Magnusson & Stattin, 1998), individual development is marked by a continual restructuring of existing patterns and—through the facilitation and constraint of the biological through sociocultural levels of the total person–environment system—the emergence of new structures and processes (i.e., of developmental novelty). In other words, as also specified within the Thelen and Smith (1998) dynamic systems theory, *novelty* in structures and processes, in forms and patterns, arises through principles of system self-organization. Indeed, *self-organization* is a guiding principle within the developmental systems theory proposed by Magnusson. Thus, development, novelty, arises in the living world because the parts of the organism produce each other and, as such, through their association create the whole (Magnusson & Stattin, 1998).

Also consistent with the theories of Gottlieb (1997), Thelen and Smith (1998), and others (Lerner, 1978, 1991, 1996; Schneirla, 1957; Tobach & Greenberg, 1984), is Magnusson's view (1995, 1999a, 1999b; Magnusson & Endler, 1977) of the character of the relation among the components of this system: That is, holistic interaction is synonymous with *dynamic interaction*. Indeed, Magnusson and Stattin (1998, p. 701) noted that, "Dynamic interaction among operating factors is a fundamental characteristic of the processes of all living organisms *at all levels* . . . from the interaction that takes place between single cells in the early development of the fetus . . . to the individual's interplay with his or her environment across the life span."

Magnusson (1995, 1999a, 1999b, Magnusson & Stattin, 1998) noted that there are two key concepts that are involved in understanding the character of dynamic interaction: *reciprocity* and *nonlinearity*. Magnusson and Stattin (1998) pointed to data on the mutual influences of parents and children (e.g., Lerner et al., 1995) as the best illustration of reciprocity in the person–environment system. Similar to our discussion of Schneirla's (1957) idea of circular functions (Chapter 6), Magnusson and Stattin noted that reciprocity occurs in parent–child interactions as the behaviors of each person in the relationship act as an influence on the behavior of the other person and, at the same time, change as a consequence of the influence of the other person's behavior.

As do Thelen and Smith (1998), Magnusson (1995, 1999a, 1999b; Magnusson & Stattin, 1998) noted that nonlinearity is the prototypic characteristic of the relationship among constituents of the person–environment system. Nonsystems perspectives typically approach scholarship with the perspective that the relationship among variables is linear and, as well, that linear relations among variables that are identified by appraising differences between people may be generalized to the relations that exist among variables within a person (Magnusson & Stattin, 1998). However, increases (or decreases) in one variable are not always accompanied by proportional increases (or decreases) in another variable, either across people or within individuals. That is, rather than finding such linear changes to be ubiquitous, changes in one variable may be accompanied by disproportionate changes in another variable. Such relationships are curvilinear in character and, for instance, may take the form of "U"- or inverted "U"- shaped functions. For example, low levels of stress may not provide enough impetus to elicit high levels of performance on a given task or skill; high levels of stress may overwhelm the person and produce performance "paralysis" rather than high-level performance; but moderate levels of stress may be associated with the greatest likelihood of high-level performance (Magnusson & Stattin, 1998; Strauss, 1982).

Together, the notions of reciprocity and nonlinearity associated with dynamic interaction underscore the *bidirectional causality* involved in the developmental system envisioned by Magnusson (1995, 1999a, 1999b), and return us to the point that his model challenges the key concepts of nonsystems approaches to human development, even insofar as fundamental notions, such as the definition of the concept of "variable," are concerned. For instance, within the system of bidirectional, or configural, causality, such as the one seen in Figure 7.1:

> The concepts of independent and dependent variables, and of predictors and criteria, lose the absolute meaning that they have in traditional research, which assumes unidirectional causality. What may function as a criterion or dependent variable at a certain stage of a process may, at the next stage, serve as a predictor or independent variable. (Magnusson & Stattin, 1998, p. 702)

Moreover, Magnusson's theory changes the emphasis in developmental science from one of a search for information that will allow generalizations to be made about how variables function across individuals to one of attempting to understand how variables function within the person.

That is, because of the nonlinear relation among variables within the individual and because the individual's "internal" distinctiveness is both a product and a producer of his or her distinct pattern of exchanges with the other levels of organization within the total person–environment system, *individual differences* are a fundamental feature of human development. Indeed, in order to understand the development of the individual, one must identify the particular factors that are pertinent to his or her life and the specific ways these factors are organized and operate within him or her (Magnusson & Stattin, 1998). In short, "developmental changes do not take place in single aspects isolated from the totality. The total individual changes in a lawful way over time; individuals, not variables, develop" (Magnusson & Stattin, 1998, p. 727).

The complexity of this person-centered analysis is underscored when, as Magnusson (1995, 1999a, 1999b; Magnusson & Stattin, 1998) explained, one understands that the contextual component of the person–environment system is as multifaceted and individualistic as are the levels of organization having their primary loci within the individual (e.g., biology, cognition, personality, and behavior). That is, the *context* refers to:

> The total, integrated, and organized system, of which the individual forms a part, consists of a hierarchical system of elements, from the cellular level of the individual to the macro level of environments. . . . In actual operation, the role and functioning of each element in the total person–environment system depend on its context *within each level.* Each level of the system is simultaneously a totality seen in relation to lower levels, and a subsystem in relation to higher levels. Systems at *different levels* are mutually interdependent. (Magnusson & Stattin, 1998, p. 705)

Magnusson and Stattin (1998) depicted the complexity of these contextual components of the person–environment system by noting that the environment may be differentiated on the basis of its physical and social dimensions, and that a person may be influenced by either the actual and/or the perceived features of these two dimensions. Either dimension may serve as either a source of stimulation for behavior and/or a resource for information. In addition, environments may differ in the extent to which they provide an optimal context for healthy development, and in regard to the extent to which they serve over time as a basis for developmental change (i.e., as a *formative* environment; Magnusson & Stattin, 1998), or as a source for a specific behavior at a particular point in time (i.e., as a *triggering* environment; Magnusson & Stattin, 1998).

In addition, environments may be differentiated on the basis of their proximal or distal relationship to the person. For instance, the family or the peer group may constitute proximal contexts for the person, whereas social policies pertinent to family resources (e.g., policies regarding welfare benefits for poor families) may be part of the distal context of human development (cf. Bronfenbrenner & Morris, 1998).

Conclusions

When the complexity of the environment is coupled with the multiple dimensions of the person (e.g., his or her biology; mental system; subconscious processes; values, norms, motives, and goals; self-structures and self-perceptions; and behavioral characteristics; Magnusson and Stattin, 1998), the need for a holistic, integrated theory of the developmental system is apparent. This system must be engaged in order to understand the course of human development and, as well, to enhance or optimize it. Consistent with our earlier discussions (Chapter 5) of the implications of plasticity for intervention to enhance the course of human life, Magnusson and Stattin (1998) saw the need to involve all levels of the person and the system to not only design a comprehensive scientific research agenda but also to devise strategies to apply developmental science in ways that would promote positive human change:

> The holistic interactionistic view on individual functioning and development, as advocated here, implies that in the development of societal programs for intervention and treatment, the total person–environment system must be considered, not single problems of individual functioning and single risk factors in the social context. . . . Multiple agencies, programs, and initiatives must be integrated if the breadth of the person–context system is to be adequately engaged. (p. 740)

Thus, Magnusson's ideas about holistic interaction underscore the integral connection between science and application involved in a developmental systems perspective. His views of the scientific and societal utility of such theories are consistent with, and buttressed by, the ideas of other developmental systems theorists. Another significant instance of such a theory—one also spanning the research–application continuum and stressing the ideas of holism advanced by Magnusson—has been developed by Seymour Wapner and his colleagues over the course of the last half century (e.g., Wapner, 1969, 1977, 1981, 1987, 1995; Wapner & Demick, 1992, 1998, 1999; Werner & Wapner, 1949, 1952). It is useful to turn to a discussion of Wapner's ideas.

WAPNER'S HOLISTIC, DEVELOPMENTAL, SYSTEMS-ORIENTED PERSPECTIVE

Seymour Wapner (1981, 1987; Wapner & Demick, 1990, 1998, 1999) has developed a developmental systems theory that seeks to understand the "human in relation"; that is, the person as he or she interacts with all the levels of his or her context across the course of the entire life span. To devise such a broadly applicable theory, Wapner has explicitly attempted to synthesize features of both organismic and contextual world views.

As I discussed in Chapter 3 and as argued by Overton (1984) as well, Wapner (1986, 1987; Wapner & Demick, 1998) also believes that it useful to "violate" Pepper's (1942) proscription against "mixing metaphors" and trying to integrate ideas associated with different world views. Accordingly,

Seymour Wapner

Wapner formulated a theory that integrates the ideas of synthesis and holism fundamental to organicism and the dynamic interaction of contextualism, wherein "Relations among the aspects of the whole are not conceived of as involving mutual influences of antecedent–consequent causation. Instead the different aspects of wholes co exist as intrinsic and inseparable qualities of the whole" (Altman & Rogoff, 1987, p. 25).

Moreover, as in the other instances of developmental systems theory that are linked to such organismic–contextual integration—most notably, the probabilistic–epigenetic ideas of Schneirla (1957) and Gottlieb (1997), as well as in my own version of developmental systems theory—developmental contextualism (see Chapter 8, and Lerner, 1978, 1991, 1996, 1998b)—Wapner's synthesis of the organismic and contextual philosophies is linked to a commitment to the idea of levels of integration in human development. That is, Wapner (1986, 1987; Wapner & Demick, 1998) rejects reductionism and, quite specifically, biological reductionism. Rather, than viewing developmental events as epiphenomena or as by-products of other phenomena (e.g., genes), as in biological reductionism (e.g., Plomin, 1986, 2000; Rowe, 1994; Rushton, 1999), Wapner contends that phenomena at any one level of organization affect and are affected by phenomena at all other levels.

Given, then, this integrative orientation to developmental science, Wapner synthesized three key ideas within the developmental systems theory he forwarded: holism, development, and systems-orientation. The theory according to Wapner and Demick (1998)

is *holistic,* insofar as it assumes that all part processes—biological/physical, psychological (cognitive, affective, valuative), sociocultural—are interrelated; *developmental,* insofar as it assumes, in keeping with the orthogenetic principle (Werner, 1957), that development proceeds from a relative lack of differentiation toward the goal of differentiation and hierarchic integration of organismic functioning; and *systems-oriented* insofar as the unit of analysis is the *person-in-environment,* where the physical/biological (e.g., health), psychological (e.g., self-esteem), and sociocultural (e.g., role) levels of organization of the *person* are operative and interrelated with the physical (e.g., natural and built environment), interpersonal (e.g., friend, relative), and sociocultural (e.g., regulations and rules of society) levels of organization of the *environment.* (p. 761)

Accordingly, to Wapner (1987, 1995; Wapner & Demick, 1998, 1999), the unit of analysis within

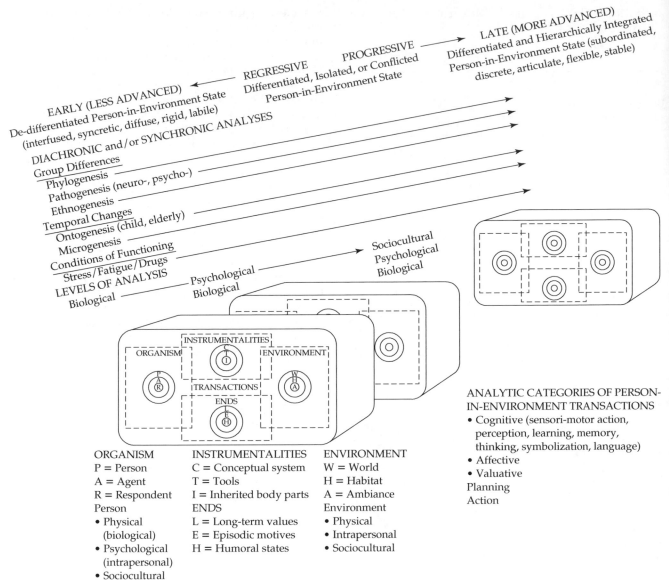

FIGURE 7.2
A holistic, developmental, systems-oriented approach to person-in-environment functioning.

Source: S. Wapner and J. Demick (1998, p. 767). Developmental analysis: A holistic, developmental, systems-oriented perspective. In R. M. Lerner (Vol. Ed.), *Handbook of Child Psychology: Vol. 1. Theoretical models of human development* (pp. 761–805). W. Damon. (Series Ed.) New York: Wiley. Copyright © 1998 by John Wiley & Sons, Inc. Reprinted with permission.

this theory is the organism-in-environment system. He specified that the organism and the environment are the structural components of this system and that they are related through *transactions,* that is, by exchanges involving experience (cognitive, affective, and valuative) and action, and possessing dynamic components characterized by ends (or goals) and means (or instrumentalities; Wapner, 1987, 1995; Wapner & Demick, 1998, 1999). Figure 7.2 presents an illustration of this complex system.

Person-in-Environment Functioning Within the Holistic, Developmental System

Consistent with the ideas of Gottlieb (1997), Magnusson (2000), Schneirla (1957), and Thelen and Smith (1998), Wapner and Demick (1998, 1999) noted that the organism-in-environment system represented in this figure reflects the integration of levels of organization. The least complex level is termed the *respondent-in-ambience* system, and involves reflexlike reactions of the organism to

Jack Demick

ambient stimulation. Wapner and Demick (1998, p. 767) noted that whereas "biological drives, sensory systems, and locomotor systems are clearly evident in these respondents, means and ends are more difficult to identify."

The next higher level in the system is termed the *agent-in-habitat* system, and involves the organism transacting with a context comprised of social and nonsocial objects. There is a goal for such transactions: satisfaction of episodic motives, such as the attainment of food or attaining a relationship with a mate. These goals are accomplished through the use of instrumentalities such as tools (Wapner, 1986, 1987, 1995; Wapner & Demick, 1998, 1999).

The most complex level in the system is the *person-in-world* system. Here, the person is shaped by his or her culture, and transacts with a context composed of sociocultural objects such as educational, religious, and political institutions and family and kinship rules. Both short- and long-term goals are involved in these transactions and, to Wapner (1986, 1987; Wapner & Demick, 1998), values are always a part of these ends. In addition, instrumentalities used in these transactions involve the formulation of plans and the use of conceptual systems, such as language or mathe-

matics (Wapner, 1987, 1995; Wapner & Demick, 1998, 1999).

Figure 7.2 illustrates, as well, the idea that there exist several analytic categories of experience, ones involving cognition, affect, and values, and of planning and action. In addition, the figure depicts progressive and regressive change, both presented in terms of the orthogenetic principle (Werner, 1957). Moreover, the figure displays the idea that the analyses of the system may proceed diachronically (across time) or synchronically (within time) and may involve the assessment of differences between groups, changes within individuals across time, or different conditions or states of the organism; these analyses can occur on one or more levels of organization (biological, psychological, and/or sociocultural).

The person-in-environment system that Wapner envisioned operates in accord with the principles of dynamic equilibrium, for instance, as we have noted that Thelen and Smith (1998) described. Indeed, consistent with the views of these other developmental scientists, Wapner and Demick (1998) noted that, within the dynamic equilibria of the person-in-environment system:

> Ongoing person-in-environment relations may be disturbed or perturbed by a change in the organism, in the environment, or in both. This may make for dramatic qualitative changes in the relations among system components (organism, environment, transactions, means, ends). Moreover, following perturbation of the organism-in-environment system, the reestablishment of a new dynamic equilibrium or ongoing state directed toward accomplishing goals is assumed to take place. (p. 771)

The goals of the actor, of the person within the person-in-environment system, introduce a *teleological-directedness* (Wapner & Demick, 1998, p. 773) to the holistic system. However, this teleology is not one of a suprasystem agent, or system designer giving form, organization, or direction to the system from a vantage point outside of it. Rather, teleology here is meant to reflect the fact that humans, especially at the level of the *person-in-world* system, have goals and intentions and use means to enact the ends they have selected. Humans' active transactions with their world, predicated on their goals and intentions (on their *teleological prospections*, if you will), are part of the self-organizational influences within the developmental system.

Conclusions

We will discuss models of such intentional behavior; for example, the Baltes and Baltes (1990) model of "selection, optimization, and compensation," in Chapter 9, in the context of reviewing systems-oriented theories that stress the central role of human action in the self-organization of the person–context developmental system (e.g., Brandtstädter, 1998, 1999). Here, we should note that by bringing the goals and intentions of the active individual into the levels of organization integrated within the holistic developmental system theory he has developed, Wapner is asserting the importance for understanding human development not only of cognition, affect, and action but also of values, aspirations, and hopes.

By incorporating these features of human functioning into his theory, Wapner is being consistent with his interest in forwarding a comprehensive and integrative theory of human development. His interest in valuation is central in his theory because he believes that all dimensions of psychological functioning—and critically ones involving valuing, planning, and acting with instrumentalities to attain one's planned ends—need to be synthesized in order to understand the rich panoply of person-in-environment transactions that are involved in healthy development—what he terms *adaptation* (Wapner, 1986, 1987; Wapner & Demick, 1998)—across life.

To promote such adaptation—conceived of as *optimal* relations between the person and his or her environment (Wapner & Demick, 1998)—Wapner conceives of actions that foster the person's altering self to fit the context, altering the context to fit the person, or mutual accommodations between person and context. In this view of the components that may be included in attempts to promote optimal development in people, Wapner's theory underscores again the use of developmental systems ideas for application. This link will be evident as well in the last instance of developmental systems theory we consider in this chapter, the perspective of Ford and Lerner (1992).

FORD AND LERNER'S DEVELOPMENTAL SYSTEMS THEORY

Ford and Lerner (1992) provided both a general overview of the guiding assumptions, or key design criteria, for a developmental systems theory and, as well, their specific ideas about human development. Ford and Lerner characterized human development as open, self-regulating and self-constructing system. Both their general design criteria and the specific formulation of developmental systems that

Donald H. Ford

they provided, are quite consistent with the ideas found in the theories of Gottlieb (1997), Magnusson (1995, 1999), Thelen and Smith (1998), and Wapner (1986, 1987), which should be familiar to readers by this point in the chapter. It is useful to describe, first, Ford and Lerner's (1992) specific conception of the human development system.

Human Development as a Living System

In regard to Ford and Lerner's (1992) specific formulation of developmental systems theory, they conceptualized a system as an organization wherein the functioning of each component is at least in part influenced by the collective state of the entire organization. As such, they saw a system as an entity wherein the cooperation of components both preserves the configuration of its structures and functions and, as a consequence of dynamic equilibrium, restores structure and function after perturbations (across fluctuations). They indicated that all biological (living) entities possess such systemic organization (Ford & Lerner, 1992) and that, as well, such systems are open ones (i.e., as explained also by Thelen and Smith, 1998); they "exchange material, energy, and/or information with their contexts" (Ford & Lerner, 1992, p. 95).

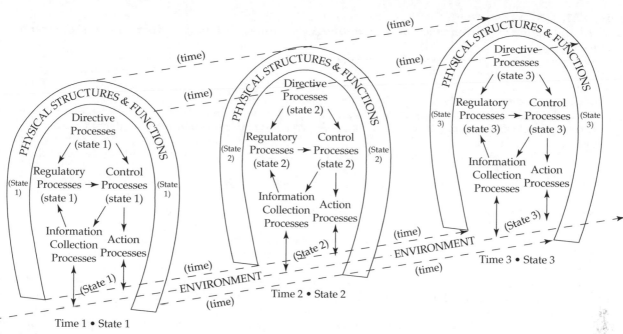

FIGURE 7.3

A prototypical representation of the dynamic nature of control systems. The component structure and processes are continually interacting among themselves and with their environment. The content of those activity configurations, called states, will vary and change across time as a function of their changing environment and of the internal dynamics of the system.

Source: D. H. Ford and R. M. Lerner (1992). Develpomental systems theory: An integrative approach (pp. 88–90). Copyright © 1992 by Sage Publications. Reprinted with permission.

As such, and underscoring the negentropic character of open, living systems, Ford and Lerner (1992) noted that such systems

> can become larger, more complex, and more elaborate because they can obtain and use additional resources from their contexts and transmit materials and information into their environments. Through such exchanges, moreover, they can alter the context and organization of their contexts. (p. 95)

As a consequence of these characteristics, open, living systems are self-constructing, self-regulating entities that, through their functioning, produce novelty—development—across time.

A depiction of the self-regulation—or *control system*—involved in open, living systems is presented in Figure 7.3. The figure presents interactions of the system components and processes both among themselves and with the environment within which the system is embedded. The configuration of these exchanges at any point in time are termed *states,* and the figure illustrates that these states vary across time in relation to internal system dynamics and the interactions with the context.

Moreover and consistent with the other developmental systems theories discussed in this chapter, Ford and Lerner (1992) explained that several

self-organization processes are involved in this control system and, together, these produce a dynamic equilibrium within the system. To illustrate, Ford and Lerner (1992) noted that:

> When a person reaches for an object, his or her mind establishes the goal (directive processes), the nervous system organizes the necessary movement pattern (control processes), and the body carries out the movements (action processes). The eye and muscle senses collect information about the accuracy of the action (information collection processes), the mind compares that with the desired result (regulatory processes), and initiates movement adjustments to ensure the desired result. (p. 98)

Based on this example, Ford and Lerner (1992) explained that:

> It is not necessary for the control system to anticipate, identify, and measure all the factors that might perturb its successful operation. That would be impossible. As long as the control system can compare current with desired states and make adjustments to reduce the discrepancy it doesn't need to know the nature of the perturbing influences. Because perturbations are frequently occurring and there is a time lag between the perturbation and the corrective action, the system will always oscillate around the exact values toward which it is directed. This kind of

TABLE 7.1
The Ford and Lerner (1992) Summary of the Guiding Assumptions, or Design Criteria, for Developmental Systems Theory

1. There are variables from multiple, qualitatively distinct levels of analysis or levels of organization involved in human life and development. These must operate in organized patterns to produce the coherent unitary functioning of the person-in context on which both life and development depend.
   a. The individual as a dynamic unit is to be understood as a complex, multilevel organization of biological structures plus biological and psychological–behavioral processes embedded and fused in dynamic interaction with multilevel environments.

2. Individuals' functioning and development result from a dynamic interaction within and between levels of organization of multiple, qualitatively different variables.
   a. The dynamic interactions among variables are in the form of reciprocal or mutually causal relationships through which the functioning of and changes in any variable are influenced by the organization of the set of variables in which it is embedded. This may be called a causal field of variables.
   b. The maintenance of stability as well as change and development result from the organization or configuration of variables rather than solely or even primarily through the operation of single variables.
   c. Changes in the dynamic organization of variables between and within levels constitute the basic nature of human development.

3. Each human differs from every other human in their genetic endowment, in the environments in which her or she is embedded during their lifetime, and in the dynamic interactions through which genetic and environmental variables are fused in their influence on behavior and development.
   a. A person's biological characteristics make possible their psychological–behavioral potentials through biological constraining and facilitating influences, but do not strictly determine the person's psychological–behavioral functioning and development. Similarly, a person's environments make possible sets of functional and developmental possibilities but do not strictly determine which are actualized.
   b. The flow of dynamic interactions among environmental and genetic–biological variables promotes and produces individuality in both developmental pathways and outcomes.

4. Human development displays relative plasticity so there is no single, ideal developmental pathway for any person.
   a. The dynamic interactions of one's genetic endowment and environments provide constraining and facilitating conditions or boundaries within which one's development occurs. Those boundaries are, themselves, dynamic because both one's environment and the nature of one's genetic processes vary and change across a lifetime.
   b. Within those dynamic boundaries there are multiple though not unlimited potential developmental pathways for any individual (i.e., development is multidimensional and multidirectional). The range of plasticity, of potential developmental pathways, may differ within and between components and levels such as biological, psychological, and social (e.g., the development of one's heart may be constrained to fewer possibilities than the development of one's cognitive capabilities).
   c. The nature of the constraining and facilitating conditions and of a person's potential developmental pathways change in both predictable and unpredictable ways, making development open ended and probabilistic rather than preordained and rigidly deterministic. Both chance and necessity play a role.

5. Individuals influence their own development through their own functioning in several ways. In that sense, humans are self-organizing and self-constructing.
   a. People process their world in unique ways so that the same environmental conditions may have different developmental influences from one person to another and for the same person from one occasion or developmental period to another.
   b. People are proactive as well as reactive. They selectively engage specific contexts and specific aspects of those contexts from among their potential environments. Through their actions, they alter their actual and potential environments, thereby influencing the nature of the environmental variables that may influence them.
   c. Person–context dynamics result from circular functions within and between levels of organization through which the person's characteristics and behaviors influence the feedback the environment provides, which, in turn, influences the person's characteristics and behaviors. This process is continuous although the content of the circular functions will vary.
   d. The social context is of special importance in human development, and people influence and stimulate changes in one another through their patterns of circular functions.

continues

TABLE 7.1
The Ford and Lerner (1992) Summary of the Guiding Assumptions, or Design Criteria, for Developmental Systems Theory (continued)

6. Individuals not only function to establish and maintain coherent intraperson organization so they can function effectively as a unit, but they also function to establish and maintain coherent person-context patterns of organization so they can function effectively as a component of their larger contexts.

   a. Establishing a goodness-of-fit between their personal characteristics and their contexts is a dynamic, continuing process since both persons and environments vary. The extent to which a person successfully matches his or her personal characteristics and functioning to the demands and opportunities of his or her contexts is an indicator of competence and a major influence on the content of the circular functions with his or her contexts.

Note. D. H. Ford and R. M. Lerner (1992). Developmental systems theory: An integrative approach. (pp. 88–90). Copyright © 1992 by Sage Publications. Reprinted with permission.

stable pattern of variability within boundaries is called a *dynamic equilibrium* or *steady state*. . . . Thus a person's life is never a steady hum (equilibrium), but, rather, it is more like a symphony (a dynamic equilibrium). (pp. 98–99)

Moreover, as emphasized by Wapner (1986, 1987; Wapner & Demick, 1998), a person's psychological characteristics—his or her thoughts, feelings, values, goals, and actions with instrumentalities—play an essential part in creating this dynamic equilibrium and, through the person–context fusions involved in it, create a basis for the self-construction of developmental change (novelty) across life. Indeed, the self-constructing abilities of humans are the defining characteristic differentiating living systems from nonliving control systems (e.g., the computers involved in the "automatic pilot" of a modern jet plane). The biological, psychological, and sociocultural characteristics of humans are reciprocally involved in providing humans with their self-regulatory, self-constructing capacities.

Through the fusion of these levels of organization, each level both produces humans' self-constructing capabilities and, in turn, is a product of them. Ford and Lerner (1992) noted that these self-constructing properties of the human development system have been labeled *autopoiesis*. Moreover and reflecting the ideas about developmental systems presented earlier in the chapter, they agreed with the view that the living systems of humans "are autonomous, nonlinear, dissipative, active, open, thermodynamic systems that persist, adapt, evolve, reproduce, and construct themselves" (Yates & Iberall, 1973, p. 17).

Design Criteria for Developmental Systems Theory

In short, Ford and Lerner's (1992) conception of the living, human development system reflects their commitment to the ideas of dynamism, self-organization, novelty, and the integration of levels of organization that have been hallmarks of the other instances of developmental systems discussed in this chapter. In introducing their specific developmental systems theory, Ford and Lerner (1992) presented a table summarizing the guiding assumptions of any developmental systems theory and, then, used this table as a template against which to judge the features of their own formulation. They contended that this table reflected the internal, logical coherence of the assumptions of developmental systems theories and, as such, constituted design criteria for any such theory of development (and, in fact, they argued, for "any adequate theory of development"; Ford & Lerner, 1992, p. 87).

Not surprisingly, given the consistency between the six design criteria presented in their table and the ideas their theory shares with the other developmental systems theories we have discussed, the points in the table, reproduced here as Table 7.1, constitute a useful summary of the key features of such theories of human development. Moreover, recognition of the commonality among developmental systems theories provides a useful introduction to some integrative comments about the dimensions and implications of developmental systems theory for basic and applied scholarship in human development.

FROM DEVELOPMENTAL SYSTEMS THEORIES TO APPLIED DEVELOPMENTAL SCIENCE

In our discussion of the history of concepts and theories of human development (Chapter 2), I noted that the editor of the third, 1970 edition of the *Handbook of Child Psychology*, Paul Mussen, presaged what today is abundantly clear about the contemporary stress on systems theories of human development. That is, it may be recalled that Mussen (1970, p. vii) said, "the major contemporary empirical and theoretical emphases in the field of developmental psychology . . . seem to be on *explanations* of the psychological changes that occur, the mechanisms and processes accounting for growth and development," and, thus, alerted developmental scientists to a burgeoning interest not in either structure, function, or content per se but to change, to the processes through which change occurs, and, thus, on the means through which structures transform and functions evolve over the course of human life.

Today, Mussen's vision has been crystallized. The cutting-edge of contemporary developmental theory is represented by systems conceptions of process, of how structures function and how functions are structured over time. Thus, as reflected in the theories reviewed in this chapter, developmental systems theories of human development are not tied necessarily to a particular content domain—although particular empirical issues or substantive foci (e.g., motor development, successful aging, wisdom, extraordinary cognitive achievements, language acquisition, the self, psychological complexity, or concept formation) may lend themselves readily as exemplary sample cases of the processes depicted in a given theory.

Furthermore, the theories we have reviewed illustrate that the power of developmental systems theories lies in their ability not to be limited by (or, perhaps better, be confounded by an inextricable association with) a unidimensional portrayal of the developing person (e.g., the person seen from the vantage point of only cognitions, emotions, or stimulus–response connections; see Piaget, 1970; Freud, 1949; Bijou & Baer, 1961, respectively). Thus, in developmental systems theories the person is neither biologized, psychologized, nor sociologized. Rather, the individual is "systemized," that is, his or her development is embedded within an integrated matrix of variables derived from multiple levels of organization; development is conceptualized as deriving from the dynamic relations among the variables within this multitiered matrix.

Developmental systems theories use the polarities that engaged developmental theory in the past (e.g., nature–nurture, individual–society, biology–culture; Lerner, 1976, 1986), but not to "split" depictions of developmental processes along conceptually implausible and empirically counterfactual lines (Gollin, 1981; Overton, 1998), or to force counterproductive choices between false opposites;

rather, these issues are used to gain insight into the integrations that exist among the multiple levels of organization involved in human development. These theories are certainly more complex than their one-sided predecessors; however, they are also more nuanced, more flexible, more balanced, and less susceptible to extravagant, or even absurd, claims (i.e., that "nature," split from "nurture," can shape the course of human development; that there is a gene for altruism, militarism, intelligence, and even television-watching; or that when the social context is demonstrated to affect development, the influence can be reduced to a genetic one; e.g., Hamburger, 1957; Lorenz, 1966; Plomin, 1986, 2000; Plomin et al., 1990; Rowe, 1994; Rushton, 1987, 1988, 1997, 1999).

These mechanistic and atomistic views of the past have been replaced, then, by theoretical models that stress the dynamic synthesis of multiple levels of analysis, a perspective having its roots in systems theories of biological development (Cairns, 1998; Gottlieb, 1992; Kuo, 1930, 1967, 1976; Schneirla, 1956, 1957; von Bertalanffy, 1933). In other words, development, understood as a property of systemic change in the multiple and integrated levels of organization (ranging from biology to culture and history) comprising human life and its ecology, is an overarching conceptual frame associated with the theoretical models of human development that we have reviewed in this chapter.

Accordingly, the power of these theories lies in the multilevel and, hence, multidimensional design criteria they impose on concepts (and research) pertinent to any content area about, or dimension of, the person. As illustrated by the above depiction of the multilevel, changing matrix representing the system involved in development, this power of a developmental systems perspective is constituted by four interrelated, and in fact "fused" (Tobach & Greenberg, 1984) components of such theories:

1. Change and relative plasticity.

2. Relationism and the integration of levels of organization.

3. Historical embeddedness and temporality.

4. The limits of generalizability, diversity, and individual differences.

Although these four conceptual components frame the contemporary set of developmental systems theories within the field of human development (Lerner, 1998a), each has a long and rich tradition in the history of the field (Cairns, 1998). For instance, Cairns (1998) described James Mark

Baldwin's (1897) interest in studying development-in-context, and, thus, in integrated, multilevel, and, hence, interdisciplinary scholarship. These interests were also shared by Lightner Witmer, the founder in 1896 of the first psychological clinic in the United States (Cairns, 1998; Lerner, 1977). As well, Cairns describes the conception of developmental processes—as involving reciprocal interaction, bidirectionality, plasticity, and biobehavioral organization (all emphases in current developmental systems theories)—as integral in the thinking of the founders of the field of human development. For instance, Wilhelm Stern (1914; see Kreppner, 1994) stressed the holism that is associated with a developmental systems perspective about these features of developmental processes. In addition, other contributors to the foundations and early progress of the field of human development (e.g., John Dewey, 1916; Kurt Lewin, 1935, 1954; John B. Watson, 1928) stressed the importance of linking child development research with application and child advocacy—a theme of very contemporary relevance (Zigler, 1999) and one that we have seen to be explicitly associated with some of the instances of developmental systems theories we have discussed in this chapter.

Although, as noted, the concepts involved in each of the four thematic components of contemporary theories are interrelated, it is useful to begin to discuss each separately. This discussion has several purposes. First, it serves as a means to integrate the ideas discussed in each of the theories reviewed in this chapter, and, as well, in the several instances of developmental systems theories that exist. In turn, this integration enables us to better understand the links between developmental systems theories and other theoretical formulations that draw from such models in order to depict key features of development across the life span (e.g., person–context relations, successful aging, or intentions and goal-directed behavior). Moreover, this integration also enables us to understand more clearly the dimensions of difference between developmental systems theories and theoretical formulations that diverge significantly from them, most prominently, theories that take nature, biological reductionistic approaches to development. Finally, this summary allows us to expand on previous points about the linkage between developmental systems theory and research and application in human development.

Change and Relative Plasticity

We have noted that developmental systems theories stress that the focus of developmental understanding must be on (systematic) change. This focus is required because of the belief that the potential for change exists across (a) the life span and (b) the multiple levels of organization comprising the ecology of humans. Although it is also assumed that systematic change is not limitless (e.g., it is constrained by both past developments and by contemporary ecological or contextual conditions), developmental systems theories stress that relative plasticity exists across life (Lerner, 1984).

There are important implications of relative plasticity for understanding the range of intraindividual variation that can exist over ontogeny (Fisher, Jackson, & Villarruel, 1998) and, in turn, for the application of development science. For instance, we have discussed that the presence of relative plasticity legitimates a proactive search across the life span for characteristics of people and of their contexts that, together, can influence the design of policies and programs promoting positive development (Birkel, Lerner, & Smyer, 1989; Fisher & Lerner, 1994; Lerner & Hood, 1986). For example, the plasticity of intellectual development, that is a feature of a systems view of mental functioning, provides legitimization for educational policies and school- and community-based programs aimed at enhancing cognitive and social cognitive development (Dryfoos, 1994; Villarruel & Lerner, 1994); such implications for the design of policies and programs stand in marked contrast to those associated with mechanistic, genetic reductionistic theories that suggest that genetic inheritance constrains intellectual development among particular minority and/or low-income groups (Herrnstein, 1973; Herrnstein & Murray, 1994; Jensen, 1969, 1980; Rushton, 1987, 1988).

Relationism and the Integration of Levels of Organization

Developmental systems theories stress that the bases for change, and for both plasticity and constraints in development, lie in the relations that exist among the multiple levels of organization that comprise the substance of human life (Schneirla, 1957; Tobach, 1981). These levels range from the inner–biological, through the individual–psychological and the proximal social relational (e.g., involving dyads, peer groups, and nuclear families), to the sociocultural level (including key macro-institutions such as educational, public policy, governmental, and economic systems), and the natural and designed physical ecologies of human development (Bronfenbrenner, 1979; Bronfenbrenner & Morris, 1998; Riegel, 1975). These tiers are structurally and functionally integrated, thus, underscoring the use of a developmental systems view of the levels involved in human development.

We have noted that such a developmental systems perspective promotes a *relational* unit of analysis as a requisite for developmental analysis: Variables associated with any level of organization exist (are structured) in relation to variables from other levels; the qualitative and quantitative dimensions of the function of any variable are shaped, as well, by the relations that the variable has with ones from other levels. Unilevel units of analysis (or the components of, or elements in, a relation) are not an adequate target of developmental analysis; rather, the relation itself—the interlevel linkage—should be the focus of such analysis (Fisher et al., 1998; Lerner, 1991; Riegel, 1975).

Moreover, relationism and integration have a clear implication for unilevel theories of development: At best, such theories are severely limited, and inevitably provide a nonveridical depiction of development, due to their focus on what are, essentially, main effects embedded in higher-order interactions (e.g., see Walsten, 1990); at worst, such theories are neither valid nor useful. Accordingly, neither biogenic theories (e.g., genetic reductionistic conceptions such as behavioral genetics or sociobiology; Freedman, 1979; Plomin, 1986; Rowe, 1994; Wilson, 1975), psychogenic theories (e.g., behavioristic or functional analysis models; Baer, 1970, 1976; Bijou, 1976; Bijou & Baer, 1961; Skinner, 1938), nor sociogenic theories (e.g., "social mold" conceptions of socialization; Homans, 1961; and see Hartup, 1978, for a review) provide adequate theoretical frames for understanding human development).

Thus, neither nature nor nurture theories provide adequate conceptual frames for understanding human development (cf. Hirsch, 1970; Lewontin, 1992). For instance, theories that stress critical periods of development (e.g., Ainsworth et al., 1978; Bowlby, 1969; Erikson, 1959, 1968; Lorenz, 1965, 1966), that is, periods of ontogeny constrained by biology (e.g., by genetics or by maturation), are seen from the perspective of theories that stress relationism and integration as conceptually flawed (and empirically counterfactual).

Moreover, many nature–nurture interaction theories also fall short in this regard; many theories of this type still treat nature and nurture variables as separable entities, and view their connection in manners analogous to the interaction term in an analysis of variance (e.g., Bijou, 1976; Erikson, 1959; Plomin, 1986; cf. Gollin, 1981; Hebb, 1970; Walsten, 1990). The theories discussed in this chapter move beyond the simplistic division of sources of development into nature- and nurture-related variables or processes; they see the multiple levels of organization that exist within the ecology of human development as part of an inextricably fused developmental system.

Historical Embeddedness and Temporality

The relational units of analysis of concern in developmental systems theories are understood as change units. The change component of these units derives from the ideas that all of the levels of organization involved in human development are embedded in the broadest level of the person–context system: history. That is, all other levels of organization within the developmental system are integrated with historical change. Relationism and integration mean that no level of organization functions as a consequence of its own, isolated action. Each level functions as a consequence of its fusion (its structural integration) with other levels (Gottlieb et al., 1998; Tobach & Greenberg, 1984). History—change over time—is incessant and continuous, and it is a level of organization that is fused with all other levels. This linkage means that change is a necessary and inevitable feature of variables from all levels of organization. In addition, this linkage means that the structure, as well as, the function, of variables changes over time.

An illustration of the temporality of developmental change occurs in regard to secular trends in child and adolescent physical and physiological maturation (Garn, 1980; Katchadourian, 1977; Tanner, 1991). Since 1900, children of preschool age have been taller on an average of 1.0 centimeter and heavier on an average of 0.5 kilogram per decade (Katchadourian, 1977). In turn, changes in height and weight occurring during the adolescent growth spurt have involved gains of 2.5 centimeters and 2.5 kilograms, respectively (Falkner, 1972; Katchadourian, 1977). In addition, there has been a historical trend downward in the average age of menarche. Among European samples of youth there was a decrease of about 4 months per decade from about 1840 to about 1950 (Tanner, 1962, 1991). This rate seems to have slowed down, but has not stopped (Marshall & Tanner, 1986; Tanner, 1991). Within American samples, however, the decline in age of menarche seems to have stopped in 1940. Since that time the expected (mean) age of menarche among European–American samples has been 12.5 years. In Japan, the most dramatic secular trend has been evidenced. From the immediate post-World War II years until about 1975, there was a decline of 11 months a decade in the average age of menarche (Marshall

& Tanner, 1991). These temporal changes in the biological maturation of youth are linked to historical improvements in health and nutrition in their respective nations, variation in turn associated with socioeconomic and technologic changes in their societies. Simply, biological structure and function and societal structure and function are linked systemically across history.

Indeed, at the biological level of organization, one prime set of structural changes across history is subsumed under the concept of evolution (Gould, 1977; Lewontin, 1981; Lewontin, Rose, & Kamin, 1984); of course, the concept of evolution can also be applied to functional changes (Darwin, 1872; Gottlieb, 1992). In turn, at more macro levels of organization many of the historically linked changes in social and cultural institutions or products are evaluated in the context of discussions of the concept of progress (Nisbet, 1980).

The continuity of change that constitutes history can lead to both intraindividual (or, more generally, intralevel) continuity or discontinuity in development—depending on the rate, scope, and particular substantive component of the developmental system at which change is measured (Brim & Kagan, 1980; Lerner, 1986, 1988; Lerner & Tubman, 1989). Thus and reflecting the dynamic equilibrium concept within developmental systems theories, continuity at one level of analysis may be coupled with discontinuity at another level; quantitative continuity or discontinuity may be coupled with qualitative continuity or discontinuity within and across levels; and continuity or discontinuity can exist in regard to both the processes involved in (or the "explanations" of) developmental change and in the features, depictions, or outcomes (i.e., the "descriptions") of these processes (Cairns & Hood, 1983; Lerner, 1986).

In sum, since historical change is continuous, temporality is infused in all levels of organization (Elder, 1998; Elder, Modell, & Parke, 1993). Accordingly, the temporality involved in contemporary theories of human development necessitates change-sensitive measures of structure and function *and* change-sensitive (i.e., longitudinal) designs (Baltes, Reese, & Nesselroade, 1977; Brim & Kagan, 1980). The key questions vis-à-vis temporality in such research is not whether change occurs; rather, the question is whether the changes that do occur make a difference for a given developmental outcome (Lerner, Skinner, & Sorell, 1980).

Given that the study of these changes will involve appraisal of both quantitative and qualitative features of change, which may occur at multiple levels of organization, there is a need to use both quantitative and qualitative data collec-

tion and analysis methods, ones associated with the range of disciplines having specialized expertise at the multiple levels of organization at which either quantitative or qualitative change can occur (Shweder et al., 1998). In essence, then, the concepts of historical embeddedness and temporality indicate that a program of developmental research adequate to address the relational, integrated, embedded, and temporal changes involved in human life must involve multiple occasions, methods, levels, variables, and cohorts (Baltes, 1987; Lerner, 1986, 1991; Schaie & Strother, 1968).

Temporality, Basic Process, and Application in Human Development

A development systems perspective, and the implications it suggests for research, through concepts such as temporality, may seem descriptively cumbersome; inelegant (if not untestable) in regard to explanations of individual and group (e.g., family) behavior and development; and, as a consequence, of little use in the formulation of interventions (policies or programs) aimed at enhancing individual and social life. In response to such criticism, I would argue that, in the face of the several profound historical changes in the lives of children and their families that have occurred across the last century (e.g., see Elder et al., 1993; Hernandez, 1993), it would seem, at best, implausible to maintain that the nature of the human life course has been unaffected by this history. For example, it is not plausible to assert that: (a) the historical changes that have resulted in an average age of menarche of 12.5 years in America—that is, an age when girls, although they may be capable of sexual reproduction, typically do not have the cognitive or behavioral capacity to assume the responsibilities that may accrue from such behavior; are not related to (b) historical increases in the United States in rates of engagement in high-risk sexual behaviors, teenage pregnancy, childbearing, and one-parent teenage families (Dryfoos, 1990; Hernandez, 1993; Lerner, 1995). Accordingly, it would seem necessary to adopt some sort of developmental systems perspective in order to incorporate the impact of such historical changes, and of the contemporary diversity it has created, into the matrix of covariation considered in developmental explanations and the interventions that should, at least ideally, be derived from them (Lerner & Miller, 1993).

Yet, it would be traditional in developmental psychology to assert that the historical variation and contemporary diversity of human (individual and group) development was irrelevant to understanding *basic* processes. Indeed, within developmental psychology, the conventional view of basic process, whether involving cognition, emotion, personality, or social behavior, is that it is a function generalizable across time and place. I believe, however, that data such as those presented by Elder et al. (1993) and Hernandez (1993)—which document the profound impact of historical change on individual and family life over the course of just the last two centuries—constitute a serious challenge to the ontological presuppositions that have grounded this view of basic process and, as such, of developmental psychology's theory and research about people's ontogenies.

Can learning, cognition, and emotional life, and the brain and neuroendocrine systems underlying these functions, be argued to occur invariantly in the context of the differing economic, nutritional, and medical resource environments, and of the different systems of work, school, and family relationships, that have occurred over the course of the last century and that, today, are involved in the diverse social contexts (e.g., families) of America and the world? Can developmental psychology, with a historical record of minimal attention to history (Elder et al., 1993), context (Bronfenbrenner, 1979), and diversity (Graham, 1992; Lerner, 1991), contend that the atemporal and acontextual study of the individual is an appropriate or adequate focus of its inquiry?

I believe the answers to these questions are "no," and that, quite simply, the traditional view of basic process found in developmental psychology (i.e., the prototypic view for much of the last 50 to 60 years) cannot be defended in the face of the historical and contextual variation characterizing American individuals and families across the past century. Indeed, without adequate tests of, and evidence for, its presuppositions about the irrelevance of temporality, context, and diversity for its view of basic process, the field of developmental psychology fails in even an attempt to represent veridically the course of human life (Cairns, 1998).

By weaving historical change and contextual specificities into the matrix of causal covariation that shapes human developmental trajectories, I believe that a developmental systems perspective reconstitutes the core process of human development from a reductionistic and individualistic process to a synthetic, or multilevel integrated process. That is, a developmental systems perspective stresses temporality and relationality and the field, or configural, view of causality previously noted (Ford & Lerner, 1992; Overton, 1998). Through the seemingly simple step of integrating historical change, contextual variation, and individual developmental change, a developmental systems perspective provides a paradigmatic departure from the psychogenic, biogenic, or reductionistic environmentalist models of causality that have undergirded the theories of human development that have been prevalent during most of this century (Gottlieb, 1992; Lerner, 1986, 1991). These theories typify a reductionism and contextual insensitivity which occurs because developmental psychologists are traditionally focused on psychogenic views of the course of human development (Dannefer, 1984; Meyer, 1988).

Such a psychogenic, or exclusively individualistic perspective, has led numerous developmental psychologists, and perhaps especially those who study cognitive functioning, to take the a priori position that any phenomenon of individual behavior and development that interacts with the context is not a basic psychological process; this same orientation has resulted in the contention that information about temporal or interindividual variation is not relevant to the understanding of basic process. Accordingly, the several "revolutions" that have occurred over the last 150 years in the nature of the family context of American children's development (e.g., involving decreases in family size; changes in maternal and paternal employment patterns; a different set of structures, for instance, single-parent ones, characterizing American families; and the spread of youth poverty; Hernandez, 1993) have not been seen by the psychogenicists populating developmental psychology as relevant to the nature or study of basic process.

However, the historical changes and contextual variation that characterize America's children and families challenge this position, not only by presenting ontologically revolutionary ideas to developmental psychologists, but also by promoting epistemological revisions among those who have studied child development through unidisciplinary lenses. As noted by Cahan, Mechling, Sutton-Smith, and White (1993, p. 210), "if childhood is not everywhere and everyplace the same—and the anthropologists and social historians have been amply demonstrating to us that it is not—then the meaning and object of all forms of psychological research have to be reconsidered." Accordingly, a multiplicity of qualitative and quantitative methods—ones associated with the several disciplines that have demonstrated this temporal and relational specificity of child development—must be used to construct the knowledge of the multiple levels of organization that are involved in the system linking children and contexts (Shweder et al., 1998). In turn, use of these methods in relation to contextually sensitive theory affords an empirically richer focus on classic issues in the study of personality (e.g., regarding individual differences) and cognition (e.g., regarding learning) that have concerned developmental psychologists across this century.

In short, I believe that a developmental systems view of the historical and developmental ecology of individual and family life helps reduce the incidence of what Elder et al. (1993, p. 6) termed the "blindness to social history and context" prevalent in much of psychology and, even, sociology, a blindness which, to paraphrase them (1993, p. 7) has envisioned the child as embedded in the atemporal and acontextual realm of abstract developmental theory. This is, to say the least, a curious conceptual stance for a field seemingly focused on change.

The Limits of Generalizability, Diversity, and Individual Differences

The temporality of the changing relations among levels of organization means that changes that are seen within one historical period (or time of measurement) and/or with one set of instances of variables from the multiple levels of the ecology of human development, may not be seen at other points in time (Baltes et al., 1977; Bronfenbrenner, 1979). What is seen in one data set may be only an instance of what does or what could exist. Accordingly, contemporary systems theories focus on diversity—of people, relations, settings, and times of measurement (Lerner, 1991, 1995, 1996).

Individual differences within and across all levels of organization are seen as having core, substantive significance in the understanding of human development (Baltes et al., 1998; Lerner, 1991, 1995, 1996). Diversity is the exemplary illustration of the presence of relative plasticity in human development (Fisher et al., 1998; Lerner, 1984). Diversity is also the best evidence that exists of the potential for change in the states and conditions of human life (Brim & Kagan, 1980).

Moreover, the individual structural and functional characteristics of a person constitute an important source of his or her development (Brandtstädter, 1998, 1999; Csikszentmihalyi & Rathunde, 1998; Lerner, 1982; Lerner & Busch-Rossnagel, 1981). The individuality of each person promotes variation in the fusions he or she has with the levels of organization within which the person is embedded. For instance, in discussing Schneirla's (1957) notion of circular functions in ontogeny (Chapter 6), I noted that the distinct actions or physical features of a person promote differential actions (or reactions) in others toward him or her. These differential actions, which constitute

feedback to the person, shape, at least in part, further change in the person's characteristics of individuality (Lerner & Lerner, 1989; Schneirla, 1957).

For instance, several studies of American adolescents report that pubertal maturation negatively alters the nature of the social interactions between youth and their parents, for example, at the height of pubertal change more conflict and greater emotional distance is seen (e.g., Hill et al., 1985a, 1985b; Holmbeck & Hill, 1991; Steinberg, 1987, 1990; Steinberg & Hill, 1978). However, these findings have been derived in large part from research with homogeneous, European-American samples of adolescents and their families (Brooks-Gunn & Reiter, 1990). Accordingly, when diversity is introduced into the data base used for understanding the links between pubertal change and adolescent–parent relationships, a much more complicated—and richer and more interesting—pattern is evident. Among samples of Latino (primarily Mexican-American) boys and their families, pubertal maturation brings youth *closer* to their parents (Molina & Chassin, 1996). Puberty among these Latino youth is associated with greater parental social support and less intergenerational conflict than is the case either for correspondingly mature European-American samples (where the completely opposite effect of puberty on family relations is seen) or for Latino youth prior to or after their maturation.

In essence, racial/ethnic, cultural, and developmental diversity must be understood systematically in order to appreciate the nature and variation that exists within and across time in human behavior and development. In other words, individual differences arise inevitably from the action of the development system; in turn, they move the system in manners that further elaborate diversity. It is useful to discuss in more detail the nature and import of individuality in human development.

Implications for Research and the Application of Developmental Science

A developmental systems perspective involves the study of active people providing a source across the life span of their individual developmental trajectories; this development occurs through the dynamic interactions people experience with the specific characteristics of the changing contexts within which they are embedded (Brandtstädter, 1998). This stress on the dynamic relation between the individual and his or her context results in the recognition that a synthesis of perspectives from multiple disciplines is needed to understand the multilevel (e.g., person, family, and community) integrations involved in human development. In addition, to understand the basic process of human development—the process of change involved in the relations between individuals and contexts—both descriptive and explanatory research must be conducted within the actual ecology of people's lives.

In the case of explanatory studies, such investigations by their very nature constitute intervention research. The role of the developmental researcher conducting explanatory research is to understand the ways in which variations in person–context relations account for the character of human developmental trajectories, life paths that are enacted in the "natural laboratory" of the "real world." Therefore, to gain understanding of how theoretically relevant variations in person–context relations may influence developmental trajectories, the researcher may introduce policies and/or programs as, if you will, "experimental manipulations" of the proximal and/or distal natural ecology; evaluations of the outcomes of such interventions become a means to bring data to bear on theoretical issues pertinent to person–context relations and, more specifically, on the plasticity in human development that may exist, or that may be capitalized on, to enhance human life (Csikszentmihalyi & Rathunde, 1998; Lerner, 1984). In other words, a key theoretical issue for explanatory research in human development is the extent to which changes—in the multiple, fused levels of organization comprising human life—can alter the structure and/or function of behavior and development.

Life itself, of course, an intervention. That is, the accumulation of the specific roles and events a person experiences across life—involving normative age-graded events, normative history-graded events, and nonnormative events (Baltes et al., 1998; Baltes, Reese, & Lipsitt, 1980)—alters each person's developmental trajectory in a manner that would not have occurred had another set of roles and events been experienced. The interindividual differences in intraindividual change that exist as a consequence of these naturally occurring interventions attest to the magnitude of the systematic changes in structure and function—the plasticity—that characterizes human life.

Explanatory research is necessary, however, to understand what variables, from what levels of organization, are involved in particular instances of plasticity that have been seen to exist. In addition, such research is necessary to determine what instances of plasticity may be created by science or society. In other words, explanatory research is

needed to ascertain the extent of human plasticity or, in turn, the limits of plasticity (Baltes, 1987; Baltes et al., 1998; Lerner, 1984). From a developmental systems perspective, the conduct of such research may lead the scientist to alter the natural ecology of the person or group he or she is studying. Such research may involve either proximal and/or distal variations in the context of human development (Lerner & Ryff, 1978); but, in any case, these manipulations constitute theoretically guided alterations of the roles and events a person or group experiences at, or over, a portion of the life span.

These alterations are indeed, then, interventions: They are planned attempts to alter the system of person–context relations that constitute the basic process of change; they are conducted in order to ascertain the specific bases of, or to test the limits of, particular instances of human plasticity (Baltes, 1987; Baltes & Baltes, 1980; Baltes et al., 1998). These interventions are a researcher's attempt to substitute designed person–context relations for naturally occurring ones in an attempt to understand the process of changing person–context relations that provide the basis of human development. In short, then, basic research in human development is intervention research (Lerner et al., 1994).

Accordingly, the cutting-edge of theory and research in human development lies in the application of the conceptual and methodological expertise of human development scientists to the natural ontogenetic laboratory of the real world. Although the focus of our discussion in Chapter 18 is the implications for developmental research methodology of concepts and theories of development, here, in regard to the specific import of developmental systems notions, it is useful to suggest that multilevel, and hence, multivariate, and longitudinal research methods must be used by scholars from multiple disciplines to derive, from theoretical models of person–context relations, programs of "applied research"; these endeavors must involve the design, delivery, and evaluation of interventions aimed at enhancing—through scientist-introduced variation—the course of human development (Birkel, Lerner, & Smyer, 1989).

This relationism and contextualization has brought to the fore of scientific, intervention, and policy concerns issues pertinent to the functional import of diverse instances of person–context interactions. Examples are studies of the effects of maternal employment, marital disruption, or single-parent families on infant, child, and young adolescent development; the importance of quality day care, variation in school structure and function, and neighborhood resources and programs for the immediate and long-term development in children of healthy physical, psychological, and social characteristics; and the effects of peer group norms and behaviors, risk behaviors, and economic resources on the healthy development of children and youth.

Accordingly, as greater study has been made of the actual contexts within which children and parents live, behavioral and social scientists have shown increasing appreciation of the diversity of patterns of individual and family development that exist, and that comprise the range of human structural and functional characteristics. Such diversity—involving racial, ethnic, gender, national, and cultural variation—has, to the detriment of the knowledge base in human development, not been a prime concern of empirical analysis (Fisher et al., 1998; Hagen, Paul, Gibb, & Wolters, 1990).

Yet, there are several reasons why this diversity must become a key focus of concern in the study of human development. Diversity of people and their settings means that one cannot assume that general rules of development either exist for, or apply in the same way to, all children and families (Fisher & Brennan, 1992; Fisher & Tryon, 1990; Lerner, 1988; Lerner & Tubman, 1989). This is not to say that general features of human development do not exist, or that descriptive research documenting such characteristics is not an important component of past, present, and future scholarship. However, the lawful individuality of human behavior and development means that one should not make a priori assumptions that characteristics identified in one or even in several groups exist or function in the same way in another group. Moreover, even when common characteristics are identified in diverse groups, we cannot be certain that the individual or unique attributes of each group—even if they account for only a small proportion of the variance in the respective groups' functioning—are not of prime import for understanding the distinctive nature of the groups' development or for planning key components of policies or programs (i.e., for planning "services") designed for the groups.

Accordingly, a new research agenda is necessary. This agenda should focus on diversity and context while at the same time attending to commonalities of individual development, family changes, and the mutual influences between the two. In other words, diversity should be placed at the fore of our research agenda. Then, with a knowledge of individuality, we can empirically determine parameters of commonality and interindividual generalizability. Thus, we should no longer

make a priori assumptions about the existence of generic developmental laws or of the primacy of such laws, even if they are found to exist, in providing the key information about the life of a given person or group.

Simply, integrated multidisciplinary and developmental research devoted to the study of diversity and context must be moved to the fore of scholarly concern. Research in human development that is concerned with one or even a few instances of individual and contextual diversity cannot be assumed to be useful for understanding the life course of all people. Similarly, policies and programs derived from such research, or associated with it in the context of a researcher's tests of ideas pertinent to human plasticity, cannot hope to be applicable, or equally appropriate and useful, in all contexts or for all individuals. Accordingly, developmental and individual differences-oriented policy development and program (intervention) design and delivery must be integrated fully with the new research base for which I am calling.

The variation in settings within which people live means that studying development in a standard (e.g., a "controlled") environment does not provide information pertinent to the actual (ecologically valid), developing relations between individually distinct people and their specific contexts (e.g., their particular families, schools, or communities). This point underscores the need to conduct research in real-world settings (Bronfenbrenner, 1974; Zigler, 1999), and highlights the ideas that: (a) Policies and programs constitute natural experiments (i.e., planned interventions for people and institutions) and (b) the evaluation of such activities becomes a central focus in the developmental systems research agenda that I have described (Cairns, 1998; Lerner, 1995; Lerner, Ostrom, & Freel, 1995; Ostrom, Lerner, & Freel, 1995).

In this view, policy and program endeavors do not constitute secondary work, or derivative applications, conducted after research evidence has been complied. Quite to the contrary, policy development and implementation, and program design and delivery, become integral components of the present vision for research; the evaluation component of such policy and intervention work provides critical feedback about the adequacy of the conceptual frame from which this research agenda should derive (Zigler, in press; Zigler & Finn-Stevenson, 1992).

To be successful, this developmental, individual differences, and contextual view of research, policy, and programs for human development requires not only collaboration across disciplines but also multi-professional collaboration. Colleagues in the research, policy, and intervention communities must plan and implement their activities in a synthesized manner in order to successfully develop and extend this vision. All components of this collaboration must be understood as equally valuable, indeed, as equally essential. The collaborative activities of colleagues in university extension, in service design and delivery, in policy development and analysis, and in academic research are vital to the success of this new agenda for science and service for children, youth, and their contexts (e.g., their families, schools, and communities). Moreover, such collaborative activities must involve the communities within which such work is undertaken (Lerner & Miller, 1993; Lerner, Miller, & Ostrom, 1995; Miller & Lerner, 1994).

In other words, to enhance its ecological validity, and to provide empowerment and increased capacity among the people that we are trying to both understand and serve with our synthetic research and intervention activities, we must work with the community to codefine the nature of our research and program design, delivery, and evaluation endeavors. In short, then, we must find ways to apply our scientific expertise to collaborate with, and promote the life chances of, the people participating in our developmental scholarship. Such steps will provide needed vitality for the future progress of the field of human development.

Indeed, I believe that the future scholarly and societal significance of the field of human development lies in such application of developmental science, that is, in building a scientific enterprise that works to help envision, enact, and sustain effective policies and programs promoting the positive development of people across the life span (Zigler, in press). Accordingly, Chapter 19 is devoted to a discussion of applied developmental science.

Here, however, it is useful to note that such a focus of the scholarship of the human development field is, on the one hand, a logical and—if judged by the previously noted trends in the theoretical foci of the field—an inevitable outcome of the growth and progress developmental science has experienced as a scientific community (Cairns, 1998; Zigler, 1999). On the other hand, the four summary themes that I have reviewed in regard to developmental systems theories may lead the field to embrace a focus on (a) ecologically embedded research, (b) on testing notions of person–context relational systems, and (c) on relative plasticity—in order to appraise whether theoretically predicated changes in the nature and course of the relations people have with the proximal and distal

features of their context can alter in salutary ways the trajectories of their development.

In other words, the concepts of development embraced in developmental systems theory lead us to test our theories through intervention/action research. Simply, I believe that within the field of scholarship about human development, basic research and applied research are synthetic, indivisible endeavors.

Conclusions

A developmental systems perspective leads us to recognize that, if we are to have an adequate and sufficient science of human development, we must integratively study individual and contextual levels of organization in a relational and temporal manner (Bronfenbrenner, 1974; Zigler, 1998). If we are to serve America's citizens and families through our science and if we are to help develop successful policies and programs through our scholarly efforts, then we may make great use of the integrative temporal and relational model of the person and of his or her context that is embodied in the developmental systems perspective forwarded in contemporary theories of human development.

This theme of the linkage between science and service to society—of seeing science as an instrument of civil society (Lerner, Fisher, & Weinberg, 1997, 2000a, 2000b; Lerner, Sparks, & McCubbin, 1999, 2000)—continues to be emphasized, both in our discussion of ideas consistent with and discrepant from developmental systems theories. Although, to some, the importance of this linkage may seem to be self-evident, it is important to point out that the idea of science serving society is not uncontroversial. In fact, some scholars maintain that if science is to retain its important, and perhaps singular, stature as an objective arbiter of truth, it can best serve society by remaining independent of the social and political events of society (however, see Boyer, 1990, 1994; Whitehead, 1936).

Accordingly, in subsequent chapters, we have reason to again explore the potential "uses and abuses" of science when it is involved as an instrument of, if not civil society, then at the least of social action. Indeed, we begin to further explore this linkage between science and service in our discussion in Chapter 8 of another theoretical model associated with developmental systems theory, one developed in relation to trying to understand the bidirectional relations across the life span between individuals and their social world: developmental contextualism.

8 | *Developmental Systems Theory: The Sample Case of Developmental Contextualism*

Developmental contextualism is an instance of developmental systems theory. Consistent with the emphases on integrative (or fused) relations between individuals and contexts found in other instances of such systems perspectives (Chapter 7), the central idea in developmental contextualism is that changing, reciprocal relations (or dynamic interactions) between individuals and the multiple contexts within which they live comprise the essential process of human development (Lerner, 1986; Lerner & Kauffman, 1985).

As described in previous chapters, developmental contextualism stresses that bidirectional relations exist among the multiple levels of organization involved in human life (e.g., biology, psychology, social groups, and culture) (Bronfenbrenner, 1977, 1979; Lerner, 1986, 1991, 1996, 1998b). These dynamic relations provide a framework for the structure of human behavior (Ford & Lerner, 1992). In addition, this system is itself dynamically interactive with historical changes; this temporality provides a change component to human life (Dixon, Lerner, & Hultsch, 1991a, 1991b). In other words, within developmental contextualism a changing configuration of relationships constitutes the basis of human life—of behavior and development (Ford & Lerner, 1992).

PROBABILISTIC EPIGENESIS WITHIN DEVELOPMENTAL CONTEXTUALISM

We have noted in previous chapters that developmental contextualism takes a probabilistic–epigenetic view of biological functioning. Biological and contextual factors are considered to be reciprocally interactive. Developmental changes are probabilistic in respect to normative outcomes due to variation in the timing of the biological, psychological, and social factors (or levels) that provide interactive bases of ontogenetic progressions (e.g., Schneirla, 1957; Tobach, 1981). Indeed, we have noted that the developmental–contextual conception of development can be traced to comparative biology (Novikoff, 1945a, 1945b) and comparative psychology (e.g., Gottlieb, 1970, 1976a, 1976b; Kuo, 1967; Maier & Schneirla, 1935; Schneirla, 1957). In this literature, the probabilistic–epigenetic perspective is not used to emphasize intrinsically predetermined (or inevitable) timetables and outcomes of development; instead, the probabilistic–epigenetic perspective stresses that the influence of the changing context on development is that it makes the trajectory of development less certain with respect to the applicability of norms to the individual (Gottlieb, 1970; Tobach, 1981).

Thus, such a conception emphasizes the probabilistic character of both the directions and outcomes of development, and, in so doing, admits of more plasticity in development than do predeterministic conceptions. As we discussed in Chapter 5, it is this plasticity which necessitates a revised formulation of the continuity–discontinuity issue. The plasticity which derives from the probabilistic (yet, causal) interaction among levels makes both continuity and/or discontinuity a probabilistic feature of developmental change across life periods.

Probabilism in continuity and discontinuity is stressed because, to reiterate the ideas of Gottlieb (1970, p. 123), "behavioral development of individuals within a species does not follow an invariant or inevitable course, and, more specifically, . . . the sequence or outcome of individual behavioral development is probable (with respect to norms) rather than certain." Of course, it is possible to ask whether all instances of continuity and discontinuity have an equal probability of occurrence. As explained by Thelen and Smith (1998; see, too, Ford & Lerner, 1992), this is not the case. Within a dynamic developmental system, the dialectic between system-changing and system-constraining relations reduces the degrees of freedom available for change; thus, the potentially infinite instances of change that could exist within a dynamic, open, and living system are reduced through the self-organizing actions of the system.

In other words, development occurs in a multi-level context. The nature of the changes in this context contributes to the probabilistic character of development; but one also needs to appreciate that the organism as much shapes the context as the context shapes the organism, and that—at the same time—both organism and context constrain (or limit) the other. The processes that give humans their individuality and plasticity are the same ones that provide their commonality and constancy (Lerner, 1984, 1988).

Although there is some probability that any process or feature of development could show continuity or discontinuity, constraints on change, arising from both organism and context, make some instances of constancy and change more probable than others. This differential probability complicates the study of continuity and discontinuity because it requires not only an indication of "confidence intervals" around particular instances of continuity and discontinuity but also a specification of the likely systemic ordering of such instances.

For example, it is less likely that a large and complex social institution such as a junior high school will alter its overall curriculum or educational policies to accommodate one child's individuality than it is that a single classroom will show such change. Nevertheless, there is some possibility that a particular instance of a child's individuality (e.g., consider a child with AIDS) will evoke a general change in the junior high school. Conversely, it is less likely that the experience of instruction within a single course will alter the lives of an entire cohort of adolescents than it is that the experience of an overall high school curriculum will have that influence. Yet, as the case of East Los Angeles Garfield High School mathematics teacher, Jaime Escalante, illustrates (in the 1988 film *Stand and Deliver*), a single class, or in

this case teacher, can indeed alter the educational lives of an entire cohort of students. Thus, although a single child is more likely to influence one classroom than an entire school, and although a cohort of high school students is more likely to be influenced by an entire school curriculum than by a single course, there is, nevertheless, some probability in both cases that the less likely change will occur.

Another key point about the developmental–contextual view needs to be highlighted. Although, in attempting to explain development, both this conception and mechanistic–behavioral views conceive of the context as enveloping an organism, it is clear that they do so in distinctly different ways. Developmental–contextual theorists do not adopt a reductionistic approach to conceptualizing the impact of the context (Tobach, 1981). Instead, there is a focus on organism–context transactions (Sameroff, 1975), a commitment to using an interlevel (or relational) unit of analysis (Lerner, 1984) and, as previously emphasized, a concept of the context as composed of multiple, qualitatively different levels (e.g., see Riegel, 1975, 1976a, 1976b).

Moreover, although both the mechanistic and the developmental–contextual perspectives hold that changes in the context become part of intra-individual changes in the organism's constitution, the concept of "organism" found in the two perspectives is also quite distinct. The organism in developmental contextualism is not merely the host of the elements of a simplistic environment (e.g., as in Baer, 1976). Instead, the organism is itself a qualitatively distinct level within the multiple, dynamically interacting levels forming the context of life.

As such, the organism has a distinct influence on the multilevel context that is influencing it. The organism is an active contributor to its own development (Lerner, 1982; Lerner & Busch-Rossnagel, 1981a, 1981b; Lerner & Walls, 1999).

Probabilistic Epigenesis and Human Evolution

Clearly, from a developmental–contextual perspective, human behavior is both biological and social (Featherman & Lerner, 1985; Tobach & Schneirla, 1968). In fact, no form of life as we know it comes into existence independent of other life. No animal lives in total isolation from others of its species across its entire life span (Tobach, 1981; Tobach & Schneirla, 1968).

Indeed, in regard to humans, early human were relatively defenseless, having neither sharp teeth nor claws. Coupled with the dangers of living in the open African savanna, where much of early human evolution occurred, group living was essential for survival (Masters, 1978; Washburn, 1961). Therefore, human beings were more likely to survive if they acted in concert with the group than if they acted in isolation. Human characteristics that support social relations (e.g., attachment and empathy) may have helped human survival over the course of human evolution (Hoffman, 1978; Hogan, Johnson, & Emler, 1978; Sahlins, 1978).

Biological survival requires meeting the demands of the environment or, as I noted in previous chapters and discuss again later in the present one, attaining a goodness of fit (Chess & Thomas, 1984, 1999; Lerner & Lerner, 1983, 1989; Thomas & Chess, 1977) with the context. Because this environment is populated by other members of one's species, adjustment to (or fit with) these other organisms is a requirement of survival (Tobach & Schneirla, 1968).

Given this biological contribution to, or, better, in the terms of dynamic developmental systems, fusion with the social ecology of human development, it is not surprising to learn that several scholars having ideas associated with developmental systems theory believe that human evolution has promoted the link between biological and social functioning (Featherman & Lerner, 1985; Gould, 1977). In other words, the ontogenetic integration of human biological and social levels of organization has been shaped by the evolutionary history of humans.

The scholarship of Stephen J. Gould has provided singular contributions to the understanding of this linkage between ontogeny and phylogeny. A discussion of his ideas allows us to understand the relevance of human evolution to the dynamic person–context relations that, in developmental contextualism, propel individual development across the life span.

GOULD'S VIEWS OF ONTOGENY AND PHYLOGENY: EVOLUTIONARY BASES OF RECIPROCAL PERSON–SOCIAL CONTEXT RELATIONS

As evident from the title of his book, *Ontogeny and Phylogeny* (1977), Stephen J. Gould has had an abiding interest in detailing the relation between ontogeny and phylogeny. He contends that that "some relationship exists cannot be denied. Evolutionary changes must be expressed in ontogeny, and phyletic information must, therefore, reside in the development of individuals" (Gould, 1977, p. 2). However, this point in itself is obvious and unenlightening for Gould. What makes the study of the relation between ontogeny and phylogeny interesting and important is that there are "*changes in developmental timing* that produce *parallels* between the stages of ontogeny and phylogeny" (Gould, 1977, p. 2).

Discussing the relation between ontogeny and phylogeny may raise the hackles (read: "Haeckels") of many scientists. This may be especially true for those trained in human development, where, as discussed in Chapter 2, the recapitulationist ideas of Haeckel (e.g., 1868), especially as they were adopted by G. Stanley Hall (1904), have long been in disfavor. To recall our earlier discussion, we may note that, in simplified form, Haeckel's theory was one of *recapitulation,* by which he meant that the mechanism of evolution was *a change in the timing of developmental events such that there occurred a universal acceleration of development that pushed ancestral forms into the juvenile stages of descendants*. For example, Haeckel (1868) interpreted the gill slits of human embryos as characteristics of ancestral adult fish that had been compressed into the early stages of human ontogeny through a universal mechanism of acceleration of developmental rates in evolving lines.

It is unfortunate for the scientific study of links between ontogeny and phylogeny that people have come to equate Haeckel's recapitulation idea with all potential types and directions of evolutionary change in the timing of developmental events. This is because there is an alternative to the changes in timing specified by recapitulation, and it provides an evolutionary basis for viewing person–social context relations in a reciprocal manner. According to Gould (1977), this alternative is the key to human evolution and to human plasticity. In order to understand this alternative, we need to introduce three interrelated terms: heterochrony, neoteny, and paedomorphosis.

According to Gould (1977), evolution occurs when ontogeny is altered in one of two ways. First, evolution occurs when new characteristics are introduced, at any stage of development, which then have varying influences on later developmental stages. The second way in which evolution occurs is when characteristics that are already present undergo changes in developmental timing. This second means by which phyletic change occurs is termed *heterochrony*. Specifically, heterochrony is changes in the relative time of appearance and rate of development of characters already present in ancestors.

In human evolution, a specific type of heterochrony has been predominant; as a consequence, the changes that were associated with human plasticity occurred. The type of heterochrony that has characterized human evolution is *neoteny,* which is a slowing down, a retardation, of development of selected somatic organs and parts. Heterochronic changes are regulatory effects; that is, they constitute "a change in rate for features already present" (Gould, 1977, p. 8). Gould (1977) maintained that neoteny has been a—and probably *the*—major determinant of human evolution.

For example, as explained in greater detail later, delayed growth has been found to be important in the evolution of complex and flexible social behavior and, interrelatedly, it has led to an increase in cerebralization by prolonging into later human life the rapid brain-growth characteristics of higher vertebrate fetuses. As such, this general evolutionary retardation of human development has resulted in adaptive features of ancestral juveniles being retained. That is, a key characteristic of human evolution is *paedomorphosis,* or phylogenetic change involving retention of ancestral juvenile characters by the adult. In other words, Gould (1977) noted:

> Our paedomorphic features are a set of adaptations coordinated by their common efficient cause of retarded development. We are not neotenous only because we possess an impressive set of paedomorphic characters; we are neotenous because these characters develop within a matrix of retarded development that coordinates their common appearance in human adults . . . [and these] temporal delays themselves are the most significant feature of human heterochrony. (pp. 397, 399)

But what are some of the paedomorphic–neotenous characteristics? How do they provide an evolutionary basis of human plasticity and reciprocal person–social context relations? Gould (1977) himself answered these questions, and, in so doing, indicated that humans' evolving plasticity both enabled and resulted from their embeddedness in a social and cultural context. Gould, (1977) noted:

> In asserting the importance of delayed development . . . I assume that major human adaptations acted synergistically throughout their gradual development. . . . *The interacting system of delayed development-upright posture-large brain is such a complex:* delayed development has produced a large brain by prolonging fetal growth rates and has supplied a set of cranial proportions adapted to upright posture. Upright posture freed the hand for tool use and set selection pressures for an expanded brain. A large brain may, itself, entail a longer life span. (p. 399, italics added)

> Human evolution has *emphasized* one feature of . . . common primate heritage—delayed development, particularly as expressed in late instruction and extended childhood. This retardation has reacted synergistically with other hallmarks of hominization—with intelligence (by enlarging the brain through prolongation of fetal growth tendencies and by providing a longer period of childhood learning) and with socialization (by cementing family units through increased parental care of slowly developing offspring). It is hard to imagine how the distinctive suite of human characters could have emerged outside the context of delayed development. (p. 400)

Thus, in linking neoteny with reciprocal relations between brain development and sociocultural functioning, Gould (1977) made an argument of extreme importance for comparative–developmental and sociocultural–intergenerational analyses of human development. The role of the former type of analysis is raised in regard to species differences (heterochrony) in the ontogeny of brain organization and their import for levels of plasticity finally attained across life; the role of the latter type of analysis is raised in regard to the role of parent–child relations in promoting the child's development toward a final level of functioning characterized by plasticity. In other portions of the evolutionary biology literature and in the anthropology literature, there is support for the link suggested by Gould (1977) between plastic brain development and human sociocultural functioning.

Bidirectional Organism–Context Relations in Evolution: Paleoanthropological Perspectives

Several ideas in anthropology suggest that humans have been selected for social dependency. The course and context of evolution was such that it was more adaptive to act in concert with the group than in isolation. For example, Masters (1978) noted that early hominids were hunters. These ancestors evolved from herbivorous primates under the pressure of climatic changes that caused the African forest to be replaced with savanna. Masters speculated that our large brains (1978, p. 98), may be the (naturally selected) *result* of cooperation among early hominids and, hence, in an evolutionary sense, the human brain is a social organ. Indeed, he believed that, with such evolution, the "central problem" in anthropological analysis—that of the origin of society—may be solved. Washburn (1961) appeared to agree. He noted that the relative defenselessness of early humans (lack of fighting teeth, nails, or horns), coupled with the dangers of living on the open African savanna, made group living and cooperation *essential for survival* (Hogan, Johnson, & Emler, 1978; Washburn, 1961).

There is some dispute in anthropological theory as to whether material culture or specific features of social relations such as intensified parenting, monogamous pair bonding, nuclear family formation, and, thus, specialized sexual-reproductive behavior were superordinate in these brain-behavior evolutionary relations. For example, some paleoanthropologists currently believe that there are five characteristics that separate human beings from other hominids: large neocortex, bipedality, reduced anterior dentation with molar dominance, material culture, and unique sexual and reproductive behavior (e.g., of all primates only the human female's sexual behavior is not confined to the middle of her monthly menstrual cycle; Fisher, 1982a). Some paleoanthropologists believe that early human evolution was a direct consequence of brain expansion and material culture. However, Lovejoy (1981), among others (e.g., Johanson & Edey, 1981), believes that:

> Both advanced material culture and the Pleistocene acceleration in brain development are sequelae to an already established hominid character system, which included intensified parenting and social relationships, monogamous pair bonding, specialized sexual-reproductive behavior, and bipedality. (p. 348)

Other debates also exist. For instance, the roles that continual sexual receptivity and loss of estrus played in the evolution of human pair bonding are controversial and complex (e.g., Fisher, 1982b; Harley, 1982; Isaac, 1982; Swartz, 1982; Washburn, 1982). Such debate, however, exists in the midst of the general consensus indicated earlier: that the social functioning of hominids (be it interpreted as dyadic, familial, or cultural) was reciprocally related to the evolution of the human brain. Many evolutionary biologists appear to reach a similar conclusion.

For example, summarizing a review of literature pertaining to the character of the environment to which organisms adapt, Lewontin and Levins (1978) stressed that reciprocal processes between organism and environment are involved in human evolution; as such, this leads to a view that human functioning is one source of its own evolutionary development. Lewontin and Levins (1978) stated that:

> The activity of the organism sets the stage for its own evolution. . . . The labor process by which the human ancestors modified natural objects to make them suitable for human use was itself the unique feature of the way of life that directed selection on the hand, larynx, and brain in a positive feedback that transformed the species, its environment, and its mode of interaction with nature. (p. 78)

Moreover, not only did Lovejoy (1981) and Fisher (1982a) give graphic accounts of the history of the role of hominid social behavior in human evolution, but—in specific support of Gould's (1977) views—they also showed how the complex social and physical facets of this evolution led to human neoteny. Interestingly, whereas Fisher and (especially) Lovejoy tend to view the ecological presses that led to the evolution of social behaviors as eventuating in bipedalism and then rapid brain development, they, nevertheless, both see these links in more of a circular than a linear framework.

For instance, Lovejoy (1981) noted that it was not just that ecological changes led to social relationships, which in turn led to bipedalism, and, in turn, to brain evolution. Instead, social relationships that led to brain evolution were then themselves altered when larger-brained and more plastic organisms were involved in them; in turn, new social patterns may have extended humans' adaptational presses and opportunities into other arenas, ones fostering further changes in the brain, in social embeddedness, and so forth. Indeed, as Johanson and Edey (1981) described Lovejoy's (1981) position, it is one that requires the examination of

> the mechanism of a complex feedback loop in which several elements interact for mutual reinforcement. . . . If parental care is a good thing, it will be selected for by the likelihood that the better mothers will be more apt to bring up children, and thus intensify any genetic tendency that exists in the population toward being better mothers. But increased parental care requires other things along with it. It requires a greater IQ on the part of the mother; she cannot increase parental care if she is not intellectually up to it. That means brain development—not only for the mother, but for the infant daughter, too, for someday she will become a mother.
>
> In the case of primate evolution, the feedback is not just a simple A–B stimulus forward and backward between two poles. It is multipoled and circular, with many features to it instead of only two—all of them mutually reinforcing. For example, if an infant is to have a large brain, it must be given time to learn to use that brain before it has to face the world on its own. That means a long childhood. The best way to learn during childhood is to play. That means playmates, which, in turn, means a group social system that provides them. But if one is to function in such a

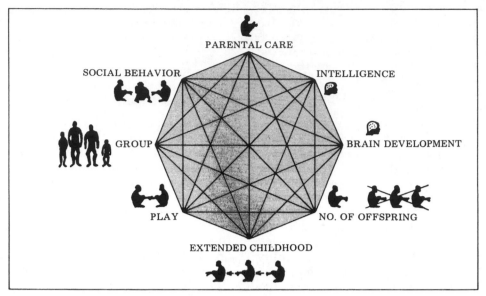

FIGURE 8.1
Components of the system of reciprocal influences that Lovejoy (1981; Johanson & Edey, 1981) believes was involved in the evolution of human neoteny and social embeddedness.

group, one must learn acceptable social behavior. One can learn that properly only if one is intelligent. Therefore social behavior ends up being linked with IQ (a loop back), with extended childhood (another loop), and finally with the energy investment and the parental care system which provide a brain capable of that IQ, and the entire feedback loop is complete.

All parts of the feedback system are cross-connected. For example: if one is living in a group, the time spent finding food, being aware of predators and finding a mate can all be reduced by the very fact that one is in a group. As a consequence, more time can be spent on parental care (one loop), on play (another) and on social activity (another), all of which enhance intelligence (another) and result ultimately in fewer offspring (still another). The complete loop shows all poles connected to all others. (pp. 325–326)

An illustration of this "complete loop," or system of reciprocal influence, is presented in Figure 8.1. This figure illustrates that the foundations of humans' plasticity evolved in a complex system of bidirectional relationships among social, ontogenetic, and neuronal variables.

Conclusions

Our analysis of the links between Gould's (1977) ideas pertinent to the role of neotenous heterochrony in the evolution of human plasticity has drawn us into a discussion of the role of reciprocal relations between organisms and their contexts in human evolution. In other words, neoteny provides

adaptive advantages for members of both older and younger generations. Considering children first, the neoteny of the human results in the newborn child being perhaps the most dependent organism found among placental mammalian infants (Gould, 1977). Moreover, their neoteny means that this dependency is extraordinarily prolonged, and this requires intense parental care for the child for several years.

The plasticity of childhood processes, which persists among humans for more than a decade, thus entails a history of necessarily close contact with adults and places an "adaptive premium . . . on learning (as opposed to innate response) . . . unmatched among organisms" (Gould, 1977, p. 401). Gould agrees with de Beer (1959) who stated that for the human:

> Delay in development enabled him to develop a larger and more complex brain, and the prolongation of childhood under conditions of parental care and instruction consequent upon memory-stored and speech-communicated experience, allowed him to benefit from *a more efficient apprenticeship for his conditions of life.* (p. 930, italics added)

The neoteny of humans, their prolonged childhood dependency on others, and their embeddedness in a social context composed of members of the older generation who both protect them and afford them the opportunity to actualize their potential plasticity allows members of a new birth cohort to adapt to the conditions and presses particular to their historical epoch.

Such development in a new cohort also has evolutionary significance for members of the older cohort. Gould (1977) pointed out that neoteny and the protracted period of dependent childhood may have led to the evolution of features of adult human behavior (e.g., parental behavior). The presence of young and dependent children requires adults to be organized in their adult–adult and adult–child interactions in order to support and guide the children effectively. Furthermore, since the period of childhood dependency is so long, it is likely that human history tended to involve the appearance of later-born children before earlier-born children achieved full independence (Gould, 1977). Gould (1977, p. 403) saw such an occurrence as facilitating the emergence of pair bonding, and further saw "in delayed development a primary impetus for the origin of the human family."

In sum, several lines of evidence—from human development, evolutionary biology, sociology, and anthropology—converge to suggest that individuals and the other significant people in their lives (for instance, and perhaps most important for human development, children and their parents) interact dynamically. In so doing, they promote their own and each other's mutual development.

Whereas our discussion in this section has highlighted evolutionary bases of such person–social context reciprocity, there are also ontogenetic, historical, and contemporary contextual features of this relationship. To use or "translate" Gould's (1977) ideas about the phylogenetic bases of dynamic person–context relations into concepts useful in understanding the role of such relations in human ontogenetic changes, it is useful to draw again on the ideas about the ontogeny of the human "psychological level" proposed by T. C. Schneirla (1957), discussed in Chapter 6. Schneirla's (1957) ideas constitute a conceptual bridge between Gould's (1977) view of human evolution and the specification of a developmental contextual theory of person–context dynamic interactions across the life span.

FROM PHYLOGENY TO ONTOGENY: A DYNAMIC INTERACTIONAL MODEL OF INDIVIDUAL–CONTEXT RELATIONS

To understand the important role that Schneirla's (1957) ideas played in the formulation of developmental contextualism, it is useful to consider the diagram presented in Figure 8.2. Employing Schneirla's (1957) terms discussed in Chapter 6, this figure illustrates what we have described as a probabilistic–epigenetic conception of development. In the figure, I use the term *maturation* to represent endogenous organism changes and the term *experience* to denote all stimulative influences acting on the organism over the course of its life span. A conception of interaction levels is used in the figure. The organism's individual developmental history of maturation–experience interactions (what I term *Level 1 development*—a term analogous to Riegel's, 1975, inner–biological development level; see Chapter 2), provides a basis of differential organism–environment interactions. In turn, differential experiences accruing from the individual developmental history of organism–environment interactions (or *Level 2 development*—a term analogous to Riegel's, 1975, individual–psychological developmental level; again, see Chapter 2), provide a further basis of Level 1 developmental individuality.

As illustrated in the figure, endogenous maturation–experience interactions are not discontinuous with exogenous organism–environment interactions. As a consequence of the timing of the interactions among the specific variables involved in an organism's maturation–experience interactions, a basis of an organism's individual distinctiveness is provided. This organism interacts differently with its environment as a consequence of this individuality. In turn, these new interactions are a component of the organism's further experience and, thus, serve to further promote its individuality. Endogenous maturation–experience relations provide a basis of organism individuality, and, consequently, differential organism–environment (exogenous) relations develop.

In sum, then, the target organism in the figure is unique because of the quality and timing of endogenous Level 1 maturation–experience interactions; but the experiences that provide a basis of Level 1 development are not discontinuous with other extraorganism experiences in influencing the target individual. The target interacts with environmental influences composed of other organisms (themselves having intraindividual Level 1 developmental distinctiveness) and of physical variables, which also show individual change over time. Indeed, all tiers—the extraorganism (social), the physical–environmental, the sociocultural, and the historical—change over time. The timing of interactions among variables within and across all tiers not only provides a distinct experiential context that affects the developing organism, but this distinctiveness is,

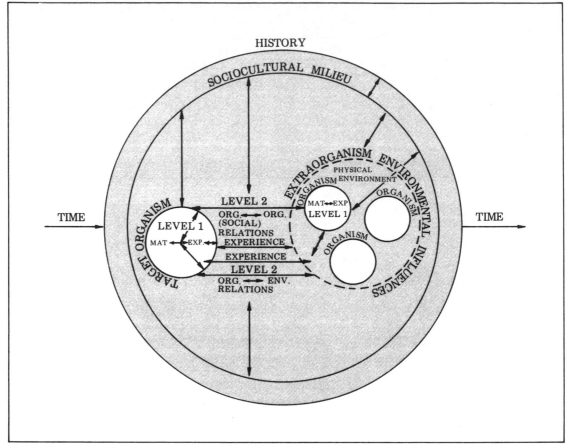

FIGURE 8.2
A dynamic interactional model of development.

itself, also shaped by the individually different organism.

Schneirla's (1957) probabilistic–epigenetic view of development is illustrated in the model shown in Figure 8.2. Just as the model in this figure serves as a means to translate the ideas about evolution presented by Gould (1977) into the ontogenetic ideas of Schneirla (1957), the model presented in Figure 8.2 may be translated into a model that specifically focuses on human development. It is this second translation that provides the parameters of developmental contextualism.

There were several conceptual issues within the field of human development that arose over the course of the last 30 to 40 years that provided the impetus of and helped to formulate the frame for this translation. It is important to discuss them.

BASES AND FEATURES OF DEVELOPMENTAL CONTEXTUALISM

Over the last four decades, the study of children and their families has evolved in at least three significant directions. These trends involve: (a) changes in the conceptualization of the nature of the person, (b) the emergence of a life-span perspective about human development, and (c) stress on the contexts of development. These trends were both products and producers of developmental contextualism. In turn, developmental contextualism promoted a rationale for a synthesis of theory and application, an integration focused on the diversity of children and on the contexts within which they develop (Fisher & Lerner, 1994a, 1994b; Lerner & Fisher, 1994).

As we noted in Chapter 2, much of the history of the study of human development prior to the mid-1970s was predicated on either organismic or mechanistic (reductionistic) models (Overton & Reese, 1973, 1981; Reese & Overton, 1970). In turn, it is accurate to say that, since the 1970s, developmental systems theories such as developmental contextualism have been increasingly prominent bases of scholarly advances in human development theory and methodology (Dixon & Lerner, 1999; Dixon et al., 1991a, 1991b; Lerner, Hultsch, & Dixon, 1983; Lerner, 1998a, 1998b; Riegel, 1975, 1976a, 1976b; Sameroff, 1975, 1983). The three previously noted themes in the study of human development define the place of developmental contextualism in theory and research over the last three decades. Accordingly, it is worthwhile to discuss each of these themes in some detail.

Children's Influences on Their Own Development

Children have come to be understood as active producers of their own development (Bell, 1968; Lerner & Spanier, 1978; Lewis & Rosenblum, 1974; Thomas, Chess, Birch, Hertzig, & Korn, 1963). These contributions primarily occur through the reciprocal relations individuals have with other significant people in their context (e.g., children with family members, caregivers, teachers, and peers).

The content and functional significance of the influences that people have on others and, in turn, on themselves, occur in relation to people's characteristics of individuality (Schneirla, 1957). Individual differences in people evoke differential reactions in others, reactions which provide feedback to people and influence the individual character of their further development (Schneirla, 1957). Accordingly, individuality—diversity among people—is central in understanding the way in which any given person is an active agent in his or her own development (Lerner, 1982, 1991; Lerner & Busch-Rossnagel, 1981a, 1981b; Lerner & Walls, 1999). In other words, diversity has core, substantive meaning and, as such, implications for all studies of human development.

To illustrate these points, note that there is an old adage that the child is father to the man. This saying means, simply, that a person's characteristics when he or she is a child relate to his or her characteristics during adulthood. However, there is another way of interpreting this saying: How

people behave and think as adults—and perhaps especially as parents—is very much influenced by their experiences with their children. Children as much rear adults as adults do them. The very fact that parents are parents makes them different adults than they would be if they were childless. But, more importantly, the specific, and often special, characteristics of a particular child influence parents in unique ways. How parents behave toward their children depends quite a lot on how their children have influenced them to behave. Such child influences are termed *child effects*.

By influencing the parents that are influencing him or her, the child is shaping a source of his or her own development. In this sense, children are producers of their own development (Lerner, 1982; Lerner & Walls, 1999), and the presence of such child effects constitutes the basis of *bidirectional* relations between parents and children. Of course, this bidirectional relation continues when the child is an adolescent and an adult. Corresponding relations exist between the person and siblings, friends, teachers, and all other significant people in his or her life. This "child–other" relation is the basic feature of the developmental–contextual relations that characterize the social creature we call a human being. To elucidate this core relation, it is useful to continue our emphasis on "child" effects (on person–context *relations* involving children), recognizing, of course, that we can readily extend other examples to include adolescents, adults, the aged, or the parents with whom the child interacts.

Child effects emerge largely as a consequence of a child's individual distinctiveness. All children, with the exception of genetically identical (monozygotic) twins, have a unique genotype (i.e., a unique genetic inheritance). Similarly, no two children, including monozygotic twins, experience precisely the same environment. However, as explained in Chapter 4, all human characteristics, be they behavioral or physical, arise from an integration (a fusion) of genes and environment (Anastasi, 1958; Lerner, 1986; Magnusson, 1996, 1999a, 1999b; Magnusson & Stattin, 1998). Given the uniqueness of each child's genetic inheritance and environment, the distinctiveness of each child is assured (Feldman & Lewontin, 1975; Hirsch, 1970). In other words, every child is unique and, therefore, individually distinct from every other child.

Child individually is represented diagrammatically in Figure 8.3 in respect to Child A (represented as a circle) and to Child B (represented as a triangle). This individuality may be illustrated

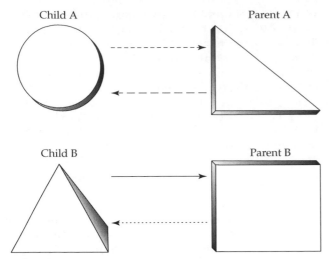

FIGURE 8.3
Parents' behaviors toward their children are related both to their own and to their children's characteristics of individuality.

by drawing on the study of temperament (Chess & Thomas, 1984; Thomas & Chess, 1977; Thomas et al., 1963). As we discuss in greater detail in Chapter 17, temperament is a characteristic of a child's behavior that describes *how* he or she acts.

For instance, all children eat and sleep. Temperament is the *style* of eating or sleeping shown by the child; if the child eats the same amount at every meal and/or gets hungry at the same time, then this child has, in regard to eating, a regular, or rhythmic, temperament. A child who gets hungry at different times of the day, or who may eat a lot or a little without any seeming predictability has in regard to eating, an arrhythmic temperament. Similarly, all children sleep. However, some children may sleep irregularly, that is, for seemingly unpredictable (at least to their parents) lengths of time, with periods of sleep being interspersed with wakeful periods of crying and fussing.

Let us say that Child A in Figure 8.3 is like this; he or she is an arrhythmic eater and sleeper. Other children might sleep and eat in a more regularly patterned way, and/or when awake they may show more smiling than crying and fussing. Let this be Child B.

The importance of these individual differences arises when we recognize that, as a consequence of their individuality, children will present different stimulation to parents. Child A and Child B present different stimuli to their parents as a

consequence of their respective eating and sleep– wake patterns. The experience for a parent having a pleasant, regularly sleeping child, who is also predictable in regard to eating habits, is quite different from the experience for a parent who has a moody, irregularly sleeping and eating child. The different stimulation provided by Child A and Child B is also represented in Figure 8.3, by the small-dashed and solid-lined arrows going from Child A to Parent A and from Child B to Parent B, respectively.

The effect of the child's stimulation of the parent depends, in part, on the parent's own characteristics of individuality. However, to explain this point it helps to consider the second theme in the literature that helped crystallize the developmental–contextual view of human development.

Development as a Life-Span Phenomenon

Throughout the history of its genesis in philosophy and science, the study of human development has involved the articulation of several "life-span perspectives" (for reviews of the history of these ideas, see Baltes, 1979, 1983). However, it is the formulation developed by Schaie (1965, 1970), Baltes (1968, 1987, 1997; Baltes et al., 1998, 1999), and Nesselroade (1970, 1977) in psychology, and the related life-course view of the human life cycle developed by Brim (Brim, 1966; Brim & Kagan, 1980a, 1980b), Riley (1976, 1979), Featherman (1980, 1983), and Elder (1975, 1979, 1980, 1998) in sociology, and by other scholars in these and other disciplines (e.g., see Hetherington, Lerner, & Perlmutter, 1988; Magnusson, 1996; Sorensen, Weinert, & Sherrod, 1986) that have been the major influences in contemporary theory and research about the bidirectional connections across life between the developing person and the changing, multiple, and integrated levels of his or her context.

As is discussed in greater detail in Chapter 9, the life-span perspective, as specified by Baltes (1979, 1983, 1987, 1997; Baltes et al., 1998, 1999), is associated with the developmental–contextual model of human development (Lerner, 1984, 1986; Lerner & Kauffman, 1985). To understand this connection, it is important to note that the emergence of interest during the 1970s and 1980s in a life-span perspective about human development led to the understanding that development occurs in more than the childhood or adolescent years (Baltes, 1968, 1987; Block, 1971; Brim & Kagan, 1980a, 1980b; Elder, 1974, 1980; Featherman, 1983; Riley, 1979; Schaie, 1965).

The import of this point for the development of the developmental–contextual model of human development is that parents as well as children may be seen to develop as distinct individuals across life (Lerner & Spanier, 1978). For instance, parents develop both as adults in general and, more specifically, in their familial (e.g., spousal) and extrafamilial (e.g., vocational or career) roles (Vondracek, Lerner, & Schulenberg, 1986). Indeed, the influence of a child on his or her parents will depend in part on the prior experience the adult has had with the parental role and on the other roles in which the parent is engaged (e.g., worker, adult–child, and caregiver for an aged parent) (Hetherington & Baltes, 1988).

Thus, a person's unique history of experiences and roles, as well as his or her unique biological (e.g., genetic) characteristics, combine to make him or her unique—and with time, given the accumulation of the influences of distinct roles and experiences—increasingly more unique across the course of life (Lerner, 1988). This uniqueness is the basis of the specific feedback a parent gives to his or her individual child.

Parents who are stimulated differentially may be expected to differentially react to, or *process* (e.g., think and feel about), the stimulation provided by their child. Child A might evoke feelings of frustration and exasperation, and thoughts of concern in his or her parents (Brazelton, Koslowski, & Main, 1974; Lewis & Rosenblum, 1974). In addition, especially among first-time parents, it is possible that parents might wonder if they will have the personal and marital resources to handle such a child (Chess & Thomas, 1984). We might expect, however, that the thoughts and feelings evoked in parents by Child B might be markedly different. Certainly, the parents of Child B would be better rested than Child A's parents. When their child was awake, they would have a child with a more regularly positive mood, and this would also present less stress on them as parents and as spouses Figure 8.3 also illustrates the presence of different types of reactions by the parents of Child A and Child B. The individual reaction of Parent A is represented as a right triangle, whereas the individuality of Parent B is represented as a rectangle.

The individuality of these parental reactions underscores the idea that parents are as individually distinct as are their children. Not all parents of an irregularly eating and sleeping, moody child will react with concern and/or frustration. Similarly, some parents will be stressed by even the most regular, predictable, and positive of children. Such parental individuality makes child effects more complicated to study. However, at the same time, parental individuality underscores the uniqueness of each child's context. Simply, then, it may be expected that, as a consequence of the different stimulation received from their children, and in relation to their own characteristics of individuality, parents will provide differential feedback to their children.

Such differential feedback may take the form of different behavior shown to children by parents and/or of different emotional climates created in the home (Brazelton et al., 1974). For instance, the parents of Child A might take steps to alter his or her eating and sleep–wake patterns. In regard to sleeping, they might try to cut naps short during the day so that the child will be more tired in the evening. In addition, during the time when they are appraising the success of their attempts to put the child on an imposed schedule, a general sense of tenseness might pervade the household, They might wonder: "Will we have another sleepless night?" or "Will we be too tired to be fully effective at work?"

In essence, then, Figure 8.3 also illustrates the presence of differential feedback by the parents of Child A and Child B (see the large dashed and dotted arrows going from Parent A to Child A and from Parent B to Child B, respectively). This feedback becomes an important part of the child's experience, and is distinct in that it is based on the effect of the child's individuality on the parent. Thus, the feedback serves to further promote the child's individuality.

Circular Functions and Bidirectional Socialization

The reciprocal child–parent relations involved in child effects constitute what we have noted in Chapter 6 is termed by Schneirla (1957) a *circular function* in individual development: Children stimulate differential reactions in their parents, and these reactions provide the basis of feedback to the children, that is, return stimulation that influences their further individual development. These circular functions underscore the point that children (and adolescents, and adults) are producers of their own development and that people's relations to their contexts involve bidirectional exchanges (Lerner, 1982; Lerner & Busch-Rossnagel, 1981b). The parent shapes the child, but part of what determines the way in which the parent does this is the child himself or herself.

Children shape their parents—as adults, spouses, and, of course, as parents per se—and, in so doing, children help organize feedback to themselves, feedback that contributes further to their individuality and, thus, starts the circular function all over again (i.e., returns the child effects process to its first component). Characteristics of behavioral or personality individuality allow the child to contribute to this circular function. Bornstein's (1995b) "specificity principle" underscores the individuality of person-context relations that are at the core of these circular functions. Writing in regard to infancy, he notes that "The specificity principle states that specific experiences at specific times exert specific effects over specific aspects of infant growth in specific ways" (Bornstein, 1995b, p. 21).

The idea of circular functions needs to be extended; that is, in and of itself, the notion is mute regarding the specific characteristics of the feedback (e.g., its positive or negative valence) a child will receive as a consequence of his or her individuality. In other words, to account for the specific character of child–context relations, the circular functions model needs to be supplemented; this is the contribution of the goodness-of-fit model.

The Goodness-of-Fit Model

Just as a child brings his or her characteristics of individuality to a particular social setting, there are demands placed on the child by virtue of the social and physical components of the setting. These demands may take the form of:

1. Attitudes, values, or stereotypes that are held by others in the context regarding the person's attributes (either his or her physical or behavioral characteristics.

2. The attributes (usually behavioral) of others in the context with whom the child must coordinate, or fit, his or her attributes (also, in this case, usually behavioral) for adaptive interactions to exist.

3. The physical characteristics of a setting (e.g., the presence or absence of access ramps for the motorically handicapped) require the child to possess certain attributes (again, usually behavioral abilities) for the most efficient interaction within the setting to occur.

The child's individuality, in differentially meeting these demands, provides a basis for the spe-

cific feedback he or she gets from the socializing environment. For example, considering the demand "domain" of attitudes, values, or stereotypes, teachers and parents may have relatively individual and distinct expectations about behaviors desired of their students and children, respectively. Teachers may want students who show little distractibility, but parents might desire their children to be moderately distractible, for example, when they require their children to move from television-watching to dinner or to bed. Children whose behavioral individuality was either generally distractible or generally not distractible would, thus, differentially meet the demands of these two contexts. Problems of adjustment to school or to home might, thus, develop as a consequence of a child's lack of match (or of goodness-of-fit) in either or both settings. Within the study of human development, the concept of goodness-of-fit has been advanced by several different scholars concerned with the systemic relations between individuals and the settings within which they live and develop.

The contributions of Jacquelynne Eccles. Through a focus on young adolescents and their transition from elementary school to either junior high or middle school, Jacquelynne Eccles and her colleagues (e.g., Eccles, 1991; Eccles & Harold, 1996; Eccles, Lord, & Buchanan, 1996; Eccles &

Jacquelynne Eccles

Midgley, 1989; Eccles, Midgley, Wigfield, Buchanan, Reuman, Flanagan, & MacIver, 1993; Fuligni, Eccles, & Barber, 1995; Midgley, Feldlaufer, & Eccles, 1989a, 1989b) have offered a theoretically nuanced and (empirically) highly productive approach to understanding the significance of person–context fit for development. Eccles and her colleagues have demonstrated the importance for achievement motivation and academic achievement of goodness-of-fit between young adolescents (in regard to their level of development) and their school environment. For instance, there may be effects of the transition from elementary school to junior high school or middle school on students' academic performance or on their academic feelings and motivation that may be due, in part, to the poorness-of-fit between the students' orientation to learning and the organization and curriculum of the junior high or middle school (Eccles & Midgley, 1989; Eccles et al., 1996; Eccles, Wigfield, Midgley, Reuman, MacIver, & Feldlaufer, 1993).

To account for such findings, Eccles and colleagues (1996) explained that the theory of person–environment fit is embedded within this work and proposed that:

> Behavior, motivation, and mental health are influenced by the fit between the characteristics individuals bring to their social environments and the characteristics of these social environments. Individuals are not likely to do very well, or be very motivated, if they are in social environments that do not fit their psychological needs. (p. 254)

Accordingly, this model of person–context fit led Eccles and colleagues (1996, p. 254) to predict that:

> If the social environments in the typical junior high school do not fit very well with the psychological needs of adolescents, then person–environment fit theory predicts a decline in the adolescents' motivation, interest, performance, and behavior as they move into this environment. (p. 254)

Eccles and colleagues noted that there is considerable "evidence that such a negative change in the school environment occurs with the transition to junior high school" (1996, p. 254) and that:

> The nature of these environmental changes, coupled with the normal course of individual development, is likely to result in a developmental mismatch so that the "fit" between the early adolescent and the classroom environment is particularly poor, increasing the risk of negative motivational outcomes, especially for adolescents who are already having difficulty succeeding in school academically. (p. 258)

The contributions of Thomas and Chess and Lerner and Lerner.   Thomas and Chess (1977, 1980, 1981, 1999; Chess & Thomas, 1984) and Lerner and

Lerner (1983, 1989) have forwarded ideas and conducted research consistent with the approach to person–context fit that has been taken by Eccles and her colleagues. Thomas and Chess and Lerner and Lerner have found that if a child's characteristics of individuality provide a goodness-of-fit (or match) with the demands of a particular setting, adaptive outcomes will accrue in that setting. Those children whose characteristics match most of the settings within which they exist receive supportive or positive feedback from the contexts and show evidence of the most adaptive behavioral development. In turn, of course, poorly fit, or mismatched, children, those whose characteristics are incongruent with one or most settings, appear to show alternative developmental outcomes.

What are the precise competencies a child must possess to attain a good fit within and across time? To competently attain an adaptive fit, a child must be able to evaluate appropriately: (a) the demands of a particular context, (b) his or her psychological and behavioral characteristics, and (c) the degree of match that exists between the two. In addition, other cognitive and behavioral skills are necessary. The child has to have the ability to select and gain access to those contexts within which there is a high probability of match and to avoid those contexts where poor fit is likely. In addition, in contexts that cannot usually be selected (e.g., family of origin or assigned elementary school class) the child has to have the knowledge and skills necessary either to change him- or herself to fit the demands of the setting or, in turn, to alter the context to better fit his or her attributes (Mischel, 1977; Snyder, 1981). In most contexts, multiple types of demands will impinge on a person, and not all of them will provide identical presses. As such, the child needs to be able to detect and evaluate such complexity, and to judge which demand it will be best to adapt to when all cannot be met.

In short, as the child's competency in self-regulation, or "agency" (Bakan, 1966) developes he or she will be able to become an active selector and shaper of the contexts within which he or she develops (Brandtstädter, 1998, 1999; Eccles, Early, Frasier, Belansky, & McCarthy, 1997; Heckhausen, 1999). Thus, with such agency, it will become increasingly true that the child "rears" his or her parents as much as they do him or her.

The literatures on "child effects" and on the lifespan perspective promote a concern with individual differences, variation in developmental pathways across life, and the developmental–contextual idea that changing relations between the person and his or her context provide the basis, across life, of the individual's unique repertoire of physical, psychological, and behavioral characteristics (Lerner, 1991). The recognition of this link between person and context was a product and a producer of the third theme that emerged in the study of human development since the 1970s.

Development in Its Ecological Context

The study of children and their parents became increasingly "contextualized," or placed within the broader "ecology of human development," during the last three to four decades (Bronfenbrenner, 1977, 1979; Bronfenbrenner & Morris, 1998; Elder, 1974, 1998; Garbarino, 1992; Pepper, 1942). In Chapter 2, we discussed the important contributions made by Urie Bronfenbrenner to the appreciation among developmental scientists of the ecology of human development. Although we discuss Bronfenbrenner's ideas in greater detail in Chapter 9, it is important to note here that the focus on the ecology that Bronfenbrenner's ideas promoted involved a concern with the "real life" situations within which children and families exist. This focus was associated with the study of the bidirectional relations between the family and the other social settings within which children and parents function (e.g., the workplace, the welfare office, the day-care center, the Medicaid screening office, and the formal and the nonformal educational and recreational settings present in a neighborhood or a community) (Lewis & Feiring, 1978; Lewis & Rosenblum, 1974).

In order to understand how the social context contributes to bidirectional person–context relations, we should reiterate that a child is *not* best thought of as merely similar to all other children, or as simply different from others in respect to only one, or even just a few, characteristics. Instead, individual differences exist in respect to numerous characteristics. To illustrate, Figure 8.4 divides the child into components reflecting some of the several dimensions of individuality that exist. The "slice" labeled "Etc." is used to indicate that there are numerous other characteristics of individuality that might be mentioned. The "slice" labeled "Developmental Level" is used to indicate that all of the child's characteristics of individuality change over time.

I have illustrated how at least some of these changes occur through the bidirectional relations the child has with his or her parents. However, what I have not illustrated to this point is that parents are also made up of multiple dimensions of individuality which, as with the child, develop across time (e.g., see Baltes, 1987). The multiple dimensions of the parent are also presented in Figure 8.4, along with arrows to indicate the bidirectional relations which exist between the child and his or her parent.

Another point not yet illustrated is that the parent–child relationship does not exist in isolation. Both the child and the parent have other social roles. These roles lead both children and parents into social relationships with other groups

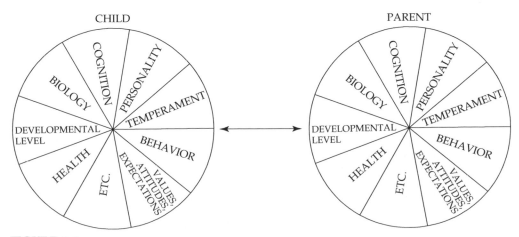

FIGURE 8.4
There are multiple dimensions involved in the bidirectional relationships between a child and a parent.

of people (i.e., with other social "networks"). We have noted that the life-span perspective (Baltes, 1987; Baltes et al., 1998, 1999) emphasizes that parents are also spouses, adult children of their own parents, workers, and neighbors. Children may also be siblings, and friends of other children; and as they progress through childhood and, later, adolescence, they become students and often at least part-time employees, respectively. The sorts of relationships in these other social networks in which children and parent engage when "outside" of their role of child or parent, respectively, can be expected to influence the parent–child relationship (Bronfenbrenner, 1977, 1979).

A child's poor performance at school may influence his or her behavior in the home, and especially, may alter the quality of the parent–child relationship. In turn, a problematic home situation—as is experienced by children in families wherein parental abuse or neglect of the child occurs—will affect the child's relationships with peers, teachers, and other family members (Baca Zinn, & Eitzen, 1993; Belsky, Lerner, & Spanier, 1984).

In regard to parents, strain in the spousal relationship can occur if the adult spends too much energy in his or her parental caregiving role (J. Lerner, 1994). For instance, a child's unpredictable sleep pattern and negative mood when awake can severely tax his or her parents' energy. Energy and time needed for parents to be good spouses to each other, therefore, may not be available. In addition, the fatigue caused by the demands of parental roles can be expected to influence parents' performance in the workplace (J. Lerner, 1994). It is difficult for people who have been up all night caring for a crying infant to be at their best at work the next morning. In turn, of course, problems at work can be brought home. Parents whose energies are significantly depleted outside the home may not have the stamina during the evening to be attentive, patient parents to their children (or attentive, emotionally supportive spouses for their mates).

Thus, bidirectional relationships exist between the child and the parent (Bornstein & Tamis-Le Monda, 1990; Lerner & Lerner, 1987); and these relationships are reciprocally related to the other social networks within which the dyad exists and to the broader societal and cultural context. For example, studying mother–infant dyads in the United States, France, and Japan, Bornstein and colleagues (1992) found both culture-general and culture-specific patterns of maternal responsiveness to characteristics of infant individuality

(e.g., in regard to activity level, exploration, and vocalization).

Levels of Embeddedness in the Ecology of Human Development

We have emphasized that the core idea in developmental contextualism is that the organism (organismic attributes or, most generally, biology) and context cannot be separated (Gottlieb, 1991, 1992; Lerner, 1984; Magnusson, 1999a, 1999b; Magnusson & Stattin, 1998; Thelen & Smith, 1998; Tobach, 1981). Both are fused across all of life, and, thus, across history. One way to begin to illustrate just what is involved in this relation, even for one person, is to consider the diagram presented in Figure 8.5 (see Lerner, 1984, 1986). Here, I continue to use the representations introduced in Figure 8.4 to depict an individual child and parent. As before, the mutual influence between child and parent, their fusion with each other, is represented in the figure by the bidirectional arrows between them.

It is important to indicate at this point that we may speak of dynamic interactions between parent and child that pertain to either *social* or *physical* (i.e., biological or physiological) relations. For example, in regard to social relationships, the parent "demands" attention from the child, but the child does not show it; this "lights" the parent's "short fuse" of tolerance; he or she scolds the child, who then cries; this creates remorse in the parent and elicits soothing behaviors from him or her; the child is calmed, snuggles up to the parent, and now both parties in the relationship show positive emotions and are happy (for data pertinent to such parent–child relationships, see Tubman & Lerner, 1994).

I may also illustrate dynamic interactions which involve not only the exchange of "external" social behaviors but also involve biological or physiological processes. For example, parental religious practices, rearing practices, or financial status may influence the child's diet and nutritional status, health, and medical care. In turn, the contraction of an infectious disease by either parent or child can lead to the other member of the relationship contracting the disease. Moreover, the health and physical status of the child influences the parent's own feelings of well-being and his or her hopes and aspirations regarding the child (Finkelstein, 1993).

Thus, the child's physiological status and development are not disconnected from his or her behavioral and social context (in this example,

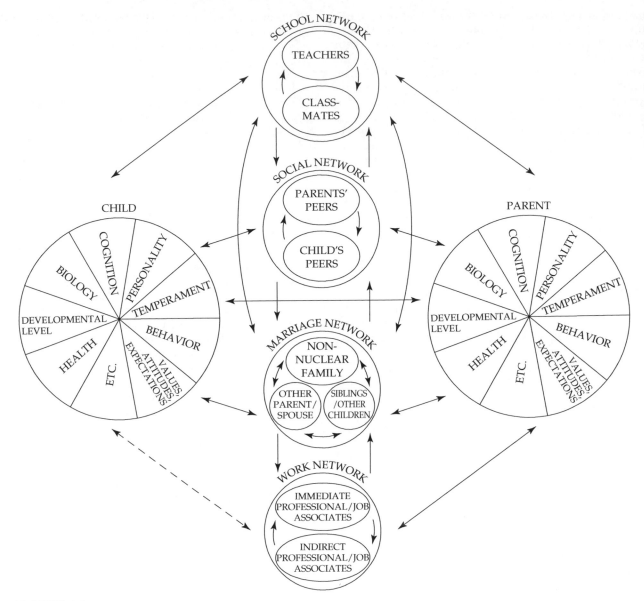

FIGURE 8.5
Parent–child relations are influenced by the interpersonal and institutional networks within which parents and children are embedded.

parental) functioning, and development (e.g., see Finkelstein, 1993; Ford & Lerner, 1992; Howard, 1978). The inner and outer worlds of the child are fused and dynamically interactive. In addition, of course, the same may be said of the parent and, in fact, of the parent–child relationship. Each of these foci—child, parent, or relationship—is part of a larger, enmeshed *system* of fused relations among the multiple levels which compose the ecology of human life (Bronfenbrenner, 1979).

For instance, illustrated in Figure 8.5 is the idea that both parent and child are embedded in a broader social network, and that each person has reciprocal reactions with this network. This set of relations occurs because both the child and the parent are much more than just people playing only one role in life. As already emphasized, the child may also be a sibling, a peer, and a student; the parent may also be a spouse, a worker, and an adult child. All of these networks of relations are embedded within a particular community, society, and culture. And, finally, all of these relations are continually changing across time, across history. Simply, for all portions of the system of person–context or biology–environment relations envisioned in developmental contextualism, change across time is an integral, and, indeed, inescapable, feature of human life.

Thus, Figure 8.5 illustrates that, within and among each of the depicted networks, one may conceive of bidirectional relationships as existing among the people populating the network. A child effect may function, in a sense, like a small pebble thrown into a quiet lake. It can prompt a large ripple. In turn, of course, the reverse of this possibility can occur. Events in settings lying far beyond

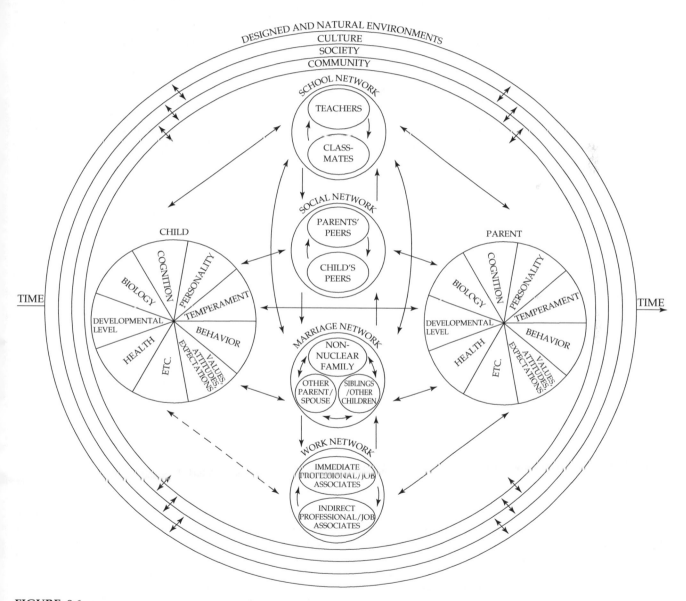

FIGURE 8.6
The developmental contextual view of human development: Parent–child relations, and interpersonal and institutional networks, are embedded in and influenced by particular community, societal, cultural, and designed and natural environments, all changing across time (across history).

the child—parent relationship can influence it. For instance, the resources in a community for child day care during the parent's working hours, the laws (e.g., regarding tax exemptions), or social programs available in a society supporting day care, and the cultural values regarding families who place their infants in day care, all exert an impact on the quality of the parent—child relationship.

Moreover, as I have just noted, the child—parent relationship, and the social networks in which it is located, are embedded in still larger community, societal, cultural, and historical levels of organization. These relations are illustrated in Figure 8.6, which presents the complete depiction of developmental contextualism. Time—history—cuts through all levels of the system. This feature of the figure is introduced to remind us that, as with the people populating these social systems, change is always occurring. Diversity within time is created as change across time (across history) introduces variation into all the levels of organization involved in the system depicted in Figure 8.6.

In other words, people develop, the family changes from one having infants and young children, to one having teenagers, to an "empty nest": The children have left the home of their parents to live elsewhere and very likely to start their own families. Similarly, communities, societies, and cultures also change (Elder, 1974, 1998; Elder, Modell, & Parke, 1993; Garbarino, 1992; Hernandez, 1993). In addition, each of these multiple "levels" is embedded in the natural and human-designed physical ecology, a physical world that, of course, also changes. Changes at one or more of these levels produce changes in the other levels as well, given their bidirectional connections.

Finally, since history "cuts through" all levels of organization (Baltes, 1987, 1997; Elder, 1974, 1998; Elder et al., 1993) the character of parent—child relations, of family life and development, and of societal and cultural influences on the child—parent—family system are influenced by both "normative" and "nonnormative" historical changes (Baltes, 1987) or, in other words, by "evolutionary" (i.e., gradual) and "revolutionary" (i.e., abrupt) (Werner, 1957), historical changes. In sum, this system of multiple, interconnected, or "fused" (Tobach & Greenberg, 1984) levels constitutes the integrated organization involved in the developmental contextual view of human development (Lerner, 1986, 1991, 1996, 1998b).

APPRAISING DEVELOPMENTAL CONTEXTUALISM

The bidirectional relations depicted in Figure 8.6 (as well as in Figure 8.2, from which Figure 8.6 has been derived) may be regarded as "translations" of the phylogenetic relationships represented in Figure 8.1 into relationships that stress ontogenetic relations. However, it is important to emphasize several things about Figure 8.6 (and also Figure 8.2). First, the figure is only descriptive of the relations that theory and research (e.g., Baltes et al., 1998, 1999; Bronfenbrenner & Morris, 1998; Elder, 1979, 1998; Gottlieb, 1997; Lerner, 1998b; Lewis, 1997; Magnusson, 1999a, 1999b; Magnusson & Stattin, 1998; Schneirla, 1957; Thelen & Smith, 1998; Thomas & Chess, 1997, 1999; Tobach & Schneirla, 1968; Wapner & Demick, 1998) have noted as being involved in person—context relations.

Let me also stress that I do not believe that it would be useful or even possible to do research testing the figure as a whole. Instead, the use of this or similar representations (e.g., see Figures 7.1, 7.2, and 7.3) of person—context relations is to guide the selection of individual and ecological variables in one's research and to provide parameters about the generalizability of one's findings. That is, this representation should remind us that we need to consider whether the results of a given study may be generalized beyond the particular individual and ecological variables we have studies, and applied to other community, societal, cultural, and historical contexts.

In addition, I would like to emphasize that the representation is a useful guide to theory development. What I take from this and other such illustrations of developmental systems models (e.g., Ford & Lerner, 1992; Gottlieb, 1997; Wapner & Demick, 1998) is that there needs to be three components of theory-guided research studying person—context relations. First, one needs to have some conceptualization of the nature of the attributes of the person one is interested in studying. Second, one must have some conceptualizations of the feature of the person's context one wishes to explore and a rationale for why this portion of the context is pertinent to the individual attribute one is assessing. Third, and most important, one needs some conceptualization of the *relation* between the individual attribute and the contextual feature. To illustrate this point, it is useful to discuss one way in which individual development and social change may be linked within developmental contextualism.

The Individual as a Component of Social Change

A key implication of the model presented in Figure 8.6 is that there is a systematic connection between individual development and social changes; this connection becomes evident if one recognizes that the set of individually different and differentially developing organisms living at any one point in time constitute, in effect, a major component of the social context and, in part, social change, respectively. In other words: (a) if each person may be characterized at any one point in time as possessing both the Level 1 and Level 2 individuality displayed in Figure 8.2, (b) if these characteristics of individuality change systematically as a consequence of each person being reciprocally embedded in a context with other individually different people, and (c) if the set of all people surrounding a given target person represents elements of that person's social world, then (d) this set defines a key feature of the social context and the changes in this set constitute a major parameter of social change.

This analysis gives both the social context and social change two important features. First, it gives them an inherent developmental quality; this arises as a consequence of the social context being composed of developing organisms. Second, this analysis again underscores the contributions of the individual person. First, the individual affects other people (i.e., elements of the social context) and, hence, elicits feedback to him- or herself. Second, the individual is—in respect to any other target organism—a key element of the social context.

Finally, this analysis provides a rationale for integrating the study of contextual variables marked by concepts such as "cohort effects," "normative, history-graded influences," and "nonnormative events" (see Baltes et al., 1980) into a comprehensive view of developmental processes. Such concepts are similar in that they are concerned with effects on development other than those prototypic of contributions made by individual organisms; these contextual influences are part of the extraindividual context (including the physical environment) depicted in Figures 8.2 and 8.6. Such influences attempt to mark contextual events that provide commonality across people—events that shape the experiences of groups of individuals living at particular historical moments. In terms of the present conceptualization, the contextual experiences marked by these terms make up an important component of the Level 2 stimulative influences represented in Figure 8.2, and of

the social, cultural, physical, ecological, and—ultimately—historical levels of organization displayed in Figure 8.6. Such historical influences serve to make organisms living in a context at a given time systematically alike. As such, these components of the developmental–contextual system are key shapers of the social context with which individuals transact.

Conclusions

Developmental contextualism reflects the ideas of dynamic interaction, levels of integration, and self-organization associated with other instances of open, living, developmental systems theories of human development (e.g., see Chapter 7). As such, scholarship framed by such a model eschews reductionism, unilevel assessments of the individual, and time-insensitive and atemporal analyses of human development. Instead, integrative/holistic, relational, and change-oriented research focused on the individual-in-context relation (e.g., Magnusson, 1985, 1999a, 1999b; Magnusson & Stattin, 1998) is promoted.

Moreover, such research, necessarily embedded in the actual ecology of human development (Bronfenbrenner & Morris, 1998), has another significant feature—its import for actions (e.g., intervention programs and policies)—that may enhance human development. It is important to expand on these points about the relation of developmental contextualism to human development research and application.

IMPLICATIONS OF DEVELOPMENTAL CONTEXTUALISM FOR RESEARCH AND APPLICATION

In essence, (a) individuality (diversity), (b) change, involving both the individual and the context; and, as a consequence, (c) further individuality, are the essential features of human development within developmental contextualism. Given that the multiple levels of change involved in person–context relations may involve individuals at any point in their lives—whether they are infants or young children, on the one hand, or adults (and acting in roles such as parents, spouses, or teachers), on the other, it is possible to see why a developmental–contextual perspective provides a useful frame for studying development across the life span.

The possibility that bidirectional relations exist across the life span among all the levels shown in Figure 8.6 represents a formidable state of complexity, but one which behavioral and social science theory and research must address. If scholarship does not cope with this complexity, then neither research nor application will be adequate. That is, research inattentive to the complexity of person–context relations will be deficient in that either it will fail to appreciate the substantive nature of individual, familial, or relationship variation and/or it will mistakenly construe variation around some (potentially, specifically inapplicable) mean level as, at best, error variance (Lerner, 1991, 2002). In turn, applications—policies and/or programs (that are at least ideally) derived from research (Lerner & Miller, 1993)—will be insufficiently fit with the needs of the specific people intended to be served by these interventions, *if* it is the case that these activities are insufficiently informed by knowledge about the specific characteristics of individuality of these groups.

However, developmental contextualism offers an alternative to this situation. It does so by stressing the importance of a focus on diversity and context for integrated research and application. The fusion of levels in developmental contextualism means that changes at one level are producers and products of changes at others and, therefore, that human development is characterized by the potential for systematic change—by plasticity—at any point in the course of life (Lerner, 1984, 1998b).

Nevertheless, we have stressed that structures and functions at each level of this integrated system of relations both constrain and limit change as well as promote it, and we have explained (see Chapter 5, and, as well, Thelen & Smith, 1998) that this ubiquitous synthesis between the constraining and affording of change means that plasticity is a relative and not an absolute feature of human life. As a consequence, it is taken as a given that plasticity is not limitless but that, nonetheless, individual–context relations may be found, or may be created, to alter the course of human life. In short, the presence of relative plasticity indicates that means may be found to change systematically at least some structural or functional component of any target "entity" (i.e., any component of an individual, group, or institution) embedded within the system of integrated levels constituting human life (Lerner, 1984).

Furthermore, no two people (even those from monozygotic multiple births) will experience the same temporal sequence of person–context relations across their lives. Consequently, interindividual differences in intraindividual change trajectories are the rule in human development.

Diversity and context are superordinate concerns within developmental contextualism. A focus on diversity provides a sample of the plasticity of human developmental paths. A focus on context affords some understanding of how changes at interindividual and extraindividual levels are both producers and products of human plasticity. A concern with both diversity and context elevate to "center stage" the importance of a focus on the individual, on both the general and lawfully unique features of his or her developmental trajectory, and on the role of this singular individual—as he or she dynamically interacts with the context—in being an active producer of his or her own development (Lerner, 1982; Lerner & Busch-Rossnagel, 1981b; Lerner & Walls, 1999; Scarr & McCartney, 1983).

The Life-Span Application of Developmental Contextualism

For any functional component of the changing person–context relations that constitute the developmental process (e.g., for cognitive functioning), a developmental–contextual analysis would suggest assessments ranging from (a) the contributions of other within-level functions (e.g., personality or emotional functioning) to the diversity of changes in the target function (i.e., in this example, intraindividual interactions between cognition and emotion or personality would be assessed), and (b) the contributions of "naturally occurring" (i.e., ecologically valid) interlevel relations (involving either interindividual or extraindividual interactions) to diversity of target function changes; to (c) the contributions of designed interindividual or extraindividual relations to such change.

Exploration of the contributions of ecologically valid relations enables a demonstration of the range of plasticity that does exist, given the sampled array of intraindividual, interindividual, or extraindividual relations. In turn, appraisal of the diversity of changes that are produced by a given set of designed relations provides some indication of the range of plasticity that might exist. Here, in this point, lies a key basis for the synthesis between theory and application associated with developmental systems theories in general (Chapter 7) and with developmental contextualism in particular (Lerner & Fisher, 1994).

As explained in Chapter 7, designed relations between the person and the context, when they are embedded in the actual ecology of human development, constitute developmental interventions (Birkel, Lerner, & Smyer, 1989). These interventions, first, represent critical means to test propositions about the causal network of person–context covariation believed to be involved in the process of developmental change. Second, these interventions constitute simulations of the individual and contextual conditions that may be used to promote human plasticity in desired or valued directions; they represent a means to explore how to move the prototypic array of human diversity to within an "optimal" (or at least a more enhanced) range.

Basic Versus Applied Research

Education and training in the disciplines involved in the study of human development have traditionally involved a distinction between basic and applied research. As is the case with other areas of behavioral and social science, this division rests on the view that the basic researcher pursues "pure" problems; that is, he or she studies the variables involved in the core processes of behavior and development. These processes are seen to account for the structure and/or function of target phenomena and, as such, understanding their character allows one to go beyond description and attain an appreciation of the causes (the explanations) of development. In short, the basic researcher explains how development works in the world of the experimental, or at least the controlled, situation.

Applied research has been seen as involving study of the functioning of one or more basic processes as they are embedded in their "natural state" (i.e., in the actual ecology of human life). The goal of such research has been seen to be the identification of the ways in which basic knowledge can be used, or must be modified, to design and deliver interventions. The applied researcher studies how development actually happens in the ecology of human life. In other words, the distinction between basic and applied research is that the former endeavor may be cast as the pursuing of "knowledge for its own sake." Within such a view, applications from basic research arise from serendipity, whereas in applied research intervention is the core focus.

It is fair to say that a status hierarchy has existed in academe regarding the distinctions between basic research and applied (or intervention) research. Colleagues engaged in endeavors labeled *basic research* have been typically afforded ascriptions of "pure scientists" and positions of high academic standing. Whatever the history, or current standing, of such appraisals in academe in general, in regard to the study of human development, the rationale for distinctions between basic and applied research are quite fuzzy and rapidly eroding (Fisher & Lerner, 1994a, 1994b; Lerner, 1991; Lerner & Tubman, 1990).

The bases of this dissolution of divisions between research aimed at understanding basic processes, on the one hand, and research studying development in the ecologically valid settings of human life, on the other, have arisen in the theoretical and empirical literatures associated with the study of development across the life span (e.g., Baltes, 1987; Featherman, 1983; Lerner, 1984, 1986), especially when it has been coupled with a developmental systems or, more specifically, with a developmental–contextual perspective (Lerner, 1998a, 1998b).

A vision for such an integration of basic and applied research, one linking developmental scholarship with progress and policies, was articulated almost three decades ago by Bronfenbrenner (1974). Bronfenbrenner argued that engagement with social policy not only enhances developmental research but, consistent with the developmental–contextual perspective, also augments understanding of key theoretical issues pertinent to the nature of person–context relations.

Accordingly, Bronfenbrenner (1974) noted that:

> In discussions of the relation between science and social policy, the first axiom, at least among social scientists, is that social policy should be based on science. The proposition not only has logic on its side, but what is more important, it recognizes our proper and primary importance in the scheme of things. The policymakers should look to us, not only for truth, but for wisdom as well. In short, social policy needs science. My thesis in this paper is the converse proposition, that, particularly in our field, science needs social policy—needs it not to guide our organizational activities, but to provide us with two elements essential for any scientific endeavor—vitality and validity. (p. 1) . . . I contend that the pursuit of [social policy] questions is essential for the further development of knowledge and theory on the process of human development. Why essential? (p. 2) . . . [Because] issues of social policy [serve] as points of departure for the identification of significant theoretical and scientific questions concerning the development of the human organism as a function of interaction with its enduring environment—both actual and potential. (p. 4)

There are several possible foci for developmental scholarship, and for using such work to serve individuals and communities, that may be associated with Bronfenbrenner's (1974) vision.

Potential Scholarly and Service Themes

Together, the previously noted facets of developmental–contextual scholarship in the study of children, youth, and contexts suggest several important themes for research, for the training of developmental scientists, and for applying developmental science in the service of society. First, a developmental, individual differences perspective is required to understand *both* children and families; this perspective must focus on the relations within the family between parents and children and, as well, on the relations between each family member and the other settings within which he or she functions (e.g., children and day-care settings and parents and the workplace). In addition, the relations among settings must become a focus of developmental analysis (Bronfenbrenner, 1979; Bronfenbrenner & Morris, 1998; Magnusson & Stattin, 1998). The compilation of such information will afford a profile of the individual people and relations that comprise a specific family.

Second, the study of children and parents must become broadly contextualized. Variables from multiple levels of organization—ranging from biology and health through social institutions involving education, politics, and the economy—affect people across their lives. It is the array of these variables as they extend across life that can make each person increasingly individually distinct from others in his or her family, social group, cohort, or society (Tobach, 1981).

Moreover, the contextual and developmental approach to the study of children and their parents must emphasize diversity. There is no one developmental path that is ideal for all people. As such, a key scientific concern of scholars of children, youth, and families must be the understanding of the richness of human life reflected in racial, ethnic, gender, national, and cultural variation. Education, intervention, service, and policy endeavors should similarly emphasize the specific patterns of contextual variation associated with the diverse peoples of concern to scholars.

Third, because no one discipline or professional area has an experiential or a knowledge base (or a repertoire of methodologies) sufficient to understand this diversity, or the interrelated influences of multiple levels of analysis on children and families, a multidisciplinary and multiprofessional approach to training, research, and service is required. In other words, to study the phenomena and problems of children, youth, and families, as they function and develop in their real-life settings, and to provide effective health, family, and human policies and services, we need interdisciplinary conceptualizations and multiprofessional collaborations.

This integration should be a key facet of the mission of any academic fields aimed at advancing science and service for children, youth, and families. The knowledge base which may be generated in activities associated with such a mission may be extended into programs and services for the children and families of a state, of a nation, and—given the proper collaborative arrangements—the world.

CONCLUSIONS

Developmental contextualism is a theoretical approach to the science of, and service to, human development. Building on the integrative ideas found in Schneirla's (1956, 1957, 1959; Tobach, 1981) thinking, developmental contextualism represents a model of human life that transcends the dichotomies, or splits (Overton, 1998), found so often in the study of human development, and in social and behavioral science and society more generally, that is, splits such as, nature–nurture, organism–environment, person–context, and basic versus applied research.

From a developmental–contextual perspective, research must be conducted with an appreciation of the individual differences in human development, differences that arise as a consequence of diverse people's development in distinct families, communities, and sociocultural settings. In turn, policies and programs must be similarly attuned to the diversity of people and context in order to maximize the chances of meeting the specific needs of particular groups of people. Such programs and policies must be derived appropriately from research predicated on an integrative, multidisciplinary view of human development. The evaluation of such applications should provide both societally important information about the success of endeavors aimed at the enhancement of individuals, *and* theoretically invaluable data about the validity of the synthetic, multilevel processes posited in developmental contextualism to characterize human development.

Meeting the challenge represented by the need to merge research with policy, and with intervention design, delivery, and evaluation, will bring the study of people and their contexts to the threshold of a new intellectual era. The linkage between research, policy, and intervention that I have discussed will demonstrate to scientists that the basic processes of human behavior are ones involving the development of dynamic, reciprocal relations between individually distinct people and the specific social institutions they encounter in their particular ecological settings. As suggested in Chapter 7, such demonstrations may then enable developmental scientists to collaborate with communities to use scholarship to promote posi-

tive human development and enhance civil society (Lerner et al., 1974; Lerner, Fisher, & Weinberg, 2000a; Lerner, Sparks, & McCubbin, 1999).

As noted also in Chapter 7, we return, in Chapter 19, to the idea of integrating developmental systems theory and civil society. At this point, however, it is useful to turn to a fuller discussion of several of the key theoretical models—ones also linked to developmental systems theory—that have influenced and enhanced developmental contextualism. We consider, then, life-span, life-course, bioecological, and action theory perspectives.

9 | *Life-Span, Action Theory, Life-Course, and Bioecological Perspectives*

By the end of the twentieth century, developmental systems theory emerged as a superordinate frame for several different models of human development. As discussed in previous chapters, these instances of developmental systems theory (e.g., Ford & Lerner, 1992; Gottlieb, 1992, 1997; Lerner, 1995a, 1996, 1998b; Lewis, 1997; Magnusson, 1995, 1996, 1999a, 1999b; Sameroff, 1983; Thelen & Smith, 1998; Wapner & Demick, 1998; see, too, Feldman, 2000; Fischer & Bidell, 1998; Rogoff, 1998) may be regarded as members of the same theoretical "family": All "family members" reject nature–nurture "split" concepts of reality and causation (Overton, 1998) and, in turn, adopt a relational and integrated (or fused) conception of the multiple levels of organization involved in the ecology of human development (Schneirla, 1957; Tobach, 1981).

Accordingly, because of these common conceptual orientations, we were able to illustrate in Chapter 7 that the several instances of developmental systems theory we discussed (i.e., those of Gottlieb, 1992, 1997; Magnusson, 1995, 1996, 1999, 2000; Thelen & Smith, 1994, 1998; Wapner & Demick, 1998) approached in comparable ways issues such as (a) plasticity (i.e., the dynamism between change and constraints on change that is derived from the integrations across the levels of the developmental system), (b) the role of individuals as active agents in their own development, and (c) the importance of including the contributions of multiple levels of organization—ranging from biology through history—into one's explanations of development.

In Chapter 8, we discussed how another instance of developmental systems theory—developmental contextualism (Lerner, 1991, 1996, 1998b)—not only further demonstrated these common foci among members of this theoretical family but also provided an illustration of how a given family member may make unique additions to the conceptual "repertoire" with the developmental systems theoretical family. For instance, developmental contextualism was shown to bring to the fore ideas of children as producers of their own development (through the circular functions they have with their social context); of the "goodness-of-fit" model as a means to represent the interlevel relations that are seen as the necessary units of analysis in developmental systems' ideas of person–context relations; and of the link between basic and applied research that derives from the focus in developmental contextualism of studying the change trajectories of individuals embedded in the actual, changing ecology of human life.

Moreover, our discussion of developmental contextualism throughout the previous chapters of this book has pointed to the linkage of this perspective with—and its great intellectual debt to—other, prior or simultaneously developing instances of relational, developmental systems models. In particular, I have noted the important associations between developmental contextualism and the life-span view of human development—as elaborated in particular by Paul B. Baltes, John R. Nesselroade, and K. Warner Schaie (e.g., see Chapter 2).

The generative character of the life-span perspective was not limited to an influence on developmental contextualism. In addition, the life-span perspective was both an influence on—and was influenced by—other key members of the developmental systems theoretical family. Three family members stand out as particularly involved in this association: action theories of

John R. Nesselroade

human development, the life-course perspective, and the bioecological view of human development. Aspects of each of these four instances of developmental systems theory—the life-span, life-course, bioecological, and action theory perspectives—have been noted in prior discussions of the concepts and theories involved in the study of human development (e.g., in Chapter 2, we noted the role of some of these models in influencing the direction of the study of human development during the 1970s and 1980s). However, it is helpful here to discuss each instance of developmental systems theory in more detail. This pre-sentation provides both further illustration of the commonality of ideas shared across diverse instances of members of this theoretical family and, at the same time, enables us to underscore the unique and important contributions to theory made by each model.

Because of its central generative role in the past and present development of developmental systems models in general, and in the other instances of this family of perspectives we discuss in this chapter, we shall consider first the life-span view of human development. For more than three decades, the work of Paul B. Baltes and his colleagues has provided the core conceptual and empirical foundation for this theory of human development.

LIFE-SPAN DEVELOPMENTAL THEORY

Life-span developmental theory (Baltes, 1979a, 1979b; 1983, 1987, 1997, 1980; Baltes et al., 1998, 1999; Baltes, Reese, & Lipsitt, 1980) as stated by Baltes and colleagues (1998)

> deals with the study of individual development (ontogenesis) from conception into old age. . . . A core assumption of life-span developmental psychology is that development is not completed at adulthood (maturity). Rather, the basic premise of life-span developmental psychology is that ontogenesis extends across the entire life course and that lifelong adaptive processes are involved. (p. 1029)

In the context of these assumptions, Baltes and colleagues (1998) noted that life-span developmental theory has several scientific goals, ones that span *and integrate* the basic-to-applied continuum of interest in other members of the developmental systems theory family (e.g., developmental contextualism; see Chapter 8). That is:

> The objective of life-span psychology is: (a) to offer an organized account of the overall structure and sequence of development across the life span, (b) to identify the interconnections between earlier and later developmental events and processes, (c) to delineate the factors and mechanisms which are the foundation of life-span development, and (d) to

Paul B. Baltes

specify the biological and environmental opportunities and constraints which shape life-span development of individuals. With such information, life-span developmentalists further aspire to determine the range of possible development of individuals, to empower them to live their lives as desirably (and effectively) as possible, and to help them avoid dysfunctional and undesirable behavioral outcomes. (p. 1030)

Moreover, given the central interest in life-span developmental theory in how the individual–context relation is associated with adaptive (healthy, positive) developmental trajectories, Baltes and his colleagues (e.g., Baltes & Baltes, 1980, 1990) tested the idea that successful development involves the maximization of gains and the minimization of losses. Indeed, more generally, Baltes and Baltes (1990) hypothesized that *all* development involves an integration of loss and gain. Consistent with the notion of integrated levels, however, Baltes and colleagues (1998) noted that a person's cultural and historical niche influences his or her development— that is, his or her synthesis across ontogeny of gains (e.g., in visual acuity or native language fluency) and losses (e.g., involved in the death of neurons not involved in acuity, or in the loss of capacity to learn nonnative languages with fluency equal to that associated with one's native language).

A key illustration that Baltes and his colleagues pointed to in regard to the dynamic integration between gains and losses across the life span, and to the social and cultural embeddedness of this dynamic of individual–context relations, pertains to the fluid mechanics and crystallized pragmatics of intelligence. Baltes and colleagues (1998) explained that:

> Very much in line with the life-span dynamic between biology and culture . . . intellectual abilities that are thought to reflect the neurobiologically based mechanics of intelligence—like working memory and fluid intelligence—typically showed normative (universal) declines in functioning beginning in middle adulthood. Conversely, intellectual abilities that primarily reflect the culture-based pragmatics of intelligence—such as professional knowledge and wisdom—may show stability or even increases into late adulthood. As to the ontogenesis of intelligence, then, gains and losses . . . co-exist. (p. 1046)

Levels of Analysis in Life-Span Developmental Scholarship

To pursue the goal of life-span developmental theory, Baltes and his colleagues conducted scholarship at five levels of analysis. Baltes and

colleagues (1998) explained that the first level of analysis is the

> most distal and general one, [and] makes explicit the cornerstones and "norms of reaction" or "potentialities" . . . of life-span ontogenesis. With this approach, which is also consistent with the levels of integration notion of Schneirla, we obtain information on what we can expect about the general scope and shape of life-span development based on evolutionary, historical, and interdisciplinary views dealing with the interplay between biology and culture during ontogenesis. (p. 1035)

Baltes and colleagues (1998) further noted that:

> Levels 2 and 3 bring us closer and closer to psychological theories of individual development. . . . We begin with a general view on the overall form of gains and losses across the life span (Level 2) followed by the description of a family of metatheoretical perspective (Level 3). We argue that this family of metatheoretical perspectives is useful when articulating more specific theories of life-span development. On Level 4, we advance one concrete illustration of an overall life-span developmental theory, a theory which is based on the specification and coordinated orchestration of three processes: selection, optimization, and compensation. On Level 5 . . . we characterize life-span theory and research in such areas of psychological functioning as cognition, intelligence, personality, and the self. (p. 1035)

Table 9.1 summarizes the several theoretical ideas that Baltes and his colleagues used to frame the study of life-span development across these five levels. In presenting the theoretical ideas associated with life-span developmental theory, this table illustrates both (a) the commonality of theoretical ideas between life-span developmental theory and other instances of developmental systems theories (e.g., in regard to plasticity and to the embeddedness of development in a dynamic system comprised of levels of organization ranging from biology through culture and history), and (b) the ideas about human development that are specifically brought to the fore of human development theory by a life-span perspective (e.g., development as a lifelong process, the dynamic between gains and losses, the integration of ontogenetic and historical contextualism, and the functional dynamic between processes of selection, optimization, and compensation that is involved in successful/adaptive development).

Thus, to pursue scholarship within or across the five levels of analysis involved in life-span development theory, Baltes and his colleagues employed a set of theoretical ideas both general to developmental systems theory and, as well, unique within their specific theoretical model. To

TABLE 9.1
Family of Theoretical Propositions Characteristic of Life-Span Developmental Theory

---

Life-span development
  Ontogenetic development is a lifelong process. No age period holds supremacy in regulating the nature of development.

Life-span changes in the dynamic between biology and culture
  With age and certainly after adulthood, there is a growing gap between biological potential and individual-cultural goals. This gap is fundamental to ontogenesis as the biological and cultural architecture of life is incomplete and inevitably results in loss of adaptive functioning and eventually death.

Life-span changes in allocation of resources to distinct functions of development: Growth versus maintenance versus regulation of loss
  Ontogenetic development on a systemic level involves the coordinated and competitive allocation of resources into distinct functions: Growth maintenance including recovery (resilience), and regulation of loss. Life-span developmental changes in the profile of functional allocation involve a shift from the allocation of resources to growth (more typical of childhood) toward an increasingly larger and larger share allocated to maintenance and management of loss.

Development as selection (specialization) and selective optimization in adaptive capacity
  Development is inherently a process of selection and selective adaptation. Selection is due to biological, psychological, cultural, and environmental factors. Developmental advances are due to processes of optimization. Because development is selective and because of age-associated changes in potential, compensation is also part of the developmental agenda.

Development as gain—loss dynamic
  In ontogenetic development, there is no gain without loss, and no loss without gain. Selection and selective adaptation are space-, context-, and time-bound. Thus, selection and selective adaptation imply not only advances in adaptive capacity but also losses in adaptivity for alternative pathways and adaptive challenges. A multidimensional, multidirectional, and multifunctional conception of development results from such a perspective.

Plasticity
  Much intraindividual plasticity (within-person variability) is found in psychological development. The key developmental agenda is the search for the range of plasticity and its age-associated changes and constraints.

Ontogenetic and historical contextualism as paradigm
  In principle, the biological and cultural architecture of human development is incomplete and subject to continuous change. Thus, ontogenetic development varies markedly by historical—cultural conditions. The mechanisms involved can be characterized in terms of the principles associated with contextualism. As an illustration: Development can be understood as the outcome of the interactions (dialectics) between three systems of biological and environmental influences: Normative age-graded, normative history-graded, and non-normative (idiosyncratic). Each of these sources evinces individual differences and, in addition, is subject to continuous change.

Toward a general and functionalist theory of development: The effective coordination of selection, optimization and compensation
  On a general and functionalist level of analysis, successful development, defined as the (subjective and objective) maximization of gains and minimization of losses, can be conceived of as resulting from collaborative interplay among three components: Selection, optimization, and compensation. The ontogenetic pressure for this dynamic increases with age, as the relative incompleteness of the biology- and culture-based architecture of human development becomes more and more pronounced.

Note. From "Life-Span Theory in Human Development," by P. B. Baltes, U. Lindenberger, and U. M. Staudinger (1998). In W. Damon (Series Ed.) and R. M. Lerner (Volume Ed.), *Handbook of Child Psychology: Vol. 1. Theoretical Models of Human Development* (5th ed.), p. 1043. New York: Wiley. Copyright © 1998 by Wiley. Reprinted with permission.

illustrate how Baltes and his colleagues used the theoretical propositions summarized in Table 9.1 to conceptualize the five levels of analysis used in the study of development across the life span, consider the interest within Level of Analysis 2 in understanding the structure of gain and loss integrations across ontogeny. To appreciate the character of the developmental process involved across the life span in these integrations, Baltes and colleagues (1998) saw it necessary to investigate four dimensions of changing person—context relations:

1. An age-related general reduction in the amount and quality of biology based resources as individuals move toward old age.

2. The age-correlated increase in the amount and quality of culture needed to generate higher and higher levels of growth.

3. The age-associated biology based loss in the efficiency with which cultural resources are used.

4. The relative lack of cultural, "old-age-friendly" support structures. (p. 1041)

This example of the way in which Baltes and his colleagues used the propositions associated with life-span developmental theory to conceptualize and study developmental phenomena associated with the five levels of theoretical analysis they envisioned (in the case of this example, the gain–loss integrations of concern in the Level 2 analytic focus on individual ontogenetic processes) illustrates the use by Baltes and colleagues (1998) of ideas both common to members of the developmental systems theoretical family (e.g., in regard to life-span changes in plasticity) and specific to life-span theory (e.g., the thorough integration of sociocultural influences across the breadth of the life span).

Given the unique and important role played in life-span developmental theory of propositions specific to this instance of developmental systems theory, it is useful to discuss these features of the conceptual repertoire of this perspective in more detail. In particular, it is useful to review the ideas of Baltes and his colleagues regarding ontogenetic and historical contextualism as paradigm and the concepts of selection, optimization, and compensation. The former instance of the propositions of life-span developmental theory serves as an important conceptual bridge to life-course models of human development, whereas the latter instance is associated closely with action–theoretical accounts of human development.

Ontogenetic and Historical Contextualism as Paradigm

To illustrate the specific theoretical contributions of the life-span developmental perspective, it is useful then to first discuss how Baltes and his colleagues integrated individual ontogeny and the historical context of human development. Baltes and colleagues (1998) noted that:

> Individuals exist in contexts that create opportunities for and limitations to individual developmental pathways. Delineation of these contexts in terms of macrostructural features, like social class, ethnicity, roles, age-based passages and historical periods, is a major goal for the sociological analysis of the life course. (p. 1049)

Baltes and his colleagues offered a tripartite model for integrating ontogenetic development with features of historical change, and, thus, for synthesizing sociological approaches (e.g., Elder, 1998) and individual–psychological approaches (Hetherington & Baltes, 1988) to understand the bases of development. The three components of this model involve: (a) normative, age-graded influences; (b) normative, history-graded influences; and (c) nonnormative, life-event influences (Baltes et al., 1980).

Normative, age-graded influences consist of biological and environmental determinants that are correlated with chronological age. They are normative to the extent that their timing, duration, and clustering are similar for many individuals. Examples include maturational events (changes in height, endocrine system function, and central nervous system function) and socialization events (marriage, childbirth, and retirement).

Normative, history-graded influences consist of biological and environmental determinants that are correlated with historical time. They are normative to the extent that they are experienced by most members of a *birth cohort* (i.e., a group of people who share a common year of birth or, somewhat more broadly, a group born during a specific historical period (e.g., the "baby boom" generation of the immediate post-World War II period). In this sense, normative, history-graded events tend to define the developmental context of a given birth cohort. Examples include historic events (wars, epidemics, and periods of economic depression or prosperity) and sociocultural evolution (changes in sex-role expectations, the educational system, and child-rearing practices). Both age-graded and history-graded influences *covary* (change together) with time.

Nonnormative, life-event influences—the third system—are not directly indexed by time since they do not occur for all people, or even for most people. Rather, they are idiosyncratic in development (Baltes et al., 1998). Thus, when nonnormative influences do occur, they are likely to differ significantly in terms of their clustering, timing, and duration. Examples of nonnormative events include such items as illness, divorce, promotion, death of a spouse, and so on.

In short, variables from several sources, or dimensions, influence development. As such, life-span developmental theory stresses that human development is *multidimensional* in character. In other words, variables from many dimensions (ones ranging from biology related, age-graded events through the normative and nonnormative events constituting history) are involved in developmental change. As I have emphasized, in life-span developmental theory the relationships among the sources of contextual influence— normative, age-graded; normative, history-graded; and nonnormative, life-event—are seen as *dynamic* (i.e., *reciprocal*). They may continually change, and each influence has an effect on the others and, in turn, is affected by them.

Baltes and colleagues (1980) suggested that these three sources of influence exhibit different profiles over the life cycle. Normative, age-graded influences are postulated to be particularly significant in childhood and again in old age, whereas normative, history-graded influences are thought to be more important in adolescence and the years immediately following it; this is thought to reflect the importance of the sociocultural context as the individual begins adult life. Finally, nonnormative, life-event influences are postulated to be particularly significant during middle-adulthood and old age, promoting increasing divergence as individuals experience unique life events. Such a perspective is consonant with a concept of multidirectional development across the life span.

Baltes and colleagues (1998) concluded, in regard to the links between human ontogeny and historical change, that:

> Individual development, then, proceeds within these closely intertwined contexts of age-graded, history-graded, and nonnormative life events. None of these patterns of biologically and environmentally based influences is likely to operate independently from the other. In life-span theory these three sources of influence create the contexts within which individuals act, react, organize their own development, and contribute to the development of others. . . . Such a focus on contextualism also makes explicit the lack of full predictability of human development as well as the boundedness individuals experience as they engage in the effort to compose and manage their lives. . . . And finally, such a focus on contextualism places individual development in the context of the development of others. It is not surprising, therefore, that life-span researchers have easily embraced concepts such as collaborative development, collaborative cognition, or interactive minds. (p. 1050)

The role of the "dynamic collaborations" (Fischer & Bidell, 1998, p. 476) suggested by Baltes and colleagues (1998) to be a key part of individual development is discussed in greater detail in Chapter 14, in the context of a presentation of neo-nativist (e.g., Spelke & Newport, 1998) and dynamic, developmental systems (e.g., Fischer & Bidell, 1998; Rogoff, 1998) theoretical approaches to cognitive development. Here, however, it is important to note the interrelation between the ideas of Baltes and his colleagues regarding the interrelation of (a) ontogenetic and

historical–contextual changes, and (b) the role of individuals as active agents in their own development. This focus on the interrelation of the action of individuals on their context and of the context on individuals leads to a consideration of another key, and specific, feature of life-span developmental theory: the use of concepts of selection, optimization, and compensation within a systematic and overall theory of development across the life span.

The Baltes and Baltes Selective Optimization With Compensation (SOC) Model

For more than a decade, Margret M. Baltes, Paul B. Baltes, and their colleagues Baltes & Baltes, 1980, 1990; M. Baltes, 1987; M. Baltes & Carstensen, 1996, 1998; Baltes; 1987, 1997; P. Baltes, Dittmann-Kohli, & Dixon, 1984; Carstensen, Hanson, & Freund, 1995; Freund & Baltes, 1998, 2000; Lerner, Freund, De Stefanis, & Habermas, 2001; Marsiske, Lang, Baltes, & Baltes, 1995) have developed a model of development—selective optimization with compensation (SOC)—that is aimed at providing a systemic view of human development across the life span.

The SOC model integrates the theoretical propositions summarized in Table 9.1 and, in turn, provides a general theoretical framework for the

Margret M. Baltes

understanding of *processes of developmental regulation*—that is, the processes through which individual–context relations occur across the life span or, in other words, the processes through which individuals affect their context at the same time that their context is influencing them (Brandtstädter, 1998, 1999; Lerner & Walls, 1999). The SOC model seeks to depict these person–context processes across the different levels of analysis (ranging from the micro- to macro-levels) involved in the developmental system, across different domains of functioning (such as cognitive functioning or social relations), and across the entire life span.

In the SOC model, the three processes posed to be central to developmental regulation—selection, optimization, and compensation—are conceptualized to involve goal-selection, goal-pursuit, and goal-maintenance. Selection, optimization, and compensation need to be considered conjointly to adequately describe and understand development. For the sake of clarity, however, it is helpful to introduce each of the processes individually.

Based on the assumption that constraints and limitations of (internal and external) resources (e.g., stamina, money, and social support) are present throughout the entire life span (e.g., Baltes, 1997), the SOC model posits that the range of alternative developmental options (goals, ecologies, and domains of functioning) needs to be delineated (this action is termed "elective selection"). Selection gives direction to development by orienting and focusing resources (i.e., means to reach goals) on certain domains of functioning and preventing diffusion of resources. In order to actually achieve higher levels of functioning in the selected domains, optimization needs to take place. Optimization denotes the process of acquiring, refining, coordinating, and applying goal-relevant means or resources in the selected domains (or goals). Typical instances of optimization are (a) the acquisition and training of specific goal-related skills (e.g., engaging in weight-training to increase athletic ability, or working on test-taking skills in order to improve performance on an exam important for college admission); and (b) persistence in goal-pursuit.

Optimization describes a process of developmental regulation addressing the growth aspect of development, as optimization is geared toward achieving higher levels of functioning. Throughout the life span, however, development can be characterized as multidirectional, that is, as encompassing growth and decline (Baltes, 1997; P. B. Baltes, Lindenberger, & Staudinger, 1998; Brandtstädter & Wentura, 1994; Labouvie-Vief, 1981). The SOC model addresses the aspect of decline and

management of loss by stressing the importance of *compensation*. When loss or decline in goal-relevant means threatens one's level of functioning, it is necessary to invest resources or apply means geared toward the maintenance of functioning (Carstensen et al., 1995; Staudinger, Marsiske, & Baltes, 1995; Marsiske et al., 1995). Prototypical instances of compensation are the substitution of means or the use of external aids (e.g., help of a tutor to improve academic test performance in a particular subject area).

It is, of course, possible that compensatory efforts fail (e.g., weight-training fails to improve one's strength and athletic ability sufficiently to gain a place on a high school football team) or that their costs outweigh their gains (e.g., one learns that to have a chance to make the team, the amount of training required would mean that no other activity—including studying or social interaction—would be feasible). In such circumstances, the more adaptive response to loss or decline in goal-related means might be to restructure one's goal hierarchy (e.g., place academics ahead of football), to lower one's standards (e.g., settle for being a junior varsity football player), or to look for new goals, an action termed "loss-based selection" (e.g., here one could make weight-lifting, or body-building, a goal instead of a means). This component of selection is functionally different from elective selection as it occurs as a response to loss, most likely leading to different motivational and affective consequences (e.g., Shah, Higgins, & Friedman, 1998).

To illustrate how the SOC model may be useful in depicting the actual behaviors of people across their lives, Table 9.2 provides some examples of actions associated with selection, optimization, and compensation that are derived from the biographies of a famous athlete, scientist, and performing artist. In turn, Table 9.3 presents the specific actions individuals may take in regard to either elective or loss-based selection, optimization, or compensation. It is relevant to note that the terms used by Baltes and colleagues (1998) in this table reflect actions that may be conceptualized as consistent with what we shall discuss as "action theory."

In sum, selection refers to the development of preferences or goals, the construction of a goal-hierarchy, and the commitment to a set of goals or domains of functioning. Optimization denotes the investment of goal-related means in order to achieve higher levels of functioning. Compensation refers to the process involved in maintaining a given level of functioning in the face of loss or decline in goal-related means. Although it is

TABLE 9.2

Selective Optimization With Compensation: Biographical Examples

Source	Selection	Optimization	Compensation
Athelete Michael Jordan (Greene, 1993)	Focused only on basketball in youth excluding swimming and skating	Daily line drills and upper body training	Reliance on special footwear to deal with chronic foot injury
Scientist Marie Curie (Curie, 1937)	Excluded political and cultural activities from her life	Spent a fixed number of hours daily in isolation in her laboratory	Turned to the advice of specific colleagues when encountering scientific problems that were beyond her expertise
Concert pianist Rubinstein (Baltes & Baltes, 1990b)	Played smaller repertoire of pieces in late life	Practiced these pieces more with age	Slowed performance before fast movements (ritardando) to heighten contrast

Note. From "Life-Span Theory in Human Development," by P. B. Baltes, U. Lindenberger, and U. M. Staudinger (1998). In W. Damon (Series Ed.) and R. M. Lerner (Vol. Ed.), *Handbook of Child Psychology: Vol. 1. Theoretical Models of Human Development* (5th ed.), p. 1058. New York: Wiley. Copyright © 1998 by Wiley. Reprinted with permission.

possible to differentiate these components of SOC, successful development encompasses their coordinated integration (Freund & Baltes, 2000; Marsiske et al., 1995). For instance, optimization efforts most likely only lead to higher levels of functioning when they are focused on a delineated number of domains of functioning instead of diffused among many domains. Similarly, selection per se does not ensure high achievement if no goal-relevant means are applied (e.g., wanting to have high peer status but using no means—neither athletic nor academic success—to attain it).

Finally, the adaptiveness of compensation needs to be seen in the context of the entire goal-system (e.g., "How many other goals are there that need resources for optimization?" and "How important, relative to other goals, is a threatened goal?") and the availability of resources. It does not appear to be adaptive to put a lot of one's resources into a relatively unimportant domain of functioning at the cost of having to neglect more important goals (Freund, Li, & Baltes, 1999).

Figure 9.1 provides an illustration of the life-span character of the SOC model. The figure presents the ideas of Baltes and his colleagues about the developmental bases of selection, optimization, and compensation processes and, in turn, of their developmental outcomes. The role, then, of the SOC model within the frame of the goals that are pursued by life-span developmental theory are clear. The actions depicted in the SOC model enable individuals to engage their contexts in ways that promote their positive development across the life span.

Conclusions

Life-span developmental theory constitutes a conceptually rich and empirically productive instance of developmental systems theory. The breadth and depth of the sets of ideas of Baltes and his colleagues offer a singularly creative means to understand the dynamic links between individuals and contexts. These relations underscore the changing character of plasticity across the life span and enable individuals to play an active role throughout their lives in promoting their own, positive development.

The conceptual integrations involved in life-span developmental theory span levels of organization ranging from biology through culture and

TABLE 9.3
Selection, Optimization, and Compensation (SOC) Embedded in an Action–Theoretical Framework (after P. Baltes, M. Baltes, Freud, & Lang, 1995)

Selection (goals–preferences)	Optimization (goal-relevant means)	Compensation (means–resources for counteracting loss–decline in goal-relevant means)
Elective selection —specification of goals —evolution of goal system (hierarchy) —contextualization of goals —goal-commitment *Loss-based selection* goal(s) —search for alternate goals —reconstruction of goal hierarchy —adaptation of standards	—attentional focus —effort–energy —time allocation —practice of skills —acquiring new skills–resources —modeling successful others —motivation for self-development	—substitution of means —neglect of optimizing other means —increased effort–energy —increased time allocation —activation of unused skills–resources —acquiring new skills–resources —modeling successful others who compensate —focusing on most important —use of technical aids —use of assistance/help/therapy

Note. This specification reflects the specific explication of Baltes' general theoretical orientation, that is, from the point of view of action theory.
Source: From "Life-Span Theory in Human Development," by P. B. Baltes, U. Lindenberger, and U. M. Staudinger (1998). In W. Damon (Series Ed.) and R. M. Lerner (Vol. Ed.), *Handbook of Child Psychology: Vol. 1. Theoretical Models of Human Development* (5th ed.), p. 1056. New York: Wiley. Copyright © 1998 by Wiley. Reprinted with permission.

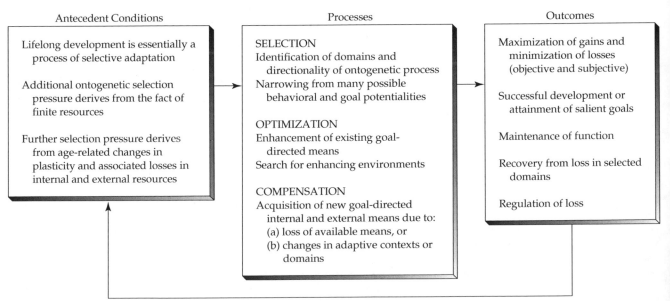

FIGURE 9.1
The life-span model of selective optimization with compensation. The essentials of the model are proposed to be universal, but specific phenotypic manifestations will vary by domain, individual, sociocultural context, and theoretical perspective.
Source: Baltes et al. (1998, p. 1055).

history and, as such, provide a means to achieve another sort of integration, one related to the five levels of analytic work pursued by life-span developmentalists. That is, life-span developmental theory provide a means to synthesize into discussions of the course of human life other instances of developmental systems theories, those spanning a range of interests from more micro, individual-level (e.g., psychological) interests to more macro, social institutional and historical interests.

For instance, we have seen that the theoretical propositions of life-span developmental theory provide an integration of models associated with historical contextualism and the individual actions taken by people seeking to pursue their immediate and long-term goals within the context of the actual ecologies of their lives. In other words, life-span developmental theory provides a means to see the integrative relevance of individual action, of the institutional/sociological setting of the life course, and of the broad ecology of human development. Accordingly, we turn now to a discussion of theories associated with each of these other domains of developmental systems theory. We proceed from the micro (action–theory perspective) to the macro (the life-course and the bioecological perspectives). However, as perhaps implied by the label attached to the last approach we consider in this chapter, and consistent with the fused character of the levels integrated within the developmental system (and as illustrated by life-span developmental theory), our discussion of the bioecological model returns us full-circle to the linkage between micro and macro levels of organization in human development.

ACTION THEORIES OF HUMAN DEVELOPMENT

Scholarship pertinent to the nature of human plasticity within developmental systems theories suggests that developmental regulation—processes involving the actions of individuals on their contexts and the actions of contexts on individuals (i.e., processes of dynamic person–context relations)—should be a key focus of inquiry in the study of human development. Action theory (Brandtstädter, 1998, 1999; Brandtstädter & Lerner, 1999) is an exemplar of an approach that is focused on these relational processes. For example, we have noted that one key instance of this theoretical approach is the Baltes and Baltes (1990) selection, optimization, and compensation (SOC) model. Table 9.3 displayed the components of the SOC

model by emphasizing the actions involved in regulating people's goal-related behaviors.

The focus on such self-regulative actions, on the ways that the "individual is both the active producer and the product of his or her ontogeny . . . [and thus on] self-regulative loops that link developmental changes to the ways in which individuals, in action and mentation, construe their personal development" (Brandtstädter, 1988, p. 807) is the essence of action perspectives about human development. Thus, the central feature of action theories is isomorphic with a key idea in the developmental–contextual version of developmental systems theory, that of individuals acting as producers of their own development (Lerner, 1982; Lerner & Busch-Rossnagel, 1981a, 1981b; Lerner & Walls, 1999). As is also illustrated by life-span developmental theory, this emphasis on the role of the active person as an agent in his or her own development exists for other instances of developmental systems theory. In fact, this central use of the idea of individual action as a source of the person's own development arises because of the importance, underscored in action theory, of the link between regulation and human plasticity.

Regulation and Plasticity in Human Development

Across their ontogeny, humans actualize a rich potential for cognitive and behavioral plasticity (Lerner, 1984). As discussed in Chapter 8, the evolutionary gains in complexity (anagenesis) that underlie human plasticity have come "at a price," however, that is, neotenous development (Gould, 1977); in other words, there is ontogenetically protracted development of humans' eventually high-level cognitive and behavioral capacities. Other organisms, whose nervous systems have ratios of association-to-sensory fibers (A/S ratios; Hebb, 1949), are more stereotyped in their eventual, final level of ontogenetic functioning (Schneirla, 1957). That is, as discussed in Chapter 6, stimulus input is highly correlated with behavioral output. These organisms are adapted to ecological niches where they can survive and reproduce despite the fact that their behavior is strictly regulated by their context. Their relatively low level of ontogenetic plasticity (and their low A/S ratio) solves the problem of the regulation of organism–context relations and, thus, of adaptation (Hebb, 1949; Schneirla, 1957).

For humans, however, the situation is quite different. As discussed by Heckhausen (1999):

The relative dearth of biologically based predetermination of behavior gives rise to a high regulatory requirement on the part of the human individual and the social system. The social and cultural system and the individual have to regulate behavior so that resources are invested in an organized and focused way, and that failure experiences lead to an improvement rather than to a deterioration of behavioral means. (p. 8)

For humans, then, the complexity of their nervous systems and the multiple levels of their contexts mean that there is no one necessarily adaptive relation between context and behavior; what behaviors are requisite for adaptation are uncertain. As a consequence, while plasticity affords vast variation in behavior, the evolutionary status of humans means that the selection of adaptive options from within the array of behaviors available to them constitutes the key challenge in human development. Thus, according to Heckhausen (1999):

> Selectivity and proneness to failure as basic challenges both result from the extensive variability and flexibility of human behavior. Other nonprimate species are far more programmed in terms of their repertoire of activities and behavioral responses to the environment, with more instinct-driven behavior and substantially more constrained behavioral options. Humans, in contrast, have evolved with the ability to adapt flexibly to a great range of environmental conditions, and in particular with the ability to generate new systems of behavior. (p. 7)

Similarly, Brandtstädter (1999) indicated that:

> A basic evolutionary feature that makes possible—and at the same time enforces—cultural and personal control of ontogeny is the great plasticity and openness of development . . . These features of human ontogeny imply adaptive potentials as well as vulnerabilities, and they have concomitantly evolved with mechanisms to cope with the latter. The capacities to create, maintain, and enact culture, and to plot the "trajectory of . . . life on the societal map" (Berger, Berger, & Kellner, 1967, p. 67), are rooted in this coevolutionary process. Generally, developmental plasticity is already implicated in the notion of culture, as far as this notion connotes the cultivation of some process that is open to modification and optimization. (p. 46)

In essence, then, the regulation by individuals of their relations with their complex and changing physical, social, cultural, and historical context is the key problem for successful development across life (Baltes et al., 1998, 1999). Arguably, the understanding of the system involved in linking individuals and contexts becomes the essential intellectual challenge for developmental science. Indeed, as noted in our earlier discussion in this chapter of the Level 2 analyses that Baltes and his colleagues pursued in order to understand the cultural embeddedness of gain–loss processes, as the biological underpinnings of human behavior recede in ontogenetic significance as people traverse their post-reproductive years, the need for humans to intentionally draw on either individual–psychological or collective (e.g., cultural) resources (means) to promote their successful development becomes both increasingly salient and, as well, the necessary target of life-span developmental analysis (Baltes & M. Baltes, 1990; M. Baltes & Carstensen, 1998).

Accordingly, to understand development as conceived of within a dynamic, developmental systems perspective and, centrally, to appreciate the role of a person's own contributions to this development, focus should be placed on the role of an individual's actions in regulating the course of engagement with the context and in fostering constancy and change (in actualizing plasticity) across life. In the theoretical and empirical scholarship associated with this action theory perspective, the work of Jochen Brandtstädter has been the most important in framing and advancing the key conceptual issues in this instance of developmental systems theory. Accordingly, we begin our discussion of action theory by considering his scholarship.

The Contributions of Jochen Brandtstädter

Brandtstädter conceptualizes actions as a means through which individuals affect their contexts and, through the feedback resulting from such actions, organize their ideas about their contexts and themselves. As a consequence of this understanding, individuals then develop a set of "guides" [i.e., motivations (e.g., intentions and goals), or regulators] for or of future actions. The outcome of this reciprocal, "action-feedback-self-organization-further action" process is, to Brandtstädter (1998, 1999), human development. Thus, action constitutes the "engine" of development and, as such, of person–context relations. As Brandtstädter (1998) explained:

> Through action, and through experiencing the consequences of our actions, we construe representations of ourselves and of our material, social, and symbolic environments, and these representations guide and motivate activities by which we shape and influence our behavior and personal development. . . . Action thus forms development, and development forms action. . . . The central tenet of an action–theoretical perspective thus holds that human ontogeny, including adulthood and later life, cannot be understood adequately without paying heed to the self-reflective

Jochen Brandtstädter

and self-regulative [bases of] . . . personal development. This should not be read to imply that individuals are the sole or omnipotent producers of their biographies. Like any other type of activity, activities related to personal development are subject to cultural, sociohistorical, and physical constraints. These constraints lie partly or even completely outside of one's span of control, but they decisively structure the range of behavioral and developmental options. Action–theoretical perspectives on development must therefore consider not only the activities through which individuals try to control their development over the life course, but also the nonpersonal or subpersonal forces that canalize such activities. (pp. 807–808)

Accordingly, Brandtstädter emphasizes the role of individuals as producers of their own development and, as such, conceives of action as both a dynamic means through which individuals regulate their linkages with their contexts and as a basis for the development of the self (see, too, Baltes, 1998, and Table 9.1). Indeed, it is the self—the person who reflects on his or her own intentions, goals, and interests and who understands, therefore, who he or she is at the moment and who he or she would like to be at some future time—that acts to regulate relations with the context.

Thus, akin to other members of the developmental systems theoretical family, action theory as conceptualized by Brandtstädter (1988, 1999)

emphasizes the fused, dynamic relations between individuals and their contexts as constituting the core process of human development. However, as is the case with other members of this theoretical family, Brandtstädter's action theory also has attributes specific to it. One key distinctive feature is the central role given to the intentionality of the individual in moderating the exchanges occurring between person and context, and the changes in development deriving from these intention-based exchanges. That is, as Brandtstädter (1998) explained, other instances of developmental systems theory have placed primary emphasis on

> development as the result of person–environment transactions, rather than as a target area of intentional action; in other words, the relation between action and development has been conceptualized primarily as a functional rather than an intentional one. (p. 826)

Although Brandtstädter (1998) noted that the functional emphasis is appropriate for the early portions of the life span (e.g., the initial infancy period), by the end of this initial phase of life, and certainly thereafter across the life span, intentionality must play a central role in moderating the individual's interactions with his or her physical and social world.

Given, then, this central role of the individual's intentions within the person–context fusions involved in the developmental system, Brandtstädter (1998) defined actions as

> behaviors that (a) can be predicted and explained with reference to intentional states (goals, values, beliefs, volitions); (b) are at least partly under personal control, and have been selected from alternative behavioral options; (c) are constituted and constrained by social rules and conventions or by the subject's representation of these contextual constraints; and (d) aim to transform situations in accordance with personal representations of desired future states. (p. 815)

Contextual and developmental constraints on action. Accordingly, to Brandtstädter, actions link the person dynamically to his or his social context. The plasticity of the individual enables him or her to regulate what he or she does, to and in the context, and to circumscribe to some extent the influence of the context on him or her. Of course, as Brandtstädter noted within his definition of action, the person's control over the context is not limitless. There are both individual and contextual constraints on action. First, on the individual level, human plasticity is, of course, not infinite (Lerner, 1984; see, too, Chapter 5) and, in any case, the level of plasticity of which a human is eventually capable must be developed (actualized) across ontogeny (Hebb, 1949; Schneirla, 1957). In turn, some features of the context are simply not under the control of individual actors (e.g., as much as we might rage against the storm, no person controls the course of a tornado or hurricane). In addition, the social and cultural context imposes rules on actions.

In fact, Brandtstädter (1998, 1999) sees two types of such rules (i.e., constitutive and regulative rules). In regard to regulative rules, Brandtstädter (1998) noted that:

> Personal action is regulated by a variety of cultural prescriptions and restrictions, and these can be more or less formal and explicit (laws, norms, customs, social expectations, and so on). Such rules delimit situationally defined zones and margins of action. The limits imposed by regulative rules, however, are not rigid; cultural laws, in contrast to natural laws, can be violated. (p. 815)

In turn, in regard to constitutive rules, Brandtstädter (1998) indicated that:

> When one considers acts or action episodes such as marrying, formulating an excuse, promising something, or taking a penalty kick, it is evident that such actions are not simply regulated, but, in a stronger sense, are constituted by rules. Through constitutive rules, certain types of action are linked inseparably to cultural institutions. (p. 815)

For instance, "without the system of constitutive rules called football, the behaviors of scoring, blocking, passing, and so on would not exist" (D'Andrade, 1984, p. 94).

The developmental capacities of the individual also constrain, or moderate, his or her interactions with the context and, especially in regard to Brandtstädter's emphasis on the centrality of intentions in developmental regulation, the person's changing cognitive capacities are particularly important in respect to possessing the ability to form intentions. For instance, Brandtstädter (1998) noted that:

> Development-related action, as we have described above, presupposes particular representational capacities. The individual must have formed goals and standards for personal developments, and must be able to evaluate the current situation with regard to these self-guides; furthermore, he or she must have acquired some knowledge about probable and possible courses of future development, and, in particular, about means and strategies for attaining personally and socially desired outcomes. Moreover, specific regulatory competencies are required for enacting self-regulatory intentions and maintaining them over longer intervals. Personal concepts of actual, desired, and possible selves (i.e., representations of how and what one is, should be, could be, and would like to be) provide the motivational basis for such processes. . . . These representations also change, and are socially expected to change in particular ways, over the life cycle. (p. 836)

Conclusions

Brandtstädter's action theory places central emphasis on an individual's intentions in his or her regulatory actions. These actions both reflect and propel development. As such, actions constitute the means through which the active individual, fused with his or her active context, actualizes his or her potential for plasticity in ways that develop, support, and elaborate the self. At the same time, Brandtstädter (1998, 1999) explained that the intentions of the self are limited in the developmental goals that can be actualized due to both individual and contextual constraints on plasticity.

Accordingly, Brandtstädter (1998) envisioned three dimensions of scholarship that should be pursued in order to understand the dynamic relations between plasticity and constraints, a relation brought to the fore of conceptual attention by an action–theoretical perspective. That is, Brandtstädter (1998) recommended that:

> In analyzing the ontogeny of intentional self-development, three basic lines of development should be considered: (a) the development of intentional action in general, and of cognitive and representational processes related to intentionality; (b) the formation of beliefs and competencies related to personal control over development; and (c) the development of the self (or self-concept) as a more or less coherent structure of self-referential values, beliefs, and standards that guides and directs self-regulatory processes. (p. 836)

Other action theorists have pursued theoretical and empirical agendas that correspond to the scholarly vision of Brandtstädter. In particular, Jutta Heckhausen (1999) has taken on the challenge of developing a program of work that addresses directly the issue of plasticity and constraints that is of concern in action theory. It is important, then, to consider her scholarship.

Jutta Heckhausen's Life-Span Theory of Control

Heckhausen (1999) extends action models of human development in a theoretically creative and empirically impressive way. Heckhausen and her colleagues have developed a life-span theory of control (e.g., Heckhausen, Dixon, & Baltes,

Jutta Heckhausen

1989; Heckhausen & Krueger, 1993; Heckhausen & Schulz, 1995; Schulz & Heckhausen, 1996). The theory and the research associated with it describe how humans—and particularly adults, given her empirical interests—regulate their behavior in the face of (a) their enormous ontogenetic potential for plasticity and (b) the biological, sociocultural, and age-normative constraints on their flexibility, that is, on their creativity in finding the means to control their behavior in ways that are desired by them and that are optimal for healthy functioning.

Heckhausen (1999) noted that across human life, these biological and ecological constraints on humans provide a developmental scaffold, both channeling behavior and making the vast range of potential behaviors that could be generated more manageable for the individual and more likely to be associated with positive outcomes. Heckhausen (1999) indicated how this dialectic between plasticity and constraints requires, on the one hand, selection of goals and investments of resources to reach them and, on the other, the compensation for failure when resource investments do not eventuate in successful (e.g., desired) outcomes.

Here, in regard to selection and compensation for failure and losses, Heckhausen's model converges with other models of successful development, such as the selection, optimization, and compensation (SOC) model (Baltes & Baltes, 1990; Freund & Baltes, 1998). However, Heckhausen's theory is distinctive in regard to the conceptualization of the way in which the dialectic between plasticity and constraints occurs.

Heckhausen (1999) explained that the enactment of this dialectic involves two processes: primary control, behaviors aimed at influencing the ecology in order to alter the context to *fit* the needs and goals of the individual; and secondary control, internal (e.g., cognitive) processes that are used to minimize losses of and failures in control and/or to maintain or even expand existing primary control capacities. Heckhausen (1999) argued that, across life, primary control striving takes primacy in human behavior, although the potential for primary control shows an inverted U-shape across ontogeny—involving a marked increase in childhood and declines in old age. As a consequence of this age-related developmental loss, individuals need to compensate by using secondary control in later life.

Heckhausen (1999) demonstrated the applicability of her theory of control through a series of conceptual presentations about: the different types of primary and secondary control strategies that may be used across life (i.e., selective primary control, selective secondary control, compensatory primary control, and compensatory secondary control); developmental goals as basic units of action; the way in which control occurs in different developmental ecologies (e.g., those differentiated by age and those that vary as a consequence of historically unprecedented sociocultural change—for instance, involving transformations in East Germany in the 1990s—after the fall of the Berlin Wall); and social comparisons as prototypic strategies for developmental regulation.

A particularly intriguing conceptual proposal Heckhausen (1999) made relates to the concept of developmental deadlines. Developmental deadlines mark the age-graded transition from favorable to unfavorable opportunities for attaining important developmental goals. Once the deadline is passed, the goal has to be given up. In what she termed an *action-phase* model of developmental regulation, Heckhausen (1999) proposed adaptively sequenced control strategies which serve predeadline urgency and postdeadline goal-disengagement. This model of deadline-related action cycles may be applied to a broad range of important developmental pursuits across the life span (e.g., regarding the "biological clock" associated with childbearing).

In addition to these conceptual contributions, Heckhausen (1999) has conducted several studies that bring empirical evidence to bear on the salience for regulation across life of primary and secondary control, and underscores the role of both facets of control for understanding life-span adaptability, and, particularly, adaptation during portions of ontogeny (e.g., old age) wherein behavioral means may become increasingly compromised due to age-associated losses.

In sum, Heckhausen's theory of life-span control provides at least three other important contributions. First, and reflecting key ideas as well in life-span developmental theory (Baltes et al., 1998, 1999), Heckhausen's (1999) ideas extend action–theoretical conceptions by offering an innovative and empirically supported set of ideas about the gains and losses that characterize humans' attempts to regulate their behavior across life.

Second, Heckhausen's (1999) theory constitutes a rich set of ideas for further research about control across the life span and in regard to different ecological settings. For example, Heckhausen offered several ideas that pertain to portions of life other than adulthood. To illustrate, she explained why future scholarship "should systematically investigate individual's regulatory behavior in life-course settings that are rich in . . . long-term/short-term or interdomain conflicts" (Heckhausen, 1999, p. 195), and, thus, suggested the importance of her model for elucidation of the purported conflicts in (or at least the connections among) the parent–family and friend–peer group social relationships that occur during adolescence. In turn, she also suggested the importance of studying "developmental regulation in individuals who lead exceptional lives" (Heckhausen, 1999, p. 195). In fact, an illustration of the use of action theory for such an analysis was provided by Baltes and colleagues (1998) in regard to the SOC model, and has been previously presented in Table 9.2. Given the person–context relational focus of action theory, such scholarship might focus on gifted or disabled children, adolescents, or adults, on the one hand, or on individuals embedded in nonnormative contexts such as abusive homes, inner-city gangs, or war-torn villages, on the other.

Third, Heckhausen (1999) provided a compelling theoretical frame and a research base for the use of ideas about control in applied scholarship aimed at understanding the bases of successful and failed attempts to regulate behavior across life. Her presentation may motivate developmental scientists to identify the ways in which processes of primary and secondary control may be promoted across life to enable individuals to optimize their plasticity in manners that eventuate in successful development.

Conclusions

Action theory provides a means to understand the dynamic relations between individuals and their contexts that exist across the life span. From the point in ontogeny when cognitive development is sufficiently advanced to form intentions and/or to devise strategies for primary or secondary control, and then for the rest of the life span, individuals may influence their social world that is influencing them.

However, as both Brandtstädter and Heckhausen emphasize, the actualization across the life span of an individual's capacity for plasticity sufficient to enable him or her to act in ways realizing his or her intentions or exerting his or primary control is not limitless. Human action is plastic but it is also constrained. The features of, and the historical changes in, the physical and social contexts of human development represents a source of behavior across life that constrains or circumscribes human development. In addition, of course, the social system within which the person lives may promote particular directions—particular courses or trajectories—of development across life.

Indeed, this linkage between individual action and the social context is the essence of the process of developmental regulation of concern in action theory. In addition, such regulation is a core interest within developmental systems theory in general and, as well, within the instances of such theories discussed in this chapter. For instance, the paradigmatic linkage between ontogeny and historical–contextual levels was seen to be a key proposition in the life-span developmental theory of Baltes and his colleagues (e.g., see Table 9.1).

Accordingly, to understand the integrations among the levels of the developmental system that comprise the action context for human development, we must include a discussion of the social system within which people develop and of the historical/contextual focus used to specify the role of the social world within the developmental system. This social system approach to human development has been termed *life-course theory* and the scholarship of Glen H. Elder, Jr. has been central in understanding the importance of the life course in influencing the character of human development—the transitions in social situations or institutions involved in people's lives and the shaping of the trajectory of human life by its embeddedness in the institutions of society. As such, we focus on Elder's scholarship in our discussion of the life-course perspective.

GLEN H. ELDER, JR. AND LIFE-COURSE THEORY

Glen H. Elder, Jr. (e.g., 1974, 1975, 1980, 1998, 1999) has been the major contributor to theory and research framed by what may be termed the life-course theory of human development. As envisioned by Elder (1998), this theory is predicated on the following proposition:

> Human lives are socially embedded in specific historical times and places that shape their content, pattern, and direction. As experiments of nature or design, types of historical change are experienced differentially by people of different ages and roles. . . . The change itself affects the developmental trajectory of individuals by altering their life course. (p. 969)

The life-course theory of human development has emerged over the last 30 years, based on theoretical and empirical contributions derived from three general areas of scholarship. As shown in Figure 9.2, these areas are the study of:

1.   Social relations, for example, involving scholarship about the study of self (i.e., as in action theory), social roles, role transitions (i.e., from student to worker,

Glen H. Elder, Jr.

Social Relations	Life-span Concepts of Development	Age and Temporality
Self and other self-esteem, self efficacy	Psychosocial stage, adult stages of development	Anthropology of age, age grades, expectations, concepts of age status identity, proscriptive and prescriptive age norms
Social roles, status, role-playing	Multi-directionality of development	
Role transitions and sequences	Human personality the long way, as life-long process	History of childhood and the family
Socialization as role/ social learning	Selective optimization with compensation	Cohorts—Birth cohorts and social change, structural lag
Life cycle of social roles, generational succession	Life review, autobiographical memory	Age and life-course variations
Social exchange, networks, capital	Relative plasticity	Transitions and trajectories
	Life structure	
	Developmental tasks	
	Individuals as producers of own development	

FIGURE 9.2
The emergence of life-course theory (1960s to present): research traditions and their concepts.
Source: Elder (1998, p. 952).

or from married with no children to parenthood), and the linkages among generations (i.e., involving children, parents, and the parents of the parents—or the grandparents).

2.   Life-span developmental theory, for instance, as we have discussed earlier in this chapter in regard to the work of Baltes and his colleagues (e.g., in regard to their interest in the paradigmatic understanding of the integration of ontogenetic and historical contextualism) and also in Chapter 2 (e.g., involving not only the work of Baltes but also the contributions of Schaie and Nesselroade).

3.   Age and temporality, involving birth cohort, age, and the role of normative and nonnormative historical variation (e.g., see the discussion of these influences on human development, discussed earlier in this chapter, in the ideas associated with life-span developmental theory, as presented in Table 9.1).

Thus, as was the case in regard to action theory and life-span developmental theory, life-course theory shares common interests and origins with other members of the developmental systems theoretical family. Specifically, life-course theory shares with the two other instances of developmental systems theory discussed to this point in this chapter some common intellectual roots and conceptual attributes.

Elder (1998), in recounting these roots of life-course theory, explained that this perspective emerged, often in collaboration with life-span developmental theory, to meet three interrelated sets of conceptual and empirical challenges to devising an integrated and dynamic view of the entire course of human life. A first challenge was to extend the theoretical frame used to study people from a child-focused view that only emphasizes development or growth to one that is useful across the life span, and, thus, one encompassing development and aging, growth, and decline, or gain and loss. A second challenge was to employ such a frame to develop a set of concepts for depicting the changes and the organization of changes in humans' lives across their ontogenies and, as well, across different historical events and eras. The third challenge was to use these concepts about ontogeny and history to integrate human lives with the changing social contexts within which each individual and all birth cohorts live across their life spans. Thus, Elder (1998) noted that:

> The emergence of life-course theory and its elaboration over the past 30 years can be viewed in terms of prominent challenges to developmental studies that questioned traditional forms of thought and empirical work. They include: (a) the necessity for concepts of development and personality that have relevance beyond childhood and even adolescence; (b) the need for a way of thinking about the social patterning and dynamic of lives over time, as they relate in particular to developmental processes; and (c) the increasing recognition that lives and developmental trajectories may be transformed by a changing society.
>
> Social theories of relationships and age converged in the 1960s with emerging concepts of life-span development to produce a theoretical orientation to the life course. More than any other theoretical initiative, life-span developmental psychology has responded to the first challenge by advancing a conceptual orientation on human development and personality across the life span. One result is a concept of ontogenetic development in which social structures and cultures merely establish behavioral settings. By contrast, life-course theory views human development as a coactive process in which sociocultural, biological, and psychological forces interact over time. Social structures and cultures are constituent elements in the developmental process. The individual plays an important role in shaping the life course and development, though choices and initiatives are always constrained by social forces and biological limitations. (pp. 982–983)

Accordingly, Elder (1998) believes that life-course theory adds value to life-span developmental theory through providing a productive means to address the second and third challenges to devising a dynamic model of the breadth of human development. He sees life-course theory as enabling scholars to move beyond an additive or simple interactional view of the social system within which development unfolds. Rather, life-course theory synthesizes the social systems into the actual constitution of the structures and functions comprising human development. The means through which this integration is seen to occur in life-course theory is one that is also emphasized in life-span developmental theory (Baltes et al., 1998, 1999) and in action theory (Brandtstädter, 1998, 1999), that is, through the selective and intentional regulative actions of individuals, functioning as producers of their own development. Through this vision of the contribution of life-course theory, Elder (1998) believes that this perspective addresses the other two challenges involved in devising a comprehensive understanding of human development. Elder (1998) explained that:

> In concept . . . the individual life course provides a response to the second challenge, a way of thinking about life patterns or organization. Lives over time do not merely follow a sequence of situations or person–situation interactions. Instead the life course is conceived as an age-graded sequence of socially defined roles and events that are enacted and even

recast over time. It consists of multiple, interlocking trajectories, such as work and family, with their transitions or changes in states. People generally work out their life course in relation to established, institutionalized pathways and their regulatory constraints, such as the curricula or tracks of a school, the age-graded expectations of a family, and the work careers of a firm or culture.

The individual life course, developmental trajectories and transitions (as psychobiological continuities and change), and established pathways are key elements in the life-course study of child development. Any change in the life course of individuals has consequences for their developmental trajectory, and historical change may alter both by recasting established pathways. . . . By placing people in historical locations, life-course theory has oriented research to the third challenge, to understand the process by which societal changes make a difference in the primary worlds and development of children. (pp. 982–983)

Accordingly, both because of its evolution in intellectual proximity to the also evolving theory of life-span development, the two perspectives have come to rely on very similar ideas about the dynamics of individuals and contexts in the development of the structures and functions comprising the course of human life. Moreover, through this collaboration Elder also draws on action–theoretical concepts (which, or course, life-span developmental theory does as well), and emphasizes the role of the active individual in the construction of life-course changes. Indeed, as a consequence of these linkages, Elder (1998) adopts a theoretical view of developmental process that is completely consistent with both life-span developmental theory, with action theory, and with the other instance of developmental systems theory we have discussed in previous chapters. Elder (1998) stated that:

Human development in life-course theory represents a process of organism–environment transactions over time, in which the organism plays an active role in shaping its own development. The developing individual is viewed as a dynamic whole, not as separate strands, facets or domains, such as emotion, cognition, and motivation. (p. 951–952)

Thus, as did Baltes and colleagues (1998), Elder saw human development as an interpersonally relational—a dynamically collaborative (Fischer & Bidell, 1998; Rogoff, 1998), social—process. Hence, as is the case with all instances of developmental systems theory we have discussed, there are important commonalities among members of this theoretical family. In addition, we have seen that each member of the family has specific theoretical features associated with it. In fact, the distinctive features of life-course theory are associated with the link that Elder (1998) draws between individual development and the social relationships within which the person's ontogeny is dynamically collaborative.

Constructing the Life Course

We have noted that Elder (1998) specified that the substantive roots of life-course theory lie in the integration of scholarship pertinent to life-span developmental theory, social relations, and age and temporality. As such, in meeting the challenge of developing a model that enables individual lives to be interrelated with their changing social settings, theorists elaborating a life-course perspective would be expected to draw on ideas from these three domains of scholarly influence. Elder (1998) explained that in fact such conceptual integration exists. Elder (1998) noted that there are four central principles in life course theory. These are

(1) the interplay of human lives and development with changing times and places; (2) timing of lives; (3) interdependence of human lives, including the relation between social and developmental trajectories; and (4) human agency in choice-making and actions. (p. 961).

In explaining these principles, Elder (1998) indicated that:

The first principle of historical time and place asserts that (1) the life course of individuals is embedded in and shaped by the historical times and places they experience over their life time. This principle also reflects the premise that developmental trajectories are changed by changing the life course. The extent to which this occurs depends in part on the nature of the change. The second principle of timing expresses the fundamental bond between age and time; that (2) the developmental impact of a life transition or event is contingent on when it occurs in a person's life. Social age, for example, refers to the age at which people enter and leave particular roles. Timing may also be expressed in terms of biological events and transitions, such as puberty, whether relatively early or late.

The third principle . . . states that (3) lives are lived interdependently and that social and historical influences are expressed through this network of shared relationships. Social roles expose individuals to the stresses and strains of others, as well as to the possibility of social support. The fourth principle on human agency reflects an enduring premise of biographical studies on the constructionist role of individuals in shaping their life course. . . . It states that (4) individuals construct their own life course through the choices and actions they take within the constraints and opportunities of history and social circumstances. The principle expresses the dynamic relation between people and social roles in life course theory. Social roles and situations are selected and shaped by people, but they also constrain behavior, as do internal forces. (pp. 961–962)

Accordingly, in Elder's (1998) view, the life course is constructed through the sorts of dynamic actions—the person–context regulations—that we have discussed as being of central interest within action–theoretical accounts of human development (Brandtstädter, 1998, 1998; Heckhausen, 1999). What Elder's (1998) view of the life course adds to this focus is the idea that the life course is constructed through the *simultaneous* contribution of (a) these actions, (b) made by individuals dynamically interacting with other individuals, while (c) embedded in a context changing along three temporal dimensions: "life" or "ontogenetic" time (one's age from birth to death), "family" time (one's location within the flow of prior and succeeding generations), and "historical" time (the social and cultural system that exists in the world when one is born and the changing circumstances regarding this system that occur during one's life). That is, Elder (1998) pointed out that:

The life course is age-graded through institutions and social structures, and it is embedded in relationships that constrain and support behavior. In addition, people are located in historical settings through birth cohorts and they are also linked across the generations by kinship and friendship. . . . Both the individual life course and a person's developmental trajectory are interconnected with the lives and development of others. (pp. 951–952)

The postulation of a dynamic integration between an individual's regulatory actions and a social system constituted by the people, social institutions, and historical events that vary across these three temporal dimensions provides, for Elder (1998), a means to represent the life course of an individual. As such, Elder's (1998) vision results in a theoretical system of singular creativity and enormous value to developmental systems theories of human development. His theory merges within a given person the micro (ontogenetic biological, behavioral, and psychological) and macro (social system) level of organization that are held to be fused within developmental systems theory. In explanation of this model, Elder (1998) indicated that:

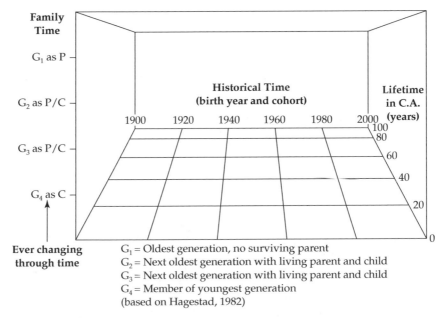

FIGURE 9.3
Life-course trajectories in three-dimensional space: life, family, and historical time.
Source: Elder (1998, p. 949).

A skeletal life course for a person can be mapped in the three-dimensional space of life, family, and historical time (Figure 9.3). Historical time of birth, coupled with passage through the age structure, define particular life trajectories on the grid of history and age. Persons born in 1920, 1940, and 1960 follow the age gradient, though divergent paths may arise from the variable relation between age and events/roles. Historical events, such as war and economic recession, may alter the correlation between life events and age, or change their temporal arrangements—for example, full-time employment may come after first marriage in the lives of World War II servicemen. Another source of variation is the unstable path of family time. Figure 9.3 lists four generations on the family timetable, but the number and pattern of the generations can vary sharply across a single life span. (p. 949)

One's birth year is the point of entry into the social system. As one enters this system, the life course is constructed by one's location along the three temporal dimensions displayed in Figure 9.3. That is, Elder (1998) noted that:

> Birth year indicates historical time, and chronological age acquires the meanings of social timing and life stage. Birth cohorts provide a link between historical change and the life course. . . . Birth year or date of entry into a system (such as school graduation or marriage) locates the individual according to historical time and related social changes; with age peers in the cohort, this person is exposed to a particular segment of historical experience as he or she moves across the sequence of age-graded roles. (p. 948)

In short, then, the model presented in Figure 9.3 constitutes a means to integrate an individual's life into the social system from the moment of his or her birth. Birth provides for his or her immediate membership into (a) a familial flow of generations, and (b) a society that exists at a given point in history with its extant but evolving set of institutions, roles, and socially defined life pathways. Accordingly, Elder (1998) explained that:

> The individual life course and its relation to developmental trajectories represent a common meeting ground for life-course theory and developmental science, with its "perspective on individual functioning that emphasizes the dynamic interplay among processes that operate across time frames, levels of analysis, and contexts". . . . Building on advances since the 1960s, life-course theory has uniquely forged a conceptual bridge between developmental processes, the life course, and ongoing changes in society, one based on the premise that age places people in the social structure and in particular birth cohorts. (p. 953)

Conclusions

Life-course theory adds a significant and unique dimension to the set of concepts associated with developmental systems theories. Building on the ideas associated with other members of this theoretical family—and, most prominently, life-span developmental theory and, to a somewhat lesser but nevertheless significant extent, action theory—Elder's (1998) view of the life course provides a dynamic means to integratively bring the social system into the ontogeny of individuals.

There is always the danger that, when scholars whose training or interests are in a discipline (such as sociology, anthropology, or history) more macro than those disciplines having focal units of analysis involving individuals (e.g., psychology) or even units more molecular than individuals (e.g., genes, as may be the case in some branches of biology), the course of an individual life may be interpreted in "sociogenic" terms, that is, by exclusive reference to the institutions of society, the rules of culture, or the events of history. Just as we would wish to avoid the alternative conceptual "danger," of a psychogenic or a biogenic interpretation of the life span of a person, such a sociogenic view of human development would not be theoretically desirable (in regard, at least, to the perspective of human development advanced by developmental systems theory) or empirically supportable. At best, an incomplete view of the course of life would be provided by a sociogenic appeal to macro institutional influences, in the same way that an incomplete picture of human life would be derived from a psychogenic appeal to, for instance, cognitive functioning in and of itself, or from a biogenic reliance on genes. Just as Overton (1998) has cautioned scholars of human development to "avoid all splits," we can offer a similar warning: Avoid all interpretations of human development that are based on the hegemony of one disciple over all others.

The enormous significance of Elder's formulation of life-course theory, then, is that he is able to weave the importance of macro, social system influences into the development of individuals in a manner that is neither disciplinarily "isolationist" (or hegemonist) nor simply additive. Elder's scholarship is an exemplar of the relationism, the multilevel fusions, that define a developmental systems perspective. He brings the social system to human development, *not* as a context for development but—in the essence of what is sought for in developmental systems theory—as part of the very constitutive fabric of human ontogeny.

Elder provides a standard against which other theorists interested in a nonreductionist, synthetic view of development may measure the quality of their contributions. There is at least one scholar whom I am certain that Elder and I would agree meets this standard. Urie Bronfenbrenner has, for a half century, provided a vision for—and a rich theoretical and empirical literature supportive of—the seamless integration of all levels of organization within the ecology of human development. Accordingly, we now turn to his contributions.

URIE BRONFENBRENNER'S BIOECOLOGICAL THEORY OF DEVELOPMENTAL PROCESSES

In Chapter 2, we reviewed the important contributions Urie Bronfenbrenner made through the 1970s and early 1980s in regard to an understanding of the importance of the context of human development. In his 1979 book, *The Ecology of Human Development*. Bronfenbrenner explained the importance for human ontogeny of the interrelated ecological levels, conceived of as nested systems, involved in human development.

As explained in Chapter 2, Bronfenbrenner described the *microsystem* as the setting within

Urie Bronfenbrenner

which the individual was behaving at a given moment in his or her life and the *mesosystem* as the set of *microsystems* constituting the individual's developmental niche within a given period of development. In addition, the *exosystem* was composed on contexts that, although not directly involving the developing person (e.g., the workplace of a child's parent), nevertheless had an influence on the person's behavior and development (e.g., as may occur when the parent has had a stressful day at work and, as a result, has a reduced capacity to provide quality caregiving to the child). Finally, the *macrosystem* is the superordinate level of the ecology of human development; it is the level involving culture, macro-institutions (such as the federal government), and public policy. The *macrosystem* influences the nature of interaction within all other levels of the ecology of human development.

Bronfenbrenner's (1979) formulation had a broad impact on the field of human development, promoting considerable interest through the 1980s in the role of the ecological system in texturing the life course of individuals. Yet, by the end of the that decade and into the 1990s, Bronfenbrenner indicated that he was not pleased by the nature of his contribution to either theory, research, or policy applications pertinent to enhancing the ecology of a child's life to promote his or her positive development. For instance, in 1989 Bronfenbrenner observed that:

> Existing developmental studies subscribing to an ecological model have provided far more knowledge about the nature of developmentally relevant environments, near and far, than about the characteristics of developing individuals, then and now. . . . The criticism I just made also applies to my own writings. . . . Nowhere in the 1979 monograph, nor elsewhere until today, does one find a parallel set of structures for conceptualizing the characteristics of the developing person. (p. 188)

Bronfenbrenner believes, as do other theorists drawn to developmental systems notions of human development, that *all* the levels of organization involved in human life are linked integratively in the constitution of the course of individual ontogeny. Although his 1979 book made an enormous contribution to such a conception of human development, through giving scholars conceptual tools to understand and study the differentiated but integrated levels of the context of human development, Bronfenbrenner recognized that this theory would be incomplete until he included in it the levels of individual structure and function (biology, psychology, and behavior) fused dynamically with the ecological systems he described. Accordingly,

Bronfenbrenner and his colleagues (e.g., Bronfenbrenner, in press; Bronfenbrenner & Ceci, 1993, 1994a, 1994b; Bronfenbrenner & Morris, 1998) have, for more than a decade, worked to integrate the other levels of the developmental system, starting from biology, psychology, and behavior, into the model of human development he was formulating. The span of the levels he seeks to synthesis in his model—biology through the broadest level of the ecology of human development—accounts for the label, *bioecological,* that he attaches to the model. In short, Bronfenbrenner (in press; Bronfenbrenner & Morris, 1998) has sought, at this writing for more than 10 years now to bring the features of the developing person into the ecological system he has elaborated.

Thus, as Bronfenbrenner describes it, the defining properties of the model that has emerged from this scholarship involves four interrelated components:

1. The developmental *process,* involving the fused and dynamic relation of the individual and the context.

2. The *person,* with his or her individual repertoire of biological, cognitive, emotional, and behavioral characteristics.

3. The *context* of human development, conceptualized as the nested levels, or systems, of the ecology of human development he has depicted (Bronfenbrenner, 1977, 1979).

4. *Time,* conceptualized as involving the multiple dimensions of temporality that we have noted that Elder (1998) explained are part of life-course theory.

Together, these four components of Bronfenbrenner's formulation of bioecological theory constitute a process-person-context-time (or PPCT) model for conceptualizing the integrated developmental system and for designing research to study the course of human development. That is, Bronfenbrenner believes that just as each of the four components of the PPCT model should be included in any adequate conceptual specification of the dynamic, human development system, so, too, must research appraise all four components of the model to provide data that are adequate for understanding the course of human development.

Indeed, neither research nor theory could exclude the developmental process, the person and the context integrated by this process, or the changes over time that occur as a consequence of this process and still hope to have a full depiction of the dynamics of development within the developmental system. Accordingly, in describing the PPCT model, Bronfenbrenner and Morris (1998) noted that Bronfenbrenner must explain the

> four principal components and the dynamic, interactive relationships among them . . . the first of these, which constitutes the core of the model, is Process. More specifically, this construct encompasses particular forms of interaction between organism and environment, called proximal processes, that operate over time and are posited as the primary mechanisms producing human development. However, the power of such processes to influence development is presumed, and shown, to vary substantially as a function of the characteristics of the developing Person, of the immediate and more remote environmental Contexts, and the Time periods, in which the proximal processes take place. (p. 994)

In regard to the three remaining defining properties of the model—person, context, and time—Bronfenbrenner and Morris (1998, p. 994) noted that they give priority in their scholarship to defining the biopsychosocial characteristics of the "person," since, as noted by Bronfenbrenner in 1989, his earlier formulations of the model (e.g., Bronfenbrenner, 1979) left a gap in regard to this key feature of the theory. As a consequence, Bronfenbrenner and Morris (1998) noted in regard to these person characteristics, that:

> Three types of Person characteristics are distinguished as most influential in shaping the course of future development through their capacity to affect the direction and power of proximal processes through the life course. The first are dispositions that can set proximal processes in motion in a particular developmental domain and continue to sustain their operation. Next are bioecological resources of ability, experience, knowledge, and skill required for the effective functioning of proximal processes at a given stage of development. Finally, there are demand characteristics that invite or discourage reactions from the social environment of a kind that can foster or disrupt the operation of proximal processes. The differentiation of these three forms leads to their combination in patterns of Person structure that can further account for differences in the direction and power of resultant proximal processes and their developmental effects. (p. 995)

Consistent with the integrative character of development systems theory, Bronfenbrenner and his colleagues point out that, when the characteristics of the person component of the bioecological model is expanded in this way, the result is a richer understanding of the context—the ecological system—with which the developing person is fused. Thus, as explained by Bronfenbrenner and Morris (1998):

These new formulations of qualities of the person that shape his or her future development have had the unanticipated effect of further differentiating, expanding, and integrating the original 1979 conceptualization of the environment in terms of nested systems ranging from micro to macro. . . . For example, the three types of Person characteristics outlined above are also incorporated into the definition of the microsystem as characteristics of parents, relatives, close friends, teachers, mentors, coworkers, spouses, or others who participate in the life of the developing person on a fairly regular basis over extended periods of time. (p. 995)

Indeed, Bronfenbrenner redefines the character of the microsystem to link it centrally to what he regards as the "center of gravity" (Bronfenbrenner & Morris, 1998, p. 1013)—the biopsychosocial person—within his theory as it has now been elaborated. That is, although, as in 1979, he sees the ecology of human development as "the ecological environment . . . conceived as a set of nested structures, each inside the other like a set of Russian dolls" (p. 3), he magnifies his conception of the innermost, microsystem structure within this ecology by incorporating the activities, relationships, and roles of the developing person into this system. That is, Bronfenbrenner (1994) noted that:

> A microsystem is a pattern of activities, social roles, and interpersonal relations experienced by the developing person in a given face-to-face setting with particular physical, social, and symbolic features that invite, permit, or inhibit, engagement in sustained, progressively more complex interaction with, and activity in, the immediate environment. (p. 1645)

What may be particularly significant to Bronfenbrenner in this expanded definition of the microsystem is he includes not only the person's interactions with other people in this level of the ecology but also the interactions the person has with the world of symbols and language (with the semiotic system)—a component of ecological relationships that action theorists also believe is especially important in understanding the formulation of intentions, goals, and actions (cf. Brandtstädter, 1998, 1999). Bronfenbrenner and Morris (1998) noted that:

> The bioecological model also introduces an even more consequential domain into the structure of the microsystem that emphasizes the distinctive contribution to development of proximal processes involving interaction not with people but with objects and symbols. Even more broadly, concepts and criteria are introduced that differentiate between those features of the environment that foster versus interfere with the development of proximal processes. Particularly

significant in the latter sphere is the growing hecticness, instability, and chaos in the principal settings in which human competence and character are shaped—in the family, child-care arrangements, schools, peer groups, and neighborhoods. (p. 995)

Finally, Bronfenbrenner noted that the emphasis on a redefined and expanded concept of the microsystem leads to the last defining property of the current formulation of his theory of human development. Bronfenbrenner and Morris (1998) indicated that

> the fourth and final defining property of the bioecological model and the one that moves it farthest beyond its predecessor [is] the dimension of Time. The 1979 Volume scarcely mentions the term, whereas in the current formulation, it has a prominent place at three successive levels—micro-, meso-, and macro-. Microtime refers to continuity versus discontinuity within ongoing episodes of proximal process. Mesotime is the periodicity of theses episodes across broader time intervals, such as days and weeks. Finally, Macrotime focuses on the changing expectations and events in the larger society, both within and across generations, as they affect and are affected by, processes and outcomes of human development over the life course. (p. 995)

As we have noted, Bronfenbrenner and Morris (1998) indicated that the inclusion of a temporal dimension in the current model draws on the work of Elder (1998), discussed previously, in regard to the multiple dimensions of time that are involved in linking the ecology of human development (or the social system, in the terms of Elder, 1998) to individual development. Thus, as is the case in regard to the other instances of developmental systems theory that we have reviewed in this chapter, Bronfenbrenner's theory integrates ideas unique to his model with those associated with other members of the developmental systems theoretical family.

Conclusions

Bronfenbrenner's bioecological model is, in at least two senses, a living system (Ford & Lerner, 1992). First, the theory itself depicts the dynamic, developmental relations between an active individual and his or her complex, integrated, and changing ecology. In addition, the theory is itself developing (e.g., see Bronfenbrenner, in press), as Bronfenbrenner seeks to make the features of the theory more precise and, as such, a more operational guide for PPCT-relevant research about the dynamic character of the human development process.

At this writing, the bioecological model has developed to include two propositions. Both of these sets of ideas promote a dynamic, person–context relational view of the process of human development. As explained by Bronfenbrenner and Morris (1998), Proposition 1 of the bioecological model states that:

> Especially in its early phases, but also throughout the life course, human development takes place through processes of progressively more complex reciprocal interaction between an active, evolving biopsychosocial human organism and the persons, objects, and symbols in its immediate external environment. To be effective, the interaction must occur on a fairly regular basis over extended periods of time. Such enduring forms of interaction in the immediate environment are referred to as proximal processes. Examples of enduring patterns of proximal process are found in feeding or comforting a baby, playing with a young child, child–child activities, group or solitary play, reading, learning new skills, athletic activities, problem solving, caring for others in distress, making plans, performing complex tasks, and acquiring new knowledge, and know-how. (p. 996)

Thus, in the first proposition in his theory, Bronfenbrenner emphasizes a theme found in the other instances of developmental systems theory we have discussed in this chapter—the role of the active individual as an agent in his or her own development. In fact, the idea of the contribution of the individual to the developmental process is also present in the second proposition of bioecological theory. That is, the second proposition of the model (Bronfenbrenner & Morris, 1998) specifies that:

> The form, power, content, and direction of the proximal processes effecting development vary systematically as a joint function of the characteristics of the developing person; of the environment—both immediate and more remote—in which the processes are taking place; the nature of the developmental outcomes under consideration; and the social continuities and changes occurring over time through the life course and the historical period during which the person has lived. (p. 996)

As is evident from the two propositions, Bronfenbrenner regards proximal processes as the primary sources of development, an assertion that is compatible with the several versions of action theory discussed in this chapter (Baltes & Baltes, 1990; Brandtstädter, 1998, 1999; Heckhausen, 1999). That is, in all of the proximal processes described by Bronfenbrenner in the first proposition of the bioecological model, goal-selections, intentions, developing means to engage goals, the primacy of primary control, and the importance of compensatory behaviors and/or of secondary control may be involved. In turn, the propositions also point to the fusions across the developmental system described by Bronfenbrenner as providing the dynamism that enables the proximal processes to drive the developmental system.

Finally, as we have noted, the role of the individual, as an active agent in his or her own development, is central in the bioecological model. Bronfenbrenner and Morris (1998) asked their readers to:

> Note that characteristics of the person actually appear twice in the bioecological model—first as one of the four elements influencing the "form, power, content, and direction of the proximal process," and then again as "developmental outcomes"; that is, qualities of the developing person that emerge at a later point in time as the result of the joint, interactive, mutually reinforcing effects of the four principal antecedent components of the model. In sum, in the bioecological model, the characteristics of the person function both as an indirect producer and as a product of development. (p. 996)

In sum, then, as has been the case in all of the instances of developmental systems theory we have discussed in this chapter, and as emphasized almost a half century ago by Schneirla (1957), the active, developing individual is seen by Bronfenbrenner as a central force of his or her own development. This contribution to the process of development is made by a synthesis, an integration, between the active person and his or her active context.

CONCLUSIONS: FROM DEVELOPMENTAL SYSTEMS TO NATIVISM

In the view of the theories discussed in this chapter, as well as of the other instances of developmental systems theory reviewed in Chapters 4 through 8, individuals are part of a fused, multilevel, dynamic system. The key to understanding development from the perspective of these theories is in the notion of integrative levels, for example, as in Level 1 of life-span developmental theory (Baltes et al., 1998) and, in turn, as formulated by Schneirla (1957), and earlier by Novikoff (1945a, 1945b). Simply, then, and as noted in several places in our discussion, a key idea involved in these models of the dynamics of the developmental system is to "avoid all splits" (Overton, 1998).

However, as we have also seen throughout the previous chapters, this integrative view of the nature and nurture of human development has not been, and at this writing is still not, the only theoretical formulation used to understand the contributions that different levels of organization make to human development. Rather, split conceptions continue to exist in the study of human development and, although we have noted in previous chapters that there have been and are some exclusively nurture versions of split conceptions (e.g., Bijou, 1976; Bijou & Baer, 1961; Gewirtz & Stingle, 1968; Hayes, 1993; Morris, 1993; White, 1970), the split conceptions most frequently employed at this writing emphasize the primary role of nature variables in human development.

Just as a range of developmental systems theories exist, so, too, is there a range of such "split," nativist theories that have been and continue to be used in the study of human life. As we discuss in Chapters 10 through 14, these theories range from ones embracing an extreme, hereditarian view of the basis of human behavior and development (e.g., Plomin, 2000; Rowe, 1994; Rushton, 1999) to, in turn, conceptions that reject such thoroughly reductionistic, genetic determination but, nevertheless, cast themselves as neonativist; they do so as a consequence of their belief in the presence of intrinsic structures that organize human psychological and behavioral development (e.g., Spelke & Newport, 1998).

As we discuss these nativist theories we shall see that, in all cases, they possess significant, indeed fatal, conceptual flaws. In addition, in all cases, ideas associated with developmental systems theory provide us with information useful in critiquing nativist theory. Accordingly, our exploration of nativist ideas across the next five chapters inevitably brings us back to understanding the importance of a dynamic, developmental systems view of human development.

10 | *Nature Approaches to Human Development: Behavioral Genetics*

Many experimental biologists outside of the bio-medical–industrial complex are just now coming (back) to grips with the facts of epigenesis; with the profound mystery that developmental biology is, with the poverty of gene programs as an explanatory device; and with a crisis defined by the realization that an increasingly deficient theory of developmental genetics is the only *theory currently available. The question remains: if biologists are starting to learn this lesson, will the psychologists be far behind?*

—Richard C. Strohman (1993, p. 101)

Genes are part of the developmental system in the same sense as other components (cell, tissue, organism), so genes must be susceptible to influence from other levels during the process of individual development.

—Gilbert Gottlieb (1992, p. 167)

In Chapters 6 through 9, we discussed theories of human development that are predicated on dynamic, relational, and systems perspectives. The complexity involved in the depictions of development found in these theories can be daunting to scholars, both in regard to the conceptual difficulties involved in integratively understanding the multiple levels of organization fused within the developmental system and in respect to the methodological challenges involved in using such theories as a frame for research. If challenging to scholars, such theories are often seen as virtually impossible to grasp by nonspecialists (the "person in the street," to Horowitz, 2000, p. 8) and/or by media representatives. Both groups may gravitate toward "single-variable stories" (Horowitz, 2000, p. 3) about human development—such as "genes cause behavior" (e.g., see Rushton, 1999)—in order to understand or communicate about people's lives, respectively.

Such a simplistic—a distortingly simplistic—alternative to developmental systems theories of human development is embodied in the field of behavior genetics. As explained by Horowitz (2000):

> Against the media popularity of single-variable stories, the science itself is moving inexorably toward greater and greater data-driven, integrative theoretical complexity. An exception to this is behavioral genetics. In contrast to the dynamic nonlinear interactive models full of reciprocity between and among levels and variables, behavioral genetics presents a relatively non-dynamic linear additive model that tries to assign percentages of variance in behavior and development that can be attributed to genes. The enterprise rests on the assumption that genetic influence can be expressed as a value accounting for a portion of the variance in a nondynamic linear equation for predicting behavioral functioning and furthermore, that the individual experiences of shared and nonshared environments can be assessed inferentially by the degree of biological relatedness of individuals without empirical observations of experience (Hoffman, 1991; Horowitz 1993).
>
> Behavioral genetics involves a relatively simplistic approach when compared with the kinds of dynamic systems theories currently being elaborated. Perhaps that is why, in the mode of wanting simple answers to simple questions, behavior genetic reports are so media attracting. (p. 3)

What then is the field of behavior genetics? What is the view of human development it presents? How does it seek to support this view? Does it represent a viable, "nature" alternative to dynamic and integrative developmental systems conceptions of human development in general or of particular facets of human development (e.g., intelligence) more specifically? This chapter and the next one address these questions. To begin this discussion, we turn to a definition of this field.

THE DEFINITION OF THE FIELD OF BEHAVIOR GENETICS

According to Robert Plomin (2000, p. 30), a prolific contributor to the behavior genetics literature, "Behavioural genetics is the genetic study of behaviour, which includes quantitative genetics (twin and adoption studies) as well as molecular genetics (DNA studies) of human and animal behaviour broadly defined to include responses of the organism from responses measured in the brain such as functional neuroimaging to self-report questionnaires." Plomin, DeFries, and McClearn (1980) indicated that "Behavioral genetics lies at the interface between genetics and the behavioral sciences" (p. 12), and Plomin (1986) noted that "Behavioral geneticists explore the etiology of individuality, differences among individuals in a population" (p. 5). Plomin (1986) explained that "The three basic methods used in human behavioral genetics are family, twin, and adoption studies" (p. 11).

Across all of these methods, the goal of behavior genetic analysis is to separate (partition) the variation in a distribution of scores (e.g., for a personality trait, temperamental characteristic, or intelligence) into the proportion due to genes and the proportion due to the environment. Although behavior geneticists admit that genes and environments may be correlated and/or may interact, they most typically seek to compute a score (termed a *heritability coefficient*) that (in its most frequently used form) denotes the independent contribution of genetic variance to the overall differences in the distribution of scores for a given individual characteristic.

For such heritability scores to be meaningful, the methodologies of behavior genetics rest on a model of gene function that considers the possibility that genetic contributions are independent of (not correlated or interactive with) the context within which genes exist. However, genes do not work in the way that behavior geneticists imagine.

Fatal Flaws in the Behavior Genetics Model of Gene Function

As illustrated in the epigraph by Strohman (1993), as well as in the writings of other molecular geneticists (e.g., Ho, 1984; Müller-Hill, 1988), and cell biologists (McEwen, 1997, 1998, 1999; Meaney et al., 1988), more generally, molecular biologists do not place credence in the model of genetic function involved in behavioral genetics. In fact, Venter and his colleagues (2001), the group that successfully mapped the sequence of the human genome, emphasize that there are two conceptual errors that should not be made in the face of the advances they and other scientists are making in understanding the structure and functional consequences of the human genome. They stress that "There are two fallacies to be avoided: determinism, the idea that all characteristics of the person are 'hard-wired' by the genome; and reductionism, the view that with complete knowledge of the human genome sequence, it is only a matter of time before our understanding of gene functions and interactions will provide a complete causal description of human variability" (Venter et al., 2001, p. 1348).

Contemporary thought in molecular genetics thus rejects the idea that genes are structures that act *on* supragenetic levels; instead, these scientists adopt the dynamic, developmental systems view noted in the epigraph by Gottlieb (1992) and discussed in Chapter 7 (e.g., Ford & Lerner, 1992; Lerner, 1998b; Lewis, 1997; Magnusson, 1995, 1991, 2000; Magnusson & Stattin, 1998; Smith & Thelen, 1993; Thelen & Smith, 1994, 1998). This view emphasizes the integration—or fusion—of genes *with* the other levels of organization that comprise the person and his or her context. In such dynamic systems, the specific features of the interactions of the processes associated with these

Robert Plomin

multiple levels create both the individuality of behavior at any point in time *and* the integrated character of human functioning that gives behavior its generality and cross-time predictability (Lerner, 1978; Smith & Thelen, 1993; Thelen & Smith, 1998).

In essence, we have in the field of behavior genetics (e.g., Plomin, 1986, 2000; Rowe, 1994) the use of a model of genetic structure and function that is specifically rejected by those scientists who study the structure and action of genes directly (e.g., Venter et al., 2001). This rejection occurs because the field of behavioral genetics not only employs a counterfactual and scientifically atavistic conception of the role of genes in human development (Ho, 1984; Strohman, 1993), but also because behavior genetics is a viewpoint with a conceptually flawed and empirically deficient view of the developmental process and, as well, involves the conflation of description and explanation.

For instance, in regard to process, the structural account of genetic action offered by behavior genetics suffers from the flaws of all structural accounts of development; that is, as explained by Thelen and Smith (1994, 1998; Smith & Thelen, 1993), such conceptions are inherently incomplete. These views do not explain individual behavioral performance (actions), other than to express empirically unsubstantiated confidence that in some way genetic structures translate—through the levels of cells, tissues, organs, the individual, and his or her actual context—into real-time actions.

For example, without any specification of the pathways of influence from genes to behaviors, Rowe (1994) asserted that:

> Genes can produce dispositions, tendencies, and inclinations, because people with subtly different nervous systems are differently motivated . . . [and] given enough environmental opportunities [for selection of environments], the ones chosen are those most reinforcing for a particular nervous system created by a particular genotype . . . the direction of the growth curve of development, and the limit ultimately attained, is set in the genes. (p 91)

However, because behavior geneticists believe that genetic structure transcends and is independent of real-time actions, an adequate, empirically verifiable account of actual individual-in-context behavior is beyond theoretical range (Smith & Thelen, 1993). Moreover, because of the inability to explain individual performance, of actual individual-in-context behavior, behavior genetics, like other structural theories (Smith & Thelen, 1993), cannot explain the global order of behavior or developmental change itself.

In turn, in regard to the conflation of description and explanation, behavior genetics describes variability in trait *distributions* in a specific sample, and then explains the distribution it has observed by reference to a label it has applied to one (or the other) of the "sources" of the variability—genes or environment. Not only is this reification an instance of the nominal fallacy, but also—to paraphrase the parody of structural explanations presented by Smith and Thelen (1993, p. 159)—the cause of the distribution of interindividual differences in a trait distribution is merely an abstract description of the trait distribution itself: Behavior genetics describes the variability in a distribution, labels it with a fancy "source" term (i.e., heritability), and then imputes that there is a gene, or set of genes, that explains the distribution.

To illustrate, Rowe (1994) noted that "understanding the growth and development of a single individual has been confused with understanding the origin of different traits in a population" (p. 3). However, this confusion about the distinction between interindividual differences and intraindividual change (see Chapter 5), as well as the problem of the conflation of description and explanation, exists in behavior genetics. On the basis of heritability data, writers such as Rowe (1994) seamlessly slide from talking about descriptive "sources" of variation within a trait distribution into talking about the genetic basis of individual development [i.e., about the "causal influence on such child outcomes as intelligence, personality, and psychopathology" (p. 1)].

It will be important to return again to the problems raised in behavior genetics by the conflation of description and explanation. Here, however, it is necessary to note that one key basis of the lack of an adequate treatment in behavior genetics of performance, developmental sequence and process, as well as the distinction between description and explanation, is that these conceptual problems are coupled in behavior genetics with a lack of an adequate theoretical understanding both of supragenetic intraorganism processes (Gottlieb, 1991, 1992, 1997; Gottlieb et al., 1998) and of extraorganism contextual or ecological processes (Bronfenbrenner & Ceci, 1994; Horowitz, 2000; Lewis, 1997; Magnusson, 1999, 2000; Sameroff, 1983; Thelen & Smith, 1998). Accordingly, in behavior genetics, there is a failure to adequately measure the "environment" or ecology (Hoffman, 1991) of human development. In short, to paraphrase Goldberger (1980), in his discussion of Hearnshaw's (1979) account of the scientific fraud perpetrated by behavior geneticist, Cyril Burt, in regard to the study of the heritability of intelligence (see Chapter 11 for a discussion of this sorry episode in the history of social and behavioral science), behavior geneticists have methods that give them a lot of numbers but very little sensible or useful data about human development.

THE EMPEROR'S NEW CLOTHES

That these egregious conceptual and methodological problems exist is not news, not even in psychology. Hirsch (e.g., 1970, 1976a, 1976b, 1990a, 1990b, 1997) has written repeatedly about these problems for about a quarter of a century, and Schneirla (1956, 1957), Kuo (1967, 1970, 1976), Lehrman (1953, 1970), Tobach (1981; Tobach & Greenberg, 1984; Tobach & Schneirla, 1968), Gottlieb (1970, 1983, 1992), Bronfenbrenner (1979, 1989; Bronfenbrenner & Ceci, 1994), and others such as Collins, Maccoby, Steinberg, Hetherington, and Bornstein (2000); Ford and Lerner (1992); Horowitz (2000); Lerner (1978, 1984, 1986, 1991); Lewis (1997); Magnusson (1999a, 1999b; Magnusson & Stattin, 1998), Overton (1998), and Thelen and Smith (1994, 1998; Smith & Thelen, 1993) have contributed consonant commentaries both

Lawrence Steinberg

prior to and during the period of Hirsch's still ongoing work.

Yet, despite this criticism by their colleagues in the field of psychology, as well as by the lack of credence given to behavior genetics by molecular geneticists—as well as by eminent population geneticists (e.g., Feldman & Lewontin, 1975) and evolutionary biologists (e.g., Gould, 1981)—many psychologists continue to act *as if* behavioral genetics provides evidence for the inheritance of behaviors as varied as intelligence (Jensen, 1969, 1998), parenting (Scarr, 1992), morality (Wilson, 1975), temperament (Buss & Plomin, 1984), television watching (Plomin, Corley, DeFries, & Faulker, 1990), and even the role in human development of the "environment" (Harris, 1998; Plomin, 1986, 2000; Plomin & Daniels, 1987; Rowe, 1994)! It should be noted that "environment" is the too general, and now outmoded, term used by behavior geneticists to refer to the context, or the ecology, of the dynamic system of person–context relations that characterizes human development (e.g., Bronfenbrenner, 1979; Bronfenbrenner & Ceci, 1994; Bronfenbrenner & Morris, 1998; Thelen & Smith, 1998).

The breadth and depth of these continuing criticisms of behavior genetics have been somewhat invisible or, at least, ignored by Plomin (2000, p. 30), who claimed that "The controversy that

Andrew Collins

Marc Bornstein

To illustrate, in a critique of the explanatory model and method associated with behavior genetic analyses of parent behaviors and the effects of parenting on child and adolescent development, Collins and colleagues (2000) noted that:

> Large-scale societal factors, such as ethnicity or poverty, can influence group means in parenting behavior—and in the effects of parenting behaviors—in ways that are not revealed by studies of within group variability. In addition, highly heritable traits also can be highly malleable. Like traditional correlational research on parenting, therefore, commonly used behavior–genetic methods have provided an incomplete analysis of differences among individuals. (p. 220)

Accordingly, Collins and colleagues (2000) concluded:

> Whereas researchers using behavior–genetic paradigms imply determinism by heredity and correspondingly little parental influence (e.g., Rowe, 1994), contemporary evidence confirms that the expression of heritable traits depends, often strongly, on experience, including specific parental behaviors, as well as predispositions and age-related factors in the child. (p. 228)

swirled around behavioural genetics research during the 1970s has largely faded. During the 1980s and especially during the 1990s, the behavioural sciences became much more accepting of genetic influence."

This view is wrong in at least two ways. First, the controversy regarding the legitimacy of behavioral genetics—both as a conceptual frame for understanding the role of genes in behavioral development and as a methodology for studying the role of genes in behavioral development—has not diminished at all. One need only note the controversy associated with the publication of *The Bell Curve* (Herrnstein & Murray, 1994) (see Chapter 11 for a discussion of some of this controversy) or the criticisms leveled at the hereditarian views of J. Philippe Rushton (1996, 1997, 1999), which rely heavily on information derived from behavior genetics, to recognize that Plomin's (2000) "declaration of victory" is an inadequate attempt to either ignore or deny the persisting flaws of behavior genetics theory and method identified by scientists from numerous disciplines (e.g., see the critiques published throughout the 1990s and into the twenty-first century by Collins et al., 2000; Gottlieb, 1997; Hirsch, 1997; Horowitz, 2000; Lerner & von Eye, 1992; Lewontin, 2000; Peters, 1995; Strohman, 1993; Winston, 1996, 1997).

Second, Plomin rewrites history by stating that it was not until the 1990s that behavioral science accepted the role of genes in behavioral development. For well more than a half century (e.g., Anastasi, 1958; Maier & Schneirla, 1935; Novikoff, 1945a, 1945b; Schneirla, 1956, 1957), genes have been accepted as part of the developmental system that propels human life across time. The issue is not the one that Plomin points to, then, that of accepting that genes are involved in development. Instead, the issue is *how* do genes contribute to development. Plomin's (2000) approach and that of other behavior geneticists (e.g., Rowe, 1994) involves a split, nature–reductionist treatment of this issue. Most contemporary developmental scientists take an integrated, relational developmental systems approach to the issue (see Chapters 6 to 9, and 14).

In fact, Plomin (2000) conceptually approaches the vacuity of the behavior genetics approach at least as it has been pursued through the twentieth century. Although he maintains that "Twin and adoption research and genetic research using nonhuman animal models will continue to thrive" in the twenty-first century (Plomin, 2000, p. 30), Plomin perhaps admits to the serious flaws in this approach to understanding the role of genes in behavioral development when he acknowledges that. "The greatest need is for quantitative genetic research that goes beyond heritability, that is, beyond asking whether and how much genetic factors are important in behavioral development" (Plomin, 2000, p. 31). Plomin (2000) then continued by asking a series of important questions about the role of genes in behavioral development: "How do genetic effects unfold developmentally? What are the biological pathways between genes and behaviour? How do nature and nurture interact and correlate?" (p. 31). Unfortunately, he was seeking answers to these questions through the flawed model and methods of behavior genetics and never explored the potential usefulness of developmental systems approaches. Nevertheless, such exploration would be very useful because Plomin (2000) admitted that it would be a major mistake

> to think that genes determine outcomes in a hard-wired, there's-nothing-we-can-do-about-it way. For thousands of rare single-gene disorders. Such as the gene on chromosome 4 that causes Huntington's disease, genes do determine outcomes in this hard-wired way. However, behavioral disorders and dimensions are complex traits influenced by many genes as well as many environmental factors. For complex traits, genetic factors operate in a probabilistic fashion like risk factors rather than predetermined programming. (p. 33)

Thus, ultimately, Plomin (2000) admitted that a probabilistic, nature–nurture relation is involved in accounting for the role of genes in behavioral development. Still, his views about single-gene disorders reflect an ahistorical conception of such problems of human development. That is, in respect to other such single-gene disorders (e.g., as involved with phenylketonuria [PKU]), genetic research has found means to counteract the problems produced by the genetic inheritance, and has thus shown that a hard-wired genetic influence is not that hard-wired after all (Scriver & Clow, 1980a, 1980b). As such, Plomin maintains a narrow view of the probabilistic developmental system; it apparently does not include the ingenuity of scholars to capitalize on the plasticity within the developmental system and to demonstrate that what might seem to be hard-wired is in reality amenable to change as a consequence of its embeddedness within a dynamic system. Nevertheless, in admitting to the importance of a probabilistic system in behavioral development, Plomin (2000) is, in actuality, defeating his own, split approach to the nature and nurture of behavioral development.

Moreover, other scholars are not as convinced as is Plomin (2000) that the various methodologies he associates with behavior genetics will generate useful data. For example, Collins and colleagues (2000) noted that:

> One criticism is that the assumptions, methods, and truncated samples used in behavior—genetic studies maximize the effects of heredity and features of the environment that are different for different children and minimize the effects of shared family environments. . . . A second criticism is that estimates of the relative contributions of environment and heredity vary greatly depending on the source of data . . . heritability estimates vary considerably depending on the measures used to assess similarity between children or between parents and children. . . . The sizable variability in estimates of genetic and environmental contributions depending on the paradigms and measures used means that no firm conclusions can be drawn about the relative strength of these influences on development. (pp. 220–221)

Similarly, and again counter to Plomin's (2000) assertion that the controversy surrounding behavior genetics faded by the 1990s, Horowitz (2000) noted that:

> One sees increasing skepticism about what is to be learned from assigning variance percentages to genes. . . . The skepticism is informed by approaches that see genes, the central nervous system and other biological functions and variables as contributors to reciprocal, dynamic processes which can only be fully understood in relation to sociocultural environmental contexts. It is a perspective that is influenced by the impressive recent methodological and substantive advances in the neurosciences. (p. 3)

An Example From the Neurosciences: The Work of Suomi

The cutting-edge study of the neurosciences within the developmental systems perspective noted by Horowitz (2000) is exemplified by the work of Stephen J. Suomi. Suomi and his colleagues (1997, 2000; Bennett ct al., in press) has sought to identify how genes and context fuse within the developmental system and, as such, because of the close genetic similarity of rhesus moneys to humans, he has studied such organisms as a means to provide a model for the investigation of this system. In one recent instance of this long-term research program, Suomi (2000; Bennett et al., in press) found that young rhesus monkeys show individual differences in their emotional reactivity (or "temperament," see Chapter 17). Some young monkeys are highly reactive (e.g., they become quite excited and agitated when they experience environmental stress; i.e., separation from their mothers). Other monkeys show low reactivity in such situations

Stephen J. Suomi

Moreover, Suomi (2000; Bennett et al., in press) found that the interaction between the serotonin transporter genotype and early experience not only influences rhesus monkey behavior but also brain chemistry regarding the use of serotonin. Despite having a high-reactivity genotype, the monkeys whose early life experiences were with the low-reactivity foster mothers had brain chemistry that corresponded to monkeys with a low-reactivity genotype. Accordingly, Suomi (2000) concluded that:

> The recent findings that specific polymorphisms in the serotonin transporter gene are associated with different behavioral and biological outcomes for rhesus monkeys as a function of their early social rearing histories suggest that more complex gene–environment interactions actually are responsible for the phenomenon. It is hard to imagine that the situation would be any less complex for humans. (p. 31)

Conclusions

Clearly, many human developmentalists do not believe the causal "storyline" of behavior genetics. Nevertheless, "research" in behavior genetics—studies that, in effect, involve obtaining samples of people with differing degrees of biological relatedness and applying, typically, state-of-the-art measures of traits and inadequate measures of the ecology of human development (Bronfenbrenner & Ceci, 1994; Hoffman, 1991)—is well funded and widely disseminated, both through articles in the best scientific journals and in books produced through excellent publication houses.

But, behavior genetics is really like the story of the emperor's new clothes. Despite the positive regard some researchers hold for this area, there is actually "nothing there." The naked truth is that conceptual errors and misapplied models—no matter how often repeated or published—do not by dint of their numbers make for an adequate contribution to science. To understand both the conceptual problems of the split, nature–mechanistic model of human development of behavior genetics and the several limitations of the scientific methods it uses to try to support this model, it is necessary to turn to an analysis of the construct that is the cornerstone of behavior genetics: heritability. There is pervasive misunderstanding and misapplication of this concept, and it is important to understand how it should and should not be used.

We begin our discussion of the concept of heritability in this chapter. In Chapter 11, we extend this discussion in relation to an analysis of the

(i.e., they behave calmly in the face of such separation). Suomi (2000; Bennett et al., in press) discovered that these individual differences in behavior are associated with different genetic inheritances related to the functioning of serotonin, a brain chemical involved in neurotransmission and linked to individual differences in such conditions as anxiety, depression, and impulsive violence.

In order to study the interrelation of serotonergic system genes and environmental influences on behavioral development, Suomi (2000; Bennett et al., in press) placed high or low reactivity rhesus young with foster rhesus monkeys who were also either high or low in emotional reactivity. When young monkeys with the genetic inheritance marking high reactivity were reared for the first 6 months of life with a low-reactivity mother, they developed normally (i.e., despite their genes they did not show high reactivity, even when removed from their foster mothers and placed in a group of peers and unknown adults). In fact, these monkeys showed a high level of social skill (e.g., they took leadership positions in their group). However, when young monkeys with this same genetic marker for high reactivity were raised by high-reactivity foster mothers, they did not fare well under stressful conditions and proved socially inept when placed in a new social group.

problematic use of heritability research in regard to a specific characteristic of human development: intelligence.

USES AND MISUSES OF THE CONCEPT OF HERITABILITY

If developmental scientists are interested in measuring a certain individual (e.g., psychological) construct or characteristic of people, such as intelligence, they will often formulate a test to measure this characteristic or trait. Now, if a group of people is given such an intelligence test, it is very unlikely that they will all get the exact same score. Rather, some will score low, some high, and some intermediate. The scores of the group will form a distribution, ranging from high to low. (This is similar to what happens when we, as students, take several tests in a course over a semester and our test scores distribute themselves from high to low.)

If we are interested in representing the way the group functioned on the test in general (or if we want to know how we are doing overall in the course), the first thing we might opt to do is find the mean (the average) score of the distribution. To do this, we would simply add up all the individual scores in the distribution and divide this total by the number of scores in the distribution.

Second, we might want to know about the distribution of scores per se. In other words, not everyone in our group got the same score. Rather, within the group there was *variation*. Many people scored near the group mean, a few scored way above it, and a few scored way below it. Statistical analysis would allow us to represent the amount of variation in a distribution through the use of the term *variance* (σ^2). The magnitude of the variance would indicate how much or how little variation in test scores occurred in the distribution.

Heritability as a Means for "Partitioning" the Sources of Variance in a Distribution of Scores

For the purposes of understanding the concept of heritability, it is important to recognize that, in regard to this concept, the key question is not how much variation is present in a distribution of scores, but rather what is the source of the variance (i.e., of the differences between peopl in their scores). In regard to the concept of heritability, we would want to know how much of the variation in the test scores making up the distribution was due to variation in the gene distribution of the people tested and how much was due to variation in their environments. The goal of a heritability analysis, then, is to separate—"partition"—the variance in a distribution of scores into differences associated with genetic differences, and differences associated with environmental differences across people.

Since we have a distribution of scores, this means that there are differences among the people in our population in their test scores. We may ask several questions—all similar in purpose—about these differences. Why do these people differ? Why do they vary? What is the source of the variation between them? How much of this variation may be attributed to genetic differences between them? How much to environmental differences between them? What percentage of these differences between these people—what proportion of this variance involves genetic differences between them? What percentage of these differences between people may be attributed to the corresponding gene differences (i.e., the corresponding gene distribution)? Note that here we are asking what proportion of the test differences between people corresponds to the *gene differences* between people; we are *not* asking about how much of a given single person's test score is determined by his or her genes. (It should be clear that these are two different questions.) We should keep this distinction in mind and see that since these are two different questions, we can in no way answer the second question by coming to an answer for the first.

Defining and Calculating Heritability

Whenever we answer questions such as the first one—when we try to find out how much of the variation between people is due to gene differences between them—we are addressing questions that will lead us toward the calculation of heritability. Such questions inquire about what proportion of variation in a group of people (a population that has been measured for a particular psychological characteristic) is related to the gene variation among these people. In other words, heritability is "the percentage of variability attributable to genotype" (Pianka, 1978, p. 11). It is an estimate of variation in genes, not of commonality. Although it will be important to note again that, if a human trait were underlain by genes common to all people in a group, the estimated heritability index for that trait would be zero (e.g., Collins et al., 2000; Hirsch, 1997), we should stress here that, consistent with our previous discussion of heritability, we may define this concept as the proportion of trait variation in a population that is attributable to genetic variation in that population. For the purposes of our discussion in this chapter, we may symbolize heritability by the term h^2.

Now, if all the variation in a trait (such as intelligence) could be attributed to the concomitant variation within the gene distribution of the population under study, then no variation whatsoever in the trait would be due to environmental variation. Thus, in such a case, the value for environmental variation in the population would be zero and, accordingly, h^2 would equal one, or $+1.0$. Alternatively, if no trait variation could be attributed to genetic variation, all the trait variation in the population would have to be a function of environmental variation in the population. Therefore, in this case, h^2 would equal zero, or 0.0. Thus, we see that h^2 values can range anywhere from zero to plus one, increasing in proportion to the extent that the population's genetic variation accounts for the trait variation. Typically, however, the heritability of a trait falls somewhere within this zero-to-plus-one range.

A heritability score can be calculated in several ways. Basically, the main thrust of all calculation methods is to determine the degree to which a specific population of organisms has responded to being bred for the expression (the degree of presence) of some trait (Hirsch, 1970). For example, let us say that a particular population of organisms (e.g., a specific population of fruit flies, *Drosophila*) can be distributed in terms of a particular trait (e.g., the tendency to move toward light). If the distribution of this trait in this population remains the same despite any changes in the genetic similarity of the parents of these flies, then heritability would equal zero. That is, if the genes transmitted to the offspring making up our fly population could be varied and this transmission did not differentially affect the population's trait distribution, then heritability would equal zero. This would be the case because, if changes in the genetic similarities or differences among the parents do not lead to any variation in the population's trait distribution, then genetic variation within the population does not contribute to the variation in this population's trait distribution, and h^2 would equal zero.

However, if in another population of *Drosophila* similarly distributed in terms of a particular trait, the genes transmitted by the parents do lead to a change in the population's trait distribution, then, obviously, genetic variation within the population does account for some of this variation; therefore, in this case, the heritability value would be greater than zero. The exact numerical value of heritability would thus be determined by calculating the magnitude of the relationship between (the correlation for a given trait that existed for) the parents and their offspring comprising the population under study.

Variation in the Estimates of Heritability of Human Characteristics

From these illustrations, we should recognize an essential point. Heritability values for the same trait vary in relation to the particular populations under study. That is, the heritability for the same exact trait may be plus one in one population, zero in another, and somewhere between these two scores in yet another population. Therefore, it should be clear that *heritability is a property of populations and not of traits* (Hirsch, 1963). Thus, a trait in an individual cannot be appropriately spoken of as of being heritable; one cannot correctly speak of the trait intelligence as being heritable. Rather, heritability only refers to the extent to which genetic variation among the members of a specific population of organisms accounts for the trait distribution in that population. Jensen (1969) made the same point. In discussing the appropriateness of applying the concept of heritability to a population of people and the inappropriateness of such application to any individual within that population, Jensen (1969) stated:

> Heritability is a population statistic, describing the relative magnitude of the genetic component (or set of genetic components) in the population variance of the characteristic in question. It has no sensible meaning with reference to a measurement or characteristic in an individual. A single measurement, by definition, has no variance, (p. 42)

Hence, heritability describes something about a group and not anything about an individual. Heritability relates to the source of differences among people in a population; it says nothing about a given psychological trait within any person in that population. Accordingly, although the claim, that if a trait is heritable it is therefore inherited, seems so obvious as to border on a tautology, or an assertion true by definition, nothing could be further from the truth: *The demonstration of heritability says nothing about the extent to which a trait is inherited* (Lerner, 1992b; Lerner & von Eye, 1992, 1993). In fact, evidence for heritability cannot be taken as evidence for the common possession of a particular set of genes. Moreover, there is no connection between the concept of heritability and the idea that a human's characteristics are caused by one or more genes!

Heritability Does NOT Mean Inherited

From our discussion so far, it is clear that heritability is a far less meaningful, more limited piece of information than most people seem to realize (Hirsch, 1970, p. 72). Most importantly, we should recognize that *heritability does not mean genetically determined*. Nevertheless, the assonance between the terms "heritability" and "inherited" (Hirsch, 1997) suggests one reason why the concept may be used in a confused and confusing manner. Indeed, for several reasons heritability *is* a difficult, confusing concept.

At first blush, it would seem to pertain to the extent to which something is inherited, that is, is based in the genes. For instance, if one were told that "intelligence is 80% heritable" (Jensen, 1969), it might be reasonable to take this to mean that 80% of intelligence was genetically "determined"— that a given person's intelligence was largely (80%) shaped by his or her genes and that something else (environment) shaped the small percentage remaining.

The seemingly reasonable interpretation that high heritability means that, as we have noted that Rushton (1999, p. 60) claimed, "the differences are inborn and the environment has no effect" is a claim often made by some scientists, members of the media, and governmental policy-makers (e.g., see Horowitz, 2000). Nevertheless, this interpretation of heritability is *completely incorrect*.

However, in pertaining only to differences *between* people, heritability has absolutely nothing to do with the extent to which anything—be it genes or environment—determines characteristics *within* an individual. Heritability only refers to the extent to which differences between people in a specific characteristic can be summarized by genetic differences between these people.

Lerner and von Eye (1992) provided a technical explanation of this claim, and noted that, despite the dazzling statistical pyrotechnics often involved in the computation of heritability estimates (e.g., Molenaar, Boomsma, Neeleman, & Dolan, 1990), these statistics, nevertheless, still only describe the extent to which interindividual differences in a trait distribution measured at one point in time and under one particular set of environmental conditions are associated with interindividual differences in gene distributions. These analyses say *nothing* about the trait per se. They say nothing about the role of genes in causing the interindividual differences in the trait distribution. Most certainly, they say nothing about the role of genes in providing a basis for the development of the trait within the person (e.g., see Hirsch, 1990a, 1990b, 1997). As such, Horowitz (2000) concluded that:

> The data reported in behavioral genetics studies involving degrees of relationships among twins, siblings, and biologically unrelated individuals are in themselves interesting, even if it is doubtful that these relationships tell us anything about the direct and unmediated impact of genes. (p. 3)

Nevertheless, despite the clear fact that heritability does not mean inherited (Hirsch, 1997), people building their scientific careers around the production of heritability analyses cast their work *as if* it, in fact, provided some understanding of the separate *and causal* role of genes in human behavior and development (Hirsch, 1990a, 1997). This "nature as separate from nurture" work cannot achieve such a partition; indeed, the entire idea of this work—of separating the contribution of nature from nurture in the causation of an individual's behavior—is simply counterfactual.

Yet, whatever the motivations of hereditarians for perpetuating the causal misuse of the concept of heritability, they often manifest lapses in language—for example, moving from describing factors associated with interindividual differences in a trait distribution to advancing genetically causal explanations for the behavior itself (e.g., see Rowe, 1994; Rushton, 1990). Indeed, as noted by Gottlieb (1992), "Although population thinkers tell us that, strictly speaking, h^2 and e^2 refer to sources of individual *differences* among phenotypes, as a matter of fact in actual practice these measures are often applied to a causal understanding of the outcome of individual development as well" (p. 117). Moreover, Gottlieb goes on to note that, "If h^2 actually was useful for estimating genetic constraints or limitations on developmental outcomes, it would have some value, but it is widely agreed by geneticists themselves that h^2 cannot be interpreted in that way (Feldman & Lewontin, 1975), although individual scientists may now and again lapse into thinking in those terms (e.g., Gottesman & Shields, 1982)" (Gottlieb, 1992, p. 118).

For instance, Plomin and colleagues (1990) conducted a behavior genetic study of individual differences in television viewing in early childhood in order to "explore the etiology of individual differences" (p. 372). Plomin and colleagues contended that their data provide evidence of a "genetic influence" (p. 371) on television viewing, and used phrases that often becloud the distinction between interindividual differences in a behavior and the behavior itself and, invariably, cast their descriptive information as if genetic causality had been demonstrated: "The remarkable result is the evidence for significant genetic influence . . . inherent proclivities of children are in part responsible for differences in the amount of time they choose to watch television" (p. 376).

From the vantage point of the scholarship presented by Gottlieb (1992), the interpretation Plomin and colleagues (1990) gave of their data is not correct. Quite simply, it is counterfactual to contend that nature is separable from nurture, and counterproductive (to say the least) to devise statistical methods to model this imaginary (or, at best, hypothetical) situation; but, most important, genes do not, in reality, function in the manner that behavior geneticists (or sociobiologists; see Chapter 13) must have them work if their "storylines" about the influence of nature are to attain even face validity. As Gottlieb (1992) pointed out:

> The actual role of genes (DNA) is not to produce an arm or a leg or fingers, but to produce protein (through the coactions inherent in the formula DNA ↔ RNA ↔ protein). The protein produced by the DNA ↔ RNA ↔ cytoplasm coaction then differentiates according to coactions with other cells in its surround. Thus, differentiation occurs according to coations *above the level of DNA ↔ RNA ↔ coactions* (i.e., at the supragenetic level). (pp. 164–165)

High Heritability Does Not Rule Out Environmental Influences

In addition to a high heritability score *not* indicating that a characteristic is caused by genes, a high heritability score also does *not* mean—despite what Rushton (1999, p. 60) erroneously insisted—that a characteristic is unavailable for influence by the environment. Implicit in all we have said about heritability up to this point has been the assumption that the environments of the populations under study have been constant and unvarying.

Of course, except under specially and artificially designed conditions that are *sometimes* possible to achieve with *Drosophila* but not with humans, environmental conditions can be expected to vary. Thus, it is possible that h^2 might equal one for a population reared under a given set of environmental circumstances and might equal zero for that same population reared under a different set

of environmental circumstances. If this is the case, then h^2 values are obviously affected by environment, and one can in no way speak of h^2 as telling anything about genetic determination. Accordingly, as Hirsch (1970) cautioned, heritability is only an estimate of the proportion of phenotypic variation of a trait that can be attributed to genetic variation in some *particular generation of a specific population under one set of environmental conditions*. Similarly, Jensen (1969, p. 43) stated that heritability estimates "are specific to the population sampled, the point in time, how the measurements were made, and the particular test used to obtain the measurements."

To give an example of how misleading heritability interpretations can be in regard to understanding the role of environmental influences, let us consider an imaginary example. Suppose a society had a law pertaining to eligibility for government office. The law was simply that men could be elected to such positions and women could not. Consider what one would need to know in order to completely and correctly divide a group of randomly chosen people from this society into one of two groups. Group 1 would consist of those who had greater than a zero percent chance of being elected to a leadership post and Group 2 would consist of those who had no chance. All that one would need to know to make this division with complete accuracy was whether a person possessed an XX pair of chromosomes or an XY pair. In the first case, the person would be a female (since possession of the XX chromosome pair leads to female development). In the second, the person would be a male. One could, thus, correctly place all possessors of the XY pair into the "greater than zero chance" group and all possessors of the XX pair into the "no chance" group.

In this example, then, *all* the differences between people with respect to the characteristic in question—eligibility for office—can be summarized by genetic differences between them, that is, possession of either the XX or the XY chromosome pair. In this case the heritability of "being eligible" would be 1.0. In other words, in this society eligibility is 100% heritable. But, by any stretch of the imagination, does this mean that the eligibility characteristic is inherited, or that the differences between men and women with respect to this characteristic are genetic in nature? Is there a gene for "eligibility," one that men possess and women do not?

Of course, the answers to these questions is no. Although heritability in this case is perfect, it is social ("environmental") variables—laws regarding what men and women can and cannot do—that determine whether someone has a chance of being elected. Indeed, if the law in question were changed, and women were then allowed to hold office, then the heritability of the eligibility characteristic would—probably rather quickly—fall to much less than 1.0.

The research of Guo (1999) is instructive to discuss here, in that it extends empirically this imaginary example about electability. Documenting the actual computational problems in the estimation of heritability in human populations, Guo (1999) simulated the calculation of heritability in the absence of any genetic differences. Consistent with the "electability" example, Guo (1999) found that, despite the lack of genetic differences, it was still possible to obtain values for heritability!

Hebb (1970) offered another useful example of the problems associated with the measurement and interpretation of heritability, one drawing on a "modest proposal" put forth by Mark Twain:

> Mark Twain once proposed that boys should be raised in barrels to the age of 12 and fed through the bung-hole. Suppose we have 100 boys reared this way, with a practically identical environment. Jensen agrees that environment has *some* importance (20% worth?), so we must expect that the boys on emerging from the barrels will have a mean IQ well below 100. However, the variance attributable to the environment is practically zero, so on the "analysis of variance" argument, the environment is not a factor in the low level of IQ, which is nonsense. (p. 578)

In Hebb's example, environmental had no *differential* effect on the boy's IQs; presumably in all boys it has the same (severely limiting) effect. In having this same effect, environment could contribute nothing to differences between the boys. No differences—or variation—existed in the environment, and so the environment could not be said to contribute anything to differences between people. Yet, it is also obvious that environment had a major influence on the boys' IQ scores. Even with IQ heritability equal to +1.0, the intelligence of each of the boys would have been different had he developed in an environment other than a barrel.

A third example is based on the research of Partanen and colleagues (1966). These researchers analyzed data from 172 monozygotic and 557 dizygotic male twin pairs. All participants were alcohol users. The aim of the study was to estimate the degree to which alcohol abuse is genetically determined. When measured by frequency of alcohol consumption, alcohol abuse seems to have at least a modest genetic component (heritability 0.40). However, if one uses the amount of alcohol consumed on each occasion, the heritability estimate drops considerably (to 0.27). A third measure of alcohol abuse—the number of citations and other social conflicts resulting from drinking—yields a heritability estimate of 0.02. Thus, judgments concerning heritability can depend largely on the definition and operationalization of the behavior under study. In addition, the confusion between commonality and variability can lead to misinterpretation.

High Heritability Does Not Speak to Developmental Process

Given the above considerations, it is clear that *high heritability does not mean developmental fixity*. A high estimate of heritability means that environment does not contribute very much to *differences* among people in their expression of a trait; yet environment may still provide an important (although invariant) source of the expression of that trait, for instance in determining the average level of a trait shown by people in a given group.

From Hebb's (1970) example we see clearly that although heritability may be high, the characteristic in question may still be influenced by the environment. Even when environment contributes nothing to *differences* between people in a population, this fact does not mean that the population characteristic is fixed by heredity or that it is unavailable to environmental influence. As Hebb well points out, while contributing nothing to differences between people, environment can still be a uniformly potent source of behavioral development and functioning within each of the people in a group.

A related point has been made by Lehrman (1970). When geneticists speak of a trait as heritable, all they mean is that one is able to predict the trait distribution in the offspring of a group on the basis of knowing the trait distribution in the parent group. One can predict the distribution of eye color in the offspring generation merely by knowing the distribution of eye color among the parents. Thus, while geneticists may use the term hereditary or inherited as interchangeable with the term heritable, they are not, by such usage, making any statements about the *process* involved in the development of this trait. In other words, the geneticist is not saying anything at all about the way that nature and nurture serve as sources of a heritable trait. Thus, the geneticist is not saying anything about the extent to which the expression of the trait may change in response to environmental modification.

In short, a geneticist would not say that a highly heritable trait cannot be influenced by the environment. Rather, the geneticist would probably recognize, as we now must, that even if the heritability of a trait is +1.0, an almost infinite number of expressions (phenotypes) of that trait may be expected to develop as a result of an interaction with the almost infinite number of environments to which any one genotype may be exposed.

Those who equate heritability with genetic determination assume that as the magnitude of heritability increases from zero to +1.0, less and less can be done through environmental modifications to alter the expression of the trait. Correspondingly, they assume that if heritability is low, more room is left for alteration of the trait by means of environmental manipulation (Rushton, 1999). This argument is fallacious. As noted by Scarr-Salapatek (1971):

> The most common misunderstanding of the concept "heritability" relates to the myth of fixed intelligence: if h^2 [heritability] is high, this reasoning goes, then intelligence is genetically fixed and unchangeable at the phenotypic level. This misconception ignores the fact that h^2 is a population statistic, bound to a given set of environmental conditions at a given point in time. Neither intelligence nor h^2 estimates are fixed. (p. 1128)

In short, whatever the level reached by an estimate of heritability, environmental variation may be a (or the) key causative factor. In addition, it is clear that high heritability does not mean developmental fixity. If the social context changes, one cannot be certain if any information one has about heritability still applies.

Conclusions

We should be able to now recognize that the limited information conveyed by an estimate of heritability has little potential generalizability due to the facts that a particular heritability estimate can be used only in reference to one particular generation of a particular population that is reared in a specific, invariant environment. In addition, Hirsch (1970) reports that when a heritability estimate is made on a population more than once—that is, when repeated measurements of h^2 are taken—some studies report that h^2 increases, others report that it decreases, and still others report that h^2 varies randomly. Thus, in addition to its other limitations, h^2 seems to fluctuate in a largely unpredictable manner from one time of measurement to the next. In psychological parlance, this is termed *unreliability*. This is a devastating, seemingly fatal, flaw. If a measurement does not come out to be the same value from one time of testing to the next (which means that the measurement is not reliable), what confidence can we place in that measurement? If we cannot even measure a concept reliably, of what use is it? And if a concept cannot be measured reliably, can we justifiably make any social or educational policies on the basis of such measurement? I think the answer to these questions is no.

Thus, a heritability estimate is not what it may *seem* to be. In addition, we shall now consider information that will suggest that heritability may not even be a good measurement of what it is *supposed* to be. Indeed, as we see in Chapter 11, where we discuss the controversies surrounding the use of heritability estimates in understanding the "nature and nurture" of intelligence, there is considerable support for Hirsch's view (1970, p. 74) that, in regard to human intelligence, "the plain facts are that in the study of man a heritability estimate turns out to be a piece of 'knowledge' that is both deceptive and trivial." Moreover, both in this chapter and in the following one, we review evidence that indicates that a heritability estimate is a problematic statistic. It is important to understand the technical (statistical) problems associated with heritability research in order to fully appreciate the myriad shortcomings of behavior genetics and why any purported evidence it presents for the split, hereditarian view of behavioral development is "more apparent than real."

STATISTICAL AND OTHER METHODOLOGICAL PROBLEMS IN THE COMPUTATION OF HERITABILITY

Several statistical and other technical (methodological) problems associated with the determination of heritability are important to note (Hirsch, 1970, 1976, 1990a, 199b; Hirsch, McGuire, & Vetta, 1980; Lerner, 1986; McGuire & Hirsch, 1977; Wahlsten, 1990). A key problem arises in regard to differences between the concept of broad heritability (H^2) and the concept of narrow heritability (h^2). To understand these concepts, we should recognize that the contributions of variation in heredity and environment to the variance in a given behavior such as general intelligence, temperament, or personality, might be expressed in several ways.

Hereditary and environmental variance can relate to behavioral variance separately and independently. In such a case, what one contributes is unrelated to what the other contributes. Each may be labeled as a *main effect,* in the conventional analysis of variance (ANOVA) sense of the term. Alternatively, the contributions of hereditary variance and environmental variance may interact, again in the conventional analysis of variance meaning of the term. Finally, heredity–environment (or genotype–environment) correlation occurs when hereditary (genotype) and environmental differences covary. Together, the concepts of main, interactional, and correlational contributions of hereditary and environmental variation allows the concepts of broad heritability (H^2) and narrow heritability (h^2) to be distinguished and the statistical problems associated with them to be noted.

Feldman and Lewontin (1975), in distinguishing between broad heritability and narrow heritability, indicated that heritability, in the broad sense, is the term used for the proportion of all variance that is partitioned into the genetic variance in an analysis of variance of genetic and environmental sources. For instance, there is a contribution that is made by individual alleles (this is termed *additive variance*), a contribution that is made by pairs of homologous (similar) alleles at a given locus (location) of the genome (this is termed *dominance variance*), and a contribution that is made by combinations of nonhomologous loci (termed *epistatic variance*). Heritability, in the narrow sense, is the proportion of the phenotype variance that is additive genetic variance (Feldman & Lewontin, 1975).

Feldman and Lewontin (1975) noted however, that this variance analysis cannot be used in the study of problems of human population genetics. They indicated:

> In problems concerning the population genetics of human behavioral traits, the existence of a variance contribution from genotype–environment interaction and a genotype–environment correlation have long been recognized as major difficulties. On the one hand, the obvious problems these cause for estimation of [narrow heritability] have led to the use of the [broad heritability] in discussion of such characters. On the other hand, as was implied by Falconer (1960) and emphasized by Moran (1973) and Layzer (1974), the very existence of genotype–environment correlation precludes the valid statistical estimation of the genotypic, environmental, and interaction contributions to the phenotypic variance. That is because correlation makes it impossible to know how much of the phenotype similarity arises from similarity of genotype and how much from similarity of the environment. Thus in human population studies, where experimental controls are either impossible or unethical, statistical inference about the heritability of traits that are phenotypically plastic is invalid. (p. 1164)

In other words, then, H^2 is the proportion of the total variation in a given behavior that may be attributed to the sum of (a) the independent genetic variation (i.e., the main effect of hereditary variance) and (b) the variance due to genotype–environment correlation (McGuire & Hirsch, 1977, p. 46). H^2 is of little interest in genetics (McGuire & Hirsch, 1977), primarily because it does not allow the contribution of genotype variance per se to be disentangled from environmental variance; and, of course, such separation is an objective of heritability analyses in the first place.

Narrow heritability (h^2) is simply the proportion of variance in behavior that may be attributed solely to the main effect of hereditary (genotypic) variance; that is, h^2 is the hereditary variance that exists independent of, and thus that merely separately adds to, environmental variance (McGuire & Hirsch, 1977). It is the determination of h^2 toward which most heritability analysis is aimed. But there, especially in the case of the analysis of such variation in human behavior, lies the rub. It is in human heritability analysis, and the calculation of h^2, that the statistical and methodological problems inherent in this work arise.

It makes sense to attribute through heritability analysis (and the calculation of h^2) variation in some behavior to variation in heredity *only* if the contributions of heredity and of the environment are additive (Wahlsten, 1990). If the heredity and environment interact, the calculation of heritability is quite problematic (Bullock, 1990; Feldman & Lewontin, 1975; McGuire & Hirsch, 1977; Wahlsten, 1990). However, in assessing heritability among humans, the statistical techniques used to determine whether there is evidence for heredity–environment interaction (analysis of variance or its equivalent, multiple regression) are not as sensitive to the presence of interactions as they are to the independent (and, hence, additive) influences of heredity and environment. In other words, these statistical techniques cannot as readily detect the presence of interactions as they can the presence of main effects (Wahlsten, 1990).

This problem is especially apparent when these statistical tests are used with relatively small numbers of observations, and it is unfortunately the case that such small samples are generally the rule in social and behavioral science studies involving the calculation of heritability (Wahlsten, 1990). Thus, the smaller the sample used in a study, the greater the likelihood of the statistical test being unable to identify an interaction that is actually present. In such situations, the inference that an interaction between heredity and

Douglas Wahlsten

environment does not exist, and that in turn the contributions of these two factors involve only main, and, therefore, additive effects is incorrect. As a consequence, heritability estimates, and any conclusions based on them, are similarly misconceived.

However, if a large sample of observations exists, other methodological problems occur. If a scientist is interested in determining how much variance in a behavior is accounted for by variance in what people inherit versus what they experience in their environment, it is imperative that the nature of the specific heredity involved in the group under study be completely certain. If one wants to determine the extent to which variation in children's intelligence is accounted for by the genes provided to children by their mothers and fathers, as compared to the environments provided by these parents, one must be certain to measure the intelligence of children and their actual biological mothers and fathers. As Hirsch and colleagues (1980, p. 236) have argued, "A sine qua non for the study of heredity is proof positive of the presumed biological relationship, i.e., ascertainment of the biological validity of the designated kinships, such as parent–offspring, sibling, etc."

Unfortunately, however, heritability studies have not included controls for presumed biological relatedness. The absence of controls for presumed

biological relatedness makes one uneasy about presuming that in all studies involving estimates of the contribution of genes to behavioral resemblance between, for instance, children and parents, accurate designations of biological relatedness have occurred. Such concerns are magnified when, in the few studies including such controls, evidence exists that substantial proportions of the people labeled as "biological parent" are, in fact, unrelated biologically to the children in question. For instance, Hirsch and colleagues (1980) were able to determine, through blood testing, the actual biological relationships between parents and children within a subsample of 38 of the 112 families they studied. In 13% of the families in this subsample, there were children who could not have been the biological offspring of at least one of the putative parents in the family. Similarly, Philipp (1973; Hirsch, 1990a; Hirsch et al., 1980), reporting evidence derived from comparable analyses done on samples from the United Kingdom, noted that there were data disqualifying as the presumed fathers 30% of the husbands within the families being studied.

When correct information regarding biological relatedness is unavailable to the researcher who is appraising heritability, literal miscalculations and inferential errors abound. Such concerns have led Kempthorne (1990, p. 139), a quantitative genetic analyst, to view that "most of the literature on heritability in species that cannot be experimentally manipulated, for example, in mating, should be ignored." In a similar vein, population geneticists Feldman and Lewontin (1975, p. 1164) have concluded that "Certainly the sample estimate of heritability, either in the broad or narrow sense, but most especially in the broad sense, is nearly equivalent to no information at all for any serious problem of human genetics."

Thus, what heritability estimates at best provide (and *only* in a case involving additive genotypic variation, large sample sizes, compelling evidence for no genotype–environment interaction or correlation, and valid evidence for the relevant biological relatedness) is an estimate of the extent to which genetic differences (variation) within a given group are associated with differences (variation) in the scores for a trait measured among people in that group at a specific time in their lives.

In sum, then, heritability estimates describe only characteristics of a distribution of scores; they describe only a feature of differences between people. Such estimates say nothing about the trait itself. Such estimates, in particular, say nothing about the genetic and/or environmental determination (or cause) of the trait *within* any person in a group. Certainly, from such an estimate of *between*-people differences (which is what heritability is), one cannot legitimately make any statements about how humans have been selected for the homogenous presence of a trait (Lewontin, Rose, & Kamin, 1984). Indeed, as we noted earlier, to the extent such homogeneity exists, heritability must be low, due to lack of variation (Collins et al., 2000; Hirsch, 1997).

The Problem of Genotype–Environment Correlation

It is instructive here to focus on one key statistical problem that exists in regard to the estimation of a heritability coefficient. This statistical problem is present due to genotype–environment correlations.

As noted by Feldman and Lewontin (1975), one of the scientists who has dealt with this point has been Layzer (1974). Writing in regard to the controversy about the heritability of intelligence, a debate we discuss in Chapter 11, Layzer (1974) indicated that he assumes that:

> Some meaningful estimate of IQ heritability—high or low, rough or accurate—can be extracted from the reams of published statistics and that refinements of current techniques for gathering and analyzing test data may be counted on to yield increasingly reliable estimates. These propositions are by no means self-evident, however, and one of my purposes here is to demonstrate that they are actually false.
>
> This conclusion rests upon two arguments:
>
> One concerns the limitations of conventional heritability analysis, the other the validity of IQ scores as phenotypic measurements. Contrary to widely held beliefs, (i) heritability analysis does not require the genotype–environment interaction to be small, and (ii) a high phenotypic correlation between separated monozygotic twins does not, in general, imply that the genotype–environment interaction is small. If genotype–environment interaction does contribute substantially to the phenotypic value of a trait (as there are strong biological reasons for supposing in the case of phenotypically plastic traits), then a necessary and sufficient condition for the applicability of heritability analysis is the absence of genotype–environment correlation. This condition is rarely, if ever, met for behavioral traits in human populations. The second argument is that IQ scores contain uncontrollable, systematic errors of unknown magnitude. (p. 1259)

While we shall have reason to refer later to Layzer's (1974) analysis of the errors of measurement found in IQ scores, let us focus here on his treatment of the genotype–environment correlation problem. Using the label G for genotype and E for environment, Layzer (1974) argued

> that G and E can be unambiguously defined if, and only if, genotype–environment correlations are absent. Even then, however, a certain practical ambiguity persists. Genetic differences may influence the development of a trait in qualitatively distinct ways. For example, the curves labeled x_1, x_2, and x_3 in Figure 10.1 have different thresholds, different slopes, and different final values. Heritability estimates do not take such qualitative distinctions into account. Thus, if the environmental variable y is distributed in a narrow range about the value as illustrated in Figure 10.1, h^2 is close to unity. Yet in these circumstances the phenotypic variable could reasonably be considered to be largely environmental in origin since it is much greater than the phenotypic variance that would be measured in an environment ($y = y^2$) that permitted maximum development of the trait, consistent with genetic endowment. (p. 1260)

Layzer (1974) then noted that plant and animal geneticists *can* minimize genotype–environment correlation by *randomizing environments*: thus, such researchers can take a step that is, according to Layzer, *indispensable* for the application of heritability analysis, since without such randomization there is just no means to disentangle genetic and environmental contributions to phenotypic variances. But this step is not done in IQ heritability research. Layzer (1974) explained:

> The applicability of heritability analysis does not, as is commonly assumed, hinge on the smallness of the interaction term (R) relative to the terms G and E in Fisher's decomposition of the phenotypic

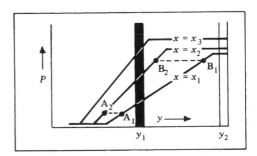

FIGURE 10.1
Phenotypic value (P) of a hypothetical metric trait as a function of an environmental variable (x) for three values of a genotypic variable (y). A_1 and A_2 (also B_1 and B_2) indicate individuals with a common phenotypic value but distinct genotypes x_1 and x_2, respectively.
Source: Layzer (1974, p. 1260).

value. In fact, one may reasonably assume on biological grounds that genotype–environment interaction makes a substantial contribution to the phenotypic value of every phenotypically plastic trait, except in populations where the ranges of genetic and environmental variation are severely restricted. Even so, heritability analysis can be applied to phenotypically plastic traits, provided that the relevant genetic and environmental variables are statistically uncorrelated. When this condition is not satisfied, the contributions of interaction to phenotypic variances and covariances cannot, in general, be separated from the contributions of genotype and environment, and heritability analysis cannot, therefore, be applied meaningfully.

In adult subpopulations, IQ and environment are well known to be more or less strongly correlated. Since differences in IQ are undeniably related to genetic differences (although not, perhaps, in a very simple way), one may safely assume that genotype–environment correlation is significant in adult subpopulations and in subpopulations composed of children reared by their biological parents or by close relatives. Hence, no valid estimate of IQ heritability can be based on data that refer to such subpopulations.

Yet data of precisely this kind make up the bulk of the available material, and many published heritability estimates have been based on them. Burt (1966), Jensen (1969), and Herrnstein (1971) for example, all cite kinship correlation data as evidence for a high value of h^2. (p. 1263)

As I have noted, we see in Chapter 11 that these interpretative problems are linked to others associated with the work of hereditarians when they discuss the heritability of IQ. Here, however, we should note that the existence of genotype–environment correlation presents a seemingly insurmountable problem in studies of the heritability of any human characteristic. Analyses of the heritability of human characteristics that rely on data sets wherein such correlations exist, therefore, result in flawed estimates. However, the problem of genotype–environment correlation is not the only one precluding a scientifically useful analysis of the heritability of human characteristics. Another major problem is presented by the arrays (sets) of genotypes and environments that are sampled in studies of the heritability of human characteristics.

Problems of Genotype and Environment Sampling

Feldman and Lewontin (1975) made the obvious point that, in quantitative human characteristics (such as IQ or personality scores), differences in phenotypes can be caused by both genotypes and

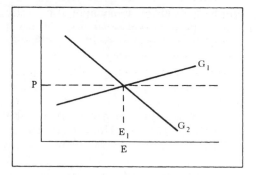

FIGURE 10.2
Phenotype P plotted against an environmental variable E. If the environments are symmetrically distributed around E_1 there is no average effect of genotype. If there is an excess of G_1 in the population the average phenotype will be constant, as represented by the horizontal dashed line.
Source: Feldman and Lewontin (1975, p. 1166).

environments. However, the not-so-obvious point for which they argue is that these two causes of variation cannot be separated by an analysis of variance and its summary statistic, heritability. They indicated that this situation occurs because the variance analysis and the calculation of heritability are done in regard to a particular set of genotypes and environments in a specific population and are studied at a specific point in time. They argued that this set is usually a biased sample of the full range of genotypes and environments that exist (Feldman & Lewontin, 1975).

The diagram presented in Figure 10.2 illustrates this point they offered. This figure illustrates a norm-of-reaction wherein the phenotype (P) is represented as a function of two genotypes (G_1 and G_2). Feldman and Lewontin (1975) explained:

Obviously, both genotype and environment influence the phenotype in this example. However, if the environments are symmetrically distributed around E_1 [Figure 10.2], there will appear to be no average effect of genotype, while if the population is weighted toward an excess of G_1, the average phenotype across environments will be constant, as is shown by the dashed line. Thus the environmental variance depends on the genotypic distribution, and the genotypic variance depends on the environmental variance. This very important interdependence means that, for a character like IQ, where the norm of reaction, the present genotype distribution, and the present environmental distribution are not known, we cannot predict whether an environmental change will change the total variation. Lewontin

(1970) gives an extreme example of the latter difficulty where all the variation between two populations is environmental, despite a heritability of 1.0 within each. (pp. 1166–1167)

We saw earlier that Hebb (1970), in his example from Mark Twain about raising boys to the age of 12 in a pickle barrel, made a point similar to the one forwarded by Lewontin (1970) and Feldman and Lewontin (1975). In Hebb's (1970) example, we noted that because the environment was precisely the same for all boys it could not contribute to any variance in their IQ scores. Nevertheless, Hebb's example also illustrates that, although not contributing to variance in scores, the environment (e.g., development in a pickle barrel or, more realistically, under conditions of persistent and pervasive poverty; Lerner, 1995) can influence scores for human characteristics (e.g., IQ scores). That is, it is clear that even with IQ heritability equal to +1.0, the intelligence of each of the boys would have been different had he developed in an environment other than a pickle barrel.

Accordingly, even if the heritability of IQ for a given group were +1.0, then alterations in their environmental experiences could still favorably alter the distribution of their IQ scores. Hence, *high* h^2 *does not mean developmental fixity*. A high h^2 estimate means that environment does not contribute very much to differences among people in their expression of a trait; yet environment may still provide an important (although invariant) source of the expression of that trait.

Interestingly, Jensen (1973) made a point that is consistent with Hebb's (1970) example and, as well, with Hirsch's (1970) criticisms of the heritability concept. Jensen (1973) noted that some people who interpret heritability estimates apparently believe that:

> There is an inverse relationship between heritability magnitude and the individual's improvability by training and teaching; this is to say, if heritability is high, little room is left for improvement by environmental modification, and conversely, if heritability is low, much more improvement is possible. Hirsch is quite correct in noting a possible fallacy that may be implicit in this interpretation of heritability. . . . (pp. 55–56)

Jensen (1973) explains this fallacy by noting that:

> First of all, the fact that learning ability has high heritability surely does not mean that individuals cannot learn much. Even if learning ability had 100 percent heritability it would not mean that individuals cannot learn, and therefore the demonstration of learning or the improvement of performance, with or

without specific instruction or intervention by a teacher, says absolutely nothing about heritability. But knowing that learning ability has high heritability does tell us this: if a number of individuals are all given equal opportunity—the same background, the same conditions, and the same amount of time—for learning something, they will still differ from one another in their rates of learning and consequently in the amount they learn per unit of time spent in learning. That is the meaning of heritability. It does not say the individuals cannot learn or improve with instruction and practice. It says that given equal conditions, individuals will differ from one another, not because of differences in the external conditions but because of differences in the internal environment which is conditioned by genetic factors. (pp. 56–57)

Hence, in both Hebb's and Jensen's statements we see the view that although heritability may be high, the characteristics in question may still be influenced by environment. In turn, we also see that even when conditions are "equal"—*and in actuality this could probably never occur*—and the differences that people will still assuredly manifest are attributable to genetic factors, this genetic influence is still not absolute, not environment-independent. Even when differences are due to internal differences, such sources are only conditioned by genetic factors; that is, such genetic factors only contribute to this internal environmental source. Clearly, then, when environment contributes nothing to the *differences* between people in population, their gene distribution accounts for these differences; but this, again, does not mean that the population characteristic is fixed by heredity or that it is unavailable to environmental influence. As both Hebb and Jensen pointed out, although contributing nothing to differences between people, environment can still be a uniformly potent source of behavior development and functioning within each of the people in a group. We have noted that both Lehrman (1970) and Scarr-Salapatek (1971a) made consistent points.

In short, there seems to be some consensus with the view of Feldman and Lewontin (1975) that, despite the level that is reached by an estimate of heritability, environmental variation may be a (or the) key causative factor; in addition, there seems to be general consensus with a key implication of their view that high heritability does not mean developmental fixity. Moreover, there are other implications of the Feldman and Lewontin (1975, 1976) position. One other important one, which may also be derived from Figure 10.2, is that holding either the environment or the genotype constant does not lead necessarily to a decrease in the

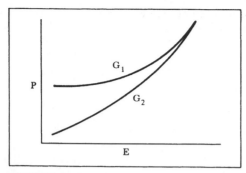

FIGURE 10.3
Phenotype *P* plotted against an environmental variable *E*. If the environments are
weighted to the left, there is a strong genotypic effect. If the environments are
weighted to the right, the genetic variation
is reduced.

Source: Feldman and Lewontin (1975, p. 1166)

total variance. To illustrate Feldman and Lewontin (1975) noted that:

> Fixing genotype G_2 (and thus eliminating the genetic
> variance) increases the total variance because G_2 is
> more susceptible to environmental change. It is also
> easy to construct graphs like Figure 10.2 in which
> environmental change improves the phenotype of
> both G_1 and G_2 but decreases the proportion of the
> variance that is genetic.
>
> Figure 10.3 is a case such that, if the environ-
> ments are weighted to the left, analysis of variance
> shows a strong genotypic effect. If the environments
> are weighted toward the right, thus producing im-
> provement in both phenotypes, the proportion of
> variation that is genetic is reduced. This situation is
> ignored by both Jensen (1969) and Herrnstein
> (1971), whose discussion does not take account of
> this possible form of genotype–environment interac-
> tion. (p. 1166)

In short, Feldman and Lewontin (1975) argued
that an estimate of heritability does not necessarily accurately portray the character of environmental and genotypic variation causally
involved in the differences in the scores for any
given human characteristic. Moreover, in pointing to some of the major methodological shortcomings involved in heritability research as a
consequence of the inadequate appraisal of
the environment, Feldman and Lewontin underscored a central problem in this hereditarian
approach, that is, the critically flawed conceptualization and measurement of the context of human development.

BEHAVIOR GENETICS INVOLVES AN IMPOVERISHED CONCEPT OF, AND AN INADEQUATE MEASUREMENT MODEL FOR, THE ECOLOGY OF HUMAN DEVELOPMENT

Behavior genetics merges a counterfactual view of
gene action with a naive and impoverished understanding of the ecology of human development. A
key example of these deficits occurs in regard to
the book by David Rowe (1994), *The Limits of
Family Influence: Genes, Experience, and Behavior.*

Rowe (1994) stated that his central idea was
that "broad differences in family environments,
except those that are neglectful, abusive, or without opportunity—may exert little influence on
personality development over the life course"
(p. 1). However, he also claimed that his "book's
thesis [is] shared family environments have little
effect on developmental outcomes" (p. 4).

Thus, according to Rowe (1994), it does not matter (except in extreme circumstances) whether
family "environments" are, across children, different or common (i.e., "shared"): It is his thesis that
in neither case does "environment" influence

David C. Rowe

developmental outcomes (see, too, Scarr, 1992). There are several problems with this stance, ones prototypic of the behavior genetics approach to the environment.

A key one is that Rowe (1994) failed to recognize that family influences can have a strong influence on individual development—perhaps especially when there is no variation in them (i.e., when they are shared equally across children). Elder's (1974) classic work on the effects of family economic hardship on children developing during the Great Depression is one excellent case in point. Another is provided by the recent work of Conger, Elder, and their colleagues (e.g., Conger, Conger, Elder, Lorenz, Simons, & Whitbeck, 1992; Conger, Lorenz, Elder, Melby, Simons, & Conger, 1991; Ge, Conger, Lorenz, Elder, Montague, & Simons, 1992) linking family economic hardship to adolescent distress, adjustment, and problems of substance use. Yet, because such invariant ecological influences contribute nothing to the variance across children or adolescents, their effects may be underestimated—*especially* when the ANOVA analytic techniques used in behavior genetics are ill-advisedly employed to estimate environmental contributions—a point we have seen made by Hebb (1970) and by Feldman and Lewontin (1975).

Another example of the problematic view of the context of human development used by Rowe (1994) occurred when he explained what he meant by the term *socialization science*. Here, Rowe seems to be referring to an area of social and behavioral science that is predicated on the view that characteristics of the ecology of human development, such as culture, socioeconomic status, family milieu, and nonnormative life events, may have some causal influence on human development. He claimed that socialization science "may miss entirely which experiences are influential for personality development, and in many cases these may be experiences we cannot grasp to change our children's lives" (Rowe, 1994, p. 5).

Of course, causal influences may not be identified in a given study. But, such omission would seem to be especially likely when—*as is typically the case in behavior genetics*—the context of human development is represented by, or better reduced to, a single score on a personality or intelligence test. For instance, consider behavior genetic studies using adoption designs. Here, assessments of the relative contributions to child outcomes of: (a) the conception through point-of-adoption family context provided by a biological parent versus (b) the family context of an adopting parent to child outcomes, are indexed by differences in the relations (e.g., by dif-ferences between correlations) in trait scores for the biological parent and child compared to the adopting parent and child (cf. Hoffman, 1991). To illustrate, in discussing how the influence of selective placement in adoptions can be understood, Rowe (1994, p. 39) noted that "its quantitative strength is the correlation between the trait as measured in the biological parent (usually the unwed mother of the adoptee) and as measured in the adoptive parent."

Such adoption studies underestimate the possible contribution to the variance of context *and* of dynamic person–context relations, and at the same time overestimate the contribution of genetic variance, because:

1.   Variance due to intrauterine contextual influences (and typically also to post-birth, pre-adoption contextual influences) is not measured and is attributed instead to genetic variance; in fact, Rowe (1994, p. 34) admitted that "all the accidents of embryological development are unshared; they can affect siblings differently, because each child has a different birth history."

2.   Data sets of trait correlations involving different degrees of biological family resemblance represent findings to-be-explained; the presence of correlations does not prove anything about the role of genes or of genetic differences in causing the correlations.

3.   The multiple levels of organization comprising the ecology of human development (Bronfenbrenner, 1979, 1989; Bronfenbrenner & Ceci, 1994) cannot even begin to be measured by a single trait measure, or even by a multivariate array of trait measures. To the contrary, and as again illustrated by the work of Elder (1974) and Conger (e.g., Conger et al., 1991, 1992; Ge et al., 1992), multilevel–multivariate representations of the context are needed to adequately represent the ecology of human development.

The reason that Rowe (1994) omitted these theoretical and empirical contributions to the study of the context of human development is that behavior genetics is theoretically anachronistic. In splitting genes from environment, in divorcing the genes from the developmental system in which they are fused (Gottlieb, 1997; Horowitz, 2000; Thelen & Smith, 1998), Rowe focuses on the "environment" of human development though a lens that reduces the scope of his vision and has him looking at past theories instead of contemporary ones (Lerner, 1998a). That is, to Rowe (1994), the theories that are seen as relevant to the context, or ecology, of human development or, in his terms, that represent the breadth of "socialization science" are Freudian theory (pp. 9–10), early Behaviorism (pp. 10–12), and social learning theory (pp. 12–13), as represented by two references to the work of Bandura (1965, 1971). Bandura's (1986) later work—which is dynamically interactional and developmental—is not mentioned.

Indeed, nowhere in Rowe's (1994) book, or in another hereditarian book written by Rushton (1999), is there an appreciation of this complex ecology of human development or, even more surprisingly, of the major theoretical contributions that have occurred over about the last 30 years in the understanding of context in human development and of the dynamic systems linking the individual to his or her multilevel context (e.g., Baltes et al., 1998, 1999; Brim & Kagan, 1980; Bronfenbrenner, 1979, 1989; Bronfenbrenner & Morris, 1998; Elder, 1980, 1998; Elder, Modell, & Parke, 1993; Ford & Lerner, 1992; Gottlieb, 1983, 1991, 1992, 1997; Horowitz, 2000; Lerner, 1978; 1986, 1991; Levine & Fitzgerald, 1992; Lewis, 1997; Magnusson, 1996, 1999a, 1999b; Sameroff, 1975, 1983; Thelen & Smith, 1998; Wapner & Demick, 1998).

Moreover, the absence of reference to dynamic developmental systems theory is a particularly striking omission, given Rowe's (1994) "biological orientation" and the fact that it was in biology (von Bertalanffy, 1933) and later in comparative psychology (e.g., Gottlieb, 1976, 1991, 1992; Kuo, 1976; Schneirla, 1957; Tobach, 1971, 1981) where such perspectives had much of their genesis and (and continue to have) influence. As we have discussed in prior chapters, developmental systems theories constitute an integrative and dynamic alternative to the sort of nature-mechanistic, split conceptions represented by behavior genetics.

THE DYNAMIC, DEVELOPMENTAL SYSTEMS "ALTERNATIVE" TO BEHAVIOR GENETICS

It is useful to reiterate briefly the character of the developmental process found in the dynamic developmental systems perspective discussed in prior chapters. As explained by Gottlieb (1992), the key "conception is one of a totally interrelated, fully coactional system in which the activity of genes themselves can be affected through the cytoplasm of the cell by events originating at any other level in the system, including the external environment" (Gottlieb, 1992, pp. 144–145). As

such, Gottlieb (1992, 1997) and other developmental systems theorists (e.g., Thelen & Smith, 1998) emphasize that neither genes nor the context by themselves cause development. The fusion among levels within the integrated developmental system means that relations among variables—not splits between nature and nurture—constitute the core of the developmental process.

Accordingly, although hereditarians argue that biological contributions are isomorphic with genetic influences (e.g., Rushton, 1999), this equivalence is not seen as veridical with reality from the perspective of developmental systems theory. For instance, although some hereditarians see constitutional variables (e.g., relating to brain volume, head size, size of reproductive organs, and stature) as all based on heredity (Rushton, 1999), within developmental systems (Horowitz, 2000):

> "Constitutional" is not equivalent to "genetic," and purposely so. Constitutional includes the expressed functions of genes—which, in themselves require some environmental input—but constitutional includes the operations of the central nervous system and all the biological and environmental experiences that impact organismic functioning and that make constitutional variables part of the dynamic change across the life span as they affect the development of and the decline of behavior. (p. 8)

In short, developmental science and developmental scientists should stop engaging in the pursuit of theoretically anachronistic and counterfactual conceptions of gene function. Indeed, significant advances in the science of human development will rest on embedding the study of genes within the multiple, integrated levels of organization comprising the dynamic developmental system of person–context relations.

As noted by Thelen and Smith (1994, 1998; Smith & Thelen, 1993), pursuing this dynamic interactionist, developmental systems perspective will surely be an arduous path, one likely filled with conceptual and empirical difficulties, mistakes, and uncertainties. Nevertheless, there is more than sufficient reason to continue to pursue this approach to behavioral development.

First, the nature–mechanistic approach of behavior genetics fails completely as an adequate theoretical or empirical approach to understanding human development. Second, and to paraphrase the epigraph by Strohman (1993, p. 101) that opened this chapter, we have no better option available than to pursue a dynamic developmental systems approach. And third, great progress is being made. To appraise this progress it is useful to review the ideas of Frances Degen Horowitz (2000).

The Contributions of Horowitz to Understanding the Importance of Developmental Systems Theories

Summarizing the status at the beginning of the twenty-first century of theory and research pertinent to developmental systems perspectives, Horowitz (2000) noted that there exists

> extremely important information about structural plasticity in neuro-psychological function. Most critically, this structural and functional plasticity across developmental time is being tied directly to the amplifications and constraints of the social/cultural contexts that determine the opportunities that children and adults have to experience and to learn. (p. 3)

To help frame these data, Horowitz (2000, p. 4) introduced a model of the dynamic developmental system, reproduced in Figure 10.4, that she notes corresponds to those of other developmental systems theorists (e.g., Gottlieb et al., 1998). Indeed, reference to the model in Figure 10.4 will remind readers of the figures presented in Chapters 6 through 9 to illustrate the several instances of developmental systems theories discussed in those chapters. As such, Horowitz (2000) indicated that:

> In this model, as in some of the others, the assumption is made (supported by data) that from the moment of conception development is influenced by constitutional, social, economic and cultural factors and that these factors, furthermore, continue in linear and nonlinear relationships, to affect development across the life span, with development broadly defined to accommodate both the increase and decrease in ability and function. (p. 4)

Moreover, in the context of presenting her model of the human developmental system, Horowitz (2000) compared the approach to developmental analysis represented by hereditarian approaches to behavior development, such as behavior genetics, with the approach pursued in the sorts of theories represented by the model in Figure 10.4. While recognizing the attractiveness to the "average person" and the media of the simplistic answers provided by nature-oriented theorists, Horowitz (2000) observed that:

> The conundrum for many is to explain the regularities of the postnatal emergence of the normal universal species-typical behaviors in each individual child despite the seeming variations in the gross nature of environments. The nativists answer is recourse to instincts, to predetermined, architecturally and genetically driven explanations both for the species as a whole and for the individuals in particular (Chomsky, 1965; Pinker, 1994; Spelke, Breinlinger, Macomber, & Jacobsin, 1992; Spelke & Newport, 1998). To the Person in the Street these explanations seem to provide the simple answers to simple questions though the nativist position is by no means simplistic and the position is often supported by very interesting data.
>
> The alternative view and, I believe, the more compelling view is to consider that within all the gross environmental variations there is present the essential minimal experience necessary for the acquisition—the learning—of the basic universal behaviors of our species. There is a growing agreement that universal behaviors and physical structures are not built into the organism but that humans are, at the very least, evolutionary primed to take advantage of the transactional opportunities provided by what Brandtstädter (1998) sees as the universal physical and social ecologies available to all normal human organisms—the kinds of transactional opportunities so beautifully analyzed by Thelen and her colleagues with respect to early motor development (Thelen & Ulrich, 1991). As a result of these transactional experiences, the forms and function of the universal developmental domains are constructed, whether as described in Thelen's dynamic systems approach to motor development (Thelen & Smith, 1994; Thelen & Ulrich, 1991), in Katherine Nelson's (1996) powerful

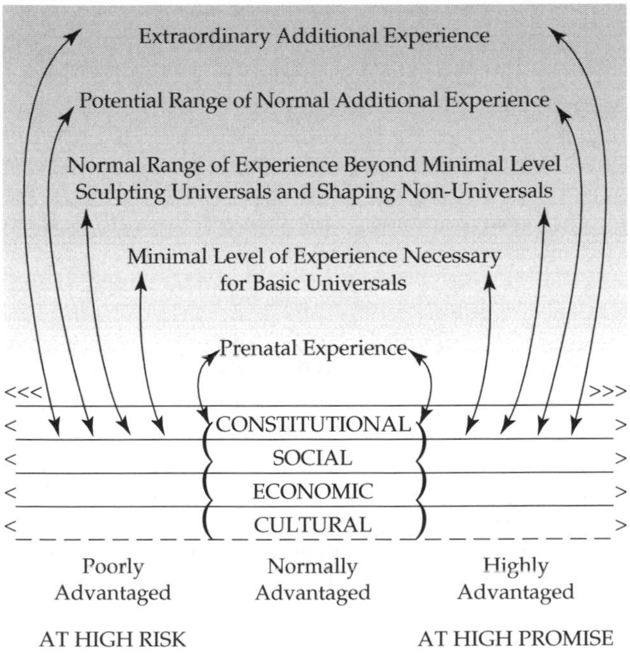

Extraordinary Additional Experience

Potential Range of Normal Additional Experience

Normal Range of Experience Beyond Minimal Level Sculpting Universals and Shaping Non-Universals

Minimal Level of Experience Necessary for Basic Universals

Prenatal Experience

<<<   >>>

<   CONSTITUTIONAL   >
<   SOCIAL   >
<   ECONOMIC   >
<   CULTURAL   >

Poorly   Normally   Highly
Advantaged   Advantaged   Advantaged

AT HIGH RISK   AT HIGH PROMISE

FIGURE 10.4
A depiction of the constitutional, social, cultural, and economic sources of influence on development with respect to the nature of experience and in relation to the circumstances of advantage, risk, and promise.
Source: Horowitz (2000, p. 4).

analysis and synthesis of the role of language in cognitive development, or in Kurt Fischer's notion of the "constructive web" and his attempts to document the linear and nonlinear mechanisms involved in the construction and development of the hierarchies of skills (Fischer, 1980; Fischer & Bidell, 1998). (p. 5)

Conclusions

Given the myriad theoretical and methodological problems associated with behavior genetics, little can be gained either for advancing the science of human development or for adequately informing or serving Horowitz's (2000) "Person in the Street" by continuing to invest resources in the behavior genetics approach. Indeed, there seems to be compelling reasons to make human and financial investments elsewhere given, on the one hand, the counterfactual view of genetic activity inherent in behavior genetics and the several insurmountable conceptual and computational problems involved in the derivation of heritability estimates and, on the other hand, the availability of the theoretically rich and empirically productive developmental systems alternatives to hereditarian approaches such as behavior genetics.

Frances Degen Horowitz

I believe, then, that both science and society may be well served by embarking on the scholarly path envisioned by Horowitz (2000): We should begin to devote our theoretical and research efforts to the exploration of the dynamic developmental system depicted by her and others (e.g., Collins et al., 2000; Ford & Lerner, 1992; Lerner, 1991; Levine & Fitzgerald, 1992; Lewis, 1997; Sameroff, 1983; Smith & Thelen, 1993; Thelen & Smith, 1994, 1998). This observation leads to my concluding points.

FROM SCIENCE TO SOCIAL POLICY AND SOCIAL ACTION

The conceptualization of genes and, superordinately, of nature as separable from nurture, found within behavior genetics is known—at least among molecular geneticists and some developmental and/or comparative scientists—to be counterfactual. Yet, the field associated with this conceptual mistake continues to flourish. Indeed, as we see in Chapters 11 through 13, despite a continuing failure by hereditarians to demonstrate the scientific validity of their nature–mechanistic ideas, new versions of the same flawed ideas continue to arise and attract research funding and media attention (e.g., Herrnstein, 1971; Herrnstein & Murray, 1994; Jensen, 1969, 1998; Lorenz, 1942, 1965; Rushton, 1996, 1999; Wilson, 1975).

Scholars in the field of human development must, therefore, confront several questions as a consequence of this curious situation: How did the biological, social, and behavioral sciences that attempt to contribute to the understanding of human behavior and development arrive at this point? Why do we not just declare that the "emperor has no clothes?" Why, instead, do we award grants and journal space to work having this fatal conceptual flaw?

Most important, why do we allow such mistaken reductionistic and mechanistic thinking to influence both science and social policy? In turn, why do we not more generally embrace policies informed by the scientifically valid alternative, developmental systems models of the role of biology–context relations?

In response to these questions, I believe that we can acknowledge, on the one hand, that behavior genetics *has* helped social and behavioral science recall that both biology and context must be considered in any adequate theory of human development. On the other hand, however, I believe it is appropriate at this point in the history of the field of human development to reject the oversimplified and incorrect view of context and of biology, respectively, found in behavior genetics. We are at a point in the science of human development where we must move on to the more arduous task of understanding the integration of biological and contextual influences in terms of the developmental system of which they are a dynamic part. This change in scientific attention is important for reasons of both the production of adequate developmental scholarship and the generation of useful social policy.

To illustrate, I may note that for Rowe (1994), as for other behavior geneticists as well (e.g., Plomin, 1986, 2000), as long as variance can be partitioned, there is a belief that genes can be shown to give rise to any aspect of human functioning, even the environment in which the individuals—the "lumbering robots" (Dawkins, 1976)—housing the genes are embedded. For instance, Rowe (1994, p. 5) asserted that "the measures we label as environmental (including such central ones as social class) may hide genetic variation." And how do genes create the environment? To Rowe (1994, p. 90), "The answer is that the genes may construct a nervous system—and that hormones and neurotransmitters may then motivate behaviors resulting in the dramatic redesign of an environment. The way a beaver will restructure its environment is as genetically shaped as its flat tail and keen hearing." Thus, Rowe's (1994) answer, which is his description of a process termed *niche picking,* illustrates not only the mechanism and reductionism of behavior genetics but also the acontextual, asystemic, superficial, and even magical, thinking about developmental process that exists within the field of behavior genetics.

Moreover, it is in the incautious dissemination of work based on such thinking wherein pernicious implications for social policy can arise (Lerner, 1992a). Rowe (1994) argued that:

> My thesis here is that social class may capture not variation in rearing and environmental social background, but instead variation in genes. This idea returns genes to socialization science by a back door—*by the very variable (social class) thought to have liberated social science from hereditarian thinking!* (p. 135)

Rowe's (1994) idea is redolent of the late nineteenth- and early twentieth-century. Social Darwinists in America and Europe (Proctor, 1988; Tobach, Gianutsos, Topoff, & Gross, 1974).

In particular, and as discussed in Chapter 12, his idea is consistent with the thinking involved in the German "racial hygiene" movement during this period (Proctor, 1988). Here, writers such as Alfred Ploetz, Wilhelm Schallmayer, Karl Binding, and Alfred Hoche maintained that members of low socioeconomic status groups—among other "weaker" members of society (e.g., the chronically sick or the lame)—were in their respective societal niches because of the inheritance of particular (i.e., "inferior") genes (Lerner, 1992a; Proctor, 1988).

At this point, however, any similarity to the thinking of Rowe (1994) disappears. This is because these racial hygienists went on to recommend that, if the overall health of society were to be improved, then policies must be instituted to rid society of these inferior genes. For instance, social programs and health care could be denied to the people possessing these genes and, as a result, they would have neither the economic, social, or medical resources to long survive on their own (Proctor, 1988). As a consequence, it was thought that these policies would—in perhaps only a generation or two—eliminate poverty as well as the weak, medically fragile, or handicapped. Simply, then, it was argued that the overall health of the German people would be enhanced because the carriers of the inferior genes would not be present to reproduce.

While again underscoring my belief that Rowe (1994) would find such policy recommendations reprehensible, my point is that the assertion that social class differences are due to genetic differences has been used in the past to justify horrible, and indeed criminal, social policies and political actions (Lifton, 1986; Müller-Hill, 1988; Proctor, 1988). Moreover, ideas about genetic differences are influencing social policy today. Recall our discussion in Chapter 7 about the linkage that former NIMH Director, Frederick K. Goodwin, drew between violent behavior among nonhuman primates and the presence of violence among urban males (Psychological Science Agenda, 1992), and his assertion that these youth have lost the social controls humans have had imposed by civilization over thousands of years of evolution (Psychological Science Agenda, 1992).

Given the use to which they may be put, it is my belief that when assertions about the genetic basis of social class (or racial, ethnic, gender, or sexual orientation) differences are based on such weak theory and data, as I believe they are in the case of the behavior genetic arguments and evidence offered by Rowe (1994), then I think that much greater caution must be exercised by scientists. Scientists are part of the world they study. I believe all scientists have a responsibility, even if it ends up being based in some cases only on enlightened self-interest, to disseminate their ideas in ways cognizant of the potential policy actions they might evoke.

Indeed, and to close on a point of agreement with Rowe (1994), scientists, as citizens, might serve both their science and society best by working with other sectors of their community "to try to understand how things really work and what levers for change may exist in them" (p. 224). However, from my perspective, in order to understand how things really work will require knowledge far beyond that which could be gained from partitioning variance into genetic and environmental components. We will need knowledge about all the levels of organization that comprise the ecology of human development and, as well, and perhaps most critically, about the dynamic system of developmental relations that comprise this ecology.

To obtain such knowledge we must go beyond the limits of any one area of scholarship. Indeed, we will have to go beyond the limits of academe. How things really work in the real world involves people from all walks of life. In the end, then, each of our perspectives is limited. To effect important and sustained social changes through our actions, communities of scholars in concert with communities of citizens will have to coalesce to learn how desired individual, family, and societal changes can be created.

In such efforts, we would do well to heed the advice of Horowitz (2000) in regard to how, in the face of the simplistically seductive ideas of hereditarianism, we must find the will to act in a manner supportive of social justice. Horowitz (2000) noted that:

> If we accept as a challenge the need to act with social responsibility then we must make sure that we do not use single-variable words like genes or the notion of innate in such a determinative manner as to give the impression that they constitute the simple answers to the simple questions asked by the Person in the Street lest we contribute to belief systems that will inform social policies that seek to limit experience and opportunity and, ultimately, development, especially when compounded by racism and poorly advantaged circumstances. Or, as Elman and Bates and their colleagues said in the concluding section of their book *Rethinking Innateness* (Elman et al., 1998), "If our careless, under-specified choice of words inadvertently does damage to future generations of children, we cannot turn with innocent outrage to the judge and say 'But your Honor, I didn't realize the word was loaded.'" (p. 8)

The challenge Horowitz articulates is one that is quite real for human development scientists who have been involved in trying to provide ideas and evidence countering the behavior genetics approach to intelligence. The issues involved in this area of controversy are the focus of our discussion in Chapter 11.

11 | *Nature Approaches to Development: The Sample Case of Intelligence and the Work of Sir Cyril Burt and Arthur Jensen*

In the late 1960s, the different average group scores of African-American and European-American children on intelligence tests (i.e., scores that reflected the computation of an "intelligence quotient" or IQ) became a point of major public concern. The mean (i.e., the arithmetic average) difference between these two groups is often reported to be as high as 15 IQ points (e.g., Jensen, 1980; Rushton, 1999; Scarr-Salapatek, 1971a, 1971b) in favor of the European-American children. That is, on standardized intelligence tests, European-American children as a group typically score higher than do African-American children as a group. However, this does not mean that African Americans always do worse on IQ tests than do European Americans. In fact, as Jensen (1973) pointed out:

> Although the average IQ of the Negro population of the United States, for example, is about one standard deviation (i.e., 15 IQ points) below that of the white population, because of the disproportionate sizes of the Negro and white populations, there are more whites with IQs below the Negro average than there are Negroes. (p. 16)

Until the late 1960s, psychologists in the United States interpreted these group differences in IQ scores as being environmentally based. That is, stress was placed on the cultural disadvantages of African Americans; and the leading hypothesis was that a complex of environmental factors associated with poverty—a complex as yet largely undefined—

prevents a child from achieving optimum development (Scarr-Salapatek, 1971a, 1971b). Such environmental disadvantage, it was argued, accounts for the inferior performance of African American children on standardized IQ tests. In essence it was hypothesized that it is not African-American children but their environments that are deficient.

Assuredly, no one could argue against the point that African Americans as a group have experienced a history of inferior and possibly even pernicious environmental circumstances. In fact, in our discussion of social stereotypes in Chapter 4, we saw how environmentally based social attitudes may have a destructive effect on African-Americans' intellectual development. Accordingly, psychologists working with the "environmental-differences" hypothesis have attempted to determine the nature of the environmental variables that led African-American children to inferior performance on IQ tests. They have also contributed to social projects designed to ameliorate African-Americans' environmental disadvantages (e.g., Project Head Start).

THE GENETIC-DIFFERENCES HYPOTHESIS

What brought the IQ score differences between African Americans and European Americans to the general public's attention was that an alternative hypothesis, suggested by Arthur R. Jensen (1969), was offered for investigation. Writing in the *Harvard Educational Review,* Jensen (1969) proposed a genetic-differences hypothesis as an alternative to the aforementioned environmental-differences explanation of the IQ differences between African Americans and European Americans. Jensen suggested that if behavior and characteristics of behavioral functioning (such as intellectual behavior, as indexed by IQ) can be measured and found to have a genetic component, then such behavior can be regarded as no different from other human characteristics, at least insofar as a genetic viewpoint is concerned. Moreover, he asserted that "there seems to be little question that racial differences in genetically conditioned behavioral characteristics, such as mental abilities, should exist, just as physical differences" (Jensen, 1969, p. 80).

This hypothesis, in one form or another, has remarkable persistence in Western culture. For instance, Herrnstein and Murray (1994) and Rushton (1999) reiterated it over a quarter century after Jensen (1969) presented his formulation of the idea—despite, as we discuss in this chapter, the broad and thorough documentation of the egregious conceptual and methodological flaws associated with it. Indeed, Gould (1981, 1996) noted that the idea of genetically based intellectual differences between "racial" groups has not only had a

Arthur R. Jensen

long record of presentation after Jensen (1969) but also a history of more than 100 years before him.

Thus, in 1969, Jensen was only the latest in a long series of scholars contributing to a hereditarian view of the psychological and social differences between racial groups. Accordingly, after reviewing several lines of evidence bearing on the general idea of race differences in intelligence and their possible sources, Jensen (1969) advanced

> a not unreasonable hypothesis that genetic factors are strongly implicated in the average Negro–white intelligence difference. The preponderance of the evidence is, in my opinion, less consistent with a strictly environmental hypothesis than with a genetic hypothesis, which, of course, does not exclude the influence of environment or its interaction with genetic factors. (p. 82)

Thus, Jensen proposed what J. Philippe Rushton (1999), a strong advocate of nature-based race differences, termed a *hereditarian* argument (i.e., that the differences in mean IQ between African Americans and European Americans are not largely due to differences in environmental opportunity but to differences in the gene distributions for these groups) (Scarr-Salapatek, 1971a). In his attempt to support this hypothesis, Jensen presented empirical data bearing on the racial difference in IQ scores and interrelated these findings with data bearing centrally on the concept of heritability.

As discussed in Chapter 10, heritability refers to the proportion of a group's individual differences in a trait (e.g., a psychological characteristic such as intelligence) that is due to the individual genetic differences in that group. If a group of people is given an intelligence test, not everyone in the group will get the same score; there will be differences between people. Simply, heritability is a concept that indicates the percentage (or proportion) of these differences in intelligence test scores that can be attributed to (accounted for by) genetic differences between these people.

Jensen argued that IQ is a highly heritable trait—that is, that individual differences (variation *among* people) in IQ scores within a group are mostly due (e.g., 80%) to the genetic variation in that group. In other words, he pointed out that about 80% of the differences between the people in certain groups are attributable to genetic differences among these people. Therefore, because of these relations, it might seem tenable to argue that because heritability appears to be a genetic concept, the IQ differences between African Americans and European Americans are, in turn, genetically based. Of course, Jensen recognized that most of the studies done to assess the heritability of intelligence had been done on European-American individuals; such estimates—of how much of the differences in IQ scores between members of specific populations can be attributed to genetic differences between these people—cannot be appropriately applied to other populations. Thus, Jensen (1973) pointed out:

> Although one cannot formally generalize from *within*-group heritability to *between*-groups heritability, the evidence from studies of within-group heritability does, in fact, impose severe constraints on some of the most popular environmental theories of the existing racial and social class differences in educational performance. (p. 1)

Thus, although Jensen recognized that it was not perfectly legitimate to attempt to apply heritability findings derived within groups of European Americans to an analysis between these European-American and African-American groups, he still believed that the findings with European Americans were impressive enough to cast doubt on the environmental-differences hypothesis.

As such, Jensen (1969) offered for consideration a hereditarian, genetic-differences hypothesis. He proposed this hypothesis in an attempt to explain why major educational intervention programs such as Head Start were apparently failing in the attempt to raise the IQs of both African-American and European-American lower-class children.

Moreover, Jensen's (1969, 1972) ideas were linked to appeals to consider the import of his hypothesis for the control of the breeding (the reproduction) of what he termed "Negro Americans." We discuss, in Chapter 12, the link between hereditarian claims about the genetic bases of racial differences in mental and behavioral functioning and appeals for selective breeding of humans (i.e., for eugenics). To preview this discussion, we may note here that the work of Konrad Lorenz exemplified the call for such linkages (e.g., Lorenz, 1940a, 1940b, 1943a, 1943b, 1965, 1966). However, Jensen (1969, 1972) held eugenic ideas consistent with those of Lorenz. For instance, Jensen (1969) suggested that:

> Is there a danger that current welfare policies, unaided by eugenic foresight could lead to the genetic enslavement of a substantial segment of our population? The possible consequences of our failure seriously to study these questions may well be viewed by future generations as our society's greatest injustice to Negro Americans. (p. 95)

This issue was of such concern to Jensen that he republished this statement 3 years later (Jensen, 1972).

Given, then, the quite significant scientific and social policy implications that Jensen associated with his hypothesis—implications also noted by reviewers (Goldberger & Manski, 1995; Hirsch, 1997) of later work (Hernstein & Murray, 1994) that drew on Jensen (1969) as a basis for much the same arguments about the genetic bases of race differences in IQ scores—it is important to assess the logical and methodological features of Jensen's hypothesis. Let us follow Hirsch's (1970) analysis of the reasoning used in formulating this hypothesis, and, thus, of the implication that African Americans are genetically inferior to European Americans in intellectual capacity:

1. First, a trait (such as intelligence) is defined.

2. A means of measuring this trait is devised; a psychological test, designed to measure the trait (intelligence), is constructed. Needless to say, if another definition of the trait were offered, and if other tests of the trait were constructed and used, the empirical expression of the trait could be expected to be different. The possibility that the use of different intelligence tests could lead to different findings in terms of African-American–European-American differences in intelligence is important. Intelligence tests do not correlate with each other perfectly; that is, the scores for the same individual on two different intelligence tests are often not exactly equivalent. Therefore, if other tests are given to African-American and European-American populations—tests not standardized exclusively on European-American, middle-class populations, for example, but rather tests that take into account the specificities of the African-American cultural milieu—then the status of racial differences in IQ might be different. Holding the tenability of this point in abeyance, however, let us assume for argument's sake that the same test is used to measure the trait expression in people.

3. Through a series of studies of test scores for this trait done on populations comprised of people of various degrees of kinship (relationship), the heritability of this trait is estimated.

4. Different racial populations are then tested, and their performances on this test of the trait are compared.

5. If the racial populations differ on the test, then because the heritability of the trait measured by the test is now known (and in the case of intelligence has been found to be high), the racial population with the lower mean score is considered to be genetically inferior. (p. 69)

Harrington (1975, 1988) demonstrated crucial flaws in the reasoning associated with Jensen's (1969) hypothesis and, as well, with the scientific procedures/methods pursued to support this reasoning. Harrington (1975, 1988) provided a compelling experimental demonstration showing

> that the very assumptions and procedures employed in psychometric test construction ensure minority-group inferiority and principal-group superiority in testing outcome. With several races ("homogeneous lines") of rats combined in various proportions to comprise different populations (i.e., the same race was a plurality in one, a minority in another, absent in a third, and of intermediate proportions in still other populations), standard psychometric procedures were used to select items to construct a separate intelligence test for each population. When all tests were administered to each race, the test performance of a race was found to be positively correlated with the proportional representation of that race in the base population on which a test had been standardized; that is, races received higher scores on tests derived from populations in which they comprised a plurality and lower scores on others from populations in which they were a minority or absent. (Harrington, 1975, p. 709)

Harrington (1975) interpreted this study as indicating that:

> Generalisation from these data to man is direct and not analogical: the experiment was an empirical test of common psychometric assumptions and procedures. Generalisation is therefore to those assumptions and procedures. The implications are far ranging. Majorities will score higher than minorities as a general artifact of test-construction procedures. Theoretical approaches which ignore the existence of genetic–environment interactions ignore a significant source of individual and of group variation. (p. 709)

On the basis of his formulation of the genetic-differences hypothesis, Jensen (1969) thus suggested that the failure of early intervention programs was due to the high heritability of IQ (see, also, Scarr-Salapatek, 1971a, 1971b). Moreover, because to at least some reviewers of Jensen's ideas (see Jensen, 1973) it was erroneously assumed that high heritability of a trait indicates that the trait is minimally available to environmental influence (see Chapter 10 for a discussion of why this is an incorrect assumption), it followed that (a) because IQ is a highly heritable trait, the environment can have little influence in affecting the expression of that trait; and (b) therefore programs such as Head Start, that attempt to present alternative environmental influences to some children, have little effect because the target of influence is IQ.

The hereditarian, genetic-differences hypothesis is both complex and important; its evaluation is the major burden of the rest of this chapter. In order to evaluate it, we have to understand the limitations of the concept of heritability discussed in Chapter 10 and the specific problems associated with appraising the heritability of intelligence.

ESTIMATING THE HERITABILITY OF INTELLIGENCE

How does one find data pertinent to the inheritance of a human characteristic such as intelligence? Intelligence, if it is inherited, is not believed by *any* scholar to derive from the inheritance of a single pair of genes (Plomin, 1986, 2000; Rushton, 1999). That is, neither nature- nor nurture-oriented scholars contend that a child inherits his or her intelligence by the pairing of just two *alleles* at conception (an allele is a particular form of a gene; the presence of different alleles is responsible for genetic variation), one from the mother and one from the father. Rather, if intelligence is inherited it is a *polygenic* (many-gene) type of inheritance. In addition, intelligence is quite a *plastic* human characteristic; plasticity here refers to the fact that intelligence can take many values (it is a continuous variable), and as such it is distinct from such human characteristics as sex, which, of course, takes only two basic values (male and female; i.e., sex is a discrete variable).

Moreover, study of this polygenic and plastic human characteristic is complicated by the fact that for obvious ethical (and less obvious but important technological) reasons, one cannot do true experimental studies of the relative effects of genes and environment on human intelligence. Such a true experiment might involve holding genes constant and seeing if environmental variation led to changes in IQ scores. If it did, then hereditarians would see this as a problem for their perspective (Rushton, 1999). If it did not—if despite environmental variability a particular set of genes was invariantly related to a particular IQ score—then support for a nature position would be claimed by hereditarians. In turn, one could vary genes, or actually genetic similarity among people, and see if, in comparable environments, any differences are obtained in IQ scores. If such variation was associated with IQ score differences, then hereditarians would contend that support for a nature view was provided. Alternatively, if such genetic variation was not associated with IQ score differences—if, despite differences in genes, people in comparable environments had corresponding IQ scores—then support for the hereditarian position would be diminished.

But, as I have noted, such manipulations cannot be done for ethical and technological reasons. For instance, how could one hold all potentially significant features of the human environment constant? However, variations may naturally occur that present conditions comparable to a true experiment. For example, some children are born as monozygotic (MZ) twins; that is, as noted earlier, after the ovum is fertilized by the sperm, the one zygote that is formed splits into two genetically identical zygotes. Typically, such MZ twins not only have identical genotypes but also quite similar environments; that is, they are usually reared in the same home by the same parents. Thus, for most MZs there is a genes–environment correlation. Imagine, however, that one could locate a group of MZs who were immediately separated after birth (e.g., because of maternal death or because of financial stresses on the family) and placed in two radically different environments. If, despite the twins' rearing in separate and distinct environments, their IQs were quite similar, this would be seen as evidence in support of the hereditarian position (Rushton, 1999). Similarly, if one assessed the naturally occurring resemblance among all types of genetically related people—for instance, MZs, dizygotic twins (i.e., twins born of the same pregnancy but developed from two different fertilized eggs), cousins, and unrelated people—and found that as genetic resemblance decreased (as it does in the above ordering) IQ resemblance also decreased, then that might seem to lend additional support to the hereditarian position.

Although data from true experiments of the role of genes and environment in human intelligence do not exist, approximations (albeit limited ones) of such studies, ones constituting purportedly "natural experiments" (Gould, 1981) do exist. In the main, these data were the ones most relied on by Jensen (1969). Information from such studies provided the key information from which he derived the heritability estimate of 0.8 for human intelligence. As such, let us evaluate the data used by Jensen and others (e.g., Eysenck, in Eysenck & Kamin, 1981a) in these heritability estimates. Here, it is important for both historical and substantive reasons to focus on the role that the writings of Sir Cyril Burt made to the database relied on by Jensen (1969) to discuss the heritability of intelligence.

Although Jensen relied on many data sets pertinent to family resemblance in genes and in IQ scores, he relied most centrally on the information reported by Sir Cyril Burt (1883–1971), who during his lifetime was one of the world's most famous and celebrated psychologists. Burt was the official psychologist of the London County Council for 20 years, where his responsibilities included administration and interpretation of mental tests in the London schools (Gould, 1981, 1996). After this, from 1932 to 1950, he held the most influential professorial chair in psychology in Great Britain, the one in University College, London. For his accomplishments in science and service he was knighted and then, in 1971, given the prestigious Edward Lee Thorndike Award of the American Psychological Association.

During his long career, Burt published numerous papers reporting his research on family resemblance and IQ (e.g., Burt, 1955, 1966). In particular, Burt's work involved reports of assessments of a relatively large sample (i.e., large considering their seeming rarity) of MZs reared apart (e.g., Burt, 1955, 1958, 1966; Conway, 1958). The findings that Burt reported from this research were such as to lend strong support to the hereditarian position.

Thus, not only because of his positive scientific reputation but also because of the scope of his research and the nature of his findings, Burt's reports were heavily relied on by Jensen (1969). As such, in order to begin our evaluation of the scientific database used in support of the heritability of IQ, and of the genetic-differences hypothesis, let us first turn our attention to the work of Cyril Burt.

THE WORK OF SIR CYRIL BURT

Why were the Burt data of such importance to Jensen's (1969) argument and to any assertion that most of the variance in intelligence is associated with one's genotype? The evolutionary biologist Stephen J. Gould (1981) in his typically engaging style, answered these questions by noting:

> If I had any desire to lead a life of indolent ease, I would wish to be an identical twin, separated at birth from my brother and raised in a different social class. We could hire ourselves out to a host of social scientists and practically name our fee. For we would be exceedingly rare representatives of the only really adequate natural experiment for separating genetic from environmental effects in humans—genetically identical individuals raised in disparate environments.
>
> Studies of identical twins raised apart should therefore hold pride of place in literature on the inheritance of IQ. And so it would be but for one problem—the extreme rarity of the animal itself. Few investigations have been able to rustle up more

than twenty pairs of twins. Yet, amidst this paltri-ness, one study seemed to stand out: that of Sir Cyril Burt (1883–1971).

During his long retirement, Sir Cyril published several papers that buttressed the hereditarian claim by citing very high correlation between IQ scores of identical twins raised apart. Burt's study stood out among all others because he had found fifty-three pairs, more than twice the total of any previous attempt. It is scarcely surprising that Arthur Jensen used Sir Cyril's figures as the most important datum in his notorious article (1969) on supposedly inherited and ineradicable differences in intelligence between whites and blacks in America.

The story of Burt's undoing is now more than a twice-told tale. Princeton psychologist Leon Kamin first noted that, while Burt had increased his sample of twins from fewer than twenty to more than fifty in a series of publications, the average correlation between pairs for IQ remained unchanged to the third decimal place—a statistical situation so unlikely that it matches our vernacular definition of impossible. (pp. 234–235)

It is useful to review the information that Kamin (1974) found as he reviewed Burt's (1955, 1958, 1966; Conway, 1958) publications. This information reveals so many major problems with Burt's work that a close and fair scrutiny of it will indicate that "the apparent evidence for IQ heritability will evaporate to nothing" (Kamin, 1974, p. 35).

Kamin (1974) noted that the Burt study would seem to be impressive and important in several ways. Not only did it purport to study more twin pairs than any of the other three similar studies for which quantitative evidence was available when Kamin did his review (i.e., the studies by Juel-Nielsen, 1965; Newman, Freeman, & Holzinger, 1937; and Shields, 1962), but also the Burt study reported the largest correlation between the separated MZ twins. These two features of the Burt study (its larger sample and the higher correlation found) are displayed in Table 11.1, which also presents the corresponding information for the other three studies reviewed by Kamin (1974). Kamin noted, too, that the most important—and a unique feature of Burt's (1955, 1958, 1966) study—is that it claims to provide quantitative evidence that the environments in which the separated twins were reared were not at all correlated.

If the environments of the separated twins were correlated, one might be able to attribute any similarity in their IQ scores to the experience of being reared in comparable settings; however, if there was no similarity between their environments, then it is argued that only their genetic similarity could account for any correspondence in their IQs. We should recall a point about the computation of heritability discussed in Chapter 10, that is, that for the hereditarian position to be supported, it is also important that genotype not *interact* with environment. If such interactions occurred, they would diminish the impact of genes alone in the determination of IQ scores. Later in this chapter, we return to the issue of whether it is possible to determine—*in studies of human intelligence*— whether genotype and environment are uncorrelated, or whether they do not interact. If one cannot empirically demonstrate these two points or if one cannot legitimately assume the two points to be the case, then it would not be possible to assert unequivocally that it was primarily genetic similarity that provided the basis for correspondences in IQ scores. Here, however, we should reemphasize the point that Burt's study was unique in offering quantitative evidence that the environments of the separated MZ twins were uncorrelated. In short, there seemed to be several quite distinct and important attributes of Burt's (1955, 1958, 1966) study, and because of these "assets," it is clear why Burt's study played such a central role in Jensen's (1969) argument.

But what of the scientific adequacy of Burt's "data"? Kamin (1974) noted that Burt's study of

TABLE 11.1
IQ Correlations in Four Studies of Separated MZ Twins

Study	Test	Correlation	Number of pairs
Burt (1955, 1958, 1966)	"Individual Test"	0.86	53
Shields (1962)	Dominos + 2 × Mill Hill	0.77	37
Newman, Freeman, and Holzinger (1937)	Stanford-Binet	0.67	19
Juel-Nielsen (1965)	Wechsler	0.62	12

Source: Adapted from Kamin (1974, p. 35).

separated MZ twins was part of a larger research effort aimed at accumulating IQ data for several categories of biological relationships (e.g., parent–child and uncle–nephew). Over the years, as the sample size for each category of biological relationship grew, the correlations were reported in a series of publications. But here is where the purported scientific importance of Burt's data begins to unravel. Kamin (1974) indicated that the series of publications by Burt

contain virtually no information about the methods employed in testing IQ, but the correlations were usually reported to three decimal places. They were astonishingly stable, seeming scarcely to fluctuate as the sample size was changed. Two forms of such stability are illustrated in Table 11.2, which reproduces data contained in Burt's 1955 and 1966 reports.

The intelligence correlations were reported in three forms: for "group test," for "individual test," and for "final assessment." There is, as we shall see, much ambiguity concerning what these terms mean.

This remarkable stability also characterized the unknown "group test" of intelligence which Burt administered to his separated MZ twins. Table 11.3 reproduces the correlations reported by Burt on that test for MZ twins reared apart, and for MZ twins reared together. The table includes data from a 1958 paper by Burt and a 1958 paper by Conway, as well as data from Burt's 1955 and 1966 papers. The sample sizes increased over time by 32 pairs for MZs reared apart, and 12 pairs for MZs reared together. There is a minor perturbation which simultaneously afflicted both correlations in late 1958, but a benign Providence appears to have smiled upon Professor Burt's labors. When he concluded his work in 1966,

his three decimal place correlations were back to where they had been in the beginning. The 1943 paper had contained his first reference to separated MZs. Then, for 15 pairs, the correlation had been reported as 0.77.

Burt, often without specific acknowledgment, employed "adjusted assessments" of IQ rather than raw test scores. The reader must be sharp-eyed to detect this on occasion. The 1956 Burt and Howard paper reported correlations for "assessments of intelligence" for 963 parent–child pairs, 321 grandparent–grandchild pairs, 375 uncle–nephew pairs, etc. The term "assessments" was not defined, and the description of procedure is characteristic of Burt. "The sources for the latter [assessments], the procedures employed, and the results obtained have already been described in previous publications (Burt, 1955, and refs.)." The Burt and Howard paper, which has been very widely read and cited, goes on to fit a mathematical–genetic model of inheritance to the reported correlations. The fit is excellent.

The reader who troubles to refer to the 1955 paper will discover that many of the 1956 results were not reported there, and he will also discover that the entire description of procedure is contained in a footnote. The footnote includes the following sentence: "For the assessments of the parents we relied chiefly on personal interviews; but in doubtful or borderline cases an open or a camouflaged test was employed." That sentence bears pondering. The scores of children, on the other hand, were "based primarily on verbal and non-verbal tests of intelligence . . . transformed into standard scores . . . for each age converted to terms of an IQ scale. Whatever ambiguity exists in the case of children, clearly the intelligence of adults was simply guessed at in the course of a personal interview. The spectacle of Professor

TABLE 11.2
Correlations Reported by Burt

	Siblings reared apart		DZs reared together	
	1955 (N = 131)	1966 (N = 151)	1955 (N = 172)	1966 (N = 127)
Intelligence				
Group test	0.441	0.412	0.542	0.552
Individual test	0.463	0.423	0.526	0.527
Final assessment	0.517	0.438	0.551	0.453
School attainment				
Reading, spelling	0.490	0.490	0.915	0.919
Arithmetic	0.563	0.563	0.748	0.748
General	0.526	0.526	0.831	0.831
Physical				
Height	0.536	0.536	0.472	0.472
Weight	0.427	0.427	0.586	0.586

Note. N refers to number of pairs, as reported by Burt.
Source: Kamin (1974, p. 37).

TABLE 11.3
Correlations for MZ Twins, "Group Test" of Intelligence

Source	Twins reared apart	Twins reared together
Burt, 1955	0.771 ($N = 21$)	0.944 ($N = 83$)
Burt, 1958	0.771 ($N = $ "over 30")	0.944 ($N = $?)
Conway, 1958	0.778 ($N = 42$)	0.936 ($N = $?)
Burt, 1966	0.771 ($N = 53$)	0.944 ($N = 95$)

Source: Kamin (1974, p. 38).

Burt administering a camouflaged test of intelligence to a London grandparent has considerable comic merit, but it does not inspire scientific confidence. The only reported IQ correlation between uncle and nephew in the entire scientific literature appears to be Burt's, obtained in this survey in this way.

The same survey was cited by Burt and Howard in 1957, who in reply to a critic stressed that "in each of our surveys, assessments were individually obtained for a representative sample of parents, checked, for purposes of standardization, by tests of the usual type." The 1955 footnote is cited. There is some ambiguity in the meaning of "for purposes of standardization"; but it is entirely clear that over two years Professor Burt's memory had magically transmuted "doubtful or borderline cases" to "a representative sample of parents." The "open or a camouflaged test" of 1955 had become by 1957 "tests of the usual type." Professor Burt, we may conclude, was not always precise in his use of language. The procedural ambiguities are no less marked in the case of Burt's 53 pairs of separated MZ twins. These cases had been gradually accumulated over a period of some 45 years. The most explicit and extended discussion of the twin data was given in Burt's 1966 paper. That paper indicates that all the twins had been separated before the age of 6 months, but it contains no information about the extent or duration of separation. There is no information about the sexes of the twin pairs, nor is their age at testing indicated. They were all, however, "children," and except in three cases "the tests were applied in school." Three very early cases had been dropped from the sample because of a relatively late age of separation. There were, "in the initial survey," some children outside London "originally tested by the local teacher or school doctor, but these have all been since retested by Miss Conway." We are not told whether Miss Conway's test results corresponded to the teachers', nor whether discrepancies were averaged, or handled in some other way. (pp. 37–40)

Because of these egregious scientific deficits in Burt's (1955, 1958, 1966) study, Kamin (1974,

p. 41) summarized by simply indicating that "we do not know what was correlated with what in order to produce the coefficient of .77" between MZ twins reared apart (as shown in Table 11.3). In sum, I agree with Kamin's (1974) overall appraisal that:

> The conclusion seems not to require further documentation, which exists in abundance. The absence of procedural description in Burt's reports vitiates their scientific utility. The frequent arithmetical inconsistencies and mutually contradictory descriptions cast doubt upon the entire body of his later work. The marvelous consistency of his data supporting the hereditarian position often taxes credibility; and on analysis, the data are found to contain implausible effects consistent with an effort to prove the hereditarian case. The conclusion cannot be avoided: The numbers left behind by Professor Burt are simply not worthy of our current scientific attention. (p. 47)

Reactions to Kamin's (1974) Analysis and Subsequent Developments

Many of Burt's supporters and/or advocates of the hereditarian position, in regard to this issue, reacted unfavorably to Kamin's (1974) work (for a detailed history of this reaction, see Hirsch, 1981). For example, some of those sympathetic to Burt's position denigrated Kamin's competence and claimed that his motives in writing his critique were purely political. For example, Hans J. Eysenck, whose own work in this area we consider shortly, wrote to Burt's sister and said that (quoted in Gould, 1981):

> I think the whole affair is just a determined effort on the part of some very left-wing environmentalists determined to play a political game with scientific facts. I am sure the future will uphold the honor and integrity of Sir Cyril without any question. (p. 234)

In turn, some of Burt's defenders acknowledged that Burt's work and publications may have included some errors, but attributed this to the poor memory and unfortunate carelessness of an aging and infirm scholar (e.g., Jensen, 1974; see, also, Gould, 1981, 1996, and Hirsch, 1981, for a discussion of this reaction).

But on October 24, 1976, Oliver Gillie, medical correspondent of the London *Sunday Times,* wrote a front-page story with the headline "Pioneer of IQ Faked His Research Findings," which presented information that, as Gould (1981) put it

> elevated the charge from inexcusable carelessness to conscious fakery. Gillie discovered, among many other things, that Burt's two "collaborators," a Margaret Howard and a J. Conway, the women who supposedly collected and processed his data, either never existed at all, or at least could not have been in contact with Burt while he wrote the papers bearing their names. These charges led to further reassessments of Burt's "evidence" for his rigid hereditarian position. Indeed, other crucial studies were equally fraudulent, particularly his IQ correlations between close relatives (suspiciously too good to be true and apparently constructed from ideal statistical distributions, rather than measured in nature (Dorfman, 1978), and his data for declining levels of intelligence in Britain. (p. 235)

The Burt issue may be resolved by the findings made and conclusions drawn in a biography of him written by L. S. Hearnshaw (1979) and authorized by Burt's sister before the "scandal" about Burt began to appear. As summarized by Goldberger (1980), prior to beginning work on the biography Hearnshaw's assessment of Burt was

> almost wholly favorable. But as he worked through the large collection of Burt's writings, correspondence, memoranda, diaries, lecture notes, and other material made available to him, Hearnshaw "became convinced that the charges against Burt were, in their essentials, valid."
>
> Herewith some specifics. First, on the separated identical twins, "no data were collected between 1955 and 1966," the period during which Burt claimed to have increased his sample size from 21 pairs to 53 pairs. (On my reading, there is no evidence that the first 21 pairs were any more real.) Second, on the mystery women: "of the more than forty 'persons' who contributed reviews, notes and letters to the journal during the period of Burt's editorship, well over half are unidentifiable, and judging from the style and content of their contributions were pseudonyms for Burt. Howard and Conway were members of a large family of characters invented."
>
> Third, and most intriguing, on the list of individual IQ scores and social class for the 53 pairs of separated identical twins: Christopher Jencks, having seen the summary-statistics from this sample in

Burt's publications, wrote in December 1968 to ask for the individual figures in order to undertake some regression analysis for his book in progress, *Inequality.* (Jensen, who had many visits and discussions with Burt, never attained that advanced level of curiosity.) Seven weeks later, Burt sent the list with a covering letter which began, "I apologize for not replying more promptly; but I was away for the Christmas vacation, and college (where the data are stored) was closed until the opening of term."

But Hearnshaw reports, "As a matter of fact Burt had not been away for Christmas; his data were not stored at college; and the college had only been closed for a week. . . . According to his diary Burt spent the whole week from 2 January 1969 onwards 'calculating data on twins for Jencks.' . . . Had the IQ scores and social class gradings been available they could have been copied out in half an hour at the most. So quite clearly the table of IQ scores and social class gradings was an elaborately constructed piece of work." (I confess to some sympathy with Burt at this point: at the age of 86, he was faced with the task of making up 53 pairs of numbers consistent with the mean, standard deviation, and correlation coefficient which he had previously published.)

On the cross-tabulation of fathers' and sons' IQs by social class, Hearnshaw reviews the evidence and finds that "there is no doubt that Burt's reporting of his sources and methods was grossly inadequate, and little doubt that the data he possessed had been subjected to a good deal of 'adjustment.'" (Here Hearnshaw left one avenue of investigation unexplored. In *Science* [29 September 1978], D. D. Dorfman gave a persuasive demonstration that the source of Burt's table was the formula for the bivariate normal distribution function rather than a representative sample of British men.)

Hearnshaw's study of Burt's private papers thus documents what would have been apparent to any thoughtful reader of Burt's public papers: while his figures may have been numbers, they were surely not data. It is remarkable that they passed as data—indeed as crucial data—for so many years. (p. 62)

Indeed, Goldberger's (1980) last point was also raised by Gould (1981) in his own comments about the Hearnshaw (1979) biography. Gould noted that the discovery of such seemingly obviously flawed data "does not touch the deeper issue of why such patently manufactured data went unchallenged for so long, and what this will to believe implies about the basis of our hereditarian presuppositions" (Gould, 1981, p. 236).

One point that is obviously implied is that the power of this presupposition may lead those holding it to misrepresent and distort information. As a case in point, Hirsch (1981) noted that the "balance sheet on Burt" published by the British Psychological Society (Gillie, 1980, p. 12):

documents the following "falsehoods" propounded by . . . Jensen in the attempt to "cover-up" the Burt scandal:

1. Jensen said that Professor Hearnshaw had "located some of the identical twins reared apart, tested by Burt and Margaret Howard." This is quite untrue.

2. Jensen suggested that I was related in some way to Professor William Stephenson, a student of Burt who had quarreled with him. This is untrue.

3. Jensen said that Margaret Howard was a faculty member of the Mathematics Department of the University of London yet there is absolutely no evidence for this.

4. Finally, Jensen attributed political motives to all Burt's detractors, whether or not he had met them, saying that "anyone who has had any contact with them, or even lunch with them knows . . . in the first 15 minutes." However, Jensen had never met the Clarkes nor me. And if he could tell me my own political position after 15 minutes I would be grateful because I am not clear what it is myself. (p. 31)

Earlier, in his discussion of "Burt's Missing Ladies" in *Science*, Gillie (1979, p. 1036) documented another Jensen fabrication. "Conway's case is . . . curious. No one . . . knows anything . . . about her . . . Jensen has given her the name Jane . . . but I can find no documentary evidence for this forename." (Hirsch, 1981, p. 31).

In sum, the directions in which people's hereditarian presuppositions may lead them reflects, as some reviews of Jensen's (1969) work (e.g., Hirsch, 1975) have noted, the bankruptcy of science when it is conducted without adequate scholarship. A situation may result wherein scholarly scrupulosity is lost in the presence of gross misrepresentations of facts (Hirsch, 1975, 1976a, 1976b; see, too, Goldberger & Manski, 1995). As such, we may conclude that the events following Kamin's (1974) presentations about Burt's study did nothing to diminish the appropriateness of Kamin's conclusions. In fact, Gillie's reports (1976, 1979, 1980) and Hearnshaw's biography (1979) buttressed Kamin's (1974) view that Burt's "evidence" was not evidence at all. Indeed, although we will not treat the other three studies that Kamin (1974) reviewed (Juel-Nielsen, 1965; Newman, Freeman, & Holzinger, 1937; Shields, 1962) in any detail here, the data they provide—although not faked—do not provide any better evidence for high IQ heritability. Thus, Kamin (1974) closed his review of these studies with a position with which I must agree:

The four separated MZ twin studies reviewed in this chapter led Professor Jensen (1970, p. 146) to conclude: "The overall intraclass correlation . . . 824 . . . may be interpreted as an upper-bound estimate of the heritability of I.Q. in the English, Danish, and North American Caucasian populations sampled in these studies." The conclusion of our own review is vastly different. We have seen that Burt's data, reporting by far the strongest hereditarian effects, are riddled with arithmetical inconsistencies and verbal contradictions. The few descriptions of how the data were collected are mutually inconsistent, as are the descriptions of "tests" employed. The "assessments" of IQ are tainted with subjectivity. The utter failure to provide information about procedural detail can only be described as cavalier. There can be no science that accepts such data as its base.

To the degree that the case for a genetic influence on IQ scores rests on the celebrated studies of separated twins, we can justifiably conclude that there is no reason to reject the hypothesis that IQ is simply not heritable. (pp. 66–67)

OTHER DATA IN SUPPORT OF THE HEREDITARIAN POSITION

Data from MZ twins reared apart may be the best, but are not the only evidence that may be used to support the hereditarian position. These less-direct potential bases of support have been reviewed by Goldberger (1980; see, too, Goldberger & Manski, 1995), Gould (1981, 1996), Kamin (1974, 1980), and Layzer (1974, 2000). These reviewers do not lead us to alter our position regarding the apparently minimal level of support for the hereditarian position. Nevertheless, it is useful to bolster this conclusion by briefly discussing other lines of work purporting to provide evidence for the hereditarian position.

Correlations Between IQ and Amplitude and Latency of Evoked Potentials

Hans J. Eysenck (1979, 1980), whose views about the Burt "case" we noted earlier, has been a strong advocate of the hereditarian position. In his 1979 book, *The Structure and Measurement of Intelligence*, Eysenck made the claim that culture-bound intelligence tests are appropriate for selection/admission of students into schools because "we're often justified in assuming considerable uniformity in cultural background among candidates" (1979, p. 23). However, Eysenck (1979) provided no support for this belief in cultural uniformity.

What he did do was describe evidence that a feature of brain functioning that, he believes, is not influenced by cultural variables is highly related to scores on culture-bound tests. The feature of brain functioning on which he focuses is "evoked cortical potentials," an index of the brain's activity in response to stimulation. Eysenck claimed that evoked cortical potentials with higher amplitude and shorter latencies indicate greater or more efficient processing of stimulus input. Thus, for instance, he would expect a high negative correlation between latency of response and IQ score, a finding that would indicate that people with higher IQs processed information more rapidly. Such is the nature of the findings that Eysenck reported.

However, Dorfman (1980) noted:

> The figures that he displays in support of a strong correlation are taken from Ertl's early work which even Eysenck admits "suffered from technical and methodological deficiencies" (p. 50). He then asserts that Shucard and Horn have also obtained "quite sizable correlations between AEP's [averaged evoked potentials] and IQ" (p. 50). In fact, those investigators reported a correlation of only 0.24 for fluid intelligence and an absence of correlation for crystallized intelligence in the article cited by Eysenck. He also presents data from "our own laboratories" collected in about 1973. No details are given and no reference is made to any relevant publications in scholarly journals. (p. 643)

In 1980, Eysenck again misrepresented the character of the literature pertaining to the correlation between IQ and evoked cortical potentials. Gould (1980) wrote a review of a book of Jensen's (*Bias in Mental Testing,* 1980), wherein Gould criticized the evidence in support of a strong biologically based general factor of intelligence. Commenting on Gould's (1980) review, Eysenck (1980) asserted:

> One line of evidence which has become very important in recent years, and which supports the hypothesis of the strong general factor of intelligence, is work with non-cognitive tests, such as measures of reaction time, speed and sensory discrimination, and in particular EEG evoked potentials. None of these are tainted by cultural factors, and all are reactions to simple sensory stimuli, yet they all correlate highly with IQ as measured by traditional tests. In our own recent work, EEG evoked potentials show correlations with Wechsler IQ as high as does the Wechsler IQ with, say, the Binet IQ. In other words, non-cognitive tests of this kind, which aim to disclose the biological basis of intelligence, correlate as highly with IQ tests as these correlate with each other. (p. 52)

Eysenck (1980) did not cite any specific scientific literature that supports these claims. Fortunately, however, although Eysenck (1980, p. 52) characterized Gould as "little more than an amateur in this field" and noted that being able to

adequately review books on psychology requires "a degree of knowledge and expertise which outsiders simply do not possess," it was Gould who cited the relevant studies and, as such, let the data speak for themselves. Gould (1980) indicated that Eysenck (1980) contended

> that IQ would be affirmed as a measure of "intelligence" if it correlates strongly with basic, neurological reactions of the brain that cannot (so he claims) be attributed to cultural or environmental differences. These include: (1) reaction time (in which an experimenter measures how long it takes a subject to react to a stimulus—time from seeing a flashing light to pushing a button, for example); and (2) EEG evoked potentials (in which an experimenter attaches electrodes to a subject's head and records the timing and intensity of electrical responses within his brain to various stimuli). Eysenck then makes a specific claim about such studies that they correlate as highly with IQ tests as various IQ tests correlate with each other. Ignoramus that I am, I dare not venture into this area of psychological professionalism. So let me, instead, simply cite the contrary opinions of an expert namely, Arthur Jensen. In *Bias in Mental Testing,* the book that I reviewed, Jensen summarizes [p. 314] many studies on the correlation of Wechsler IQ with Binet IQ, the two tests that Eysenck chooses as his standard. Average correlation is 0.77 for Binet with the Wechsler adult scale (WAIS) and 0.80 for Binet with WISC (Wechsler Intelligence Scale for Children). These high correlations are scarcely surprising since all these tests use similar material, and are constructed with the same end in mind.
>
> On the correlation of IQ with reaction time (an area of Jensen's primary research), Jensen writes [p. 691]: "Neither I nor anyone else, to my knowledge, has been able to get correlations larger than about -0.4 to -0.5 between choice RT [reaction time] and IQ, with typical correlations in the -0.3 to -0.4 range, using reasonable-sized samples." (The correlations are appropriately negative because short reaction time is supposed to accompany more intelligence. But they are much lower than the 278Wechsler–Binet correlation, not equal to it as Eysenck claims. The correlation coefficient, by the way, is a peculiar statistic with a highly asymmetrical distribution that compresses differences at the upper end and magnifies them at the lower end. Thus, a correlation of 0.4 is not "half as good" as one of 0.8, but substantially less intense.)
>
> Jensen is even more dubious about the literature on evoked potential, for he writes [p. 709]: "The AEP average evoked potential and IQ research picture soon becomes a thicket of seemingly inconsistent and confusing findings, confounded variables, methodological differences, statistically questionable conclusions, unbridled theoretical speculation, and, not surprisingly, considerable controversy." The only correlations he cites between IQ tests and evoked

potentials average −0.28 with none higher than −0.35 (again, appropriately negative since less time between a stimulus and responding brain waves supposedly records more intelligence—but again vastly less than the Wechsler–Binet correlation, not equal to it). The −0.28 may be statistically "significant," but vernacular and statistical meanings of the word "significant" are quite unrelated. A statistically "significant" correlation is not necessarily a strong one, but only one that can be adequately discriminated from a value of zero, or no correlation.

The relevant measure, in this case, is the coefficient of determination, or r^2 (the correlation coefficient times itself). An r of −0.28 means that variation in evoked potential accounts for a whopping 8 percent (−0.28) (−0.28, or 0.0784) of the variation in measured IQ! Jensen then casts further doubt upon the literature of evoked potentials [p. 709]: "Visual and auditory AEPs seem to yield quite different, even contrary results, visual latencies usually being negatively correlated with IQ, and auditory latencies being positively correlated. The directions of correlations also seem to flip-flop according to whether the IQs of the sample involved in the study are distributed mostly in the below-average range or mostly in the above-average range of IQs."

But even if the correlations were as high as Eysenck claimed, what would it mean? It wouldn't validate a notion of inborn general intelligence. Who can say that childhood nutrition (both gastronomical and educational) does not affect the growing brain and induce variation equally recorded by reaction time and performance on mental tests? (pp. 52–53)

In sum, the contention that some measure of cortical activity provides an index of biological functioning "untainted" by cultural factors is not a sound one. In turn, the purported evidence that measures of evoked cortical potentials are highly correlated with measures of IQ is as illusory as Burt's data about IQ resemblance among MZ twins reared apart. Neither Burt's study (1955, 1958, 1966; Conway, 1958) nor Eysenck's assertions (1979, 1980) provide adequate scientific data to support the hereditarian position.

Reviews of Familial Studies of Intelligence After the Burt "Scandal"

Both before and after the Burt "scandal" surfaced, several summaries were published of the world literature on IQ correlations between relatives. For instance, Erlenmeyer-Kimling and Jarvik (1963) published such a review that, unfortunately, included Burt's reports on MZ twins reared apart as well as his reports on the correlations found for people of other types of relationship (e.g., uncle–nephew correlations). Later reviews

Matthew McGue

were published by Roubertoux and Carlier (1978), Plomin and DeFries (1980), Bouchard and McGue (1981), Herrnstein and Murray (1994), and Rushton (1999). The review by Bouchard and McGue (1981) is comprehensive and was also subjected to peer review prior to its publication in the prestigious scientific journal, *Science*. Thus, to evaluate the quality of the evidence for the genetic determination of intelligence, it is useful to consider this review in some detail.

The results of the Bouchard and McGue (1981) review are summarized in Table 11.4. The table summarizes their analysis of 111 studies that reported family resemblances in intelligence. Across these studies there were 526 familial correlations based on 113,942 pairings. Table 11.4 summarizes those correlations between both biological and adoptive relatives by using a vertical bar to indicate the median correlation for each type of relationship (e.g., MZ twins reared together, MZ twins reared apart, etc.). In addition, a small arrow is used to indicate the correlation by a simple genetic model of no dominance, no assortative mating, and no environmental effects. The reason Bouchard and McGue (1981, p. 1055) displayed the predictions derived from such a model is that such a model "provides a noncontroversial pattern against which to compare the results of various familial groupings. Different investigators will undoubtedly fit different models to the data."

TABLE 11.4
Familial Correlations for IQ

	No. of correlations	No. of pairings	Median correlation	Weighted aver. age	χ^2 (d.f.)	χ^2 d.f.
Monozygotic twins reared together	34	4,672	0.85	0.86	81.29 (33)	2.41
Monozygotic twins reared apart	3	65	0.67	0.72	0.92 (2)	0.41
Midparent–midoffspring reared together	8	410	0.73	0.72	2.66 (2)	1.3
Midparent–offspring reared together	8	992	0.475	0.50	8.11 (7)	1.1
Dizygotic twins reared together	41	5,546	0.58	0.60	94.5 (40)	2.31
Siblings reared together	69	26,473	0.45	0.47	403.6 (64)	6.3
Siblings reared apart	2	203	0.24	0.24	.02 (1)	0.02
Single parent–offspring reared together	32	8,133	0.385	0.42	211.0 (1)	6.8
Single parent–offspring reared apart	4	814	0.22	0.22	9.61 (3)	3.20
Half-siblings	2	200	0.35	0.31	1.55 (1)	1.5
Cousins	4	1,176	0.145	0.15	1.02 (2)	0.5
Nonbiological sibling pairs (adopted/natural pairings)	5	345	0.29	0.29	1.93 (4)	0.41
Nonbiological sibling pairs (adopted/adopted pairings)	6	369	0.31	0.34	10.5 (5)	2.1
Adopting midparent–offspring	6	758	0.19	0.24	6.8 (5)	1.3
Adopting parent–offspring	6	1,397	0.18	0.19	6.64 (5)	1.3
Assortative mating	16	3,817	0.365	0.33	96.1 (15)	6.4

Note. The vertical bar in each distribution indicates the median correlation; the arrow, the correlation predicted by a simple polygenic model.
Source: Bouchard and McGue (1981, p. 1056).

The issue of modeling these data is a key one, and later in this chapter I discuss whether it is possible to adequately model genetic effects on human intelligence using family resemblance data and, if so, whether such a model has ever been used. Here, however, note that the reason it is important to present a model of the inheritance of intelligence is that without the use of a model one cannot appraise the extent to which a given set of correlations supports a hereditarian view of intelligence. In other words, the model here serves as a template; it specifies the nature of the family correlations that would occur if genetic similarity alone accounted for any observed correlations. Obtained correlations are then compared to what is predicted in the model, and to the extent that the model is useful the empirical findings will match the predictions made by the model. Thus, to support a hereditarian position, it is crucial that the model be a conceptually and technically (i.e., mathematically) appropriate means to portray the role of genes in human intelligence.

To anticipate our forthcoming discussion, the inadequacy of such models is the fatal flaw with using family resemblance data, such as in Table 11.4. However, we should note here that Bouchard and McGue (1981) interpreted the pattern of average correlations displayed in Table 11.4 as being consistent with what would be predicted with a model of "polygenic inheritance. That is, the higher the proportion of genes two family members have in common, the higher the average correlation between their IQs" (p. 1055). But, as Bouchard and McGue (1981) pointed out and as we, too, shall see, there are many features of the information presented in Table 11.4 that diminish the strength of their interpretation. First, "the individual data points are quite heterogeneous" (p. 1055) within any category of family resemblance. This means that for a group of relatives of a common type of relationship (e.g., MZs reared together or MZs reared apart), their invariant degree of genetic resemblance is not invariantly related to a given degree of IQ resemblance! Although some of this variability may be produced by differences across studies in the tests used to assess intelligence, Bouchard and McGue (1981, p. 1056) reported, "We do not have sufficient data to determine whether the magnitude of the familial correlation is moderated by the specific test used."

Thus, it remains quite plausible that, within a given category of genetic resemblance, environmental interactions moderate levels of IQ resemblance. In addition, we should note that the heterogeneity of "within-genetic-resemblance-category family member" correlations presents a

formidable problem for those who seek to model genetic influences on human intelligence through the use of such data (Goldberger, 1979).

Here, we should emphasize that there are additional features of the information in Table 11.4 that mitigate the power of a genetic model and that, in turn, implicate the role of the environment. For instance, Bouchard and McGue (1981) pointed out that DZ twins of the same sex have more similar IQs than do DZ twins of the opposite sex. They saw this as possibly reflecting a social effect wherein same-sex DZ twins are treated more similarly by their parents than are opposite-sex DZ twins.

In addition, Bouchard and McGue (1981) noted that the weighted average correlation for 34 correlations reported on 4,672 MZs *reared together* was 0.86, and that 79% of the 34 correlations were above 0.80. They concluded that such a finding "convincingly demonstrates the remarkable similarity of monozygotic twins" (Bouchard & McGue, 1981, p. 1057); but we must expand this conclusion to underscore the point that these findings are for MZs reared in the same environment. Not only do these twins share the same genotype but they are also of the same sex (and recall that DZs of the same sex have higher IQ resemblances than do opposite-sex DZs) and are born at the same time. Moreover, the weighted average correlation for MZs reared apart is 0.72 and Bouchard and McGue (1981, p. 1056) recognized that this value "is much less than that found for the monozygotic twins reared together, the differences suggesting the importance of between-family environmental differences." However, Bouchard and McGue (1981, p. 1056) said that "at the same time, the magnitude of this correlation would be difficult to explain on the basis of any strictly environmental hypothesis."

Of course, developmental systems theorists (e.g., Gottlieb, 1997; Horowitz, 2000; Magnusson, 1999a, 1999b; Overton, 1998; Thelen & Smith, 1998) would agree about the uselessness of a *strictly* environmental hypothesis. In turn, I would assume that, except for the most ardent genetic reductionists, most supporters of the hereditarian position would not dispute the uselessness of a *strictly* genetic hypothesis (e.g., see Plomin, 2000). Nevertheless, I must disagree with Bouchard and McGue's (1981) implication that the weighted average of 0.72 for IQ resemblance among separated MZs provides good support for the hereditarian position. There are two reasons for my disagreement. First, Bouchard and McGue (1981) obtained the weighted correlation of 0.72 from the reports of three separate investigations. That is, Burt's "data" were deleted and they were left with test results from three other studies on 65 pairs of MZs reared apart. Were these the three studies summarized by Kamin (1974) and noted in Table 11.1 of this chapter? Bouchard and McGue (1981) did not indicate in their review the particular three studies they used to identify the 65 cases and obtain the weighted correlation of 0.72. The three studies (other than Burt's) noted in Table 11.1 of this chapter (Juel-Nielsen, 1965; Newman, Freeman, & Holzinger, 1937; Shields, 1962) have a combined sample of 68. It may be that all or some of the data from one or all of these three studies were part of the data of the unknown three studies summarized by Bouchard and McGue (1981). Unfortunately, we cannot tell from their review if this is the case. Given the inadequate scientific characteristics (Kamin, 1974) of the studies by Juel-Nielsen (1965), Newman, Freeman, and Holzinger (1937), and Shields (1962), however, we can have no confidence in the accuracy of the weighted correlation of 0.72 *if* these studies in any way contributed to the weighted correlation. In turn, given the methodological problems of studies of MZs reared apart (Kamin, 1974), we should in any event be particularly cautious about relying on such studies unless all their research procedures are fairly and openly evaluated; such evaluation was not part of the report by Bouchard and McGue (1981; e.g., see Footnote 8, pp. 1058–1059).[1]

Indeed, the particular methodological problems of studies of MZ twins reared apart are the second reason for my disagreement with Bouchard and McGue (1981). These problems have been, of course, discussed by Kamin (1974) and Farber (1981; see, also, Gruber, 1981), who did a reanalysis of all the major studies of MZs reared apart, excluded the doubtful cases (e.g., those of Burt) according to clear and objective criteria, and then attempted to evaluate the information provided by the remaining sample of 95 MZs reared apart. Farber (1981) noted that, across the several studies she reviewed, about 90% of the twin pairs were *selected for inclusion in the study on the basis of known similarities between them.* In other words, MZs who were not similar (along dimensions of interest to the researcher) were systematically and intentionally excluded from the study. Farber estimated that currently there are about 600 pairs of MZ twins being reared apart in the United States alone. Thus, the technique of *a priori* systematic exclusion of dissimilar separated MZs is not only incongruent with an unbiased and objective scientific analysis but also the sample so obtained cannot be representative of the larger population of separated MZs that seems to exist. That is, the group that has been studied is probably only a small proportion of the population of separated MZs that exists (i.e., those who were sufficiently similar); the level of correspondence seen with

---

[1] On October 18, 1983, I wrote Professor Bouchard about the three studies of MZ twins reared apart summarized in his article with McGue. My request for information read:

"I am writing in regard to your paper with Matthew McGue in Science (1981, Volume 212, pages 1055–1059), "Familial studies of intelligence: A review." On page 1056 (column 2, paragraph 2) you note that, "After deleting the Burt data we are left with test results on but 65 pairs of monozygotic twins reared apart, as reported in three separate investigations." I would appreciate learning of the references for these three studies and of the numbers of MZ pairs assessed in each study.

"Thank you very much for your help in this matter. . . ."

About a month later my original letter was returned to me. On the bottom of it someone—I assume Professor Bouchard—had handwritten the following message: See Book reviewed in attached paper—also Taylor, H. *The IQ Myth,* Ruter 1980. Poor book. I have a critique which will appear in *Intelligence.*

There was no signature. However, reprints of four papers were enclosed (1) the Bouchard and McGue (1981) paper, about which I had inquired in my October 18 letter to Professor Bouchard; (2) a book review by Duncan (1982) of the Eysenck and Kamin (1981) book, *The Intelligence Controversy;* the review did not identify the three studies by Bouchard and McGue (1981), although Kamin's (1974) reanalysis of the Juel-Nielsen (1965) data was critiqued; (3) a book review by Bouchard (1982) of the Farber (1981) book, *Identical twins reared apart: A reanalysis;* this review also did not identify the three studies cited by Bouchard and McGue (1981), although Farber's (and Kamin's, 1974) reanalyses of the Newman, Freeman, and Holzinger (1937) and the Shields (1962) data are critiqued; and (4) an article by David T. Lykken (1982), wherein Lykken identifies (Table 1, p. 362) "the four major studies of monozygotic twins reared apart." One of these studies is the Minnesota Study (1981), of which Professor Bouchard is the principal investigator. The other three studies are the ones identified by Kamin (i.e., Newman, Freeman, & Holzinger, 1937; Shields, 1962; and Juel-Nielsen, 1965). However, the numbers of MZ pairs noted by Lykken as being in these studies are 19, 44, and 12, respectively; this results in a total number of 75 pairs, which is 10 pairs more than the number cited for the three studies summarized in Bouchard and McGue and 7 pairs more than the number cited by Kamin (1974) for these same three studies.

Although none of the above four articles sent to me explicitly identifies the three articles summarized in the Bouchard and McGue (1981) paper, we may presume they are indeed the ones also reviewed by Kamin (1974). In fact, Professor Robert Plomin, a prominent behavior geneticist, whose work was discussed in Chapter 10, indicated to me (personal communication, January, 1984) that this was the case.

these inappropriately sampled (and, typically, inappropriately assessed; Kamin, 1974) pairs *overestimates* any actual similarity that exists in this population in general. Simply put, researchers seeking similarity excluded those pairs who did not have it and then, when assessing the remaining pairs for similarity, they "discovered" it.

It is interesting that Bouchard and McGue (1981) seemed to recognize this problem with twin research, but *only* for DZ twins. They noted, "The greater similarity of dizygotic twins than of other siblings is most often interpreted as a reflection of greater environmental similarity. It is also likely that bias in the recruitment of dizygotic twins for study is in the direction of increasing psychological similarity" (Bouchard & McGue, 1981, p. 1056). However, a similar recruitment bias may occur with MZs reared apart, and may account for the resemblance in their IQ scores. Bouchard and McGue (1981) failed to indicate this possibility, despite the evidence that exists in support of it (Farber, 1981).

Farber (1981) also reported that, even with the separated MZs studied, there is evidence for the ubiquitous role of environmental influences. She noted that greater separation between the MZs tended to be linearly related to greater disparities in their IQ scores. In turn, most separated MZs come from lower-class and lower-middle-class families and are quite often adopted by families of similar socioeconomic standing or by relatives; thus, although separated, the MZs have similar environments. As a consequence, "The range of environments in which the twins develop is thus reduced, and as the great geneticist Theodosius Dobzhansky pointed out, reducing the variability of the environment increases estimates of heritability" (Gruber, 1981, p. 22). Thus, as Kamin (in Eysenck & Kamin, 1981b) pointed out, in such a case of comparable rearing environments, the increased estimate of the inheritance of intelligence is an artifact and the score resemblance could be determined as much by environment as by genes.

The problems with the determination of estimates of the degree to which the variance in IQ scores is due to variance in genes, that is, the problems with estimating the heritability of IQ, is important to focus on later. Here, we should simply note that the confidence one may place in the weighted correlation of 0.72 reported by Bouchard and McGue (1981) as being an accurate estimate of the IQ resemblance of separated MZ twins is not at all great. That this correlation provides useful scientific support for the hereditarian position is far from certain.

Indeed, other information found in Table 11.4 argues against the hereditarian position. For instance, Bouchard and McGue (1981) noted that DZs are more similar than other biological siblings; this suggests not only that the DZs' common birth puts them into a socializing environment at the same time, but also it suggests that this context may treat them similarly. Bouchard and McGue also pointed out that the IQs of adoptive parents were also consistently related to the IQs of the adopted children; this relation suggests that environmental similarity can lead to some IQ resemblance between people. Thus, Bouchard and McGue (1981) concluded that "the data clearly suggest the operation of environmental effects" (p. 1058).

In turn, they concluded that it is "indisputable" that "the data support the influence of partial genetic determination for IQ" (Bouchard & McGue, 1981, p. 1058). Of course, genes are part of the integrated developmental system (Gottlieb, 1997; Horowitz, 2000; Magnusson, 1999a, 1999b; Thelen & Smith, 1998) and, as such, there is no reason to dispute the broad claim that genes are involved in providing some material basis for such human functioning. Indeed, both in our discussion of Anastasi's (1958) position in Chapter 4 and throughout our discussion of developmental systems theories (in Chapters 7 through 9), I have argued that all human behavior derives from (the fusion of) genes and context. However, I have argued that the data reviewed by Bouchard and McGue (1981) provide far less scientifically useful and/or certain support for a strong hereditarian view of the bases of IQ than may be taken from initial inspection of Table 11.4. Indeed, the last statements made by Bouchard and McGue (1981) seem to support my conclusion. First, they noted that it is "dubious" (p. 1058) whether the data are informative about the precise strengths of the genetic effect. Second, they pointed out that "the large amount of unexplained variability within degrees of relationship, while not precluding attempts to model the data, suggests that such models should be interpreted cautiously" (Bouchard & McGue, 1981, p. 1058).

CONTINUING MISUSES OF THE HERITABILITY CONCEPT IN THE DISCUSSION OF RACE DIFFERENCES IN INTELLIGENCE

Despite the cautions forwarded by Bouchard and McGue (1981) about the difficulty of modeling the heritability of intelligence, in the decades following their work other hereditarians either ignored their warnings or misunderstood the problems involved in this area of research. For example, Rushton (1999) demonstrated that he either completely misunderstood the meaning of heritability or that he simply used the concept in a scientifically inaccurate way. He asserted that:

> Heritability is the amount of variation in a trait due to the genes. A heritability of 1.00 means that the differences are inborn and the environment has no effect. A heritability of zero (0.00) means that the trait is controlled by the environment and not at all by the genes. A heritability of .50 means that the differences come from both the genes and the environment. (p. 60)

However, behavior geneticists such as Plomin (1986, 2000) and Plomin and colleagues (1980) explained the meaning of heritability in a manner that indicates that Rushton's (1999) interpretation of the concept is egregiously incorrect. Indeed, for more than 60 years, behavior geneticists have understood that, whatever heritability represents, it is not a construct that represents what Rushton (1999) claims.

For instance, the behavior geneticist, J. C. De-Fries (1967, p. 324) explained that Lush (1940) first defined the term "heritability" "as the fraction of the observed variance which was caused by differences in heredity." He continued "This fraction is a statistic describing a particular population. It can be made larger or smaller if either the numerator or the other ingredients in the denominator can be altered. Thus it may vary from population to population for the same characteristic and may vary from one characteristic to another even in the same population." Thus it was explicitly stated in 1940 that heritability is a function of both the trait and the population in which it is measured, a point which has been emphasized by workers in behavior genetics (Hirsch, 1963; Hadler, 1964).

Given that Rushton's definition departs so significantly from the one used by the behavior geneticists on whose scientific authority he so heavily relies, one may wonder whether Rushton (1999) either failed to consult these hereditarian authors about the correct technical interpretation of heritability or opted to define this concept in a manner which gives it a significance that fits his theory but is without conceptual or empirical foundation. No less of an authority on genetics than Luca Cavalli-Sforza, professor in the Department of Genetics at Stanford University, raised a similar question in regard to the sort of "scholarship" represented by the work of Rushton. Cavalli-Sforza and Cavalli-Sforza (1995) in a paper that reviews the research base for statements about the (high) heritability of IQ, noted that:

> Researchers who might be called "IQ hereditarians" are in general reporting high heritabilities for IQ without any information on how these calculations have been obtained, or why the other papers here cited have been ignored. It is unlikely that they were not seen or read; they are published in well-known scientific journals . . . it is possible that the IQ enthusiasts who do not cite these seminal papers are aware of them but did not understand them. This is not as incriminating as the possibility that they did not cite them because they are at odds with their own strongly hereditarian conclusions. (p. 280)

Indeed, Cavalli-Sforza and Cavalli-Sforza (1995) noted that the literature ignored by Rushton (1999) and others (e.g., Herrnstein & Murray, 1994; Jensen, 1969, 1998), including the work of Cavalli-Sforza, found much lower heritabilities than those reported by the "IQ enthusiasts" (Cavalli-Sforza & Cavalli-Sforza, 1995; Hirsch, 1997). Thus, when Rushton (1999, p. 69) contended that "Arthur Jensen's 1998 book, *The g Factor,* shows that indeed race difference [sic] are higher on high heritability tests. Such tests show greater White–Black differences even for toddlers," one cannot have any assurance that such a claim is based on a complete and even-handed review and analysis of the published literature (cf. Hirsch, 1997).

Indeed, these problems exist not only with Rushton (1999) but also, as Hirsch (1997, pp. 215–220) documented in precise detail, with the book, *The Bell Curve,* of Herrnstein and Murray (1994), a publication that he sees as lacking any scientific scrupulosity. To illustrate, Hirsch (1997) pointed out that Herrnstein and Murray (1994, p. 628) contend that there is *unanimous* conclusion among scholars that "no bias against blacks in educational and occupational prediction has been found." Hirsch pointed out that Herrnstein and Murray cite Hartigan and Wigdor (1989) as an example of this consensus. However, when Hirsch (1997, p. 219) read this reference he found that Hartigan and Wigdor (1989) reached the entirely opposite conclusion! Hirsch (1997) noted that their:

> Analysis of the impact of selection on minority and nonminority applicants demonstrates that in the absence of score adjustments, minority applicants who could perform successfully on the job will be screened out of the referral group in greater proportions than are equivalent majority applicants. Conversely, majority applicants who turn out not to perform successfully will be included in the referral group in greater proportions than equivalent minority applicants. (p. 7)

Charles Murray

Goldberger and Manski (1995) pointed also to the several conceptual and methodological flaws in the Herrnstein and Murray (1994) book. For instance, Goldberger and Manski (1995) noted that the entire line of argument presented in the book

> is tainted by two misconceptions. Heritability is not a measure of parent–child resemblance in IQ, nor is it a biological parameter that sets limits on the effectiveness of policy. (p. 764)

Moreover, Goldberger and Manski (1995) pointed to several fatal flaws in the scientific methods used by Herrnstein and Murray (1994) to support their misconceived argument. To support their ideas about the significance of the heritability of IQ scores for understanding human development, and thus about the genetic basis of intelligence, Herrnstein and Murray (1994) reported analyses from the National Longitudinal Survey of Youth (NLSY) pertinent to trying to determine whether socioeconomic status (SES) or IQ test scores (indexed by the Armed Forces Qualifying Test, AFQT), measured in 1980, are "more important" as determinants of various social behaviors, measured in the NLSY in 1990. Goldberger and Manski indicated several problems with using AFQT scores to measure cognitive ability and SES to index a child's social environment. In addition, Goldberg and Manski (1995) noted

Herrnstein and Murray measure AFQT and SES scores in qualitatively different units and that the statistical procedures used to address this problem (i.e., standardization procedures using statistics termed "beta weights")

> accomplishes nothing except to give quantities in noncomparable units the superficial appearance of being in comparable units. This accomplishment is worse than useless—it yields misleading inferences. (p. 769)

Accordingly, Goldberger and Manski (1995) concluded that:

> We find no substantively meaningful way to interpret the empirical analyses in Part II of *The Bell Curve* as showing that IQ is "more important" than SES as a determinant of social behaviors. (p. 769)

Thus, whether one is reading Herrnstein and Murray (1994), Jensen (1969, 1998), or Rushton (1996, 1997, 1999) about the heritability of IQ and the inherited racial differences in intelligence that are purported to be reflected by such "information," one must be mindful of the problems with their presentations identified by scholars such as Hirsch (1997), Cavalli-Sforza (1995), and others (e.g., Kamin, 1974; Lewontin, 2000). In fact, one may find it useful and quite appropriate to heed the strong caution explicit in the comment of Wahlsten (1981) that:

> So widespread are errors in this literature that the critical reader now has good reason to doubt every article published on this topic and to check the arithmetic, algebra and original references before seriously considering the "findings" and conclusions. The pitifully low standards of scholarship of many who write on heredity and IQ are scandalous and unforgivable. (p. 33)

Although Wahlsten presented this view more than two decades ago, the work of Hirsch (1997) reminds us that Wahlsten's observations are still, alarmingly, true at the time of this writing.

Conclusions

The egregiously poor scientific work associated with the conduct of heritability research in regard to human intelligence involves unreliable and invalid uses of the concept. In addition, technical problems exist in the computation of the heritability statistic itself. In regard to these technical problems, I noted earlier that, in order to use data such as those presented in Table 11.4 to determine the extent to which variation in IQ scores is related to variation in genes, some mathematical model of the role of genes and of environmental has to be formulated. While the result of the application of such a model with a given set of data (e.g., those in Table 11.4) enables a heritability coefficient to be computed in regard to data such as those reviewed by Bouchard and McGue (1981), it is in such computation that major conceptual and technical (mathematical) complications arise. We turn now to a discussion of these problems.

THE CALCULATION OF THE HERITABILITY OF INTELLIGENCE: MODELS AND MISTAKES

Since the publication of Jensen's (1969) article in the *Harvard Educational Review,* there have been repeated discussions in the literature about the concept of heritability, about the applicability of the concept to assessments of the genetic contribution to human intelligence, and about the scientific usefulness of the mathematical models used to estimate heritability (e.g., Eysenck & Kamin, 1981a, 1981b; Feldman & Lewontin, 1975, 1976; Frankel, 1976; Goldberger, 1979; Gottlieb et al., 1998; Gould, 1980, 1981, 1996; Havender, 1976; Hirsch, 1970, 1981, 1997; Jensen, 1973, 1976, 1980; Kamin, 1974; Layzer, 1974; Morton, 1976; Plomin & DeFries, 1976; Scarr-Salapatek, 1971a, 1971b). In Chapter 10, we reviewed some of the discussions in regard to the uses and misuses of the heritability concept. We noted that these discussions highlighted the points that the concept of heritability is a complex one, and is not necessarily what it seems to be (i.e., it is *not* an index of the extent to which heredity is a basis of any characteristic *within* a given person; Hirsch, 1997). We also noted in Chapter 10 that estimates of heritability are not always formulated appropriately. As we now discuss, this problem may be especially the case in regard to human intelligence.

Problems of Generalizing Heritability Estimates

After the publication of Jensen's (1969) article, several reviewers identified a problem of inappropriate generalization in Jensen's analysis (e.g., Feldman & Lewontin, 1975; Gould, 1980; Hirsch, 1970; Lewontin, 1976). That is, Gould (1980) made the point that:

> The value of heritability within either the white or the black population carries no implication whatever about the causes for different average values of IQ between the two populations. (A group of very short

people may have heritabilities for height well above 0.9, but still owe their relative stature entirely to poor nutrition.) *Within and between group variation are entirely different phenomena;* this is a lesson taught early in any basic genetics course. Jensen's conflation of these two concepts marked his fundamental error. (p. 38; italics added)

Similarly, Feldman and Lewontin (1975) noted that:

> We are unable to make any inferences from between-group differences and within-group statistics about the degree of genetic determination of the between-group differences. In other words, the concept of heritability is of no value for the study of differences in measures of human behavioral characters between groups. (p. 1167)

Moreover, when Lewontin (1973) calculated the genetic diversity within populations, within races between populations, and between races, he found that 85% of human genetic diversity is accounted for by variation between people within populations. Only about 6% of human genetic diversity was found to be attributable to variation between races (Lewontin, 1973).

In addition to inappropriate attempts to generalize a within-group heritability estimate between groups, there is an additional instance of inappropriate generalization. People who attempted to use h^2 as an indication of genetic determinacy appear to be involved in asking and attempting to answer the question "how much?" This is one of the two questions that we have seen Anastasi (1958) reject as illogical. In essence, they ask, "How much heredity and how much environment go into the determination of intelligence?" or "Which of the two is more important in determining intelligence?" However, as we know, answering this question is both logically impossible and inappropriate.

This significance of this issue has been explained by Hirsch (1970). As he explained, people working from this orientation typically test a population on the intelligence trait at a single time in their development. In then making a heritability estimate, all that is being done is a determination or the relative proportions of the variation between the individuals in the population that can be assigned to genetic and environmental variation. That is, the reason that a distribution exists is that, as we have seen, by definition individuals differ from each other in their scores on the test for that trait. All that h^2 does, then, is provide an estimate of how much of these *between-individual differences* is due to genetic variation and how much is due to environmental variation.

People mistakenly use these values, however, to estimate how much of the expression of the tested trait *within a single individual* of that population is determined by heredity and environment. Between-individual data are applied to purported within-individual phenomena. Thus, not only is an attempt to ask "How much of each?" illogical, but also the collected data can in no way be used appropriately to begin to address the question. As Hirsch emphasized, people taking this approach "want to know how instinctive is intelligence *(with)in* the development of a certain individual, but instead they measure differences *between* large numbers of fully, or partially, developed individuals" (1970, p. 7; italics added).

The apparent confusion of those people taking this approach is further complicated. We have seen that the norm-of-reaction concept leads us to recognize that all individuals in the world, no matter to what race they belong, can be expected to have a unique, individual genotype. In addition, we recognize the impossibility of ever determining, with any degree of exactness, a human's norm-of reaction (or as Hebb, 1949, would term it, intelligence A). Moreover, because of genotypic uniqueness, members of the same racial group cannot be appropriately equated in order to attempt to assess a racial group's norm-of-reaction. In fact, such a concept makes no sense. Even if it did, however, an exposure of each population genotype to the range of possible environments with which it could interact in order to assess phenotypic variability would remain a theoretical and practical impossibility. There is, then, absolutely no empirical or theoretical basis for any general statement assigning fixed proportions to the contributions of nature and nurture to the intellectual development of a single individual (Hirsch, 1970), *much less within every individual in an entire group of people!* Indeed, Jensen (1969, p. 42) stressed, "There is no way of partitioning a given individual's IQ into hereditary and environmental components, as if a person inherited, say, 80 points of IQ and acquired 20 additional points from his environment. This is, of course, nonsense."

Thus, heritability estimates may not be generalized between populations and they are meaningless and irrelevant for determining the roles of heredity and environment within a given individual. There is one final and very important, albeit quite technical, problem with heritability estimates. That is, you will recall Bouchard and McGue's (1981) warning that the family resemblance data they reviewed (which are summarized in Table 11.4) presented formidable problems for devising useful mathematical procedures (models) to appraise the heritability of human intelligence. These problems may be even more severe than Bouchard and McGue (1981) indicated.

Problems With Modeling Heritability

Perhaps the most penetrating analysis of the problems encountered when attempting to devise models with which to estimate heritability from a set of family resemblance data has been presented by Goldberger (1979). He addressed these problems by noting:

> About 1970, a consensus had developed among experts that the genetic component of IQ variance was very high, about 80 percent. In part the consensus was based upon common sense. As one correspondent, the geneticist C. O. Carter, later put it, "It is I think evident to any experienced and unprejudiced observer that the major part of the variation in intellectual ability in school children in Britain is genetic" (*The Times*, 3 November 1976). In greater part, however, the consensus was based on the fitting of statistical models to sets of IQ kinship correlations.
> I will be concerned with model fitting rather than with common sense. (p. 327)

To begin to address the issue of model fitting, Goldberger (1979) devised a table wherein each column gave a set of IQ kinship correlations that arose when various pairs of relatives were given IQ tests and their scores were then correlated. Table 11.5 presents this information. In this table it may be seen that the IQ correlation decreases as the biological and/or social "distances" increase.

Model Fitting

As we have discussed (in regard to the views of Feldman & Lewontin, 1975, 1976), in order to partition the variance in IQ scores into genetic and environmental components from data such as those in Table 11.5, one uses some statistical model. The genetic and environmental variance components appear as unknown *parameters* (statistical portions of the model), and these parameters are adjusted to best fit the data. Table 11.6, which is also taken from Goldberger (1979), presents the estimates of the modeled environmental and genetic variance components that have been derived from the major attempts at such work. The column numbers in Table 11.6 correspond to those of Table 11.5.

Goldberger (1979) noted that the column headed "Jinks and Fulker (1970) UK" refers to modeling work done in the United Kingdom that uses seven of Cyril Burt's kinship correlations (and that finds h^2_B to be 0.83). Of course, these figures were recognized by Goldberger (1979) to be inadmissible and scientifically useless, given the errors and dishonesty associated with them. But Goldberger (1979) noted that both Eysenck and Jensen claimed that

TABLE 11.5
IQ Kinship Correlation Sets Used in Various Studies

Type of relationship	Jinks and Fulker (1970) UK	Eaves (1975) UK	Eaves (1975) US	Eaves (1972) US	Jencks (1977) US	Rao, Morton, and Yee (1976) US	Rao and Morton (1978) US
	(1)	(2)	(3)	(4)	(5)	(6)	(7)
Identical twins reared together	0.92	0.92	0.97	—	0.91	0.89	0.84
Identical twins reared apart	0.87	0.87	0.75	—	0.67	0.69	0.68
Siblings reared together	0.53	0.53	0.59	0.38	0.53	0.52	0.52
Siblings reared apart	0.44	0.44	—	—	—	—	0.25
Parent and biological child reared together	—	0.49	0.55	—	0.48	0.48	0.48
Parent and biological child reared apart	—	—	0.45	—	0.41	—	0.41
Adoptive siblings	0.27	0.27	0.38	—	0.36	0.25	0.32
Adoptive parents	—	0.19	0.28	—	0.23	0.23	0.23
Grandparents	—	0.33	—	—	—	—	—
Uncles	—	0.34	—	—	—	—	—
First cousins	—	0.28	—	0.14	—	—	—
Second cousins	—	0.16	—	0.07	—	—	—
Third cousins	—	—	—	0.03	—	—	—
Spouses	0.39	0.39	0.57	0.46	0.50	0.50	0.51

Note. Several kinships that were distinguished in the studies are combined here for simplicity: "Sibling" includes fraternal twins along with ordinary siblings. "Adoptive sibling" includes adoptive-adoptive pairs along with adoptive-natural pairs. In column (4) the entries were calculated by Goldberger from the ANOVA tables in Eaves (1977). In column (5) the entries were assembled by Goldberger from various pages in Jencks (1972).
Source: Goldberger (1979, p. 328).

even after Burt's "data" were discarded, modeling using other data would confirm the estimates derived from Burt's study. For instance, Goldberger (1979, p. 329) noted that Eysenck wrote:

> [I]t is noteworthy that many different approaches have resulted in very similar estimates [of IQ heritability] usually centering around the 80 percent mark, although the range of uncertainty gives a lower bound of something like 60 percent and an upper one of 90 percent or thereabouts. [*The Times,* 12 November 1976]

and

> There is ample evidence for the genetic determination of intelligence. . . . [The] studies are remarkably congruent in the conclusions they allow us to come to. It is typical that opponents are vocal mainly in the pages of newspapers, in the letter columns of popular magazines, or in other non-technical places. . . . Critics seem to fight shy of the technical literature, or the essential examination of the totality of the evidence. [*The Times,* 8 November 1976]

On various subsequent occasions, Eysenck restated his scholarly concern in such distinguished "technical" journals as *New Society* (11 November 1976), *New Scientist* (25 November 1976), *Encounter* (January 1977), and *The Bulletin of the British Psychological Society* (1977).

Eysenck placed particular weight on the contributions of the Birmingham school of biometrical genetics, represented by J. L. Jinks, D. W. Fulker, and L. J. Eaves. Jensen, on the other hand, placed particular weight on the contributions of the Honolulu school, represented by N. E. Morton and D. C. Rao, writing:

> It is noteworthy that a leading American geneticist, Professor Newton Morton, has made a detailed statistical comparison of British kinship correlations (most all of them from Burt's studies) with those of all the parallel studies done by American investigators, and he finds the differences between the two sets of results to be statistically nonsignificant. . . . Morton writes: "Whatever errors may have crept into his (i.e., Burt's) material, they do not appear to be systematic." . . . The scientific weight of all the massive and newer evidence and modern quantitative genetic analyses, in numerous studies by independent investigators using somewhat different methods, now far surpass that of Burt's own pioneer research. Yet the evidence *sans* Burt leads *in toto* to essentially the same general conclusions: . . . in accounting for individual differences in IQ, genetic factors considerably outweigh the existing environmental influences. [*The Times,* 9 December 1976]

But, despite Eysenck's and Jensen's claims, Goldberger (1979) showed, in Table 11.6, that

TABLE 11.6
Components of IQ Variance as Estimated in Various Studies

	Jinks and Fulker (1970) UK	Eaves (1975) UK	Eaves (1975) US	Eaves (1977) US	Jencks (1972) US	Rao, Morton, and Yee (1976) US		Rao and Morton (1978) US		Eaves model fitted to Rao and Morton data US
						Children	Adults	Children	Adults	
	(1)	(2)	(3)	(4)	(5)	(6)		(7)		(8)
Genetic	83	85	68	60	45	67	21	69	30	58
Additive	62	65	35	60	32	67	21	69	30	31
Nonadditive	21	20	33	0	13	0	0	0	0	27
Environmental	17	15	32	40	35	19	66	51	70	42
Common	9	7	29	0	—	9	51	16	55	26
Specific	8	8	3	40	—	10	15	15	15	16
Covariance	0	0	0	0	20	14	13	0	0	0
Total	100	100	100	100	100	100	100	100	100	100
Kinships	7	14	9	4		11		16		10
Parameters	4	4	4	2	No formal fitting	8		9		4
X²/d.f.	2.1	14	1.5	0.6		0.9		4.4		1.0

Source: Goldberger (1979, p. 330).

when Burt's "data" are discarded, a picture quite different from the one portrayed by Eysenck emerges. Indeed, the picture is quite blurred (Goldberger, 1979). First, he noted that in the data sets presented in Table 11.5 "the entry for a kinship is not a correlation observed in a single sample, but rather an average across several samples taken at various times and places. For example, in Column 3, the entry of 0.38 for adoptive siblings is actually an average of the figures found in seven adoption studies, the original correlations having ranged from 0.06 to 0.65" (Goldberger, 1979, p. 333). We have seen also in Table 11.4 that the family resemblance data reviewed by Bouchard and McGue (1981) had similar evidence for considerable within-category heterogeneity. Given this heterogeneity, the clarity of any of the models' estimates becomes quite dim. Indeed, Goldberger (1979) summarized the usefulness of the modeling attempts represented in Tables 11.5 and 11.6 by indicating that:

> Enough of the structure has been exposed that we can assess the plausibility of the models. Ignorance of genetics need not deter us, because the models involve as much social science theorizing as genetic theorizing. How marriages take place, how adoption agencies operate, how parents raise their children, how brothers and sisters educate one another—all those processes are reflected in the biometrical–genetic models.
>
> I call attention to two such pieces of theorizing that are incorporated in the Birmingham and Honolulu models. (1) Identical twins share just as much IQ-relevant experience as ordinary siblings do, no more. That happens despite the fact that identical twins are of the same age and sex, while ordinary siblings may differ in age and sex. (2) Adoption agencies place children in families randomly drawn from the population at large. That happens even though every adoption study shows that adoptive parents rank high on virtually every socioeconomic and psychological measure.
>
> If those pieces of theorizing are unbelievable, then the parameter estimates provided by Birmingham and Honolulu (and by me in column [8] of Table 11.6) should not be believed either. For the assumptions are critical rather than incidental ones. If ordinary siblings share less IQ-relevant experience than identical twins do, then the difference between the IQ correlations for those two kinships is partly attributable to environment. If adoptive families span a reduced range of environments, then the IQ correlations among adoptive kin understate the common environment variance in the population at large. Both pieces of theorizing tilt the estimated balance from environment to genes. To explain the persistent use of such assumptions, we need only recognize that without them the models would be indeterminate. If less restrictive, and hence more plausible,

specifications were made, the number of unknown parameters would approach and soon exceed the number of observations. Implausible assumptions are needed to identify the parameters and produce the estimates, and thus to keep the model-fitters happy. However, estimates produced in that manner do not merit the attention of the rest of us. (p. 336)

CONCLUSIONS

As discussed in Chapter 10, heritability research in general, and as illustrated in the present chapter, particularly as it has been done in relation to IQ, has involved advancement of fallacious arguments and misapplication of data (see Layzer, 1974). At best, heritability is a concept of extremely narrow utility. If misunderstood and misapplied, it leads to the assumption that high heritability means developmental fixity—that the expression of a highly heritable trait cannot be altered through environmental changes—that the trait is simply innate and unavailable to environmental influence (Lehrman, 1970). However, in previous chapters, we have indicated that no psychological trait is preorganized in the genes and unavailable to environmental influence. Our assessment of the implications of the

David Layzer

question "how?" makes such an assertion simply implausible.

Thus, any alleged genetic difference (or "inferiority") of African Americans based on the high heritability of intelligence would seem to be an attribution built on a misunderstanding of concepts basic to an appropriate conceptualization of the nature–nurture controversy. An appreciation of the interactive interrelation of heredity and environment, of the parameters of how they in fact interact, of the norm-of-reaction concept, and of the meaning, implications, and limitations of the concept of heritability should lead us to an important conclusion. *All our considerations strongly suggest that the genetic-differences hypothesis of racial differences in IQ makes little compelling scientific sense.* The heritability (in the sense of developmental fixity) of intelligence, or of any other psychological trait for that matter, must be recognized as a psychological unreality. Such terms have, at best, so little scientific utility as to make them functionally worthless (see Layzer, 1974, 2000).

Hence, in a review of the scientific and mathematical status and bases of the calculation of heritability analyses of IQ, Layzer (1974) argued that there are significant cultural differences between African Americans and European Americans in today's society that speak against any attempt to evaluate race differences in IQ scores (even with so-called culture-free tests). Layzer (1974) stated:

> The definition of IQ has no theoretical context or substratum. Tests of IQ measure what they measure. They are precisely analogous to physical readings made with a black box—a device whose internal working is unknown. Because we do not know what an IQ test or a black box is supposed to measure or how it works, we cannot know to what extent measurements carried out on different subjects are comparable or to what extent they are influenced by extraneous factors. Thus, IQ scores contain uncontrollable, systematic errors of unknown magnitude.
>
> This helps to explain why different investigators frequently report such widely differing estimates of the same IQ correlation. For example, reported estimates of the parent–child correlation range from .2 to .8, whereas estimates of the correlation between same-sex dizygotic twins range from .4 to .9 (Erlenmeyer-Kimling & Jarvik, 1963). According to Jensen (1973), there are no objective criteria (other than sample size) for weighting discrepant estimates of the same correlations.
>
> Because the definition of IQ is purely instrumental, it fails to confer the most essential attribute of a scientific measurement—objectivity. To measure a subject's Stanford-Binet IQ, one must administer a specific test in a specific way under specific conditions. By contrast, a well-equipped physics laboratory does not need to have replicas of the standard meter and the standard kilogram to measure length and mass, and the physicist or biologist is free to devise his own techniques for measuring such quantities. Systematic discrepancies between measurements of the same quantity are never ignored in the physical and biological sciences, because they signal the presence of unsuspected systematic errors or of defects in the theory underlying the measurements.
>
> IQ scores also differ from conventional measurements in that they have no strict quantitative meaning. The IQ is an index of rank order on a standard test, expressed according to a convenient but essentially arbitrary convention (Stevens, 1946). In effect, the intervals of the IQ scale are chosen in such a way as to make the frequency distribution of test scores in a reference population approximately normal, but other methods of defining the scale could claim equal prior justification.
>
> These considerations show that IQ scores are not phenotypic measurements in the usual sense. (p. 1262)

These general problems with IQ tests complicate the issues involved in making any valid statements about the genetic basis of IQ differences between the races. Given, then, the additional problems with the calculation of heritability estimates that we have reviewed, it is clear why Layzer believes that "the only data that might yield meaningful estimates of narrow heritability are phenotypic correlations between halfsibs reared in statistically independent environments. No useful data of this kind are available" (Layzer, 1974, p. 1265). It is possible to conclude:

> Under prevailing social conditions, no valid inferences can be drawn from IQ data concerning systematic genetic differences among races or socioeconomic groups. Research along present lines directed toward this end—whatever its ethical status—is scientifically worthless.
>
> Since there are no suitable data for estimating the narrow heritability of IQ, it seems pointless to speculate about the prospects for a hereditary meritocracy based on IQ. (p. 1266)

Moreover, writing about a quarter century later, Layzer (2000) continued to see theoretical and computational misconceptions of biometrical "IQists." After noting these problems, Layzer (2000) asked:

> How have biometricians who analyze IQ scores managed to occupy themselves for so many decades with strictly meaningless questions? The answer—or at least the most polite part of the answer—lies in their failure to formulate their mathematical model correctly. (p. 2)

Accordingly, Layzer (2000) concluded that:

> Biological, psychological, and sociological considerations make it seem highly implausible that IQ test scores could have the additive structure biometricians posit. For this reason alone, it seems to me that biometric studies of IQ are scientifically bankrupt. (p. 2)

Both Hirsch (1981, 1997) and Feldman and Lewontin (1975) reached congruent conclusions. For instance, Hirsch (1981) noted:

> Failure conceptually to appreciate and to integrate three fundamentals of biology—individuality, interaction and norm of reaction throughout ontogeny—underlies the confusion. Individuality is a consequence of the fact that members of diploid, bisexual, cross-fertilizing species are genotypically unique. Moreover, although it is a platitude to say that heredity and environment *interact* to produce the phenotype, it is that interaction of unique genotypes with environments which thwarts a simple systems approach. . . . Not only do genotypes differ in response to a common environment, but one genotype varies in response to different environments. The latter property is called norm of reaction. Interaction and norms of reaction describe aspects of the complex genotype–phenotype relationship. The latter focuses on the developmental outcomes of a single genotype replicated in different environments. The former includes the latter and considers at one time many genotypes and many environments. For an array of genotypes replicated in various sets of environmental conditions, it calls attention to how, out of the variety of possible distributions of phenotypic outcomes, the particular one obtained will depend on which genotype develops under which conditions.
>
> The key to "establishing the relative roles of heredity and environment" has been believed erroneously to be the heritability estimate. But heritability estimates cannot be made for human intelligence measurements, because the heritability coefficient is undefined in the presence of either correlation or interaction between genotype and environment, both of which occur for human intelligence. When correlation exists, either (1) between genetic and environmental contributions to trait expression, or (2) between environmental contributions to trait expression in both members of a parent–child or sib pair, heritability is not defined. Furthermore, when heritability can be defined, for example in well-controlled plant and animal breeding experiments, it has *no* relevance to measured differences in average values of trait expression between different populations: heritability estimates throw no light upon intergroup comparisons! Also, heritability estimates provide no information about ontogeny and are thus irrelevant to the formulation of public policy on education and social conditions.
>
> None of the statements about proportional contributions of heredity and environment to the determination of level of "intelligence" or of many other human traits can be either substantiated or disproven by any conceivable observations. (p. 33)

In turn, Feldman and Lewontin (1975) indicated:

> The problem we have been examining is the degree to which statistical structures can reveal the underlying biological structure of causation in problems of human quantitative genetics. We must distinguish those problems which are by their nature numerical and statistical from those in which numerical manipulation is a mere methodology. Thus, the breeding structure of human populations, the intensities of natural selection, the correlations between mates, the correlations between genotypes and environments, are all by their nature statistical constructs and can be described and studied, in the end, only by statistical techniques. It is the numbers themselves that are the proper objects of study. It is the numbers themselves that we need for understanding and prediction.
>
> Conversely, relations between genotype, environment, and phenotype are at base mechanical questions of enzyme activity, protein synthesis, developmental movements, and paths of nerve conduction. We wish, both for the sake of understanding and prediction, to draw up the blueprints of this machinery and make tables of its operating characteristics with different inputs and in different milieus. For these problems, statistical descriptions, especially one-dimensional descriptions like heritability, can only be poor and, worse, misleading substitutes for pictures of the machinery. There is a vast loss of information in going from a complex machine to a few descriptive parameters. Therefore, there is immense indeterminacy in trying to infer the structure of the machine from those few descriptive variables, themselves subject to error. It is rather like trying to infer the structure of a clock by listening to it tick and watching the hands. At present, no statistical methodology exists that will enable us to predict the range of phenotypic possibilities that are inherent in any genotype, nor can any technique of statistical estimation provide a convincing argument for a genetic mechanism more complicated than one or two Mendelian loci with low and constant penetrance. Certainly the simple estimate of heritability, either in the broad or narrow sense, but most especially in the broad sense, is nearly equivalent to no information at all for any serious problem of human genetics. (pp. 1167–1168)

Conclusions About the Study of Heritability and Intelligence

It seems clear that the evidence for the genetic basis of intelligence and/or for racial/ethnic/social class differences in IQ that is derived from heritability estimates is more "apparent" to hereditarians than it is "real" to scientists using appropriate conceptual and methodological lenses. Perhaps the ephemeral quality of evidence based on heritability estimates is a reason why some behavior geneticists refuse to allow other qualified scholars or appropriate public forums to examine their data (Hirsch, personal communication, September 1, 2000).[2]

Given, then, the poor quality of the evidence in support of the hereditarian position, we may agree with the conclusion of Kempthorne (1978) that:

> The heredity–IQ controversy has been a "tale full of sound and fury, signifying nothing". To suppose that one can establish effects of an intervention process when it does not occur in the data is plainly ludicrous. Mere observational studies can easily lead to stupidities, and it is suggested that this has happened in the heredity–IQ arena. The idea that there are racial–genetic differences in mental abilities and behavioral traits of humans is, at best, no more than idle speculation. (p. 1)

Similarly, Jacquard (1983) noted that:

> The need for great rigour exists particularly in the case of research projects which have serious implications for us all; this is the case when psychologists study the "heritability of intellectual aptitudes." They should take the precaution of systematically defining in a precise way the sense in which they use the word "heritability," they should also state whether the assumptions under which this word can be used hold true in their studies. It is highly probable that most of the time this exercise in rigour would lead them to the conclusion that none of the three parameters proposed by geneticists can be of any use in solving their problems. (p. 476)

Comparable ideas have been forwarded by Moran (1973).

In sum, then, it is perhaps appropriate to end our presentation of the controversy over the nature and nurture of intelligence with the summary statement about this topic offered by Hirsch (1970), since his ideas have been quite important in the clarification of the issues:

> The relationship between heredity and behavior has turned out to be one of neither isomorphism nor independence. Isomorphism might justify an approach like naive reductionism, independence a naive behaviorism. Neither one turns out to be adequate. I believe that in order to study behavior, we must understand genetics quite thoroughly. Then, and only then, can we as psychologists forget about it intelligently. (p. 81)

From Behavior Genetics to Sociobiology

I agree with Hirsch that human developmentalists should understand the role of genes in development quite thoroughly. I agree with Hirsch (1970) as well that we must not just forget about the role of genes in human development. We should seek to understand how genetic functioning is embedded within (integratively fused in) the dynamic, developmental system involved in human life across ontogeny.

There is, as well, another reason not to forget about genes. As we have seen (in Chapter 10) Horowitz (2000) caution, and as I noted at the beginning of this chapter, scholars with nature–mechanistic conceptions will not forget about genes; they will insist that in explaining human development genetic reduction and nature–nurture

---

[2] To illustrate, on June 22, 1995, Cardiss Collins, a member of the United States Congress from Illinois, and the then ranking minority member of the Committee on Government Reform and Oversight, wrote Professor Robert Plomin, requesting copies of his twin data sets and some data analyses he has conducted that were pertinent to his claims about heritability. Congresswoman Collins wrote:

Dear Professor Plomin,

As Chairwoman of the U.S. House of Representatives' Subcommittee on Commerce, Consumer Protection, and Competitiveness, during the 102nd and 103rd Congresses, I reviewed the evidence in support of claims of substantial genetic influence in psychological measures used by the Data Analysis Working Group of the National Collegiate Athletic Association.

I have been advised by several scientists that your heritability claims have potentially far reaching implications, and I am particularly interested in receiving your twin data sets and the mean squares which underlay your claims. Would you please supply all relevant data and models as soon as possible for my review.

I appreciate your help and cooperation. If you have any questions regarding the above, please contact Mr. . . . of my staff at . . .

Sincerely,

CARDISS COLLINS
Member of Congress

Professor Plomin did not comply with the request of Congresswoman Collins (Hirsch, personal communication, September 1, 2000).

splits make eminent sense and reflect empirical reality (e.g., Rowe, 1994; Rushton, 1999). Thus, as evidence by the recurring articulation of hereditarian positions (e.g., Rushton, 1999), history teaches us that nature conceptions will not go away even though they are shown repeatedly to be scientifically "fatally flawed."

In fact, as we now discuss in the next two chapters, even if a given nativist conception is found to be untenable in one historical era, it may resurface in a subsequent period, perhaps with a different label but with an invariant core conceptual perspective about the role of genes in human development. Accordingly, in Chapter 12, we discuss the ideas of Konrad Lorenz in regard to the hereditarian concept of "instinct." Although much of Lorenz's (1943, 1966) work was found to be conceptually and empirically flawed (e.g., Lehrman, 1953; Schneirla, 1966), we will see in Chapter 13 that many of the ideas that Lorenz emphasized resurfaced in the 1970s and 1980s in the context of sociobiological theory.

12 | *Nature Approaches to Development: Konrad Lorenz and the Concept of "Instinct"*

The ultimate wisdom is always the understanding of instinct.
  —Hitler (*Mein Kampf,* 1925, pp. 244–245)

I am by inheritance obsessed with eugenics.
  —Konrad Lorenz (1974, p. 20)

Konrad Zacharias Lorenz (1903–1989) was the foremost proponent of a branch of biology termed *ethology,* which involves the study of the evolutionary, and it is thus argued, the hereditary bases of animal behavior. Lorenz's ethological work was built around his conceptualization of the notion of "instinct," a conceptualization that was a key intellectual basis of the hereditarian theory of behavior and development termed *sociobiology* (Wilson, 1975). Historian Robert Richards (1987, p. 528) explained that Lorenz "gave conceptual and empirical shape to the modern science of ethology, the science which has been further elaborated into (and . . . Wilson believes absorbed by) sociobiology."

As suggested by his influence on the field of sociobiology, Lorenz's contribution to science were numerous and highly valued by many scholars. In fact, with two other eminent ethologists—Nikolaas Tinbergen and Karl von Frisch—Konrad Lorenz was awarded the Nobel Prize for Medicine or Physiology in 1973. The award was given for his ethological theory and research regarding instinctual behavior in animals, particularly precocial birds (i.e., birds that walk or swim efficiently immediately after hatching).

As discussed in Chapter 6, Lorenz (1965) used the term *imprinting* to describe such birds' social attachment to, and following along after, the first moving object they saw after hatching. Usually this "object" was a member of their own species, typically their mother, and the newly hatched birds would follow after this other bird. Upon reaching sexual maturity later in their lives, the birds would try to mate with another such social object, in this case another bird of their own species.

Lorenz (1965) attempted to demonstrate the fixed nature of imprinting by showing that following and, later, mating behaviors could be directed to virtually any living organism, as long as it was the first moving object a newly hatched bird saw in the first critical hours after its birth. Birds could be made to imprint on boots or even on Lorenz himself. Numerous introductory psychology texts accompany their discussions of imprinting with a photograph of a somewhat stooped and kindly appearing Dr. Lorenz, an elderly man with white hair and beard, being followed by a troop of young goslings.

LORENZ'S CONCEPTION OF "INSTINCT"

According to Lorenz (1965), the imprinting phenomenon was an instance of instinctual behavior in animals. Beginning in his earliest publications (e.g., Lorenz, 1932/1970, 1935, 1937a, 1937b), Lorenz was concerned with the concept of instinct. Following the "discovery" by Oskar Heinroth of such phenomena, Lorenz (1932/1970) noted "that there are motor patterns of constant form which are performed in exactly the same manner by every healthy individual of a species." He presented five criteria for determining whether an observed pattern of behavior reflected "inherited drives of fixed behaviors."

Konrad Lorenz

Lorenz's (1937a, 1943/1954) criteria for an instinctual behavior pattern (see Richards, 1987) were:

1. Appearance of the behavior pattern in virtually all individuals of a species.

2. Appearance of the behavior pattern in species members who were reared in experimentally controlled isolation (i.e., who were (purportedly) deprived of experience.

3. Complexity of the behavior pattern (i.e., the learning capacity of the individual should not be sufficient for the acquisition of the behavior pattern yet the behavior pattern is present).

4. Appearance, or "release," of the behavior pattern either at inappropriate times or in incomplete ways (e.g., a bird may try to build a nest outside of the mating season).

5. Fixity and rigidity (i.e., stereotype and nonplasticity) of the behavior pattern—in other words, the behavior pattern takes the same form whenever it appears.

According to Lorenz (1937a, 1937b), an instinctual behavior pattern could occur in one of two ways. First, an instinct could be observed when the

individual experienced a specific "releasing" stimulus—that is, when the organism encountered a certain stimulus that "triggered" a given instinct—or, second, the instinct could be released in a seemingly spontaneous manner (Lorenz, 1937a). To explain these bases for the occurrence of an instinctual behavior pattern, Lorenz (1937a, 1937b, 1965; see, too, Richards, 1987) posited the existence of an "innate releasing mechanism" (IRM), a hypothetical mechanism believed to involve a set of receptor cells that released the instinctual behavior pattern when activated by a specific environmental stimulus.

More specifically, Lorenz saw as instinctual certain inherited properties of nervous system structures (Lehrman, 1970). Some groups of neurons, he claimed, have specific instinctive properties built into them (Lehrman, 1970). The structures obtain these properties directly from the organism's genetic inheritance, from the "interaction of the species with its environment during evolution . . . [that is,] by mutation and selection, a method analogous to learning by trial and success."

According to Lorenz (1937a, 1965), experience over the course of an organism's life (its ontogeny) has no role in the shaping (the development) of this neural structure. Instead, as Lehrman pointed out, the key innate feature of such a neural structure is "its ability to select, from the range of available possible stimuli, the one which specifically elicits its activity, and thus the response seen by the observer" (Lehrman, 1970, p. 24).

A classic example of a "fixed action," or instinctual, pattern deriving from an IRM involves the male three-spined stickleback fish (Lorenz, 1965; Richards, 1997). When this fish encounters another male three-spined stickleback with a red belly, the fish displays a set of behaviors indicative of threat; however, when the fish encounters a female with a swollen (but nonred) belly, the male displays the behavior pattern indicative of mating. Similarly, greylag geese display a fixed action pattern involving escape responses when they encounter a whitetailed eagle, the only flying predator that is a danger to these geese (Lehrman, 1970). However, the instinctual escape response can also be released if the goose is exposed to any object gliding slowly and silhouetted against the sky (Lorenz, 1965; Richards, 1987).

Thus, more than one specific stimulus can engage the IRM and release an instinct. Indeed, as noted, fixed action patterns can occur "spontaneously,"—that is, if the appropriate releasing stimulus has not been encountered for some period of time, then (apparently because of an accumulation of energy associated with the instinct and/or the IRM) the fixed action pattern "might go off in vacuo, as if dammed energy burst through containing valves" (Richards, 1987, p. 531). Because of this "spontaneous release" feature in IRMs, Lorenz (1965) came to view instincts not as sets of reflexes but as drives, as constructs having motivational properties. That is, Lorenz believed animals sought out stimuli that would release their instincts, which would dissipate the energy associated with the instincts that had presumably been built up (Lorenz, 1937b). In other words, Lorenz was saying that, unlike a reflex, wherein one behaves automatically, instincts have motivational properties: instincts drive one to engage in particular behaviors.

Criticisms of Lorenz's Conception of "Instinct"

Throughout his writings, Lorenz did not divorce himself from a commitment to the IRM concept, or from the belief that certain stimulus conditions can release, even in humans, a quite complex fixed action pattern (e.g., involving aggression and "militant enthusiasm") (Lorenz, 1965, 1966). However, his concept of instinct evolved in ways other than changing from a reflexlike construct to a motivational construct. Lorenz changed his conception of instinct, at least in part, in response to criticisms from several comparative psychologists.

For instance, some of the flaws in Lorenz's ideas were discussed in Chapter 6, in relation to the work that comparative psychologist T. C. Schneirla (1956, 1957) and his colleagues (e.g., Lehrman, 1953) did to counter hereditarian concepts such as Lorenz's view of instinct. Other scholars added to Schneirla's (1956, 1957) criticisms of Lorenz's concept of instinct, for instance, by pointing to the artificial and simplistic distinction Lorenz (1965) drew between instinct and learning (e.g., Hebb, 1949; Lehrman, 1970). That is, Lorenz (1965) often seemed to equate or subsume all nonevolutionary experience with the term "learning," when there are actually many more ways in which experience can influence behavior. For example, diseases, natural events (e.g., storms and earthquakes), wars, famine, dietary regimens, technological changes, and social and political policies, laws, and cultural movements can all influence behavior—even though those phenomena are not readily subsumed under the concept of "learning."

Scholars also objected to problems with experimental isolation studies (Lehrman, 1970). For instance, in such studies the researcher can deprive the animal of only some experiences, since it is not possible to deprive a living organism of all experience; even a dark box is an environment, although potentially noxious. Thus, an isolation experiment can tell us only that a particular experience is not necessary for a certain behavior; we can never determine from such a procedure that experience per se is not involved (Hebb, 1949).

Lorenz's (1937a, 1965) concept of instinct was also criticized for ignoring the problem of development across life, at least as far as the presence of the IRM was concerned. The issue of how genes, which are chemicals, interact with cells, tissues, organs, and the environment to "build" across life the neural structures involved in the IRMs is never adequately discussed by Lorenz (1937a, 1965, 1966; cf. Schneirla, 1956, 1957, 1966). Furthermore, Lorenz's concept of IRM was seen as problematic because it had an element of nonfalsifiability to it: An instinct was released either under specific environmental stimulus conditions or in the absence of them (Lehrman, 1970).

Lorenz's Responses to His Critics

In response to such criticisms, Lorenz contended in his 1965 book, *Evolution and Modification of Behavior*:

> What is preformed in the genome and inherited by the individual is not any "character," such as we can see and describe in a living organism, but a limited range of possible forms in which an identical genetic blueprint can find its expression in phenogeny. . . . The term "innate" should never, on principle, be applied to organs or behavior patterns, even if their modifiability should be negligible. (p. 1)

Thus, Lorenz was arguing that it is not the behavior pattern, no matter how fixed it may seem, that is instinctual; rather, it is the "range" of the behaviors involved in the instinct that is innate. In other words, what is preformed in, or built into, the genome (the set of genes received or inherited at conception) is information about the forms of a given behavior that are possible for the species. Moreover, this conception of "instinct as information" requires the involvement of the environment in order for the presence of a behavior within the range of the instinct to be in evidence. This need for "nurture" in order to identify features of "nature" arises because, Lorenz (1965) contended, the environment is involved in the:

> "Decoding" of genome-bound information . . . [and as a consequence] contrasting of the "innate" and the "learned" as mutually exclusive concepts is undoubtedly a fallacy. (p. 79)

Lorenz (1965) believed that by conceptualizing the information genes contain about such behavior patterns (instead of fixed action sequences) as innate, he had addressed the criticisms of his purportedly simplistic division between "instincts" and "learning." Of course, it is not possible to observe this innate information. One can see only behavior, which, Lorenz (1965) contended, is not instinctual per se but rather the product of "morphological ontogeny producing structure . . . and . . . of trial-and-error behavior exploiting structure as a teaching apparatus." (p. 79)

In my view, however, as a consequence of his new 1965 conception of instinct, Lorenz replaced one set of problems with another. He gave up the five observational criteria for identification of instinctual behavior patterns and defined instinct as a nonempirical construct, which cannot be known directly. Information about the range of forms can only be inferred from behaviors that, by his own insistence, are not (however) independent of experience, or "learning."

The changes Lorenz introduced into his conception of "instinct" in 1965 led him away from the stance of an empirical scientist. His statements about the instinct concept became increasingly less linked to clear observational criteria and, as such, took on more of the character of an intuitive construct (Richards, 1987, p. 530). Nevertheless, an interest in the instinct concept spanned Lorenz's entire career, and he continued to be an advocate for the importance of the construct for understanding both animal and human behavior. Indeed, this advocacy was based on Lorenz's belief that human civilization was at risk because of phenomena associated with certain types of changes in instinctual patterns (Lorenz, 1974a).

Lorenz's Application to Humans of His Concept of "Instinct"

As a committed Darwinist, Lorenz (1965, 1966, 1974a, 1974b) believed that instincts were shaped by evolution, by natural selection. Instincts— whether defined behaviorally or through reference to genome information—afford, then, survival; their function is to allow the organism to "fit" the demands of the natural environment within which the particular set of behaviors, or range of forms—comprising the instinct has been selected. In this vein, Lorenz (1965) contended:

> Some information underlying an individual's behavior has indeed been "preformed" by the species. . . . It becomes all too easy to overlook the survival function of behavior altogether and, therewith, the

selection pressure which caused its mechanisms to evolve. To anyone tolerably versed in biological thought, it is a matter of course that . . . any function of . . . survival value . . . must necessarily be performed by a very special mechanism built into the organic system in the course of its evolution. (p. 13)

Therefore, according to Lorenz (1965), instincts allow the organism to survive within the natural surroundings within which the instinct has been selected. The essence of instincts is to allow a fit with the demands of the environment within which the instinct evolved.

But what happens if and when individuals are taken from the environments within which their instincts have been naturally selected? What are the implications for survival when an organism finds itself in a setting other than the one within which its instincts evolved to fit? It is with these questions—involving the implications of taking individuals out of their natural selection environment and placing them in a tamer and more domesticated and civilized setting—that much of Lorenz's scholarship, beginning in the 1930s and engaging him for much of the remainder of his life, was concerned.

This central theme in the work of Lorenz has been the focus of reviews by philosopher Theodora Kalikow (1978a, 1978b, 1983). Kalikow (1978a, 1983) adopted this focus because of her view that Lorenz interwove political ideology with his scientific focus, which was the discussion of the nature of instincts among domesticated animals or among humans "encountering" civilization. Kalikow (1983) stated:

> Ideology played a triple role in Lorenz's speeches and writings during the years from 1938 to 1943. (1) He saw changes in the instinctive behavior patterns of domesticated animals as symptoms of decline. (2) He assumed a homology between domesticated animals and civilized human beings, that is, he assumed there must be similar causes for effects assumed to be similar, and he further believed that civilization was in a process of "decline and fall." Finally, (3) he connected the preceding concerns to racial policies and other features of the Nazi program. (p. 39)

Kalikow (1983) also drew a distinction between Lorenz's early and later work:

> As examination of Lorenz's writings from before and after World War II shows that (1) and (2) have remained as features of his work, while (3) has disappeared, at least in its overt manifestations. (p. 39)

In other words, then, Lorenz (1940b, 1974a; see, too, Richards, 1987) offered the hypothesis that human biological degeneration has been brought about through domestication. According to this hypothesis, the instinctual behaviors of "civilized," urban human beings, behaviors that evolved to fit more rural settings, have become increasingly more diseased and degenerate. Akin to the domestication-induced degeneracy that, he believed, afflicts animals reared away from their natural, or wild, setting, Lorenz (1940b, 1974a) contended that modern society's protection of humans from natural selection has resulted in the degeneration of human beings both intellectually and morally (Richards, 1987).

As noted in the epigraph beginning this chapter, Lorenz admitted that, through his inheritance, he was obsessed with eugenics (Lorenz, 1974b; in Cox 1974). Thus, if Kalikow's (1983) views are correct, the focus Lorenz (1937a, 1937b, 1965, 1966, 1974a) adopted for his work on instincts is redolent of the Social Darwinist/racial hygienist thinking that was part of the intellectual, social, and political milieu of Germany before the Third Reich (Kalikow, 1978a, 1983; Lifton, 1986; Müller-Hill, 1988; Proctor, 1988). But are Kalikow's (1983) views of the conflation of science and politics in Lorenz's work correct? If so, was there a connection between Lorenz's scientific and political writings? Did his scientific beliefs shape his political ones? Did political ideology affect the quality of his scientific work?

In Chapter 2, we discussed the ubiquitous connections between scholars' philosophies of science and their theoretical and empirical work. In addition, in Chapter 5 we noted the linkage between assumptions about constancy and change in human development and the empirical identification by a scientist of continuity or discontinuity in development. Accordingly, it would not be unusual for any scholar—Lorenz, or me for that matter—to have one aspect of his or her intellectual life commingle with other aspects (cf. Lewontin, 1992, 2000). Indeed, humans, as living, open, and relational systems, may be marked by such integration.

Moreover, as a part of human life, one inevitably integrated with other facets of human behavior and development, science is not independent of politics. Scientists often lobby political leaders to garner support for and funding of their areas of research. Most scientific organizations have staff whose assignment is to work with governmental bodies to promote or protect the funding of their domain of scholarship. In turn, political pressures on governmental bodies may result in politicians increasing or decreasing support for politically sensitive or controversial areas of research (e.g., early-life intervention, fetal tissue research,

human cloning, day-care effects, family leave, or sex education). In the case of political issues resulting in support for a given line of scholarship, it is most clear that scientific theory and research may serve political purposes. The "fate" of such lines of scholarship (e.g., whether they continue to attract governmental funding) may hinge, then, on the political context.

As such, the questions I am raising here about Lorenz's work are not ones that criticize him per se for manifesting a situation wherein one facet of his beliefs influences another. In addition, I am not faulting him per se because there may have been a connection in his work between science and politics. Rather, the questions I am raising are directed at understanding whether such connections existed and, if so, how they may have affected his theoretical ideas about human development *and* about the social uses or applications he and others saw—and some may still see—for such ideas. If, as I discuss at the end of this chapter and again in Chapter 13, there is a strong connection between Lorenz's ideas and sociobiological thinking, then we may legitimately question whether any of the science–politics connections relevant to Lorenz's work are also pertinent to sociobiology.

To address these questions, let us first review the "evidence" Kalikow (1983) and others (e.g., Chorover, 1979; Eisenberg, 1972) marshaled in support of the contention that Lorenz's 1938–1943 writings—his work during the Nazi political era—combined science and politics. We then consider an analysis of Kalikow's (1983) views presented by Richards (1987), the historian who has been most critical of Kalikow's (1983) interpretation of Lorenz's Nazi-era writings. Finally, we note the themes in Lorenz's writings that appear to have been carried beyond World War II and discuss the connection between the biological-determinist views of Lorenz and those found among contemporary sociobiologists.

THE NAZI-ERA WORK OF LORENZ

The National Socialist German Workers' Party (abbreviated as the NSDAP or simply as the Nazi Party) controlled Germany and, eventually, much of western and eastern Europe from January 30, 1933, when Adolf Hitler became Chancellor of Germany, to May 7, 1945, when Germany surrendered unconditionally to the Allied forces to end World War II in Europe. Throughout this period, the career of Konrad Lorenz flourished.

Many of Lorenz's writings pertinent to his commitment to Nazi racist ideology and policies have been identified and translated by Kalikow (1978a, 1978b, 1983), although other scholars have drawn attention to Lorenz's "Brown past" [i.e., his participation in Nazi party ("Brown Shirt") activities] (e.g., Chorover, 1979; Eisenberg, 1972; Lerner, 1992a; Lewontin, 1984; Lifton, 1986; Nisbett, 1977; Proctor, 1988). However, it was Kalikow (1983) who, in searching the records of the Berlin Document Center, found that Lorenz had applied for membership in the Nazi party on May 1, 1938, and was accepted (and given membership number 6170554) on June 28, 1938. Lorenz, then, was a scientist with doctoral degrees in medicine and zoology and, as well, was literally a card-carrying member of the Nazi party. It seems reasonable to inquire about the extent to which biological science and National Socialist ideology and policies were combined in Lorenz's work.

As I have noted, throughout his career, Lorenz (1937a, 1937b, 1965, 1966, 1974a, 1975) was concerned with the degeneration of instincts brought about by the domestication of animals with inferior genes. As indicated in Chapter 2, this theme has had time-honored status in German biological-determinist writings, since at least the period of Ernst Haeckel (1876, 1891, 1905) and the "Monist League" that he started in order to bring scholars from different fields together to use one set of ideas—Darwinian thinking about evolution—to understand all areas of biological, social, and cultural life (Gasman, 1971; Proctor, 1988; Stein, 1987). However, it was in 1938 that Lorenz first presented his views on how domestication was associated with human degeneration (Kalikow, 1983), at a meeting of the German Psychological Association in a paper titled "Deficiency Phenomena in the Instinctive Behavior of Domestic Animals and Their Social Psychological Meaning" (his presentation was published in 1939). First, Lorenz discussed the connection between instincts in animals and instincts in humans. Second, and sounding the theme first raised by Haeckel (1876, 1891, 1905), Lorenz talked about how the domestication-induced degeneracy of instinctual behavior threatens the survival of the German people—the *Volk*. Third, he discussed how differences between, in his terms, the genetically fit and the genetically unfit (and degenerate) are manifested—one way being that fit people appraise beauty and aesthetic appeal as associated with the fit and not with the unfit. Fourth and again similar to Haeckel, Lorenz (1939) argued that judgments of good and bad, or of moral or

immoral, are associated with the hereditarily fit and the hereditarily unfit, respectively (Kalikow, 1983, pp. 58–61).

For instance, with respect to the connection between instincts in animals and humans, Lorenz (1939; translated by Kalikow, 1983) contended:

> What ought to be compared, in these inferences from animals to human beings, are the *hereditary* changes in the system of innate species-specific behavior patterns, changes that arise in animals in the course of domestication and in human beings in the course of the civilization process. These two processes, seen from the standpoint of the biologist, have much in common. (pp. 58–61)

In regard to the threat to the survival of the *Volk* caused by this biological degeneracy, Lorenz (1939; translated by Kalikow, 1983) stated:

> The similarity of the biological foundations makes it quite believable that these parallels, which extend to the smallest details of human and animal behavior, are not just superficial analogies, but are founded on underlying causes. Thus, through a closer investigation of the behavior of domestic animals, we may hope to further our understanding of the biological causes of many menacing decay phenomena in the behavior of civilized human beings. (pp. 58–61)

Finally, in regard to the connection between innate goodness and badness and the presence of hereditarily fixed social behaviors that are either fit or not fit, respectively, Lorenz (1939; translated by Kalikow, 1983) argued:

> Even the observer striving for complete objectivity cannot stop himself from evaluating the decay of social behavior patterns negatively, even in animals. This is even more the case with respect to our conspecifics. For humans we mean by "good" and "bad" really nothing other than "complete with respect to innate social behavior patterns" and the opposite of this. If a person in fact detachedly exhibits a thoroughly social behavior, but does this not according to feeling, or instinctively, but calculatingly, and we see through this, we never feel this person to be "good." Our instinctive evaluation thus really relates to the presence of absolutely specific *hereditary properties* in our conspecifics. (pp. 58–61)

Lorenz (1939) closed by cautioning that the carriers of "bad" hereditary properties can degenerate the health of the *Volk* "like the cells of a malignant tumor." This phrasing is a metaphor that was employed by a group of Nazi-era scientists working expressly on improving the biological fitness of the *Volk*—a group who were termed *racial hygienists* (Proctor, 1988). The aforementioned metaphor was directed expressly at Jews, who were seen by the Nazis as the nonhuman "anti-race." Given this threat, Lorenz (1939) made what must have been seen as the necessary call for social action, again quite similar to the appeals of other National Socialist physicians (Lifton, 1986; Müller-Hill, 1988; Proctor, 1988). Lorenz contended that those who possess fit instinctual patterns must capitalize on their aesthetic/valuational reactions to those who possess unfit, degenerating genes (Kalikow, 1983, p. 61). Using these reactions to recognize the unfit, the fit must *eliminate* the unfit in order to ensure the "racial health and power" of the *Volk*. Specifically, in closing his 1939 publication, Lorenz (1939, pp. 146–147; translated by Kalikow, 1978a) argued:

> This high valuation of our species-specific and innate social behavior patterns is of the greatest biological importance. In it as in nothing else lies directly the backbone of all racial health and power. Nothing is so important for the health of a whole *Volk* as the elimination of "invirent types": those which, in the most dangerous, virulent increase, like the cells of a malignant tumor, threaten to penetrate the body of a *Volk*. This justified high valuation, one of our most important hereditary treasures, must however not hinder us from recognizing and admitting its direct relation with Nature. It must above all not hinder us from descending to investigate our fellow creatures, which are easier and simpler to understand, in order to discover facts which strengthen the basis for the care of our holiest racial, *Volk*ish and human hereditary values. (pp. 174–175)

In short, as did Hitler (1925) and Haeckel (1876, 1891, 1905) before him, Lorenz (1939) saw the mission of race purification—protecting the *Volk* from the "malignant tumor" threatening it by the presence of genetic inferiors—to have cosmic, mystical, and, indeed, holy characteristics.

In 1940, Lorenz published a paper titled "Systematics and Evolutionary Theory in Teaching" in the journal *Der Biologe* (*The Biologist*) (Lorenz, 1940a), expanding on the themes of his 1939 publication and emphasizing, as had racial hygienists in Germany (e.g., Ploetz, 1895), that the natural selection process had been eroded by modern civilization and that this erosion was the basis of the degeneration process threatening the survival of the *Volk*. Lorenz (1940a; translated by Kalikow, 1983) cautioned:

> Whether we share the fate of the dinosaurs or whether we raise ourselves to a higher level of development, scarcely imaginable by the current organization of our brains, is exclusively a question of biological survival power and the life-will of our *Volk*.

Today especially the great difference depends very much on the question whether or not we can learn to combat the decay phenomena in *Volk* and in humanity which arise from the lack of natural selection. In this very contest for survival or extinction, we Germans are far ahead of all other culture-*Volks*. (p. 63)

Given the nature of the journal in which the paper was published, it is not surprising that Lorenz (1940a) sounded this caution about the need to combat the "decay phenomena" endangering the *Volk* and that he complimented his fellow Germans (although he himself was Austrian) for having the wherewithal to be winning this fight (through the racial policies of the National Socialist state), for example, including Hitler's "final solution" to the Jewish problem, a policy that involved mass extermination in the service of genocide.

As Kalikow (1983) explained, *Der Biologe* was an organ of the Biology Section of the National Socialist Teachers' League, and its editorial board members came from such politically correct organizations as the National Socialist University Teachers' League, the SS, and the Race-Political Department of the Nazi party. Given the striking similarity between the views expressed by Lorenz and those promulgated by Nazi physicians and politicians, and given the nature of the publication in which Lorenz presented his views, it is difficult to determine whether this 1940 article is a scientific statement or a Nazi political statement. If the article was meant as only a scientific statement, then at the very least one can wonder whether another publication outlet would have been more appropriate.

The article in *Der Biologe* (Lorenz, 1940a) is not the only one of Lorenz's Nazi-era publications to have a combined scientific and political message. In another paper published in 1940, "Domestication-Caused Disturbances in Species-Specific Behavior," appearing in the *Zeitschrift für angewandte Psychologie und Charakterkunde* (*Journal of Applied Psychology and Personality*), several reviewers of Lorenz's work (e.g., Chorover, 1979; Evans, 1974; Kalikow, 1983; Nisbett, 1977) and Lorenz himself (Lorenz, 1974b, in Cox, 1974) admitted that the most explicit Nazi-oriented statements are made in regard to his interpretation of domestication-induced degeneracy. Indeed, Lorenz (1940b) included at the end of that paper a section entitled "Practical Applications" (Kalikow, 1983): Throughout the paper, however, Lorenz repeated his themes of the danger of racial degeneration, the erosion of natural selection factors, and the need to applaud the National Socialist state's endeavors to institute their own selection measures and thereby exterminate the cancerous cell—the aesthetically ugly and the ethically evil—from the midst of the *Volk*. Lorenz (1940b; translated by Kalikow, 1978a) stated that the paper addressed the question whether the life-conditions of civilization and of domestic animal behavior contain factors that encourage mutations and continued:

> This problem receives its particular importance first through the knowledge that among the most dangerous and race-hygienically most damaging decay phenomena in the social behavior of civilized people are those which have their precise equivalents in the "domestication characteristics" of many domestic animals, and which, in all probability, depend on the same causes. On the answering of the question about these causes, however, depend the counter-measures to be taken. If there should be mutagenic factors, their recognition and elimination would be *the most important task of those who protect the race,* because the continuing possibility of the novel appearance of people with deficiencies in species-specific social behavior patterns constitutes a danger to *Volk* and race which is more serious than that of a mixture with foreign races. The latter is at least knowable as such and, after a one-time elimination of breeding, is no longer to be feared. If it should turn out, on the other hand, that under the conditions of domestication no increase in mutations takes place, but the mere removal of natural selection causes the increase in the number of existing mutants and the imbalance of the race, then race-care must consider an even more stringent elimination of the ethically less valuable than is done today, because it would, in this case, literally have to replace all selection factors that operate in the natural environment. (p. 176)

Later in the paper, Lorenz (1940b; translated by Eisenberg, 1972) expanded on this argument, especially in regard to how to deal with the threat posed by the "ethically less valuable":

> The only resistance which mankind of healthy stock can offer against being penetrated by symptoms of degeneracy is based on the existence of certain innate schemata. . . . Our species-specific sensitivity to the beauty and ugliness of members of our species is intimately connected with the symptoms of degeneration, caused by domestication, which threaten our race. . . . Usually, a man of high value is disgusted with special intensity by slight symptoms of degeneracy in men of the other race. . . . In certain instances, however, we find not only a lack of this selectivity . . . but even a reversal to being attracted by symptoms of degeneracy. . . . Decadent art provides many examples of such a change of signs. . . . The immensely high reproduction rate in the moral imbecile has long been established. . . . This phenomenon leads everywhere . . . to the fact that socially inferior human material is enabled . . .

to penetrate and finally to annihilate the healthy nation. The selection for toughness, heroism, social utility . . . must be accomplished by some human institution if mankind, in default of selective factors, is not to be ruined by domestication-induced degeneracy. The racial idea as the basis of our state has already accomplished much in this respect. The most effective race-preserving measure is . . . the greatest support of the natural defenses. . . . We must— and should—rely on the healthy feelings of our Best and charge them with the selection which will determine the prosperity or the decay of our people. (p. 124)

Also, Lorenz (1940b; translated by Chorover, 1979) expanded:

> [that is, charge them with] the extermination of elements of the population loaded with dregs. Otherwise, these deleterious mutations will permeate the body of the people like the cells of a cancer. (p. 105)

Continuing the analogy between the presence of cancer cells within a body and the presence of a group of people within a society, Lorenz (1940b; translated by Fraser in Müller-Hill, 1988) maintained:

> There is a certain similarity between the measures which need to be taken when we draw a broad biological analogy between bodies and malignant tumors, on the one hand, and a nation and individuals within it who have become asocial because of their defective constitution, on the other hand. . . . Any attempt at reconstruction using elements which have lost their proper nature and characteristics is doomed to failure. Fortunately, the elimination of such elements is easier for the public health physician and less dangerous for the supra-individual organism, than such an operation by a surgeon would be for the individual organism. (p. 14)

Because Lorenz (1940b) called so clearly for reliance on the selection policies of "the Best" of Nazi Germany and for the extermination of elements of the population permeated with "dregs," and a more severe elimination of the morally inferior, it is difficult to reconcile his claim of 34 years later "that they meant murder when they said 'selection' was beyond the belief of anyone. I never believed the Nazi ideology" (Lorenz, 1974b, in Cox, 1974). It is puzzling, to say the least, that someone who called for "elimination" and "extermination" is surprised that those whose selection practices he congratulated exterminated those selected for eliminations. And for someone to claim that he never believed in Nazi ideology, when his publications make claims about biological determinism and call for social policies that dovetail precisely with the explicit details of such ideology, would seem to be a remarkable coincidence. The contradiction that might appear to exist between Lorenz's Nazi-era statements, and his postwar, later-life recollections of his wartime thoughts and meanings, are only compounded when we learn about his other publications during the Nazi period.

In a 1943 article titled "The Innate Forms of Possible Experience," published in the *Zeitschrift für Tierpsychologie* (*Journal of Animal Psychology*), Lorenz (1943a; translated by Kalikow, 1983) reiterated his concept of the links between domestication-produced racial degeneration and aesthetic value judgments about what is ugly, and, therefore, about what is threatening and dangerous (and, hence, "bad," in the moral sense) for society:

> If one systematically goes through the—on close observation—astonishing short list of the characteristics which clearly produce the ugly in human beings and animals, one comes to the result that they are all relational characteristics which in *human beings* indicate domestication—or civilization-caused decay phenomena. If the ugly is to be represented in art, the artist accordingly resorts, not to any old arbitrary distortions of the human ideal Gestalt, but with great regularity to the few typical characteristics of domestication. Classic Greek sculpture represented Silenus as the opposite of the god-and-hero-type, always pinch-headed, with pot-belly and too-short limbs, . . . and in just the same way the traditionally ugly Socrates is always pictured as a chondrodystrophic. (p. 68)

The image Lorenz (1943a) presented of the genetically degenerate and exemplary ugly person is remarkably akin to the depiction of the Jew presented in drawings found in Nazi-publisher Julius Streicher's rabidly anti-Semitic "newspaper," *Der Stürmer,* as well as in various elementary school primers and children's books Streicher published at the time Lorenz was writing these papers. Figure 12.1 presents two illustrations from Streicher's publications depicting Jews (in contrast to Aryans—the race of the German *Volk*) as conforming closely to the characteristics Lorenz contended exemplified the domestication-induced degenerate ugly (e.g., "pot-belly and too-short limbs"; Kalikow, 1983, p. 68).

Still other Nazi-era papers by Lorenz, consistent with Nazi ideology and social policy, appeared repeatedly between 1938 and 1943. For instance, another 1943 paper, "Psychology and Phylogeny" (Lorenz, 1943b; translated by Kalikow, 1978a), appearing in a volume edited by G. Heberer (*Die Evolution der Organismen* [The Evolution of Organisms]), draws connections between domestication-induced degeneration phenomena in animals

FIGURE 12.1
Taken from a racist primer published by Julius Streicher in 1936, *Trust No Fox in the Green Meadow and No Jew on His Oath,* these illustrations depict Jewish adults and children being expelled from a school (above) and from a town (below) as Aryan children look on and/or jeer. As is typical in Streicher's publications, Jews are drawn as potbellied and as having limbs that are too short, features that Lorenz claimed exemplified the domestication-induced degenerate ugly.

Source: Illustrations reproduced in Time-Life Books, *The New Order* (Alexandria, Va.: Time-Life, 1980), p. 105

and humans and concludes that this "scientific" evidence has clear and necessary racial–political implications:

> A domestic goose will mate nonchalantly with any gander, while the mating of the wild form is dependent on a vast quantity of complicated [and innate] "betrothal customs." In human beings, on the other hand, the expansion of [innate] schemata leads to the race-politically highly undesirable increase in the rate of reproduction of the inferior classes. . . . No inevitable "logic of time" brings the "senescence"

of culture-nations with it, as Spengler believed—rather it is factors in the environment, which are concrete, accessible to experiment, and thus certainly possible to combat. The race-political necessity of their immediate, precise investigation is obvious. (pp. 177–178)

Thus, to Lorenz, the need to interrelate hereditarian ideas about race and political necessities was obvious.

Given such a perspective, the need to take political action was clear to Nazi Germany (even if it meant the extermination of a people). Perhaps, this is why Rudolf Hess, the Deputy Führer of Nazi Germany, contended at a mass meeting that "National Socialism is nothing but applied biology" (cited in Lifton, 1986, p. 31).

Conclusions

Given, then, this sample of Lorenz's Nazi-era writings, it is possible to conclude that at least from the time Lorenz joined the Nazi party in 1938 through 1943, when he entered military service for the Third Reich, Lorenz's papers (e.g., 1939, 1940a, 1940b, 1943a, 1943b) contained consistent themes that increasingly more clearly and stridently appeared to combine his science with his racist–political views, views that were entirely consonant with other statements by National Socialist scientists that merged politics and "scientific" Nazi racial hygiene ideology (Lifton, 1986; Müller-Hill, 1988; Proctor, 1988).

Common among Lorenz's Nazi-era papers was the theme of domestication-induced degeneracy; of aesthetically repulsive and immoral genetic misfits multiplying at dangerous rates in society because of the erosion of natural selection; of the need, therefore, to rely on "the Best" of the *Volk* to institute selection measures to fight the threat to the race posed by these hereditarily unfit "cancers"; and of the need for these state-designed selection measures to involve elimination—extermination—of these degenerate "dregs."

The consistent repetition of these themes in several papers spanning a half-decade cannot be interpreted as simply a temporary or minor aberration of a scientist toying with the implications of his work for political ideology and social policy. It seems, rather, to be the work of a person energetically explaining the important congruence between his science and his politics, a person who wants to demonstrate to his audience how his theory and research coalesce to give credibility to National Socialist biological-determinist ideology and legitimacy to Nazi racial policies.

This conclusion is clearly predicated on the scholarship of Kalikow (1978a, 1978b, 1983), who provided the seminal work documenting the linkage between Lorenz's scientific views and National Socialist ideology. However, Kalikow's (1983) view of this linkage has been questioned by Richards (1987), in his authoritative and acclaimed book, *Darwin and the Emergence of Evolutionary Theories of Mind and Behavior* (1987). It is, therefore, important to review and evaluate Richards's (1987) discussion of Kalikow's (1978a, 1978b, 1983) interpretation of Lorenz's Nazi-era work. This discussion also helps to clarify the nature of Lorenz's work during World War II and aid us in understanding the ideas Lorenz presented after the end of the war.

THE SCIENCE AND POLITICS OF LORENZ'S WORK: EVALUATING THE EVIDENCE

According to Richards (1987), Kalikow (1978a, 1978b, 1983) maintained that Lorenz's (e.g., 1939, 1940a, 1940b, 1943a, 1943b) ideas about domestication-induced human degeneracy are tied both to the thinking of Haeckel (1876, 1891, 1905) and the politics of the Nazis. Influenced by the work of Gasman (1971), who also argued that the Nazi "biological mission" was promoted by the Social Darwinism of Haeckel, Kalikow (1983) found in Haeckel (and other Monist League members), in National Socialist ideology, and in the writings of Lorenz four sets of ideas:

1. A biological view of the world, a world in which the laws of nature and the laws of society are the same.

2. The belief that human evolution has been moving with constancy until the present era, in which high reproduction rates and "humanistic" attitudes toward the less fit put the human race at risk for survival.

3. The belief that there is a one-to-one relationship between outer human appearance and internal moral value (i.e., "what is beautiful is good") and that the Aryan race, which exemplifies the pinnacle of this correspondence, has its ancestry among the ancient Greeks.

4. The idea that evolution is the creative force in the world, a notion that replaces the belief that God is the creator and shaper.

Richards (1987) presented several reasons why the links Kalikow (1978a, 1978b, 1983) saw among the Haeckelian/Monist League views, National Socialist ideology, and Lorenz's ideas may be more apparent than real. One reason is "nondistinctiveness"—that the first two sets of ideas are present in the general literature on evolution whereas the last two sets were common at the turn of the nineteenth century. Thus, Richards (1987) dismissed Kalikow's (1983) arguments regarding convergence among the three positions in regard to the four sets of ideas by contending, "If such vague similarities suffice here, we should all be hustled to the gallows" (Richards, 1987, p. 533).

One may question, however, whether the similarities Kalikow (1983) found are as vague as Richards (1987) portrayed. Furthermore, one may ask whether there is support for the convergence among the three positions in addition to the four sets of ideas noted by Kalikow. An examination of the other reasons that Richards rejected Kalikow's ideas allows us to address these questions.

Richards's (1987) second reason for disagreeing with Kalikow's (1983) linkage of the three positions is that the intellectual influence of Haeckelian/Monist League views on National Socialist ideology was not a completely clear one. That may certainly be the case, but there is little reason to expect that the hodgepodge of concepts, the opportunistic twisting of the motley set of ideas that constitutes the corpus of Nazi ideology, should show a neat and logical pattern of influence. For instance, Ralph Manheim (1925, 1927/1943), translator of the most frequently cited English version of Hitler's (1925) magnum opus, *Mein Kampf* (*My Struggle*), indicated in his notes to that edition that Hitler never attempted to systematize his knowledge and, instead, relied largely on disjointed facts. Manheim (1925; Manheim, in Hitler, 1925, 1927/1943) indicated that:

> Even where he is discussing theoretical matters like "the state," "race," etc., he seldom pursued any logic inherent in the subject matter. He makes the most extraordinary allegations without so much as an attempt to prove them. Often there is no visible connection between one paragraph and the next. (pp. xi–xii)

In short, if Nazi ideology was not a logical and coherent system, it is not appropriate to make the presence of a coherent pattern of influence a criterion for linkage between Haeckelian/Monist League views and Nazi ideology.

Accordingly, in order to understand the "intellectual influences" on Nazi ideology, Hitler's (1925) presentation in *Mein Kampf* and the succeeding tracts by Nazi ideologues may best be scrutinized for the sources that (not necessarily logically or correctly) are reflected in them. For instance, whereas both Richards (1987) and Kalikow (1983) noted that evolutionary theory was not fully accepted in the Third Reich, it is known that Hitler was influenced by German Social Darwinist/racial hygiene thinking. For example, the eminent molecular geneticist Benno Müller-Hill (1988) noted that while Hitler was imprisoned in Landsberg Prison in 1923, he read the textbook by Baur, Fischer, and Lenz (1927), *Grundriss der menschlichen Erblicbkeitslehre und Rassenhygiene* (*The Principles of Human Heredity and Racial Hygiene*). Subsequently, Hitler (1925) incorporated racial ideas into *Mein Kampf,* which he was preparing during his imprisonment (Müller-Hill, 1988).

Thus, whereas all features of evolutionary thinking are not necessarily present in Hitler's writings, we do find the idea of selection by a "wise" but ruthless nature (i.e., by a nature making hard but appropriate choices); the notion that a hardened race of high accomplishment will eventually emerge under such conditions; and the view, present in German Social Darwinist/racial hygiene writings, that societal interference with this process will permit the weak and the sick ("lives unworthy of life"; Binding & Hoche, 1920) to survive and the quality of the race to be thereby diminished (Proctor, 1988). Hitler (1925, 1927/1943) wrote:

> Nature herself in times of great poverty or bad climatic conditions, as well as poor harvest, intervenes to restrict the increase of population of certain countries or races; this, to be sure, by a method as wise as it is ruthless. She diminishes, not the power of procreation as such, but the conservation of the procreated, by exposing them to hard trials and deprivations with the result that all those who are less strong and less healthy are forced back into the womb of the eternal unknown. Those whom she permits to survive the inclemency of existence are a thousandfold tested, hardened, and well adapted to procreate in turn, in order that that process of thoroughgoing selection may begin again from the beginning. By thus brutally proceeding against the individual and immediately calling him back to herself as soon as he shows himself unequal to the storm of life, she keeps the race and species strong, in fact, raises them to the highest accomplishments.
>
> At the same time the diminution of number strengthens the individual and thus in the last analysis fortifies the species.
>
> It is different, however, when man undertakes the limitation of his number. He is not carved of the same wood, he is "humane." He knows better than the cruel queen of wisdom. He limits not the conservation of the individual, but procreation itself. This

seems to him, who always sees himself and never the race, more human and more justified than the opposite way. Unfortunately, however, the consequences are the reverse:

> While Nature, by making procreation free, yet submitting survival to a hard trial, chooses from an excess number of individuals the best as worthy of living, thus preserving them alone and in them conserving their species, man limits procreation, but is hysterically concerned that once a being is born it should be preserved at any price. This correction of the divine will seem to him as wise as it is humane, and he takes delight in having once again gotten the best of Nature and even having proved her inadequacy. The number, to be sure, has really been limited, but at the same time the value of the individual has diminished; this however, is something the dear little ape of the Almighty does not want to see or hear about.
>
> For as soon as procreation as such is limited and the number of births diminished, the natural struggle for existence which leaves only the strongest and healthiest alive is obviously replaced by the obvious desire to "save" even the weakest and most sickly at any price, and this plants the seed of a future generation which must inevitably grow more and more deplorable the longer this mockery of Nature and her will continues. (pp. 131–132)

The link between the German Social Darwinists/racial hygienists and Hitler's (1925) ideology is underscored by the consistency between the recommendations Binding and Hoche made regarding the treatment of the weak, lame, and ill in their 1920 book *Die Freigabe der Vernichtung lebensunwerten Lebens* (*The Sanctioning of the Destruction of Lives Unworthy to Be Lived*) and Hitler's (1925) views in *Mein Kampf*. Hitler (1925, 1927/1943) said:

> It is a half-measure to let incurably sick people steadily contaminate the remaining healthy ones. This is in keeping with the humanitarianism which, to avoid hurting one individual, lets a hundred others perish. The demand that defective people be prevented from propagating equally defective offspring is a demand of the clearest reason and if systematically executed represents the most humane act of mankind. It will spare millions of unfortunates undeserved sufferings, and consequently will lead to a rising improvement of health as a whole. . . . The right of personal freedom recedes before the duty to preserve the race. (p. 255)

Hitler turned these ideas into policy (e.g., involving the "forced euthanasia" of German children) when he assumed power (Lifton, 1986). But to Hitler (1925)—and to at least some proponents of the Haeckelian/Monist League views, as well as to Lorenz (1940b, 1966) during both the Nazi era and more than two decades after it—forced euthanasia programs were not the best way to "prune the weak" and move the race in the direction a wise and ruthless Nature would select. Rather, it was through warlike behavior—aggression, struggle, and killing of other humans—that such selection will occur. Thus, according to Hitler (1925, 1927/1943):

> There will be but two possibilities [,] either the world will be governed according to the ideas of our modern democracy, and then the weight of any decision will result in favor of the numerically stronger races, or the world will be dominated in accordance with the laws of the natural order of force, and then it is the peoples of brutal will who will conquer, and consequently once again not the nation of self-restriction.
>
> No one can doubt that this world will some day be exposed to the severest struggles for the existence of mankind. In the end, only the urge for self-preservation can conquer. Beneath its so-called humanity, the expression of a mixture of stupidity, cowardice, and know-it-all conceit, will melt like snow in the March sun. Mankind has grown great in eternal struggle, and only in eternal peace does it perish. (p. 135)

Similarly, Heinrich Ziegler (1893), a founding member of the Monist League, argued:

> According to Darwin's doctrine war has been of the greatest importance for the general progress of the human race, since the physically weaker, the less intelligent, and the morally degenerate must make way for the stronger and better developed people. . . . If one accepts the insights of modern science, he must see war between different races or people as a form of the struggle for existence in the human race. (pp. 168–169)

Lorenz (1966), in turn, noted:

> It is quite typical of man that his most noble and admirable qualities are brought to the fore in situations involving the killing of other men, just as noble as they are. . . . Aggression, far from being the diabolical, destructive principle that classical psychoanalysis makes it out to be, is really an essential part of the life-preserving organization of instincts. (pp. 251, 248)

Hitler's (1925) idea of racial greatness through eternal struggle, and Ziegler's (1893) notion of racial war as a feature of the human race's struggle for existence, converge with Lorenz's 1966 view that aggression is life-preserving and that, by acting on his aggressive instincts, man [sic] has often attained nobility and other admirable characteristics.

Such linkages among the ideas of Hitler, the Monist League literature, and Lorenz are not consistent with Richards's (1987, p. 533) view that only "vague similarities" exist across the three positions. Moreover, although Richards (1987) pointed out that the Monist League had a pacifist, socially liberal orientation, such a general stance does not gainsay either Ziegler's (1893) conception of the race-preserving function of war or the possibility that individual scientists may be personally committed to a pacifist political ideology and yet committed as scientists to a belief about the inevitable, or even instinctual, basis of human aggression. Indeed, this is just the stance Lorenz (1966) took in his book *On Aggression,* in which he argued that to avoid the release of instinctual "militant enthusiasm," society must find means to discharge aggression in innocuous ways.

In short, the linkages Kalikow (1983) drew appear to be real, perhaps even beyond the extent she posited. For instance, although Kalikow (1983) pointed out that the Nazis did not share with either Haeckel (1876, 1891, 1905) or Lorenz (1965, 1966) the commitment to evolution per se as the creative force in the world, we have seen in Hitler's (1925) *Mein Kampf* an emphasis in National Socialist ideology on the selective and shaping force of nature and on several ideas associated with German Social Darwinist/racial hygiene thinking, and quite notably the notion of domestication-induced degeneracy. Indeed, Richards (1987) indicated that some National Socialist ideologues did, in fact, eulogize Haeckel, crediting him with providing scientific support for ideas central to the Nazis' biologized view of the world.

Nevertheless, although Richards (1987) himself provided some evidence for the links between Nazi ideology and Haeckelian/Monist League views, he offered two additional reasons why Kalikow (1983) is mistaken in making this dyad a triad by adding the views of Lorenz. Richards (1987) pointed out that Lorenz never cited Haeckel's work as supportive of his own, and that Lorenz held that the key facet of Haeckel's theory of heredity—the idea of the inheritance of acquired characteristics—was scientifically unsound. Neither of these objections to Kalikow's (1983) argument seems strong, however.

Kalikow's (1983) point appears to be more that Lorenz's ideas were consistent with the views found within the general orientation of Haeckel and the Monist League, and not that Lorenz adopted either all of these ideas or any of the ideas of a particular member of the league—including (as it seems) Haeckel. Indeed, the above presentation of converging quotes from Hitler (1925), Ziegler (1893), and Lorenz (1966) suggests that there is some corre-

spondence between the views of Lorenz and at least one prominent member of the Monist League. In addition, both Richards (1987) and Kalikow (1983) pointed out that Lorenz's (1937a, 1937b) original formulation of "instinct" followed the conceptual lead of Ziegler (1893). Furthermore, Kalikow (1983) and, earlier, Nisbett (1977) noted that Lorenz's early interest in evolutionary biology was prompted by his reading a book by Wilhelm Boelsche (1906), cofounder of the Monist League, titled *Die Schöpfungstage* (*The Days of Creation*).

Perhaps because of the nature of these last two points made in argument against Kalikow's (1983) position, Richards (1987) concluded his analysis of her position by interpreting the historical record of Lorenz's Nazi party affiliation and of his publication record (from 1938–1943) during the era of the Third Reich as "a gossamer thread by which to tie Lorenzian biology to the Nazis" (Richards, 1987, p. 535). However, Richards (1987) did not deny that Lorenz wrote papers consistent with National Socialist ideology, but only claimed that such papers represent Lorenz's "few occasions of public Nazi association" (Richards, 1987, p. 535). One must, therefore, decide how often a person must make a public commitment, in speeches and/or in writing, to a given ideology before that person can be justifiably linked with it. Perhaps what is operating in Richards's stance on this issue is a commitment to the Frankonian proverb "Amol schad' kan Malda nix," "Once does not do a maiden any damage."[1]

In any case, Richards (1987) did conclude that "Lorenz [in 1940] undoubtedly descended to accommodate some of his biological views to the ideology of his time and place" and that "at this point in Lorenz's career, certain well entrenched evolutionary ideas happened to intersect with despicable Nazi dogma" (pp. 535–536). Thus, Richards appeared to come full circle to admit Kalikow's (1983) point about the convergence of Lorenzian and Nazi "biology," and he left one to wonder only about the pervasiveness of the association and Lorenz's enthusiasm for it.

In regard to pervasiveness, we have the historical record provided by Kalikow (1978a, 1978b, 1983), as well as by some other authors (e.g., Müller-Hill, 1988). Regarding enthusiasm, it may be (as Richards, 1987, speculated) that, had the Weimar Republic survived, the main features of Lorenz's work would have remained the same. Indeed, we have seen that the racial ideas found in Nazi ideology had a long history antedating the

---

[1] I am grateful to Professor Alexander von Eye for pointing out this proverb to me.

Third Reich, and that history might have involved Lorenz in some other manner had the events of 1933–1945 not taken place. Nevertheless, it is difficult to gainsay Lorenz's enthusiasm for Nazi ideology when we learn that in his 1940 paper in *Der Biologe,* Lorenz (1940a) called it "one of the greatest joys of [his] life" to have converted a student to "our concept of the world (Weltanschauung)"— that is, to National Socialism (translated by Fraser in Müller-Hill, 1988).

In my view, then, there seems to be both appearance and reality to Kalikow's (1978a, 1978b, 1983) views of the linkage between Lorenz's writings during the Nazi era and the biologized world view of National Socialist politics. Moreover, Kalikow's interpretation of the connection between themes in the writings of Lorenz and in Nazi ideology is underscored when the continuity between the key theoretical ideas found in Lorenz's Nazi-era writings and his post–Nazi-era work is recognized. It is, therefore, useful to focus on this continuity, and also to explain its important role in legitimizing more contemporary biological determinist claims such as those found in sociobiology.

LORENZ'S WORK AFTER WORLD WAR II

Throughout his scholarly career, Konrad Lorenz maintained a central interest in the role of evolution, and of heredity, in animal and human behavior, focusing on the importance of instincts in understanding such behaviors as social attachment, aggression, and moral or ethical functioning. Morality may involve not only behaving in particular ways but also knowing right from wrong, and good from bad. Given this connection between morality and knowledge, we can also understand Lorenz's career-long interest in the evolutionary basis of humans' knowledge or of their cognitive system (Lorenz, 1941, 1974).

All these themes in Lorenz's scholarly work are indisputably appropriate arenas for academic intellectual endeavor. His continuity of interest in these topics could be evidence of an admirable scholarly commitment to long-term programmatic research, research that would be regarded as of scientific interest per se if we were to judge it in isolation from the theoretical ideas from which it sprang. But, if his work involved a merger of scientific and racist political ideas, his continuity of interest might tell us as much about enduring political agendas as scientific ones. If little has

changed in Lorenz's core scientific political message, other than the deletion after World War II of Nazi terminology to present the message, then one must be skeptical (at the least) about Lorenz's (1974b; in Cox, 1974) claim that his involvement with the Nazis and their ideology was merely a foolish, "naive error":

> Like a fool I thought I could improve them [the Nazis and their ideology], lead them to something better. It was a naive error. (p. 20)

The issue we need to address, then, is whether: (a) the message in the writing of the Nazi-era Lorenz was a combined scientific–racist one whereas the message after the Nazi era has been solely scientific; or (b) the messages have remained essentially the same, with only the Nazi-era terminology omitted.

If a case can be made for the second alternative, the implications for present-day science and social policy would be considerable, in light of the scientific eminence Lorenz enjoyed and the credibility and respect thereby accorded his work. That is, politicians and policymakers could get the impression that there is broad-based scientific acceptance of biological-determinist thinking that at its core has pejorative, racist–political aims. The resulting danger would be that these policymakers might promote social policies that are consistent with those particular assertions of biological determinism. For example, interpretations that the bases of criminality and immorality are genetically based would come to the fore. It might, therefore, seem that devoting resources to prevention programs or to programs that sought to promote positive development among people who possessed such genes would not be economically prudent or scientifically realistic.

The most straightforward way to decide about the continuity or discontinuity in Lorenz's core message is to refer to his own post–Nazi-era statements. Has the tune really changed, or has the song only been given a new name? Continuity alone in the topics Lorenz studies is not enough to make a decision; we must see whether his stance on the key theoretical theme in his work, if one exists, has been altered appreciably.

There *is* a core theme uniting Lorenz's Nazi-era and post–Nazi-era work: the threat posed by domestication-induced degeneration of human instincts for the survival and further evolution of human moral, or ethical, being and thus for the future survival or progress of civilization. It is my belief that Lorenz's post-World War II interpretation of this theme continued to be identical to that in his Nazi-era papers, reviewed earlier in the chapter. Lorenz may have claimed that he never believed Nazi ideology, and that he saw his use of it as a "naive error." However, he never apologized or claimed regret for the *interpretations* he made—which were consistent not only with Nazi ideology but also, as I have noted, with the ideas of pre–Nazi- and Nazi-era German Social Darwinists, eugenicists, and racial hygienists such as Haeckel, Ploetz, Schallmayer, Binding, Hoche, and Lenz (see Proctor, 1988). Indeed, the only specific facet of his message for which I can find an apology is his choice of *terminology;* he did not apologize for the underlying ideas the particular terms conveyed. Lorenz (1974a; in Cox, 1974) said:

> In retrospect, I deeply regret having employed the terminology of the time . . . which was subsequently used as a tool for the setting of horrible objectives. (p. 20)

However, perhaps revealing of the actual continuity in the core, underlying theme of his work, Lorenz admitted in 1974 that, as indicated by the epigraph at the beginning of this chapter, he was intrigued with eugenics to the point of obsession.

We might expect to find, therefore, that the only changes in Lorenz's views about the threats posed to civilization by domestication-induced genetic degeneracy are in the way the views are phrased. Although this is partly the case, one can also find a continuing ideological and terminological emphasis on changing the distortions of natural selection that modern civilization's domestication practices have wrought; on the genetic basis of morality, of the human sense of good and bad; on the decay brought about in this instinctual capacity by domestication phenomena; on the fact that some people have genes for good morality and/or ethics and that others have ethically bad genes; and on the inevitable need for elimination (if not extermination) procedures to protect society against further degeneration.

For instance, Lorenz (1954; translated by Kalikow, 1983) equated domestication phenomena with deleterious mutations and pathologies and indicated that civilization's interference with (or removal of) natural selections processes was responsible for the appearance of such phenomena:

> One might possibly be inclined to think that environmental conditions . . . have favored homologous mutations. However, this would definitely seem to be a false assumption; instead the blame for the appearance of these characters seems to be exclusively due to the removal of natural selection. . . . Domestication-induced alterations of instinctive behavior are, by nature, processes bordering closely on pathological events. (p. 70)

Moreover, as in the Nazi era, the postwar Lorenz (1954) indicated that this domestication-induced genetic degeneracy occurs in humans as a consequence of modern civilization's interference with naturally selected instinctual behavior patterns. Lorenz (1950; translated by Kalikow, 1978b) contended:

> With every organism that is plucked out of its natural environment and placed in novel surroundings, behaviour patterns occur which are neutral or even detrimental for the survival of the species. . . . Modern man represents such an animal, torn from his natural environmental niche. . . . The flowering of human culture has so extensively changed the entire ecology and sociology of our species that a whole range of previously adaptive endogenous behavior patterns have become not only non-functional but extremely disruptive. (p. 184)

To Lorenz (1950, 1954), then, instinctive behavior patterns arose as naturally selected adaptations to humans' premodern context. These instincts are fixed patterns of action; they are not flexible (or plastic) in and of themselves, and they are not available for modification either in or through the action of an altered environment. Thus, when humans find themselves in the radically new setting of modern civilization, they are in twofold peril: (1) Their previously adaptive instincts may no longer be useful in the new setting, and (2) the removal of natural selection from the new setting will allow degenerative instincts (what Lorenz terms *deleterious mutations* and *pathologies*) to survive and be reproduced.

The Example of Human Aggression

Lorenz's views regarding aggression provide an instructive example of how an instinctual pattern that purportedly evolved to facilitate human survival may undermine it in the context of modern civilization. In his 1966 book, *On Aggression,* Lorenz described humans' aggression as involving instinctual "militant enthusiasm," an inherited vestige of their past and an instinctual response that allowed the individual to respond, with confederates in his or her group, to threats from organisms outside the community. Indeed, Lorenz (1966) saw such an instinctual pattern as one that, with no thought involved, allowed communities of even fully evolved humans to survive:

> To the humble seeker of biological truth there cannot be the slightest doubt that human militant enthusiasm evolved out of a communal defense response of our prehuman ancestors. The unthinking single-mindedness of the response must have been of high

survival value even in a tribe of fully evolved human beings. It was necessary for the individual male to forget all his other allegiances in order to be able to dedicate himself, body and soul, to the cause of the communal battle. (p. 270)

Lorenz (1966) contended that with changes in cultural development the "object" that is defended by the militant enthusiasm instinct may change as well. For example, in early human evolution, the immediate group may have been the object toward which a threat would have elicited militant enthusiasm, whereas among contemporary humans the nation or an abstract idea (i.e., "democracy") may elicit the instinct (Lorenz, 1966). Whatever the object, Lorenz believed two points were certain. First, the object that is salient in a culture becomes so "by a process of true Pavlovian conditioning plus a certain amount of irreversible imprinting," and, second, culture owes a great debt to militant enthusiasm, because "without the concentrated dedication of militant enthusiasm neither art, nor science, nor indeed any of the great endeavors of humanity would ever have come into being" (Lorenz, 1966, pp. 270–271).

Although all these positive outcomes of civilization derive from the instinctual aggression of human beings, civilized humans are not, in Lorenz's (1966) view, entirely in control of whether these outcomes will materialize. Because militant enthusiasm is an instinct that attaches to an object through irreversible imprinting and reflexlike learning or conditioning in early life, negative outcomes of the instinct's release and attachment to a cultural object (outcomes such as war) may occur. Thus, in speaking of whether militant enthusiasm will, in fact, lead to positive social outcomes, Lorenz (1966) contended:

> Whether enthusiasm is made to serve these endeavors, or whether man's most powerfully motivating instinct makes him go to war in some abjectly silly cause, depends almost entirely on the conditioning and/or imprinting he has undergone during certain susceptible periods of his life. There is reasonable hope that our moral responsibility may gain control over the primeval drive, but our only hope of its ever doing so rests on the humble recognition of the fact that militant enthusiasm is an instinctive response with a phylogenetically determined releasing mechanism and that the only point at which intelligent and responsible supervision can get control is in the conditioning of the response to an object which proves to be a genuine value under the scrutiny of the categorical question. (p. 271)

Lorenz (1966), then, offered hope that, if civilization recognizes the instinctive nature of aggression, future generations can be attached to cultural objects subserving the most prized and positive achievements, and also the moral responsibility, of human beings. Indeed, in *On Aggression,* he described what he believes are "simple and effective" ways of "discharging aggression" in an "innocuous manner" through attempting to "redirect it at a substitute object" and suggests that sports may be particularly useful in such attempts to channel militant enthusiasm in nondestructive ways (Lorenz, 1966).

What if instinctual aggression is not redirected by civilization? What if militant enthusiasm is released and attached to an object that is associated with war? Given the instinctual, reflexive, and irreversible character that Lorenz attributed to human aggression, there is little a person or group can do if early experience leads militant enthusiasm to be associated with negative—dangerous and destructive—outcomes.

It is possible to view this "double-edged sword" character of human aggression in a historical context. On the one hand, the instinctual and reflexive character of militant enthusiasm can be controlled in the future, if society presents appropriate imprinting, conditioning, and redirection, so there is hope that aggressive instincts can subserve moral and positive aims. On the other hand, Lorenz's (1966) formulation excused the past: If society did not recognize the evolutionarily determined, instinctual nature of aggression, and if, therefore, a cohort of people were exposed in their early youth to an inappropriate object, they are not morally culpable for having had their instinct released by this object. Knowing now that human aggression is instinctual may make the leaders of society morally responsible for building programs for the future that will involve the nondestructive release of instinctual aggression (e.g., through sports programs). However, current groups of adults cannot be blamed if leaders of the society they experienced as children did not act in this responsible manner. In short, it is possible to interpret Lorenz's formulation of instinctual militant enthusiasm as excusing the past—perhaps, more specifically, his past—while providing hope for the future.

This interpretation is bolstered when one reviews Lorenz's (1966) ideas about "the stimulus situation which releases" militant enthusiasm. Lorenz contended that there were four stimulus conditions that led to the appearance of militant enthusiasm; and when militant enthusiasm appeared in this way, Lorenz believed it occurred with a degree of certainty equivalent to an inborn reflex such as an eyeblink (van der Dennen, 1987). Lorenz (1966) argued:

Militant enthusiasm can be elicited with the predictability of a reflex when the following environmental situations arise. First of all, a social unit with which the subject identifies himself must appear to be threatened by some danger from outside. . . . A second key stimulus which contributes enormously to the releasing of intense militant enthusiasm is the presence of a hated enemy from whom the threat to the above "values" emanates. This enemy, too, can be of a concrete or of an abstract nature. It can be "the" Jews, Huns, Boches, tyrants, etc., or abstract concepts like world capitalism, Bolshevism, fascism, and any other kind of ism; it can be heresy, dogmatism, scientific fallacy, or what not. . . . A third factor contributing to the environmental situation eliciting the response is an inspiring leader figure. . . . A fourth, and perhaps the most important, prerequisite for the full eliciting of militant enthusiasm is the presence of many other individuals, all agitated by the same emotion. (pp. 272–273)

That Lorenz's (1966) specification of the four eliciting conditions of instinctual militant enthusiasm parallels the social conditions he and other members of his generation experienced during the Nazi era is striking. The four stimulus conditions correspond to, respectively, (1) the German *Volk,* threatened by the danger of biological annihilation by the (2) hateful (diseased, criminal, and biologically degenerate) Jew. The *Volk* will be protected by (3) the inspiring leader, the Führer, Hitler, who will (4) inflame the emotions of all members of the superior, Aryan race and thus elicit actions—militantly enthusiastic actions—aimed at totally destroying the arch, biological enemy of the *Volk,* the Jew.

It is a remarkable coincidence that Lorenz (1966) would be able to report, more than 20 years after the end of World War II, that there was scientific "evidence" for the existence of a reflex in humans that, in effect, freed the German people from any guilt in following Hitler. Indeed, it is bordering on the incredible that Lorenz "discovered" an instinctual reflex whose path of elicitation paralleled exactly the social events involved in Hitler's "war against the Jews" (Dawidowicz, 1975). We humans certainly cannot be guilty if we possess a knee-jerk reflex, since we were "designed" by evolution to possess such an automatic reaction.

In the same sense, it would be consistent with Lorenz's (1966) argument to assert that the people of Nazi Germany could not help but follow Hitler once their "militant enthusiasm" reflex was imprinted and conditioned in the manner that occurred during the Third Reich. In other words, who could fairly blame the German people for the militant enthusiasm with which they murdered the Jews—and other targets of Nazi murder such as Gypsies, communists, homosexuals, the handicapped, Catholic clergy, and political opponents (Proctor, 1988)—if they were acting in the unthinking, irreversible, and reflexive manner that Lorenz said was the case with instinctual military enthusiasm?

Is There a "Militant Enthusiasm" Instinct?

But what if the notion of "instinct," as a hereditarily predetermined, genetically fixed and immutable set of behaviors, is a scientific fiction? What if the very behaviors that Lorenz described as genetically predetermined to emerge are neither inevitable nor immutable? What if there is no instinctual reflex such as militant enthusiasm—and thus no evolutionarily preprogrammed apologia for Nazi genocide? What if, even in the fish or the bird, much less the human being, nurture can alter both the nerve cells and the behaviors purportedly associated with instincts? In short, what if the supposedly predetermined and fixed genes–nerve cells–behavior connection is neither predetermined nor fixed but instead a readily modifiable, "plastic" linkage? Then social policies and programs designed to redirect innate militarism would be time and money misspent. The error in such policies and programs is that they are based on the assumption of an evil (or at least undesirable) basic nature for human beings, and if this assumption is wrong, then the programs that follow from it have no justification.

What can be wrong with promoting social policies and programs to diminish aggression and militarism? Even if those behaviors are not really instinctual, humans do engage in them all too often. Would the time and money spent on such programs then be wasted or unjustified? There are at least three reasons why they would. First, by building social programs to counter the occurrence of a scientific fiction, one is legitimating the use of what is, in effect, a lie in order to shape social policy.

Second, the efforts directed at deriving policies based on a scientific "lie" divert limited resources from scientifically supportable policies, which may actually be less pessimistic than the predetermined, instinctual views of Lorenz. The social-policy implications of this instance of Lorenz's views about "instinct" was perhaps best presented in a review of *On Aggression* written by Schneirla (1966):

It is as heavy a responsibility to inform man about aggressive tendencies assumed to be present on an inborn basis as it is to inform him about "original sin," which Lorenz admits in effect. A corollary risk is advising societies to base their programs of social training on attempts to inhibit hypothetical innate aggressions, instead of continuing positive measures for constructive behavior. (p. 16)

Thus, if nature and nurture are both equally involved in shaping human behavior, programs to develop positive and/or valued social behaviors may be designed proactively. There would be no need to have to expect only the worst and have as the only option the design of "containment or rechanneling" programs to constrain the undesirable but inevitable behaviors.

Third, when one legitimates a scientific lie for use in shaping social policy, one is creating a potential for the lie to be used again in other policy areas. If humans are instinctually militaristic, might they also be controlled by other instincts? Can we not find instincts or, in other words, innate or inborn behavioral differences to account for differences between African Americans and European Americans (e.g., in intelligence), between men and women (e.g., in their sexuality and family orientations), and between the socially privileged and the socially powerless (e.g., in their resources and life options)? We certainly can, and, as colleagues of Schneirla pointed out, the biological-determinist thinking exemplified by Lorenz has been used to legitimate not only militarism but also racism, sexism, and Social Darwinism (Tobach, Gianutsos, Topoff, & Gross, 1974).

The view of human nature exemplified by Lorenz leads to a pessimistic, and, indeed, bleak, view of our social world: Humans have evolved to possess genes that inevitably give them specific behaviors. Some of these behaviors (e.g., aggression) are shared by all people because evolution has provided all humans with an almost identical array of genes (i.e., an almost equivalent genotype). There are, of course also differences in genotypes, and to Lorenz (1965, 1966) it is those differences that are the basis of the most socially important (in my view, pernicious) implication of his concept of instinct.

Some differences are obvious—for instance, between men and women (females have two "X" chromosomes, and men have one "X" and one "Y" chromosome). Other differences may be more subtle and complex, reflecting the differing evolutionary histories of particular groups. In all cases, however, Lorenz, as a committed Darwinist, would hold that genetic differences are outcomes of differences in the history of selection experienced by the groups in question.

The social policy implications of these genetic differences arise when, in Lorenz's (1965, 1966) view, the different selection histories involve civilization's attempts to domesticate and permit the continued survival of individuals who, under the conditions of natural selection, would not otherwise have survived. This point brings us back to the issue of domestication-induced degeneracy, a theme of central concern to Lorenz during the Nazi era. Let us focus on this topic within Lorenz's post-World War II writings.

SELECTION AND ETHICAL DEGENERATION IN MODERN CIVILIZATION

In *Civilized Man's Eight Deadly Sins* (1974a), Lorenz spelled out the perils to modern human beings quite specifically and warned: "If the progressive infantilism and the increasing juvenile delinquency are, as I fear, signs of genetic decay, humanity as such is in grave danger. In all probability, our instinctive high valuation of goodness and decency is the only factor today exerting a fairly effective selection pressure against defects of social behavior" (p. 58). Thus, to Lorenz in 1974, domestication had eroded humans' sense of the normal: their ability to tell the difference between pathological and nonpathological, or between good and healthy versus bad and unhealthy. Moral or ethical deterioration, then, was an outcome of domestication phenomena.

Is such ethical degeneration essentially the result of a generalized decline in the genes of all humans, or are there individual differences? Is the threat more a matter of some individuals carrying inferior genes—genes that produce moral and ethical degeneracy? Simply, did the post–Nazi-era Lorenz (1974a) believe, as did the Nazi-era Lorenz (e.g., 1939, 1940a, 1940b, 1943a, 1943b), that some people have ethically inferior genes and some have ethically superior ones? Did the postwar Lorenz continue to believe that the "moral imbeciles" that threatened the health and survival of the *Volk* in the 1940s (Lorenz, 1940b) also exist in post–World War II society? If so, did they put in peril the survival of all nondegenerate humanity, if not the German *Volk*?

Ultimately, the key question is: "What did Lorenz believe must be done to protect humanity against such a threat?" Did he make recommendations redolent of Nazi-era selections and eliminations, albeit perhaps not using the "unfortunate terminology" of that era? Did he once again call on the best among us—those with their instinctual ethics intact—to help create selection procedures aimed at restoring the natural order? In my view, the answers to these last questions are yes.

Lorenz (1975) wrote:

> Selection is and always has been the main creative and developing agent, from the molecular stage at the very beginnings of life up to the process of gaining knowledge by falsification of hypotheses. . . . By the very achievements of his mind, man has eliminated all those selecting factors which have made that mind. It is only to be expected that humaneness will presently begin to decay, culturally and genetically, and it is not surprising at all that the symptoms of decay become progressively more apparent on all sides. . . . The genetic "domestication" of civilized man is, I am convinced, progressing quite rapidly. Some cardinal symptoms which are present in most of our domestic animals are an increase in size and the hypertrophy of eating as well as of sexual activity. That all three of these symptoms have noticeably increased in man during the short span of my own life, is, to say the least, alarming. . . . Equally widespread is the quantitative increase of eating and sexual drive, accompanied in both cases by a loss of selectivity in releasing mechanisms. One has only to go to a beach where many urbanized people are bathing to note the rapidly increasing incidence of fat boys and young men or to look at a great modern illustrated paper in order to be confronted with both symptoms in a thoroughly alarming manner. . . . Of course, I do not know for sure that these symptoms are genetic, they may well be cultural, at least in part, but that does not matter much. Cultural development is analogous to genetical evolution in so many areas that the causal distinctions become immaterial as regards the phenomenon here under discussion, except that cultural processes are not less, but more dangerous because of their incomparably greater speed. . . . I am convinced that it is one of technocracy's most insidious stratagems to avoid all coercive methods and rely on kind-seeming reinforcements alone. . . . I do not think that a healthy philosophy of values can develop without a sense not only of what is good but also of what is evil. It is my chief reproach against the ideology of the pseudodemocratic doctrine that it tends to eradicate, throughout our whole culture, the sense of values on which alone the future of humanity depends. . . . I do not believe that the death penalty or incarceration are able to prevent our genetic stock from decay; in fact there is nothing left in civilized society which could prevent retrograde evolution *except our nonrational sense of values,* which I still believe and hope can take a decisive hand in human evolution, both genetic and cultural. . . . There is such a thing as good and evil, there are decent guys and there are scoundrels and the difference between them is indu-

bitably partly genetic. No living system can exist without elimination, however humanely it can be brought about and however much one tries not to make it appear as a punitive measure. . . . We *know* that evolution stops on its way upward and steps backward when creative selection ceases to operate. Man has eliminated all selective factors except his own nonrational sense of values. We must learn to rely on that. (pp. 126–128)

This passage underscores quite clearly Lorenz's continuing belief in the genetic basis of society in general, and in the hereditary determination of either the ethical value or the ethical worthlessness of people in particular. As did Haeckel (1876, 1891, 1905), Lorenz (1940b, 1975) saw both genetic and cultural evolution as essentially interchangeable, if not identical, processes that have a mystical, or at least nonrational, component which imbues only certain people with a proper sense of values. In addition, I believe that Lorenz saw in 1975, as he did in 1940, the need to rely on the moral responses of the people who have their innate ethical values intact to lead society. We must rely on them to bring civilization back to the path of healthy evolution from which it has been diverted—given the loss of natural selection processes and, instead, the institution of "kind-seeming reinforcements," a phrase reminiscent of Ploetz's (1895; see, too, Lenz, 1930) characterization of the "misguided" humanitarian social programs that allowed the genetically unfit to survive and reproduce.

Moreover, as did Haeckel (1876, 1891, 1905) and the Nazi-era racial hygienists (Baur et al., 1921; Lenz, 1930), Lorenz (1975) called for the institution of "creative selection" procedures, which we may infer should be conducted by those with the best values. What these procedures should involve is not specified. However, I have noted that Lorenz criticized technocracy's avoidance of coercive methods and insisted on the need for elimination procedures beyond the death penalty and incarceration to ensure the continued existence of human beings. These views, frankly, are too consistent with his writings and those of other Nazi-era racial hygienists to lead one to conclude anything other than the continuity of a core theme.

Finally, although Lorenz (1975) was apparently flirting momentarily with environmental, or cultural, causation, he ultimately continued to take a hereditarian stance consistent with the biological-determinism of the Nazi racial hygienists: Even if one were to label society's problems as cultural and not biological in origin, with close analysis one would learn that any causal distinction becomes unimportant. Because of the ontological and material priority of biological processes over cultural processes, the latter ones can be reduced to the former; as such, therefore, at the core, the differences between good and bad people are biological.

If there could be any remaining doubt that Lorenz (1975) continued to insist on the biological basis of morality and ethics and on the possibility of sorting people into good and bad groups, or ethically superior and inferior groups, on the basis of their environmentally immutable genetic inheritance, then some of his own statements should remove this doubt. Shortly after Lorenz was awarded the Nobel Prize, an article by a freelance writer living in Munich, Vic Cox, appeared in the March 1974 issue of *Human Behavior*. Titled "A Prize for the Goose Father," it summarized Lorenz's career, contained excerpts from an interview with him, and discussed Lorenz's Nazi past and current thinking and work. As part of that article, Cox quoted a passage from Lorenz's 1940 publication on "Domestication-Caused Disturbances in Species-Specific Behavior," an article (Lorenz, 1940b) that we have discussed and cited earlier in this chapter.

In two places on page 19 of Cox's (1974) article the passage was quoted. In both places the quote was incorrect, containing a small typographical error in one word which, nevertheless, changed the meaning of the passage. The passage was misquoted to read that Lorenz called for "a more severe elimination of the ethnically inferior than has been done so far" (Cox, 1974, p. 19), although as noted in my own quote from this same article (see page 302), Lorenz actually said: "an even more stringent elimination of the ethically less valuable than is done today."

An extra "n" had been added to the word "ethical," to make the word "ethnical." Thus, we may infer that, in 1940, Lorenz called for elimination, indeed, the "extermination," of people who were ethically inferior by virtue of their genes, but that he did not call for the elimination of any particular ethnic groups that because of their "race" may have been carriers of inferior genes. My inference about Lorenz's meaning is supported by his own words. Lorenz wrote a letter to *Human Behavior* to correct the typographical error and to clarify the views the misquoted passage represented. The letter, appearing in the September 1974 issue, reads in its entirely as follows (Lorenz, 1974c, p. 6):

> I thank you very much for the readiness to correct what was obviously more an error of the printer than of the editor. However, I beg you to realize that changing ethical into ethnical ("A Prize for the Goose Father," March 1974) makes me appear a rabid racist, which I never was. I never believed in any ethnical superiority or inferiority of any group of human beings, though I strongly hold that ethical inferiority of individuals due to heredity or to bad upbringing (lack of motherly love during the first year of life) is indeed a reality, which has to be taken seriously.
>
> I should highly appreciate it if you could include that in the intended correction.
>
> Prof. Dr. Konrad Lorenz, Altenberg, Austria. (p. 6)

Although Lorenz (1974c) thus insisted he was not a racist, claiming that he had never believed there was a group of humans who by virtue of their "ethnical" heredity are inferior, he did believe in 1974, and in the Nazi period, that there was a group of humans who, by virtue of their ethical heredity, were inferior. It was this group—the moral imbeciles and dregs discussed in 1940—that should be eliminated, Lorenz believed. Such a fine conceptual distinction about who is and who is not to be the target of such "special treatment" (to use the Nazi euphemism for extermination) provided little comfort to the men, women, and children who were sent to the gas chambers and crematoria. In addition, Lorenz's conceptual distinction between ethnical and ethical has little historical validity, given the fact that Nazi Germany equated ethical degeneracy with membership in a particular ethnic group (i.e., Jews).

LORENZ AND SOCIOBIOLOGY

The core message of the Lorenz of the post-World War II era is, therefore, not conceptually different from that of the Lorenz of the Nazi era. There is continuity in his views of the basic causes of both individual behavior and the social order: they are evolutionarily based, genetic causes. There is also continuity in his beliefs about the basis of social problems and the threats to civilization: the erosion of natural selection; the reproduction, therefore, of hereditary moral inferiors who otherwise would have not survived; and the degeneracy in healthy instinctual patterns produced by the domestication of these inferiors. Ultimately, there is also continuity in the remedies Lorenz sees as requisite for saving civilization: We must rely on the nonrational ethical responses of the genetically—ethically superior among us and charge them with creating selection procedures to replace the eroded natural selection ones, and thereby eliminate the threat that domestication-induced ethical degeneracy poses to our healthy genetic stock.

Given what I regard as the quite evident Nazi-era/post–Nazi-era continuity in the core message of Konrad Lorenz, it is extremely puzzling that he received the world's most prestigious scientific award. Nevertheless, when other biological-determinist positions were then promulgated, the broad scientific and societal legitimization of biological-determinist ideology that the Nobel Prize provided could not help but impart to that ideology, for scientists and citizens alike, an aura of believability and the impression that this was on the cutting-edge advance of "normal science." This creation of a biological-determinist Zeitgeist (spirit of the times) may have contributed in part to the broad scientific and social attention E. O. Wilson received in 1975, when he announced the presence of the new, synthetic discipline of sociobiology (see Chapter 13).

The affinity between the work of Lorenz and that of contemporary sociobiologists is highlighted by the frequent citations of Lorenz's work in the sociobiological literature, citations usually made approvingly and in the service of marshaling support for one or another sociobiological idea (e.g., Barlow, 1980; Dawkins, 1976; Freedman, 1979; Konner, 1982). In addition, this reliance on Lorenz's work has led some contemporary sociobiologists to go out of their way to defend Lorenz against often unnamed critics and vaguely described criticism.

For instance, sociobiologist Melvin Konner, in his 1982 book, *The Tangled Wing,* praised one of Lorenz's Nazi-era papers ("*Der Kumpan in der Umwelt des Vogels*" [The Companion in the Bird's World, 1935]), reminds the reader that Lorenz was a Nobel Prize recipient, and then, in what is clearly a non sequitur, asserts that people are incorrect if they judge Lorenz only on his late (but uncited) popular writings or on the (undescribed) comments of his (unnamed) critics: "It is a magnificent paper, not only informative and convincing, but sweeping, incisive, beautiful. Reading it gives an impression very similar to that gained by reading Freud's early anatomical writings: that one has been very wrong to judge Lorenz only by his late popular writings, or worse, secondhand, by the opinions of his critics" (Konner, 1982, p. 124).

Among the several problems with Konner's (1982) vague defense of Lorenz is the marked continuity between the topics, themes, and opinions found in the writings of Lorenz published in the Nazi era and in the post-Nazi era: there was little change in Lorenz's views about domestication-induced degeneracy, about selection, and about the genetic basis of moral worth and moral degeneracy. Simply, Konner (1982) proposed a division of Lorenz's work that cannot be supported by a close analysis of Lorenz's views across this span of time. What Konner's (1982) remarks do suggest, however, is that perhaps sociobiologists may look approvingly on the core ideas of Lorenz because his ideas are similar to the ideas they themselves promote. In the next chapter, I consider these latter, sociobiological ideas in more detail and draw further parallels with the work of Lorenz.

Nature Approaches to Development: Sociobiology

In 1975, E. O. Wilson published a book that announced the "new" scientific discipline of sociobiology. Wilson (1975a) contended that sociobiology would be the "master" synthetic discipline, a field enveloping all of behavioral and social science.

In this chapter, arguments forwarded by Wilson (1975a, 1975b, 1980) and others (e.g., Rushton, 1999) in support of this synthetic role for sociobiology are evaluated, especially as these ideas have been advanced in regard to understanding human behavior and development. In particular, this chapter focuses on sociobiological claims pertinent to features of behavior central to human reproduction, parenting, and child caregiving. My discussion draws on and extends prior discussions of sociobiological ideas (Barlow & Silverberg, 1980; Caplan, 1978; Kitcher, 1985; Lerner, 1992; Lerner & von Eye, 1992, 1993; Lewontin et al., 1984), especially in regard to issues relevant to human development and to the provision of an alternative to sociobiological views of the role of biology in human development, one based on a developmental systems perspective.

THE SCIENTIFIC GOALS OF SOCIOBIOLOGY

Wilson's (1975a, 1975b, 1980; Lumsden & Wilson, 1981) claims about sociobiology, as well as corresponding assertions made by others (Konner, 1982; MacDonald, 1988), have both found support and application (Rushton, 1987, 1988a, 1988b, 1990, 1991, 1995, 1996, 1999) and evoked strong criticism (Barlow & Silverberg, 1980; Caplan, 1978; Kitcher, 1985; Lerner, 1992a; Lerner & von Eye, 1992, 1993), even among those who associated themselves with the "new synthesis." For instance, according to Dunbar (1987):

Wilson created the impression that sociobiology was on the verge of replacing most of the disciplines in the social and behavioral sciences. This, of course, is arrant nonsense since sociobiology does not, of itself, deal with much of the subject matter of these disciplines. (p. 51)

However, Dunbar (1987) went on to defend the importance of Wilson's views for social and behavioral science:

Wilson was, none the less, right to emphasize the importance of sociobiology in relation to these disciplines. What it in fact does . . . is to provide a unifying umbrella under which these disciplines can interact on common ground. (p. 51)

It is the mechanism through which this unification is purported to occur that concerns us first. As noted in previous chapters, this mechanism bears on the nature–nurture controversy.

Genetic Determinism as Sociobiology's Key to Interdisciplinary Integration

In Wilson's (1975a) view, the "unifying umbrella" provided by sociobiology is the ubiquitous influence of genes on all facets of individual and social behavior and development. Indeed, Wilson's (1975a, 1975b) views exemplify a key conception of genetic determinism—thorough genetic reductionism. The complexity of all social behavior and development and, indeed, all human culture (Lumsden & Wilson, 1981) can be reduced to a few simple genetic principles.

The core idea, however, is one of "gene reproduction." To Wilson (1975a, 1980), Dawkins (1976), and other sociobiologists (Barash, 1977; Freedman, 1979; MacDonald, 1988), the essential, core purpose of human life is only to reproduce genes. As Konner (1982, p. 265) put it, "A person is only a gene's way of making another gene." Similarly, Dawkins (1976,

E. O. Wilson

p. ix) sees humans as only "survival machines"—robot vehicles blindly programmed to preserve the selfish molecules known as genes."

Simply put, all of human development reduces ultimately to gene reproduction and, as such, a human organism "does not live for itself" (Wilson, 1975a, p. 3). Instead, the organism's primary function is not even to produce other organisms per se. Rather, Wilson (1975a) claimed that the primary purpose of an organism is to produces genes. In fact, the organism is seen as only the temporary carrier of genes (Wilson, 1975a, p. 3); through reproduction, the organism "transports" genes to another organism which, in turn, transports the genes to another organism, and so on.

According to this view, humans have not evolved to produce other people, but only to replicate some of their particular complement of genes. Humans' life spans represent only a relatively short period within the vast temporal span of evolution. During this time they provide a temporary "house," or a transport, for the genes carried within them. Given this machinelike view of the "human as transport," it is clear why Dawkins (1976, p. 21) could see humans merely as "lumbering robots

(housing genes that) created us, body and mind; and their preservation is the ultimate rationale for our existence."

Given this core, "gene reproduction" principle, it is also evident why Dawkins (1976) considered genes to be selfish. Genes are "concerned" with nothing other than self-replication, with reproducing themselves over and over, as many times as possible. Simply, then, in this view humans are really just (seemingly complex) duplicating machines. Their mating rituals, their family relationships, and their cultural institutions are all inventions in the service of gene reproduction.

This core genetic principle of life leads to several other ideas about how genes influence individual behavior and the social world. The more copies of one's genes one can send out into the world, then, in the terms of sociobiology, the more one is increasing one's *inclusive fitness*. In other words, the more copies of itself a genotype can transport into another generation of "gene reproducers" the greater is its inclusive fitness.

This concept derives from the sociobiological view that natural selection is the essential vehicle through which evolutionary change occurs (Dawkins, 1976; Wilson, 1975a). However, not all genes are able to compete equally in the face of the fierce and rigorous challenges imposed by the natural environment; only the most aggressive genotypes will succeed in this struggle for survival. It is here, in the link between sociobiological ideas regarding inclusive fitness and aggression, that, as discussed in Chapter 12, the ideas of Konrad Lorenz (1940a, 1940b, 1965, 1966, 1974, 1975) play an important role in the shaping of sociobiological thinking.

SOCIOBIOLOGY AND HUMAN AGGRESSION

A parallel arises between the views of sociobiologists (Dawkins, 1976; Konner, 1982) and the ideas of Konrad Lorenz. As discussed in Chapter 12, Lorenz (1966) saw human aggression as both inevitable and inherent in the human genome—to the point of providing for innate "militant enthusiasm." To Lorenz, not only do the genes of humans make them aggressive, but also the "highest form" of humans should be the most aggressive—the most militaristic—because such action reflects the presence of genes that have succeeded most in the struggles of natural selection. Similarly, in the sociobiological world of selfish genes, and the robotic "survival machines" that house them, aggression functions to allow genes to enhance their inclusive fitness; "blind" (i.e., unthinking, and machinelike) aggression allows genes to eliminate anything in the environment that interferes with their reproduction.

Thus, to Lorenz (1966) and to sociobiologists (e.g., Konner, 1982), selfish—indeed, ruthless—human aggression is the cornerstone of genes' control over human functioning. The most successful genes— the "best" of evolution, if you will (Lorenz, 1940b)— will be the most successful at ruthless aggression. They will be the most selfishly directed to maximizing their presence in the gene pool and, at the same time, to minimizing the genes of others. Of this blind, ruthless, militant aggression, Dawkins (1976) said:

> To a survival machine, another survival machine (which is not its own child or another close relative) is part of its environment, like a rock or a river or a lump of food. It is something that gets in the way, or something that can be exploited. It differs from a rock or a river in one important respect: it is inclined to hit back. This is because it too is a machine which holds its immortal genes in trust for the future, and it too will stop at nothing to preserve them. Natural selection favours genes which control their survival machines in such a way that they make the best use of their environments. This includes making the best use of other survival machines, both of the same and other species. (p. 71)

Similarly, and redolent of Lorenz's (1966) views in his book, *On Aggression,* Konner (1982) explained:

> I believe in the existence of innate aggressive tendencies in humans (p. 203) . . . if we are ever to

control human violence we must first appreciate that humans have a natural, biological tendency to react violently as individuals or as groups, in certain situations. (p. xviii)

According to Lorenz (1966), these innate violent reactions are elicited in a reflexlike manner among either individuals or groups. The reflex occurs when members of an in-group are threatened by members of an out-group. Similarly, we have noted that Dawkins (1976) contended that selfish genes impel humans to act aggressively against survival machines other than those of their own, close genetic group, and Wilson (1975a; see also Flohr, 1987, p. 199) likewise believes that fear of (and hatred toward) an out-group (xenophobia) is innate in humans. For example, in his book, *On Human Nature,* Wilson (1978) wrote of "hidden biological prime movers," and contended that:

> In all periods of life there is (a) . . . powerful urge to classify other human beings into two artificially sharpened categories. We seem able to be fully comfortable only when the remainder of humanity can be labeled as members versus nonmembers, kin versus nonkin, friend versus foe. (p. 70)

In sum, all genotypes must struggle arduously to include as many copies of themselves as possible in the gene pool. However, within sociobiological thinking all genotypes are not "created equal"; that is, whereas all genotypes strive to maximize their inclusive fitness, genotypes differ in what is termed in sociobiology *gametic potential,* (i.e., the potential of a genotype to replicate itself). Differences in gametic potential are associated with the differences that exist between males and females.

Richard Dawkins

SEX DIFFERENCES IN GAMETIC POTENTIAL

Within sociobiology, it is held that men and women differ in their potential for transmitting copies of their genes into the future. For example, as claimed by Konner (1982, p. xviii), "as now seems clearly demonstrated, there are biological reasons why women, like other primate females, have a weaker aggressive tendency than males." Since aggression is the key, according to sociobiologists, to getting one's genotype reproduced maximally, it follows that women, lacking an aggressive ability sufficient to compete with men, must evolve some other strategy to enhance their inclusive fitness. The strategy that women use derives completely, sociobiologists contend, from the nature of the specialized cells used by women to transmit copies of their genes to future generations.

Genotype copies are contained in gametes, that is, sperms and ova. Both types of gametes function to maximize the inclusive fitness of the genotypes they carry. However, the two types of gametes have a different potential for such reproduction—due to the anatomical and physiological differences between the "lumbering robots"—men and women—housing these gametes. Men, who—it is of more than passing interest to note—were the founders and leading proponents of sociobiology, can generate a large number of genotype copies. Their gametes can be "sent forth to multiply" quite readily—millions can be sent out with each ejaculation. Thus, in the terms of sociobiology, their "gametic potential" is great, given that there is—at least theoretically—a ready, large pool of recipients of their gametes. Freedman (1979) put this idea as follows:

> Since mammalian males produce many more sperm than females produce ova, any given male has far greater potential for producing offspring. He is also more inclined to compete with other males over the "scarce" resource, females. (p. 2)

Simply put, then, any male has a greater potential for enhancing his inclusive fitness than any female, given males' greater gametic potential. Moreover, males must have, in general, a more aggressive genotype than females, because they must compete for access to the female gamete, viewed as a "resource" for the deposit of the males' sperm. Such competition is, of course, highly desirable in the view of sociobiologists, because it ensures that the most aggressive genotypes—those best suited to succeed against the struggles of natural selection—will reproduce most often.

In turn, the genotypes of females impel women to try to reproduce in quite a different way. One might understand the origin and development of this "alternative," female reproductive strategy if one asks these questions:

> Given the vast difference in reproductive potential, and if the point of life is to actualize such potential, is it not reasonable to expect that on the average the male pattern of courtship will differ from the female? Might nature not have arranged it so that men are ready to fecundate almost any female and that selectivity of mates has become the female prerogative? (Freedman, 1979, p. 12)

In answer to such questions, van den Berghe and Barash (1977) noted:

> Human females, as good mammals who produce a few, costly and therefore precious, offspring, are choosy about picking mates who will contribute maximally to their offspring's fitness, whereas males, whose production of offspring is virtually unlimited, are much less picky. (p. 813)

Gametic Potential and Social and Sexual Development

What does the sexes' different gametic potential imply for understanding male and female social behavior and development? Given the selfishness of genes and the single-minded direction of the duplicating machines housing them, men develop sexual mores dictating the acceptability (if not the appropriateness) of multiple sexual partners. Indeed, van den Berghe and Barash (1977) argued that the different gametic potential of men and women explains

> the widespread occurrence in human societies of polygamy, hypergamy, and double standards of sexual morality. There is another related reason for the sexual double standard in such things as differential valuation of male and female virginity and differential condemnation of adultery: marital infidelity of the spouse can potentially reduce the fitness of the husband more than that of the wife. Women stand to lose much less if their husbands have children out of wedlock than vice versa (p. 813). . . . In addition, a woman will, at a maximum, produce some 400 fertile eggs in her lifetime, of which a dozen at most will grow up to reproductive age, while a man produces millions of sperm a day and can theoretically sire hundreds of children. Not surprisingly, females tend to go for quality, and males for quantity. (p. 814)

Moreover, given the large number of offspring they can potentially produce, a male's parental investment in any one is quite small. Unfortunately for the recipients of males' genetic copies—women—their gametic potential is quite different, and so, too, is their parental investment. They can replicate themselves at most every 9 months. Even with multiple births, a woman cannot replicate her genes as much in a lifetime as a man can in a short period of time. Therefore, according to sociobiologists, a woman's investment in her offspring is much greater than is a man's. Moreover, sociobiologists also contend that because women cannot reproduce very frequently, women will not be motivated toward frequent copulation with multiple partners. Instead, it is believed that women need to protect their offspring and assure their survival, and that this need should motivate them to keep their impregnators bound to them. As a consequence, the view of sociobiologists is that females develop monogamous sexual behaviors and a devotion to childbearing and rearing. Van den Berghe and Barash (1977) argued:

> For a woman, the successful raising of a single infant is essentially close to a full-time occupation for a couple of years, and continues to claim much attention and energy for several more years. For a man, it often means only a minor additional burden. . . . (M)ost societies make no attempt to equalize parental care; they leave women holding the babies. (p. 813)

Lest anyone contend that the different moral, sexual, and social developments of men and women are merely products of socialization, Barash (1977, p. xv) argued that the sex differences in gene reproduction strategy explain "why women have almost universally found themselves relegated to the nursery, while men derive the greatest satisfaction from their jobs." Van den Berghe and Barash (1977, p. 815) further noted that "ethnographic evidence points to different reproductive strategies on the part of men and women, and to a remarkable consistency in the institutionalized means of accommodating these biological predispositions." Van den Berghe and Barash (1977), therefore, concluded:

> Men are selected for engaging in male–male competition over resources appropriate to reproductive success, and women are selected for preferring men who are successful in that endeavor. Any genetically influenced tendencies in these directions will necessarily be favored by natural selection. (p. 814)

Dawkins (1976) embellished these ideas by contending that women's exploitation by men is biologically determined. He argued that the sexes' behavioral developments are differentiated not only by the different number of sex cells that can be used for genotype reproduction but also by the different size of their respective sex cells:

> The sex cells or "gametes" of males are much smaller and more numerous than the gametes of females . . . it is possible to interpret all the other differences between the sexes as stemming from this one basic difference. (p. 152)

> Sperms and eggs . . . contribute equal numbers of genes, but eggs contribute far more in the way of food reserves: indeed sperms make no contribution at all, and are simply concerned with transporting their genes as fast as possible to an egg. . . . Female exploitation begins here. (p. 153)

Sex differences in the gametic potential and size of the gametes result not only in female exploitation in general but, in particular, in the legitimization of extramarital sex for males, but not for females, and of the use of violence toward wives who have extramarital sexual relations. To explain these sex differences, Freedman (1979) argued:

> We have to assume that cultural universals reflect those aspects of our species that were evolutionarily derived (evolved). Male promiscuity is universally winked at because there is nothing much we can do about it, and Kinsey's (Kinsey et al., 1953) main findings appear to be descriptions of the species: males must have "frequent outlets" for sex, whether heterosexual or homosexual; whereas many females can go for long periods without copulation or masturbation. . . . And this difference appears to hinge on the difference in gametic potential that we have been discussing. (p. 19)

> As in the gelada baboon, in humans female jealousy is based not on the male's sex act with another woman but on his potential attachment to the latter. . . . Male jealousy is rather different. . . . It does not make evolutionary sense for the male to invest in a child not possessing his genes and the murderous jealousy exhibited by a cuckolded male is biologically sensible. Furthermore, the cuckold's retribution can strike either the female or the male cheater . . . and most legal systems (perhaps all patrilineal systems) wink at the ensuing violence. (pp. 20–21)

Dawkins (1976) extended across the life span the idea of the biological basis of men's promiscuous sexual interests. He offered both "a possible explanation of the evolution of the menopause in females" (p. 136) and, at the same time, an account of the sociobiological basis of the existence of what are colloquially (and pejoratively) termed "dirty old men":

> The reason why the fertility of males tails off gradually rather than abruptly is probably that males do not invest so much as females in each individual child anyway. Provided he can sire children by young women, it will always pay even a very old man to invest in children rather than in grandchildren. (p. 136)

Conclusions: Genetic Determinism and Human Development

In the sociobiology advanced by Wilson (1975a, 1975b), men—impelled mechanistically by their genes—are oriented to seek sexual relations with as many women as possible, to achieve more and more copies of their genes, and to not be overly devoted to or concerned with any one or any few given "replicates." Women in contrast, are oriented to remain monogamous in order to maximize the probability that their relatively few replicates will survive. In essence, then, men and women are genetically impelled to differ in ways that are consistent with traditional (i.e., stereotypic) sex-role patterns.

As did Freud (1923) and later Erikson (1968), Wilson's (1975a, 1975b) sociobiology in effect holds that "anatomy is destiny" regarding key features of behavioral development—ones involving reproduction, parenting, child caregiving, and sexuality. In other words, Wilson (1975a, 1975b), Dawkins (1976), Freedman (1979), and other sociobiologists (e.g., Barash, 1977; Konner, 1982; MacDonald, 1988; Rushton, 1999) built a natural edifice encompassing the very core of all human behavior and development—the reproduction of men and women, the character of the family, and the survival of the species. Any notions of nurture or of nature–nurture fusion as sources of key features of human behavior are mere fictions if genes work in the way that sociobiology requires, that of selfish, goal-directed, and intentional agents. According to sociobiology, after other, more superficial "causes" of human behavior are stripped away (e.g., "causes" involved in an individual's development such as cognition or social values), genes provide the ultimate basis for human functioning: the replication of genotypes.

According to this conception, the social world does not interact with humans' genes, much less act as an alternative source for human development. Instead, according to sociobiologists, our social world—human mores (e.g., regarding sexual permissiveness or monogamy), social institutions (such as marriage and the family), and, indeed, all of human culture—is nothing other than the outcome of strategies laid down by humans' genes for their own replication. Sociobiologists have complete faith in the inevitable reducibility of human behavior to the functioning of selfish genes.

Akin to Lorenz (1966), this genetic–determinist view has necessarily xenophobic and ruthlessly (if not militantly) selfish implications for society. The faith in genetic determinism and reductionism maintained by sociobiologists is expressed by Dawkins (1976) in his claim that "It can be perfectly proper to speak of 'a gene for behavior so-and-so' even if we haven't the faintest idea of the chemical chain of embryonic causes leading from gene to behaviour" (pp. 65–66). Dawkins (1976) also stated "Be warned that if you wish, as I do, to build a society in which individuals cooperate generously and unselfishly towards a common good, you can expect little help from biological nature" (p. 3).

To what extent is this sociobiological view of human development, and of society, supported by scientific evidence? Asked another way, what

scientific evidence do sociobiologists draw on to legitimate their claims, and how adequate is this evidence? We now turn to an examination of these key questions.

EVALUATING SOCIOBIOLOGICAL CLAIMS

Given Wilson's (1975a, p. 4) original definition of sociobiology as "the systematic study of the biological basis of all social behavior," it may seem surprising, and perhaps contradictory, to learn that Wilson (1980, p. 296) also contended that "contrary to an impression still widespread among social scientists, sociobiology is not the theory that human behavior has a genetic basis." Perhaps, Wilson (1980) was just playing with words. Perhaps, he meant that sociobiology is not a "theory" but only a "perspective," or merely a rather general framework within which to systematically study the biological and, therefore, ultimately, the genetic basis of all social behavior. Whether his statement pertaining to social scientists' mistaken impressions about sociobiology rests on a difference in meaning between the phrases "the theory that . . ." and "the systematic study of . . . ," Wilson's own words show that sociobiology is the study of the role of the connection between genes and human social behavior. He (1980), in fact, used the term *sociobiological theory* to represent this linkage. Wilson (1980) claimed:

> Real sociobiological theory allows no less than three possibilities concerning the present status of human social behavior: (a) During the rapid evolution of the human brain, natural selection exhausted any genetic variability of the species affecting social behavior, so that today virtually all human beings are identical with respect to behavioral potential. In addition, the brain has been "freed" from these genes in the sense that all outcomes are determined by culture. The genes, in other words, merely prescribe the capacity for culture. (b) Genetic variability has been exhausted, as in (a). But the resulting uniform genotype predisposes psychological development toward certain outcomes as opposed to others. In an ethological sense, species-specific human traits exist and, as in animal repertories, they have a genetic foundation. (c) Genetic variability still exists, and, as in (b), at least some human behavioral traits have a genetic foundation.

> Having identified these alternatives, and stressed the freedom of the discipline of sociobiology from the necessity of any particular outcome, I can now add that the evidence appears to lean heavily in favor of alternative (c). (p. 296)

In the case of each of the given options—(a), (b), and (c)—stress is given to the links among evolution, genetic variability, and human development and society. However, if sociobiologists have spent a good deal of time exploring the first two of the three options, such work has not found its way into the published literature. Hence, Wilson is correct in asserting that to the extent that "evidence" exists in support of any of the three options, it does so in regard to option (c). Yet, support for (c) does not exist because the three options have been repeatedly subjected to comparative scientific analyses. Rather, the preponderance of published sociobiological work—at least insofar as the human literature is concerned—has taken as its "working assumption" option (c). The "evidence" derived from such work constitutes not a test of competing hypotheses but, rather, an attempt to bring empirical observations to bear on a demonstration of a guiding presupposition.

That is, given what are quite well-known facts of genetic variability (McClearn, 1981; see Chapter 4), it would be nothing short of preposterous to conduct a scientific investigation predicated on the idea that genetic variability does not exist. As a consequence, we do not believe it plausible that either Wilson or other sociobiologists are not fully aware of this quite basic evidence about the existence of immense human genetic variability. Consequently, it is equally difficult to envision that any serious scientific attention could be paid by sociobiologists to options (a) or (b). Therefore, these two options cannot be, and, as we have indicated, are not treated as, viable counters to (c). Instead, this last conception is the only one actually pursued scientifically by sociobiologists. But, given that no alternatives are really comparatively tested, such pursuit is more a demonstration of how empirical phenomena coincide with a conceptual presupposition than a critical test of theoretical options.

How do such demonstrations proceed? Three types of evidence have been invoked. It is useful to examine each type separately.

Comparisons of Humans and Nonhumans: The Concept of Homology

One way in which sociobiologists demonstrate that human social behavior is constrained by evolutionarily shaped genes is to draw parallels between the behaviors of humans and nonhuman animals. If the behaviors of distinct species can be described similarly, it is argued that there must be some evolutionary connection, or conti-nuity, between them. A common evolutionary pathway for a physical structure or a behavioral function in distinct species is termed a *homology*. Simply, then, sociobiologists argue that if the characteristics of two species can be described in a common way, evidence is present of homologous evolution. The positing of such homology is offered as proof that the characteristics in question are controlled, or constrained, by evolutionarily shaped genes.

The use of such "evidence" is exemplified in the writing of Freedman (1979) and Rushton (1999, 2000). For instance, in attempting to document his views that human males' gametic potential gives rise to sexually promiscuous behavior—in order to increase their opportunities to garner the "scarce resource" of females' ova—whereas human females' gametic potential makes them more monogamous, Freedman found homologies between fruit flies, rhesus monkeys, and South American jungle-dwelling, polygynous humans. Freedman (1979) argued that in all species:

> Females tend to cluster about an average number of young whereas males form a greatly skewed curve, some very successful, many not successful at all. And, since most mammals are polygynous . . . this tendency may characterize the entire class Mammalia. (p. 13)

Freedman (1979, p. 14) carried his argument one step further. By again using what he regarded as common behavioral descriptions across species, he attempted to provide an evolutionary and genetic account not only for inevitable human male promiscuity but also for the genetically preordained urge to seek sexual relations with other females even to the point of forcing oneself onto them (i.e., committing rape) (Freedman, 1979). First, Freedman (1979) cites the work of Grzimek (1972) that:

> In spring, when the gonads are at the peak of their development, there are attempts to "rape" strange females in the mallard and pintail and a few other species (Grzimek, 1972, p. 270). (p. 14)

Second, Freedman made an inference about the "promiscuous, polygynous intentions" of ducks and, finally, drew a conclusion about the insatiable, continuous, and carnal search by human males for females with whom to copulate. Freedman (1979) contended:

> It would appear that if the mallard drake had his way his would be a polygynous species and, in fact, one does occasionally see a consortship of two females and a male. In our own species and our own culture, I am asserting nothing startling when I

point out that with sexual maturity, most heterosexual males are in constant search of females, and if inhibited about sexual contact, they fantasize almost continuously and fairly indiscriminately about such contact . . . adolescent males in our culture frequently experience life as a nearly continuous erection—spaced by valleys of depression that accompany sexual disappointment. (p. 14)

Are these descriptions, and those by other sociobiologists (Barash, 1977; Wilson, 1975a), of purportedly comparable human and nonhuman social behavior, satisfactory proof of the evolutionary and genetic bases of human behavior? Does apparent descriptive similarity establish evolutionary homology? The answer to both of these questions is no, for several reasons, not the least of which is the difficulty of accumulating sound scientific evidence of common evolutionary descent when only physical attributes are being considered (Atz, 1970; Gould, 1980). The task is even more problematic in the case of behavioral characteristics, as even very similar behaviors (a) may be manifestations of quite different processes, and/or (b) may serve different functions (Bitterman, 1965, 1975; see Chapter 5 as well).

In regard to (a), it is a truism that one can describe similar behaviors across even vastly different species. For instance, as discussed in Chapter 5, insects, fish, rats, and humans all "learn"; that is, in members of each of these species, systematic and relatively permanent changes in behavior occur in relation to experience. Nevertheless, the ways in which these species learn—the processes of learning—vary considerably. For example, it would be difficult to contend that thought processes play a part in the learning of insects at any point in their lives. In turn, it would be equally difficult to argue that cognition does not enter into human learning for anything other than the earliest years of the life span, and even in early human infancy cognition may play a role (Piaget, 1970).

Accordingly, although experience-based changes occur in all animals' adjustment to the environment, this similarity is at best evidence for an analogy, not a homology (Atz, 1970; Schneirla, 1957). In other words, different processes may subserve analogous functions. But to claim that such descriptive analogies are indicative of common evolutionary histories is, at best, naive, and, at worst, poor scholarship. Dunbar (1987) was frank in admitting this limitation in sociobiological scholarship:

> Many of those who were influential in promoting the sociobiological perspective . . . (e.g., E. O. Wilson) tend to be unaware of the more sophisticated nature of the behaviour of higher organisms and are apt to regard even advanced mammals simply as scaled-up insects. (p. 53)

In turn, and in regard to the aforementioned point (b), the presence of identical behaviors in different organisms does not constitute proof for even common function or purpose. To illustrate, the reasons that male mallard ducks might force copulation upon a female of their species are certainly distinct from those involved when a human male rapes a human female. Indeed, to label both the male duck's behavior and the actions of the human male with the same term (rape) seems to trivialize, through biological reductionism, what is certainly a complex and violent human act, one that current scholars point out may not even be a behavior predicated in any way on sexuality or sexual feelings (Sunday & Tobach, 1985).

Can Freedman (1979), Barash (1977), or other sociobiologists who argue for homology on the basis of such cross-species descriptions, contend that the devaluation of women in many sectors of modern society, and the legitimization of violence as a means of exercising social (and political control), do not enter into the primary causation of forced copulation by human males and/or that they enter as well into the basis of such behaviors in ducks? I think not. Simply stated, the mere portrayal of behaviors in two species as appearing comparable is no proof at all of their common evolutionary heritage. Nor is it any proof at all regarding the extent to which such behaviors are genetically constrained or produced.

Indeed, this conclusion seems to have been reached by Wilson (1980) himself. He noted that:

> We cannot rest the hypothesis of genetic constraint in human social behavior on the indirect evidences of homology. (p. 297)

If the sociobiologists' behavioral homologies do not constitute adequate proof for the genetic basis of human social behavior, what then does? Two other types of evidence have been offered, pertaining to the concepts of heritability and adaptation. We first consider heritability.

Sociobiology and Heritability Analyses

The myriad conceptual and methodological problems associated with heritability analyses of human behavior have been discussed in Chapters 10 and 11. We need not reiterate here the information we reviewed about the counterfactual view of genetic functioning, the flawed reasoning, and the methodological shortcomings associated with heritability research to note that, in relying on heritability as a source of support for their hereditarian views, sociobiologists are, in effect, relying on no evidence at all (e.g., Hirsch, 1997).

Nevertheless, Wilson (1980) argued that data from heritability research supported the third of the three possible theoretical options upon which sociobiology rests. This was the notion that genetic variability exists and, as such, that at least some human behavioral traits have a genetic foundation. Accordingly, Wilson (1980) saw that heritability research not only supported the presence of genetic variability but also that it did so in a manner supporting the hereditarian claims of sociobiology. This seemingly straightforward perspective evokes, in actuality, a thicket of conceptual confusion.

First, we have noted that sociobiologists do not have to look to behavior genetics to document the clear fact that genetic variability exists (see Chapter 4). In fact, behavior genetics and its use of research about heritability does not provide proof about the presence of human genetic variability—molecular genetics and population genetics does this; rather, heritability analysis capitalizes on (begins with the acknowledged fact of) genetic variability and then seeks to partition this variability into hereditary and environmental sources (see Chapters 10 and 11).

Second, however, sociobiologists' reliance on the findings of heritability research as offering support for their views is completely ill-conceived. Sociobiologists wish to talk about behavioral characteristics (i.e., traits) that are common to a species. The task of the sociobiologist is to show scientifically that such traits uniformly and unequivocally characterize the subgroups of humans in question (e.g., males and females), and do so because of the possession of evolutionarily based genetic "directives" for genotype reproduction.

Stated simply, sociobiologists wish to demonstrate that some human traits (i.e., ones common to a given group and dealing with that group's reproductive strategy and, hence, inclusive fitness), have a genetic basis. In other words, sociobiologists want to demonstrate the common, or invariant, inheritance of these traits but, in relying on evidence from the study of heritability, they are using information that capitalizes not on commonality of inheritance but on its variability!

In essence, then, sociobiologists are trying to claim support for the importance of invariant heredity for human characteristics by pointing to evidence that shows there is variation in heredity. Hirsch (1997) made a similar point. Hirsch noted (1997, p. 210) that "The misleading picture that emerged in *Sociobiology* was that heritability is the very essence of evolution." This depiction of the connection between sociobiology and evolution was flawed, Hirsch (1997) argued because:

> Wilson was downright irresponsible in his failure to emphasize the inherent contradiction in this picture, namely that the important characters have the lowest heritabilities. In the words of his own source "characters with the lowest heritabilities are those most closely connected with reproductive fitness, while the characters with the highest heritabilities are those that might be judged on biological grounds to be the least important determinants of natural fitness" (Falconer, 1960, p. 167). (p. 210)

Similarly, Collins and colleagues (2000) pointed out that "genetic factors that are highly important in a behavior do not show up in a study of heritability of that behavior because the genetic factor is uniform for all members of a population. Thus, analyzing the variation of a factor within a population does not provide exhaustive information concerning either the genetic or the environmental contributions to the factor" (p. 220).

Accordingly, there are insurmountable logical, conceptual, methodological, and empirical problems involved in sociobiologists' reliance on data derived from heritability research for evidence in support of their hereditarian claims. As such, neither this line of "evidence" nor that provided by work associated with the concept of homology can be used by sociobiologists to support their ideas about human behavior and development. There is, then, only one possible line of evidence left for them to use to document the validity of their ideas: adaptation. Let us consider it.

Are Adaptations Everywhere?

A cornerstone of the sociobiological "method" is to offer explanations in the vein of Rudyard Kipling's "Just-So Stories" of how particular social behaviors, or differences among people in their social status or roles, came to be (Gould, 1980). As recounted by Gould (1980):

> Rudyard Kipling asked how the leopard got its spots, the rhino its wrinkled skin. He called his answers "just-so stories." When evolutionists try to explain form and behavior, they also tell just-so stories—and the agent is natural selection. Virtuosity in invention replaces testability as the criterion for acceptance. (p. 258)

According to Gould (1980), this unacceptable scientific procedure led the biologist von Bertalanffy (1969) to complain:

> If selection is taken as an axiomatic and a priori principle, it is always possible to imagine auxiliary

hypotheses—unproved and by nature unprovable—to make it work in any special case. . . . Some adaptive value . . . can always be construed or imagined. . . . I think the fact that a theory so vague, so insufficiently verifiable and so far from the criteria otherwise applied in "hard" science, has become a dogma, can only be explained on sociological grounds. Society and science have been so steeped in the ideas of mechanism, utilitarianism, and the economic concept of free competition, that instead of God, selection was enthroned as ultimate reality. (p. 11)

According to both Gould (1980) and von Bertalanffy (1969), the key feature of sociobiological "just-so stories" is that these current arrangements in society are adaptations; that is, adaptations are changes that enhance fitness, that have been shaped by natural selection, over the eons of human evolution to have this function, and that are now represented in the human genotype. Yet, it is the key element in these arguments—the presence of an adaptation, of a change in fitness—that all too often remains a scientifically unverified, post hoc story.

Indeed, as admitted by Dunbar (1987):

A simple statement that X increases the fitness of those that perform it explains nothing: it is strictly tautologous for improving fitness is what every sociobiological explanation implicitly assumes. What we need to know—and this is the heart of any sociobiological explanation—is: How does it increase fitness?

It is the transparent failure to answer this question that has left so many sociobiologists open to criticisms of "Just-So" story-telling and unscientific practice. Since we necessarily have to rely on comparative observations rather than experimental manipulation when tackling evolutionary problems, we are particularly exposed to this kind of accusation. The only way to avoid it is to provide as watertight a case as is possible by showing that proximate problems of survival or reproduction are in fact resolved when individuals behave in a specified way, and that efficient solutions to these problems will result in increased contributions to the species' future gene pool. This will not always be easy, but, unless it can be done, sociobiological explanations will always be open to skeptical doubts, particularly where these doubts are fuelled by political or religious conviction. (p. 50)

Despite these explanatory difficulties, sociobiologists see adaptations—changes in fitness "designed" by (or, actually, "resulting" from) natural selection—as being everywhere. And, in the view of sociobiologists, these changes in fitness, because they are adaptations, are optimizations. That is, as argued as well by nineteenth-century social Darwinists (Tobach et al., 1974), natural selection results in genetically based features that are the "time-tested," best possible outcomes of humans' evolutionary history.

According to sociobiologists, then, that which exists is an adaptation: Humans' social behaviors and the niches they occupy in the social hierarchy have been shaped by natural selection to take their present form. As claimed succinctly by Konner (1982, p. 18), "An organism has characteristics, they must have been selected for or they wouldn't be here now."

Given this centrality of the concept of adaptation in sociobiologists' thinking, we may ask whether there is the direct, uniform, and singular pathway that sociobiologists infer from evolution, through natural selection, to adaptation and the present character of people and society. We may also ask precisely why presenting a story—which is a possible scenario of the way natural selection *could have* resulted in a given feature of human behavior—is not sufficient to establish scientifically that just such a history transpired.

The concept of "exaptation." The work of Gould and Vrba (1982) is quite relevant to these issues. They tried to provide a new term in evolutionary biology in order to clarify some important, but confusing, uses of the term *adaptation*. Gould and Vrba noted that one meaning of adaptation is the shaping of a feature of the organism (e.g., a physical attribute or a behavior) by natural selection for the function it now performs. A second meaning is a more static one, and refers to the immediate way in which a physical feature or a behavior enhances the organism's current ability to fit its context. This second meaning does not take into account the historical origin of the feature, but only whether the organism's physical or behavioral characteristics help it to meet the current demands of its environment.

Gould and Vrba (1982) cited Williams (1966) as adhering to the first definition of adaptation. Williams (1966, p. 6) contended that one should speak of adaptation only when one can "attribute the origin and perfection of this design to a long period of selection for effectiveness in this particular role." Bock's (1979) views illustrate the second definition of adaptation. Bock indicated that "an adaptation is . . . a feature of the organism . . . which interacts operationally with some factor of its environment so that the individual survives and reproduces" (p. 39).

Gould and Vrba (1982) claimed that a confusion, therefore, exists regarding a central concept in evolutionary theory—adaptation. This conflict exists because the single term "adaptation" has been used when, in fact, there are different criteria for the historical basis of a given organism's feature and for its current use. Darwin (1859) himself may have seen this potential confusion:

> The sutures in the skulls of young mammals have been advanced as a beautiful adaptation for aiding parturition, and no doubt they facilitate, or may be indispensable for this act; but as sutures occur in the skulls of young birds and reptiles, which have only to escape from a broken egg, we may infer that this structure has arisen from the laws of growth, and has been taken advantage of in the parturition of the higher animals. (p. 197)

In other words, while Darwin saw the necessity of unfused sutures in the skulls of young mammals, he was uncertain about labeling the unfused sutures as adaptations, because the unfused sutures were not built by selection to function as they now do in mammals (Gould & Vrba, 1982). But if the unfused sutures are not adaptations, if they were not shaped by natural selection, what are they and where did they come from? Clearly, a new term must be used to rectify the confusion, and Gould and Vrba (1982, p. 6) provided one. They suggested that such characters evolved for other usages (or for no function at all), and were later "coopted" for their current role. They termed such characters *exaptations*. The characters are fit for their current role (i.e., they are "aptus"), but they were not designed by natural selection for this role, therefore, they are not ad aptus (pushed toward fitness by natural selection).

To illustrate, it is useful to consider exaptation pertinent to the features of microevolution. This illustration of exaptation indicates how this concept may account for a feature of the genome that, to those committed to an adaptationist program, might appear anomalous. Gould and Vrba (1982) pointed out that:

> For a few years after Watson and Crick elucidated the structure of DNA, many evolutionists hoped that the architecture of genetic material might fit all their presuppositions about evolutionary processes. The linear order of nucleotides might be the beads on a string of classical genetics: one gene, one enzyme; one nucleotide substitution, one minute alteration for natural selection to scrutinize. We are now, not even 20 years later, faced with genes in pieces, complex hierarchies of regulation and, above all, vast amounts of repetitive DNA. High repetitive, or satellite, DNA can exist in millions of copies: middle-repetitive DNA, with its tens to hundreds of copies, forms about one quarter of the genome in both *Drosophilo* and *Homo*. What is all the repetitive DNA for (if anything)? How did it get there? (p. 101)

Some of the repeated DNA may be conventional adaptations, selected for a role in regulation (e.g., the repeated copies may bring previously separated parts of the genome into new, aptative interrelation). However, there is too much repetitive DNA for such direct adaptation to account for all of it. A second, traditional (i.e., adaptationist program-oriented) basis for the presence of so much repeated DNA has been forwarded. This suggestion is that repetitive DNA exists because it is needed for *future* evolution, that is, it exists to provide for a "flexible future"; for instance, nonused, redundant copies are free to alter because their adaptative product is still being produced by the remaining DNA copies (e.g., Cohen, 1976; Kleckner, 1977). However, this second argument is teleological because it permits future needs to determine present circumstances.

Whereas Gould and Vrba (1982) claimed that future uses are quite significant consequences of repeated DNA, the potential future use cannot be held to empirically determine the prior status of the genome. In turn, the concept of exaptation capitalizes on the idea that repeated DNA may, indeed, have a significant future use but does so without recourse to teleological, "final cause" explanations. And in making these contributions, the concept of exaptation furthers understanding of how features of the genome provide a basis for plastic microevolutionary processes. Gould and Vrba (1982) explained that:

> Defenders of the second tradition understand how important repetitive DNA is to evolution, but only know the conventional language of adaptation for expressing this conviction. But since utility is a future condition (when the redundant copy assumes a different function or undergoes secondary adaptation for a new role), an impasse in expression develops. To break this impasse, we might suggest that repeated copies are nonapted features available for cooptation later, but not serving any direct function at the moment. When coopted, they will be exaptations in their new role (with secondary adaptive modifications if altered).

> What then is the source of these exaptations? According to the first tradition, they arise as true adaptations and later assume their different function. The second tradition, we have argued, must be abandoned. A third possibility has recently been proposed (or rather, better codified after previous hints): perhaps repeated copies can originate for no adaptive reason that concerns the traditional Darwinian level of phenotypic advantage (Orgel & Crick, 1980; Doolittle & Sapienza, 1980). Some DNA elements are transposable: if these can duplicate and move, what is to stop their accumulation as long as they remain invisible to the phenotype (if they become so numerous that they begin to exert energetic constraint upon the phenotype, then natural selection will eliminate them)? Such "selfish DNA" may be

playing its own Darwinian game at a gene level, but it represents a true nonaptation at the level of the phenotype. Thus, repeated DNA may often arise as a nonaptation. Such a statement in no ways argues against its vital importance for evolutionary futures. When used to great advantage in that future, these repeated copies are exaptations. (p. 11)

In other words, and crucial for a synthesis of micro- and macro-evolutionary processes, Gould and Vrba (1982) claimed that there exists an "enormous pool" of nonaptations and that this pool must be the source, the "reservoir," of most evolutionary flexibility. They noted that:

> We need to recognize the central role of "cooptability for fitness" as the primary evolutionary significance of ubiquitous nonaptation in organisms. In this sense, and at its level of the phenotype, this nonaptive pool is an analog of mutation—a source of raw material for further selection.
>
> Both adaptations and nonaptations, while they may have non-random approximate causes, can be regarded as randomly produced with respect to any potential cooptation by further regimes of selection. Simply put: all exaptations originate randomly with respect to their effects. Together, these two classes of characters, adaptations and nonaptations, provide an enormous pool of variability, at a level higher than mutations, for cooptation as exaptations [and provide for] . . . the flexibility of phenotypic characters as a primary enhancer of or damper upon future evolutionary change. Flexibility lies in the pool of features available for cooptation (either as adaptations to something else that has ceased to be important in new selective regimes, as adaptations whose original function continues but which may he cooted for an additional role, or as nonaptations always potentially available). The paths of evolution—both the constraints and the opportunities—must be largely set by the site and nature of this pool of potential exaptations. Exaptive possibilities define the internal contribution that organisms make to their own evolutionary future. (pp. 12–13)

In sum, the concept of exaptation, and the limitations it imposes for the notion of adaptation as the sole process by which evolution occurs, present formidable conceptual and empirical problems for sociobiological thinking. The existence of exaptive processes indicates that evolution is considerably more plastic than sociobiology would imply. This plasticity is highlighted by those objections to the adaptationist program that involve the specification of the causal role played by the developing organism, and especially by its dynamic interactions with its context, in influencing the course of evolution.

The role of the organism in its own evolution. A clear implication of Gould and Vrba's (1982) revised terminology is that not all instances of fitness are adaptations; that is, not all features of an organism's structure and function that are aptational have this character as a consequence of being shaped by natural selection. Such a possibility, if supported, would serve to weaken what Gould and Lewontin (1979) labeled the "adaptationist program," that is, the position, reflected in the earlier quote by Konner (1982, p. 18), that a feature's current aptational character implies historical shaping by natural selection for that character.

Lewontin (1981) discussed the adaptationist "program" and its conventional use of the concept of adaptation. As do Gould and Vrba (1982), Lewontin (1981) saw problems with this view of adaptation; in essence, he saw the view as deficient because it ignores the active, constructive role the organism plays in its own adaptation. The organism shapes the context to which it adapts, and, hence, there is a reciprocal, multilevel (i.e., fused) relation between organism and context (e.g., Ford & Lerner, 1992; Gottlieb, 1997; Lerner & Walls, 1999; Magnusson, 1999a, 1999b; Thelen & Smith, 1998). Thus, Lewontin's (1981) criticisms of the conventional use of the concept of adaptation is associated with a view of the organism compatible with a developmental systems conception of human development. Specifically, Lewontin (1981) noted:

> Organisms . . . by their own life activities determine which aspects of the outer world make up their environment. Organisms change the environment by their activities . . . they "construct" environments. The problem is that the concept of adaptation has been extended metaphorically from its valid domain of describing individual, short-term, goal-directed behavior to other levels . . . it is pure metaphor, ideologically molded by the progressivism and optimalism of the nineteenth century, to describe numbers of chromosomes, patterns of fertility, migrations, and religious institutions as "adaptations." . . . It is not simply that some evolutionary process can be described as nonadaptive, but that the entire framework is in question. Whether we look at the fossil record or at living species, we do not see them as "adapting," but as "adapted." But how can that be? How is it that, if evolution is a process of adapting, organisms always seem to be adapted. It may be more illuminating to see organisms as changing and, in the process, as reconstructing the elements of the outer world into a new environment that is sufficient for their survival. (p. 245)

For example, summarizing the literature pertaining to the character of the environment to which organisms adapt, Lewontin and Levins (1978) stressed that reciprocal processes between organism and environment are involved in human evolution, supporting the view that human functioning is one source of its own evolutionary development. Lewontin and Levins (1978) stated that:

> The activity of the organism sets the stage for its own evolution . . . the labor process by which the human ancestors modified natural objects to make them suitable for human use was itself the unique feature of the way of life that directed selection on the hand, larynx, and brain in a positive feedback that transformed the species, its environment, and its mode of interaction with nature. (p. 78)

Consistent with the position of Lewontin (1981) and Lewontin and Levins (1978) regarding the problems with the "adaptationist program," Gould and Vrba (1982) contended that recognition of the potential presence of exaptative features leads one to recognize that previously nonaptative (note, *not* preadaptive) features may be present and may be coopted for fitness—a recognition that provides a key for plasticity in evolutionary processes and for the role of individuals' own organismic characteristics in their development. Gould and Vrba (1982) indicated:

> Flexibility lies in the pool of features available for cooptation. . . . The paths of evolution—both the constraints and the opportunities—must be largely set by the size and nature of this pool of potential exaptations. Exaptive possibilities define the "internal" contribution that organisms make to their own evolutionary future. (pp. 12–13)

The concept of exaptation leads to the understanding that the processes involved in evolution are plastic ones, and that plasticity involves organisms' active contributions to their own evolutionary change (e.g., Brandtstädter, 1998, 1999; Gottlieb, 1983, 1997; Lerner & Walls, 1999). As such, exaptation is a concept consistent with a key theme in the developmental systems "alternative" to a hereditarian view of the role of biology in human development (e.g., Ford & Lerner, 1992; Gottlieb, 1997; Lerner & Walls, 1999; Magnusson, 1999a, 1999b; Thelen & Smith, 1998). According to this alternative, it is possible to envision how processes exist that contribute to the plasticity of people's functioning, processes that allow people to play a role in the ontogeny—and, through a concept introduced by Gottlieb (1987), in the phylogeny as well—of their own flexible characteristics.

Developmental systems and the role of the concept of "behavioral neophenotypes" in evolutionary change. As described by Lewontin (1981), it is possible to view the organism as other than just the host of its evolutionarily provided genes, and it is likewise possible to view the importance of the organism's activity across ontogeny as more than just the maturationally predetermined unfolding of

hereditarily fixed progressions. The key alternative view is one that sees biological and contextual factors as reciprocally interactive; as such, developmental changes are probabilistic in respect to normative outcomes due to variation in the timing of the biological, psychological, and social factors that provide interactive bases of ontogenetic progressions (e.g., Schneirla, 1957; Tobach, 1981).

As discussed in previous chapters, this view has been labeled as probabilistic epigenetic by Gottlieb (1983), and developed by him (Gottlieb, 1970, 1976, 1983, 1991, 1992, 1997; Gottlieb et al., 1998) and earlier by Schneirla (1956, 1957) and Tobach and Schneirla (1968). Probabilistic epigenesis constitutes a defining feature of developmental systems theories, and the fusions among levels of organizations within the system that it reflects provides the basis of plasticity in development across the human life span (e.g., Ford & Lerner, 1992; Gottlieb, 1997; Magnusson, 1999a, 1999b; Thelen & Smith, 1998). As we have just noted, Lewontin (1981) indicated what such plasticity in development may mean for altering the course of evolution. In turn, Gottlieb (1987) also provided a quite intriguing discussion of the role of plastic developmental functioning in shaping evolutionary change.

Although biologists such as Garstang (1922), de Beer (1930), and Goldschmidt (1933) previously argued that developmental changes may lead to evolution, they also believed that a genetic change or a mutation was necessary to create the developmental changes. Gottlieb (1987), however, argued for an evolutionary pathway in which ontogenetic development leads to evolutionary change and, quite significantly, where "genetic change is a secondary or tertiary consequence of enduring behavioral changes brought about by nongenetic alterations of species-typical development" (p. 267). Gottlieb's conception draws on a notion introduced by Kuo (1967), of behavioral neophenotype, that is, a behavioral innovation, or ontogenetic novelty, made possible by the plasticity of the organism and its probabilistic, dynamic interactions with its context.

Gottlieb contended that a behavioral neophenotype is likely the first step in an evolutionary sequence that proceeds from behavioral change, to morphological change, to genetic change. More specifically, the emergence of a behavioral neophenotype encourages new environmental relationships that, in turn, bring out latent possibilities for morphological and physiological changes. Gottlieb (1987) noted that somatic mutation, cytoplasmic alteration, or change in gene regulation may also take place at this point, however, an alteration of structural genes need not take place in this secondary stage of the process. However, a change in genes or in gene frequency does occur in the third stage, wherein as a consequence of long-term geographic or behavioral isolation (i.e., separate breeding populations), such alteration takes place.

Because of the plasticity that exists in organisms (and especially ones with larger relative brain size such as humans; Gottlieb, 1987), a plasticity textured by the probabilistic, dynamic interactions they have across ontogeny with their context, an evolutionary pathway is created that is inconsistent with the conception of evolutionary change found in evolutionary epistemology and in the associated predetermined–epigenetic view of organism change. Thus, on the basis of both this contribution to evolution by organism development, and the implications of the concept of exaptation, we may conclude that the key features of sociobiological thinking are severely scientifically limited. Evolution processes are not, therefore, just comprised of phylogenetically continuous changes that, by virtue of the antecedent and independent effects of the physical world, shape via natural selection particular cognitive structures, reproductive strategies, or parent–child relations. The particular set of behavioral or social features present in a person, social group, or culture cannot be judged as contributing to or diminishing the survival of the human species by virtue of the adaptationist assertion that the features have or have not been shaped and selected for fitness.

Conclusions About the Presence of Evidence in Support of the Sociobiological View of Human Development

As was the case in regard to the lines of evidence relating to the concept of homology and to the use of heritability research data, the third line of evidence relied on by sociobiologists—an adaptationist storyline to explain what are purported to be genetically based differences in individual and social development—fails. "Just-so stories" (Gould, 1980) about human evolutionary history are used to substitute superficial descriptions for in-depth explanations (Piaget, 1979); alternative paths to current fitness (or aptation) are excluded from scientific consideration or analysis.

Equally serious problems arise in regard to the other two lines of evidence relied on by sociobiologists—involving the inappropriate postulation of homologies between nonhuman and human animals and the misuse of the concept of heritability. These logical and empirical problems reveal the weak scientific basis of the sociobiological viewpoint. The severity of these problems suggests

that sociobiological thinking has little relevance for the understanding of human behavior and development in general, or for individual or group differences in particular.

Nevertheless, the scientific vacuity of sociobiological ideas about human development has not deterred some writers from using these ideas to propose theories about the evolutionary basis of individual and/or group differences in numerous features of human development (e.g., MacDonald, 1994, 1998; Rushton, 1988a, 1988b, 1996, 1999), for example, sexuality, intelligence, criminality, and parenting. It is useful to present and evaluate an example of this type of work in order to illustrate the quality of the evidence that sociobiologists use to make pronouncements about the hereditary basis of group differences in human development.

To provide this illustration, I focus on the work of arguably the most visible of the hereditarian writers who use sociobiology to explain group differences in human behaviors: J. Philippe Rushton (e.g., 1999). In Chapter 11, we noted the problems associated with Rushton's (1999) interpretation of heritability data. Here, we focus on his views about human evolution and the quality of the scientific work he does to support his ideas.

THE WORK OF J. PHILIPPE RUSHTON

Rushton's (1997) work rests on a split view of the nature–nurture issue. In fact, he not only splits genes from context in his attempts to explain human development but also he sees a split between the people whose work is associated with hereditarian versus developmental systems conceptions, a split that divides—in his view—good from poor scientists. That is, Rushton (1997) proposed a hermeneutical versus race-realist division to reflect this split between scientists. Rushton (1997) noted that:

> Most of those engaged in the serious study of race today do so from either the "hermeneutical" or the "race-realist" perspective. At one extreme, those I have termed "hermeneuticists" approach race as an epiphenomenon, a mere social construction, with political and economic forces as the real causal agents worthy of study. Rather than research race, hermeneuticists research those who do. At the other end of the forum, those I term the "race-realists" view race as a natural phenomenon to be observed, studied, and explained. Alternative and intermediate positions certainly exist, but the most heated debate currently takes place

J. Philippe Rushton

between advocates of the two polar positions. The hermeneutical approach relies on textual, historical, and political analysis; the race-realist approach is empirical and employs a panoply of scientific methodologies, including surveys, psychometrics, and genetics. Because the hermeneutical viewpoint sees inexorable links between theory and practice, its writings are often prescriptive and assume an advocacy position. The race-realist viewpoint is descriptive and typically avoids prescribing policy. To their opposite numbers, hermeneuticists come across as muddled, heated, and politically committed to "antiracism"; the race-realists come across to their opponents as cold, detached, and suspect of hiding a "racist" agenda. (p. 78)

In effect, this instance of Rushton's split conception is actually one of labeling hermeneuticists as "obfuscating politically correct ad hominemists" and seeing race realists as "objective crusaders for scientific and social truth." It may be, however, that this characterization hoists Rushton "on his own petard." To see if it does, we turn to a discussion of the ideas and methods Rushton uses to seek and present "truth."

Rushton's Tripartite Theory of Race, Evolution, and Behavior

Rushton (1999) proposed a tripartite racial view of human evolution, one which purports to show that in regard to characteristics of human functioning linked to successful development (e.g., high intelligence and occupational achievement, good parenting and caregiving skills, and low criminality), the three racial groups he identified (what he terms "Orientals," "Whites," and "Blacks") differ significantly. Although Rushton (1999) never defined the concept of "race," he noted that there are:

> Three major cases: *Orientals* (East Asians, Mongoloids), *Whites* (Europeans, Caucasoids), and *Blacks* (Africans, Negroids). To keep things simple, I will use these common names instead of scientific ones and will not discuss subgroups within the races.
>
> On average, Orientals are slower to mature, less fertile, and less sexually active, have larger brains and higher IQ scores. Blacks are at the opposite end in each of these areas. Whites fall in the middle, often close to the Orientals. (p. 18)

There are numerous, and well-known data sets contradicting Rushton's all-too-facile divisions. For instance, consider the variable that Rushton (1999) considered to be the most clearly linked to the biological and, hence, evolutionary differences between the racial groups he described, that is, reproductive maturation. For example, he noted that "races tend to differ in the age when they reach milestones such as the end of infancy, the start of puberty, adulthood, and old age" (Rushton, 1999, pp. 27–28) and that "Blacks reach sexual maturity sooner than Whites, who in turn mature sooner than Orientals. This is true for things like age at first menstruation, first sexual experience, and first pregnancy" (Rushton, 1999, p. 30). Rushton failed to attend to abundant information which indicates unequivocally that his assertion is simply incorrect.

To illustrate, Rushton (1999) ignored Hiernaux's (1968) data showing that pubertal maturation (i.e., age of menarche, the age of the first menstrual cycle) among Africans can vary from as low as 12.4 years to as high as 18.8 years; as such, the maturation of some Africans is substantially slower than those of many groups of Asians and Europeans studied by Hiernaux (1968). In turn, Tanner (1973, 1991) reported a secular trend wherein the time of pubertal maturation decreased over the course of the twentieth century for numerous groups of Europeans, for European Americans, and for Asians (e.g., Japanese). In fact, the latter group showed the most dramatic decrease in time of maturation for all groups studied by Tanner (1991). In describing trends after World War II, he noted that "in improving postwar conditions, there was a decline of some 11 months per decade until 1975, when the trend leveled out to practically zero" (Tanner, 1991, p. 638). Thus, pubertal maturation is a quite plastic phenomenon, responsive to the nutritional and medical resources present in the ecology of developing individuals.

The data reflecting such plasticity directly contradict the tripartite differences specified by Rushton (1999). As such, *either* Rushton is open to criticism for weak and inadequate scholarship as a consequence of his not knowing of data sets that have been quite prominent in the biological and human development literatures for more than 40 years, *or* he is open to criticism for biased and inadequate scholarship as a consequence of failing to acknowledge that his ideas are convincingly contradicted by strong, countervailing data. In either case, Rushton's (1999, p. 96) self-congratulatory assertion that "I have not ignored any important studies" is simply incorrect. Indeed, Winston (1997) explained that Rushton makes similar "errors" in regard to his claiming support for his tripartite racial theory from data about the brain size of the three "racial groups" Rushton (1997, 1999) described (cf. Peters, 1995; Winston, 1996).

Rushton's Ideas About Different Reproductive Strategies Across Race Groups

Despite the inadequate scholarship that characterizes the evidentiary basis for his claims, Rushton (1999) went on to propose that the bases for the reproductive and associated behavioral differences he associated with the three racial groups he discussed lies in the different "reproductive strategies" characterizing them. He described a continuum of reproductive strategies wherein "At one end of this scale are r-strategies that rely on high reproductive rates. At the other end are K-strategies that rely on high levels of parental care" (p. 24).

The different strategies depicted across this continuum are useful in biology to depict the reproductive rates of separate species (that are trying to survive and reproduce in diverse ecological niches (Johanson & Edey, 1981). For instance, a sponge, living and reproducing on the ocean floor, will produce literally thousands of offspring during a given reproductive cycle, and this rate will increase the probability of a few offspring withstanding the harsh currents and otherwise dangerous ecology of the ocean bottom for a period sufficient for their survival and eventual perpetuation of the species. In turn, given elephants' enormous nutritional needs during their lengthy prenatal gestation period and postnatal years, the probability of offspring survival is enhanced when a small number, most typically one, offspring, is produced during a reproductive cycle.

Thus, the r−K distinction is useful for describing differences between species in how their rate of reproduction fits the ecological niche within which they live. However, there is no validity for applying this concept to differences *within* a species in the reproductive rates of different individuals or groups. Yet, this is an error that Rushton (1999) made, and, in fact, admitted that he did! He noted that the r−K "scale is generally used to compare the life histories of different species of animals. I have used it to explain the small but real differences between the human races" (Rushton, 1999, p. 24).

Hence, Rushton (1999) misapplied the r−K distinction in two ways. First, he took a concept that describes differences between species and applied it to differences within a species *without any biological evidence of the validity of such an application*. Nevertheless, without any documentation, Rushton (1999, p. 103) asserted that, in response to the question of whether his r−K concept applied only to differences between species and not to within-species differences, "It applies to both."

Second, Rushton used a descriptive concept to explain differences within a species—and his explanation was that, basically, the group he called "Blacks" represent an evolutionarily less-advanced form of organism, in that their reproductive strategy is more closely aligned with more "primitive," r-like organisms. Indeed, Rushton (1999) used his r−K explanation to account for purported differences between "Orientals" and "Whites," who he claimed are more "K-selected" and "Blacks," who he contends are more r-selected," in their investment in their children.

He indicated that, "Highly K-selected men invest time and energy in their children rather than the pursuit of sexual thrills. They are "dads" rather than "cads" (Rushton, 1999, p. 24). Moreover, Rushton (1999, pp. 35−36) asserted—*without any citation whatsoever to bolster his statements*—that "In Africa, the female-headed family is part of an overall social pattern. It consists of early sexual union and the procreation of children with many partners. It includes fostering children away from home, even for several years, so mothers remain sexually active. . . . In Black Africa and the Black Caribbean, as in the American underclass ghetto, groups of pre-teens and teenagers are left quite free of adult supervision."

Amazingly, Rushton (1999) showed no awareness (e.g., through discussion or even mere citation) of the rich literature pertinent to the African American family (e.g., Demo, Allen, & Fine, 2000; McAdoo, 1977, 1991, 1993a, 1993b, 1995, 1998, 1999; McCubbin et al., 1998). This literature presents data providing a point-for-point contradiction of Rushton's undocumented assertions. Accordingly, when Rushton (1999, p. 105) asserted that "scientists have a special duty to examine the facts and tell the truth," one may wonder whether he included himself within the group held to this standard. In any case, it seems clear, from the evaluations that have been made of the quality of the "data" Rushton forwarded regarding his ideas, that the "truth" was not being told by either the data he presented or the interpretations he made of his data.

Evaluations of Rushton's Evidence

Although we have—both in this chapter and in Chapter 11—noted the numerous criticisms that have been forwarded in regard to the theory of and data presentations made by Rushton, it is useful to consider a critique of the breadth of the evidence he has presented in regard to his ideas. Cernovsky (1997) noted that Rushton's studies of racial differences (e.g., Rushton, 1988a, 1998b, 1990, 1991a, 1991b, 1995), as well as those of other researchers working to support his findings (e.g., Lynn, 1993)

> are noteworthy for their excessive reliance on very low correlation coefficients from obsolete data sets to postulate causal relationships. When a given method produces findings inconsistent with their . . . views, they conveniently switch to a different method. An independent statistical re-examination of the same source of data by others may produce dramatically different results. (p. 1)

To illustrate, Cernovsky and Litman (1993) reanalyzed the data that Rushton (1990) used to demonstrate that there were significant race differences (involving what Rushton termed "Mongoloid," "Caucasoid," and "Negroid" groups) across nations in crime rates (e.g., involving homicide, rape, and serious assault). The data, Rushton (1990) claimed, indicated that the Negroid group had higher rates of crime than did either of the other two groups. However, Cernovsky and Litman (1993) found that the race differences reported by Rushton (1990) were not strong and, in fact, were largely weak and inconsistent. Not only did Rushton (1990) *not* present any evidence why these small differences among races should be considered genetic in origin but also Cernovsky and Litman (1993) found that, in Rushton's own data, reliance on race to predict an individual's likelihood of committing a crime "would result in an absurdly high rate (99.9%) of false positives" (p. 31).

Similarly, Gorey and Cryns (1995) reassessed some of the data that Rushton used (1988, 1990, 1991, 1995) to illustrate the evolutionary and genetic deficits of "Negroids" in regard to intelligence, rate of physical maturation, personality and temperament, sexuality, and social/familial organization. However, the results of Gorey and Cryns' (1995) independent analysis of these data contradicted Rushton's characterization of the support provided for his hereditarian views of race differences. Gorey and Cryns found that the "relationships are very close to zero and some are in the opposite direction than postulated by Rushton" (Cernovsky, 1997, p. 2).

To illustrate some of the problems with Rushton's interpretation of the literature, we may note that Rushton (1990) cited the assessment of Beals, Smith, and Dodd (1984) of the relations between brain weight and race as providing support for his contention that "Negroids" have lower brain weights than do the other two race groups Rushton considers. Yet, Cernovsky and Litman (1993) noted that the statistical conclusions of Beals and colleagues (1984) "are the opposite of his own: brain weight is *not* primarily related to race" (p. 35). In addition, Cernovsky and Litman (1993) indicated as well that Rushton "selectively reports data confirming his theory . . . this renders the data reported in (his work) *worthless* for generalization" (p. 35).

In addition, Cernovsky (1992) noted that Rushton's (e.g., 1988, 1990, 1991) information suffers from conceptual and methodological flaws, for example, relating to his ignoring environmental effects such as secular trends (e.g., as in Tanner, 1991); statistical problems, associated with interpreting data with restricted ranges or with the overinterpretation of low correlations; and either omitting contradictory information from the literature he reviewed or (as we have seen in regard to Gorey and Cryns, 1995) interpreting contradictory information as supportive of his ideas.

Conclusions About the Quality of Rushton's Hereditarian Views of Race Differences

Given the numerous dimensions of critical scientific problems associated with Rushton's work, we may agree with Cernovsky's (1995) view that:

> Although Rushton's writings and public speeches instill the vision of Blacks as small-brained, oversexed criminals who multiply at a fast rate and are afflicted with mental disease, his views are neither based on a bona fide scientific review of literature

nor on contemporary scientific methodology. His dogma of bioevolutionary inferiority of Negroids is not supported by empirical evidence. (p. 677)

In sum, given this quality of work that Rushton (1999) employed to document his views, I believe we must reach a conclusion about Rushton's scholarship that is reflected in Cernovsky's (1997) view, that:

> Rushton's racial theory is logically inconsistent, built on methodologically obsolete procedures, and is not supported by credible data sets selected in an objective manner. (p. 4)

As is the case with the other lines of evidence that intend to provide sociobiological evidence in support of the genetic basis of human behavior and development (relating to homology, heritability, and adaptation), Rushton's work reduces to no evidence at all.

CONCLUSIONS: IS NATIVISM "DEAD?"

In this and the preceding three chapters we have reviewed several different approaches to nature/hereditarian conceptions of human development. All approaches—behavior genetics theory, the assessment of the heritability of intelligence, the study of instincts, and sociobiology—involve nature–nurture split concepts. Each has been seen to have critical conceptual and methodological problems associated with it.

Despite these problems, we have seen that these nativistic ideas have an impressive and perhaps even surprising (given the repeated demonstration of their egregious flaws) record of maintaining a presence in the field of human development. As Horowitz (2000) explained (see Chapter 10), the simplicity of the hereditarian answer to the questions of the "Person In the Street" about

human development (i.e., "The answer is that it is in your genes") continues to be attractive to people and seen as newsworthy to the media. Often, neither the "Person in the Street" nor the media have patience for more complex answers (e.g., "The answer depends on the particular history of fusions within the developmental system").

In turn, scientists may continue to be attracted to hereditarian ideas because of a commitment to theoretical parsimony, that is, an interest in trying to explain development through the use of the smallest possible number of theoretical statements and, perhaps as well, a belief in Occam's razor, the idea that the simplest of competing explanations should be preferred to more complex ones. Often, theories that reflect these two features—parsimony and simplicity—are seen as the most "elegant" in science.

Accordingly, given both the theoretical and practical reasons that are associated with attraction to hereditarian ideas, it is likely that other versions of such formulations will continue to be forwarded. As a consequence, and as Lewontin cautioned, the "price" we must pay for the continued possible use of such conceptions is the need to remain vigilant about their appearance. We must be prepared to discuss the poor science they reflect and the inadequate bases they provide for public policy and applications pertinent to improving human life (see, too, Schneirla, 1966; Tobach, 1994). We must be ready to suggest alternatives, such as developmental systems views, to hereditarians views of research about and applications for human development.

In the next chapter, we discuss a sample case of theoretical "elegance" associated with ideas that, although not reflective of the extreme hereditarian views of sociobiologists, do constitute a new approach—a neo-nativist one—to a key facet of human function: cognition and its development. In turn, we also consider alternatives to neo-nativist ideas that are linked to ideas associated with developmental systems' conceptions of human development.

14 | *Cognition and Development: From Neo-Nativism to Developmental Systems*

As emphasized in previous chapters, the nature–nurture issue is at the core of philosophical and theoretical debates about the character of human development. Indeed, across substantive domains ranging from those associated with intraindividual levels of organization (e.g., temperament and personality) to those linked with social behaviors (e.g., parenting), we have considered scholars' ideas pertinent to nature, nurture, interactional, and relational, developmental systems perspectives.

Across these discussions, intelligence has been a major sample case. Arguably, because of the centrality of intellectual functioning in: depicting the defining features of human behavior and development; evolutionary, adaptive (and aptive; Gould & Vrba, 1982) change; ontogenetic adjustments to (fits with) the demands of the social and cultural setting; and understanding individual differences in human performance and achievement. Designing interventions aimed at enhancing such behavior, variables and processes related to intelligence have been major concerns of scholars of human development.

The interest in intellectual development is not restricted, however, to studying scores on intelligence tests, and attempting to ascertain whether hereditarian or developmental systems ideas are more useful in understanding the bases of variance in such scores. Rather, intelligence is seen as an instance of a broader domain of human functioning that is labeled "cognitive." Although, at this writing, the extreme nativism found in the works of Rushton (1999), Rowe (1994), or Plomin (2000) would be subscribed to by relatively few scholars of human development (e.g., see Collins et al., 2000, Horowitz, 2000, and prior chapters in this volume for discussions of why these views are largely and increasingly rejected), there is considerable current interest in a set of ideas about cognitive development that may be characterized as "neo-nativist" (e.g., Keil, 1998; Spelke & Newport, 1998). Not surprisingly, given the history of debate regarding the nature–nurture issue, the ideas of neo-nativist scholars are countered by a range of ideas associated with interactional or developmental systems models of human development (Feldman, 2000; Fischer & Bidell, 1998; Rogoff, 1998; Thelen & Smith, 1998).

Accordingly, to further illustrate the dimensions of the nature–nurture debate, and to discuss in more detail a central facet of human development, we consider in this chapter ideas about cognition and development associated with theories ranging from neo-nativism to developmental systems. To start this discussion, it is useful to note the set of characteristics that may be labeled as "cognitive."

COGNITION AND DEVELOPMENT: DEFINITIONS AND DOMAINS

Cognition refers to thought, consciousness, and knowing, and the study of cognition involves an appraisal of the processes involved in the acquisition (or development) and the utilization of knowing. The study of cognition involves at least six interrelated areas of inquiry (cf. Eisenberg, 1998; Kuhn & Siegler, 1998; Lerner, 1998a; Sigel & Renninger, 1998).

First, scientists who study cognition are interested in the study of cognitive *processes* [i.e., the changes in the variables (or components) of the structure and function of knowing]. Representative topics of concern in this area of cognitive science are perceiving, thinking, memory, information processing, reflective functioning, executive decision making, consciousness, meta-cognition (i.e., thinking about one's thinking), and problem solving (e.g., Aslin, Jusczyk, & Pisoni, 1998; Bertenthal & Clifton, 1998; DeLoache, Miller, & Pierroutsakos, 1998; Keil, 1998; Kellman & Banks, 1998; Klahr & Mac Whinney, 1998; Schneider & Bjorklund, 1998).

Second, cognitive scientists are interested in cognitive *abilities,* that is, the array of areas of skill or expertise about which individuals may know (e.g., mathematical knowledge, verbal knowledge, spatial knowledge, or knowledge about social relationships, music, art, etc.). Representative topics here are representation, intelligence, creativity, talent, giftedness, language, and literacy (e.g., Adams, Treiman, & Pressley, 1998; Bloom, 1998; Csikszentmihalyi & Rathunde, 1998; Mandler, 1998; Maratsos, 1998; Winner, 1996; Woodward & Markman, 1998). Moreover, the different structures of such abilities (e.g., Case, 1998; Fischer & Bidell, 1998; Gelman & Williams, 1998), or the different forms of expression of abilities, for instance, the different types of intelligence that might exist (e.g., Ferrari & Sternberg, 1998; Gardner, 1993a, 1993b, 1993c, 1998; Sternberg, 1985, 1988), are of interest to cognitive scientists.

Third, scholars are interested in *motivation* and cognition, that is, the conditions under which processes are activated or abilities enacted. Examples of topics of interest here include achievement and/or mastery motivation, curiosity, exploration, and novelty seeking (e.g., Brandtstädter, 1998, 1999; Dweck, 1975, 1998; Dweck & Leggett, 1988; Eccles, 1985; Eccles & Wigfield, 1995; Heckhausen, 1999).

Fourth, cognitive scientists are also interested in *achievement* (i.e., the outcomes of the enactment of cognitive processes and abilities). Examples of such interest include educational achievement, social status/occupational attainment, and creative and athletic achievement (e.g., Ames & Ames, 1989; Eccles, 1991; Ginsberg, Klein, & Starkey, 1998; Strauss, 1998).

Fifth, scholars are interested in the *contributions* to society of cognitive functioning, that is, there is an interest in how cognitive abilities or achievements may enable people to enhance their own lives and the quality of life of their families, communities, and society (e.g., Damon, 1997; Eisenberg & Fabes, 1998; Turiel, 1998). For instance, how might cognitive development in regard to the understanding of computer technology or the attainment of high levels of moral reasoning or moral development enable individuals to contribute positively to their own, their family's, and their community's well-being?

Sixth, scholars are interested in the *context* of cognition. Scholars here may be concerned with the role of the ecology of human development—for instance, in regard to culture (e.g., Shweder et al., 1998)—in shaping the human mind. As well, scholars may be interested in how cognitive functioning enables the person to negotiate his or her everyday tasks and demands (e.g., Rogoff & Lave, 1984) or to interact effectively in a social world (Flavell & Miller, 1998; Rogoff, 1998).

The breadth and depth of the scholarship associated with these domains of cognitive science is enormous. For example, reviews of this scholarship have filled one complete volume (Kuhn & Siegler, 1998) of the four-volume, fifth edition of the *Handbook of Child Psychology* (Damon, 1998) and, as well, significant portions of the other three volumes (Eisenberg, 1998; Lerner, 1998a; Sigel & Renninger, 1998)—with each volume exceeding 1,000 pages in length! Moreover, in regard to the focus of this chapter on the neo-nativist versus developmental systems debate in regard to cognition and development, it is important to note that there are also numerous instances of distinct neo-nativist (e.g., Gelman & Williams, 1998; Spelke & Newport, 1998) or developmental systems ideas (e.g., Fischer & Bidell, 1998; Rogoff, 1998; Thelen & Smith, 1998; Wapner & Demick, 1998) being used to frame this scholarship. Accordingly, the goal of this chapter cannot be to exhaustively represent each of the instances of these perspectives; rather, it is to discuss exemplary cases of this neo-nativist through developmental systems range of ideas in order to understand the dimensions of, and suggest possible resolutions for, the debate engaging these perspectives. It is useful to begin this discussion with the key features of neo-nativism, as represented in the ideas of two of the leading spokespeople for this view of development, Elizabeth S. Spelke and Elissa L. Newport (1998).

FEATURES OF NEO-NATIVISM

Spelke and Newport (1998) took an approach to the study of cognition and development that distinguishes between nature and nurture as sources of the development of knowledge. They cast this contrast *not* in terms of neo-nativism

Elissa L. Newport

person)]. For instance, Spelke and Newport (1998) asked:

> Which of our concepts are inherent in our minds, and which are abstracted from our experience of the world around us? What aspects of human knowledge are present at the beginning of life, and what aspects emerge thereafter? (p. 275)

and, when recasting this general, nature (nativism) versus nurture (empiricism, experience, learning) "split" concept of the sources of human development into a specific domain of cognitive functioning—(i.e., perception)—Spelke and Newport (1998) further questioned:

> To what extent does perception of the world depend on the nature of the perceptual systems with which humans are endowed? In what ways does perception result from the shaping effects of experiences gained by observing the world and acting on it? (p. 285)

Other scholars writing about the neo-nativist versus the empiricist views of cognitive development depict the debate in terms that correspond to those used by Spelke and Newport. For instance, Keil (1998) also characterized the dimensions of debate in regard to selected features of early cognitive development, for instance, infant causal reasoning, as involving either an empiricist

versus developmental systems but, rather, in regard to neo-nativism versus *empiricism,* which they regarded as a view of cognitive development opposing biological or hereditarian ideas and stressing instead the role of experiences located in the environment outside of the individual as the source of development. Thus, they organized their discussion of cognition through an explicit split between nature and nurture as sources of development. Spelke and Newport (1998) stressed that:

> The nativist–empiricist dialogue . . . rests on the thesis that human knowledge is rooted partly in biology and partly in experience, and on the promise that successful explanations of the development of knowledge will come from attempts to tease these influences apart. (p. 323)

Accordingly, Spelke and Newport (1998) saw the attributes of mental life as either inherent in biology *or* derived from "experience," which they interpreted as events in the observable (empirical) world surrounding the individual and (somehow) independent of events within the individual [i.e., his or her biological processes (which—it should be noted—are also "experiences" as they occur, but are regarded as exclusively internal to the

Elizabeth S. Spelke

perspective or a neo-nativist view involving the idea that the child might be initially endowed with specific modes of explanatory ability. That is, reflecting the split between nature and nurture we have seen espoused, too, by Spelke and Newport (1998) and, as well, equating the empiricist position with the mechanism of learning, Keil (1998) noted that:

> The nativist argues that humans are endowed with a handful of modes of construal that have come to be useful through evolution, even if they were not originally selected for. . . . The empiricist posits an extraordinarily sensitive learning device that abstracts away multiple and distinct clusters of causal patterns right from the start in infancy and uses them to constrain all later learning. (p. 380)

In short, and in distinction from the integrative, developmental systems perspectives about the nature–nurture issues discussed in earlier chapters (e.g., Gottlieb, 1997; Magnusson, 1999a, 1999b; Thelen & Smith, 1998), within the view of human development found among proponents of neo-nativism, "Person and environment are partitioned into separate groups of factors instead of being treated as *dynamic collaborators* in producing activities" (Fischer & Bidell, 1999, p. 476, italics added).

We have reason to return later in this chapter to the concept of "dynamic collaborators," when we discuss the scholarship of Rogoff (1998) in regard to the role of collaborations with other people and within culture as a basis of an individual's cognitive development. Here, however, it is useful to illustrate how the split orientation to asking questions about the bases of cognitive development that is found in neo-nativism frames the approach to studying specific domains of functioning. To provide this illustration, we turn to the three types of explanation that Spelke and Newport (1998) saw as possible in regard to the development of action:

> Developmental changes could depend on (a) learning processes that shape the child's actions in accord with environmental constraints; (b) the maturation of action systems whose structure is determined by intrinsic developmental processes; or (c) action capacities that are constant over development, but whose expression is first masked and then revealed by changing extrinsic factors. (p. 277)

Thus, the basis of the development of action is regarded as lying within one of three individual- (or personological-) level explanations, explanations which separate learning and environmental influences from intrinsic and maturational sources.

Indeed, even in the third possible explanation suggested by Spelke and Newport (1998), wherein both maturation and extrinsic factors are suggested as possibly involved in cognitive development, and, thus, where it may be thought that an "interaction" between nature and nurture is being posited, there is in fact no causal status given to extrinsic factors in the development of action. Rather, the "interaction" that is suggested is one wherein the role given to experiential factors is only to "unmask," or lift the "veil" off of, the intrinsic, native capacity.

Conclusions

As reflected in the aforementioned conception of the basis of action, there are at least three important dimensions of neo-nativism introduced by Spelke and Newport (1998). First, there is a commitment to splitting nature from nurture. Their position involves a search for native, or intrinsic, abilities or competencies, versus a reliance on the environment external to the individual, on experience, or on what is construed as the process through which experience of the world outside of the organism exerts its influence on the individual, that is, "learning."

It is important to note, however, that the view of learning reflected in this neo-nativist concept is not the view of learning found within a developmental systems perspective. What presumptively is the process described by neo-nativists as "learning" is a function of the person having its locus at the individual–psychological level of organization. Some developmental systems-oriented theorists, who see cognitive developments and, for instance, learning, as an interpersonal, collaborative process (e.g., Baltes & Staudinger, 1996; Cole, 1996; Damon, 1996; Rogoff, 1998; Staudinger & Baltes, 1996; Wertsch, 1985) might not agree with the location of learning at the individual level of organization. Moreover, such theorists would emphasize the key point that, within a developmental systems perspective, learning is a part of a system involving both more molecular and more molar levels of organization, each having their own focal functions. As with learning, these functions play necessary but, by themselves, insufficient roles in texturing the changing developmental system and accounting for developmental change (Lerner, 1995b). Learning is no more or no less important than any other focal function at any level of organization, then, in providing a basis of human thought and action. In contrast to the view taken within the split conception of nature and nurture involved in the nativist–empiricist controversy, the developmental systems view of learning is that it is only one part of one level of the developmental system. If learning has an influence on one or more levels of the developmental system—and, specifically, if learning is involved in the development of cognitive abilities—it exerts this "influence" only through being part of an integrated system of multilevel relations (Lerner, 1995b). Learning plays a role through the "dynamic collaborations" (Fischer & Bidell, 1998, p. 476), previously noted.

A second feature of neo-nativist thinking reflected in the ideas of Spelke and Newport (1998) is the belief that there exist innate capacities that organize or structure cognitive functioning independent of experience external to the individual (i.e., in the environment within which the person is embedded). Thus, Spelke and Newport claimed that there is a disjuncture between inner and outer levels of organization and the change processes—the internal and the external "experiences"—that are involved in these levels. This instance of the neo-nativist split is completely inconsistent with decades of accumulated evidence about the organism–context integrative character of biological and physiological functioning (e.g., Gottlieb, 1983, 1997; Gottlieb et al., 1998; Lewontin, Rose, & Kamin, 1984; Magnusson, 1995, 1996, 1999a, 1999b; Petersen & Taylor, 1980; Schneirla, 1956, 1957; Tobach, 1981). Moreover, the biologically counterfactual view of cognitive development results in the neo-nativist proposal that there exist cognitive structures that have arisen innately, that is, independent of the reciprocal system of dynamic, person–context actions that characterizes the material and functional basis of human behavior and development.

Third, the innate capacity envisioned by Spelke and Newport is believed to be always present, even in the youngest individual. However, Spelke and Newport claimed that this intrinsic capacity is not always seen in actual performance; external experience may hide the actual, native competence of the individual. However, in principle, if the correct observational (methodological) conditions for observation could be arranged, then the ubiquitously present native ability could be demonstrated.

As discussed in Chapters 2 and 3, there are philosophical and metatheoretical reasons for the formulation of these features of neo-nativism. In addition, there are also important data-based reasons for this view of cognitive development. Indeed, to account for the three key features of the position articulated by Spelke and Newport (1998), it is useful to consider the bases of neo-nativism that are associated with research about cognitive development. These research bases pertain to the presence of variability in the development of human cognitive abilities.

VARIABILITY IN COGNITIVE DEVELOPMENT: ISSUES AND ANSWERS

No one doubts that the ebb and flow of human behavior as it exists within its natural ecology of people's lives constitutes a formidable degree of complexity. Scientists, of course, try to understand this complexity and find models that afford understanding of the within- and across-time variability in human functioning. Nevertheless, in any area of scholarship, and certainly cognitive development would be one such field of study, the variation and interrelation among variables involved in human development represent a difficult-to-conceptualize level of complexity, one that leads scientists to "often retreat into oversimplification and stereotyping" (Fischer & Bidell, 1998, p. 468). As a consequence, scientists may not appreciate that "people's activities are embodied, contextualized, and socially situated— understood in terms of their ecology . . . as well as their structure. . . . Action in context is the center of who people are and how they develop" (Fischer & Bidell, 1998, p. 468). Instead, they may be prone to find "solutions" to the puzzle of human variability through seeking to find, or at least to formulate (hypothesize), structures of the individual (at neural, cognitive, or behavioral levels) that reduce complexity by "extracting" the particular function or activity of the person (i.e., his or her cognition) from the context.

Such reductionistic tools of analysis may be useful as long as the scientist does not *reify* these disembodied structures. Reification would involve treating the simplification tools as having a reality separate from the person–context system from which they have been "extracted" (Fischer & Bidell, 1998). If such reification occurs, then the scientists would make the error of using a tool that was invented to just describe a limited (i.e., a reduced) view of the variation in function as a means to explain this very same variation. Fischer and Bidell (1998) explained that, in the study of the variability in human cognitive development, just such mistakes of reductionism and reification have combined to create the neo-nativist view.

Fischer and Bidell (1998, p. 493) explained that neo-nativism arose over the past several decades as a theoretical means to account for research findings about the variability that exists in cognitive development. To a great extent, the research that has identified this variability was predicated on an interest among cognitive scientists to test ideas associated with the stage theory of cognitive development proposed by Jean Piaget (1950, 1960, 1970). As is discussed in greater detail in Chapter 15, one of the key points about which Piaget's (1950, 1960, 1970) stage theory of cognitive development has been criticized is that there is much more variation in cognitive abilities that would be expected on the basis of his theory (Feldman, 2000; Fischer & Bidell, 1998). Key bases of neo-nativism arose, then, from the identification of such variability and from the ensuing search for an alternative to Piaget's theory.

Piaget's theory characterizes cognitive development as being organized on the basis of four successive, general stages of thought. Each stage is believed to represent a general structure that gives wholeness, unity of functioning, and integration to all domains of cognitive ability present within the stage; this is, each stage is regarded by Piaget as an general operating system (Feldman, 2000), and, as such, Piaget used the concept of "structures as a whole," "*structures d'ensemble*," to describe this domain-general system. Thus, if a general stage of development such as that described by Piaget accounted for cognitive functioning within a given period of life, then in all domains of cognitive ability (e.g., depth perception, language, or concepts of causality) there should be a comparable level of development.

However, a general stage model such as Piaget's would not seem to be adequate in the development of cognition if there were more variability in cognitive development than Piaget's stage theory would suggest (Feldman, 2000; Fischer & Bidell, 1998; Spelke & Newport, 1998). Evidence for this variability would exist if, at the same point in development, individuals showed functioning in one domain that was more or less advanced than functioning manifested in another cognitive domain; if young children or even infants could be shown to possess cognitive abilities that were purportedly prototypic of the cognitive functioning of older children; or if domain-specificity and not domain-generality (i.e., "*structures d'ensemble*") were evident in cognitive development. Current data provide compelling support for the presence of such domain-specific variability (e.g., Feldman, 2000; Gelman & Williams, 1998; Spelke & Newport, 1998) and, in fact, there is a consensus among cognitive scientists that domain-specificity is the "rule" in the development of cognitive abilities (Fischer & Bidell, 1998).

Accordingly, neo-nativism has developed as a response to (as a way of dealing with) this domain-specific variability. That is, Fischer and Bidell (1998) noted that:

> Another theoretical response to the discovery of variability has been the neo-nativist movement (Carey & Gelman, 1991; Fodor, 1983; Gelman & Gallistel, 1978), which has come to represent a major theoretical alternative to stage theory within the structure-as-form paradigm. With the elimination of the [Piagetian] concept of structure as stages of formal logic, the other predominant concept of structure— innate formal rules—seems to be the only remaining alternative, so long as one remains within the structure-as-form paradigm. Unfortunately, the concept of innate formal rules has the same fundamental limitation as its sister concept of formal logic: As a static conception of structure, it cannot adequately account for the variability that arises from dynamic human activity (Bidell & Fischer, 1996; Fischer & Bidell, 1991). Perhaps as a result of this limitation, neo-nativist researchers have focused on selected effects of cognitive variability that seem to support the existence of innate competences. For the most part, they have not attempted to deal with the extensive variability found in performance. Indeed, the modern father of this movement, Noam Chomsky (1965, 1986), specifically rejects the evidence of variability in language, asserting that it is illusory and that the "real" truth is that all people speak the same fundamental language. (p. 493)

Indeed, in regard to Chomsky's theory, Fischer and Bidell (1998) indicated that:

> Chomskian linguistic competence theory tries to account for human linguistic behavior on the basis of a few innate rules. It has been notoriously unable, however, to account for either the variations of human languages (Chinese is different from English!) or the highly variable everyday communication skills that individuals develop within and across diverse settings. (p. 476)

Simply, then, the split conception of nature and nurture, the purported discontinuity between within-organism and extra-organism experiences, and the resulting notion of intrinsic abilities as contextually independent structures, results in neo-nativists adhering to a biologically counterfactual and reified reductionist concept of the forms (the intrinsic abilities) involved in cognitive development. This reification is furthered by the research methods used by neo-nativists. That is, the method through which neonativists focus on cognitive abilities is flawed.

As is discussed in Chapter 18, developmental scientists need to be certain that the methods they use to identify a psychological, behavioral, or social characteristic are accurate, that they constitute a means to get a true or *valid* measure of the characteristic. There are many ways to establish a method's validity, but one key issue pertinent to all approaches involves establishing that the depiction of the characteristic, or construct, under study is a reflection of the actual construct and not just of the method used to measure it. For example, if we were interested in measuring aggression in a group of children, we might measure this characteristic by interviewing children about whether they behave aggressively with friends or by observing children interacting on the playground and recording any instances of aggression that occurred. We would want to be certain that any conclusions we reached about the aggressive tendencies of children were reflective of their actual characteristics and not due to the limitations of the methods we employed to measure aggression [e.g., on interviews people may misrepresent their behavioral tendencies, and the behaviors seen on a playground may not be generalizable to behavior in all arenas of behavioral interaction (e.g., at home or in the classroom)]. Similarly, scores derived from a measure of cognitive ability (e.g., knowledge of number, or knowledge that objects have a permanent existence apart from the person observing them) may reflect true differences in the characteristic or the variance may be due to how the ability is measured.

We do not want to confuse differences in the scores for an ability that are due to its actual character with differences due to the method used to assess the construct. One way of avoiding such confusion is through *"triangulation,"* that is, using two different methods to assess the same construct (e.g., an interview and a behavioral observation). If both methods provide a comparable depiction of the construct, then one would be in a better position to assert that the construct is being represented in a valid way than would be the case if the two methods provided nonconverging depictions of the characteristic.

When one uses only one method to identify an attribute (e.g., a cognitive ability among, say, young infants) one cannot be certain that the "presence" (or "absence") of the ability is not an artifact of the method used to measure it. If, in addition, one method is used at one age to identify an ability and, at another age, another method is used to identify an ability, then one does not know if either method provides a valid depiction of the

ability. Furthemore, even if one did know that each method was valid at the age at which it was used, this would *not* mean that the two methods measured the same ability at the different age levels or, if they did, whether they measured the ability in an equivalent manner. For instance, one method might be more sensitive to differences in the ability than the other; for example, behavioral observations may provide a better depiction of aggressive tendencies among 4-year-olds than would interviews with children of the same age.

However, when there is no triangulation at either age level, the researcher cannot say anything certain about whether it is the ability or just method variance that is being assessed; whether one age is being assessed in a valid way and the other is not; or whether the same cognitive ability is actually being appraised at the different ages.

Accordingly, let us say that one theory (e.g., that of Piaget, 1950, 1960, 1970) predicts that a cognitive ability (e.g., knowledge that objects have a permanent existence apart from their perception by a person) should not be present at a given age level. In turn, let us also say that another theory (e.g., neo-nativism) predicts that this same ability should be present at this age level. To test these alternative predictions, researchers should: (a) Find, through triangulation, methods that *each* theory would accept as a valid means to measure the ability; and (b) Establish that the measures used by the two theories provide an *equivalent* index of the ability. If either of these two steps is not taken, then the competing predictions cannot be tested adequately. As such, a serious scientific error would occur if one asserts that evidence for one's preferred theory exists on the basis of using a method that neither has been shown via triangulation to be valid nor has been demonstrated to provide equivalence of measurement with a measure from the competing theoretical position.

This error would be compounded if, on the basis of findings associated with this inadequate approach to measurement, one concluded that evidence for the existence of the ability was present. Such a conclusion would constitute an assertion, that a cognitive structure existed, made on the basis of data from a method of unknown validity.

In short, a reification through the use of a flawed, a biased, methodology—a problem that we may term *methodologism*—would exist in such a circumstance. In other words, without evidence that a construct exists independent of the method that observes it, there is a confound between a method and a construct; a researcher cannot determine if the construct would be found to exist if another method was used to measure the construct. If one insists that a construct—an intrinsic ability, for example—exists by virtue of a single method, and if one does not triangulate the existence of the construct by verifying its presence through another method, then one is in effect reifying the concept through an incomplete methodological appraisal of the concept.

Fischer and Bidell (1998) noted that such a "methodologism" occurs in many neo-nativist research studies. That is, they noted that if neo-nativists can find methods that reveal a behavior that is akin to one found with other methods among older individuals, then the data derived from the method is used to argue for the presence of an innate ability. As Fischer and Bidell (1998) explained:

> During the debate over stage theory, many studies have followed the pattern illustrated in Gelman's (1972) number conservation research. Researchers introduced techniques for simplifying Piagetian task materials and procedures, and provided modeling, training, and other forms of support to children. They thus demonstrated severe violations of Piaget's age norms for logical concepts such as classification and spatial reasoning (Donaldson, 1978) and seriation (Bryant & Trabasso, 1971), in addition to conservation. The manipulations typically had the effect of driving the age of acquisition downward from Piaget's findings. Neo-nativist researchers overlooked the fact that it is equally possible to introduce more complex, less supportive conditions to drive the age of acquisition upward beyond Piaget's norms (Bidell & Fischer, 1992; Halford, 1989). (p. 493)

The methodologism associated with the neo-nativist research described by Fischer and Bidell (1998) leads, then, to a belief that there are data indicating that the reductionistic tools (the hypothesized native structures) used to address the variability of cognitive development have a separate, contextually disembedded existence. This existence is used, then, to propose that an inborn competence exists for domain-specific cognitive abilities. Thus, Fischer and Bidell (1998) indicated that:

> Based on findings such as these, neo-nativist researchers have advanced what Fischer and Bidell (1991) have referred to as the *argument from precocity*. The argument runs like this: If behaviors that are sometime s associated with a concept like object permanence can be made to appear much younger than in earlier research, then the concept in question must be present innately. This argument has led to claims of innate determination for a growing list of concepts, including conceptions of gravity and inertia

(Spelke, 1991), Euclidean geometry (Landau, Spelke, & Gleitman, 1984) and numerical abstraction (Starkey, 1992). However, the argument from precocity contains important logical flaws, all related to the failure to consider the full range of variability involved in developmental phenomena.

> The argument from precocity takes advantage of the selective focus on downward variation in the age of acquisition. Baillargeon's [1987] task and procedures were dramatically different from the more complex method of assessment used by Piaget. In place of independent problem solving in which the infant must actively search for an object hidden in several successive places, Baillargeon substituted a simple look toward one of two stimulus arrays. These conditions simplify the task so greatly that it shifts from a conceptual task to one of perceptual anticipation. Indeed, Mareschal and his colleagues (1995) showed that a neural-network model of the situation could solve a similar task with only such a simple perceptual strategy.

> The net effect of such simplification is to drive the age of acquisition downward by several months to its lowest limit and ignore the gradual epigenetic construction that is involved in all conceptual development. The research thus creates the impression that an object concept appears very early, although the more complex behaviors described by Piaget still develop at the usual later ages. The selective focus on one early age for one behavior obscures the constructive mechanisms and makes it seem that the concept of object permanence has suddenly leaped up, fully formed, at 3 1/2 months of age. How could such early development arise except through innate concepts?

> Unfortunately, this neo-nativist perspective does little to further the understanding of development. To preserve a static model of psychological structures as innate rule systems, it gives up the widely accepted principle of self-organization in the construction of knowledge, and it makes no attempt to deal with the pervasive evidence of variation of many kinds. Development disappears as innate "concepts" emerge abruptly in the first few months of life. (p. 494)

In short, then, the attempt to address the domain-specific variability in cognitive development through the nature–nurture splitting approach taken by neo-nativists is associated with problems of reductionism and of methodologically driven reification. The theory and research associated with the neo-nativist view of cognitive development results, then, in the belief that even the youngest of human infants possesses an inborn and unchanging cognitive competence in at least some domains of cognitive functioning. This belief is linked quite centrally to the notions of biological determinism and of developmental process associated with neo-nativism, and as a consequence, it is important to discuss the belief of intrinsic competence in more detail.

The Thesis of Unchanging Competence

Spelke and Newport (1998) made a distinction between competence and performance. An individual may possess a cognitive capacity but, because of environmental constraints, he or she may not manifest this competence. Indeed, Spelke and Newport (1998) claimed that the "thesis of unchanging competence that fails, at some times in development, to be revealed in performance" (p. 282) enables scholars of human development:

> To attribute abilities to children, rather than simply describing changes with age in what children happen to do in particular circumstances . . . it allows scientists to move from a description of behavior to an account of the underlying neural or mental states that make behavior possible. (p. 280)

The Spelke and Newport thesis of unchanging competence indicates that a revealed capacity is native to the individual. They suggested that "many developing capacities do not emerge by trial-and-error learning but in accord with an intrinsically paced schedule" (p. 283). Again, then, splitting the sources of development into native versus learned, they argued that competence can be present before it is reflected in performance and, as a consequence, "prior to any shaping by the demands of performance" (Spelke & Newport, 1998, p. 283).

For example, in reviewing data pertinent to comparative research on the development of depth perception, Spelke and Newport (1998) concluded that:

> Experiments resolve one question that has long been central to the nativist–empiricist dialogue: Neither humans nor other animals need to learn to perceive a stable, three-dimensional world. These findings do not imply, however, that depth perception is impervious to visual experience. (p. 289)

Thus, it is clear that Spelke and Newport, in drawing this conclusion, in effect equate "learning" with the purported causal process that would be operational if the context of the organism or, at least, the organism's experience of the context, would influence depth perception. It is also clear that Spelke and Newport see depth perception as an example of a native competence that does not require learning for its existence. Moreover, they believe that learning can only affect the manifestation of depth perception.

In short, then, on the basis of their views of native structures, neo-nativists advance a concept of inborn and, hence, unchanging competence and, as well, formulate a distinction between the presence of a cognitive ability and its enactment— its performance—in the behavioral repertoire of an individual. Simply, the concept of native ability is associated within neo-nativism with a model distinguishing between competence and performance.

Thus, in describing the neo-nativist concept of native competence and its link to the competence–performance distinction, Fischer and Bidell (1998) noted that:

> According to this view, an individual's specific activities in a situation are essentially divorced from the structures that govern them. These structures exist somewhere in the background and serve a limiting function: They determine the upper limit on the range of actions possible at a given time, but they leave open the specific action that will take place. Competence/performance theories are somewhat broader than innate competence theories because they do not necessarily require that psychological structures exist innately—only that they exist separately from the actions that instantiate them. The dynamics of construction of activities leading to wide variation are completely lost. (p. 495)

The particular action that occurs depends on the specific domain of ability (e.g., depth perception, knowledge of object permanence) of focus in a given study. That is, the competence–performance distinction made in neo-nativist theory is related to and complicated by the treatment within this approach of domain-specific ability. To understand the problems in neo-nativism that derive from the use made of the competence–performance distinction and the domain specificity of innate structures, it is useful to note that Fischer and Bidell (1998) indicated that:

> According to domain specificity theory, psychological processes are not organized in universal structures, but within limited domains that can include content areas such as spatial, linguistic, or mathematical reasoning, or groups of similar tasks such as problem solving or analogical reasoning tasks. . . . The domain specificity concept escapes the problem of having to explain patterns of variability —for example, the differences in age of acquisition across different logical concepts—*by simply asserting that they do not have to be explained,* because cognition is organized locally and should not be expected to show cross-domain consistency. . . . Consequently, the concept of domain specificity in itself does not provide a model of psychological structure. It simply acknowledges the fact of variability while sidestepping a systematic account of its origins. In some ways, this acknowledgment has represented an advance for a field once dominated by stage theory. However, to the extent that domain specificity theory creates the illusion of having solved the problem of variation, it may represent a theoretical detour. Simply to acknowledge that variability across domains exists does not

provide explanations for particular patterns of variability. . . . Although domain specificity theory provides important recognition of developmental variability, it offers no conception of structure to explain the variability across domains. (pp. 492–493)

Hence, given these problems, Fischer and Bidell (1998) concluded that:

> Domain specificity, innate competence, and competence/performance models share the same fatal limitations as the [Piagetian] logical stage models they were meant to replace. Although the newer models do not make the cross-domain claims that stage models did, they nevertheless retain a conception of psychological structure as some kind of static form existing separately from the behavior it organizes. Whether such static forms are seen as universal logics or domain-specific modules, they offer accounts only of stability in the organization of behavior while ignoring or marginalizing variability. The challenge for contemporary developmental psychology is not to explain away evidence of variability in performance. Instead, researchers need to build models of psychological structure . . . that provide methods and concepts to explain both the variability and the stability in the organization of dynamic human activity. (pp. 495–496)

In essence, then, Fischer and Bidell suggested that instead of a notion of developmental system-independent structures pertinent to specific domains of cognitive ability that exist in static, unchanging form, developmental science should develop a means to conceptualize and study cognitive abilities as parts of a dynamic system of organism–context relations. We discuss later in this chapter, the ideas forwarded by Fischer and Bidell (1998) to provide such a developmental systems approach to the study of the development of cognitive abilities. Here, however, we should note that a key implication of the point raised by Fischer and Bidell is that neo-nativism and developmental systems approaches to the conceptualization of cognitive structure differ in regard to the character of the developmental process they see as integral in the genesis of specific domains of cognitive ability. The different views of developmental process associated with the two theoretical positions are associated with contrasts in the understanding of the role of genes in development and in the concept of epigenesis.

Native competence and developmental process. Despite the problems with the neo-nativist concepts of domain specificity, innate competence, and competence–performance, other cognitive scientists following the neo-nativist approach to cognitive development provide ideas that extend those of Spelke and Newport regarding the meaning of

Rochel Gelman

the concept of "native competence" and the conception of "innateness" that it reflects. To illustrate, Gelman and Williams (1998, p. 583) asserted, "learning is the product of behavioral mechanisms with elaborated internal structures that have evolved to guide domain- and species-relevant learning" and Keil (1998) agreed, noting that:

> Nativists and empiricists disagree, but not on the premise that one organism has something built in that enables acquisition of a behavior or of knowledge while another does not. That very weak version is uninteresting . . . the real debate is whether one organism achieves greater learning successes than another organism because its mind is generally more cognitively capable or because it has specialized structures tuned to learn a specific kind of knowledge. (p. 385)

Keil (1998) indicated that the issue of whether there are such knowledge-specific structures is the issue of "domain specificity," and went on to indicate that:

> Empiricists and nativists disagree on how far "upstream" the domain-specific specializations must be for knowledge acquisition to proceed successfully. If there is nothing but general laws of association beyond the sense organs, then we have a strong empiricist view. If specialized systems are tuned to building up representations for abstract aspects of specific domains, such as social interactions, or moral beliefs, or language, that is a strong nativist position. . . . In short, although there may be disagreements about how to distinguish levels, there can be little question that they should be distinguished or that, in concert with domain specificity, nativists and empiricists

primarily disagree on the extent to which biases for specific information go beyond those in effect at the levels of sensory tranducers. (p. 386)

Accordingly, Keil (1998) saw a difference between neo-nativists and the group of scholars opposing them who, as did Spelke and Newport (1998), Keil (1998) characterized as "empiricists" (i.e., scholars purportedly focused on learning as the alternative to innateness). The difference Keil saw is in whether domain-specific structures in the brain, arising independent of learning, account for the acquisition in life of particular cognitive abilities (ranging from specific features of language to moral and socioemotional behaviors). As suggested earlier, I would differ with Keil's (1998) characterization of the two interpretative "camps" in this debate as nativist and empiricist. I would label them not as nativist and empiricist but, instead, as those adhering to split conceptions of nature versus nurture and those adhering to integrative, relational ideas associated with dynamic developmental systems theories. However, I would agree with Keil (1998) that the controversy that exists between the two groups is one involving the *process* through which human cognitive abilities are developed. Indeed, Keil (1998), in terms characteristic of the nature–nurture split, characterized this difference of perspective about developmental process by noting that:

> It takes only a little reflection to realize that nativists and empiricists often do not disagree on whether something can be learned, but on how it is learned. (p. 387).

To illustrate how the developmental systems view of process differs from the neo-nativist version of how cognitive abilities are developed, we may recall that in Chapter 6 we discussed the ideas of Schneirla (1957) regarding the phylogenetic differences among species in the eventual levels of stereotypy or plasticity reached at the highest levels of their ontogenetic development. In that discussion, we used Hebb's (1949) notions regarding the ratio of association fibers to sensory fibers (the A/S ratios) in the brains of organisms at different psychological levels to suggest a structural basis for the presence of these eventual functional differences across the ontogenies of different species.

Both neo-nativists and developmental systems theorists would agree that species at different psychological levels possess different levels of brain complexity (e.g., as represented by differences in their respective A/S ratios). They would agree, as well, that variation in brain complexity would be associated with eventual ontogenetic differences in the relative plasticity in behavior attained by different organisms. Thus, neither Schneirla's (1957) nor Hebb's (1949) ideas would evoke much controversy here.

However, what may be controversial is the basis of the "defining" structural and functional characteristics of a given species. Hereditarian, or what we may term *traditional* nativists, suggest that the differences across species in their structural characteristics and in their eventual functional abilities lie in the maturational ground plan given by evolution and specified in the genes of these organisms. Neo-nativists reject the genetic determinism of the traditional nativists, and instead suggest that evolution has given impetus to an endogenously active system that instantiates the species-typical structures and functions, and that—somehow—this instantiation occurs independent of both precise genetic specification *or* influence by experiences having loci in the environment within which the organism lives.

However, it is this means of instantiation that introduces for neo-nativists a host of conceptual problems that, on the one hand, involve the espousal of mutually contradictory statements (an unintentional embracing, if you will, of Aristotle's "law of the excluded middle") and, on the other hand, lead neo-nativists ineluctably if unwillingly to a position requiring the adoption of a dynamic, developmental systems orientation in order to account for the species-typical cognitive abilities of humans.

To understand the self-contradictions in neo-nativism, it is important to note that it is not clear from Spelke's and Newport's (1998) treatment of the concept of native, unchanging competence in specific domains of cognitive abilities what, specifically, is the "nature" of nativism. When an attribute of cognitive functioning, such as visual perception (e.g., in regard to depth), is regarded to be an instance of a native competence, it is possible to construe the attribute as an example of the sort of hereditarian, genetic determinism found in the ideas of Rushton (1999) and Rowe (1994). Spelke and Newport (1998) were quite clear that neo-nativists explicitly and unequivocally disavow such genetic determinism. They rejected any equation between their view of nativism and the notion of a reductionist, hereditarian, genetic determination of cognition.

But it is this very rejection—a rejection to which I also clearly subscribe—that creates complications for neo-nativist theory. As we now discuss, the nature–nurture split associated with neo-nativism creates a logical problem for this view when, as Spelke and Newport (1998) emphasized, the idea of genetic determination is rejected.

Neo-Nativism and Genetic Determination

Spelke and Newport (1998) stressed that nativist explanations of cognitive development do not imply that cognition (e.g., visual perception) is genetically determined. They explained that:

> In classical discussions of nativism in visual perception, the concept of innateness did not, of course, refer to genetic specification, but rather to the existence of structured developmental outcomes that arise in the absence of experience of a visible environment. (p. 291)

Thus, from this statement, what Spelke and Newport might have meant by the term "innate" is *only* that the neuronal structures that enable visual functioning develop independent of visual experience. That is, the implication of this statement is *not* that experience—interactions between the developing organism and the environment—is not fundamental in the development of the structures involved in visual perception, but rather that only some types of experiences, ones involving vision, are not a part of these interactions.

If this interpretation of the Spelke's and Newport's (1998) statement were correct, then neo-nativism would reduce to a theoretical position that claims that not all the experiences involved in an organism's history of interactions with its context have equal potential to shape the course of development. In the case of visual perception, their view might be, then, that, surprisingly and in fact counterintuitively, visual experiences are not a necessary part of the history of biology—context (or organism—environment) interactions that build the neuronal "apparatus" that enable visual functioning (e.g., perception of depth). Thus, neo-nativism, in denying genetic determination of cognitive functioning, would be an area of scholarship that (a) *described* cognitive characteristics that developed independent of some, but not all, experiences (e.g., as explained by Anastasi, 1958, at a minimum the organism would still need a history of supportive and facilitative experiences to enable its physical structures to develop in a healthy and species-typical manner); but that (b) explained development through recourse to some version, some model, of organism—environment interaction.

Of course, it is very unlikely that this interpretation would be accepted by Spelke's and Newport (1998, p. 291) as being correct. Although I later suggest that, in actuality, their position ends up in fact, acknowledging a position closely akin to the one noted in "b," previously mentioned, we have noted that Spelke and Newport forwarded a view of development wherein *all* experience lying outside of the organism is required to be independent of the genesis of intrinsic competence, of domain-specific ability. There could be, then, no privileged status given to nonvisual experience if the neo-nativist position is to remain an internally coherent position. That is, if Spelke and Newport are to avoid self-contradiction then, as with visual experience, nonvisual exogenous (extraorganism) experience must be seen as causally irrelevant for intrinsic abilities.

If, then, a view of the interactive role of external experience *cannot* be incorporated into neo-nativism, how is it possible to explain the presence of innate abilities without recourse to a claim of genetic determination? Especially because the neo-nativist position is predicated on a nature—nurture split, it seems puzzling, to say the least, that neither nature (genes) nor nurture (the environment and experience exogenous to the organism) are seen as being involved in the genesis of intrinsic structures.

What makes native structures native if not genes? The answer that Spelke and Newport provided returns them, albeit perhaps unintentionally, to the very genetic determination they wished to disavow. To understand this problem in their explanatory system, it is important to note that Spelke and Newport (1998) stated that:

> The existence of innate perceptual mechanisms that are not genetically specified undermines recent arguments that perceptual abilities cannot be innate because the human genome does not contain enough information to specify the connections on which those abilities depend (e.g., Edelman, 1987; Thelen & Smith, 1994). Direct genetic specification is not the only process that can produce visual mechanisms that operate prior to one's first encounters with the visual world. Indeed, the central accomplishments of recent research in developmental neurobiology are to reveal a host of *epigenetic* processes through which neural structures develop in accord with a species-typical plan, without either shaping by the environment external to the organism or detailed genetic instructions. These *epigenetic* processes may contribute not only to the development of depth perception but also to the development of object perception. (p. 291, italics added)

It is clear from this statement that Spelke and Newport turned to epigenesis as a means to explain the emergence of neural structures that are involved in one or more instances of cognitive functioning. Yet, their reliance on epigenesis as a means to explain what they still chose to term *innate* abilities is problematic in multiple ways. First, Spelke and Newport implied that the critics of neo-nativist thinking (e.g., Thelen & Smith, 1994; see, too, Chapter 7) are incorrect in their rejection of innateness because the critics equate the concept of "innateness" with the idea of genetic determination (not an unreasonable equation, given the long history and active present use of just such a linkage).

Nevertheless, although agreeing with critics that genetic determination is not a viable explanation of perception, Spelke and Newport claimed that their critics are mistaken in believing that visual perception is not, therefore, innate. Spelke and Newport based their view of the shortcomings of their critics on the fact that there is abundant evidence that *epigenetic* processes are involved in the development of perceptual ability and that, as a consequence, there is support for the belief that perceptual abilities are innate. This argument is flawed in several respects. These flaws derive from the problematic conception of epigenesis involved in neo-nativism.

Neo-Nativism and the Concept of Epigenesis

On the one hand, it is ironic that Spelke and Newport faulted their critics for failing to appreciate the importance of epigenetic processes when it is, in fact, the case that their critics have been among the "champions" of the use of epigenesis as a concept that serves to counter nativist, hereditarian thinking (e.g., see Thelen & Smith, 1994, 1998; and see, too, Gottlieb, 1970, 1983, 1991, 1992, 1997; Gottlieb et al., 1998). On the other hand, however, it seems clear that the version of epigenesis that Spelke and Newport forwarded, is *not* the one used by their critics.

That is, as explained in Chapter 3, a distinction may be drawn between predetermined and probabilistic versions of epigenesis. Predetermined epigenesis (e.g., Hamburger, 1957) admits that development is characterized by qualitative changes but sees these changes as arising completely independent of experience and as having their basis in the genome of the organism. Experience plays a role in predetermined epigenesis, but only insofar as it speeds up or slows down the intrinsically, that is, genetically determined, ground plan for development (e.g., see Erikson, 1959, and Chapter 16). Thus, in essence, predetermined epigenesis is an instance of a nature–nurture split conception. Probabilistic epigenesis—the version of epigenesis used by Thelen and Smith (1994, 1998) and other developmental systems-oriented critics of nativist ideas (e.g., Gottlieb, 1997; Magnusson, 1999a, 1999b; see, too, Chapter 7)—stresses the fusion of internal and external levels of organiza-

tion, and thus specifies that organismic characteristics of the individual are influenced by and are influences on the experiences encountered across the life span (e.g., Schneirla, 1956, 1957; Tobach, 1981; Tobach & Greenberg, 1984).

However, Spelke and Newport *cannot* mean probabilistic epigenesis when they point to epigenesis as a source of innate abilities because: (1) probabilistic epigenesis stresses the fusion of organismic endogenous and exogenous environmental influences (Gottlieb, 1970, 1983, 1997), and Spelke and Newport explicitly reject such a linkage as involved in the development of intrinsic competence (and, indeed, if they accepted the reality of such a fusion, they would contradict the very neo-nativist concept of development they wish to forward); and (2) subscription to probabilistic epigenesis involves an explicit rejection of the possibility that structures arise in the experience-independent manner described by Spelke and Newport (e.g., see Fischer & Bidell, 1998; Thelen & Smith, 1998). In turn, however, Spelke and Newport would not really want to subscribe to a predetermined epigenetic view of epigenesis because this version of epigenesis explicitly relies on the genetic determination (e.g., Erikson, 1959; Hamburger, 1957) that Spelke and Newport disavow. However, if they cannot turn to either probabilistic or predetermined epigenesis, they have no other epigenetic view to which to turn. They are, then, faced with an enormous—if not insurmountable—explanatory problem. Because there are no versions of epigenesis left to consider as a basis for intrinsic abilities, Spelke and Newport cannot explain the presence of these abilities.

In short, we have noted that as a consequence of the methodologism associated with its measures of early-life cognitive abilities, neo-nativism encounters problems in the descriptions made of intrinsic abilities. When coupled now with the explanatory dilemma faced in regard to not being able to embrace either extant interpretation of epigenesis, the resulting set of conceptual problems that neo-nativism must resolve to be regarded as a viable theoretical view of cognitive development are, to say the least, formidable. Accordingly, it is important to discuss further the issues raised by Spelke's and Newport's (1998) claim that epigenetic processes allow them to adhere to a nativist view of intrinsic abilities while, at the same time, rejecting the conceptually and empirically flawed notion of genetic determinism. Is there any way that Spelke and Newport can maintain what seems to be a set of contradictory views (rejection of the fusions of probabilistic epigenesis, rejection of the genetic determinism of predetermined epigenesis, and acceptance of the presence of innate cognitive competence)?

To begin to address this question, it is useful to point out that not all cognitive scientists sympathetic with a neo-nativist position conceive of epigenesis in precisely the same way as did Spelke and Newport (1998). For instance, Gelman and Williams (1998) noted that:

> With rare exception, any genetic developmental program carries with it extensive requirements for interactions with environments that can nurture, support, and channel the differentiation of adult structure. In the absence of those environments, the program will almost certainly fail. The same is surely true for skeletal mental structures; the existence of a primordial input-structuring mechanism does not guarantee that related knowledge will spring forth full blown the moment the individual encounters a single example of the requisite environment. Without opportunities to interact with, learn about, and construct domain-relevant inputs, as well as to practice components of relevant action plans, the contributions of skeletal structures will remain unrealized, or will lead to atypical developments. It follows that learners must encounter opportunities to interact with and assimilate relevant supporting environments. . . . It also follows that variability is a characteristic of any learning, whether about core domains that benefit from skeletal structures or non-core domains that do not. (p. 584)

Gelman and Williams (1998) thus cast the epigenetic process in a manner that regards genetic and environmental sources of cognitive development as separate domains, albeit necessarily and inextricably interactive ones. Nevertheless, it seems clear that Spelke and Newport, to maintain their position, could not agree with Gelman and Williams (1998). Spelke and Newport could not include within their theoretical position the sort of foundational, causal role for the thorough organism–context interactions that Gelman and Williams described. Instead, if Spelke and Newport adhered to the specification of epigenesis described by Gelman and Williams, then they could not at the same time logically adhere to a neo-nativist view of the role in cognitive development of the individual's interactions with the internal and external experiences in his or her world. That is, Spelke and Newport (1998) saw as discontinuous the endogenous and exogenous experiences of the organism, and contended that exogenous experiences play a role in cognitive development only insofar as they enable intrinsic competence to be revealed. As such, Spelke and Newport could not embrace the thorough, interactionist (but note, *not* fused) view of epigenesis embodied in the position

taken by Gelman and Williams (1998) and, at the same time, see the genesis of native competencies as independent of a continuity of inner- and outer-organism experiences interacting causally in a system with the developing individual.

Accordingly, Spelke and Newport (1998) *must* follow more closely the predetermined, as opposed to the probabilistic, version of epigenesis, in order to maintain a neo-nativist position, although this version of epigenesis will lead them directly into an unwanted alliance with the genetic determinism they (quite appropriately) reject as counterfactual and empirically empty. Nevertheless, the fact that they, indeed, link themselves with the predetermined view of epigenesis can be supported by their aforementioned statement (p. 291), wherein they stressed the presence of an "intrinsic plan" and emphasize that "experience external to the organism" is irrelevant to the development of the neural structures in question. As suggested in the view of Gelman and Williams (1998, p. 584), and contrary to the ideas about epigenesis embraced by Spelke and Newport, a probabilistic–epigenetic perspective would question the possibility of an impenetrable disconnection of experiences external to and internal in the organism and, as well, would argue that the course of species-typical development derives from the dynamic developmental relations between the organism and the multilevel ecological niche within which it exists.

It seems quite evident, then, that Spelke and Newport align themselves with the predetermined–epigenetic position, both because of the theoretical requirements of neo-nativism and, as such, as a consequence of their resulting commitment to a belief in intrinsic plans that arise independent of exogenous experience. This alignment, however, is the basis of the contradictory, internally inconsistent conception used by Spelke and Newport to explain cognitive development. That is, I have emphasized that, although they adopt a view of epigenesis that separates external and internal experiences (as if there were a membrane around the organism that was not permeable in regard to at least some ecological influences), and rely on the presence of an intrinsic ground plan to account for epigenetic change, Spelke and Newport also explicitly rejected "detailed genetic instructions" (p. 291), or genetic determination more generally, as the basis for epigenetic change. Unfortunately, then, they have excluded from their framework the precise explanatory mechanism—genetic determination—that is used by predetermined–epigenetic theorists (e.g., Erikson, 1959; Hamburger, 1957) to account for developmental change.

In short, Spelke and Newport cannot have it both ways. They cannot, on the one hand, reject the probabilistic–epigenetic view of organism–experience fusions that are integral in a dynamic, developmental system, and that are used to explain the succession of changes involved in the ontogeny of any feature of an individual's functioning and, at the same time, reject the explanatory device (genetic determination) used in the predetermined–epigenetic alternative to probabilistic epigenesis. As noted, there are no versions of epigenesis left and, as such, Spelke and Newport must either (a) accept the dynamic view of organism–environment fusions and, in so doing, accept as well that neo-nativism is a failed theoretical position; or (b) accept the genetic determinism of predetermined epigenesis, although they recognize that a hereditarian view of development is fatally flawed. Spelke and Newport are, then, between a theoretical "rock and a hard place." Embracing either version of epigenesis will destroy the viability of their theoretical model.

Spelke and Newport find themselves in this theoretically nonviable position because they wish to retain a split conception between neo-nativist and "empiricist" views of cognitive development; thus they are drawn to a version of epigenesis that is based on just such a split between nature and nurture. Although, as they implicitly recognize, in eschewing genetic determination as a basis of cognitive development, the debate is not really one of neo-nativism versus a theoretical system that stresses "learning" as an empiricist alternative to nativist thinking. Rather, and as stressed in the previous chapters of this book, the debate is one between genetic determinists and epigeneticists. However, where Spelke and Newport go awry is in not recognizing that, in effect, the distinction between the two versions of epigenesis, predetermined and probabilistic, reduces to a debate between a nature–nurture split conception that stresses the primacy of genetic determination (predetermined epigenesis) and an integrative, relational view which "heals" the nature–nurture split and proposes a dynamic, developmental system view of human development (Overton, 1998).

In sum, the organism–environment fusions that are a part of probabilistic epigenesis cannot be admitted into the neo-nativist perspective forwarded by Spelke and Newport (1998) *if* they are to maintain a view that claims that at least some experiences—ones external to the organism—are not relevant to cognitive development. The only version of epigenesis to which they can turn to make such a claim is predetermined epigenesis. However, they are not comfortable with the genetic determination involved in this version of epigenesis and so they reject this defining feature of the position. As such, Spelke and Newport are left with an empty version of epigenesis, that is, one that cannot adequately explain the very developments that Spelke and Newport seek to account for by their reliance on the concept of epigenesis.

There is little that remains left, then, in the conceptual repertoire of neo-nativism to represent the presence of intrinsic cognitive abilities. Arguably, all that in fact does remain is a view of the importance of within-organism activities, or self-generated experiences, promoting neuronal growth and organization. Given, then, that this concept may be the only means through which neo-nativism may be retained as a viable theoretical position, it is important to understand this view of experience.

The Concept of Experience Within Neo-Nativism

Given the abandonment of genetic determination as a means to explain brain development and, in turn, the rejection of a fused, organism–environment, dynamic developmental systems notion of epigenesis to account for such change, Spelke's and Newport's (1998) conception of innate cognitive abilities rests on their ability to account for the development of structures and functions through the organism's encounter with experiences, but only ones that are somehow completely endogenous to, and completely independent of, exogenous influences. However, given that Spelke and Newport do not take recourse to a dynamic developmental system to account for endogenous organism activity and for the brain developments that might arise from such internal experiences, they are left with nothing more than noting that endogenous activity exists (which it certainly does) but without a means to explain the presence and developmental course of this activity.

Moreover, although Spelke and Newport (1998) noted that there is a "species typical, intrinsic plan" (p. 291) for such development, the fact that they rejected genetic determination leaves them with no way of explaining how this plan gets inside of the organism or why it is enacted in the sequence that it follows; they are left with reifying, from the observation that species-typical patterns exist, the presence of a nonexplained (and, given their rejection of both genetic determination and dynamic, developmental systems, an unexplainable) plan. Simply, Spelke and Newport are left with claiming that a pattern of endogenous activities exists because a pattern of endogenous activities exists.

Perhaps even more problematic, however, is the fact that Spelke and Newport (1998) did not forward adequate evidence that supports the existence of external environment-independent endogenous experiences or activities. Instead, Spelke and Newport (1998) noted (p. 299) that they agree with the proposal made by Elman and colleagues (1998) that "an ability be considered 'innate' if it develops independently of the external environment, regardless of the epigenetic processes involved." It may be, however, that no such case of innateness exists, given the impossibility of ruling out that the chance that external experiences may be found that influence the organism's endogenous activity (e.g., the growth and organization of neuronal structures).

In fact, despite their claims that there is evidence that such exogenous-experience independent activity exists (e.g., Radic, 1977; Shatz, 1992), Spelke and Newport (1998, p. 298) also supported the views (e.g., of Gallistel, 1990) that innateness does "not imply that highly elaborate special-purpose neural machinery is preformed in the newborn's brain" or that cognitive ability "is impervious to experience." More critically, given their subscription to Edelman and colleagues' (1998) definition of innateness, Spelke and Newport recognized that there *is* a connection between the endogenous (brain) activities linked to internal *and* to external experiences. Spelke and Newport (1998) stated that:

> Studies in developmental neurobiology reveal that the neural connections underlying binocular functioning arise in animals not by genetic specification but by patterns of endogenously generated activity. Moreover, *the same activity-dependent processes that shape the brain in the absence of visual experience also shape the brain in response to visual experience.* (p. 298, italics added)

Thus, it appears that the Spelke and Newport (1998) theoretical position is once again undercut by the acceptance of the very continuity between endogenous and exogenous experience that they denied in their other statements about exogenous experience. Other ideas introduced by Spelke and Newport implicate further this more elaborate role of exogenous experience and, as such, lead Spelke and Newport to the threshold of a dynamic, developmental systems theory view of experience.

Experience, language, and evolutionary biases. The importance of experience is evident even in

the area of cognitive development wherein the "evidence for innate factors . . . is extremely strong" (Spelke & Newport, 1998, p. 299), that is, language development. That is, in contradiction to the hypothesis that there is a critical period (see Chapters 5 and 6) in language development (e.g., Lenneberg, 1967), wherein, after a particular, experience-independent maturationally determined age limit was passed, new languages could not be learned, Spelke and Newport (1998) indicated that:

> It is thus perhaps more accurate to say that human language learning shows a sensitive period, rather than a critical period (although virtually every behavior displaying maturational changes in plasticity also shows them in a less-than-absolute form, so such a distinction may not be worth making). (p. 304)

Thus, Spelke and Newport hedged a bit in regard to whether the evidence of sensitive periods in human language learning is really, in effect, evidence for the critical period notion that they disavowed. However, their equivocation indicates that they missed a crucial point about what the presence of a sensitive period, as opposed to a critical one, means in regard to the role of organism-experience interactions in the development of behavior. As discussed in Chapter 5, the plasticity that is involved in a sensitive period means that there are person–environment relations— experiences—that can promote change. A sensitive period also means that biology alone is not sufficient to account for the presence of behavior and that, therefore, when we see a particular behavior arising across a wide range of environmental conditions, we should not fall prey to the temptation to say that the behavior in question must be innate in that it develops no matter what the environmental circumstances may be. The presence of evidence in support of a sensitive period means that there are some environmental conditions that may be introduced to change the behavior in question, albeit that they may be atypical ones for the organism and/or difficult or expensive to introduce (Bruer, 1999; Clarke & Clarke, 1976; Columbo, 1982; MacDonald, 1985; Nelson, 1999). Given the infinity of environments within which an organism may interact, the presence of a period of sensitivity in the development of a feature of cognitive functioning means that what is likely to exist is still only a miniscule sample of the individual–context relationships and of their outcomes that, through planned interventions or naturally occurring variation, might arise.

Spelke and Newport (1998) argued that humans are "biased" learners in regard to language, in that the:

> Acquisition of language is not a slavish reproduction of environmental forms; rather it is the systematization and reorganization of these forms into patterns, according to the native tendencies of learners. (p. 306)

However, the presence of sensitive periods in language learning indicates that these "native tendencies" do not exist independent of individual–context relations that help forge a developmental system producing species-typical changes in language. That is, a native tendency or a bias in learning is not equal to innateness, in the sense of a structure or function arising independent of influence from an ecological context providing internal and external experiences that are fused with the organism in shaping its development.

For instance, humans are "biased" in regard to the portions of the visual spectrum or the auditory rage to which sensitivity exists. Moreover, the structure of visual experiences are "biased" by the fact that humans' eyes are at the front of their heads, as compared, for instance, to the sides. That humans have evolved to possess these functional and structural characteristics is not in question. And, if such an evolutionary heritage, which of course is the outcome of *experiences* interacting with organisms over the course of phylogeny, is all that is meant by innateness, then neo-nativism would reduce to nothing more than a field of scholarship that seeks to describe the ways in which evolutionary change has affected ontogenetic change. Such a focus is an important one, nonetheless, and it is one that has engaged and continues to engage biologists (e.g., Gould, 1977) and comparative and developmental scientists (e.g., Aronson et al., 1972; Gottlieb, 1992), including those scholars interested in using dynamic, developmental systems notions to understand the course of development (e.g., Gottlieb, 1997; Gottlieb et al., 1998).

In fact, Spelke and Newport (1998) may have adopted just such a view of neo-nativism. For instance, in discussing the facts of language development, they called for "a theoretical account involving evolutionary specialized developmental mechanisms of some type" (pp. 299–300). Similarly, Keil (1998) noted that scholarship in the field of cognitive science has resulted in the view that "humans have a special endowment tailored to facilitate . . . the ability to acquire and use language . . ." (p. 366). When viewed independent of the nativist–empiricist controversy, these views

are nothing more remarkable than a claim that humans have evolved in a manner that, given the necessary supportive and facilitative environmental conditions (Anastasi, 1958), will result in the development of particular species-typical structures and functions.

For instance, just as bats, when they develop in interaction within supportive and facilitative (i.e., "species typical") contextual conditions, develop the capacity to move through their environment using a radarlike sense of locomotion, and just as dogs, when they develop in interaction with species-typical ecological conditions, have the capacity to hear tones outside of the normal auditory range to which humans are sensitive, humans, when they develop within the context of an ecology supportive and facilitative for their healthy functioning, will develop language. It is not remarkable or controversial, then, that there are evolutionarily based differences in the structural characteristics and functional capacities of different organisms.

If this account is what is meant by neo-nativism (i.e., biased or, perhaps better, shaped by evolution), then what is meant by innateness in this perspective is that the history of organism–environment relations (i.e., that phylogeny) is important in the ontogenetic development of a particular cognitive ability. As we have noted that Keil (1998) also claimed, such an assertion is neither controversial nor particularly important. Moreover, such a conception—of evolutionary influence—does not deny the role of organism–environment interactions in ontogeny in actualizing, through dynamic, self-organizational features of the developmental system (Thelen & Smith, 1998), the structures or functions associated with evolutionary heritage. In fact, as discussed in Chapter 7, these system properties can result in the very "biases"—or, in the terms of dynamic systems models, attractor states—in which neo-nativists are interested.

In sum, Spelke and Newport (1998) placed primary theoretical importance on maintaining a split between the internal and external world of the developing organism in order to retain the viability of a neo-nativist view of the bases of cognitive abilities. Nevertheless, experiential histories of organism–environment interaction are admitted into the ideas that Spelke and Newport forwarded in regard to the phylogenetic and ontogenetic bases of cognitive development. Spelke and Newport (1998) recognized that, across the life span, brain activity (e.g., neural growth and organization), and, of course, the very survival or the organism itself, involves experiences acting within the individual that are not discontinuous from (i.e., independent of or disconnected with) experiences external to the corporal being of the individual. In turn, the history of organism–environment experiences specific to a species shaped the structures that provide the material foundation for cognitive functioning and, as well, evolved as structures and functions that are instantiated over the life span by a continuity of experiences having loci both internal and external to the individual.

Conclusions

A neo-nativist view of cognitive development becomes a position that in several respects is an internally inconsistent conception of development. Whereas, at one level, neo-nativism attempts to maintain an outmoded split between nativism and empiricism, on another level this split is rejected in the service of forwarding epigenesis as the basis of developmental change. In turn, although explicitly rejecting genetic determinism as a basis for what is termed innate, neo-nativism aligns itself with a version of epigenesis (i.e., predetermined epigenesis) that relies on genetic determination to explain the course of organismic development.

Moreover, while operationalizing "innateness" of cognitive development as involving abilities that arise independent of experiences external to the individual, neo-nativism ultimately acknowledges that there is continuity between internal and external experiences. Indeed, even in domains wherein the contention of innateness is claimed to be strongest, for example, human language learning, the presence of sensitive periods in development attest to the role of individual–experience relations as fundamental in development.

Furthermore, the experience of organism–environment interactions enters into cognitive development in yet another way, one that Spelke and Newport (1998) stressed themselves. Experiential differences may create differences between people in the manifestation of (or levels reached in) cognitive development. That is, they noted that scholarship about the nature and nurture of cognitive development has no relevance to accounts of the sources of individual differences in knowledge or cognitive abilities. Contrary to the assertions of hereditarians such as Rushton (1999), Rowe (1994), and Plomin (2000), Spelke and Newport (1998) pointed out that:

> The claim that some body of knowledge is innate in the human species does not entail, or even suggest,

that *differences* in knowledge and cognitive performance between different members of the species are innate as well. Individual differences in knowledge and cognitive processes may depend wholly on differences in the opportunities available to different people to elaborate on their common, biologically given knowledge systems. (p. 327)

Thus, ultimately, neo-nativism involves the role of individual–experience interactions both in regard to within-person changes and in respect to between-person differences in such change.

In sum, the neo-nativist view, when its conceptions and contradictions are "unpacked," enables one to see a rich role for the experience of a history of dynamic and systemic individual–context relations. In fact, it is possible to offer views of cognitive development that constitute dynamic, developmental systems alternatives to neo-nativist ideas. In Chapter 7, we discussed one of these alternatives, the theory of Thelen and Smith (1998) and, in the present discussion, we noted some of the ways in which this view contrasted with neo-nativism. To illustrate the generality of the alternative to neo-nativism represented by dynamic, developmental systems theories it is useful to consider another instance of such alternatives, one provided by Kurt W. Fischer.

As has been illustrated already, Fischer and his colleagues (e.g., Thomas R. Bidell) have provided detailed criticism of the neo-nativist position. In addition, they offer a dynamic, developmental systems formulation to counter it.

FISCHER'S THEORY OF DYNAMIC DEVELOPMENT OF PSYCHOLOGICAL STRUCTURES IN ACTION AND THOUGHT

For several decades, Kurt W. Fischer (e.g., 1980, 1987; Fischer & Bidell, 1991, 1998; Fischer & Pipp, 1984; Fischer & Rose, 1994) has formulated a theory of human development that focuses on the dynamic relations between the person and his or her context. As a consequence, Fischer views developmental structures as active entities organizing these person–context relations. Not surprisingly, given the previously noted criticisms Fischer and his colleagues (e.g., Fischer & Bidell, 1998) have forwarded in regard to neo-nativist thinking, a key impetus for the development of his theory has been to devise a means to treat the variability that exists in human cognitive development in a manner

Kurt W. Fischer

that avoids the problems of reductionism and reification associated with neo-nativism.

Accordingly, Fischer and Bidell (1988) noted that the core issue confronting contemporary developmental theory

> is the problem of how to account for the tremendous variability in developmental phenomena. . . . The static notion of stage structure, which dominated theories of cognitive development from its inception as a field of study through the early 1980s, has proven incapable of accounting for the massive and growing evidence of both variation and consistency: wide-ranging variability within and across individuals in the age of acquisition of logical concepts across domains and contexts, systematic sequences in the order of acquisition of many of these concepts and their components, and high synchrony in development of some concepts under some conditions. (p. 470)

As we have noted, neo-nativism represents one means to deal theoretically with the variability in cognitive development. However, we have noted that Fischer and Bidell (1998) criticized neo-nativist accounts because such views have

> selectively focused on one consequence of variability—the downward variation in age of onset for concepts like conservation or object permanence that can be achieved with modified methods or simplified

tasks. . . . Scholars in this movement have focused only on the downward variation in age, without considering the complementary, widely observed pattern of increase in age of onset for many tasks and assessment conditions. (p. 470)

Moreover, compounding this problem of selective attention among neo-nativist scholars is the tendency in neo-nativist approaches (Fischer & Bidell, 1998)

> toward reductionism, a view of mind and science that seeks to explain action and thought entirely in terms of lower-level processes such as genes, neural activity, and biochemical processes, extracting them out of their natural contexts and isolating them as if they were not interrelated. . . . Conceiving of development in terms of genetically unfolding brain structures, or similar reductionist explanations, has led to the erroneously rooted view of cognitive structures as static forms. (pp. 470–471)

As we have noted, however, Fischer and Bidell (1998) not only provided a critique of neo-nativism but also offered an alternative to it, one based on a dynamic, developmental systems approach to understanding cognitive abilities. Fischer and Bidell (1998) explained that:

> A new view of cognitive structure as a property of *dynamic systems* instead of static forms is beginning to emerge from a growing number of research and theoretical efforts across the field . . . dynamic systems theories aim to understand the underlying relations among complex processes that give rise to orderly patterns of variability—stabilities within the variations—dynamic systems theories focus directly on explaining and modeling processes of change in complex systems . . . [with] psychological structure as the organizational property of dynamic systems of activity. (p. 471)

Accordingly, to provide an alternative to the reductionism and reification associated with the positing of native competence and of the conceptual split between nature and nurture within which such a contextually disembodied entity is presumed to exist, Fischer and Bidell presented a theory of psychological structure that is predicated on the features of a dynamic, living system (cf. Ford & Lerner, 1992; Sameroff, 1983; Thelen & Smith, 1998). In explaining their view of this system, Fischer and Bidell (1998) noted that:

> All living systems—whether biological, psychological, or social—must be organized to function. A living organism that becomes sufficiently disorganized dies. A disorganized society collapses. A disorganized mind leaves a person helpless in the face of everyday problems. This organizational aspect of living systems is what we call *structure,* a dynamic

patterning and relating of components that sustain the organized activities that define life and living things. . . . To say that a system is structured or organized implies that specific relations exist among its parts, subsystems, or processes . . . dynamic structure exists only where relationship exists, and structures comprise sets of intrinsic relations among the parts of a system that provide its specific type of organization. . . . In order to flourish, living systems must be more than just organized. They must be dynamic. Systems must constantly move and change if they are to carry out their functions and maintain their integrity. A system that becomes static—unable to change and adapt to varying conditions—will quickly perish. . . . For living systems, the dynamic is self-organization. Living systems are agentic or self-moving: they change and adapt as a result of self-regulation and self-organization. . . . A living system is involved in multiple relations with other living and nonliving systems, and they are part of its dynamics. Their influence functions through the living system's self-regulation and self-organization. . . . This agency and dynamism lead naturally to variability in systems. (p. 472)

The sort of dynamic, developmental systems view of human development proposed by Fischer and Bidell (1998) results in a conception of cognitive structure that stands in marked contrast to the view of cognitive structure found in neo-nativism. In neo-nativism, structure exists independent of and prior to the activity of the organism, and this structure is argued to arise through innate, experience-independent means. In turn, in Fischer's and Bidell's conception, structure and activity are inextricable, fused components of the integrated, organism–context relations that constitute the developmental system. Thus, in contrasting the neo-nativist versus the dynamic, developmental systems views of cognitive structure, Fischer and Bidell (1998) noted that:

Traditional static conceptions of psychological structure are closely related to a widespread cultural metaphor for development—a ladder. Development is conceived as a simple linear process of moving from one formal structure to the next, like climbing the fixed steps of a ladder. It matters little whether the steps of the ladder are conceived as cross-domain stages, levels of a domain-specific competence, or points on a psychometrically based scale. In each case, the beginning point, sequence of steps, and end point of the developmental process are all linear and relatively fixed, forming a single ladder. With such a deterministic, reductionist metaphor, it is difficult to represent the role of constructive activity or differential contextual support because there appears to be no choice of where to go from each step. The richness

of children's development of narrative skills, including the variability in their skills across contexts, is simply lost with the ladder metaphor. Development means just moving to the next step.

An alternative metaphor for development that includes variability as well as stability in development, is the constructive web (Bidell & Fischer, 1992a; Fischer, Knight, & Van Parys, 1993). The metaphor of a web is useful for dynamic models because it supports thinking about active skill construction in a variety of contexts as well as types of variability. Unlike the steps in a ladder, the strands in a web are not fixed in a determined order but are the *joint product* of the web builder's constructive activity and the supportive context in which it is built (like branches, leaves, or the corner of a wall, for a spider web). . . . The separate strands in a web represent the various pathways along which a person develops. (p. 473)

Thus, Fischer and Bidell integrated the notion of developmental strands found in the organismic philosophy of science (Pepper, 1942; see Chapter 3) with the richness of variations present in the context of human development (again, see Pepper, 1942, and Chapter 3). As a result, they proposed a process of dynamic, person–context relations that reflects the features of fusion and reciprocal relationships involved in the probabilistic–epigenetic view of developmental process (Gottlieb, 1970, 1983, 1997; Gottlieb et al., 1998). The dynamism of this integrated, multilevel system synthesizes continuity and discontinuity, constancy and change, and structure and variability. That is, as Fischer and Bidell described it, the weblike system they envisioned gives rise to dynamically developing, integrative structures. Fischer and Bidell (1998) explained that such:

Structure is simply the actual organization of dynamic systems of activity. Instead of a separately existing entity, such as a logical stage dictating behavior, or a preformed capacity awaiting actualization, psychological structure is one of many qualities or properties of human activity systems. Because real systems of activity are dynamic—constantly moving, adapting, and reorganizing—they must be dynamically structured. Variability is a natural consequence of system dynamics, and because systems are organized, the variability is not random but patterned. These patterns of variability provide the key to understanding and modeling the dynamic structure of psychological systems because they reflect not only the potential for mobility and change but also the limits on change inherent in each system's organization. Just as geologists have modeled the structures of coastal evolution and biologists have modeled the structures of evolution of living species, developmental psychologists can analyze the intrinsic connection between structure and variation in order to build models that reflect the true complexity and dynamics of developmental processes. (pp. 477–478)

According to Fischer and Bidell (1998), as well as to other theorists who use developmental systems notions to frame their developmental scholarship (e.g., Ford & Lerner, 1992; Gottlieb, 1997; Magnusson, 1995, 1996, 1999a, 1999b; Sameroff, 1983; Thelen & Smith, 1998; Wapner & Demick, 1998), *all* facets of human behavior develop with this system. However, specifically in regard to the development of human cognition, Fischer and Bidell (1998) stated that:

> Because the human mind is a type of living system, it can be understood in terms of the principles of living systems, including structure, relationship, agency, and dynamics. From this perspective, psychological structure is defined as the organizational property of dynamic systems of activity, both mental and physical. Systems of activity, like other living systems, must be organized to function properly, to maintain themselves and adapt to variation in useful ways. This organization involves relationships among the biological, psychological, and social systems that contribute to any given activity. In agency, people set goals (and regulate their own activities in terms of those goals) with respect to the many systems relationships in which they are embedded. The result of all this complexity is a self-regulated dynamic system of activities in which psychological organization varies widely while at the same time showing important kinds of order and stability within the variation. (p. 472)

In sum, instead of positing the innate existence of structures that provide an external-environment-independent competence, the dynamic, developmental system depicted by Fischer and Bidell gives rise to structures through a process of organism–environmental fusions. The structures created through this fusion integrate the capacities for constancy and change that are requisite for a living entity to survive. Fischer and Bidell labeled these structures *dynamic skills*.

This concept is perhaps the one that serves as the best point of contrast between the neo-nativist idea of cognitive structure as an experimentially disembodied, intrinsic competence and the dynamic, developmental systems view of structure as an active, integrated link between the person and his or her multilevel context. Accordingly, it is important to discuss the concept of dynamic skills in more detail.

The Concept of Dynamic Skill

Fischer and Bidell's view of dynamic developmental systems requires that the concept of cognitive structure that they employ can, at one time, be used to understand several different manifestations of the variability that exists in cognitive development: the range of cognitive abilities that exists in human development, and its emergence within and across time; the convergence in ontogeny of particular cognitive developments; and the relatively general, species-specific sequence across ontogeny of changes in cognitive ability. However, to be consistent with the probabilistic–epigenetic view of developmental process involved in developmental systems theory, Fischer and Bidell need to propose a concept of structure that accounts for these dimensions of variability in relation to a fused, multilevel developmental system involving reciprocal relations between the developing person and his or her active context.

In the view of Fischer and Bidell, the concept of dynamic skill provides just such an integrative structure. That is, Fischer and Bidell (1998) envisioned a skill as

> a capacity to act in an organized way in a specific context. Skills are thus both action-based and context-specific. People don't have abstract, general skills. Instead, skills are always skills *for* some specific context of activity: a skill for riding a bicycle, a skill for tennis, or a skill for interpersonal negotiation. Skills do not spring up fully grown from preformed rules or logical structures; they are built up gradually through the practice of real activities in real contexts, and are then gradually extended to new contexts through this same constructive process (Fischer & Farrar, 1987; Fischer & Granott, 1995).
>
> The concept of skill is also helpful in conceptualizing the relations among various psychological, organismic, and sociocultural processes because skills draw on and integrate all of these components. It helps to cut through artificial dichotomies between mind and action, memory and planning, or person and context. A skill—say, for storytelling—draws on and unites systems for emotion, memory, planning, communication, cultural scripts, speech, gesture, and so forth. Each of these systems must work in concert with the others for an individual to tell an organized story to specific other people in a particular context, in a way that it will be understood and appreciated. In place of concepts of isolated processes or modules that obscure relations among cooperating systems, the concept of dynamic skill facilitates the study of relations among collaborating systems and the patterns of variation they produce.
>
> Skills are not composed atomistically but are necessarily integrated with other skills . . . the components of living systems not only depend on one another but participate in one another. . . . For living systems, conceptions of structure must reflect the interparticipation of one system in another. Systems of activities are central parts of living systems, especially complex systems such as human beings. (pp. 478–479)

Thus, to Fischer and Bidell (1998) the "unit" of cognitive structure is not an internal and intrinsic entity, arising innate and thus independently of exogenous experience. Rather, the unit within their system—the dynamic skill—is a structure that influences and is influenced by the set of interlevel relations ongoing within the developmental system.

Accordingly, a dynamic skill is a means through which the inner and outer worlds of the developing person become dynamically (i.e., reciprocally and developmentally) linked. A dynamic skill, then, both enables the person to act on his or her world while, simultaneously, it reflects the impact of all levels of the world (family, community, culture, and history) on the person. Indeed, Fischer and Bidell (1998) discussed the cultural embeddedness of a dynamic skill by noting that:

> Skills are context-specific and are culturally defined. . . . The context specificity of skills is related to the characteristics of integration and interparticipation because people build skills to participate with other people directly in specific contexts for particular sociocultural systems. In turn, people internalize (Wertsch, 1979) or appropriate (Rogoff, 1993) the skills through the process of building them for participating in these contexts, and as a result, the skills take on cultural patterning. (p. 479)

Moreover, given that skills represent this bidirectional linkage between the inner and outer levels of organization comprising the developmental system and, as well, constitute the means through which the active individual influences (as well as is influenced by) his or her social context, it is clear that for Fischer and Bidell (1988):

> Skills are self-organizing. Part of the natural functioning of skills is that they organize and reorganize themselves. . . . The self-organizing properties of living systems also go beyond maintenance to include self-organization and mutual regulation in the growth of new, more complex systems. (p. 479)

Thus, the concept of dynamic skills represents a view of an active individual engaging his or her active world. The person envisioned in the theoretical position presented by Fischer and Bidell is not just the "host" of the innate structure somehow placed in his or her head by an innate process of indeterminate epigenetic character; rather, the person is an active constructor of the cognitive abilities that give him or her the competence to stay the same or change, as the requirements of his world impinge on him or her, and do so through dynamic structures that bridge the inner and outer worlds of the living, developmental system. Accordingly, Fischer and Bidell (1998) noted that:

> Skills are organized in multilevel hierarchies. As skills grow, they are constructed through a process of coordination. . . . As skills and other living systems become integrated, subsystems subordinate themselves, of necessity, to new forms of organization and mutual regulation. The newly formed systems represent higher levels of organization in the specific sense that the component systems must conform to the regulatory demands and maintenance needs of the larger entity if the system as a whole is to survive. . . . Dynamic systems in general develop via a process of active coordination of component systems. (p. 480)

In sum, dynamic skills link the active person in a dynamic relation with his or her changing world. The probabilistic–epigenetic system—the developmental web, in the terms of Fischer and Bidell (1998)—that is a product and a producer of these skills embeds the person in a process that enables him or her to be an active agent in his or her own development. This agency occurs through dynamic collaborations with the components of his or her context, including other people and the products of these other people, for example, their dynamic skills, and the social institutions, culture, and the designed ecology they construct (e.g., Brandtstädter, 1998, 1999; Bronfenbrenner, in press; Bronfenbrenner & Morris, 1998; Lerner & Busch-Rossnagel, 1981a; 1981b; Lerner & Walls, 1999; Rogoff, 1998). Fischer and Bidell (1998) indicated that:

> The constructive web provides a metaphor for the construction of skills that facilitates reconceptualizing psychological structure in dynamic terms. . . . Building a web is a self-organizing process in which various activities must be coordinated and differentiated. The strands in a web are the joint product of the person's constructive activity and the contexts in which skills are built, including the other people that coparticipate in building them. (p. 480)

Conclusions

Fischer and Bidell (1998) offered an alternative to the neo-nativist view of cognitive development that places the genesis of cognitive abilities *not* within the head of the developing person, and certainly *not* centered in intrinsic structures that are purported to exist independently of organism–context activity and of endogenous experience. The Fischer and Bidell (1988) conception of cognitive structures is one associated with a probabilistic–epigenetic view of person–context relations and, as such, relies on the "dynamic collaborations" between the person and his or her world to understand the character of cognitive development.

Accordingly, Fischer and Bidell see cognitive development as a fully relational process. This relationism involves all levels of organization in the developmental system, and includes, therefore, the general, but abstract, linkage between all endogenous and exogenous stimulation and, as well, more specific and concrete linkages between a person and others in his social world. A growing theoretical and empirical literature underscores the importance of such person-to-person "dynamic collaborations" in cognitive development. The scholarship of Barbara Rogoff exemplifies this work. Accordingly, to illustrate the importance for cognitive development of the integrative, dynamic developmental system described by Fischer and Bidell, it is useful to discus the ideas of Rogoff pertinent to the social collaborations that are involved in cognitive development.

Barbara Rogoff

ROGOFF'S CONCEPTION OF COGNITION AS A COLLABORATIVE PROCESS

Neo-nativists place learning and/or cognitive development within the "head" of the individual. Denying the relevance for the development of intrinsic abilities of exogenous experience, neo-nativists believe that the variables or processes involved in the genesis of cognitive competence are intraindividual ones. In contrast, scholars following a developmental systems view stress the relations among all the intraindividual and interindividual levels of organization involved in the developmental system and, as such, see these levels dynamically collaborating (Fischer & Bidell, 1998) in the development of cognition.

Critically, to Rogoff (1998) these levels contributing to the development of an individual's cognition include those involving other people (e.g., families, peer groups, communities, and cultures). At this writing, the idea that more than an individual alone is involved in the development of his or her cognitive competence "is still new to many cognitive developmentalists. For some, it is a foreign concept to think of cognition as something other than an individual activity. For others, the idea of cognition involving social processes is comfortable, but somewhat inchoate" (Rogoff, 1998, p. 680). Nevertheless, as noted above, the idea that an individual's intellectual abilities, learning, or cognitive capacities involve interindividual relationships, association embedded within a sociocultural context, has been gaining increasing currency in the study of human development

(e.g., Baltes & Staudinger, 1996; Cole, 1985; Cooper, 1980; Damon, 1984; Leont'ev, 1981; Rogoff & Chavajay, 1995; Staudinger & Baltes, 1996; Valsiner, 1998; Vygotsky, 1978; Wertsch, 1981, 1985), especially among scholars attracted to the use of developmental systems perspectives (e.g., Baltes et al., 1998, 1999; Rogoff, 1998). Indeed, using Vygotsky's (1978; see, too, Chapter 2) concepts of development to describe the emerging emphasis on cognition as an interpersonally and socioculturally collaborative process, Rogoff (1998) noted that:

> The paradigm shift required to move from thinking of cognition as a property of individuals to thinking of cognition as an aspect of human sociocultural activity (without attempting to locate the process only in individuals) is at the edge of the "zone of proximal development" of the field at this point. (p. 680)

Rogoff (1998) noted, however, that this emerging, cutting-edge concern with the interpersonal and contextual bases of an individual's cognitive competence did not begin at the end of the twentieth century, with the advent of developmental systems theories coming to the fore of theoretical interest in human development in general (e.g., Lerner, 1998a) and in cognitive development in particular (e.g., Feldman, 2000; Fischer & Bidell, 1998; Thelen & Smith, 1998). Rather, the idea of cognition as a collaborative process arose at the beginning of the twentieth century, through the contributions of Vygotsky (e.g., 1927/1982, 1933/1966, 1978) and Piaget (e.g., 1923, 1950, 1952, 1954). That is, Rogoff (1998, p. 680) noted that the former theorist used cultural/theoretical ideas to argue "that individual development was an aspect of cultural/historical activity," while the latter one contended that cognitive development occurred "through co-operation as individuals attempt to resolve conflicts between their perspectives." Moreover, Rogoff (1998) explained that:

> One of the key commonalities between the cultural/historical and Piagetian approaches to cognition as a collaborative process is an emphasis on achievement of shared thinking. In the process of everyday communication, people share their focus of attention, building on a common ground that is not entirely shared (for each person works with a somewhat unique perspective). To engage in shared endeavors, there must be some common ground, even to be able to carry out disputes. . . . Mutual understanding between people in communication has been termed *intersubjectivity*, a process that occurs *between* people; it cannot be attributed to one person or the other in communication . . . . Some modification in the perspectives of each participant are necessary to understand the other person's perspective. The modifications can be seen as the basis for development—as the participants adjust to understand and communicate, their new perspectives involve greater understanding and are the basis for further growth. (pp. 681–682)

Within this interpersonal and culturally embedded frame, Rogoff described several means through which interpersonal relations influence the cognitive development of an individual. For instance, Rogoff (1998) noted that:

> Cognitive development occurs as new generations collaborate with older generations in varying forms of interpersonal engagement and institutional practices. For example, in some communities, conversation between adults and young children is common, but children seldom have the opportunity to observe and participate in adult activities; in other communities, engagement between adults and young children occurs in the context of children's involvement in the mature activities of the community, but not in peer-like conversation. . . . The topic of cognition as a collaborative process necessarily includes all such forms of collaboration. (p. 680)

Moreover, Rogoff (1998, p. 681) described the importance of the aid that experts in a given knowledge domain give to "novices" in that domain, and explained that the use by experts of various techniques to support the learning of novices (e.g., tutoring, scaffolding of concepts, or adjustment of learning supports to match the needs novices have

for assistance) promotes learning through enactment of "the mutual roles of children and adults in structuring adult-child interaction" in the service of cognitive development. In turn, Rogoff (1998) explained the significant role that child-to-child (peer) interaction plays as well in the development of an individual's cognitive capacity. Rogoff (1998) indicated that:

> How peers assist each other in learning addresses concepts . . . [such as] . . . collaboration in peer play and child caregiving, the role of similarity of status in collaborative argumentation, and peers' facilitation of each other's learning in classrooms. It also includes consideration of how children and the adults and institutions that work with them learn to collaborate. (p. 681)

In fact, given the embeddedness of child–adult and child–child learning in a socioculturally shaped institutional context, Rogoff (1998) pointed out that:

> Collaboration involves groups larger than dyads and includes specialized asymmetrical as well as symmetrical roles between participants, discord as well as harmony, and collaboration among people of different eras and locations. (p. 681)

As a consequence of this diversity of social players, of the roles they enact, and the behaviors they manifest, collaboration

> is a process that can take many forms, whether intended or accidental, mutual or one-sided, face-to-face, shoulder-to-shoulder, or distant, congenial or contested; the key feature is that in collaboration, people are involved in others' thinking processes through shared endeavors. (Rogoff, 1998, p. 728)

Conclusions

Rogoff (1998) advanced a concept of cognitive development that richly capitalizes of the idea of dynamic collaborations advanced by Fischer and Bidell (1998) to depict the thorough, interlevel integrations that constitute the process of human development depicted within developmental systems theories. By explaining how the dynamic collaborations within the developmental system are significantly instantiated by interpersonal, intergenerational, and person-institutional relationships, all embedded with the sociocultural moment, Rogoff (1998)

> goes beyond regarding the individual as a separate entity that is the base unit of analysis to examine sociocultural activity as the unit of analysis, with examination of the contributions of individual, interpersonal, and community processes. Thus, analysis

goes beyond the individual and the dyad to examine the structured relations among people in groups and in communities, across time.

With sociocultural activities as the units, analysis emphasizes the purposes and dynamically changing nature of events. Analysis examines the changing and meaningful constellations of aspects of events, not variables that attempt to be independent of the purpose of the activity. Central to analysis of cognition as a collaborative process is a focus on the shared meaning in endeavors in which people engage in common. Cognition is not conceptualized as separate from social, motivational, emotional, and identity processes—people's thinking and development is conceived as involved in social relations, with purpose and feeling central to their involvement in activities, and transformation of their roles as a function of participation. (p. 729)

In short, the ideas of Rogoff (1998) help transform the concept of cognitive development from a phenomenon seen, within neo-nativist theory, to have exclusive, endogenous bases to one linked dynamically to other people and to the social institutions and cultures created by their activity. Indeed, individuals' own actions, in concert with the other levels of the dynamic developmental system that they influence and are influenced by, are brought to the fore of concern in the developmental systems theoretical perspective exemplified by Rogoff's (1998) perspective.

Her ideas, like those of other cognitive theorists exploring the use of developmental systems notions (e.g., Baltes et al., 1998, 1999; Feldman, 2000; Fischer & Bidell, 1998; Magnusson, 1996, 1999a, 1999b; Overton, 1998; Sameroff, 1983; Thelen & Smith, 1998; Wapner & Demick, 1998), underscore the importance of approaching the description and explanation of cognitive phenomena from a perspective that integrates (that does not split) the levels of organization comprising the ecology of human development. Indeed, the idea of "levels of integration" (instead of "split levels") emphasized (at this writing) more than a half century ago by Schneirla (1956, 1957; Maier & Schneirla, 1935), seem to be an idea of renewed attractiveness to scholars of cognitive development.

CONCLUSIONS

If the past is at all prelude, then it seems safe to predict that the study of cognitive development will, as it did across the twentieth century, be likely to continue to engage the interest and energy of scholars of human development across the

Deanna Kuhn

twenty-first century. However, I believe that it is likely that the admonition of Overton (1998) to "avoid all splits" will become very much a rallying cry of scientists interested in both richly describing and in adequately explaining the features of cognitive development.

Levels of Integration and the Explanation of Cognitive Development

As illustrated by the discussion in this chapter and the preceding ones (i.e., Chapters 10–13), approaches to development that are predicated on split notions of nature and nurture—either those associated with hereditarian conceptions of development or with neo-nativist ones—fail on several logical, theoretical, and empirical grounds. In turn, theories that integrate levels, and do so within a frame provide by dynamic, developmental systems ideas, appear at this writing to succeed on these very same grounds. It may be, then, that such theories will be the ones that prove most engaging to cognitive developmentalists throughout the twenty-first century.

A similar prediction was made by Deanna Kuhn, in the afterword she provided to the second volume of the fifth edition of the *Handbook of Child Psychology* (Damon, 1998). Specifically, Kuhn (1998) indicated that:

One prediction, however, is that we will demand of future theories that they account for more than a very narrow range of phenomena, particularly those tied to a specific task, even if they account for those phenomena quite well. We also can predict that future theories will be more inclusive than past ones, not only in incorporating multiple mechanisms as suggested earlier, but also in integrating multiple levels of explanation. At the moment, progress is being made in constructing accounts of cognitive development at the neurological level; at the level of action systems and perceptual systems; as well as at the various cognitive levels of representational systems, knowledge, strategies, information processing mechanisms, and metacognitive awareness and control. Social systems represent yet another level of explanation. It is a misconception to treat these explanatory accounts as alternatives . . . recognizing the coexistence of all of these different levels of explanation should remind us that it is in fact one individual who incorporates these systems—from the physical and molecular to the teleological and reflec-

tive—and that ultimately these levels of explanation must be integrated. (p. 981)

There is in fact evidence that Kuhn's (1998) predictions are already being confirmed and, indeed, not only in the treatment of new, dynamic developmental systems theories but, as well, in regard to the reconceptualization of more traditional approaches to the understanding of cognitive development, for example, Piagetian stage theory. In Chapter 15, we consider Piaget's stage theory, along with other instances of stage theory approaches to human development (i.e., the theories of Lawrence Kohlberg and Sigmund Freud). In the discussion and evaluation of all theories, but especially Piaget's, we will see the use made of dynamic, developmental systems ideas (e.g., by Feldman, 2000) to both critique and extend the conceptions of development found in stage theories of human development.

15 | *Stage Theories of Development*

In previous chapters, we discussed the historical bases and philosophical underpinnings of the key conceptual issues of human development (e.g., the nature–nurture and the continuity–discontinuity controversies). In relation to these conceptual issues we, in addition, reviewed various theoretical approaches to human development. The approaches included various mechanistic–nurture positions [e.g., the behaviorist ideas of Skinner, (1971, and of Bijou & Baer, 1961), mechanistic–nature positions (e.g., the hereditarian ideas associated with behavior genetics [e.g., Plomin, 2000], the study of instincts [e.g., Lorenz, 1965], and sociobiology [e.g., Rushton, 1999]), and developmental-systems conceptions of (e.g., Ford & Lerner, 1992; Gottlieb, 1997; Magnusson, 1999a, 1999b, Schneirla, 1957; Thelen & Smith, 1998; Wapner & Demick, 1998). These groups of theories do not, however, exhaust the range of theoretical approaches that can and have been used to understand the course of human development.

As we noted in previous discussions (e.g., in the review in Chapter 2 of the history of concepts of development) and as we note again in this and the following two chapters, these additional approaches also relate to the core conceptual issues of human development and, as well, to the ideas associated with the various theoretical models we have already discussed. Nevertheless, these additional approaches—stage theories, the differential approach, and the ipsative approach—merit separate discussion. These three approaches, and especially the stage theory approach, have been major conceptual orientations to theory building in the field of human development (e.g., Emmerich, 1968; Muuss, 1996). Stage theories have attempted to depict universal features of development, features applicable to all humans. In turn, differential approaches have sought to identify features of development common to specific groups of people. Ipsative approaches have begun their analysis of

human development by seeking to find characteristics of human development that might be unique to individuals.

As previously implied, in the study of human development, considerably more conceptual analysis and discussion have been associated with the stage theory approach than with either the differential or the ipsative approaches. Thus, we shall focus on the stage approach first. The next two chapters discuss, respectively, the differential and ipsative approaches.

THE STAGE THEORY APPROACH TO DEVELOPMENT

The stage approach to developmental theory may also be simply termed the *developmental approach* or the *classical approach,* perhaps because it was systematized first historically. Accordingly, we will use the terms *stage theory, classical theory,* and *classical developmental theory* interchangeably.

As is discussed later in this chapter, various theorists who have used this approach have considered different aspects of development (e.g., the development of cognition, morality, and personality). Nevertheless, all classical developmental theories have specific, common characteristics. All of these theories hold that all people pass through a series of qualitatively different levels (stages) of organization and that the ordering of these stages is invariant. To a developmental stage theorist, there are *universal* stages of development. If people develop, they will pass through all these stages, and they will do so in a fixed order. Moreover, the ordering of the stages is held to be invariant; this means that people cannot skip stages or reorder them.

Let us use the stages in Freud's (1949) theory as an example. As is discussed in greater detail later in this chapter, Freud postulated that there are five stages in development: the oral, anal, phallic, latency, and genital stages. Freud held that if a person develops, he or she will pass through all these stages; he believed that all of the stages apply to a given person's development and, in fact, to all people's development. Moreover, Freud contended that the order of these stages is the same for all people. Thus, it would be theoretically impossible for someone to skip a stage; one could not go right from the oral stage to the phallic stage; instead one would have to develop through the intermediary stage, the anal stage. Similarly, one cannot reorder the sequence; thus, one could not go from the oral to the phallic stage and then to the anal stage. In essence, according to Freud, all people who develop must pass through each stage in the specified, invariant sequence.

The Definition of a Developmental Stage

But what are these entities that develop in an invariant sequence? Answering this question—and arriving, therefore, at a definition of a developmental stage—is a far from uncomplicated and uncontroversial issue. Indeed, several distinct and quite diverse theoretical stage or stage-related formulations have been forwarded in attempts to characterize human development across the life span. Runyan (1980) commented on the breadth of the formulations that have been forwarded. He noted:

> The search for useful ways of conceptualizing the course of human lives has been a long and difficult one, approached from many different theoretical perspectives, each with distinct assets and limitations. To provide a partial list, the life course has been conceptualized as a sequence of episodes and proceedings (Murray, 1938, 1959); a sequence of tasks or issues (Erikson, 1963); a sequence of stages (Levinson et al., 1978; Loevinger, 1976); a sequence of transitions (Lowenthal, Thurnher, & Chiriboga, 1975); a sequence of personality organizations (Block, 1971); a sequence of changing environments and organismic responses (Skinner, 1953); a sequence of dialectical operations (Riegel, 1975); a sequence of person–situation interactions (Baltes & Schaie, 1973); and a sequence of behavior-determining, person-determining, and situation-determining processes (Runyan, 1978). The life course has also been conceptualized from sociological and social–structural perspectives that focus more on roles, life-long socialization, age norms, and the flow of populations through socially and historically structured pathways (e.g., Clausen, 1972; Elder, 1975, 1977; Neugarten & Datan, 1973; Riley, Johnson, & Foner, 1972). (p. 951)

Still other dimensions of diversity exist in the stage-related formulations that have been applied to understanding human development across life. For instance, as we illustrate with our discussions later in this chapter, major developmental stage theorists describe changes across much, if not all, of the life span, and they focus on broad-based changes—for example, on the nature of individuals' psychosexual conflicts (e.g., Erikson, 1950; Freud, 1949) or on individuals' cognitive structuring of the world (e.g., Bruner, 1964; Piaget, 1954). In turn, theorists have offered stagelike descriptions of more circumscribed domains of development (e.g., Case, 1984, 1992a, 1992b; Davison et al., 1980; Feldman, 1994, 1995, 2000; Fischer, 1980; Fischer & Bidell, 1998; Gardner, Kornhaber, & Wake, 1996; Kohlberg, 1968; Selman, 1976; Siegler, 1978, 1981; von den Daele, 1975).

Some theorists have opted to investigate relatively specific areas of ability, such as problem-solving skills (e.g., Siegler, 1981) and social–cognitive development (e.g., Selman, 1976; Turiel, 1978). In addition, these theorists have tried to define patterns of change more precisely by limiting their focus of study, by delineating smaller and more circumscribed increments of developmental change, and by identifying procedures for measuring developmental change. Some of these theorists, for instance, have described specific sequences of development and have argued against the existence of pervasive underlying structures and homogeneous functioning across different domains of behavior. For instance, as noted in Chapter 14, Fischer (1980; Fischer & Bidell, 1998) portrayed development as the acquisition of sequences of skills in different domains of functioning.

A final complication we may note here is that there exist several terms in the developmental literature that may relate to the stage concept. However, theorists differ in regard to the way terms are used in relation to stage theories. As Glasersfeld and Kelley (1982) observed:

> In the field of developmental psychology we find ambiguity and occasional confusion with regard to the use of the terms *stage* and *level*. The confusion is compounded by the terms period and phase which some authors freely interchange. (p. 152)

Similar problems have been identified by Campbell and Richie (1983) and by Wohlwill (1973), who noted the confusion that exists between the concepts of stage and sequence. One key point to be derived from these discussions is that although all developmental stages involve a sequence (of invariantly ordered qualitative changes in an organism's structures), not all sequences involve developmental stages. For example, the sequence of changes in motor behaviors that has been described by Shirley (1933) describes "steps" along a path of physical maturation; such "steps" do not involve the theoretical specification of qualitative structural changes (Wohlwill, 1973). A second key point to abstract from these discussions is that whatever is meant by stage is not merely an increase in the quantity of behaviors or skills; rather, a conception encompassing other, more abstract, changes is involved in the use of this term. It is the nature of such a conception that we seek here to understand.

In sum, we are faced with the breadth and depth of a diverse theoretical literature that attempts to use the idea of stage and/or some stage-like notions—(i.e., "period," "phase," or "level") (Campbell & Richie, 1983; Glasersfeld & Kelley, 1982; Wohlwill, 1973)—in formulations designed to characterize human development. Our task is to extract from this literature the key features of, and/or issues involved in formulating, a definition of a developmental stage. Fortunately, being able to draw on the scholarship of other developmentalists who have taken on this task (e.g., Feldman, 2000; Flavell, 1971, 1972; Flavell & Wohlwill, 1969; Kessen, 1962; Wohlwill, 1963, 1973) somewhat simplifies our work.

As a consequence of the analyses in this literature, I believe it is useful to start our discussion of this definitional issue by noting that, in their most general sense, developmental stages are seen as portions of the life span that are qualitatively different from each other. That is, each stage in a given theoretically specified sequence represents a qualitatively different organization—or, more precisely, a qualitatively different *structure*—from every other stage. In fact, the existence of qualitative, structural differences among portions of life is the basis of the stage formulation. That is, the reason why one portion of time in development is labeled as one stage and another portion of time is labeled as another stage, is that it is believed that within each of the two periods something qualitatively different exists. If different portions of development were not qualitatively different, there would seem to be no reason to maintain that they were, in actuality, different portions of development. Thus, it is necessary for the classical theorist to posit the existence of qualitatively distinct stages.

Joachim Wohlwill (1973) underscored this view by noting that the concept of stage "is most profitably reserved for modal interrelationships among two or more *qualitatively* defined variables, variables developing apace" (p. 192, italics added). He

Joachim Wohlwill

added that "conceptual links among these behavioral dimensions allow each stage to be defined in terms of a set of behaviors sharing some feature in common. In other words, 'stage' is taken as a construct within a *structurally defined system,* having the property of unifying a set of behaviors" (Wohlwill 1973, p. 192, italics added). Thus, in Wohlwill's view, the presence of qualitatively distinct and integrative structures differentiates one period of life from another.

In discussing the stage-related properties of cognitive development, John Flavell (1971) offered a compatible conception of stage; but he also added more elements to the definition. Flavell asked what would be revealed if one could take a psychological X-ray in order to evaluate all the cognitive items present in a child who is said to be at a given stage of development ("item" is used here to refer to such things as concepts, rules, or, in fact, any cognitive "element"). Flavell's (1971) conception of stage led him to say four things about these items. First, he claimed that the items do not exist in an unrelated manner, as elements isolated one from the other. Rather, they interact with each other and can accordingly be said to be organized into cognitive structures. Second, Flavell (1971) contended that "the items and their structural organizations are qualitatively rather than just quantitatively different from those defining previous stages of the child's cognitive evolution; they are genuine developmental

John Flavell

novelties, not merely more efficient or otherwise improved versions of what had already been achieved" (pp. 422–423).

Thus, in stressing that qualitative structural distinctiveness is a key defining attribute of stages, Flavell (1971) took a position consonant with that of Wohlwill (1973). As noted, Flavell added two other statements to these first two in order to present what he saw as the key attributes of stages. However, even in regard to his first two statements, he introduced some qualifications that complicate the conception of stage he put forward.

First, as seen in his quoted second statement, Flavell raised the issue of the role of quantitative changes in development and their relation to the qualitative structural changes that define a stage as an ontogenetically novel period in life. The presence of qualitative change does not deny the presence of quantitative change, and vice versa. Both exist in development; and, in fact, it may be that if one focused on *how* people develop from one stage to the next (i.e., if one focused on *stage transitions*), one would see "that processes which either remain the same or only change quantitatively could directly or indirectly facilitate the qualitative changes we observe" (Flavell 1971, p. 425; see also Flavell & Wohlwill, 1969). Indeed, we note later in this chapter that within the stage theories we discuss—that is, the theories of Piaget, Kohlberg, and Freud, which are all major developmental stage theories—a role for invariance is specified. All theorists posit that the functioning of a constant *qual-*

itatively unchanging process is the basis of a person's movement from one stage to the next; that is, from the continual application of a qualitatively constant *functional invariant* (i.e., a process that always functions in the same way) qualitative changes occur, stage transitions take place. In Piaget's (1970) and in Kohlberg's (1978) theories the "equilibration process" is the functional invariant accounting for stage transition. In Freud's (1949) theory, the libido model plays this role. In addition, in the stage theory of Erikson (discussed in Chapter 16), his idea of the "maturational time table" has this function.

Thus, it seems that to specify what is changing in development and, more basically, how this change comes about, one must posit the existence of a constant. Indeed, in a more general sense, how could change be detected unless there were some constancy against which to appraise it (Lerner, 1984)?

A second complication Flavell (1971) introduced into his first two definitional statements concerns the idea that a stage involves the organization and interrelation of specific (i.e., qualitatively distinct) items into a structure. Flavell noted that, to use the term *structure* correctly, there must be at least two items or elements linked by at least one relationship. But Flavell contended that there exist two other properties of a structure. He claimed that a structure provides a "common underlying basis of a variety of superficially distinct, possibly even unrelated-looking behavioral acts" (Flavell, 1971, p. 443). We have seen this view also taken by Wohlwill (1973), who added that stages are "systematic forms of *interpatterning* among sets of developmental responses" (p. 191). However, Flavell (1971) also contended that structures involve organizations of items that are "relatively stable, enduring affairs, rather than merely temporary arrangements" (p. 443). This property of a structure is likely to generate more controversy than the others that Flavell suggested. There are at least two reasons for this.

One is that "relatively stable," "enduring," and "temporary" are not fixed or standardly agreed-on time spans. Different theorists are free to attach time spans to these terms in almost any manner they wish or, at the very least, with enough of a range that what is seen as nonenduring by one theorist may be viewed as quite stable by another. For example, a structure prototypic of an infant's early cognitive functioning for 3 to 6 months may be seen by a scholar theorizing about the early years of life as a relatively stable organization (and given this theorist's frame of reference, it is). However, a theorist who is concerned with the scope of the entire life span (e.g., Erikson, 1959, 1963) might contend that such a structure was short-lived and, at best, only transitory. Moreover, even short-lived structures, such as those that are studied by comparative psychologists concerned with "transitory ontogenetic adaptations" (Gottlieb, 1983), may be of great importance for the development and, indeed, the survival of an organism.

A second reason why controversy may exist in regard to using the length of time a given organization exists as a criterion of a structure is that stage theorists do not see "time spent" within a given stage as a key property of a stage or of development in general. As we note again later, although developmental stage theorists typically do not pay a great deal of attention to the topic of individual differences in development, one way (of the two) in which people are held to differ is in their rate of development through stages. This implies, then, that the relative duration of the existence of a stage-specific structure is largely irrelevant in defining a stage as such.

Further controversy about how to define a stage is seen when we turn to the last two statements Flavell (1971) offered in regard to his view of the properties of a stage of development. The third feature of a stage Flavell noted is that as soon as a stage is said to exist, this means that any given item involved in that stage functions at its "peak level" of efficiency—that is, it shows an adult-level state of proficiency. Flavell noted that this means, for example, that as soon as a child could perform the mathematical operation of multiplication in respect to a given set of objects, then the child "was capable of performing this particular concrete operation on all sets of classes and in all the task settings that he would ever be capable of" (Flavell, 1971, p. 423). Moreover, as the fourth statement he made in regard to his conception of stages, Flavell noted that all the items involved in a given stage make this abrupt transition—from not being present or functional to being present and immediately functional at an adultlevel—simultaneously; that is, he said that a fourth feature of stages is that all items involved in a stage become linked to it as soon as a person enters that stage.

Obviously Flavell's last two statements (1971) about what he believed to be a prototypical conception of stage are ideas that bring the issue of stage transition into the definition of stage per se. That is, Flavell (1971) noted that his last two statements assert that a person cannot be in a stage in a partial, ambiguous, or qualified way, "either in the sense of having only a rudimentary

command of some given operation (third assertion) or in the sense of possessing only some of those operations at a given time (fourth assertion)" (p. 423). Although Flavell was clear that he proposed his statements in an admittedly overdrawn fashion (particularly in respect to the third and fourth statements), it is, nevertheless, the case that many developmentalists do subscribe to such a rather strict view of stage (e.g., Gibson, 1969; Pinard & Laurendeau, 1969). As such, issues of transitions, or developments, between and within stages are issues that must be dealt with in attempting to define a stage.

The third statement that Flavell (1971) forwarded may be understood as a concern with the issue of *"abruptness,"* that is, in this context the term means that "the development of individual stage-specific items is characteristically abrupt rather than gradual; that is, there is a zero-order transition period between the initial appearance of each item and its state of functional maturity" (Flavell, 1971, p. 425). In turn, the fourth statement that Flavell (1971) forwarded may be understood as a concern with *"concurrence";* that is, "The various items which define a given stage develop concurrently (i.e., in synchrony with one another)" (Flavell, 1971, p. 435). Let us consider these two issues separately.

The Issue of "Abruptness": What Is the Nature of Stage Transition?

What happens to people as they progress through the various stages within a particular sequence? Specifically, what happens to the qualitatively distinct characteristics of a first stage when the person passes into a qualitatively different second stage?

Flavell (1971) noted that there are several ways of answering such a question. One may envision, or formulate models of, types of transitions from one stage to the next. These models may vary along a dimension anchored, at one extreme, by complete abruptness of change and, at the other, by complete gradualness of change (an extreme wherein, if it existed for a given theory, the idea of stage—as a novel period of life, one having structures special only to it—would probably lose all meaning). However, whereas a model of stage transition located at the extreme-gradualism end of the abruptness–gradualism dimension would, in effect, be a nonstage model of development, a model of stage transition located at the extreme-abruptness end of this dimension would be a nondevelopmental model of stages.

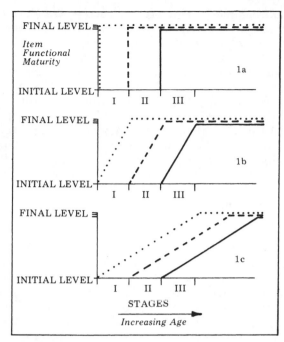

FIGURE 15.1
Three models of stage transitions. The developmental course of individual stage-specific items varies in relation to the model's location along a dimension of "abruptness-gradualism" of transition.

Source: Adapted from Flavell (1971, p. 426).

Such an extreme-abruptness model of development is depicted in Figure 15.1a, an illustration adapted from Flavell (1971). Flavell explained why the extreme-abruptness model illustrated in Figure 15.1a is, in actuality, an nondevelopmental and, indeed, a quite static model of stage. Flavell (1971) noted that in this model one is characterized as being "in" a particular stage of development

> because and just so long as, one *continues* to behave in some particular fashion; developmental *changes* in behavior are largely relegated to the "period of transition" from one stage to the next. If these "periods of transition" are taken to be of essentially null duration . . . , the view that stages emerge abruptly rather than gradually, leads logically to the rather paradoxical conclusion that the individual spends virtually all of his childhood years "being" rather than "becoming" . . . the termination of any stage is defined not by the cessation of developmental change in the stage-specific item (this change having both commenced and ceased at the *beginning* of the stage), but simply by the abrupt emergence of the succeeding stage. (pp. 426–427)

Flavell (1971) went on to note that this model

> has much to commend it on formal grounds. It lends a meaning to "stage" that is conceptually clear, theoretically strong, operationally useful, and quite congruent with the ordinary language meaning of that term. Unfortunately, that developing system we call the child just does not seem to conform to it [therefore] Model 15 "a" can immediately be ruled out of contention. (p. 428)

And indeed it *is* out of contention. No major developmental stage theorist takes such an abrupt view of stage transition—although it is the case that such abruptness is, as noted, part of the "stereotyped" view of stages (Flavell, 1971) and that some critics of stage theory (e.g., Bandura, 1977; Mischel & Mischel, 1976) have attributed such a conception to stage theories in the criticisms they have made. For example, Davison and colleagues (1980), in discussing the stage concept in theories of cognitive development, noted:

> Such critics have assumed that stage theories imply that there will be a patterning to a subject's stage score. All of them will be zero except one, the stage at which the subject reasons. Actually the stage theorists . . . do not say that people reason at only one stage. Their theories are more complicated than is assumed by the critics. These more complicated stage theories, however, can imply that there will be a patterning to subjects' stage scores, but not the simple patterning that would occur if subjects reason at only one stage. (pp. 121–122)

The patterning to which Davison and colleagues (1980) referred is explicitly recognized by stage theorists, for example in their use of concepts such as "stage mixture"—a notion indicating that people exist simultaneously at several different stages. We return later to this notion. Here, however, we should stress that in the extant major developmental stage theories, a model of abrupt stage progression such as that in the first model of Figure 15.1 is *not* used; stage progression is never held to be an all-or-none event. That is, people do not progress from one stage to another overnight. It is not the case that one day a person goes to sleep in Stage 1 and the next day awakens in qualitatively different Stage 2. Development is not held to be a series of qualitative leaps, of saltatory, steplike functions. Rather, transitions from one stage to the next are gradual; they take place slowly over time.

For example, one way of determining if a person is at a particular stage in development is to see if the person shows behaviors consistent with what we would expect from knowledge of that particular stage. If the person does not show such behaviors, we could say that the person has not developed into that stage. On the other hand, however, just because a person does show responses representative of a particular stage of development does not mean that the person has fully developed into that stage, that the stage is completely and comprehensively associated with his or her behavior. Because people progress from one stage to another gradually, they will, therefore, show behaviors that are representative of more than one stage at the same time. In other words, because stage progression is not an all-or-none process, but rather is one that takes place gradually over time, we would expect a person to show behavior representative of more than one stage of development at the same time.

How, then, may we determine what stage a person is in? Clearly, one behavior or even a few would not be a sufficient sample to allow us to determine unequivocally a person's representative stage of development. Rather, it is necessary to get a large sample of the person's behaviors. Once we know what behaviors are representative of which stages of development, we have to observe many instances of the person's behavior. Only then can we make a stage determination. Then we may know within which stage the majority of the person's behaviors fall. Thus, we are determining to which stage most of the person's behaviors relate. By determining the most frequently occurring (i.e., the modal) behavior, we are finding out what stage best represents the person's level of development.

Hence, whenever we say that a person is at a particular stage of development, we are saying this on the basis of the person's most frequently occurring (modal) behaviors. We are not saying that a person at a particular stage of development is functioning only at that one stage; in fact, as we have seen, we would expect quite the opposite to be the case. Yet, if we are judicious enough to obtain a large sample of a person's behaviors, we will also be able to ascertain the stage that is most representative of his or her behaviors.

In sum, whenever we speak of a person as being at a particular stage of development, we are making a relative, not an absolute, statement—a statement that should ideally be based on that person's modal response pattern. We are saying that relative to other stages of development, the person's modal behavior is representative of a particular stage. In other words, people may function at more than one developmental level at a time, and attributing the status of a particular stage to a person should be based on a large sample of behaviors and then a determination of the person's

modal behaviors. However, if people also simultaneously possess attributes of more than one stage as a consequence of less than completely abrupt transitions between stages, then we need to inquire into the form that may be taken by these more gradual stage changes. Thus, it is useful to refer to the other models illustrated in Figure 15.1.

Figure 15.1b represents a model of stage transition wherein the functional maturity of a stage-specific item increases gradually throughout the stage. Development of this item continues until the very end of the stage, when full maturity is reached. However, at the endpoint of the stage the items specific to the next stage are beginning their development. Therefore, Flavell (1971) noted that in this model the endpoint of a stage is defined by the completion of development of its own items and by the initiation of development of the items of the next stage. Thus, in this model a stage is not a static state of being. Rather it is a state of constant "becoming." The stage's own items are becoming more developed (i.e., functionally mature) throughout the stage and, while this achievement is being attained, the stage is also a period of preparation for the development of the items of the next stage.

This view of stage transition is found in Piaget's (1955) own writings. As translated by Flavell (1971), Piaget indicated that "a stage thus comprises both a level of *preparation,* on the one hand, and of *achievement,* on the other" (Piaget, 1955, p. 35). Flavell (1971, p. 427) himself noted that "a stage here is not a state but a process—it is *itself* the "period of transition."

However, models can be formulated that are even more extreme in their emphasis on the gradualness of development. One such model, formulated by Flavell (1971), is represented in Figure 15.1c. In this model, a stage's items do not reach complete functional maturity within the stage with which they are modally associated or, in other words, with the stage within which the major proportion of their development occurs. In this third model, an item's development can continue into subsequent stages. Thus, a feature of development present in this model, but not in the other two suggested by Flavell (1971), is that items from two different stages can be developing at the same time. An item from a former stage can be completing its development in a subsequent stage while, at the same time, items from that subsequent stage can also be developing.

Flavell (1971) observed that because the three models illustrated in Figure 15.1 lie on a continuum of abruptness–gradualness, it is possible to formulate models representative of other points along this continuum. A general implication of this observation is that there may be several different ways to conceptualize the characteristics of stage transition. Indeed, scholars other than Flavell (1971) have formulated different sets of models, or schemes, of stage transition (e.g., Emmerich, 1968; van den Daele, 1969, 1974; Wohlwill, 1973). Despite starting from perhaps different conceptual bases, because these scholars deal with the same issues addressed by Flavell (1971), their schemes of transition are often substantially compatible.

To illustrate another approach to the topic of the ways in which stage transitions may occur, and to indicate this compatibility among scholars, let us consider the views of Walter Emmerich (1968), a scholar whose work has clarified issues pertinent not only to the stage approach but also to the differential and the ipsative approaches we consider in the next two chapters. As such, we have reason to return again to Emmerich's views. Here, however, let us note only Emmerich's ideas regarding stage transition.

Emmerich claimed that one of three things may happen to the characteristics (or "items," in Flavell's, 1971, terms) of a previous stage when a person develops into the next stage. He pointed out that the first thing that could happen when a person completes a transition from one stage of development into the next is that the characteristics of the first stage become completely displaced. This is the most extreme view of what may happen when transition from one stage to the next is complete. This component of Emmerich's first alternative is compatible with the outcome of abrupt change depicted in Flavell's (1971) first model. That is, both views hold that when transition is complete, the person will be completely newly organized and the characteristics of the previous stage will be lost. However, there is no requirement in Emmerich's first alternative that the change from Stage 1 to 2 be totally abrupt. That is, even this radical transition may take place gradually over time; and accordingly, even in this case the person will show evidence of behavioral characteristics of both developmental stages while the transition is still occurring.

In the second type of transition, the later stage becomes the dominant level of functioning, but the behavioral characteristics of the previous stage are still seen. This possibility is similar to the general notions of gradual stage transition already discussed, and it is a view consonant with features of the second and third models illustrated by Flavell (1971). However, this second alternative suggested by Emmerich (1968) places greater emphasis on stage development as a modal phenomenon. This alternative, then, stresses the notion that current stages are dominant in that behaviors representative of that stage are most frequent. However, although they do occur at a lower frequency than the modal behaviors, the behavioral characteristics of earlier stages are not lost. In fact, it is sometimes held that under some circumstances the lower-frequency behaviors can, for a time, become dominant in frequency (Emmerich, 1968, p. 674).

The third possibility is similar to the second. Here, however, when the new stage has fully emerged, the behavioral characteristics of the earlier stage do not typically occur. That is, the characteristics of the new stage will be the only characteristics that are typically seen. The characteristics of the earlier stage lie dormant, or are latent, and are not typically seen. In certain special circumstances, however, the earlier characteristics may emerge (Emmerich, 1968, p. 674).

In sum, scholars such as Flavell (1971) and Emmerich (1968), among others (e.g., Feldman, 2000; van den Daele, 1969, 1974; Wohlwill, 1973), suggested several types of transitions that may occur between the stages proposed within developmental stage theories. Different stage theories may opt for any one of these alternatives. Of course, the difficulty for the researcher who wants to test these different alternatives lies in measuring the differences that each alternative predicts. It would be difficult to discriminate among these three types of transitions because, in any event, all the transitions take place gradually. Hence, by the time a given stage has almost completely displaced a previous stage as a person's dominant level of functioning, another stage may be beginning to displace this now-dominant stage.

Because of this stage mixture (Turiel, 1969), stage development is very complex, and it is most difficult to ascertain which model or scheme of stage transition best fits the data (i.e., best characterizes development). However, this very complexity is the major point of our present discussion. Because of the gradual nature of stage transition, a person functions at more than one qualitatively different stage at the same time. Thus, stage mixture is an essential component of any adequate stage theory of development and is a key feature of an appropriate conceptualization of a developmental stage.

We have noted, however, that at least one other concept—that of concurrence—needs to be evaluated in respect to its role as a feature of the definition of stage. We have seen that the concept of abruptness with which we have just dealt pertains to the issue of the development—the transitions—between stages. We also noted that the concept of concurrence pertains to the issue of development within a stage. Let us turn, then, to a consideration of this last concept.

The Issue of "Concurrence": Is There Synchrony in the Development of the Items Within a Stage?

Is the time course of the development of the stage-specific items that define a stage common across all these items? "Being in" a stage means possessing certain stage-specific attributes. But does this mean, too, that all items begin and end their development at the same time? These questions are involved in considering the concept of concurrence.

The best answer to these questions seems to be "no." Time differences are typically, indeed almost invariably, found in the attainment of the different attributes (or items) that are specific to a stage (Flavell, 1971). In fact, we note later in this chapter that such lacks of concurrence are quite specifically included in the ideas of some stage theorists. For instance, in our discussion below of Piaget's theory, we see that his notion of *décalage* (Piaget, 1950, 1970) is used to refer to systematic time differences in the cognitive attainment of particular stage-specific concepts. Accordingly, and although the point is not held without some exceptions (e.g., Pinard & Laurendeau, 1969), we may agree with Flavell (1971) that *complete* concurrence is not a requirement of a developmental stage theory, be it Piaget's (1950, 1970) or any other.

Wohlwill (1973) appeared to agree with this point but added some important qualifications, noting:

> That despite *the undeniable fact of asynchrony,* a considerable degree of order and regularity—or, to put it another way, of constraints on the forms which the interrelationships of developing elements of a structure may take—still obtains. (p. 239, italics added)

In other words, despite a lack of complete concurrence, the elements or items of a stage do not develop in a completely haphazard fashion. For instance, just as one may model the nature of developments, or transitions, between stages as varying along an abruptness–gradualness continuum (Flavell, 1971), one may model the nature of developments, or concurrences, within a stage as involving differing degrees of concurrence (or synchrony). Wohlwill (1973) formulated some models

representing different degrees of concurrence, and they are summarized in Table 15.1.

Thus, Wohlwill's (1973) position is akin to Flavell's (1971): A concept of stage necessarily involves relative concurrence. However, absolute concurrence is neither a theoretical requirement of developmental stage theories nor is it empirically ubiquitous. Wohlwill (1973) summarized his position by noting that his

> underlying assumption is that in certain areas of development, particularly in the cognitive realm, but not necessarily confined to it, there exist regulating mechanisms that modulate the course of the individual's development so as to ensure a degree of harmony and integration in his functioning over a variety of related behavioral dimensions. The mechanism might be thought of in part as a mediational generalization process, permitting acquisitions in one area, for example number conservation, to spread both to equivalent aspects of different concepts (e.g., conservation of length) and to different aspects of the same concept (e.g., cardinal–ordinal correspondence). The result is the formation of a broad structural network of interrelated concepts appearing, not all at once to be sure, but within a fairly narrowly delimited period, with further progress along any component concept or dimension being assumed to be deferred till the consolidation of this network—that is, the attainment of the "stage." Stage development thus provides for relative consistency of behavior, economy in the acquisition of new responses, and harmony and interrelatedness in the development of diverse concepts or skills across successive levels. (p. 192)

In sum, we may abstract from the controversy surrounding the conception of developmental stages a definition of a developmental stage as a component of a sequence of qualitative structural reorganizations. Between-stage developments are never completely abrupt, and there is no complete concurrence or synchrony in the within-stage development of the elements or items comprising a specific stage.

Finally, we may note that in positing the universal applicability of the stages they describe—that is, the invariant applicability of the stages to all people—stage theorists are proposing features of development that are common to all people. Thus, such theories describe the development of the *generic* human being, the general case of humanity, and accordingly the laws of development proposed by stage theorists are laws that apply to all individuals. Such laws are termed *nomothetic* laws. That is, the stage-theory approach is concerned with the postulation of general (group, nomothetic) laws of development—laws that apply to the

TABLE 15.1

Degrees of Within-Stage Concurrence or Synchrony: Wohlwill's Models of Developmental Stages, Arranged in Order of Complexity of Interrelationship Among Component Sequences

Model	Major hypothesis	Implications for concepts of stages
IA: Synchronous progression	Changes in level for all sequences occur in synchrony	Structural network tying together ordered sequences of responses at equivalent levels, with developmental progression occuring in unison in all sequences, linked in one rigid system
IIA: Horizontal décalage, convergent	Changes in level occur in synchrony, with exceptions for certain sequences, taking the form of staggered progression	Structural network integrating ordered sequences of responses atequivalent levels, with sequence-specific or extraneous factors resulting in temporary lags between systems at intermediary levels
IIB: Horizontal décalage, divergent	As in IIA above	As in IIA above, except that sequence-specific or extraneous factors have cumulative effect, with progressively widening gaps between sequences
III: Reciprocal interaction	Changes in level occur in synchrony, with exceptions for certain sequences, taking the form of intersecting developmental functions	Structural network integrating ordered sequences of responses atequivalent levels, with interdependence among particular sequences resulting in temporary perturbations in developmental timetable
IV: Disequilibration-stabilization	Attainment of levels of stage consolidation occurs synchronously for all sequences, separated by intermediary levels marked by behavior oscillation; irregular relationships among sequences	Structural network representing nodes at which ordered sequences of response become functionally integrated, with developmental progression occurring in fluid fashion between these nodes

Note. From *The Study of Behavioral Development* (p. 206), by J. F. Wohlwill, 1973, New York: Academic Press. Copyright © 1973 by Academic Press. Reprinted with permission.

generic human being. Such laws stand in contrast to idiographic laws, that is, laws that pertain to an individual.

Individual Differences Within Stage Theories

Despite their overriding attention to laws that characterize all people, stage theorists do recognize that people differ. However, they hold these individual differences to be relatively minimal. That is, stage theorists maintain that there are only two ways in which people may differ (Emmerich, 1968). First, as we noted earlier, people may differ in their *rate of progression* through the stages, in how fast they develop. It may take one individual 1 year and another individual 2 years to pass through the same stage, but all people pass through the same stages in the same order.

The second way that people may differ within developmental stage theories is in the *final level of development* they reach. Not all people go through all the stages—for example, because of illness or death, the development of such people stops. The point is, however, that as far as the development of such people goes, it will necessarily be in accord with the specified stage progression; if these people had developed, they would have progressed through the stages in accordance with the specified sequence. In sum, according to stage theory, people may differ in how *fast* they develop (rate of stage progression) and in how *far* they develop (final level of development reached).

Relation of Concepts of Development to Stage Theories

We have seen that the stage concept is used to denote an ordered, qualitative structural change in development. It should be clear that such an approach to development contrasts fundamentally with perspectives that describe developmental change as quantitative or incremental—that is, as occurring only continually and gradually, and involving only the addition of "molecular" (e.g., stimulus–response) units to the behavioral repertoire (e.g., Bijou, 1976; Bijou & Baer, 1961). Such mechanistic approaches typically take a nurture-oriented, empirical–behaviorist or a nurture-oriented, theoretical–behaviorist approach to conceptualizing behavioral changes. In the empirical–behaviorist approach, for instance, the processes through which behaviors are shaped, and through which an increasing number of skills are acquired, are seen to involve an individual's

response to contingencies in the external environment (e.g., Bijou & Baer, 1961).

A key basis of this difference between developmental stage theorists and such nurture–mechanistic theorists is, as noted in Chapter 3, that stage theories of development are predicated on a commitment to an organismic philosophy of science (see Reese & Overton, 1970). Within this tradition, the characterization of the nature of development is an idealized one, and it provides a formal conceptual metric against which observed behavioral changes are compared in order to ascertain whether a given change constitutes development (e.g., see Kaplan, 1966, 1983).

From this organismic perspective, there are two key components of a developmental analysis. First, a stage theory must provide descriptions of the stages themselves—that is, descriptions of the structural properties of each stage in the sequence. Second, a stage theory must posit mechanisms by which the individual progresses through these stages. However, the difference with nurture–mechanistic positions arises because these stages—and the progression through them—are explained by concepts different than those associated with the system of explanation employed in nurture–mechanistic views of development (e.g., Bijou, 1976; Brainerd, 1978, 1979). Specifically, these stage components of development are explained from the perspective of formal causality (e.g., see Berndt, 1978; Buss, 1979; Ford & Lerner, 1992; Neimark, 1978; Olson, 1978; Overton, 1998). The role of formal causality in developmental stages has, however, not often been understood or appreciated by mechanistically- and nurture-oriented developmentalists—who either prefer to focus solely on notions of efficient causality (Bijou, 1976; Bijou & Baer, 1961) or who cannot appreciate the idea that there may be a useful notion of causality other than efficient cause (Brainerd, 1978, 1979). In short, the concern with formal cause within stage theory stands in contrast to the focus on efficient cause in nurture–mechanistic approaches to development. This difference stands as a key contrast between the two types of formulations.

Stage theorists take stands on developmental issues other than those pertinent to causality, however, and it should be clear at this point where stage theorists stand in terms of at least some of the concepts we have considered in earlier chapters (e.g., the continuity–discontinuity issue). By definition, stage theorists consider development to include qualitatively discontinuous phenomena. In specifying that the sequential emergence of qualitatively different levels of functioning characterizes development, stage theorists are defining development as being qualitatively discontinuous.

On the other hand, we have noted that stage theorists also recognize that there are certain laws that function invariantly across a person's life span. Hence, the postulation of such functional invariants indicates that most stage theorists recognize that development is characterized by continuity as well as discontinuity. In short, even though stage theorists define development as being qualitatively discontinuous, continuous laws that exist throughout development are also recognized. Consistent with the ideas of Werner (1957), development involves a *synthesis* of processes making a person the same across life with processes making a person different across life.

Second, stage theorists—committed to an organismic philosophy of science—to differing extents take an interactionist viewpoint in respect to the nature–nurture controversy. Thus, to some extent, all stage theorists look at an interaction between intrinsic (nature) and extrinsic (nurture) variables in accounting for behavioral development. However, different theorists put differing degrees of emphasis on nature and nurture factors. Thus, Piaget (1950, 1970) put greater emphasis on an interaction between nature and nurture factors than did Freud (1949) and Erikson (1963, 1964), who placed greater emphasis on nature variables and viewed the nurture variables as either facilitators or inhibitors of primarily intrinsic emergences (Emmerich, 1968; Kohlberg, 1963). For example, we see in Chapter 16 that Erikson (1959, 1963) placed a good deal of emphasis on the "maturational ground plan" that he claimed exists in all people. Thus, to Erikson, although a child must interact within society in order to develop normally, the stage emergences that characterize a child's development are primarily maturational in origin; they will emerge and exert a particular influence on development independent of the character of the child's interactions in society.

Moreover, just as stage theorists differ to some extent on the specifics of the nature–nurture interaction, they also differ about the critical-periods issue. It may be said that, in one sense, all stage theorists support a critical-periods notion, in that in each qualitatively different stage something unique is developing. This unique development, which gives the stage its qualitative distinctiveness, is by definition supposed to be developing at this particular point. Because stage theorists define development as comprising qualitatively distinct phenomena that arise in a universal, invariant sequence, they, therefore, maintain that not all periods in development have equal potentiality for any particular development. Thus, each specific stage has its own specific emergence, which by its very existence serves to define that period in ontogeny as a stage. In this sense, each stage has its own critical development.

Yet, different stage theorists have different ideas about "how critical is critical." Given the different views about stage transition that we have discussed, and, therefore, the different models of transition to which stage theorists may adhere, it is understandable that they disagree about the implications for later development of inappropriate development within a given stage. For some stage theorists, if one does not develop what one should develop in a given stage, one will never have another chance for such development (e.g., Erikson, 1959, 1968). Thus, each given stage of development is truly critical, in that, if one does not develop appropriately within a given period, irreversible unfavorable implications will be inevitable. Such extreme views will be illustrated later in this chapter by the theory of Freud and, in Chapter 16, by the theory of Erikson.

In addition, as might be surmised from these differences of opinion, stage theorists also differ about the source of critical periods. Just as different stage theorists place contrasting emphases on nature and nurture factors in explaining the interactive basis of development, they correspondingly place different emphases on these factors in accounting for the critical nature of different stages. Those theorists who lay greater emphasis on nature (maturational) factors in accounting for stage development similarly place greater stress on maturation as the source of the criticality of critical periods.

Conclusions

All stage theorists present theories that speak to the various core conceptual issues of development. In this chapter, we consider three of the most prominent stage theories of psychological development: those of Piaget, Kohlberg, and Freud. In addition, Anna Freud's (1969) extension of her father's theory (Freud, 1949) is also be considered. Although these theories deal with different aspects of the developing person, they have certain similarities. Whether talking about the development of cognition (Piaget), moral reasoning (Kohlberg), or psychosexual development (Freud), these theorists all hold that all people who develop pass through the stages specified in the theory in an invariant sequence. These stages represent universal sequences of development—that is, qualitatively different developmental levels through which all people must pass in the same order if they are to develop. As noted earlier, the essential ways in which people are thought to differ, from a classical stage point of view, are in the final level of development they reach (how far they eventually develop) and in the amount of time it takes them to move from one stage to the next (how fast they develop).

The stage theories we consider in this chapter are also similar in that they take definite stands on the major conceptual issues we have considered in earlier chapters. Thus, these stage theories take a more or less interactionist viewpoint on the nature–nurture controversy. Similarly, they make specific statements about the continuity and the discontinuity of behavioral development, noting that development is, in part, characterized by qualitatively different phenomena across ontogeny.

In turn, the stage theorists also maintain that there are continuous elements in development. Consistent with the organismic notions advanced by Heinz Werner (1957), the stage theorists considered in this chapter more or less explicitly view development as a dialectical process, an organismic synthesis of the discontinuous and continuous variables affecting development. In short, then, although we see that Piaget, Kohlberg, and Freud often talked about different aspects of the developing person, they did so within the context of some markedly similar views about the nature of psychological development.

I should reemphasize here a point made earlier in regard to my purposes in reviewing the theories of development discussed in this chapter, as well as in other chapters of this book. My goal is not to present an in-depth description of each theory. This could not readily be accomplished within the confines of one chapter, since there are literally dozens (and in many cases hundreds) of books devoted to each theory alone; moreover, to learn what a particular theorist says, it is best to read his or her own words (i.e., to read primary sources) rather than a brief review in a secondary source. Thus, my goals are to indicate the relationships between key conceptual issues in development and exemplars of each of the major types of theories of development, and to show how these issues pertain both to the features of one theory *and* to the sorts of research derived from or related to it. Let us turn, then, to a consideration of each of the above theorists' ideas; we begin with the developmental theory of cognition of Jean Piaget.

PIAGET'S DEVELOPMENTAL THEORY OF COGNITION

Jean Piaget was born in Switzerland in 1896. He died there in 1980. The young Piaget was quite intellectually precocious; for example, he published his first scientific paper at the age of 10, and while still a teenager he published so many high-quality research papers on mollusks (sea-dwelling organisms such as oysters and clams) that he was offered the position of curator of the mollusk collection in a Geneva museum (Flavell, 1963). As a culmination of these early research interests, Piaget received his doctorate in the natural sciences at the advanced age of 22!

Although his doctorate was in the natural sciences, Piaget maintained broad intellectual interests. Thus, soon after receiving his degree in 1918, he found himself involved with work in psychology. In addition, he maintained an active interest in epistemology, an area of inquiry concerned with the philosophy of knowledge. Perhaps, it seemed to Piaget that the best way to understand knowledge was to study how it develops. In any event, he began to study the development of cognition in his own children. Piaget's first books resulted from

Jean Piaget

these initial studies. What he began to devise, then, in his first endeavors, was a developmental theory of cognition—rather than a cognitive theory of development. He viewed cognition as a developmental phenomenon rather than viewing all development as a cognitive phenomenon.

In terms of Piaget's theory, the study of cognitive development can be defined as the study of knowledge and of the mental processes involved in its acquisition and utilization (Elkind, 1967). Moreover, as we have said, Piaget came to his interest in cognitive development from his training in natural science and interest in epistemology. Thus, not only is his theory influenced by these intellectual roots but also, as he himself pointed out (see Flavell, 1963), he never took a course in psychology or even passed a test in the subject! Most of us forgive Piaget this limitation. He is one of the two (the other is Freud) unquestioned geniuses who have ever contributed to the field. However, like Freud, and due most probably to his doctoral training, Piaget's theory has a strong biological basis. To begin our assessment of Piaget's theory, then, let us first consider his views concerning the biological basis of intelligence.

Stage-Independent Conceptions

Although Piaget's theory is a stage theory, he advanced several important conceptions relevant to all stages of cognitive development. That is, Piaget proposed certain stage-independent conceptions, principles of cognitive development that apply to all stages of development. These are general laws of development that continually function to provide a source of cognitive development throughout ontogeny. To understand them, we must first focus on the biological basis of Piaget's theory.

According to Piaget, *cognition* and *intelligence,* terms we treat as synonymous for our purposes here, are just instances of a biological system. Digestion, respiration, and circulation are also examples of biological systems. Intelligence, according to Piaget, is a biological system just like any of those mentioned, governed by the laws that govern any other biological system; the functions and characteristics of the biological system "cognition" are identical to those involved in the organism's digestive, respiratory, and circulatory systems.

Like all biological systems, then, cognition has two basic aspects that are always, invariantly, present and functioning: *organization* and *adaptation.* Cognition always functions within an organization, and it is always an adaptive system—that is, its functioning allows the organism to adapt to its environment; it has survival value.

The functional invariants of organization and adaptation are present throughout the organism's development; they are general characteristics of cognitive functioning applicable to any and all points in the organism's ontogeny. Although he recognized the fundamental importance of both of these general laws of cognitive functioning, Piaget chose to devote the major portion of his theorizing to the second functional invariant, adaptation. By focusing on how cognitive development allows the organism to adapt to its environment—to survive—we can understand the dynamic interrelation between the organism and its environment; this interrelation provides a source of intellectual development.

According to Piaget, the process of adaptation is divided into two complementary component processes: *assimilation* and *accommodation.* Both of these processes are always involved in the functioning of cognition to allow the organism to adapt to its environment.

Assimilation

Let us first consider assimilation. This concept is used in a manner identical to that used in any biological discussion (i.e., when a cell assimilates food). It takes the food in through its membrane and breaks it down to fit its needs. In other words, when food is taken into a cell, it does not retain its original form or structure but is altered; it is converted into energy and water, for example, in order to fit the already existing cellular structure. Thus, when a cell assimilates food, it alters it in order to integrate it into its already existing characteristics. Hence, Piaget indicated, "From a biological point of view, assimilation is the integration of external elements into evolving or completed structures of an organism" (1970, pp 706–707).

Cognitive assimilation functions in a similar manner. Let us imagine that a child has knowledge of a particular stimulus object, say an isosceles triangle like the one presented Figure 15.2a. Now the child is presented with another triangle, a right triangle like the one presented in Figure 15.2b.

How may the child know what this second stimulus object is? If the child assimilates, the external object (the right triangle) will be integrated into the child's already existing cognitive structure; knowledge of that object will be distorted, or

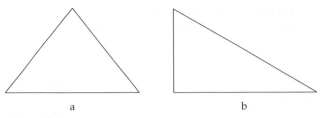

FIGURE 15.2
An isosceles triangle (a) and a right triangle (b).

altered, so that the object will take the form of an isosceles triangle. When assimilation occurs the person distorts reality by changing the external object to fit the subject (i.e., to fit the already existing internal structure of the subject).

Thus, an infant may have knowledge of its mother's breast. It has gained this knowledge through its *actions* on this external stimulus object. The infant has sucked on its mother's nipple and has developed an internal cognitive structure pertaining to this action-based knowledge. The infant "knows" the mother's breast through the actions it performs in relation to it. Hence, the subject has an internal structure, derived from its actions on an external stimulus, which allows it to know that stimulus. Thus, objects are known through the actions performed on them. In other words, to Piaget the basis of knowledge lies in action.

When, however, the infant discovers its thumb and begins to suck on it, knowledge of this other external stimulus may be gained by assimilating it into the already existing action-based cognitive structure. That is, instead of changing its cognitive structure in order to know this new object, the infant may act on the thumb as it did the nipple, thus integrating the thumb into the already existing cognitive structure pertaining to the mother's breast. We may say that the infant alters its actions on the thumb or rather fits its actions on the thumb—so as to incorporate these actions into an already existing cognitive structure. Thus, the infant would be changing the object to fit, or match, the structure of the subject; the infant would be assimilating.

Accommodation

As we have already noted, however, there is a process that is the complement of assimilation. This process is termed *accommodation*. Instead of the subject's altering the external object to match his or her internal cognitive structure (assimila-

tion), accommodation involves the altering of the subject to fit the object. For example, think of two people seated very comfortably on a rather small sofa. A third person comes along and asks to sit down. Either or both of the already seated people would have to alter their positions on the sofa to accommodate this third person. The people seated on the sofa would have to change their already existing structure to incorporate this intrusion by an external stimulus. They will have to accommodate, to change themselves, to fit with the external object.

Thus, cognitive accommodation involves the altering of already existing cognitive structures in the subject to match new, external stimulus objects. Rather than changing the object to fit the subject, accommodation involves changing the subject to fit the object. In the triangle example we already offered, accommodation would involve an alteration of the child's cognitive structure pertaining to triangles. Instead of altering the right triangle to fit in with the existing isosceles-triangle cognitive structure, the child would change the existing structure; he or she would accommodate by now changing the structure to include knowledge of both isosceles and right triangles.

Similarly, the infant could accommodate to its thumb rather than assimilate it. Instead of acting on the thumb as it did on its mother's nipple, hence, assimilating the thumb through integrating it into an already existing cognitive structure, the infant could incorporate different actions through an alteration of its own already existing cognitive structure. The infant would suck differently on the thumb than how he or she sucks on the nipple. The infant could, therefore, alter his or her cognitive structure to include its differential actions on this new object, thus gaining a new knowledge. By the subject's altered actions on the different object (the thumb), a corresponding alteration in the subject's cognitive structure would occur. Rather than matching the object to the subject, in this case the subject—through differential action—would match the object. Hence, accommodation would have occurred.

Equilibration

Why are assimilation and accommodation complementary processes? Piaget answered this question by postulating what he believed to be a fundamental factor in development. He termed this factor *equilibration*. Piaget proposed that an organism's adaptation to its environment involves a balance, an equilibrium, between the activity of the organism on its environment and the activity of the environment on the organism.

When an organism acts on its environment, it incorporates the external stimulus world into its already existing structure (assimilation); alternatively, when the environment acts on the organism, the organism is altered in order to adjust to the external stimulus world (accommodation).

Hence, Piaget proposed that a balance must be struck between these two tendencies. In essence, he hypothesized that there is an intrinsic orientation in the organism to balance its actions on the environment with the environment's actions on it. In order for the organism to be adaptive, it must be able to incorporate the environment into its already existing structure and to adjust itself to fit the exigencies imposed on it by the environment. Piaget proposed that, if the organism is to be adaptive, neither of these two tendencies must always override the other. An equilibration between these two tendencies is needed in order for the organism to be adaptive.

Hence, for every assimilation there must be a corresponding accommodation. One process must balance the other. Just as the subject changes the object to fit its internal structure, the internal structure of the subject must be changed to fit the object. Thus, according to Piaget, equilibration is the balance of interaction between subject and object (Piaget, 1952). There is an inherent tendency in the organism to equilibrate, to balance between assimilation and accommodation. This tendency exists because of its fundamental biological significance; that is, it is the basis of an organism's adaptation to its environment. Thus, as Piaget (1970) stated:

> Cognitive adaptation, like its biological counterpart, consists of an equilibrium between assimilation and accommodation. As has been shown, there is no assimilation without accommodation. But we must strongly emphasize the fact that accommodation does not exist without simultaneous assimilation either. (p. 708)

In essence, Piaget proposed that there is a general, biologically based adaptive tendency that applies to the organism throughout its development. This factor—equilibration—is the moving force behind all cognitive development. There must be a balance between subject and object, between assimilation and accommodation. Whenever the organism alters the environment to incorporate it into its already existing internal structure, there must also be a compensatory alteration of the organism's structure to match the objects in its external environment. There must be a balance in action—the basis of all knowledge—between the organism and its environment.

Functional (Reproductive) Assimilation

If, as we have seen, cognitive development tends to move toward a balance—an equilibration—between assimilation and accommodation, then why does cognitive development not just stop when such a balance is reached? Why, after the infant assimilates its mother's nipple and then accommodates to its thumb, does cognitive development not simply stop there? If equilibration is the endpoint, or goal, of cognitive development, why does such development continue after a given equilibration is reached?

It is not enough to argue that there are many things that impinge on the infant's world that necessitate further assimilations (and ensuing accommodations). If the infant is in equilibrium, there would seem to be no reason to bother with other impinging stimuli.

Let me make an analogy. Most of us have a favorite food. For example, let us suppose that we cannot resist cheeseburgers. Whenever we have the opportunity to eat a cheeseburger we do so. (We "assimilate" as many cheeseburgers as we can.) However, let us imagine that we have just finished a holiday dinner at our grandmother's home. If we were offered a cheeseburger now, we certainly would not assimilate it; we would be more likely to turn away, protesting the inappropriateness of more food at that time. We would be in gastronomical equilibrium and would not bother with any food stimuli that we would otherwise assimilate.

Of course, we do not remain in gastronomical equilibrium forever. Rather, our digestive system continues to function, and as a result food is assimilated and we are no longer in equilibrium. Similarly, we do not appear to remain in cognitive equilibrium. Thus, the problem according to Piaget is how to account for continuing cognitive development while maintaining that equilibrium is the point toward which all cognitive development tends.

To address this problem, Piaget specified that there exist several other aspects of assimilation. Discussion of one of these—*functional* (or *reproductive*) *assimilation*—will illustrate how cognitive development continues to progress. In essence, the concept of reproductive assimilation refers to the fact that any cognitive structure brought about through assimilation will continue to assimilate. That is, it is the nature of assimilatory functioning to continue to assimilate. This is the case for any biological system; although a biological system may be in equilibrium, this balance is necessarily temporary because the system must continue to function if its adaptive role is to be maintained. (Although ingested food may place the digestive system in equilibrium, such balance is transitory since the food must necessarily be assimilated if digestion is to continue to subserve its adaptive function.) The cognitive system works like any other biological system. When a simple cognitive structure is developed on the basis of assimilation—such as that involved in our example of the infant's sucking on its mother's nipple—it continues to assimilate; it functions to reproduce itself. That is, such structures "apply themselves again and again to assimilate aspects of the environment" (Flavell, 1963, p. 55). Thus, the concept of functional (or reproductive) assimilation indicates that it is a basic property of assimilatory functioning to continue to assimilate. (In the same way, it is a basic property of the digestive system to continue to digest.)

Hence, any equilibrium that the infant establishes will be only transitory. The child assimilates and then accommodates and reaches an equilibrium. But cognitive development goes on to higher and higher developmental levels. This happens because reproductive assimilation occurs even though an equilibrium is reached. Thus, the child assimilates other components of the environment, which in turn require compensatory accommodation. Thus, an equilibrium is again reached, but this, too, is short-lived because a disequilibrium will inevitably result when the child continues to assimilate. As before, this assimilation will be balanced by a corresponding accommodation, again establishing a transitory equilibrium. Thus, because of the disequilibrium resulting from the child's continued functional assimilation, higher and higher levels of cognitive development are attained.

Schematically, the steps in this continuous process of cognitive development may be seen as (a) *assimilation,* (b) *accommodation,* which results in (c) *equilibration,* (d) *reproductive assimilation,* resulting in (e) *disequilibrium,* which necessitates a return to accommodation (step b) and a repetition of the sequence.

Hence, the occurrence of disequilibrium (through the process of reproductive assimilation) provides the source of cognitive development throughout all stages of life. In other words, with the postulation of this model Piaget offered a set of stage-independent concepts about cognitive development; that is, these concepts apply at all stages of cognitive development. They represent general laws of development applicable to the development of cognition throughout all stages. In fact, these stage-independent concepts account for the person's continual cognitive development. With this understanding, then, let us now turn to a consideration of Piaget's stage-dependent concepts.

Stage-Dependent Concepts: The Stages of Cognitive Development

There are four stages in Piaget's theory. They span the age range from birth through adolescence (with no fixed point associated with the end of the last stage, since it is presumed to continue throughout adulthood).

The Sensorimotor Stage

The first stage of cognitive development in Piaget's theory is the sensorimotor stage. Although the age limits of any stage may vary from individual to individual, we may suggest rough boundaries for each stage. Thus, the sensorimotor stage may be held to last from birth through 2 years of age.

When the child is born and thus begins his or her sensorimotor stage, he or she enters the world with what Piaget termed *innate schemes*. Piaget's use of the term *innate* does not mean that he claimed that these "schemes" are unavailable to experiential influences. In fact, Piaget was quite aware of the necessity of conceptualizing development within an interactionist model. Hence, by "innate schemes" Piaget meant "congenital schemes"—schemes that are present at birth.

But what is a scheme? A *scheme* according to Piaget, is the essential component, the main building block, of cognitive development. It is an organized sensorimotor action sequence. By this term, then, Piaget referred to a structure:

1. That has an organization.

2. That has a sensory, or input, component that is, a component comprising stimulation derived from the external environment.

3. That has a motor component that is, a component comprising, in part, some output component like a muscular movement.

4. That some action on the environment follows the sensory portion of this structure.

5. That the components of this structure function in a sequential order; that is, there is a sequence to the organized sensory and motor actions that occur.

It may seem to you that a scheme resembles what we typically term a *reflex*. In fact, the schemes that the child is born with—as well as the schemes existing throughout this first stage—may conveniently be thought of as reflexive in nature. Like a reflex, a scheme is a rigid cognitive structure. That is, although the development of schemes throughout the sensorimotor stage represents considerable development in the child's cognitive functioning, at the same time, the existence of schemes during this period tends to place limitations on the child's cognition. As we soon see, schemes tend to be unidirectional; that is, the direction of the sequence involved in the scheme is always the same. Thus, a scheme is in many ways analogous to a reflex. For example, in an eyeblink reflex a puff of air would always precede and lead to an eyeblink. Schemes are also unidirectional in that the motor component of their sequences cannot be reversed.

In essence, when we say that the newborn enters the world with a complement of innate schemes, we may think of this as the beginning of the sensorimotor stage, characterized by the presence of birth of an assortment of reflexes, or sensorimotor structures. Such innate schemes may be illustrated by the grasping reflex; the infant will grasp an object placed in its palm tightly. Another example would be the Babinski reflex, a backward curling and fanning of the toes in response to tactile stimulation of the sole of the foot. (This reflex, by the way, disappears early in ontogeny due to the development of portions of the brain; in fact, the presence of this reflex in an older child is an indication of brain damage.) Yet another example of an innate reflex, or scheme, would be the rooting reflex. Here, if the infant's cheek is stimulated—say by lightly running a finger from the bottom of the ear to the corner of the mouth—the infant will turn its head in the direction of the stimulation and promptly begin to suck. This is obviously an adaptive reflex. It is typically the mother's nipple that so stimulates the infant, and head-turning and sucking actions will increase the infant's proximity to the mother's nipple and, hence, food. In sum, then, the infant enters the world with a complement of innate schemes.

However, these schemes do not remain innate for long. That is, they do not retain their original structures. In functioning for the very first time, they change. They begin to assimilate from the environment and hence become *acquired schemes*. In other words, once the scheme functions it does so by assimilating. This, of course, changes its structure and requires a complementary accommoda-

tion. Then, because of functional or reproductive assimilation, the structure of the scheme continues to change.

To understand how schemes develop throughout the sensorimotor stage and how the concomitant cognitive developments are attained through these alterations in schematic structure, we must point out some other facets of the sensorimotor stage. First, Piaget divided this stage into six sequential periods. Within each period, the concept of circular reaction is involved.

A *circular reaction* refers to one repetition or a series of repetitions of a sensorimotor response. The first response in any of these series is always new to the infant. When a scheme first functions, the infant cannot anticipate its specific results; the results were not intended before the response was made. The important aspect of a circular reaction comes about, however, after this first response is made. Because of reproductive assimilation the infant will tend to repeat this new, chance adaptation over and over (Flavell, 1963, p. 93). Simply, a circular reaction involves the repetition of a given scheme's functioning.

Thus, the first period of the sensorimotor stage involves the alteration of the infant's innate schemes to acquired schemes. Again, this alteration—this bringing into existence of initial acquired schemes—comes about through the functioning of reproductive assimilation. In period two of this stage, circular reactions are involved with and affect the infant's body itself; these circular reactions are termed *primary*. In period three, the infant's circular reactions come to involve objects in the outside world, such as toys or mobiles hanging over the crib; these circular reactions are termed *secondary*.

To this point in the sensorimotor stage, one could use the phrase "out of sight, out of mind" to describe the infant's cognitive development. The infant interacts with objects in the external world as if their existence depended on their being sensed (Piaget, 1950). When objects are not in the infant's immediate sensory world, the infant acts as if they do not exist. In other words, infants are egocentric; there is no differentiation between the existence of an object and the sensory stimulation provided by that object (Elkind, 1967).

Although all stages of cognitive development contain functioning that may be described as egocentric, overcoming this sensorimotor egocentrism will involve the child's most important cognitive attainment during this stage. We may think of all of the remaining periods within the sensorimotor stage as involving the elaboration of schematic structures that subserve the crucial function of allowing the infant to know that there is object permanency in the world (i.e., that objects continue to exist even when he or she is not observing them).

We may think of numerous instances of the infant's apparent lack of a scheme of object permanency. Before a certain point in cognitive development, games, such as peek-a-boo, hold the child's attention. The child acts as if the person playing peek-a-boo with him or her appears and disappears throughout the game by going into and passing out of existence. Thus, the person jumps in and out of the child's immediate sight and, when the person is in the reappearing phase, the child responds with "surprise" (a smile or a laugh). Similarly, if an attention-getting toy or object is brought in and out of the child's sight, then at these initial points in cognitive development the child will not follow the object (e.g., visually) when it leaves his or her immediate sensory world. It is only after a series of circular reactions, involving many different objects, that the child is finally able to represent an object that is not in its immediate sensory world. Only after repeatedly acting on objects does the child become able to represent these objects internally.

Thus, as a consequence of these repeated sensorimotor actions, resulting in an internalized representation of an object, the child comes to know that an object exists even though he or she is not perceiving it. The child has *conquered the object* (Elkind, 1967). The child's egocentrism has diminished enough—the child has decentered enough now—to know the difference between an object and the sensory impression it makes. This *representational ability,* this ability to represent an absent object internally and, thus, to act as if one knows it continues to exist, constitutes the major cognitive achievement of the sensorimotor stage. It is an achievement enabling the infant to progress to the ensuing stage of cognitive development.

The Preoperational Stage

The age range associated with this second stage is usually from 2 through 6 years of age. The major cognitive achievements in this stage involve the elaboration of the representational ability that enabled the child to move from the sensorimotor stage to the present one. In the preoperational stage, true systems of representation, or symbolic functioning, emerge. In fact, Elkind (1967) termed this stage the period of *the conquest of the symbol.*

The most obvious example of the development of representational systems in this stage is language.

Here the child's use of language develops extensively, as words are used to symbolize objects, events, and feelings. There are also other indications of this representational ability. During this stage of life, we see the emergence of symbolic play; for example, the child uses two crossed sticks to make an airplane or uses his or her finger to make a gun. In addition, we see the emergence of delayed imitation; for example, the child sees someone perform an act (e.g., Daddy smoking a pipe and pacing across the room) and then imitates the act hours later.

Although cognitive development in the preoperational stage does have positive characteristics—by virtue of the fact that such elaborate systems of representational ability do develop—it also has limitations. The child in this stage is also egocentric, but here the egocentrism takes a form different from that seen in the previous stage. The child now has the ability to symbolize objects with words, to use words to refer to objects. But, at the same time, the child fails to differentiate between the words and the things the words refer to. For example, the child believes that the word representing an object is inherent in it, that an object cannot have more than one word that symbolizes it (Elkind, 1967). The child does not know that an object and the word symbolizing the object are two independent things. The child does not differentiate between symbols and what the symbols refer to (Elkind, 1967).

This type of egocentrism has several consequences. One is that the child acts as if words carry much more meaning than they actually do (Elkind, 1967). For instance, it is not uncommon to see a child in this stage of development ask someone for the "thing" and act as if enough information has been conveyed to the other person to have the request fulfilled. Since the child does not differentiate between symbols and their referents, he or she thinks the word belongs to (inheres in) the object.

A broader consequence of this egocentrism is the child's inability to hold two aspects of a stimulus or situation separately in mind at the same time. That is, the child does not differentiate between objects and the words that refer to them and thus joins, or merges, these two dimensions of a stimulus: the object and the symbol. This failure suggests a more general lack of ability to take into account two different aspects of a stimulus array at the same time. One indication of this general inability may be found in the preoperational child's failure to show conservation ability.

Conservation refers to the ability to know that one aspect of a stimulus array has remained

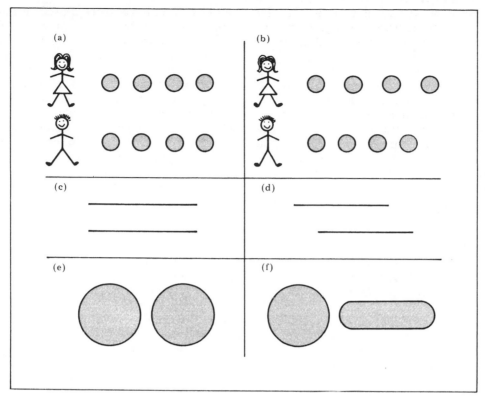

FIGURE 15.3
Examples of tests of number conservation (a and b), length conservation (c and d), and mass conservation (e and f).

unchanged, although others have changed. To understand this concept, let us imagine that we present a 5-year-old with two dolls, a "mommy" doll and a "daddy" doll. We then take four marbles and place them in a row beside the mommy doll, and we place four more marbles beside the daddy doll in positions directly corresponding to the mommy doll's marbles. Our materials would look like those in Figure 15.3a. Now, if we show the 5-year-old these materials arranged in this way and ask, "Which doll has more marbles to play with, the mommy doll or the daddy doll?," the child will most probably say that both dolls have the same amount of marbles to play with. However, if we spread out the mommy doll's marbles in the full view of the child (but leave the daddy doll's marbles in their original position), so that we have an arrangement that looks like Figure 15.3b, and then ask which doll has more, the preoperational 5-year-old will answer that the mommy doll has more.

What we see from this example, then, is the inability to conserve number. The child does not know that one aspect of the stimulus array—the number of marbles—has remained unchanged, al-

though another aspect of the array—the positioning of the marbles—has changed. It would seem that the child cannot appreciate these two dimensions of the stimulus array at the same time. A cognitive error is made because, in not being able to put these two dimensions in their proper interrelation, the child fails to know that the movements of the mommy doll's marbles can be reversed and the marbles can be put back into the original arrangement. As we learn when we discuss the next stage of cognitive development—the concrete operational stage—the child cannot yet understand this *reversibility*. The child's thought is still dominated by schemes, and as we have seen, such structures are rigidly unidirectional. Thus, although we spread out the marbles right in front of the child, the child will still maintain that the altered array has more marbles. We might even return the array to its original form and again ask which doll has more. The child will now probably say, once again, that they both have the same amount, and even if we repeat these steps several times the child's answers might correspondingly alternate between "same" and "more."

The lack of conservation ability seen with the quantitative dimension of number applies, too, to other quantitative aspects of stimuli. Thus, if we present two equal lengths of rope—as in Figure 15.3c—and ask which rope is longer, the child will probably answer that the ropes are equal in length. If, however, we move the location of one of these pieces of rope—as in Figure 15.3d—and repeat the question, the child will now probably claim that one piece of rope is longer than the other. Similarly, if we take two equal-sized pieces of clay and roll them up into balls of equal size and shape and present them to the child—as in Figure 15.3e—the child will most likely say that each ball contains the same amount of clay. If, however, we reshape one of these clay balls into a sausage—as in Figure 15.3, again doing this right in full view of the child, and then ask which ball contains more clay, the child's answer will be different; the child will now probably say that the sausage-shaped piece contains more clay. In this example, we see an instance of the inability to show conservation of mass. The child does not know that one aspect of the stimulus array—its mass—remains the same although another aspect of the array—its shape—is altered.

In sum, then, the preoperational child generally does not show conservation ability; this manifests itself not only in respect to quantitative aspects of stimuli such as mass, length, and number but also to other quantitative aspects of stimuli, such as area and volume. Thus, although the preoperational child's thought has progressed well beyond that of the sensorimotor child—due mostly to extensive representational abilities—the preoperational child's cognition still has the aforementioned limitations. However, as the cognitive conflicts produced by being unable to differentiate between symbols and the objects they refer to increase, and as instances of the inability to simultaneously appreciate two different aspects of a stimulus array similarly increase and cause conflict, the child must accommodate more and more. As the equilibrations and the disequilibrations involved in this process occur, the child's cognitive structure will be altered. When enough alteration has taken place, the child will enter into the next stage of cognitive development.

The Concrete Operational Stage

Up to the point that a child enters the concrete operational stage (which spans a period from about 6 years through 11 or 12 years of age), the child's cognitive structure is composed predominantly of schemes. However, because a scheme is a unidirectional structure, the child is generally unable to simultaneously appreciate contrasting aspects of a stimulus array. This limitation, as we have seen, is illustrated by the lack of conservation ability. Preoperational thought thus limits a child in not providing the ability to reverse various physical events. That is, if we, as adults, see two balls of clay and decide that each contains an equal amount of clay, we would continue to maintain this even if one of the balls were reshaped to look like a sausage. If this were done we would know—without having to see the action performed—that by reversing the action of reshaping the clay we would be back to the original two clay balls. Because nothing was added to or subtracted from either ball—because reshaping does not alter the mass—we would assert that both pieces contain the same amount of clay.

The emergence of *operational structures* gives the child this ability. An operation is an internalized action that is reversible. As opposed to schemes, operations allow the person to know that actions can be counteracted by reversing them. Moreover, operational thought, as internalized actions, do not require a person having to see the action of rolling the sausage back into a ball to know that the clay can be returned to its original shape. We can just think of this action. Our thoughts about concrete, physical actions do not depend on our actually seeing these actions. We can reverse the actions in our heads and come to the same conclusion about them as if we actually, concretely viewed them. We can "see them in our mind's eye."

Thus, the emergence of operational cognitive ability extends the child's capacity to deal with the world. Because thought is now reversible—because the child can now appreciate the reciprocity in concrete actions on and with physical stimuli—the concrete operational stage is the period in which the child begins to show the conservation abilities lacking in the preoperational stage. Moreover, because operations are internalized actions, the child's cognitive abilities are also extended in that now he or she need not actually see actions performed in order to know about them. Thus, the child now has cognitive structures that enable him or her to think about the actions of the world without actually having to experience these actions. Simply, operations extend the scope of action by internalizing it.

But despite the great cognitive accomplishments inherent in the concrete operational stage, thought in this stage also has its limitations. Notice that the label for this stage is concrete operational. What this denotes is that although thought is operational, it is bound by concrete, physical reality. Although the child can deal with objects internally (i.e., without having to actually experience them) these actions and objects must have a concrete, real existence. Things or events that are counterfactual—that are not actually represented in the real world—cannot be understood by the concrete operational child.

An illustration of this point, which is offered by Elkind (1967), is helpful. Suppose someone asks you to imagine that coal is white, and then further asks you to indicate what color coal would be when burning at its hottest. Most probably you would have an answer to this counterfactual question. You might think that since coal is actually black and when burning at its hottest is white, then if it were white, it would be black when burning at its hottest. The point here is not the particular solution, but the fact that you can deal with the counterfactual question. The concrete operational child, on the other hand, cannot do this. For example, the response of the concrete operational child might typically be, "But coal is black!" (Elkind, 1967). In essence, then, a major limitation of concrete operational thought is that it is limited to thinking about concrete, real things.

There are also other limitations of concrete thought. As Elkind (1967) pointed out, the concrete operational child is also egocentric. Here, however, the egocentrism takes the form of an inability to differentiate between actions and objects experienced directly and actions and objects the child thinks about. We have seen that the child's thought is now independent of experience, so that he or she can now deal with an action whether it is experienced or just thought about. However, the child fails to distinguish between knowledge gained through experience and knowledge gained from thought alone. If given some information about a physical situation (say, a scientific problem) and asked to give a solution to the problem, the child will not have to see the actual physical objects in order to reach a solution; instead, he or she will think about it and form an answer, a hypothesis. But the child will not recognize that the answer is just a hypothesis, just one possible solution to the problem. Rather, the child will think that the answer is one and the same with the physical situation. The child will not see any difference between what he or she thinks and what is! Even if the child's ideas about experience are challenged and/or evidence is presented contradicting those ideas, the child will not alter the answer, but will just reinterpret the opposing evidence to fit into his or her ideas (Elkind, 1967).

Unable to think counterfactually, and equating perceived and actual reality, the child cannot recognize that his or her thoughts about reality represent only hypotheses; that they are arbitrary: that they are not necessarily imposed by, or part of, reality but are just one of many possible interpretations of reality. Thus, a child is egocentric in failing to view thoughts and experience as two independent phenomena. With further cognitive development, however, the child attains the ability to think counterfactually, to see that thoughts about reality and reality are different. Hence, the child's final stage of cognitive development begins.

The Formal Operational Stage

The last stage of cognitive development in Piaget's theory is termed the *formal operational stage*. It begins at about 11 or 12 years of age and, according to Piaget (1972), continues for the rest of life. It is because of the lower age limit typically associated with this stage in both theory and research (see Neimark, 1975) that the study of formal operations is linked with the period of adolescent development.

In the formal operational stage, thought becomes hypothetical in emphasis. Now discriminating between thoughts about reality and actual reality, the child comes to recognize that his or her thoughts about reality have an element of arbitrariness about them, that they may not actually be real representations of the true nature of experience. Thus, the child's thoughts about reality take on a hypothetical "if, then" characteristic: "*If* something were the case, *then* something else would follow." In forming such hypotheses about the world, the child's thought can be seen to correspond to formal, scientific, logical thinking. This emergence accounts for the label applied to this stage—the formal operational stage.

Another perspective on the quality of this stage is provided by Neimark (1975). She explained the distinctive quality of adolescent thought by noting:

> Although the properties and relations at issue during the concrete operational stage are abstract in the sense of being derived from objects and events, they are still dependent upon specifics of the objects and events from which they derive; that is, they are empirically based abstractions rather than pure abstractions. In this sense the elements of concrete operational thought are "concrete" rather than "abstract" or "formal." On the other hand, propositions, the elements of formal operational thought, are abstract in the sense that the truth value of a statement can be freed from a dependence upon the evidence of experience and, instead, determined logically from the truth values of other propositions to

which it bears a formal, logical relationship. This type of reasoning, deriving from the form of propositions rather than their content, is new in the development of the child: Deductive rather than inductive thought. (pp. 547–548)

In other words, because the concrete operational child can only form abstractions relevant to phenomena or problems that exist, thoughts about a given topic cannot be integrated with *potentially* relevant but nonempirical (that is, hypothetical) aspects of the problem. In this sense, mental operations are not coordinated, and the child cannot reach solutions by means of general theories or by the postulation of all possible solutions to a problem (Wadsworth, 1971). In turn, the formal operational person does show these qualities of thought.

Thus, to be able to deal with all potentially relevant aspects of a problem, a person has to be able to *transform* (i.e., alter, or rearrange) the problem so as to contend with all its possible forms. The cognitive structure that characterizes formal operations allows such complete transformations. Piaget termed this structure the *INRC group* (Inhelder & Piaget, 1958; Piaget, 1950, 1952, 1970). That is, all transformations of a problem may be obtained though the application of the components of this group: identity, negation, and reciprocal and correlative transformations. Simply, one can think of all the aspects of a problem by, for instance, recognizing the problem in terms of its singular attributes (an identity transformation), canceling the existence of the problem (a negation operation), taking its opposite (a reciprocal transformation), or relating it to other problems (a correlative transformation).

To illustrate, Piaget and Inhelder (1969, pp. 97–98) described an "experiment relating to the conservation of liquids in which the contents of glass A were poured into a narrower glass B or a wider glass C." When asked if B or C has the same, more, or less water than A, a child might address this question through identity ("Nothing has been taken away or added"; Piaget & Inhelder, 1969, p. 98); through negation ("You can put the water in B back into A where it was before", Piaget & Inhelder, 1969, p. 98); through reciprocity ("The water is higher, but the glass is narrower, so it's the same amount", Piaget & Inhelder, 1969, p. 98); or through correlation (e.g., "A ball of clay could be rolled into a sausage but that wouldn't change how much clay you had.").

It is possible to illustrate further the functioning of the formal operational thought structure by describing some of the tasks used to assess whether children show this type of thought. For instance, one of these tasks tests *combinatorial*

thought. To explain the meaning of this term, Piaget and Inhelder (1969) described a task wherein a child is presented with five jars, each containing a colorless liquid. Combining the liquids from three particular jars will produce a color, whereas any use of the liquids from either of the other jars will not produce a color. The child is shown that a color can be produced but is not shown which combination will do this.

Concrete operational children typically try to solve this problem by combining the liquids two at a time, but after combining all pairs or possibly trying to mix all five liquids together, their search for the workable combination usually stops. However, the formal operational child will explore all possible solutions, typically testing all possible combinations of two and three liquids until a color is produced.

Tasks involving certain types of *verbal problems* cannot usually be solved without formal operational ability (Piaget & Inhelder, 1969; Wadsworth, 1971). One such verbal problem is represented by the question, "If Jane is taller than Doris, and is shorter than Francine, who is the shortest of the three?" (Wadsworth, 1971). Although concrete operational children may be able to solve an analogous problem (e.g., one dealing with sticks of various lengths) when the elements of the problem (the sticks) are physically present, abstract verbal problems are usually not solved until formal operations have emerged.

Another task, the *pendulum problem,* also illustrates the quality of formal operational thought. A pendulum can be made to swing faster by shortening the string holding it. Conversely, it can be made to swing slower by lengthening the string. Concrete operational children typically adjust the *weight* of a pendulum when asked to alter its speed (Wadsworth, 1971). Alternatively, they may adjust string length and weight simultaneously and attribute any change in speed to the weight alteration (Wadsworth, 1971). However, in the formal operational period, children separate weight and string length, deal with them separately (e.g., through a reciprocity transformation), and show knowledge that it is string length that is the variable relevant to the speed of swinging (Inhelder & Piaget, 1958).

In short, only the coordinated use of all these transformations allows all potentially applicable aspects of a problem to be dealt with. It is not until the INRC group is established that the person possesses a cognitive structure appropriate for dealing with pure abstraction—with a set of all the propositions pertinent to a problem—which is the "object" of thought in the formal operational stage. In addition to these assets of formal operational thought, there are also important limitations of thinking in this stage. As in other stages, these limitations relate to egocentrism, and to the special features of egocentrism that characterize the person who, normatively at this time in life, is in the adolescent period of development.

Adolescent egocentrism: The contributions of David Elkind. Because anything and everything can become the object of the adolescent's newly developed abstract and hypothetical cognitive ability, the person may not only recognize his or her own thoughts as only one possible interpretation of reality but also may come to view reality as only one possible instance of a potentially unlimited number of possible realities. The concrete predomination of what is real is replaced by the abstract and hypothetical predomination of what can be real. All things in experience are thought about hypothetically, and even the adolescent's own thoughts can become objects of his or her hypothesizing.

In other words, one can now think about one's own thinking. Since the young person spends a good deal of time using these new thought capabilities, the person's own thought processes thereby become a major object of cognitive concern. This preoccupation, or *centration* on one's own perspective, leads, however, to a limitation of the newly developed formal operational thought. It leads to egocentrism within the formal operational stage.

The scholarship of David Elkind (1967) has been most important in advancing understanding of egocentrism within the formal operational stage. He labeled the egocentrism of this stage *adolescent egocentrism*. Elkind saw such egocentrism as having two parts.

First, we have seen how the adolescent' own thoughts come to dominate his or her thinking. Because of this preoccupation, the adolescent fails to distinguish, or discriminate, between his or her own thinking and what others are thinking about. Being preoccupied with self and not making the above discrimination, the adolescent comes to believe that others are as preoccupied with his or her appearance and behavior as he or she is (Elkind, 1967). Thus, the adolescent constructs an *imaginary audience*.

As an illustration of the functioning of the imaginary audience, and of some emotional consequences of this cognitive development, think back to your early-adolescent days. Assuredly, some new fad—perhaps in regard to a particular style of clothing—sprang up among your peers. Some adolescents were perhaps stuck with wearing the old, outdated style and were literally afraid to be seen in public. They were sure that as soon as

David Elkind

they appeared without the appropriate clothes, everyone would notice the absence.

There is a second component of adolescent egocentrism. The adolescent's thoughts and feelings are experienced as new and unique by him or her. Although to the adolescent they are, in fact, new and unique, the young person comes to believe that they are *historically* new and unique. That is, the adolescent constructs a *personal fable,* the belief that he or she is a one-of-a-kind individual—a person having singular feelings and thoughts.

Here, too, it is easy to think of an illustration of the personal fable. Think back to your early-adolescent years and your first "love affair": No one had ever loved as deeply, as totally—no one had ever felt the intense compassion, the devotion, the longing, the overwhelming fulfillment that you felt for your one true love! Then remember a few days or weeks later, when it was over. The pain, the depression, the agony—no one had ever suffered as deeply, no one had ever been so wrongfully abused, so thoroughly tortured, so spitefully crushed by unrequited love! You sat in your room, unmoving. Your mother would say, "What's wrong with you? Come and eat." The inevitable answer: "You don't understand. What do you know about love?"

Although the formal operational stage is the last stage of cognitive development in Piaget's theory, the egocentrism of this stage diminishes over the course of the person's subsequent cognitive functioning. According to Piaget (Inhelder &

Piaget, 1958; Piaget, 1969, 1972), the adolescent decenters through interaction with peers and elders and—most importantly—with the assumption of adult roles and responsibilities: "The focal point of the decentering process is the entrance into the occupational world or the beginning of serious professional training. The adolescent becomes an adult when he undertakes a real job" (Inhelder & Piaget, 1958, p. 346).

In sum, Piaget (1950, 1970, 1972) claimed that with the attainment of formal operations, the person has reached the last stage of cognitive development. According to Piaget and his followers, no new cognitive structures emerge over the course of life (Flavell, 1970; Piaget, 1972); however, the person may change through a differentiation or specialization of abilities within the common formal structure (Neimark, 1975; Piaget, 1972). By way of summary, Table 15.2 presents the four stages in Piaget's theory and shows the cognitive achievements and limitations involved in each stage.

Conclusions

What we have seen is that Piaget offerred a theory of cognitive development that includes both continuous, stage-independent phenomena and discontinuous, stage-dependent phenomena. Piaget's is an organismic account of development; he viewed development as the outcome of organism–environment interactions and, hence, as an active, self-generated process. Action—the action of the organism on the environment and the action of the environment on the organism—is the basis of cognitive development. The disequilibriums continually caused by these actions provide the moving force of cognitive development, and the changes brought about by this process are characterized by developmental stages.

Although a stage theorist, Piaget did not view the person as making abrupt modal transitions from one stage of development to the next. Rather, as is true of other stage theorists, he recognized in several ways that people function at more than one stage of development at the same time. For instance, children do not gain the ability to make conservations in all quantitative dimensions at one time. Rather, number and length conservations appear first, area conservation appears later, and volume conservation typically develops last. Thus, in some areas of cognitive functioning, a child may show behaviors indicative of the preoperational stage, whereas in other areas the child may show evidence of concrete operational functioning. Thus, stage transition becomes a matter of shifts in modal type of functioning.

Moreover, through his concept of décalage, Piaget also recognized the fact that people fre-

TABLE 15.2
Piaget's Stages of Cognitive Development

Stage	Approximate age range	Major cognitive achievements	Major cognitive limitations
Sensorimotor	Birth to 2	Scheme of object permanency	Egocentrism: lack of ability to differentiate between self and external stimulus world
Preoperational	2–6 or 7	Systems of representation: symbolic functioning for example, language, symbolic play, delayed limitation	Lack of conservation ability. Egocentrism: lack of ability to differentiate between symbol and object
Concrete operational	6 or 7–12	Ability to show experience-independent thought (reversible, internalized actions) Conservation ability	Egocentrism: lack of ability to differentiate between thoughts about reality and actual experience of reality
Formal operational	≥12	Ability to think hypothetically, counter factually, and propositionally	Egocentrism: imaginary audience, personal fable

quently show similar cognitive phenomena at different points in their ontogeny. Piaget termed a repetition of a cognitive phenomenon that takes place within the same, single stage of development and involving a single, general level of functioning a *horizontal décalage*. The circular reactions that occur throughout the sensorimotor stage are illustrations of horizontal *décalage*. In addition, repetitions of the same phenomena at different stages of development are termed by Piaget *vertical décalage* (Flavell, 1963, pp. 21–22). Showing conservation ability at two different stages of development is an instance of vertical *décalage,* as is the continuous functioning of reproductive assimilation across ontogeny.

Thus, although different stages of development have different stage-specific laws governing their functioning, vertical *décalage* suggests that there are laws general to all level of functioning. This, then, is the second "compromise" between the organismic and the mechanistic philosophies of science discussed in Chapter 3. This is the general-and-specific-laws compromise. That is, there are phenomena at all ontogenetic levels that can be understood by one or a common set of laws or principles; however, this does not alter the fact that each level may also be governed by specific laws whose specificity, in fact, serves as the criterion for calling a stage a stage. Thus, Piaget, in agreement with Werner, saw both continuity and discontinuity as characteristic of developmental processes. Piaget's recognition of stage mixture as characterizing cognitive development and functioning is an indication of his understanding of the modal nature of stage transition and his belief in the orthogenetic nature of cognitive development.

Accordingly, while Piaget presented a theory of cognitive development that shares important features with other major theories of human development, several of the ideas particular to his theory have been subjected to quite specific criticism. It is important to consider these criticisms.

David Henry Feldman

CRITIQUING AND RECONSTRUCTING PIAGET'S STAGE THEORY: THE CONTRIBUTIONS OF DAVID HENRY FELDMAN

We have noted earlier in this chapter that stage theories in general have been subjected to criticism (e.g., Emmerich, 1968; Wohlwill, 1973). In addition, Piaget's theory has been the target of specific criticism (e.g., Brainerd, 1978; Case, 1984; Feldman, 1980a, 1980b, 1994; Ginsberg & Opper, 1979; Neimark, 1975). David Henry Feldman (2000) discussed many of the criticisms that have been made in regard Piaget's stage theory (e.g., Brainerd, 1978). He also evaluated the responses of some of the scholars working from within a Piagetian perspective who have suggested that the stages be dropped from the theory in order to maintain the usefulness of the general, stage-independent features of the theory (e.g., Karmiloff-Smith, 1992; Montangero, 1985).

However, in addition to clarifying the dimensions of problems associated with Piagetian approaches to developmental stages, Feldman (2000) offered creative formulations that enable stages of cognitive development consonant with Piagetian thinking to be retained in developmental science, but in manners that are theoretically less problematic and (potentially) empirically richer. It is useful, then, to use Feldman's scholarship as a means to understand both some of the major theoretical problems that are associated with Piaget's theory and some of the ways in which these problems may be transcended.

Criticisms of Piaget's Theory

Piaget (1950, 1960, 1970) described each of the stages within his theory as representing an overall general operating system (Feldman, 2000). He used the idea of "structures as a whole," "*structures d'ensemble*," to describe this overall system.

However, Feldman (2000) noted that it is difficult to prove the existence of structures as a whole when the behavior (the cognitive functioning) that is observed is rarely consistent with theoretical prescriptions. Moreover, Feldman (2000) observed that, if, in response to the problems associated with the structures as a whole concept, the stages are dropped from Piaget's theory, then another problem would be introduced into the theory. That is, the theory would not be able to account for qualitative change—for novelty—in development. As discussed in Chapter 7, the emergence of novelty is a key focus in developmental theories, especially those that are framed by a dynamic systems perspective (e.g., Thelen & Smith, 1998), and Piaget (1971) himself agreed with the importance of the concept of novelty for his theory. Thus, if a stage theory eliminated the concept of stage from its conceptual repertoire, it would lose the defining feature of its approach to novelty.

Feldman (2000) also noted that other, stage-independent concepts found in Piaget's theory—in particular the equilibration model—although clearly pointing to a part of the person–context relations involved in cognitive functioning, are not sufficient to account for either novelty—the defining characteristic that makes one type of functioning distinct from another—or the change from one instance of novelty to another (i.e., stage progression). Feldman (2000) pointed out that:

> While it is almost certainly true that equilibration or something very much like equilibration is involved in the extension, adjustment, elaboration and transformation of structures for comprehending and interpreting the world, it is not at all clear how such processes could account for the appearance of a set of structures as broad, interconnected, qualitatively advanced, and dramatically improved as is true of each of the stages succeeding Sensorimotor behavior. (p. 6)

Thus, Feldman (2000) identified a key problem with the emergence of novelty within Piaget's theory: the "miraculous transition" problem. That is, there is no adequate means through which to explain the emergence of the integrated, qualitative features that characterize the structures as a whole of a given stage.

Furthermore, Feldman (2000) noted that the miraculous transition problem between stages is compounded by a lack of clarity about within-stage changes, about how progressions within a stage lead the individual through a stage and into a succeeding one. In addition, the depiction of the characteristics of within-stage functioning are too general to account for, or even recognize, the presence of individual differences (e.g., Neimark, 1975). In this regard, Feldman (2000) noted that:

> Piaget's theory is of course notorious for being oblivious to individual differences. . . . In Piaget's rarified theoretical space, there exists only "epistemic subjects," minds disembodied from the rough and tumble of day to day existence, unmarked and uninfluenced by ambient variations in experience. The developing mind was supposed to make its way ineluctably toward mature thought regardless of gender, cultural context, historical period, nutritional input, training, or even biological variations unless they proved to be very extreme indeed (e.g., Down syndrome). (pp. 7–8)

An example of the lack within Piaget's theory of sufficient attention to individual differences occurs in regard to the formal operational stage. There is evidence, for instance, that the emergence of a formal operational thought structure is not a characteristic of all people. As reviewed by Neimark (1975), studies done with older adolescents and adults in Western cultures show that not all individuals attain the level of formal operations (e.g., see Dale, 1970; Martorano, 1977; Papalia, 1972; Tomlinson-Keasey, 1972).

Thus, generalizations about the course of formal operations across the life span within a culture are tentative, but so, too, are such statements when made from a cross-cultural perspective. As summarized by Neimark (1975), people in many cultural settings do not attain formal operational abilities at the average, early-adolescent time that is typical within Western cultural settings (e.g., Douglas & Wong, 1977). In fact, in some non-Western groups there is a failure to ever attain such thinking ability, and Piaget (1969, 1972) himself noted such failures.

Given, then, the problems of within-stage developmental change and the lack of sensitivity to individual differences in the stages described by Piaget, Feldman (2000) concluded that:

> Only the sensori-motor period has a carefully delineated within-stage sequence of six levels from the innate reflexes of looking, listening, grasping and sucking to the beginnings of symbolic thought that appear near the end of the second year of life" (p. 10). . . . The stages are simply too broad and are

intended to cover too large an age span . . . to be plausible in the absence of more fine grained internal roadmaps through them. Indeed, the persistently difficult problems of structures as a whole and where they come from (the miraculous transition problem) has been exacerbated by the scale of the stages and the fact that they seem to appear out of nowhere in most accounts. (p. 19)

Reconceptualizing Piagetian Stages

Although clearly well aware of the problems associated with Piaget's stage theory, Feldman (2000) drew on the work of other cognitive developmentalists (e.g., Case, 1984, 1992a, 1992b; Fischer & Bidell, 1998; Fischer & Pipp, 1984), as well as on his own prior scholarship (e.g., Feldman, 1971, 1980a, 1980b, 1982, 1994, 1995; Feldman & Fowler, 1997), to revise Piaget's four stages of cognitive development in a manner that retained essential features of the stage concept and in a manner responsive to the critiques forwarded about the theory. Feldman (2000) made this contribution by drawing on concepts associated with dynamic, developmental systems ideas (e.g., Ford & Lerner, 1992; Thelen & Smith, 1998).

For instance, drawing on the notion of integrative levels (e.g., Schneirla, 1957), Feldman (2000) proposed a concept of *situated activity,* wherein the *relation* of the activity of the person and the activity of the context becomes the focus of cognitive functioning, as opposed to a focus on within-person symbolic processing. Similarly, Feldman (2000) used the concept of *recursive sequences* (i.e., "a repeating sequence that can be found in more than one place, a kind of loop where the last event in the previous set becomes the first event in the succeeding set, often with a parameter or parameters shifting as the pattern repeats itself over and over again"; Feldman, 2000, p. 16) to depict the changes that occur within the system as a consequence of situated activity.

Feldman (2000) noted, then, that his approach to reconceptualizing Piagetian stages reoriented the theory from an individualistic, within-the-person formulation to a relational and integrative perspective, one that overcame the "split" between internal and external reality (cf. Overton, 1998). Accordingly, Feldman (2000) pointed out that:

Instead of focusing on the processing of information where action is inside the head and where there is a clear demarcation between what is inside and what is outside the mind of the epistemic subject, the situated approach focuses on the ontology of its interactions. The situated paradigm does not decompose the system under study by function but rather by activity. It uses the activity patterns as the categories under study. The situationalist approach is called "enactivism" because it studies the subject as enacting activity patterns that have been differentiated through the history of structural couplings between the subject and its environment. (p. 26)

Cognitive development is propelled through the relationism and integration between the actions of the individual and the situational, or contextual, levels of the developmental system envisioned by Feldman. For example, there is an integration of actions involving the "internal," cognitive world of the person, the maturational changes in the person's brain structure and function (e.g., see Gottlieb, 1992, 1997; Gottlieb et al., 1998), and the particular features of the diverse context within which he or she is embedded. Thus, development occurs via a history of recurring sequences in the biological, psychological, and ecological levels of the system; as more (different portions/features) of the system becomes engaged in this manner, novelty of cognitive structure emerges. Stages are "constructed,"—stages that constitute more dynamic, systems versions of those proposed by Piaget. That is, Feldman (2000) noted that:

The main recursive pattern involves dividing each of the four stages roughly into two halves. An "active construction phase" is followed by an "active extension and application phase" for each of the Piagetian stages. The turning point from construction to application is marked by a "taking of consciousness" process, indicating that the system is generally complete and available to the child, who in turn is aware of the added power of the new system. (p. 31)

Accordingly,

The basic approach to revising the stages of Piaget is to set them as a sequence of recurring efforts to construct overall systems for understanding the world, punctuated by achieving a satisfactory system at about the halfway point of each stage, a "taking of consciousness" recognizing that the system is fully operational, a period devoted to extending and applying the system as widely as possible, followed by increasingly confronting the system's limitations during the latter part of the stage, and finally reaching the point where a new system is apprehended as an acceptable alternative to the prevailing system. Then, starting the basic construction process begins again to build a new, more advanced system; this is where the last phase of the current stage and the first phase of the succeeding stage are simultaneously occurring. Underlying each of the major transitions are a set of maturational changes in the brain and central nervous system that are made possible by the child's activities and that enable the child to construct the next stage's structure. (Feldman, 2000, p. 31)

In sum, Feldman (2000) brought Piagetian theory to a new plane of development through the use of developmental systems notions in describing a four-stage sequence involving the integration of biological, psychological, and sociocultural levels of organization. His formulation addresses many of the key theoretical problems, that he and others have identified as part of Piaget's stage formulations, through inventing an alternative formulation that proposes a "recursive, two-substage process that divides each stage in half" (Feldman, 2000, p. 81).

Conclusions

As illustrated by Feldman's (2000) scholarship, Piaget's theory continues at this writing to be a provocative, engaging formulation. His ideas have elicited theoretical and empirical efforts to defend and/or transcend both his stage ideas and his stage-independent notions. For instance, Piaget's ideas have stimulated scholars to search for stages of cognitive development that might emerge after formal operations or, more generally, to assess changes in adult cognition from a developmental perspective influenced by Piaget (e.g., Kramer, 1989; Labouvie-Vief, 1994; Sinnott, 1989). Similarly, Piaget's ideas have engaged scholars who have been interested in ascertaining whether his theory can be extended or applied to other domains of individual behavior and development.

One example of such an extension exists in regard to the theory proposed by Lawrence Kohlberg. We turn now to a consideration of this theory.

KOHLBERG'S STAGE THEORY OF THE DEVELOPMENT OF MORAL REASONING

Before detailing the features of Lawrence Kohlberg's stage theory, it is useful to note the many reasons why morality is of major scientific concern. Most developmental theorists see morality as a basic dimension of a person's adaptation to his or her world (Eisenberg & Fabes, 1998). Although different theorists define moral behavior and development in markedly distinct ways, all

Lawrence Kohlberg

ideas about moral functioning suggest an adjustment by the person to the social world, an adjustment that serves the dual purpose of fitting the person to his or her society, and at the same time, contributing to the maintenance and perpetuation of that society.

Thus, moral development appears to be a basic component of human adaptation and societal survival. This view is reflected in the position taken by Hogan and Emler (1978):

The capacity of human groups to survive and to extend their domination over the environment is a direct reflection of their ability to solve the problems of social organization and cultural transmission.

Most scholars who have thought seriously about these problems have concluded that they are rooted largely, if not mainly, in the moral socialization of the group. The great social philosophers of recent times—Emile Durkheim, Karl Marx, Max Weber, L. T. Hobhouse, and Sigmund Freud—have all taken the view that human societies are at the core embodiments of moral orders. If we wish to understand that uniquely human invention, culture, we must analyze the relation of the individual to this moral issue. (p. 200)

However, despite this general agreement, there are substantial theoretical differences involved in the specification of this bidirectional relation.

Thus, one should understand the different meanings attached to the term *moral development* in order to place Kohlberg's theory of the development of moral reasoning in its proper theoretical perspective.

Definitions of Moral Development

Despite the practical and scientific importance given to moral functioning, there is no consensus about what constitutes such functioning. What is morality? How does one know if a person is or is not moral? When and how does morality develop, and what are the changes that people go through as they show this development? Theories derived from nature, nurture, and various interactionist or relational conceptions discussed in previous chapters provide different answers to these questions. Indeed, three major types of theories of moral development are present in the current study of human development: theories that stress the role of *nature, nurture,* or the *interaction* between person and context.

Freud's Nature-Oriented Theory

Sigmund Freud's (1949) psychoanalytic theory of psychosexual stage development is discussed next in this chapter. Both to presage this discussion and to reflect our present concern with alternative theoretical views of moral development, suffice it to say here that Freud (1949) took a weak interactionist stance regarding nature and nurture and, as such, saw each stage emerging in an intrinsically determined, universalistic manner. Accordingly, all people experience an oedipal conflict in their third psychosexual stage (the phallic stage). The successful resolution of this conflict will result in the formation of the structure of the personality Freud labeled the *superego*. This structure has two components, the ego ideal and the conscience. The latter represents the internalization into one's mental life of society's rules, laws, codes, ethics, and mores. In short, by about 5 years of age (with the end of the phallic stage), superego development will typically be complete. When this occurs, the person's conscience will be formed as much as it ever can be, and this in turn means that by about 5 years of age the person will have completed his or her moral development.

Of course, there are reasons for incomplete moral development. Freud (1949) specified that females did not experience the same type of conflict in the phallic stage as did males. Males were

thought to develop based on an emotional reaction termed *castration anxiety;* females, not having an identical genital structure, developed based on an emotional reaction termed *penis envy*. Freud held that only castration anxiety could eventually lead to full superego development (and, hence, conscience formation). Because of their biologically fixed anatomical difference, females could never have complete conscience formation. Females would never be as morally developed as males (Bronfenbrenner, 1960).

In addition, moral development could be hampered by particular experiences occurring within the third psychosexual stage (e.g., absence of an appropriate same-sex model might lead to an inability to resolve the oedipal conflict). However, because such experiences are moderated in their possible influence on the basis of whether they occur within the third stage, such experiences are shaped by the nature of the person. Hence, Freud's view of moral development is a nature-based view, and one that emphasizes the completion of moral development in early childhood.

We may underscore here two attributes of Freud's psychoanalytic view of moral development. First, Freud would identify a person as morally developed or not morally developed on the basis of whether that person showed behavior consistent with society's rules. Because of the internalization involved with conscience formation, Freud would only be able to know when a person had completed this formation on the basis of behavioral consistency with these external social rules. Accordingly, to Freud (1949), moral development involves increasing behavioral consistency with society's rules, and as soon as a person shows such behavioral congruence (at about 5 years of age), he or she is completely morally developed. This conception indicates, then, that as long as two people—say a 5-year-old and a 20-year-old—show an identical response in a moral situation, they are identically morally developed.

This observation raises a second point about Freud's views on morality. Freud did not deal with the content of behavior. He did not concern himself with whether a particular response in a situation should be judged as moral in some universalistic sense. Rather, as long as the response conforms to the particular rules of the society, then that response shows internalization, conscience formation, and thus moral development. Hence, because different societies can and do prescribe different sorts of rules for behavior, Freud said there is no universal moral behavior. Rather, what is seen as moral behavior is defined *relative* to a particular society.

In short, Freud's nature-based view focuses on response consistency with society's rules as an index of moral development and takes a *moral relativism* stance about the ethical appropriateness of any given behavior. Interestingly, a theoretical position often diametrically opposed to Freud's takes an identical stance regarding moral responses and moral relativism. That is, some nurture-based social-learning theories converge with psychoanalytic conceptions of moral development.

Nurture-Oriented Social-Learning Theories

Some social-learning theorists see behavior as a response to stimulation (Davis, 1944; McCandless, 1970). Such responses may arise either from external environmental sources, such as lights, sounds, or other people, or from internal bodily sources, such as drives (McCandless, 1970). Nevertheless, in either case, responses become linked to stimulation on the basis of whether reward or punishment is associated with a particular stimulus–response connection (Bijou & Baer, 1961). Those responses leading to reward stay in the person's behavioral repertoire, whereas those associated with punishment do not. The social environment determines which responses will or will not be rewarded, and as such, behavior development involves learning to emit those responses leading to reward and not to emit those responses leading to punishment.

Although different social-learning theorists vary in regard to the details of how such learning takes place (e.g., Bandura & Walters, 1963; Davis, 1944; McCandless, 1970; Sears, 1957), there is general consensus that development involves behavior that increasingly conforms to social rules. Thus, the comparability of this position with Freud's is evident. Moreover, it is clear that behavioral development and moral development are virtually indistinct. There is no qualitative difference between behavior labeled as moral and behavior labeled as social, personal, or anything else for that matter. All behavior follows the principles of social learning, and as such, all behavior involves the conformity of the person's responses to the rules of society.

Thus, like all classes of behavior, moral development involves increasing response consistency to the rules of society; and because there is an *arbitrary* relation between a response and a reward — that is, any particular society may reward any given behavior — there are no responses that necessarily (universally) *have* to be rewarded. Hence, any response may be defined as moral in a given society, and this means that a morally relativistic

stance is taken by the previously noted social learning theorists. By focusing on how nurture processes come to control a person's behavior, these social-learning theorists derive a conception of moral development that, like the nature-based psychoanalytic one, stresses increasing response consistency with society's rules as the index of moral change. This view also takes a morally relativistic stance regarding the content of moral behavior.

Although basing their views on quite distinct ideas about the *basis* of response conformity to societal rules, both psychoanalytic and social-learning theorists would judge that if a young child and an adult emitted the same response in a moral situation, they would, therefore, be equally morally developed. Moreover, theorists from both persuasions might say that if the killing of certain people were condoned in a particular society and, in fact, rewarded (e.g., the murder of Jews by Nazi Germany or the institutionalized killing of some female infants in some primitive societies), this would be morally acceptable behavior insofar as that society was concerned. That is, because of moral relativism, any society may establish any behavior as moral.

Structural Cognitive Developmental Theories

Another view of moral development became increasingly prominent in American social science during the latter half of the twentieth century. This conception not only rejected the focus on responses as an index of moral development but also stressed that a *universalistic* view of moral development must be taken.

Rejecting moral relativism, this view might lead to the claim that those societies that condone killing of other humans are, in fact, immoral societies. This third type of theory is based on the work of Jean Piaget. It was, however, more prominently advanced by theorists who, working from a cognitive developmental position like Piaget's, expanded his initial conceptions.

Piaget (1965) became a major contributor to the topic of moral development by offering a theory that, consistent with his general theory of cognitive development, saw a child's morality as progressing through phases. That is, he saw the child as having "two moralities," as progressing through a two-phase sequence. However, the target of concern in this sequence is not behavior that might require moral action, but rather it is *reasoning* about moral responses in such situations. Thus, in his major statement of his views regarding moral development, Piaget (1965, p. 7) cautioned readers that they will find "no direct analysis of child morality as it is practiced in home and school life or in children's societies. It is the moral judgment that we propose to investigate, not moral behavior."

Kohlberg (1958, 1963a, 1963b), Turiel (1969, 1998), and other followers of the cognitive–developmental view (e.g., Colby, 1978; Colby et al., 1983) believed that there must be a focus on reasoning and not on responses, because the same moral response may be associated with two quite distinct reasons for behavior. Unless one understands the reasons why people believe an act is moral or not, one will be unable to see the complexity of moral development that actually exists (Turiel, 1969, 1998).

On the basis of his research, Piaget (1965) formulated two phases of moral reasoning development in children. In the first phase, labeled *heteronomous morality*, the child is objective in his or her moral judgments. An act is judged right or wrong solely in terms of its consequences. If one breaks a vase, a child in this phase would judge one as morally culpable, regardless of whether the breaking was accidental. This type of judgment is based, Piaget claimed, on the child's moral realism. Rules are seen as unchangeable, externally (i.e., societally) imposed requirements for behavior; these rules are imposed by adults on the child and require unyielding acceptance. Such a "relationship of constraint" is seen as necessary because punishment for disobedience to rules is seen as an automatic consequence of the behavior. In short, acts are objectively judged as good or bad, and if a bad act is committed, there will be *imminent justice* (i.e., automatic, immediate punishment).

However, in the second phase, labeled *autonomous morality*, children become subjective in their moral judgments. This means that, when judging the moral rightness or wrongness of an act, children take intentions into account. If one breaks a vase out of spite or anger, one would be judged morally wrong. But if one breaks the vase because of clumsiness, no moral culpability would be seen. This second type of judgment, Piaget claimed, is based on the child's *moral rationality*. Rules are seen as outcomes of agreements between people in a relation not of social constraint but rather of cooperation and autonomy. That is, each person is an equal in such a relation, and as such, rules are made in relation to the mutual interest of those involved. Thus, acts are judged good or bad in terms of the principles of this "contract." Whatever punishment is associated with violation of contract rules is determined by humans and is not a consequence of some reflexive, automatic punisher.

Accordingly, although a 7-year-old and an 18-year-old might behave in similar ways in a moral situation—for example, neither might cheat on a test or steal from a friend—the similar responses would not mean that the reasons underlying the responses were similar. The younger person might not cheat or steal simply because of a belief that he or she would be physically punished for it. However, the 18-year-old might see such reasoning as "immature." Here the reason for not stealing might involve an implicit agreement among friends to respect each other's rights and property. The fact that there may be physical punishment associated with stealing would be irrelevant to a reason based on such a conception of mutual trust. Thus, according to Piaget, because of the presence of such different types of moral reasoning, the 7-year-old and the 18-year-old would not have similar levels of moral development, despite their similar responses.

In short, Piaget (1965) believed that all people pass through these two phases of moral reasoning. In other words, he suggested a sequence that first involves an objective and concrete morality based on constraints imposed by the powerful (e.g., adults) on the nonpowerful (e.g., children). Second, a subjective morality follows, based on an abstract understanding of the implicit contracts involved in relationships marked by cooperation and autonomy.

Piaget's denial of the importance of focusing just on the moral response and his stress on an ordering to moral reasoning represented an approach to the study of moral development that was quite distinct from the morally relativistic, response-centered approaches of psychoanalysis and social-learning theory. As such, it stimulated considerable interest among developmental researchers, especially because it offered a provocative framework for assessing changes in morality beyond the level of early childhood. However, the interest it stimulated soon led to Piaget's theory being replaced as the focus of developmental research inquiry. Following Piaget's general cognitive–developmental–theoretical approach, Lawrence Kohlberg (1958, 1963a, 1963b) obtained evidence that Piaget's two-phase model was not sufficient to account for all the types of changes in moral reasoning through which people progressed. Kohlberg devised a theory involving several stages of moral-reasoning development in order to encompass all the qualitative changes he discerned. Interest in moral development in the 1960s and 1970s was centered on assessing the usefulness of Kohlberg's universalistic theory. Problems with the specifics of his theory, issues that will be noted later, have led in more recent years to a waning of interest in Kohlberg's work and, instead, to a focus on other approaches to moral thought and behavior (e.g., Damon, 1997; Eisenberg & Fabes, 1998; Turiel, 1998). Nevertheless, because of its historical importance, both as a creative and provocative alternative to behavior-focused conceptions of moral development *and* as an instance of the application of cognitive developmental theory to a critical domain of social and cultural significance, it is useful to discuss Kohlberg's theory.

Features of Kohlberg's Theory of Moral-Reasoning Development

Kohlberg's theory of moral development, like Piaget's, is based on the idea that by focusing only on the response in a moral situation, one may ignore important distinctions in people's moral reasoning at different points in their life span. These reasoning differences, in fact, may give different meaning to the exact same response at various developmental levels. Because the response alone does not necessarily give a clue about underlying reasoning, "an individual's response must be examined in light of how he perceives the moral situation, what the meaning of the situation is to the person responding, and the relation of his choice to that meaning: The cognitive and emotional processes in making moral judgments" (Turiel, 1969, p. 95).

Because of these issues, Kohlberg rejected response-oriented approaches to understanding development and chose to investigate the reasons underlying moral responses (Kohlberg, 1958, 1963a). He devised a way to find the underlying reasons through his construction of a moral-development interview. Information from this interview provided the data for the theory he formulated. As such, to understand the empirical origin of Kohlberg's ideas, one must consider his method of studying moral reasoning.

Kohlberg's Method of Assessing Moral Reasoning

To study moral reasoning, Kohlberg devised a series of stories, each presenting imaginary moral dilemmas. We will present one such story (see Colby et al., 1983) and then evaluate the features it offers in providing a technique for assessing moral reasoning:

> One day air raid sirens began to sound. Everyone realized that a hydrogen bomb was going to be dropped on the city by the enemy, and that the only way to survive was to be in a bomb shelter. Not everyone

had bomb shelters, but those who did ran quickly to them. Since Mr. and Mrs. Jones had built a shelter, they immediately went to it where they had enough air space inside to last them for exactly five days. They knew that after five days the fallout would have diminished to the point where they could safely leave the shelter. If they left before that, they would die. There was enough air for the Joneses only. Their next door neighbors had not built a shelter and were trying to get in. The Joneses knew that they would not have enough air if they let the neighbors in, and that they would all die if they came inside. So they refused to let them in.

So now the neighbors were trying to break the door down in order to get in. Mr. Jones took his rifle and told them to go away or else he would shoot. They would not go away. So he either had to shoot them or let them come into the shelter.

What features of this story make it a moral dilemma? First, like all of Kohlberg's moral dilemma stories (Turiel, 1969), the story presents the listener with a conflict. In this particular story, the conflict involves the need to choose between two culturally unacceptable alternatives: killing others so that you may survive or allowing others, yourself, and your family to die. The story presents a dilemma because it puts the listener in a conflict situation in which no response is clearly the only conceivably acceptable one. As such, the particular response is irrelevant. What is of concern is the reasoning used to resolve the conflict. Thus, Kohlberg would ask the listener not just to tell him *what* Mr. Jones should do, but *why* Mr. Jones should do it.

Thus, Kohlberg would first ask, "What should Mr. Jones do?" Next he would ask, "Does he have the right to shoot his neighbors if he feels that they would all die if he let them in because there would not be enough air to last them very long? Why?" Then, "Does he have the right to keep his neighbors out of his shelter even though he knows they will die if he keeps them out? Why?" And finally Kohlberg would ask, "Does he have the right to let them in if he knows they will all die? Why?"

On the basis of an elaborate and complicated system for scoring the answers people give to questions about this and other dilemmas in his interview (Kohlberg, 1958, 1963a; Kurtines & Greif, 1974), a system which has undergone considerable revision (Colby et al., 1983), Kohlberg classified people into different reasoning categories. This classification led him to formulate the idea that there existed a sequence in the types of reasons people offered for their responses to moral dilemmas. The types of moral reasoning people used passed through a series of qualitatively different stages. However, contrary to the two cognitive developmental phases Piaget (1965) proposed, Kohlberg first (1958, 1963a) argued that there are six stages in the development of moral reasoning and asserted that these stages were divided into three levels, with each level being associated with two stages. Kohlberg (1976, 1978) and his collaborators (Colby, 1978, 1979; Colby et al., 1983) later revised the theory, believing that they had evidence for the existence of only five stages; that is, in the revised theory, the last level had only one stage. In addition, with the stages redefined, new systems of scoring moral development were developed. Nevertheless, in both the initial and the latter version of the theory, both the levels and the stages within and across them are seen to form a universal and invariant sequence of progression.

It is useful to describe the stages and levels in both the initial and the latter formulations of Kohlberg's theory. Such a presentation illustrates the active character of developmental theory, and the fact that such theories are not "carved in stone" but are themselves developing sets of ideas. Kohlberg and his associates revised the theory because of research evidence and conceptual criticism that could not be addressed well by the theory as it stood initially.

No age limits are typically associated with Kohlberg's stages or levels. However, because in both versions of the theory the first stage does seem to rest on some minimal representational ability, we may presume it does not emerge prior to the preoperational period of Piaget's theory (i.e., somewhere between 2 and 6 or 7 years of age). Moreover, many of the subsequent stages of moral reasoning seem to be dependent on formal operational thinking (Kohlberg, 1973). As such, they may be expected to be involved more typically with adolescence and adulthood, at least insofar as Western culture is concerned (Simpson, 1974).

Levels and Stages in the Former Version of Kohlberg's Theory of Moral-Reasoning Development

Kohlberg's (1958, 1963) earlier formulation of his theory included three levels of moral reasoning development. There were two stages within each level.

Level 1: Preconventional moral reasoning. The first two stages of moral reasoning emerge within the first level. Although these two stages involve qualitatively different thought processes about moral conflicts, they do have a general similarity. For both stages a person's moral reasoning in-

volves reference to external, physical events and objects—as opposed to such things as societal standards—as the source for decisions about moral rightness or wrongness.

Stage 1: Obedience and punishment orientation—The reference to external, physical things is well illustrated in this first stage of moral development. Kohlberg saw this stage as being dominated by moral reasoning involving reference merely to obedience or punishment by powerful figures. Thus, an act is judged wrong or right if it is or is not associated with punishment. Reasoning here is similar to what we have seen involved in Piaget's first phase of moral reasoning. In Stage 1, a person reasons that one must be obedient to powerful authority because that authority is powerful—it can punish you. Acts, then, are judged as not moral only because they are associated with these external, physical sanctions.

Stage 2: Naively egotistic orientation—Reference to external physical events is also made in this stage. However, an act is judged right if it is involved with an external event that satisfies the needs of the person or, sometimes, the needs of someone very close to the person (e.g., a father, mother, husband, or wife). Thus, even though stealing is wrong—because it is associated with punishment—reasoning at this level might lead to the assertion that stealing is right if the act of stealing is instrumental in satisfying a need of the person. For example, if the person was very hungry, then, in that instance, stealing food would be seen as a moral act.

Although this second stage also involves major reference to external, physical events as the source of rightness or wrongness, the perspective of self-needs (or, sometimes, the needs of significant others) is also brought into consideration (albeit egocentrically). Thus, the development in this second stage gradually brings about a transition of perspective, a perspective involving other people. This transition then leads to the next level of moral reasoning.

Level 2: Conventional moral reasoning. In this second level of moral reasoning, the person's thinking involves reference to acting as others expect. Acts are judged right if they conform to roles that others (i.e., society) think a person should play. An act is seen as moral if it accords with the established order of society.

Stage 3: Good-person orientation—Here, the person is oriented toward being seen as a good boy or a good girl by others. The person sees society as providing certain general, or stereotyped, roles for people. If you act in accord with these role prescriptions, you will win the approval of other people, and, hence, you will be labeled a good person. Thus, acts that help others, that lead to the approval of others, or that simply should—given certain role expectations by society—lead to the approval of others will be judged as moral.

Stage 4: Authority and social order maintenance orientation—A more formal view of society's rules and institutions emerges in this stage. Rather than just acting in accord with the rules and institutions of society to earn approval, the person comes to see these rules and institutions as ends in themselves. That is, acts that are in accord with the maintenance of the rules of society and that allow the institutions of social order (e.g., the government) to continue functioning are seen as moral. The social order and institutions of society must be maintained for their own sake; they are ends in themselves. A moral person is one who "does his or her duty" and maintains the established authority, social order, and institutions of society. A person is not moral if his or her acts are counter to these goals.

Reasoning at this level involves a consideration of a person's role in reference to society. In addition, at Stage 4, in contrast with Stage 3, moral thinking involves viewing the social rule to do one's duty as the basis of being moral; however, this thinking may lead the person to consider the alternative, or the reverse, side of the issue. The person may begin to think about what society must do in order for it to be judged as moral. If and when such considerations begin to emerge, the person will gradually make a transition into the next level of moral reasoning.

Level 3: Postconventional moral reasoning. This is the last level in the development of moral reasoning. Moral judgments are made in reference to the view that there are arbitrary, subjective elements in social rules. The rules and institutions of society are not absolute, but are relative. Other rules, equally as reasonable, may have been established. Thus, the rules and institutions of society are no longer viewed as ends in themselves, but as being subjective. Such postconventional reasoning, which is related to formal operational thinking—and thus to adolescence as well—also develops through two stages.

Stage 5: Contractual legalistic orientation—In this stage, similar to Piaget's (1965) second phase, the person recognizes that a reciprocity, an implicit contract, exists between self and society. One must conform to society's rules and institutions (do one's duty) because society, in turn, will do its duty and provide one with certain protections. Thus, the institutions of society are not seen as ends in themselves but, instead, as part of a contract.

From this view, a person would not steal because this would violate the implicit social contract, which includes mutual respect for the rights of other members of the society.

Thus, the person sees any specific set of rules in society as somewhat arbitrary. But one's duty is to fulfill one's part of the contract (e.g., not to steal from others), just as it is necessary for society to fulfill its part of the contract (e.g., it will provide institutions and laws protecting one's property from being stolen). The person sees an element of subjectivism in the rules of society, and this recognition may lead into the last stage of moral reasoning development.

Stage 6: Conscience, or principle, orientation—Here there is more formal recognition that societal rules are arbitrary. One sees not only that a given implicit contract between a person and society is a somewhat arbitrary, subjective phenomenon but also that one's interpretation of the meaning and boundaries of such a contract is necessarily subjective. One person may give one interpretation to these rules, whereas another person may give a different interpretation. From this perspective, the ultimate appeal for moral judgments must be made to one's own conscience.

The person comes to believe that there may be rules that transcend those of specific given social contracts. Since a person's own subjective view of this contract must be seen as legitimate, a person's own views must be the ultimate source of moral judgments. One's conscience, one's set of personal principles, must be appealed to as the ultimate source of moral decisions. To summarize, Stage 6 reasoning involves an appeal to transcendent universal principles of morality, rules that find their source in the person's own conscience.

Levels and Stages in the Revised Version of Kohlberg's Theory of Moral-Reasoning Development

In the revised version of the theory (Colby, 1978; Colby et al., 1983; Kohlberg 1976, 1978), there were again three levels of moral reasoning development, generally labeled as in the former version. The last level, however, includes only one stage. The first two levels each have two stages. The major change in the theory is in the definition of these five stages. They focus on the person's social perspective *moving toward increasingly greater scope* (i.e., including more people and their institutions) *and greater abstraction* (i.e., moving from physicalistic reasoning to reasoning about values, rights, and implicit contracts). The levels are seen in essentially the same way as in the former version; however, the characteristics of each stage within each level have been changed in the ways I have described.

Level 1: Preconventional.

Stage 1: Heteronomous morality—Here the person has an egocentric point of view. The person does not consider the interests of others or recognize that they differ from his or her interests; the person does not relate to others' point of view. Actions are considered physically rather than in terms of the psychological interests of others. There is a confusion of authority's perspective with one's own.

Stage 2: Individualism, instrumental purpose, and exchange—Here the person has a concrete individualistic perspective. The person is aware that everybody has interests to pursue and that these can conflict. From this perspective, right is relative.

Level 2: Conventional.

Stage 3: Mutual interpersonal expectations, relationships, and interpersonal conformity—Here, the perspective of the individual exists in relationships with other individuals. The person is aware of shared feelings, agreements, and expectations which take primacy over individual interests— and he or she relates points of view through the concrete "golden rule" of putting oneself "in the other person's shoes." The person does not yet consider a generalized system perspective.

Stage 4: Social system and conscience—Here, the person differentiates the societal point of view from interpersonal agreements or motives. At this stage, the person takes a point of view of the system that defines roles and rules and considers individual relations in terms of the roles they play in the system.

Level 3: Postconventional or principled.

Stage 5: Social contract or utility and individual rights—This stage may also be termed the *prior-to-society perspective*. The rational individual is aware of values and rights prior to social attachments and contracts. Such a person integrated perspectives by formal mechanisms of agreement, contract, objective impartiality, and due process. He or she considers moral and legal points of view. The person recognizes that these sometimes conflict, and may find it difficult to integrate them.

Characteristics of Moral Reasoning Stage Development

Kohlberg and his associates (e.g., Colby, 1978, 1979; Colby et al., 1983; Turiel, 1969) did more than just describe the ordering and nature of

Eliot Turiel

these stages. They have also attempted to describe the nature of intraindividual *change* from one stage to another. Turiel (1969), for example, noted that development through the stages of moral reasoning is a gradual process. Transition from one stage to another is not abrupt; rather, movement is characterized by gradual shifts in the most frequent type of reasoning given by a person over the course of development. Stage movement is characterized, then, by gradual shifts in the modal type of reasoning given by a person over the course of development. As illustrated in our discussion of Piaget's concept of décalage, such stage mixture means that at any given time a person will be functioning at more than one stage.

Accordingly, one must have a large sample of instances of a person's moral reasonings in order to accurately determine that person's stage of moral reasoning. Only such a large sample will allow one to discover the modal (i.e., the most frequently occurring) type of reasoning the person uses to make moral decisions. Although research and writing by some psychologists interested in moral development (e.g., Bandura & McDonald, 1963) have not attended to the existence and implications of stage mixture, Turiel (1969) claimed that stage mixture is an ever-present facet of the developmental processes involved in moral reasoning.

In addition, Turiel (1969) indicated that stage mixture is a necessary component of the development of moral reasoning. From a cognitive developmental perspective, changes in moral reasoning level should come about as a result of disequilibrium, which of course would necessitate the reestablishment of equilibrium. Turiel (1969) demonstrated that when children are exposed to reasoning at a level one stage higher than their own, disequilibrium is caused. That is, the child perceives a contradiction between his or her own level of moral reasoning and the next higher one, and the conflict produced by this recognition is the product of disequilibrium. In order to achieve equilibration, the child must accommodate to this higher stage, and this results in the child's movement toward a higher stage of moral reasoning.

But how is the child able to perceive a discrepancy between his or her own reasoning and reasoning that is from one stage higher and, thus, not modally the child's? Turiel suggested that the answer involves stage mixture. Since the person is functioning at more than one stage at the same time, reasoning structures available from the higher stage enable the person to perceive the discrepancy. Stage mixture, then, is not only a ubiquitous component of moral reasoning development but also a necessary component. As Turiel said, "Stage mixture serves to facilitate the perception of contradictions, making the individual more susceptible to disequilibrium and conse-

Anne Colby

quently more likely to progress developmentally" (1969, p. 130).

Data reported by Colby and colleagues (1983) provided support for the presence of stage mixture. Kohlberg (1958) studied a group of males who had been followed longitudinally since origi-

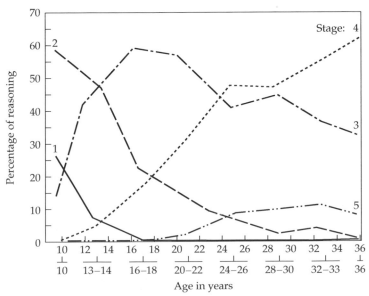

FIGURE 15.4
Mean percentage of reasoning at each stage for each age group.
Source: Colby et al. (1983).

nal testing. When first tested, the people ranged from late childhood to middle adolescence. Figure 15.4 presents the percentage of reasoning at each of five stages of development for the various age levels through which the people progressed over the course of the study. For example, at the 10-year-old level, most moral reasoning was at Stage 2, but there were several instances of reasoning at other stages. In turn, at the 36-year-old level, most reasoning was at Stage 4, but reasoning at several other stages is also evident.

Of course, people may experience differing degrees of cognitive conflict—and, therefore, disequilibrium—in their lives. Accordingly, they may pass through the stages of moral reasoning at different rates—if in fact they pass through them at all. Thus, different people are likely to reach different levels of moral thinking at any one time in life. This last observation leads beyond just description of the attributes of Kohlberg's theory. We are led to consider whether his formulations are useful for indicating what processes lead or do not lead to advances in moral reasoning. Indeed, we may consider more generally the overall utility of Kohlberg's theory.

Evaluating Kohlberg's Theory

Evaluations of Kohlberg's work can be classified into two areas. First, there are those who have considered Kohlberg's method of evaluating moral reasoning development. Second, there are those who have tried to determine whether moral reasoning follows the stage-like sequence Kohlberg formulated. Evidence from the first area of evaluation resulted in scholars being quite cautious about generalizing information about moral reasoning derived from the use of Kohlberg's interview. Although consideration of information relevant to the second area supported the idea that there are qualitative changes across life in moral reasoning, the data also indicated that the changes were not completely consistent with the order suggested in Kohlberg's theory.

To illustrate the evaluations arising in regard to methodological issues, it is useful to note that Kurtines and Greif (1974) identified several major problems with how scores were derived from Kohlberg's interview, problems relating to a lack of standardization in the administration of the interview and to subjectivity and ambiguity in scoring. Similarly, Eisenberg-Berg (1976) indicated that all dilemmas in the interviews pertained only to constraint situations (i.e., to a person's being pressured by two moral values affecting himself or herself). Prosocial issues, such as risking one's

own life to save someone else's, were never evaluated (cf. Eisenberg & Fabes, 1998).

In turn, the role of culture in shaping moral reasoning has been a basis for evaluating Kohlberg's method (e.g., Shweder, 1982, Shweder et al., 1998; Turiel, 1998). In one early critique of this sort, Simpson (1974) noted that the interview dilemmas and the scoring system for them were culturally biased, that is, morality was seen from an American viewpoint, and as such, only those answers that were consistent with American moral values were scored as moral. For example, Simpson (1974) noted that one typical dilemma contrasts *property rights* with the *value of human life.* A man's wife is dying of a disease for which a pharmacist has developed a cure. However, the drug is quite expensive, and because the man cannot afford it, he breaks into the pharmacy to steal the pharmacist's property (the drug) so that his wife may be saved.

Simpson saw cultural bias in the content and scoring of this dilemma. First, not all cultures have notions of property rights that would make the situation a dilemma. She noted that "The Americans who believe that one has a right to anything one can pay for and that taxes on income and private property and restrictive use laws are wrong or bad have very little content in common with members of a culture where little or no property is seen as private and rights over it are group rights and held in common" (Simpson 1974, p. 96). Simpson noted, too, that the scoring attached to this interview story is also biased in that Kohlberg (1971, p. 174) claimed that "anyone who understands the values of life and property will recognize that life is morally more valuable than property." Simpson contended that this view not only falsely reflects actual moral practice even in the United States but also reflects a lack of appreciation of the nature of other cultures.

First, she noted that in America it is human life, and not all life, that is seen as sacred. However, even the value of human life may be secondary to other values. Those who kill or rape others are often put to death, and insofar as property is concerned, those "who steal secrets from the government to give to other governments" (Simpson, 1974, p. 97) are liable in times of war to receive the death penalty. In turn, in cultures such as that of the Eskimo, it was appropriate to kill the aged or newborns because they might consume resources needed for the survival of the major part of the group. Similarly, Gilligan (1982) argued that Kohlberg's theory was also sex biased. She noted that Kohlberg developed the stages in his theory from the responses of males to his interview questions, and that the resulting content of his stages and the scores generated for maturity of moral reasoning did not give sufficient attention to the "voice" of females (a "voice," Gilligan contended, which gave greater weight to interpersonal and caring issues as opposed to the more interpersonal justice ones stressed in Kohlberg's system). As a consequence, Gilligan (1982) argued that Kohlberg underestimated the moral development of females.

Most research has not supported Gilligan's claims, in that, females' and males' moral development scores within Kohlberg's system are comparable (Brabeck, 1983; Turiel, 1998). For instance, in an analysis of several studies of gender differences in moral orientation (Jaffe & Hyde, 2000), both men and women were found to use the same modes of moral reasoning (i.e., both groups employed care and justice reasoning). Nevertheless, Gilligan's point—that there are ways to conceptualize moral reasoning development other than the one presented by Kohlberg—is a useful one, especially when seen in relation to the criticisms leveled by Simpson (1974) and Kurtines and Greif (1974).

Moreover, in regard to empirical appraisals of Kohlberg's theory, although there is strong evidence for the existence of an age-associated development toward principled reasoning, the weight of available data suggests that the sequence of such change does not appear as inevitable as Kohlberg predicted. That is, one the one hand, data collected in the longitudinal study conducted by Kohlberg

and his colleagues (Colby et al., 1983) provided support for the view that people from late childhood to the early part of the middle-adult years go through the stages of moral reasoning in the manner Kohlberg specifies. Figure 15.5, derived from Colby and colleagues (1983), shows a smooth, continuous increase from age 10 to 36 in the average moral maturity score derived from responses to the dilemmas of the interview, and Table 15.3 shows that there is an age-associated increase in the percentage of people reasoning at each of the succeeding stages.

Data other than those provided by Kohlberg and his colleagues also suggest an age-associated progression toward principle- or intention-based, as opposed to consequence-based, moral reasoning (e.g., Davidson, Robbins, & Swanson, 1978; Edwards, 1974; Eisenberg-Berg, 1979; Hewitt, 1975; Jadack, Hyde, Moore, & Keller, 1995; Keasey, 1974; Lourenço, 1990; Perry & McIntire, 1995; Walker & Taylor, 1991; Weiner & Peter, 1973). However, other data indicate that young children can be trained to use intentions in making moral judgments (Hill & Enzie, 1977) and that, even without explicit training, children as young as kindergarten-age youth take intentions into account when making moral judgments (Elkind & Dabek, 1977).

In turn, and as implied by the criticisms of Kurtines and Greif (1974), the method one uses to measure moral development is related to whether one finds evidence for the use of intentions in

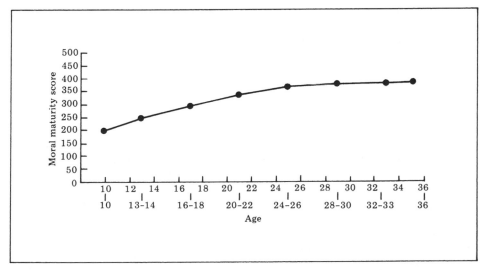

FIGURE 15.5
Mean moral maturity score for each group.
Source: Colby et al. (1983).

TABLE 15.3

Percentage of Subjects of Each Age Group at Each Stage

Global stage	Age (years)							
	10	13–14	16–18	20–22	24–26	28–30	32–33	36
1/2	47.6	8.1	2.2	0	0	0	0	0
2	33.3	16.2	11.1	0	0	0	0	0
2/3	14.3	56.8	17.8	9.4	8.0	0	0	0
3	4.8	16.2	44.4	31.3	12.0	16.2	8.7	0
3/4	0	2.7	24.4	40.6	48.0	51.4	47.8	44.4
4	0	0	0	18.8	16.0	18.9	30.4	44.4
4/5	0	0	0	0	16.0	13.5	13.0	11.1
Mcsn MMS	189	246	290	327	357	361	369	375
SD MMS	31.4	37.7	43.7	36.1	49.1	42.3	41.5	25.6
N	21	37	46	33	25	38	23	9

Note. From "A Longitudinal Study of Moral Judgment," by A. L. Colby, J. Kohlberg, J. Gibbs, & M. Lieberman (1983). *Monographs of the Society for Research in Child Development, 48,* p. 46. Copyright © 1983 by Society for Research in Child Development. Reprinted with permission.

making moral judgments (Chandler, Greenspan, & Barenboim, 1973; Feldman et al., 1976). Moreover, and as implied by the criticisms of Simpson (1974), there is evidence that cultural influences, rather than age- or stage-related variation, is associated with changes in moral development scores (White, Bushnell, & Regnemer, 1978). In turn, fluctuation in moral judgments occurs in relation to the time of testing during which assessments of moral development are made (Kuhn, 1976).

In sum, although information about the intentions involved in an act can be and is increasingly used from early childhood through the adult years in making moral judgments, this information is used at young ages and may not follow the stage-like order suggested in Kohlberg's theory. Although scholars have attempted to support Kohlberg's theory in the face of such evidence (e.g., Colby, 1978; Kuhn, 1976; Turiel, 1998), many of the problems identified by the critics of Kohlberg's theory remains unaddressed. Simply, then, it is appropriate to conclude that, in contradiction to what would be expected on the basis of Kohlberg's theory, both methodological variables and substantive ones (relating to gender, culture, experience/training, or time of testing) may influence moral judgments.

Conclusions

Kohlberg's theory of moral reasoning development is not, at this writing, a major frame for research in moral development theory or research (e.g., see Damon, 1997; Eisenberg & Fabes, 1998; Turiel, 1998), due in large part to the conceptual, methodological, and empirical problems associated with it. Nevertheless, his work continues to texture the scholarship about morality that is being conducted by contemporary scholars. That is, contemporary research *does* reflect Kohlberg's concern with people's reasons for moral action and his stress on developmental changes that may be associated with thought—and behavior—related to moral functioning (Damon, 1997; Eisenberg & Fabes, 1998; Turiel, 1998).

Turiel (1998) summarized the contemporary status and contribution of Kohlberg's theory by noting that:

> Kohlberg's influence on subsequent research and theories is, in important respects, separate from the influence of his particular formulation of stages of moral development, or even from the theoretical viewpoint he espoused. Many advance alternative theoretical paradigms . . . many propose formulations divergent from that of Kohlberg. Yet, Kohlberg has influenced discourse about the psychology of moral development in several ways. One is that there is greater recognition of the need to ground psychological explanations in philosophical considerations about morality. . . . Another of these influences is that in many current formulations . . . investigators now think that children are, in an active and positive sense, integrated into their social relationships with adults and peers, and that morality is not solely or even primarily an external or unwanted imposition on them. (pp. 867–868)

Accordingly, as is the case for Piaget, Kohlberg's influence on contemporary thought extends beyond the specifics of his theory. This broad influence is true as well for the next stage theorist we discuss, Sigmund Freud. Indeed, it is arguably the case that no theory of human development has had a more general influence on Western cultural thought than that of Freud.

FREUD'S STAGE THEORY OF PSYCHOSEXUAL DEVELOPMENT

Sigmund Freud was born in Freiberg, Moravia in 1856 and died in London in 1939. He lived most of his life, however, in Vienna, where in 1881 he obtained his medical degree. Although thus able to practice medicine, Freud became a research physician after graduation and undertook a series of studies of the nervous system. However, Freud was forced to leave the university setting and his neurological research; although he had shown himself to be an excellent scientific researcher, he was unable to support his family on the basis of the limited income given to low-status faculty members, and he was unable to receive faculty advancement because of the anti-Semitism that was prevalent in Austrian universities at that time. Freud thus left university life and entered medical practice.

Freud began this private practice as an associate of another physician, Joseph Breuer. Breuer

Sigmund Freud

had been working to a great extent in the treatment of hysteria, a disease believed to afflict only women because it was held that the source of the disease was damage to the uterus. Breuer had successfully treated this disorder through the application of what he termed the "talking cure" (Boring, 1950). Breuer hypnotized his patients and allowed them to talk about the emotional events associated with their difficulty. Thus, through use of this *catharsis* or emotional release, Breuer was able to cure his hysterical patients. Freud readily adopted this method but soon modified its use. He found it equally, if not more, effective to allow his patients to talk completely freely about whatever was on their minds. Thus, by supporting such *free association* in his patients, Freud found that the same emotional releases could be produced without the use of hypnosis. Freud soon found that once such emotions were released, his patients would talk about things that they themselves thought they had forgotten.

With this use of the free association method, Freud was able to get his patients to reveal to him, and to themselves, what he termed *repressed* memories. These were memories of unpleasant feelings (affects or emotions) or events that patients had experienced and—because of their negative emotional valence—had actively kept out of their awareness. Because of the negative affective connotation of these experiences, they had repressed the memory of them; they had actively kept these unpleasant memories in an area of their mind, the unconscious, that contained only material normally not present in awareness. Thus, through the use of such methods as free association, as well as a subsequent method he developed—dream interpretation—Freud was able to discover the repressed, emotion-laden memories stored in the unconscious of his patients. He was also giving himself the major tools for the method of therapy he was developing and discovering information for his theory of development and personality. Thus Freud's practice resulted in two things: a method of treatment of emotional, or neurotic, disorders, termed *psychoanalysis,* and a psychoanalytic theory of development.

Freud's methods allowed him to ascertain his patients' repressed memories. He saw that most of these memories were of events that had occurred very early in the lives of his now-adult patients. In fact, he discovered that these events occurred in the first 5 years of their lives. On the basis of these retrospective accounts by adult patients of their early years of life, Freud was able to formulate a theory of affective (or emotional) development. To understand the characteristics of this theory, it is useful to first deal with a concept central in all the developments that concerned Freud. This is the concept of libido.

The Concept of Libido

Freud was trained as a scientist and, understandably, was influenced by work in many areas of scientific inquiry, including the field of physics. In that field, notions relating to the concept of physical energy were being investigated, and one such idea—the law of the conservation of energy—appears to have had a profound influence on Freud's thinking. This principle states that physical energy can neither be created nor destroyed, but only transformed. For example, in the human visual system, energy in the form of light rays is transformed into chemical energy (when light hits the retina of the eye), which in turn becomes electrical energy (when the chemicals decompose and cause nerve-cell firing to occur). When this electrical energy reaches the appropriate area of the brain, we experience vision.

Freud saw a parallel between the transformation of energy in the physical world and events that occur in people's mental life. That is, Freud hypothesized that humans are really just complicated energy systems (Hall, 1954). By this he meant that human mental life is energized just as other physical systems are energized. Human mental life, he hypothesized, is governed by its own energy, and this human mental (or psychic) energy he termed *libido*.

To Freud, libido could not be created or destroyed. Humans are born with a finite amount of libido. Instead of this psychic energy being transformed into another type of energy, an alternative type of transformation was seen to take place: Libido changes its area of localization within the body over the course of development. Thus, people are born with psychic energy, libido—which energizes their psychological functioning, enabling them to perform such functions as thinking, perceiving, and remembering. But, although a person is born with a finite amount of libido, this libido is transformed throughout the course of a person's development in that it changes its area of localization within the body.

This alteration in bodily location is the essential determinant of a person's developmental stages. The law governing the movement of the libido is the factor accounting for developmental stage progression. Analogous to Piaget's equilibration model, libido movement is the continual process underlying stage development. But before we turn to a consideration of how libidinal movement accounts for stage progression, let us first consider some implications of the fact that libido is centered in different bodily areas, or zones, at different times in development.

As we have noted, libido is energy. This energy is not held to be distributed evenly across all parts of the body. Rather, at different points in time, it is thought to be localized in specific bodily zones. When energy is present in a zone, all the person's libido is concentrated in that one bodily area. Such an accumulation of energy would lead to an excessive amount of tension if there were not some way for this energy-produced tension to be released. Freud specified, however, that such excessive tension could be avoided, that it could be released, if stimulation were applied to the appropriate bodily area. For example, if one's libido were centered in the area of the mouth, then stimulation of this zone would release tension. An unpleasant feeling-state (tension) would be gotten rid of, and in turn a pleasurable feeling (tension reduction) would occur. We may term this tension reduction resulting from appropriate stimulation *gratification*. Stimulation of the appropriate bodily zone would provide libidinal gratification.

The area of the body wherein the libido is centered is termed an *erogenous zone*. (This term implies sexual arousal, but we will see that Freud had a broad view of what "sexual" meant.) Sexual gratification was seen as involving not only the genital areas (although at specific stages, it did mean this) but also any bodily area wherein the libido was centered was an erogenous zone of the body and was therefore, capable of providing as much sexual gratification as that provided by any other such zone. Accordingly, such sexual gratification could be obtained through appropriate manipulation and stimulation of that area (Hall, 1954).

In sum, Freud said that a person's libido "travels" to different zones of the body over the course of development and, depending on where the libido is centered, the person may receive sexual gratification from stimulation to that area. That is, such stimulation would give pleasure to the person in that it would diminish the tensions that tend to accumulate in such an erogenous zone due to the focusing of libido there. Hence, Freud conceptualized in this way the means through which people's emotions were gratified. In turn, we may also see how a person's emotions cannot be gratified. If the appropriate stimulation to a bodily area does not occur, then an unpleasant feeling-state will remain. Freud believed that such an event would have a profoundly negative effect on the person's emotional/sexual (or psychosexual) development. To understand these effects, we need to consider the sequences that Freud postulated as characterizing the changes in bodily localization of the libido.

The Psychosexual Stages

Freud saw the libido as changing its site of bodily localization several times in the course of development. Hence, several psychosexual stages resulted from this libidinal movement.

The Oral Stage

Freud believed that the location of the libido at a particular point in a person's development follows the sequence of what he saw to be invariant, universal stages. According to Freud, the emergence of these stages is primarily maturationally determined, but the effects of these emerging stages on a person's psychosexual functioning are dependent on the specifics of that person's experience.

Accordingly, Freud postulated that the first erogenous zone in development is the oral zone. Here, the libido is centered in the mouth region, where it remains for approximately the first year of the child's life. The infant at this stage obtains gratification through stimulation of this oral area, which can occur in two ways. The infant can bring things into its mouth and suck on them, or later, when teeth develop, the infant can bite on things. The first portion of the oral stage, therefore, can be thought of as the oral incorporative (or oral sucking) period. Again, stimulation appropriate for the obtaining of gratification would involve sucking on things such as the mother's nipple or the thumb.

We have indicated, however, that it is possible for such sexual gratification not to occur. For example, an infant might be deprived of some needed oral stimulation because of frequent or prolonged mother absence. When the infant's attempts to obtain appropriate stimulation are blocked (or frustrated) serious problems in the infant's psychosexual development may ensue. If such frustration is extensive enough, *fixation* may occur. That is, there may be an arrest of libidinal development. Some of the infant's libido will remain fixed at the oral zone; when the infant develops to the next stage—in accordance with its maturational timetable—all the libido that could have moved on to the next erogenous zone will not now do so. Thus, some libido will always be tied into the person's oral zone, fixated there for the rest of life. Such an oral fixation during the oral

stage will mean that, for the rest of his or her life, the person will attempt to obtain the gratification missed earlier. To put it another way, the emotional and/or psychosexual problems the person has as an adult will be based on these early, stage-specific fixations.

Accordingly, a fixation in the incorporative portion of the oral stage might result in an adult who is always attempting to take things in, to acquire things (Hall, 1954). This might manifest itself through attempts to acquire wealth or power or, more obviously, through the taking in of excessive amounts of food. Other examples might be an older child who relentlessly sucks on his or her thumb or an adult who chain smokes.

Alternatively, a fixation in the oral biting period of the oral stage might result in an adult who continually uses orality to be aggressive. Thus, someone who constantly makes "biting remarks" about others (e.g., an extremely sarcastic or cynical person) might be seen to be fixated in the oral biting portion of the oral stage.

The Anal Stage

From about the end of the first year of life through the third year, the libido is centered in the anal region of the body. Here, the child obtains gratification through exercise of the anal musculature, the muscles opening and closing the anal sphincters allowing the fecal waste products to be let out or kept in. In this stage, we may also speak of two subperiods: an anal explusive period, wherein the child obtains gratification from loosening his or her anal musculature and allowing the feces to leave; and an anal retentive period, wherein gratification is obtained through keeping the feces in.

Fixations may result also from frustrating experiences in this stage. For example, because this stage usually corresponds in Western culture to the time in which people are toilet trained, anal expulsive fixations may result from too-severe toilet training. This may result in an adult who "lets everything hang out"—a messy, disorderly, wasteful, or excessively demonstrative person (Hall, 1954). Alternatively, an anal retentive fixation might result in an adult who is excessively neat and orderly. Such an adult might also be seen to be "uptight," keeping everything in including his or her emotions.

The Phallic Stage

Here, for the first time in our discussion of psychosexual development, we must distinguish between the development of boys and of girls. Although for both sexes the phallic stage, which spans from about the third through the fifth years, involves the moving of the libido to the genital area, it is necessary to discuss the sexes separately because of the structural differences in their genitalia.

The male phallic stage.   The libido has moved to the boy's genital area. Here, sexual gratification is obtained through manipulation and stimulation of the genitals. Although masturbation would certainly provide a source of such gratification, Freud believed that the boy's mother is the person most likely to provide this stimulation. Because the mother is providing this stimulation, the boy comes to desire his mother sexually. That is, the boy experiences incestuous love for his mother. However, at the same time, he recognizes that his father stands in the way of the fulfillment of his incestuous desires. This recognition arouses considerable negative feeling toward the father in the boy.

This complex of emotional reactions Freud labeled the *Oedipus complex.* Oedipus was a character in Greek mythology who (unknowingly) killed his father and then married his mother. Freud saw a parallel between this myth and events in the lives of all humans. Freud believed that the stages of his theory are universally applicable to all humans and, further, that phenomena occurring within each stage—such as the Oedipus complex—are biologically imperative. They are biologically based developments and, hence, cannot be avoided, although their effects on the person's psychosexuality are dependent on experience. Thus, all males experience an Oedipus complex; all experience incestuous love for their mother and feelings of antagonism toward their father.

However, when the boy realizes that the father is his rival for the mother's love, a new problem is presented. The boy comes to fear that the father will punish him for his incestuous desires and that this punishment will take the form of castration. Thus, as a result of his Oedipus complex, the boy experiences castration anxiety. Because of the power of this castration anxiety, the boy gives up his incestuous desires for his mother and, in turn, identifies with his father, a phenomenon termed "identification with the aggressor" (Bronfenbrenner, 1960).

This identification with the father is a most important development for the young boy. As a result of this identification, the boy comes to model himself after the father. That is, the boy forms a structure of his personality that Freud terms the *superego.* As noted earlier, the superego has two components. The first, the *ego-ideal,* is the repre-

sentation of the perfect, or ideal, man (the "father figure"), and the second is the *conscience,* the internalization of society's standards, ethics, and morals. Thus, as a result of castration anxiety, the boy models himself after his father and in so doing becomes a "man" in his society. That is, the modeling, or identification, process results in the formation of the superego, whose ego-ideal component represents the internalization of the attributes that are required to become an ideal man in society. Moreover, as a result of this process, the boy develops a conscience, the second superego component, and as discussed earlier in this chapter, this internalization brings about moral development in the boy (Bronfenbrenner, 1960).

At many points in this complex series of events, experiences can unfavorably alter the outcome of this stage. For example, if for some reason the boy does not successfully resolve his Oedipus complex, he may not give up his love for his mother. Thus, as an adult he may be inordinately tied to her, or he may in fact identify with her instead of with his father. If this event occurs, the male might incorporate the mother's superego; this might express itself in the choice of a sexual partner when the boy reaches adulthood. Part of the mother's ego-ideal involves the type of person she wants or has as a mate. Whatever her preference, however, the point is that she chooses a male as a mate and as a sexual partner. The young boy who adopts his mother's ego-ideal might also choose a male sexual partner when an adult. Thus, according to Freud, one possible outcome of an unresolved Oedipus complex would be male homosexuality. However, it should be noted that there is no scientifically reliable empirical evidence in support of this hypothesis.

The female phallic stage.   Freud himself was never fully satisfied with his own formulation of the female phallic stage (see Bronfenbrenner, 1960). Here, too, the libido moves to the genital area, and gratification is obtained through manipulation and stimulation of the genitals. Although presumably it is the mother who provides the major source of this stimulation for the girl, the girl (for reasons not perfectly clear even to Freud himself) falls in love with her father. Then, analogous to what occurs with boys, she desires to possess her father incestuously but realizes that her mother stands in her way. At this point, however, the similarity with male development is markedly different.

The female is afraid that the mother will punish her for the incestuous desires she maintains toward the father. Although it is possible that the girl first fears that this punishment will take the form of castration, her awareness of her own genital structure causes her to realize that in a sense she has already been punished. That is, the girl perceives that she does not have a penis but only an inferior organ (to Freud, at least), a clitoris.

Hence, the girl is unable to resolve her oedipal conflict in the same way as the male does. The male experiences castration anxiety and this impels him to resolve his Oedipus complex. However, because the girl does not have a penis, she cannot very well fear castration. Thus, the girl experiences only a roughly similar emotion; she experiences *penis envy*. The girl envies the male his possession of a genital structure of which she has been deprived.

The effect of penis envy is, however, to impel the girl to resolve her oedipal conflict. She relinquishes her incestuous love for her father and identifies with her mother. This phenomenon is termed "anaclitic identification" (Bronfenbrenner, 1960). As a result of this identification, the girl then forms the superego component of her personality, which again is composed of the ego-ideal (here, the ideal female, or "mother figure") and the conscience. However, to reiterate a point made earlier in this chapter, Freud believed that only castration anxiety could lead to complete superego development, and thus, because females experience penis envy and not castration anxiety, they do not attain full superego development. This lack, Freud believed, takes the form of incomplete conscience development. In short, to Freud (1949), females are never as morally developed as males.

Finally, as with males, difficulties in the female's phallic stage could have profound effects on adult psychosexual functioning. Thus, in a manner analogous to that discussed for males, Freud believed that female homosexuality could result from extreme difficulties occurring in the female's phallic stage. Again, however, there is no scientifically reliable empirical support for this hypothesis.

The Latency Stage

After the end of the phallic stage—at about 5 years of age—the libido submerges, in a manner analogous to that of an iceberg. The libido is not localized in any body zone from the end of the phallic stage until puberty occurs, for example, at about 12 years of age in many contemporary Western nations (Tanner, 1991). Freud said that the libido is latent. Because it does not localize itself in any bodily zone until puberty, no erogenous zones emerge or exist.

The Genital Stage

At puberty, the libido again emerges. Once more it emerges in the genital area, but now it takes a mature (or adult) form. If the person has not been too severely restricted in his or her psychosexual development in the first 5 years of life, adult sexuality may now occur. Sexuality can now be directed to heterosexual union and reproduction. Although remnants (or traces) of the effects of the earlier stages may significantly affect the person at this time in life, it is only when the genital stage emerges that the person's libido can be gratified through directing it into reproductive functions.

An Evaluation of Freud's Ideas

Freud described five stages involved in the development of one's psychic energy. This libido, he claimed, changes its bodily localization over the course of development, and this change determines where in the body tensions are built up (through the presence of the libido in one concentrated area) and how these tensions may be diminished. That is, where the libido is centered determines how the person may be gratified.

Thus, psychosexual development and modes of psychosexual gratification involve the stage-dependent alteration of libido localization. Moreover, since anything that can adversely affect adult psychosexual functioning seems to have to occur in the first three stages, one major implication of Freud's theory is that the first 5 years of life are most crucial for adult psychosexual functioning.

Accordingly, for Freud, the form of development after childhood (i.e., the form of adolescent and adult life) was determined in early life. To him, the first 5 years of life, involving the first three psychosexual stages, were critical stages for functioning in later life. As such, Freud's concerns with adolescence and adulthood were only secondary. The behaviors in these periods were shaped in earlier life and, if one wanted to understand an adolescent or an adult, one had to deal with the fixations, conflicts, and frustrations that had occurred in the first 5 years of that person's life.

Several objections can be raised to these conclusions from Freud's ideas. Freud was a critical-periods theorist. As such, he saw nature as having a primary role in development, independent of the contribution of nurture. As discussed in prior chapters, such a conception has significant logical and empirical shortcomings. Moreover, one may object to Freud's ideas because of the sources of information he used to form his ideas.

That is, although Freud believed his stages to be biologically based and universal, Freud had a very biased source of "data." He worked in Victorian Europe, a historical period noted for its repressive views about sexuality. As a practicing psychiatrist, his main source of data was the memories of *adult* neurotic patients, people who came for treatment of emotional and behavioral problems interfering with their everyday functioning. Freud used his psychoanalytic therapy methods to discover the source of his patients' emotional problems. Through work with such patients, he attempted to construct a theory of *early* development. But these patients were adults from one particular historical period—and were not children. Thus, Freud constructed a theory about the early development of all children without actually observing any children.

Freud's adult patients reconstructed their early, long-gone pasts through retrospection. With Freud's help they tried to remember what had happened to them when they were 1, 2, or 3 years of age. This is how Freud obtained the information to build his theory. But it is quite possible that adults may forget, distort, or misremember events from their long-ago past. Therefore, because his data were unchecked for failures of early memories, the possibility that he obtained biased information cannot be discounted. Furthermore, Freud's patients cannot necessarily be viewed as representative of other nonneurotic Victorian adults or, for that matter, of all other humans living during other times in history.

Thus, one may question whether Freud, if he were working today, would devise the same theory of psychosexual development. For example, would Freud today find females viewing their genital structure as inferior and thus experiencing penis envy? Would he still maintain that females are not as morally developed as males, and would he find no evidence of psychosexual functioning during the years of latency?

Finally, even if one were to ignore all the above criticisms, one might question whether Freud's ideas represented all the possible developmental phenomena that could occur in each stage of life. Is latency necessarily a period of relative quiet, a time when few significant events occur for the child? Is adolescence just a time when events in preceding life make themselves evident? Or are there characteristics of adolescence that are special to that period? Interestingly, although accepting most of Freud's ideas as correct, it was other psychoanalytically oriented thinkers who led the way in showing that Freud's depiction of developmental phenomena within and across stages was incomplete. Erikson (1959, 1963), for instance, showed that by attending to the demands placed on the individual by society as the person developed, important phenomena could be identified in latency, in adolescence, and across the rest of the life span as well. Similarly, Anna Freud (1969) said that if one focused on events that occurred only at puberty, one would see special characteristics of the adolescent period.

Erikson and Anna Freud did not so much contradict Freud as they transcended him. Both reached this point not by adding anything new to Freud's basic ideas, but rather by focusing on the implications of one aspect of Freud's theory to which he himself did not greatly attend—the role of the ego in human development. If we consider Freud's ideas about the structure of personality, we can understand how the focus taken by Anna Freud represents a revision of her father's ideas. In addition, this presentation presages the ideas of Erikson, discussed in Chapter 16.

Structures of the Personality

Freud believed that the human personality is made up of several different mental structures. We have noted that one of these structures, the superego, arises out of the resolution of the oedipal conflict. Another of these, termed the *id,* was defined by Freud as an innate structure of the personality. The id "contains" all the person's libido. The id is thus involved in all of the person's attempts to obtain pleasure, or gratification, through appropriate stimulation. In fact, because the id is the center for the libido, and because the libido creates tensions that require appropriate stimulation, resulting in pleasure, Freud said that the id functions in accordance with the *pleasure principle.* Thus, in emphasizing the implications of the gratification of libidinal energy, Freud emphasized the implications of the biologically based id on human functioning.

However, in addition to the superego and the id, Freud specified a third structure of the personality, the *ego.* The function of the id is solely to obtain pleasure. Thus, the id compels a person in the oral stage to seek appropriate stimulation (e.g., the mother's nipple). When the stimulation is not available, the id functions in a particular way that Freud termed the *primary process.* Simply, the primary process is a fantasy, or imagining, process. When the mother's nipple is not present, the child imagines that it is there. But such fantasies are not sufficient to allow the child to obtain appropriate stimulation. One cannot just fantasize. One must interact with reality. Accordingly, another structure of the personality—the ego—is formed, and the sole function of the ego is to adapt to reality, to allow the person actually to obtain needed stimulation and, hence, to survive.

Because the ego develops only to deal with reality, to allow the person to adjust to the demands of the real world and, hence, to survive, Freud said the ego functions in accordance with the *reality principle*. The ego has processes that enable it to adjust to and deal with reality. This *secondary process* involves such factors as cognition and perception. Through the functioning of these processes, the ego is capable of perceiving and knowing the real world, and, thus, of adapting to it.

Although Freud spoke about the implications of all three of the structures of the mind—the id, the ego, and the superego, the sum of which constitute a person's personality structure—he emphasized the implications of the id on human functioning. Thus, in describing human psychosexual development, Freud was viewing human beings as essentially governed by inner biological and psychological variables. On the other hand, Freud did not spend a good deal of time discussing the implications of the ego. This focus is what was provided by Anna Freud (and by others, e.g., Erikson 1959, 1963).

Anna Freud: Adolescence as a Developmental Disturbance

In agreement with her father, Anna Freud (1969) noted that all structures of the personality are present when the ego and the superego form to join with the innately present id. Moreover, like her father, she believed that all three of these structures are present by the end of the third psychosexual stage—the phallic stage—or in other words, by about the end of the fifth year of life.

Both of the Freuds contended that when all structures are present, they present different directives to the person. The id only "wants" pleasure (gratification). It is not concerned with either survival or morality. The superego, at the other extreme, contains the conscience and cares nothing for pleasure. Only morality (and a stern Victorian view of it at that!) is important. Thus, whereas the id might pressure the person for sexual gratification, the superego would condemn the person for such a desire. The ego, however, has to balance these two counterdirected types of pressures.

Anna Freud

The ego's only function is survival. It must defend itself from dangers to that survival, whether those dangers are from within or without. The conflict between the id and the superego represents a danger to survival. If the person spent all of his or her time in conflict about action, there would be no energy left to deal with the demands placed on the person from outside the self (e.g., from society). Accordingly, the ego develops defense mechanisms, that is, ways to avoid dealing with at least one set of the conflicting demands imposed from within. Such avoidance would rid the person of the internal conflict, and "free up" energy for dealing with external adaptive demands.

The defense mechanisms developed by the ego (mechanisms like *repression, rationalization, substitution,* and *projection*) involve taking the pressures imposed by the id and placing them in a particular area of the mind—the *unconscious*. This area contains material most difficult to bring into awareness (into the conscious). The reason that the id pressures are defended against, and not those of the superego, is that the latter's pressures represent the demands and rules of society. If one got rid of these demands—internalized as one's conscience—this would mean getting rid of one's morality. We term people who apparently have no internalized morality, who do not obey rules of society, *sociopaths*. Typically, society has severe sanctions against sociopaths, often defining their behavior as illegal and sometimes imprisoning them. Accordingly, it would not be adaptive for the ego to put the superego in the unconscious, and so it is the id material that is placed in this area of the mind.

According to both Freuds, the typical person establishes a balance among the id, ego, and super-ego by 5 years of age. By the time latency has been reached, ego defenses appropriate for dealing with all pressures (or drives) from the id have been established. The person is, thus, in equilibrium. However, although people may differ in regard to the character of this balance, depending on events in the first three stages of life, Anna Freud (1969) claimed that all people will have their balance *destroyed* in adolescence.

Unlike her father, Anna Freud saw adolescence as a period in life presenting demands for the person that are not *just* those relating to earlier life. These demands involve new pressures being put on the ego, and they require new adaptational solutions for the person. The new demands on the ego are universal, she contended, because the pressures that create them are also universal. To understand this, let us consider the special alterations that Anna Freud (1969) associated with adolescence.

Alterations in Drives

With puberty comes an adult genital drive. Thus, the balance among the id, ego, and superego is upset as this new feeling-state comes to dominate the person's being. Because this alteration is an inevitable, universal one, Anna Freud argued that an inescapable imbalance in development occurs. As such, adolescence is necessarily a period of *developmental disturbance*. Although for theoretical reasons that differ from theorists such as G. Stanley Hall (1904), Anna Freud also said that adolescence is a period of storm and stress.

In short, because of the universal emergence of the genital drive at puberty, the adolescent is necessarily involved "in dangers which did not exist before and with which he is not accustomed to deal. Since, at this stage, he lives and functions still as a member of his family unit, he runs the risk of allowing the new genital urges to connect with his old love objects, that is, with his parents, brothers, or sisters" (A. Freud, 1969, p. 7). Because such incestuous relations are not condoned in any known culture (Winch, 1971), some defense against them must be established. The genital alteration thus requires a personality alteration.

Alterations in Ego Organization

Anna Freud claimed that the new drive throws the person into upheaval. It causes unpredictable behavior, as the person tries out all the formerly useful defenses to deal with the new drive. This, she contended, puts strain on the person because what is involved is using a set of mechanisms balanced for one state on another, quantitatively greater and qualitatively different state. As such, not only does the adolescent try more of the same defenses but also he or she eventually forms new types of mechanisms. For example, in relation to the new cognitive abilities that emerge in adolescence, the adolescent comes for the first time to use highly abstract, intellectual reasons to justify his or her behavior. This new ego-defense mechanism is thus termed *intellectualization*. However, such alterations are still not sufficient to resolve the adolescent disturbance.

Alterations in Object Relations

Despite the new ego defenses, the danger of inappropriately acting out the genital drive is so great that "nothing helps here except a complete discarding of the people who were the important love objects of the child, that is, the parents" (A. Freud, 1969, p. 8). Indeed, the new defenses are useful in helping the adolescent to alter the relations he or she has had with these "love objects." Defenses like intellectualization often involve quite involved rationales for why the parents are "stupid," are "ineffective," or possess "useless beliefs and conventions" (A. Freud, 1969, p. 8). Of course, in moving away from parents as the major object of social relations, the adolescent does not necessarily become nonsocial. To the contrary, in fact, there is a last alteration that follows from the break in ties with parents.

Alterations in Ideals and Social Relations

When the adolescent has broken the ties with the parents, he or she has also rejected the attitudes, values, and beliefs formerly shared with them. Anna Freud argued that the adolescent is thus left without social ties or ideals. Substitutes are found for both of these in the peer group, she suggested. Moreover, these new social relations may be "justified" on the basis of shared ideology (e.g., in accordance with the intellectualization defense, adolescents might say that the peers understand them whereas parents do not). More importantly, attachment to the peer group provides a mechanism wherein the new genital drive—which started all alterations initially—may be dealt with in a setting less dangerous to the adolescent's adaptation than the family setting.

An Evaluation of Anna Freud's Ideas

Anna Freud, her father, and others who use nature bases for their ideas share the limitations of such an orientation. Because she saw the alterations of adolescence as biologically imperative and, hence, universal, Anna Freud clearly described adolescence in terms that acknowledge little plasticity within people and few differences between people. She was led to a depiction of adolescence as necessarily stormy and stressful.

However, such statements simply are not consistent with a vast amount of existing data. Contrary to what she indicated, we noted in Chapter 1 that the data of Bandura (1964), Douvan and Adelson (1966), and Offer (1969) clearly indicate that most young people (a) do not have stormy, stressful adolescent periods, (b) do not break ties with parents, (c) continue to share the ideals of their parents, and (d) choose friends who, like themselves, have ideals consistent with those of their parents (see, too, Lerner, 2002). By taking a weak interactionist stance in regard to the nature–nurture issue, both Sigmund and Anna Freud were led to describe human development in a manner inconsistent with the known character of the transition that occurs from childhood to adolescence.

However, it should be recognized that although problems exist in his formulations pertaining to the universal nature of the psychosexual stages, the cultural bias of his theory, and the nature of the methods he used to obtain information relevant to his formulations, Sigmund Freud did posit an extremely influential view of emotional development. Moreover, his views have had considerable heuristic significance, influencing other psychoanalytically oriented scholars—for example, Anna Freud and Erik Erikson—as well as scientists working from a more mechanistic perspective, for example, Miller and Dollard (1941). Thus, despite the problems and limitations of Freud's theory, we do see that he provided the field of human development with a provocative and influential—if not readily empirically testable—stage theory of aspects of emotional development.

CONCLUSIONS ABOUT STAGE THEORIES

With our analysis of Freud's theory, we have seen three instances of stage theories of human development. These positions are similar in that they all view development as proceeding through a series of qualitatively different levels of organization. Moreover, although these stage theorists thus see development, in part, as being qualitatively discontinuous, they also include notions of continuity. That is, they posit general as well as specific laws. Hence, according to Piaget and Kohlberg it is disequilibrium that continuously accounts for stage progression, whereas to Freud it is the continual movement of libido. Finally, to differing extents, these three positions share an organismic, interactionist view of behavioral development; in differing ways these three theorists see the outcomes of development resulting from an interaction between the organism's characteristics and the characteristics of its experience.

However, the approach to interaction found in these theories is not the same as the one associated with dynamic, developmental systems formulations, for example, as embodied in the concept of "fusion" (Tobach & Greenberg, 1984) and found in the models discussed in Chapters 7, 8, 9, and 14 (e.g., Fischer & Bidell, 1998; Gottlieb, 1997, 1998; Thelen & Smith, 1998). Indeed, the theoretical and empirical problems associated with the conception of interaction found in the stage theories discussed in this chapter is one key reason why scholars such as Feldman (2000) have used notions associated with developmental systems theory to recast the approach to stage development used in Piagetian theory. As is discussed in Chapter 16, an analogous use of ideas linked to developmental systems theories has been made by Côté (e.g., 1996, 2000; Côté & Levine, 1997, 2000) to revise the stage conception found in Erikson's (1959) neo-psychoanalytic theory.

The work of Côté is useful to note here because although stage theories have been discussed separately from our consideration of other approaches to the conceptualization of human development, these conceptualizations are not necessarily mutually exclusive with these other approaches. Indeed, as we next consider in Chapter 16, the differential approach to the study of behavioral development, we note that it is possible to combine both stage and differential concepts into one integrated theory of development. This integration is evident in the developmental theory of Erik Erikson. A follower of Freud, Erikson, however, went beyond both Sigmund and Anna Freud in his refocusing of psychoanalytic theory.

16 | *The Differential Approach*

The differential approach to development begins by posing what is basically an empirical question: "How in the course of development do groups of people become assorted into subgroups, subgroups which are differentiated on the basis of status and behavior attributes?" (Emmerich, 1968, p. 671). In its most basic form, the differential approach to development is primarily empirical rather than theoretical; it uses particular research methods to study differences among groups of people and individuals within these groups. Thus, the differential approach does not necessarily connote any given theoretical point of view; it can be used by people with various theoretical perspectives.

The main focus of the differential approach is to discover how people become sorted into subgroups over the course of their development. Subgroups are formed, or differentiated, on the basis of one of two types of attributes. The first type is *status attributes*. Status attributes are characteristics that place people in particular demographic categories or groups, such as those based on age, sex, race, religion, and socioeconomic status (SES). A differentiation of people into subgroups on the basis of age, sex, and race is illustrated in Figure 16.1.

Obviously, however, there is nothing really developmental about differentiating a group of people on the basis of their status attributes. The developmental component of the differential approach arises when people are further differentiated on the basis of the second type of attribute, *behavioral attributes*.

Behavioral attributes may be considered as bipolar behavioral, or psychological, dimensions. For example, a behavioral attribute would be any dimension such as:

Extraversion–introversion.
Dominance–submission.
Aggression–passivity.
High activity level–low activity level.

Independence–dependence.
Basic trust–mistrust.

A behavioral attribute is really a continuum that has opposite traits, or characteristics, at either end. A differential researcher using the term *behavioral attribute,* then, is referring to behavioral or psychological attributes conceptualized along a bipolar continuum. For instance, behavioral attributes such as independence–dependence or high activity level–low activity level are seen as bipolar traits running along a continuum, and people grouped toward one end of each of the continua might be termed independent or high-active, whereas people grouped toward the other end of the continua might be termed dependent or low-active, respectively.

The goal of a scientist using the differential approach for the study of psychological development would thus be to discover the subgroups into which people become assorted across ontogeny on the basis of both their behavioral and status attributes. The differential researcher would choose some behavioral attributes (e.g., aggression–passivity and independence–dependence), as well as some selected status attributes (e.g., age groups—5-year-olds and 10-year-olds—and sex groups) for study and then try to discover how people in these groups become differentiated in the course of development.

For instance, the researcher would ask questions to see whether the 5-year-old boys as a subgroup are located at different points along the aggression–passivity and the independence–dependence continua than are the 5-year-old girls. The researcher would also ask these same questions of the 10-year-old male and female subgroups. Thus, in relation to the status attributes of age and sex, the researcher would be able to determine whether these people form subgroups located at different points along the behavioral dimensions. The researcher would be able to see, for instance, if 5-year-old girls as a

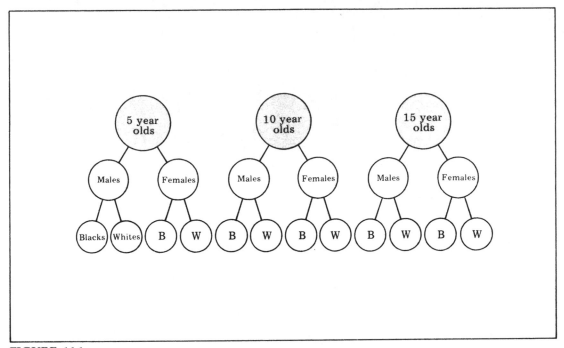

FIGURE 16.1
A group of people differentiated into subgroups on the basis of the status attributes of age, sex, and race.

subgroup are more or less aggressive than 5-year-old boys; for that matter, the researcher would be able to see how each subgroup compares with every other subgroup in terms of relative location along each of the bipolar dimensions studied.

The design of such an inquiry is illustrated in Figures 16.2(a) and 16.2(b); some imaginary results are depicted in order to illustrate the aforementioned points. In this figure we see that the four subgroups differentiated on the basis of status attributes are also differentiated on the basis

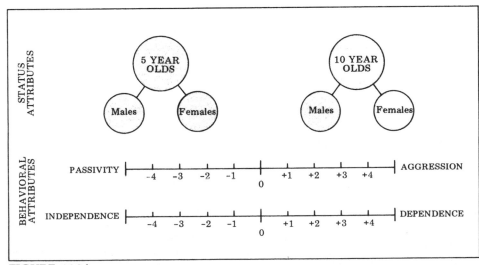

FIGURE 16.2A
Design of a differential study of the relation of two status attributes to two behavioral attributes.

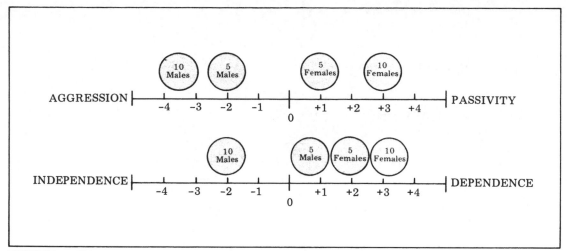

FIGURE 16.2B
Some imaginary findings of the study illustrated in Figure 16.2a.

of their location along the bipolar behavioral dimensions. That is, the subgroups occupy different spaces on these dimensions.

INDIVIDUAL DIFFERENCES WITHIN THE DIFFERENTIAL APPROACH

The differential approach is primarily concerned with groups—or better with subgroups—of people. Accordingly, in attempting to ascertain how such subgroups become differentiated with development, the differential approach is concerned with discovering nomothetic laws. Those taking the differential approach do not necessary posit universal group laws of development, and they are thus different from the nomothetically oriented stage theorists. Yet, differential researchers are concerned with nomothetic laws insofar as they are concerned with ascertaining the variables that predict how groups are differentiated into subgroups over the course of development.

However, differential researchers are more interested than are stage theorists in ascertaining the dimensions of individual differences in development. Consistent with how they conceptualize subgroup differences, they define individual differences in terms of people's different locations along various bipolar dimensions. Just as subgroups have different locations along each of these dimensions, so do individuals. In turn, each individual may also have his or her own location in multidimensional space. This is illustrated in Figure 16.3

for two individuals, each of whom takes up a different space along each of the four dimensions shown. In sum, within the differential approach individuality is defined as one's location in multidimensional space (Emmerich, 1968, p. 678).

THE STUDY OF DEVELOPMENT WITHIN THE DIFFERENTIAL APPROACH

Although the differential approach can be used simply as an empirical approach within which to consider development, it can also be combined with specific theoretical formulations. For example, as discussed in more detail later in this chapter, Erik H. Erikson, primarily a stage theorist, employed a differential formulation within each of his "eight stages of man" (Erikson, 1959, 1963). Similarly, just as stage theorists may use the differential approach within their qualitatively discontinuous theoretical point of view, other theorists may use differential ideas within theoretical approaches that stress continuity throughout development (e.g., Cattell, 1957). The point here is that the differential approach does not constitute a perspective mutually exclusive from other approaches.

In regard to the empirical use of the differential approach, a researcher may have no previously formulated ideas about whether development is characterized by, for instance, developmental stages and/or by continuity or discontinuity. The researcher may thus adopt the differential

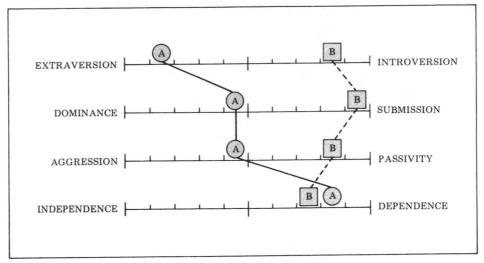

FIGURE 16.3
Individuality within the differential approach. Individuals A and B have different locations on each of the four dimensions.

approach in order to see which of these concepts best describes the development of certain subgroups of people.

Particular types of research methodology and statistical analyses of results—for example, statistics that can readily show how many dimensions are needed to characterize subgroups of people—are typically utilized by differential researchers. Thus, such statistical procedures as correlational analysis, factor analysis, or cluster analysis are used. These procedures have common bases and, when used within the context of the differential approach, a common goal. Their intent is to see how variables—composed of status and behavioral attributes—group together over the course of development.

For example, do the same groups of behavioral attributes characterize females when they are 5, 10, 15, and 20 years of age (e.g., Block, 1971)? Or do the dimensions that must be used to group females of different ages differ over the course of development? Such questions are addressed by statistical procedures such as those previously mentioned. For instance, factor analysis, one of the more sophisticated of these procedures, would be used to discern whether the number of dimensions that differentiated the groups stayed the same or changed over time, and whether the group of behavioral attributes that related to each other at Time 1 in development remained in the same relation at Time 2 (Baltes & Nesselroade, 1973).

To specify the exact details of these statistical procedures is beyond the purposes of the present discussion. Nevertheless, a simplified illustration of the use of these procedures within the differential approach will clarify and convey their utility. Suppose a researcher is studying boys and girls aged 5, 10, and 15 years. In relation to these status attributes (age and sex), the researcher wishes to learn how these people form into subgroups on the basis of 50 behavioral attributes, 50 bipolar dimensions (e.g., aggression—passivity or dominance—submission). The researcher labels the 50 variables by their number and measures each of the research participants on each of the variables. The resear-cher next performs a factor analysis on each of the age–sex subgroups; that is, the researcher statistically analyzes the scores on the variables (the behavioral attributes) to determine whether some of them seem to have a high degree of relationship (thus, forming a factor) while not similarly relating to the other variables. The researcher finds that, for both the 5-year-old males and females, the same variables seem to group together, that is, the scores on each of the first 20 variables are consistent (correlated) with each other but are not so related to any of the remaining 30 variables.

Thus, the first 20 variables form a factor. Similarly, the next 15 variables form a second factor, and the last 15 variables form a third factor. As such, the 5-year-old males and females are found to be similarly differentiated on the basis of three similar groupings of variables. The structure of the relationship among the variables—*the factor structure*—is the same. With both subgroups of youth the same variables cluster together.

This finding may not mean, however, that the males and females have identical sets of scores on each of the variables within a factor. Suppose that Factor 1 is aggression–passivity and that some of the behavioral bipolar dimensions comprised by this factor are:

Looks for fights–stays away from fights.

Teases others–gets teased.

Yells when bothered–is quiet when bothered.

Other variables within the factor are similar to these, and thus the researcher might reasonably opt to give this factor a name such as "aggression–passivity." In order for each of the variables in this factor to relate to each other and thus form a factor, we would expect the scores on the variables within the factor to be consistent. For instance, we would expect a person scoring high (or low) on one variable in the factor to score similar-ly high (or low) on each of the other variables. Thus, regardless of whether a subgroup scores high and/or low on all of the variables, the variables would form a factor as long as the scores of all the people in the subgroup were highly inter-related (i.e., they showed high levels of covariation). The same factor could be obtained for both the 5-year-old boys and girls even if each group's scores were not identical. For instance, the boys could have higher aggression scores than the girls on all the variables comprising the factor. Of course, this would not mean that boys and girls do not vary among themselves. The point here is that the boys may vary along the aggression–passivity continuum at points closer to the aggression end of the continuum than do girls.

With these findings about the factor structure of the 5-year-old males and females, the differential researcher may proceed to assess developmental changes or consistencies in the 10- and 15-year-old subgroups. In doing so, the researcher will necessarily be addressing some of the core conceptual issues of psychological development—the continuity–discontinuity and the stability–instability issues.

Continuity–Discontinuity

When looking at results across age levels, the differential researcher will be primarily concerned with whether the subgroup differentiations found at earlier age levels (e.g., with the 5-year-olds) remain the same or change at older age levels. If the same variables seem to relate to each other in the same way at all age levels, this is continuity. If, however, differences from earlier patterns are found, this is discontinuity. Specifically, the differential researcher may find continuity if, for example, the same number of factors, comprised by the same variables, exist in the older subgroups (Baltes & Nesselroade, 1973). Alternatively, discontinuity may be discovered if, for example, a different number of factors exists within the older subgroups. In addition, discontinuity may be found even if the same factors exist but different behavioral attributes comprise the factors. That is, bipolar dimensions not included in earlier age-level factors may be related to older age-level factors or vice versa.

In Figure 16.4, we see an imaginary example of such differential research, illustrating the discovery of both continuity and discontinuity using this approach. Continuity exists between both the 5-year-old male and female subgroups and both the 10-year-old male and female subgroups. The same number of factors exists in each subgroup and, in addition, the variables comprised by each factor remain the same. However, discontinuity exists between the 10- and 15-year-old subgroups. With the males, the same number of factors still exists at both age levels, but the meaning of the factors is different because different variables make up the factors of the 15-year-old males as compared with the 10-year-old males. With the females, discontinuity also exists. Here, however, the reason is primarily the emergence of a new factor among the 15-year-old females.

Stability–Instability

In addition to being able to determine whether the same variables account for differentiation throughout development (continuity–discontinuity), the differential researcher is able to determine whether a person's rank on a variable, and on a factor within his or her subgroup, remains the same or changes with time. Each subgroup is, of course, composed of individuals who have scores on each of the measured variables. Although these scores may be similar, it will still be possible to rank-order all of the individuals in a subgroup, from high to low. Thus, a person's rank for a variable may change with development; as we have seen in Chapter 5, when such a change relative to one's reference group occurs, we term this *instability*. If a person's rank on a variable remains the same across time, we term this *stability*.

Consistent with what we have said in Chapter 5, Emmerich (1968, pp. 676–677) pointed out that

| | 5 YEAR OLDS | | 10 YEAR OLDS | | 15 YEAR OLDS | |
	Males	Females	Males	Females	Males	Females
	Variables		Variables		Variables	
FACTOR A	1–20	1–20	1–20	1–20	1–15	1–20
FACTOR B	21–35	21–35	21–35	21–35	16–30	16–25
FACTOR C	36–50	36–50	36–50	36–50	31–50	26–40
FACTOR D						41–50

FIGURE 16.4
An example of hypothetical findings of differential research, illustrating both continuity (between 5 and 10 years of age) and discontinuity (between 10 and 15 years of age).

any thorough analysis of development from the differential point of view must consider the continuity–discontinuity and stability–instability issues at the same time. As illustrated in Chapter 5, any combination of continuity–discontinuity and stability–instability may occur. In reference specifically to the differential approach, Emmerich (1968, p. 677) pointed out that:

(1) *Continuity and stability* may occur when the factors (and the variables within them) remain the same for subgroups from time 1 to time 2 and, accordingly, individuals' rankings within their respective subgroups remain unaltered.

(2) *Continuity and instability* may occur when the factors (and the variables within them) remain the same for subgroups from time 1 to time 2 but, despite this consistency, individuals' rankings within their respective subgroups change.

(3) *Discontinuity and stability* may occur when factors (and/or the variables within them) are altered for subgroups from time 1 to time 2 but, despite these changes, individuals are ranked in similar ways within these new subgroupings.

(4) *Discontinuity and instability* may occur when the factors (and/or the variables within them) change for subgroups from time 1 to time 2 and individuals' rankings are accordingly altered.

We have reason to return to some of these possible interrelations later in this chapter, in order to understand the results of a specific instance of

research done with a differential approach—the longitudinal study of Kagan and Moss (1962). Here, however, let us review the relation of the differential approach to the conceptual issues of development we dealt with in earlier chapters.

RELATION OF CONCEPTS OF DEVELOPMENT TO THE DIFFERENTIAL APPROACH

We have seen that those researchers employing a differential approach deal primarily with the continuity–discontinuity and stability–instability issues, and that the differential approach may be interrelated with other approaches to the understanding of development. When this approach is interrelated with stage theories of development, as in the case of Erikson's (1959, 1963) theory of psychosocial development, the stage formulation, in a sense, takes theoretical precedence. That is, when Erikson uses differential formulations within the context of his stage theory, the continuity–discontinuity of behavioral development does not remain an empirical question; rather, development is held to proceed through eight qualitatively different stages.

The interrelation by Erikson of the stage and differential approaches does not alter the substance of the differential approach. As more of an approach to the study of development, rather than a theoretical view of development, the differential approach does not maintain an a priori position relative to the continuity–discontinuity issue. Moreover, it in no way addresses the nature–nurture issue or related issues. That is, the differential approach in no way offers formulations that specify the sources of differential developmental subgroupings; rather, in its use within the context of contrasting theoretical perspectives, it can be integrated with virtually any position on a nature-oriented to a nurture-oriented conceptual continuum.

Conclusions

The differential approach to the study of behavioral development considers how people become sorted into various subgroups over the course of their development. Researchers taking such an approach are concerned with the developmental interrelations among selected status and behavioral attributes. This concern may be expressed either in primarily theoretical terms or as a primarily empirical interest. Researchers employing differential concepts as components of their theoretical writings may specify how specific status attributes will be interrelated with specific behavioral attributes. Such theoretical attempts may first posit particular status attributes and then specify, along with each status attribute, characteristics that are thought of in behavioral-attribute terms, for example, characteristics thought of as bipolar trait dimensions (e.g., activity–passivity).

Differential researchers whose orientation is primarily empirical do not a priori specify the exact interrelation of these attributes. They certainly may have theoretical orientations that affect their choices of particular status and behavioral attributes for study, and they certainly may make predictions about how status and behavioral attributes will interrelate. However, they are primarily concerned with empirically discovering or verifying these interrelations. Thus, this approach attempts to ascertain empirically how people become differentiated into subgroups over the course of their development. In this chapter, we consider examples of both the theoretical and empirical uses of the differential approach to psychological development. First, as an example of how differential concepts may be put to use within a given theoretical context, we consider the theory of Erik Erikson. Next, we consider an instance of the empirical use of the differential approach through our review of the classic work

of Jerome Kagan and Howard Moss (1962). Let us now consider the developmental theory of Erik Erikson.

ERIK H. ERIKSON'S STAGE AND DIFFERENTIAL THEORY OF PSYCHOSOCIAL DEVELOPMENT

Erik H. Erikson was a psychoanalytically oriented stage theorist who, following Sigmund Freud (1949, 1954), proposed a stage theory of human emotional development. But, in addition, within each of the eight stages of development that Erikson specified, we see the inclusion of an emotional crisis in development which is conceptualized in differential terms.

Erikson combined both stage and differential concepts of development and provided a theoretical account of the development of human beings

Erik H. Erikson

across their entire life span. In other words, Erikson saw development *within* each of the eight stages of his theory as involving a person's location along a stage-specific differential dimension; in addition, the location one attains on a dimension within any later stage of development is influenced by one's location(s) in previous stages.

Of course, Erikson's primary use of differential notions as theoretical constructs does not obviate the fact that research may be derived from his theory. Moreover, this research is also of a differential character; that is, the research derived from Erikson's stage-differential theory leads empirically to the differential categorization of people into subgroups on the basis of status attributes such as "stage" and/or sex. Thus, after we review the features of Erikson's stage-differential theory, we consider several lines of differential research derived from it. It is useful to begin our discussion by referring to some of the events in Erikson's life.

A Brief Biographical Sketch

Erik H. Erikson (1902–1994) was born in Frankfurt, Germany and moved to the United States in the early 1930s. While still a young man, Erikson served as tutor to the children of some of Sigmund Freud's associates. Working in this capacity, Erikson came under the influence of both Sigmund Freud and his daughter Anna. Accordingly, Erikson received training in psychoanalysis and, after moving to the United States and settling in the Boston area, he soon established his expertise in the area of childhood psychoanalytic practice.

Through his practice, as well as through the results of some empirical investigations (see Erikson, 1963), Erikson began to evolve a theory of affective—or emotional—development that complemented the theory of Sigmund Freud. Erikson's theory altered the essential focus of psychoanalytic theorizing from a focus on the id to one on the ego. To understand this alteration, let us first consider some of Sigmund Freud's views about the mental structures that comprise the human personality.

The Id and the Ego

As indicated in Chapter 15, Freud's theory emphasized the biologically based components of a person's psychosexual development. That is, he emphasized an interrelation between inner, biologically imperative presses and psychological functioning. Simply, Freud stressed the effects of the human inner–biological level on human psychology. In the terminology of psychoanalysis, this stress is illustrated by Freud's emphasis on the biologically based id on psychological functioning.

In Chapter 15, we saw that Freud specified several different mental structures comprising the human personality. To review this discussion briefly, we noted that one of these structures, the superego, arises out of the resolution of the oedipal conflict. Other personality structures were held to exist, however, and, as we discussed, Freud termed these the id and the ego.

Although Freud spoke about the implications of all three of the structures of the mind, we have seen that he emphasized the implications of the id for human psychological functioning. Freud did not spend a good deal of time discussing the implications of the ego. Erikson provided this focus.

Implications of the Ego

When one turns one's focus from the id to the ego, one immediately recognizes the necessity of dealing with the society in which the person is developing. The function of the ego is survival, or adjustment to the demands of reality. That reality is shaped and presented by the society in which the person is developing. An appropriate adjustment to reality in one society, which allows the person to survive, might be inefficient or even totally inappropriate in another society. Hence, when we say that the child is adapting to reality, we are saying, in effect, that the child is adapting to the demands of his or her particular society. How the ego fulfills its function of reality adaptation will, necessarily, be different in different societies.

For instance, although it is held that all infants pass through the same oral stage and need to deal with reality in order to obtain the appropriate oral stimulation, the way they obtain it may be different in different societies. In one society, for example, there may be prolonged breastfeeding by the mother. Here, the infant need only seek the mo-ther's breast, which may never be very far away, in order to obtain the needed oral stimulation (Super & Harkness, 1981). In another society, however, infants may be weaned relatively early. A few days after birth the mother might return to work and leave the infant in the care of a grandparent or older sibling (see DuBois, 1944). Although the latter infant still needs oral stimulation, different adjustments to reality will have to be made than those that will be made in the case of the former infant. We see, then, that the specifics of a child's society must be understood when we consider the implications of the ego's functioning. In some societies, learning to hunt, fish, and make arrowheads is necessary for survival. In other contexts, such skills are not as useful as learning to read, write, do arithmetic, and program a computer.

Thus, society, the roles it evolves, and the process of socialization within society are all components of adaptive individual and social functioning. According to Erikson, the aspect of the person that attains the competency to perform these individual–social linkages is the ego, that element of the personality believed in psychoanalytic theory to be governed by the reality principle. Regardless of whether one chooses to talk of an ego as being involved in these linkages, a person must attain the skills requisite for survival in his or her society.

It is clear that the demands placed on the person (or the ego) are not constant across life. Although society may expect certain behaviors from its adult members—behaviors that both maintain and perpetuate society—similar behaviors are not expected from infants, children, and (in some societies) adolescents. In other words, the adaptive demands on an infant are not the same as those on a child, an adolescent, or an adult. Rather, such demands are age-graded (Baltes, 1987). One must understand the person's social context to understand the specific, age-associated adaptational demands placed on him or her.

Such a conclusion was reached by Erikson. Along with other psychoanalysts who practiced after Sigmund Freud (e.g., Anna Freud), Erikson believed that Freud had not given sufficient attention to the implications of the ego for human psychological functioning. When such attention was given, however, it seemed clear that humans are not only biological and psychological creatures but also social creatures. According to Erikson, a child's psychological development can be fully understood only within the context of the society in which the child is growing up. Perhaps we can see why Erikson's most famous book is titled *Childhood and Society* (1963).

In sum, Erikson changed the focus of Freud's psychoanalytic theory by giving primary consideration to the implications of the ego rather than the id. Although Erikson also dealt with the development of affect (or feelings) his alteration in theoretical focus broadened the scope of Freud's theory beyond just concern with the psychosexual stages of development. Erikson's theory stresses the interrelation of the ego and the societal forces affecting it; thus, rather than being concerned with biologically based psychosexual development, Erikson was concerned with a person's *psychosocial* development throughout life. He saw that

human emotional development involves far more than only psychosexual development.

As psychosocial development proceeds, the ego has to continuously alter to meet the changing, age-graded demands of society. At each stage of psychosocial development, new adjustment demands are placed on the ego and, accordingly, new emotional crises emerge. Hence, Erikson's consideration of the ego and society led him to the formulation of stages of development different from those of Freud, and to the formulation of psychosocial emotional crises specific to each stage of development. It is these emotional crises that are conceptualized in differential terms and that, accordingly, allow us to use Erikson's theory as an instance of the interrelation of stage and differential theories of development. In order to understand both Erikson's use of these concepts and the details of his theory of psychosocial development, let us consider the eight stages of ego development he specified. As a necessary introduction to these stages, however, we must focus on Erikson's epigenetic principle and his concomitant concept of critical periods. The former notion provides us with Erikson's model for stage transition, whereas the latter indicates the central importance of each stage for effective, integrated psychosocial functioning.

ERIKSON'S EPIGENETIC PRINCIPLE

As the ego develops, new adjustment demands are continually placed on it by society. The ego must adapt to these new demands if healthy or optimal development is to proceed. Yet, when new adjustment demands are placed on the developing ego, new ego capabilities must be gained in order for these demands to be met; each new societal demand requires a different adaptation by the ego, that is, a different capability to be developed—if the ego is to continue to develop optimally. Simply, healthy ego development involves appropriate, age-graded adjustments to the demands of society.

Society alters its specifications for adaptive behavior at different times in a person's life. In infancy, society (specifically, the family) expects "incorporation" from an infant. All that an infant must do in order to be deemed socially adaptive is to be stimulated by caregivers and to consume food from caregivers. We would not expect a person of this age to do much more than this. Certainly, we would not expect the infant to get a summer job or follow career goals. We might, however, expect such behavior from an 18-year-old. Indeed, if all one did during one's summer vacation from college was to take in stimulation (from the sun) and incorporate food (from the kitchen), this would not be considered appropriate behavior by one's parents.

Thus, a behavior deemed adaptive at one time in life is not going to be seen as similarly functional over the rest of life. Rather, new behaviors must emerge. Although we still have to be incorporative at age 18, we also have to do more. Identity-related behaviors (i.e., behaviors related to finding an adult role to play in society) may come to predominate at this time of life. Unless one shows these behaviors, and shows them to sufficient degrees, one may be judged as unadaptive. One may not meet the demands of his or her society. In short, a person must always meet the societally shaped demands of his or her world, but these demands are altered continually across the person's life span.

A similar conception was advanced by Robert Havighurst (1951, 1953, 1956), who believed that as people progress across their life spans, they must master certain tasks at different portions of life. He termed such change-related requirements *developmental tasks* and noted that the specific tasks that occur at each particular portion of life arise out of particular combinations of pressures from inner–biological (e.g., physical maturation), psychological (e.g., aspirations in life), and sociocultural (e.g., cultural expectations) influences (Havighurst, 1956). These pressures require an adjustment on the part of the person. Because of the fact that, at different times in the life span, the combination of pressures from each of the levels is different, then at each successive portion of life a distinct set of adjustment demands is placed on the developing person. Consequently, Havighurst (1953) maintained that developmental tasks occur at specific periods in life and that the successful meeting of these tasks resulted in happiness and success at meeting future tasks; however, failure to meet developmental tasks resulted in unhappiness, problems in meeting future tasks, and societal disapproval.

In other words, as each new demand is placed on the ego, a new crisis must be faced. Can the ego meet the demands of the society by developing this new capability? Can it, thus, continue to function adaptively? In essence, psychosocial development involves the development of the ego's emerging capabilities to meet society's demands; it involves the person's attempts to resolve the emotional crises provoked by these changing demands. Hence, each new demand placed on the ego causes an emotional crisis, a new adjustment challenge. If the ego develops the appropriate ca-

pabilities, the crisis will be successfully resolved and healthy development will proceed. In turn, if the appropriate ego attributes are not developed, negative emotional consequences will ensue. Of course, for this view to be of use, infants must be capable of manifesting a range of emotional reactions, and research indicates that they are (Hiatt, Campos, & Emde, 1979; Izard et al., 1980; MacDonald & Silverman, 1978; Saarni, Mumme, & Campos, 1998). For example, Izard and colleagues (1980) reported that 1- to 9-month-old infants can reliably be shown to express at least eight different emotions (interest, joy, surprise, sadness, anger, disgust, contempt, and fear).

But how does the ego develop the appropriate capabilities to deal with the changing demands of reality and, hence, to effectively resolve the concomitantly changing emotional crises? To use Erikson's (1959, p. 52) terms, "How does a healthy personality . . . accrue . . . increasing capacity to master life's outer and inner dangers . . . ?" To address this question, Erikson offered an *epigenetic principle*. As defined by Erikson, "This principle states that anything that grows has a ground plan, and that out of this ground plan the *parts* arise, each having its *time* of special ascendancy, until all parts have arisen to form a *functioning whole*" (1959, p. 52).

Thus, to account for healthy ego development, Erikson offered a principle that is basically maturational in its emphasis. This predetermined–epigenetic principle asserts the existence of a maturational ground plan, a timetable, for ego development. According to Erikson, various capabilities make up a fully developed ego. These capabilities are not, however, present or fully developed at birth. Rather, each part of the ego has a particular period of time, or stage, in the life span when it must develop if it is ever to do so. When one capability is developing, the focus of development is centered around this function. However, when the next stage of development comes about, again in accordance with a maturationally fixed timetable of development, the focus of development has switched to this next stage. This pre-determined–epigenetic, maturationally fixed alteration in developmental focus is represented schematically in Figure 16.5.

In sum, Erikson (1959) proposed a stage theory of psychosocial development. In this formulation, the emergence of each stage of development—of each ego part—is fixed in accordance with a maturational timetable. Because each stage involves the development of a specific ego capability, a person has only a limited time to develop each stage-

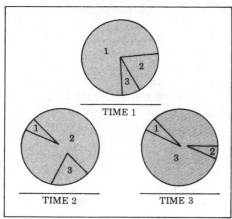

FIGURE 16.5
Schematic representation of maturationally fixed alterations in developmental focus. Here, we see a developmental pattern involving three parts of a whole; each part has its own time period of ascendancy.

specific capability. Time is limited because the timetable of development will move on to the next stage, regardless of whether the necessary capability is developed. Thus, according to Erikson (1959), each stage of psychosocial development is a *critical period.*

It should be noted, however, that other interpretations exist of the strength of Erikson's commitment to a concept of critical periods within his theory (e.g., see Chapter 6; and Muuss, 1996; Sorell & Montgomery, in press). For instance, some of these interpretations draw on Erikson's later writings (e.g., Erikson, 1982; Erikson & Kivnick, 1986), and some leading scholars of Erikson's work (e.g., see Sorell & Montgomery, in press) see Erikson as having recast his ideas in order to emphasize the recurrence and reworking during later stages of development (e.g., adulthood) of issues (e.g., identity) that were the foci of earlier periods of the life span (e.g., adolescence). Sorell and Montgomery (in press) regard the admission of such reworking into his scheme of development as evidence of a less rigid concept of critical periods then found, for instance, in classical psychoanalytic theory (e.g., Freud, 1954).

Critical Periods of Psychosocial Development

Because stage development is governed by a predetermined–epigenetic, maturational timetable, a

person *must* develop what is supposed to be developed in each stage of development or else there will *never* be another chance. The timetable of development will move on, and another part of the whole, another capability, will be in *its* time of as-cendan-cy. Thus, each stage of psychosocial development is critical in that if the appropriate capability does not develop when it is supposed to, two things will happen. First, that capability is doomed as a completely adequate entity. The potential for its optimal development will be lost. Second, if what was necessary in order for healthy ego development to proceed did not develop, the rest of development will be unfavorably altered. When all parts of the whole should have formed a synthesized, functioning whole, the person will be lacking the complete, or adequate, development of one ego part, one ego capability. Because, according to Erikson, there are no second chances in development, once part of one's ego fails to appropriately develop one will never, be able to regain it, and the rest of development will be unfavorably altered. Hence, to the extent that this ego capability is not developed sufficiently, the person will be ineffective in dealing with reality. In this sense, the second outcome of inappropriate development within each critical period of development is neurotic, as opposed to healthy, personality development.

In short, Erikson proposed that ego development proceeds through eight stages of psychosocial development. In each stage, a different ego capability must be developed in order for healthy ego development to proceed. Developments within each psychosocial stage are critical for the final development of a fully integrated, whole ego. Such an ego will have all the capabilities necessary to meet all the societal demands imposed on it. Thus, within each stage of development, the component emotional crisis—which Erikson conceptualized in differential terms—must be successfully resolved in order for healthy ego development to proceed.

Stages of Psychosocial Development

As a follower of Freudian psychoanalysis, Erikson saw the stages of psychosocial development as complementary to Freud's psychosexual stages. Accordingly, the id-based psychosexual stages exist, but they do so along with the ego-based psychosocial stages. Although these psychosocial stages have some similarity to the psychosexual stages, they go beyond them in that they constitute stages in the ego's continual functioning.

Stage 1: The Oral-Sensory Stage

Freud's first stage of psychosexual development is termed the oral stage. In that stage, the infant is concerned with obtaining appropriate stimulation in the oral zone. Erikson believed, however, that when one's focus shifts to the ego, one sees that the newborn infant is not merely concerned with oral stimulation. Rather, the infant has newly entered the world, and, therefore, all its senses are being bombarded with stimulation—its eyes, ears, nose, and all other sense-receptor sites. Thus, in order to begin to deal effectively with the social world, the infant must be able to incorporate all this sensory information effectively. Erikson termed this psychosocial stage the *oral*-sensory stage, and in so doing he indicated that the ego must develop the capability of dealing with the wealth of sensory stimulation constantly impinging on it.

However, the need to deal with all this stimulation evokes a stage-specific emotional crisis for the infant. If the infant experiences the sensory world as relatively pleasant or benign, one sort of emotion will result. Alternatively, if the child's sensory stimulation experiences are negative or harsh, another type of feeling will result. If the infant has relatively pleasant sensory experiences, he or she will come to *feel* that the world is a relatively benign, supportive place—that it will not hurt or shock him or her. According to Erikson, then, the infant will develop a sense of basic trust. If, however, the infant experiences pain and discomfort, he or she will feel that the world is not supportive—that there is pain and danger in the world. Here, the infant will develop a sense of mistrust.

The infant thus faces an emotional crisis, precipitated by the nature and quality of the sensory world he or she attempts to incorporate. The infant will develop a sense of basic trust in the world or a sense of mistrust. It is this emotional crisis that Erikson conceptualized in differential terms. The emotional crisis, then, is between *basic trust* versus *mistrust*. (We may delete the words "a sense of" for the sake of brevity of presentation, with the understanding that they are always to be applied to all of the alternative stage-specific sets of feelings.) Erikson thought of these two alternative feelings as forming a behavioral attribute. That is, they represent bipolar, alternative endpoints along a single dimension. Erikson would represent the emotional crisis of basic trust versus mistrust as: basic trust—mistrust. The ends of this bipolar continuum represent the alternative emotional outcomes of this stage of psychosocial

development. In other words, Erikson stressed the point that people do not, and should not, develop *either* complete basic trust or complete mistrust. Rather, a given person will develop a feeling that falls somewhere *along* this dimension.

If a person develops complete trust, Erikson pointed out, that would be as unadaptive as developing complete mistrust—the person would not recognize the real dangers that exist in the world (e.g., the person would never look when crossing the street because of a belief that no driver would ever hurt him or her, or the person might never strive to provide for him- or herself because he or she feels that the world will surely do that). On the other hand, however, a person on the far end of the mistrust side of the continuum would never venture interactions with the world, feeling that the world would assuredly hurt him or her. In a sense, we might say that such a person would have absolutely no hope; he or she would feel that there would be no chance of anything but pain resulting from his or her interactions with (his or her incorporations of) the world.

Thus, we see that it is necessary to develop a feeling that lies somewhere between the two endpoints of the bipolar continuum. If one develops more trust than mistrust, Erikson believed that healthy ego development will proceed. If, however, one develops greater mistrust than trust, then unhealthy, unoptimal ego development will proceed. Having a feeling located closer to the trust end of the continuum means that the ego has developed the appropriate incorporative capabilities to allow it to effectively deal with the world's sensory input. Having a feeling located closer to the other side of the continuum means that the appropriate ego capabilities have not developed. Importantly, of course, one can develop a location at any point along this continuum.

In other words, for this first status attribute—the oral-sensory psychosocial stage of development—a ratio of basic trust–mistrust greater than 1.0 will result in healthy ego development. For any status attribute (stage of development), a behavioral attribute location that results in a ratio (from positive end to negative end) greater than 1.0 means that the appropriate ego capabilities have developed, whereas a corresponding ratio less than 1.0 means that the appropriate ego capabilities have not developed.

We see that each stage of psychosocial development may be construed as a status attribute, and that within each status attribute there exists an emotional crisis that is conceptualized as a bipolar dimension, as a behavioral attribute. One's location along this dimension defines the extent to which one has successfully resolved the emotional crisis precipitated by the reality demands put on the ego at this stage of development; thus, the location reflects the extent to which the appropriate ego capability has been developed. Further, this location will affect the ego's functioning as the child enters the next stage of psychosocial development.

Stage 2: The Anal-Musculature Stage

Freud's second stage of psychosexual development is termed the anal stage. Here, we may remember from Chapter 15 that the infant obtains gratification through the exercise of his or her anal musculature. According to Erikson, however, psychosocial development involves the other muscles of the body as well. Here, then, psychosocial development involves developing control over all of one's muscles, not just those involved in psychosexual development. Analogous to use of his anal muscles, the infant must learn when to hold on to and when to let go of all his or her bodily muscles (Erikson, 1963). He or she must develop the capability of being able to control his or her overall bodily movements.

Accordingly, if the child feels that he or she is in control of his or her own body—that he *himself* or she *herself* can exert this control over himself or herself—the child will develop a sense of autonomy. To the extent that the child can control his or her own movements, he or she will feel autonomous. On the other hand, if the child finds him- or herself unable to exert this independent control over his or her own bodily musculature, if he or she finds that others have to do what he or she feels expected to do him- or herself, then the child will develop a sense of shame and doubt: The child will feel shame because he or she is not showing the ability to control his or her own movements (e.g., bowel movements and/or movements involved in feeding himself or herself), and this may evoke disapproval from significant other persons—parents.

Moreover, because the child experiences this inability to control him- or herself, he or she will feel doubt about his or her capabilities to do so. The child feels shame because he or she experiences that others do things for him or her that both the child and these others feel the child should be doing for him- or herself. Thus, feeling shame about this lack of effectiveness, the child further doubts whether he or she has the capability to perform these expected functions. In sum, the second bipolar psychosocial crisis is one of *autonomy* versus *shame and doubt.*

Stage 3: The Genital-Locomotor Stage

Here, if the child has appropriately developed within the anal-musculature stage and gained the ability to control his or her own movements, he or she will have a chance to use these abilities. This third psychosocial stage corresponds to Freud's psychosexual phallic stage. Although Erikson did not dismiss the psychosexual implications of the Oedipal conflict, he specified that such a development also has important psychosocial implications. That is, if the child is successfully able to resolve the Oedipal conflict, he or she must begin to move away from the parental figures. He or she must begin to employ the previously developed self-control over his or her muscles, take his or her own steps into the world, and thereby break his or her Oedipal ties. Erikson said that society expects the child not to remain "tied to the mother's apron strings," but, rather, to locomote (walk off) independently and thereby eliminate such attachments. The child him- or herself must be able to move freely in interaction with the environment.

Accordingly, if the child can move in the world without a parent's guiding or prodding, he or she will develop a sense of initiative. He or she will feel able to decide when to use his or her locomotor abilities to interact with the world. On the other hand, if the child does not do this, if he or she remains tied to the parent for directives about the exercise of his or her locomotor functioning, he or she will not feel a sense of initiative. Rather, the child will feel a sense of guilt. That is, the child's Oedipal attachments will remain relatively intact, and to the extent that they continue to exist while society simultaneously expects the child to show evidence of their abolishment, he or she will feel guilt.

Thus, in this stage, a child will develop either toward *initiative* or *guilt,* and again, of course, this emotional crisis is conceptualized as a bipolar dimension. People should develop toward the initiative side of this emotional attribute continuum so that the ratio of initiative to guilt is greater than one.

Stage 4: Latency

Freud did not pay much attention to the psychosexual latency stage because of his belief that the libido is submerged; consequently, the stage had little if any psychosexual importance for him. However, Erikson attached a great deal of psychosocial importance to the latency years. Erikson claimed that, in all societies, children begin at this stage to learn the tasks requisite for being adult members of society. In our society, this psychosocial directive takes the form of the child's being sent to school. In other societies, this same psychosocial orientation may take the form of teaching the child to farm, cook, hunt, or fish.

Accordingly, if the child learns these skills well, if he or she learns what to do and how to do it, he or she will develop a sense of industry. The child will feel that he or she knows what to do to be a capably functioning adult member of society. He or she will feel able to be industrious, that he or she has the capability to *do*. On the other side of the continuum lies the feeling associated with failures in these psychosocial developments. If the child feels that he or she has not learned to capably perform the requisite tasks of his or her society (while feeling that others around him or her *have* acquired this), the child will feel a sense of inferiority. Thus, to the extent that children feel that they have developed the requisite skills of their society, they will develop feelings toward either *industry* or *inferiority*.

Stage 5: Puberty and Adolescence

This stage of development corresponds to the genital stage of psychosexual development in Freud's theory. Erikson, too, was concerned with the implications of the emergence of a genital sex drive occurring at puberty. But, as with the previous stages of psychosocial development, Erikson here looked at the broader, psychosocial implications of all the physical, physiological, and psychological changes that emerge at puberty.

Numerous changes occur when a person enters puberty. In fact, one may even suggest that every dimension of the person undergoes a quantitative and/or qualitative change. With puberty comes the emergence of the secondary sexual characteristics (e.g., pigmented pubic hair, changes in the voice, changes in bodily muscle and fat distributions, menarche and breast development for females, or the first ejaculation and pigmented facial hair for males). There are even changes in the primary sexual characteristics, the genitalia; for instance, in males, there is a thickening and an elongation of the penis. Moreover, the person now has a sexual drive—a genital capacity—and this evokes new bodily sensations that have to be dealt with and understood. Furthermore, the person's mental structures also undergo a qualitative change at about this time. As we have seen in our discussion of Piaget's theory in Chapter 15, the person at this time begins to think differently; formal operations emerge, and this means that the person will become predominantly centered on him- or herself (we have seen this centration termed adolescent egocentrism; Elkind, 1967). In addition, the person will think about him- or herself abstractly and hypothetically.

Erikson saw all these changes occurring with puberty as presenting the adolescent—for this is the label that contemporary society now attaches to the person (Lerner, 2002)—with serious psychosocial problems. The child has lived for about 12 years and has developed a sense of who he or she is and of what he or she is and is not capable. If the child has developed successfully, he or she will have developed more trust than mistrust, more autonomy than shame and doubt, more initiative than guilt, and more industry than inferiority. In any event, all the feelings the child has developed have gone into giving him or her a feeling about who he or she is and what he or she can do. Now, however, this knowledge is challenged. The adolescent now finds him- or herself in a body that looks and feels different, and further finds that he or she is thinking about these things in a new way. Thus, all the associations the adolescent has had about him- or herself in earlier stages may not be relevant to the new person he or she now has become.

Accordingly, the adolescent asks him- or herself a crucial psychosocial question: Who am I? Moreover, at precisely the time when the adolescent feels unsure about this, society begins to ask the adolescent related questions. For instance, in Western society, the adolescent must now begin to take the first definite steps toward career objectives (e.g., deciding whether to enter college preparatory courses). Society asks adolescents what role they will play in society and wants to know when these soon-to-be-adult persons will contribute to its maintenance (e.g., Hamilton, 1994). Society wants to know what *socially prescribed set of behaviors*—behaviors functioning for the adaptive maintenance of society—will be adopted. Such a set of behaviors is a role, and, thus, the key aspect of the adolescent dilemma is that of finding a role. Yet, how can one know what one can do and wants to do to contribute to society (and to meet its demands) if one does not know who one is?

In summary, this question—Who am I?—is basically a question of self-definition, necessitated by the emergence of all the new feelings and capabilities experienced during adolescence (e.g., the sex drive and formal thought), as well as by the demands placed on the adolescent by society. The adaptive challenge of finding a role one can be committed to, and, thus, achieving an identity, is the most important psychosocial task of adolescence. Erikson termed the emotional upheaval provoked by this challenge the *identity crisis*. To resolve this crisis and achieve a sense of identity, Erikson (1959) saw it necessary to attain a complex synthesis between psychological processes and societal goals and directives (Erikson, 1959). That is, to achieve identity the adolescent must find an orientation that fulfills the attributes of the self while being consistent with society's expectations. As such, this orientation must be both individually and socially adaptive. That is, such a role cannot be something that is self-destructive (e.g., sustained fasting) or socially unacceptable (e.g., criminal behavior). Erikson termed the adoption of a role such as the latter *negative identity formation* and noted that although such roles exist in most societies, they have—by definition—severe sanctions associated with them.

Thus, in trying to find an orientation to life that meets both individual and societal demands, the adolescent is searching for a set of behavioral prescriptions—a role—that fulfills the biological, psychological, and social demands of life. To put it another way, a role represents a synthesis of biological, psychological, and social adaptive demands. This is why Erikson (1959, 1963) saw ego identity as having these three components.

To find such an identity, the adolescent must discover what he or she believes in, what his or her attitudes and ideals are. These factors, which can be said to define one's *ideology,* provide an important component of one's role. When we know who we are, we know what we do, and when we know what we do, we know our role in society.

Along with any role (e.g., wife, father, student, teacher, engineer, or physician) goes a set of orientations toward the world that serve to define that role. These attitudes, beliefs, and values give us some idea of what a person engaged in a particular role in society thinks of and does. Thus, there is an ideology that serves to define a societal role. We know fairly well what the ideology of a Catholic priest is and how it is similar to and different from the ideology associated with a professional soldier, professional artist, or professional politician. The point is that along with any role goes a role-defining ideology. To solve one's identity crisis, one must be committed to a role, which in turn means showing commitment toward an ideology. Erikson (1963) termed such an emotional orientation *fidelity*.

If the adolescent finds his or her role in society, if he or she can show commitment to an ideology, the adolescent will have achieved a sense of identity. Alternatively, if the adolescent does not find a

role to play in society, he or she will remain in the identity crisis. The adolescent might typically complain of not knowing "where I'm at" or of being unable to "get my head together." In an attempt to resolve this crisis, the adolescent may try one role one day and another the next, perhaps successfully—but only temporarily—investing the self in many different things. Accordingly, Erikson maintained that if the adolescent does not resolve the identity crisis, he or she will feel a sense of *role confusion* or *identity diffusion*. These two terms denote the adolescent's feelings associated with being unable to show commitment to a role and, hence, to achieve a crisis-resolving identity.

Several possibilities exist for an adolescent who is in his or her identity crisis. One is to simply adopt a readily available role supplied by society. For instance, the adolescent could go into his or her father's or mother's business, enter military service, or get married and define him- or herself as a husband or wife. Another possible route would be to adopt an identity also readily available but deemed socially unacceptable by society (e.g., one could become a delinquent). We have noted that Erikson terms such an occurrence negative identity formation.

Finally, instead of finding a role first, one could adopt an ideology. That is, one could show intense commitment to some set of beliefs (e.g., those associated with some current social cause) and, thus, achieve a feeling of having a role. Because ideology and role go hand in hand, if one adopts an ideology, one must, therefore, have a role. One would be someone who stands for that cause, and this would give a feeling of having found one's role. Thus, one would feel "older now"; one would feel that one had moved past one's identity crisis. Perhaps, however, because such a solution does not represent a true internalization of a role, this intense commitment to an ideology and the concomitant sense of being "older now" are not enduring. One might become disillusioned with the ideology; then, if one develops further and finally achieves an actual identity, one might look back at these previous commitments and feelings as immature. Indeed, as Bob Dylan (1964) wrote in his song, *My Back Pages,* "Good and bad, I defined these terms, so clear, no doubt, some how. But I was so much older then. I'm younger than that now."

In sum, it may be seen that the identity crisis of adolescence is provoked by individual changes in the person and societal changes toward the person; the identity crisis can only be resolved through commitment to a role balancing the individual and social demands raised by these changes. The terms *crisis* and *commitment* become hallmarks of the fifth stage of psychosocial development. Yet, not only is the adaptive struggle in this stage preceded by events in earlier stages, but also its outcome is influenced by them. As Constantinople (1969) pointed out:

> In order to achieve a positive resolution of the identity crisis, the adolescent must sift through all of the attitudes toward himself and the world which have occurred over the years with the resolution of earlier crises, and he must fashion for himself a sense of who he is that will remain constant across situations and that can be shared by others when they interact with him. (p. 358)

Furthermore, the identity the adolescent attains as a consequence of the psychosocial crises preceding and during adolescence will influence the rest of the life span. According to Erikson, self-esteem is a feeling about the self that tends to remain constant across life and, thus, gives the person a coherent psychological basis for dealing with the demands of social reality. In one essay in which he cast the notion of identity in terms of self-esteem, Erikson (1959) said:

> Self-esteem, confirmed at the end of a major crisis, grows to be a conviction that one is learning effective steps toward a tangible future, that one is developing a defined personality within a social reality which one understands. (p. 89)

Constantinople (1969) elaborated that in adolescence:

> This self-esteem is the end product of successful resolutions of each crisis; the fewer or the less satisfactory the successful resolutions, the less self-esteem on which to build at this stage of development, and the greater the likelihood of a prolonged sense of identity diffusion, of not being sure of who one is and where one is going. (p. 358)

Where one is going is on to the early portion of one's adulthood. There, yet another psychosocial crisis will be faced. As implied, its successful resolution, as well as that of the remaining crises of the adult years, will rest on the attainment of an adequate identity.

Stage 6: Young Adulthood

In this and the last two psychosocial stages, Erikson departed from the psychosexual model and provided a description of the psychosocial stage changes involved with the rest of the human life span. Thus, after the adolescent years, the person enters into young adulthood and accordingly is faced with a new set of psychosocial requirements.

In young adulthood, the person is oriented toward entering into a marital union. The person should by now have achieved an identity and should know who he or she is. The society now requires the person to enter into an institution that will allow the society to continue to exist. Accordingly, the formation of a new family unit must be established (e.g., through marriage). The young adult must form a relationship with another person that will allow such an institution to prosper. This psychosocial directive, however, leads the person into another emotional crisis.

Erikson argued that to enter into and successfully maintain such a relationship, a person must be able to give of him- or herself fully. Such openness and complete give-and-take is not limited, according to Erikson, to sexual relations. Rather, Erikson meant that by giving of oneself fully, all the facets of one person (e.g., feelings, ideas, goals, attitudes, and values) must be unconditionally available to the other; moreover, the person must be unconditionally receptive to these same things from the partner. Accordingly, to the extent that one can attain such interchange, one will feel a *sense of intimacy*. Again, this is not limited to sexual intimacy but includes the mutual interchange of both partners' most intimate feelings, ideas, and goals.

If, however, one has not achieved an identity in Stage 5 and, thus, does not have a total sense of self (to give of completely), then, of course, one will not be able to achieve this sense of intimacy. One cannot give of one's self if one does not have a self to give. Thus, rather than being able to have a complete mutual interchange, one will be restricted in what one is capable of giving. Accordingly, there are limits to intimacy with another; if one cannot (for whatever reason) share and be shared, then one will feel a *sense of isolation*.

Erikson's theorizing provides a suggestion about why divorce may occur in contemporary society. Perhaps, people enter into marriage unions with the expectation of finding their identities. They expect to define themselves through marriage and, thus, discover who they are. However, because, according to Erikson, less than two identities can never be made to equal two identities, such people will be disillusioned by marriage. Instead of finding out who they are, they experience feelings of isolation. Although they are now joined with another person, this union—this other person—is a disappointment. This other person has not provided them with what they expected—an identity—and this union has instead brought on feelings of being alone.

Stage 7: Adulthood

If a successful, intimate union has been formed, however, the person can now attempt to meet the next set of psychosocial requirements, the ones presented by adulthood. In this stage, society requires the person to play the role of a productive, contributing member of society. Farmers must grow crops, artists must paint pictures, and professors must generate ideas (and publications).

Accordingly, if the person is successfully playing the role society expects, if he or she is contributing and producing what is expected, then the person will have a *sense of generativity,* a feeling that he or she is performing his or her role appropriately. The person will feel he or she is being generative. On the other hand, if the person finds that he or she is not fulfilling the requirements of his or her role, if the person is not producing as he or she should, the person will feel a *sense of stagnation.* The person will find that his or her output is below expectations.

Traditionally, American society has drawn important distinctions between men and women in the behaviors in which they may engage (Block, 1973). As such, how men and women achieve feelings of generativity has been different. Whereas men's generative feelings could be achieved through engaging in professional or business activities, women's generational feelings traditionally could be attained only through the generation (or production) of children (J. Lerner, 1994). Women who chose not to have children or opted for entering the "men's world" (of business or professionalism) were negatively evaluated by society and were viewed as inappropriately fulfilling women's roles (Block, 1973). Such pejorative orientations toward women obviated the possibility of women making their maximal contribution to our society. This situation is, of course, changing (Hernandez, 1993), and Erikson pointed out that well it should. If women are limited to the production of children as their only way of attaining this needed feeling of generativity, then, Erikson believed, eventually our society and the world will be faced with a severe problem: overpopulation.

Thus, in addition to the moral and human-rights reasons for widening women's roles in society, Erikson provided us with a psychological and an ecological reason for this alteration. Women must, he argued, be allowed to channel their generational behavior in other directions—to fulfill their generational feelings in all possible ways—if society is to survive; and thus society must come to view this change as appropriate. The choice for women should not remain one of child-bearing versus having a feeling of stagnation. If this choice is not altered, then we will enter into a most dangerous spiral. More and more people will be produced, and they in turn will produce more and more people.

However, Erikson's ideas may not be as egalitarian as they may seem at initial inspection. Although Erikson believed that women should engage in roles other than wife and mother, he did *not* believe women and men should engage in the same exact set of roles and/or play roles in the exact same ways.

Sex differences in ego development. There are obvious differences between the sexes. Structural differences in primary and secondary sexual characteristics and functional differences in reproduction are universal contrasts between males and females. Only women can *menstruate, gestate* (carry children), and *lactate* (breastfeed). Only men can *impregnate* (Money & Ehrhardt, 1972).

Erikson (1964, 1968), as well as Freud (1923), suggested that personality and social functioning are innately tied to the physical and physiological characteristics of males and females. Such a *nature* view says that there are inevitable differences between the sexes, because there are universal biological contrasts between them. Just as it is biologically adaptive (for species survival) to engage in male or female reproductive functions; it is also "biologically imperative" (Freud 1923, 1949) to engage in those personal behaviors that are innately linked to one's biological status as a male or female. It is in this sense that sex differences in personality and social relations are seen as universal. According to proponents of this position such as Erikson (1964, 1968), *anatomy is destiny!*

Erikson's theory of inner and outer space. As I have indicated, Erikson (1959, 1963) believed that healthy or adaptive ego development requires a synthesis of the biological, psychological, and societal demands placed on the person. At each stage of ego development, the person is placed in a psychosocial crisis that can best be dealt with through such a synthesis, or integration.

In adolescence, the identity crisis can only be resolved adequately through the attainment of a role. Such a role must involve the adoption of a set of behaviors and an ideology that allow the individual to contribute to society in a biologically appropriate way. Erikson (1964, 1968) believed that because males and females differ in terms of their physiological functions and reproductive organs, there will be different implications for role adoption. In other words, because of the basic biological differences between men and women, they will necessarily have to adopt different role-related behaviors and ideologies in order to be psychosocially "healthy." Thus, for Erikson (1964, 1968), the anatomical and physiological differences between the sexes relate directly to differences in ego development:

> Many of the testable items on the long list of "inborn" differences between human males and females can be shown to have a meaningful function within an ecology which is built, as any mammalian ecology must be, around the fact that the human fetus must be carried inside the womb for a given number of months, and that the infant must be suckled or, at any rate, raised within a maternal world best staffed at first by the mother (and this for the sake of her own awakened motherliness, as well) with a gradual addition of other women. (Erikson, 1968, p. 281)

The inner-space orientation of females. Thus, Erikson saw women's reproductive role as the dominant force in shaping their ego identities. However, his idea is more pervasive than this. He argued that, because of their anatomical structure and the biological demand for carrying and nurturing the child of a man, women's whole sense of self is necessarily involved with motherhood and mothering. Erikson (1968) said:

> The stage of life crucial for the emergence of an integrated female identity is the step from youth to maturity, the state when the young woman, whatever her work career, relinquishes the care received from the parental family in order to commit herself to the love of a stranger and to the care to be given to his and her offspring. (Erikson, 1968 p. 265)

According to Erikson, identity development in females moves in the direction of being a wife and a mother. Accordingly, Erikson believed that, to fulfill her biologically based role appropriately, an adolescent female must be oriented to her inner space. To bear children in fulfillment of her biological directive, a female must be oriented toward incorporation—toward bringing a man's penis into her *inner space,* into her body. Only through such *incorporation* can the woman create a situation allowing adaptation. Only through incorporation can she create within herself the child that will fulfill her biological destiny. Because of this biologically based orientation to inner space, the female will undergo identity-formation processes different from the male's. The behaviors females will be committed to, or show fidelity toward, will be markedly different than those of males. Indeed,

by asking some rhetorical questions, Erikson (1968) argued that regardless of whether a woman chooses a career outside marriage (as we have seen he, in fact, espoused in order to avoid overpopulation), at her core the woman is always disposed to, and indeed dominated by, her orientation toward being a mother and mothering. Erikson (1968) said:

> But how does the identity formation of women differ by dint of the fact that their somatic design harbors an "inner space" destined to bear the offspring of chosen men and, with it, a biological, psychological, and ethical commitment to take care of human infancy? Is not the disposition for this commitment (whether it be combined with a career, and even whether or not it be realized in actual motherhood) the core problem of female fidelity? (p. 266)

To become a mother and to engage in mothering, a female obviously needs a male. Thus, her inner-space incorporative orientation leads to an interpersonal orientation. She needs to admit a male to her inner space so that her biologically imperative psychosocial role can be achieved. In short, because of her inner-space demands, a female becomes interpersonally oriented to search for a man to incorporate. Although a female can prepare for this before she meets a particular male, she must keep her identity somewhat open in order to adjust herself to the specific characteristics of the particular male she attracts. Erikson (1968) noted:

> Young women often ask whether they can "have an identity" before they know whom they will marry and for whom they will make a home. Granted that something in the young woman's identity must keep itself open for the peculiarities of the man to be joined and of the children to be brought up, I think that much of a young woman's identity is already defined in her kind of attractiveness and in the selective nature of her search for the man (or men) by whom she wishes to be sought . . . womanhood arrives when attractiveness and experience have succeeded in selecting what is to be admitted to the welcome of the inner space "for keeps." (p. 283)

A female needs to attract a male in order that a biologically adaptive incorporation into her inner space may occur. Thus, a female is dependent on a male for the attainment of her identity, because without a literal, (or at least symbolic) incorporation of the penis, she cannot attain her requisite role. Indeed, all her psychosocial activities are directed toward this fulfillment of inner-space pressures. In fact, Erikson (1968) said: "But since a woman is never not-a-woman, she can see her long-range goals only in those modes of activity which include and integrate her natural dispositions" (p. 290).

In sum, Erikson saw a female's inner-space, incorporative *mode of functioning* as making her committed to a role involving interpersonal orientations and dependency on others. Because of the invariant biological basis of these relations, Erikson appears to be taking a weak interactional, and, hence, nature-based, view of the basis of females' ego development. Indeed, Erikson (1968) is quite explicit about this stance:

> Am I saying, then, that "anatomy is destiny"? Yes, it is destiny, insofar as it determines not only the range and configuration of physiological functioning and its limitation but also, to an extent, personality configurations. The basic modalities of woman's commitment and involvement naturally also reflect the ground plan of her body. (p. 285)

If "anatomy is destiny" for females, it must also be so for males. Yet, the different structure of male reproductive organs leads to quite different implications for them.

The outer-space orientation of males. According to Erikson (1968), males must also use their reproductive organs in ways consistent with their biological roles. If they are to use their bodies appropriately, they cannot be incorporative. Rather, they must seek to *intrude upon* (or enter into) objects external to their own bodies. They must be oriented to *outer space* and develop an *intrusive mode* of dealing with the environment outside themselves in order to use their bodies for reproduction. Although Erikson believed that a female needs a male, either literally or symbolically, in order to attain an appropriate identity, the reverse is not the case for males: A man does not need a woman in order to be a man. Instead, the outer-space orientation of men requires only that they develop ego capabilities allowing for intrusion on target objects outside the body. Although such objects may be females, they need not be. As long as any object in the environment is being successfully intruded on—or, in other words, *dominated, manipulated,* or *controlled*—then (at least symbolically) the male is conforming adaptively to his outer-space, intrusive mode of functioning.

Thus, as long as males are oriented toward, and effective in, gaining dominance over objects in their outer space, they are behaving in a biologically appropriate manner. Indeed, whereas the inner-space orientation of females leads to an inevitable *press* toward being a mother and mothering, males' outer-space orientation leads to quite distinct behaviors. Because appropriate use of the body involves intrusion upon any objects external

to the self, the male does not need another person to show this orientation. Thus, the adaptive male should develop an independent, *individual* orientation. In fact, if the male depended on others in any way for his psychosocial functioning, this would mean he was not dominating his outer space but, instead, that he was dependent on objects external to himself.

In contrast with a female, whose basic "unit" of reproduction—the ovum—must passively wait for the male's sperm for impregnation and, thus, fulfillment of the inner space, the male must play an active role in life to meet the demands of the outer space (Erikson, 1968). That is, if sperm are not active and mobile, then reproduction will not occur. Analogously, if males do not show behaviors that are effective, independent, and active manipulations of their environment, they cannot fulfill the demands of their outer space. Thus, roles allowing for these behaviors are appropriate for males.

In sum, the linkage between differences in reproductive anatomy and physiology and differences in the personality and social behavior of males and females is a nature-based and, hence, invariant linkage in Erikson's (1964, 1968) view. The biological basis of these differences is construed to mean that females' identities must, at their core, be oriented to being a mother or to mothering (e.g., through being a nurse or teacher of young children—roles that are traditionally associated with women in Western culture; Block, 1973), whereas males' identities must, at their core, involve mastery of the external world. These sex differences not only reflect the different ways the genitals of the two sexes are structured but also they mirror the function of the reproductive cells of each sex. Additionally, they pervade each sex group's entire orientation to the world.

Furthermore, Erikson believed that childhood play behaviors reflect the psychosocial preparation of the person for a role consistent with his or her anatomical and physiological characteristics. As evidence, Erikson (1968) reported that when he asked a group of 10- to 12-year-old males and females from the Berkeley Guidance Study to construct scenes with materials such as dolls and blocks, they portrayed scenes consistent with their respective genital structures. Although not instructed in any way about what sort of scene to construct, males built scenes figuratively related to an intrusive penis, or an organ attaining or losing its erect state. Females' scenes were symbolically related to their vaginal opening or to their internal genitalia. Erikson's (1968) report and interpretation of these data are instructive:

> Girls' enclosures consist of low walls, i.e., only one block high, except for an occasional *elaborate doorway*. These interiors of houses with or without walls were, for the most part, expressly *peaceful*. Often, a little girl was playing the piano. In a number of cases, however, the interior was *intruded* by animals or dangerous men. Yet the idea of an intruding creature did not necessarily lead to the defensive erection of walls or closing of doors. Rather the majority of these intrusions have an element of humor and pleasurable excitement.
>
> Boys' scenes are either houses with elaborate walls or facades with *protrusions* such as cones or cylinders representing ornaments or cannons. There are *high towers,* and there are entirely exterior scenes. In boys' constructions more people and animals are *outside* enclosures or buildings, and there are more *automotive* objects and animals *moving* along streets and intersections. There are elaborate automotive *accidents,* but there is also traffic channeled or arrested by the policeman. While *high structures* are prevalent in the configurations of the boys, there is also much play with the danger of *collapse* or downfall; *ruins* were exclusively boys' constructions.
>
> The male and female spaces, then, were dominated, respectively, by height and downfall and by strong motion and its channeling or arrest; and by static interiors which were open or simply enclosed, and peaceful or intruded upon. It may come as a surprise to some and seem a matter of course to others that here sexual differences in the organization of a play space seem to parallel the morphology of genital differentiation itself; in the male, an external organ, erectable and intrusive in character, serving the channelization of mobile sperm cells; in the female, internal organs, with vestibular access, leading to statically expectant ova. (pp. 270–271)

Conclusions. In sum, Erikson believed that to be appropriately generative men and women had to adopt, and be productive in, roles that were shaped by their "nature," that is, by the pressures to reproduce that were imposed on them by their sex and represented by their genital structure. As did Freud (1923), Erikson believed that anatomy was destiny insofar as healthy identity and generativity were concerned.

Although women did not have to be mothers per se, and thus did not have to *actually* reproduce to meet the demands of the adolescent and adult stages of psychosocial development, Erikson believed that they had to adopt roles that were at least symbolically related to mothering in order to develop in healthy manners during these two stages of life. If women did not, either literally or symbolically, express generativity to others in their role behavior they would not develop in a healthy manner as they moved toward their final stage of psychosocial development.

Stage 8: Maturity

In this stage of psychosocial development, the person recognizes that he or she is reaching the end of his or her life span. If the person has successfully progressed through his or her previous stages of development—if he or she has experienced more trust than mistrust, more autonomy than shame and doubt, more initiative than guilt, more industry than inferiority, and if he or she has had an identity, an intimate relationship, and has been a productive, generative person—then the individual will face the final years of life with enthusiasm and eagerness. The person will be childlike, said Erikson, in his or her enthusiasm for life. Thus, Erikson argued that he or she will feel a *sense of ego integrity*. The person will feel that he or she has led a full and complete life.

Alternatively, if the person has not experienced these events—if, for example, he or she has felt mistrustful, ashamed, guilty, and inferior, and has felt a sense of role confusion, isolation, and stagnation—then he or she will not be enthusiastic about these last years of his or her life. Rather, the person will, perhaps, feel cheated or bitter. The person might be "childish" in his or her behavior, as if trying to go back to earlier years and attain the feelings that he or she never experienced. In this case, Erikson said, the person would feel a *sense of despair*. The person would feel that time was running out and that he or she had not gained everything from life that he or she needed.

Conclusions

Erikson's theory of ego development involves changes encompassing the human life span. His theory represents a synthesis between psychoanalytically based, classical stage notions and an explicit differential orientation to development. Erikson's (1959, 1963) theory has, at least in the last three or more decades, led to more research in developmental psychology than has any other psychoanalytically oriented theory (Lerner, 2002; Muuss, 1996).

This research considers both the stagelike and differential features of Erikson's ideas and focuses to a great extent on the ideas Erikson forwarded about identity development. A discussion of this research provides an illustration of how theories such as his may be "translated" into research, and allows us to evaluate the several key conceptual issues of development associated with his ideas.

Research Related to Erikson's Theory: How Does Identity Develop in Adolescence?

For at least the last 30 years, scholars have conducted hundreds (and perhaps thousands) of investigations of identity during adolescence. This emphasis is not surprising, given the importance of this concept in (potentially at least) explaining how young people may or may not become healthy, contributing members of society. What may be surprising, however, is that still, after all this research, there remains relatively few sound studies that actually measure identity development across the span of the adolescent years (Grotevant, 1998).

Instead, beginning in the late 1970s to early 1980s, much of the research about identity focused on different statuses an adolescent may attain during the identity crisis—statuses that, as we soon discuss, may involve the attainment of an identity (in at least one of two different ways), remaining in a state of crisis, or being actively engaged in a search for identity (Marcia, 1980). Accordingly, in order to appreciate contemporary understanding of the nature of identity in adolescence, it is important to discuss research that has tested Erikson's theory.

Research About Erikson's Theory of Ego Development

Given the theoretical importance attached in Erikson's theory to the emergence of the identity crisis in adolescence, it is surprising to learn that relatively little research has been reported about the study of ego identity in *early* adolescence. Paradoxically, it is the late adolescent period, when one would expect most of the changes which should have occurred to have been completed, wherein most research activity has been directed (e.g., Archer & Waterman, 1991; Marcia, 1980, 1991; Schiedel & Marcia, 1985; Waterman, 1982).

This research has typically provided interesting and useful information about the nature of role search (see Archer & Waterman, 1991; Marcia, 1991) and, as well, about how the family context and interactions with parents facilitate the exploration of roles (Adams & Jones, 1983; Grotevant, 1998; Grotevant & Cooper, 1985). However, this research has been focused on a too advanced portion of adolescence to provide data pertinent to early adolescence as a period of role confusion and search for self.

Moreover, the findings which exist about ego identity in late adolescence indicate (theoretically surprisingly) that identity change rather than invariant stable identity achievement seems to be the rule (Archer & Waterman, 1991). For example, in a large and classic study involving an assessment of the presence of stagelike qualities in adolescent development, Constantinople (1969) tested more than 900 male and female college students from the University of Rochester. There were consistent increases in the successful resolution of identity from the freshman year to the senior year across participants and from one year to the next within groups of participants. However, only males showed consistent decreases in the scores for identity diffusion. Changes in scores for the other crises did not always decrease or increase in accordance with Erikson's theory. Thus, Constantinople's (1969) data provide, at best, only partial support for Erikson's theory of ego development.

Other data also contradict Erikson's theory. For instance, college students, by the end of their college experience and the presumed beginning of their early adulthood stage of psychosocial development, do not invariably show stable identity achievement (Archer & Waterman, 1991; Waterman, 1982). Indeed, adolescents' feelings and ideas about themselves seem to change in several directions. For example, in the Early Adolescence Study (Petersen, 1987), some aspects of self-esteem increased across early adolescence, others decreased and still others showed curvilinear changes across age.

Diversity in the nature of the ego identity crisis has also been found by researchers (Archer & Waterman, 1991; Marcia, 1964, 1966, 1980, 1991). Although gender differences are part of this diversity, they do not coincide with Erikson's theory of the identity development differences between males and females.

In a series of provocative studies of different identity "statuses" among adolescents, James Marcia (1964, 1966, 1980, 1991) hypothesized that resolutions of the adolescent identity crisis involved more than just identity versus role confusion (or identity diffusion). Marcia believed that a more diverse pattern existed, and that to accurately ascertain the adolescent's identity status, a youth's feelings of both crisis and commitment to a role should be measured.

Marcia (1966) found evidence for four identity statuses. As Erikson (1959, 1963, 1968) said, two of these statuses were held by adolescents who either had achieved identity or who were in a state of identity diffusion. The former group had had a crisis period but now showed commitment to an occupation and to an ideology. The latter group may or may not have had a crisis; however, their defining characteristic was their lack of commitment. Moreover, they were not concerned about this lack of commitment.

The first of the two other statuses Marcia identified he labeled as *Moratorium*. Students here were in a crisis and had, at best, vague commitment to an occupation or to an ideology. However, Moratorium status adolescents were actively trying to make commitments. They were in a state of search. The last identity status Marcia identified was termed *Foreclosure*. Adolescents in this status had never experienced a crisis. Yet they were highly committed. Marcia found that they had adopted the identities their parents had wanted them to take and that they had done so with little or no question and with no crisis.

Marcia (1991) summarized the evidence in support of the existence of the four identity status categories (e.g., from Marcia et al., 1985). He noted that current research evidence indicates that Identity Achievers are cognitively flexible, have higher levels of moral reasoning than youth in the other ego identity status categories, and are more capable of intimate relations than are people in the other status categories. These youth are also less neurotic and more extroverted and conscientious than are those in other ego identity categories (Clancy & Dollinger, 1993). They are also more attached to their mothers (but not their fathers) than are other youth (Benson, Harris, & Rogers, 1992).

In turn, youth in the Moratorium category have conflicting needs to conform and to rebel, have ambivalent relationships with their parents, and are seen by other people as intense, and often annoyingly so (Marcia, 1991). For instance, adolescents who are actively engaged in identity exploration are likely to be characterized by self-doubt, confusion, and conflicts with parents (Kidwell et al., 1995).

In turn, youth in the Foreclosure category are high in authoritarianism, enmeshed in their families, and cognitively rigid (Marcia, 1991). They are also not open to new experiences (Clancy & Dollinger, 1993) and tend to have an extrinsic religious orientation (Markstrom-Adams & Smith,

James Marcia

1996). Moreover, more so than youth in other identity status categories, youth who maintain their foreclosure status over a 2-year period of their late adolescence have been found to seek a lot of nurturance from others and to have a lot of memories of seeking security early in their lives (Kroger, 1995).

Finally, people in the Identity Diffusion status have lower levels of moral reasoning than youth in other categories, feel alienated from their parents, and are less capable of intimate relations than are youth in the other categories. Both these youth, and moratorium ones as well, are more neurotic and less conscientious than youth in other age-identity categories (Clancy & Dollinger, 1993). Both moratorium and diffusion youth are also less likely to be attached to their mothers and fathers (Benson et al., 1992).

Furthermore, Archer (1991) found that whereas males and females do not differ in their location during adolescence within any of the four ego identity status categories specified by Marcia (1991), there are some gender differences that occur in regard to the domains of social behavior that contribute to a person's identity status (Archer, 1985, 1989; Whitbourne & Tesch, 1985).

For instance, Archer (1985) found no gender differences in regard to the domains of vocational choice, religious beliefs, and sex-role orientation, differences that would occur if Erikson's theory of gender differences in identity development were to be supported. Moreover, Archer (1985) found that males are more likely to be in a Foreclosed status, and females in a Diffusion status, in regard to political ideology. In addition, in regard to family and career priorities and sexuality, females are more likely to be in either the Achievement or the Moratorium categories whereas males are more likely to be in the Foreclosure or the Diffusion categories.

In sum, much of the research about identity development in adolescence does not provide data supportive of Erikson's ideas about stage progression or the differences between male and female-identity development. However, whether one views Erikson's theory as valid—and scholars disagree about this evaluation (e.g., see Lerner, 2002; Muuss, 1995)—there is virtually no debate about the service Erikson provided in directing the study of human development—especially in adolescence—to a differential focus on the individual as illustrated by the concept of identity.

Some Concluding Comments About Erikson's Theory

We have seen that Erikson described eight stages in the psychosocial development of human beings, and within each of these eight stages, Erikson conceived of an emotional crisis, conceptualized in differential terms. That is, although each of the stages may be thought of as a separate status attribute, each concomitant emotional crisis is conceptualized as a bipolar trait dimension. A person develops a feeling within each stage that lies somewhere between the endpoints of each feeling dimension. Thus, each of these bipolar dimensions may be thought of as representing a behavioral attribute. In turn, because a person may develop a feeling at any particular location along each of these continua, a person's individual psychosocial developmental pattern may be represented as his or her location in this multidimensional feeling-space. Table 16.1 presents the eight psychosocial stages in Erikson's theory, along with the bipolar emotional crisis associated with each stage.

In sum, then, Erikson used differential concepts to theoretically conceptualize people's psychosocial development. He used his stages as analogous to status attributes, and, in addition, he specified

theoretically the existence of differentially conceptualized emotional crises within these stages. Thus, through our presentation of Erikson's theory, we have seen how a differential approach to the understanding of psychosocial development may be employed within what is primarily a theoretical framework. Although I would take issue with several of Erikson's specific formulations on the basis of the discussions in prior chapters about the probabilistic–epigenetic position on the nature–nurture controversy—and although my preceding research reviews have tended not to support the nature ideas derived from Erikson's (1959) essentially predetermined–epigenetic theory (and, instead, seem consistent with ideas associated with the developmental systems notions pertinent to person–context relations)—Erikson's theory is still important. It represents a unique integration of stage and differential conceptualizations of human development within a theory that attempts to describe aspects of development across the entire life span.

Moreover, Erikson's theory continues to attract the interest of contemporary scholars concerned with topics such as identity, gender and sex role development, and socialization. As a consequence, Erikson's theory is a vital, "living," formulation, one that evolved in Erikson's own thinking toward the end of his life (e.g., Erikson, 1982; Erikson, Erikson, & Kivnick, 1986) and in the work of scholars interested in both the life-span nature of identity and in contemporary, developmental systems views of the life span (e.g., Côté, 1993, 1996, 1997, 2000; Côté & Allahar, 1996; Côté & Levine, 1987, 1997, 2000; Sorell & Montgomery, in press; Spencer, 1999; Spencer, Dupree, & Hartmann, 1997).

For instance, the work of Côté (e.g., 1996, 2000; Côté & Levine, 1997, 2000) provides an integration of Eriksonian ideas with concepts pertinent to developmental contextualism (e.g., Lerner, 1995a, 1998b). Similarly, an integrative approach to the understanding of the role of multiple levels of the context on ethnic identity has been undertaken by Margaret Beale Spencer and colleagues (e.g., Cunningham & Spencer, 1996; Spencer, 1999; Spencer et al., 1997; Swanson, Spencer, & Petersen, 1998). Drawing from developmental systems conceptions, Spencer developed a "phenomenological variant of ecological systems theory" (PVEST) to study the identity-development process among ethnically diverse youth. For example, much of this work has been directed to understanding identity development among African-American male adolescents. Thus, we may, at this writing, be in the midst of an exciting and important period of neo-Eriksonian

TABLE 16.1
Erikson's Theory of Psychosocial Development

Psychosocial stage	Bipolar emotional crisis		
	A sense of	Versus	A sense of
1. Oral-sensory	basic trust	_____	mistrust
2. Anal-musculature	autonomy	_____	shame, doubt
3. Genital-locomotor	initiative	_____	guilt
4. Latency	industry	_____	inferiority
5. Puberty and adolescence	identity	_____	role confusion
6. Young adulthood	intimacy	_____	isolation
7. Adulthood	generativity	_____	stagnation
8. Maturity	ego integrity	_____	despair

theoretical elaboration and integration with other key ideas about human development (e.g., see Muuss, 1996; Sorell & Montgomery, in press).

I have said, however, that the differential approach may also be utilized as a primarily empirical mode of investigating the phenomena of psychological development. Thus, one may employ research methods that allow people who possess different status attributes to be differentiated into subgroups on the basis of studied behavior attributes. Hence, the use of such methods will allow one to make an empirical determination of the developmental interrelation of status and behavioral attributes. Although numerous examples exist of such an empirical use of the differential approach, we now consider one of the major examples of such work, the longitudinal study by Kagan and Moss (1962).

James E. Côté

Margaret Beale Spencer

THE KAGAN AND MOSS STUDY OF BIRTH TO MATURITY

In their 1962 book, *Birth to Maturity,* Jerome Kagan and Howard Moss reported the results of a *longitudinal study* of psychological development. As noted already at several points in our discussion, longitudinal research involves the study of the same group of people over the course of their development. Through such repeated measurement, the researcher obtains data that allow an assessment of the continuity–discontinuity and/or the stability–instability of the developing behaviors being studied. Accordingly, studies that have a long duration (like those of Kagan & Moss, 1962) are suited for studying these issues.

However, longitudinal studies are difficult to do and, although they provide the important asset of enabling intraindividual change to be assessed (Baltes, Reese, & Nesselroade, 1977; Magnusson & Casaer, 1992), they usually have important limitations. As I discuss in greater detail in Chapter 18, it is difficult to obtain a large group of people who are willing to submit to repeated, and often intensive, psychological investigation. Accordingly, longitudinal samples are usually comprised of a small number of people, and these people can be presumed to be different from other people in important ways. After all, these people are willing to take part in a long-term psychological investigation of their own lives. Thus, longitudinal samples may not be representative of any larger population. This makes results from such a study difficult to generalize to other groups of people.

In addition, longitudinal studies are expensive, both in terms of money needed to pay for ongoing research costs and because of the great deal of time it obviously takes to do such studies. As the years go by, some participants may drop out (possibly making the sample even more undrepresentative), or, in one way or another, the researchers themselves may drop out of the study. In addition, repeated measurements with the same participants may allow practice to affect responses.

Yet, despite these limitations, longitudinal studies seem suited for assessing the continuity–discontinuity and/or the stability–instability of selected behaviors. Indeed, as noted, longitudinal assessment is the *only* means by which we can study intraindividual change.

The expense, difficulty, and requisite commitment involved in longitudinal research allows one to recognize why major longitudinal studies of human development are relatively few in number (Magnusson & Casaer, 1992). Our consideration of

the Kagan and Moss study allows us to focus on one of the most important major longitudinal studies of psychological development. Let us now turn to a consideration of the methods that Kagan and Moss used to assess the development of various psychological phenomena from birth to maturity.

The Methods of the Kagan and Moss Study

Kagan and Moss (1962) presented a summary of the results of a longitudinal study of personality development that began in 1929 and continued through the late 1950s. Because Kagan and Moss believed that "only systematic longitudinal observations can discover those behaviors that are marked for future use and those that will be lost along the way" (1962, p. 1), they employed longitudinal observations to assess personality development. Thus, children enrolled in the Fels Research Institute's longitudinal population during the years between 1929 and 1939 were selected for such repeated observations. In this way, 89 children (44 boys and 45 girls) were selected for study. Participants were mainly from the Midwest, Protestant, white, of middle-class backgrounds, and the children of relatively well-educated parents. In other words, among the differential status variables that Kagan and Moss considered were, of course, age and sex; in addition, religion, socioeconomic status, and parents' educational backgrounds were also considered.

Obviously, not everyone who develops has the above status characteristics. Thus, we see that one limitation of the Kagan and Moss longitudinal study is that the sample is not representative of broader populations. Accordingly, although we may be unsure about the extent to which we may generalize the specific results of the Kagan and Moss study, we may at least expect the findings to provide us with some interesting (if tentative) suggestions about the general course of personality–behavioral development. For instance, the biased samples inevitably involved in longitudinal studies may limit generalizations about mean levels of behavior, but they may not be similarly restrictive in regard to learning about basic processes and/or the structure of developmental changes.

Sources of Data

The major purpose of the Kagan and Moss study was to discover the interrelation of selected status variables (primarily, age and sex) and various behavioral dimensions. Through such an interrelation, an indication of the relation between psychological development in childhood and adult psychological functioning might be discovered. Accordingly, information about the participants was gathered in a manner that allowed the information to be divided into two broad age periods.

The initial information about the children pertained to their development from birth through early adolescence. The children were administered various intelligence and personality tests, and these assessments were combined with observations of them in their homes, their nurseries and, later, their schools and day camps. In addition, assessments of the children's mothers were made and teacher interviews were conducted. Through these procedures, data allowing for the measurement of many different variables across the first 14 years of life were obtained. Each variable was conceptualized as representing a differential (behavioral) dimension, with endpoints lying at 1 and 7. For example, for the variable "dependency," a score of 7 might indicate high dependency and a score of 1 might indicate low dependency. A person's score could fall anywhere along this dimension.

Before interrelation between these attributes began, the status variable of age was further reconceptualized. Instead of differentiating their participants continuously (i.e., into 14 consecutive age groups, one year to the next), Kagan and Moss reduced the first 14 years of data into four consecutive and overlapping age periods: birth to 3 years (infancy and early childhood); 3 to 6 years (preschool); 6 to 10 years (early school years); and 10 to 14 years (preadolescent and early adolescent years). In sum, for the first 14 years of their participants' lives, status variables such as age period and sex were interrelated with several psychological variables, each conceptualized as 7-point behavioral attribute dimensions.

Of the 89 participants studied in their first 14 years of life, 71 participated in the second phase of data gathering. When they returned, from about mid-1957 through late 1959, they were between 19 and 29 years of age. Thus, a final age period (i.e., adulthood) was now introduced into the stu-dy. Again, these participants had to be tested and measured to ascertain their locations along the various psychological dimensions under study.

Kagan and Moss then had a considerable a-mount of data bearing on the psychological development and later adult functioning of a group of people, a group whose development from birth to maturity had been longitudinally studied. They began the arduous process of interrelating these measurements in their attempt to discover how

these people were differentiated into various subgroups over the course of their development. They began to analyze their information in order to discover how development in the first 14 years of life (the first four age periods) related to the psychological functioning of the adult.

Did behaviors seen early in life remain present throughout the remaining childhood years, and further, did early behavior relate in any way to the psychology of the developed adult? How did one's multidimensional location throughout childhood relate to one's multidimensional location as an adult? Let us now turn to the results of the Kagan and Moss study to see how the information they obtained answered such questions.

The Status Variables of Age Period and Sex

Perhaps the most consistent finding obtained by Kagan and Moss was that many of the childhood behaviors shown in the third age period (the early school years, from 6–10 years of age) were fairly good predictors of similar early adulthood behaviors (Kagan & Moss 1962, p. 266). Similarly, a few behaviors seen in the second age period (the preschool years, from 3–6 years of age) were also related to theoretically similar adult behaviors.

Thus, such adult behaviors as dependency (on the family) or anxiety (in social interactions) seemed to be related to analogous behavior/personality characteristics in these early or middle-childhood periods. In this way, Kagan and Moss found that knowledge of a child's position on a given variable at a particular age period in the child's life allowed one to make at least some predictions about that child's related adult functioning.

In other words, the person's position along some dimensions seemed to remain stable, and in turn, because these same variables seemed to characterize the person at these different age periods in his or her life, at least some continuity of personality development seemed to exist. Accordingly, Kagan and Moss concluded that such findings offered support to "the popular notion that aspects of adult personality begin to take form during early childhood" (1962, pp. 266–267).

Despite such overall continuity in personality development, however, an important qualification must be made. In addition to the fact that changes in the status variable of age period were often associated with continuity in the expression of various behavior/personality attributes, another status variable (i.e., sex) affected this relation. Kagan and Moss found that age-period continuity in various behavioral characteristics was essentially dependent on whether that behavior was consistent with traditional sex-role standards (Block, 1973; Broverman et al., 1972).

For example, degrees of childhood passivity and childhood dependency remained continuous for adult women but were not similarly continuous for adult men. Kagan and Moss argued that traditional sex-role standards in Western culture place negative sanctions on passive and dependent behaviors among males. Studies of stereotypes about the ideal masculine figure in Western society find that the most positively evaluated male figure is one who is viewed as dominant, aggressive, and instrumentally effective (e.g., Block, 1973; Broverman et al., 1972). Men who do not display such characteristics are negatively evaluated (Lerner & Korn, 1972). Kagan and Moss believed, however, that no corresponding negative sanctions about such behaviors exist for women in Western society. Thus, the authors found continuity between childhood passivity and dependency and adult passivity and dependency for females. A similar relation for males was not found.

On the other hand, through an analogous argument we might expect aggressive, angry, and sexual behaviors to be continuous for males but not continuous for females. In fact, such a finding was obtained. For example, "Childhood rage reactions and frequent dating during preadolescence predicted adult aggressiveness and sexual predispositions, respectively, for men but not for women" (Kagan & Moss, 1962, p. 268).

Of course, certain behaviors could be expected to remain similarly continuous for both sexes. Intellectually oriented behaviors (e.g., attempting to master schoolwork) and sex-appropriate interest behaviors (e.g., fishing for males or knitting for females) are consistent with traditional sex-role standards for either sex. Society approves such behaviors among members of both sexes. Accordingly, Kagan and Moss found that such behaviors showed a marked degree of continuity for both sexes from their early school years through their early adulthood.

In sum, Kagan and Moss found overall age continuity for at least some personality–behavior characteristics. For many of these characteristics, one could predict the adult's type of functioning through knowledge of his or her functioning in respect to conceptually consistent childhood variables. Yet, whether such overall continuity was found depended on whether a particular behavior was consistent with traditional societal sex-role standards. Those behaviors that were consistent with sex-role standards remained continuous; for those that were not, discontinuity was seen.

Kagan and Moss (1962) summarized this portion of their results by stating:

> It appears that when a childhood behavior is congruent with traditional sex-role characteristics, it is likely to be predictive of phenotypically similar behaviors in adulthood. When it conflicts with sex-role standards, the relevant motive is more likely to find expression in theoretically consistent substitute behaviors that are socially more acceptable than the original response. In sum, the individual's desire to mold his overt behavior in concordance with the culture's definition of sex-appropriate responses is a major determinant of the patterns of continuity and discontinuity in his development. (p. 269)

The Sleeper Effect

These results present an important illustration of the potential empirical outcomes derived from the longitudinal application of the differential approach. However, the longitudinal method provides the opportunity for finding other types of results. For instance, it may be the case that an important event occurs early in a person's life, and that the event will provide a cause for some of the person's behaviors; however, this effect may not be seen right away. Simply, "there may be a lag between a cause and open manifestation of the effect" (Kagan & Moss, 1962, p. 277). In other words, one may see a *sleeper effect* in development.

The Kagan and Moss method was well suited for the discovery of such sleeper effects. Through their repeated measurements of the same people over the course of their development, Kagan and Moss could ascertain whether a behavior or event measured early in a person's life, although not showing effects at middle periods, was highly related to similar behavior found in later adult life.

Three instances of a sleeper effect in development occurred in the Kagan and Moss study. First, among males, passivity and fear of bodily harm measured in the first age period (0–3 years) were found to be better predictors of a conceptually similar adult behavior (e.g., love-object dependency) than were other measurements of the childhood behaviors. Thus, males who were passive and feared bodily harm in their first 3 years of life (and, thus, may be surmised to have been dependent on their mothers for support and protection) were found to be similarly dependent on their love objects (e.g., their wives) when they reached adulthood. Yet, measurements of passivity and fear of bodily harm in the other three childhood/adolescent age periods did not predict adult male dependency.

Although one may attempt to account for this finding through reference to possible problems in the measurement of dependency (perhaps the measures used during the intervening periods were not sensitive enough to measure dependency adequately), one may also speculate that this sleeper effect is an instance of what Kagan and Moss (1962; and see Kagan, 1980, 1983; and Chapter 5) saw as an instance of *heterotypic* continuity. That is, the underlying basis of behavior (e.g.,the motive that causes behavior) may remain the same (i.e., there is explanatory continuity) although the overt behavior linked to the cause (i.e., fear of bodily harm or dependency on one's love object) may change across life (i.e., there is descriptive discontinuity). Simply, heterotypic continuity is an instance of what was discussed in Chapter 5 as the coupling of explanatory continuity and descriptive discontinuity. It may be contrasted with *homotypic* continuity, where there is descriptive and (at least presumably) explanatory continuity.

Thus, as an illustration of heterotypic continuity, we may interpret the first instance of a sleeper effect found by Kagan and Moss (1962) as reflecting descriptive quantitative discontinuity. That is, for some males, there was an abrupt change in their measured dependency-related behaviors between the first age period and the next three, and, in turn, between these three periods and the adult period. It is these two abrupt changes that represent descriptive quantitative discontinuity. Yet, because, in the first period of years, behavior measurements *were* predictive of adult behavior measurements, and because these two sets of measurements seem to be reflective of analogous behavioral tendencies, one may say that the same underlying personality characteristic was expressed in these two measurements. Thus, one may interpret the relation between the two widely separated age periods as being reflective of explanatory qualitative continuity and speculate that perhaps factors related to differential social situations can account for this complex finding.

Perhaps descriptive quantitative discontinuity was seen because the dependency-related behaviors measured in the first period and in adulthood were measures of the male in relation to a female (mother and wife, respectively), whereas the measures of dependency-related behaviors in the intervening three age periods were measures of the male in relation to his peers (presumably mostly other males). Because we know that such dependency-related behaviors are negatively sanctioned for males in Western culture (Block, 1973; Broverman et al., 1972), it may be the case that although the personality characteristic remained present, it

was not manifested in the later-childhood—adolescent age periods. Presumably, these periods involved major interaction with males and not females. Admittedly, this is speculation, but the point is that the discovery of sleeper effects in development, through the application of longitudinal differential methodology, provides rich bases for future research.

A similarly interesting sleeper effect was also found with females, when some measures of the mother's behavior toward the child during the first 3 years of the child's life were related to various aspects of the child's own adolescent and adult functioning. If mothers had critical attitudes toward their daughters during the first age period (0–3 years), this was highly predictive of adult achievement behavior on the part of the daughter. However, a similar attitude in the middle three age periods was not related to such adult female behavior. Similarly, maternal protection of the female child during the child's first 3 years of life was related to a conceptually consistent adult female behavior on the part of the daughter (e.g., withdrawal from stress), whereas similar maternal behaviors during the child's later age periods were not related to these adult female behaviors. Thus, through these findings, we see that Kagan and Moss were able to discover events and/or behaviors that occurred early in a child's life that—although not relating to similar behaviors in immediately succeeding age periods—did relate highly to later, adult functioning.

Conclusions

The application of a longitudinal differential approach allowed Kagan and Moss (1962) to discern some important ways in which people may become differentiated into subgroups over the course of their development. Although their specific results are certainly provocative, as previously noted, they are difficult to generalize to broader populations of people. Yet, their methods and findings do suggest the importance of employing a longitudinal strategy if one wants to discover the continuities and discontinuities in a child's development.

A cross-sectional approach might not have been able to uncover the fact that sex-appropriate behaviors in a child seem to be destined for continuity, whereas sex-inappropriate behaviors seem to be discontinuous. Moreover, a cross-sectional approach certainly would not have been able to discover the sleeper effects involved in particular children's development. Because a cross-sectional study assesses different children at different ages, it would not have been possible, for example, to discover that when a female has a protective mother in her first 3 years of life, she will show withdrawal from stress as an adult.

Despite the wealth of empirical findings that are possible from longitudinal differential studies, such studies do have their limitations. We have noted some of these in earlier discussions in this chapter, and we will have reason to refer to these points again in Chapter 18.

Here, however, it is useful to note that, as illustrated by the uses made of differential ideas both by Erikson (1959, 1963, 1968) and Kagan and Moss (1962), this approach to development may be employed to enrich both developmental theory and research. In contrast to developmental stage theories, wherein a priori theoretical stands are taken relative to the continuity—discontinuity and nature—nurture issues, a preset orientation to these issues are not necessarily the case within the differential approach. The next conceptual approach to development that we consider—the ipsative approach—also lends itself to such conceptual and empirical utility. We discuss the ipsative approach in the next chapter.

17 | *The Ipsative Approach to Development*

In an *ipsative* analysis, an individual is compared to him- or herself, as opposed to being compared to other people. As compared with the stage and differential approaches to developmental psychology, the ipsative approach is much more *idiographic* in orientation. Idiographic laws are regularities associated with an individual instead of a group, and the goal of the ipsative approach is to discover individual (rather than group) laws or regularities of behavioral development. Those opting for an ipsative approach might argue that the nomothetic laws of individual behavioral development, which apply only to groups and not to the individuals within them, are meaningless; they would, thus, try to ascertain the variables involved in an individual's development. If these findings could then be applied to larger groups of people (e.g., to better understand any qualifications in the application of group laws to individuals), so much the better for the science of human development. However, if the findings of ipsative research indicated that group laws were too general to be useful for understanding the character of an individual's life course, then again so much the better for science. Here, the contribution would be, however, that scientists would not be misled by relatively vacuous general principles of human functioning.

In short, the rationale for an ipsative analysis of development is that the variables providing the bases of human functioning may coalesce in each person in a unique way. As such, laws of behavioral and psychological functioning that apply only to groups may have no direct meaning for a given individual's functioning, although they may constrain that individual's social interpersonal behaviors.

Accordingly, development at the individual level must be understood, and the ipsative approach to development considers intraindividual consistencies and changes in the development of the person (Emmerich, 1968). The approach asks whether the variables that comprise the individual remain the same or change throughout the individual's ontogeny.

It should be noted that scholars from diverse theoretical perspectives have argued for the need for ipsative analyses of human behavior. For example, the need for such analyses may derive from an individual's unique genotype and genotype–environment interaction (Hirsch, 1970), from the person's individual reinforcement history (Bijou, 1976; Bijou & Baer, 1961), or from the person's unique interrelation of his or her temperament attributes (Chess & Thomas, 1984, 1996, 1999; Thomas & Chess, 1977, 1980) or his or her personality organization (Allport, 1937; Block, 1971). It should be noted, however, that although all such theorists would agree that ipsative analyses are necessary to describe an individual's functioning, not all would agree that idiographic laws need to be used to account for intraindividual uniqueness. For example, Bijou and Baer (1961) might argue that although each person would have a unique reinforcement history and would, therefore, have a unique response repertoire, the laws governing the acquisition of any of the responses (e.g., laws of associative learning or conditioning) are applicable to all organisms.

When ipsative analyses are used in developmental research, however, the scientist seeks to understand the makeup of the individual in two ways. First, an attempt is made to ascertain the specific *attributes* (e.g., behavioral or psychological variables) that make up the person (Emmerich, 1968) over the course of development. These attributes may be characteristics such as personality traits (e.g., dependency or aggression), temperamental styles (e.g., high activity level or low threshold of responsivity), or, in fact, any set of psychological–behavioral variables. Moreover, these attributes may be unique to the person or common among many people (like the personality traits illustrated previously). In any event, the first task of the ipsative approach is to find out what attributes comprise the individual, to discover the individual's attribute repertoire across development. For example, a researcher may be interested in discovering a person's values. Accordingly, the researcher might discover that, at age 15, a given person was comprised of four values (e.g., values about one's body, about sexuality, about education, and about religion); whereas at age 25, an additional two values had become part of this person's value *attribute repertoire* (e.g., values about a career and raising a family).

Second, attributes certainly have an organization. Some attributes may be central in that they serve to organize other attributes, whereas others may be subordinate. Alternatively, we may think of the organization of attributes in terms of attribute clusters. For instance, some attributes may be grouped together whereas others may not. By analogy, one might view this attribute organization in terms of intraindividual attribute factors. In fact, one form of factor analysis—P-technique factor analysis—is aimed at identifying intraindividual factors (Nesselroade, 1983); in other words, P-technique factor analysis provides an ipsative analysis of the structure of attributes that exists within a single person over the course of his or her development. Later in this chapter, we discuss still another method used to study the development of intraindividual structures—that is, the Q-sort methodology used in Block's longitudinal study (1971).

However, no matter which particular data analysis technique is used, a person may be found to have several personality attributes clustered together, and these attributes may be independent of, for example, the person's cluster of value attributes and temperamental attributes. Moreover, within a particular cluster, a specific attribute may be superordinate. Thus, the sexuality value may be superordinate to a person at a particular time in life, with all other values subordinate, at least if they are viewed in terms of the overriding importance of the sexual value. In any event, the second task of the ipsative approach is to attempt to understand a person's *attribute interrelation* across development, how the attributes comprised by the person are related to each other over the course of the person's life.

To illustrate, suppose an individual has three types of value attributes—relating to religiosity, sexuality, and economic resource attainment. Though it is possible that these same three values may make up the person's attribute repertoire at different times in life, the values may be interrelated differently over time. For instance, at age 17,

the person's sexuality value may be most important (superordinate), with the others subordinate. This attribute interrelation may stay the same over time, but it might also change. For instance, at age 38, the economic resources value may be superordinate and the sexuality value not as important—it has now fallen to second-order importance, perhaps; however, the religiosity value may maintain its previous intraindividual position. Still later, however, perhaps at age 67, these same three values may still make up the person's repertoire, but once again they are interrelated differently. Thus, at this age, the person's religious value may be most important, whereas the economic resources value has fallen to second place and the sexuality value to third place.

In sum, those taking an ipsative approach to the study of development seek to discover the regularities involved in an individual's development by attempting to find the person's attribute repertoire—those characteristics comprising the person—and attribute interrelation—the intraindividual organization of these attributes. Thus, the ipsative problem in development is to discern intraindividual consistencies and changes in attributes and their organization over the course of an individual's development.

Let us illustrate how, in an ipsative analysis, one may identify how a person may change over the course of development as a function of new attributes existing in his or her repertoire. Consider the attribute repertoire depicted in Figure 17.1. Here, we see that at Time 1 the person was comprised of seven attributes (a–g), whereas at Time 2, three new variables (h–j) are in the repertoire.

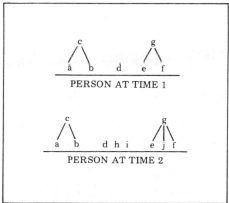

FIGURE 17.1
An example of ipsative change. The person's attribute repertoire changes from Times 1 to 2.

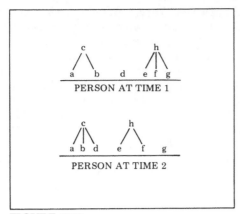

FIGURE 17.2
An example of ipsative change. The attributes in a person's repertoire are interrelated differently at Times 1 and 2.

Even if the attributes in a person's repertoire remain the same in development, the person may change if the attributes are interrelated differently over time. This second type of change that can be identified by the ipsative intraindividual approach to development is depicted in Figure 17.2. Here, we see that although the same number of attributes exists in the person's repertoire at Times 1 and 2 in development, the interrelation of the attributes is different at these two times. At Time 1, attributes a, b (subordinate), and c (superordinate) cluster together, as do attributes e, f, g, and h. Attribute d does not cluster with either of these two groups. At Time 2, however, the organization of the attributes is different. Here, we see that attribute d now clusters along with attributes a, b, and c, whereas attribute g has now become independent of the attribute cluster composed of e, f, and h.

Of course, *both* the number of attributes in the person's repertoire and the attribute interrelation may change over the course of development. If the attribute repertoire changes, then of course the person will have changed; but even if the attribute repertoire remains the same, the person can still change through a change in the attribute interrelation. Either or both of these changes may constitute an individual's development.

INDIVIDUAL DIFFERENCES WITHIN THE IPSATIVE APPROACH

It should be clear that individual differences are the essence of the ipsative approach. The goal of this approach is to ascertain laws or regularities lying closer to the idiographic than to the nomothetic end of an idiographic–nomothetic continuum (Block, 1971). Thus, the concern in this approach is to identify laws applying to an individual's development. Accordingly, a result of an ipsative analysis may be the formulation of highly specific generalizations about the course of an individual's development. Analysis begins at the level of the individual because, it is held, general laws of development may not apply equally to all individuals. Hence, within this perspective one should first understand how the individual develops before one tries to understand how large groups of individuals develop.

In stressing this view, however, those taking an ipsative approach are not denying either the validity or the necessity for study of general laws of development. Rather, they are stressing a different aspect of the problem of developmental analysis. They are trying to first understand the role of the individual in his or her own development. Accordingly, they would suggest that particular attributes of a person may be unique, but they would not disregard the possibility that other attributes of the individual may be similar to those of other individuals. Thus, the stress of the ipsative approach is not that all people are *completely* different, but rather that in order to understand all of the phenomena of development, one must deal with the particular intraindividual features of development.

There are other issues that may be raised in respect to the focus of the ipsative approach on the individual and on intraindividual differences over time—instead of on interindividual differences within time, as is more often the focus with nomothetically oriented approaches. First, theorists differ as to the ability of idiographic laws to account for substantial proportions of the variance in behavioral development, both absolutely and especially in comparison to nomothetic laws.

A second scientific issue is that the interpretation of the individual differences described in ipsative analyses is open to debate. Do such individual differences reflect qualitatively unique, individual laws or only quantitative (and perhaps "error") variance around some more general (group or universal) law? If the former is the case, then both basic research and more applied endeavors of assessment and intervention need to focus primarily on the individual, deferring for secondary analysis any focus on the group or general laws. If the latter is the case, then given the practical problems (of cost and time) of designing and implementing plans for separate assessment of every individual, it may be that the appropriate role of basic research is to remain focused on designing research to assess general laws. Similarly, if the latter is the case, the same practical problems of cost and time would suggest that those interested in applied issues should be primarily concerned with assessments and interventions aimed at the more general components of human functioning.

DEVELOPMENTAL CHANGES WITHIN THE IPSATIVE APPROACH

We have seen that, within the ipsative approach, people may change through development on the basis of changes in their attribute repertoire and/or their attribute interrelation. But are such intraindividual changes systematic? Do they follow a predictable pattern or are they unique to each and every individual? In other words, are there any principles that may be used to understand the nature of the intraindividual changes constituting development?

The scholarship of Emmerich (1968, pp. 679–681), allows the answer to all these questions to be "yes." Although Emmerich pointed out that, traditionally, there was little evidence of systematic ipsative developmental theorizing, he suggested that a principle exists that allows such conceptualization to proceed. This is a general, regulative principle of development, describing the course of developmental changes *whenever* development occurs. This principle is one we are familiar with—Werner's *orthogenetic principle*.

As discussed in Chapter 5, the orthogenetic principle holds that whenever development occurs, it proceeds from a state of globality and lack of differentiation to a state of differentiation, integration, and hierarchical organization. Individuals, of course, develop. Therefore, we would expect the orthogenetic principle to hold for the intraindividual development of a person. It would imply that no matter what the specific attribute repertoire of a person may be, the developmental changes in this attribute repertoire follow a specific, systematic course. All changes in a person's intraindividual attributes would proceed in accordance with the orthogenetic principle.

Hence, even if all individuals were completely unique in the repertoires of attributes they possessed, the development of the interrelations of their attributes would still be in accord with the descriptions provided by the orthogenetic principle. Therefore, we would expect that as an individual develops from Times 1 to 2, his or her attribute repertoire and attribute interrelation would develop along specific, systematic lines. Specifically, we would expect that:

1.   An individual's attribute repertoire would be relatively global and undifferentiated at Time 1 in development but more differentiated at Time 2. In other words, as an individual develops, new and more differentiated attributes should emerge in his attribute repertoire. Thus, in terms of the ipsative attribute repertoire, the orthogenetic principle suggests that *discontinuity* should characterize development. Differentiated attributes should emerge from global attributes.

2.   An individual's attribute interrelation would change, increasing in hierarchical integration with development. At Time 1, a person's attribute interrelation would be less integrated, less hierarchically organized than at Time 2. Thus, in terms of the ipsative attribute interrelation, the orthogenetic principle suggests that *continuity* should characterize development. The attribute interrelation should become increasingly more hierarchically organized over the course of an individual's development.

In sum, we see that when the orthogenetic principle is applied to intraindividual development, ipsative development may be held to follow certain systematic changes. There will be discontinuous changes when the person develops from Times 1 to 2 in his or her ontogeny because the attribute repertoire will go from a state of globality to a state of differentiation. In addition, there will be continuous changes when the person develops from Times 1 to 2, because the attribute interrelation will become increasingly more hierarchically organized.

RELATION OF CONCEPTS OF DEVELOPMENT TO THE IPSATIVE APPROACH

We have seen that when the ipsative approach is interrelated with the orthogenetic principle, the ipsative approach takes a clear position on the continuity–discontinuity issue. As discussed in Chapter 5, the orthogenetic principle implies the existence of both continuity and discontinuity in development and, accordingly, when this principle is applied to the ipsative approach, this approach also characterizes development as having both continuous and discontinuous components. Thus, when this interrelation is achieved, the continuity–discontinuity issue does not remain an empirical issue for those taking the ipsative approach but, instead, becomes a theoretical issue; those taking this approach would now maintain that development is both continuous and discontinuous in character.

The ipsative approach also has specific applicability to the nature–nurture issue. We have seen that an essential consideration of the ipsative approach is the role of the laws governing the individual. This focus leads, in my view, to a concern with the contribution the individual makes to his or her own development. This point may be explained by reference to our discussion of the ideas of Schneirla (1957), presented in Chapter 6. As Schneirla (1957) suggested, the experience–maturation interaction that provides the source of all individuals' development functions to give each person a lawfully singular set of behavioral characteristics; this behavioral individuality provides, then, a third source of the individual's development through the establishment of circular functions and self-stimulation in ontogeny.

Thus, ipsatively oriented researchers, in focusing on a person's behavioral individuality, can ascertain how the individual—in interaction with his or her environment—provides a source of his or her own development. Thus, such researchers would necessarily be taking an interactionist stance in respect to the nature–nurture controversy; and they would, by attempting to discover the contributions of the individual to his or her own development, be ascertaining important evidence bearing on this aspect of the nature–nurture interaction. Later in this chapter, we review two ipsatively oriented studies—one by Thomas and his colleagues (1963, 1968) and the other by Block (1971)—which bear on this argument.

Here, however, we should note that another notion involved in the ipsative approach is in accord with a stress on person–environment interactions. We have noted that the ipsative approach recognizes that although it is possible for people to have completely unique attribute repertoires, it is also possible for people to have attribute repertoires that are very similar, if not identical. Accordingly, from an ipsative point of view, we may identify people who have similar attribute repertoires at Time 1 in their development and study them longitudinally i.e., across time. Some of these people will remain similar at Time 2, whereas others will be different. Thus, by focusing on the different types of person–environment interactions these people experienced, we may discover how specific interactions provide a source of an individual's development. By discovering the laws that

function to change people who were similar at Time 1 into people who either remained similar or were different at Time 2, we may learn about the specific characteristics of organism–environment interactions that enable the person to provide a third source of his or her behavioral development.

Alternatively, of course, we could also focus on people who had different attribute repertoires and/or interrelations at Time 1 and study those people who remained different or became similar at Time 2. By assessing the organism–environment interactions of these groups we might further discover how the characteristics of the individual in interaction with his or her environment provide a source of the individual's own development. In short, the ipsative approach takes a stand on the continuity–discontinuity issue and can be potentially useful in providing information about nature–nurture interactions as a source of development.

CONCLUSIONS

The ipsative approach to human development assesses intraindividual consistencies and changes in the attribute repertoire and the attribute interrelation of a person over the course of development. As opposed to the relatively more nomothetically oriented stage and differential approaches, the ipsative approach is relatively more idiographic in orientation. That is, it seeks to understand the laws that govern an individual's behavior; it attempts to formulate highly specific generalizations, those potentially applicable to the development of a single individual.

However, in seeking to understand the variables involved in an individual's development, those taking an ipsative point of view are not necessarily formulating specific laws of development applicable only to that given person (Block, 1971). Rather, they stress that an understanding of the individual is a necessary basis for any more general understanding. Although the field of human development must be concerned with ascertaining nomothetic (or group) laws as well as idiographic laws, those taking this point of view suggest that the science would suffer if the former were emphasized to the exclusion of the latter. General laws of development may not apply equally (or at all) to all the individuals in a group. Hence, one must also understand intraindividual laws if one wants to get a full account of development. In other words, one must understand the contributions that an organism's own individuality makes toward its own development in order to comprehend development more fully.

Accordingly, a basic orientation of the ipsative approach is an assessment of the role of the organism's own characteristics in its own development. An organism's lawful, systematic characteristics of individuality provide an important source of that organism's own development. This is a key reason why those taking an ipsative point of view seek to assess an individual's attribute repertoire and the concomitant interrelation of this repertoire over the course of the individual's development. Although not necessarily denying the validity of other approaches to the study of human development (e.g., the stage approach), the ipsative approach suggests that these other orientations are incomplete because they do not pay sufficient attention to the organism's lawful (and potentially unique) characteristics of individuality and the contributions of this individuality to the organism's own development.

The ipsative approach lends itself, then, to a developmental systems analysis of human development, at least insofar as, following Schneirla (1957), it involves the idea that the organism's own characteristics play an active role in its own development. Yet, despite the similarities between the ipsative approach and other developmental systems-oriented positions, relatively little systematic developmental research has been conducted from an essentially ipsative point of view. However, as previously noted, we may discuss two

Stella Chess

major, longitudinal studies of development that do bear on the ipsative point of view. One study, the New York Longitudinal Study, has been conducted by Alexander Thomas and Stella Chess, and their collaborators (e.g., Herbert Birch,

Herbert G. Birch

Alexander Thomas

Margaret Hertzig

Margaret Hertzig, and Sam Korn). A second study, conducted by Jack Block, involves reanalyses of two longitudinal data sets derived from research conducted at the Institute of Human Development at the University of California, Berkeley. These two studies represent classic examples of ipsative research about human development in the literature, and they have especially important theoretical and practical implications. As such, the rest of this chapter reviews their features and implications.

Sam J. Korn

This review serves several purposes. First, it gives us some knowledge and appreciation of how major studies of human development are initially conceptualized. Second, it illustrates how human development researchers move from conceiving of a study to implementing it. Third, it illustrates the problems often encountered in developmental research and some ways in which human development researchers seek to address these problems. Fourth, our discussion allows us not only to appreciate two major ipsative studies of development but also to make some more general statements about conceptions of the role of organismic individuality in development. Let us begin our discussion with a review of the New York Longitudinal Study.

THE THOMAS AND CHESS "NEW YORK LONGITUDINAL STUDY"

The New York Longitudinal Study (NYLS) began in 1956 in New York City and continues through the time of this writing. The major sample in the study involves a longitudinal assessment of a sample of 133 males and females from their first days of life onward. Although, of course, it is essential for us to understand the methods, findings, and implications of this study, we must first focus on the theoretical issues that led to the study. Only by beginning there can we understand the rationale for the entire NYLS and, thus, see why the study took the form that it did.

Why Are Children Different?

Any human development researcher would, of course, admit that children are different. We have seen, for example, that both stage and differential approaches to the study of child development incorporate concepts of individuality into their respective systems. Thus, any debate about developmental individuality does not focus on whether children are different. Rather, it concerns either the ways in which children differ (e.g., stage theorists say children may differ in their rates and final levels of development, whereas differential researchers conceptualize individuality as one's location in multidimensional space) or the sources of differences. In other words, people may recognize all children as having individual characteristics, and yet they may debate about the sources of these differences.

If such a debate seems reminiscent of the controversy surrounding the nature–nurture issue dealt with in earlier chapters, this is because nature–nurture is precisely the issue involved in such debate. Arguments about the source of behavioral individuality have traditionally involved either a *hereditarian* viewpoint or an *environmentalist* viewpoint. Those taking a hereditarian view (e.g., Sheldon, 1940, 1942) have essentially stressed inborn sources of individuality, which are thought to be largely genetic in origin and apparently unavailable to environmental influence. Those taking an environmentalist position (e.g., Bijou & Baer, 1961) have stressed stimulus–response relationships, acquired through the empirical laws of conditioning. In its extreme, this position views people as malleable balls of clay. Where the genetically oriented hereditarians stress that a person enters the world as an already formed ball, the environmentalists opposingly argue that the person enters the world with little but the potential to be completely shaped by stimulus–response relations. Thus, the environmentalists suggest that instead of different genetic inheritances being the source of individuality, different—although lawfully identical stimulus–response relations provide the source of individuality.

Furthermore, we have seen that such organismic individuality may have profound influences on the organism's own development. We have seen that Schneirla (1957), in describing a "third source" of development, indicated that an organism's characteristics of individuality, which arise out of its unique maturational–experiential interaction, stimulate differential reactions on the part of the other organisms in the organism's environment. These differential reactions then feed back to the organism, providing an additional source of the organism's experience and, thus, contributing to the organism's development.

Because Thomas and colleagues (1963, 1968, 1970) subscribed to this probabilistic–epigenetic view, they rejected both the hereditarian and environmentalist views of behavioral individuality. Rather, they conceptualized the source of a child's characteristics of individuality as being the interaction between the organism's intrinsic and extrinsic factors; further, because of the theoretical implications of this integrative point of view, they sought to ascertain the role that such behavioral individuality plays in contributing to a child's development. Thus, the Thomas and colleagues (1963, p. 1) study was "concerned with identifying characteristics of individuality in behavior during the first months of life and with exploring the degree to which these characteristics are persistent and influence the development of later psychological organization."

Because of this theoretical point of view, Thomas and colleagues believed it was necessary to focus on intraindividual consistencies and changes in the characteristics of a child over the course of development. Such an ipsative analysis would yield, they believed, information regarding the contribution that such behavioral individuality makes to the child's own development. In other words, such an assessment of the contributions and implications of a child's individually different *style of behavioral reactivity*—the child's style of responding or reacting to the world—might supply important information bearing on unanswered but crucial problems of child development.

Implications of the Thomas and Colleagues Theoretical Position

I have developed the general theoretical stance of Thomas and his colleagues through addressing the question, "Why are children individually different?" An exploration and empirical assessment of this point of view would seem to have important theoretical implications. That is, if the Thomas and colleagues view of the source and implications of behavioral individuality is correct, some revisions in our thinking about both hereditarian and environmentalist views would be warranted. In addition, the approach and findings of Thomas and colleagues (1963) might have implications for other controversies in child-development study. For instance, as Thomas and Chess (1970) suggested, an approach such as theirs might provide answers about such important developmental questions as:

> Why do youngsters exposed to the same kind of parental influences so often show markedly different directions of personality and development? . . . Why do some parents who show no evidence of any significant psychiatric disturbances and who provide a good home for their children sometimes have a child with serious psychological disturbances? Why do the rules for childcare in feeding, weaning, toilet training and so on never seem to work equally well for all children, even when applied by intelligent and conscientious mothers? (p. 531)

Clearly, we see the theoretical suggestion that some portion of the answers to these questions must lie in the fact that children have important characteristics of individuality. These individual differences serve to promote two things. First, different children will have different reactions to the same environmental stimulus situation. The probabilistic–epigenetic viewpoint, as described by Schneirla (1957; see Chapter 6), suggests that, as a result of an organism's unique maturation—experience interaction, the organism will develop its own characteristics of individuality. The presence of such individuality means that although an identical stimulus may impinge on two different children, the resulting reaction may not be the same. For example, one child might react intensely to a loud noise, whereas another may hardly react at all. Thus, because of such individual differences in a child's style of reactivity, what might be a part of the *effective stimulus environment* for one child (i.e., a stimulus in the child's environment that evokes a reaction) may not be part of the effective environment for another.

Second, because the same environmental event (e.g., a particular parental child-rearing practice) will have different effectiveness for different children, such differential reactivity characteristics will differently influence others in the child's environment. Because different children may be expected to interact differently, each individual child will influence even similarly acting parents in different ways. The child who reacts intensely to even the slightest noise will certainly evoke parental responses different from those that would be evoked by a child who showed hardly any response at all to noise. Thus, one's characteristic style of reactivity to the world will differentially influence and stimulate other people in one's world. The reactions from these other people will, in turn, provide a further component of the child's stimulus-world. Because such experiences play an integral role in affecting the child's further development, we see that here, too, the child's style of reactivity plays an active contributory role in the child's own development.

To represent a child's style of reactivity, Thomas and Chess (1977) used the term *temperament,* by which they meant only the person's style of behavior—*how* he or she does whatever is done. When studying personality, one may focus on *what* people do (the content of the behavioral repertoire), *why* they do it (the motivation underlying components of the behavioral repertoire), or on *how* they do it. As we have just noted, it is this last component of individuality (or personality) that Thomas and Chess (1977) studied and labeled as *temperament.* To illustrate, because all people engage in eating, sleeping, and toileting behaviors, the absence or presence of such contents of the behavior repertoire would not differentiate among them. But whether these behaviors occur with regularity (i.e., rhythmically) or with much or little intensity, might serve to differentiate among people.

Although the New York Longitudinal Study was initiated just as a study of temperamental individuality, like other major longitudinal studies it has become an extremely rich and diverse data set. Thus, the data on temperament are embedded in a wealth of other longitudinal data pertinent to, for example, other personality variables (e.g., anxiety, adjustment, or self-image), cognitive development and academic achievement, family structure and function, parent–child relations, the development of clinical symptoms, peer relationships, the development of sexuality, drug use and abuse, vocational interests and career development, and health and physical development (e.g., see Chess & Thomas, 1984, 1996, 1999; Thomas & Chess, 1970, 1977, 1980). Moreover, these data were obtained through the use of several different methodological strategies (e.g., parental interviews, child interviews, home observations, school observations, teacher interviews, and standardized personality and cognitive tests).

Accordingly, with a database as rich and complex as the New York Longitudinal Study, we can do no more than provide an overview of the methodological and substantive features of the study, especially because this data set extends over almost a half-century of people's lives and is still an active investigation. That is, at this writing, the participants are still being followed. Accordingly, in order to discuss the uses of the data found in this study, we must consider how Thomas and colleagues (1963) translated their theoretical concerns about organism individuality and temperament into a longitudinal research investigation.

From Theory to Research

Given the basic theoretical rationale for the Thomas and colleagues study, it may provide data bearing on the use of the probabilistic–epigenetic/developmental systems perspective. That is, the importance of a focus on a child's characteristics of temperamental individuality should be illustrated. If the contributions of a child's temperamental individuality are to be found consistent with the study's theoretical rationale, then Thomas and colleagues will have demonstrated not only that such behavioral style may play a role in the child's behavior at a given point in life but also that such individuality contributes to the child's functioning over the course of development. Accordingly, in order to translate their theoretical ideas into empirical facts, Thomas and colleagues had to do several things.

First, of course, they had to have some idea how to measure individual characteristics of temperament. They had to know exactly what behaviors or aspects of behavior constitute such behavioral style and how to measure these behaviors in children as they develop. Second, they had to find out the extent to which children's individual temperament styles remained individually different or similar at various points in their development.

Third, they had to continually assess the ways in which such individuality (to the extent that it was found to exist) continued to provide an important source of the child's development. Thus, they had to ascertain how children with different temperamental styles interacted differently with the world over the course of their development, and how such differential interactions continued to provide a source of the child's development. Given these requirements, it is clear why Thomas and colleagues had to study their research participants longitudinally.

In sum, we see both the theoretical rationale of the Thomas and colleagues study and the general manner in which this theoretical viewpoint must be translated into an empirical procedure in order for the ideas to be tested. Let us turn now to a consideration of the methodology of the Thomas and colleagues study.

THE METHOD OF THE THOMAS AND COLLEAGUES NYLS

The New York Longitudinal Study (NYLS) is one of the longest ongoing longitudinal studies. Indeed, its founders (i.e., the psychiatrists Alexander Thomas and Stella Chess) continue at this writing to be actively involved in the project (e.g., Chess & Thomas, 1999). Although there has been continuity in the major staff of the NYLS, there has been an evolution in the interests of these scientists and, thus, in the features and foci of the study. These constancies and changes in the study (a prototypic phenomenon of research continuity–discontinuity, by the way, in major longitudinal studies; Magnusson & Casaer, 1992) may be evidenced by a discussion of the samples in the NYLS and the data available about them overtime.

Characteristics of the NYLS Samples

The NYLS involves several samples (Thomas et al., 1968). Two are relevant to our present discussion. First, what may be termed the *core sample*

of the NYLS is composed of 133 children (66 males and 67 females). Over 99% of the sample is European American. The sample has been an especially committed, cooperative one. The sample members have been followed from their early infancy to today—their adulthood. Begun in 1956, sample recruitment was completed 6 years later. Originally, the sample consisted of 136 children, but in the early portion of the study three children were dropped. The remaining 133 children were followed into their adult life and, at the last occasion of full-sample data collection (in 1989), 128 of the individuals participated. Prior to this last wave of data collection, all 133 individuals participated in each wave of data collection. Thus, the data from the core NYLS sample provide a depiction of the life courses of a group of people from early infancy to young adulthood that is remarkably unbiased by selective attrition.

The families of the core sample are of middle- or upper-middle-class backgrounds. Almost all parents were born in the United States. Throughout the study, information has been obtained about the parents (e.g., regarding career, health, employment, and marital status). Forty percent of the mothers and 60% of the fathers have both college educations and postgraduate degrees, and less than 10% have no college education at all. The parents of the core sample are predominantly Jewish (78%) and the remainder are Catholic (7%) and Protestant (15%). Eighty-four families are involved. Forty-five have one child participating in the study (although these families may have more than one child), 31 have two, 6 have three, and 2 families have four children participating in the study.

The NYLS has also included a population of a contrasting socioeconomic background. This sample was involved in a second study, which was initiated in 1961; it involved 98 children (50 males and 48 females) of working-class Puerto Rican parents. These families were mostly intact and stable; 86% lived in low-income public housing projects in New York City. This group was longitudinally followed from 1961 to 1968, with the same general approach to data collection and analysis as in the core NYLS sample.

Features of the NYLS Data Set

A longitudinal study that has extended over the course of almost a half-century, and one that has included a core sample as well as auxiliary ones, obviously contains considerable data. For example, for the core sample, there is demographic information about the parents and the family, including educational and employment history, the structure of the family, and the type of residence in which the family resided. Families recruited into the study during the end of pregnancy or shortly after the birth of the children, also made available the mothers' obstetrical histories (e.g., complications during pregnancy), birth information (e.g., use of medication), and neonatal information (e.g., weight and length).

In addition, starting in the first few months of life, parents were interviewed periodically (e.g., every 3 months in the children's first year of life) about the children's behaviors in numerous content areas (e.g., sleeping, feeding, bathing, toileting, mobility, social responsivity, and sensory functioning). Along with this interview, parents were asked questions pertaining to responsibilities for daily child care and details of daily living. For the first 2 years of the study, these interviews represented the major source of information about the children. However, after this age, the data set has included several other sources of information about them.

That is, as the children became older, data collection was expanded to include the other contexts within which they interacted. As the children entered nursery school or elementary school, detailed teacher interviews were conducted about the children's adaptation and overall functioning, and classroom observations of the child were made. Both interviews and observations were done periodically throughout the school years. In addition, psychometric measures (e.g., IQ tests) of cognitive functioning, standardized achievement-test scores, and school grades were also obtained throughout the school years.

In addition, there was an evaluation of the home environment of the children and of any special environmental circumstances (e.g., separations, divorces, remarriages, or deaths). Information also existed about any significant handicaps possessed by the children; and in those cases where behavioral and/or emotional disorders were identified, there were additional psychometric data and clinical psychiatric evaluations.

In adolescence and early adulthood, interviews were conducted separately with both the children and their parents. These interviews were structured much like the earlier ones, with additional questions about new spheres of functioning (i.e., college plans, career goals, and sexual and social functioning).

In turn, the procedure for data collection for the Puerto Rican sample was similar to that in the core sample; that is, birth history and family demographics were initially gathered. Subsequently,

throughout the 7 years (1961–1968) of data collection, detailed parental interviews about the children's psychological and social functioning were conducted, and direct observations of the children's behavior were made. In addition to this information, data about the home environment and any significant events that had occurred were periodically obtained. As in the core sample, once the children attended school, teacher interviews, classroom observations, and grades and achievement scores were collected. IQ data also existed for this sample.

In my presentation of the NYLS, I am obviously not able to discuss every analysis reported on each of the longitudinal samples. One reason precluding such an attempt is the great productivity of Thomas and Chess and their associates (e.g., Chess & Thomas, 1984, 1996, 1999; Chess, Thomas, & Birch, 1965, 1966; Thomas et al., 1963; Thomas & Chess, 1970, 1977, 1980, 1981; Thomas, Chess, & Birch, 1968, 1970; Thomas, Chess, & Korn, 1982). Our discussion focuses primarily on the core sample and, for comparative purposes, at times on the Puerto Rican sample. Finally, although we need to draw on diverse information in the NYLS data set, given the theoretical concerns of Thomas and his colleagues with the role of organismic individuality in development, the major data we draw on are those pertinent to temperament.

However, our interest in temperament raises a question that confronted Thomas and Chess when they initiated the NYLS. Let us consider it.

WHAT IS TEMPERAMENT?

Today, research on temperament is a rich and nuanced field of study (e.g., Kagan, 1998; Rothbart & Bates, 1988). However, at the time of the inception of the NYLS there existed no acceptable definition of the dimensions of a child's temperament. Although other researchers (e.g., Sheldon, 1940, 1942) had provided definitions of temperament (or behavioral style), these had been linked to hereditarian theoretical conceptions and were, thus, unacceptable to the probabilistic–epigenetic orientation of Thomas and his colleagues (1963; Thomas & Chess, 1970). Accordingly, although Thomas and his colleagues wanted to study objectively the aspects of a child's behavioral style, they had no preformed ideas about what constituted such aspects. They knew that they wanted to concern themselves with the how rather than the what of behavior, but they were uncertain about how to measure it in any precise way. They had no preconceived ideas about what sort of different characteristics comprised a child's temperament.

Simply, the immediate crucial conceptual problem that faced Thomas and colleagues as they began the NYLS was that, although they knew generally what aspect of a child's development they wanted to study (characteristics of temperament), they did not know what constituted the various aspects of temperament. In terms of the ipsative approach, they did not know what attributes were comprised by the child's intraindividual attribute repertoire. The dilemma faced by Thomas and colleagues was, as already implied, associated with a second unanswered question.

How Does One Measure Temperament?

Even more basic than this definitional problem was the problem of the measurement of temperament. Assuming for the moment that Thomas and colleagues knew the particular attributes of temperament in which they were interested, how were they going to go about obtaining measures of these attributes? Where was the information about the development of the child's temperament going to come from?

This problem was complicated by the fact that the researchers felt it, crucial to obtain measures of the child's temperament in all situations in which the child engaged. There were two reasons for this. First, Thomas and Chess (1977) believed that the significance of a child's particular characteristics of temperamental individuality lay in how they fit with what other people in the child's world wanted from the child. They believed that if a child fit well with most of the situations, or contexts, in which he or she found him- or herself, then healthy development would proceed; poorly fit children, however, would not show healthy adjustment.

This idea may be recognized as the "goodness-of-fit" model discussed in prior chapters. We have reason to discuss this model and the NYLS data relevant to it again later in this chapter. Here, we should note that the second reason for the Thomas and colleagues' interest in assessing the child in multiple contexts was that if their concern was with ascertaining how the child did *whatever* he or she did, and not just with how he or she went about doing *certain* things (i.e., those things that might be involved in a once-a-month experimental assessment session), Thomas and colleagues would have had to observe the child's temperamental style continuously. They would have had to observe the child each and every day of the child's life. Thus, observations could not have been limited to those at Thomas and colleagues' laboratory but, instead, would have had to also include observations of the child in the real, nonlaboratory world.

A possible way to obtain such observations would be to hire and train a large set of observers to live in each child's household around the clock and, thus, observe and rate the child in how he or she does everything. Such a procedure presents problems, however. The hiring and training of, for example, 133 observers (one for each core sample child) would be economically prohibitive. Moreover, probably three times as many observers would have to be hired, since the observers would probably work no more than 8 hours a day. Furthermore, few if any families would allow one (not to mention three) people to enter their homes permanently to observe each and every interaction made by their child. Thus, how were Thomas and colleagues going to obtain the necessary continuous, total observations of each of the children?

Fortunately, someone did exist who observed the child continuously, who at no cost to the researchers lived with the child daily and who always worked a 24-hour day. This, of course, was the child's parent (and typically, in the NYLS families, the mother). Hence, the Thomas group decided to use each child's parent as the observer of the child's temperament. Thus, through interviews with each parent, the researchers were able to obtain the needed information about the child's style of reactivity in all daily interactions with the world. Because the parent continually observed the child, an appropriately designed interview of the parent could turn these observations into data about the child's developing temperament.

Problems of Data Accuracy

We have noted that after the children were about 2 years of age, data from parental interviews were regularly supplemented with data from other people (e.g., teachers were interviewed and, as the child got older, he or she was also interviewed). In addition, data collected with methods other than interviews (e.g., through nursery-school observations) were also included after 2 years of age. However, a reliance on parental interviews continued to exist throughout childhood, and such reliance presented problems. Obviously, one would not be quick to nominate a child's parent if one wanted an objective description or appraisal of the child. Such parental observations hold the danger of being subjectively biased.

Thomas and colleagues decided that there was a way to avoid the subjectivism typically involved in parental reports. The interview of each parent was structured so that *descriptions,* rather than *interpretations,* of behavior were elicited. Although the interviewer recorded both interpretations and descriptions, only descriptions were considered for use as data. At times, when parents insisted on interpreting rather than describing, the interviewer carefully reworded, rephrased, or repeated the question so as to obtain in each case a step-by-step description of the behavior in question. This insistence on description rather than interpretation was illustrated by Thomas and colleagues (1963) in the following example of a segment of a parental interview:

> *Interviewer:* "What did the baby do the first time he was given cereal?"
>
> *Parent:* "He couldn't stand it."
>
> *Interviewer:* "What makes you think he disliked it? What did he do?"
>
> *Parent:* "He spit it out and when another spoonful was offered he turned his head to the side." (p. 25)

Thus, when questions were asked about bathing or meeting new people, for example, and the parent responded with an interpretation (e.g., "He likes to be bathed," or "She is afraid of new people"), the interviewer always insisted on a description. The only answers used for data about temperament were those that responded to the question, "What did the child do?"

In this way, Thomas and his group took a first step toward ensuring that the data derived from parental interviews were accurate. However, other steps were also followed. In Chapter 15, we saw that one of the major limitations of Sigmund Freud's method was that he obtained retrospective accounts of the early lives of his adult patients. He asked adults to reconstruct their long-gone past by remembering back to their early years of development. Such retrospections may be biased through such factors as selective remembering or forgetting, or distortion.

Similarly, biases could enter into the parental responses Such retrospective accounts are less accurate than *prospective* descriptions, descriptions of a child's behavioral development given at about the same time the behavior is occurring. Thus, the Thomas group used prospective interviews, conducted at 3-month intervals during the child's first year of life. For example, the first interview occurred when the child was about 3 months old and the parent was used to provide information about the child's temperamental development during these first 3 months; the second interview, conducted when the child was 6 months old, was used to obtain temperamental information about his or her fourth, fifth, and sixth months of life. After the first year, subsequent interviews were conducted at 6-month intervals for the second year of life. Generally, yearly interviews were conducted for periods beyond the first 2 years.

Further steps were taken to ensure data accuracy. A loss of accuracy could have resulted from the researchers' scoring of these parental interview responses. Because of the large number of response descriptions resulting from each of the several interviews with each of the many parents, different people were used to score and interpret these answers. The researchers had to be sure that each different person would score the same responses in the same way and, moreover, that the same person would always score the same response in the same way; if such consistency was not achieved, considerable inaccuracy would have been introduced into the information. To check for such consistencies, the researchers had different people score the same set of parental responses and had the same people score the same parental responses twice (after a 3-month interval had gone by). In both cases, there was over 90% agreement between the two sets of responses.

In sum, we see that after taking several necessary steps to ensure the accuracy of their data, Thomas and colleagues were able to conclude that they had consistent, accurate descriptions of the children's development. However, they still did not have an indication of what constituted the temperamental attribute repertoire of the children in their sample. Although they now considered that they had accurate, consistently scored information describing the "how" of children's behavior in the world, they did not know the particular aspects of temperament that were present. What were the variables, or attributes, comprising each child's temperamental repertoire? Although such knowledge was contained in their already obtained information, they then had to tease this knowledge out. Let us consider how they went about ascertaining this knowledge and what, in fact, they discovered.

The Attributes of Temperament

Thomas and colleagues did not have any predetermined theoretical notions concerning what the attributes of temperament were. Accordingly, the researchers could not decide deductively what particular temperamental attributes should be derived from their data; they could not say that because their theory about temperament said "x," there should be evidence of a particular attribute of temperament.

Moreover, the Thomas group wanted to avoid limiting the analyses of the interviews to a scoring of just one or two possible temperamental attributes; this methodological route would clearly introduce the possibility of ignoring large or important aspects of the data. On the other hand, there was so much information contained in the interviews that some categorization of the descriptions was necessary. One had to score, or place, the various parental descriptions into categories in order to reduce the vast number of bits of data; however, at the same time, one did not want to produce as many different categories as there were bits of information. Thomas and colleagues wanted to move from data to more general organizational categorizations; they wanted to induce (discover) categories in the data that would organize it. In consultation with their collaborator, Herbert G. Birch, a former student of T. C. Schneirla, they decided to focus on characteristics of behavior that had been identified across numerous species (e.g., approach–withdrawal or rhythmicity of biological functions) (Thomas, personal communication, 1995).

Accordingly, using these behaviors as a frame, a sample of parental interviews was read and, by a review and discussion of the contents of these interviews, Thomas and colleagues were able to identify nine categories of temperament that reflected several of the behaviors suggested by Birch. As such, Thomas and colleagues were able to identify nine attributes of temperament that could be reliably scored and into which the various behavioral descriptions in the interviews could be placed.

Although there was evidence in some of the parental descriptions for temperamental attributes other than the nine on which the Thomas group focused, the group decided to concentrate on the nine attributes of temperament induced by the aforementioned method because these nine attributes were present in all of the interview data. The nine attributes were:

1. *Activity level:* This category refers to descriptions of the child's motor behavior (muscle functioning). Such descriptions answered several questions: Was the child highly active all the time or were low levels of general activity seen? Did the child move around a lot or a little when eating, playing, sleeping, and so on?
2. *Rhythmicity:* This category refers to the cyclicality or regularity of behavior. Was the

child's behavior very predictable? For example, did the child sleep for 4 hours, wake for 4 hours, sleep for 4 hours? Did the child always eliminate 1 hour after eating or always get hungry at the same time? Or was the child's behavior irregular? Did the child sleep for 7 hours, wake for 2, then perhaps sleep for 3, but then wake for 5? Did he or she sometimes eliminate right after eating and sometimes hours after? Was he or she sometimes hungry a short time after eating, whereas at other times he or she might go for hours without getting hungry?

3. *Approach or withdrawal:* Did the child tend to move toward (approach) new stimuli (e.g., toys or people) or move away (withdraw) from all such stimuli?
4. *Adaptability:* Did the child tend to adjust easily to new situations (after his or her initial approach or withdrawal response was made), or did the child tend to take a good deal of time to adjust to new situations and stimuli?
5. *Intensity of reaction:* This attribute refers to the strength of a response. Whenever the child responded to a situation or stimulus, was this response indicative of a high level of energy? Did the child respond with vigor or with little energy? For example, did the child tend to whimper rather than scream loudly when crying?
6. *Threshold of responsiveness:* A threshold refers to the smallest amount of energy necessary to evoke a response. If, for example, a noise has to be very loud for it to bother you, then you have a high threshold; if even a pin dropping causes you to react, you have a low noise threshold. This category, then, relates to the child's general threshold for responding.
7. *Quality of mood:* Was the child generally pleasant and friendly? Did he or she smile and laugh a lot and, thus, have a positive mood? Or was the child's behavior generally unpleasant? Did he or she cry and frown a lot and, thus, have a negative mood?
8. *Distractibility:* Once the child was engaged in a given behavior (e.g., watching television), was it very easy to alter this behavior (e.g., by calling him or her to dinner)? That is, was the child easily or highly distractible in that external stimulation would easily change his or her ongoing behavior? Or was the child hard to distract? Was it difficult to change his or her ongoing behavior through introduction of another stimulus to the situation? Did the child, thus, show low distractibility?
9. *Attention span and persistence:* How long did the child tend to stay at a given behavior in which he or she was engaged? Did he or she tend

to persist in doing a task for a long time, or did he or she stay with one task for a few minutes or so and then move to another task, and then another? If the child tended to stay with tasks for a long time, he or she would have a long (or high) attention span. He or she would be persistent. If the reverse were true, then he or she would have a short (or low) attention span. He or she would not show high persistence.

These categories comprise the nine attributes of temperament identified by Thomas and colleagues (1963). Note that the nine categories refer to descriptions of the "how," the style, of behavior. They refer to how a child goes about doing the behaviors in which he or she engages. Thus, the nine attributes make up a description, rather than an interpretation, of the dimensions of a child's style of behavioral reactivity to the world. The parental descriptions of how the child behaved in respect to such content topics as sleep, feeding, toilet training and toilet activities, bathing, grooming, meeting other people, playing, learning rules, talking, and so on, were used by Thomas and colleagues to obtain a broad sample of descriptions of the child's characteristics of reactivity; these descriptions were then placed in one of the nine categories of temperament that the Thomas group identified. Each of these nine attributes was scored on a 3 point scale. For example, for threshold of responsiveness, a child could be scored as having a low threshold, a high threshold, or a moderate threshold. The nine attributes of temperament and the three levels of scoring (or rating) for each attribute are presented in Figure 17.3.

In terms of the ipsative approach, the attribute repertoire of temperament for any given child would be made up of the child's "score" on each of the nine attributes. Because a child's score on one dimension would not necessarily affect his or her score on any other attribute, the attribute interrelation of the repertoire could be different for different children. In other words, with the identification and scoring of the nine attributes of temperament, Thomas and colleagues defined a temperamental-attribute repertoire that could exist differently in different children; that is, different children could have different scores on the various attributes; therefore, of course, the interrelation of the attributes would then be different for these different children. One child might combine a low threshold with high activity and a positive mood, whereas another child might combine a moderate threshold with low activity and a negative mood.

RESULTS OF THE NYLS

Was this, in fact, the case? Did different children show different attribute repertoires? Were different

ATTRIBUTE OF TEMPERAMENT	POSSIBLE "SCORES" FOR EACH ATTRIBUTE		
Adaptability	/ adaptive /	variable /	nonadaptive /
Rhythmicity	/ regular /	variable /	irregular /
Activity level	/ high /	moderate /	low /
Approach—Withdrawal	/ approach /	variable /	withdrawal /
Threshold	/ high /	moderate /	low /
Intensity	/ intense /	variable /	mild /
Mood	/ positive /	variable /	negative /
Distractibility	/ yes /	variable /	no /
Attention span; persistence	/ high /	variable /	low /

FIGURE 17.3
The nine attributes of temperament found by Thomas and colleagues (1963), and the possible "scores," or ratings, for each attribute.

attribute interrelations seen? Did the children's repertoires remain the same as they developed? To address these questions, let us consider some of the results of the NYLS.

Temperamental Individuality in Infancy and Childhood

As I have discussed, the NYLS is an ongoing longitudinal project. The data from the study are still being analyzed, and the children of the project are still being studied, although these children are now—at this writing—almost all in their forties, and many have children of their own. Accordingly, we have a rich and extensive database from which to draw in order to address the issues of whether children possess individually distinct temperament repertoires and/or interrelations of these repertoires and of what the developmental course of temperament might be. However, for clarity of presentation we shall not try to present all pertinent data in this vast data set. Instead, we shall focus on what are quite representative results— those describing intraindividual consistencies and changes in the individual's temperamental attribute repertoire and repertoire interrelation over the course of the first 10 years of development (Chess & Thomas, 1984, 1996, 1999; Chess, Thomas, & Birch, 1965; Thomas & Chess, 1970, 1977, 1980, 1981; Thomas, Chess, & Birch, 1968, 1970; Thomas et al., 1963).

The first task of data analysis for Thomas and colleagues (1963) was to determine whether children did, in fact, possess individually different temperamental repertoires in early infancy. Second, the group had to determine the developmental course of such individuality. The first major finding, then, was that children do show individually different temperamental repertoires and interrelations; moreover, these individual differences in temperament do become distinct— they can be discerned—even in the first few weeks of the child's life. Although some children tend to be similar in their temperamental styles— a point whose implications we later consider—different arrays of scores for each of the different attributes were found. Thus, particularly for the attributes of activity level, threshold, intensity, mood, and distractibility, marked individual differences in temperamental repertoires were evident (Thomas et al., 1963, p. 57).

Moreover, these individually different temperamental styles were not systematically related either to the parents' method of childrearing or the parents' own personality styles (Thomas et al.,

1970). This finding indicates not only that children are individually different but also that these characteristics of individuality are not simply related to what a parent does to a child or to a parent's own personality characteristics.

The second major finding of the NYLS is that these characteristics of individuality, first identified in the child's first 3 months of life, tend to remain relatively continuous in the child over the course of later years. For example, one may look at a child's most frequent score for each of his various nine temperamental attributes. That is, although in various instances a child may score high, moderate, or low in threshold, most of the ratings might be one of these scores, for example, high. If one looks at these scores, one sees that the child's temperament tends to remain in the same category over his or her childhood years; for example, the preponderance of his or her threshold scores across life tends to be high (Thomas et al., 1963, p. 71). Moreover, the child's other scores, both within a particular attribute category and between the different attribute categories, tend to remain similar over the course of the first 10 years of life as well. This finding indicates not only that the child's attribute repertoire tends to remain fairly consistent but also that the attribute interrelation tends to remain consistent. The expression of such temperamental similarity over the course of the first 10 years of life is illustrated in Table 17.1. This table displays two ratings for each of the nine categories of temperament, along with behaviors indicative of the consistency in temperament at each of the age periods ranging between 2 months through 10 years of age.

We may conclude that, to a great extent, a child is born with an individually different temperament and that this individuality tends to remain with the child over the course of his or her first 10 years of life. The ipsative longitudinal study of the Thomas group indicates that individually different attribute repertoires and attribute interrelations characterize the individual over the course of his or her childhood development. These findings, of course, have important theoretical implications for probabilistic–epigenetic ideas about development, as well as important practical implications. However, before turning to a consideration of these implications, it is useful to consider some other aspects of the results of the study. Although children were found to be characterized by individually different temperamental styles, we have also said that certain characteristics of temperament tended to be similar in some

TABLE 17.1

Illustrations for Ratings of the 9 NYLS Temperamental Attributes at Ages 2 Months Through 10 Years

Temperamental quality	Rating	2 Months	6 Months	1 Year
Activity level	High	Moves often in sleep. Wriggles when diaper is changed.	Tries to stand in tub and splashes. Bounces in crib. Crawls after dog.	Walks rapidly. Eats eagerly. Climbs into everything.
	Low	Does not move when being dressed or during sleep.	Passive in bath. Plays quietly in crib and falls asleep.	Finishes bottle slowly. Goes to sleep easily. Allows nail-cutting without fussing.
Rhythmicity	Regular	Has been on four-hour feeding schedule since birth. Regular bowel movement.	Is asleep at 6:30 P.M. every night. Awakes at 7:00 A.M. Food intake is constant.	Naps after lunch each day. Always drinks bottle before bed.
	Irregular	Awakes at a different time each morning. Size of feedings varies.	Length of nap varies; so does food intake.	Will not fall asleep for an hour or more. Moves bowels at a different time each day.
Distractibility	Distractible	Will stop crying for food if rocked. Stops fussing if given pacifier when diaper is being changed	Stops crying when mother sings. Will remain still while clothing is changed if given a toy.	Cries when face is washed unless it is made into a game.
	Not distractable	Will not stop crying when diaper is changed. Fusses after eating even if rocked.	Stops crying only after dressing is finished. Cries until given bottle.	Cries when toy is taken away and rejects substitute.
Approach/Withdrawal	Positive	Smiles and licks washcloth. Has always liked bottle.	Likes new foods. Enjoyed first bath in a large tub. Smiles and gurgles.	Approaches strangers readily. Sleeps well in new surroundings
	Negative	Rejected cereal the first time. Cries when strangers appear.	Stays away from strangers. Plays with new toys only after some time.	Stiffened when placed on sled. Will not sleep in strange beds.
Adaptability	Adaptive	Was passive during first bath; now enjoys bathing. Smiles at nurse.	Used to dislike new foods; now accepts them well.	Was afraid of toy animals at first; now plays with them happily.
	Not adaptive	Still startled by sudden, sharp noise. Resists diapering.	Does not cooperate with dressing. Fusses and cries when left with sitter.	Continues to reject new foods each time they are offered.

(continues)

TABLE 17.1
(continued)

Temperamental quality	Rating	2 Months	6 Months	1 Year
Attention span and persistence	Long	If soiled, continues to cry until changed. Repeatedly rejects water if he wants milk.	Watches toy mobile over crib intently. "Coos" frequently.	Plays by self in playpen for more than an hour. Listens to singing for long periods.
	Short	Cries when awakened but stops almost immediately. Objects only mildly if cereal precedes bottle.	Sucks pacifier for only a few minutes and spits it out.	Loses interest in a toy after a few minutes. Gives up easily if she falls while attempting to walk.
Intensity of reaction	Intense	Cries when diapers are wet. Rejects food vigorously when satisfied.	Cries loudly at the sound of thunder. Makes sucking movements when vitamins are administered.	Laughs hard when father plays roughly. Screamed and kicked when temperature was taken.
	Mild	Does not cry when diapers are wet. Whimpers instead of crying when hungry.	Does not kick often in tub. Does not smile. Whimpers and moves when temperature is taken.	Does not fuss much when clothing is pulled on over head.
Threshold of responsiveness	Low	Stops sucking on bottle when approached.	Refuses fruit he likes when vitamins are added. Hides head from bright light.	Spits out food he does not like. Giggles when tickled.
	High	Is not startled by loud noises. Takes bottle and breast equally well.	Eats everything. Does not object to diapers being wet or soiled.	Eats food he likes even if mixed with disliked food. Can be left easily with strangers.
Quality of mood	Positive	Smacks lips when first tasting new foods. Smiles at parents.	Plays and splashes in bath. Smiles at everyone.	Likes bottle; reaches for it and smiles. Laughs loudly when playing peekaboo.
	Negative	Fusses after nursing. Cries when carriage is rocked.	Cries when taken from tub. Cries when given food she does not like.	Cries when given injections. Cries when left alone.

Temperamental quality	Rating	2 Years	5 Years	10 Years
Activity level	High	Climbs furniture. Explores. Gets in and out of bed while being put to sleep.	Leaves table often during meals. Always runs.	Plays ball and engages in other sports. Cannot sit still long enough to do homework.
	Low	Enjoys quiet play with puzzles. Can listen to records for hours.	Takes a long time to dress. Sits quietly on long automobile rides.	Likes chess and reading. Eats very slowly.

(continues)

TABLE 17.1
(continued)

Temperamental quality	Rating	2 Years	5 Years	10 Years
Rhythmicity	Regular	Eats a big lunch each day. Always has a snack before bedtime.	Falls asleep when put to bed. Bowel movement regular.	Eats only at mealtimes. Sleeps the same amount of time each night.
	Irregular	Nap time changes from day to day. Toilet training is difficult because bowel movement is unpredictable.	Food intake varies; so does time of bowel movement.	Food intake varies. Falls asleep at a different time each night.
Distractibility	Distractible	Will stop tantrum if another activity is suggested.	Can be coaxed out of forbidden activity by being led into something else.	Needs absolute silence for homework. Has a hard time choosing a shirt in a store because they all appeal to him.
	Not distractible	Screams if refused some desired object. Ignores mother's calling.	Seems not to hear if involved in favorite activity. Cries for a long time when hurt.	Can read a book while television set is at high volume. Does chores on schedule.
Approach/withdrawal	Positive	Slept well the first time he stayed overnight at grandparents' house.	Entered school building unhesitatingly. Tries new foods.	Went to camp happily. Loved to ski the first time.
	Negative	Avoids strange children in the playground. Whimpers first time at beach. Will not go into water.	Hid behind mother when entering school.	Severely homesick at camp during first days. Does not like new activities.
Adaptability	Adaptive	Obeys quickly. Stayed contentedly with grand-parents for a week.	Hesitated to go to nursery school at first; now goes eagerly. Slept well on camping trip.	Likes camp, although homesick during first days. Learns enthusiastically.
	Not adaptive	Cries and screams each time hair is cut. Disobeys persistently.	Has to be hand led into classroom each day. Bounces on bed in spite of spankings.	Does not adjust well to new school or new teacher; comes home late for dinner even when punished.
Attention span and persistence	Long	Works on a puzzle until it is completed. Watches when shown how to do something.	Practiced riding a two-wheeled bicycle for hours until he mastered it. Spent over an hour reading a book.	Reads for two hours before sleeping. Does homework carefully.
	Short	Gives up easily if a toy is hard to use. Asks for help immediately if undressing becomes difficult.	Still cannot tie his shoes because he gives up when he is not successful. Fidgets when parents read to him.	Gets up frequently from homework for a snack. Never finishes a book.

(continues)

TABLE 17.1
(continued)

Temperamental quality	Rating	2 Years	5 Years	10 Years
Intensity of reaction	Intense	Yells if he feels excitement or delight. Cries loudly if a toy is taken away.	Rushes to greet father. Gets hiccups from laughing hard.	Tears up an entire page of homework if one mistake is made. Slams door of room when teased by younger brother.
	Mild	When another child hit her, she looked surprised, did not hit back.	Drops eyes and remains silent when given a firm parental "No." Does not laugh much.	When a mistake is made on a model airplane, corrects it quietly. Does not comment when reprimanded.
Threshold of responsiveness	Low	Runs to door when father comes home.	Always notices when mother puts new dress on for first time. Refuses milk if it is not ice-cold.	Rejects fatty foods. Adjusts shower until water is at exactly the right temperature.
	High	Can be left with anyone. Falls to sleep easily on either back or stomach.	Does not hear loud, sudden noises when reading. Does not object to injections.	Never complains when sick. Eats all foods.
Quality of mood	Positive	Plays with sister; laughs and giggles. Smiles when he succeeds in putting shoes on.	Laughs loudly while watching television cartoons. Smiles at everyone.	Enjoys new accomplishments. Laughs when reading a funny passage aloud.
	Negative	Cries and squirms when given haircut. Cries when mother leaves.	Objects to putting boots on. Cries when frustrated.	Cries when he cannot solve a homework problem. Very "weepy" if he does not get enough sleep.

Note. From "The Origin of Personality," by A. Thomas, S. Chess, and H. G. Birch, 1970, *Scientific American, 223.* Copyright © 1970 by Scientific American, Inc. Reprinted with permission.

children. That is, for some children—although not for all—certain attribute scores on one dimension tended to occur at the same time as certain other attribute scores on other dimensions. Let us see the implications and meaning of such occurrences.

Temperamental Types

Among some children, scores on some temperamental attributes tended consistently to go along with scores on some of the other attributes. That is, a cluster, or grouping, of attribute scores was found for some children. For instance, for some children, low thresholds tended to go along with high adaptability and high attention spans. In fact, Thomas and colleagues were able to identify three such temperamental clusters. Some children had one type of temperamental attribute grouping, whereas other children possessed another type. These three types were given different labels to describe the temperamental patterns of the children who possessed them.

The Easy Child

Some children were characterized by a temperament composed of a positive mood, high rhythmicity, low- or moderate-intensity reactions, high adaptability, and an approach orientation to new situations and stimuli. About 40% of the children in the NYLS sample possessed this temperamental type (Thomas, Chess, & Birch, 1970). Such children slept and ate regularly as infants, were generally happy, and adjusted readily to new people and events. As older children, they also adjusted easily to changing school requirements and adapted and participated easily in games and other activities. Hence, the Thomas group labeled such a child as *easy* because such a child obviously presents few difficulties to raise. Such a child is easy to interact with.

As we see later, when we consider the data in the NYLS pertinent to the goodness-of-fit model, it is the implications of the child's temperamental style for social interaction with others that provide the significance of a given temperamental style for the child's healthy psychosocial functioning. Simply, the functional significance of a temperament type (i.e., the significance for healthy or unhealthy behavior and development) lies in the impact of the type on other people.

The Difficult Child

In contrast to the easy (to interact with) child, there is the child who possesses a temperamental style that makes for difficult interactions. These children are characterized by low rhythmicity, high-intensity reactions, a withdrawal orientation to new situations and stimuli, slow adaptation, and a negative mood. About 10% of the NYLS children had this temperamental type. As infants they ate and slept irregularly, took a long time to adjust to new situations, and were characterized by a great deal of crying. To say the least, such a child would be difficult for a parent to train or a teacher to educate. Such a child would even be difficult just to interact with. Parents and teachers would have to show both tolerance and patience in order to have favorable interactions with such children.

The Slow-To-Warm-Up Child

Here, we find a child who has a low activity level, a withdrawal orientation, slow adaptability, a somewhat negative mood, and relatively low reaction intensities. Such children comprised 15% of the NYLS sample (Thomas, Chess, & Birch, 1970).

These children would also present interaction difficulties and problems for their parents and teachers. It would take some time to get such a child involved in new activities and situations, and similarly, the child's slow adaptability and somewhat negative mood would suggest that the slow-to-warm-up child would not interact favorably with new people. Clearly, the temperamental characteristics of this type of child would provide a basis for parental and teacher interactions different from that of easy children.

One indication of the different functional significance of these three types of temperamental styles is found in the proportion of children in each temperamental group who eventually developed behavioral problems severe enough to call for psychiatric attention. Of the total number of children in the Thomas and colleagues project, 42% were seen (i.e., screened) at one time or another for the presence of such problems. (This high percentage is due, probably in large part, to the fact that the NYLS parents had free access to the advice of Stella Chess in regard to any behavioral or emotional problems in their children; this opportunity may have elevated the proportion of parents who would seek out a psychiatrist for advice or treatment of their children.)

About 70% of the difficult children developed behavior difficulties, whereas only 18% of the easy children did so; the proportion of slow-to-warm-up children who developed such problems was between these two groups. Thus, each of the three temperamental types found among the NYLS sample children seemed to have a different significance for the quality of behavioral functioning.

The various temperamental-attribute scores of the easy, difficult, and slow-to-warm-up children are presented in Table 17.2. From this table and our preceding discussion, we may infer that the distinct temperamental styles associated with these three types might have different implications for healthy psychosocial functioning because of their import for social interaction. That is, easy children are easy because they are not hard people with whom to interact; they possess the temperamental attributes that many parents and teachers might desire in children. In turn, difficult children are difficult by virtue of the fact that it is hard to interact with them; they possess temperamental attributes that many parents and teachers might not want, desire, or prefer in children.

A study by Gordon and Thomas (1967) illustrates these ideas. Gordon and Thomas (1967) found that kindergarten teachers were able to

TABLE 17.2
Temperamental Attributes of the Easy, Difficult, and Slow-To-Warm-Up Child

Type of child	Activity level	Rhythmicity	Distractibility	Approach/ Withdrawal	Adaptability
	The proportion of active periods to inactive ones.	Regularity of hunger, excretion, sleep, and wakefulness.	The degree to which extraneous stimuli alter behavior.	The response to a new object or person.	The ease with which a child adapts to changes in his environment.
"Easy"	Varies	Very regular	Varies	Positive approach	Very adaptable
"Slow to warm up"	Low to moderate	Varies	Varies	Initial withdrawal	Slowly adaptable
"Difficult"	Varies	Irregular	Varies	Withdrawal	Slowly adaptable

Type of child	Attention span and persistence	Intensity of reaction	Threshold of responsiveness	Quality of mood
	The amount of time devoted to an activity, and the effect of distraction on the activity.	The energy of response regardless of its quality of direction.	The intensity of stimulation required to evoke a discernible response.	The amount of friendly, pleasant, joyful behavior as contrasted with unpleasant, unfriendly behavior.
"Easy"	High or low	Low or mild	High or low	Positive
"Slow to warm up"	High or low	Mild	High or low	Slightly negative
"Difficult"	High or low	Intense	High or low	Negative

Note. From "The Origin of Personality," by A. Thomas, S. Chess, and H. G. Birch, 1970, *Scientific American, 223.* Copyright © 1970 by Scientific American, Inc. Reprinted with permission.

rate their students in respect to their temperamental styles. The teachers were also asked to estimate the intelligence of these students, and Gordon and Thomas independently measured these children's intelligence. It was found that the teachers distorted the students' intelligence; that is, the teacher ratings of intelligence were biased by the students' temperamental styles. For instance, children who had temperaments similar to that of the easy child were rated as more intelligent than children who had temperamental styles similar to the slow-to-warm-up child. Yet, these estimates tended to represent an overestimation of the easy children's intelligence and an underestimation of the slow-to-warm-up children's intelligence. It is reasonable to assume that teachers will interact differently with children they believe

to be brighter than with children they believe to be duller. For example, they may attempt to provide remedial work for the "duller" children and might leave the "brighter" children alone to work by themselves more often. The presence of temperament-related distortion suggests that different children, possessing different temperamental types, will experience different interactions with their teachers over the course of their educational development; these different interactions are based, in part at least, on the different meanings attached by teachers to different child temperament styles (Pullis & Caldwell, 1982).

Thus, if the functional significance of a child's easy, difficult, or slow-to-warm-up temperamental style lies in the impact the style has on the child's social context, it is important to understand the nature of the relations between the child's temperament and his or her social settings. Such understanding is the goal of those who use the goodness-of-fit model. We turn now to a discussion of this model, and the NYLS data pertinent to it.

The Goodness-of-Fit Model

We may recall from our discussions of the nature–nurture controversy in previous chapters that both a person and his or her context will be individually distinct as a consequence of the unique combination of genotypic and phenotypic features of the person and of the specific attributes of his or her context. The presence of such individuality is central to understanding the goodness-of-fit model. We have noted that as a consequence of characteristics of physical individuality (e.g., in regard to body type or facial attractiveness) (Adams, 1991; Lerner, Lerner, & Jovanovic, 1996; Perkins & Lerner, 1995; Sorell & Nowak, 1981) and/or of psychological individuality (e.g., in regard to conceptual tempo or temperament (Chess & Thomas, 1999; Kagan, 1966, 1998; Rothbart & Bates, 1998; Thomas & Chess, 1977)— children promote differential reactions in their socializing others; these reactions may feed back to children, increase the individuality of their development milieu, and provide a basis for their further development. As we have seen, Schneirla (1957) termed these relations circular functions. It is through the establishment of such functions in ontogeny that people may be conceived of as producers of their own development (Brandtstädter, 1998, 1999; Lerner & Busch-Rossnagel, 1981a, 1981b; Lerner & Walls, 1999). However, this circular functions idea needs to be extended because it is mute regarding the specific characteristics of the feedback (e.g., its positive or negative valence) a child will receive as a consequence of his or her individuality.

We have noted that a basis of the feedback a child receives comes from his or her fit with the demands placed on the child by virtue of the physical and/or social components (i.e., by the significant others) in the setting, or in the "context" in other terms (Lerner & Lerner, 1983, 1989). If a given temperament attribute is congruent with the demands of a significant other (e.g., a parent), we expect positive adjustment (adaptation), whereas if that same attribute is incongruent with such demands, we expect negative adjustment.

To illustrate, let us consider the case of the child in his or her family context and of the psychosocial and physical climate promoted by the parents.

Parents can vary in their cognitive and behavioral attributes (e.g., in regard to their child-rearing attitudes and parenting styles) (Baumrind, 1971; Collins et al., 2000; Grotevant, 1998); parents can vary, too, in the physical features of the home they provide. These parent-based psychosocial and physical characteristics constitute presses for, or demands on, the child to adapt (Lerner & Lerner, 1989). Similarly, parent characteristics are "translated" or "transduced" into demands on the child (Lerner & Lerner, 1989).

As explained earlier, these demands may first take the form of attitudes, values, or expectations held by parents (or in other contexts by teachers and/or peers) regarding the child's physical or behavioral characteristics. Second, demands exist as a consequence of the behavioral attributes of parents (or, again, of teachers and/or peers); these people are significant others with whom the child must coordinate, or fit, his or her behavioral attributes for adaptive interactions to exist. Third, the physical characteristics of a setting (such as the noise level of the home) constitute contextual demands. Such physical presses require the child to possess certain behavioral attributes for the most efficient interaction within the setting to occur. The child's individuality in differentially meeting these demands provides a basis for the feedback he or she gets from the socializing environment.

Considering the demand "domain" of attitudes, values, or expectations, teachers and parents may have relatively individual and distinct expectations about behaviors desired of their students and children, respectively. Teachers may want students who show little distractibility, because they would not want attention diverted from the lesson by the activity of other children in the classroom. Parents, however, might desire their children to be moderately distractible (e.g., when they require their children to move from television watching to dinner or to bed). Children whose behavioral individuality was either generally distractible or generally not distractible would, thus, differentially meet the demands of these two contexts. Problems of adjustment to school or to home demands might develop as a consequence of a child's lack of match, or "goodness-of-fit," in either or both settings.

In short, the key idea within the goodness-of-fit model is that adaptive psychological and social functioning do not derive directly from either the nature of the person's characteristics of individuality per se or the nature of the demands of the contexts within which the person functions. Instead, if a person's characteristics of individuality fit or exceed the demands of a particular setting, *adaptive outcomes* (i.e., those associated with good personal adjustment and positive social interaction) in that setting will accrue. If the characteristics are incongruent with (i.e., fall short of) the demands of a setting, then personal maladjustment and/or negative social functioning will occur.

TESTS OF THE GOODNESS-OF-FIT MODEL IN THE NYLS

Much of the research literature supporting the use of the goodness-of-fit model is derived from the Thomas and Chess (1977; Chess & Thomas, 1996, 1999) NYLS. Let us consider, then, the contribution of these data from the NYLS.

Within the NYLS data set, information relevant to the goodness-of-fit model exists as a consequence of the multiple samples present in the project. We have noted that the NYLS core sample is composed of 133 middle-class, mostly European American children of professional parents and that, in addition, a sample of 98 New York City Puerto Rican children of working-class parents has been followed for about 7 years. Each sample was studied from at least the first month of life onward. Although the distribution of temperamental attributes in the two samples was not different, the import of the attributes for psychosocial adjustment was quite disparate. Two examples may suffice to illustrate this distinction.

First, let us consider the impact of low regularity or rhythmicity of behavior, particularly in regard to sleep–wake cycles. The Puerto Rican parents studied by Thomas and Chess (1977; Thomas et al., 1974) were quite permissive. No demands in regard to rhythmicity of sleep were placed on the infant or child. Indeed, the parents allowed the child to go to sleep at any time the child desired and permitted the child to awaken at any time as well. The parents molded their schedule around the children. Because parents were so accommodating, there were no problems of fit associated with an arrhythmic infant or child. Indeed, neither within the infancy period nor throughout the first 5 years of life did arrhythmicity predict adjustment problems. In this sample, arrhythmicity remained continuous and independent of adaptive implications for the child (Korn, 1978; Thomas et al., 1974).

In the middle-class families, however, strong demands for rhythmic sleep patterns were maintained. Thus, an arrhythmic child did not fit with parental demands, and consistent with the goodness-of-fit model, rhythmicity was a major predictor of problem behaviors both within the infancy years and across time through the first 5 years of life (Korn, 1978; Thomas et al., 1974).

It should be emphasized that there are at least two ways of viewing this finding. First, consistent with the idea that children influence their parents, we may note that sleep arrhythmicity in their children resulted in problems in the parents (e.g., through their reports of stress, anxiety, and anger) (Chess & Thomas, 1984, 1996, 1999; Thomas et al., 1974). Such an effect of child temperament on the parent's own level of adaptation has been reported in other data sets; for instance, infants who had high thresholds for responsiveness to social stimulation, and, thus, were not easily soothed by their mothers, evoked intense distress reactions in their mothers and a virtual cessation of maternal caregiving behaviors (Brazelton, Koslowski, & Main, 1974). Thus, it is possible that the presence of such child effects in the NYLS sample could have altered previous parenting styles in a way that constituted feedback to the child that was associated with the development of problem behaviors in him or her.

In turn, a second interpretation of this finding arises from the fact that problem behaviors in the children were identified initially on the basis of parental report. Thus, it may be that irrespective of any problem behavior evoked in the parent by the child and/or of any altered parent–child interactions that thereby ensued, one effect of the child on the parent was to increase the probability of the parent labeling the child's temperamental style as problematic and so reporting it to the NYLS staff psychiatrist. Unfortunately, the current state of analysis of the NYLS data do not allow us to discriminate between these obviously nonmutually-exclusive possibilities.

However, what the data in the NYLS do allow us to indicate is that the parents in the middle-class sample took steps to change their arrhythmic children's sleep patterns; and as most of these arrhythmic children were also adaptable, and since temperament may be modified by person–context interactions, low rhythmicity tended to be discontinuous for most children. That the parents behaved to modify their children's arrhythmicity is also an instance of a child effect on its psychosocial context. That is, the child "produced" in his or her parents alterations in parental caregiving behaviors regarding sleep. That these child effects on the parental context fed back to the child and influenced his or her further development is consistent with the previously noted finding that sleep arrhythmicity was discontinuous among these children.

Thus, in the middle-class sample, early-infant arrhythmicity tended to be a problem during this time of life but proved to be neither continuous nor predictive of later adjustment problems. In turn, in the Puerto Rican sample, infant arrhythmicity was not a problem during this time of life, but it was continuous and—because in the Puerto Rican context it was not involved in poor fit—it was not associated with adjustment problems in the child in the first 5 years of life. Of course, this is not to say that the parents in the Puerto Rican families were not affected by their children's sleep arrhythmicity; as with the parents in the middle-class families, it may be that the Puerto Rican parents had problems of fatigue and/or suffered marital or work-related problems due to irregular sleep patterns produced in them as a consequence of their child's sleep arrhythmicity; however, again, the data analyses in the NYLS do not indicate this possible child effect on the Puerto Rican parents.

The data do allow us to underscore the importance of considering fit with the demands of the psychosocial context of development, in that they indicate that arrhythmicity did begin to predict adjustment problems for the Puerto Rican children when they entered the school system. Their lack of a regular sleep pattern interfered with their getting sufficient sleep to perform well in school and, in addition, often caused them to be late to school (Korn, 1978; Thomas et al., 1974). Thus, before the age of 5 only one Puerto Rican child presented a clinical problem diagnosed as a sleep disorder. However, almost 50% of the Puerto Rican children who developed clinically identifiable problems between ages 5 and 9 were diagnosed as having sleep problems.

Another example may be given of how the differential demands existing between the two family contexts provide different presses for adaptation. This example pertains to differences in the demands of the families' physical contexts.

As noted by Thomas and colleagues (1974), as well as by Korn (1978), overall there was a very low incidence of behavior problems in the Puerto Rican sample children in their first 5 years of life, especially when compared to the corresponding incidence among the core sample children. However, if a problem was presented at this time among the Puerto Rican sample, it was most likely to be a problem of motor activity. In fact, across the first 9 years of their lives, of those Puerto Rican children who developed clinical problems, 53% presented symptoms diagnosed as involving problematic motor activity. Parents complained of excessive and uncontrollable motor activity in such cases.

However, in the core sample, only one child (a child with brain damage) was characterized in this way.

We may note here that the Puerto Rican parents' reports of "excessive and uncontrollable" activity in their children does constitute, in this group, an example of a child effect on the parents. That is, a major value of the Puerto Rican parents in the NYLS was child "obedience" to authority (Korn, 1978). The type of motor activity shown by the highly active children of these Puerto Rican parents evoked considerable parental distress, given their perception that their children's behavior was inconsistent with what would be emitted by obedient children (Korn, 1978).

Of course, if the middle-class parents had seen their children's behavior as excessive and uncontrollable, it may be that—irrespective of any major salience placed on the value of child obedience—problems would have been evoked in them, and feedback to the children would have ensued. Thus, an issue remains as to why the same (high) activity level should evoke one set of appraisals among the Puerto Rican parents but quite another set among the middle-class parents (i.e., in the latter group no interpretation of "excessive and uncontrollable" behavior was evoked). Similarly, one may ask why high activity level is closely associated with problem behavior in the Puerto Rican children and not in the middle-class children. I believe that the key information needed to address these issues relates to the physical features of the respective groups' homes.

In the Puerto Rican sample, the families usually had several children and lived in small apartments. Even average motor activity, therefore, tended to impinge on others in the setting. Moreover, and as an illustration of the embeddedness of the child—temperament—home—context relation in the broader community context, I may note that even in the case of the children with high activity levels, the Puerto Rican parents were reluctant to let their children out of the apartment because of the actual dangers of playing on the streets of East Harlem.

In the core sample, however, the parents had the financial resources to provide large apartments or houses for their families. There were typically suitable play areas for the children both inside and outside the home. As a consequence, the presence of high activity levels in the home of the core sample did not cause the problems for interaction that they did in the Puerto Rican group. Thus, as Thomas and colleagues (1968, 1974) emphasized the mismatch between temperamental attribute and physical environmental demand accounted for the group difference in the import of high activity level for the development of behavioral problems in the children.

Chess and Thomas (1999) reviewed other data from the NYLS, and from independent data sets that tested their temperament–context, goodness-of-fit model. The conclusions of the Chess and Thomas (1999) review are consistent with the results of the NYLS tests of the goodness-of-fit model that I have reviewed. Both the Chess and Thomas (1999) review and my discussion allow the inference that, at a given point in development, neither children's attributes per se nor the demands of their setting per se are the key predictors of their adaptive functioning. Instead, the *relation* between the child and his or her context—one described by the goodness-of-fit model—seems most important in home and school settings. This conclusion leads to some important practical implications. However, before we turn to these implications of the results of the NYLS let us first consider the theoretical implications of this important ipsative longitudinal study of child development.

Theoretical Implications of the NYLS

The results of the Thomas and colleagues NYLS indicate that children have present at birth characteristically individual, or unique, attributes of temperament. That is, children tend to show stylistically different reactive repertoires to the stimuli and situations with which they interact. This individual pattern of reactivity is presumed to arise out of an interaction between the intrinsic and extrinsic variables that provide a source of the child's development. In other words, on the basis of the child's individual organismic–experience dynamic interaction, the child develops characteristics of individuality, which are furthered on the basis of interactions between this individually different child and his or her environment. In fact, we have seen that because the child does have such characteristically different attributes of reactivity, he or she will react to a given environmental situation differently than will another individually different child. Thus, because different children can be expected to react differently to the same environmental situation, these differential reactions will differentially influence significant other persons in their respective environments; and these influences on others are consistent with what would be expected on the basis of the goodness-of-fit model. Similarly, these different reactions in significant others will then feed back to the child and provide a further experiential source of his or her own development.

Thus, even if parents attempt to provide the same child-rearing environment for their different children, and even if such parents possess markedly similar personalities, such parental similarities will not have the same effect on different children. Because a child's temperament is, at least, in part unrelated to his or her parents' personalities and child-rearing practices (Thomas, Chess, & Birch, 1970), this suggests: (a) That such parental–environmental variables cannot be viewed as the *only* source of a child's temperament, and (b) that the same environment will have a different effect on different children.

One may not, then, focus solely on either hereditary or experiential sources of influence if one wants to deal accurately with the actual source of individuality and development. Rather, one must study hereditary sources, prenatal and perinatal sources and influences, and later, life-course experiences, all of which may interact to contribute to the development of the individual (Thomas et al., 1963, p. 81).

In sum, the results of the Thomas and colleagues NYLS indicate that:

1.   Extremely early in their lives children appear to possess, and to maintain, characteristically different patterns of reactivity, or temperament; this individuality is believed to find its source in the interactions of the intrinsic and the extrinsic factors affecting the development of organisms. The functional significance of this individuality lies in the relation between the child and his or her context.
2.   Because of this interactively based individuality, different children will react differently even to the same environmental influences. Thus, the same stimulus will not have the same effect on different children, and any analysis of behavioral development that attempts to account for development simply by reference to stimulus factors is inappropriate, naive, and destined to remain incomplete (Scarr, 1982; Scarr & McCartney, 1983).
3.   On the basis of the child's individuality and the circular feedback functions that arise out of this individuality (Schneirla, 1957)—functions that are consistent with the goodness-of-fit model—the child must be viewed as playing an active, participatory role in his or her own development (Lerner, 1982; Lerner & Busch-Rossnagel, 1981b; Lerner & Walls, 1999).

Thus, the ipsative study of the Thomas group has found results consistent with the dynamic developmental systems perspective we have been stressing throughout this book. Consistent with other such theories (e.g., Ford & Lerner, 1992; Gottlieb, 1970, 1983, 1997; Schneirla, 1957; Thelen & Smith, 1998), the child's development was seen by Thomas and colleagues (1963) as finding its source in a fusion between the child's organismic characteristics and the characteristics of experience; hence, the organism itself plays an active, contributory role in its own development. We are able to draw similar conclusions from the second major ipsative study of development we discuss in this chapter, the study by Block (1971). However, before we turn to this study, let us first consider the important practical implications of the Thomas and colleagues NYLS.

Practical Implications of the NYLS

Many parents consult various how-to books about childrearing to gain information about how to raise their children. Often such books tell the parent what a child is like at a particular age period and what child-rearing practices to employ. One important practical implication of the NYLS is that such cookbook approaches to childrearing are inappropriate.

Because children are individually different, because they possess characteristically different and potentially continuous attributes of reactivity, one may not appropriately make generalized statements about what children at a particular age level are like. One may not imply that a given type of rearing procedure will work equally well with all children. Although children do share general, age-related characteristics, they also possess important characteristics of individuality. Thus, a child-rearing book must help parents understand that, to an important extent, their child is an individual person (see Chess, Thomas, & Birch, 1965).

Moreover, the cookbook approach to childrearing is also inappropriate because, again, one cannot accurately specify how a general method of child-rearing will affect all children. Since children have individually different temperamental repertoires, they will not react in the same way to the same rearing procedure. Different children will react differently to the same exact procedure. For instance, adoption by the parents of a fixed schedule of feeding may work well for an easy child but might prove unfavorable for either a difficult or slow-to-warm-up child.

Another practical implication of the Thomas and colleagues study relates to parental responses to children's development. If emotional or behavioral problems arise in a child, the typical parental response is guilt. Perhaps because the parents believe an environmentalist doctrine—that anything a child becomes is solely an outcome of his or her environmental experiences (e.g., Watson, 1928)—the parents feel that they are responsible for the child's problems. They feel guilt because they believe that they are responsible for their child not only in a moral sense—which, of course, one may maintain that they *are*—but also in a behavioral-determinacy sense. They believe that they are the major environmental determinants of their child's behavior, and in turn they believe that the environment provides a primary source of their child's behavioral development.

Such parents are not aware of the fact that the child plays an active contributory role in his or her own development (Lerner, 1982; Lerner & Busch-Rossnagel, 1981a, 1981b; Lerner & Walls, 1999). It is perhaps to help parents overcome ill-founded guilt that Stella Chess (personal communication, 1978) was fond of saying that "All parents are environmentalists until they have their second child!" Thus, parental guilt is misdirected if they do not understand that a child's behavioral or emotional problems arise, in part, from an interaction between the child's temperament and conflicting environmental demands. For instance, whereas it is easy to imagine that almost any environmental circumstance would be adapted to by an easy child, a difficult child would probably have interactional difficulties with almost any environment.

Hence, parents should not feel guilty. Rather, they should be made aware of the importance of understanding the implications of their child's individuality, and they should attempt to alter their procedures to achieve a more favorable interaction between the child's temperamental characteristics and their child-rearing practices.

In summarizing the implications of their work for both theory and practice in psychiatry, Thomas, Chess, and Birch (1970) said:

> Theory and practice in psychiatry must take into full account the individual and his or her uniqueness: how children differ and how these differences act to influence their psychological growth. A given environment will not have the identical functional meaning for all children. Much will depend on the temperamental makeup of the child. As we learn more about how specific parental attitudes and practices and other specific factors in the environment of the child interact with specific temperamental, mental, and physical attributes of individual children, it should become considerably easier to foster the child's healthy development. (p. 109)

Some Concluding Comments

With this specification of the practical implications of the NYLS, we may see how this ipsative study of development may be used to understand the complexities of human development and to apply this understanding in order to enhance the lives of children and families (Chess & Thomas, 1984, 1996, 1999; Thomas et al., 1965, 1970). Although the ipsative approach, as represented in the work of the Thomas group is quite different in its procedural orientation from either the stage or the differential approaches, we have seen that the Thomas and colleagues approach to ipsative analysis addresses similar issues of development. Thus, consistent with the general organismic, interactionist theoretical positions found in the ideas of stage theorists (e.g., Piaget, Kohlberg), the Thomas and colleagues ipsative approach provides evidence for the interactive basis of human development and supports probabilistic epigenetic notions about the important role that the individual him- or herself plays in his or her own development.

As previously noted, the importance of a focus on individuality in attempting to understand development, and the use of an ipsative approach in implementing this focus, are illustrated in the second major study that we consider in this chapter. We turn, then, to our discussion of the research of Block (1971).

BLOCK'S STUDY OF *LIVES THROUGH TIME*

For more than one-half century, the Institute of Human Development at the University of California, Berkeley, has been one of the leading centers in the United States for the long-term longitudinal study of human development (for discussions of centers of excellence in Europe for the longitudinal study of human development, see, too, Magnusson, 1996, 1999a, 1999b). The multidisciplinary group of scientists, who have worked at the Institute of Human Development (IHD) over this period, have been prolific in regard to the important theoretical, methodological, and empirical contributions they have made to the study of human development across the life span (e.g., Bayley, 1949; Block, 1971; Eichorn et al., 1981; Elder, 1974, 1999; Haan, 1974, 1977; H. Jones, 1938, 1939a, 1939b, 1958; Jones & Bayley, 1950; Livson & Pesking 1967, 1980; Macfarlane, 1938a, 1938b; Mussen & Jones, 1957; Tuddenham, 1959).

Jack Block

Two major longitudinal studies conducted by the scientists at the IHD provide the database for the second ipsatively oriented research project we discuss in this chapter—the research project conducted by Jack Block (with the collaboration of Norma Haan), entitled "Lives Through Time" (1971). That is, Block used the data from two IHD longitudinal studies "to trace, more closely than before, the ways of personality development and change from adolescence to adulthood" (1971, p. 2). Block (1971) reorganized, recorded, and reanalyzed the already collected data from these two IHD studies in order to indicate

> the importance of studying personality development and personality change in a differentiated way, of identifying and understanding the alternative paths along which people evolve over time. (p. 1)

By addressing this issue, Block not only provided a demonstration of the usefulness of an ipsative approach to understanding personality in a more refined, singular way but also showed that when sound and creative scientific procedures are followed, substantial use can be made of existing longitudinal data (i.e., of a longitudinal data archive) in the study of human development.

The first of the longitudinal studies that Block drew on was started in 1929 by Jean Macfarlane and involved the quite intensive study of people (and their families) from their infancy through their childhood, adolescence, and into their adulthood. These people were intensively studied as a consequence of their placement in what was termed a *guidance group*—a group whose families had agreed to participate in an in-depth long-term study of normal children. The 74 children who were involved in this long-term longitudinal enterprise (and who were studied in Block's 1971 research) are referred to as the Berkeley Guidance Study (BGS) children. The second longitudinal study that Block employed was started by Harold Jones in 1932. Here, children were studied from the fifth grade onward. The sample was drawn from the Oakland, California area, and, therefore, the 97 children who were involved in this longitudinal study (and who were part of Block's 1971 research) are referred to as the Oakland Growth Study (OGS) children.

Both the BGS and the OGS children took part in repeated, often quite time-consuming testing sessions over much, if not most, of their lives; we have to recognize that such commitment may not be present among all people, and that—as is true of *all* samples in long-term longitudinal research—issues of representativeness, bias, and generalizability are present. However, as Block (1971) well argued, one must live with such problems because the long-term longitudinal "approach can respond to questions regarding psychological development not otherwise scientifically accessible" (p. 1). Indeed, without longitudinal research such as Block's (1971), the conditions, causes, and consequences of constancy and change—of continuity and discontinuity—could not be described or understood. Let us turn, then, to a discussion of Block's study to discern how his ipsative approach allows one to understand the nature and implications of individual constancies and changes across life.

The Orientation of the Study

Block wanted to combine the BGS and the OGS samples in order to increase his sample size and, thus, the power of his statistical analysis and ability to discern possible subgroups of people whose personality development was of a particular type. Because the OGS sample was not studied until late childhood/early adolescence (i.e., they were recruited in the fifth grade), it was not possible to fully combine the samples (i.e., to use information from the BGS prior to the adolescent period). Thus, Block's study is, as previously noted, an assessment of personality development from adolescence to adulthood—that is, from junior high

school to the time the participants of the study were established in their families and their careers. Consistent with contemporary views of the adolescent period (e.g., Lerner, 2002; Lerner & Galambos, 1998; Petersen, 1988) as one in which substantial personality and social development and change may occur, Block (1971) argued that:

> Contrary to the view still largely held within psychoanalysis, with its emphasis on the irreversible and determinative significance for character formation of the first few years, adolescence is a time of considerable change and considerable consequence. Contrary to the cumulative, continuous view of personality evolvement held within reinforcement theory, which heavily influences the field of developmental psychology, adolescence is a time often of dramatic personality flux, consolidation, and redirection. (p. 2)

Thus, Block asserted, as we have discussed in previous chapters (e.g., in regard to the ideas of Brim & Kagan, 1980, and Bruer, 1999), that the course of life is not irrevocably set in the early years. He also argued (and his study provides evidence) that there is often individually distinct changing—as well as constancy—across the years following childhood.

Accordingly, although he did not deny the relevance of nomothetic laws or the usefulness of nomothetic analyses, Block (1971) believed that:

> Developmental psychology has been hampered in its progress to date because, in its preferred world, it has staked much and clung too long to the assumption of uniformity of relationships . . . the presumption . . . that all people develop in the same way . . . [and that] in the main, temporal correspondence or stability is to be expected if measurement has been adequate and important, central variables are considered. (p. 10)

Thus, although "normative trends and continuities in personality development" have been emphasized in previous work, Block (1971) stressed that:

> The emphasis in the present work, to achieve more complete understanding is upon consideration of *different life trends* and the significance of *personality changes* for later behavior and adjustment. (p. 10)

Block contended that life paths that differ in kind and direction, as well as in rate, represent an idea antithetical to a nomothetic one, which emphasizes universal laws that apply to all people. But as we discussed earlier in this chapter, from an ipsative perspective "universal applicability and lawfulness need not go together" (Block, 1971, p. 11). In addition, the presence of laws of development pertinent to one or relatively few people does not deny that there are features of these people's development to which universal laws may apply. In fact, I also noted earlier in this chapter that—despite the potentially unique intraindividual developmental courses of different people—it may be that the structural development of any individual life trajectory may be capable of description by the orthogenetic principle (Block, 1982; Lerner, 1978; Wapner & Demick, 1998; Werner, 1957). Indeed, it may be that individual ontogenesis is characterized by a synthesis of singular (idiographic) and generic (nomothetic) developments (Block, 1971; Lerner, 1984; Wapner & Demick, 1998). Such a possibility led Block (1971) to posit that development is best viewed as neither idiographic nor nomothetic, but rather as a phenomenon that may be identified as existing along a continuum anchored at its extremes by the concepts of nomothetic and idiographic development.

Block (1971) marshaled considerable evidence in support of this notion, which is reminiscent of the often-cited observation of Kluckhohn and Murray (1948, p. 35) that, in certain respects, every person is (a) like all other people (e.g., the orthogenetic principle may be used to describe any person's structural pattern of change), (b) like some other people (e.g., people's personality development may be divisible into subgroupings on the basis of their sex, race, ethnicity, child-rearing experiences, etc.), and (c) like no other person (e.g., the particular constellation of personality or behavior attributes possessed by a person may be singular to him or her). To understand how Block (1971) was able to provide data illustrating all three of these features of development, we must discuss his research methodology.

Methods of Research

When one wants to study intraindividual change across a substantial portion of the life span, one has at least two major options. One can plan one's own study and select participants, methods, measures, and times (ages) of observation. Then, one can implement these plans and—for instance, if one is concerned with intraindividual change from early adolescence through middle adulthood—begin the 20 year or so process of conducting one's study. On the other hand, one can turn to one of the relatively few longitudinal data archives that exist and try to address one's interest by capitalizing on these already existing data (e.g., see Colby, 1997; Lachman & James, 1997). Of course, the characteristics of the participant population, the methods, and measures, as well as the ages of observation, may not match ideally with what one desires. In fact, as Block (1971) found—and as

I believe is generally the case in regard to broad-based, long-term longitudinal archives—data available for one participant may not be exactly the same as that available for any other participant in the archive; some participants miss testing sessions, others supply additional information (e.g., letters, school reports, or hospital records) and still others are simply more cooperative than others.

However, if the longitudinal archive is rich in depth and breadth of coverage, if the researcher is willing to live with methodological features he or she would not have wanted, and if the unevenness of data across participants can be surmounted through the researcher's conceptual and methodological ingenuity, the advantages in time (and cost) of using an archive to address one's concerns may be greater than those to be gained by initiating a new study. In fact, given the extreme commitment in time and money of such an enterprise, as well as the difficulty in locating and maintaining a longitudinal sample for a substantial portion of the life span, the practical reality may be that if questions of long-term constancy and change are to be addressed, a researcher has no recourse *other* than to use a longitudinal archive.

If such a decision is indeed taken, then the procedures of Block—who himself was faced with these methodological issues and chose to use the IHD archival data—serve as excellent examples to follow. Block was faced with issues involving the participants, measures, methods, and incommensurate data across participants. Let us discuss these issues and see how Block dealt with them.

Participants

We have already seen some of the characteristics of the BGS and the OGS samples. Let us note some others which underscore the fact noted earlier—that longitudinal samples tend to have characteristics different from those that would be seen in a random sample of the population. Both IHD groups were, in general, brighter than average, although the BGS group scored somewhat higher. The mean IQ score of the BGS participants was 123 (standard deviation = 15.99), and the mean IQ of the OGS participants was 116 (standard deviation = 11.81). Moreover, within both the BGS and OGS groups, there tended to be a greater-than-typical representation of families of higher socioeconomic standing. In addition, for 81% of the participants, their families were intact through their adolescence.

Finally, we should note again that the way in which Block made sure that at least the age periods were commensurate across both groups was to study only the junior-high-school-to-adulthood age range. This left him with 171 participants, about equally divided in regard to sex (e.g., 84 males and 87 females were studied into adulthood), but this sample was much smaller than the original one of 212 for the OGS group and 248 for the BGS group. Accordingly, sample attrition is a problem in this study; this means that not only may results be difficult to generalize precisely to a broader population but also that we do not know the extent to which the 171 participants—who remained in the study from early adolescence through adulthood—provide data comparable to what could be derived from the 289 participants who did not remain in the study.

The Nature of the Longitudinal Archive

We have already noted that the IHD archives did not provide exactly the same information for each of the participants. This lack of equivalence presented a problem that manifested itself in several ways. First, Block (1971) noted that at least some data were missing for a great number of participants. Second, across the years the procedures needed to test participants changed; this made it difficult to determine whether differences over time were due to developmental or methodological changes. Third, across the two IHD samples (BGS and OGS), there was some difference in conceptual frame of reference; in turn, Block approached the research with a set of concepts that differed from those of either the original BGS or the original OGS researchers. This difference in conceptual orientation means that the variables of interest to the original IHD scientists, and about which data were collected, were not necessarily those of greatest interest to Block. For example, he noted that in the 1920s and 1930s, when the BGS and the OGS were initiated, there was major interest in such relatively overt and practically applicable variables as "leadership" and "behavior problems"; at the time of Block's (1971) research, however, major interest was in more covert variables such as "identity formation" and "ego mechanisms."

Another problem Block faced pertaining to the nonequivalence of data across participants arose from the presence of considerable naturalistic data about each participant. That is, in addition to the quantitative tests and measures for each participant, there was anecdotal information about each participant regarding his or her behavior at home, in school, or in peer groups. In addition, news clippings (if any) about participants were included, as well as records of any informal encounters they had with IHD staff members.

Lastly, Block (1971) noted, "Unpredictable events happen, and people react complexly" (p. 35). That is, nonnormative events occur in the lives of some people (e.g., death, divorce, and sudden illness) and these may influence the course of development in major ways. Information about these events was also in the participants' files, and because different people have different histories of life events, this represents a major basis of lack of equivalent information across participants.

In sum, the IHD archives provided a rich source of quantitative and qualitative information about each participant. However, this richness—which existed in regard to both the BGS and OGS samples at the early-adolescent (junior high school), middle-adolescent (high school), and adulthood (the fourth decade of life) age levels—was not present in exactly equivalent ways across participants. Block wanted to discern what, if any, differentiated patterns of personality development existed across the early-adolescent-to-adulthood age range; more specifically, he wanted to identify potentially distinct patterns of constancy and change in personality development from the first measurement time (early adolescence) to the second (middle adolescence), and from the second to the third (adulthood). But how could he score, or rate, the available data to address this concern in a manner that would allow him to know whether differences in personality development were "real" or merely a reflection of the fact that the different sorts of information about each participant made likely different depictions of personality change? Block needed to find a way to rate the different sets of information so as to provide comparable databases for each participant; only then could he begin to see whether personality developed in a differentiated or a universal way. The means Block took to address this issue resulted in the main data of the Lives Through Time study and, in addition, constituted his ipsative methodological approach to understanding personality development.

The Q-Sort Procedure

Block assembled a group of 27 clinically experienced mental health professionals (11 males and 16 females). These clinicians served as a panel of "judges," or raters, of the participants' personalities. That is, at least two, and typically more, of these judges read through a complete file on a given participant for one of the three age periods in question (early or middle adolescence or adulthood). Each judge then independently contributed ratings of the participant's personality via the Q-sort procedure.

As described by Block (1971):

> The Q-sort procedure is simply a set of mildly techni-
> cal rules for the scaling of a group of personality-de-
> scriptive variables (Q items) vis-à-vis a particular
> individual, so that the ultimate ordering of the Q
> items expresses well the judge's formulation of the
> personality of the individual being evaluated. (p. 37)

The Q-items Block (1971) presented to the
judges to rate the participants during their adulthood was a version of the California Q-set (CQ-
set), which was developed by Block (1961). There
are 100 items in the CQ-set. Some of these are "is
critical, skeptical, not easily impressed"; "basically
submissive"; "has warmth; is compassionate"; "responds to humor"; "has fluctuating moods"; and "is
verbally fluent; can express ideas well."

Corresponding versions of the CQ-set were used
to rate the participants as adolescents. That is, a
104-item adolescent CQ-set was used by the
judges to assess adolescent personality structure
and dynamics. Ninety items in the adolescent CQ
parallel those in the CQ-set used to rate the participants as adults (Block, 1971). Some representative items are "seeks reassurance from others";
"feels satisfied with self"; and "questing for meaning, self-definition, or redefinition."

Finally, a 63-item interpersonal Q-set was used
by judges to rate the participants' behavior, during
adolescence, in regard to peer-group relations,
attitudes toward parents, and differential behavior with peers and with adults. Some representative items are "participant (S) respects his
parents"; "is competitive with peers"; and "is dependent on peers."

But how does a judge use a given Q-set to formulate his or her ratings of a participant? After
reading a file and formulating an impression of the
participant, the judge—in order to quantify his or
her impressions—is instructed to

> order the Q items into a designated number of cate-
> gories and, most important, with an assigned num-
> ber of items placed in each category. At one end of the
> judgmental continuum are placed those items most
> characteristic of the person being described or most
> "salient" in describing him. At the other end of the
> continuum are placed the items most uncharacteris-
> tic or most "salient" in a negative sense in formulat-
> ing the personality description of the designated
> subject.
> Conventionally, the Q items are printed separately
> on cards, a convenience which permits easy arrange-
> ment and rearrangement until the desired ordering
> is obtained. After the sorting, the placement of
> each item is recorded. The categories into which the
> judge has placed the Q statements are themselves
> numbered, from 9 through 1, with 9 by convention

referring to the most characteristic end of the continuum and the number 1 to the least characteristic
end. For each item, the number of the category in
which it was placed is recorded as that item's value
in the personality description. With the data entered
in this fashion ready for subsequent analysis, the
procedure is completed. (Block, 1971, p. 38)

Thus, despite missing data, procedural
changes, new conceptual foci, or the differential
presence of life-event data, judges, after reading
a file, rate each participant on a set of Q-items
that are consistent across participants at a given
age period. To illustrate, with the CQ-set used by
the judges to rate the participants as adults, the
100 items are required to be sorted into nine categories: Five items (cards) must be placed into
category 1; 8 into Category 2; 12 into Category 3;
16 into Category 4; 18 into Category 5; 16 into
Category 6; 12 into Category 7; 8 into Category 8;
and 5 into Category 9. Scores of 1 through 9, respectively, are assigned to the cards put into each
of the above categories. Similarly, the 104 items
of the adolescent CQ-set are required to be distributed among the nine categories according to
the following distribution: 6, 9, 13, 15, 18, 15, 13,
9, and 6.

The judges were instructed by Block to formulate their ratings from an ipsative frame of reference. That is, for each Q-item it was the judge's
task to appraise "the saliency or the decisiveness
of the item in shaping or characterizing" (Block,
1971, p. 46) that particular participant's personality. Thus, the placement of an item into a category
(1 through 9) was not made on the basis of how a
given participant compared to any other participant. Rather, the placement of an item was made
by "comparing the participant against himself or
herself." That is, how important was this item, as
compared to the others used to constitute the participant's personality, in *shaping* the participant's
personality? Thus, ratings were intraindividual.
As we saw in respect to the Thomas group (1977)
NYLS, wherein nine categories of temperament
were used to characterize all participants, Block's
(1971) use of the Q-sort procedure "imposed," or
defined, the attribute repertoire for each participant (i.e., the 100- or 104-item Q-set used to rate
the participants as adults and as adolescents, respectively, constituted each participant's attribute
repertoire). However, it was the judges' ratings
(and the ratings' statistical analyses, e.g., factor
analyses) that determined the attribute interrelation of the participants.

In sum, by using the Q-sort procedure, Block
(1971) was able to move the IHD archival data set
from one providing incommensurate information

across participants to one allowing for a common set of ratings at each of the three age levels studied. Thus, application of Q-sort methodology allowed Block to capitalize on the richness present in the IHD archive.

However, as with virtually any methodological strategy, the use of the Q-sort method exists along with its limitations. Thus, the Q-sort procedure has liabilities as well as assets. For example, given the requirements of sorting Q-items in a fixed frequency distribution, there is an imposed (and negative) expected average correlation among the items; that is, the statistically conventional null hypothesis which here would be that there is no correlation among the items (i.e., that there is no personality structure discernible in the ratings of the Q-items) does not hold for Q-items rated by the Q-sort procedure (J. R. Nesselroade, personal communication, September 1982). This nonzero and, in fact, negative expected average correlation makes difficult the interpretation of the significance levels of correlation coefficients, which are typically judged for their statistical significance on the basis of whether they differ from an expected correlation of zero (i.e., from the null hypothesis of "no correlation").

In addition to this statistical issue, a conceptual one may be raised. Mischel (1983) noted that the Q-items are not all conceptually independent. That is, putting a given item into one category (e.g., Category 9, which indicates high salience in depicting the person) means that other items are likely to be rated with similar salience levels. In turn, if a Q-item might "carry" other Q-items with it, this also suggests that there may be items that, for reasons of a "negative carrying effect," may be placed in a category far from the item in question. For instance, in the adult CQ-set, placement of Item 57 ("is an interesting, arresting person") in a category of a given salience may imply that Item 88 ("is personally charming") be placed in the same or in a close-by category, and that Item 48 ("aloof, keeps people at a distance; avoids close interpersonal relationships") be placed further away.

Block (1971) was, of course, aware of these potential problems with the Q-sort procedure, and he took steps to address them. Thus, he trained his judges extensively to avoid making stereotypic ratings. In addition, he instructed them that they could rate conceptually similar items in distinct ways. Finally, his use of multiple judges for each participant meant that reliable composite ratings could be (and indeed were) formed. In addition, the presence of multiple judges meant that a participant's scores were not a product of the biases (e.g., the implicit personality theory or stereotype) of a single judge (although the possible effect of a common stereotype across judges—as in Broverman, 1972—cannot be ruled out). Thus, although Block acknowledged that his results were, of course, a function of his particular method of assessment, he did not believe his findings were merely an artifact of his method. Block (1971) stated:

> Although the results are inevitably a function of the variable set employed, this variable set appears to have sufficient degrees of freedom so that personality diversities can be manifested. Thus, the dependency of the relationships found upon the particular Q items employed is not methodologically bothersome. The limitation, to the extent it exists, is the limit on current ways of viewing personality rather than a deficiency of a particular method. (p. 114)

But what are the results found by Block? What evidence exists for the presence of stability and for change? What evidence is there that personality develops in other than a nomothetic, universal fashion? To answer these questions, we turn to a presentation of some of the key results of Block's research.

THE FINDINGS OF BLOCK'S (1971) STUDY

Block's findings are presented in well over 200 pages of his 1971 book. As a consequence, we may here consider only a summary of some of the key findings of his data analyses. It should be noted that these analyses are complicated as well as numerous. Although Block strived to analyze his data in as straightforward a manner as possible, the large number of variables he had to deal with simultaneously required that some relatively sophisticated multivariate procedures be used to reduce the complexity of the data.

For example, the adolescent CQ-set included 104 variables and the adult CQ-set had 100 variables. Thus, to reduce the complexity of dealing with interrelationships among so many variables, Block in many cases used factor analysis as a multivariate data-analysis technique with which to identify patterns of relationships among variables. We see that factor analysis was used, for instance, to identify particular types of personality development. Before considering these types, however, it is useful to discuss other bases of differential personality development that were found in the data.

Sex Differences in Personality Attributes Studied Over Time

Block first sought to ascertain whether the men in the sample followed courses of personality development that differed from those of the women in the sample. Simply, he was concerned with whether, *in general,* the sex of the participant was associated with differential patterns of personality constancy and change. Of course, to address this concern Block had to specify what he meant by pattern, type, or category of continuity or of change. To define such types or categories of continuity or change, Block had to deal with three features of developmental change in his data.

1. *Correspondence:* This facet of change refers to the correlation between personality attributes (Q-items) studied at one time (e.g., early adolescence) and those same attributes studied at a second time (e.g., middle adolescence).

2. *Salience level:* This facet of development refers to the mean (average) level of the rating given to personality attributes. The higher the rating, the more salient that attribute in depicting the person.

3. *Salience heterogeneity:* This facet of development refers to the dispersion (variation) among salience levels. Here, the concern is with whether attributes have similar (homogeneous) or dissimilar (heterogeneous and, therefore, dispersed) salience levels.

Using these three components of development, Block generated seven categories of continuity and change. Figure 17.4 lists these categories and, in addition, diagrammatically portrays their meaning. For each of the seven categories presented in the figure, the statistical criteria used by Block (1971) to define the category are shown. For each category, there is a presentation of the statistical criterion for either (1) correspondence, expressed as a correlation coefficient (r) calculated between two measurement times; and/or (2) salience level,

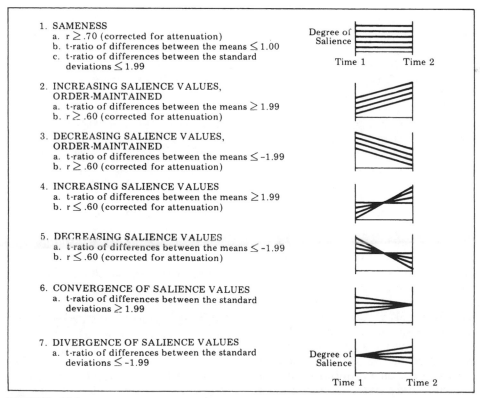

1. SAMENESS
   a. $r \geq .70$ (corrected for attenuation)
   b. t-ratio of differences between the means ≤ 1.00
   c. t-ratio of differences between the standard deviations ≤ 1.99

2. INCREASING SALIENCE VALUES, ORDER-MAINTAINED
   a. t-ratio of differences between the means ≥ 1.99
   b. $r \geq .60$ (corrected for attenuation)

3. DECREASING SALIENCE VALUES, ORDER-MAINTAINED
   a. t-ratio of differences between the means ≤ -1.99
   b. $r \geq .60$ (corrected for attenuation)

4. INCREASING SALIENCE VALUES
   a. t-ratio of differences between the means ≥ 1.99
   b. $r \leq .60$ (corrected for attenuation)

5. DECREASING SALIENCE VALUES
   a. t-ratio of differences between the means ≤ -1.99
   b. $r \leq .60$ (corrected for attenuation)

6. CONVERGENCE OF SALIENCE VALUES
   a. t-ratio of differences between the standard deviations ≥ 1.99

7. DIVERGENCE OF SALIENCE VALUES
   a. t-ratio of differences between the standard deviations ≤ -1.99

FIGURE 17.4
The criteria employed by Block (1971) to define categories of continuity and change.
Source: Block (1971, p. 63)

expressed as a *t*-ratio between means derived from two measurement occasions; and/or (3) salience heterogeneity, expressed as a *t*-ratio of differences between the standard deviations (as a measure of variability) associated with the means derived from two measurement occasions.

Using these categories, we may turn now to the issue of whether males in general showed a different pattern of personality continuity or change than did females. We should note that the time interval between Measurement Times 1 and 2—that is, from junior high school (JHS) to senior high school (SHS)—was only 3 years. However, the time interval between Measurement Times 2 (SHS) and 3 (adulthood) was about 20 years. Thus, we might expect that if change were found, it would be more evident among both sexes between Times 2 and 3 than between Times 1 and 2. This was, in fact, found to be the case. For both sexes, there were more Q-items in the sameness and order-maintained categories across the JHS–SHS period than across the SHS–adulthood period. However, women tended to change more than men; in the Time 2–Time 3 comparison, 48 Q-items showed significant changes for women, whereas only 31 Q-items showed such changes for men.

But what were the specific patterns of continuity and change found for men and women? Table 17.3 shows some of the Q-items for which significant personality continuities and changes were found within the IHD male and female samples studied by Block (1971). This is an admittedly complicated table. Nevertheless, it is possible to summarize some of the trends in personality development it displays. For males, the JHS–SHS period was marked by continuity with respect to Q-items related to expressiveness, personal resiliency, and a cognitive orientation; there were changes in this period as well, and these changes were in regard to Q-items related to cognitive concerns, sexual interest, and dependence. In turn, the males' SHS–adulthood period was marked by continuity in respect to such attributes as cognitive orientation and dependability, and by change in such attributes as self-assurance, aggressiveness in interactions, and preoccupation with somatic concerns.

For females, the JHS–SHS period was marked by a continuity in expressiveness, a concern for interpersonal relatedness, and a cognitive orientation, and by change in regard to an intensification of reflecting on life, an increase in heterosexual interests, and greater interpersonal deviousness. In turn, the SHS–adulthood period showed continuity for females in respect to a passive/conforming versus expressive/aggressive orientation and,

in respect to a cognitive–intuitive orientation; change was seen in respect to movement toward a "psychological-mindedness" (e.g., introspectiveness) and toward a culturally stereotypical definition of femininity (see the discussion of this stereotype in Chapter 16).

In sum, by the time the IHD participants reached adulthood they had shown, from early adolescence on, substantial sex differences in their patterns of personality continuities and change. As Block (1971) concluded, these sex differences were as much reflective of stereotypic cultural pressures regarding sex-roles as they were of biological pressure. Thus, the IHD males became more goal oriented and self-satisfied and, in addition, changed in the direction of becoming less esthetically reactive, less responsive to humor, less straightforward, and more narrow in their interests. In turn, the IHD women became more psychologically minded and showed greater tenderness in close interpersonal relationships; in addition, they showed more esthetic orientation, more protectiveness, and more sympathy. In short, as we saw in our discussion of the Kagan and Moss (1962) study, Block's (1971) study indicates that both constancy and change characterize people's development across life, and that sex is an important differential variable in such development; sex differences in personality development exist, and they often reflect culturally stereotypic sex-role prescriptions.

Block (1971) pointed out, however, that this pattern of sex differences in development reflects only a general trend in the IHD sample. Not all males showed the same pattern of personality development and, similarly, not all females followed an identical course of personality development. Indeed, Block posited that there may be as much, if not more, within-sex as between-sex variation. Block was, in fact, quite correct about this point. Although we may profitably discuss numerous other facets of Block's (1971) data, let us turn to the findings that provide evidence for the presence of different kinds, or types, of personality development within both males and females.

Different Courses of Personality Development Among the IHD Males and Females: Block's Typological Approach

As we noted earlier, Block contended that personality development was a phenomenon that existed at some midway point on a continuum whose endpoints were idiographic and nomothetic. Block's view translates into the contention that although,

TABLE 17.3
Some of the Q Items for Which Significant Personality Continuities and Changes Were Found Within the IHD Male and Female Samples Studied by Block (1971)

Category of continuity and change	Males		Females	
	JHS–SHS	SHS–adulthood	JHS–SHS	SHS–adulthood
1. Sameness	Arouses liking Turned to for advice Warm Socially perceptive Plus ten additional items	Values intellectual matters Verbally fluent	Values intellectual matters Aesthetically reactive Overcontrolled Undercontrolled Plus ten additional items	No items met the criterion for this category
2. Increasing salience, order maintained	High intellectual capacity Philosophically concerned High aspiration level Questing for meaning	Dependable Prides self on objectivity	Philosophically concerned Questing for meaning Deceitful Basic hostility	Wide interests Values intellectual matters Philosophically concerned Submissive
3. Decreasing salience, order maintained	Dependable Fantasizes Extrapunitive Thin-skinned Plus two additional items	Intellectual capacity Aesthetically reactive Undercontrolled Fantasizing	Dependable Productive Arouses liking Warm Plus four additional items	Rebellious Intellectual capacity
4. Increasing salience	Calm Interesting Affected Eroticizing Interested in opposite sex	Feels satisfied with self Philosophically concerned Fastidious Overcontrolled Plus nine additional items	Distrustful Affected Interested in opposite sex	Introspective Straightforward Cheerful Feels guilty Plus thirteen additional items
5. Decreasing salience	Self-defensive Projective Favors status quo Fearful Plus three additional items	Responds to humor Interesting Sensuous Lacks personal meaning Plus seven additional items	Express hostile feelings directly	Fantasizing Sensuous Undercontrolled Power-oriented Plus eighteen additional items
6. Convergence	No items converged	Productive Eroticizes Interested in opposite sex Physically attractive	No items converged	Expressive Responds to humor Intellectual capacity Dependable Plus nine additional items

(continues)

TABLE 17.3
(continued)

Category of continuity and change	Males		Females	
	JHS–SHS	SHS–adulthood	JHS–SHS	SHS–adulthood
7. Divergence	Affected Favors status quo Calm Philosophically concerned	Self-defensive Somatizes Brittle Expresses hostile feelings directly Plus two additional items	Prides self on objectivity Interesting Questing for meaning Deceitful Plus three additional items	Introspective Satisfied with self Evaluates situation in motivational terms Arouses nurturance Plus four additional items

Note. From *Lives Through Time* (pp. 66–68, 70, 72–73), by J. Block, 1971, Berkeley, CA: Bancroft by Bancroft Books, Inc.

on the one hand, there may be no one completely universal (nomothetic) course to personality development, on the other hand, there should not be completely singular development either. People are not completely alike, but everyone is not completely different from everyone else. Thus, although there may not be one universal pattern of personality development, there may be coherent subgroups of people (i.e., people who have a particular pattern of personality development, one shared by some but not all others). Indeed, Block's (1971) identification of sex differences in the personality development of the IHD sample illustrates two general subgroupings; the male type of personality development and the female type. However, as noted, Block believed that grouping just by sex did not provide a sufficiently fine discrimination for the course of personality development. He believed that several different *types* of personality development might exist among males and females.

Block (1971) defined a type "as a subset of individuals characterized by a reliably unique or discontinuously different pattern of covariation across time with respect to a specifiable (and nontrivial) set of variables" (pp. 109–110). He believed that the reliable identification of types would help researchers accept the view "that the nomothetic, monolithic view of personality functioning is gross, misguided, and outworn" (p. 110).

Block's procedure to identify reliably different personality types is perhaps the best illustration of the ipsative character of his research. The Q-sort procedure involves the intraindividual

distribution of a set of Q-items, such that one achieves an ordering of items—from those highly salient (or characteristic) to those of low saliency—*within* a person. Block (1971, p. 114) believed that this "ordering of variables . . . [is the] sufficient basis for defining the personality configuration of a subject." In order to have an empirical indication of the presence of a resemblance in the order of Q-items for different people sufficient to categorize them as having the same type of personality, Block calculated product–moment correlation coefficients among the orderings found for the IHD participants. He then factor-analyzed the resulting matrix of correlations in order to see whether types emerged as the results of these analyses.

As Block noted, factor analysis is a multivariate statistical procedure for reducing the complexity of a set of relationships. The procedure allows one to estimate the number of dimensions to which some (larger) set of relationships (e.g., correlations) may be reduced; the procedure, of which there exist many varieties, allows one to discern the structure that exists in a matrix of relationships. For instance, in a correlation matrix involving 100 variables (all related each to the other), there are too many interrelations to summarize without some attempt at reduction of this complexity. Factor analysis might reveal, however that the relationships in the matrix could be described by reference to only a relatively few higher-order relationships, or "factors." For example, it may be that one group of 20 of the items correlate highly with each other but do not relate highly to any other items; that another group of 20 items similarly interrelate highly among themselves but not highly with any other items; and so forth. Thus, it may be, in this example, that the 100-item correlation matrix could be reduced to a 5-factor structure. That is, there may be five groupings of items—five dimensions—each with 20 items, that constitute the factor structure for that matrix.

Thus, factor analysis, when used to analyze correlations among items (or variables), can reveal how variables form together to form factor dimensions. However, one can also apply factor analysis to a matrix of correlations among people—that is, the sort of matrix that Block (1971) generated when he intercorrelated the IHD participants' ordering of Q-items. When factor analysis is used to analyze correlations among people, *factor types* are derived, and one may interpret these types as the categories into which different people may be placed. The technical term for this type of factor analysis—one that identifies clusters, or types, of people (as opposed to clusters, or "types," of variables)—is Q-factor analysis. This type of person-centered approach to understanding human development has been discussed more generally in Chapter 7 in regard to the holistic person–context interaction theory forwarded by David Magnusson and his colleagues (e.g., Magnusson, 1995, 1999a, 1999b; Magnusson & Stattin, 1998).

In regard to Block's data analytic approach, it may be noted that he performed one Q-factor analysis for the IHD males and another for the IHD females. As he expected, evidence was found within each sex-group for different personality types. In fact, although a relatively few participants in each sex-group did not have personality structures clearly classifiable into a given type, most participants fell rather well into one of the Q-factor-analysis-derived categories. Block identified five male types and six female types. The labels associated with these types are presented in Table 17.4. Let us discuss briefly some of the key features of the course of personality development associated with each of these male and female types.

The Male Types

For each of the five male types identified by Block, we shall note some of the Q-items found to be most characteristic of their personalities at each of the three times of measurement.

1.   *The Ego Resilients:* During JHS, Q-items found to be highly characteristic of Ego Resilient males were "dependable, productive, ambitious, bright, values intellectual matters, likable, has a

TABLE 17.4

Types of Personality Development Identified by Block (1971) in the IHD Male and Female Samples

Male types	Female types
1. Ego Resilients	1. Female Prototypes
2. Belated Adjusters	2. Cognitive Copers
3. Vulnerable Overcontrollers	3. Hyperfeminine Repressives
4. Anomic Extraverts	4. Dominating Narcissists
5. Unsettled Undercontrollers	5. Vulnerable Undercontrollers
	6. Lonely Independents

wide range of interests, verbally fluent, poised, straightforward, sympathetic, and interesting" (Block, 1971, p. 139). Many of these items were found in SHS to remain as highly characteristic of these males. Similarly, in adulthood, these males continued to be highly characterized by such items. In short, throughout the JHS–SHS–adulthood period, these males were characteristically goal-oriented and individually and interpersonally effective people. As Block (1971, p. 149) put it, the Ego Resilient male "was blessed with more than his share of native intelligence, good health, and physical endowment . . . [he] has been favored by circumstance from the beginning and he did not muff his opportunities."

2.   *The Belated Adjusters:* During JHS, Q-items found to be highly characteristic of Belated Adjuster males were "basically hostile, withdraws when frustrated, self-indulgent, self-defeating, bothered by demands, extrapunitive, brittle, projective, and negativistic" (Block, 1971, p. 151). However, the presence of this relatively negative set of items began to diminish by SHS. Although these males were still characterized by items such as "gives up and withdraws when frustrated, negativistic, and testing of limits," Block noted that these participants became significantly *more* warm, aware of their impression on others, valuing of intellectual matters, internally consistent, and *less* irritable, extrapunitive, hostile, and self-indulgent. The more positive picture of these males found in SHS was evident also in their adulthood assessments. Items found to be characteristic of these males were "dependable, sympathetic, giving, protective, productive, likable, warm, calm, straightforward, cheerful, and internally consistent." Thus, the Belated Adjusters show substantial change from JHS to adulthood.

They develop from being what Block (1971, p. 158) described as a "nasty adolescent" that is, an adolescent marked by "narcissistic, sulky, fitful, and fickle" behavior, to being an adult who is cheerful, parental, relaxed, a steady worker—in short, a contributing member of society.

3.   *The Vulnerable Overcontrollers:* During their JHS period, the Vulnerable Overcontroller males had Q-items that characterized their personalities as "overcontrolled, aloof, thin-skinned, ruminative, uncomfortable with uncertainty, and distrustful." Many of these attributes continued to characterize these males in SHS; for instance, they were still overcontrolled, distrustful, aloof, and uncomfortable with uncertainty. In addition, they were seen now to be critical, emotionally bland, delaying of action, and guilty. Similarly, in adulthood, these males were characterized along similar lines—for example, they were aloof, basically hostile, self-defensive, thin-skinned, ruminative, distrustful, and uncomfortable with uncertainty. They also felt cheated and victimized by life and were self-defeating, projective, and submissive.

Thus, although there is continuity from JHS to adulthood in these males' overcontrolled, "uptight," anxious, and introverted characteristics, and in their uneasiness in interpersonal situations, there seems to also be some change. Block (1971) noted that by adulthood there has been a "cost" for the lifetime of over-control. These males are barely tolerable to themselves. The Vulnerable Overcontroller has been now defeated by life, and he "is exposed to his despairs, confronted with his failures, and is resourceless before them" (Block, 1971, p. 168).

4.   *The Anomic Extroverts:* Males who were categorized as Anomic Extroverts were characterized in JHS as gregarious, masculine, assertive, likable, cheerful, poised, and conventional. This outgoing interpersonal style shows continuity into SHS. These males continued to be gregarious, assertive, and cheerful; in addition, they became emotionally involved with members of the same sex, had a rapid personal tempo, tested limits imposed on them, and were undercontrolled.

By the time of their adult testing, a major change occurs with these males, however. The prototypic male they seemed as JHS adolescents (e.g., gregarious, cheerful, and vigorous), and to a great extent as SHS adolescents as well (e.g., they remained gregarious, but in addition they changed to show undercontrol), is not now apparent. As adults, they are characterized by such Q-items as "uncomfortable with uncertainty, basically hostile, self-defensive, repressive, brittle, irritable, conventional, and moody." Block (1971) described

these males, as adults, as having a repressive character structure and a sense of anomie; that is, he noted that they lack personal meaning and an inner life, and that they are suspicious, bitter, and valueless.

5.   *The Unsettled Undercontrollers:* During their JHS period, the Unsettled Undercontroller males were rebellious and covertly hostile with adults. Indeed, these males perceived their parents as restraining their activities and viewed their family life as conflicted. In turn, with peers, they were talkative, attention-getting, initiating of humor, and assertive. The relatively negative characteristics seen in JHS tended to become accentuated in SHS, when these males were characterized as being rebellious, hostile toward others, thin-skinned, self-defeating, undercontrolled, irritable, bothered by demands, and negativistic; in addition, they showed fluctuating moods and lacked a sense of meaning in life. Rebelliousness, moodiness, and undercontrol continued to characterize these males when they were assessed as adults. In addition, however, they were rated as talkative, interesting, rapid in tempo, and bright.

Thus, Block characterized these males, as adults, as impulsive and unsettled. In essence, these males showed a continuity in their being rebellious and undercontrolled.

The Female Types

As noted in Table 17.4, Block identified six female types. As with the male types, we shall note some of the Q-items found to be most characteristic of the personalities of each type at each time of measurement.

1.   *The Female Prototypes:* In JHS, the Q-items rated to be characteristic of the Female Prototype females were "likable, poised, cheerful, gregarious, dependable, warm, productive, giving, sympathetic, straightforward, fastidious, physically attractive, socially perceptive, turned-to-for-advice and reassurance, protective, and aware of her social stimulus value" (Block, 1971, p. 190). In SHS, many of these same attributes continued to characterize the females; in addition, seemingly compatible items ("responsive to humor, talkative, and feminine") were also seen to characterize them. Similarly, there was continuity into adulthood for many of the JHS and SHS attributes. In addition, the attribute of "overcontrolled" was seen to characterize these women.

Block (1971) saw these females as having needs and capacities that were highly congruent with the prototypic societal demands and values regarding women's roles (see Chapter 16). Thus, these females showed substantial continuity from JHS to adulthood and are, as adults, at ease with themselves and others and are optimistic, nurturant, and attractive people.

2. *The Cognitive Copers:* During JHS, the females categorized as Cognitive Copers were characterized as overcontrolled, thin-skinned, aloof, distrustful, and basically hostile; in addition, they felt guilty, fearful, and victimized, and they were bothered by demands, uncomfortable with uncertainty, ruminative, self-defensive, and tended to fantasize. This essentially negative depiction in early adolescence may be expected to bode ill for these females. However, in SHS, these females were seen as having a high degree of intellectual capacity and as being dependable and productive; in addition, they were also seen to continue to be overcontrolled and to be hostile toward others and judgmental in regard to human conduct.

Thus, perhaps as a means of coping with their negative characteristics, these females were found, in SHS, to combine positive cognitive attributes with those other personality characteristics seen in JHS. This cognitive emphasis was found to be more prominent in adulthood. Here, these females were seen as having high intellectual capacity, as valuing intellectual matters, and as verbally fluent; in addition, these females were rated as dependable, introspective, ambitious, esthetically reactive, and as valuing their independence. Thus, as Block (1971) described her, the Cognitive Coper "blossomed with the years, going from inadequacy in adolescence to an admirable competence as an adult" (p. 209).

3. *The Hyperfeminine Repressives:* In JHS, females in the Hyperfeminine Repressive category were rated, as the label implies, as feminine and repressive. In addition, they were seen as dependable, but as uncomfortable with uncertainty, and as people who compared themselves to others. In SHS, these females continued to be characterized as feminine, calm and relaxed in manner, sympathetic, and accepting of their dependency. In addition, these females favored the status quo and continued to show something of a repressive characteristic in that they handled anxiety and conflicts by attempting to exclude them from awareness.

It is this repressive characteristic that implied potential problems for these females and, indeed, their adult personality characteristics seem essentially negative. They were seen as basically hostile, brittle, self-defensive adults who—as in JHS—were uncomfortable with uncertainty and, in addition, were distrustful, thin-skinned, aloof, irritable, self-defeating, extrapunitive, moody, and negativistic. They felt cheated and victimized by life, were bothered by demands put on them, and had concerns about their bodily integrity. Thus, although showing only a moderate and certainly not a unique set of personal inadequacies in adolescence, the Hyperfeminine Repressive became in adulthood "a characterological shambles, unhappy, self-pitying [and] explosively but ineffectively reactive to frustrations" (Block, 1971, p. 218).

4. *The Dominating Narcissists:* In JHS, the Dominating Narcissist females were characterized as both self-indulgent and self-defensive. In addition, they were interested in the opposite sex, they eroticized, and they were undercontrolled. They were also rebellious, extrapunitive, assertive, and conventional. They expressed hostile feelings directly. In SHS, these females continued to be self-indulgent and self-defensive as well as eroticizing and extrapunitive. However, in addition, they were seen as irritable, bothered by demands, and distrustful.

In adulthood, the Dominating Narcissists were characterized by Q-items that suggested both continuity and change between SHS and their later lives. The items associated with these females during adulthood were "assertive, power-oriented, proffers advice, condescending, and expresses hostile feelings directly." In addition, they were rated as socially poised, straightforward, and as feeling satisfied with themselves. Block saw continuity in these females' aggressive, direct, interpersonal style, and a personality characterized by condescension, self-indulgence, and undercontrol. However, these women became highly poised adults, a manner quite distinct from the pushy and "nasty" characteristics seen in adolescence.

5. *The Vulnerable Undercontrollers:* During their JHS period, the Vulnerable Undercontroller females were characterized as talkative, self-dramatizing, and self-indulgent. In addition, they were seen as pushing the limits imposed on them, and as changeable and undercontrolled. In SHS, these females continued to be seen as undercontrolled, and their fluctuating mood was consistent with their changeable style in early adolescence. In addition, the females tended toward fantasizing and identified and romanticized individuals and causes. They enjoyed sensuous experiences, were facially and gesturally expressive, and sought reassurance from others. Finally, they were rated as brittle (i.e., vulnerable to being easily hurt).

As adults, these females continued to seek reassurance from others and were submissive to and aroused nurturance in others. They also continued to be emotionally changeable (i.e., moody); in addition, they were concerned about their bodies, were self-defeating, and felt a lack of personal meaning in their lives. Block (1971) summarized the changes involved in these females' personality development from early adolescence to adulthood as involving a "move toward a personal unpleasantness and undercontrol in adolescence and on to a pathetic self-unsureness in adulthood" (p. 236).

6.   *The Lonely Independents:* In their JHS period, the Lonely Independent females were seen as assertive, ambitious, and as valuing independence. In addition, they were seen as interesting and expressive young adolescents. In SHS, these females were still characterized as valuing their own independence and autonomy, ambitious, and interesting. In addition, they valued intellectual matters and, in fact, had a high degree of intellectual capacity. However, they were now seen as rebellious, irritable, and bothered by demands imposed on them, and critical and introspective. In their adulthood, these females continued to value their independence and to have high intellectual capacity. However, they also continued to be bothered by demands on them, and in addition they were seen now as basically hostile, skeptical, aloof, and distrustful. They felt cheated and victimized by (and felt a lack of personal meaning in) their lives.

Thus, over their early-adolescence-to-adulthood period, these females experienced a continuity in their self-assertiveness and desire for autonomy. However, an increasingly more prominent social unconnectedness came to characterize them, and by adulthood they felt cheated by a life that held no personal meaning for them.

Conclusions

As noted earlier, there are several other quite significant features of Block's (1971) findings that we might review. However, I believe that the details we have presented are sufficient to allow us to see the merit of Block's approach to studying development *and* the substantive importance of his findings. His concern with the individual distinctiveness of people's lives led him to employ a longitudinal ipsative analysis of the changing intraindividual salience of a large set of personality attributes. His approach illustrates, then, the usefulness of merging a conceptual concern about individuality with a method of analysis designed to allow one to focus directly on what is developing within a person. Moreover, the *Lives Through Time* research stands as an excellent example of

the use that can be made of a rich longitudinal archive by a capable and creative scientist (cf. Lachman & James, 1997).

The substantive import of Block's (1971) research is equally noteworthy. First, Block's findings amply demonstrate that both constancy *and* change characterize development. For all of the 11 (5 male and 6 female) personality types that Block identified, we have seen instances of constancy from one time of measurement to the next; at the same time, and within the same personality type, we have seen instances of change as well.

Thus, as noted in Chapter 5, both continuity and discontinuity exist simultaneously across life periods. Debate, then, should *not* be focused on which one is present. Rather, developmental science must ask more appropriate—but more difficult—questions: "What are the bases and implications of the synthesis of continuity and discontinuity at particular times of life (and for particular types of people)?" and "What are the conditions under which constancy and/or change will be seen in a particular developmental process at a given point in time?"

A second major substantive contribution of Block's (1971) research is the identification of the different courses of personality development present in the IHD sample. As we have seen also in respect to the Thomas and Chess (1977) NYLS, the presence of numerous distinct courses of development across life speaks to the empirical limitations and conceptual difficulties of any completely nomothetic, universalistic view of human development. People exist as distinctive and, in many ways, singular entities. Block's data, along with those of other scientists sensitive to ipsative analysis and the relative singularity of development across life (e.g., Chess & Thomas, 1996, 1999; Lerner, 1982; Nesselroade, 1983, 2000; Thomas & Chess, 1977; Thomas et al., 1963), serve to underscore the importance of focusing on each individual's attribute repertoire and the intraindividual changes in the content and structure of that repertoire over the course of life. Through such a focus, the organizing role of the individual, as a central contributor to his or her own development, may best be understood.

FROM THEORY TO RESEARCH AND APPLICATION

In sum, across the last three chapters, we have seen that the ipsative, the differential, and the stage approaches represent contrasting orientations to the study of development. Yet, all approaches forward concepts that bear on the core conceptual issues of development. These approaches—along with the other theoretical views of human development we have discussed across previous chapters—provide different ideas about the bases of development; and accordingly, the empirical questions and concomitant research studies done by those concerned with each respective approach are different. Similarly, the ideas the different theories present regarding how developmental science may be applied, and the conditions of continuity and change (e.g., regarding plasticity) that must occur for such applications to be feasible, differ as well across theories.

Nevertheless, all of the approaches to the conceptualization of development do provide us with ideas, and eventually with empirical observations, that are useful in attempting to understand the complexities of human development, and to use this understanding in applications aimed at enhancing the course of life. Accordingly, in the following chapters we, first, in Chapter 18, discuss the methodological implications for human development research that are associated with the conceptual and theoretical ideas we have discussed throughout this book. Second, in Chapter 19, we discuss the import of theoretical and research methodology issues for the application of developmental science across the life span.

18 | *Methodological Issues in the Study of Human Development*

Change and, especially, developmental change is difficult to study empirically. Methods used to study developmental change are predicated on theoretical specification of the nature of development and on the assumptions one derives from theory about: (a) units of analysis (e.g., individual–psychological variables or *relations* between variables from different levels of analysis, (b) levels of organization involved in developmental change (e.g., genes, organism, social relationships, or culture), and (c) the role of time and temporality (history) in indexing such change (Baltes, Reese, & Nesselroade, 1977). In other words, developmental theories vary in regard to the units of analysis and the levels of organization used to study people across time. This variation is linked to differences in the approach to research taken by scholars following different theories of development. It is useful to illustrate this linkage between theory and research.

Given the stress throughout this book on developmental systems theories, such as developmental contextualism, we use the implications of these theories for research methods and applications to provide this example. A key point made in this illustration is that, within the frame for empirical scholarship provided by developmental systems theory, there is a blurring of the distinction between basic and applied research.

IMPLICATIONS OF DEVELOPMENTAL SYSTEMS THEORY FOR RESEARCH METHODS AND APPLICATION

Developmental systems models stress that reciprocal changes among levels of organization are both products and producers of the reciprocal changes within levels. In the view of such scholars, *relations*—between individuals and contexts—are the units of analysis in their research. As such, the multiple levels of organization involved in these relations comprise the domain of inquiry of concern to these scholars.

For example, over time, parents' "styles" of behavior and rearing influence children's personality and cognitive functioning and development. In turn, the interactions between personality and cognition constitute an emergent "characteristic" of human individuality that affects parental behaviors and styles and the quality of family life (e.g., Lerner, 1982; Lerner & Busch-Rossnagel, 1981b; Lerner, Castellino et al., 1995; Lewis, 1997).

As explained in Chapter 7, to gain understanding of—or, in other words, to generate explanatory data about—how variations in person–context relations may influence actual or to-be-actualized developmental trajectories, researchers may act to change either the proximal and/or distal natural ecology of people's development. These actions (which, as explained in earlier chapters, may—depending on their level of organization—constitute policies on programs) constitute tests of ideas about how person–context linkages are involved in shaping the course of human development (e.g., Bronfenbrenner et al., 1996), and elucidate the plasticity in human development that may exist, or that may be capitalized on through interventions, to enhance human life.

Accordingly, as noted in Chapter 7, developmental systems-oriented theory and research in human development provides the basis for a model of applied developmental science (Fisher et al., 1993; Fisher, Jackson, & Villarruel, 1998; Fisher & Lerner, 1994).

The link between developmental systems theory and applied developmental science is discussed again in Chapter 19. Here, however, we may note that in the integrative basic–applied research perspective brought to the fore by a developmental systems perspective policy development and implementation, and program design and delivery, become integral components of research; the evaluation component of such policy and intervention work provides a critical feedback about the adequacy of the conceptual frame from which this research agenda should derive. This conception of the integration of multidisciplinary research endeavors centrally aimed at the diversity of individuals and contexts, with policies, programs, and evaluations is illustrated in Figure 18.1.

Conclusions

Research predicated on developmental systems theory must be conducted with an appreciation of the dynamic relation, or the fusion, between the person and the specific array of distinct family, community, and sociocultural settings constituting his or her individual developmental trajectory. As a consequence, such research must involve individual difference (diversity-) and change-sensitive measures, designs, and analyses (e.g., multivariate, longitudinal research should be conducted with measures having equivalence across age and other individual difference dimensions). In addition, such research should involve both structural and measurement models that include indices of the person–contexts relations theoretically relevant for a given study of the developmental system.

In turn, applications of such research (e.g., public policies or community-based programs) must be similarly attuned to the diversity of people and context in order to maximize the chances of meeting the specific needs of particular groups of people at particular times in their lives (Lerner, 1993b, 1995; Lerner & Miller, 1993; Lerner, Miller et al., 1994; Lerner, Terry, McKinney, & Abrams, 1994). Indeed, given the multilevel and multipurpose orientation of such scholarship—involving the integrated understanding of the basic, relational processes of human development and the application of knowledge about human development to enhance the course of people's lives—it may be important to involve both quantitative and qualitative measures in a given study, especially given the diversity of basic science and applied sciences audiences to which the findings of such research might be directed.

For instance, scholars will find it important to see methodological triangulation of measures (i.e., two distinct measures of the same concept are

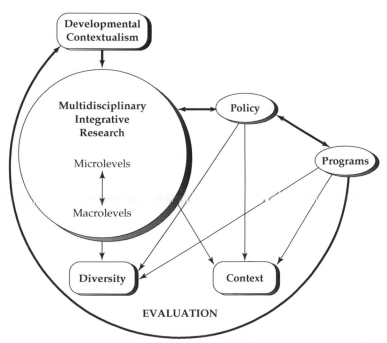

FIGURE 18.1
The conception of the integration of multidisciplinary research endeavors centrally aimed at diversity and context, with policies, programs, and evaluation.

shown to be related to each other; Baltes et al., 1977), and, when such convergence is actualized across quantitative and qualitative domains, they are all the more impressive. In turn, some policy-makers may be more oriented to qualitative (e.g., case study) reports of human development, especially when they "bring to life" individual "stories" of development that might be masked by perhaps more abstract quantitative analyses of group data. Although the developmental systems-oriented researcher will want to be certain that such data can be defended in regard to its generalizability and its consistency with quantitative appraisals, he or she may be well served to understand the usefulness of rich ("thick") qualitative analyses in marshaling a policy and funding constituency for his or her work.

In sum, as illustrated by the prescriptions for research methods associated with developmental systems theory, the ideas comprising any theory of development provide a frame for making decisions about: (a) what measures will be appropriate for and sensitive to detect the sorts of changes (e.g., continuous and/or discontinuous and/or quantitative and/or qualitative) that may occur in regard to the units of analysis specified by the theory, (b) what designs are appropriate to and valid for the observation of such change, and (c) what data analysis techniques usefully exploit the change information present in a data set.

In short, theory-predicated decisions must be made about how data derived from change-sensitive measures and designs may be generated in order to provide information that fully informs theory-based studies of developmental change. Such decisions must be made within the context of the frame provided by a specific philosophical approach to the attainment of knowledge about development or, in fact, about any feature of the natural world (Kaufmann, 1969). This approach is termed *the scientific method*.

THE SCIENTIFIC METHOD AND THE METHODS OF SCIENCE

To use theory within the scientific study of human development, scholars must link their concepts of development with procedures that enable *empirical* (observable) evidence to be brought to bear on their ideas about developmental change. A commitment to using observations (i.e., a commitment to empiricism) in order to gain knowledge is the hallmark of science (Kaufmann, 1968;

and see Chapter 2). This philosophical aproach (i.e., this epistemology) is termed the scientific method, and it represents the belief that to be useful in science—for information to be regarded as valid or true—knowledge must be empirically verifiable.

There are, of course, other routes to knowing. For example, theologians may appeal to faith as a basis for knowing and, in fact, may specify that spiritual knowledge does not require empirical confirmation of its validity or truth. Indeed, to have faith means, in this context, that no empirical information is needed to recognize something as true or valid. Thus, a faith-based epistemology is antithetical to an appeal to empiricism.

However, when functioning as a scientist, a person would use the scientific method of knowing to identity what is true or valid. Within the scientific method, then, knowledge must be proven correct through observations. To be useful in science, a statement would have to be linked to some empirical statement that could verify it and/or, critically, that could falsify it (Lakatos, 1978a, 1978b; Popper, 1959). Indeed, if there were no observations that could possibly be used to falsify a statement, then—given the epistemology of the scientific method—that statement would not be of any use or value in science.

As a consequence, in order to provide support for their ideas, scientists must make statements (e.g., propose hypotheses) that can be verified and falsified through empirical observations. As such, scientists need to find means to make such empirical observations. The means scientists use to make such observations are their methods of their science—the instruments, tools, and procedures for making observations of the subject matters in their field of science. Some scientists may use microscopes to study cells, others may use machines that provide scans of the living brain, others may employ telescopes to explore galaxies, and still others may administer questionnaires to make observations of the attitudes and values of children, adolescents, or adults. However, in all cases, scientists use method of observations (the methods of their particular science) because of their commitment to the scientific method. In other words, because of the scientific method (of knowing) scientists employ the methods of (their specific) science to make observations that bear on the verifiability and falsifiability of their ideas.

Accordingly, we may inquire into the array of methods used by developmental scientists to obtain observations that enable them to test statements associated with their theories. Clearly, the methods of science used by a developmental scientist testing one theoretical position may not be identical to the methods employed by a scientist following another theoretical tradition. For instance, in Chapter 15, we discussed social learning (e.g., Bandura & McDonald, 1963), psychoanalytic (e.g., Freud, 1954), and cognitive developmental (e.g., Kohlberg, 1978) theories of the development of morality. We noted that, whereas followers of the first two theoretical traditions would employ methods (e.g., in regard to the measures they would use) that would enable them to obtain observations about the *behaviors* displayed in situations involving moral choices, followers of the third theoretical approach would eschew the measurement of behavior. Instead, they would seek to take measures of the *reasons* people made whatever moral choices they enacted. However, despite such differences among human development researchers, all would—as a consequence of being concerned with development across life in moral functioning (whether it involved behavior and/or reasoning)—want to have observations that could detect changes across ontogeny (or, at least, the portions of it that concerned them).

In essence, then, by virtue of their common interest in development, that is, independent of their particular theoretical orientation, a generalization that may be made in regard to all scholars of human development is that they are interested in the description, explanation, and optimization of change. These changes may involve (a) successive characteristics of behavior that emerge across ontogeny (e.g., in regard to the course of changes in childhood in moral functioning or to the multiple transitions framing the adolescent period), (b) induced changes in affective, cognitive, or behavioral functioning that result from program or policy interventions, or (c) changes related to variations in learning and achievement that derive from revisions of educational curricula or classroom practices.

However, regardless of whether associated with descriptive and/or explanatory developmental research, concern with such instances of change is unified by a common interest in systematic, organized, and successive (or, in some cases, progressive) changes, as opposed to random or disorganized change. In other words, all human development researchers, whether concerned with the description, explanation, or promotion of organized, systemic, and successive change, are interested in development and concerned with the methods that are available to study it.

Conclusions

Any theory of human development must be tied to the examination of data in order for it to have a use in science. It is important, then, to understand the character of the methods available to developmental scientists to obtain the particular types of observations relevant to their specific ideas about development. Indeed, such specification of the methods of science is useful because many people do not understand what scientists do and why what they do is "scientific."

Without such information, it is often difficult to evaluate the claims made by scientists or to reconcile what may appear to be conflicting information provided by them. For instance, without knowledge of the methodological differences between psychoanalytic and cognitive developmental researchers in the respective measurements they use to assess moral functioning, it would be hard to reconcile the difference between the psychoanalytic claim that moral development is complete by 5 years of age (e.g., Freud, 1954) and the cognitive developmental claim that moral development ordinarily continues well into the adult years of life (Colby et al., 1983; Kohlberg, 1978).

Moreover, there are other complications that arise when trying to explain the methods of developmental science to people. Most people accept the fact that physicists, chemists, and astronomers are scientists, and do not raise questions about whether their work, in fact, reflects the appropriate practice of science. On the other hand, when it comes to the study of human development, there is often skepticism expressed about whether the work of researchers in these areas actually reflects the enactment of science.

Typically, one thinks of a scientist as a person in a white lab coat, toiling over test tubes and charts and "experimenting." Certainly, some scientists do these things; and some of them study human development. Yet, a scientist—and science—are not defined by what one wears or where one works. Rather, science is defined by whether the person adheres to the scientific method, a commitment to empiricism as the epistemological route to knowing. However, empiricism does not alone define the scientific method. The scientific method builds on empiricism to entail other key attributes, attributes that help frame the methods that any specific instance of science will use to pursue its empirical goals. Accordingly, to help us understand the key dimensions of the methods used in the scientific study of human development, it is useful to understand the key attributes of the scientific method.

CHARACTERISTICS OF THE SCIENTIFIC METHOD

I have noted that all scientists—whether they are physicists, chemists, biologists, sociologists, psychologists, or human developmentalists—are scientists because they work in accordance with the scientific method. I have stressed that when scholars speak of the "scientific method" they are not referring *per se* to a particular way of doing research (e.g., using test tubes in a laboratory to assess the combination of chemicals, studying the speed of particles in a nuclear accelerator, or observing infants as they interact with their mothers in the natural setting of the home). Rather, building on the essential attribute of the scientific method—empiricism—the scientific method involves a series of steps taken by a scholar to assure that what he or she observes (no matter how it is observed) is accurate and able to be verified by other researchers. In other words, the scientist adheres to certain principles to be certain that what he or she learns from research—his or her knowledge—is information that anyone else, following the same procedures, would have observed.

When something is *empirical* it is capable of observation, and although any "fact" that enters into the knowledge base of science must, in some way, be observable (it must in some manner be empirical), not everything that is observable becomes a "fact" of science. That is, scientists do not just observe anything. Rather, there is a *purpose* to their observations. For example, they may want to see if observations about parent–child relations are consistent with the idea of storm and stress during adolescence (see Chapter 1) or the purpose of their observations may be to learn whether certain types of parenting (e.g., authoritative ones; Baumrind, 1971; Collins et al., 2000) are associated with healthy development among youth.

To fulfill the purposes of their observations, scientists do not observe behavior haphazardly. Rather, scientists arrange an order or sequence for their observations. They observe *systematically*. Moreover, if scientists' systematic and purposeful observations are accurate, then, if other scientists follow their procedures, they should be able to make the same observations. In other words, scientific observations must be *replicable*.

In addition, in order for replication to occur, scientists cannot keep their observations secret. If scientists do not *communicate* their observations to other scientists (e.g., through publications in journals or books, or through presentations at scientific conferences), there cannot be any hope of independent and objective replication (and, thus, verification of the accuracy of the scientist's observations).

When a scientist's observations are communicated, the scientific community (other scientists working in the same area of research) can then work to verify and/or correct the work of the scientist. In order words, through communication within the scientific community, science has the characteristic of *self-correction*.

Finally, then, when an observation has been subjected to communication, replication, and correction it may enter the knowledge base of an area of science. In this way, then, science is a *cumulative* endeavor, a community process whereby knowledge is shared, verified, and integrated by the group of scholars working on a particular problem of concern to them.

In sum, then, the seven characteristics of the scientific method (Kaufmann, 1969) are: observation (empiricism); purposefulness; systematicity; replicability; communication; self-correction (by the scientific community); and cumulativeness. As I have emphasized, all areas of science share these characteristics.

Conclusions

The manner—the specific empirical procedures—through which a scientist makes observations is dependent on the subject matter of his or her investigation. How one observes the molecules of a particular gas under a specific temperature differs from the way one observes 15-year-old adolescents interacting at a shopping mall. Accordingly, it is important to discuss the ways in which scientists interested in the study of human development make their observations.

It is a complex task to obtain data useful in the study of human development across the life span. Obviously, observation at multiple times of life are needed. But how are such observations to be made in ways that will be of use to scientists studying human development? This key question raises the issue of what scientific methods of investigation are available to human developmentalists.

For a scientist to know something about the development of humans, people must be examined, questioned, interviewed, or in some way observed. One cannot rely *just* on what one believes or wants to believe about behavior. Rather, one's beliefs must be tested by determining whether they are supported when actual behavior is studied. The set of specific procedures by which a science makes observations and collects and examines data may be termed its *research methods*.

However, there are several problems typically encountered in applying the scientific methods available for research on human development. From a developmental systems perspective, we believe that variables from multiple levels of organization contribute to development and that, as a consequence, development may take many forms and directions. To observe such plasticity, it is unlikely that any one means of observing development would be appropriate for all contexts, times, or people. Indeed, there are many research methods that may be used study development. And although each method has its special advantages, each also has limitations.

In order to understand the range of methods that may be used in the study of development and to become sensitive to the problems in existing data and the dangers such problems present for future data collection, this discussion is organized in two parts. First, the variety of research methods that can be used to study development is discussed. Second, general problems in research, especially those in human development research, are considered. Ways to avoid such problems are also suggested.

As I have already stressed, a general theme throughout this presentation is that the method one uses depends on issues of theoretical interest. In other words, I argue that the questions one asks about development determine what methods one ought to use. It should not be the case that the questions one asks are determined by the particular method one likes to use. Theory should determine method and not the other way around.

Finally, however, we note that theory and its related research do not exist in a social vacuum. A scholar of human development obviously works in a specific society at a specific time in history. Thus, research must be conducted in accordance with the strictest ethical standards appropriate within the researcher's social, cultural, and historical contexts. Accordingly, a key feature of our discussion in this chapter is the ethical standards for developmental research.

We see, then, that as much as research needs theory (to organize and understand knowledge and to lead to the generation of new knowledge), theory needs research (to provide tests, substantiations, and revisions of theory). Because of its importance, the student of human development should be familiar with the dimensions of developmental research, the problems and issues of such research, and in turn, the problems that may exist in attempting to interrelate these empirical concerns with theoretical issues.

As I have noted, these facets of the research endeavor are complex. Yet, their understanding is necessary for a complete appreciation of the discipline, as well as for an elucidation of some of the theoretical issues we have considered in previous chapters. Because of their complexity, we attempt to present the dimensions of developmental research within a framework that may facilitate their comprehension. We discuss the developmental research dimensions described by McCandless (1967, 1970).

DIMENSIONS OF RESEARCH METHODS IN HUMAN DEVELOPMENT

For many years, Boyd McCandless (1915–1975) was an active contributor to the literature of developmental psychology; he contributed both theoretical and research papers and also spoke to the issues, problems, and aspects of developmental research per se. It is this last portion of McCandless's writings that concerns us here.

McCandless described (1967, 1970) four dimensions of developmental research. That is, it is possible to place any developmental study on a particular location along each of four continua. In Chapter 16, I noted that the differential approach to human development defines individuality as a person's location in multidimensional space. As will be recalled, this definition means that any

Boyd R. McCandless

particular person occupies his or her own individual space on each of a number of bipolar attribute dimensions. Similarly, a given developmental study possesses its own location along each of four dimensions. These four dimensions—or attributes—of developmental research describe the various continua along which any developmental study may vary. Thus, by describing and understanding the characteristics of each of these research attribute dimensions, one will be able to see where any given developmental study fits into the total scheme of possible developmental research.

Location at one point on one dimension does not necessarily imply a similar location on the other dimensions. The fact that any one study could fall along different points of each dimension means that an almost limitless array of strategies of research is available to the developmental researcher. To see this variety let us turn to the first dimension of developmental research methods.

The Normative–Explanatory Dimension

McCandless (1967, 1970) typically presented the four dimensions of developmental research he discussed in a particular order. However, there is no necessary sequence. All are equally important to consider. The normative–explanatory dimension is presented first for historical reasons. As discussed in Chapter 2, human development was, until the 1950s, a largely *descriptive* discipline aimed at finding norms of behavior. Increasingly since that time, however, there has been a shift to a focus on theoretical issues, and, hence, a concern with research aimed at *explaining* behavior change. Because this dimension pertains to a major historical shift in science, it is considered first.

Normative studies are those that describe the typical (mean, median, or modal) behavior of people of particular age levels and specific populations. Norms *describe* characteristics (e.g., behaviors and physical attributes) that may be expected to be seen among specific groups of people (e.g., 6 year-old, poor, European-American males, 25-year-old middle class Latino women from Mexico, etc.) in particular situations (e.g., public school classrooms) or under specific circumstances (e.g., living in working-class, urban settings in the eastern United States). Thus, normative research might be aimed at describing the average height or weight for European-American, middle-class, 13-year-old males and females from the midwestern United States. Indeed, norms such as these have been obtained.

Barnett and Einhorn (1972) reported that the average height for 13-year-old males is 61.3 inches

and for 13-year-old females 62.2 inches. Similarly, the average weight for these two groups is 98.6 pounds and 105.5 pounds, respectively. In both height and weight, the average early adolescent female has higher scores that the average early adolescent male.

By providing typical descriptions of characteristics, norms are useful in indicating what may be expected to occur in groups of people at particular points in their development. Thus, if we look at the height and weight norms for 18-year-old males and females, we see that the average male height is 70.2 inches and the average weight is 144.8 pounds. The corresponding measures for 18-year-old females are 64.4 inches and 126.2 pounds. Thus, for 18-year-olds, there is a reversal of what was seen at age 13. By looking at the growth norms for these two age levels, we can expect that the average late-adolescent male will be taller and heavier than the average late-adolescent female.

These height and weight norms were published in 1972. Corresponding norms, collected earlier and later in history, indicate that what was average for a particular group of adolescents at a particular age has changed across history (Garn, 1980; Tanner, 1991). Accordingly, not only does normative research give the researcher an appreciation of the developmental characteristics of people over the course of their lives but, also, as norms are repeatedly collected over history, they allow the researcher to see the interrelation of individual development with sociocultural change.

But why do norms change over either individual or historical time? Why do height, weight, and, in addition, age of menarche typically change from early to late adolescence? Why have adolescents tended to be taller across history? Why do some researchers believe that such trends are ending (Tanner, 1991)? Physical maturation obviously is associated with ontogenetic changes in height, weight, and pubertal alterations in bodily characteristics and functions (e.g., those associated with puberty; Katchadourian, 1977). In turn, and as we noted in Chapter 13, the "secular trends" (Tanner, 1991) in these attributes of adolescent maturation have been associated with historical changes involving improvements and/or stability of adequate delivery of nutritional resources and health care. Addressing questions about the bases (reasons) for norms allows us to distinguish between descriptions and explanations of behavior. Normative research does not explain why behavior changes in the typical manner that it does.

Such explanation is the goal of studies that lie toward the explanatory end of this first dimension. *Explanatory* studies attempt to account for the "why" of social change and behavioral development. Such studies, however, clearly depend on the identification of norms. After all, if researchers do not have any ideas about how to describe the typical occurrence of the behavior under study, they will have difficulty explaining it. Thus, norms are necessary for explanatory research. However, norms are not sufficient in and of themselves; they just present a catalog of descriptions, a collection of unaccounted-for facts.

Then, where do explanations come from? As emphasized in preceding chapters, explanations come from theory. Researchers attempt to integrate the norms of development within a particular theoretical formulation. They devise an empirical test of their theory, carry out this test, and in this way determine whether their explanation is valid. Thus, theory is useful in that it provides a basis for doing the type of research that will allow for an accounting of the facts of a discipline. In this regard, McCandless (1970) stated:

> Norms, while essential and of interest to all, are concerns for the pragmatist. Developmental psychologists . . . are likely to be pragmatists and empiricists. This may be why there are so many facts—and of them there are many about which thoughtful scholars are skeptical—and so few explanations. It is for this reason that . . . an attempt is made to maintain a conceptual orientation. It seems more promising to depend on theory for explanation than on mere collection of facts. (p. 42)

To illustrate McCandless's view, it is useful to note again a point made in Chapter 11 in regard to normative differences in the IQ scores of African-American and European-American children and adolescents (e.g., Loehlin, Lindzey, & Spuhler, 1975). European American samples have higher average scores than African American samples. Various theories have been advanced to explain this difference (Burt, 1966; Gould, 1981, 1996; Hirsch, 1970, 1997a, 1997b; Jensen 1969, 1973; Rushton, 1999), and one such interpretation rests on social-class and cultural differences between the groups. To simplify for purposes of illustration, the gist of this explanation is that variables that exist in different sociocultural settings account for the difference in IQ. For instance, differences in health, nutrition, and quality of education explain why the average African-American youth, who is more likely than the average European-American youth to be in a sociocultural setting that has lower levels of these variables (Hernandez, 1993; Huston, 1991), scores lower on IQ tests. The average African-American youth is not as well educated, well fed, or healthy as the average European-American youth. If it

were found that normative IQ differences disappeared for particular samples of African Americans and European Americans, who were equated on such variables, then the aforementioned explanation of the basis of the norms would find support. Indeed, evidence supporting this explanation has been presented (Kagan, 1969).

In sum, the first dimension of research sorts studies on the basis of the relative emphasis on either description or explanation. When the latter type of study is done, the researcher attempts to relate one set of observations (the normative ones, the descriptions) to another set of observations in particular ways. That is, the researcher will argue that *if* the descriptions are to be explained by a particular theory, *then* certain relations between the described behaviors and other, independently observed behaviors should be seen. If social-class differences explain IQ differences, then particular changes in social class-related variables (e.g., increased quality of education) should be related to certain changes (i.e., increases) in IQ scores.

In essence, in explanatory studies the researcher makes a prediction, or forms a hypothesis, about how the variables are related to each other. Many different types of data collection techniques are available to the researcher testing such hypotheses. The range of techniques is associated with the second dimension of research.

The Naturalistic–Manipulative Dimension

There are many different, useful ways in which scientists may obtain data. The choice of a data collection technique is determined partly by an interest in avoiding *reactivity*—an unwanted influence on a research participant's responses. Reactivity exists when a participant's behavior or responses are influenced by the fact that he or she is participating in a research study. One useful way of avoiding reactivity while studying development is to go into the real world to observe behavior. Observation of behavior as it occurs in its natural setting is termed *naturalistic observation*. In such observation, the researcher avoids manipulation of the ongoing behavior. Rather then deciding what to observe, the researcher attempts to find behavior as it naturally exists.

Such naturalistic observation has real-world or *ecological validity,* because it is an observation of behavior as it *actually* exists in its true ecology. If we want to see how aggressive behavior exists among 12-year-olds when they are playing, a good way to find this out is to observe 12-year-olds at play!

There are three general types of naturalistic observation. A first type is termed *nonobtrusive measures*. Much research can be done without directly observing, testing, or taking to people. There are data all around us, waiting to be collected, and we often do not even know it. Whenever we use data that already exist in our environment, we are using *nonobtrusive* measures.

There are numerous examples of such research studies (Webb, Campbell, Schwartz, & Sechrest, 1996). Reading habits on campus could be studied by examining wear and tear on library books; sexual attitudes could be examined by reading the graffiti on bathroom walls; divorce could be researched by analyzing records available at the county courthouse. We could study radio-listening preferences by having auto mechanics find out the stations to which car radios are automatically preset. And popular versus unpopular magazines in libraries or waiting rooms could be determined by looking at which ones collected the most dust.

A second type of naturalistic observation is termed *participant observation*. This technique is used mostly by sociologists and anthropologists to discover the nature of social relationships in real-life settings. In this type of research, the researcher becomes a part of the setting for weeks, months, or even a year or two, and systematically observes what he or she sees and hears. The participant observer may also do some informal interviewing and may supplement his or her observations with other data available in the setting. The researcher usually writes up very comprehensive notes each day about what was said and about what happened in the setting. These notes are carefully analyzed later. Many important social science studies have used this technique because it allows the researcher to observe social phenomena firsthand. This technique, however, has not been used widely in psychological studies of human development.

The second type of naturalistic observation is more structured. Psychologists, in particular, often wish to examine the relationship between a very small number of variables in a given study. Thus, it might be necessary to focus on a relatively limited set of specific behaviors of interest; for instance, in a naturalistic study of preschool children playing in a sandbox, one might focus on observing whether children play by themselves, interact positively (e.g., share) or interact negatively (e.g., show verbal or physical aggression). Given such a targeted focus, the researcher would systematically observe only those behaviors of interest.

Although it is clear that such an observational technique gives the researcher an excellent chance of discovering how behavior really occurs, it also has some limitations. A behavior of interest (e.g., verbal aggression) may occur at infrequent or irregular intervals, and the researcher may not be able to attend to everything that is possible to observe—even with the help of such apparatus as videotape recorders.

Moreover, such observations are sometimes difficult to use as a basis for explanations. For example, suppose a researcher is interested in how adolescents form dating relationships and wants to know whether people of similar levels of physical attractiveness tend to form relationships with each other. If the researcher chooses to study such development with the use of structured naturalistic observations, he or she might go out and find an appropriate sample of adolescents and then watch them, for example, at a high school social event (e.g., a dance). Of course, a good deal of behavior might be occurring at a very rapid pace. To try to cope with such an enormous input of information, the researcher might look at the adolescents for only 30 seconds at a time, and then only at 5-minute intervals. Moreover, a wide-angle-lens camera might be used to record these observations. However, despite these techniques, the researcher must avoid manipulating the behavior of the youth if the study is to remain naturalistic. Thus, if too few adolescents are forming new relationships—for example, by dancing repeatedly with one another or by leaving the dance together—the researcher does not intervene to increase the frequency of the behavior of interest.

Indeed, because no planned intervention in behavior occurs in naturalistic observation, the researcher cannot cancel out or control for the influences of other variables that might relate to the formation of relationships. For example, things other than the physical attractiveness of a potential partner might influence relationship formation in adolescence. Such things as prior acquaintance, mutual friends, or even dancing ability could determine whether one person repeatedly dances with or leaves with another. Since the researcher cannot control the role of such other potentially influential variables, it is sometimes difficult to use structured naturalistic observations to support explanations. For example, it would be difficult to assert that people of similar physical attractiveness levels formed relationships in adolescence, because even if sufficient observations of relationship formations occurred, and comparable physical attractiveness levels did seem to link people together, the researcher would not be able to tell whether attractiveness (or another possible but uncontrolled-for influence) was the key determinant.

As another example, suppose a psychologist is interested in the development of aggression in 5-, 6-, and 7-year-olds. If the psychologist chooses to study such development with the use of naturalistic observations, he or she would simply go out and find an appropriate sample of children and then sit down and watch them, for example, at play in a schoolyard. It is possible, however, that after days of such observations, the researcher could have few, if any, observations relevant to the behavior of interest. Although this instance is unlikely in the case of aggressive responses, one may easily think of behaviors that do not occur frequently or regularly. For instance, to use a somewhat unusual topic for developmental inquiry but, nonetheless, a legitimate one, suppose the researcher is interested in observing masturbatory behaviors among these children. Even after days of intense naturalistic observation, the occurrences of such behaviors among this age group of children—and within the free-play situation—would be expected to be extremely low.

In any event, the researcher using this technique would not necessarily be able to make any statements about the variables in the children's development that provided a source of whatever behavior he or she was attempting to observe. Rather, the researcher might be only able to describe a particular sequence of events. Although such a description has the virtue of having ecological validity, because of the lack of control over the observations, the data obtained by the researcher may be unsystematic, of a frequency limiting the potential generalizability of any findings, and of a sort that does not allow for more than descriptive appraisals of the developing behavior.

In sum, the lack of control over behavior—in terms of its frequency and its influence by other variables—is one reason why naturalistic observation cannot be the only observational technique in developmental research. Another reason is that there are some features of development (e.g., thoughts, values, and motives) that are not readily available for naturalistic observation.

Controlled and Experimental Observations

Some changes in behavior that are of interest require more controlled observational techniques. The child might be put into a situation that maximizes the likelihood that the researcher will see the relevant behavior. The presence or level (e.g., amount, intensity) of variables that could potentially influence the relevant behavior, but that are not of current interest, would be controlled in the research, or excluded altogether.

Researchers who opt for techniques that allow more control over their observations are conducting research toward the *manipulative* end of the dimension. When the research situation is controlled by the researcher, but the behavior of the person is not directly manipulated, we label this *controlled observation.* In *experimental observation,* on the other hand, maximum control over observations and direct manipulation of behaviors are involved. It is useful to discuss controlled and experimental observations in more detail.

Controlled observations.   Rather than studying behavior based on observations of its occurrence in the ecologically valid ("real world"), the methods of controlled observation can be employed to increase the likelihood of observing the behavior of interest. This goal is sought by controlling the situation in which the behavior will take place.

To illustrate controlled observation, again suppose that a researcher is interested in seeing whether adolescents form relationships in school on the basis of similar levels of physical attractiveness. Now, using controlled observation to address this interest, the researcher might place a group of adolescents unacquainted with each other in a classroom in order to form two-person study groups to examine a topic about which they have little background. The researcher could have observers rate the physical attractiveness of the people and see who paired up with whom. In this study, then, the researcher has exerted greater control over his or her observations. Although no attempt has been made to manipulate (i.e., change) the adolescents' behaviors *directly,* the situation within which the adolescents interact has been controlled, and even some characteristics of adolescents within the situation have been arranged.

As another example, imagine that a researcher believes that physical aggression in 8-year-olds does not occur very frequently and yet wants to study this behavior. He or she might see the advantage of controlled observation. Suppose that two 8-year-olds are placed in a room with a very attractive video game which can be used by only one youth at a time. After putting the children in this situation for a very short time, we might expect to see some aggression as we defined it.

Controlled observation allows the scientist to influence the observations because he or she controls and manipulates the situation. Situations are chosen on the basis of their likelihood of "producing" the behavior of interest. Yet, this technique also has a disadvantage: By itself it allows the scientist directly to manipulate the situation alone, not the behavior of the people in the study. One knows that a certain type of behavior may be expected to occur in this standard, controlled situation with some certain degree of regularity; but one may not know what in the situation influenced the behavior to take the form that it took.

Controlled observation can, nevertheless, provide *normative* information; that is, by having people respond in standard, controlled situations, we learn what behavior to expect in such situations. In fact, when scientists use a special type of controlled observation technique—known as a *psychological test*—important normative information about such aspects of functioning as intelligence, attitudes, values, goals, and personality may be discovered.

Controlled experiments. In the controlled experiment, one exercises as much control over the situation as possible. One manipulates conditions such that only the variables whose effects on behavior one wants to ascertain would vary, and this variation itself is also controlled. Everything else that could possibly affect the behavior of interest would be either held constant in all conditions or balanced across the research conditions. In other words, one would (ideally) control any variation in the situation that could influence the behavior of interest.

To the extent that the researcher is successful in designing an experiment that enables him or her to infer that all the variation in the behavior he or she observes is due to the manipulations he or she has performed, the experiment is said to have *internal validity* (Baltes et al., 1977). Such validity does not mean, however, that the results of the experiment can be generalized to situations having characteristics other than those precisely identical to those of the experiment. Indeed, if the results of an experiment can be generalized to other situations unlike those of the experiment, the study is said to have *external validity* (Baltes et al., 1977).

Thus, the controlled experiment is the observational technique that gives the researcher the best understanding of the basis of people's behavior *in a particular situation.* In other words, in a controlled experiment the scientist actually attempts to manipulate all events that he or she believes will influence the person's behavior, and this means that, besides controlling a situation, the researcher also controls exactly what happens to the person in the situation. Such control is used to see what will result when people are exposed to certain, specific events. The goal is to establish a cause–effect relationship, and the researcher

hopes to find evidence that "a change in X will cause (have the effect of) a change in Y." In an experiment, the researcher tries to control the important influencing factors that act on the participants of the study; of course, what the participants do *depends* on them.

To illustrate, a researcher might conduct an experiment to determine whether high school students "learn" (operationally defined as success in memorizing a list of words) better when everything is quiet versus when music is playing. The researcher might ask: How will different students learn if one-half are stimulated with (or distracted by) contemporary music while trying to study, whereas the other half are not stimulated (or distracted) by sound at all? The researcher would then randomly assign students to the two groups and expose them to the different events—either the "music" or the "quiet" stimulation. The researcher would be interested in observing whether differences in learning (memory of the words on the list) resulted between students exposed to one condition as opposed to the other. In an experiment, then, the researcher tries to see if the person's behavior can be affected, or changed, as a consequence of the different conditions that the researcher manipulates.

Independent variable—The condition that the researcher chooses to vary, that is, the various events with which the researcher stimulates the participants, is called the *independent variable*. A *variable* may be defined as anything that can change. Noise (or sound level), age, height, intelligence, amount of tenseness, and years in college are all variables. Anything that can change (or vary) in terms of how much of it exists is a variable. An independent variable is something which the researcher chooses to vary through intentional manipulation in an experimental study of development. This variable is "independent" of the participant's behavior. It is what the researcher chooses to manipulate.

In a "true" experiment, the researcher chooses the levels (e.g., intensity and duration) of the variables he or she will vary, and assigns research participants randomly to these conditions (e.g., music or quiet, as in the aforementioned learning study). However, and perhaps especially in studies of human development, researchers may be interested in studying the role of variation in variables that have levels that they can select but that they cannot control, in the sense of being able to randomly assign participants to the levels of these variables. A key example in developmental research is age. Other often used examples are sex and race/ethnicity. A researcher may be interested in studying learning among 5- and 6-year-old, Latino and African-American boys and girls. However, the researcher cannot randomly assign a child to be age 5 or 6, a boy or a girl, or African American or Latino. Thus, when a study is designed using such variables, it is not a true experiment. It is termed a *quasi-experiment* (Campbell & Stanley, 1963).

Dependent variable—Although the independent variables, or the stimulus conditions, are chosen by the researcher for manipulation and are, thus, independent of the participants, their effects on the participants' behaviors are not independent of the participants. How the participants behave in response to the different stimulations they receive *depends* on them, and in an experiment the behavior shown in response to an independent variable's stimulation is termed the *dependent variable*.

In an experiment, the scientist alters a specific stimulus—the independent variable—to see its effect on the dependent variable (i.e., the participants' *responses* to the various stimuli). As in our example, the researcher manipulates the background sound stimulus (music or quiet) to see what effect this change will have on the students' learning. In this illustrative experiment, then, the level of background sound is the independent variable, and the resulting degree of participant learning (list memorization) constitutes the dependent variable.

Controls. Controlling the independent variable to which participants are exposed is important, but the researcher also has to control many other variables. In fact, in an ideal instance of the aforementioned learning experiment, the only thing that can be different between the two groups of students is that one studies with music playing whereas the other studies in a quiet environment. Any other stimulus which, if varied, could have some effect on the students' responses (on the dependent variable) must not be allowed to vary (e.g., intelligence, educational background, familiarity with the items on the list, age, health status, hearing ability, temperament, etc.). Only through control will the researcher be sure that any changes in the participants' learning are due *only* to the changes in the independent (stimulus) variable.

Thus, the scientist would want to make sure that such things as these other instances of potentially relevant variables previously noted (e.g., age, intelligence, etc.) were not different before the study was conducted. If the scientist found differences in how well students learned when stimulated with music versus quiet, he or she would want to be sure that such differences were due to this different stimulation between the two groups and did not arise because one group was composed of, say, 12-year-olds whereas the other group was composed of, say, 20-year-olds, or because one group consisted of very bright students whereas the other group contained students of average intelligence. If such differences existed between the two groups, the researcher could not be sure that the differences found in the dependent variable were, after all, really due only to the variations introduced by the independent variable.

Unless an experiment is properly controlled, the differences could just as easily have been due to age, intelligence, or educational differences. When an experiment is properly controlled, the researcher can make sound determinations of what caused the variations in the dependent variable.

Controlled experimental observations have an advantage not found with either naturalistic observation or controlled observation. When the scientist observes how changes in the independent variable affect the students' behaviors, he or she may state that, given the internal validity of the investigation, the difference in the participants' behaviors was the result of the different conditions to which they were exposed. In other words, experimental observation allows the researcher to discover a basis of a particular behavior within the specific situation used for study.

Suppose that the group that studied with quiet learned better than the group that studied with music. Given all the proper controls, the researcher examining this difference could now say that the basis of the different levels of learning seen in the experiment was the different sound stimulation given the two groups. Hence, experimental observations allow the researcher to discover bases of studied behavior within a controlled experimental setting.

The controlled experiment also has disadvantages, however. The results of an experiment tell us only the effect of a specific stimulus on a certain behavior in one specific situation. We cannot necessarily apply these results to a different situation, where perhaps other stimuli may be used and/or other things may or may not be controlled. We cannot just assume external validity. Thus, we cannot easily apply results of one experiment to other experimental situations *unless* everything about the two situations is identical.

Moreover, in ecologically valid settings, everything is not as controlled as it is in an experiment. Things vary naturally, and because many variables stimulate a person at the same time (instead of one at a time), each of these variables may affect behavior singularly or in combination. Although experimental observations give us important information about a basis for behavior in a specific situation, that situation is rarely identical to events in ecologically valid settings. Hence, we must apply or "generalize" the results of controlled experimental observations cautiously to such contexts.

It may be concluded that observational techniques always involve a trade-off. One trades precise control over behavior for ecological validity when one uses the naturalistic observation method; on the other hand, one loses such validity when one gains control through manipulation in controlled or experimental observations. However, both types of observational techniques are needed. The researcher who begins with manipulated, controlled observations may recognize the necessity of seeing if and how the results may actually occur in the natural world. The naturalistic observer, on the other hand, may find it necessary to move into the laboratory and make controlled observations in order to verify the impressions of behavior gained in the field setting and attempt to understand the independent effects of particular variables on specific behaviors.

In sum, a disadvantage of experimental observation—that it may not have ecological validity—is an advantage of naturalistic observaton. On the other hand, the disadvantage of naturalistic observation—that it cannot easily discover a basis of a behavior—is an advantage of the controlled experiment. Ideally, a researcher interested in discovering the most accurate information about behavior should try to move back and forth between these two methods of scientific observation, observing reality in the natural world but testing hypotheses carefully under controlled conditions. Actually, researchers tend to use one or the other of the foregoing types of observation; or, because of the disadvantages associated with each technique, they may choose yet another type of method of observation.

Questionnaires and Interviews

Observational techniques are most useful when social interaction or behavior is of interest, and when such behavior is ethically open to scientific scrutiny. However, different techniques may be needed if (a) there is no overt social interaction or behavior to observe, (b) the behavior is not one that may readily or ethically be seen through observation, or (c) the presence of a researcher when the behavior of interest is occurring would influence that behavior in a way that would not have occurred had the researcher not been present.

An example of the first problem would be if the researcher was interested primarily in feelings, attitudes, values, or recollections of earlier events. In regard to the second problem, researchers may not study behaviors that harm or embarrass their research participants. Thus, trying to observe certain behaviors directly (e.g., sexual acts) might be prohibited. In addition, some behaviors (e.g., those associated with adolescent car accidents) are not often readily available to naturalistic observation, and for obvious ethical reasons cannot be "controlled" by the researcher. Furthermore, other events occur only once in life (e.g., menarche or the loss of virginity), and at times and in situations making them unavailable for direct observation. Indeed, if a researcher went beyond the bounds of ethics and tried to be present at such an event, it is certain that the person's reactions would differ from what they would have been had the researcher been absent.

The presence of the researcher is the third problem with making direct observations. Often, there are issues and behaviors of interest to the researcher of human development that cannot be directly observed by him or her because doing so would distort the behavior. Sexual interactions among people are obvious examples of the sort of behavior that would be distorted if a researcher were present. However, drug use and alcohol consumption, voting behavior, and certain types of parent–child interaction (e.g., such as may occur in child-abusing or child-neglectful homes) are other examples of social interaction and behavior that could be influenced by the presence of an outside observer.

Thus, because of the difficulties involved in direct observation, other methods are sometimes used. These take the form of questionnaires and interviews. These techniques involve written or verbal responses to questions. A questionnaire is usually self-administered but may be completed in a group setting with the questions read out loud. Interviews may be conducted in face-to-face settings, by telephone, or by other means. Both questionnaires and interviews can have fixed-choice questions, in which the possible answers are specified, or open-ended questions, in which any answer is possible and the precise response given by the respondent is recorded. Questionnaires and interviews are the techniques of *survey research*.

There are numerous issues in development that can only be studied through the use of survey research methods. For instance, as previously noted, survey research is most valuable when one is interested in people's reports or recollections, values, attitudes, or other unobservable information.

For example, whereas few people would allow their sexual behavior to be observed daily, more people might provide anonymous information on a questionnaire about their sexuality. Indeed, when aspects of behavior may not be ethical or easy to investigate, questionnaires or interviews may be the method of choice. In addition, since anonymity can be assured, questionnaires may often be answered very honestly and accurately. Interviews allow the respondent and researcher to get better acquainted, and the technique allows the researcher to probe issues or change directions in the midst of data collection. Furthermore, such methods allow the researcher to study large numbers of people in a shorter time than is often permitted by direct behavioral observation and to collect data on a large number of variables in a short time span. For instance, if a questionnaire has both written questions and answers, one scientist may obtain information from several hundred people at the same time.

However, responses to questionnaires and interviews are not expected to perfectly reflect behavior as it would occur if directly observed. Without a direct assessment of the correspondence between actual behavior and reported behavior, one cannot be certain of how well reports of behavior agree with actual behavior. People might forget, distort, or really not know the answers to various items in these instruments. Although it is possible to take steps to assess how much distortion takes place in people's answers, this is difficult. For example, one could compare people's answers to questions about their behavior with their actual behavior. However, often the unavailability of such direct observation of behavior is, as noted, the reason that indirect assessment devices are used in the first place.

Another potential problem with this method is that researchers may include questions which make certain answers more likely than others or, in asking questions during an interview, the behavior of researchers may bias the participants' answers to questions. For instance, a researcher who establishes a warm rapport with a person may elicit answers that differ from those elicited by a cold and/or hostile interviewer.

In sum, then, as with all other research techniques, questionnaires and interviews have assets and limitations. Again there is a trade-off. One is able to investigate behaviors not readily available for observation, but one has to use techniques whose correspondence with the actual behaviors of interest is often uncertain. Yet, because of their assets, such methods tend to be among the most frequently used by social scientists (Cattell, 1973), and researchers have sought to overcome

the disadvantages of such techniques. For instance, techniques have been developed to measure people's tendency to lie on questionnaires, and scientists have attempted to devise ways to "screen" the actual purpose of the questions from the participant, or at least make it hard to guess. Finally, one additional value that these techniques have is their ability to be combined with other (e.g., behavioral observation) techniques (Parke, 1978). For instance, one could see whether a person's attitudes or values, as measured by a questionnaire, changed as a consequence of various experimental manipulations.

Conclusions About Methods of Observation

There are, then, several different ways in which a scientist may observe behaviors associated with human development. However, a special observational task is presented to a scientist concerned with studying development. As explained in Chapter 1, development involves change. Change—an alteration over time in some characteristic of the person—cannot be observed by studying a person only once. To observe change, at least two points in time must be involved.

Accordingly, in order to study human development, researchers must plan (or design) their observations to encompass two or more occasions. In other words, measures related to development must be taken on at least two occasions in order to determine whether a change has, in fact, occurred. There are several ways in which researchers may design observations over time in order to obtain information about developmental change.

In sum, with the various forms of data-collection techniques available to a researcher, a variety of potential strategies are available for observing people. Although every method has specific strengths and weaknesses, any method may be used depending on the nature of the research question being investigated. But what determines the issue addressed in a given research effort? There is some rationale for every research effort, and this question is addressed by the third dimension of developmental research.

The Atheoretical–Theoretical Dimension

This dimension of developmental research identifies studies on the basis of their relative emphasis on (or specification of) theory as the basis of the research. There may be various reasons that lead researchers to conduct a particular study. Some research may be done simply on the basis of interest in some particular phenomenon. The researchers may be curious about the way something develops. They may have a hunch about some aspect of development. Or they may simply want to see what happens when a variable is manipulated or assessed.

In addition, research may be used as a way of solving a practical problem (McCandless, 1970). One key instance of such a problem (discussed in Chapter 19) pertains to how to design and enact systematic and sustained actions to promote positive development in people. As noted earlier in this chapter, such actions are termed *developmental interventions*—planned attempts to alter the course of development. Often, these developmental interventions take the form of community-based programs of action designed to prevent problem behaviors and, in turn, promote positive behaviors in members of the community (e.g., children, youth, and parents). The "practical" research topic that arises in relation to these programs involves *evaluation,* that is, empirical procedures to ascertain whether programs are effective in meeting their objectives (to prevent problems or promote positive behaviors) and/or if means may be found to improve the program and capacity of the community to sustain it (e.g., Fetterman, Kaftarian, & Wandersman, 1996; Jacobs, 1988; Jacobs & Kapuscik, 2000; Lerner, 2002; Lerner, et al., 1999). Thus, evaluation research is aimed at addressing the practical problems of proving (e.g., to funders, to policymakers) that a program is effective, improving a program, and building community capacity to maintain effective programs.

As is discussed in Chapter 19, although programs should, under ideal circumstances, have a "theory of change," that is, a theory of how the components of (the actions involved in) the intervention should enhance development, many community-based programs do not have a clear or explicit theory on which its actions are predicated (Roth et al., 1997, 1998). In turn, although some approaches to evaluation research (e.g., Jacobs, 1988) are developmental in nature and are structured in a manner consistent with developmental systems theory (Jacobs & Kapuscik, 2000), many instances of evaluation research do not have such a theoretical base. Instead, many evaluations use quantitative and qualitative research procedures to address the immediate and practical problems of proving that a program is effective and, simultaneously, of improving its performance.

Thus, in many cases, program evaluations are instances of atheoretical research. As such, this research is not based on statements drawn from a theory (hypotheses), and the researcher's ideas, when tested, will not necessarily support, clarify, or refute a theory.

Rather, atheoretical research is, by definition, carried out on a theory-independent basis. Although such research may be found to have some relevance to theory after it is completed, this is usually not intended. In fact, the data from such an atheoretical study may end up being just a bit of scientific data that has no meaning or relevance to any given theoretical formulation.

Because of such potential limitations for the study of human development, theoretically relevant research is stressed in this book. As indicated in our historical review of the changing emphases in the study of human development, studies based on theoretical conceptions of development may be seen as most useful in advancing the science. The data resulting from such research are expected to have some direct relevance for understanding development. As I have stressed, the purpose of theory is to integrate existing knowledge and obtain new knowledge. New knowledge results from the test of hypotheses derived from such theories. Thus, theory-related research always has the promise of providing information that expands our understanding of development.

The Ahistorical–Historical Dimension

How does one study the effects of several influences on human development across the life span? The issue is how can one design research to measure intraindividual change, or individual development, as that development is influenced by many variables. Although the preceding discussion presented different observational techniques for studying development, there was no statement about how these techniques could be used in an investigation of the character of developmental change. This concern is addressed in the discussion of the fourth dimension of developmental research. It is this dimension that determines whether a research effort is or is not a developmental one. It is this dimension that sorts studies on the basis of their relative concern with change.

Some studies are concerned with behavior at one particular time in a person's development. In such studies, there may be no interest whatsoever in how the behavior came to take the form that it does at this point in development or in what form this behavior may take later. Such studies may be termed *ahistorical,* because behavior is studied at only one point in time (McCandless, 1970). For instance, a particular study might be concerned with the effects of a certain type of social reinforcement on aggression in 10-year-olds. If the study is ahistorical in its orientation, it will not be concerned about how the child's earlier development contributed to this relation or about the future status of this relation.

However, as research becomes more concerned with the origins and the future course of behavior, it moves closer to the historical end of the continuum. Thus, historical research is concerned not only with the status of a relationship between two or more variables at a particular point in development but also with the basis of that relation as well as the future status of that relation. Historical researchers wants to know what variables in the 10-year-old's developmental history provided a basis for the relation between reinforcement and aggression, and what implications the relation at age 10 has for later adolescent and adult relations between social reinforcement and aggression. In short, then, historical research is concerned with the change in behavior over time.

Without historical investigation, basic issues of development could not be studied empirically. The developmentalist would be unable to determine either the continuity–discontinuity or the stability–instability of behavior. Thus, although an ahistorical study allows us to know the relations among the variables (e.g., of sex, social class, race, and IQ) at a given age, for example, it in no way allows us to know anything about the previous or eventual interrelations among these variables. A historical research study is, thus, the most appropriate for developmental inquiry. However, although there are several ways to design historical research, not all such research designs are, in fact, equally useful for developmental research.

Indeed, although there have been three types of historical designs typically noted by developmentalists, none of these conventional methods is completely adequate for developmental research. These three conventional research designs—termed the *longitudinal, cross-sectional,* and *time-lag designs*—each has important uses but also some limitations when applied to developmental research. Because of the need to understand the uses and limits of conventional research designs for studying change, the next section focuses on the nature of design in developmental research. Here, however, let us make some final statements about the ideas presented in this section of the chapter.

Conclusions

McCandless's framework for describing the possible dimensions of developmental research allows us to see the ways in which such research may vary. Developmental research is, thus, multifaceted; there are several dimensions along which a given study may vary, and, hence, the developmental researcher has available a large array of techniques and approaches with which to obtain information about psychological development. The usefulness of these dimensions of research, then, is to allow us to appreciate the many forms that developmental research may take, the many research emphases that may be stressed in such research, and the assets and limitations of each of these approaches to the study of human development. As a summary of these dimensions, Table 18.1 presents the endpoints of each of these four

TABLE 18.1
Four Dimensions of Studies in Human Development Research

1. Normative Studies _____ (Descriptions of averages, frequencies, and norms behavior.)	Explanatory Studies (Assessment of the causes or bases of behaviors.)
2. Naturalistic Studies _____ (Studies of people in their actual "real life" [ecologically valid] settings.)	Manipulative Studies (Conditions of the setting are controlled—e.g., as in a laboratory setting. The design of such research is often experimental.)
3. Atheoretical _____ (Studies designed to answer practical problems, verify casual observations, or satisfy curiosity.)	Theoretical (Studies designed to test ideas—hypotheses—derived from a theory.)
4. A historical _____ (Studies of relations among variables that have been measured at the same time. No assessment of the antecedents and/or the consequences of the relations that exist at one point in time.)	Historical (Studies of the antecedents and/or consequences of behavior, a focus on the history of the behavior.)

Source: Based on McCandless (1967, p. 60).

dimensions of developmental research, along with some brief descriptions of their meaning.

DESIGNS OF DEVELOPMENTAL RESEARCH

Many people who attempt to understand an individual's development do so by specifying age-related developmental progressions. An example is attributing storm and stress to the adolescent stage of life (see Chapter 1). Although age-related, or "stage," progressions may be one source of a person's change, they are not the only processes that provide a basis for change. For example, if a major event occurred in society at a particular time, for instance, the impeachment of President Clinton in the late 1990s, the Watergate political crisis of the 1970s, the assassination of President John F. Kennedy in 1963, or the 1929 stock market crash, behaviors of people might be affected despite the stage or age of development they were in. If one were measuring attitudes toward government during the impeachment process or during Watergate, the events in society at this time of measurement may have influenced children, adolescents, and adults: As such, it is possible that time of measurement, as well as, age-related phenomena, can influence development.

In addition to age and time, history may also affect change. Again imagine that attitudes toward government were being measured and that the participants of the study were people born during the Great Depression in the United States. During this historical era, many of the institutions that provided economic security to American citizens (e.g., banks) failed, and existing governmental policies were not able to deal with this situation. Accordingly, it may be expected that people born in the 1920s who experienced the effects of the depression during childhood might have developed differently than people born well before or well after this historical era. Indeed, research has found this to be true (Elder, 1974, 1998, 1999).

A *cohort* is a group of persons experiencing some event in common. People born in a given year are members of a particular *birth cohort*. By virtue of being in a particular birth cohort, one may have specific experiences that might not be part of the experiences of people born in other historical eras. Such birth-cohort-related influences can affect the character of behavior that people show across their lives. People who were children during the Great Depression may continue to be more wary about the stability of the economy and

the ability of the government to safeguard citizens than may people who were children during eras of affluence, high employment, and prosperity (e.g., the late 1950s or 1990s in the United States). Because of membership in a certain birth cohort, people may continue to differ from those of other cohorts, no matter at what age they are measured or what exists in the sociocultural setting at a particular time of measurement.

It may be seen that there are at least three components of developmental change. *Birth-cohort-related* events, as well as *time of measurement* and *age-related phenomena,* can contribute to developmental changes. Recognizing that reference is always made to phenomena that change in relation to these components, we label these components *age, time,* and *cohort* for convenience. Thus, when intraindividual change is seen from one point in the life span to another, one must be able to determine how processes associated with each of these three components may influence change.

Until the late 1960s (Baltes, 1968; Schaie, 1965), the three most popular designs of developmental research did not allow for an adequate determination of the contributions of these three components. The three designs—the longitudinal, cross-sectional, and time-lag method—typically involve a *confounding* of two of the three components of change. When a variable is confounded, its influence on behavior cannot be separated from that of another variable that could be influencing behavior at the same time.

For instance, if one wanted to know whether males or females could score higher on a test of reading comprehension, one would not want all the males to be college-educated and all the females to be only grade-school-educated. It is known that education level can influence reading comprehension as well as can sex-related variables. If one did not equate the two sex-groups on education level (if one did not "control" for the contributions of education), then one would not know whether differences between the groups were influenced by their sex or by their educational disparities (or some combination of the two). Thus, sex would be confounded with education. In other words, one could not determine the separate influences of the two variables because these variables were confounded. Any study that involves such a confounding has a serious methodological flaw.

Unfortunately, the three commonly used designs for developmental research confound two of the three aforementioned components of developmental change and, as a consequence, their utility is limited. Table 18.2 presents the particular confounding factors in each of these designs.

TABLE 18.2
Some Characteristics of Longitudinal, Cross-Sectional, and
Time-Lag Designs of Developmental Research

Design	Study involves	Confounded components of developmental change
Longitudinal	One birth cohort	Age with time
Cross-sectional	One time of measurement	Age with birth cohort
Time-lag	One age	Time with birth cohort

Reference to this table is useful as the discussion turns to an explanation of the characteristics of each of these designs and an explanation of why they confound what they do.

The Longitudinal Design

The *longitudinal design* (also known as a *panel design*) involves observing the same group of people at more than one point in time. The main asset of this approach is that because the same people are studied over time, the similarities or changes in behavior (i.e., intraindividual change) across their development can be seen directly. However, this method, particularly as it involves repeated observations of the same people over an extended period of time, has some limitations.

It obviously takes a relatively long time to do some longitudinal studies. If researchers wanted, for instance, to do a longitudinal study of personality development from birth through late adolescence, they would have to devote about 20 years of their own lives to such a research endeavor. Such a commitment would be expensive as well as time consuming, and, thus, it may easily be seen why relatively few long-term longitudinal studies have been done.

Other limitations of longitudinal studies pertain to the nature of the people studied and problems with the measurements that may be used. Not everyone would be willing to be a participant in a study that required their being continually observed over the course of many months or years of their lives. Hence, samples in such studies often tend to be small. Those people who are willing to take part may not be representative of most people. Thus longitudinal studies often involve unrepresentative, or "biased," samples. Results of such studies may not be easily applied, or "generalized," to a broader population. In addition, longitudinal samples typically become increasingly biased as the study continues. Some people drop out of participation, and one should not assume that those

people that do remain are identical to the former group. After all, the group that stays may be different just by virtue of the fact that they continue to participate.

Another problem with longitudinal studies is that, after some time, people may become used to the tests of their behavior. They may learn "how to respond," or they may respond differently than they would have if they had never been exposed to the test. Hence, the meaning of a particular test to the participants may be altered over time through its repeated use with the same sample. Such an occurrence would make it difficult to say that the same variable was actually being measured at different times in the participants' lives.

Often, the purpose of using this design is to determine the developmental time course for a particular type of behavior or psychological function. One also wants information that may be applied to understanding development about future generations of people. Yet, with a longitudinal study, one is only studying people who are born in one historical era and who are measured at certain points in time. One does not know whether findings about this one cohort can be generalized to people in other cohorts.

A confounding of age and time exists when one cohort is studied. Because a longitudinal study involves assessing one particular cohort of people (e.g., a group of males and females born in 1980), such people can be 15 years of age at only one time of measurement (in this case, 1995). Thus, their behavior at age 15 may be due to age-related phenomena or to phenomena present at the time of measurement (or to both). Similarly, members of one birth cohort can only be 20-years-old at one time of measurement. Thus, as noted in Table 18.2, age and time are confounded in a longitudinal study. One does not know whether the results of a longitudinal study can be applied to other 15- or 20-year-olds who are measured at other times.

Hence, the findings about development that one gains from a longitudinal study may reflect age-related changes *or,* alternatively, they may reflect only characteristics of people born and studied at particular points in time. In a longitudinal study, one does not know whether the findings are due to universal rules, or "laws," of development (i.e., rules that describe a person's development no matter when it occurs), to particular historical events that may have influenced the research participants, the particular times the participants are measured, *or* to some combination of all these influences.

To summarize, although longitudinal studies are useful for describing development as it occurs in a group of people, such studies have expense, sampling, and measurement problems; they may present results not applicable to similarly aged people who grew up in different historical eras or who were measured at different points in time. Because of such problems, alternatives to the longitudinal method are often used.

The Cross-Sectional Design

The most widely used developmental research design is the *cross-sectional design.* Here, different groups of people are studied at one point in time, and, hence, all observations can be completed relatively quickly. The design is less expensive than longitudinal research and requires less time. Because of these characteristics, some have argued that the method allows for a very efficiently derived description of development. However, there are important limitations of cross-sectional research.

If one wanted to study the development of aggression in individuals who range in age from 2 to 20 years, one could use the cross-sectional method. For example, instead of observing one group of people every year for 18 years, groups of individuals at each age between 2 and 20 could be observed at one point in time.

However, it is difficult to control fully and adequately for all variables that may affect behavior differences. One may not be certain whether differences between the various age groups are reflections of real age changes or merely reflections of the groups not being really identical to begin with. Sometimes, to ensure some degree of comparability, the researcher attempts to match the individuals on a number of important variables other than age. However, such comparability is difficult to achieve. Moreover, although it is possible to get less biased, more representative samples for cross-sectional research than it is for longitudinal studies (people may cooperate more readily because they are only committed to being

observed or interviewed once), this better sampling may still not lead to a useful description of the components of developmental change. This failure occurs because of a flaw in the rationale for the use of a cross-sectional method instead of a longitudinal one.

The expectation for some cross-sectional studies is that they will yield results comparable to those obtained from studying the same group of people over time—and that they will do so more efficiently—as long as the only differences among cross-sectional groups are their ages. However, despite how adequately participants are matched, it is rarely true that the results of cross-sectional and longitudinal studies are consistent (Schaie & Strother, 1968).

For example, when studying intellectual development with a cross-sectional design, most researchers report that highest performance occurs in the early twenties or thirties and considerable decreases in performance levels occur after this period (e.g., Horn & Cattell, 1966). With longitudinal studies of these same variables, however, often no decrease in performance is seen at all. In fact, some studies (e.g., Bayley & Oden, 1955) have found some increases in performance levels into the fifties. As has been pointed out, it may be suggested that the nature of the participants typically used in a longitudinal design is considerably different from that of participants used in a cross-sectional study.

Longitudinal studies, as has also been noted, may be composed of a select sample to begin with and, as the study proceeds, some people will drop out. Such attrition may not be random. Rather it may be due to the fact that subjects of lower intellectual ability leave the study. Hence, in the example of research on intellectual development, this bias could account for lack of decreases in performance levels. In addition, as Schaie and Strother (1968) pointed out, many of these longitudinal studies have not assessed intellectual development in the sixties and seventies—the age periods during which the greatest performance decreases have been seen in cross-sectional studies (e.g., Jones, 1959). Thus, comparisons of age-associated changes found with the two methods are not appropriate.

On the other hand, cross-sectional samples have not escaped criticism. Schaie (1959) argued that such samples do not give the researcher a good indication of age-associated changes because it is difficult to control for extraneous variables in the samples used to represent people of widely different age ranges.

Although these arguments may appropriately be used to reconcile the differences (or perhaps to explain them away), Schaie (1965) suggested that these arguments miss an essential point: They do not show a recognition of an essential methodological problem involved in the consideration of longitudinal and cross-sectional designs. Just as longitudinal studies are confounded (between age and time), cross-sectional studies are also confounded. As seen in Table 18.2, the confounding is between age and cohort. Because the two types of studies involve different confounding, it is unlikely that they will reveal the same results.

The confounding of age and cohort that exists in cross-sectional studies occurs because, at any one time of measurement (e.g., 1999), people who are of different ages can only be so because they were born in different years. To be 20 in 1999, one has to have been born in 1979, whereas to be 25 at this time of measurement, one has to be a member of the 1974 birth cohort. Consequently, because cross-sectional studies focus only on one time of measurement, there is no way of telling whether differences between age groups are due to age-related changes or to differences associated with being born in historically different eras.

To summarize, like the longitudinal method, the cross-sectional method has important limitations. Because of these shortcomings, it is difficult to decide whether longitudinal or cross-sectional designs give a more useful depiction of developmental changes. Both designs may potentially introduce serious, but different, distortions into measures of developmental changes. This is perhaps the major reason why information from the two techniques is often not consistent (Schaie & Strother, 1968). Similarly, data derived from a third type of design for developmental research, the time-lag design, are not necessarily consistent with those of the former two. This is because yet another type of confounding is involved.

The Time-Lag Design

Although not as frequently used in research as the cross-sectional or longitudinal designs, the time-lag design allows a researcher to see differences in behavior associated with particular ages at various times in history. That is, in contrast to focusing on one cohort or one time of measurement, the time-lag design considers only one age level and looks at characteristics associated with being a particular age at different times in history.

For example, earlier in this chapter, when differences between the 1970s and earlier decades in the normative height and weight of 13-year-olds were discussed, a time-lag design was actually being indicated. When the focus of research is to determine the characteristics associated with being a particular age (e.g., 15-years-old) at different times of measurement (e.g., 1970, 1980, 1990, and 2000), a time-lag design is implied.

Of course, such a design involves cross-sections of people and has all the problems of control, matching, and sampling associated with such designs. But there are also additional problems. As indicated in Table 18.2, because only one age is studied at different times, the different groups are members of different birth cohorts. Thus, in a time-lag design, time and birth cohort are confounded, and one does not know, for example, if the behaviors of 15-year-olds studied at two points in time are associated with events acting on all people—no matter what their age—at a particular test time or with historical events associated with membership in a specific cohort.

In sum, the three types of conventional developmental research designs do not allow for unconfounded assessment of the contributions of the age, time, and cohort components of developmental change. Because of these shortcomings, it is difficult to decide which method gives a more useful depiction of developmental changes. Each method may potentially introduce different distortions into measures of developmental change. As already noted, this is perhaps the major reason why information about developmental changes derived from these techniques is often not consistent (Schaie & Strother, 1968). Although each design has some advantages, the problems of each limit the ability of developmental researchers to adequately describe how individual, sociocultural, or historical variables can influence change.

This point might lead some to conclude that a bleak picture exists for the study of human development, because the three conventional designs of developmental research have some methodological problems. But, of course, no research method is without its limitations—a point I have noted before and return to again later in this chapter. As such, my view is that all the conventional designs of developmental research may be used to enhance understanding if they are employed with a recognition of their limitations. These limitations, however, can be transcended by the use of still other designs, designs that are described in the following section. Although these designs also have their limitations (e.g., they typically require large samples of people and are quite expensive to implement), they offer a useful alternative to traditional approaches.

The use of these designs has been made clear through the work of K. Warner Schaie (1965), Paul B. Baltes, and John R. Nesselroade (Baltes,

1968; Nesselroade & Baltes, 1974). Schaie (1965) demonstrated how the conventional methods were part of a more general developmental model for developmental research design. Presentation of this model allowed him to offer a new type of approach to designing developmental research. These are the sequential methods of developmental research.

Sequential Strategies of Design

The problems of confounding involved in the cross-sectional, longitudinal, and time-lag designs may be resolved, Schaie (1965) argued, through the use of sequential methods. By combining features of longitudinal and cross-sectional designs, the researcher may assess the relative contributions of age, cohort, and time in one study, and know what differences (or portion of the differences) between groups are due to age differences, cohort (historical) differences, or time-of-testing differences. In addition, a sequential design allows these sources of differences to be determined in a relatively short period of time.

Research based on sequential designs is complex, due in part to the usual involvement of multivariate (many variable) statistical analyses and the numerous measurements that have to be taken of different groups. But a simplified example of such a design may be offered. It will suggest how use of such a design allows the developmental researcher to avoid the potential confounding involved with traditional cross-sectional and longitudinal approaches.

Basically, a sequential design involves the remeasurement (i.e., the longitudinal assessment) of a cross-sectional sample of people after a given fixed interval of time has passed. A researcher selects a cross-sectional sample composed of various cohorts and measures each cohort longitudinally (with the provision that each set of measurements occurs at about the same point in time for each cohort). In addition, if, for example, three times of testing are included (as the longitudinal component of the design), then control cohort groups (assessed, for instance, at the second and/or the third testing times) may be used to control for (to assess) any retesting effects. Hence, this design calls for obtaining repeated measures from each of the different cohort groups included in a given cross-sectional sample, and obtaining data from retest control groups to assess effects of retesting. The researcher is, thus, in a position to make statements about the relative influences of age, cohort, and times of measurement on any observed developmental functions in the results.

Cross-sectional and longitudinal sequential designs consist of sequences of either simple cross-sectional or longitudinal designs. The successive application of these strategies permits us to describe the extent to which behavior change is associated with age- or history-related influences. Figure 18.2 provides a contrast between the simple and sequential strategies. The top portion of the figure shows the simple cross-sectional and longitudinal designs described earlier, whereas the bottom portion of the figure shows the two sequential strategies. Cross-sectional sequences involve successions of two or more cross-sectional studies completed at different times of measurement. Longitudinal sequences involve successions of longitudinal studies begun at different times of measurement. The strategies differ in that cross-sectional sequences involve independent measures on different individuals, whereas longitudinal sequences involve repeated measures of the same individuals. In practice, one can apply both strategies simultaneously. In any event, the application of sequential strategies permits the discrimination of within- and between-cohort sources of change, thus, increasing the scope of one's descriptive efforts.

To see how this approach to the design of developmental research works, it is useful to consider a sample design of such a sequential study. Such a design is presented in Table 18.3 and recast in the form of a matrix in Figure 18.3. Different cohort levels are composed of different groups of people born at different historical periods (1954, 1955, 1956, or 1957). Thus, at the time of the first testing (for this design, 1970), the study has the attributes of a cross-sectional study. Indeed, there are three such cross-sectional studies in this particular design—one for each time of measurement (see Figure 18.3). However, the sequential feature is introduced when these same participants are again measured in 1971 and 1972. Thus, for each cohort, there is now a longitudinal study. As seen in Figure 18.3, each cohort in a sequential design of this sort is involved in its own short-term longitudinal study (there are four of these in the design shown in Figure 18.3). In addition, it should be noted that the diagonals of the design matrix of Figure 18.2 represent time-lag studies; people of the same age are studied at different times. Thus, a sequential study involves all combinations of observations of other designs in one integrated matrix of observations.

With such a matrix, the researcher can answer a number of questions involving the potentially interrelated influences of cohort, age, and time. Referring to Table 18.3 and Figure 18.3, for example,

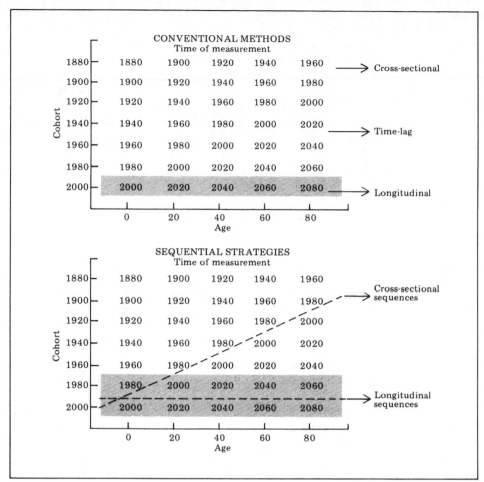

FIGURE 18.2
Illustration of simple cross-sectional, longitudinal, and time-lag designs (*top*) and cross-sectional and longitudinal sequences (*bottom*).

Source: Baltes, Reese, and Nesselroade (1977).

TABLE 18.3
The Design of a Sequential Study

Birth cohort	Time of measurement 1	Age at time 1	Time of measurement 2	Age at time 2	Time of measurement 3	Age at time 3	Time of measurement of retest control group	Age of control group
1957	1970	13	1971	14	1972	15	1972	15
1956	1970	14	1971	15	1972	16	1972	16
1955	1970	15	1971	16	1972	17	1972	17
1954	1970	16	1971	17	1972	18	1972	18

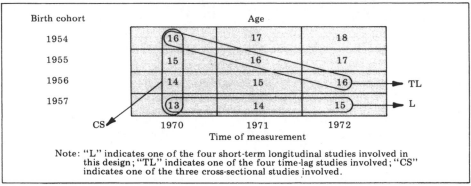

FIGURE 18.3
The design of a sequential study put into the form of a matrix.

if the cohort composed of people born in 1955 underwent changes between Times of Measurement 1 and 2 and were found to be different at age 16 from the people in the 1954 cohort group when they were 16, then there must be some historical difference between these two cohort levels. In other words, if differences are due simply to age-related changes, then people of the same age should perform the same no matter what cohort they are from or when they are measured. A younger cohort group should perform similarly to an older cohort group as members of each group age, if there are no historical differences between cohorts and if time of testing does not matter. Again, from Table 18.3 and Figure 18.2, the 1957 cohort should show a level of performance on its second measurement comparable to that of the first measurement for the 1956 cohort *if* there are no historical differences between the generations.

In turn, if time of testing were a source of change, then people should respond the same despite their age or cohort. If events in 1972 were the strongest influence on behavior, then one should see that people of all cohorts represented in Table 18.3 and Figure 18.3 respond the same way.

Finally, of course, if birth cohorts were of most importance, then people of a particular cohort should respond in a given way no matter what age they are and no matter at what time they are measured. As illustrated by the example of children born in the Great Depression (Elder, 1974, 1988, 1999), membership in a particular cohort would override influences due to age or time of measurement.

In addition, it should be mentioned that by including groups of participants to be tested for the first time at the end of the study (see Table 18.3), sequential researchers provide a way to judge the effects of repeated use of the measuring instruments, noted earlier. If participants in the core sample did not respond differently as a consequence of their having been repeatedly measured (e.g., by the same personality or IQ tests), then their behavior at the end of the study should be comparable to a group of participants matched with them in every way except for the fact that no repeated testing was given. If there are differences, however, between the core sample and these "retest" controls, then there are statistical techniques available to researchers to measure the effects of retesting (Nesselroade & Baltes, 1974).

Despite the complexity of data analysis and the more complex research design and reasoning process associated with it, the sequential approach has advantages not associated with other techniques. It allows for the unconfounding of the age, time, and cohort components of developmental change in one descriptive effort. As such, it allows the contributions of variables associated with multiple levels of influence to be evaluated adequately.

In fact, although sequential research studies are relatively few in number, one such study may be presented here in order to illustrate the use of sequential designs for assessments of development. Indeed, the design illustrated in Table 18.3 and Figure 18.3 was used because it corresponds to the one used by Nesselroade and Baltes (1974) in their sequential study of adolescent personality development.

A Sequential Study of Adolescent Personality Development

Noting that most conceptions of adolescent personality development suggest that age-related progressions are influential in this period of life,

Nesselroade and Baltes (1974) argued that historical (cohort) and specific sociocultural (time) influences may also be involved. As such, they applied longitudinal sequential methodology to see how these three components contributed to changes in personality in the period from 1970 to 1972.

About 1,800 West Virginia male and female adolescents were measured in 1970, 1971, and 1972. These adolescents were from birth cohorts 1954 to 1957, and thus—as in Table 18.3 and Figure 18.3—ranged in age at the time of first measurement from 13 to 16 years of age. Personality questionnaires and measures of intelligence were administered to these participants.

Contrary to what is stressed by those theorists who focus on personological components of adolescent development (e.g., Anna Freud, 1969), Nesselroade and Baltes found that change at this time of life was quite responsive to sociocultural–historical influences. In fact, age by itself was not found to be a very influential contributor to change. Rather, for these groups of adolescents, developmental change was influenced more by cultural changes over the 2-year historical period than by age-related sequences.

For instance, adolescents as a whole, despite their age or birth cohort, decreased in "superego strength," "social–emotional anxiety," and achievement during the 1970 to 1972 period. Moreover, most adolescents, regardless of age or cohort, increased in independence during this period.

Accordingly, the Nesselroade and Baltes (1974) data show that it was the time at which all these differently aged adolescents were measured that was most influential in their changes. Perhaps due to the events in society of that time (e.g., events associated with the Vietnam War) all adolescents performed similarly in regard to these personality characteristics. Despite where they were developmentally (in regard to age) upon "entering" the 1970 to 1972 historical era, members of different cohorts changed in similar directions, due presumably to events surrounding them at the times they were tested.

Without sequential methodology, the importance of the specific sociocultural setting at that time could not have been suggested. This implication is supported by data obtained from other sequential studies that have shown the influence of birth cohort on intellectual development in children (Baltes, Baltes, & Reinert, 1970) and adults (Schaie, Labouvie, & Buech, 1973). Consistent with developmental systems notions, these data suggest that to understand developmental change, one should consider the relation among individual and sociocultural–historical processes.

Conclusions

We have seen that there are several ways in which to design developmental research and that each type of design has both methodological assets and limitations. Indeed, I have made a similar point in regard to any study of development, located at any point along each of the four dimensions of developmental research we have discussed in this chapter; that is, any particular method has both some uses *and* some limitations.

However, in addition to such method-specific problems, we should note that all developmental studies have the danger of being biased or faulty if certain general issues of method are not confronted and dealt with. These issue may involve how the actual data of the study are obtained. Whereas certain data collection procedures may be appropriate, others may yield data with serious problems of interpretation. If one collects data in wrong or biased ways, little confidence may be placed in such data; such data will be of little use to science. Hence, although all research has methodological problems that must be recognized and dealt with, there are some methodological issues of particular relevance to developmental psychological research.

These methodological problems of developmental research—also reviewed by McCandless (1970)—caution us about the many safeguards that must be taken to ensure that the data give as accurate a representation as possible of the facts of development. If these potential methodological problems are recognized and successfully dealt with, the researcher will have confidence not only in the accuracy of the data but also in the interpretations drawn from them. Let us turn, then, to some of the important methodological problems of developmental research.

SOME GENERAL METHODOLOGICAL PROBLEMS OF DEVELOPMENTAL RESEARCH

McCandless (1970) detailed several of the prominent methodological problems of developmental research. The first one he noted is contamination.

Contamination

When data are contaminated, they are influenced by variables other than those being studied. That is, the results of the study may not solely be due to the actual relations among the variables investigated. Contamination may occur in several ways.

In some studies, participants are tested successively, one after the other. If one participant reveals the intent of the study to a succeeding participant, or in some way tells the later participant what to expect, this revelation might influence the second participant's responses. If the second participant's behavior is influenced by this information, then his or her responses would not solely be due to the variables being studied.

Researchers also may contaminate their own data. Suppose a researcher believes that there is a relationship between an adolescent's body type and his or her personality or temperament. To test this belief, the researcher might develop a method to rate body type and temperament. However, it is possible that, if the researcher him- or herself does both of these ratings for all the participants, any relation discovered between body type and temperament might be contaminated by the researcher's hypothesis about this relationship.

To illustrate this possibility, the work of William Sheldon (1940, 1942) may be noted. Sheldon developed a theory relating a person's type of physique to the person's temperament. He specified that there are three essential components of body build and that it is possible to characterize the body in terms of their relative contributions. Thus, some people are predominantly fat—their bodies are composed essentially of adipose (fat) tissue. Other people's bodies are composed mainly of muscle and bone tissue—they have athletic-looking bodies. Finally, still other people's bodies are essentially composed of neither fat nor muscle tissue but of nervous-system tissue—such a body build would appear thin and linear.

Sheldon also specified that certain types of temperament go along with each of these three body types. He then devised ways to measure the body builds and temperaments of his participants (4,000 Harvard University male undergraduates). However, Sheldon himself performed both of these sets of measurements. He rated body build and then, even though he knew the hypothesized relation between body build and temperament, he rated temperament. Thus, there is the strong possibility that the high relation Sheldon found between these two sets of ratings was contaminated.

Of course, Sheldon did not intentionally set out to contaminate his ratings. Such errors may often occur among well-trained but perhaps unvigilant researchers. Hence, researchers must take precautions to ensure that their research participants' responses are not affected by anything extraneous to the research situation. Furthermore, the relations found among their data should not be influenced by their own hypotheses. In science, a question should not determine the answer.

Researcher Effects on Subject Responses

Another related type of methodological problem involving the researcher occurs when the investigator unintentionally affects the responses of his or her participants. These researcher effects have been investigated by Rosenthal (1966), who suggested that such errors may play an important part in much research.

Suppose one wants to conduct a study of the attitudes of European American adolescents toward African American people and chooses to use the interview method. Each adolescent sits alone with the researcher in a small cubicle to conduct the interview. If the interviewer were African American, he or she might get verbal responses from the respondents that are different from what might be obtained if he or she were European American. European-American adolescents may be more candid about expressing any hostile or negative racial attitudes when interviewed by a European-American person than when interviewed by a African-American person. Thus, in this example, the researcher's race might affect the answers of the respondent.

Another, perhaps more subtle, example of the researcher affecting participants' responses may be seen in the following illustration. Suppose a researcher wants to study the differential effects of a particular type of instructional technique on students who do below-average schoolwork and students who do above-average schoolwork. Obviously, the researcher would want to control everything in the research situation that might conceivably affect the participants' responses. Thus, beside the fact that one group is slow learning and the other fast learning, all other between-group factors should be equivalent. Yet, it is possible that the researcher may unknowingly interact with the two groups in different ways. For instance, the researcher may spend more time presenting the instructional technique to one group than the other, or he or she might be warmer with one group than with the other. Such actions would mean that the conditions between the two groups are not, in fact, identical and that, if differences between the groups are found, they might reasonably be due to the differential effects of the researcher's different behaviors toward the two groups.

Although it is difficult to determine when such researcher effects enter into the participants' responses, the developmental researcher should always be aware of the potential of such bias, and should design the method of the study with safeguards. For instance, in the example of the racial attitude study, the researcher might want to use two interviewers, one African American and one European American, in order to control and test for any possible biasing effects introduced by the race of the researcher. In the second example, a standardized presentation of the instructional techniques might be given, perhaps through the use of a videotape.

Reconstruction Through Retrospection

There are many ways to obtain information about the events that characterize people's development. In Chapter 15, the method used by Freud (1949) was discussed. By asking his adult neurotic patients to recall the events of their early childhood, Freud reconstructed their developmental histories. However, it was noted that such a method has a strong potential for introducing serious problems into one's data. Events may be recalled incorrectly, partially forgotten, distorted, or even lied about. However, there is usually no way to check on these distortions. With the retrospective method, the actual events and interactions are not being observed empirically, but are merely being reconstructed through use of a subjective verbal account.

Thus, when one reconstructs the past developmental history of a person through retrospection—by having the respondent look back on his or her life and recall previous events—one is using a subjective, and perhaps distorted, account of developmental history. Hence, the reconstruction-through-retrospection method is a limited way of obtaining information about the events that characterize people's development. Because the data collected through this method may be inaccurate, and because it is difficult to determine the level of inaccuracy, theories and inferences drawn on the basis of such information may have limitations.

However, in Chapter 17, we saw an example of another way of obtaining information about the events that characterize people's development— the prospective-construction method used by Thomas and colleagues (1963) in their longitudinal study of the development of temperament. In this method, behavior is measured at or about the very time it occurs. Hence, any constructions or representations of the course of development are based on reports of behavior as it is currently developing. Thus, this prospective method offers more useful

empirical data whose accuracy may be objectively verified; for example, the correspondence between the verbal reports and behavioral observations can be examined.

Faulty Logic

Another important problem in developmental research is presented when the investigator uses faulty reasoning techniques in interpreting data. In fact, such faulty reasoning may actually influence the design of the study itself and the method used to collect data.

Although faulty logic is by no means unique to developmental research, it does play an all-too-prominent role in such investigations. The potential problem may be illustrated by offering the following syllogism:

1. Boats float on water.

2. X is floating on water.

3. X is a boat.

Obviously, this is an example of faulty logic. On the basis of the initial premise, one cannot exclude the possibility that things other than boats float on water; thus, it is not logical to conclude that just because X floats on water, X is a boat. However, if one asserts that boats *and only* boats float on water, then it *would* follow from this premise that X is a boat.

Although it is clear that the first syllogism is not logical, it is possible to just alter the words of the syllogism (the content) and leave the structure of the logic (or lack of logic) intact. Thus, a second syllogism might be:

1. Infants deprived of their mother's breast milk in the first year of life overeat at age 15.

2. John, a 15-year-old, overeats.

3. Therefore, John was deprived of his mother's breast milk during the first year of his life.

Clearly, this conclusion also does not follow from the premise. There may be sources of overeating among 15-year-olds other than breast milk deprivation. Yet, when this logically faulty syllogism is cast in terms of developmental events between mother and child, it somehow all too often acquires an air of believability. The assertion that John's overeating is due to (unseen) breast milk deprivation in the first year of life is as lacking in logic as the syllogism concerning X being a boat.

Perhaps, one reason for such faulty logic in developmental research is that development per se deals with sequential or time-ordered events. There may be the belief that *post hoc ergo propter hoc,* "after the fact, therefore because of the fact." That is, when events occur sequentially, there may be a tendency to infer that if B happens after A, then A must be a source of B. However, such inferences also rest on faulty logic. If a traumatic event occurs early in a person's development, and years later some neurotic disorder emerges, it is simply not logical to assert that the trauma was *the* source—or even *a* source—of the later neuroticism. Although such a relation might actually exist, the mere fact that the trauma was followed by the neuroticism does not represent a logically necessary reason for the conclusion that the trauma is a source of the neuroticism. The neuroticism's emergence might have occurred in any event, and so, in general, it is merely an instance of faulty logic to assert that when one event follows another in development, the former is a source of the latter. Clearly, no one would reasonably assert that if he or she rose at 4:00 A.M. every day and then, with astonishing predictability, the sun rose just a few hours later, that his or her personal rising was the source of the sunrise. Yet, when similar faulty reasoning is couched in terms of sequential events that occur over the course of development, such lack of logic may all too often slip by unnoticed.

As previously noted, such faulty logic in interpretation of results may find its way into the methodological design of developmental research. A researcher may wish to ascertain the developmental source of a particular behavior. Thus, the researcher might collect data about events that occurred during the first few years of a child's life and relate this information to data collected at a later time in the child's life. If a relation between these early and later measures is found—perhaps expressed in terms of a correlation coefficient—the researcher might infer that the early behavior provided a source of the later behavior. Yet, we have seen that sufficient information was not obtained to make this inference logically necessary.

A related logical problem involved in developmental research occurs in regard to what are termed *follow-up* versus *follow-back* designs. The former design is also termed a *prospective design* (as illustrated by the Thomas and colleagues, 1963, study procedures) and the latter design is also termed a *retrospective design.*

In a follow-back design, a researcher identifies a contemporaneous instance of behavior among a sample and tries to ascertain whether the members of the sample had some common, earlier experience. For example, suppose a researcher finds that, among 100 men incarcerated for sexually violent crimes, all had been physically abused in the first 5 years of life. If the researcher concludes, therefore, that early abuse is an general antecedent (e.g., a cause) of later sexual violence, he or she is making a logical error.

Follow-back (retrospective) data do not reveal how many people who have an experience at one point in development show a given behavior at a later time in life. Such data are provided through follow-up (prospective) designs. For instance, in such a design, children who experience early physical abuse would be followed to adulthood, and the proportion of abused children who eventually became incarcerated for sexual violence would be determined. It is not logical to assume that, because most men incarcerated for sexual violence were abused as children, that as a consequence most men who were abused as children end up as people who commit sexually violent acts.

As another instance of the lack of logic that may occur with follow-back designs, we may note that all people who end up with Ph.D. degrees graduated from high school at an earlier point in their lives. However, not all people who graduate from high school go on to earn a Ph.D. degree.

In sum, throughout this book we have pointed out instances of faulty logic used in relation to the concepts and theories of development we have been discussing. Our discussions of the concept of heritability (in Chapters 10 and 11) and the notion of instinct (in Chapter 12) indicated how some developmentalists often use faulty logic in their discussions of these topics. Accordingly, the student of human development must be aware of this problem and be ready to recognize such faulty logic when it occurs.

Inadequate Definition of Concepts

This problem pertains to how researchers define and measure the concepts they are investigating. A *concept* is a term used to represent some aspect of the physical or social world. Concepts, of course, may be more or less abstract. Thus, a concept used to represent such things as cars, wagons, and trains—that is, the concept of vehicle—might be considered relatively concrete. The empirical referents of the concept (whatever is being referred to) are generally understood. Other relatively concrete concepts might be animal, body, or height. Yet, not all concepts are similarly concrete. Some concepts do not have commonly understood empirical referents. Thus, when psychologists use concepts such as aggression, learning, or personality, it is absolutely necessary that they specify precisely what they mean. Then, anyone interested in the researcher's work, will know exactly what is meant by the use of a term. If such *operational definitions* are not used, however, considerable communication problems may result. Two different researchers may be studying the same phenomenon, but if they define and measure it differently, their results may not be comparable. If they do not communicate these different meanings clearly, this lack of comparability may never be recognized.

For example, suppose a researcher is interested in studying the "generation gap." What exactly does the term mean? On a simple level, one may suppose that it refers to a set of differences that allegedly exist between young people and their parents. But this definition is not sufficient because it does not specify what the differences are. Are the differences referred to by this term differences in the physical appearances of the generational groups (e.g., in their respective styles of dress and hair lengths)? Or, does one mean divisions between the generations in their support for radical political causes? Or, does one mean differences between the generations in attitudes about such issues as drug use, sexual behavior, and racism?

If researchers anchor their concepts in precise, empirical terms, considerable confusion may be avoided. For example, in the aforementioned example of learning under conditions of music versus quiet, learning was operationalized through the ability to memorize a list of information. The results of such research may not be applicable to learning operationalized in regard to ability to solve math problems, crossword puzzles, verbal analogies, or other tasks of cognitive functioning.

However, as long as researchers take pains to define clearly what they mean by their use of any concept and design their study with such clear definitions in mind, any confusion about the use of the same term to represent different things may be eliminated. To a great extent, researchers may define things as they wish, as long as they anchor their definitions in understandable, empirical referents. Once this is done, any possible differences in what is meant by a particular concept may be recognized and understood.

Sampling

Another methodological problem deals with obtaining participants for developmental research

and making inferences about development based on results from a particular sample. If one wants to do a study of the racial attitudes of European-American and African-American 5-year-olds, one obviously needs groups of European-American and African-American 5-year-olds to study. The procedures used to obtain such samples will affect the conclusions one can appropriately make from the data.

Ideally, one might like to measure the attitudes of all such children. However, this is clearly an economic and practical impossibility. Therefore, the researcher must often draw a sample from the larger population, that is, a group of persons from the population that may feasibly be studied. Through the study of this sample, the researcher hopes to obtain results that can be generalized to the entire population.

Thus, the researcher must be sure that the sample used is representative of the entire population. If the sample is not representative, if it is *biased,* then he or she may not appropriately infer that results obtained with the sample are characteristic of the entire population. For example, if the researcher conducting a study of racial attitudes among 5-year-old African Americans and European Americans chooses as his or her sample European-American and African-American children from a small, southern, United States city, then it would be inappropriate to infer that such children were representative of all European-American or African-American children living elsewhere.

Standard procedures are available for obtaining unbiased samples. With *probability sampling,* all persons in the population have a known, nonzero chance of falling in the sample. In *nonprobability sampling,* not everyone in the population of interest may have a chance of being sampled.

There are three types of probability sampling. In *simple random sampling,* everyone in the population has an equal chance of being selected. Drawing names from a hat and using a computer to generate random selections are examples of simple random sampling.

Stratified sampling involves proportionately dividing the population according to the categories of a variable of interest, and then randomly sampling from within those categories. For example, if race is an important variable in the study and only 10% of the population is African American, then one would obtain only one African-American respondent for every nine European American respondents, using simple random sampling techniques. By using stratified sampling, one could choose equal numbers of African Americans and

European Americans for comparison, even though their numbers in the population were different.

The third type of probability sampling is *cluster* (or *area*) *sampling*. This technique involves dividing a state (e.g., into areas). First, areas (e.g., counties) are sampled, then areas within these areas (e.g., towns) are sampled again. Then, after a specified number of towns have been sampled, individuals or households within the towns may be sampled further. Thus, a statewide study could be conducted by sending observers or interviewers to only a few communities.

There are also three types of nonprobability sampling. *Availability* samples are often used in research in human development, and, unfortunately, they do not necessarily allow for great generalization. Availability sampling involves using whoever is available for the research—whoever is around and volunteers to participate.

Judgmental (or *purposive*) *sampling* is similar, except that the researcher chooses participants who fit a specific definition for the study. If, for example, the researcher wanted to study contraceptive use among adolescent females, he or she might look specifically for sexually active females between the ages of 14 and 18. There would be no guarantee, however, that the girls found would be representative of others.

Quota sampling, the third type of nonprobability sampling, involves the selection of individuals on the basis of whether they can be used to fill a predetermined quota that is set up to represent the population in question. For example, the researcher might want to do a national study without the great expense associated with probability samples. He or she might try to construct a sample that appears to be representative of the nation as a whole by establishing quotas of certain numbers of African Americans and European Americans; Jews, Protestants, and Roman Catholics; males and females; the college-educated and those with high school educations or less; and married and unmarried adults. Any person can be selected for the sample as long as he or she fills the quota. The sampling ends when all the quotas have been met, and those selected are then studied. This method is often used by national polling organizations and can be quite accurate, even though it is a nonprobability method.

However, although such procedures are well known to all researchers, it is still often the case that studies are done with knowingly biased, unrepresentative samples. Why? To answer this question, we must recognize that there are often ethical, economic, and practical problems that interfere with the researcher's desire to obtain a truly representative, unbiased sample. For example, it should be obvious that not all 5-year-old African-American and European-American children are available for the researcher to sample form. The researcher is located in a particular part of the country, and only children living in that area are usually potentially available for study. Even then, however, not all these children may be available. School authorities may not want or be able to allow a researcher to enter the school to study the children there. Even if a school does cooperate, all the appropriately aged children in that school may not be available for study.

In any human development study, the researcher is ethically bound to obtain the informed consent of those responsible for the child to study the child. Usually, then, the parents will have to be fully informed of the intent of the study in terms that they are capable of understanding (i.e., the researcher may not relate the purpose of the study in highly technical and complex terms, incomprehensible to the average layperson); the parents must then give their consent for their child's participation. In this way, the researcher is taking one necessary step to ensure that the rights and safety of the participants are not being violated. Of course, although other such steps must be taken (e.g., the researcher may not do a study that he or she even suspects will in any way harm the child), the fact that only volunteer participants may be used limits the representativeness of any sample. In other words, only some population strata will be even potentially available for any researcher to study; only some groups of children will be potentially available within those strata; and only some children will be available within those groups.

Of course, a good researcher will still apply appropriate sampling techniques even within such an unrepresentative sample. Yet, because of the seemingly inescapable sampling problems involved in developmental research, any researcher must be aware that any inferences made on the basis of results obtained with such samples are limited. We saw that there were important sampling problems in the Kagan and Moss (1962) longitudinal study (Chapter 16), the Thomas and colleagues (1963) New York Longitudinal Study (Chapter 17), and the research reported by Block (1971) in the *Lives Through Time* monograph (Chapter 17), which limited the generalizations that could be made from the respective data sets.

Thus, sampling is always a problem in developmental research. The investigator must always be aware of these problems of sampling, and in fact, because of absolutely necessary ethical restrictions—imposed on developmental researchers by themselves—more sampling problems are introduced. For instance, the ethical standards for research with children that have been developed by the Society for Research in Child Development represent a significant instance of such rules of conduct. These ethical principles are presented in Table 18.4.

In sum, the results of any developmental study are limited to the extent that biased sampling procedures interfere with obtaining a representative sample. Accordingly, the results of any such study may be generalized to such broader populations only with extreme caution. Thus, because of methodological problems of sampling, the researcher always encounters a related problem—that of generalization.

Overgeneralization

It may be concluded that if limitations imposed on developmental research by sampling are not recognized, the researcher may try to interpret the study's results as being more representative than they actually are. As noted by McCandless (1970), there are other types of overgeneralization. The results of a particular study might indicate that there exist small but reliable differences between two groups. Yet, the researcher may speak of the differences as if they reflected wide disparities between the groups. If such statements occur, one may also term this *overgeneralization.*

For instance, suppose that a particular researcher is interested in the attitudes that adolescent males and females maintain about their own bodies. To study such body concepts, the researcher might ask a large group of adolescent males and females to rate several body characteristics (e.g., arms, legs, face, body build, height, and general appearance) in terms of how important each is in determining the personal satisfaction with his or her body's appearance (e.g., Lerner, Karabenick, & Stuart, 1973). Now suppose that female adolescents have a mean importance rating for the face of 4.20 (on a 5-point scale, with 5.0 being extremely important), and the corresponding rating for the male adolescents is 3.95. Because of the fact that many adolescents' responses went into the calculation of these means, and, thus, that only small differences are needed for statistically significant differences to occur, the researcher might find that such a small difference between males and females is noteworthy. However, such *statistical* significance may not correspond to *psychological* significance. Can one say that on the basis of only a 0.25 point difference (out of a possible 4-point difference) this one aspect of adolescent females' body concept is considerably different from adolescent males' body concept? Probably not, and in fact, if such an assertion were made, it might be seen as an instance of overgeneralization.

Other types of overgeneralization also exist. Suppose that, in the previous study, the researcher is also interested in learning what parts of the male body are most important to females in deciding that a male is attractive, and what parts of the female body are most important to males in deciding that a female is attractive. The researcher can again ask the adolescent males and females to rate each of the body parts, but this time in terms of its importance for establishing the attractiveness of the opposite sex. Suppose that it is found that females rate general appearance as the most important characteristic of the male's body in determining male attractiveness, whereas males rate the face as the most important part of the female's body in determining a female's attractiveness. Would the researcher be justified in concluding that when adolescent males go about choosing a female for a dating partner they make their judgments on the basis of the female's face, and that when females choose a male dating partner they make their judgments on the basis of the male's general appearance? May these ratings be generalized to choice of partners in dating situations? Because the findings of the study pertain to ratings obtained about females and males in general, not about choices of dating partners, such a generalization would appear unwarranted.

As McCandless indicated, "applying findings gathered in one situation to circumstances different in essential characteristics" is an instance of unsound generalization (1970, p. 55). Whenever one applies specific results to situations that may be different in important ways, one is guilty of overgeneralization.

To avoid unsound overgeneralization, researchers must be wary of attempting to (a) extend their results to situations different from those actually beared on by their data, (b) attribute more meaning, clarity, or significance to their results than are actually indicated, and (c) apply their findings to groups of people not actually represented in their sample (McCandless, 1970). The human development researcher must also recognize that because of sampling, situational, and, thus, interpretational problems, the body of existing knowledge in the discipline may not be applicable to many groups of people. The "facts" of development, obtained through considerable research work, may in any event not be reflective of the "facts" for all people.

TABLE 18.4
Ethical Standards for Research With Children

Principle 1. Non-harmful procedures: The investigator should use no research procedure that may harm the child either physically or psychologically. The investigator is also obligated at all times to use the least stressful research procedure whenever possible. Psychological harm in particular instances may be difficult to define; nevertheless, its definition and means for reducing or eliminating it remain the responsibility of the investigator. When the investigator is in doubt about the possible harmful effects of the research procedures, consultation should be sought from others. When harm seems inevitable, the investigator is obligated to find other means of obtaining the information or to abandon the research. Instances may, nevertheless, rise in which exposing the child to stressful conditions may be necessary if diagnostic or therapeutic benefits to the child are associated with the research. In such instances careful deliberation by an Institutional Review Board should be sought.

Principle 2. Informed consent: Before seeking consent or assent from the child, the investigator should inform the child of all features of the research that may affect his or her willingness to participate and should answer the child's questions in terms appropriate to the child's comprehension. The investigator should respect the child's freedom to choose to participate in the research or not by giving the child the opportunity to give or not give assent to participation as well as to choose to discontinue participation at any time. Assent means that the child shows some form of agreement to participate without necessarily comprehending the full significance of the research necessary to give informed consent. Investigators working with infants should take special effort to explain the research procedures to the parents and be especially sensitive to any indicators of discomfort in the infant. In spite of the paramount importance of obtaining consent, instances can arise in which consent or any kind of contact with the participant would make the research impossible to carry out. Non-intrusive field research is a common example. Conceivably, such research can be carried out ethically if it is conducted in public places, participants' anonymity is totally protected, and there are no foreseeable negative consequences to the participant. However, judgments on whether such research is ethical in particular circumstances should be made in consultation with an Institutional Review Board.

Principle 3. Parental consent: The informed consent of parents, legal guardians or those who act *in loco parentis* (e.g., teachers, superintendents of institutions) similarly should be obtained, preferably in writing. Informed consent requires that parents or other responsible adults be informed of all the features of the research that may affect their willingness to allow the child to participate. This information should include the profession and institution affiliation of the investigator. Not only should the right of the responsible adults to refuse consent be respected, but also they should be informed that they may refuse to participate without incurring any penalty to them or to the child.

Principle 4. Additional consent: The informed consent of any persons, such as schoolteachers for example, whose interaction with the child is the subject of the study should also be obtained. As with the child and parents or guardians informed consent requires that the persons interacting with the child during the study be informed of all features of the research which may affect their willingness to participate. All questions posed by such persons should be answered and the persons should be free to choose to participate or not, and to discontinue participation at any time.

Principle 5. Incentives: Incentives to participate in a research project must be fair and must not unduly exceed the range of incentives that the child normally experiences. Whatever incentives are used, the investigator should always keep in mind that the greater the possible effects of the investigation on the child, the greater is the obligation to protect the child's welfare and freedom.

Principle 6. Deception: Although full disclosure of information during the procedure of obtaining consent is the ethical ideal, a particular study may necessitate withholding certain information or deception. Whenever withholding information or deception is judged to be essential to the conduct of the study, the investigator should satisfy research colleagues that such judgment is correct. If withholding information or deception is practiced, and there is reason to believe that the research participants will be negatively affected by it, adequate measures should be taken after the study to ensure the participant's understanding of the reasons for the deception. Investigators whose research is dependent upon deception should make an effort to employ deception methods that have no known negative effects on the child or the child's family.

(continues)

TABLE 18.4
(continued)

Principle 7. Anonymity: To gain access to institutional records, the investigator should obtain permission from responsible authorities in charge of records. Anonymity of the information should be preserved and no information used other than that for which permission was obtained. It is the investigator's responsibility to ensure that responsible authorities do, in fact, have the confidence of the participant and that they bear some degree of responsibility in giving such permission.

Principle 8. Mutual responsibilities: From the beginning of each research investigation, there should be clear agreement between the investigator and the parents, guardians or those who *act in loco parentis,* and the child, when appropriate, that defines the responsibilities of each. The investigator has the obligation to honor all promises and commitments of the agreement.

Principle 9. Jeopardy: When, in the course of research, information comes to the investigator's attention that may jeopardize the child's well-being, the investigator has a responsibility to discuss the information with the parents or guardians and with those expert in the field in order that they may arrange the necessary assistance for the child.

Principle 10. Unforeseen consequences: When research procedures result in undesirable consequences for the participant that were previously unforeseen, the investigator should immediately employ appropriate measures to correct these consequences, and should redesign the procedures if they are to be included in subsequent studies.

Principle 11. Confidentiality: The investigator should keep in confidence all information obtained about research participants. The participants' identity should be concealed in written and verbal reports of the results, as well as in informal discussion with students and colleagues. When a possibility exists that others may gain access to such information, this possibility, together with the plans for protecting confidentiality, should be explained to the participants as part of the procedure of obtaining informed consent.

Principle 12. Informing participants: Immediately after the data are collected, the investigator should clarify for the research participant any misconceptions that may have arisen. The investigator also recognizes a duty to report general findings to participants in terms appropriate to their understanding. Where scientific or humane values justify withholding information, every effort should be made so that withholding the information has no damaging consequences for the participant.

Principle 13. Reporting results: Because the investigator's words may carry unintended weight with parents and children, caution should be exercised in reporting results, making evaluative statements, or giving advice.

Principle 14. Implications of findings: Investigators should be mindful of the social, political and human implications of their research and should be especially careful in the presentation of findings from the research. This principle, however, in no way denies investigators the right to pursue any area of research or the right to observe proper standards of scientific reporting.

Principle 15. Scientific misconduct: Misconduct is defined as the fabrication or falsification of data, plagiarism, misrepresentation, or other practices that seriously deviate from those that are commonly accepted within the scientific community for proposing, conducting, analyzing, or reporting research. It does not include unintentional errors or honest differences in interpretation of data.

The Society shall provide vigorous leadership in the pursuit of scientific investigation that is based on the integrity of the investigator and the honesty of research and will not tolerate the presence of scientifc misconduct among its members. It shall be the responsibility of the voting members of Governing Council to reach a decision about the possible expulsion of members found guilty of scientific misconduct.

Principle 16. Personal misconduct: Personal misconduct that results in a criminal conviction of a felony may be sufficient grounds for a member's expulsion from the Society. The relevance of the crime to the purposes of the Society should be considered by the Governing Council in reaching a decision about the matter. It shall be the responsibility of the voting members of Governing Council to reach a decision about the possible expulsion of members found guilty of personal misconduct.

Note. From the *Society for Research in Child Development Directory of Members, 1999–2000,* pp. 283–284. Ann Arbor, MI: Society for Research in Child Development.

For example, due both to an intense interest in studying child development and the difficulty of readily obtaining samples of children to study, many university and other research institutions set up laboratory schools in the early decades of the twentieth century. Many of the "facts" of development (at that time, mostly "normative facts") were obtained through the study of children at these schools. Yet, in many cases, these children were often the children of the university faculty or the personnel of the institute. Hence, they were primarily European-American, middle-class children of highly educated parents. Certainly, although the "facts" of development of such children are important, these "facts" may not be generalizable to all other children. Most children do not have parents who are professors or researchers. Many children are not European American, and many children do not come from middle-class backgrounds. Thus, the "facts" of development derived from such samples may be highly biased and unrepresentative. Bronfenbrenner (1977, 1979) made a similar point.

In recognition of this problem, research in human development over the few decades has focused increasingly on other populations (Fisher, Jackson, & Villarruel, 1998). Hence, the field of human development is today increasingly moving away from being a area of scholarship focused only on European-American, middle-class children of highly educated parents. Studies of diverse groups of people are being conducted in an attempt to broaden the basis of our knowledge of development in all strata of society (McLoyd, 1998; Spencer & Dornbusch, 1990). Moreover, the increase of scope has not been limited to diverse people in one nation (e.g., the United States). There is growing theoretical and empirical attention to the need to study other societal and cultural settings (e.g., see Shweder et al., 1998). The facts of development found in one nation may not be generalizable to the development of people in all countries, and, hence, there is a need for and a growing concern with cross-cultural studies of development.

Conclusions

As research broadens to embrace the diversity of people and their contexts, the field of human development will move toward providing a body of knowledge about the development of all people. Thus, as research in human development focuses increasingly on the diversity of human life and, as well, pursues the longitudinal study of people with rigorous methods that are able to depict with veridicality the changing relations between individuals and their contexts, the "job" of de-

velopmental scholars—which is already quite complex—will become even more difficult.

Moreover, if such scholarship is conducted within a frame provided by developmental systems theory, then the developmental researcher must be able to collaborate across disciplines and, in turn, with members of communities outside of higher education. Indeed, and specially from a developmental systems perspective, the developmental researcher must be able to synthesize basic and applied foci of research into his or her scholarly agenda.

It is accurate to say that, at this writing, many contemporary developmental researchers, although subscribing to such an approach to scholarship (e.g., Lerner, 1998a), see future generations of human development scientists as more likely than members of their own cohort of scholars to have the capacity to fully pursue such integrative and collaborative careers (Lerner & Fisher, 1994). Indeed, for this reason, there is great interest among current researchers in human development in training—educating—the next generation of developmental scholars (e.g., Fisher, Murray, & Sigel, 1996; Ralston et al., 1999).

FROM RESEARCH TO TRAINING

At this writing, few scholars have been trained in both the basic and applied dimensions of human developmental science. However, not only does the developmental systems theoretical frame suggest the importance of such training (Fisher & Lerner, 1994; Lerner & Fisher, 1994) but also there is obviously a compelling societal need for policies and programs predicated on sound knowledge of human development. Accordingly, it is important to discuss some of the issues that must be addressed in order to create cohorts of human developmental scholars prepared to address the scholarly *and* societal issues pertinent to understanding and enhancing human development across the life span.

Building on our discussion in prior chapters of the developmental systems theoretical bases for the study of human development, I believe that training in human developmental science must inculcate the ability to empirically identify—to validly and reliably measure—change in the person–context system. At a *minimum,* such expertise requires knowledge of:

1. Classical versus developmental issues in test theory, and techniques pertinent to establishing measurement equivalence across both person and contextual variables.

2. The concepts of external and internal validity and of convergent and divergent validation.

3. Strategies for triangulation within and across both quantitative and qualitative methods.

4. Multivariate versus univariate conceptions and analyses of change.

5. The nature of developmentally sensitive, descriptive and explanatory, research designs aimed at generating observations pertinent either to the identification of general developmental trajectories or to specific developmental issues (e.g., partitioning developmental variance into cohort-, age-, or time-related influence).

6. Methods and data analytic techniques affording the identification of the fused contributions of heredity and environment to developmental change.

7. Methods and data analytic techniques affording the study of learning processes through the use of either group and/or individual approaches.

8. The nature of developmental explanation and the role of structural models and measurement models in the study of change.

9. Methodological issues of design and analysis pertinent to discriminating between intraindividual change and interindividual differences, especially in intraindividual change.

10. Ethical issues in developmental research, and the rights and responsibilities of the scholar—to his/her career, profession, discipline, institution, and community.

In addition, students need to gain experience in conducting a range of developmental research, involving different observational techniques (o.g., naturalistic and controlled observations; questionnaires, interviews, and surveys; and experimental–quasi-experimental studies) and alternative research designs (e.g., cross-sectional, longitudinal, and sequential). Students also need training in the development, management, and analysis of data sets pertinent to these research experiences. In addition, students need to gain experience in the publication/grant submission and peer review process. They need to be trained to write and submit research reports based on the studies they conduct; and they need to gain experience in revising and resubmitting their work for rereview (e.g., they

need to learn how to construct a letter to an editor—or a grant review panel—explaining how their revision responded to criticisms of an earlier draft). In turn, students need to gain experience as reviewers of others' work. Finally, students should be given an understanding of: (a) scholarly collaboration and coauthorship, (b) piecemeal publication and "careerism," (c) grantsmanship, (d) duties of authors, reviewers, and editors, (e) mentorship: faculty–student and senior faculty–junior faculty relationships, (f) diversity, and (g) community collaboration and outreach: conducting research that is relevant, durable, affordable, sustainable, feasible, and palatable to communities (Jensen, Hoagwood, & Trickett, 1999; see Chapter 19 for a fuller discussion of this point).

CONCLUSIONS

There are certainly other elements of methodological training that must be included within a program training human development scholars to conduct their science in a manner that furthers understanding of basic process and has value for application. Moreover, there are certainly several different ways in which each of the recommendations for training previously noted may be implemented.

However, despite how such training may be defined or pursued, in all training—and in all research—conducted in human development, care must be taken to treat the participants of research—youth, parents, other family members, and all people involved in the lives of research participants—in a humane, caring, and responsible manner. This requirement is the reason why ethical principles, such as those presented in Table 18.4, must be followed (Fisher, 1993, 1994, 1997; Fisher & Brennan, 1992; Fisher et al., 1995, 1996; Fisher & Fyrberg, 1994; Fisher, Hoagwood, & Jensen, 1996; Fisher & Tryon, 1990).

In addition, there is increasing acceptance of the view that developmental science must be devoted simultaneously to understanding and enhancing the life chances of all people. There is growing interest in developmental scientists using their research (methodological) abilities to devise means to apply developmental science in the service of promoting the positive development of individuals, families, and communities (Fisher et al., 1993; Fisher & Lerner, 1994; Lerner et al., 1999; Lerner, Fisher, & Weinberg, 2000a, 2000b). In short, there is a growing interest in applied developmental science. We discuss this facet of developmental scholarship in Chapter 19.

19 | *Applied Developmental Science*

. . . the very meaning of things known is wrapped up in relationships beyond themselves. Thus, unapplied knowledge is knowledge shorn of its meaning. Careful shielding of a university from the activities of the world around is the best way to chill interest and to defeat progress.

—Alfred North Whitehead (1936, p. 267)

The latter part of the twentieth century was marked by public anxiety about a myriad of social problems, some old, some new, but all affecting the lives of vulnerable children, adolescents, adults, families, and communities (Fisher & Murray, 1996; Lerner, 1995; Lerner & Galambos, 1998; Lerner, Sparks, & McCubbin, 1999). For instance, in America, a set of problems of historically unprecedented scope and severity emerged. These included issues of economic development, environmental quality, health and health care delivery, and, ultimately, of people—of children, youths, and families (e.g., involving poverty, crime, and violence; drug and alcohol use and abuse; unsafe sex; and school failure and dropout).

Indeed, in the latter portion of the twentieth century and into the present one, and across both the United States and in other nations, infants, children, adolescents, and the adults who cared for them continued to die—from war and criminal violence, drug and alcohol use and abuse, unsafe sex, and hunger and poor nutrition (Dryfoos, 1990; Hamburg, 1992; Hernandez, 1993; Huston, 1991; Lerner, 1995a; Lerner & Fisher, 1994; Schorr, 1988, 1997). And, if people were not dying, their life chances were being squandered—by civil unrest and ethnic conflict, famine, environmental challenges (e.g., involving water quality and solid waste management), school failure (including underachievement and dropout), crime, teenage pregnancy and parenting, lack of job opportunities and preparedness, prolonged welfare dependency, challenges to their health (e.g., lack of immunization,

inadequate screening for disabilities, insufficient prenatal care, and lack of sufficient infant and childhood medical services), and the sequelae of persistent and pervasive poverty (Dryfoos, 1990; Huston, 1991; Huston, McLoyd, & Garcia Coll, 1994; Lerner, 1995a; Lerner et al., 1999; Lerner & Fisher, 1994). These issues challenged the resources and the future viability of civil society in America and throughout the world (Lerner, Fisher, & Weinberg, 2000a, 2000b).

The potential role of scientific knowledge about human development in addressing these issues resulted in growing interest and activity in what has been termed *applied developmental science*. As articulated, for example, by scholars such as Celia B. Fisher (Fisher & Lerner, 1994a, 1994b), Richard A. Weinberg (e.g., Lerner, Fisher, & Weinberg, 1997, 2000a, 2000b), Lonnie R. Sherrod (e.g., 1999a, 1999b), Jacquelynne Eccles (1996), and Ruby Takanishi (1993), and as discussed in prior chapters (e.g., Chapter 18), applied developmental science (ADS) may be seen as scholarship that is predicated on a developmental systems theoretical perspective. ADS seeks to advance the integration of developmental research with actions that promote positive development and/or enhance the life chances of vulnerable children, adolescents, young and old adults, and their families. Given its roots in developmental systems theory, ADS challenges the usefulness of decontextualized knowledge and, as a consequence, the legitimacy of isolating scholarship from the pressing human problems of our world.

Researchers and the institutions within which they work (e.g., universities) are part of the developmental system, of the context, that ADS tries to understand and to enhance. As such, ADS emphasizes the importance of scholar/university–community partnerships as an essential means of contextualizing knowledge and, through the embedding of scholarship about human development within the diverse ecological (community) settings

Celia B. Fisher

Lonnie R. Sherrod

within which people develop, of fostering bidirectional relationships between research and practice. Within such relationships, developmental research both guides and is guided by the

Richard A. Weinberg

outcomes of community-based interventions (e.g., public policies or programs aimed at enhancing human development).

The people in the communities served by the work involved in ADS are certainly "experts" in the character of life in their neighborhoods and communities. Accordingly, in order to conduct research that is useful to community members, scholars and universities must engage the collaboration of these experts. That is, two "expert" systems—universities and communities—must work together to apply science in a manner that advances knowledge and, at the same time, is useful to and valued by people, as they live their lives in their actual families, schools, businesses, religious institutions, civic organizations, and communities. Universities and communities must learn together, then, how best to use their respective knowledge to enhance the course of human development.

However, such colearning is a process that is difficult to actualize. This difficulty occurs, in part, because faculty members and universities have not ordinarily possessed sufficient humility to learn from community members (Lerner & Simon, 1998a, 1998b). In addition, this difficulty occurs because the traditional model of higher education and faculty scholarship has not seen the knowledge possessed by communities as relevant to their own areas of expertise (Lerner & Simon, 1998a, 1998b).

American universities have been modeled on the nineteenth-century German university—wherein community-disengaged, independently working scholars pursued "ethereal" knowledge (i.e., knowledge that was seen as not contingent on the extant sociocultural context pertinent at a given historical moment; Lynton & Elman, 1987). Historically, the more decontextualized the knowledge, the higher its value (Bonnen, 1986, 1998).

However, across the world, contemporary intellectual and, as well, societal forces have been moving university scholars—whether they are in the role of teacher, researcher, and/or administrator—to consider ideas about the existence or validity of decontextualized knowledge, and about the legitimacy of the disciplinary and sociocultural isolation associated both with such knowledge and with research predicated on it. These issues have been discussed in diverse scholarly fields and have involved the elaboration of concepts related to developmental systems. As illustrated by discussions in prior chapters, examples of these discussions have occurred in:

1. The physical sciences—involving concepts such as quantum mechanics (Zukav, 1979), chaos (Gleick, 1987), and dissipative systems and entropy (Prigogine, 1978).

2. Evolutionary biology—involving concepts such as exaptation (Gould & Vrba, 1982), self-selection (Lewontin & Levins, 1978), and behavioral neophenotypes (Gottlieb, 1992).

3. The social and behavioral sciences—involving concepts such as individual–environment dialectics (Riegel, 1975, 1976a, 1976b, the ecology of human development (Bronfenbrenner, 1979; Bronfenbrenner & Morris, 1998), developmental systems (Ford & Lerner, 1992; Magnusson, 1999a 1999b; Sameroff, 1983; Thelen & Smith, 1998; Wapner & Demick, 1998), and the home economics–human ecology vision of integrative (community-collaborative, multidisciplinary, and multiprofessional) scholarship (Bubolz & Sontag, 1994; Lerner, De Stefanis, & Ladd, 1998; Lerner, Miller, & Ostrom, 1995; Miller & Lerner, 1994).

Together, these concepts have provided an intellectual grounding for calls for the application of developmental science (Fisher et al., 1993; Fisher & Brennan, 1992; Fisher & Lerner, 1994a; 1994b; Fisher & Tryon, 1990; Lerner & Fisher, 1994; Lerner et al., 1997, 2000a, 2000b), and have also created a burgeoning interest in linking

scholarship and "outreach," that is, the use of university expertise to address topics of concern to communities in manners that these communities define as important and valuable (Kennedy, 1999; Lerner & Simon, 1998a, 1998b; Schorr, 1997).

The growth of such "outreach scholarship" has fostered a scholarly challenge to prior conceptions of the nature of the world (Cairns, Bergman, & Kagan, 1998; Overton, 1998; Valsiner, 1998). The idea that all knowledge is related to its context has promoted a change in the typical ontology within current scholarship (i.e., as discussed in prior chapters this change has emerged as a focus on "relationism" and an avoidance of "split" conceptions of reality—such as nature–nurture; Overton, 1998). This ontological change has helped advance the view that all existence is contingent on the specifics of the physical and social cultural conditions that exist at a particular moment of history (Overton, 1998; Pepper, 1942). As a consequence, changes in epistemology have been associated with this revision is ontology: Contingent knowledge can only be understood if relationships are studied.

Accordingly, any instance of knowledge (e.g., the core knowledge of a given discipline) must be integrated with knowledge of: (a) the context surrounding it and (b) the relation between knowledge and context. Thus, knowledge that is disembedded from the context is not basic knowledge. Rather, knowledge that is relational to its context (e.g., to the community) as it exists in its ecologically valid setting (Trickett, Barone, & Buchanan, 1996) is basic knowledge. As such, social–behavioral scientists have increasingly become intent on learning to integrate what they know with what is known of and by the context (e.g., of and by the community; Fisher, 1997a, 1997b). This view underscores the importance of colearning collaborations between scholars and community members becoming a part of the knowledge generation process (Higgins-D'Alessandro, Fisher, & Hamilton, 1998; Lerner & Simon, 1998a, 1998b).

In sum, the significant changes that have occurred in the way in which social and behavioral scientists, in general, and human developmentalists, in particular, have begun to reconceptualize their roles and responsibilities to society is in no greater evidence than in the field of applied developmental science (Fisher & Murray, 1996; Lerner et al., 2000a, 2000b). Human developmental science has long been associated with laboratory-based scholarship devoted to uncovering "universal" aspects of development by stripping away contextual influences (Cairns et al., 1998; Hagen, 1996).

However, the mission and methods of human development are being transformed into an applied developmental science devoted to discovering diverse developmental patterns by examining the dynamic relations between individuals within the multiple embedded contexts in which they live (Fisher & Brennan, 1992; Fisher & Lerner, 1994; Fisher & Murray, 1996; Horowitz & O'Brien, 1989; Lerner et al., 2000a, 2000b; Morrison, Lord, & Keating, 1984; Power, Higgins, & Kohlberg, 1989; Sigel, 1985).

A DEFINITION OF APPLIED DEVELOPMENTAL SCIENCE

In the late 1980s, scholars from several disciplines (ones associated with the American Psychological Association, the Society for Research in Child Development, the Society for Research on Adolescence, the International Society for Infant Studies, the Gerontological Society of America, the National Black Child Development Institute, and the National Council on Family Relations) came to the realization that issues of child and youth development, family structure and function, economic competitiveness, environmental quality, and health care were interdependent, and, thus, required creative and integrative research to understand and the design, deployment, and evaluation of innovative public policies and intervention programs to improve. Moreover, as a consequence of the presence of the interrelated problems confronting global society, over the last decade, there has been an increasing societal pressure for universities and for the scholars within them to design and deliver knowledge applications addressing the problems of individuals and communities across the life span (Boyer, 1990, 1994; Chibucos & Lerner, 1999; Ralston et al., 1999).

These applications involve the ability to understand and assist the development of individuals who vary with respect to cultural and ethnic background, economic and social opportunity, physical and cognitive abilities, and conditions of living (e.g., in regard to their family, neighborhood, community, and physical settings). Moreover, infants at biological or social risk (e.g., due to being born into conditions of poverty), gifted children or those with developmental disabilities, adolescents considering health-compromising behaviors, single- and dual-worker parents, the frail elderly, and ethnic minority and impoverished families are just some of the populations requiring applications of knowledge based on the work of scholars—in

fields such as psychology, sociology, nursing, human ecology–human development, social work, criminology, political science, medicine, biology, anthropology, and economics—who adopt a developmental perspective to their science.

The multiplicity of disciplines called on to apply their scientific expertise in the service of enhancing the development of individuals, families, and communities has resulted in a collaboration among the aforementioned learned societies. These groups organized a "National Task Force on Applied Developmental Science" in order to synthesize research and applications aimed at describing, explaining, and promoting optimal developmental outcomes across the life cycle of individuals, families, and communities.

To accomplish these objectives, the National Task Force defined the nature and scope of applied developmental science (ADS). The Task Force forwarded these definitions in the context of convening a national conference (at Fordham University, in October, 1991), on "Graduate Education in the Applications of Developmental Science Across the Life Span." The conference inaugurated ADS as a formal program of graduate study and specified the key components involved in graduate education in ADS (Fisher et al., 1993).

The National Task Force indicated that the activities of ADS span a continuum of knowledge generation to knowledge application which includes, but is not limited to:

1. Research on the applicability of scientific theory to growth and development in "natural," (i.e., ecologically valid) contexts.

2. The study of developmental correlates of phenomena of social import.

3. The construction and utilization of developmentally and contextually sensitive assessment instruments.

4. The design and evaluation of developmental interventions and enhancement programs.

5. The dissemination of developmental knowledge to individuals, families, communities, practitioners, and policymakers through developmental education, written materials, the mass media, expert testimony, and community collaborations.

This articulation of ADS activities by the several scholarly societies involved in the National Task Force has, in a sense, involved the rearticulation of the philosophy, the scholarly, and the outreach agenda of the land-grant university (Bonnen, 1998;

Kellogg Commission on the Future of State and Land-Grant Universities, 1999; Lerner & Miller, 1993; Miller & Lerner, 1994; Ralston et al., 1999). In addition, ADS has involved an embracing of an approach to scholarship that merges basic and applied research within an integrated developmental system (i.e., developmental systems theory) (Lerner et al., 2000a, 2000b; see Chapters 7, 8, and 18).

Accordingly, consistent with a developmental systems perspective, applied developmental scientists seek to synthesize research and outreach in order to describe, explain, and enhance development in individuals and families across the life span (Fisher & Lerner, 1994). Fisher and her colleagues (Fisher et al., 1993) characterized the "principles," or core substantive features, of applied developmental science (ADS) in terms of the following five conceptual components:

1. The first component is the temporality of change; there is a temporal component to individuals, families, institutions, and community experiences. Some components remain stable over time; other components may change. The temporality of change has important implications for research design, service provision, and program evaluation.

2. The second component is sensitivity to individual differences and within-person change. What this means is that interventions must take into account individual differences, which means the diversity of racial, ethnic, social class, and gender groups.

3. The third component involves the centrality of context in terms of individual families and of family development. Context exists at all levels—biological, physical–ecological, sociocultural, political, economic, etc.—and invites systemic approaches to research and program design and implementation.

4. The fourth component is an emphasis on (descriptively) normative developmental processes, and on primary prevention and optimization—on the promotion of positive development—rather than on remediation.

5. The fifth component is respect for the bidirectional relationship between knowledge generation and knowledge application.

Moreover, given the developmental systems perspective involved in applied developmental science, scholars in this field assume:

There is an interactive relationship between science and application. Accordingly, the work of those who generate empirically based knowledge about development and those who provide professional services or construct policies affecting individuals and families is seen as reciprocal in that research and theory guide intervention strategies and the evaluation of interventions and policies provides the bases for reformulating theory and future research. . . . As a result, applied developmental [scientists] not only disseminate information about development to parents, professionals, and policy makers working to enhance the development of others, they also integrate the perspectives and experiences of these members of the community into the reformulation of theory and the design of research and interventions. (Lerner & Fisher, 1994, p. 7)

Conclusions About the Concept of Applied Developmental Science

Applied developmental science is a view of outreach scholarship predicated on seeing the world as a "system." This view may require helping faculty see beyond their disciplinary-based perspectives and understand the changing interrelations among levels of organization that comprise human systems. That is, to address adequately the serious problems faced by today's communities, research must involve more than just assembling researchers from different disciplines. Such an approach typically results in a simple layering of investigations and publications—faculty from each discipline approach a topic with their own theory and method, and report their findings separately or in an edited collection of articles.

Pursuing this traditional paradigm has built the scholarly careers of numerous generations of faculty. However, ADS suggests that this paradigm is not adequate for meeting the needs of our communities. What is required is an effort to pursue an integrative or, even better, a "fused" approach to research, such as the one embodied in the developmental systems approach to research discussed in Chapter 18. By conducting integrated research, scholarship that focuses on the interactions of levels of organization studied by different disciplines, the heretofore disconnected insights of different disciplines may be merged into a useful, synthetic knowledge base that may guide the development of public policies and human development-enhancing programs.

That is, to enhance the ecological validity of their scholarship and to provide empowerment based on increased capacity among people, applied developmental scientists try to both understand and serve society with synthetic research and intervention (e.g., program- and policy-related) activities. These scholars seek to work with the community to define the nature of research and program design, delivery, and evaluation endeavors. Thus, applied developmental scientists seek ways to apply their scientific expertise to collaborate with, and promote the life chances of, the individuals, social groups, and communities participating in developmental scholarship. The key challenge in such efforts is to generate scientifically rigorous evaluations of the usefulness of the policies and the programs associated with such ADS and, as well, to use such information in the day-to-day operation of programs (Fetterman, Kaftarian, & Wandersman, 1996; Higgins-D'Alessandro et al., 1998; Jacobs, 1988; Ostrom, Lerner, & Freel, 1995; Weiss & Greene, 1992).

To understand how such community-collaborative scholarship may be enacted, it is useful to discuss an example of an application of ADS to program and policy efforts in a specific area of joint scholarly and community concern. Given the enormous, historically unprecedented challenges that we noted are facing the children and adolescents (i.e., the youth) of the United States and the world (Lerner, 1995a, 2002; Lerner & Galambos, 1998), it is both conceptually useful and socially important to discuss work pertinent to applied developmental science efforts aimed at promoting positive youth development through program and policy innovations. Accordingly, we focus on ADS-related efforts to promote such development, first, through a discussion of programs (interventions) intended to enhance the healthy development of young people and, second, through a discussion of how policies pertinent to such development may be formulated and implemented.

A SAMPLE CASE OF APPLIED DEVELOPMENTAL SCIENCE: 1. DEFINING AND EVALUATING YOUTH PROGRAMS

Programs are planned and systematic attempts to either (a) *reduce* (or *ameliorate*) the presence of an emotional, behavioral, or social problem, (b) *prevent* such problems from occurring, or (c) *promote* positive, healthy behaviors among people. These outcomes can be summarized by "five Cs": Competence, Connection, Character, Confidence, and Caring (or Compassion; Carnegie Council on Adolescent Development, 1989; Lerner, 1995; Lerner et al., 1999, 2000a, 2000b; Little, 1993). These five attributes represent five clusters of individual attributes (e.g., intellectual ability and social and behavioral skills; positive bonds

with people and institutions; integrity and moral centeredness; positive self-regard, a sense of self-efficacy, and courage; and humane values, empathy, and a sense of social justice, respectively).

Little (personal communication, April, 2000) noted that when these five "Cs" are present, a sixth "C" emerges, that is "contribution." That is, Little observed that when the five sets of outcomes are developed, young people have the orientation to contribute to civil society. Civil society is constituted by the institutions of society (including governmental and nongovernmental organizations, public services, and the public problem solving roles of businesses) that integrate the rights of people in free societies with the responsibilities of citizens to maintain those rights (O'Connell, 1999). In other words, civil society promotes democratic institutions, social justice, and an equality of opportunity ("a level playing field") for all people in society. Contributions to civil society—the "sixth C"—is enhanced through the intergenerational effects youth who possess the other "Cs" initiate in regard to the rearing of subsequent generations of citizens, that is, through the parenting of their own children (Bornstein, 1995).

Rick R. Little

Programs that seek to develop these attributes in youth (e.g., in individuals during the first two decades of life) constitute attempts to optimize the lives of people by building up their strengths. In addition, such programs reflect an abiding concern for youth well-being, employ principles of effective youth programs (i.e., principles that we discuss in detail later), and are committed to going beyond traditional intervention (e.g., remediation or alleviation of problems) or preventive interventions and, in turn, stress skill and competency development (Roth et al., 1997).

Stephen F. Hamilton (1999) provided a comprehensive definition of positive youth development programs. His definition reflects three interrelated facets of such programs, that is, (a) the conception of the process of youth development used by proponents of such programs, (b) the approach to programming associated with this conception and, finally (c) the characteristics of programs or organizations that use such an approach. Hamilton's (1999) three-part definition of positive youth development programs is presented in Table 19.1.

In regard to all three types of programs (i.e., problem reduction, problem prevention, and positive development promotion) the work undertaken constitutes attempts to *intervene* into the course of a person's development, to change the person's life for the better. Intervention programs may be conducted by professionals trained to use particular methods (e.g., psychotherapy or group interactions) or they may be presented to youth through community-based club or organizations (e.g., YMCA, 4-H, Boys and Girls Clubs, or Scouting).

Representative Focal Issues of Youth Programs

The behaviors, or targets, of youth programs vary. Interventions may be aimed at externalizing and/or internalizing problems and may use methods that focus primarily on the individual or the developmental system within which the youth is embedded; that is, in addition to the individual adolescent, the program may involve his or her peer group, family, school, or community. For example, in regard to externalizing behaviors, interventions that focus primarily on the individual exist in regard to problems of alcohol use and abuse (e.g., Marlatt et al., 1998), smoking (e.g., Prince, 1995), conduct disorders (e.g., Ansari, Gouthro, Ahmad, & Steele, 1996; Mann-Feder, 1996), social skills (e.g., Thompson, Bundy, & Broncheau, 1995), and delinquency (e.g., Richards & Sullivan, 1996). In addition, interventions that involve the developmental system exist in regard to such problems as juvenile delinquency (e.g., Battistich, Schaps, Watson, & Solomon, 1996; Chamberlain & Reid, 1998; Henggeler et al., 1997), alcohol use and abuse (e.g., Johnson et al., 1996; Richards-Colocino, McKenzie, & Newton, 1996), violence (e.g., Corvo, 1997; Henggeler et al., 1996), and drug use (e.g., Battistich, Schaps, Watson, & Solomon, 1996; Gottfredson, Gottfredson, & Skroban, 1996; Johnson et al., 1996; LoSciuto, Rajala, Townsend, & Taylor, 1996, Richards-Colocino, McKenzie, & Newton, 1996).

Similarly, in regard to internalizing behaviors, interventions that focus primarily on the individual exist in regard to such problems as depression (e.g., Field, Grizzle, Scafidi, & Schanberg, 1996), anger (e.g., Kellner & Tutin, 1995), and suicide (e.g., Cotgrove, Zirinsky, Black, & Weston, 1995; Kerfoot, Harrington, & Dyer, 1995). In addition, interventions that involve the developmental system exist in regard to such problems as anxiety (e.g., Kendall & Southam-Gerow, 1996), conduct disorders (e.g., Mann-Feder, 1996), or multiple "emotional problems" (e.g., Wassef et al., 1996). In addition, some systems-level efforts focus on multiple, internalizing and externalizing problems, for instance, on several health needs (Gullotta & Noyes, 1995) or emotional and behavioral problems (e.g., Dolan, 1995; Wassef, Collins, Ingham, & Mason, 1995).

Stephen F. Hamilton

TABLE 19.1
Positive Youth Development: Hamilton's Three-Part Definition

Hamilton (1999) envisioned positive youth development as a process, as a philosophy of or an approach to youth programming, and as a specific type of organization or program. Therefore, the three parts of his definition specify that youth development is:

1. A natural process: The growing capacity of a young person to understand and act upon the environment

Youth development (synonymous in this sense with child and adolescent development) is the natural unfolding of the potential inherent in the human organism in relation to the challenges and supports of the physical and social environment. People can actively shape their own development through their choices and interpretations. Development lasts as long as life, but youth development enables individuals to lead a healthy, satisfying, and productive life, as youth and later as adults, because they gain the competence to earn a living, to engage in civic activities, to nurture others, and to participate in social relations and cultural activities. "The Five Cs" are a useful summary of the goals of youth development: Caring/compassion, competence, character, connection, confidence. The process of development may be divided into age-related stages (infancy, childhood, adolescence, and smaller divisions of these stages) and into domains (notably physical, cognitive, social, emotional, and moral).

2. A philosophy of or an approach to programming: Active support for the growing capacity of young people by individuals, organizations, and institutions, especially at the community level

The youth development approach is rooted in a commitment to enabling all young people to achieve their potential. It is characterized by a positive, asset-building orientation, building on strengths rather than categorizing youth according to their deficits. However, it recognizes the need to identify and respond to specific problems faced by some youth (e.g., substance abuse, involvement in violence, premature parenthood). The most important manifestation of youth development as a philosophy or approach is the goal of making communities better places for young people to grow up. Youth participation is essential to the achievement of that goal.

3. Programs and organizations: A planned set of activities that foster young people's growing capacity

Youth development programs are inclusive; participation is not limited to those identified as at risk or in need. They give young people the chance to make decisions about their own participation and about the program's operation, and to assume responsible roles. They engage young people in constructive and challenging activities that build their competence and foster supportive relationships with peers and with adults. They are developmentally appropriate and endure over time, which requires them to be adaptable enough to change as participants' needs change. Youth development is done with and by youth. Something that is done to or for youth is not youth development, even though it may be necessary and valuable. Youth development organizations exist specifically for the purpose of promoting youth development. Some other organizations operate youth development programs but have other functions as well. Programs to prevent or treat specific problems stand in contrast to youth development programs; however, problem-oriented programs may incorporate youth development principles by acknowledging participants' strengths and the wider range of issues they must cope with and by giving participants a strong voice in the choice to participate and in the operation of the program.

Note. Hamilton (1999).

Moreover, in programs that seek to promote positive development there may be efforts that focus either on the individual level (i.e., attempts to enhance cognitive and ego development may adopt such an orientation) (e.g., Faubert, Locke, Sprinthall, & Howland, 1996) or on the developmental system. Examples here include programs that seek to enhance self-esteem (e.g., Jurich & Collins, 1996), adolescent–parent relations or family strength (e.g., Gavazzi, 1995), or health (e.g., Brack, Brack, & Orr, 1996; Emshoff et al., 1996).

Whatever the focus of an intervention program might be—whether it is an individual adolescent or includes features of his/her developmental system, or whether the interest is on reducing or preventing one or more internalizing and/or externalizing behaviors or in promoting one or several facets of positive development—every program must, in some way, consider three key issues. These issues are effectiveness, scale, and sustainability (Little, 1993). To understand these issues it is useful to focus first on the issue of effectiveness.

Program Effectiveness

Does a program accomplish its aims? For example, does it reduce youth violence? Does it prevent unsafe sexual behaviors? Does it enhance self-esteem among adolescents? If a program achieves what it is intended to achieve, it is *effective*. It is a program that is valid for its intended purpose.

Program effectiveness is often difficult to determine (Jacobs, 1988; Jacobs & Kapuscik, 2000). For example, young people are not randomly assigned to programs. Instead, they enter a program for particular reasons, reasons based on their past experiences and/or current life circumstances. For instance, adolescents are in a drug reduction program because they use drugs; they are in a violence prevention program because there is a risk that they will engage in violence; or they are in a positive youth development program because they live in a community that has the resources to provide such a potentially beneficial experience to its young people. Because of the reasons youth enter into a program, it may not be possible to determine whether changes in youth behavior that occur over the course of their participation in the program are due to who they were when they started the program or the program itself.

Program Evaluation

Procedures—termed *evaluations*—are used to ascertain that changes in participants are due to the program, that programs are effective, and that programs attain their goals (Connell, Kubisch, Schorr, & Weiss, 1995; Fetterman, Kaftarian, & Wandersman, 1996; Jacobs, 1988; Jacobs & Kapuscik, 2000; Millett, 1996; Lerner, Ostrom, & Freel, 1995; Ostrom, Lerner, & Freel, 1995). Evaluations try to *prove* that any changes youth experience over the course of their participation in a program are due to the program itself and not due, for example, to the factors that involved them in drugs in the first place, factors that led them to be "at risk" for violence, or factors that gave them the opportunity to live in a community that provided programs promoting positive development. Evaluations aimed at proving that a program is effective are often termed *outcome* or *summative* evaluations.

Evaluations also try to *improve* the quality of the program as it is being conducted. Here, the evaluator will try to determine whether the program can be improved—whether midcourse corrections can be made to the program so that better efforts at promoting self-esteem or preventing violence can be made. For instance, if the "theory" of developmental change used by program planners involves the idea that more police need to be present on the streets of the community in order to reduce youth violence, the evaluator may monitor whether such presence is, in fact, increasing; if not, then he or she may work with the community to create conditions that would allow greater community policing. The evaluator would not wait for a final determination of violence reduction to be made prior to taking the step of involving more police in the community. Rather, before any outcomes are seen, efforts would be made to improve the work involved in the delivery of the program. For this reason, evaluations that seek to improve programs are often also called *formative* evaluations. Because they seek to enhance the process through which a program provides its services, such evaluations may also be termed *process* evaluations.

Evaluations also try to *empower* the people who are delivering the program and, as well, those who are participating in it (e.g., the youths themselves). A key goal of evaluators of contemporary youth programs—especially of those programs that are located in communities, those that were begun and are continued through the efforts of members of the community [as compared to trained professionals (e.g., psychologists, social workers, nurses, or physicians)] is to increase capacity among community members to both prove and improve the program (Connell et al., 1995; Fetterman et al., 1996; Jacobs, 1988; Jacobs & Kapuscik, 2000; Millett, 1996; Ostrom et al., 1995). These *empowerment evaluations* (Fetterman et al., 1996) are seen as critical to enact if the community is to use evidence of program effectiveness to bring the program to all the youths who need it and to maintain the program over time. Such goals for a program pertain to the issues of scale and effectiveness, respectively.

Program Scale and Effectiveness

As we shall discuss later, there is a good deal of knowledge about the characteristics of effective youth programs. There is knowledge about how to prove that programs are effective and there is knowledge about how to improve the quality of programs as they are in the process of being conducted. In addition, there is growing knowledge about how to empower communities through evaluation (Connell et al., 1995; Fetterman et al., 1996; Jacobs, 1988; Jacobs & Kapuscik, 2000; Millett, 1996; Ostrom et al., 1995).

However, even if programs are know to be effective they may not be reaching all the youth for whom they are appropriate, for whom they could have positive benefits. This a problem of program *scale*. Often, we do not know the number of youth that would be appropriate for a given program. For instance, if a YMCA modern dance program or an after-school basketball program involves a dozen youth, we may not know whether greater skill attainment could be developed in the participants if the maximum number of youth in the program were eight or, in turn, if equivalent skill attainment could be achieved among youth even if the program size was increased to 20 youth.

In turn, we may have information that more people could benefit from a program; for instance, we might know that a program that sends visitors to the homes of adolescent mothers to help improve their skills as parents is effective, but that only 50% of the youths eligible for the program participate in it. We might not know, however, why we cannot involve all eligible youth in the program. We may not know the psychological, social, economic, and political reasons that keep youth from participating in the program. Alternatively, we might understand that there are economic reasons that keep the adolescent mothers out of home-visiting programs (e.g., they have to work and are not available when the program is offered), but we may not know how to change the social system (e.g., by developing labor law policies regarding flexible working hours or time off from work for program participation) in a manner that would enable the program to be brought to scale.

If there is a lot of scholarship to conduct about program scale, there is even more to learn about *program sustainability*. A sustained program is one that is maintained over time. Most programs—especially community-based ones—are not sustained over long periods of time. Many programs are initiated through "start-up" grants made by government agencies or private, philanthropic foundations. In turn, many programs are initiated by university faculty who have obtained a grant to demonstrate that a particular intervention they have invented is effective. In either case, after the start-up funds have run out or the demonstration project is completed, the project usually ends—if not immediately, then after a relatively short period (e.g., Dryfoos, 1998; Hamburg, 1992; Lerner, Sparks, & McCubbin, 1999; Little, 1993; Schorr, 1988, 1997). This lack of sustainability occurs even for programs that have been proven through evaluations to be effective (Little, 1993).

Toward a New Research Model for Youth Programs

The National Institute of Mental Health (NIMH) is a federal government agency that has funded many demonstration projects pertinent to reducing or preventing problems of youth development. Recently, some of the leaders of NIMH have suggested that the predominant research model used to conduct evaluations may be flawed; its use may be the reason that effective youth programs have not been sustained (Jensen, Hoagwood, & Trickett, 1999).

Jensen and colleagues (1999) described two distinct models of research pertinent to the promotion of positive youth development that have been pursued through grants provided by units within the National Institutes of Health (NIH) (e.g., NIMH and the National Institute of Child Health and Human Development [NICHD]). The first model has been predominant in American social and behavioral science, and is termed by Jensen and colleagues (1999) the "Efficacy Research" model. The key question addressed by research conducted within the frame of this model is: "What works under optimal, university-based, research conditions?"

Peter Jensen

Studies using this model are aimed at determining what is maximally effective under "optimal" (i.e., university-designed, as opposed to "real-world") conditions, in regard to: (a) preventing the onset of behavioral or emotional problems, (b) ameliorating the course of problems after their onset, and (c) treatment of problems that have reached "clinical" severity. Jensen and colleagues (1999) noted that the results of the studies conducted within the frame of this model indicate that effective preventive interventions for several high risk behaviors and/or outcomes are possible.

However, a second model of research exists, although it has not received the literally hundreds of millions of dollars of NIH support given to efficacy research. Indeed, this second model has been rarely used and poorly funded. This second model is one of "outreach" research; it is research conducted in "real-world" community settings.

The key question addressed in this model is: "What works that is also: 1. palatable; 2. feasible; 3. durable; 4. affordable; and 5. sustainable in real-world settings?" Jensen and colleagues (1999) concluded that, when this question is asked, the answer in regard to prevention or positive youth development programs is "very few (if any), indeed."

Kimberly Hoagwood

Edison Trickett

Jensen and colleagues (1999) argued that the federal government must move, and it is, in fact, now moving, to support outreach research, to change the answer to the last-noted question to "many, if not most." To create this sea change in the way scholars conduct their research, Jensen and colleagues (1999) recognized that new, more effective partnerships had to be created between universities and communities. Jensen and colleagues (1999) believed that there had to be a qualitative change in the way universities interact with communities in regard to identifying ways to promote positive youth development (see, too, Eccles, 1996; McHale & Lerner, 1996). Table 19.2 presents the ideas suggested by Jensen and colleagues (1999) and others (e.g., Chibucos & Lerner, 1999; Eccles, 1996; McHale & Lerner, 1996) about how universities and communities can collaborate in sustaining effective youth-serving programs.

Typically, after start-up funds end or the expertise possessed by university faculty has left the community, the members of the community do not have the capacity to identify new resources to sustain the program. In addition, they may not have the skills to conduct the program themselves — especially in manners that will enable them to both continue to improve the program and, in turn, to prove to potential funders that they are

Francine Jacobs

effectively changing youth for the better (Jacobs, 1988; Lerner, Ostrom, & Freel, 1995, 1997; Ostrom et al., 1995; Weiss & Greene, 1992).

Because of the need to assist community program leaders in developing such capacities, increasingly greater attention has been paid, in recent years, to empowerment approaches to evaluation (Fetterman et al., 1996). Arguably, the most useful of these approaches has been developed by Francine Jacobs (1988; Jacobs & Kapuscik, 2000). In her "Five Tier Model" of evaluation, Jacobs provided the means for a community to develop a stronger program in regard to both the proving and improving dimensions of evaluation. Table 19.3 summarizes the Jacobs "Five Tier Model."

Conclusions About Defining and Evaluating Youth Programs

Youth programs vary in numerous ways. They differ in their emphasis on problem reduction or prevention, or in their attempts to promote positive development. They also differ in their emphasis on changing an individual (or one of his/her behaviors) versus changing both the individual and some portion of his/her developmental system (e.g., his

---

TABLE 19.2
Sustaining Effective Youth-Serving Programs: Ideas for Building University–Community Collaborations

Jensen and colleagues (1999) pointed out that effective university-community collaborations in support of positive youth development should be based on several specific principles. These include:

1. An enhanced focus on the relevance of research to the actual ecology of youth (Bronfenbrenner, 1979; Bronfenbrenner & Morris, 1998; Hultsch & Hickey, 1978). We have to study youth in the actual settings within which they live as opposed to contrived, albeit well-designed, laboratory-type studies.
2. Incorporating the values and needs of community collaborators within research activities (Kellogg Commission on the Future of State and Land-Grant Universities, 1999; Richardson, 1996; Spanier, 1997, 1999).
3. Understanding and measuring both the intended and the unintended outcomes of an intervention program for youth and their context and to measuring these outcomes.
4. Flexibility to fit local needs and circumstances, that is, an orientation to adjust the deign or procedures of the research to the vicissitudes of the community within which the work is enacted (Jacobs, 1988).
5. Accordingly, a willingness to make modifications to research methods in order to fit the circumstances of the local community.
6. The embracing of long-term perspectives, that is, the commitment of the university to remain in the community for a time period sufficient to see the realization of community-valued developmental goals for its youth.

In addition, Chibucos and Lerner (1999), Ebata (1996), Eccles (1996), Fitzgerald et al. (1996), Lerner and Simon (1998), McHale et al. (1996), McHale and Lerner (1996), Peterson (1995), Small (1996), Weinberg and Erikson (1996), Zeldin (1995), and Zeldin and Price (1995) proposed ideas that allow several other principles to be forwarded, including:

7. A commitment by both the university and the community to learn from each other (to co-learn) about what is required to enhance the lives of particular youth; and
8. Humility on the part of the university and its faculty, so that (a) true co-learning and collaboration among equals can occur; and (b) cultural integration is achieved and, through this, the university and the community recognize and appreciate each other's perspective.

Note. Based on Jensen et al. (1999).

TABLE 19.3
Francine Jacobs' Five-Tier Model of Program Evaluation

Level/title	Purposes of evaluation	Audiences	Tasks	Kinds of data to collect/analyze
TIER ONE Needs Assessment	1. To document the size and nature of a public problem 2. To determine unmet need for services in a community 3. To propose program and policy options to meet needs 4. To set a data baseline from which later progress can be measured 5. To broaden the base of support for a proposed program	1. Policy-makers 2. Funders 3. Community stakeholders	1. Review existing community, county and state data 2. Determine additional data needed to describe problem and potential service users 3. Conduct "environmental scan" of available resources 4. Identify resource gaps and unmet need 5. Set goals and objectives for interventions 6. Recommend one program model from range of options	1. Extant data on target population; services currently available 2. Interviews with community leaders 3. Interviews or survey data from prospective participants 4. Information about similar programs in other locations
TIER TWO Monitoring and Accountability	1. To monitor program performance 2. To meet demands for accountability 3. To build a constituency 4. To aid in program planning and decision-making 5. To provide a groundwork for later evaluation activities	1. Program staff and administrators 2. Policy-makers 3. Funders 4. Community stakeholders 5. Media	1. Determine needs and capacities for data collection and management 2. Develop clear and consistent procedures for collecting essential data elements 3. Gather and analyze data to describe program along dimensions of clients, services, staff, and costs	1. MIS (management information system) data; collected at program, county and/or state level 2. Case material; obtained through record reviews, program contact forms, etc.
TIER THREE Quality Review and Program Clarification	1. To develop a more detailed picture of the program as it is being implemented 2. To assess the quality and consistency of the intervention 3. To provide information to staff for program improvement	1. Program staff and administrators 2. Policymakers 3. Community stakeholders	1. Review monitoring data 2. Expand on program description using information about participants' views 3. Compare program with standards and expectations 4. Examine participants' perceptions about effects of program 5. Clarify program goals and design	1. MIS monitoring data 2. Case material 3. Other qualitative and quantitative data on program operations, customer satisfaction, and perceived effects; obtained using questionnaires, interviews, observations, and focus group

(continues)

TABLE 19.3
(continued)

Level/title	Purposes of evaluation	Audiences	Tasks	Kinds of data to collect/analyze
TIER FOUR Achieving Outcomes	1. To determine what changes, if any, have occurred among beneficiaries 2. To attribute changes to the program 3. To provide information to staff for program improvement	1. Program staff and administrators 2. Policymakers 3. Community stakeholders 4. Funders 5. Other programs	1. Choose short-term objectives to be examined 2. Choose appropriate research design, given constraints and capacities 3. Determine measurable indicators of success for outcome objectives 4. Collect and analyze information about effects on beneficiaries	1. Client-specific data; obtained using questionnaires, interviews, goal attainment scaling observations, and functional indicators 2. Client and community social indicators 3. MIS data
TIER FIVE Establishing Impact	1. To contribute to knowledge development in the field 2. To produce evidence of differential effectiveness of treatments 3. To identify models worthy of replication	1. Academic and research communities 2. Policymakers 3. Funders 4. General public	1. Decide on impact objectives based on results of Tier Four evaluation efforts 2. Choose appropriately rigorous research design and comparison group 3. Identify techniques and tools to measure effects in treatment and comparison groups 4. Analyze information to identify program impacts	1. Client-specific data; obtained using questionnaires, interviews, goal attainment scaling, observations, and functional indicators 2. Client and community social indicators 3. MIS data 4. Comparable data for control group

Note. Adapted from Jacobs, F. (1988). The Five-Tiered Approach to evaluation: Context and implementation. In H. Weiss and F. Jacobs (Eds.), *Evaluating family programs.* Hawthorne, NY: Aldine de Gruyter.
Source: Jacobs, F. H. and Kapuscik, J. L. (2000). Making it count: Evaluating family preservation services. Medford, MA: Tufts University, Eliot-Pearson Department of Child Development.

or her family or peer group, or the public policies affecting youth). Finally, they differ in regard to their emphasis on, or approach to, the issues of evaluation, scale, and sustainability. Together, all these dimensions of difference make the picture of contemporary youth programs quite complex.

Themes of Contemporary Youth Programs

There are, however, some themes that characterize contemporary discussions of youth programs. Focus on these themes allows us to reduce the complexity involved in understanding youth programs to a few key concepts. First, most scholars

and practitioners want to prevent problems before their occurrence. Although the plasticity of human development (see Chapter 5) means that we may always remain optimistic about finding some intervention to reduce problem behaviors, it is both more humane and more cost effective to prevent problems from occurring than to wait for them to develop before acting.

In turn, although we would always want, therefore, to take steps to ensure that we are effective in developing and delivering preventive programs, we may want to focus more on the promotion of positive development than on the prevention of negative outcomes (e.g., Furstenberg & Hughes,

Karen J. Pittman

1995; Lerner, 1993b, 1995a; Moore & Glei, 1995; Oden, 1995). Several scholars (e.g., Benson, 1997; Lerner et al., 1999; Pittman, 1996) have emphasized that prevention is not the same as *provision: Preventing a problem from occurring does not, in turn, guarantee that we are providing youths with the assets they need for developing in a positive manner.*

Simply, as Pittman (1996) emphasized, problem free is not prepared. Not having behavioral problems (e.g., not using drugs and alcohol or not engaging in crime or unsafe sex) is not equivalent to possessing the skills requisite to productively engage in a valued job or other role in society. Preventing negative behaviors is, then, not the same as promoting in youth the attributes of positive, healthy development.

Accordingly, as noted by several scholars (e.g., Benson, 1997; Benson et al., 1998; Blyth & Leffert, 1995; Leffert et al., 1998; Lerner et al., 1997, 1999, 2000a, 2000b; Roth & Brooks-Gunn, 2000; Roth et al., 1998; Scales et al., 2000; Scales & Leffert, 1999), to succeed in the development of prepared and productive youth, communities need to proactively provide resources to young people to ensure that they develop the five "Cs" of positive youth development.

However, preventing problems does not provide these assets. What does, then, provide them?

The Promotion of Developmental Assets

What, then, is required for the promotion of positive development in our nation's young people? Peter L. Benson and his colleagues at Search Institute in Minneapolis claimed that the application of "assets" is needed (Benson, 1997; Benson, Leffert, Scales, & Blyth, 1998; Leffert, Benson, Scales, Sharma, Drake, & Blyth, 1998; Scales & Leffert, 1999). They stressed that positive youth development is furthered when actions are taken to enhance the strengths of a person (e.g., a commitment to learning, a healthy sense of identity), a family (e.g., caring attitudes toward children and rearing styles that both empower youth and set boundaries and provide expectations for positive growth), and a community (e.g., social support, programs that provide access to the resources for education, safety, and mentorship available in a community) (Benson, 1997).

Accordingly, Benson and his colleagues claimed there are both internal and external attributes that comprise the developmental assets needed by youth. Through their research, they have identified 40 such assets, 20 internal ones and 20 external ones. These attributes are presented in Table 19.4.

Peter L. Benson

TABLE 19.4
40 Developmental Assets

External	*Support*	1. *Family support*—Family life provides high levels of love and support.
		2. *Positive family communication*—Young person and his or her parent(s) communicate positively, and young person is willing to seek advice and counsel from parent(s).
		3. *Other adult relationships*—Young person receives support from three or more nonparent adults.
		4. *Caring neighborhood*—Young person experiences caring neighbors.
		5. *Caring school climate*—School provides a caring, encouraging environment
		6. *Parent involvement in schooling*—Parent(s) are actively involved in helping young person succeed in school.
	Empowerment	7. *Community values youth*—Young person perceives that adults in the community value youth.
		8. *Youth as resources*—Young people are given useful roles in the community.
		9. *Service to others*—Young person serves in the community one hour or more per week.
		10. *Safety*—Young person feels safe in home, at school, and the neighborhood.
	Boundaries and Expectations	11. *Family boundaries*—Family has clear rules and consequences and monitors the young person's whereabouts.
		12. *School boundaries*—School provides clear rules and consequences.
		13. *Neighborhood boundaries*—Neighbors take responsibility for monitoring young people's behavior.
		14. *Adult role models*—Parent(s) and other adult model positive, responsible behavior.
		15. *Positive peer influence*—Young person's best friends model positive, responsible behavior.
		16. *High expectations*—Both parent(s) and teachers encourage the young person to do well.
	Constructive Use of Time	17. *Creative activities*—Young person spends three or more hours per week in lessons or practice in music, theater, or other arts.
		18. *Youth programs*—Young person spends three hours or more per week in sports, clubs, or organizations at school and/or in community organizations.
		19. *Religious community*—Young person spends one or more hours per week in activities in a religious institution.
		20. *Time at home*—Young person is out with friends "with nothing special to do" two or fewer nights per week.
Internal	*Commitment to Learning*	21. *Achievement motivation*—Young person is motivated to do well in school.
		22. *School engagement*—Young person is actively engaged in learning.
		23. *Homework*—Young person reports doing at least one hour of homework every school day.
		24. *Bonding to School*—Young person cares about his or her school.
		25. *Reading for pleasure*—Young person reads for pleasure three or more hours per week.
	Positive Values	26. *Caring*—Young person places high value on helping other people.
		27. *Equality and social justice*—Young person places high value on promoting equality and reducing hunger and poverty.
		28. *Integrity*—Young person acts on convictions and stands up for her or his beliefs.
		29. *Honesty*—Young person "tells the truth even when it is not easy."
		30. *Responsibility*—Young person accepts and takes personal responsibility.
		31. *Restraint*—Young person believes it is important not to be sexually active or to use alcohol or other drugs.

(continues)

TABLE 19.4
(continued)

Social Competencies	32.	*Planning and decision making*—Young person knows how to plan ahead and make choices.
	33.	*Interpersonal competence*—Young person has empathy, sensitivity, and friendship skills.
	34.	*Cultural competence*—Young person has knowledge of and comfort with people of different cultural/racial/ethnic backgrounds.
	35.	*Resistance skills*—Young person can resist negative peer pressue and dangerous situations.
	36.	*Peaceful conflict resolution*—Young person seeks to resolve conflict nonviolently.
Positive Identity	37.	*Personal Power*—Young person feels he or she had control over "things that happen to me."
	38.	*Self-exteem*—Young person reports having high self- esteem.
	39.	*Sense of purpose*—Young person reports that "my life has a purpose."
	40.	*Positive view of personal future*—Young person is optimistic about her or his personal future.

Note. Benson et al. (1998).

Benson and his colleagues found that the more developmental assets possessed by an adolescent the greater the likelihood of his or her positive, healthy development. For instance, in a study of 99,462 youths in Grades 6 through 12 in public and/or alternative schools from 213 cities and town in the United States who were assessed during the 1996 to 1997 academic year for their possession of the 40 assets presented in Table 19.1, Leffert and colleagues (1998) found that the more assets present among youth the lower the likelihood of alcohol use, depression/suicide risk, and violence. Figures 19.1, 19.2, and 19.3 taken from the research of Leffert and colleagues (1998) present these findings.

For instance, Figure 19.1 displays the level of alcohol use risk for youth in Grades 6 to 8 combined and for youth in Grades 9 to 12 combined. As shown in this figure, in both grade groupings alcohol risk decreases with the possession of more assets. Youth with zero to 10 assets have the highest risk, followed by youth with 11 to 20 assets, youth with 21 to 30 assets, and youth with 31 to 40 assets. Thus, consistent with Benson's (1997) view of the salience of developmental assets for promoting healthy behavior among young people, both the trend lines represented in the figure, and the fact that the last group has the lowest level of risk, shows the importance of the asset approach in work aimed at promoting positive development in our nation's children and adolescents.

Moreover, the data summarized in both Figures 19.2 and 19.3 replicate the trends seen in Figure 19.1—for males and females in regard to depression/suicide risk in the case of Figure 19.2 and for combinations of males and females in different grade groupings in regard to violence risk in the case of Figure 19.3. This congruence strengthens the argument for the critical significance of a focus

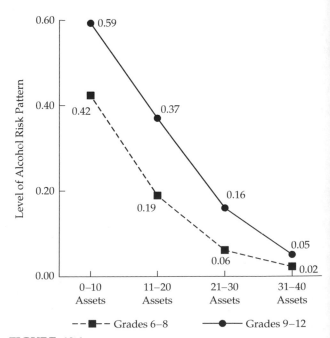

FIGURE 19.1
The effect of grade × asset level interaction on alcohol risk pattern.
Source: Leffert et al. (1998).

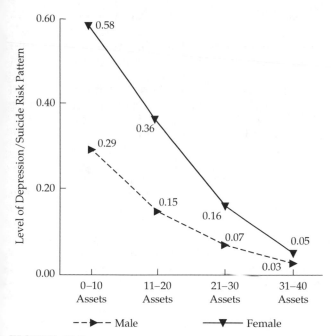

FIGURE 19.2
The effect of sex × asset level interaction on depression/suicide risk pattern.

Source: Leffert et al. (1998).

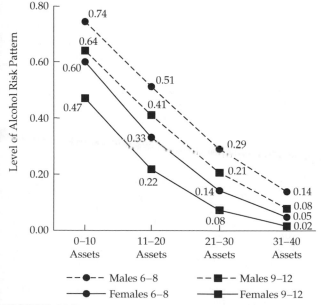

FIGURE 19.3
The effect of grade × sex × asset level interaction on violence risk pattern.

Source: Leffert et al. (1998).

on developmental assets in public policy discussions about building a national youth policy aimed at the promotion of positive youth development.

There are other data sets that support the importance of focusing on developmental assets in both understanding the bases of positive youth development and using that knowledge to inform the policy-making process. Luster and McAdoo (1994) sought to identify the factors that contribute to individual differences in the cognitive competence of African American children in the early elementary grades. Using data from the National Longitudinal Study of Youth (NLSY), and consistent with an asset-based approach to promoting the positive development of youths (Benson, 1997; Scales & Leffert, 1999), they found that favorable outcomes in cognitive and socioemotional development (operationalized as attainments within the top quartile of the sample they studied) were associated with high scores on an "advantage index." This index was formed by scoring children on the basis of the absence of risk factors (e.g., pertaining to poverty or problems in the quality of the home environment) and the presence of more favorable circumstances in their lives.

As an illustration of their findings, Luster and McAdoo (1994) reported that, whereas only 4% of the children in their sample who scored low on the advantage index had high scores on a measure of vocabulary, 44% of the children who had high scores on the measure of developing under favorable circumstances also had high vocabulary scores. Similar contrasts between low and high scorers on the advantage index were found in measures of math achievement (14 vs. 37%, respectively), word recognition (0 vs. 35%, respectively), and word meaning (7 vs. 46%, respectively).

Findings reported by Luster and McAdoo (1996) extended those of Luster and McAdoo (1994). Seeking to identify the factors that contribute to individual differences in the educational attainment of African American young adults from low socioeconomic status, Luster and McAdoo (1996) found that assets associated with the individual (cognitive competence, academic motivation, and personal adjustment in kindergarten) and the context (parental involvement in schools) were associated longitudinally with academic achievement and educational attainment.

In short, the individual and contextual assets of youth are linked to their positive development. These data legitimate the idea that the enhancement of such assets will be associated with the promotion of positive youth development. Benson and his colleagues (e.g., Scales et al., 2000) linked these assets for positive youth development to effective, community-based programs. That is, in their research, Benson and his colleagues found that (Scales et al., 2000):

> Time spent in youth programs appeared to have the most pervasive positive influence in [being a] . . . predictor of . . . thriving outcomes . . . [G]ood youth programs provide young people with access to caring adults and responsible peers, as well as skill-building activities than can reinforce the values and skills that are associated with doing well in school and maintaining good physical health. (p. 43)

Accordingly, because of the importance of youth programs for enabling developmental science to be applied in manners that transcend prevention and enable the promotion of positive youth development, it is important to understand the principles behind, and characteristics of, such programs.

Developing Effective Programs for Youth

If programs are to be successful in addressing the combined individual and contextual influences on youth problems and, in turn, if they are to be associated with positive youth development, it is reasonable to believe that they must engage both of these levels (individual and context) (Benson, 1997; Lerner, 1995a; Pittman, 1996; Pittman & Irby, 1995; Pittman, Irby, & Cahill, 1995; Trickett, Barone, & Buchanan, 1996; Wassef, Collins, Ingham, & Mason, 1995; Whalen & Wynn, 1995). In other words, whether aimed at drug use (e.g., Rohrback et al., 1994), alcohol use (e.g., Maguin, Zucker, & Fitzgerald, 1994; Wagenaar & Peery, 1994); aggression and delinquency (Guerra & Slaby, 1990); school problems (Switzer et al., 1995); or socioeconomic disadvantage (Furstenberg & Hughes, 1995), effective programs engage the system of individual and contextual variables affecting youth development.

By involving multiple characteristics of the young person [i.e., his or her developmental level, knowledge of risk taking, intrapersonal resources (e.g., self-esteem, self-competence, beliefs, and values), and interpersonal management skills (e.g., being able to engage useful social support and prosocial behaviors from peers)] successful risk prevention programs may be developed (Levitt, Selman, & Richmond, 1991). However, the programs I am describing are more than programs focusing on diminishing risk. They emphasize the strengths and assets of young people, that is, their capacities for positive development, their possession of attributes—*protective factors*—that keep them moving forward in a positive developmental path.

Protective factors—which are individual attributes (e.g., self-esteem, religious values and knowledge, skills, and motivation to do well) and contextual attributes (e.g., the experience of having authoritative parents and a socially supportive, prosocial peer group) have been identified as integral in the healthy development of young people (e.g., Browne & Rife, 1991; Feldman, 1995; Jessor et al., 1995; Stiffman, Church, & Earls, 1992). These protective factors are, in essence, the assets for healthy development that are described by the Search Institute (Benson, 1997; Scales & Leffert, 1999). Focus on these assets provides a means to envision the key features of successful youth programs.

That is, promoting the role of assets, or protective factors, in youth programs is associated with healthy adolescent development. As summarized in the report of the Carnegie Council on Adolescent Development, *Great Transitions: Preparing Adolescents for a New Century* (Carnegie Corporation of New York, 1995), programs that build the assets of positive youth development help adolescents meet the enduring human needs of youth. That is, if they are to develop into healthy and productive adults, all youths need to:

> (1) Find a valued place in a constructive group; (2) Learn how to form close, durable human relationships; (3) Feel a sense of worth as a person; (4) Achieve a reliable basis for making informed choices; (5) Know how to use the support systems available to them; (6) Express constructive curiosity and exploratory behavior; (7) Find ways of being useful to others; and (8) Believe in a promising future with real opportunities. (Carnegie Corporation of New York, 1995, pp. 10–11)

Moreover, the Carnegie Corporation of New York (1995) report went on to note that:

> Meeting these requirements has been essential for human survival into adulthood for millennia. But in a technologically advanced democratic society—one that places an increasingly high premium on competence in many domains—adolescents themselves face a further set of challenges. They must: (1) Master social skills, including the ability to manage conflict peacefully; (2) Cultivate the inquiring and problem-solving habits of mind for lifelong learning; (3) Acquire the technical and analytic capabilities to participate in a world-class economy; (4) Become ethical persons; (5) Learn the requirements of responsible citizenship; and (6) Respect diversity in our pluralistic society. (p. 11)

What sorts of programs meet these needs? What features should be included in a youth-serving program to make it effective?

Key Features of Effective Youth Programs

Numerous scholars, practitioners, advocates for youths and policymakers have studied and discussed effective youth programs (e.g., Benson, 1997; Carnegie Corporation of New York, 1995; Damon, 1997; Dryfoos, 1990, 1998; Hamilton, 1999; Lerner, 1993b, 1995a; Lerner & Galambos, 1998; Little, 1993; Pittman, 1996; Roth et al., 1997; Schorr, 1988, 1997). Although all contributors to this discussion may have their own ways of phrasing their conclusions, it is possible to provide an overview of the ideal features—the *best practices*—that should be integrated into effective positive youth development programs. These features of best practice involve coordinated attention to each youth's characteristics of individuality and to the specifics of his or her social context. Accordingly, programs that are effective in promoting positive youth development:

1. Are predicated on a vision of positive youth development (e.g., the "Five Cs" of positive youth development) (Hamilton, 1999; Lerner et al., 1999) and have clear aims (goals) for the program.

2. Focus on the assets of youth and on the importance of their participation in every facet of the program—including its design, conduct, and evaluation.

3. Pay attention to the diversity of youth and their families, communities and cultural contexts. Both the special strengths and the particular needs of youth and their contexts need to be of central concern.

4. Assure that the program represents a safe space for youth and that it is accessible to them. Such a setting should also provide youths with a context within which they can use their time constructively.

5. In recognition of the interrelated challenges facing youth, integrate the assets for positive youth development that exist within the community. Such integration involves collaborations (partnerships) among all youth-serving organizations and contributions by families, peers, and schools.

6. Provide, through the presence of safety, accessibility, and collaboration, broad, sustained, and integrated services to youth and a "seamless" social support system across the community.

7. In recognition of the importance of caring adult–youth relations in healthy adolescent development, provide training to adult leaders. For instance, useful training may involve enhancing sensitivity to diversity and providing information about the principles of positive youth development.

8. Emphasize the development of life skills, competency, caring, civic responsibility, and community service or, in other words, the "Five Cs" of positive youth development.

9. Are committed to program and evaluation and strengthening the use of research in the design, delivery, and evaluation of the program. The role of university–community partnerships is important here.

10. Advocate for youth. Although programs do not (and arguably should not) be partisan, they should provide a clear voice to policymakers across the political spectrum about the importance of investing in positive youth development.

In essence, then, there are multiple features of person and context that should be combined to design and deliver a program that effectively promotes positive youth development. Building on the general developmental characteristics of the period—involving identity and family, peer, and institutional (e.g., school and work) contextual levels—these programs, when also attuned to the specific characteristics and needs of the youth and his or her setting, will help the adolescent not just avoid the development of risk behaviors. In addition, positive youth development may be promoted.

Conclusions About Effective Youth Programs

We may be optimistic about the likely success of prevention efforts if we design and deliver these programs in the context of keeping in mind that no one, single or isolated, effort is apt to succeed, given the multiple interrelated challenges facing youths (Dryfoos, 1990, Roth et al., 1997). Thus, a coordinated set of community-based programs, aimed at both individuals and their contexts, is required for success; these programs should begin as early as possible and should be maintained for as much of the adolescent years as possible. No one effort, not even a comprehensive one, can continue to prevent the appearance of risk across all of this period.

Clearly, then, means may be found to capitalize on the potentials and strengths of all youth, their families, and communities and, through meeting their developmental needs, promote their positive development. However, if the knowledge we have about how to promote positive development is to reach the maximum number of youth possible in a sustained manner, we need to marshall the resources of society in the service of designing programs consistent with our vision for young people. To attain this end, scholars of youth development must engage public policy and policymakers in the support of effective programs for youth (Hamburg & Takanishi 1996; Lerner, 1995a; Lipsitz, 1991; Ralston et al., 1999). The ideas we have reviewed about building effective youth programs do have rather clear implications for public policy. The engagement of such policies is another key feature of the work of scholars engaged in ADS.

A SAMPLE CASE OF APPLIED DEVELOPMENTAL SCIENCE: 2. PUBLIC POLICY FOR YOUTH DEVELOPMENT PROGRAMS

Public policies represent standards, or rules, for the conduct of individuals, organizations, and institutions (Lerner, 1995; Lerner et al., 1999). As such, policies structure our actions; they let others know how they may expect us to function in regard to particular substantive issues. In addition, policies reflect what we value, what we believe, and what we think is in our best interests. Simply, policies indicate the things in which we are invested and about which we care.

If we value our youth, we will promote public policies that enable effective programs to be designed and sustained for all youths that need them. We know how to design effective programs. Our task now is to formulate a set of social rules (i.e., policies) that will enable our values about youths to be translated into effective actions. But why, specifically, do we need a policy for our nation's youth? What will occur if we continue to be without such a policy?

Why Do We Need a Youth Policy?

Youth constitute 100% of the future human and social capital upon which our nation must depend. The healthy rearing of children has often been identified as the essential function of the family (Bowman & Spanier, 1978; Lerner & Spanier, 1980). As such, although family policy is not isomorphic with child or youth policy (e.g., family policies may involve aged adults living in retirement and without children or grandchildren), it is arguably the case that there are no policy issues of greater concern to families than those that pertain to the health of welfare of their children.

Society has charged the family with the primary responsibility for rearing children; indeed, the family was "invented" as the institution that could best raise children in a safe, healthy, and effective manner, that is, with effectiveness, operationalized, both historically and in an evolutionary sense (Johanson & Edey, 1981; Lerner, 1984; Lerner & Spanier, 1978, 1980), as producing citizens committed to the maintenance and perpetuation of society. Thus, the family is the key institution contributing to civil society (Lerner, 1984; Lerner & Spanier, 1978, 1980; Lerner, Sparks, & McCubbin, 1999). In this sense, *family policies represent societal principles or strategies for furthering civil society through the nurturance and socialization of children by families*. If families are effective institutions, children will become productive and committed members of society.

Nevertheless, despite the crucial connection between families, children, and civil society, it is still the case that, today, all too many people do not see the need for public policies enabling families to strengthen the lives of their children (Lerner et al., 1999; Ralston et al., 1999). America is a prime case-in-point. In the United States, there is no comprehensive and integrated national policy pertinent to all of its nation's children (Hahn, 1994). To the contrary, many Americans see youth problems as associated with other people's children. Their stereotyped image of the "at-risk" or poor child is of a minority youth living in the inner city. Yet, the probability that an American child or adolescent will be poor—and, thus, experience the several "rotten outcomes" (Schorr, 1988) of poverty—does not differ in regard to whether that youth lives in an urban or a rural setting (Huston, 1991). Moreover, the incidence of risk behaviors among American youths (Dryfoos, 1990, 1994) extends the problems of United States children and adolescents far beyond the bounds associated with the numbers of the nation's poor or minority children.

For these reasons alone, there appears to be ample reason for the development of a national youth policy pertinent to all of America's children and adolescents. However, there are additional reasons. Just as we may be concerned with developing better policies for sustaining and/or enhancing

American agricultural, industrial, manufacturing, and business interests, it would seem clear that we must not lose sight of the need to sustain the communities—and the people—involved in the production, distribution, *and* the consumption of the products of the economy.

Still, we often neglect the fact that problems of rural and urban youth—problems that are similarly structured, similarly debilitating, and similarly destructive of America's human capital—diminish significantly the nation's present and future ability to sustain and enhance the nation's economic productivity. Clearly, then, both from the standpoint of the problems of children and adolescents and from the perspective of enlightened self-interest within America's industrial, agricultural, business, and consumer communities, policies need to be directed to enhancing youth development, to preventing the loss of human capital associated with the breadth and depth of the problems confronting its children and youths. Accordingly, let us continue to use the United States as an illustration of why it is crucial to have a comprehensive public policy pertinent to positive youth development.

David Hamburg

Problems Resulting From the Absence of a National Youth Policy

Despite the historically unprecedented growth in the magnitude of the problems of America's youth (e.g., Dryfoos, 1990; Hamburg, 1992; Lerner, 2002; Lerner & Galambos, 1998), and of the contextual conditions that exacerbate these problems (e.g., changes in family structure and function and in youth poverty rates) (Hernandez, 1993; J. Lerner, 1994), there have been few major policy initiatives taken to address these increasingly more dire circumstances. Indeed, as Hamburg (1992) noted:

> During the past three decades, as all these remarkable changes increasingly jeopardized healthy child development, the nation took little notice. One arcane but important manifestation of this neglect was the low research priority and inadequate science policy for this field. As a result, the nature of this new generation of problems was poorly understood; emerging trends were insufficiently recognized; and authority tended to substitute for evidence, and ideology for analysis. Until the past few years, political, business, and professional leaders had very little to say about the problems of children and youth. Presidents have tended to pass the responsibility to the states and the private sector. State leaders often passed the responsibility back to the federal government on the one hand or over to the cities on the other. And so it goes. (p. 13)

As a result of this "treatment" of social policy regarding the nation's children and adolescents, the United States has no national youth policy per se (Hahn, 1994). Rather, policies, and the programs associated with them, tend to be focused only on the family [e.g., Aid for Dependent Children (AFDC) or the Personal Responsibility and Work Opportunity Reconciliation Act (PRWORA)] and not on youths per se (Corbett, 1995; Huston, 1991; Morelli & Verhoef, in press; Zaslow et al., 1998). As such, although these policies may influence the financial status of the family, they may not readily affect and certainly they fail to emphasize, youth development. That is, these policies do not focus on the enhancement of the capacities and the potentials of America's children and adolescents. For instance, a policy or program that provides a job for an unemployed single mother, but results in the placement of her adolescent child in an inadequate afterschool care environment for extended periods of time, may enhance the financial resources of the family; however, it may do so at the cost of placing the child in an unstimulating and, possibly, detrimental environment (Lerner et al., 1999).

Accordingly, if we are to substantially reduce the current waste of human life and potential caused by the problems confronting contemporary

American youth, new policy options must be pursued, ones that focus on children and adolescents and emphasize positive youth development and not only amelioration, remediation, and/or deterrence of problems. Thus, as argued by Pittman and Zeldin (1994):

> The reduction of problem behaviors among young people is a necessary policy goal. But it is not enough. We must be equally committed to articulating and nurturing those attributes that we wish adolescents to develop and demonstrate. (p. 53)

Accordingly, it may be argued that it is critical we develop a national policy that is aimed at promoting the positive development of youth. What would such a policy look like?

Possible Features of a National Youth Policy

The Carnegie Council of New York (1995, pp. 13–14) is once again quite helpful. In the *Great Transitions* report, they offerred five policy directions that, if followed, will marshal the resources needed to enhance the lives of the youth of America. The recommendations for policy that the Council forwards are: "1. Reengage families with their adolescent children; 2. Create developmentally appropriate schools for adolescents; 3. Develop health promotion strategies for young adolescents; 4. Strengthen communities with young adolescents; and 5. Promote the constructive potential of the media."

This last recommendation is crucial. A chapter in a textbook, such as the present one, may serve as a means to broaden your understanding of the nature of youth problems and the effective means that exist to address them. However, other ways of disseminating this information must be found. Most people in our nation do not study human development. Instead, most get their information about youth development not from science or scholarship, but from their relatively limited personal experience and from the media.

If we are to rally the resources of the nation around the needs of youths, we must convince our fellow citizens that these resources will not be wasted if they are invested in the programs we envision. The media can help tell this story—which is one, if a balanced view is presented, of hope and potential—to all segments of society.

Still other ideas exist about the important features of youth policy. Benson (1997) and Pittman and Zeldin (1994) emphasized that policy must focus on promoting positive features of youth development, and not on the deterrence of negative characteristics. As described by Benson (1997),

assets must be marshaled to promote the competencies and potentials of youth, and to develop and evaluate programs designed to promote these positive attributes. Accordingly, policy must go beyond two necessary but not sufficient goals—first, of "meeting basic human needs [through ensuring] economic security, food, shelter, good and useful work, and safety" (Benson, 1997, p. xiii) for youths and the members of their families; and second, targeting and reducing, or even eliminating "the risks and deficits that diminish or thwart the healthy development of children and adolescents. Guns, unsafe streets, predatory adults, abuse, family violence, exclusion, alcohol and other drugs, racism, and sexism are among the threats" (Benson, 1997, pp. xiii–xiv). Policy must add the third component (i.e., assets) that is crucial for building a strong young person supported through positive relationships with his/her family and community. Indeed, as Benson and colleagues (1998) noted:

> Ultimately, the most critical question is how communities can be supported to integrate and simultaneously pursue strength—building in three community infrastructures—economic, service delivery, and development. The goal of this integration is to develop a combination of policy, resources, and actions, which will meet basic human needs, reduce threats to human development, provide humane and effective access to services, and promote healthy development. (p. 156)

Implementing Policy: The Potential of Community Program–ADS Collaborations

How might we develop a system to implement the policy objective of delivering these assets to youth in the communities within which they live? Although there are certainly numerous answers to this question, an obvious principle we may use to formulate any answer is to build on the existing assets associated with such delivery. A prominent instance of such an asset is the youth-serving organizations and programs that exist in virtually all communities in America.

Whether the community-based programs in a particular community are ones associated with national organizations such as 4-H, the YMCA, Scouting, Little League, or Boys and Girls Clubs, or with the thousands of community-specific, "grassroots" organizations that are present in the communities of the United States (e.g., across America, more than 17,500 organizations have the mission of providing community-based, comprehensive, and/or integrated programs for youth; Roth et al., 1997), many scholars and advocates for youth believe that it is important to capitalize on the important role played by these youth-serving organizations in attempting to build a system to deliver assets that enhance the life chances of youths (cf. Carnegie Corporation, 1992; Dryfoos, 1990; National Research Council, 1993; Schorr, 1988). That is, advocates for the support and sustainability of youth-serving programs argue that policies must promote the financial health, and broad acceptance, of community-based youth organizations (Pittman & Zeldin, 1994).

Such acceptance involves support of the socialization experiences and youth services provided by these organizations. Moreover, acceptance can be enhanced by the collaborative expertise of applied developmental scientists to conduct the outreach scholarship (e.g., the evaluation research) needed to prove and improve the programs of these organizations and to empower program participants to sustain actions effective in promoting positive youth development.

In fact, when applied developmental scientists have engaged in such evaluations of community-based youth programs they have been able to identify the conditions under which these programs may be effective and, as such, provide ideas for the specific features of program that policymakers could support with some confidence.

For example, in the most comprehensive review to date of the evaluation research evidence pertinent to programs aimed at promoting positive youth development, Roth and colleagues (1997, 1998) noted that the extant evaluation database for such programs is quite limited, in regard to both the quantity (the number) of evaluations that have been conducted and the quality of the research that has been involved. Nevertheless, despite these limitations, it is possible to conclude that if programs are implemented well, positive youth development can be promoted (Roth et al., 1997). In particular, Roth and colleagues found that the more features of the "positive youth development" framework possessed by a program, the more likely it was to promote positive youth outcomes. In addition, they indicated that caring adolescent–adult relations are central for program effectiveness, and that program sustainability is related to program effectiveness. Longer-term programs that engage youths across the adolescent years are most effective (Roth et al., 1997).

There is additional evidence that the confidence placed in the programs offered by youth-serving organizations is warranted. Scales and Leffert (1999) also reviewed the results of evaluations of such youth programs. They found that involvement in effective youth programs is associated with several significant indicators of positive youth development,

including increased self-esteem, popularity, sense of personal control, and identity development. In addition, youths in such programs show better development of life skills, leadership skills, decision-making skills, and public-speaking ability (Scales & Leffert, 1999). Moreover, Scales and Leffert (1999) reported that there is an association between participation in effective youth programs, and increased dependability and job responsibility; better communication with family members; fewer instances of problems of loneliness, shyness, and hopelessness; and decreased involvement in risky behaviors such as drug use and juvenile delinquency.

Conclusions

Accordingly, youth programs, when they adhere to the principles of effective programming ("best practice") previously discussed, are essential assets in a coordinated effort to promote positive youth development. The translation involved in turning such community programs into policy is predicated on the view that the promotion of youth development is not the exclusive province of any single organization or agency (Dryfoos, 1990; Hamburg, 1992; Schorr, 1988). To the contrary, an integrated, community-wide effort is necessary both to foster positive youth development through such programs (Dryfoos, 1990; Hamburg, 1992; Schorr, 1988) and to evaluate the success of these efforts (Jacobs, 1988; Jacobs & Kapuscik, 2000). That is, given the evidence that exists about the outcomes of positive youth development programs, it is reasonable to conclude that public policy must move from a focus on just building effective programs to also building cohesive and effective communities (National Research Council, 1993; Pittman & Zeldin, 1994).

Hamburg (1992) made a similar point. He suggested three policy initiatives that, together, would enhance the capacity of communities to (a) provide comprehensive and integrated services that (b) promote positive youth development through (c) the provision of effective programs delivered by a well-trained staff. Thus, Hamburg (1992) noted that he would:

> First, use federal and state mechanisms to provide funding to local communities in ways that encourage the provision of coherent, comprehensive services. State and federal funding should provide incentives to encourage collaboration and should be adaptable to local circumstances.
>
> Second, provide training programs to equip professional staff and managers with the necessary skills. Such programs would include training for collaboration among professionals in health, mental health,

education, and social services, and would instill a respectful, sensitive attitude toward working with clients, patients, parents, and students from different backgrounds.

Three, use widespread evaluation to determine what intervention is useful for whom, how funds are being spent, and whether the services are altogether useful. (p. 166)

Similarly, a report by the National Research Council (1993) noted that building supportive communities for youth faced with the destruction of their life chances

will require a major commitment from federal and state governments and the private sector, including support for housing, transportation, economic development, and the social services required by poor and low-income residents. (p. 239)

Furthermore, Pittman and Zeldin (1994) emphasized that for youth development programs to attain sustained successes—across the span of individual lives and across multiple generations—issues of individual and economic diversity must be clearly and directly confronted. Specifically, poverty and racism must be a continued, core focus of social policy. We must continue to be vigilant about the pernicious sequelae of poverty among children and adolescents, the vast overrepresentation of minority youth among the ranks of our nation's poor, and the greater probability that minority youth will be involved in the several problem behaviors besetting their generation.

In short, the policy recommendations forwarded by Pittman and Zeldin (1994), Hamburg (1992), Benson (1997), Lerner and colleagues (1999), and the National Research Council (1993) stress the importance of comprehensive and integrative actions linking youth, families, programs, evaluation research, and policymakers. These actions involve, then, both proximal community participation and the contributions of broader segments of the public and private sectors and of community-based evaluations aimed at demonstrating the conditions under which positive youth development may be promoted (Damon, 1997).

In sum, ADS, as an instance of outreach scholarship, contributes to the community-collaborative linkage between scholarship and policies and programs aimed at enhancing the capacity of individuals and communities to contribute to civil society. As a consequence, ADS is attracting the increasing interest of both policymakers (e.g., Kennedy, 1999; Thompson, 1999) and the private (Overton & Burkhardt, 1999; Sherrod, 1999b) and public funders (Jensen, Hoagwood, & Trickett, 1999) of such work.

By providing such collaborative knowledge, scholars are making, by definition, value-added contributions to the community; they are promoting social justice by facilitating the development and utilization in the community of abilities (i.e., power) to take action pursuant to controlling the future of community members' individual and collective lives. Brought to scale, this empowerment institutionalizes the democratization on which civil society depends (O'Connell, 1999).

APPLIED DEVELOPMENTAL SCIENCE AND THE FUTURE OF AMERICAN CIVIL SOCIETY

As previously noted, civil society rests on integrative contributions by all sectors and institutions of a nation in support of social justice. Such contributions to civil society would assure that there is a "level playing field" for individuals to pursue lives marked by positive and healthy contributions to self, family, and community. To maintain and perpetuate such actions, social functioning that supports civil society must be transformed into public policy.

Applied developmental science may act as an instrument for the promotion of civil society by (a) ADS-oriented scholars conducting research that engages public policy and (b) such scholars working to promote in their institutions a sustained commitment to engaging their communities in collaborative actions that merge research and service in support of civil society (Kellogg Commission, 1999).

Accordingly, ADS research may engage public policy by ascertaining whether current local, state, and federal policies are supported by or run counter to research evidence and by providing empirical grounding for policies (Jensen et al., 1999). Studies can be made of programs and policies already in place or of the likely impacts of actions that may be developed into policies (Jensen et al., 1999).

If such ADS scholarship and the institutions within which such work is conducted are to contribute to the enhancement and future maintenance of civil society, they must aid policymakers in developing principles or strategies (i.e., policies) that enable all families to produce children capable of, and committed to, contributing to self and society in a positive and integrated way. In other words, in the superordinate sense of enabling civil society to be maintained and perpetuated, all families with children—no matter what their particular structure may be (e.g., families wherein two biological parents rear children, families wherein stepparents are involved in childrearing, families with adopted children, or single-parent families)—have the responsibility of socializing the next generation in ways that allow children to become productive and committed members of society. Any society, then, needs to develop rules (policies) that enable such contributions to be made by the diverse families that exist within it (Lerner et al., 1999).

A model of how civil society is furthered through the family's effective nurturance and socialization of children is presented in Figure 19.4. This figure summarizes the results of several studies conducted within an ADS-related perspective (e.g., Benson, Leffert, Scales, & Blyth, 1998; Leffert et al., 1998; Scales, Benson, Leffert, & Blyth, 2000), as well as, the views found in other, related scholarly publications (e.g., Benson, 1997; Damon, 1997; Dryfoos, 1998; Lerner et al., 1999; Scales & Leffert, 1999; Schorr, 1997). This literature describes (a) the essential functions required

for families to promote positive development in their children, (b) the resources necessary for families to transform their functional characteristics into valued child outcomes, and (c) the elements of these positive youth outcomes (i.e., the features of healthy youth development).

Thus, the figure indicates that public policies should be aimed at ensuring that families have the capacity to provide for children's boundaries and expectations, fulfillment of physiological and safety needs, a climate of love and caring, the inculcation of self-esteem, the encouragement for growth, positive values, and positive links to the community. The programs that derive from these policies should ensure that the resources that families need to nurture and socialize children in this manner are available. These resources would give children a healthy start, a safe environment, freedom from prejudice and discrimination, an education resulting in marketable skills, and opportunities to "give back" to their communities—to volunteer and serve.

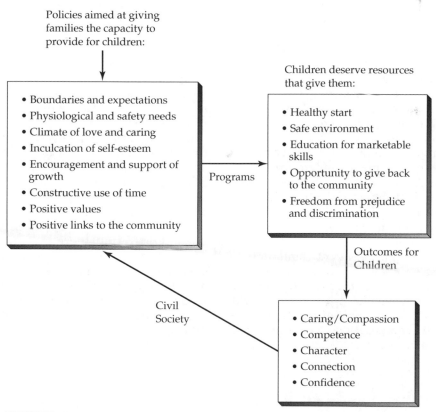

FIGURE 19.4
A model of a national youth policy: the integration of families, children, and civil society.
Source: Lerner, Fisher, and Weinberg (2000a), p. 16.

If programs are effective in delivering these resources, then several positive developmental outcomes will accrue among children—the "five Cs" will be inculcated and the "sixth C"—contribution to civil society—will emerge from them. Then, as indicated in the model displayed in Figure 19.4, the enhancement of civil society, in turn, influences the family and the young people reared within it. As young people grow up in families providing the orientation to self and society displayed in the figure, they will take on the behaviors that the policies and associated programs were designed to inculcate. Thus, the model indicates that the growth of civil society will occur through facilitating the nurturing and socialization function of families.

CONCLUSIONS

Ultimately, we must all continue to educate ourselves about the best means available to promote enhanced life chances among all of our youth and families, but especially among those whose potential for positive contributions to civil society is most in danger of being wasted (Dryfoos, 1990, 1998; Hamburg, 1992; Lerner et al., 1999; Schorr, 1988, 1997). The collaborative expertise of the research and program delivery communities can provide much of this information, especially if it is obtained in partnership with strong, empowered communities. Policies promoting such coalitions could become an integral component of a national youth and family development policy aimed at creating caring communities with the capacity to further the healthy development of children and families (Jensen et al., 1999; Kennedy, 1999; Overton & Burkhardt, 1999; Sherrod, 1999a; Spanier, 1999; Thompson, 1999).

Clearly, the key fuel to enable a model for a national youth and family policy to work is one that builds on the existing assets of communities. These assets are the current inventory of building blocks for civil society in America. Accordingly, they must be employed to build the programs that will be associated with the enactment of the model displayed in Figure 19.4. Facilitation of such program

development consists of key operational ways ADS may contribute to civil society (e.g., through technical assistance, asset mapping, needs assessment, issues identification, demonstration research, participatory action research, and evaluation research). In this way, developmental scholars can do what they have been trained to do (i.e., scholarship about the course of human life), but they can do it in the context of collaboration with communities.

These partnerships, if facilitated and rewarded by an engaged university (Kellogg Commission, 1999; Spanier, 1997, 1999), will enable scholars and their community collaborators to enhance social justice and contribute to civil society. As such, these collaborations will model how universities may be part of a multi-institutional system that is changing American society by moving it in the direction of greater equity and access to democratizing resources for all its diverse citizens.

Given the enormous, indeed historically unprecedented, challenges facing the families of America and the world, perhaps especially as they strive to raise healthy and successful children capable of leading civil society productively, responsibly, and morally across the twenty-first century (Benson, 1997; Damon, 1997; Lerner, 1995a; Lerner et al., 2000a, 2000b), there is no time to lose in the development of such collaborations. The field of human development has an opportunity, through the publication of its applied developmental science research, to serve both scholarship and the communities, families, and people of our world.

By integrating policies and programs sensitive to the diversity of nations, their communities, and their people, by combining the assets of our scholarly and research traditions with the assets of our people (Benson, Leffert, Scales, & Blyth, 1998; Leffert et al., 1998; Scales & Leffert, 1999), we can improve upon the often-cited idea of Kurt Lewin (1943) that there is nothing as practical as a good theory. We can, through the application of developmental science, serve our world's citizens and demonstrate that there is nothing of greater value to civil society than a science devoted to using its scholarship to improve the life chances of all people.

References

Abravanel, E. (1968). The development of intersensory patterning with regard to selected, spatial dimensions. *Monographs of the Society for Research in Child Development, 33, 2*, 118.

Adams, G. R. (1977). Physical attractiveness research: Toward a developmental social psychology of beauty. *Human Development, 20*, 217–239.

Adams, G. R. (1991). Runaways, negative consequences for. In R. M. Lerner, A. C. Petersen, & J. Brooks-Gunn (Eds.), *Encyclopedia of adolescence* (pp. 947–950). New York: Garland Publishing.

Adams, G. R., Day, T., Dyk, P., Frede, E., & Rogers, D. (1992). On the dialectics of pubescence and psychosocial development. *Journal of Early Adolescence, 12*, 348–365.

Adams, G. R., & Jones, R. M. (1983). Female adolescents' identity development: Age comparisons and perceived childrearing experiences. *Developmental Psychology, 19*, 249–256.

Adams, M. J., Treiman, R., & Pressley, M. (1998). Reading, writing, and literacy. In W. Damon (Series Ed.), I. E. Sigel, & K. A. Renninger (Vol. Eds.), *Handbook of child psychology: Vol. 4. Child psychology in practice* (5th ed., pp. 275–355). New York: Wiley.

Ainsworth, M. D. S., Blehar, M. C., Water, E., & Wall, S. (1978). *Patterns of attachment*. Hillsdale, NJ: Erlbaum.

Alexander, C. N., & Langer E. J. (Eds.). (1990). Higher stages of human development. New York: Oxford University Press.

Allport, G. W. (1937). *Personality: A psychological interpretation*. New York: Holt.

Altman, I., & Rogoff, B. (1987). World views in psychology: Trait, interactional, organismic and transactional perspectives. In D. Stokols & I. Altman (Eds.), *Handbook of environmental psychology* (pp. 7–40). New York: Wiley.

Ames, C., & Ames, R. (Eds.). (1989). *Research on motivation in education: Goals and cognitions*. New York: Academic Press.

Anastasi, A. (1958). Heredity, environment, and the question "how?" *Psychological Review, 65*, 197–208.

Anderson, P. W. (1972). More is different. *Science, 177*, 393–396.

Ansari, A. A., Gouthro, S., Ahmad, K., & Steele, C. (1996). Hospital-based behavior modification program for adolescents: Evaluation and predictors of outcome. *Adolescence, 31*(122), 469–476.

Anthony, J. (1969). The reaction of adults to adolescents and their behavior. In G. Caplan & S. Lebovici (Eds.), *Adolescence*. New York: Basic Books.

Archer, S. L. (1985). Identity and the choice of social rules. *New Directions for Child Development, 30*, 79–99.

Archer, S. L. (1989). Adolescent identity: An appraisal of health and intervention. *Journal of Adolescence, 12*, 341–343.

Archer, S. L. (1991). Identity development, gender differences in. In R. M. Lerner, A. C. Petersen, & J. Brooks-Gunn (Eds.), *Encyclopedia of adolescence* (pp. 522–524). New York: Garland Publishing.

Archer, S. L., & Waterman, A. S. (1991). Ego development. In R. M. Lerner, A. C. Petersen, & J. Brooks-Gunn (Eds.), *Encyclopedia of adolescence* (pp. 295–300). New York: Garland Publishing.

Aronson, L. R., Tobach, E., Lehrman, D. S., & Rosenblatt, J. S. (Eds.). (1970). *Development and evolution of behavior: Essays in memory of T. C. Schneirla*. San Francisco, CA: W. H. Freeman.

Aronson, L. R., Tobach, E., Rosenblatt, J. S, & Lehrman, D. S. (Eds.). (1972). *Selected writings of T. C. Schneirla*. San Francisco, CA: W. H. Freeman.

Aslin, R. N., Jusczyk, P. W., & Pisoni, D. B. (1998). Speech and auditory processing during infancy: Constraints and precursors to language. In W. Damon (Series Ed.), D. Kuhn, & R. S. Siegler (Vol. Eds.), *Handbook of child psychology: Vol. 2. Cognition, perception, and language* (5th ed., pp. 147–198). New York: Wiley.

Atz, J. W. (1970). The application of the idea of homology to behavior. In L. R. Aronson, E. Tobach, D. S. Lehrman, & J. S. Rosenblatt (Eds.), *Development and evolution of behavior: Essays in memory of T. C. Schneirla* (pp. 53–74). San Francisco, CA: W. H. Freeman.

Baca Zinn, M., & Eitzen, D. S. (1993). Diversity in families (3rd ed.). New York: HarperCollins College Publishers.

Baer, D. M. (1970). An age-irrelevant concept of development. *Merrill-Palmer Quarterly of Behavior and Development, 16,* 238–245.

Baer, D. M. (1976). The organism as host. *Human Development, 19,* 87–89.

Baer, D. M. (1982). Behavior analysis and developmental psychology: Discussant comments. *Human Development, 25,* 357–361.

Baillargeon, R. (1987). Object permanence in very young infants. *Cognition, 20,* 191–208.

Bakan, D. (1966). *The duality of human existence.* Chicago, IL: Rand McNally.

Baldwin, J. M. (1897a). *Mental development in the child and the race.* New York: Macmillan Publishing.

Baldwin, J. M. (1897b). *Social and ethical interpretations in mental development: A case study in social psychology.* New York: Macmillan Publishing.

Baltes, B. B. & Dickson, M. W. (2001). Using the life-span models in industrial/organizational psychology: The theory of selective optimization with compensation. *Applied Developmental Science, 5,* 51–62.

Baltes, M. M. (1987). Erfolgreiches altern als ausdruck von verhaltenkompetenz und unweltqualität. In C. Niemitz (Ed.), *Der mensch im zusammenspiel von anlage und umwelt* (pp. 353–377). Frankfurt: Suhrkamp.

Baltes, M. M., & Carstensen, L. L. (1996). The process of successful ageing. *Ageing and Society, 16,* 397–422.

Baltes, M. M., & Carstensen, L. L. (1998). Social-psychological theories and their applications to ageing: From individual to collective. In V. L. Bengtson & K. W. Schaie (Eds.), *Handbook of theories of ageing* (pp. 209–226). New York: Springer.

Baltes, P. B. (1968). Longitudinal and cross sectional sequences in the study of age and generational effects. *Human Development, 11,* 145–171.

Baltes, P. B. (1979a). Life-span developmental psychology: Some converging observations on history and theory. In P. B. Baltes & O. G. Brim, Jr. (Eds.), *Life-span development and behavior* (Vol. 2, pp. 255–279). New York: Academic Press.

Baltes, P. B. (1979b). On the potential and limits of child development: Life-span developmental perspectives. *Newsletter of the Society of Research in Child Development,* 1–4.

Baltes, P. B. (1983). Life-span developmental psychology: Observations on history and theory revisited. In R. M. Lerner (Ed.), *Developmental psychology: Historical and philosophical perspectives* (pp. 79–111). Hillsdale, NJ: Erlbaum.

Baltes, P. B. (1987). Theoretical propositions of life-span developmental psychology: On the dynamics between growth and decline. *Developmental Psychology, 23,* 611–626.

Baltes, P. B. (1997). On the incomplete architecture of human ontogeny: Selection, optimization, and compensation as foundations of developmental theory. *American Psychologist, 52,* 366–380.

Baltes, P. B., & Baltes, M. M. (1980). Plasticity and variability in psychological ageing: Methodological and theoretical issues. In G. E. Gurski (Ed.), *Determining the effects of ageing on the central nervous system* (pp. 41–66). Berlin: Schering AG (Oraniendruck).

Baltes, P. B., & Baltes, M. M. (1990). Psychological perspectives on successful aging: The model of selective optimization with compensation. In P. B. Baltes & M. M. Baltes (Eds.), *Successful aging: Perspectives from the behavioral sciences* (pp. 1–34). New York: Cambridge University Press.

Baltes, P. B., Baltes, M. M., & Reinert, G. (1970). The relationship between time of measurement and age in cognitive development of children: An application of cross-sectional sequences. *Human Development, 13,* 258–268.

Baltes, P. B., Baltes, M. M., & Reinert, G. (1970). The relationship between time of measurement and age in cognitive development of children: An application of cross-sectional sequences. *Human Development, 13,* 258–268.

Baltes, P. B., & Brim, O. G., Jr. (Eds.). (1984). *Life-span development and behavior* (Vol. 6). New York: Academic Press.

Baltes, P. B., Cornelius, S. W., & Nesselroade, J. R. (1978). Cohort effects in behavioral development: Theoretical and methodological perspectives. In W. A. Collins (Ed.), *Minnesota symposia on child psychology* (Vol. 11, pp. 1–63). Hillsdale, NJ: Erlbaum.

Baltes, P. B., Dittmann-Kohli, F., & Dixon, R. A. (1984). New perspectives on the development of intelligence in adulthood: Toward a dual-process conception and a model of selective optimization with compensation. In P. B. Baltes & O. G. Brim, Jr. (Eds.), *Life-span development and behavior* (Vol. 6). New York: Academic Press.

Baltes, P. B., Featherman, D. L., & Lerner, R. M. (Eds.). (1986). *Life-span development and behavior* (Vol. 7). Hillsdale, NJ: Erlbaum.

Baltes, P. B., & Kliegl, R. (1992). Further testing of limits of cognitive plasticity: Negative age differences in a innemonic skill are robust. *Developmental Psychology, 28,* 121–125.

Baltes, P. B., Lindenberger, U., & Staudinger, U. M. (1998). Life-span theory in developmental psychology. In W. Damon (Series Ed.) & R. M. Lerner

(Vol. Ed.), *Handbook of child psychology: Vol. 1. Theoretical models of human development* (5th ed., pp. 1029–1144). New York: Wiley.

Baltes, P. B., & Nesselroade, J. R. (1973). The developmental analysis of individual differences on multiple measures. In J. R. Nesselroade & H. W. Reese (Eds.), *Life-span developmental psychology: Introduction to research methodological issues* (pp. 219–251). New York: Academic Press.

Baltes, P. B., Reese, H. W., & Lipsitt, L. P. (1980). *Life-span developmental psychology, 31,* 65–110.

Baltes, P. B., Reese, H. W., & Nesselroade, J. R. (1977). *Life-span developmental psychology: Introduction to research methods.* Monterey, CA: Brooks/Cole.

Baltes, P. B., & Schaie, K. W. (Eds.). (1973). *Life-span developmental psychology: Personality and socialization.* New York: Academic Press.

Baltes, P. B., & Schaie, K. W. (1973). On life-span developmental research paradigms: Retrospects and prospects. In P. B. Baltes & W. K. Schaie (Eds.), *Life-span developmental pyschology: Personality and socialization.* New York: Academic Press.

Baltes, P. B., & Schaie, K. W. (1974). Aging and IQ: The myth of the twilight years. *Psychology Today, 7,* 35–40.

Baltes, P. B., & Schaie, K. W. (1976). On the plasticity of intelligence in adulthood and old age: Where Horn and Donaldson fail. *American Psychologist, 31,* 720–725.

Baltes, P. B., Smith, J., & Staudinger, U. M. (1992). Wisdom and successful aging. In T. B. Sonderegger (Ed.), *Nebraska Symposium on Motivation* (Vol. 39, pp. 123–167). Lincoln, NE: University of Nebraska.

Baltes, P. B., & Staudinger, U. M. (Eds.). (1996) *Interactive minds: Life-span perspectives on the social foundation of cognition.* New York: Cambridge University Press.

Baltes, P. B., Staudinger, U. M., & Lindenberger, U. (1999). Lifespan psychology: Theory and application to intellectual functioning. In J. T. Spence, J. M. Darley, & D. J. Foss (Eds.), *Annual Review of Psychology* (Vol. 50, pp. 471–507). Palo Alto, CA: Annual Reviews.

Baltes, P. B., & Willis, S. L. (1982). Plasticity and enhancement of intellectual functioning in old age: Penn State's Adult Development and Enrichment Program (ADEP). In F. I. M. Craik & S. E. Trehub (Eds.), *Aging and cognitive processes* (pp. 353–389). New York: Plenum Publishing.

Bandura, A. (1964). The stormy decade: Fact or fiction? *Psychology in the School, 1,* 224–231.

Bandura, A. (1965). Influence of models' reinforcement of contingencies on the acquisition of imitative responses. *Journal of Personality and Social Psychology, 1,* 589–595.

Bandura, A. (1971). *Social learning theory.* Morristown, NJ: General Learning Press.

Bandura, A. (1977). Self-efficacy: Toward a unifying theory of behavioral change. *Psychological Review, 84,* 191–215.

Bandura, A. (1978). The self system in reciprocal determinism. *American Psychologist, 33,* 344–358.

Bandura, A. (1986). *Social foundations of thought and action: A social cognitive theory.* Englewood Cliffs, NJ: Prentice-Hall.

Bandura, A., & McDonald, F. (1963). The influence of social reinforcement and the behavior of models in shaping children's moral judgement. *Journal of Abnormal and Social Psychology, 67,* 274–281.

Bandura, A., & Walters, R. H. (1963). *Social learning and personality development.* New York: Holt, Rinehart & Winston.

Barash, D. P. (1977). *Sociobiology and behavior.* New York: Elsevier.

Barlow, G. W. (1980). The development of sociobiology: A biologist's perspective. In G. W. Barlow & J. Silverberg (Eds.), *Sociobiology: Beyond nature/nurture* (pp. 3–34). Boulder, CO: Westview Press.

Barlow, G. W., & Silverberg, J. (Ed.). (1980). *Sociobiology: Beyond nature/nurture? Reports, definitions, and debate.* Boulder, CO: Westview Press.

Barnett, H. L., & Einhorn, A. H. (Eds.). (1972). *Pediatrics* (15th ed.). New York: Appleton-Century-Crofts.

Barraclough, C. A. (1966). Modifications of CNS regulation of reproduction after exposure of prepubertal rats to steroid hormones. *Recent Progress in Hormone Research, 22,* 503–539.

Basser, L. S. (1962). Hemiplegia of early onset and the faculty of speech with special reference to the effects of hemispherectomy. *Brain, 85,* 427–460.

Bateson, P. P. G. (1964). Effects of similarity between rearing and testing conditions on chicks' following and avoiding responses. *Journal of Comparative and Physiological Psychology, 57,* 100–103.

Bateson, P. P. G. (1966). The characteristics and context of imprinting. *Biological Reviews, 41,* 177–220.

Bateson, P. P. G. (1979). How do sensitive periods arise and what are they for? *Animal Behavior, 27,* 470–486.

Bateson, P. P. G. (1983). The interpretation of sensitive periods. In A. Oliverio & M. Zapella (Eds.), *The behavior of human infants* (pp. 57–70). New York: Plenum Publishing.

Battistich, V., Schaps, E., Watson, M., & Solomon, D. (1996). Prevention effects of the Child Development Project: Early findings from an ongoing multisite demonstration trial. *Journal of Adolescent Research, 11*(1), 12–35.

Bauer, E., Fischer, E., & Lenz, F. (1927). Grundriss der menschlichen Erblicheitslehre und Rassenhygiene (Vol. 1, 3rd ed.). Munich, Germany: J. F. Lehmann.

Baumrind, D. (1971). Current patterns of parental authority. *Developmental Psychology Monographs, 4*, No. 1, Part 2.

Baumrind, D. (1972). An exploratory study of socialization effects on Black children: Some black–white comparisons. *Child Development, 43*, 261–267.

Baxter, B. (1966). Effect on visual deprivation during postnatal maturation of the electroencephalogram of the cat. *Experimental Neurology, 14*, 224–237.

Bayley, N. (1949). Consistency and variability in the growth of intelligence from birth to eighteen years. *Journal of Genetic Psychology, 75*, 165–196.

Bayley, N., & Oden, M. H. (1955). The maintenance of intellectual ability in gifted adults. *Journal of Gerontology, 10*, 91–107.

Beach, F. A. (1950). The Snark was a Boojum. *American Psychologist, 5*, 115–124.

Beals, K. L., Smith, C. L., & Dodd, S. M. (1984). Brain size, cranial morphology, climate, and time machines. *Current Anthropology, 25*, 301–330.

Bell, R. Q. (1968). A reinterpretation of the direction of effects in studies of socialization. *Psychological Review, 75*, 81–95.

Bell, R. Q., & Harper, L. V. (1977). *Child effects on adults*. Hillsdale, NJ: Erlbaum.

Belsky, J., Lerner, R. M., & Spanier, G. B. (1984). *The child in the family*. Reading, MA: Addison-Wesley.

Belsky, J., & Tolan, W. J. (1981). Infants as producers of their own development: An ecological analysis. In R. M. Lerner & N. A. Busch-Rossnagel (Eds.), *Individuals as producers of their own development: A life-span perspective* (pp. 87–116). New York: Academic Press.

Bennett, A. J., Lesch, K. P., Heils, A., Long, J., Lorenz, J., Shoaf, S. E., Champoux, M., Suomi, S. J., Linnoila, M., & Higley, J. D. (in press). Serotonin transporter genotype and early experience interact to influence nonhuman primate CNS serotonin turnover. *Molecular Psychiatry*.

Benson, M. J., Harris, P. B., & Rogers, C. S. (1992). Identity consequences of attachment to mothers and fathers among late adolescents. *Journal of Research on Adolescence, 2*(3), 187–204.

Benson, P. L. (1997). *All kids are our kids: What communities must do to raise caring and responsible children and adolescents*. San Francisco, CA: Jossey-Bass.

Benson, P. L., Leffert, N., Scales, P. C., & Blyth, D. A. (1998). Beyond the "village" rhetoric: Creating healthy communities for children and adolescents. *Applied Developmental Science, 2*(3), 138–159.

Berg, P. (1981). Dissections and reconstructions of genes and chromosomes. *Science, 213*, 296–303.

Berger, P. L., Berger, P. L., & Kellner, H. (1967). *The homeless mind: Modernization and unconsciousness*. New York: Random House.

Berndt, T. J. (1978). Stages as descriptions, explanations, and testable constructs. *The Behavioral and Brain Sciences, 2*, 183–184.

Bertentahal, B. I., & Clifton, R. K. (1998). Perception and action. In W. Damon (Series Ed.), D. Kuhn, & R. S. Siegler (Vol. Eds.), *Handbook of child psychology: Vol. 2. Cognition, perception, and language* (5th ed., pp. 51–102). New York: Wiley.

Bidell, T. R., & Fisher, K. W. (1992). Beyond the stage debate: Action, structure, and variability in Piagetian theory and research. In R. Sternberg & C. Berg (Eds.), *Intellectual development* (pp. 100–140). New York: Cambridge University Press.

Bidell, T. R., & Fisher, K. W. (1996). Between nature and nurture: The role of human agency in the epigenesis of intelligence. In R. Sternberg & E. Grigorenko (Eds.), *Intelligence: Heredity and environment* (pp. 193–242). Cambridge, England: Cambridge University Press.

Bijou, S. W., (1976). *Child development: The basic stage of early childhood*. Englewood Cliffs, NJ: Prentice-Hall.

Bijou, S. W., & Baer, D. M. (1961). *Child development: A systemic and empirical theory* (Vol. 1). New York: Appleton-Century-Crofts.

Bijou, S. W., & Baer, D. M. (1967). *Child development: Readings in experimental analysis*. New York: Appleton-Century-Crofts.

Bijou, S. W., & Baer, D. M. (1975). *Child development: Universal stage of infancy* (Vol. 2). Englewood Cliffs, NJ: Prentice-Hall.

Binding, K., & Hoche, A. (1920). *Die Freigabe der vernichtung lebensunwerten lebens (The Sanctioning of the destruction of lives unworthy to be lived)*. Leipzig, Germany: F. Meiner.

Binet, A., & Simon, T. (1905a). Sur la necessite d'etablir un diagnostic scientific des etats inferieurs de l'intelligence. *L'Annee Psychologique, 11*, 162–190.

Binet, A., & Simon, T. (1905b). Methodes nouvelles pour le diagnostic du niveau intellectuel des anormaux. *L'Annee Psychologique, 11*, 191–244.

Birch, H. G., & Lefford, A. (1963). Intersensory development in children. *Monographs of the Society for Research in Child Development, 28*(5), 89.

Birch, H. G., & Lefford, A. (1967). Visual differentiation, intersensory integration, and voluntary motor control. *Monographs of the Society for Research in Child Development, 32*(2), 110.

Birkel, R., Lerner, R. M., & Smyer, M. A. (1989). Applied developmental psychology as an implementation of a life-span view of human development. *Journal of Applied Developmental Psychology, 10,* 425–445.

Bitterman, M. E. (1960). Toward a comparative psychology of learning. *American Psychologist, 15,* 704–712.

Bitterman, M. E. (1965). Phyletic differences in learning. *American Psychologist, 20,* 396–410.

Bitterman, M. E. (1975). The comparative analysis of learning. *Science, 188,* 699–709.

Blakemore, C., & Van Sluyters, R. C. (1974). Reversal of the physiological effects of monocular deprivation in kittens: Further evidence for a sensitive period. *Journal of Physiology, 248,* 663–716.

Block, J. (1961). *The Q-sort method in personality assessment and psychiatric research.* Springfield, IL: Charles C. Thomas.

Block, J. (1971). *Lives through time.* Berkeley, CA: Bancroft.

Block, J. (1982). Assimilation, accommodation, and the dynamics of personality development. *Child Development, 53,* 281–295.

Block, J. H. (1973). Conceptions of sex roles: Some cross-cultural and longitudinal perspectives. *American Psychologist 28,* 512–526.

Block, J. H., & Block, J. (1980). The role of ego-control and ego-resiliency in the organization of behavior. In W. A. Collins (Ed.), *Minnesota Symposia on Child Psychology* (Vol. 13, pp. 89–101). Hillsdale, NJ: Erlbaum.

Bloom, B. S. (1964). *Stability and change in human characteristics.* New York: Wiley.

Bloom, L. (1998). Language acquisition in its developmental context. In W. Damon (Series Ed.), D. Kuhn, & R. S. Siegler (Vol. Eds.), *Handbook of child psychology: Vol. 2. Cognition, perception, and language* (5th ed., pp. 309–370). New York: Wiley.

Blyth, D. A., & Leffert, N. (1995). Communities as contexts for adolescent development: An empirical analysis. *Journal of Adolescent Research, 10*(1), 64–87.

Bock, W. J. (1979). A synthetic explanation of macroevolutionary change—a reductionistic approach. *Bulletin of the Carnegie Museum of Natural History, 13,* 20–69.

Bodmer, W. F., & Cavalli-Sforza, L. L. (1976). *Genetics, evolution and man.* San Francisco, CA: W. H. Freeman.

Boelsche, W. (1906). *Die Schopfungstage: Umrisse zu einer Entwicklungsgeschichte der Natur.* Dresden, Germany: Reissner

Bolles, R. C. (1967). *Theory of motivation.* New York: Harper & Row.

Bonnen, J. T. (1986). A century of science in agriculture: Lessons for science policy. *American Journal of Agricultural Economics, 68,* 1065–1080.

Bonnen, J. T. (1998). The land-grant idea and the evolving outreach university. In R. M. Lerner & L. A. K. Simon (Eds.), *University-community collaborations for the twenty-first century: Outreach scholarship for youth and families* (pp. 25–71). New York: Garland Publishing.

Boring, E. G. (1950). *A history of experimental psychology* (2nd ed). New York: Appleton-Century-Crofts.

Bornstein, M. H. (Ed.). (1995a). *Handbook of parenting, Vol. 3. Status and social conditions of parenting.* Mahwah, NJ: Erlbaum.

Bornstein, M. H. (1995b). Parenting infants. In M. H. Bornstein (Ed.), *Handbook of parenting* (Vol. 1, pp. 3–39). Mahwah, NJ: Erlbaum.

Bornstein, M. H., Tamis-LeMonda, C. S., Tal, J., Ludemann, P., Toda, S., Rahn, C., Pêcheux, M., Bornstein, M., & Bruner, J. S. (Eds.). (1989). *Interaction in human development.* Hillsdale, NJ: Erlbaum.

Bornstein, M. H., Tamis-LeMonda, C. S., Tal, J., Ludemann, P., Toda, S., Rahn, C. W., Pêcheux, M. G., Azuma, H., & Vardi, D. (1992). Maternal responsiveness to infants in three societies: The United States, France, and Japan. *Child Development, 63,* 808–821.

Bouchard, T. J., Jr. (1982). Identical twins reared apart: Reanalysis or pseudoanalysis. Review of: S. L. Farber (1981). *Identical twins reared apart: A reanalysis.* New York: Basic Books. *Contemporary Psychology, 27,* 190–191.

Bouchard, T. J., Jr., & McGue, M. (1981). Familial studies of intelligence: A review. *Science, 212,* 1055–1059.

Bower, T. G. R. (1966). Slant perception and shape constancy in infants. *Science, 151,* 832–834.

Bowlby, J. (1969). *Attachment and loss: Vol. 1. Attachment.* New York: Basic Books.

Bowman, H. A., & Spanier, G. B. (1978). *Modern marriage* (8th ed.). New York: McGraw-Hill.

Boyer, E. L. (1990). *Scholarship reconsidered: Priorities of the professoriate.* Princeton, NJ: The Carnegie Foundation for the Advancement of Teaching.

Boyer, E. L. (1994, March 9). Creating the new American college. *The Chronicle of Higher Education*, A48.

Brabeck, M. (1983). Moral judgment: Theory and research on differences between males and females. *Developmental Review, 3,* 274–291.

Brack, C., Brack, G., & Orr, D. P. (1996). Adolescent health promotion: Testing a model using multidimensional scaling. *Journal of Research on Adolescence, 6*(2), 139–149.

Brainerd, C. J. (1978). The stage question in cognitive–developmental theory. *The Behavioral and Brain Sciences, 2,* 173–182.

Brainerd, C. J. (1979). Further replies on invariant sequences, explanation and other stage criteria. *The Behavioral and Brain Sciences, 2,* 149–152.

Brandtstädter, J., & Lerner, R. M. (Eds.). (1999a). *Action and self-development: Theory and research through the life-span.* Thousand Oaks, CA: Sage.

Brandtstädter, J., & Lerner, R. M. (1999b). Development, action, and intentionality: A view of the issues. In J. Brandtstädter & R. M. Lerner (Eds.), *Action and self-development: Theory and research through the life-span* (pp. ix–xx). Thousand Oaks, CA: Sage.

Brandtstädter, J. (1998). Action perspectives on human development. In W. Damon (Series Ed.) & R. M. Lerner (Vol. Ed.), *Handbook of child psychology: Vol. 1. Theoretical models of human development* (5th ed., pp. 807–863). New York: Wiley

Brandtstädter, J. (1999). The self in action and development: Cultural, biosocial, and onotgenetic bases of intentional self-development. In J. Brandtstädter & R. M. Lerner (Eds.), *Action and self-development: Theory and research through the life-span* (pp. 37–65). Thousand Oaks, CA: Sage.

Brandtstädter, J., & Wentura, D. (1994). Veränderungen der Zeit- und Zukunftsperspektive in Übergang zum höheren Erwachsenenalter: Entwicklungspsychologische und differentielle Aspekte. *Zeitschrift für Entwicklungspsychologie und Pädagogische Psychologie, 26,* 2–21.

Brazelton, T. B., Koslowski, B., & Main, M. (1974). The origins of reciprocity: The early mother–infant interaction. In M. Lewis & L. A. Rosenblum (Eds.), *The effect of the infant on its caregivers.* New York: Wiley

Breland, K., & Breland, M. (1961). The misbehavior of organisms. *American Psychologist, 16,* 681–684.

Brent, S. B. (1978). Individual specialization, collective adaptation and rate of environment change. *Human Development, 21,* 21–33.

Bridgman, A., & Philips, D. (Eds.). (1996). *Child Care for low income families: Directions for research: Summary of a workshop.* Washington, DC: National Academy Press.

Brim, O. G., Jr. (1996). Socialization through the life cycle. In O. G. Brim, Jr., & S. Wheeler (Eds.), *Socialization after childhood: Two essays* (pp. 1–49). New York: Wiley.

Brim, O. G., Jr., & Kagan, J. (Eds.). (1980a). *Constancy and change in human development.* Cambridge, MA: Harvard University Press.

Brim, O. G., Jr., & Kagan, J. (1980b). Constancy and change: A view of the issues. In O. G. Brim, Jr., & J. Kagan (Eds.), *Constancy and change in human development* (pp. 1–25). Cambridge, MA: Harvard University Press.

Brim, O. G., Jr., & Ryff, C. D. (1980). On the properties of life events. In P. B. Baltes & O. G. Brim, Jr. (Eds.), *Life-span development and behavior* (Vol. 3, pp. 367–388). New York: Academic Press.

Broca, P. (1861). Sur le volume et la forme du cerveau suivant les individus et suivant les races. *Bulletin de la Société de Anatomie de Paris, 2,* 139–207, 301–321, 441–446.

Broca, P. (1862a). Sur les proportions relatives du bras, de l'avant bras et de la clavicule chez les nègres et les européens. *Bulletin de la Société de Anatomie de Paris, 3,* Pt. 2, 13.

Broca, P. (1862b). Sue la capacité des crânes parisiens des diversew époques. *Bulletin Société d'Anthropologie Paris, 3,* 102–116.

Broca, P. (1862c). Sur les projections de la tête et sur un nouveau procédé de céphalométrie. *Bulletin Société d'Anthropologie Paris, 3,* 32 pp.

Bronfenbrenner, U. (1960). Freudian theories of identification and their derivatives. *Child Development, 31,* 15–40.

Bronfenbrenner, U. (1963). Developmental theory in transition. In H. W. Stevenson (Ed.), *Child psychology: Sixty-second yearbook of the National Society for the Study of Education* (Pt. 1, pp. 517–542). Chicago, IL: University of Chicago Press.

Bronfenbrenner, U. (1974). Developmental research, public policy, and the ecology of childhood. *Child Development, 45,* 1–5.

Bronfenbrenner, U. (1977). Toward an experimental ecology of human development. *American Psychologist, 32,* 513–531.

Bronfenbrenner, U. (1979). *The ecology of human development: Experiments by nature and design.* Cambridge, MA: Harvard University Press.

Bronfenbrenner, U. (1989). Ecological systems theory. In R. Vasta (Ed.), *Six theories of child development: Revised formulations and current issues* (pp. 185–246). Greenwich, CT: JAI Press.

Bronfenbrenner, U. (1983). The context of development and the development of context. In R. M. Lerner (Ed.), *Developmental psychology: Historical and philosophical perspectives*. Hillsdale, NJ: Erlbaum.

Bronfenbrenner, U. (1994). Ecological models of human development. In T. Husen & T. N. Postletwaite (Eds.), *International encyclopedia of education* (2nd ed., Vol. 3, pp. 1643–1647). Oxford, England: Pergamon Press/Elsevier Science.

Bronfenbrenner, U. (In press). The bioecological theory of human development. In N. J. Smelser & P. B. Baltes (Eds.), *International encyclopedia of the social and behavioral science*. Oxford, England: Elsevier.

Bronfenbrenner, U., & Ceci, S. J. (1993). Heredity, environment, and the question "How?" A new theoretical perspective for the 1990s. In R. Plomin & G. E. McClearn (Eds.), *Nature, nurture, and psychology* (pp. 313–324). Washington, DC: American Psychological Association.

Bronfenbrenner, U., & Ceci, S. J. (1994). Nature–nurture reconceptualized in developmental perspective: A bioecological model. *Psychological Review, 101,* 568–586.

Bronfenbrenner, U., & Crouter, A. C. (1983). The evolution of environmental models in developmental research. In W. Kessen (Series Ed.) & P. H. Mussen (Vol. Ed.), *Handbook of child psychology: Vol. 1. History, theory, and methods* (4th ed., pp. 357–414). New York: Wiley.

Bronfenbrenner, U., McClelland, P., Wethington, E., Moen, P., & Ceci, S. J. (1996). *The state of Americans: This generation and the next*. New York: Free Press.

Bronfenbrenner, U., & Morris, P. A. (1998). The ecology of developmental process. In W. Damon (Series Ed.) & R. M. Lerner (Vol. Ed.), *Handbook of child psychology: Vol. 1. Theoretical models of human development* (5th ed., pp. 993–1028). New York: Wiley.

Bronson, F. H., & Desjardins, C. (1970). Neonatal androgen and adult aggressiveness in female mice. *General and Comparative Endocrinology, 15,* 320–325.

Brooks-Gunn, J. (1987). Pubertal processes in girls' psychological adaptation. In R. M. Lerner & T. T. Foch (Eds.), *Biological–psychocial interactions in early adolescence: A life-span perspective* (pp. 123–153). Hillsdale, NJ: Erlbaum.

Brooks-Gunn, J., & Petersen, A. C. (1983). *Girls at puberty: Biological and psychosocial perspectives*. New York: Plenum Publishing.

Brooks-Gunn, J., & Reiter, E. O. (1990). The role of pubertal processes in the early adolescent transition. In S. Feldman & G. Elliott (Eds.), *At the threshold: The developing adolescent* (pp. 16–53). Cambridge, MA: Harvard University Press.

Broverman, I. K., Vogel, S. R., Broverman, D. M., Clarkson, F. E., & Rosenkrantz, P. S. (1972). Sex-role stereotypes: A current appraisal. *Journal of Social Issues, 28,* 59–78.

Brown, D. D. (1981). Gene expression in eukaryotes. *Science, 211,* 667–674.

Brown, R. T. (1974). Following and visual imprinting in ducklings across a wide age range. *Developmental Psychobiology, 8,* 27–33.

Browne, C. S., & Rife, J. C. (1991). Social, personality, and gender differences in at-risk and not-at-risk sixth-grade students. *Journal of Early Adolescence, 11,* 482–495.

Bruer, J. T. (1999). *The myth of the first three years*. New York: Free Press.

Bruner, J. (1964). The course of cognitive growth. *American Psychologist, 19,* 1–15.

Bubolz, M. M., & Sontag, M. S. (1993). Human ecology theory. In P. G. Boss, W. J. Doherty, R. LaRossa, W. R. Schumm, & S. K. Steinmetz (Eds.), *Sourcebook of family theories and methods: A contextual approach* (pp. 419–448). New York: Plenum Publishing.

Buhler, C. (1928). *Kindheit und jugend*. Leipzig, Germany: Hirzel.

Buhler, C. (1933). *Der menschliche Lebenslauf als psychologisches Problem*. Leipzig: Hirzel.

Bullock, D. (1990). Methodological heterogeneity and the anachronistic status of ANOVA in psychology. *Behavioral and Brain Sciences, 13,* 122–123.

Burt, C. (1955). The evidence of the concept of intelligence. *British Journal of Educational Psychology, 25,* 159–177.

Burt, C. (1958). The inheritance of mental amility. *American Psychologist, 13,* 1–15.

Burt, C. (1966). The genetic determination of differences in intelligence: A study of monozygotic twins reared together and apart. *British Journal of Psychology, 57,* 137–153.

Burt, C., & Howard, M. (1957). The relative influence of heredity and environment on assessments of intelligence. *British Journal of Statistical Psychology, 10,* 103.

Burton, L. M. (1990). Teenage childbearing as an alternative life-course strategy in multigeneration black families. *Human Nature, 1*(2), 123–143.

Buss, A. H., & Plomin, R. (1984). *Temperament: Early developing personality traits*. Hillsdale, NJ: Erlbaum.

Buss, A. R. (1979). On the four kinds of causality *The Behavioral and Brain Sciences, 2,* 139.

Cahan, E., Mechling, J., Sutton-Smith, B., & White, S. H. (1993). The elusive historical child: Ways of knowing the child of history and psychology. In G. H. Elder, J. Modell, & R. D. Parke (Eds.), *Children in time and place: Developmental and historical insights* (pp. 192–223). New York: Cambridge University Press.

Cairns, R. B. (1998). The making of developmental psychology. In W. Damon (Series Ed.) & R. M. Lerner (Vol. Ed.), *Handbook of child psychology: Vol. 1. Theoretical models of human development* (5th ed., pp. 419–448). New York: Wiley.

Cairns, R. B., Bergman, L. R., & Kagan, J. (Eds.). (1998). *Methods and models for studying the individual: Essays in honor of Marian Radke-Yarrow*. Thousand Oaks, CA: Sage.

Cairns, R. B., & Cairns, B. D. (1994). *Lifelines and risks: Pathways of youth in our time*. New York: Cambridge University Press.

Cairns, R. B., & Hood, K. E. (1983). Continuity in social development: A comparative perspective on individual difference prediction. In P. B. Baltes & O. G. Brim, Jr. (Eds.), *Life-span development and behavior* (Vol. 5, pp. 301–358). New York: Academic Press.

Campbell, D. T., & Stanley, J. C. (1963). *Experimental and quasi-experimental designs for research*. Chicago, IL: Rand McNally.

Campbell, R. L., & Richie, D. M. (1983). Problems in the theory of developmental sequences. *Human Development, 26,* 156–172.

Capaldi, E. J., & Proctor, R. W. (1999). *Contextualism in psychological research? A Critical Review*. Thousand Oaks, CA: Sage.

Capitanio, J. P., & Leger, D. W. (1979). Evolutionary scales lack utility: A reply to Yarczower and Hazlett. *Psychological Bulletin, 86,* 876–879.

Caplan, A. L. (1978). *The sociobiology debate*. New York: Harper & Row.

Carey, S., & Gelman, R. (Eds.). (1991). *The epigenesis of mind: Essays on biology and cognition*. Hillsdale, NJ: Erlbaum.

Carlson, R. (1972). Understanding women: Implications for personality theory and research. *Journal of Social Issues, 28,* 17–32.

Carnegie Corporation of New York. (1992). *A matter of time: Risk and opportunity in the non-school hours*. New York: Carnegie Corporation of New York.

Carnegie Corporation of New York. (1995). *Great transitions: Preparing adolescents for a new century*. New York: Carnegie Corporation of New York.

Carnegie Council on Adolescent Development. (1989). *Turning points: Preparing American youth for the twenty-first century*. Washington, DC: Carnegie Council on Adolescent Development.

Carstensen, L. L., Hanson, K. A., & Freund, A. (1995). Selection and compensation in adulthood. In R. A. Dixon & L. Bäckman (Eds.), *Compensating for psychological deficits and declines: Managing losses and promoting gains* (pp. 107–126). Hillsdale, NJ: Erlbaum.

Case, R. (1984). The process of stage transition: A neo-piegetian development. In R. J. Sternberg (Ed.), *Mechanisms of change* (pp. 19–44). San Francisco, CA: W. H. Freeman.

Case, R. (1985). *Intellectual development: Birth to adulthood*. New York: Academic Press.

Case, R. (1992a). Neo-piegetian theories of intellectual development. In H. Beilin & P. B. Pufall (Eds.), *Piaget's theory: Prospects and possibilities* (pp. 61–107). Hillsdale, NJ: Erlbaum.

Case, R. (1992b). *The mind's staircase: Exploring the conceptual underpinnings of children's thought and knowledge*. Hillsdale, NJ: Erlbaum.

Case, R. (1998). The development of conceptual structures. In W. Damon (Series Ed.), D. Kuhn, & R. S. Siegler (Vol. Eds.), *Handbook of child psychology: Vol. 2. Cognition, perception, and language* (5th ed., pp. 745–800). New York: Wiley.

Cattell, R. B. (1957). *Personality and motivation: Structure and measurement*. New York: World.

Cattell, R. B. (1966). Psychological theory and scientific method. In R. B. Cattell (Ed.), *Handbook of multivariate experimental psychology* (pp. 1–18). Chicago, IL: Rand McNally.

Cavalli-Sforza, L. L., & Cavalli-Sforza, F. (1995). *The great human sasporas: The history of diversity and evolution* (first published in 1993 in Italy by Arnoldo Mondadori, Editore Spa, Milano as *Chi siamo: La storia della diversita umana,* translated into English by Sarah Horne, English postscript 1995 by Luigi Luca Cavalli-Sforza). Menlo Park, CA: Addison-Wesley.

Cernovsky, Z. Z. (1992). J. P. Rushton on negroids and caucasoids: Statistical concepts and disconfirmatory evidence. *The International Journal of Dynamic Assessment and Instruction, 2*(2), 55–67.

Cernovsky, Z. Z. (1995). On the similarities of American blacks and whites. *Journal of Black Studies, 25*(6), 672–679.

Cernovsky, Z. Z. (1997). Statistical methods and behavioral similarities of blacks and whites. Paper presented at the 58th Annual Convention of the Canadian Psychological Association. Toronto, Canada.

Cernovsky, Z. Z. & Litman, L. C. (1993). Reanalyses of J. P. Rushton's crime data. *Canadian Journal of Criminology, 35*(1), 31–36.

Chamberlain, P., & Reid, J. B. (1998). Comparison of two community alternatives to incarceration for chronic juvenile offenders. *Journal of Consulting and Clinical Psychology, 66*(4), 624–633.

Chandler, M. J., Greenspan, S., & Barenboim, C. (1973). Judgements of intentionality in response to videotaped and verablly presented moral dilemmas: The medium is the message. *Child Development, 44,* 315–320.

Chapman, M. (1988a). *Constructive evolution: Origins and development of Piaget's thought.* Cambridge, England: Cambridge University Press.

Chapman, M. (1988b). Contextuality and directionality of cognitive development. *Human Development, 31,* 92–106.

Chess, S., & Thomas, A. (1984). *The origins and evolution of behavior disorders: Infancy to early adult life.* New York: Brunner/Mazel.

Chess, S., & Thomas, A. (1996). *Temperament: Theory and practice.* New York: Brunner/Mazel.

Chess, S., & Thomas, A. (1999). *Goodness-of-fit: Clinical applications from infancy through adult life.* Philadelphia, PA: Brunner/Mazel.

Chess, S., Thomas, A., & Birch, H. G. (1965). *Your child is a person.* New York: Viking.

Chess, S., Thomas, A., & Birch, H. G. (1966). Distortions in developmental reporting made by parents of behaviorally disturbed children. *Journal of Child Psychiatry 5,* 226–234.

Chibucos, T., & Lerner, R. M. (Eds.). (1999). *Serving children and families through community–university partnerships: Success stories.* Norwell, MA: Kluwer.

Chomsky, N. A. (1965). *Aspects of the theory of syntax.* Cambridge, MA: MIT Press.

Chomsky, N. A. (1966). *Cartesian linguistics.* New York: Harper & Row.

Chomsky, N. A. (1986). *Knowledge of language: Its nature, origin, and use.* Westport, CT: Praeger.

Chorover, S. L. (1979). *From genesis to genocide.* Cambridge, MA: MIT Press.

Chow, K. L., & Stewart, D. L. (1972). Reversal of structural and functional effects of long-term visual deprivation in the cat. *Experimental Neurology, 34,* 409–433.

Clancy, S. M., & Dollinger, S. J. (1993). Identity, self, and personality: I. Identity status and the five-factor model of personality. *Journal of Research on Adolescence, 3*(3), 227–245.

Clark, G. H. (1957). *Thales to Dewey.* Boston, MA: Houghton-Mifflin.

Clarke, A. M., & Clarke, A. D. B. (Eds.). (1976). *Early experience: Myth and evidence.* New York: Free Press.

Clausen, J. A. (1972). The life-course of individuals. In M. W. Riley, M. Johnson, & A. Foner, (Eds.), *Aging and society: Vol. 3. A sociology of age stratification.* New York: Sage.

Cohen, S. (1976). Transposable genetic elements and plasmid evolution. *Nature, 263,* 731–738.

Colby, A. (1978). Evolution of a moral-developmental theory. *New Directions for Child Development, 2,* 89–104.

Colby, A. (1979). Presentation at the center for advanced study in the behavioral sciences summer institute, July, on "Morality and moral development."

Colby, A. (1997). Forward. In M. E. Lachman & J. B. James (Eds.), *Multiple paths of midlife development.* Chicago, IL: University of Chicago Press.

Colby, A. L., Kohlberg, J., Gibbs, J., & Lieberman, M. (1983). A longitudinal study of moral judgment. *Monographs of the Society for Research in Child Development, 48,* 200.

Cole, M. (1996). Interacting minds in a life-span perspective: A cultural/historical approach to culture and cognitive development. In P. B. Baltes & U. M. Staudinger (Eds.), *Interactive minds: Life-span perspectives on the social foundation of cognition* (pp. 59–87). New York: Cambridge University Press.

Collins, C. (1995, June 22). Letter from Cardis Collins, U.S. House of Representatives to Professor R. Plomin, The Pennsylvania State University. In J. Hirsch Papers, University of Illinois Archives, No. 15/19/22.

Collins, W. A. (1982). *The concept of development: The Minnesota Symposia on Child Psychology* (Vol. 15). Hillsdale, NJ: Erlbaum.

Collins, W. A., Maccoby, E. E., Steinberg, L., Hetherington, M. E., & Bornstein, M. H. (2000). Contemporary research on parenting: The case for nature and nurture. *American Psychologist, 55*(2), 218–232.

Colombo, J. (1982). The critical period concept: Research, methodology and theoretical issues. *Psychological Bulletin, 91,* 260–275.

Conger, R. D., Conger, K. J., Elder, G. H., Jr., Lorenz, F. O., Simons, R. L., & Whitbeck, L. B. (1992). A family process model of economic hardship and adjustment of early adolescent boys. *Child Development, 63,* 526–541.

Conger, R. D., Lorenz, F. O., Elder, G. H., Jr., Melby, J. N., Simons, R. L., & Conger, K. J. (1991). A process model of family economic pressure and early adolescent alcohol use. *Journal of Early Adolescence, 11,* 430–449.

Connell, J. P., Kubisch, A. C., Schorr, L. B., & Weiss, C. H. (1995). *New approaches to evaluating community initiatives: Concepts, methods, and contexts.* Washington, DC: Aspen Institute.

Connolly, K. (1972). Learning and the concept of critical periods in infancy. *Developmental Medicine and Child Neurology, 14,* 705–714.

Constantinople, A. (1969). An Eriksonian measure of personality development in college students. *Developmental Psychology, 1,* 357–372.

Conway, J. (1958). The inheritance of intelligence and its social implications. *British Journal of Statistical Psychology, 11,* 171–190.

Corbett, T. (1995a). Changing the culture of welfare. *Focus, 16,* 12–22.

Corvo, K. N. (1997). Community-based youth violence prevention: A framework for planners and funders. *Youth & Society, 28*(3), 291–316.

Côté, J. E. (1993). Foundations of a psychoanalytic social psychology: Neo-Eriksonian propositions regarding the relationship between psychic structure and cultural institutions. *Developmental Review, 13,* 31–53.

Côté, J. E. (2000). *Arrested adulthood: The changing nature of maturity and identity.* New York: New York University Press.

Côté, J. E., & Allahar, A. L. (1996). *Generation on hold: Coming of age in the late twentieth century.* New York: New York University Press.

Côté, J. E., & Levine, C. (1987). A formulation of Erikson's theory of ego identity formation. *Developmental Review, 7,* 273–325.

Côté, J. E., & Levine, C. G. (1997). Student motivations, learning environments, and human capital acquistion: Toward an integrated paradigm of student development. *Journal of College Student Development, 38*(3), 229–243.

Côté, J. E., & Levine, C. G. (2000). Attitude versus aptitude: Is intelligence or motivation more important for postive higher-educational outcomes? *Journal of Adolescent Research, 15*(1), 58–80.

Cotgrove, A., Zirinsky, L., Black, D., & Weston, D. (1995). Secondary prevention of attempted suicide in adolescence. *Journal of Adolescence, 18,* 569–577.

Cox, V. (1974). A prize for the Goose Father. *Human Behavior, 3,* 17–22.

Crawford, M. L., Blake, R., Cool, S. J., & von Noorden, G. K. (1975). Physiological consequences of unilateral and bilateral eye closure in macaque monkeys: Some further observations. *Brain Research, 84,* 150–154.

Cronbach, L. J. (1975). Beyond the two disciplines of scientific psychology. *American Psychologist, 30,* 116–127.

Csikszentmihalyi, M., & Rathunde, K. (1998). The development of the person: An experiential perspective on the ontogenesis of psychological complexity. In W. Damon (Series Ed.) & R. M. Lerner (Vol. Ed.), *Handbook of child psychology: Vol. 1. Theoretical models of human development* (5th ed., pp. 635–684). New York: Wiley.

Cumming, E., & Henry, W. E. (1961). *Growing old: The process of disengagement.* New York: Basic Books.

Cunningham, M., & Spencer, M. B. (1996). The Black male experiences measure. In R. L. Jones (Ed.), *Handbook of tests and measurements for black populations* (pp. 301–307). Hampton, VA: Cobb & Henry.

Curtiss, S. (1977). *Genie: A psycholinguistic study of a modern day "wild child."* New York: Academic Press.

Curtiss, S., Fromkin, V., Rigler, M., Rigler, D., & Krashen, S. (1975). An update on the linguistic development of Genie. In D. Dato (Ed.), *Developmental psycholinguistics: Theory and applications* (pp. 145–157). Washington, DC: Georgetown University Press.

Cynader, M., Berman, N., & Hein, A. (1976). Recovery of function in cat visual cortex following prolonged deprivation. *Experimental Brain Research, 25,* 139–156.

Dale, L. G. (1970). The growth of systematic thinking: Replication and analysis of Piaget's first chemical experiment. *Australian Journal of Psychology, 22,* 277–286.

Damasio, A. R., & Damasio, H. (1996). Making images and creating subjectivity. In R. R. Llinas & P. S. Churchland (Eds.), *The mind-brain continuum: Sensory processes* (pp. 19–27). Cambridge, MA: MIT Press.

Damon, W. (1996). The lifelong transformation of moral goals through social influence. In P. B. Baltes & U. M. Staudinger (Eds.), *Interactive minds: Life-span perspectives on the social foundation of cognition* (pp. 198–220). New York: Cambridge University Press.

Damon, W. (1997). *The youth charter: How communities can work together to raise standards for all our children.* New York: Free Press.

Damon, W. (Ed.). (1998). *Handbook of child psychology* (5th ed.). New York: Wiley.

D'Andrade, R. G. (1984). Cultural meaning systems. In R. A. Shweder & R. A. Le Vine (Eds), *Culturre theory: Essays on mind, self, and emotion* (pp. 88–119). Cambridge, England: Cambridge University Press.

Dannefer, D. (1984). Adult developmental and socialization theory: A paradigmatic reappraisal. *American Sociological Review, 49,* 100–116.

Darwin, C. (1859). *The origin of species by means of natural selection or the preservation of favoured races in the struggle for life.* London, England: J. Murray.

Darwin, C. (1872). *The expression of emotions in man and animals.* London, England: J. Murray.

Datan, N., & Ginsberg, L. H. (Eds.). (1975). *Life-span developmental psychology: Normative life crises.* New York: Academic Press.

Datan, N., & Reese, H. W. (Eds.). (1977). *Life-span developmental psychology: Dialectical perspectives on experimental research.* New York: Academic Press.

Davidson, M. L., Robbins, S., & Swanson, D. B. (1978). Stage structure in objective moral judgments. *Developmental Psychology, 14*, 121–131.

Davis, A. (1944). Socialization and the adolescent personality. *Forty-third yearbook of the national society for the study of education* (Vol. 43, Pt. 1). Chicago, IL: University of Chicago Press.

Davison, M. L., King, P. M., Kitchener, K. S., & Parker, C. A. (1980). The stage sequence concept in cognitive and social development. *Developmental Psychology, 14*, 137–146.

Dawidowicz, L. S. (1975). *The war against the Jews, 1933–1945*. New York: Holt, Rinehart & Winston.

Dawkins, R. (1976). *The selfish gene*. New York: Oxford University.

de Beer, G. R. (1930). *Embryology and evolution*. Oxford, England: Clarendon Press.

de Beer, G. R. (1958). *Embryos and ancestors* (3rd ed.). Oxford, England: Clarendon Press.

de Beer, G. R. (1959). Paedomorphosis. *Proceedings of the XV International Congress of Zoology, 15*, 927–930.

DeFries, J. C. (1967). Quantitative genetics and behavior: Overview and perspective. In J. Hirsch (Ed.), *Behavior–genetic analysis*. New York: McGraw-Hill.

DeLoache, J. S., Miller, K. F., & Pierroutsakos, S. L. (1998). Reasoning and problem solving. In W. Damon (Series Ed.), D. Kuhn, & R. S. Siegler (Vol. Eds.), *Handbook of child psychology: Vol. 2. Cognition, perception, and language* (5th ed., pp. 801–850). New York: Wiley.

Demo, D. H., Allen, K. R., & Fine, M. A. (2000). *Handbook of family diversity*. New York: Oxford University Press.

de Santillana, G., & von Dechend, H. (1977). *Hamlet's mill: An essay investigating the origins of human knowledge and its transmission through myth*. Boston, MA: Godine.

Dewey, J. (1916). *Democracy and education: An introduction to the philosophy of education*. New York: Macmillan Publishing.

Dewey, J., & Bentley, A. F. (1948). *Knowing and the known*. Boston, MA: Beacon Press.

Dixon, R. A., & Lerner, R. M. (1988). A history of systems in developmental psychology. In M. H. Bornstein & M. E. Lamb (Eds.), *Developmental psychology: An advanced textbook* (2nd ed., pp. 3–50). Hillsdale, NJ: Erlbaum.

Dixon, R., & Lerner, R. M. (1999). A history of systems in developmental psychology. In M. H. Bornstein & M. E. Lamb (Eds.), *Developmental psychology: An advanced textbook* (4th ed., pp. 3–45). Mahwah, NJ: Erlbaum.

Dixon, R. A., Lerner, R. M., & Hultsch, D. F. (1991a). Maneuvering among models of developmental psychology. In P. van Geert & L. P. Mos (Eds.), *Annals of theoretical psychology* (Vol. 7, pp. 357–368). New York: Plenum Publishing.

Dixon, R. A., Lerner, R. M., & Hultsch, D. F. (1991b). The concept of development in the study of individual and social change. In P. van Geert & L. P. Mos (Eds.), *Annals of theoretical psychology* (Vol. 7, pp. 279–323). New York: Plenum Publishing.

Dixon, R. A., & Nesselroade, J. R. (1983). Pluralism and correlation analysis in developmental psychology: Historical commonalities. In R. M. Lerner (Ed.), *Developmental psychology: Historical and philosophical perspectives* (pp. 113–145). Hillsdale, NJ: Erlbaum.

Dobzhansky, T., Ayala, F. J., Stebbings, G. L., & Valentine, J. W. (1977). *Evolution*. San Francisco, CA: W. H. Freeman.

Dolan, B. (1995). A teen hot line. *Adolescence, 30*(117), 195–200.

Dollard, J., Doob, L. W., Miller, N. E., Mowrer, O. H., & Sears, R. R. (1939). *Frustration and aggression*. New Haven, CT: Yale University Press.

Dollard, J., & Miller, N. E. (1950). *Personality and psychotherapy*. New York: McGraw-Hill.

Donaldson, M. (1978). *Children's minds*. New York: Norton.

Doolittle, W. F., & Sapienza, C. (1980). Selfish genes, the phenotype paradigm, and genome evolution. *Nature, 284*, 601–603.

Dorfman, D. D. (1978). The Cyril Burt question: New findings. *Science, 201*, 1177–1186.

Dorfman, D. D. (1980). Intelligence for beginners? (Review of Hans J. Eysenck's *The Structure and Measurement of Intelligence*). *Nature, 284*, 645.

Douglas, J. D., & Wong, A. C. (1977). Formal operations: Age and sex differences in Chinese and American children. *Child Development, 48*, 689–692.

Douvan, J. D., & Adelson, J. (1966). *The adolescent experience*. New York: Wiley.

Dryfoos, J. G. (1990). *Adolescents at risk: Prevalence and prevention*. New York: Oxford University Press.

Dryfoos, J. G. (1994). *Full service schools: A revolution in health and social services for children, youth, and families*. San Francisco, CA: Jossey-Bass.

Dryfoos, J. G. (1998). *Safe passage: Making it through adolescence in a risky society*. New York: Oxford University Press.

DuBois, C. (1944). *The people of Alor*. Minneapolis, MN: University of Minnesota Press.

Dunbar, R. I. M. (1987). Sociobiological explanations and the evolution of ethnocentrism. In V.

Reynolds, V. Falger, & I. Vine (Eds.), *The sociobiology of ethnocentrism* (pp. 48–59). London, England: Croom Helm.

Duncan, C. P. (1982). Book reviews: The intelligence controversy. *American Journal of Psychology, 95,* 346–349.

Dunn, L. C. (1965). *A short history of genetics.* New York: McGraw-Hill.

Dweck, C. S. (1975). The role of expectations and attributions in the alleviation of learned helplessness. *Journal of Personality and Social Psychology, 36,* 451–462.

Dweck, C. S. (1998). The development of early self-conceptions: Their relevance for motivational processes. In J. Heckhausen & C. S. Dweck (Eds.), *Motivation and self-regulation across the life span* (pp. 257–280). New York: Cambridge University Press.

Dweck, C. S., & Leggett, E. L. (1988). A social cognitive approach to motivation and personality. *Psychological Review, 95,* 256–273.

Dylan, B. (1964). My back pages. *Another side of Bob Dylan.* New York: Columbia Records.

Eacker, J. N. (1972). On some elementary philosophical problems of psychology. *American Psychologist, 27,* 553–565.

Earls, F. (1998). Positive effects of prenatal and early childhood interventions. *JAMA, 280,* 1271–1273.

Ebata, A. T. (1996). Making university–community collaborations work: Challenges for institutions and individuals. *Journal of Research on Adolescence, 6*(1), 71–79.

Eccles, J. S. (1985). Sex differences in achievement patterns. In B. Sonderegger (Ed.), *Psychology and gender. Nebraska symposium on motication, 1984* (pp. 97–132). Lincoln, NE: University of Nebraska Press.

Eccles, J. S. (1991). Academic achievement. In R. M. Lerner, A. C. Petersen, & J. Brooks-Gunn (Eds.), *Encyclopedia of adolescence* (Vol. 1, pp. 1–9). New York: Garland Publishing.

Eccles, J. S. (1996). The power and difficulty of university–community collaboration. *Journal of Research on Adolescence, 6,* 81–86.

Eccles, J. S., Early, D., Frasier, K., Belansky, E., & McCarthy, K. (1997). The relation of connection, regulation, and support for autonomy to adolescents' functioning. *Journal of Adolescent Research, 12*(2), 263–286.

Eccles, J. S., & Harold, R. D. (1996). Family involvement in children's and adolescents' schooling. In A. Booth & J. F. Dunn (Eds.), *Family–school links: How do they affect educational outcomes?* (pp. 3–34). Mahwah, NJ: Erlbaum.

Eccles, J. S., Lord, S., & Buchanan, C. M. (1996). School transitions in early adolescence: What are we doing to our young people? In J. A., Graber, J. Brooks-Gunn, & A. C. Petersen (Eds.), *Transitions through adolescence* (pp. 251–284). Mahwah, NJ: Erlbaum.

Eccles, J. S., & Midgley, C. (1989). Stage–environment fit: Developmentally appropriate classroms for young adolescents. In C. Ames & R. Ames (Eds.), *Research on motivation in education: Goals and cognitions* (Vol. 3, pp. 139–186). New York: Academic Press.

Eccles, J. S., Midgley, C., Wigfield, A., Buchanan, C. M., Reuman, D., Flanagan, C., & MacIver, D. (1993). Development during adolescence: The impact of stage–environment fit on young adolescents' experiences in schools and in families. *American Psychologist, 48,* 90–101.

Eccles, J. S., & Wigfield, A. (1995). In the mind of the actor: The structure of adolescents' achievement task values and expectancy-related beliefs. *Personality and Social Psychology Bulletin, 21,* 215–225.

Eccles, J. S., Wigfield, A., Midgley, C., Reuman, D., MacIver, D., & Feldlaufer, H. (1993c). Negative effects of traditional middle schools on students' motivation. *Elementary School Journal, 93,* 553–574.

Eckensberger, L. H. (1989). A bridge between theory and practice, between general laws and contexts? *Psychology and Developing Societies, 1,* 21–35.

Edelman, G. M. (1987). *Neural Darwinism: The theory of neuronal group selection.* New York: Basic Books.

Edelman, G. M. (1988). *Topobiology: An introduction to molecular biology.* New York: Basic Books.

Edwards, D. A. (1970). Postnatal androgenization and adult aggressive behavior in female mice. *Physiology and Behavior, 5,* 1115–1119.

Edwards, J. B. (1974). A developmental study of the acquisitions of some moral concepts in children aged 7–15. *Educational Research, 16,* 83–93.

Eichorn, D. H., Clausen, J. A., Haan, N., Honzik, M. P., & Mussen, P. H. (1981). *Present and past in middle life.* New York: Academic Press.

Eisenberg, L. (1972). The *human* nature of human nature. *Science, 176,* 123–128.

Eisenberg, N. (Ed.). (1998). *Handbook of child psychology: Social, emotional, and personality development* (Vol. 3). W. Damon (Editor-in-Chief). New York: Wiley.

Eisenberg, N., & Fabes, R. A. (1998). Prosocial development. In W. Damon (Series Ed.) & N. Eisenberg (Vol. Ed.), *Social, emotional, and personality development: Vol. 3. Handbook of child psychology* (5th ed., pp. 1097–1149). New York: Wiley.

Eisenberg-Berg, N. (1976). The relation of political attitudes to constraint-oriented and prosocial moral reasoning. *Developmental Psychology, 12,* 552–553.

Eisenberg-Berg, N. (1979). The development of children's prosocial moral judgment. *Developmental Psychology, 15,* 128–137.

Elder, G. H., Jr. (1974). *Children of the Great Depression.* Chicago, IL: University of Chicago Press.

Elder, G. H., Jr. (1977). Family history and the life course. *Journal of Family History, 2,* 279–304.

Elder, G. H., Jr. (1975). Age differentiation and the life course. In A. Inkeles, J. Coleman, & N. Smelser (Eds.), *Annual review of sociology.* Palo Alto, CA: Annual Review.

Elder, G. H., Jr. (1979). Historical change in life patterns and personality. In P. B. Baltes & O. G. Brim, Jr. (Eds.), *Life-span development and behavior* (Vol. 2, pp. 117–159). New York: Academic Press.

Elder, G. H., Jr. (1980). Adolescence in historical perspective. In J. Adelson (Ed.), *Handbooks of adolescent psychology* (pp. 3–46). New York: Wiley.

Elder, G. H., Jr. (1998). The life course and human development. In W. Damon (Series Ed.) & R. M. Lerner (Vol. Ed.), *Handbook of child psychology: Vol. 1. Theoretical models of human development* (5th ed., pp. 939–991). New York: Wiley.

Elder, G. H., Jr. (1999). *Children of the Great Depression: Social change in life experience* (25th anniversary ed.). Boulder, CO: Westview Press.

Elder, G. H., Jr., Modell, J., & Parke, R. D. (Eds.). (1993a). *Children in time and place: Developmental and historical insights,* New York: Cambridge University Press.

Elder, G. H., Jr., Modell, J., & Parke, R. D. (1993b). Studying children in a changing world. In G. H. Elder, Jr., J. Modell, & R. D. Parke (Eds.), *Children in time and place: Developmental and historical insights* (pp. 3–21). New York: Cambridge University Press.

Elkind, D. (1967). Egocentrism in adolescents. *Child Development, 38,* 1025–1034.

Elkind, D., & Dabek, R. F. (1977). Personal injury and property damage in moral judgments of children. *Child Development, 48*(2), 518–522.

Elman, J. L., Bates, E. A., Johnson, M. H., Karmiloff-Smith, A., Parisi, D., & Plunkett, K. (1998). *Rethinking innateness: A connectionist perspective on development (neural network modeling and connectionism).* Cambridge, MA: MIT Press.

Emmerich, W. (1968). Personality development and concepts of structure. *Child Development, 39,* 671–690.

Emshoff, J., Avery, E., Raduka, G., Anderson, D. J., & Calvert, C. (1996). Findings from SUPER STARS: A health promotion program for families to enhance multiple protective factors. *Journal of Adolescent Research, 11*(1), 68–96.

Erikson, E. (1963). *Childhood and society* (2nd ed.). New York: Norton.

Erikson, E. (1964). Inner and outer space: Reflections on womanhood. In R. J. Lifton (Ed.), *The woman in America* (pp. 1–26). Boston, MA: Beacon Press.

Erikson, E. (1968). *Identity, youth, and crisis.* New York: Norton.

Erikson, E. H. (1950). *Childhood and society.* New York: Norton.

Erikson, E. H. (1959). Identity and the life cycle. *Psychological Issues, 1,* 50–100.

Erikson, E. H. (1982). *The life cycle repeated: A review.* New York: Norton.

Erikson, E. H., Erikson, J. M., & Kivnick, H. Q. (1986). *Vital involvement in old age: The experience of old age in our time.* New York: Norton.

Erlenmeyer-Kimling, L., & Jarvik, L. F. (1963). Genetics and intelligence. *Science, 142,* 1477–1479.

Esposito, N. J. (1975). Review of discrimination shift learning in young children. *Psychological Bulletin, 82,* 432–455.

Evans, R. I. (1974). Interview with Konrad Lorenz. *Psychology Today, 8,* 26 ff.

Eysenck, H. J. (1979). Genetic models, theory of personality and the unification of psychology. In J. R. Royce & L. P. Mos (Eds.), *Theoretical advances in behavior genetics.* Rockville, MD: Sijthoff and Noordhoff.

Eysenck, H. J. (1980). Jensen and bias: An exchange. *The New York Review of Books, 27,* 52.

Eysenck, H. J., & Kamin, L. (1981a). *The intelligence controversy.* New York: Wiley.

Eysenck, H. J., & Kamin, L. (1981b). *Intelligence: The battle for the mind.* New York: Macmillan Publishing.

Falconer, D. S. (1960). *Quantitative genetics.* Edinburgh: Oliver & Boyd.

Falkner, F. (1972). Physical growth. In H. L. Bennett & A. H. Einhorn (Eds.), *Pediatrics* (15th ed., pp. 233–251). New York: Appleton-Century-Crofts.

Fantz, R. L. (1958). Pattern vision in young infants. *Psychological Record, 8,* 43–47.

Fantz, R. L., Ordy, J. M., & Udelf, M. S. (1962). Maturation of pattern vision in infants during the first six months. *Journal of Comparative and Physiological Psychology, 55,* 907–917.

Farber, S. L. (1981). *Identical twins reared apart: A reanalysis.* New York: Basic Books.

Farrari, M., & Sternberg, R. J. (1998). The development of mental abilities and styles. In

W. Damon (Series Ed.), D. Kuhn, & R. S. Siegler (Vol. Eds.), *Handbook of child psychology: Vol. 2. Cognition, perception, and language* (5th ed., pp. 899–946). New York: Wiley.

Faubert, M., Locke, D. C., Sprinthall, N. A., & Howland, W. H. (1996). Promoting cognitive and ego development of African-American rural youth: A program of deliberate psychological education. *Journal of Adolescence, 19,* 533–543.

Featherman, D. L. (1980). Schooling and occupational careers: Constancy and change in wordly success. In O. G. Brim, Jr., & J. Kagan (Eds.), *Constancy and change in human development* (pp. 675–738). Cambridge, MA: Harvard University Press.

Featherman, D. L. (1983). Life-span perspectives in social science research. In P. B. Baltes & O. G. Brim, Jr. (Eds.), *Life-span development and behavior* (Vol. 5, pp. 1–57). New York: Academic Press.

Featherman, D. L. (1985). Individual development and aging as a population process. In J. R. Nesselroade & A. von Eye (Eds.), *Individual development and social change: Explanatory analysis* (pp. 213–241). New York: Academic Press.

Featherman, D. L., & Lerner, R. M. (1985). Ontogenesis and sociogenesis: Problematics for theory about development across the lifespans. *American Sociological Review, 50,* 659–676.

Featherman, D. L., Lerner, R. M., & Perlmutter, M. (Eds.). (1994). *Life-span development and behavior.* Hillsdale, NJ: Erlbaum.

Feldman, B. (1995). The search for identity in late adolescence. In M. Sidoli & G. Bovensiepen (Eds.), *Incest fantasies and self-destructive acts: Jungian and Post-Jungian psychotherapy in adolescence* (pp. 153–166). New Brunswick, NJ: Transaction Books.

Feldman, D. H. (1971). Map understanding as a possible crystalizer of cognitive structures. *American Educational Research Journal, 8,* 485–501.

Feldman, D. H. (1980a). *Beyond universals in cognitive development.* Norwood, NJ: Ablex Publishing Corp.

Feldman, D. H. (1980b). Stage and sequence: Getting to the next level. *The Genetic Epistemologist, 9,* 1–6.

Feldman, D. H. (1982). *Developmental approaches to giftedness and creativity.* San Francisco, CA: Jossey-Bass.

Feldman, D. H. (1994). *Beyond universals in cognitive development* (2nd ed.). Norwood, NJ: Ablex Publishing Corp.

Feldman, D. H. (1995). Learning and developmental in nonuniversal theory. *Human Development, 38,* 315–321.

Feldman, D. H. (2000). *Piaget's stages: The unfinished symphony.* Unpublished manuscript.

Medford, MA: Eliot-Pearson Department of Child Development, Tufts University.

Feldman, D. H., & Fowler, R. C. (1997). Second thoughts: A response to the commentaries. *New Ideas in Psychology, 15,* 235–245.

Feldman, M. W., & Lewontin, R. C. (1975). The heritability hang-up. *Science, 190,* 1163–1168.

Feldman, M. W., & Lewontin, R. C. (1976). Letters: Heritability of IQ. *Science, 194,* 12–14.

Feldman, N. S., Klosson, E. C., Parsons, J. E., Rhodes, W. S., & Ruble, D. N. (1976). Order of information presentation and children's moral judgements. *Child Development, 47,* 556–569.

Ferrari, M., & Sternberg, R. J. (1998). The development of mental abilities and styles. In W. Damon (Series Ed.), D. Kuhn, & R. S. Siegler (Vol. Eds.), *Handbook of child psychology: Vol. 2. Cognition, perception, and language* (5th ed., pp. 899–946). New York: Wiley.

Fetterman, D. M., Kaftarian, S. J., & Wandersman, A. (Eds.). (1996). *Empowerment evaluation: Knowledge and tools for self-assessment and accountability.* Thousand Oaks, CA: Sage.

Field, T., Grizzle, N., Scafidi, F., & Schanberg, S. (1996). Massage and relaxation therapies' effects on depressed adolescent mothers. *Adolescence, 31*(124), 903–911.

Finkelstein, J. W. (1993). Familial influences on adolescent health. In R. M. Lerner (Ed.), Early firstborn infants in the first six months of life: Covariation, stability, continuity, correspondence, and prediction. *Child Development, 61,* 1206–1217.

Fischer, K. W. (1980). A theory of cognitive development: The control and construction of hierarchies of skills. *Psychological Review, 87,* 477–531.

Fischer, K. W. (1987). Relations between brain and cognitive development. *Child Development, 57,* 623–632.

Fischer, K. W., & Bidell, T. R. (1991). Constraining nativist inferences about cognitive capacities. In S. Carey & R. Gelman (Eds.), *The epigenesis of mind: Essays on biology and knowledge* (pp. 199–235). Hillsdale, NJ: Erlbaum.

Fischer, K. W., & Bidell, T. R. (1998). Dynamic development of psychological structures in action and thought. In W. Damon (Series Ed.) & R. M. Lerner (Vol. Ed.), *Handbook of child psychology: Vol. 1. Theoretical models of human development* (5th ed., pp. 467–561). New York: Wiley.

Fischer, K. W., & Farrar, M. J. (1987). Generalizations about generalizations: How a theory of skill development explains both generality and specificity. *International Journal of Psychology, 22,* 643–677.

Fischer, K. W., & Granott, N. (1995). Beyond one-dimensional change: Parallel, concurrent, socially distributed processes in learning and development. *Human Development, 38,* 302–314.

Fischer, K. W., Knight, C. C., & Van Parys, M. (1993). Analyzing diversity in developmental pathways: Methods and concepts. In W. Edelstein & R. Case (Eds.), *Contributions to human development* (Vol. 23, pp. 33–56).

Fischer, K. W., & Pipp, S. L. (1984). Development of the structures of unconscious thoughts. In K. Bowers & D. Meichenbaum (Eds.), *The unconscious reconsidered* (pp. 88–148). New York: Wiley.

Fischer, K. W., & Pipp, S. L. (1984). Process of cognitive development: Optimal level and skill acquisition. In R. J. Sternberg (Ed.), *Mechanisms of cognitive development* (pp. 45–81). New York: W. H. Freeman.

Fischer, K. W., & Rose, S. P. (1994). Dynamic development of coordination of components in brain and behavior: A framework for theory and research. In G. Dawson & K. W. Fisher (Eds.), *Human behavior and the developing brain* (pp. 3–66). New York: Guilford Press.

Fisher, C. B. (1993). Integrating science and ethics in research with high-risk children and youth. *SRCD Social Policy Report, 7,* 1–27.

Fisher, C. B. (1993). Joining science and application: Ethical challenges for researchers and practitioners. *Professional Psychology—Research & Practice, 24,* 378–381.

Fisher, C. B. (1994). Reporting and referring research participants: Ethical challenges for investigators studying children and youth. *Ethics and Behavior, 4,* 87–95.

Fisher, C. B. (1997). A relational perspective on ethics-in-science decision-making for research with vulnerable populations. *IRB: A Review of Human Subjects Research, 19,* 1–4.

Fisher, C. B., & Brennan, M. (1992). Application and ethics in developmental psychology. In D. L. Featherman, R. M. Lerner, & M. Perlmutter (Eds.), *Life span development and behavior* (Vol. 11, pp. 189–219). Hillsdale, NJ: Erlbaum.

Fisher, C. B., & Fyrberg, D. (1994). Participant partners: College students weigh the costs and benefits of deceptive research. *American Psychologist, 49*(5), 417–427.

Fisher, C. B., Hoagwood, K., & Jensen, P. (1996). Casebook on ethical issues in research with children and adolescents with mental disorders. In K. Hoagwood, P. Jensen, & C. B. Fisher (Eds.), *Ethical issues in research with children and adolescents with mental disorders* (pp. 135–238). Hillsdale, NJ: Erlbaum.

Fisher, C. B., Jackson, J. F., & Villarruel, F. A. (1998). The study of African American and Latin American children and youth. In R. M. Lerner (Ed.), *Handbook of child psychology: Vol. 1. Theoretical models of human development* (5th ed., pp. 1145–1207). New York: Wiley.

Fisher, C. B., & Lerner, R. M. (Eds.). (1994a). *Applied developmental psychology.* New York: McGraw-Hill.

Fisher, C. B., & Lerner, R. M. (1994b). Foundations of applied developmental psychology. In C. B. Fisher & R. M. Lerner (Eds.), *Applied developmental psychology* (pp. 3–20). New York: McGraw-Hill.

Fisher, C. B., & Murray, J. P. (1996). Applied developmental science comes of age. In C. B. Fisher, J. P. Murray, & I. E. Sigel (Eds.), *Applied developmental science: Graduate training for diverse disciplines and educational settings* (pp. 1–22). Norwood, NJ: Ablex Publishing Corp.

Fisher, C. B., Murray, J. P., Dill, J. R., Hagen, J. W., Hogan, M. J., Lerner, R. M., Rebok, G. W., Sigel, I., Sostek, A. M., Smyer, M. A., Spencer, M. B., & Wilcox, B. (1993). The national conference on graduate education in the applications of developmental science across the life-span. *Journal of Applied Developmental Psychology, 14,* 1–10.

Fisher, C. B., Murray, J. P., & Sigel, I. E. (Eds.). (1996). *Applied developmental science: Graduate training for diverse disciplines and educational settings.* Norwood, NJ: Ablex Publishing Corp.

Fisher, C. B., & Tryon, W. W. (1990). Emerging ethical issues in an emerging field. In C. B. Fisher & W. W. Tryon (Eds.), *Ethics in applied developmental psychology: Emerging issues in an emerging field* (pp. 1–15). Norwood, NJ: Ablex Publishing Corp.

Fisher, H. E. (1982a). Of human bonding. *The Sciences, 22,* 18–23, 31.

Fisher, H. E. (1982b). Is it sex? Helen E. Fisher replies. *The Sciences, 22,* 2–3.

Fitzgerald, H. E., Abrams, A., Church, R. L., Votruba, J. C., & Imig, G. L. (1996). Applied developmental science at Michigan State University: Connecting university and community via programs for children, youth, and families. *Journal of Research on Adolescence, 6*(1), 55–69.

Flavell, J. H. (1963). The developmental psychology of Jean Piaget. New York: Van Nostrand.

Flavell, J. H. (1970). Cognitive changes in adulthood. In L. R. Goulet and P. B. Baltes (Eds.), *Lifespan developmental psychology: Research and theory.* New York: Academic Press.

Flavell, J. H. (1971). Stage related properties of cognitive development. *Cognitive Psychology, 2,* 421–453.

Flavell, J. H. (1972). An analysis of cognitive developmental sequences. *Genetic Psychology Monographs, 86,* 279–350.

Flavell, J. H. (1980). Structures, stages and sequences in cognitive development. Paper presented at the 1980 Minnesota Symposium on Child Psychology, October.

Flavell, J. H., & Miller, P. H. (1998). Social cognition. In W. Damon (Series Ed.) D. Kuhn, & R. S. Siegler (Vol. Eds.), *Handbook of child psychology: Vol. 2. Cognition, perception, and language* (5th ed., pp. 851–898). New York: Wiley.

Flavell, J. H., & Wohlwill, J. F. (1969). Formal and functional aspects of cognitive development. In D. Elkind & J. H. Flavell (Eds.), *Studies in cognitive development*. New York: Oxford University Press.

Flint, B. M. (1978). *New hope for deprived children*. Toronto, Canada: Toronto University Press.

Flohr, H. (1987). Biological bases of social prejudices. In V. Reynolds, V. Falger, & I. Vine (Eds.), *The sociobiology of ethnocentrism* (pp. 190–207). London, England: Croom Helm.

Fodor, J. A. (1983). *The modularity of mind: An essay on faculty psychology*. Cambridge, MA: MIT Press.

Ford, D. H. (1987). *Humans as self-constructing living systems*. Hillsdale, NJ: Erlbaum.

Ford, D. H., & Lerner, R. M. (1992). *Developmental systems theory: An integrative approach*. Newbury Park, CA: Sage.

Fraiberg, S. (1977). *Every child's birthright: In defense of mothering*. New York: Basic Books.

Frankel, J. (1976). Controversial areas of research. *Science, 190,* 12.

Freedman, D. G. (1979). *Human sociobiology: A holistic approach*. New York: Free Press.

Freeman, M. (1993). *Rewriting the self: History, memory, narrative*. New York: Routledge.

French, V. (1977). History of the child's influence: Ancient Mediterranean civilizations. In R. Q. Bell & L. V. Harper (Eds.), *Child effects on adults* (pp. 3–29). Hillsdale, NJ: Erlbaum.

Freud, A. (1969). Adolescence as a developmental disturbance. In G. Caplan & S. Lebovici (Eds.), *Adolescence* (pp. 5–10). New York: Basic Books.

Freud, S. (1923). *The ego and the id*. London, England: Hogarth Press.

Freud, S. (1949). *Outline of psychoanalysis*. New York: Norton.

Freud, S. (1954). *Collected works, standard edition*. London, England: Hogarth Press.

Freund, A. M., & Baltes, P. B. (1998). Selection, optimization, and compensation as strategies of life-management: Correlations with subjective indicators of successful aging. *Psychology and Aging, 13,* 531–543.

Freund, A. M., & Baltes, P. B. (2000). The orchestration of selection, optimization, and compensation: An action-theoretical conceptualization of a theory of developmental regulation. In W. J. Perrig & A. Grob (Eds.), *Control of human behavior, mental processes and consciousness: Essays in honor of the 60th birthday of August Flammer* (pp. 35–58). Mahwah, NJ: Erlbaum.

Freund, A. M., Li, K. Z. H., & Baltes, P. B. (1999). The role of selection, optimization, and compensation in successful aging. In J. Brandtstädter & R. M. Lerner (Eds.), *Action and self-development: Theory and research through the life-span* (pp. 401–434). Thousand Oaks, CA: Sage.

Fromkin, V., Krashen, S., Curtiss, S., Rigler, D., & Rigler, M. (1974). The development of language in Genie: A case of linguistic isolation beyond the "critical period." *Brain and Language, 1,* 81–107.

Fuligni, A. J., Eccles, J. S., & Barber, B. (1995). The long-term effects of seventh-grade ability groupings in mathematics. *Journal of Early Adolescence, 15,* 58–89.

Furstenberg, F. F., Jr., & Hughes, M. E. (1995). Social capital and successful development among at-risk youth. *Journal of Marriage and the Family, 57,* 580–592.

Gagné, R. M. (1968). Contributions of learning to human development. *Psychological Review, 75,* 177–191.

Gallatin, J. E. (1975). *Adolescence and individuality*. New York: Harper & Row.

Gallistel, C. R. (1990). *The organization of learning*. Cambridge, MA: MIT Press.

Galton, F. (1869). *Hereditary genius: An inquiry into its laws and consequences*. London, England: Macmillan Publishing.

Galton, F. (1883). *Inquiries into human faculty and its development*. New York: Dutton.

Garbarino, J. (1992). *Children and families in the social environment* (2nd ed.). New York: Aldine.

Garbarino, J. (1998). Children in a violent world: A metaphysical perspective. *Family & Conciliation Courts Review, 36,* 360–367.

Gardner, H. E. (1993a). *Frames of mind: The theory of multiple intelligences*. New York: Basic Books.

Gardner, H. E. (1993b). *Creating minds: An anatomy of creativity as seen through the lives of Freud, Einstein, Picasso, Stravinsky, Eliot, Graham, and Gandhi*. New York: Basic Books.

Gardner, H. E. (1993c). *Multiple intelligences: The theory in practice*. New York: Basic Books.

Gardner, H. E. (1998). Extraordinary cognitive achievements (ECA): A symbol systems approach. In W. Damon (Series Ed.) & R. M. Lerner (Vol. Ed.), *Handbook of child psychology: Vol. 1. Theoretical models of human development* (5th ed., pp. 415–466). New York: Wiley.

Gardner, H. E., Kornhaber, M., & Wake, W. (1996). *Intelligence: Multiple perspectives*. Fort Worth, TX: Harcourt Brace.

Gariépy, J. L. (1995). The evolution of a developmental science: Early determinism, modern interactionism, and a new systemic approach. *Annals of Child Development, 11,* 167–222.

Garn, S. M. (1980). Continuities and change in maturational timing. In O. G. Brim, Jr., & J. Kagan (Eds.), *Constancy and change in human development* (pp. 113–162). Cambridge, MA: Harvard University Press.

Garstang, W. (1922). The theory of recapitulation: A critical re-statement of the biogenetic law. *Journal of the Linnean Society of London Zoology, 35,* 81–101.

Gasell, A. (1928). *Infancy and human growth*. New York: Macmillan Publishing.

Gasman, D. (1971). *The scientific origins of natural socialism: Social darwinsism in Ernst Haekel and the German monist league*. New York: Elsevier.

Gavazzi, S. M. (1995). The Growing Up FAST: Families and adolescents Surviving and Thriving program. *Journal of Adolescence, 18,* 31–47.

Ge, X., Conger, R. D., Lorenz, F. O., Elder, G. H., Montague, R. B., & Simons, R. L. (1992). Linking family economic hardship to adolescent distress. *Journal of Research on Adolescence, 2,* 351–378.

Gelman, R. (1972). The nature and development of early number concepts. In H. W. Reese (Ed.), *Advances in child development* (Vol. 3). New York: Academic Press.

Gelman, R., & Gallistel, C. R. (1978). *The child's understanding of numbers*. Cambridge, MA: Harvard University Press.

Gelman, R., & Williams, E. M. (1998). Enabling constraints for cognitive development and learning: Domain specificity and epigenesis. In W. Damon (Series Ed.), D. Kuhn, & R. S. Siegler (Vol. Eds.), *Handbook of child psychology: Vol. 2. Cognition, perception, and language* (5th ed., pp. 575–630). New York: Wilcy.

Gengerelli, J. A. (1976). Graduate school reminiscence: Hull and Koffka. *American Psychologist, 31,* 685–688.

Gergen, K. J. (1973). Social psychology and history. *Journal of Personality and Social Psychology, 26,* 309–320.

Gesell, A. (1939). Charles Darwin and child development. *Scientific Monthly, 49,* 548–553.

Gesell, A. L. (1929). Maturation and infant behavior pattern. *Psychological Review, 36,* 307–319.

Gesell, A. L. (1931). Maturation and the patterning of behavior. In C. Murchison (Ed.), *Handbook of child psychology* (pp. 209–235). Worcester, MA: Clark University Press.

Gesell, A. L. (1934). *An atlas of infant behavior*. New Haven, CT: Yale University Press.

Gesell, A. L. (1946). The ontogenesis of infant behavior. In L. Carmichael (Ed.), *Manual of child psychology* (1st ed., pp. 295–331). New York: Wiley.

Gesell, A. L. (1948). *Studies in child development*. Westport, CT: Greenwood.

Gesell, A. L. (1954). The ontogenesis of infant behavior. In L. Carmichael (Ed.), *Manual of child psychology* (2nd ed., pp. 335–373). New York: Wiley.

Gesell, A. L., & Thompson, H. (1941). Twins T and C from infancy to adolescence: A biogenetic study of individual differences by the method of co-twin control. *Genetic Psychology Monographs, 24,* 3–121.

Gewirtz, J. L. (1961). A learning analysis of the effects of normal stimulation, privation and deprivation on the acquisition of social motivation and attachment. In B. M Foss (Ed.), *Determinants of infant behavior* (pp. 213–303). New York: Wiley.

Gewirtz, J. L., & Stingle, K. G. (1968). Learning of generalized imitation as the basis for identification. *Psychological Review, 75,* 374–397.

Ghiselli, E. E. (1974). Some perspectives for industrial psychology. *American Psychologist, 29,* 80–87.

Gibson, E. J. (1969). *Principles of perceptual learning and development*. New York: Appleton-Century-Crofts.

Gillie, O. (1976, October 24). Crucial data was faked by eminent psychologist. *The Sunday Times (London)*, 1–2.

Gillie, O. (1979). Burt's missing ladies. *Science, 204,* 1035–1037.

Gillie, O. (1980). Burt: The scandal and the cover-up. *Supplement to the Bulletin of British Psychological Society, 33,* 9–16.

Gilligan, C. (1982). *In a different voice: Psychological theory and women's development*. Cambridge, MA: Harvard University Press.

Ginsberg, H. P., Klein, A., & Starkey, P. (1998). The development of children's mathematical thinking: Connecting research with practice. In W. Damon (Series Ed.), I. E. Sigel, & K. A. Renninger (Vol. Eds.), *Handbook of child psychology: Vol. 4. Child psychology in practice* (5th ed., pp. 401–476). New York: Wiley.

Ginsberg, H. P., & Opper, S. (1979). *Piaget's theory of intellectual development* (2nd ed.). Englewood Cliffs, NJ: Prentice-Hall.

Glasersfeld, E. von, & Kelley, M. F. (1982). On the concepts of period, phase, stage and level. *Human Development, 25,* 152–160.

Gleick, J. (1987). *Chaos: Making a new science*. New York: Viking.

Goddard, H. H. (1912). *The Kallikak family: A study in the heredity of feeble-mindedness*. New York: Macmillan Publishing.

Goddard, H. H. (1914). *Feeble-mindedness: Its causes and consequences*. New York: Macmillan Publishing.

Goldberger, A. S. (1979). Heritability. *Economica, 46*, 327–347.

Goldberger, A. S. (1980). Review of "Cyril Burt, Psychologist." *Challenge: The Magazine of Economic Affairs, 23*, 61–62.

Goldberger, A. S., & Manski, C. F. (1995). Review Article: *The Bell Curve* by Herrnstein and Murray. *Journal of Economic Literature, 33*, 762–776.

Goldschmidt, R. (1933). Some aspects of evolution. *Science, 78*, 539–547.

Gollin, E. S. (1965). A developmental approach to learning and cognition. In L. P. Lipsitt & C. C. Spiker (Eds.), *Advances in child development and behavior* (Vol. 2, pp. 159–186). New York: Academic Press.

Gollin, E. S. (1981). Development and plasticity. In E. S. Gollin (Ed.), *Developmental plasticity: Behavioral and biological aspects of variations in development* (pp. 231–251). New York: Academic Press.

Gordon, E. M., & Thomas, A. (1967). Children's behavioral style and the teacher's appraisal of their intelligence. *Journal of School Psychology, 5*, 292–300.

Gorey, K. M., & Cryns, A. G. (1995). Lack of racial differences in behavior: A quantitative replication of Rushton's (1988) review and an independent meta-analysis. *Personality and Individual Differences, 19*, 345–353.

Gottesman, I. I., & Shields, J. (1982). *Schizophrenia: The epigenetic puzzle*. Cambridge, England: Cambridge University Press.

Gottfredson, D. C., Gottfredson, G. D., & Skroban, S. (1996). A multimodel school-based prevention demonstration. *Journal of Adolescent Research, 11*(1), 97–115.

Gottlieb, G. (1970). Conceptions of prenatal behavior. In L. R. Aronson, E. Tobach, D. S. Lehrman, & J. S. Rosenblatt (Eds.), *Development and evolution of behavior: Essays in memory of T. C. Schneirla* (pp. 111–137). San Francisco, CA: W. H. Freeman.

Gottlieb, G. (1976a). Conceptions of prenatal development: Behavioral embryology. *Psychological Review, 83*, 215–234.

Gottlieb, G. (1976b). The roles of experience in the development of behavior and the nervous system. In G. Gottlieb (Ed.), *Neural and behavioral specificity* (pp. 25–54). New York: Academic Press.

Gottlieb, G. (1983). The psychobiological approach to developmental issues. In M. M. Haith & J. Campos (Eds.), *Handbook of child psychology: Infancy and biological bases* (Vol. 2, pp. 1–26). New York: Wiley.

Gottlieb, G. (1991a). Experiential canalization of behavioral development: Theory. *Developmental Psychology, 27*, 4–13.

Gottlieb, G. (1991b). Experiential canalization of behavioral development: Results. *Developmental Psychology, 27*, 39–42.

Gottlieb, G. (1992). *Individual development and evolution: The genesis of novel behavior*. New York: Oxford University Press.

Gottlieb, G. (1997). *Synthesizing nature–nurture: Prenatal roots of instinctive behavior*. Mahwah, NJ: Erlbaum.

Gottlieb, G. (1998). Normally occurring environmental and behavioral influences on gene activity: From central dogma to probabilistic epigenesis. *Psychological Review, 105*, 792–802.

Gottlieb, G., Wahlsten, D., & Lickliter, R. (1998). The significance of biology for human development: A developmental psychobiological systems view. In W. Damon (Series Ed.) & R. M. Lerner (Vol. Ed.), *Handbook of child psychology: Vol. 1. Theoretical models of human development* (5th ed., pp. 233–273). New York: Wiley.

Gould, S. J. (1976). Grades and clades revisited. In R. B. Masterton, W. Hodos, & H. Jerison (Eds.), *Evolution, brain, and behavior: Persistent problems* (pp. 115–126). Hillsdale, NJ: Erlbaum.

Gould, S. J. (1977). *Ontogeny and phylogeny*. Cambridge, MA: Harvard University Press.

Gould, S. J. (1980). Need for achievement, career mobility, and the Mexican-American college graduate. *Journal of Vocational Behavior, 16*(1), 73–82.

Gould, S. J. (1980a). Jensen's last stand. *New York Review of Books, 27*, 38–44.

Gould, S. J. (1980b). Jensens and bias: An exchange. *New York Review of Books, 27*, 52–53.

Gould, S. J. (1981). *The mismeasure of man*. New York: Norton.

Gould, S. J. (1996). *The mismeasure of man* (revised/expanded ed.). New York: Norton.

Gould, S. J., & Lewontin, R. C. (1979). The spandrels of San Marco and the paanglossian paradigm: A critique of the adaptionist programme. In J. Maynard Smith & R. Holliday (Eds.), *The evolution of adaptation by natural selection* (pp. 581–598). London, England: Royal Society of London.

Gould, S. J., & Vrba, E. (1982). Exaptation: A missing term in the science of form. *Paleobiology, 8*, 4–15.

Graham, S. (1992). "Most of the subjects were white and middle class": Trends in published research on African Americans in selected APA journals, 1970–1989. *American Psychologist, 47*, 629–639.

Greenough, W. T., & Green, E. J. (1981). Experience and the changing brain. In J. L. McGaugh,

J. G. March, & S. B. Kiesler (Eds.), *Aging: Biology and behavior* (pp. 159–200). New York: Academic Press.

Grotevant, H. D. (1998). Adolescent development in family contexts. In W. Damon (Series Ed.) & N. Eisenberg (Vol. Ed.), *Handbook of child psychology: Vol. 3. Social, emotional, and personality development* (pp. 1097–1149). New York: Wiley.

Grotevant, H. D., & Cooper, C. R. (1985). Patterns of interaction in family relationships and the development of identity exploration. *Child Development, 56,* 415–428.

Grouse, L. D., Schrier, B. K., Bennett, E. L., Rosenzweig, M. R., & Nelson, P. G. (1978). Sequence diversity studies of rat brain RNA: Effects of environmental complexity and rat brain RNA diversity. *Journal of Neurochemistry, 30,* 191–203.

Grouse, L. D., Schrier, B. K., & Nelson, P. G. (1979). Effect of visual experience on gene expression during the development of stimulus specificity in cat brain. *Experimental Neurology, 64,* 354–335.

Gruber, H. E. (1981, March 1, 7, 8). Nature versus nurture: A natural experiment. *The New York Times Book Review,* 22–23.

Grzimek, B. (Ed.). (1972). *Animal life encyclopedia.* New York: Van Nostrand Reinhold.

Guerra, N. G., & Slaby, R. G. (1990). Cognitive mediators of aggression in adolescent offenders: Intervention. *Developmental Psychology, 26*(2), 269–277.

Gullotta, T. P., & Noyes, L. (1995). The changing of community health: The role of school-based health centers. *Adolescence, 30,* 107–115.

Gump, P. V. (1975). Ecological psychology and children. In E. M. Hetherington (Ed.), *Review of child development research* (pp. 75–126). Chicago, IL: University of Chicago Press.

Guo, S. W. (1999). The behaviors of some heritability estimators in the complete absence of genetic factors. *Human Heredity, 49,* 215–228.

Haan, N. (1974). The adolescent antecedents of an ego model of coping and defense and comparisons with Q-sorted ideal personalities. *Genetic Psychology Monographs, 89,* 273–306.

Haan, N. (1977). *Coping and defending.* New York: Academic Press.

Haan, N., & Day, D. (1974). A longitudinal study of change and sameness in personality development: Adoloescence to later adulthood. *International Journal of Aging and Human Development, 5,* 11–39.

Hadler, N. M. (1964). Heritability and phototaxis in Drosphila melanogster. *Genetics, 50,* 1269–1277.

Haeckel, E. (1868). *Naturliche Schopfungsgeschichte.* Berlin, Germany: Georg Reimer.

Haeckel, E. (1876). *The history of creation; or the development of the earth and its inhabitants by the action of natural causes.* New York: Appleton.

Haeckel, E. (1891). *Anthropogenie oder Entwickelungsgeschichte des Menschen* (4th rev. and enlarged ed.). Leipzig, Germany: Wilhelm Engelmann.

Haeckel, E. (1905). *The wonders of life.* New York: Harper.

Hagen, J. W. (1996). Graduate education in the applied developmental sciences: History and background. In C. B. Fisher & J. P. Murray (Eds.), *Applied developmental science: Graduate training for diverse disciplines and educational settings. Advances in applied developmental psychology* (pp. 45–51). Norwood, NJ: Ablex Publishing Corp.

Hagen, J. W., Paul, B., Gibb, S., & Wolters, C. (1990). Trends in research as reflected by publications in Child Development: 1930–1989. Paper presented at the Biennial meeting of the Society for Research on Adolescence. Atlanta, GA.

Hahn, A. B. (1994). Toward a national youth development policy for young African-American males: The choices policy makers face. In R. B. Mincy (Ed.), *Nurturing young Black males* (pp. 165–186). Washington, DC: Urban Institute Press.

Halford, G. S. (1989). Reflections on 25 years of Piagetian cognitive developmental psychology, 1963–1988. *Human Development, 32,* 325–357.

Hall, C. S. (1954). *A primer of freudian psychology.* New York: World Publishing.

Hall, G. S. (1883). The contents of children's minds. *Princeton Review, 2,* 249–272.

Hall, G. S. (1904). *Adolescence: Its psychology and its relations to physiology, anthropology, sociology, sex, crime, religion, and education* (Vols. 1 and 2). New York: Appleton.

Hall, G. S. (1922). *Senescence: The last half of life.* New York: Appleton.

Hamburg, D. A. (1992). *Today's children: Creating a future for a generation in crisis.* New York: Time Books.

Hamburg, D. A., & Takanishi, R. (1996). Great transitions: Preparing American youth for the 21st century—the role of research. *Journal of Research on Adolescence, 6*(4), 379–396.

Hamburger, V. (1957). The concept of development in biology. In D. B. Harris (Ed.), *The concept of development* (pp. 49–58). Minneapolis, MN: University of Minnesota Press.

Hamilton, S. F. (1994). Employment prospected as motivation for school achievement: Links and gaps between school and work in seven countries. In R. K. Silbereisen & E. Todt (Eds.), *Adolescence in context: The interplay of family, school, peers, and work in adjustment* (pp. 267–303). New York: Springer.

Hamilton, S. F. (1999). *A three-part definition of positive youth development*. Unpublished manuscript. Ithaca, NY: Cornell University.

Harley, D. (1982). Models of human evolution. *Science, 217,* 296.

Harlow, H. F. (1959). Love in infant monkeys. *Scientific American, 200,* 68–74.

Harlow, H. F. (1965). Total isolation: Effects on macaque monkey behavior. *Science, 148,* 666.

Harrington, G. M. (1975). Intelligence test may favour the majority groups in a population. *Nature, 258,* 708–709.

Harrington, G. M. (1988). Two forms of minority-group test bias as psychometric artifacts with an animal model *(Rattus norvegicus). Journal of Comparative Psychology, 102,* 400–407.

Harris, D. B. (1957). *The concept of development.* Minneapolis, MN: University of Minnesota Press.

Harris, J. R. (1998). *The nurture assumption: Why children turn out the way they do.* New York: Free Press.

Hartigan, J. A., & Wigdor, A. K. (Eds.). (1989). *Fairness in employment testing: Validity generalization, minority issues, and the general aptitude test battery.* Washington, DC: National Academy Press.

Hartup, W. W. (1978). Perspectives on child and family interaction: Past, present, and future. In R. M. Lerner & G. B. Spanier (Eds.), *Child influences on marital and family interaction: A lifespan perspective* (pp. 23–46). New York: Academic Press.

Havender, W. R. (1976). Heritability of IQ. *Science, 194,* 8–9.

Havighurst, R. J. (1948). *Developmental tasks and education.* New York: David McKay.

Havighurst, R. J. (1951). *Developmental tasks and education.* New York: Longmans.

Havighurst, R. J. (1953). *Human development and education.* London, England: Longmans.

Havighurst, R. J. (1956). Research on the developmental task concept. *School Review, 64,* 214–223.

Havighurst, R. J. (1973). Social roles, work, leisure, and education. In C. Eisdorfer & M. P. Lawton (Eds.), *The psychology of adult development and aging* (pp. 598–618). Washington, DC: American Psychological Association.

Hayes, S. C. (1993). Analytic goals and the varieties of scientific contextualism. In S. C. Hayes, L. J. Hayes, H. W. Reese, & T. R. Sarbin (Eds.), *Varieties of scientific contextualism* (pp. 11–27). Reno, NV: Context Press.

Hayes, S. C., Hayes, L. J., Reese, H. W., & Sarbin, T. R. (Eds.). (1993). *Varieties of scientific contextualism.* Reno, NV: Context Press.

Hearnshaw, L. S. (1979). *Cyril Burt, Psychologist.* New York: Cornell University Press.

Hebb, D. O. (1949). *The organization of behavior.* New York: Wiley.

Hebb, D. O. (1970). A return to Jensen and his social critics. *American Psychologist, 25,* 568.

Heckhausen, J. (1999). *Developmental regulation in adulthood: Age-normative and sociocultural constratnts as adaptive challenges.* New York: Cambridge University Press.

Heckhausen, J., Dixon, R. A., & Baltes, P. B. (1989). Gains and losses in development through adulthood as perceived by different adult age groups. *Developmental Psychology, 25,* 109–121.

Heckhausen, J., & Krueger, J. (1993). Developmental expectations for the self and most other people: Age grading in three functions of social comparison. *Developmental Psychology, 29,* 539–548

Heckhausen, J., & Schulz, R. (1995). A lifespan theory of control. *Psychological Review, 102,* 284–304.

Held, R., & Hein, A. V. (1963). Movement-produced stimulation in the development of visually guided behavior. *Journal of Comparative and Physiological Psychology, 56,* 872–876.

Hempel, C. G. (1966). *Philosophy of natural science.* Englewood Cliffs, NJ: Prentice-Hall.

Henggeler, S. W., Brondino, M. J., Melton, G. B., Scherer, D. G., & Hanley, J. H. (1997). Multisystemic therapy with violent and chronic juvenile offenders and their families: The role of treatment fidelity in successful dissemination. *Journal of Consulting and Clinical Psychology, 65*(5), 821–833.

Henggeler, S. W., Cunningham, P. B., Pickrel, S. G., Schoenwald, S. K., & Brondino, M. J. (1996). Multisystemic therapy: An effective violence prevention approach for serious juvenile offenders. *Journal of Adolescence, 19,* 47–61.

Hernandez, D. J. (1993). *America's children: Resources for family, government, and the economy.* New York: Sage.

Herrnstein, R. J. (1971). I.Q. *Atlantic Monthly, 228,* 43–64.

Herrnstein, R. J. (1973). *IQ and the meritocracy.* Boston, MA: Little, Brown.

Herrnstein, R. J. (1977). The evolution of behaviorism. *American Psychologist, 32,* 593–603.

Herrnstein, R. J., & Murray, C. (1994). *The bell curve: Intelligence and class structure in American life.* New York: Free Press.

Hess, E. H. (1973). *Imprinting.* New York: Van Nostrand Reinhold.

Hetherington, E. M. (1998). Relevant issues in developmental science: Introduction to special issue. *American Psychologist, 53,* 93–94.

Hetherington, E. M., & Baltes, P. B. (1988). Child psychology and life-span development. In E. M. Hetherington, R. M. Lerner, & M. Perlmutter

(Eds.), *Child development in life-span perpsective* (pp. 1–19). Hillsdale, NJ: Erlbaum.

Hetherington, E. M., Lerner, R. M., & Perlmutter, M. (Eds.). (1988). *Child development in life-span perspective.* Hillsdale, NJ: Erlbaum.

Hewitt, L. S. (1975). The effects of provocation, intentions, and consequences on children's moral judgements. *Child Development, 46,* 540–544.

Hiatt, S. W., Campos, J. J., & Emde, R. N. (1979). Facial patterning and infant emotional expression: Happiness, surprise, and fear. *Child Development, 50,* 1020–1035.

Hiernaux, J. (1968). Ethnic differences in growth and development. *Eugenics Quarterly, 15,* 12–21.

Higgins-D'Alessandro, A., Fisher, C. B., & Hamilton, M. G. (1998). Educating the applied developmental psychologist for university–community partnerships. In R. M. Lerner & L. A. K. Simon (Eds.), *University–community collaborations for the twenty-first century: Outreach scholarship for youth and families* (pp. 157–183). New York: Garland Publishing.

Hilgard, E. R. (1956). *Theories of learning* (2nd ed.). New York: Appleton-Century-Crofts.

Hill, J. P., Holmbeck, G. N., Marlow, L., Green, T. M., & Lynch, M. E. (1985). Menarcheal status and parent–child relations in families of seventh-grade girls. *Journal of Youth and Adolescence, 14,* 301–316.

Hill, J. P., Holmbeck, G. N., Marlow, L., Green, T. M., & Lynch, M. E. (1985). Pubertal status and parent–child relations in families of seventh-grade boys. *Journal of Early Adolescence, 5,* 31–44.

Hill, K., & Enzie, M. (1977). Interactive effects of training domain and age on children's moral judgements. *Canadian Journal of Behavior Science, 9,* 371–381.

Hinde, R. A. (1962). Sensitive periods and the development of behavior. In S. A. Barnett (Ed.), *Lessons from animal behavior for the clinician* (pp. 25–36). London, England: National Spastics Society.

Hirsch, J. (1963). Behavior genetics and individuality understood. *Science, 142,* 1436–1442.

Hirsch, J. (1970). Behavior–genetic analysis and its biosocial consequences. *Seminars in Psychiatry, 2,* 89–105.

Hirsch, J. (1975). Jensenism: The bankruptcy of "science" without scholarship. *Educational Theory, 25,* 3–27, 102.

Hirsch, J. (1976a). Jensenism: The bankruptcy of "science" without scholarship. *United States Congressional Record, Vol. 122,* no. 73, E2671-2; no. 74, E2693-5; no. 75, E2703-5, E2716-8, E2721-2.

Hirsch, J. (1976b). Review of "Sociobiology," by E. O. Wilson. *Animal Behavior, 24,* 707–709.

Hirsch, J. (1981). To "unfrock the charlatans." *Sage Race Relations Abstracts, 6,* 1–65.

Hirsch, J. (1990a). Correlation, causation, and careerism. *European Bulletin of Cognitive Psychology, 10,* 647–652.

Hirsch, J. (1990b). A nemesis for heritability estimation. *Behavioral and Brain Sciences, 13,* 137–138.

Hirsch, J. (1991). Race, genetics, and scientific integrity. *Journal of Health Care for the Poor and Underserved, 2,* 331–334.

Hirsch, J. (1997a). Some history of heredity-vs-environment, genetic inferiority at Harvard (?), and The (incredible) Bell Curve. *Genetica, 99,* 207–224.

Hirsch, J. (1997b). The triumph of wishful thinking over genetic irrelevance. *Current Psychology of Cognition, 16,* 711–720.

Hirsch, J. (1999, February 12). The pitfalls of heritability. *The Times Literary Supplement, 33.*

Hirsch, J., McGuire, T. R., & Vetta, A. (1980). Concepts of behavior genetics and misapplications to humans. In J. S. Lockard (Ed.), *The evolution of humans social behavior* (pp. 215–238). New York: Elsevier.

Hitler, A. (1925[1927/1943]). *Mein kampf* (Trans. R. Manheim). Boston, MA: Houghton-Mifflin.

Ho, M. W. (1984). Environment and heredity in development and evolution. In M. W. Ho & P. T. Saunders (Eds.), *Beyond neo-Darwinism: An introduction to the new evolutionary paradigm* (pp. 267–289). London, England: Academic Press.

Hodos, W., & Campbell, C. B. G. (1969). Scala Naturae: Why there is no theory in comparative psychology. *Psychological Review, 76,* 337–344.

Hoffman, H., & Rattner, A. (1973). A reinforcement model of imprinting. *Psychological Review, 80,* 527–544.

Hoffman, L. W. (1991). The influence of family environment on personality: Accounting for sibling differences. *Psychological Bulletin, 110,* 187–203.

Hoffman, R. F. (1978). Developmental changes in human infant visual-evoked potentials to patterned stimuli recorded at different scalp locations. *Child Development, 49*(1), 110–118.

Hogan, R., & Emler, R. H. (1978). Moral development. In M. E. Lamb (Ed.), *Social and personality development.* New York: Holt, Rinehart & Winston.

Hogan, R., Johnson, J. A., & Emler, N. P. (1978). A socioanalytical theory of moral development. *New Directions for Child Development 2,* 1–18.

Hohman, M., & LeCroy, C. W. (1996). Predictors of adolescent A. A. affiliation. *Adolescence, 31*(122), 339–352.

Hollingworth, H. L. (1927). *Mental growth and decline: A survey of developmental psychology.* New York: Appleton.

Holmbeck, G. N., & Hill, J. P. (1991). Conflictive engagement, positive affect, and menarche in families with seventh-grade girls. *Child Development, 62,* 1030–1048.

Homans, G. C. (1961). *Social behavior: Its elmentary forms.* New York: Harcourt, Brace & World.

Horn, J. L. (1970). Organization of data on life-span development of human abilities. In L. R. Goulet & P. B. Baltes (Eds.), *Life-span developmental psychology: Theory and research.* New York: Academic Press.

Horn, J. L., & Cattell, R. B. (1966). Age differences in primary mental ability factors. *Journal of Gerontology, 21,* 210–220.

Horowitz, F. D. (Ed.). (1987). *Exploring developmental theories: Toward a structural/behavioral model of development.* Hillsdale, NJ: Erlbaum.

Horowitz, F. D. (1993). Bridging the gap between nature and nurture. A conceptually flawed issue and the need for a comprehensive and new environmentalism. In R. Plomin & G. E. McClearn (Eds.), *Nature, nurture and psychology* (pp. 341–354). Washington, DC: APA Books.

Horowitz, F. D. (2000). Child development and the PITS: Simple questions, complex answers, and developmental theory. *Child Development, 71,* 1–10 (see pp. 8 and 58).

Horowitz, F. D., & O'Brien, M. (1989). In the interest of the nature: A reflective essay on the state of our knowledge and challenges before us. *American Psychologist, 44,* 441–445.

Howard, J. (1978). The influence of children's developmental dysfunction on marital quality and family interaction. In R. M. Lerner & G. B. Spanier (Eds.), *Child influences on marital and family interaction: A life-span perspective* (pp. 275–298). New York: Academic Press.

Hubbard, R. (1990). *The politics of women's biology.* New Brunswick, NJ: Rutgers University Press.

Hubel, D. H., & Wiesel, T. N. (1970). The period of susceptibility to the physiological effects of unilateral eye closure in kittens. *Journal of Physiology, 206,* 419–436.

Hull, C. L. (1929). A functional interpretation of the conditional reflex. *Psychological Review, 36,* 498–511.

Hultsch, D. F., & Dixon, R. A. (1983). The role of pre-experimental knowledge in text processing in adulthood. *Experimental Aging Research, 9,* 17–22.

Hultsch, D. F., & Hickey, T. (1978). External validity in the study of human development: Theoretical and methodological issues. *Human Development, 21,* 76–91.

Hunt, J. McV. (1961). *Intelligence and experience.* New York: Ronald Press.

Huston, A. C. (1991). *Children in poverty: Child development and public policy.* Cambridge, England: Cambridge University Press.

Huston, A. C., McLoyd, V. C., & Garcia Coll, C. (1994). Children and poverty: Issues in contemporary research. *Child Development, 65,* 275–282.

Immelmann, K., & Suomi, S. (1981). Sensitive phases in development. In K. Immelmann, G. Barlow, L. Petrinovich, & M. Main (Eds.), *Behavioral development* (pp. 395–431). New York: Cambridge University Press.

Inhelder, B., & Piaget, J. (1958). *The growth of logical thinking from childhood to adolescence.* New York: Basic Books

Isaac, G. L. (1982). Models of human evolution. *Science, 217,* 295.

Izard, C. E., Huebner, R. R., Risser, D., McGinnes, G. C., & Dougherty, L. M. (1980). The young infant's ability to produce discrete emotion expressions. *Developmental Psychology, 16,* 132–140.

Jacob, F., & Monod, J. (1961). On the regulation of gene activity. *Cold Spring Harbor Symposia on Quantitative Biology, 26,* 193–209.

Jacobs, F. (1988). The five-tiered approach to evaluation: Context and implementation. In H. B. Weiss & F. Jacobs (Eds.), *Evaluating family programs* (pp. 37–68). Hawthorne, NY: Aldine.

Jacobs, F., & Kapuscik, J. (2000). *Making it count: Evaluating family preservation services.* Medford, MA: Eliot-Pearson Department of Child Development, Tufts University.

Jacquard, A. (1983). Heritability: One word, three concepts. *Biometrics, 39,* 465–477.

Jadack, R. A., Hyde, J. S., Moore, C. F., & Keller, M. L. (1995). Moral reasoning about sexually transmitted diseases. *Child Development, 66,* 167–177.

Jaffe, S., & Hyde, J. (2000). Gender differences in moral orientation: A meta-analysis. *Psychological Bulletin, 126,* 703–726.

Jarrett, R. L. (1998). African American children, families, and neighborhoods: Qualitative contributions to understanding developmental pathways. *Applied Developmental Science, 2*(1), 2–16.

Jenkins, J. J. (1974). Remember that old theory of memory: Well forget it. *American Psychologist, 29,* 785–795.

Jensen, A. R. (1969). How much can we boost IQ and scholastic achievement? *Harvard Educational Review, 39,* 1–123.

Jensen, A. R. (1970). IQ's of identical twins reared apart. *Behavior Genetics, 1,* 133–148.

Jensen, A. R. (1972, March). A reply to Gage: The causes of twin differences in IQ. *Phi Delta Kappan,* 420–421.

Jensen, A. R. (1973). *Educability and group differences*. New York: Harper & Row.

Jensen, A. R. (1974). How biased are culture-loaded tests? *Genetic Psychology Monographs, 90,* 185–244.

Jensen. A. R. (1976a). Letters: Heritability of IQ. *Science, 194,* 6–14.

Jensen, A. R. (1976b, December 9). Heritability and intelligence. Sir Cyril Burt's findings. *The Times,* 11.

Jensen, A. R. (1980). *Bias in mental testing*. New York: Free Press.

Jensen, A. R. (1998). Jensen on "Jensenism." *Intelligence, 26,* 181–208.

Jensen, P., Hoagwood, K., & Trickett, E. (1999). Ivory towers or earthen trenches?: Community collaborations to foster "real world" research. *Applied Developmental Science, 3*(4), 206–212.

Jerison, H. J. (1978). Smart dinosaurs and comparative psychology. Paper presented at the meeting of the American Psychological Association, August, Toronto, Canada.

Jessor, R., Van Den Bos, J., Vanderryn, J., & Costa, F. M. (1995). Protective factors in adolescent problem behavior: Moderator effects and developmental change. *Developmental Psychology, 31*(6), 923–933.

Jinks, J. L., & Fulker, D. W. (1970). Comparison of the biometrical genetical, MAVA and classical approaches to the analysis of human behavior. *Psychological Bulletin, 73,* 311–349.

Johanson, D. C., & Edey, M. A. (1981). *Lucy: The beginnings of humankind*. New York: Simon & Schuster.

Johnson, K., Strader, T., Berbaum, M., Bryant, D., Bucholtz, G., Collins, D., & Noe, T. (1996). Reducing alcohol and other drug use by strengthening community, family, and youth resiliency: An evaluation of the Creating Lasting Connections program. *Journal of Adolescent Research, 11*(1), 36–67.

Jones, H. E. (1938). The California Adolescent Growth Study. *Journal of Educational Research, 31,* 561–567.

Jones, H. E. (1939a). The Adolescent Growth Study. I. Principles and methods. *Journal of Consulting Psychology, 3,* 157–159.

Jones, H. E. (1939b). The Adolescent Growth Study. II. Procedures. *Journal of Consulting Psychology, 3,* 177–180.

Jones, H. E. (1958). Problems of method in longitudinal research. *Vita Humana, 1,* 93–99.

Jones, M. C., & Bayley, N. (1950). Physical maturing among boys as related to behavior. *Journal of Educational Psychology, 41,* 129–148.

Jovanovic, J., Lerner, R. M., & Lerner, J. V. (1989). Objective and. subjective attractiveness and early adolescent adjustment. *Journal of Adolescence, 12,* 225–229.

Juel-Nielsen, N. (1965). Individual and environment: A psychiatric–psychological investigation of monozygotic twins reared apart. *Acta Psychiatrica et Neurologica Scandinavica,* Monograph Supplement 183.

Jurich, A. P., & Collins, O. P. (1996). 4-H night at the movies: A program for adolescents and their families. *Adolescence, 31*(124), 863–874.

Kagan, J. (1966). Reflection-impulsively: The generality and dynamics of conceptual tempo. *Journal of Abnormal Psychology, 71,* 17–24.

Kagan, J. (1969). Inadequate evidence and illogical conclusions. *Harvard Educational Review, 39,* 274–277.

Kagan, J. (1980). Perspectives on continuity. In O. G. Brim, Jr. & J. Kagan (Eds.), *Constancy and change in human development* (pp. 26–74). Cambridge, MA: Harvard University Press.

Kagan, J. (1983). Developmental categories and the premise of connectivity. In R. M. Lerner (Ed.), *Developmental psychology: Historical and philosophical perspectives*. Hillsdale, NJ: Erlbaum.

Kagan, J. (1998). Biology and the child. In W. Damon (Series Ed.) and N. Eisenberg (Vol. Ed.), *Handbook of child psychology: Vol. 3. Social, emotional, and personality development* (pp. 117–235). New York: Wiley.

Kagan, J., & Moss, H. A. (1962). *Birth to maturity*. New York: Wiley.

Kalikow, T. J. (1978a). Konrad Lorenz's ethological theory: Explanation and ideology, 1938–1943. *Journal of the History of Biology, 16,* 39–73.

Kalikow, T. J. (1978b). Review of civilized man's eight deadly sins, by Konrad Lorenz. *Philosophy of the Social Sciences, 8,* 99–108.

Kalikow, T. J. (1983). Konrad Lorenz's ethological theory, explanation and ideology. *Journal of the Social Sciences, 8,* 39–73.

Kamin, L. J. (1974). *The science and politics of IQ*. Potomac, MD: Wiley.

Kamin, L. J. (1980, February). Jensen's last stand. A review of Arthur Jensen *Bias in Mental Testing. Psychology Today*, 117–118, 120, 123.

Kaplan, B. (1966). The comparative–developmental approach and its application to symbolization and language in psychopathology. In T. Arieti (Ed.), *American handbook of psychiatry* (Vol. 3). New York: Basic Books.

Kaplan, B. (1983). A trio of trials. In R. M. Lerner (Ed.), *Developmental psychology: Historical and philosophical perspectives* (pp. 185–228). Hillsdale, NJ: Erlbaum.

Karmiloff-Smith, A. (1992). *Beyond modularity: A developmental perspective on cognitive science*. Cambridge, MA: MIT Press.

Katchadourian, H. (1977). *The biology of adolescence*. San Francisco, CA: W. H. Freeman.

Kaufmann, H. (1968). *Introduction to the study of human behavior*. Philadelphia, PA: Saunders.

Keasey, C. B. (1974). The influence of opinion agreement and quality of supportive reasoning in the evaluation of moral judgments. *Journal of Personality and Social Psychology, 30,* 477–482.

Keil, F. (1998). Cognitive science and the origins of thought and knowledge. In W. Damon (Series Ed.) and R. M. Lerner (Vol. Ed.), *Handbook of child psychology: Vol. 1. Theoretical models of human development* (5th ed., pp. 341–413). New York: Wiley.

Kellman, P. K., & Banks, M. S. (1998). Infant visual perception. In W. Damon (Series Ed.), D. Kuhn, & R. S. Siegler (Vol. Eds.), *Handbook of child psychology: Vol. 2. Cognition, perception, and language* (5th ed., pp. 103–146). New York: Wiley.

Kellner, M. H., & Tutin, J. (1995). A school-based anger management program for developmentally and emotionally disabled high school students. *Adolescence, 30*(120), 813–825.

Kellogg Commission on the Future of State and Land-Grant Colleges. (1999). *Returning to our roots: The engaged institution*. Washington, DC: National Association of State Universities and Land-Grant Colleges.

Kellogg, W. N., & Kellogg, L. A. (1933). *The ape and the child*. New York: McGraw-Hill.

Kempthorne, O. (1978). Logical, epistemological and statistical aspects of nature–nurture data interpretation. *Biometrics, 34,* 1–23.

Kempthorne, O. (1990). How does one apply statistical analysis to our understanding of the development of human relationships. [Comments on "Insensitivity of the analysis of variance to heredity–environment interaction"]. *Behavioral and Brain Sciences, 13,* 138–139.

Kendall, P. C., Lerner, R. M., & Craighead, W. E. (1984). Human development intervention in childhood psychopathology. *Child Development, 55,* 71–82.

Kendall, P. C., & Southam-Gerow, M. A. (1996). Long-term follow-up of a cognitive-behavioral therapy for anxiety-disordered youth. *Journal of Consulting and Clinical Psychology, 64*(4), 724–730.

Kendler, H. H., & Kendler, T. S. (1962). Vertical and horizontal processes in human concept learning. *Psychological Review, 69,* 1–16.

Kendler, T. S. (1986). World views and the concept of development: A reply to Lerner and Kauffman. *Developmental Review, 6*(1), 80–95.

Kennedy, E. M. (1999). University–community partnerships: A mutually beneficial effort to aid community development and improve academic learning opportunities. *Applied Developmental Science, 3*(4), 197–198.

Kerfoot, M., Harrington, R., & Dyer, E. (1995). Brief home-based intervention with young suicide attempters and their families. *Journal of Adolescence, 18,* 557–568.

Kessen, W. (1962). "Stage" and "structure" in the study of children. In W. Kessen & C. Kuhlman (Eds.), *Thought in the young child* (pp. 65–86). *Monographs of the Society for Research in Child Development,* 27.

Kessen, W. (1965). *The child*. New York: Wiley

Kidwell, J. S., Dunham, R. M., Bacho, R. A., & Pastorino, E. (1996). Adolescent identity exploration: A test of Erikson's theory of transition crisis. *Adolescence, 30*(120), 785–793.

Kimble, G. A. (1961). *Hilgard and Marguis' conditioning and learning*. New York: Appleton-Century-Crofts.

Kinsey, A. C., Pomeroy, W. B., Martin, C. E., & Gebhard, P. H. (1953). *Sexual behavior in the human female*. Philadelphia, PA: Saunders.

Kitcher, P. (1985). *Vaulting ambition*. Cambridge, MA: MIT Press.

Klahr, D., & MacWhinney, B. (1998). Information processing. In W. Damon (Series Ed.), D. Kuhn, & R. S. Siegler (Vol. Eds.), *Handbook of child psychology: Vol. 2. Cognition, perception, and language* (5th ed., pp. 631–678). New York: Wiley.

Klaus, M., & Kennell, J. (1976). *Maternal-infant bonding*. St. Louis, MO: C. V. Mosby.

Kleckner, J. H. (1977). Alcoholics can drink again, or can they? *Psychology, 14*(2), 6–8.

Kluckhohn, C., & Murray, H. (1948). Personality formation: The determinants. In C. Kluckhohn & H. Murray (Eds.), *Personality in nature, society, and culture*. New York: Knopf.

Kohlberg, L. (1958). *The development of modes of moral thinking and choice in the years ten to sixteen*. Unpublished doctoral dissertation, University of Chicago.

Kohlberg, L. (1963a). The development of children's orientations toward a moral order: Sequence in the development of moral thought. *Vita Humana, 6,* 11–33.

Kohlberg, L. (1963b). Moral development and identification. In H. Stevenson (Ed.), *Child psychology 62nd yearbook of the national society of education*. Chicago, IL: University of Chicago Press.

Kohlberg, L. (1968). Early education: A cognitive–developmental view. *Child Development, 39,* 1014–1062.

Kohlberg, L. (1971). From is to ought: How to commit the naturalistic fallacy and get away with it in the study of moral development. In T. Mischel (Ed.), *Cognitive development and epistemology*. New York: Academic Press.

Kohlberg, L. (1973). Continuities in childhood and adult moral development revisited. In P. B. Baltes, & K. W. Schaie (Eds.), *Life-span development psychology: Personality and socialization*. New York: Academic Press.

Kohlberg, L. (1976). Moral stages and moralization: The cognitive approach. In T. Lickona (Ed.), *Moral development and behavior: Theory, research, and social issues*. New York: Holt, Rinehart & Winston.

Kohlberg, L. (1978). Revisions in the theory and practice of moral development. *New Directions for Child Development, 2,* 93–120.

Kollar, E. J., & Fisher, C. (1980). Tooth induction in chick epithelium: Expression of quiescent genes for enamel synthesis. *Science, 207,* 993–995.

Konner, M. (1982). *The tangled wing*. New York: Holt, Rinehart & Winston.

Korn, S. J. (1978). Temperament, vulnerability, and behavior. Paper presented at the Louisville Temperament Conference, September. Louisville, Kentucky.

Kramer, D. A. (1989). Development of an awareness of contradiction across the life span and the question of postformal operations. In M. L. Commons, J. D. Sinnott, F. A. Richards, & C. Armon (Eds.), *Adult development: Vol. 1. Comparisons and applications of developmental models* (pp. 133–159). New York: Praeger.

Krashen, S. D. (1975). The critical period for language and its possible bases. *Annals of the New York Academy of Sciences, 263,* 211–224.

Kreppner, K. (1994). William L. Stern: A neglected founder of developmental psychology. In R. D. Parke, P. A. Ornstein, J. J. Rieser, & C. Zahn-Waxler (Eds.), *A century of developmental psychology* (pp. 311–331). Washington, DC: American Psychological Association.

Kroger, J. (1995). The differentiation of "firm" and "developmental" foreclosure identity statuses: A logitudinal study. *Journal of Adolescent Research, 10*(3), 317–337.

Kuhn, D. (1976). Short-term longitudinal evidence for the sequentiality of Kohlberg's early stages of moral development. *Developmental Psychology, 12,* 162–166.

Kuhn, D. (1995). Microgenetic study of change: What has it told us? *Psychological Science, 6,* 133–139.

Kuhn, D. (1998). Afterword to Volume 2: Cognition, Perception, and Language. In W. Damon (Series Ed.), D. Kuhn, & R. S. Siegler (Eds.), *Handbook of child psychology: Vol. 2. Cognition, perception, and language* (pp. 979–981). New York: Wiley.

Kuhn, D., & Siegler, R. S. (Vol. Eds.). (1998). *Handbook of child psychology: Cognition, perception, and language* (Vol. 2). New York: Wiley.

Kuhn, T. S. (1962). *The structure of scientific revolutions*. Chicago, IL: University of Chicago Press.

Kuo, Z. Y. (1930). The genesis of the cat's response to the rat. *Journal of Comparative Psychology, 11,* 1–35.

Kuo, Z. Y. (1967). *The dynamics of behavior development*. New York: Random House.

Kuo, Z. Y. (1970). The need for coordinated efforts in developmental studies. In A. Aronson, E. Tobach, D. S. Lehrman, & J. S. Rosenblatt (Eds.), *Development and evolution of behavior: Essays in memory of T. C. Schneirla* (pp. 181–193). San Francisco, CA: W. H. Freeman.

Kuo, Z. Y. (1976). *The dynamics of behavior development: An epigenetic view*. New York: Plenum Publishing.

Kurtines, W., & Greif, E. B. (1974). The development of moral thought: Review and evaluation of Kohlberg's approach. *Psychological Bulletin, 81,* 453–469.

Labouvie-Vief, G. (1981). Proactive and reactive aspects of constructivism: Growth and aging in life-span perspective. In R. M. Lerner & N. A. Busch-Rossnagel (Eds.), *Individuals as producers of their development: A life-span perspective* (pp. 197–230). New York: Academic Press.

Labouvie-Vief, G. (1994). *Psyche and Eros: Mind and gender in the life course*. New York: Cambridge University Press.

Lachman, M. E., & Jamos, J. B. (Eds.) (1997) *Multiple paths of mid-life development*. Chicago, IL: University of Chicago Press.

Lakatos, I. (1978a). *The methodology of scientific research programmes: Philosophical papers* (Vol. 1). New York: Cambridge University Press.

Lakatos, I. (1978b). *Mathematics, science, and epistemology: A philosophical papers* (Vol. 2). New York: Cambridge University Press.

Lamb, M. E. (1977a). A reexamination of the infant social world. *Human Development, 20,* 65–85.

Lamb, M. E. (1977b). Father–infant and mother–infant interaction in the first year of life. *Child Development, 48,* 167–181.

Lamb, M. E. (1977c). The development of mother–infant and father–infant attachments in the second year of life. *Developmental Psychology, 13,* 637–648.

Lamb, M. E. (1978a). Qualitative aspects of mother– and father–infant attachments. *Infant Behavior and Development, 1,* 265–275.

Lamb, M. E. (1978b). Influence of the child on marital quality and family interaction during the prenatal, perinatal, and infancy periods. In R. M. Lerner & G. B. Spanier (Eds.), *Child influences on marital and family interaction: A life-span perspective* (pp. 137–163). New York: Academic Press.

Lamb, M. E. (1998). Nonparental child care: Context, quality, correlates, and consequences. In W. Damon (Series Ed.), I. Sigel, & K. A. Renninger (Vol. Eds.), *Handbook of child psychology: Vol. 4. Child psychology in practice* (5th ed., pp. 73–133). New York: Wiley.

Lamb, M. E. (2000). The effects of quality of care on child development. *Applied Developmental Science, 4,* 1112–115.

Lamb, M. E., Thompson, R. A., Gardner, W. P., & Charnov, E. L. (1985). *Infant–mother attachment.* Hillsdale, NJ: Lawrence Erlbaum Associates.

Landau, B., Spelke, E. S., & Gleitman, H. (1984). Spatial knowledge in a young blind child. *Cognition, 16,* 225–260.

Landsell, H. (1969). Verbal and nonverbal factors in right-hemisphere speech: Relation to early neurological history. *Journal of Comparative and Physiological Psychology, 69,* 734–738.

Langer, J. (1969). *Theories of development.* New York: Holt, Rinehart & Winston.

Langer, J. (1970). Werner's comparative organismic theory. In P. H. Mussen (Ed.), *Carmichael's manual of child psychology* (Vol. 1, pp. 733–772). New York: Wiley.

Langlois, J. H., & Stephan, C. W. (1981). Beauty and the beast: The role of physical attraction in peer relationships and social behavior. In S. S. Brehm, S. M. Kassin, & S. X. Gibbons (Eds.), *Developmental social psychology: Theory and research* (pp. 152–168). New York: Oxford University Press.

Laursen, B. (1995). Conflict and social interaction in adolescent relationships. *Journal of Research on Adolescence, 5*(1), 55–70.

Layzer, D. (1974). Heritability analyses of IQ scores: Science or numerology? *Science, 183,* 1259–1266.

Layzer, D. (2000). *Comment on "Misconceptions of biometrical IQists" by C. Capron et al.* Unpublished manuscript. Cambridge, MA: Harvard University Press.

Leffert, N., Benson, P., Scales, P., Sharma, A., Drake, D., & Blyth, D. (1998). Developmental assets: Measurement and prediction of risk behaviors among adolescents. *Applied Developmental Science, 2*(4), 209–230.

Lehrman, D. S. (1953). A critique of Konrad Lorenz's theory of instinctive behavior. *Quarterly Review of Biology, 28,* 337–363.

Lehrman, D. S. (1970). Semantic and conceptual issues in the nature–nurture problem. In L. R. Aronson, E. Tobach, D. S. Lehrman, & J. S. Rosenblatt (Eds.), *Development and evolution of behavior: Essays in memory of T. C. Schneirla* (pp. 17–52). San Franciso, CA: W. H. Freeman.

Lenneberg, E. (1967). *The biological basis of language.* New York: Academic Press.

Lenneberg, E. (1969). On explaining language. *Science, 165,* 635–643.

Lenneberg, E., Nichols, I., & Rosenberger, E. (1964). Primitive stages of language development in Mongolism. In *Disorders of communication research publications* (Vol. 42). Baltimore, MD: Williams & Wilkins.

Lenz, F. (1930). Alfred Ploetz zum 70. Geburtstag am 22 August. *Archiv für Rassen- und Gesellschaftsbiologie, 24.*

Leont'ev, A. N. (1981). The problem of activity in psychology. In J. V. Wertsch (Ed.), *The concept of activity in Soviet psychology* (pp. 37–71). Armonk, NY: Sharpe.

Lerner, J. V. (1994). *Working women and their families.* Thousand Oaks, CA: Sage.

Lerner, J. V., & Lerner, R. M. (1983). Temperament and adaptation across life: Theoretical and empirical issues. In P. B. Baltes & O. G. Brim, Jr. (Eds.), *Life-span development and behavior* (Vol. 5, pp. 197–231). New York: Academic Press.

Lerner, R. M. (1969). The development of stereotyped expectancies of body build–behavior relations. *Child Development, 40,* 137–141.

Lerner, R. M. (1972). "Richness" analyses of body build stereotype development. *Developmental Psychology, 7,* 219.

Lerner, R. M. (1973). The development of personal space schemata toward body build. *Journal of Psychology, 84,* 229–235.

Lerner, R. M. (1976). *Concepts and theories of human development.* Reading, MA: Addison-Wesley.

Lerner, R. M. (1977). Biographies of DeSanctis, S., Dewey, J., Gesell, A., Goodenough, F., Locke, J., Terman, L. M., Werner, H., and Witmer, L. In B. B. Wolman (Ed.), *International encyclopedia of neurology, psychiatry, psychoanalysis, and psychology.* New York: Van Nostrand Reinhold.

Lerner, R. M. (1978). Nature, nurture, and dynamic interactionism. *Human Development, 21,* 1–20.

Lerner, R. M. (1979). A dynamic interactional concept of individual and social relationship development. In R. L. Burgess & T. L. Huston (Eds.), *Social exchange in developing relationships* (pp. 271–305). New York: Academic Press.

Lerner, R. M. (1980). Concepts of epigenesis: Descriptive and explanatory issues. A critique of Kitchner's comments. *Human Development, 23,* 63–72.

Lerner, R. M. (1982). Children and adolescents as producers of their own development. *Developmental Review, 2,* 342–370.

Lerner, R. M. (1984). *On the nature of human plasticity.* New York: Cambridge University Press.

Lerner, R. M. (1985). Individual and context in developmental psychology: Conceptual and theoretical issues. In J. R. Nesselroade & A. von Eye (Eds.), *Individual development and social change: Explanatory analysis* (pp. 155–187). New York: Academic Press.

Lerner, R. M. (1986). *Concepts and theories of human development* (2nd ed.). New York: Random House.

Lerner, R. M. (1987). A life-span perspective for early adolescence. In R. M. Lerner & T. T. Foch (Eds.), *Biological–psychosocial interactions in early adolescence* (pp. 9–34). Hillsdale, NJ: Erlbaum.

Lerner, R. M. (1988). Personality development: A life-span perspective. In E. M. Hetherington, R. M. Lerner, & M. Perlmutter (Eds.), *Child development in life-span perspective* (pp. 21–46). Hillsdale, NJ: Erlbaum.

Lerner, R. M. (1991). Changing organism–context relations as the basic process of development: A developmental contextual perspective. *Developmental Psychology, 27,* 27–32.

Lerner, R. M. (1992a). *Final solutions: Biology, prejudice, and genocide* University Park, PA: Penn State Press.

Lerner, R. M. (1992b). Nature, nurture and mass murder. *Readings: A Journal of Reviews and Commentary on Mental Health, 7*(3), 8–15.

Lerner, R. M. (1993a). Plasticity: Genetic program or developmental process? [Review of Brauth, S. E., Hall, W. S., & Dooling, R. J. (Eds.). (1991). *Plasticity of development.* Cambridge, MA: MIT Press.] *Contemporary Psychology, 11,* 1192–1194.

Lerner, R. M. (1993b). Investment in youth: The role of home economics in enhancing the life chances of America's children. *AHEA Monograph Series, 1,* 5–34.

Lerner, R. M. (1995a). *America's youth in crisis: Challenges and options for programs and policies.* Thousand Oaks, CA: Sage.

Lerner, R. M. (1995b). The place of learning within the human development system: A developmental contextual perspective. *Human Development, 38,* 361–366.

Lerner, R. M. (1996). Relative plasticity, integration, temporality, and diversity in human development: A developmental contextual perspective about theory, process, and method. *Developmental Psychology, 32*(4), 781–786.

Lerner, R. M. (Vol. Ed.). (1998a). In W. Damon (Series Ed.), *Handbook of Child Psychology: Vol. 1. Theoretical models of human development* (5th ed.). New York: Wiley.

Lerner, R. M. (1998b). Theories of human development: Contemporary perspectives. In W. Damon (Series Ed.) & R. M. Lerner (Vol. Ed.), *Handbook of child psychology: Vol. 1. Theoretical models of human development* (5th ed., pp. 1–24). New York: Wiley.

Lerner, R. M. (In press). *Adolescence: Development, diversity, context, and application.* Upper Saddle River, NJ: Prentice-Hall.

Lerner, R. M., & Brackney, B. (1978). The importance of inner and outer body parts attitudes in the self concept of late adolescents. *Sex Roles, 4,* 225–238.

Lerner, R. M., & Busch-Rossnagel, N. A. (Eds.). (1981a). *Individuals as producers of their development: A life-span perspective.* New York: Academic Press.

Lerner, R. M., & Busch-Rossnagel, N. A. (1981b). Individuals as producers of their development: Conceptual and empirical bases. In R. M. Lerner & N. A. Busch-Rossnagel (Eds.), *Individuals as producers of their development: A life-span perspective* (pp. 1–36). New York: Academic Press.

Lerner, R. M., Castellino, D. R., Terry, P. A., Villarruel, F. A., & McKinney, M. H. (1995). A developmental contextual perspective on parenting. In M. H. Bornstein (Ed.), *Handbook of parenting: Vol. 2. biology and ecology of parenting* (pp. 285–309). Hillsdale, NJ: Erlbaum.

Lerner, R. M., De Stefanis, I., & Ladd, G. T. (1998). Promoting positive youth development: Collaborative opportunities for psychology. *Children's Services: Social Policy, Research, & Practice, 1*(2), 83–109.

Lerner, R. M., & Fisher, C. B. (1994). From applied developmental psychology to applied developmental science: Community coalitions and collaborative careers. In C. B. Fisher & R. M. Lerner (Eds.), *Applied developmental psychology* (pp. 505–522). New York: McGraw-Hill.

Lerner, R. M., Fisher, C. B., & Weinberg, R. A. (1997). Applied developmental science: Scholarship for our times. *Applied Developmental Science, 1,* 2–3.

Lerner, R. M., Fisher, C. B., & Weinberg, R. A. (2000a). Toward a science for and of the people: Promoting civil society through the application of developmental science. *Child Development, 71,* 11–20.

Lerner, R. M., Fisher, C. B., & Weinberg, R. A. (2000b). Applying developmental science in the twenty-first century: International scholarship for our times. *International Journal of Behavioral Development, 24,* 24–29.

Lerner, R. M., Freund, A. M., De Stefanis, I., & Habermas, T. (2001). Understanding developmental regulation in adolescence: The use of the selection, optimization, and compensation model. *Human Development, 44,* 29–50.

Lerner, R. M., & Galambos, N. (1998). Adolescent development: Challenges and opportunities for research, programs, and policies. In J. T. Spence (Ed.), *Annual review of psychology* (Vol. 49, pp. 413–446). Palo Alto, CA: Annual Reviews.

Lerner, R. M., & Gellert, E. (1969). Body build identification, preference, and aversion in children. *Developmental Psychology, 1,* 456–462.

Lerner, R. M., & Hood, K. E. (1986). Plasticity in development: Concepts and issues for intervention. *Journal of Applied Developmental Psychology, 7,* 139–152.

Lerner, R. M., Hultsch, D. F., & Dixon, R. A. (1983). Contextualism and the character of developmental psychology in the 1970s. *Annals of the New York Academy of Sciences, 412,* 101–128.

Lerner, R. M., Iwawaki, S., Chihara, T., & Sorell, G. T. (1980). Self-concept, self-esteem, and body attitudes among Japanese male and female adolescents. *Child Development, 51,* 847–855.

Lerner, R. M., & Karabenick, S. A. (1974). Physical attractiveness, body attitudes, and self-concept in late adolescents. *Journal of Youth and Adolescence, 3,* 307–316.

Lerner, R. M., Karabenick, S. A., & Meisels, M. (1975a). Effects of age and sex on the development of personal space schemata towards body build. *Journal of Genetic Psychology, 127,* 91–101.

Lerner, R. M., Karabenick, S. A., & Meisels, M. (1975b). One-year stability of children's personal space schemata towards body build. *Journal of Genetic Psychology, 127,* 151–152.

Lerner, R. M., Karabenick, S. A., & Stuart, J. L. (1973). Relations among physical attractiveness, body attitudes, and self-concept in male and female college students. *Journal of Psychology, 85,* 119–129.

Lerner, R. M., & Kauffman, M. B. (1985). The concept of development in contextualism. *Developmental Review, 5,* 309–333.

Lerner, R. M., & Kauffman, M. B. (1986). On the metatheoretical relativism of analyses of metatheoretical analyses: A critique of Kendler's comments. *Developmental Review, 6,* 96–106.

Lerner, R. M., Knapp, J. R., & Pool, K. B. (1974). The structure of body build stereotypes: A methodological analysis. *Perceptual and Motor Skills, 39,* 719–729.

Lerner, R. M., & Korn, S. J. (1972). The development of body build stereotypes in males. *Child Development, 43,* 912–920.

Lerner, R. M., & Lerner, J. V. (1977). Effects of age, sex, and physical attractiveness on child–peer relations, academic performance, and elementary school adjustment. *Developmental Psychology, 13,* 585–590.

Lerner, R. M., & Lerner, J. V. (1987). Children in their contexts: A goodness of fit model. In J. B. Lancaster, J. Altmann, A. S. Rossi, & L. R. Sherrod (Eds.), *Parenting across the life span: Biosocial dimensions* (pp. 377–404). Chicago, IL: Aldine.

Lerner, R. M., & Lerner, J. V. (1989). Organismic and social contextual bases of development: The sample case of early adolescence. In W. Damon (Ed.), *Child development today and tomorrow* (pp. 69–85). San Francisco, CA: Jossey-Bass.

Lerner, R. M., & Lerner, J. V. (1999). Adolescence: Theoretical and empirical issues in the understanding of development, diversity, and context. In R. M. Lerner & J. V. Lerner (Eds.), *Adolescence: Theoretical foundations and biological bases of development* (pp. ix–xvii). New York: Garland Publishing.

Lerner, R. M., Lerner, J. V., & Jovanovic, J. (1996). Constitutional psychology. In A. M. Kuper & J. Kuper (Eds.), *The social science encyclopedia* (2nd ed., pp. 132–133). London, England: Routledge.

Lerner, R. M., & Miller, J. R. (1993). Integrating human development research and intervention for America's children: The Michigan State University model. *Journal of Applied Developmental Psychology, 14,* 347–364.

Lerner, R. M., Miller, J. R., Knott, J. H., Corey, K. E., Bynum, T. S., Hoopfer, L. C., McKinney, M. H., Abrams, L. A., Hula, R. C., & Terry, P. A. (1994). Integrating scholarship and outreach in human development research, policy, and service: A developmental contextual perspective. In D. L. Featherman, R. M. Lerner, & M. Perlmutter (Eds.), *Life-span development and behavior* (Vol. 12, pp. 249–273). Hillsdale, NJ: Erlbaum.

Lerner, R. M., Miller, J. R., & Ostrom, C. W. (1995). Integrative knowledge, accountability, access, and the American university of the twenty-first century: A family and consumer sciences vision of the future of higher education. *Kappa Omicron Nu Forum, 8*(1), 11–27.

Lerner, R. M., Orlos, J. B., & Knapp, J. R. (1976). Physical attractiveness, physical effectiveness, and self-concept in late adolescents. *Adolescence, 11,* 313–326.

Lerner, R. M., Ostrom, C. W., & Freel, M. A. (1995). Promoting positive youth and community development through outreach scholarship: Comments on Zeldin and Peterson. *Journal of Adolescent Research, 10,* 486–502.

Lerner, R. M., Ostrom, C. W., & Freel, M. A. (1997). Preventing health compromising behaviors among youth and promoting their positive development: A developmental contextual perspective. In J. Schulenberg, J. L. Maggs, & K. Hurrelmann (Eds.), *Health risks and developmental transitions during adolescence* (pp. 498–521). New York: Cambridge University Press.

Lerner, R. M., & Ryff, C. (1978). Implementation of the life-span view of human development: The sample case of attachment. In P. B. Baltes (Ed.), *Life-span development and behavior* (Vol. 1, pp. 1–44). New York: Academic Press.

Lerner, R. M., & Schroeder, C. (1971a). Kindergarten children's active vocabulary about body build. *Developmental Psychology, 5,* 179.

Lerner, R. M., & Schroeder, C. (1971b). Physique identification, preference, and aversion in kindergarten children. *Developmental Psychology, 5,* 538.

Lerner, R. M., & Simon, L. A. K. (1998a). The new American outreach university: Challenges and options. In R. M. Lerner & L. A. K. Simon (Eds.), *University–community collaborations for the twenty-first century: Outreach scholarship for youth and families* (pp. 3–23). New York: Garland Publishing.

Lerner, R. M., & Simon, L. A. K. (1998b). Directions for the American outreach university in the twenty-first century. In R. M. Lerner & L. A. K. Simon (Eds.), *University–community collaborations for the twenty-first century: Outreach scholarship for youth and families* (pp. 461–481). New York: Garland Publishing.

Lerner, R. M., Skinner, E. A., & Sorell, G. T. (1980). Methodological implications of contextual/dialectic theories of development. *Human Development, 23,* 225–235.

Lerner, R. M., Sorell, G. T., & Brackney, B. E. (1981). Sex differences in self-concept and self-esteem in late adolescents: A time-lag analysis. *Sex Roles, 7,* 709–722.

Lerner, R. M., & Spanier, G. B. (1978). A dynamic interactional view of child and family development. In R. M. Lerner & G. B. Spanier (Eds.), *Child influences on marital and family interaction: A life-span perspective* (pp. 1–22). New York: Academic Press.

Lerner, R. M., & Spanier, G. B. (1980). *Adolescent development: A life-span perspective.* New York: McGraw-Hill.

Lerner, R. M., Sparks, E. S., & McCubbin, L. (1999). *Family diversity and family policy: Strengthening families for America's children.* Norwell, MA: Kluwer.

Lerner, R. M., Sparks, E. S., & McCubbin, L. (2000). Family diversity and family policy. In D. Demo, K. Allen, & M. Fine (Eds.), *Handbook of family diversity* (pp. 380–401). New York: Oxford University Press.

Lerner, R. M., Terry, P. A., McKinney, M. H., & Abrams, L. A. (1994). Addressing child poverty within the context of a community–collaborative university: Comments on Fabes, Martin, and Smith (1994) and McLoyd (1994). *Family and Consumer Sciences Research Journal, 23,* 67–75.

Lerner, R. M., & Tubman, J. G. (1989). Conceptual issues in studying continuity and discontinuity in personality development across life. *Journal of Personality, 57,* 343–373.

Lerner, R. M., & Tubman, J. G. (1990). Plasticity in development: Ethical implications for developmental interventions. In C. B. Fisher & W. W. Tryon (Eds.), *Ethical issues in applied developmental psychology* (pp. 113–131). Norwood, NJ: Ablex Publishing Corp.

Lerner, R. M., & von Eye, A. (1992a). Sociobiology and human development: Arguments and evidence. *Human Development, 35,* 12–33.

Lerner, R. M., & von Eye, A. (1993). Why Burgess and Molenaar "just don't get it." *Human Development, 36,* 55–56.

Lerner, R. M., & Walls, T. (1999). Revisiting individuals as producers of their development: From dynamic interactionism to developmental systems. In J. Brandtstädter & R. M. Lerner (Eds.), *Action and self-development: Theory and research through the life-span* (pp. 3–36). Thousand Oaks, CA: Sage.

Levine, R. L., & Fitzgerald, H. E. (Eds.). (1992). *Analysis of dynamic psychological systems* (Vols. 1 and 2). New York: Plenum Publishing.

Levinson, D. J. (1978). Eras: The anatomy of the life cycle. *Psychiatric Opinion, 15,* 10–11, 39–48.

Levinson, D. J., Darrow, C. N., Klein, E. B., Levinson, M. H., & Mckee, B. (1978). *Season's of a man's life.* New York: Knopf.

Levitt, M. Z., Selman, R. L., & Richmond, J. B. (1991). The psychosocial foundations of early adolescents' high-risk behavior: Implications for research and practice. *Journal of Research on Adolescence, 1*(4), 349–378.

Lewin, K. (1935). *A dynamic theory of personality*. New York: McGraw-Hill.

Lewin, K. (1943). Psychology and the process of group living. *Journal of Social Psychology, 17,* 113–131.

Lewin, K. (1954). Behavior and development as a function of the total situation. In L. Carmichael (Ed.), *Manual of child psychology* (2nd ed.). New York: Wiley.

Lewis, M. (1972). State as an infant-environment interaction: An analysis of mother–infant behavior as a function of sex. *Merrill-Palmer Quarterly, 18,* 95–121.

Lewis, M. (1990). Development, time, and catastrophe: An alternative view of discontinuity. In P. B. Baltes, D. L. Featherman, & R. M. Lerner (Eds.), *Life-span development and behavior* (Vol. 10., pp. 325–350). Hillsdale, NJ: Erlbaum.

Lewis, M. (1997). *Altering fate*. New York: Guilford Press.

Lewis, M., & Feiring, C. (1978). A child's social world. In R. M. Lerner & G. B. Spanier (Eds.), *Child influences on marital and family interaction* (pp. 47–66). New York: Academic Press.

Lewis, M., & Lee-Painter, S. (1974). An interactional approach to the mother–infant dyad. In M. Lewis & L. A. Rosenblum (Eds.), *The effect of the infant on its caregivers* (pp. 21–48). New York: Wiley

Lewis, M., & Rosenblum, L. A. (Eds.). (1974a). *The effect of the infant on its caregivers*. New York: Wiley.

Lewis, M. & Rosenblum, L. A. (1974b). Introduction. In M. Lewis & L. A. Rosenblum, L. A. (Eds.), *The effect of the infant on its caregivers*. (pp. xv–xxiv). New York: Wiley.

Lewis, M., & Rosenblum, L. A. (Eds.). (1979). *Interaction, conversation, and the development of language* (Vol. 5). New York: Wiley.

Lewontin, R. C. (1970, March). Race and intelligence. *Bulletin of the Atlantic Scientists,* 2–8.

Lewontin, R. C. (1973). The apportionment of human diversity. *Evolutionary Biology, 6,* 381–398.

Lewontin, R. C. (1974). *Genetic basis of evolutionary change*. New York: Columbia University Press.

Lewontin, R. C. (1976). The fallacy of biological determinism. *The Sciences, 16,* 6–10.

Lewontin, R. C. (1981). On constraints and adaptation. *The Behavioral and Brain Sciences, 4,* 244–245.

Lewontin, R. C. (1992). Foreword. In R. M. Lerner (Ed.), *Final solutions: Biology, prejudice, and genocide* (pp. vii–viii). University Park, PA: Penn State Press.

Lewontin, R. C. (2000). *The triple helix*. Cambridge, MA: Harvard University Press.

Lewontin, R. C., & Levins, R. (1978). Evolution. *Encyclopedia Einaudi* (Vol. 5). Turin, Italy: Einaudi.

Lewontin, R. C., Rose, S., & Kamin, L. J. (1984). *Not in our genes: Biology, ideology, and human nature*. New York: Pantheon Press.

Liben, L. S. (Ed.). (1983). *Piaget and the foundations of knowledge*. Hillsdale, NJ: Erlbaum.

Lifton, R. J. (1986). *The Nazi doctors: Medical killing and the psychology of genocide*. New York: Basic Books.

Lips, H. M. (2001). *Sex & gender: An introduction* (4th ed., pp. 60–64). Mountain View, CA: Mayfield.

Lipsitz, J. (1991). Public policy and young adolescents: A 1990s context for researchers. *Journal of Early Adolescence, 11,* 20–37.

Little, R. R. (1993). *What's working for today's youth: The issues, the programs, and the learnings*. Paper presented at the ICYF Fellows Colloquium, Michigan State University.

Livson, N., & Peskin, H. (1980). Perspectives on adolescence from longitudinal research. In J. Adelson (Ed.), *Handbook of adolescent psychology* (pp. 47–98). New York: Wiley.

Loehlin, J. C., Lindzey, G., & Spuhler, J. N. (1975). *Race differences in intelligence*. San Francisco, CA: W. H. Freeman.

Loevinger, J. (1976). *Ego development*. San Fransisco, CA: Josey-Bass.

Looft, W. R. (1972). The evolution of developmental psychology. *Human Development, 15,* 187–201.

Looft, W. R. (1973). Socialization and personality throughout the life-span: An examination of contemporary psychological approaches. In P. B. Baltes & K. W. Schaie (Eds.), *Life-span developmental psychology: Personality and socialization* (pp. 25–52). New York: Academic Press.

Lorenz, K. (1932/1970). A consideration of methods of identification of species-specific instinctive patterns in birds. In R. Martin (Ed. and Trans.), *Studies in animal and human behavior* (pp. 57–100). Cambridge, MA: Harvard University Press.

Lorenz, K. (1935). Der Kumpan in der Umwelt des Vogels. *Journal für Ornithologie, 83,* 137–215, 289–413.

Lorenz, K. (1937a). The companion in the bird's world. *Auk, 54,* 245–273.

Lorenz, K. (1937b). Über den Begriff der Instinkthandlung. *Folia Biotheoretica, 2,* 17–50.

Lorenz, K. (1937c). Über die Bildung des Instinktbegriffes. *Die Naturwissenchaften, 25,* 189–300, 307–308, 324–333.

Lorenz, K. (1939). Über Ausfallerserscheinungen im Instinctverhalten von Haustieren und ihre socialpsychologische Bedeutung. In O. Klemm (Ed.), *Charackter und Erziehung: 16. Kongress der Deutschen Gesellschaft für Psychologie in Bayreuth* (pp. 139–147). Leipzig, Germany: J. A. Barth.

Lorenz, K. (1940a). Durch Domestikation verursachte Störungen arteigenen Verhaltens. *Zeitschrift für angewandte Psychologie und Charakterkunde, 59,* 2–81.

Lorenz, K. (1940b). Systematik und Entwicklungsgedanke im Unterricht. *Der Biologe, 9,* 24–36.

Lorenz, K. (1941). Kants Lehre vom Apriorischen im Lichte gegenwärtiger biologie. *Blätter für deutsche Philosophie, 15,* 94–125.

Lorenz, K. (1943a). Die angeborenen Formen möglicher Erfahrung. *Zeitschrift für Tierpsychologie, 5,* 235–409.

Lorenz, K. (1943b). Psychologie and stammesgeschichte. In G. Heberer (Ed.), *Die evolution der organismen* (pp. 105–127). Jena, Germany: G. Fischer.

Lorenz, K. (1950). Ganzheit und Teil in der tierischen und menschilchen Gemeinschaft. *Studium Generale, 9,* 455–498.

Lorenz, K. (1954). Psychologie und Stammesgeschichte. In G. Heberer (Ed.), *Die Evolution der Organismen* (2nd ed., pp. 105–127). Jena, Germany: G. Fisher.

Lorenz, K. (1965). *Evolution and modification of behavior.* Chicago, IL: University of Chicago Press.

Lorenz, K. (1966). *On aggression.* New York: Harcourt, Brace & World.

Lorenz, K. (1974a). *Civilized man's eight deadly sins.* New York: Harcourt Brace Jovanovich.

Lorenz, K. (1074b, September). Letter: Lorenz clarifies ideas. *Human Behavior, 6.*

Lorenz, K. (1975). Konrad Lorenz responds to Donald Campbell. In R. I. Evans (Ed.), *Konrad Lorenz: The man and his ideas* (pp. 119–128). New York: Harcourt Brace Jovanovich.

LoSciuto, L., Rajala, A. K., Townsend, T. N., & Taylor, A. S. (1996). An outcome evaluation of Across Ages: An intergenerational mentoring approach to drug prevention. *Journal of Adolescent Research, 11*(1), 116–129.

Lourenço, O. M. (1990). From cost-perception to gain-construction: Toward a Piagetian explanation of the development of altruism in children. *International Journal of Behavioral Development, 13,* 119–132.

Lovejoy, C. O. (1981). The origin of man. *Science, 211,* 341–350.

Lowenthal, M. F., Thurnher, M., & Chiriboga, D. (1975). *Four stages of life: A comparative study of women and men facing transitions.* San Fransisco, CA: Josey-Bass.

Lumsden, C. J., & Wilson, E. O. (1981). *Genes. mind. and culture.* Cambridge, MA: Harvard University Press.

Lush, J. L. (1940). Intra-sire correlations or regressions of offspring on dam as a method of estimating heritability of characteristics. *Thirty-Third Annual Proceedings of the American Society of Animal Production, 56,* 622–629.

Luster, T., & McAdoo, H. P. (1994). Factors related to the achievement and adjustment of young African American children. *Child Development, 65,* 1080–1094.

Luster, T., & McAdoo, H. P. (1996). Family and child influences on educational attainment: A secondary analysis of the High/Scope Perry Preschool data. *Developmental Psychology, 32*(1), 26–39.

Lykken, D. T. (1982). Research with twins: The concept of emergenesis. *Psycho-physiology, 19,* 361–373.

Lynn, R. (1993). Further evidence for the existence of race and sex differences in cranial capacity. *Social Behavior and Personality, 21,* 89–92.

Lynton, E. A., & Elman, S. E. (1987). *New priorities for the university: Meeting society's needs for applied knowledge and competent individuals.* San Francisco, CA: Jossey-Bass.

Maccoby, E. (1998). *The two sexes: Growing up apart, coming together.* Cambridge, MA: Harvard University Press.

MacDonald, K. (1985). Early experience, relative plasticity, and social development. *Developmental Review, 5,* 99–121.

MacDonald, K. (Ed.). (1988). *Sociobiological perspectives on human development.* New York: Springer-Verlag.

MacDonald, K. (1994). *A people that shall dwell alone: Judaism as an evolutionary group strategy.* Westport, CT: Greenwood.

MacDonald, N. E., & Silverman, L. W. (1978). Smiling and laughter in infants as a function of level of arousal and cognitive evaluation. *Developmental Psychology, 14,* 235–241.

Macfarlane, J. W. (1938a). Some finding from a ten-year guidance research program. *Progressive Education 7,* 529–535.

Macfarlane, J. W. (1938b). Studies in child guidance. I. Methodology of data collection and organization. *Monographs of the Society for Research in Child Development 3* (6, Whole No. 19).

Magnusson, D. (1980). Personality in an interactional paradigm of research. *Zeitschrift für Differentielle und Diagnostische Psychologie, 1,* 17–34.

Magnusson, D. (1981). *Toward a psychology of situations: An interactional perspective.* Hillsdale, NJ: Erlbaum.

Magnusson, D. (1985). Implications of an interactional paradigm for research on human development. *International Journal of Behavioral Development, 8,* 115–137.

Magnusson, D. (Ed.) (1988a). *Paths through life* (Vol. 1). Hillsdale, NJ: Erlbaum.

Magnusson, D. (1988b). Individual development from an interactional perspective. In D. Magnusson (Ed.), *Paths through life* (Vol. 1, pp. 3–31). Hillsdale, NJ: Erlbaum.

Magnusson, D. (1990). Personality development from an interactional perspective. In L. Pervin (Ed.), *Handbook of personality* (pp. 193–222). New York: Guilford Press.

Magnusson, D. (1995). Individual development: A holistic integrated model. In P. Moen, G. H. Elder, & K. Lusher (Eds.), *Linking lives and contexts: Perspectives on the ecology of human development* (pp. 19–60). Washington, DC: APA Books.

Magnusson, D. (1996). *The life-span development of individuals: Behavioral, neurobiological, and psychosocial perspectives. A synthesis.* Cambridge, England: Cambridge University Press.

Magnusson, D. (1999a). Holistic interactionism: A perspective for research on personality development. In L. A. Pervin & O. P. John (Eds.), *Handbook of personality: Theory and research* (2nd ed., pp. 219–247). New York: Guilford Press.

Magnusson, D. (1999b). On the individual: A person-oriented approach to developmental research. *Euorpean Psychologist, 4,* 205–218.

Magnusson, D., & Allen, V. L. (Eds.). (1983). *Human development: An interactional perspective.* New York: Academic Press.

Magnusson, D., & Cairns, R. B. (1996). Developmental science: Principles and illustrations. In R. B. Cairns, G. H. Elder, Jr., & E. J. Costello (Eds.), *Developmental science* (pp. 7–30). New York: Cambridge University Press.

Magnusson, D., & Casaer, P. (1992). *Longitudinal research on individual development: Present status and future perspectives.* Cambridge, England: Cambridge University Press.

Magnusson, D., & Endler, N. S. (1977). Interactional psychology: Present status and future prospects. In D. Magnusson & N. S. Endler (Eds.), *Personality at the crossroads: Current issues in interactional psychology* (pp. 3–31). Hillsdale, NJ: Erlbaum.

Magnusson, D., & Stattin, H. (1998). Person—context interaction theories. In W. Damon (Series Ed.) & R. M. Lerner (Vol. Ed.), *Handbook of child psychology: Vol. 1. Theoretical models of human development* (5th ed., pp. 685–759). New York: Wiley.

Maguin, E., Zucker, R. A., & Fitzgerald, H. E. (1994). The path to alcohol problems through conduct problems: A family-based approach to very early intervention with risk. *Journal of Research on Adolescence, 4,* 249–269.

Maier, N. R. F., & Schneirla, T. C. (1935). *Principles of animal behavior.* New York: McGraw-Hill.

Mailick Seltzer, M., & Ryff, C. D. (1994). Parenting across the life span: The normative and nonnormative cases. In D. L. Featherman, R. M. Lerner, & M. Perlmutter (Eds.), *Life span development and behavior* (Vol. 12, pp. 2–41). Hillsdale, NJ: Erlbaum.

Mandler, J. M. (1998). Representation. In W. Damon (Series Ed.), D. Kuhn, & R. S. Siegler (Vol. Eds.), *Handbook of child psychology: Vol. 2. Cognition, perception, and language* (5th ed., pp. 255–308). New York: Wiley.

Mann-Feder, V. R. (1996). Adolescents in therapeutic communities. *Adolescence, 31*(121), 17–28.

Maratsos, M. (1998). The acquisition of grammar. In W. Damon (Series Ed.), D. Kuhn, & R. S. Siegler (Vol. Eds.), *Handbook of child psychology: Vol. 2. Cognition, perception, and language* (5th ed., pp. 421–466). New York: Wiley.

Marcia, J. E. (1964). Determination and construct validity of ego identity status. Ph.D. dissertation. Ohio State University.

Marcia, J. E. (1966). Development and validations of ego-identity status. *Journal of Personality and Social Psychology, 5,* 551–558.

Marcia, J. E. (1980). Identity in adolescence. In J. Adelson (Ed.), *Handbook of adolescent psychology* (pp. 159–187) New York: Wiley.

Marcia, J. E. (1991). Identity and self-development. In R. M. Lerner, A. C. Petersen, & J. Brooks-Gunn (Eds.), *Encyclopedia of adolescence* (pp. 529–533). New York: Garland Publishing.

Marcia, J. E., Waterman, A. S., Matteson, D.R., Archer, S., & Orlofsky, J. (1985/1992). *Ego identity: A handbook for psychosocial research.* British Columbia, Canada: Simon Fraser University.

Mareschal, D., Plunkett, K., & Harris, P. (1995). Developing object permanence: A connectionist model. In J. D. Moore & J. F. Lehman (Eds.), *Proceedings of the Seventeenth Annual Conference of the Cognitive Science Society* (pp. 1–6). Mahwah, NJ: Erlbaum.

Markstrom-Adams, C., & Smith, M. (1996). Identity formation and religious orientation among high school students from the United States and Canada. *Journal of Adolescence, 19,* 247–261.

Marlatt, G. A., Baer, J. S., Kivlahan, D. R., Dimeff, L. A., Larimer, M. E., Quigley, L. A., Somers, J. M., & Williams, E. (1998). Screening and brief intervention for high-risk college student drinkers: Results from a 2-year follow-up assessment. *Journal of Consulting and Clinical Psychology, 66*(4), 604–615.

Marshall, W. A., & Tanner, J. M. (1986). Puberty. In F. Falkner & J. M. Tanner (Eds.), *Human growth* (2nd ed., Vol. 2, pp. 171–209). New York: Plenum Publishing.

Marsiske, M., Lang, F. B., Baltes, P. B., & Baltes, M. M. (1995). Selective optimization with compensation: Life-span perspectives on successful human development. In R. A. Dixon & L. Baeckman (Eds.), *Compensating for psychological deficites and declines: Managing losses and promoting gains* (pp. 35–79). Mahwah, NJ: Erlbaum.

Martin, E. (1991). The egg and the sperm: How science has constructed a romance based on stereotypical male–female roles. *Signs: Journal of Women in Culture and Society, 16,* 485–501.

Martorano, S. C. (1977). A developmental analysis of performance on Piaget's formal operations tasks. *Developmental Psychology, 13,* 666–672.

Mason, W. A., & Kenney, M. (1974). Redirection of filial attachments in rhesus monkeys: Dogs as surrogate mothers. *Science, 183,* 1209–1211.

Masters, R. D. (1978). Jean-Jacques is alive and well: Rousseau and contemporary sociobiology. *Daedalus, 107,* 93–105.

McAdoo, H. P. (1977). A review of the literature related to family therapy in the Black community. *Journal of Contemporary Psychotherapy, 9,* 15–19.

McAdoo, H. (1991). Family values and outcomes for children. *Journal of Negro Education, 60,* 361–365.

McAdoo, H. (1993a). Family equality and ethnic diversity. In K. Altergott (Ed.), *One world, many families* (pp. 52–55). Minneapolis, MN: National Council on Family Relations.

McAdoo, H. (1993b). The social cultural contexts of ecological developmental family models. In P. Boss, W. Doherty, & W. Schyumm (Eds.), *Sourcebook of family theories and methods: A contextual approach* (pp. 298–301). New York: Plenum Publishing.

McAdoo, H. P. (1995). Stress levels, family help patterns, and religiosity in middle- and working-class African American single mothers. *Journal of Black Psychology, 21,* 424–449.

McAdoo, H. (1998). African American families: Strength and realities. In H. I. McCubbin, E. A. Thompson, A. I. Thompson, & J. E. Fromer (Eds.), *Resiliency in ethnic minority families: African American families* (pp. 17–30). Thousand Oaks, CA: Sage.

McAdoo, H. P. (1999). Diverse children of color. In H. E. Fitzgerald, B. M. Lester, & B. S. Zuckerman (Eds.), *Children of color: Research, health, and policy issues* (pp. 205–218). New York: Garland Publishing.

McAdoo, H. P., & Crawford, V. (1991). *The Black church and family support programs. Families as nurturing systems: Support across the life span* (pp. 193–222). New York: Haworth Press.

McCall, R. B. (1981). Nature–nurture and the two realms of development: A proposed integration with respect to mental development. *Child Development, 52,* 1–12.

McCandless, B. R. (1967). *Children.* New York: Holt, Rinehart & Winston.

McCandless, B. R. (1970). *Adolescents.* Hinsdale, IL: Dryden Press.

McClearn, G. E. (1970). Genetic influences on behavior and development. In P. H. Mussen (Ed.), *Carmichael's manual of child psychology* (Vol. 1, pp. 39–76). New York: Wiley.

McClearn, G. E. (1981). Evolution and genetic variability. In E. S. Gollin (Ed.), *Developmental plasticity: Behavioral and biological aspects of variations in development* (pp. 3–31). New York: Academic Press.

McCluskey, K. A., & Reese, H. W. (Eds.). (1984). *Life-span developmental psychology: Historical and generational effects.* Orlando, FL: Academic Press.

McCubbin, H. I., Thompson, E. A., Thompson, A. I., & Futrell, J. A. (Eds.). (1998). *Resiliency in ethnic minority families: African American families.* Thousand Oaks, CA: Sage.

McEwen, B. S., (1997). Possible mechanisms for atrophy of the human hippocampus. *Molecular Psychiatry, 2,* 255–262.

McEwen, B. S. (1998). Protective and damaging effects of stress mediators. *New England Journal of Medicine, 338,* 171–179.

McEwen, B. S. (1999). Stress and hippocampal plasticity. *Annual Review of Neuroscience, 22,* 105–122.

McGraw, M. B. (1943). *The neuromuscular maturation of the human infant.* New York: Columbia University Press.

McGue, M. (1981). Familial studies of intelligence: A review. *Science, 212,* 1055–1059.

McGuire, T. R., & Hirsch, J. (1977). General intelligence (g) and heritability (HZ, h2). In I. C. Uzgiris & F. Weizmann (Eds.), *J. McV. Hunt, The structuring of experience* (pp. 25–72). New York: Plenum Publishing.

McHale, S. M., Crouter, A. C., Fennelly, K., Tomascik, C. A., Updegraff, K. A., Graham, J. E., Baker, A. E., Dreisbach, L., Ferry, N., Manlove, E. E., McGroder, S. M., Mulkeen, P., & Obeidallah, D. A. (1996). Community-based interventions for young adolescents: The Penn State PRIDE Project. *Journal of Research on Adolescence, 6*(1), 23–36.

McHale, S. M., & Lerner, R. M. (1985). Stages of human development. In T. Husen & T. N. Postlethwaite (Eds.), *The international encyclopedia of education* (pp. 2327–2331). Oxford, England: Pergamon Press.

McHale, S. M., & Lerner, R. M. (1996). University–community collaborations on behalf of youth. *Journal of Research on Adolescence, 6*(1), 1–7.

McKay, H., Sinisterra, L., McKay, A., Gomez, H., & Lloreda, P. (1978). Improving cognitive ability in chronically deprived children. *Science, 200,* 270–278.

McKusick, V. A. (1981). The anatomy of the human genome. *Hospital Practice, 16,* 82–100.

McLaughlin, B. (1977). Second language learning in children. *Psychological Bulletin, 84,* 438–459.

McLoyd, V. C. (1998). Children in poverty: Development, public policy, and practice. In W. Damon (Series Ed.), I. E. Sigel, & K. A. Renninger (Vol. Eds.), *Handbook of psychology: Vol. 4. Child psychology in practice.* New York: Wiley.

McNeill, D. (1966). Developmental psycholinguistics. In F. Smith & G. A. Miller (Eds.), *The genesis of language: A psycholinguistic approach.* Cambridge, MA: MIT Press.

Meaney, M., Aitken, D., Berkel, H., Bhatnager, S., & Sapolsky, R. (1988). Effect of neonatal handling of age-related impairments associated with the hippocampus. *Science, 239,* 766–768.

Mehler, B., (1997). Beyondism: Raymond B. Cattell and the new eugenics. *Genetica, 99,* 153–163.

Meyer, J. W. (1988). The social constructs of the psychology of childhood: Some contemporary processes. In E. M. Hetherington, R. M. Lerner, & M. Perlmutter (Eds.), *Child development in life-span perspective.* Hillsdale, NJ: Erlbaum.

Midgley, C., Feldlaufer, H., & Eccles, J. S. (1989a). Changes in teacher efficacy and student self- and task-related beliefs in mathematics during the transition to junior high school. *Journal of Educational Psychology, 81,* 247–258.

Midgley, C., Feldlaufer, H., & Eccles, J. S. (1989b). Student/teacher relations and attitudes toward mathematics before and after the transition to junior high school. *Child Development, 60,* 981–992.

Miller, J. R., & Lerner, R. M. (1994). Integrating research and outreach: Delopmental contextualism and the human ecological perspective. *Home Economics Forum, 7,* 21–28.

Miller, N. E., & Dollard, J. (1941). *Social learning and imitation.* New Haven, CT: Yale University Press.

Millet, R. A. (1996). Empowerment evaluation and the W. K. Kellogg Foundation. In D. M. Fetterman, S. J. Kaftarian, & A. Wandersman (Eds.), *Empowerment evaluation: Knowledge and tools for self-assessment & accountability* (pp. 65–76). Thousand Oaks, CA: Sage.

Mischel, W. (1977). On the future of personality measurement. *American Psychologist, 32,* 246–254.

Mischel, W. (1983). Alternatives in the pursuit of the predictability and consistency of persons: Stable data that yield unstable interpretations. *Journal of Personality, 51,* 578–604.

Mischel, W., & Mischel, H. N. (1976). A cognitive social-learning approach to morality and self-regulation. In T. Lickona (Ed.), *Moral development and behavior.* New York: Holt, Rinehart & Winston.

Misiak, H., & Sexton, V. S. (1966). *History of psychology in overview.* New York: Grune & Stratton.

Misiak, H., & Staudt, V. S. (1954). *Catholics in psychology: A historical survey.* New York: McGraw-Hill.

Mitchell, D. E. (1978). *Recovery of vision in monocularly and binocularly deprived kittens.* Paper presented at the Eleventh Symposium of the Center of the Visual Science, June. Rochester, NY.

Mitchell, D. E., Cynader, M., & Movshon, J. A. (1977). Recovery from the effects of monocular deprivation in kittens. *Journal of Comparative Neurology, 176,* 53–64.

Molenaar, P. C. M., Boomsma, D. I., Neeleman, D., & Dolan, C. V. (1990). Using factor scores to detect G × E interactive origin of "pure" genetic or environmental factors obtained in genetic covariance structure analysis. *Genetic Epidemiology, 7,* 93–100.

Molina, B. S. G., & Chassin, L. (1996). The parent–adolescent relationship at puberty: Hispanic ethnicity and parent alcoholism as moderators. *Developmental Psychology, 32,* 675–686.

Moltz, H. (1973). Some implications of the critical period hypothesis. *Annals of the New York Academy of Sciences, 223,* 144–146.

Moltz, H., & Stettner, L. J. (1961). The influence of patterned-light deprivation on the critical period for imprinting. *Journal of Comparative and Physiological Psychology, 54,* 279–283.

Money, J., & Ehrhardt, A. E. (1972). *Man and woman, boy and girl.* Baltimore, MD: Johns Hopkins University Press.

Montangero, J. (1985). *Genetic epistemology yesterday and today*. New York: Publications of the Graduate Center of the CUNY.

Moore, K. A., & Glei, D. (1995). Taking the plunge: An examination of positive youth development. *Journal of Adolescent Research, 10*(1), 15–40.

Moran, P. A. P. (1973). A note on heritability and the correlation between relatives. *Annals of Human Genetics, 37,* 217.

Morelli, G. A., & Verhoef, H. (in press). Who should help me raise my child? In C. Le Monda & L. Balter (Eds.), *Handbook of child psychology*. New York: Garland Publishing.

Morris, E. (1993). Contextualism, historiography, and the history of behavior analysis. In S. C. Hayes, L. J. Hayes, H. W. Reese, & T. R. Sarbin (Eds.), *Varieties of scientific contextualism* (pp. 137–165). Reno, NV: Context Press.

Morrison, F. J., Lord, C., & Keating, D. P. (1984). Applied developmental psychology. In F. J. Morrison, C. Lord, & D. P. Keating (Eds.), *Applied developmental psychology* (Vol. 1, pp. 4–20). New York: Academic Press.

Morton, N. E. (1976). Heritability of IQ. *Science, 194,* 9–10.

Müller-Brettel, M., & Dixon, R. A. (1990). Johann Nicolas Tetens: A forgotten father of developmental psychology? *International Journal of Behavioral Development, 13,* 215–230.

Müller-Hill, B. (1988). *Murderous science: Elimination by scientific selection of Jews, Gypsies, and others, Germany 1933–1945* (Fraser, G. R., Trans.). New York: Oxford University Press.

Murchison, C. (Ed.). (1931). *Handbook of child psychology*. Worcester, MA: Clark University Press.

Murray, H. A. (1938). *Explorations in personality*. New York: Oxford University Press.

Murray, H. A. (1959). Preparations for the scaffold of a comprehensive system. In S. Koch (Eds.), *Psychology: A study of a science* (Vol. 3). New York: McGraw-Hill

Mussen, P. H. (Ed.). (1970). *Carmichael's manual of child psychology* (3rd ed.). New York: Wiley.

Mussen, P. H., & Jones, M. C. (1957). Self-conceptions, motivations, and interpersonal attitudes of late- and early-maturing boys. *Child Development, 28,* 249–256.

Muuss, R. E. (1996). *Theories of adolescence* (6th ed.). New York: McGraw-Hill.

Muuss, R. E. (Ed.). (1975a). *Adolescent behavior and society: A book of readings* (2nd ed.). New York: Random House.

Nagel, E. (1957). Determinism in development. In D. B. Harris (Ed.), *The concept of development* (pp. 15–24). Minneapolis, MN: University of Minnesota Press.

Nash, J. (1978). *Developmental psychology: A psychobiological approach*. Englewood Cliffs, NJ: Prentice-Hall.

National Research Council. (1993). *Losing generations: Adolescents in high-risk settings*. Washington, DC: National Academy Press.

Neimark, E. D. (1975). Intellectual development during adolescence. In F. D. Horowitz (Ed.), *Review of child development research* (Vol. 4). Chicago, IL: University of Chicago Press.

Neimark, E. D. (1978). Improper questions cannot be properly answered. *The Behavioral and Brain Sciences, 2,* 195–196.

Nelson, C. A. (1999). How important are the first 3 years of life? *Applied Developmental Science, 3*(4), 235–238.

Nelson, K. (1996). *Language in cognitive development: Emergence of the mediated mind*. New York: Cambridge University Press.

Nesselroade, J. R. (1970). Application of multivariate strategies to problems of measuring and structuring long-term change. In L. R. Goulet & P. B. Baltes (Eds.), *Life-span developmental psychology: Research and theory* (pp. 193–207). New York: Academic Press.

Nesselroade, J. R. (1977). Issues in studying developemntal change in adults from a multivariate perspective. In J. E. Birren & K. W. Schaie (Eds.), *The handbook of the psychology of aging* (pp. 59–69). New York: Van Nostrand Reinhold.

Nesselroade, J. R. (1983). Implications of the trait-state distinction for the study of aging: Still labile after all these years. Presidential address to Division 20, Ninety-first Annual Convention of the American Psychological Association, August. Anaheim, California.

Nesselroade, J. R. (1988). Some implications of the trait-state distinction for the study of development over the life-span: The case of personality. In P. B. Baltes, D. L. Featherman, & R. M. Lerner (Eds.), *Life-span development and behavior* (Vol. 8, pp. 163–189). Hillsdale, NJ: Erlbaum.

Nesselroade, J. R., & Baltes, P. B. (1974). Adolescent personality development and historical changes: 1970–1972. *Monographs of the Society for Research in Child Development, 39*(154).

Nesselroade, J. R., & Baltes, P. B. (Eds.). (1979). *Longitudinal research in the study of behavior and development*. New York: Academic Press.

Nesselroade, J. R., & Ghisletta, P. (2000). Beyond static concepts in modeling behavior. In L. R. Bergman, R. B. Cairns, L. G. Nilsson, & L. Nystedt (Eds.), *Developmental science and the holistic approach* (pp. 121–135). Mahwah, NJ: Erlbaum.

Nesselroade, J. R., & Reese, H. W. (Eds.). (1973). *Life-span developmental psychology: Methodological issues*. New York: Academic Press.

Nesselroade, J. R., Schaie, K. W., & Baltes, P. B. (1972). Ontogenetic and generational components of structural and quantitative change in adult cognitive behavior. *Journal of Gerontology, 27,* 222–228.

Nesselroade, J. R., & von Eye, A. (Eds.). (1985). *Individual development and social change: Explanatory analysis*. New York: Academic Press.

Neugarten, B. L. (1964). *Personality in middle and late life*. New York: Atherton Press.

Neugarten, B. L. (Ed.). (1968). *Middle age and aging*. Chicago, IL: University of Chicago Press.

Neugarten, B. L., & Datan, N. (1973). Sociological perspective on the life cycle. In P. B. Baltes & K. W. Schaie (Eds.), *Life-span developmental psychology: Personality and socialization*. New York: Academic Press.

Neugarten, B. L., & Gutmann, D. L. (1958). Age-sex roles and personality in middle age: A thematic appreception study. *Psychological Monographs, 72* (470).

Neugarten, B. L., & Gutmann, D. L. (1968). Age-sex roles and personality in middle age: A thematic appreception study. In B. L. Neugarten (Ed.), *Middle age and aging* (pp. 58–74). Chicago, IL: University of Chicago Press.

Neugarten, B. L., Havighurst, R. J., & Tobin, S. S. (1968). Personality and patterns of aging. In B. L. Neugarten (Ed.), *Middle age and aging* (pp. 173–177). Chicago, IL: University of Chicago Press.

Newman, H. H., Freeman, F. N., & Holzinger, K. J. (1937). *Twins: A study of heredity and environment*. Chicago, IL: University of Chicago Press.

Nisbett, R. A. (1977). *Konrad Lorenz: A biography*. New York: Harcourt Brace Jovanovich.

Nisbet, R. A. (1980). *History of the idea of progress*. New York: Basic Books

Novak, M. A., & Harlow, H. F. (1975). Social recovery of monkeys isolated for the first year of life: I. Rehabilitation and therapy. *Developmental Psychology, 11,* 453–465.

Novikoff, A. B. (1945a). The concept of integrative levels and biology. *Science, 101,* 209–215.

Novikoff, A. B. (1945b). Continuity and discontinuity in evolution. *Science 101,* 405–406.

O'Connell, B. (1999). *Civil society: The underpinnings of American democracy*. Hanover, NH: University Press of New England.

Oden, S. (1995). Studying youth programs to assess influences on youth development: New roles for researchers. *Journal of Adolescent Research, 10*(1), 173–186.

Offer, D. (1969). *The psychological world of the teenager*. New York: Basic Books.

Olson, D. R. (1978). A structuralist view of explanations: A critique of Brainerd. *The Behavioral and Brain Science, 2,* 197–199.

Oppenheimer, L. (1991a). The concept of action: A historical perspective. In L. Oppenheimer & J. Valsiner (Eds.), *The origins of action: Interdisciplinary and international perspectives* (pp. 1–35). New York: Springer-Verlag.

Oppenheimer, L. (1991b). Determinants of action: An organismic and holistic approach. In L. Oppenheimer & J. Valsiner (Eds.), *The origins of action: Interdisciplinary and international perspectives* (pp. 37–63). New York: Springer-Verlag.

Orgel, L. E., & Crick, F. H. C. (1980). Selfish DNA: The ultimate parasite. *Nature, 284,* 604–607.

Ostrom, C. W., Lerner, R. M., & Freel, M. A. (1995). Building the capacity of youth and families through university–community collaborations: The development-in-context evaluation (DICE) model. *Journal of Adolescent Research, 10,* 427–448.

Overton, B. J., & Burkhardt, J. C. (1999). Drucker could be right, but . . . : New leadership models for institutional–community partnerships. *Applied Developmental Science, 3*(4), 217–227.

Overton, W. F. (1973). On the assumptive base of the nature–nurture controversy: Additive versus interactive conceptions. *Human Development, 16,* 74–89.

Overton, W. F. (1978). Klaus Riegel: Theoretical contribution to concepts of stability and change. *Human Development, 21,* 360–363.

Overton, W. F. (Ed.). (1983). *The relationship between social and cognitive development*. Hillsdale, NJ: Erlbaum.

Overton, W. F. (1984). World views and their influence on psychological theory and research: Kuhn—Lakatos—Lauden. In H. W. Reese (Ed.), *Advances in child development and behavior* (Vol. 18, pp. 194–226). New York: Academic Press.

Overton, W. F. (1991a). Historical and contemporary perspectives on developmental theory and research strategies. In R. Downs, L. Liben, & D. Palermo (Eds.), *Visions of aesthetics, the environment, and development: The legacy of Joachim Wohlwill* (pp. 263–311). Hillsdale, NJ: Erlbaum.

Overton, W. F. (1991b). The structure of developmental theory. In H. W. Reese (Ed.), *Advances in child development and behavior* (Vol. 23, pp. 1–37). New York: Academic Press.

Overton, W. F. (1991c). Metaphor, recursive systems, and paradox in science and developmental theory. In H. W. Reese (Ed.), *Advances in child de-*

velopment and behavior (Vol. 23, pp. 59–71). New York: Academic Press.

Overton, W. F. (1991d). Competence, procedures and hardware: Conceptual and empirical considerations. In M. Chandler & M. Chapman (Eds.), *Criteria for competence: Controversies in the assessment of children's ability* (pp. 19–42). Hillsdale, NJ: Erlbaum.

Overton, W. F. (1994a). The arrow of time and cycles of time: Concepts of change, cognition, and embodiment. *Psychological Inquiry, 5,* 215–237.

Overton, W. F. (1994b). Interpretationism, pragmatism, realism, and other ideologies. *Psychological Inquiry, 5,* 260–271.

Overton, W. F. (1994c). Contexts of meaning: The computational and the embodied mind. In W. F. Overton & D. S. Palermo (Eds.), *The nature and ontogenesis of meaning* (pp. 1–18). Hillsdale, NJ: Erlbaum.

Overton, W. F. (1998). Developmental psychology: Philosophy, concepts, and methodology. In W. Damon (Series Ed.) & R. M. Lerner (Vol. Ed.), *Handbook of child psychology: Vol. 1. Theoretical models of human development* (5th ed., pp. 107–187). New York: Wiley.

Overton, W. F., & Reese, H. W. (1973). Models of development: Methodological implications. In J. R. Nesselroade & H. W. Reese (Eds.), *Life-span developmental psychology: Methodological issues* (pp. 65–86). New York: Academic Press.

Overton, W. F., & Reese, H. W. (1981). Conceptual prerequisites for an understanding of stability–change and continuity–discontinuity. *International Journal of Behavioral Development, 4,* 99–123.

Padin, M. A., Lerner, R. M., & Spiro, A., III. (1981). The role of physical education interventions in the stability of body attitudes and self-esteem in late adolescents. *Adolescence, 16,* 371–384.

Papalia, D. E. (1972). The status of several conservation abilities across the life-span. *Human Development, 15,* 229–243.

Partanen, J., Brunn, K., & Markkanen, T. (1966). *Inheritance of drinking.* Helsinki, Finland: Finnish Foundation for Alcohol Studies.

Penfield, W., & Roberts, L. (1959). *Speech and brain mechanisms.* Princeton, NJ: Princeton University Press.

Pepper, S. C. (1942). *World hypotheses: A study in evidence.* Berkeley, CA: University of California Press.

Perkins, D. F., & Lerner, R. M. (1995). Single and multiple indicators of physical attractiveness and psychosocial behaviors among young adolescents. *Journal of Early Adolescence, 15,* 269–298.

Perry, C. M., & McIntire, W. G. (1995). Modes of moral judgement among early adolescents. *Adolescence, 30*(119), 707–715.

Pervin, L. A. (1968). Performance and satisfaction as a function of individual–environment fit. *Psychological Bulletin, 69,* 56–68.

Pervin, L. A., & Lewis, M. (Eds.). (1978). *Perspectives in interactional psychology.* New York: Plenum Publishing.

Peters, M. (1995a). Does brain size matter? A reply to Rushton and Ankney. *Canadian Journal of Experimental Psychology, 47,* 751–756.

Peters, M. (1995b). Race differences in brain size: Things are not as clear as they seem to be. *American Psychologist, 49,* 570–576.

Petersen, A. C. (1987). The nature of biological psychosocial interactions: The sample case of early adolescence. In R. M. Lerner & T. T. Fochs (Eds.), *Biological–psychosocial interactions in early adolescence: A life-span perspective* (pp. 35–61). Hillsdale, NJ: Erlbaum.

Petersen, A. C. (1988). Adolescent development. In M. R. Rosenzweig (Ed.), *Annual review of psychology* (Vol. 39, pp. 583–607). Palo Alto, CA: Annual Reviews.

Petersen, A. C., & Taylor, B. (1980). The biological approach to adolescence: Biological change and psychological adaptation. In J. Adelson (Ed.), *Handbook of adolescent psychology* (pp. 117–155). New York: Wiley.

Peterson, G. W. (1995). The need for common principles in prevention programs for children, adolescents, and families. *Journal of Adolescent Research, 10*(4), 470–485.

Petrinovich, L. (1979). Probabilistic functionalism: A conception of research method. *American Psychologist, 34,* 373–390.

Phelps, J. A., Davis, J. O., & Schartz, K. M. (1997). Nature, nurture, and twin research strategies. *Current Directions in Psychological Science, 6,* 117–121.

Philipp, E. E. (1973). "Discussion" in Law and ethics of AID and embryo transfer. In *Ciba Foundation symposium* (Vol. 17, new series). Amsterdam: Elsevier, Excerpta Medica.

Piaget, J. (1923). La pensee l'enfant. *Archives of Psychology, Geneva, 18,* 273–304.

Piaget, J. (1950). *The psychology of intelligence.* New York: Harcourt Brace.

Piaget, J. (1952). Autobiography. In H. S. Langfeld, E. G. Boring, H. Werner, & R. M. Yerkes (Eds.), *A history of psychology in autobiography* (Vol. 4). Worcester, MA: Clark University Press.

Piaget, J. (1952). *The origins of intelligence in children.* New York: International Universities Press.

Piaget, J. (1954). *Les relations entre l'affectivité et l'intelligence dans le developpement mental de l'enfant*. Paris, France: Centre de documentation universitaire.

Piaget, J. (1954). *The construction of reality in the child*, (M. Cook, trans.). New York: Basic Books.

Piaget, J. (1955). Les stades du development intellectuel de l'enfant et de l'adolescent. In P. Osterieth, J. Piaget, R. De Saussure, J. M. Tanner, H. Wallon, R. Zazzo, B. Inhelder, & A. Rey (Eds.), *Le probleme des stadesen psychologie de l'enfant*. Paris, France: Presses Universitaires de France.

Piaget, J. (1960). *The child's conception of the world*. Paterson, NJ: Littlefield, Adams.

Piaget, J. (1961). *Les mecanismes perceptifs*. Paris, France: Presses Universitaires de France.

Piaget, J. (1965). *The moral judgement of the child*. New York: Free Press.

Piaget, J. (1968). *Six psychological studies*. New York: Random House.

Piaget, J. (1969). The intellectual development of the adolescent. In G. Caplan & S. Lebovici (Eds.), *Adolescence: Psychosocial perspective* (pp. 22–26). New York: Basic Books.

Piaget, J. (1970). Piaget's theory. In P. H. Mussen (Ed.), *Carmichael's manual of child psychology* (3rd ed., Vol. 1, pp. 703–723). New York: Wiley.

Piaget, J. (1972). Intellectual evolution from adolescence to adulthood. *Human Development, 15*, 1–12.

Piaget, J. (1979). Relations between psychology and other sciences. *Annual Review of Psychology, 30*, 1–8.

Piaget, J., & Inhelder, B. (1956). *The child's conception of space*. London, England: Routledge & Kegan Paul.

Piaget, J., & Inhelder, B. (1969). *The psychology of the child*. New York: Basic Books.

Pianka, E. R. (1978). *Evolutionary ecology* (2nd ed.). New York: Harper & Row.

Pinard, A., & Laurendeau, M. (1969). "Stage" in Piaget's cognitive–developmental theory: Exegesis of concept . In D. Elkind & J. Flavell (Eds.), *Studies in cognitive development: Essays in honor of Jean Piaget*. New York: Oxford University Press.

Pinker, S. (1994). *The language instinct*. New York: William Morrow.

Pittman, K. (1996, Winter). Community, youth, development: Three goals in search of connection. *New Designs for Youth Development*, 4–8.

Pittman, K., & Irby, M. (1995, January 22–25, 1996). *Promoting investment in life skills for youth: Beyond indicators for survival and problem prevention*. Paper presented at the Monitoring and Measuring the State of Children: Beyond Survival, an Interactional Workshop. Jerusalem, Israel.

Pittman, K., Irby, M., & Cahill, M. (1995). *Mixing it up: Participatory evaluation as a tool for generating parent and community empowerment*. Harvard Family Research Project.

Pittman, K. J., & Zeldin, S. (1994). From deterrence to development: Shifting the focus of youth programs for African-American males. In R. B. Mincy (Ed.), *Nurturing young Black males* (pp. 45–55). Washington, DC: Urban Institute Press.

Ploetz, A. (1895). *Die Tuechtigkeit unserer Rasse und der Scutz der Schwachen. Grunlinien einer einer Rassenhygiene. Theil 1. [The excellence of our race and the protection of the weak.]* Berlin, Germany: Fischer.

Plomin, R. (1986). *Development, genetics, and psychology*. Hillsdale, NJ: Erlbaum.

Plomin, R. (2000). Behavioural genetics in the 21st century. *International Journal of Behavioral Development, 24*, 30–34.

Plomin, R., Corley, R., DeFries, J. C., & Faulker, D. W. (1990). Individual differences in television viewing in early childhood: Nature as well as nurture. *Psychological Science, 1*, 371–377.

Plomin, R., & Daniels, D. (1987). Why are children in the same family so different from each other? *Behavioral and Brain Sciences, 10*, 1–16.

Plomin, R., & DeFries, J. C. (1976). Heritability of IQ. *Science, 194*, 9–12.

Plomin, R., & DeFries, J. C. (1980). Genetics and intelligence: Recent data. *Intelligence, 4*, 15–24.

Plomin, R., DeFries, J. C., & McClearn, G. E. (1980). *Behavioral genetics: A primer*. San Francisco, CA: W. H. Freeman.

Popper, K. (1959). *The logic of scientific discovery*. London, England: Hutchinson.

Power, F. C., Higgins, A., & Kohlberg, L. (1989). *Lawrence Kohlberg's approach to moral education*. New York: Columbia University Press.

Pressey, S. L., Janney, J. E., & Kuhlen, R. G. (1939). *Life: Apsychological survey*. New York: Harper.

Prigogine, I. (1978). Time, structure, and fluctuation. *Science, 201*, 777–785.

Prigogine, I. (1980). *From being to becoming*. San Francisco, CA: W. H. Freeman.

Prince, F. (1995). The relative effectiveness of a peer-led and adult-led smoking intervention program. *Adolescence, 30*(117), 187–194.

Proctor, R. N. (1988). *Racial hygiene: Medicine under the Nazis*. Cambridge, MA: Harvard University Press.

Psychological Science Agenda. (1992, May/June). Mental health community react to Goodwin's resignation (pp. 1, 8). Washington, DC: American Psychological Association.

Pullis, M., & Caldwell, J. (1982). The influence of children's temperament characteristics on teachers' decision strategies. *American Educational Research Journal, 19,* 165–181.

Rakic, P. (1977). Prenatal development of the visual system in rhesus monkey. *Philosophical Transactions of the Royal Society of London, Series B, 278,* 245–260.

Ralston, P. A., Lerner, R. M., Mullis, A. K., Simerly, C. B., & Murray, J. B. (Eds.). (1999). *Social change, public policy, and community collaboration: Training human development professionals for the twenty-first century.* Norwell, MA: Kluwer.

Ratner, A. M., & Hoffman, H. S. (1974). Evidence for a critical period for imprinting in khaki campbell ducklings *(anas platyrhynchos domesticus). Animal Behavior, 22,* 249–255.

Reese, H. W. (1982). Behavior analysis and developmental psychology: Discussant comments. *Human Development, 35,* 352–357.

Reese, H. W. (1993). Contextualism and dialectical materialism. In S. C. Hayes, L. J. Hayes, H. W. Reese, & T. R. Sarbin (Eds.), *Varieties of scientific contextualism* (pp. 71–105). Reno, NV: Context Press.

Reese, H. W. (1995). Soviet psychology and behavior analysis: Philosophical similarities and substantive differences. *Behavioral Development, 5,* 2–4.

Reese, H. W., & Lipsitt, L. P. (Eds.). (1970). *Experimental child psychology.* New York: Academic Press.

Reese, H. W., & Overton, W. F. (1970). Models of development and theories of development. In L. R. Goulet & P. B. Baltes (Eds.), *Life-span developmental psychology: Research and theory* (pp. 115–145). New York: Academic Press.

Richards, I., & Sullivan, A. (1996). Psychotherapy for delinquents? *Journal of Adolescence, 19,* 63–73.

Richards, R. (1987). *Darwin and the emergence of evolutionary theories of mind and behavior.* Chicago, IL: University of Chicago Press.

Richards-Colocino, N., McKenzie, P., & Newton, R. R. (1996). Project success: Comprehensive intervention services for middle school high-risk youth. *Journal of Adolescent Research, 11*(1), 130–163.

Richardson, W. C. (1996). A new calling for higher education. Paper presented at the John W. Olswald Lecture, The Pennsylvania State University, University Park, PA.

Riegel, K. F. (1973). Dialectical operations: The final period of cognitive development. *Human Development, 16,* 346–370.

Riegel, K. F. (1975) Toward a dialectical theory of human development. *Human Development, 18,* 50–64.

Riegel, K. F. (1976a). The dialectics of human development. *American Psychologist, 31,* 689–700

Riegel, K. F. (1976b). From traits and equilibrium toward developmental dialectics. In W. J. Arnold & J. K. Cole (Eds.), *Nebraska Symposium on Motivation* (pp. 348–408). Lincoln, NE: University of Nebraska.

Riegel, K. F. (1977a). The dialectics of time. In N. Datan & H. W. Reese (Eds.), *Life-span developmental psychology: Dialectical perspectives on experimental research* (pp. 1–45). New York: Academic Press.

Riegel, K. F. (1977b). History of psychological gerontology. In J. E. Birren & K. W. Schaie (Eds.), *Handbook of the psychology of aging* (pp. 3–23). New York: Van Nostrand Reinhold.

Riegel, K. F. (1978). *Psychology mon amour: A countertext.* Boston, MA: Houghton-Mifflin.

Riley, M. W. (1976). Age strata in social systems. In R. H. Binstock & E. Shanas (Eds.), *Handbook of aging and the social sciences* (pp. 189–217). New York: Van Nostrand Reinhold.

Riley, M. W. (Ed.). (1979). *Aging from birth to death.* Washington, DC: American Association for the Advancement of Science.

Riley, M. W., Johnson, M. E., & Foner, A. (1972). *Aging and society: A sociology of age stratification.* New York: Sage.

Rogoff, B. (1993). Children's guided participation and participatory appropriation in sociocultural activity. In R. Wozniak & K. W. Fischer (Eds.), *Development in context: Acting and thinking in specific environments* (pp. 121–154). Hillsdale, NJ: Erlbaum.

Rogoff, B. (1998). Cognition as a collaborative process. In W. Damon (Series Ed.), D. Kuhn, & R. S. Siegler (Vol. Eds.), *Handbook of child psychology: Vol. 2. Cognition, perception, and language* (5th ed., pp. 679–744). New York: Wiley.

Rogoff, B., & Chavajay, P. (1995). What's become of research on the cultural basis of cognitive development? *American Psychologist, 50,* 859–877.

Rogoff, B., & Lave, J. (1984). *Everyday cognition: Its development in social context.* Cambridge, MA: Harvard University Press.

Rohrbach, L. A., Hodgson, C. S., Broder, B. I., Montgomery, S. B., Flay, B. R., Hansen, W. B., & Pentz, M. A. (1994). Parental participation in drug abuse prevention: Results for the midwestern prevention project. *Journal of Research on Adolescence, 4*(2), 295–318.

Rose, S. (1995). The rise of neurogenetic determinism. *Nature, 373,* 380–382.

Rosnow, R. L., & Georgoudi, M. (1986). *Contextualism and understanding in behavioral science: Implications for research and theory.* New York: Praeger.

Roth, J., & Brooks-Gunn, J. (2000). What do adolescents need for healthy development? Implications for youth policy. *Social Policy Report, XIV,* 3–19.

Roth, J., Brooks-Gunn, J., Galen, B., Murray, L., Silverman, P., Liu, H., Man, D., & Foster, W. (1997). *Promoting healthy adolescence: Youth development frameworks and programs.* New York: Teachers College, Columbia University.

Roth, J., Brooks-Gunn, J., Murray, L., & Foster, W. (1998). Promoting healthy adolescents: Synthesis of youth development program evaluations. *Journal of Research on Adolescence, 8,* 423–459.

Rothbart, M. K., & Bates, J. E. (1998). Temperament. In W. Damon (Series Ed.) & N. Eisenberg (Vol. Ed.), *Handbook of child psychology: Vol. 3. Social, emotional, and personality development* (pp. 105–176). New York: Wiley.

Roubertoux, P. & Carlier, M. (1978). Intelligence: Individual differences, genetic factors, environmental factors and interaction between genotype and environment. *Annales de Biologie Clinique, 36,* 101.

Rowe, D. C. (1994). *The limits of family influence: Genes, experience, and behavior.* New York: Guilford Press.

Runyan, W. M. (1978). The life course as a theoretical orientation: Sequences of person–situation interaction. *Journal of Personality, 46,* 569–593.

Runyan, W. M. (1980). A stage-state analysis of the life course. *Journal of Personality and Social Psychology, 38,* 951–962.

Rushton, J. P. (1987). An evolutionary theory of health, longevity, and personality: Sociobiology, and r/K reproductive strategies. *Psychological Reports, 60,* 539–549.

Rushton, J. P. (1988a). Do r/K reproductive strategies apply to human differences? *Social Biology, 35,* 337–340.

Rushton, J. P. (1988b). Race differences in behavior: A review and evolutionary analysis. *Personality and Individual Differences, 9,* 1009–1024.

Rushton, J. P. (1990a). Sex, ethnicity, and hormones. *Behavioral & Brain Sciences, 13,* 194, 197–198.

Rushton, J. P. (1990b). Why we should study race differences. *Psychologische Beitraege, 32,* 128–142.

Rushton, J. P. (1991a). Do r-K strategies underlie human race differences? A reply to Weizmann et al. *Canadian Psychology, 32,* 29–42.

Rushton, J. P. (1991b). Race, brain size, and intelligence: Another reply to Cernovsky. *Psychological Reports, 66,* 659–666.

Rushton, J. P. (1992). Cranial capacity related to sex, rank, and race in a stratified random sample of 6,325 military personnel. *Intelligence, 16,* 401–413.

Rushton, J. P. (1995). *Race, evolution, and behavior.* New Brunswik, NJ: Transaction Publishers.

Rushton, J. P. (1996). Political correctness and the study of racial differences. *Journal of Social Distress & the Homeless, 5,* 213–229.

Rushton, J. P. (1997a). Cranial size and IQ in Asian Americans from birth to age seven. *Intelligence, 25,* 7–20.

Rushton, J. P. (1997b). More on political correctness and race differences. *Journal of Social Distress and the Homeless, 6,* 195–198.

Rushton, J. P. (1999). *Race, evolution, and behavior* (Special Abridged Edition). New Brunswick, NJ: Transaction Publishers.

Rushton, J. P. (2000). *Race, evolution, and behavior* (2nd Special Abridged Edition). New Brunswick, NJ: Transaction Publishers.

Saarni, C., Mumme, D. L., & Campos, J. L. (1998). Emotional development: Action, communication, and understanding. In W. Damon (Series Ed.) & N. Eisenberg (Vol. Ed.), *Handbook of child psychology: Vol. 3. Social, emotional, and personality development* (pp. 237–309). New York: Wiley.

Sahlins, M. D. (1978). The use and abuse of biology. In A. L. Caplan (Ed.), *The sociobiology debate.* New York: Harper & Row.

Salzen, E., & Meyer, C. C. (1968). Reversibility of imprinting. *Journal of Comparative and Physiological Psychology, 66,* 269–275.

Sameroff, A. (1975). Transactional models in early social relations. *Human Development, 18,* 65–79.

Sameroff, A. J. (1983). Developmental systems: Contexts and evolution. In W. Kessen (Ed.), *Handbook of child psychology: Vol. 1. History, theory, and methods* (pp. 237–294). New York: Wiley.

Sampson, E. E. (1977). Psychology and the American ideal. *Journal of Personality and Social Psychology, 35,* 767–782.

Sampson, R., Morenoff, J., & Earls, F. (1999). Beyond social capital: Spatial dynamics of collective efficacy for children. *American Sociological Review, 64,* 633–660.

Sampson, R., Raudenbush, S. W., & Earls, F. (1997). Neighborhoods and violent crime: A multilevel study of collective efficacy. *Science, 277,* 918–924.

Sanford, E. C. (1902). Mental growth and decay. *American Journal of Psychology, 13,* 426–449.

Sarbin, T. R. (1977). Contextualism: A world view for modern psychology. In J. K. Cole (Ed.), *Nebraska Symposium on Motivation* (pp. 1–41). Lincoln, NE: University of Nebraska Press.

Scales, P., Benson, P., Leffert, N., & Blyth, D. A. (2000). Contribution of developmental assets to the prediction of thriving among adolescents. *Applied Developmental Science, 4,* 27–46.

Scales, P., & Leffert, N. (1999). *Developmental assets: A synthesis of the scientific research on adolescent development.* Minneapolis, MN: Search Institute.

Scarr, S. (1982). Development is internally guided, not determined. *Contemporary Psychology, 27,* 852–853.

Scarr, S. (1992). Developmental theories for the 1990s: Development and individual differences. *Child Development, 63,* 1–19.

Scarr, S., & McCartney, K. (1983). How people make their own environments: A theory of genotype–environment effects. *Child Development, 54,* 424–435.

Scarr-Salapatek, S. (1971a). Unknowns in the IQ equation. *Science, 174,* 1223–1228.

Scarr-Salapatek, S. (1971b). Race, social class, and IQ. *Science, 174,* 1285–1295.

Schaie, K. W. (1965). A general model for the study of developmental problems. *Psychological Bulletin, 64,,* 92–107.

Schaie, K. W. (1970). A reinterpretation of age-related changes in cognitive structure and functioning. In L. R. Goulet & P. B. Baltes (Eds.), *Life-span developmental psychology: Research and theory* (pp. 485–507). New York: Academic Press.

Schaie, K. W. (1979). The primary mental abilities in adulthood: An exploration in the development of psychometric intelligence. In P. B. Baltes & J. O. G. Brim (Eds.), *Life-span development and behavior* (Vol. 2, pp. 26–115). New York: Academic Press.

Schaie, K. W. (1984). Midlife influences upon intellectual functioning in old age. *International Journal of Behavioral Development, 7,* 463–468.

Schaie, K. W. (1994). The course of adult intellectual development. *American Psychologist, 49,* 304–313.

Schaie, K. W., Anderson, V. E., McClearn, G. E., & Money, J. (Eds.). (1975). *Developmental human behavior genetics.* Lexington, MA: Heath.

Schaie, K. W., & Geiwitz, J. (1982). *Adult development and aging.* Boston, MA: Little, Brown.

Schaie, K. W., Labouvie, G. V., & Buech, B. V. (1973). Generational and cohort-specific differences in adult cognitive functioning: A fourteen-year study of independent samples. and cohort-specific differences in adult cognitive functioning: A fourteen-year study of independent samples. *Developmental Psychology, 9,* 151–166.

Schaie, K. W., & Strother, C. R. (1968). A cross-sequential study of age changes in cognitive behavior. *Psychological Bulletin, 70,* 671–680.

Schiedel, D. G., & Marcia, J. E. (1985). Ego identity, intimacy, sex role orientation, and gender. *Developmental Psychology, 18,* 149–160.

Schneider, W., & Bjorkland, D. F. (1998). Memory. In W. Damon (Series Ed.), D. Kuhn, & R. S. Siegler (Vol. Eds.), *Handbook of child psychology: Vol 2. Cognition, perception, and language* (5th ed., pp. 467–521). New York: Wiley.

Schneirla, R. C. (1956). Interrelationships of the innate and the acquired in instictive behavior. In P. P. Grassé (Ed.), *L'instinct dans le comportement des animaux et de l'homme.* Paris, France: Mason et Cie.

Schneirla, T. C. (1957). The concept of development in comparative psychology. In D. B. Harris (Ed.), *The concept of development: An issue in the study of human behavior* (pp. 78–108). Minneapolis, MN: University of Minnesota Press.

Schneirla, T. C. (1959). An evolutionary and developmental theory of biphasic processes underlying approach and withdrawal. In M. R. Jones (Ed.), *Nebraska Symposium on Motivation* (pp. 1–42). Lincoln, NE: University of Nebraska Press.

Schneirla, T. C. (1966). Instinct and aggression: Reviews of Konrad Lorenz. *Evolution and modification of behavior* (Chicago, IL: The University of Chicago Press, 1965), and *On aggression* (New York: Harcourt, Brace & World, 1966). *Natural History, 75,* 16.

Schneirla, T. C., & Rosenblatt, J. S. (1961). Behavioral organization and genesis of the social bond in insects and mammals. *American Journal of Orthopsychiatry, 3,* 223–253.

Schneirla, T. C., & Rosenblatt, J. S. (1963). Critical periods in behavioral development. *Science, 139,* 1110–1114.

Schorr, L. B. (1988). *Within our reach: Breaking the cycle of disadvantage.* New York: Doubleday.

Schorr, L. B. (1997). *Common purpose: Strengthening families and neighborhoods to rebuild America.* New York: Doubleday.

Schulz, R., & Heckhausen, J. (1996). A life-span model of successful aging. *American Psychologist, 51,* 702–714.

Scott, J. P. (1962). Critical periods in behavioral development. *Science, 138,* 949–958.

Scriver, C. R., & Clow, C. L. (1980a). Phenylketonuria: Epitome of human biochemical genetics (first of two parts). *New England Journal of Medicine, 303,* 1336–1342.

Scriver, C. R., & Clow, C. L. (1980b). Phenylketonuria: Epitome of human biochemical genetics (second of two parts). *New England Journal of Medicine, 303,* 1394–1400.

Sears, R. R. (1957). Identification as a form of behavioral development. In D. B. Harris (Ed.), *The concept of development.* Minneapolis, MN: University of Minnesota Press.

Sears, R. R. (1975). Your ancients revisited: A history of child development. In E. M. Hetherington (Ed.), *Review of child development research* (Vol. 6, pp. 1–73). Chicago, IL: University of Chicago Press.

Secord, P. F., & Backman, C. W. (1964). *Social psychology.* New York: McGraw-Hill.

Selman, R. L. (1976). Social cognitive understanding: A guide to educational and clinical practice. In T. Lickona (Ed.), *Moral development and behavior.* New York: Holt, Rinehart & Winston.

Shah, J. Y., Higgins, E. T., & Friedman, R. (1998). Performance incentives and means: How regulatory focus influences goal attainment. *Journal of Personality and Social Psychology, 74,* 285–293.

Shatz, C. J. (1992). The developing brain. *Scientific American, 267,* 60–67.

Sheldon, W. H. (1940). *The varieties of human physique.* New York: Harper & Row.

Sheldon, W. H. (1942). *The varieties of temperament.* New York: Harper & Row.

Sherrington, C. S. (1951). *Man on his nature.* Cambridge, England: Cambridge University Press.

Sherrod, L. R. (1999a). "Giving child development knowledge away": Using university–community partnerships to disseminate research on children, youth, and families. *Applied Developmental Science, 3,* 228–234.

Sherrod, L. R. (1999b). Funding opportunities for applied developmental science. In P. A. Ralston, R. M. Lerner, A. K. Mullis, C. B. Simerly, & J. B. Murray (Eds.), *Social change, public policy, and community collaboration: Training human development professionals for the twenty-first century* (pp. 121–129). Norwell, MA: Kluwer.

Sherrod, L. R., Haggerty, R. J., & Featherman, D. L. (1993). Introduction: Late adolescence and the transition to adulthood. *Journal of Research on Adolescence, 3,* 217–226.

Shields, J. (1962). *Monozygotic twins brought up apart and brought up together.* London, England: Oxford University Press.

Shirley, M. M. (1933). *The first two years.* Minneapolis, MN: University of Minnesota Press.

Shweder, R. A. (1982). Beyond self-constructed knowledge: The study of culture and morality. *Merrill-Palmer Quarterly, 28,* 41–69.

Shweder, R. A. (1991). *Thinking through cultures: Expeditions in cultural psychology.* Cambridge, MA: Harvard University Press.

Shweder, R. A., Goodnow, J., Hatano, G., Kessel, F., LeVine, R. A., Markus, H., Miller, P., & Worthman, C. (1998). The cultural psychology of development. In W. Damon (Series Ed.) & R. M. Lerner (Vol. Ed.), *Handbook of child psychology: Theoretical models of human development* (5th ed., pp. 867–937). New York: Wiley.

Siegel, A. W., Bisanz, J., & Bisanz, G. L. (1983). Developmental analysis: A strategy for the study of psychological change. *Contributions to Human Development, 8,* 53–80.

Siegel, L. S., & Brainerd, C. J. (Eds.). (1977). *Alternatives to Piaget: Critical essays on the theory.* New York: Academic Press.

Siegler, R. S. (1978). *The origins of scientific reasoning. Children's thinking: What develops?* Hillsdale, NJ: Erlbaum.

Siegler, R. S. (1981). Developmental sequences within and between concepts. *Monographs of the Society for Research in Child Development, 46*(189).

Sigel, I. E. (1985). *Parental belief systems: The psychological consequences for children.* Hillsdale, NJ: Erlbaum.

Sigel, I. E. & Renninger, K. A. (Eds.). (1998). In W. Damon (Series Ed.), *Handbook of child psychology: Vol. 4. Child psychology in practice* (5th ed.). New York: Wiley.

Sigman, M. (1982). Plasticity in development: Implications for intervention. In L. A. Bond & J. M. Joffe (Eds.), *Facilitating infant and early childhood development* (pp. 98–116). Hanover, NH: University Press of New England.

Simmons, R. G., & Blyth, D. A. (1987). *Moving into adolescence: The impact of pubertal change and school context.* Hawthorne, NJ: Aldine.

Simmons, R., Rosenberg, F., & Rosenberg, M. (1973). Disturbances in the self-image in adolescence. *American Sociological Review, 38,* 553–568.

Simpson, E. L. (1974). Moral development research: A case study of scientific cultural bias. *Human Development, 17,* 81–106.

Sinnott, J. D. (1989). Life-span relativistic postformal thought: Methodology and data from everyday problem-solving studies. In M. L. Commons, J. D. Sinnott, F. A. Richards, & C. Armon (Eds.), *Adult development: Vol. 1. Comparisons and applications of developmental models* (pp. 239–278). New York: Praeger.

Skinner, B. F. (1938). *The behavior of organisms.* New York: Appleton.

Skinner, B. F. (1950). Are theories of learning necessary? *Psychological Review, 57,* 211–220.

Skinner, B. F. (1953). *Science and human behavior.* New York: Macmillian Publishing.

Skinner, B. F. (1956). A case history in scientific method. *American Psychologist, 11,* 221–233.

Skinner, B. F. (1966). The phylogeny and ontogeny of behavior. *Science, 153,* 1205–1213.

Skinner, B. F. (1971). *Beyond freedom and dignity.* New York: Knopf.

Small, S. A. (1996). Collaborative, community-based research on adolescents: Using research for community change. *Journal of Research on Adolescence, 6*(1), 9–22.

Smith, L. B., & Thelen, E. (Eds.). (1993). *A dynamic systems approach to development: Applications.* Cambridge, MA: MIT Press.

Snyder, M. (1981). On the influence of individuals on situations: Implications for understanding the links between personality and social behavior. *Journal of Personality, 51*(3), 497–516.

Sorell, G. T., & Montgomery, M. J. (in press). Feminist perspectives on Erikson's theory: Its relevance for contemporary identity development research. *Identity: An international journal of theory and research.*

Sorell, G. T., & Nowak, C. A. (1981). The role of physical attractiveness as a contributor to individual development. In R. M. Lerner & N. A. Busch-Rossnagel (Eds.), *Individuals as producers of their development: A* life-span perspective (pp. 389–446). New York: Academic Press.

Sorensen, B., Weinert, E., & Sherrod, L. R. (Ed.). (1986). *Human development and the life course: Multidisciplinary perspectives.* Hillsdale, NJ: Erlbaum.

Spanier, G. B. (1997a). Enhancing the capacity for outreach. *Journal of Public Service and Outreach, 2*(2), 7–11.

Spanier, G. B. (1997b). *Enhancing the quality of life for children, youth, and families.* Unpublished manuscript, The Pennsylvania State University, University Park, PA.

Spanier, G. B. (1999). Enhancing the qualty of life: A model for the 21st century land-grant university. *Applied Developmental Science, 3*(4), 199–205.

Spelke, E. S. (1991). Physical knowledge of infancy: Reflections on Piaget's theory. In S. Carey & R. Gelman (Eds.), *The epigenesis of mind: Essays on biology and cognition.* Hillsdale, NJ: Erlbaum.

Spelke, E. S., Breinlinger, K., Macomber, J., & Jacobson, K. (1992). Origin of knowledge. *Psychological Review, 99*(4), 605–632.

Spelke, E. S., & Newport, E. L. (1998). Nativism, empiricism, and the development of knowledge. In W. Damon (Series Ed.) & R. M. Lerner (Vol. Ed.), *Handbook of child psychology: Vol. 1. Theoretical models of human development* (5th ed., pp. 275–340). New York: Wiley.

Spencer, M. B. (1990). Development of minority children: An introduction. *Child Development, 61,* 267–269.

Spencer, M. B. (1999). Social and cultural influences on school adjustment: The application of an identity-focused cultural ecological perspective. *Educational Psychologist, 34,* 43–57.

Spencer, M. B., & Dornbusch, S. (1990). Challenges in studying minority youth. In S. Feldman & G. Elliott (Eds.), *At the threshold: The developing adolescent* (pp. 123–146). Cambridge, MA: Harvard University Press.

Spencer, M. B., Dupree, D., & Hartmann, T. (1997). A phenomenological variant of ecological systems theory (PVEST): A self-organization perspective in context. *Development and Psychopathology, 9,* 817–833.

Sroufe, L. A. (1979). The coherence of individual development. *American Psychologist, 34,* 834–841.

Sroufe, L. A., & Waters, E. (1977). Attachment as an organizational construct. *Child Development, 48,* 1184–1199.

Starkey, P. (1992) The early development of numerical reasoning. *Cognition, 43,* 93–126.

Stattin, H., & Magnusson, D. (1990). *Pubertal maturation in female development.* Hillsdale, NJ: Erlbaum.

Staudinger, U. M., & Baltes, P. B. (1996). Weisheit als Gegenstand psychologischer Forschung. *Psychologische Rundschau, 47,* 57–77.

Staudinger, U. M., Marsiske, M., & Baltes, P. B. (1995). Resilience and reserve capacity in later adulthood: Potentials and limits of development across the life span. In D. Chicchetti & D. Cohen (Eds.), *Developmental psychopathology: Vol. 2. Risk, disorder, and adaptation* (pp. 801–847). New York: Wiley.

Stein, G. J. (1987). The biological bases of ethnocentrism, racism, and nationalism in national socialism. In V. Reynolds, V. Falger, & I. Vine (Eds.), *The sociobiology of ethnocentrism* (pp. 251–267). London, England: Croom Helm.

Steinberg, L. (1987). The impact of puberty on family relations: Effects of pubertal status and pubertal timing. *Developmental Psychology, 23,* 833–840.

Steinberg, L. (1990). Autonomy, conflict, and harmony in the family relationship. In S. S. Feldman & G. R. Elliott (Eds.), *At the threshold: The developing adolescent* (pp. 255–576). Cambridge, MA: Harvard University Press.

Steinberg, L., & Hill, J. (1978). Patterns of family interaction as a function of age, the onset of puberty, and formal thinking. *Developmental Psychology, 14,* 683–684.

Stern, C. (1973). *Principles of human genetics* (3rd ed.). San Francisco, CA: W. H. Freeman.

Stern, W. (1914). *Psychologie der frühen Kindheit bis zum sechsten Lebensiahr.* Leipzig, Germany: Quelle & Meyer.

Sternberg, R. J. (1985). *Beyond IQ: A triarchic theory of human intelligence.* New York: Cambridge University Press.

Sternberg, R. J. (Ed.). (1988). *The nature of creativity.* New York: Cambridge University Press.

Stevens, S. S. (1946). On the theory of scales of measurement. *Science, 103,* 677–680.

Stiffman, A. R., Church, H., & Earls, F. (1992). Predictive modeling of change in depressive disorder and counts of depressive symptoms in urban youth. *Journal of Research on Adolescence, 2*(4), 295–316.

Strauss, S. (1982). *U-shaped behavioral growth.* New York: Academic Press.

Strauss, S. (1998). Cognitive development and science education: Toward a middle level model. In I. E. Sigel & K. A. Renninger (Eds.), *Handbook of child psychology: Vol. 4. Child psychology in practice* (5th ed., pp. 357–399). New York: Wiley.

Streissguth, A. P., Landesman-Dwyer, S., Martin, J. C., & Smith, D. W. (1980). Teratogenic effects of alcohol in humans and laboratory animals. *Science, 209,* 353–361.

Strohman, R. C. (1993a). Organism and experience. [Review of Lerner, R. M., *Final Solutions.* University Park, PA: Penn State Press, 1992.] *Journal of Applied Developmental Psychology, 14,* 147–151.

Strohman, R. C. (1993b). Book Reviews: *Final Solutions* (Richard M. Lerner, Penn State Press, 1992) and *Individual development and evolution: The genesis of novel behavior* (Gilbert Gottlieb, Oxford University Press, 1992). *Integrative Physiological and Behavioral Science, 28,* 99–104.

Sunday, S. R., & Tobach, E. (Ed.). (1985). *Violence against women: A critique of the sociobiology of rape.* New York: Gordian.

Suomi, S. J. (1997). Early determinants of behavior: Evidence from primate studies. *British Medical Bulletin, 53,* 170–184.

Suomi, S. J. (2000). A behavioral perspective on developmental psychopathology: Excessive aggression and serotonergic dysfunction in monkeys. In A. J. Sameroff, M. Lewis, & S. Miller (Eds.), *Hand-*

book of developmental psychopathology (2nd ed., pp. 237–256). New York: Plenum Publishing.

Suomi, S. J., & Harlow, H. F. (1972). Social rehabilitation of isolate-reared monkeys. *Developmental Psychology, 6,* 487–496.

Super, C. M., & Harkness, S. (Eds.). (1980). Anthropological perspectives on child development. *New Directions for Child Development, 8.*

Super, C. M., & Harkness, S. (1981). Figure, ground, and gestalt: The cultural context of the active individual. In R. M. Lerner & N. A. Busch-Rossnagel (Eds.), *Individuals as producers of their own development: A life-span perspective* (pp. 69–86). New York: Academic Press.

Sutton-Smith, B. (1973). *Child psychology.* New York: Appleton-Century-Crofts.

Swanson, D. P., Spencer, M. B., & Petersen, A. (1998). Identity formation in adolescence. In K. Borman & B. Schneider (Eds.), *The adolescent years: Social influences and educational challenges: Ninety-seventh yearbook of the National Society for the Study of Education, Part I* (pp. 18–41). Chicago, IL: The National Society for the Study of Education.

Swartz, D. (1982). Is it sex? *The Sciences, 22,* 2.

Switzer, G. E., Simmons, R. G., Dew, M. A., & Regalski, J. M. (1995). The effect of a school based helper program on adolescent self-image, attitudes, and behavior. *Journal of Early Adolescence, 15*(4), 429–455.

Takanishi, R. (1993). An agenda for the integration of research and policy during early adolescence. In R. M. Lerner (Ed.), *Early adolescence: Perspectives on research, policy, and intervention* (pp. 457–470). Hillsdale, NJ: Erlbaum.

Tanner, J. M. (1962). *Growth at adolescence.* Springfield, IL: Thomas.

Tanner, J. M. (1973). Growing up. *Scientific American, 229,* 34–43.

Tanner, J. (1991). Menarche, secular trend in age of. In R. M. Lerner, A. C. Petersen, & J. Brooks-Gunn (Eds.), *Encyclopedia of adolescence* (Vol. 1, pp. 637–641). New York: Garland Publishing.

Terman, L. M. (1916). *The measurement of intelligence.* Boston, MA: Houghton.

Terman, L. M. (Ed.). (1925). *Genetic studies of genius, I: Mental and physical traits of a thousand gifted children.* Stanford, CA: Stanford University Press.

Terman, L. M., & Oden, M. H. (1959). *Genetic studies of genius, V: The gifted group at mid-life.* Palo Alto, CA: Stanford University Press.

Terman, L. M., & Tyler, L. E. (1954). Psychological sex differences. In L. Carmichael (Ed.), *Manual of child psychology* (pp. 1064–1114). New York: Wiley.

Thelen, E., & Smith, L. B. (1994). *A dynamic systems approach to the development of cognition and action*. Cambridge, MA: MIT Press.

Thelen, E., & Smith, L. B. (1998). Dynamic systems theories. In W. Damon (Series Ed.) & R. M. Lerner (Vol. Ed.), *Handbook of child psychology: Vol. 1. Theoretical models of human development* (5th ed., pp. 563–633). New York: Wiley.

Thelen, E., & Ulrich, B. D. (1991). Hidden skills: A dymanical systems analysis of treadmill stepping during the first year. *Monographs of the Society for Research in Child Development, 56.*

Thomas, A., & Chess, S. (1970). Behavioral individuality in childhood. In L. R. Aronson, E. Tobach, D. Lehrman, & J. S. Rosenblatt (Eds.), *Development and evolution of behavior* (pp. 529–541). San Francisco, CA: W. H. Freeman.

Thomas, A., & Chess, S. (1977). *Temperament and development*. New York: Brunner/Mazel.

Thomas, A., & Chess, S. (1980). *The dynamics of psychological development*. New York: Brunner/Mazel.

Thomas, A., & Chess, S. (1981). The role of temperament in the contributions of individuals to their development. In R. M. Lerner & N. A. Busch-Rossnagel (Eds.), *Individuals as producers of their development: A life-span perspective*. New York: Academic Press.

Thomas, A., Chess, S., & Birch, H. G. (1968). *Temperament and behavioral disorders in childhood*. New York: New York University.

Thomas, A., Chess, S., & Birch, H. G. (1970). The origin of personality. *Scientific American, 223,* 102–109.

Thomas, A., Chess, S., Birch, H. G., Hertzig, M. E., & Korn, S. J. (1963). *Behavioral individuality in early childhood*. New York: New York University Press.

Thomas, A., Chess, S., & Korn, S. J. (1982). The reality of difficult temperament. *Merrill-Palmer Quarterly, 28,* 1–20.

Thomas, A., Chess, S., Sillen, J., & Mendez, O. (1974). Cross-cultural study of behavior in children with special vulnerabilities to stress. In D. F. Ricks, A. Thomas, & M. Roff (Eds.), *Life history research in psychopathology* (pp. 53–63). Minneapolis, MN: University of Minnesota.

Thompson, K. L., Bundy, K. A., & Broncheau, C. (1995). Social skills training for young adolescents: Symbolic and behavioral components. *Adolescence, 30*(119), 723–734.

Thompson, L. (1999). Creating partnerships with government, communities, and universities to achieve results for children. *Applied Developmental Science, 3*(4), 213–216.

Thompson, R. A., & Lamb, M. E. (1986). Infant–mother attachment: New directions for theory and research. In P. B. Baltes, D. L. Featherman, & R. M. Lerner (Eds.), *Life-span development and behavior* (Vol. 7, pp. 1–41). Hillsdale, NJ: Erlbaum.

Thorndike, E. L. (1904). The newest psychology. *Educational Review, 28,* 217–227.

Thorndike, E. L. (1905). *The elements of psychology*. New York: Seiler.

Thorpe, W. (1961). Sensitive periods in the learning of animals and man: A study of imprinting. In W. Thorpe & C. Zangwill (Eds.), *Current problems in animal behavior* (pp. 194–224). Cambridge, England: Cambridge University Press.

Timney, B., Mitchell, D. E., & Griffin, F. (1978). The development of vision in cats after extended periods of dark-rearing. *Experimental Brain Research, 31,* 547–560.

Tobach, E. (1971). Some evolutionary aspects of human gender. *Journal of Orthopsychiatry, 41,* 710–715.

Tobach, E. (1978). The methodology of sociobiology from the viewpoint of a comparative psychologist. In A. L. Caplan (Ed.), *The sociobiology debate* (pp. 411–423). New York: Harper & Row.

Tobach, E. (1981). Evolutionary aspects of the activity of the organism and its development. In R. M. Lerner & N. A. Busch-Rossnagel (Eds.), *Individuals as producers of their development: A life-span perspective* (pp. 37–68). New York: Academic Press.

Tobach, E. (1994). Personal is political is personal is political. *Journal of Social Issues, 50,* 221–224.

Tobach, E., Gianutsos, J., Topoff, H. R., & Gross, C. G. (1974). *The four horses: Racism, sexism, militarism, and social Darwinism*. New York: Behavioral Publications.

Tobach, E., & Greenberg, G., (1984). The significance of T. C. Schneirla's contribution to the concept of levels of integration. In G. Greenberg & E. Tobach (Eds.), *Behavioral evolution and integrative levels*. Hillsdale, NJ: Erlbaum.

Tobach, E., & Schneirla, T. C. (1968). The biopsychology of social behavior of animals. In R. E. Cooke & S. Levin (Eds.), *Biologic basis of pediatric practice* (pp. 68–82). New York: McGraw-Hill.

Tomlinson-Keasey, C. (1972). Formal operation in females from eleven to fifty-four years of age. *Developmental Psychology, 6,* 364.

Toulmin, S. (1981). Epistemology and developmental psychology. In E. S. Gollin (Ed.), *Developmental plasticity: Behavioral and biological aspects of variations in development* (pp. 253–267). New York: Academic Press.

Trickett, E. J., Barone, C., & Buchanan, R. M. (1996). Elaborating developmental contextualism in adolescent research and intervention: Paradigm contributions from community psychology. *Journal of Research on Adolescence, 6,* 245–269.

Trivers, R. L. (1971). The evolution of reciprocal altruism. *The Quarterly Review of Biology, 46,* 35–39, 45–47.

Tubman, J. G., & Lerner, R. M. (1994). Continuity and discontinuity in the affective experiences of parents and children: Evidence from the New York Longitudinal Study (NYLS). *American Journal of Orthopsychiatry, 64,* 112–125.

Tuddenham, R. D. (1959). The constancy of personality ratings over two decades. *Genetic Psychology Monographs, 60,* 3–29.

Turiel, E. (1969). Developmental processes in the child's moral thinking. In P. H. Mussen, J. Langer, & M. Covington (Eds.), *Trends and issues in developmental psychology.* New York: Holt, Rinehart & Winston.

Turiel, E. (1974). Conflict and transition in adolescent moral development. *Child Development, 45,* 14–29.

Turiel, E. (1978). The development of concepts of social structure: Social convention. In J. Glick & A. Clarke-Stewart (Eds.), *The development of social understanding.* New York: Gardner Press.

Turiel, E. (1998). The development of morality. In W. Damon (Series Ed.) & N. Eisenberg (Vol. Ed.), *Handbook of child psychology: Vol. 3. Social, emotional, and personality development* (pp. 863–932). New York: Wiley.

Uphouse, L. L., & Bonner, J. (1975). Preliminary evidence for the effects of environmental complexity on hybridization of rat brain RNA to rat unique DNA. *Developmental Psychobiology, 8,* 171–178.

Valsiner, J. (1998). The development of the concept of development: Historical and epistemological perspectives. In W. Damon (Series Ed.) & R. M. Lerner (Vol. Ed.), *Handbook of child psychology: Vol. 1. Theoretical models of human development* (5th ed., pp. 189–232). New York: Wiley.

van den Berghe, P. L., & Barash, D. P. (1977). Inclusive fitness and human family structure. *American Anthropologist, 79,* 809–823.

van den Daele, L. D. (1969). Qualitative models in developmental analysis. *Developmental Psychology, 1,* 303–310.

van den Daele, L. D. (1974). Infrastructure and transition in developmental analysis. *Human development, 17,* 1–23.

van den Daele, L. D. (1975). Ego development and preferential judgement in lifespan perspective. In N. Datan & L. H. Ginsburg, (Eds.), *Lifespan developmental psychology: Normative life crises.* New York: Academic Press.

van der Dennen, J. M. G. (1987). Ethnocentrism and in-group/out-group differentiation: A review and interpretation of the literature. In V. Reynolds, V. Falger, & I. Vine. (Eds.), *The sociobiology of ethnocentrism* (pp. 1–47). London, England: Croom Helm.

Venter, J. C., Adams, M. D., Myers, E. W., Li, P. W., Mural, R. J., [plus 270 others]. The sequence of the human genome. *Science, 291,* 1304–1351.

Villarruel, F. A., & Lerner, R. M. (1994). Development and context and the contexts of learning. In F. A. Villarruel & R. M. Lerner (Eds.), *Promoting community-based programs for socialization and learning: Vol. 63. New directions for child development* (pp. 3–10). San Francisco, CA: Jossey-Bass.

von Bertalanffy, L. (1933). *Modern theories of development.* London, England: Oxford University Press.

von Bertalanffy, L. (1968). *General systems theory.* New York: Braziller.

von Bertalanffy, L. (1969). Chance or law. In A. Koestler & J. R. Smithies (Ed.s), *Beyond reductionism* (pp. 59–84). London, England: Hitchinson.

Vondracek, F. W., Lerner, R. M., & Schulenberg, J. E. (1986). *Career development: A life-span developmental approach.* Hillsdale, NJ: Erlbaum.

von Eye, A. (1990a). *Statistical methods in longitudinal research: Principles and structuring change.* New York: Academic Press.

von Eye, A. (1990b). *Introduction to configural frequency analysis: The search for types and anitypes in cross-classifications.* Cambridge, England: Cambridge University Press.

von Eye, A., & Clogg, C. C. (Eds.). (1996). *Categorical variables in developmental research: Methods of analysis.* San Diego, CA: Academic Press.

von Eye, A., & Schuster, C. (2000). The road to freedom: Quantitative developmental methodology in the third millenium. *International Journal of Behavioral Development, 24,* 35–43.

von Noorden, G. K., Dowling, J. E., & Ferguson, D. C. (1970). Experimental amblyopia in monkeys: I. Behavioral studies of stimulus deprivation in amblyopia. *Archives of Ophthalmology, 84,* 206–214.

Vygotsky, L. S. (1927/1982). Istorichesskii smysl krizisa v psikhologii. In *Sobranie sochinenii* (Vol. 1). Moscow: Pedagogika.

Vygotsky, L. S. (1933/1966). Play and its role in the mental development of the child. *Vaprosy psikhologii, 12,* 62–76. [English translation: In

J. Brunner, A. Jolly, & K. Sylva (Eds.), *Play* (pp. 537–554). Harmondsworth: Penguin.]

Waddington, C. H. (1942). Canalization of development and the inheritance of acquired characters. *Nature, 150,* 563–564.

Waddington, C. H. (1957). *The strategy of genes.* London: George Allen and Unwin.

Wadsworth, B. J. (1971). *Piaget's theory of cognitive development.* New York: McKay.

Wagenaar, A. C., & Perry, C. L. (1994). Community strategies for the reduction of youth drinking: Theory and application. *Journal of Research on Adolescence, 4*(2), 319–347.

Wahler, R. G. (1980). Parent insularity as a determinant of generalization success in family treatment. In S. Salzinger, J. Antrobus, & J. Glich (Eds.), *The ecosystem of the "sick" child, implications for classification and intervention for disturbed and mentally retarded children* (pp. 187–199). New York: Academic Press.

Wahlsten, D. (1981). Review of The IQ Game by Howard F. Taylor. *Behaviorists for Social Action Journal, 3,* 33–34.

Walsten, D. (1990). Insensitivity of the analysis of variance to heredity–environment interaction. *Behavioral and Brain Sciences, 13,* 109–120.

Walker, L. J., & Taylor, J. H. (1991). Family interactions and the development of moral reasoning. *Child Development, 62,* 264–283.

Wapner, S. (1969). Organismic–developmental theory: Some applications to cognition. In J. Langer, P. Mussen, & N. Covington (Eds.), *Trends and issues in developmental theory* (pp. 35–67). New York: Holt, Rinehart & Winston.

Wapner, S. (1977). Environmental transition: A research paradigm deriving from the organismic–developmental systems approach. In L. van Ryzin (Ed.), *Wisconsin Conference on Research Methods in Behavior Environment Studies Proceedings* (pp. 1–9). Madison, WI: University of Wisconsin.

Wapner, S. (1981). Transactions of persons-in-environments. Some critical transitions. *Journal of Environmental Psychology, 1,* 223–239.

Wapner, S. (1986). *An organismic-developmental systems approach to the analysis of experience and action.* Paper presented at the conference on Holistic Approaches to the Analysis of Experience and Action, University of Catania, Sicily, Italy.

Wapner, S. (1987). A holistic, developmental, systems-oriented environmental psychology: Some beginnings. In D. Stokols & I. Altman (Eds.), *Handbook of environmental psychology* (pp. 1433–1465). New York: Wiley.

Wapner, S. (1995). Toward integration: Environmental psychology in relation to other subfields of psychology. *Environment and Behavior, 27,* 9–32.

Wapner, S., & Demick, J. (1988, October 25–27). *Some relations between developmental and environmental psychology: An organismic–developmental systems perspective.* Paper presented at the "Visions of Development, the Environment, and Aesthetics: The Legacy of Joachim Wohlwill" conference, The Pennsylvania State University, University Park, PA.

Wapner, S., & Demick, J. (1990). Development of experience and action: Levels of integration in human functioning. In G. Greenberg & E. Tobach (Eds.), *Theories of evolution of knowing. The T. C. Schneirla Conference Series* (Vol. 4, pp. 47–68). Hillsdale, NJ: Erlbaum.

Wapner, S., & Demick, J. (1992). The organismic developmental, systems approach to the study of critical person-in-environment transitions through the life span. In T. Yamamoto & S. Wapner (Eds.), *Developmental psychology of life transitions* (pp. 25–49). Kyoto, Japan: Kitaohji.

Wapner, S., & Demick, J. (1998). Developmental analysis: A holistic, developmental, systems-oriented perspective. In W. Damon (Series Ed.) and R. M. Lerner (Vol. Ed.), *Handbook of child psychology: Vol. 1. Theoretical models of human development* (5th ed., pp. 761–805). New York: Wiley.

Washburn, S. L. (1961). *Social life of early man.* New York: Wenner-Gren Foundation for Anthropological Research.

Washburn, S. L. (1982). Is it sex? *The Sciences, 22,* 2.

Wassef, A., Collins, M. L., Ingham, D., & Mason, G. (1995). In search of effective programs to address students' emotional distress and behavioral problems: Part II. Critique of school- and community-based programs. *Adolescence, 30*(120), 757–777.

Waterman, A. S. (1982). Identity development from adolescence to adulthood: An extension of theory and a review of research. *Developmental Psychology, 18,* 341–358.

Watson, J. B. (1913). Psychology as the behaviorist views it. *Psychological Review, 20,* 158–177.

Watson, J. B. (1914). *Behavior: An introduction to comparative psychology.* New York: Holt.

Watson, J. B. (1918). *Psychological care of infant and child.* New York: Norton.

Watson, J. B. (1918). *Psychology from the standpoint of a behaviorist.* Philadelphia: Lippincott.

Watson, J. B. (1924). *Behaviorism.* New York: Norton.

Watson, J. B. (1928). *Psychological care of infant and child*. New York: Norton.

Watson, J. B. (1959). *Behaviorism*. Chicago, IL: University of Chicago Press.

Watson, J. B., & Raynor, R. (1920). Conditional emotional reactions. *Journal of Experimental Psychology, 3,* 1–14.

Watson, R. I. (1967). Psychology: A prescriptive science. *American Psychologist, 22,* 435–443.

Webb, E. J., Campbell, R. D., Schwartz, R. D., & Sechrest, L. (1966). *Unobtrusive measures: Nonreactive research in the social sciences*. Chicago, IL: Rand McNally.

Weinberg, R. A., & Erikson, M. F. (1996). Minnesota's Children, Youth, and Family Consortium: A university–community collaboration. *Journal of Research on Adolescence, 6*(1), 37–53.

Weiner, B., & Peter, N. (1973). A cognitive–developmental analysis of achievement and moral judgement. *Developmental psychology, 9,* 290–309.

Weiss, H. B., & Greene, J. C. (1992). An empowerment partnership for family support and education programs and evaluations. *Family Science Review, 5,* 131–148.

Wellman, H. M., & Gelman, S. A. (1998). Knowledge acquisition in foundational domains. In W. Damon (Series Ed.), D. Kuhn, & R. S. Siegler (Vol. Eds.), *Handbook of child psychology: Vol. 2. Cognition, perception, and language* (5th ed., pp. 523–573). New York: Wiley.

Werner, H. (1948). *Comparative psychology of mental development*. New York: International Universities Press.

Werner, H. (1957). The concept of development from a comparative and organismic point of view. In D. B. Harris (Ed.), *The concept of development* (pp. 125–148). Minneapolis, MN: University of Minnesota Press.

Werner, H., & Kaplan, B. (1956). The developmental approach to cognition: Its relevance to the psychological interpretation of anthropological and ethnolinguistic data. *American Anthropologist, 58,* 866–880.

Werner, H., & Kaplan, B. (1963). *Symbol formation: An organismic–developmental approach to language and the expression of thought*. New York: Wiley.

Werner, H., & Wapner, S. (1949). Sensory-tonic field theory of perception. *Journal of Personality, 18,* 88–107.

Werner, H., & Wapner, S. (1952). Toward a general theory of perception. *Psychological Review, 59,* 324–338.

Wertsch, J. V. (1979). From social interaction to higher psychological processes: A clarification and application of Vygotsky's theory. *Human Development, 22,* 1–22.

Wertsch, J. V. (1981). The concept of activity in Soviet psychology: An introduction. In J. V. Wertsch (Ed.), *The concept of activity in Soviet psychology* (pp. 3–36). Armonk, NY: Sharpe.

Wertsch, J. V. (1985). *Vygotsky and the social formation of mind*. Cambridge, MA: Harvard University Press.

Westergaard, C. G., Mehlman, P. T., Suomi, S. J., & Higley, J. D. (1999). CSF 5-HIAA and aggression in female primates: Species and interindividual differences. *Psychopharmacology, 146,* 440–446.

Whalen, S. P., & Wynn, J. R. (1995). Enhancing primary services for youth through an infrastructure of social services. *Journal of Adolescent Research, 10*(1), 88–110.

Whitbourne, S. K., & Tesch, S. A. (1985). A comparison of identity and intimacy statuses in college students and alumni. *Developmental Psychology, 21*(6), 1039–1044.

White, C. B., Bushnell, N., & Regnemer, J. L. (1978). Moral development in Bahamian school children: A 3-year examination of Kohlberg's stages of moral development. *Developmental Psychology, 14,* 58–65.

White, S. H. (1968). The learning–maturation controversy: Hall to Hull. *Merrill-Palmer Quarterly, 14,* 187–196.

White, S. H. (1970). The learning theory tradition and child psychology. In P. H. Mussen (Ed.), *Carmichael's manual of child psychology* (3rd ed., pp. 657–702). New York: Wiley.

Whitehead, A. N. (1936). Harvard: The Future. *Atlantic Monthly, 158,* 267.

Wiesel, T. N., & Hubel, D. H. (1965). Extent of the recovery from the effects of visual deprivation in kittens. *Journal of Neurophysiology, 28,* 1060–1072.

Willems, E. P. (1973). Behavioral ecology and experimental analysis: Courtship is not enough. In J. R. Nesselroade & H. W. Reese (Eds.), *Life-span developmental psychology: Methodological issues* (pp. 195–217). New York: Academic Press.

Williams, G. C. (1966). *Adaptation and natural selection*. Princeton, NJ: Princeton University.

Willis, S. L. (1982). Concepts from life span devel-opmental psychology: Implications for programming. In M. Okun (Ed.), *Source book on programs for older adults* (pp. 3–10). San Francisco: Jossey-Bass.

Willis, S. L., & Baltes, P. B. (1980). Intelligence in adulthood and aging: Contemporary issues. In L. Poon (Ed.), *Aging in the 1980s: Psychological is-*

sues (pp. 260–272). Washington, DC: American Psychological Association.

Wilson, E. O. (1975a). *Sociobiology: The new synthesis*. Cambridge, MA: Harvard University Press.

Wilson, E. O. (1975b, December 11). For sociobiology. *New York Review of Books*, 60.

Wilson, E. O. (1975c, October 12). Human decency is animal. *New York Times Magazine*, 38–50.

Wilson, E. O. (1976). Academic vigilantism and the political significance of sociobiology. *BioScience, 183*, 187–190.

Wilson, E. O. (1980). A consideration of the genetic foundation of human social behavior. In G. W. Barlow & J. Silverberg (Eds.), *Sociobiology: Beyond nature/nurture* (pp. 295–305). Boulder, CO: Westview.

Winch, R. F. (1971). *The modern family* (3rd ed). New York: Holt, Rinehart & Winston.

Winner, E. (1996). *Gifted children: Myths and realities.* New York: University Press.

Winston, A. S. (1996). The context of correctness: A comment on Rushton. *Journal of Social Distress and the Homeless, 5,* 231–250.

Winston, A. S. (1997a). Genocide as a scientific project. *American Psychologist, 52*, 182–183..

Winston, A. S. (1997b). Rushton and racial differences: Further reasons for caution. *Journal of Social Distress and the Homeless, 6,* 199–202.

Wohlwill, J. F. (1963). Piaget's system as a source of emperical research. *Merill-Palmer Quarterly, 9,* 253–262.

Wohlwill, J. F. (1973). *The study of behavioral development*. New York: Academic Press.

Wohlwill, J. (1980). Cognitive development in childhood. In O. G. Brim, Jr., & J. Kagan (Eds.), *Constancy and change in human development* (pp. 359–444). Cambridge, MA: Harvard University Press.

Wolff, P. H. (1960). The developmental psychologies of Jean Piaget and psychoanalysis. *Psychological Issues, 2*(5).

Woodward, A. L., & Markman, E. M. (1998). Early word learning. In W. Damon (Series Ed.), D. Kuhn, & R. S. Siegler, (Vol. Eds.), *Handbook of child psycology: Vol. 2. Cognition, perception, and language* (5th ed., pp. 371–420). New York: Wiley.

Yarczower, M., & Hazlett, L. (1977). Evolutionary scales and anagenesis. *Psychological Bulletin, 84,* 1088–1097.

Yarczower, M., & Yarczower, B. S. (1979). In defense of anagenesis, grades, and evolutionary scales. *Psychological Bulletin, 86,* 880–884.

Yates, F. E., & Iberall, A. S. (1973). Temporal and hierarchical organization in biosystems. In J. Urquhart & F. E. Yates (Eds.), *Temporal aspects of therapeutics* (pp. 17–34). New York: Plenum Publishing.

Zaslow, M., Tout, K., Smith, S., & Moore, K. (1998). Implications of the 1996 welfare legislation for children: A research perspective. *Social Policy Report, Society for Research in Child Development, 12*(3).

Zeldin, S. (1995). Community–university collaborations for youth development: From theory to practice. *Journal of Adolescent Research, 10*(4), 449–469.

Zeldin, S., & Price, L. A. (1995). Creating supportive communities for adolescent development: Challenges to scholars: An introduction. *Journal of Adolescent Research, 10*(1), 6–14.

Ziegler, H. (1893). *Die Naturwissenschaft und die Socialdmokratische Theorie.* Stuttgart, Germany: Enke.

Zigler, E. (1998). A place of value for applied and policy studies. *Child Development, 69,* 532–542.

Zigler, E., & Finn-Stevenson, M. (1992). Applied developmental psychology. In M. H. Bornstein & M. E. Lamb (Eds.), *Developmental psychology: An advanced textbook* (3rd ed., pp. 677–729). Hillsdale, NJ: Erlbaum.

Zukav, G. (1979). *The dancing Wu Li masters.* New York: Bantam Books.

NAME INDEX

SUBJECT INDEX

vision, newborn, 1
visualization, 2
visual-motor flexibility, 2
vitalism, 21

Wapner's holistic, developmental, systems-oriented perspective, 179–182
Werner's contributions to continuity-discontinuity issues, 114–117
World War II, 31–33

young adulthood, 424–425
youth programs, 519–534
  effective
    developing, 532
    key features of, 533
  effectiveness of, 522
  evaluation of, 522, 525–527
  program scale for, 522–523
  public policy for, 534–538
    absence of, programs from, 535–536
    features of, 536
    implementing, 536–537
    need for, 534–535
  representative focal issues of, 520–522
  sustainability of, 523
  themes of, 527–533
  toward new research model for, 523–525

zone of proximal development, 32

PHOTO CREDITS